# Business Studies

## Third Edition

# Dave Hall • Rob Jones • Carlo Raffo

## Edited by
# Ian Chambers and Dave Gray

CPL ... Ltd

# Acknowledgements

## Dedication

To Elaine, Holly, Caitlin, Amanda Jane, Mandy, Sandra, Georgina, Rebecca, Jan, Natalie and Holly Anne for all their love and support in the writing of this book.

Cover design by Caroline Waring-Collins, illustration provided by Getty Images.
Graphics by Caroline Waring-Collins, Tim Button, Anneli Jameson and Rob Gittins.
Photography by Andrew Allen and Dave Gray.
Typing by Ingrid Hamer.
Proof reading by Mike Kidson, Heather Doyle and Tony Barnes.

## Acknowledgements

The publishers would like to thank the following for the use of photographs and copyright material. Other copyright material is acknowledged at source. Agency central p 460, Cafedirect p 784, Corel pp 210,259,329,615,728,782, Digital Stock pp 539,684, DigitalVision pp 6(b),247,306(tr),342,344,355,398,568(t),586,617,642(tl),763, EasyJet p 468, Greenshop p 730, Ian Sager pp 648,649, LocalLiberty.com p 10, Monster.co.uk p 463, PhotoArtistry p 17, Photodisc pp 26,44,66,138,153,159,183,189,190,192(tl), 211,299, 310,335,349,375,382,401,412,416,426,435,457(tl,br),481,500(l),510,520,568(bl),576,579,593,594(b),625,628,696,707,748, Pilkington Glass p 576, Renault p 694, Reg Vardy p 33, Retread Manufacturers Association p 730, Rex Features pp 19, 441,537, 549, 560,567, Richer Sounds p 581, Stockbyte pp 6(t),11,21,49,67,94,118,155,192,229,265,279,282,301,306(tl,b),314, 319,327,332, 359, 361,363,389,409,455,457(tr),469,487,497,500(r),513,517,526,562,574,594(t),597,633(t),642(tr,b),685(br),726,744,756,801, The Associated Press pp 75,86,202,203,618,776, TopFoto pp 2(l),113,147,440,493,536, Vision Express p 463.

Office for National Statistics material is Crown Copyright, reproduced here with the permission of Her Majesty's Stationery Office.

Every effort has been made to locate the copyright owners of material used in this book. Any omissions brought to the notice of the publisher are regretted and will be credited in subsequent printings.

## British Library Cataloguing in Publication Data

A catalogue record for this book is available from the British Library.

ISBN 1-902796-83-7

Causeway Press Limited
PO Box 13, Ormskirk, Lancs, L39 5HP
Contribution © Dave Hall, Rob Jones, Carlo Raffo, Ian Chambers, Dave Gray
1st impression, 1993, reprinted eight times
2nd impression, 1999, reprinted four times
3rd impression, 2004, reprinted 2004

Typesetting by Caroline Waring-Collins, Waring Collins Ltd.
Printed and bound in China GCC/02

# Contents

# Preface

Business Studies does not provide a step-by-step guide to how to be 'good at business'. There is no simple set of rules that can be applied at all times which will always be successful. However, by being analytical, rigorous and critical it may be possible to develop skills and approaches which can be useful, at certain times and in certain situations, when making business decisions. It is possible that different approaches will be used by different people in business and there may be disagreement as to which approach to take.

Business Studies is integrated and different areas of business are interdependent. There are links, for example, between:

- what is being produced and the funds available to pay for it (production and finance);
- the selling of the product and ethical considerations (marketing and ethics);
- the type of business and many aspects of its operation.

Being aware of these aspects of business will help us to understand how and why business decisions are made, and how they affect a variety of people, both within and outside the business. The aim of **Business Studies (Third Edition)** is to help those studying Business to understand business decisions and to be analytical, rigorous and critical in their business thinking. A number of features are included in the book which we believe will help this task.

Comprehensive course coverage  The book contains material which should meet the demands of a wide range of courses. These include AS/A Level, Higher Grade, GCE in Applied Business, higher education and professional courses. The book is organised into 112 units across six sections:

- objectives, strategy and the business environment;
- marketing;
- accounting and finance;
- people in organisations;
- operations management;
- external influences.

In addition there are two units on study skills and assessment at the end. There is a development in the units contained in each section which reflects progress throughout a course and the requirements of different courses.

Guidance is given on exactly how the book can be used for specific courses in **Business Studies Teachers' Guide (Third Edition)**. To allow flexibility in course construction and teaching, **Business Studies AS Level (Third Edition)** and **Business Studies A2 Level (Third Edition)** are also available. They provide the AS Level and A2 Level units in seperate books.

Flexible unit structure  The unit structure allows the lecturer or teacher greater freedom to devise the course. Business Studies teachers and lecturers often teach different aspects of the course in different orders. So, whilst there is a logical order to the book, it has been written on the assumption that teachers or lecturers and students will piece the units together to suit their own teaching and learning needs and the requirements of the course being taught.

Cross referencing has been used in many of the units. This helps the teacher, lecturer or student to follow the course as they want. It will also be useful for modular courses and courses where Business Studies is only one part of the total course. The units in the book which relate to specific aspects of business, such as marketing or accounting, can be used in specialist courses or provide a short course in that area. Cross referencing also helps to stress the integrated nature of Business Studies

and the interdependence and possible conflict that may exist in many areas.

Accessibility  The book has been written in a clear and logical style which should make it accessible to all readers. Each unit is divided into short, easily manageable sections.

A workbook  The text is interspersed with a large number of questions. The questions which appear as part of the units mostly refer to preceding information. Answers in most cases are expected to be relatively short. Questions are based on a variety of case studies, data, articles, photographs, etc. They should allow the student and teacher/lecturer to assess whether the information has been understood. Shorter 'knowledge' questions provide a means of revising each unit. A longer case study appears at the end of each unit. It draws on information contained in the whole unit and answers are expected to reflect this. The questions asked reflect the type which are set in examinations. They help students to develop knowledge, application, analysis and evaluation - the criteria used in examinations to assess responses.

**Business Studies Teachers' Guide (Third Edition)** provides suggested answers and mark schemes for the activities and questions that appear in this book.

Use of business examples, case studies and data  Modern technology has allowed much of the book to proceed from manuscript to book form in a very short period. This has meant that we have been able to use the latest statistics and business examples available. Materials used have been chosen to demonstrate appropriate arguments and theories. They should, therefore, allow students to answer questions which require knowledge of what has happened 'in recent years' or 'over the past decade', as well as questions which deal with current debates.

Study skills and assessment  The last two units in the book provide guidance on how to study and the methods of assessment used in Business Studies. They are presented in the form of a manual and are designed to be used at various stages throughout the course.

Key terms  Many units contain a key terms section. Each section defines new concepts, which appear in capitals in the text of the unit. Taken together, they provide a comprehensive dictionary of business terms.

Presentation  Great care has been taken with how the book has been presented. It is hoped that the layout of the book, the use of colour and the use of diagrams will help learning.

We would like to thank the following for their efforts in the preparation of the three editions of this book: Richard Dunill, for keeping the debate sharp and yet accessible; Ingrid Hamer for her long hours of typing; Nigel Lewis; Michael J. Forshaw and Chris Sawyer for bringing a 'real' accountant's view to the book; all staff and students at Bolton Sixth Form College, King George V College, Loreto College, and Manchester University School of Education; Diane Wallace and Steve Robertson for working on the early development of the book; Alain Anderton for sharing his style ideas.

Dave Hall     Rob Jones     Carlo Raffo
Ian Chambers     Dave Gray

# 1 Business Activity

## What is business activity?

In 2003, Kelly Watson and her daughter Ruth opened a cafe in Coventry. Both had previous experience in catering. Kelly had spent the last seven years working in a school canteen, whilst Ruth had been employed by McDonald's when she was a sixth form student. Kelly invested £9,000 to help fund the setting up of the business. They called the cafe 'The Cathedral', due to its location near to the city's famous landmark. They planned to target the student market and cathedral visitors. Before trading began they had to:

● obtain a £3,000 bank loan;
● obtain a five year lease on a suitable property;
● line the kitchen with aluminium panels to conform with health and safety regulations;
● obtain a fire certificate;
● decorate the cafe area;
● buy furniture and kitchen equipment;
● find suppliers of fresh food;
● advertise the cafe in the local university.

Kelly and Ruth had different roles to play in the business. Kelly was responsible for dealing with suppliers and preparing the food. Ruth ran the cafe area. This involved waiting on tables, taking money and socialising with the customers.

Ruth and Kelly worked very long hours. The cafe opened from 8.00 am to 7.00 pm, every day of the week except Sunday. However, it was worth it because the business became successful. The Cathedral developed a reputation for good value food and a great atmosphere. After six months they were able to employ two university students to help during busy periods.

The above case illustrates many features of business activity.

● Business activity produces an **output** – a good or service. A cafe service is being provided by Kelly and Ruth.
● Goods and services are **consumed**. Cafe customers consume the service provided by Kelly and Ruth.
● **Resources** are used up. Money, food and drinks, furniture, staff, gas and electricity are just a few of the resources used by Kelly and Ruth.
● A number of business **functions** may be carried out. Administration (the paper work), managing staff (human resources) and decisions about marketing, finance and production are some examples.
● Businesses can be affected by **external factors**. The government's commitment to increasing the numbers of students in higher education may have boosted the number of students in Coventry.

Figure 1.1 shows a diagram which illustrates the nature of business activity. All types of business may be represented by this diagram - a building society, a window cleaner, a multinational chemical company, a shoe manufacturer or the BBC.

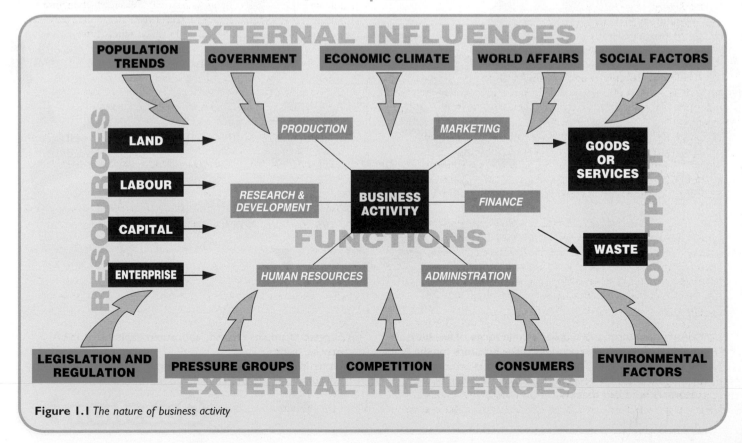

**Figure 1.1** *The nature of business activity*

# Business resources

Businesses use resources or FACTORS OF PRODUCTION in business activity. These are usually divided into four groups.

**Land** Land is not just a 'plot of land' where business premises might be located. It also includes natural resources, such as coal, diamonds, forests, rivers and fertile soil. The owners of land receive **rent** from those who use it.

Business activity uses both **renewable** and **non-renewable** resources. Renewable resources are those like fish, forests and water which nature replaces. Examples of non-renewable land resources are mineral deposits like coal and diamonds, which once used are never replaced. There has been concern in recent years about the rate at which renewable resources are being used. For example, overfishing in the North Sea has led to claims by the International Council for the Exploration of the Sea that cod stocks are now so low that fishing should stop until they recover. The number of young cod in the North Sea in early 2003 was the lowest in 20 years.

**Labour** Labour is the workforce of business. Manual workers, skilled workers and management are all members of the workforce. They are paid **wages** or **salaries** for their services. The quality of individual workers will vary considerably. Each worker is unique, possessing a different set of characteristics, skills, knowledge, intelligence and emotions.

It is possible to improve the quality of **human resources** through training and education. Human resources become more productive if money is invested by business or government in training and education.

**Capital** Capital is sometimes described as the **artificial** resource because it is made by labour. Capital refers to the tools, machinery and equipment which businesses use. For example, JCB makes mechanical diggers which are used by the construction industry. Capital also refers to the money which the owners use to set up a business (☞ unit 43). Owners of capital receive **interest** if others borrow it.

**Enterprise** Enterprise has a special role in business activity. The **entrepreneur** or businessperson develops a business idea and then hires and organises the other three factors of production to carry out the activity. Entrepreneurs also take risks because they will often use some personal money to help set up the business. If the business does not succeed the entrepreneur may lose some or all of that money. If the business is successful, any money left over will belong to the entrepreneur. This is called **profit**.

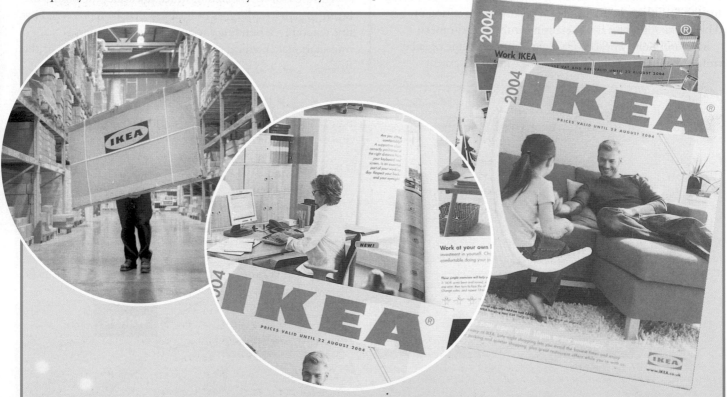

IKEA manufactures and supplies a wide range of furniture and household goods. It also provides office furniture for the home and office accessories. The company, based in Sweden, sells many of its products in flat-packs, which are assembled by customers who buy them.

(a) Suggest examples of land, labour and capital that IKEA may be using.
(b) Using IKEA's products as an example, distinguish between consumer goods and capital goods.

**Question 1**

# Business functions

Figure 1.1 showed that business activity involves a number of functions. A business is a SYSTEM - it has parts that work together to achieve an objective. The functions are all parts of the system. A business is also part of other systems such as the economic and political systems (☞ unit 9). What functions does a business carry out?

- **Production** involves changing natural resources into a product or the supply of a service. Most business resources are used up in the production process. Examples of production can be seen on a building site where houses are constructed, in a dental surgery where dental treatment is given and in a coal mine where coal is extracted.
- **Marketing** has become very important in recent years due to an increase in competition in business. It is concerned with identifying consumer needs and satisfying them. Examples of marketing activities are market research, advertising, packaging, promotion, distribution and pricing.
- The **finance** department is responsible for the control of money in a business. It has a number of important duties. This includes recording transactions, producing documents to illustrate the performance of the business and its financial position and controlling the flow of money in the business.
- Dealing with enquiries, communicating messages and producing documents for the workforce are all examples of **administrative** tasks.
- The **human resources** function involves the management of people. The personnel department looks after the welfare of the workforce, and is responsible for such things as recruitment, selection, training, appraisal, health and safety, equal opportunities, payment systems and worker disputes.
- **Research and development** (R&D) involves technical research, for example, research into a new medicine or a new production technique. R&D can be very expensive. Consequently, many businesses do not have a R&D department but rely on adapting new products and new technology developed by other companies.

In a large business these functions should be easy to identify. However, a self-employed window cleaner will also carry out these functions.

- Production - cleaning windows.
- Marketing - distributing business cards to potential customers.
- Administration - dealing with enquiries from potential customers and recording their personal details in preparation for a first visit.
- Human resources management - recruiting and supervising part time helpers during busy periods.
- Finance - keeping records of all financial transactions.

Business activity is highly **integrated**. For example, production is heavily influenced by marketing activities. If marketing is effective and more of the product is sold, then more will have to be produced. Also, the finance department, for example, will carefully watch the amount of money used by other departments.

# What does business activity produce?

All business activity results in the production of a good or a service. CONSUMER GOODS are those which are sold to the general public. They fall into two categories.

- **Durable goods** such as cookers, televisions, books, cars and furniture can be used repeatedly for a long period of time.
- **Non-durable goods** such as food, confectionery, newspapers and shoe polish are used very soon after they are purchased. Some of these goods are called **fast moving consumer goods**, such as soap, crisps and cornflakes.

CAPITAL GOODS are those goods purchased by businesses and used to produce other goods. Tools, equipment and machinery are examples of capital goods.

The supply of **services** has grown in recent years. Banking, insurance, hairdressing, car valeting and gardening are examples of this type of business activity.

Business activity also results in the production of waste materials. Most waste is useless and some waste, like radioactive nuclear waste, is very dangerous and expensive to dispose of. Some production techniques result in **by-products** (☞ unit 86) which can be sold. For example, the brewing process generates yeast which is used by the producers of Marmite.

# External factors

Business activity is affected by a number of external forces, some of which are shown in the diagram in Figure 1.1. These are beyond the control of the individual business. In some cases they constrain a firm's decisions and may prevent its growth and development.

- **The government** has a great deal of influence over business activity. In most countries the government will be in favour of business development. A **legal framework**, where all individuals abide by the law and offenders are punished, will help this. A country also needs an **infrastructure** including roads, railways, telecommunications, schools and hospitals. Some of these items may be provided by the state (☞ unit 7). Government policy can also influence business. For example, profits and many goods and services which businesses produce are taxed.
- The **economic climate** can have an impact on business activity. For example, over the period 1993-2003 the UK economy was relatively stable. Interest rates and price increases were relatively low, whilst unemployment fell steadily. These stable economic conditions allowed business activity to flourish. During this time the best performing economy in the EU was the UK's.
- **World events** can influence business activity. The attack on

**Research 'stunted by our culture of protest'**
Public opposition against high-technology and biotechnology companies has grown so strong that investors are no longer willing to support start-up companies involved in genetically modified products or those working on animals. This warning came after a survey by Grant Thornton, the business advisers. A spokesperson for the survey said that it was desperately trying to raise money in the UK for genetic modification or anything involving animals. Companies can't get enough funds and many of them are selling out to US companies. Huntingdon Life Sciences, an animal research laboratory, was forced to move its HQ to the US after intimidation by protesters.

**Flights cancelled because of strike in France**
In May 2003 travellers flying between Britain and France faced disruption to their journeys as a result of a strike by French air traffic controllers. British Airways, BMI, Ryanair, EasyJet and Aer Lingus were forced to cancel most of their flights to France. Passengers were promised refunds or free flights at a future date.

Source: adapted from the *Financial Times*, 27.5.2003.

(a) What is meant by the term 'external factors'?
(b) Identify the effects that they might have had in the above cases.

the Twin Towers in New York in 2001 and the military action against Iraq in 2003 affected a number of industries. There was a fall in the number of passengers travelling by air in many countries. This affected the aviation industry. There was also a fall in the number of holidaymakers which affected the tourist industry. It often takes many years for businesses to recover from such events. In some cases they may fail to survive and go bankrupt.

● Some individuals form **pressure groups** (☞ unit 102). For example, Transport 2000 is a pressure group that promotes ways of reducing the environmental and social impact of transport. It aims to reduce the use of cars and encourages individuals to use public transport, walk and cycle. If Transport 2000 is influential, the car industry is likely to be adversely affected.

● **Consumers' tastes** change. In recent years there has been an increase in demand for garden products. Gardens and gardening have been popularised by a number of television programmes on gardening. There has also been a rise in demand for vegetarian and vegan foodstuffs. Increasing numbers of people are opting for non-meat diets.

● Changes in **population** can affect the demand for products and the supply of workers. For example, the ageing of the population in the UK has meant increasing numbers of people aged 60 or over still looking for work. It has also given opportunities to businesses with products aimed at

this age groups, such as Saga holidays.

● Most businesses face **competition** from other firms. Rivals' activities often have an influence on their operations. Following the introduction of the National Lottery in the UK a number of firms in the gaming industry, such as Littlewoods the pools company and Ladbrokes the betting shop chain, suffered reductions in turnover.

● **Social factors** may influence business activity from time to time. For example, the roles of women in society have changed considerably in recent years. This has meant that more women have become involved in business management and business ownership. Some businesses have also been prepared to offer creche facilities as women have returned to work.

● **Environmental factors** have had a major effect on businesses in recent years. Some now use recycled materials in their manufacturing processes to reduce costs. Certain businesses have tried to manufacture products which are environmentally friendly in order to boost sales.

● **Legislation** and **regulation** may influence business activity. This may be in the form of government imposed laws, EU regulations, independent bodies set up by government to regulate industry or industry self-regulation.

## Satisfying needs and wants

The success of a business activity depends on many factors. The most important is to supply a product that consumers want to buy. Businesses must satisfy consumers' NEEDS and WANTS to be successful. People's needs are limited. They include things which are needed to survive, such as food, warmth, shelter and security. Humans also have psychological and emotional needs such as recognition and love. Wants, however are infinite. People constantly aim for a better quality of life, which might include better housing, better health care, better education, longer holidays, and more friends. Unit 9 deals with the way in which an economy attempts to satisfy people's needs.

## Markets

The **goods** and **services** produced by businesses are sold in MARKETS. A market exists when buyers and sellers communicate in order to exchange goods and services. In some cases buyers and sellers might meet at an agreed place to carry out the exchange. For example, many villages and towns have regular open air markets where buyers and sellers exchange goods and services. Also, buying and selling can be carried out over the telephone. For example, the First Direct banking facility allows customers to conduct nearly all of their banking business over the telephone. Buying and selling can also take place in shopping centres, in newspapers and magazines, through mail order, and more recently, through television and the Internet.

The goods and services of most businesses are bought by CUSTOMERS and used by CONSUMERS to satisfy their wants and needs. A business may be interested in some of the following markets.

- Consumer goods markets - where products like food, cosmetics and magazines are sold in large quantities.
- Markets for services - these are varied and could include services for individuals, such as banking, or services for industry, such as cleaning.
- Capital goods markets - where items used by other businesses are bought and sold, such as machinery.
- Labour markets - where people are hired for their services.
- The housing market - where people buy and sell properties.
- Money markets - where people and institutions borrow and lend money, such as commercial banks.
- Commodity markets - where raw materials such as copper and coffee are bought, mainly by business.

## Specialisation

One feature of modern businesses is SPECIALISATION. This is the production of a limited range of goods by an individual, firm, region or country. Specialisation can take place between firms. For example, McDonald's provides a limited range of fast foods, Ford manufactures cars, Heinz processes food products and MFI manufactures and sells

---

furniture products. Examples of regional specialisation might be Kidderminster, which specialises in carpet production, Stoke-on-Trent, which produces pottery and Kent, which is one of the country's main hop growers. Different countries also specialise. For example, it could be argued that Scotland specialises in the distilling of whisky, Saudi Arabia in oil extraction and South Africa in the supply of gold.

Specialisation within a firm is an important part of production. Departments specialise in different activities, such as marketing, purchasing, personnel and finance. People specialise in different tasks and skills. This is called the DIVISION OF LABOUR and allows people to concentrate on the task or skill at which they are best. In business, production is divided amongst workers, who each concentrate on a limited range of tasks. For example, the building of a house involves an architect to draw up the plans, a bricklayer to build the structure, a joiner to undertake woodwork, a roofer to lay the tiles etc. It is argued that the division of labour raises the productivity and efficiency of business and the economy. There is a number of reasons for this.

- Workers can concentrate on the tasks that they do best, leaving other tasks to more specialist workers.
- People's skills are improved by carrying out tasks over a long period of time. It is also possible to develop a brand new skill.
- Time is saved because workers are not constantly changing tasks, moving from one area to another or collecting new tools.
- The organisation of production becomes easier and more effective.

Specialisation, however, does have disadvantages.

- Work can become tedious and boring. This can result in poor worker motivation with the likelihood of a higher rate of absenteeism and increased staff turnover.
- Problems can also occur when one stage of production depends on another stage. If one stage breaks down, production might be halted.
- Over-specialisation can pose problems when there is a change in demand. If people are only competent in one skill they may have to retrain, causing delays in production. Some are not able to retrain and become unemployed.

## The importance of money

MONEY is anything which is generally accepted as a means of exchange. It is essential for the smooth exchange of goods and services in markets and helps specialisation.

Without money goods have to be exchanged using a BARTER SYSTEM. This involves swapping goods directly, which is inefficient. It is necessary for the wants of individuals to be perfectly matched. Searching for the perfect match in a barter deal can be very time consuming. It is also difficult to value different goods without money. In addition, giving change can be a problem when the values of the goods

---

Optos Retinal was set up by Douglas Anderson in Dunfermline in 1992. It produces retinal scanning machines. The business idea came to Douglas when he witnessed the shortcomings of eye-imaging tools after taking his young son for an eye examination. The examination process was distressing, requiring the patient to sit still for long periods with uncomfortable coloured eye drops. Anderson already owned an industrial design business and promptly instructed his design team to come up with a solution. The result was the Optomap Exam. This is a machine that uses two low-powered lasers to scan the retina at the back of the eye. It takes just a quarter of a second and does not use coloured eye drops. The images generated by the machine can be displayed instantly and sent by email to eye specialists for analysis.

So far, 630 of the machines have been installed and more than a million patients in Britain and America have benefited from the Optomap Exam. The machines are expensive, costing £70,000 each. However, Optos gives them to hospitals and surgeries and charges £25 each time they are used. In 2002 Optos was the fastest growing technology company in the country. Sales grew from £209,000 in 2000 to £3.7 million in 2002.

Source: adapted from *The Sunday Times*, 28.9.2003.

(a) Using the case as an example, explain what is meant by specialisation.
(b) Explain how Optos might benefit from specialisation.

being exchanged do not match exactly. Money also has a number of other functions. It:

- allows individuals to save some of their income and buy goods and services at a later date;
- enables all goods and services to be valued in common units, for example, a house which costs £60,000 is worth exactly 10 times more than a car which is valued at £6,000;
- allows payments to be deferred, ie goods can be bought and payment made at a later date.

There is no single definition of the money supply. No financial asset has all the characteristics or fulfils all the functions of money perfectly. In the UK, two measures tend to be used by the government. M0 is a 'narrow' measure. It includes notes and coins in circulation, cash in banks' tills and cash held for operational reasons at the Bank of England. M4 is a 'broad' measure. It includes M0 plus a wider range of financial assets. These include money held in bank accounts by the private sector and building society deposits. Cheques, debit cards and credit cards are not money. They are a means of transferring money from one account to another.

## Classification of business activity

Business activity is often classed by the type of production that takes place.

PRIMARY PRODUCTION includes activity which takes the natural resources from the earth, ie the extraction of raw materials and the growing of food. Mining, fishing, farming and forestry are examples of primary business activity. SECONDARY PRODUCTION involves manufacturing, processing and construction which transform raw materials into goods. Car production, distilling, baking, shipbuilding and office construction are examples of secondary sector activity. TERTIARY PRODUCTION includes the provision of services. Hairdressing, distribution, security, banking, theatre and tourism are all examples of business activity in this area. Other methods of classifying business include by:

- size (☞ unit 81);
- geographical area (☞ unit 88);
- sector (☞ units 6 and 7);
- ownership (☞ unit 6).

## What are the trends in business activity?

Business activity does not follow a constant pattern. Different industries grow and decline over time. In the UK some major changes have occurred in the structure of the economy. Before the Industrial Revolution most of the UK's resources were used for primary production. This included industries such as agriculture and mining. During the nineteenth century, secondary production expanded rapidly. The Industrial Revolution resulted in a growing quantity of resources being employed in manufacturing.

Figure 1.2 shows the numbers of males and females employed in manufacturing and services between 1978 and 2000.

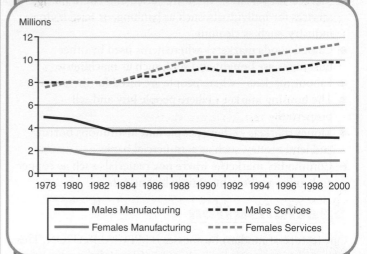

**Figure 1.2** *Employment in manufacturing and services by gender*

Source: adapted from Office for National Statistics.

(a) What evidence is there in the graph to suggest that de-industrialisation has continued throughout the period shown?

(b) Explain two possible reasons why retail services may have grown sharply in recent years.

**Question 4**

Over the last fifty years tertiary production has grown at the expense of secondary production. The decline in manufacturing is often called DE-INDUSTRIALISATION. The process of de-industrialisation has resulted in the decline of some once prosperous industries, such as shipbuilding, textiles, steel and engineering. Certain reasons have been put forward to explain the decline including:

● changes in consumer demand;
● a lack of competitiveness amongst UK manufacturers;
● increasing competition from overseas manufacturers;
● a lack of investment in manufacturing;
● trade union restrictive practices;
● unhelpful government policy.

In contrast, service industries now account for over 70 per cent of the UK's national incoome. Financial services, personal services, household services and the leisure industry are just some growth areas. For example, in the late 1990s and early 2000s the profile of the football industry was raised significantly. A number of clubs floated on the stock exchange and the amount of money flowing into the industry rose. Indeed, in 2003 a Russian billionaire took over Chelsea FC and injected millions of his own money into the club. Media interest increased, attendances at matches in the Premier League were high and commercial activities began to flourish.

The overall trend in business activity suggests a growth in services at the expense of primary and secondary production. Care needs to be taken when identifying trends from figures. For example, output in one particular service industry may be growing but employment figures may be falling. This could be because businesses in the industry are replacing workers with technology or are reorganising to reduce the workforce. However, employment figures do show clearly the changing patterns of business activity.

# key terms

**Barter system** - a system of exchange which involves the swapping of goods between individuals.

**Capital goods** - goods used to produce other goods, such as tools, equipment and machinery.

**Consumers** - individuals who use or 'consume' goods and services to satisfy their needs and wants.

**Consumer goods** - goods produced for general use by the public. They can be durable and non-durable.

**Customers** - individuals who buy goods and services supplied by businesses.

**De-industrialisation** - the decline in manufacturing.

**Division of labour** - specialisation in specific tasks or skills by individuals.

**Factors of production** - resources used by business to produce goods and services.

**Markets** - anywhere that buyers and sellers communicate to exchange goods and services.

**Money** - any substance which is generally accepted as a means of exchange.

**Needs** - human requirements which must be satisfied for survival.

**Primary production** - activities which involve the extraction of raw materials from the earth and the growing of food.

**Secondary production** - activities such as manufacturing which transform raw materials into finished goods.

**Specialisation** - in business, the production of a limited range of goods.

**System** - parts that work together to achieve an objective; a system can be a communications system, a business, an economic or a political system.

**Tertiary production** - activities which involve the provision of services.

**Wants** - human desires which are unlimited.

# Knowledge ...Knowledge...Knowledge...Knowledge...Knowledge...Know

1. What are the 4 factors of production?
2. What is the financial reward paid to each factor of production?
3. Why is capital said to be an artificial resource?
4. Describe 6 functions involved in business activity.
5. Why is business activity highly integrated?
6. Explain the difference between needs and wants.
7. What is the difference between capital and consumer goods?
8. What is meant by specialisation in business?
9. State:
   (a) 3 advantages of specialisation;
   (b) 3 disadvantages of specialisation.
10. Briefly describe the role of money in business.
11. List 10 business activities in your local town. State which of these are examples of:
    (a) primary production;
    (b) secondary production;
    (c) tertiary production.
12. What are the possible causes of de-industrialisation?

# Case study Eurocars

Sisters Gina and Toni Wilson grew up in a family that had been in the car trade for almost a century. From an early age they worked in vehicle rental, spare parts and car sales at their father's garage. After seeing the vehicle import business grow from 17,800 units in 1998 to 141,000 two years later, Gina decided to 'get a piece of the action'. She rented an office, employed one person and began importing cars from mainland Europe. Eurocars was born. After one year Gina took on her sister as sales director and appointed Stephen Hunt as managing director. Stephen was an expert at finding new cars at low prices.

The venture proved to be an immediate success. Indeed, the company expanded from their premises in Epsom, Surrey, where they had 25 cars on the forecourt, to an additional site in Cheam where they had 150 new cars and vans. They also had another 400 cars in stock in Britain and a further 1,000 in stock in mainland Europe.

The company concentrates on 'bread and butter' models rather than specialist or prestige cars. Customers are attracted by the low prices. They can save around £2,500 on the list price when buying from Eurocars. They are also reassured when they see that the cars are actually in stock. Eurocars used to sell cars to both dealers and individuals. However, they are now concentrating more on the retail trade because margins are higher.

The business is benefiting from a change in the law designed to increase competition in the sale of new cars. However, manufacturers are still trying to protect their own dealer outlets and do their best to thwart discounters such as Eurocars. For example, continental dealers often find it difficult to provide right-hand-drive UK-specification cars. 'Convertibles, for example, will be mysteriously delayed until after the summer is over', says Toni. Another problem faced by Eurocars is the amount of administration required when importing the cars. There are registration laws to deal with and payments for the cars have to be made in Euros. Also, Eurocars is vulnerable to tactical promotions used by the manufacturers' own dealers. For example, when a manufacturer announces a '£1,000 cash back' offer on a new car, it immediately affects Eurocars' business.

Source: adapted from *The Sunday Times*.

**(a) Is the business activity of Eurocars in the primary, secondary or tertiary sector? Explain your answer. (4 marks)**

**(b) Suggest examples of land, labour and capital that might be used by Eurocars. (6 marks)**

**(c) Explain:**
**(i) the type of market that Eurocars is operating in;**
**(ii) the types of customer it serves. (12 marks)**

**(d) To what extent is Eurocars affected by external factors? (18 marks)**

# 2 Starting a Business

## Setting up in business

What do ICI, Virgin, Starbucks, your nearest newsagent and the local window cleaner all have in common? At some time in the past, these businesses have been set up by their owners. Many, though not all, began as small operations. They are often started by entrepreneurs (☞ unit 3) working in a small shop or factory, or from home. Alan Sugar, the businessman behind Amstrad, started by convincing customers they really were buying the last television he had left in his flat. The Body Shop began as one retail outlet opened in Brighton by Anita Roddick, having previously sold her own cosmetics. According to Barclays Bank, 342,000 starts-up took place in 2001. This was down 15 per cent on the previous year, although slightly higher than in 1997-98.

There are certain steps involved in setting up a business. They are shown in Figure 2.1 and explained in this unit. They include deciding whether to set up in business, coming up with an idea, considering its success, planning the business, getting advice and finance, and then setting up and running the business.

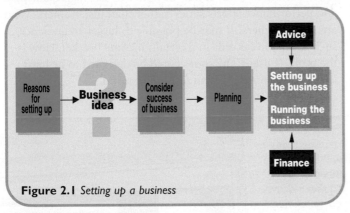

**Figure 2.1** Setting up a business

## Implications

What faces a person setting up their own business? He or she will come up against many problems and challenges. The way in which the entrepreneur works will probably be different to that of an employee. Take an example of a chef who has decided to 'go it alone' and open a cafe specialising in crepes and pancakes. At first, the chef would be uncertain about whether there is demand for this type of meal. Arguably this risk never goes away, but it is likely to be far greater at first until regular customers visit the cafe. The earnings of the chef are also likely to vary, depending on sales. Working for an employer, he would have earned a regular wage or salary.

The responsibility for the business would fall onto the owner. This means problems, from the non-delivery of ingredients to the placing of local adverts, will fall onto the chef. Even if employees are hired, the responsibility falls onto the owner. Many business people find that great personal commitment is needed. They must also be able to come up with new ideas and 'keep going' even if things get tough. This means the person must be single minded and self-sufficient.

Organisation of time is very important. He must decide what is to be done and place tasks in order of priority. He must also decide if the task can be done by someone else, ie what to **delegate.** Many people who set up in business talk about the lack of time to get things done. Working from 6am until midnight every night of the week is likely in the early stages. This places great stress on their personal and social life and their family and friends.

Entrepreneurs must also consider the skills they have and whether they are enough. Working for an employer may demand skill as a chef. This technical skill will be important to the cafe. However, the chef will also need management skills. These range from making sure that correct materials and equipment are available to having effective stock control. As workers are hired, the entrepreneur must develop personnel skills to control, motivate and organise the workforce. The owner will also need to sell himself and the company, a skill that is unlikely to be part of his role as an employee. Most people find that their technical skills are much greater than their managerial skills. It is often this lack of managerial skills which leads to problems. If a skill is needed which the entrepreneur does not have, he can:

- retrain, although there may be little time to attend a course and available courses are not always designed for specific needs;
- hire full time employees with the necessary skills;
- employ a specialist, such as an accountant, designer or market research agency, ideally for 'one off' tasks so that they do not become a full time cost;
- find a partner or take over another business. This is dealt with later.

## Reasons for setting up

Why do people set up in business?

- Independence. Some people prefer to make their own decisions and take responsibility rather than being told what to do.
- To increase rewards. People setting up their own business often believe that they will earn more than if they were working for an employer.
- As a result of redundancy. Some businesses start when an employee is made redundant and decides to use her skills in her own venture. **Redundancy payments** can be used to fund the business.
- Commitment to a product. A business may be set up to sell a new invention or because of commitment to a product. For example, James Dyson took five years and 5,127 prototypes before creating a working model of the best selling vacuum cleaner. 10 years later, after rejection by many companies, he produced the product under his own name.

- Sometimes people extend their hobbies into a business. A stamp collector may set up a small stall at local markets, for example.
- To satisfy creative needs. A worker on a production line packing biscuits may be artistic. Setting up a business to paint portraits may allow the individual to satisfy these needs.
- A person may want to work in a particular job, but can't find employment. Someone who has trained as a hairdresser or joiner may find that setting up their own business is the only alternative to being unemployed.
- An employee may be dissatisfied with their job. Setting up in business is one alternative to looking for a job with another firm.

## Getting a business idea

Anyone setting up a business must first have a business idea before they can begin. It might be a specialist shop selling items for a dolls house, a door to door hairdressing service or a company producing computers. The ideas for a business can come from many places.

- It might be an idea based on the existing skills the entrepreneur learned when doing another job.
- It might be an idea from a colleague at work or someone else in business.
- It might be an adaptation of an existing product where the entrepreneur thinks that they can do better.
- It might be a 'gap in the market' found by an entrepreneur that no other business is doing at the moment. For example, they might find that they need a product at home, but can't buy exactly what they need.
- It might be based on **market research** (☞ unit 19). It is unlikely that a new entrepreneur will have the finance to carry out detailed market research. However, simple research such as observation of customers entering a shop or a questionnaire given to a sample (☞ unit 35) of potential buyers might be possible.

## The chances of success

Many businesses that are set up fail within a few years. The Department for Trade and Industry has estimated that a quarter of all business start-ups fail within the first eighteen months and 35 per cent fail after five years. If a business is going to be a success, the entrepreneur must consider a number of factors. Any one of these factors may be important. The Showering family made fine cider at a good profit in Somerset. When they produced a high quality drink from pears, in a champagne-like bottle, and called it Babycham, they became millionaires.

Take an example of someone aiming to produce and sell training shoes. There is a number of questions that may help to make this idea into a success.

**The basic business idea** What business is the person entering and what will be sold? It may be better to sell 'high quality and performance sports shoes' rather than just 'trainers'. Who are the customers? It may be possible to target an audience, such as 25-35 year olds in a certain income bracket. How is the product used? The shoes could be designed to be hard wearing for sports, or with fashion in mind.

---

Philip Barthelemy runs a web-based Internet site, LocalLiberty.com, which allows members to exchange their DVDs and video games on a face to face and legal basis. Philip was sitting in a friend's flat one wet New Years Day, looking at his DVD collection. There were over 50 DVDs, most of which had been played only once or twice. His friend had all these DVDs, but could not make use of them. So Philip thought 'why not make use of this capital?'

People are increasingly building up DVD and video games collections. Most are played only a few times and not used again. They could be exchanged with others, so that people can then spend their money on different items. This gives them more choice. Philip argues that it also allows people to meet new acquaintances and make new friends.

Philip stopped work in his job at the end of 2002 to concentrate on his business. He estimates that he works on average 60 hours a week, which is closer to 80 at peak periods. He argues 'you have to organise your day differently' and 'get out of the comfort zone'.

Philip mainly works from home to keep costs down at the start. At the moment it's just him in the business. But this could change in future. He outsources all his main key tasks.

This wasn't Philip's first business idea. But it is the first he has been comfortable with. The business needed an initial investment to start it and funding to research the idea And it would need extra funding until money comes in regularly.

Philip also realises that he will have to be flexible to squeeze down costs as much as possible at the beginning. Philip suggests that companies like Napster and eBay had inspired him. They had been successful companies that had set up for Internet trading. It is likely that much of the work he puts in at the beginning will not be remunerated. But this is only to be expected, Philip believes.

Source: adapted from startups.co.uk.

(a) Identify the ways in which Philip got ideas for his business.
(b) Explain the implications for Philip of starting his own business.

**Question 1**

**Finding out about the market** How many products exist already? Customers may prefer other types of shoes for fashion wear or a different type of design. What are the strengths and weaknesses of the competition? It may be possible to find a gap in the market, such as trainers that can be used for hiking, water sports or with a special design feature, such as a cut away back with flexible material.

It may possible to find out about the market using market research techniques (☞ unit 19). This might be through:

● desk or secondary research to find information already gathered for another purpose. An example could be looking at a Mintel report on a particular market;

● field or primary research to gather material for a specific reason which is not collected elsewhere. An example might be a questionnaire given to possible customers.

Small or new businesses may have a restricted budget. They might only be able to carry out a small survey of their own or have limited funds to hire a market research company.

**Marketing and promotion** What price can be charged? It may be possible to undercut competitors' prices or sell initially at less than unit cost (☞ unit 26) until the product begins to sell well. Can the business compete in some other way, such as advertising? American advertisers argue that every product has a **unique selling point** or **proposition** (USP) (☞ unit 22). The business could identify this and promote it. For example, the trainers may be 'comfortable, but robust'. How will the product be sold? The producer may sell through a retailer, representative or direct to the public, for example.

Small or new businesses might have a limited budget to spend on marketing and promotion. They might decide to find relatively cheaper ways of promoting products, such as:

● advertising in local magazines and newspapers, adding their names to trade directories, sending out leaflets by direct mail, offering discounts at first to build loyalty, and setting up an Internet website;

rather than more expensive methods such as:

● advertising on television, using national magazines or publications with glossy advertisements, making use of large national advertising agencies or advertising abroad.

**People** What are the main skills needed to run the business? What skills are needed to manufacture the product? The sports shoe manufacturer may need the skills of a designer or perhaps a sports scientist before production can begin. How workers can be attracted and retained in the business must also be considered. How much do you know about legislation regarding employment? The entrepreneur will have to take into account the health and safety of employees, for example.

**Finance** How much money is needed to start up? The business person will need to work out the costs of setting up, eg rent and rates, wages, machinery, sales and distribution costs and professional fees. How much is available to invest? The business person may have savings or insurance policies which can be

Monoli spent a number years working in the insurance industry. Then she decided to act on her friends' advice and set up a restaurant in London. Friends were always telling her that she should cook for a living. They were particularly impressed with the unusual desserts and cakes which she served.

Monoli did a food hygiene and a licence trader's course when she decided to set up. Most of the funding came from herself and a non-active business partner. She attributed her success to 'common sense along with creativity in the kitchen'. However, she also argues that years of dealing with customer claims has also given her a great insight into meeting consumer needs and the single most important thing is 'the personal touch - being flexible and accommodating'. She also argues that when starting your own business you need 'an unshakeable belief in what you're aiming to do and 100 per cent commitment'. This is shown in the 80-90 hour week which she works.

The business is doing very well at the moment. There's a two week waiting list for a table on Thursdays, Fridays and Saturdays. The business offers an early evening theatre menu at reduced prices, which has proved very popular.

Customers have asked Monoli if she is going to set up another branch of the restaurant. She is considering this for the future and has asked her business partner if he wants to put more money into the business. She feels that it might take a long time before another restaurant is profitable. And can she find people with the flair to make her desserts in exactly the style of her current restaurant?

Source: adapted in part from startups.co.uk.

(a) Examine the factors that might influence the success of this business.

**Question 2**

used. According to HSBC only 50 per cent of businesses borrow from a bank. Many people use redundancy cheques or sell their house to raise finance. Over and above the initial investment, how much more will be required before cash flows into the business? The sports shoe manufacturer may have orders but no cash flowing in until goods are sold. In the meantime, bills must still be paid. Often an overdraft is negotiated with the bank to see the business through this period. What other sources of finance can be used? According to the Bank of England trade credit is twice as important as bank loans as a source of finance. If the entrepreneur approaches a third party to fund start up costs, control may be lost.

**The product or service offered** Is the product or service ready for sale? If not, how far has it been developed? It is unlikely that the sports shoe manufacturer will find a backer for the business if the idea has not yet been developed. Is the product idea safe? It may be possible to protect the idea by PATENT or COPYRIGHT before production takes place (☞ unit 87). A patent aims to protect the inventor of a new product or process. A business may apply to the Patent Office to obtain a patent. It allows a business to design, produce and sell an invention for a number of years free from competition. During this period, the invention cannot be copied by competitors.

**Is production cost effective?** The manufacturer may want to consider the way the shoe is produced, the location of production, how production is organised and the materials used. Each of these will affect the cost and speed of production.

**Risk, timescale and cost** What are the main risks involved in the venture? How can they be reduced? The producer may try the product on a small scale basis before trading or work part time while still employed to reduce risk.

# Planning

Although there are examples of businesses that just 'set up and prosper', these are limited. Most firms must plan carefully what they aim to achieve and how to do it. Answering the question 'what might make a business successful?' will help a business to produce a BUSINESS PLAN. This is a statement that outlines the way that the business will achieve its aims and objectives (☞ unit 4).

An established business may produce a business plan to show how it will obtain the funds to pay back a loan for a new piece of machinery. For a business starting up, a business plan is vital. It can be used to:

● give a clear idea of its direction and operation;
● show a bank or other institution its likely position and its ability to pay back a loan;
● identify problems that may occur to allow the business to deal with them before they can become a problem;
● highlight its strengths and weaknesses.

What is included in a business plan? Table 2.1 shows the details that might appear in the plan of a business aiming to produce and sell specialist cycle equipment.

# Getting advice

There is a variety of organisations that provide help and advice for new businesses. They range from those set up by government or private organisations to individuals with

---

Look at Figure 2.2 which shows part of a business plan of a small business selling signed and numbered limited edition artists' etchings, greetings cards and picture frames.

**Figure 2.2**

**c  Major competitors - their prices, strengths and weaknesses:**
Major competition is from 'Anystore' which has a well-known prints department, but this helps more often than not, as customers are drawn to the area and the small print gallery is cheaper.
Other competition is from all of the other shops selling gift items, but again they draw custom into the area.
Strengths of the small print gallery are:
Something for everyone at any price level. Once it is bought people cannot tell how much it costs.
Numbered handmade prints are exclusive and special, and possibly an investment for the future.
Weaknesses of the competition are that they are more expensive and less flexible. Jewellers, for instance have nothing under £18.00.

Source: *The Business Start-up Guide,* NatWest Bank.

(a) Explain how competition can:
(i) help;
(ii) harm;
the business.
(b) If an entrepreneur was applying for a loan, why might a bank manager be interested in this information?

---

**Table 2.1**

| Features | What is included | Examples |
|---|---|---|
| **The business** | Name and address of the business<br>What the business aims to achieve<br>Type of organisation | Cross-Hatchard Partnership |
| **The product or service** | What is being produced<br>What quantities will be produced<br>The proposed price | Specialist cycles<br>Average price £300 |
| **The market** | Results of research or testing<br>The size of the market<br>If the market is growing or not<br>Who will buy the product<br>Competition and their strengths and weaknesses<br>Methods of promotion and advertising | Growing demand for mountain cycles, racing cycles etc.<br>Advertising in trade journals. |
| **Personnel** | Who is involved in the business<br>What experience and skills people have | Former Raleigh workers |
| **Buying and production** | Likely costs of production<br>Who the main suppliers are<br>What benefits suppliers have | Production costs £30,000 |
| **Premises and equipment** | The type of premises<br>Location of premises and cost<br>Age, style and value of machinery<br>Replacement cost of machinery<br>How to cope with expansion | Produced on industrial estate site |
| **Profit** | Likely profit based on:<br>  * turnover (price x sales)<br>  * costs<br>Break even point. This is the quantity sold where turnover is equal to costs | Total costs = £55,000<br>At £300 need to sell 183 to break even |
| **Cash flow** | When cash will come in<br>When cash will go out<br>If payments will be cash or credit<br>Difference between cash in and cash out each month | Payment by cash and credit |
| **Finance** | How much cash owners will put in<br>How much will have to be borrowed<br>What money is needed for<br>How much borrowing will cost<br>What assets can be used as security<br>How long borrowing will be for and when it will be paid back | £5,000 put in by each of the partners |

certain skills. Advice may be in the form of:
- a telephone number, email or Internet site of a specialist who can help;
- a detailed discussion or interview on the best way to set up or run a business;
- telephone numbers, addresses or Internet sites of organisations providing funds;
- training videos or seminars;
- specialist information on markets and types of business. Where can an entrepreneur obtain help?

**Individuals** It may be possible to get advice from people who have started their own business and have been through the process of setting up. They may be able to point out what they did right or wrong and how they might do things differently. Advice about specific skills needed for running a business might come from:
- an accountant - who can give advice on accounts, book-keeping, taxation;
- a solicitor - who can give advice on the legal requirements of the business;
- an insurance adviser - who can give advice on how to protect and cover such things as equipment and employees.

**Banks** All of the main commercial banks provide advice for potential business people. This ranges from information about sources of finance to helping to draw up a business plan. An adviser can help to find out whether the business is entitled to a government or EU grant. Many banks produce folders or publications with details and guidance on setting up in business. Some also run Internet websites giving advice on how to set up.

**Government advice** The Department of Trade and Industry's (DTI) Small Business Service runs a number of initiatives aimed at helping businesses set up and small businesses that are operating. Examples include:
- Business Bridge, which provides forums where owner managers can meet and discuss problems;
- Young Enterprise, which runs business education programmes for young people;
- The Ethnic Minority Business Forum, which advises ministers on helping ethnic minority businesses;
- The Farm Business Advice Service, which offers free advice to help farm businesses grow;
- The Small Business Research Initiative, which encourages smaller businesses to participate in government research contracts;
- Enterprise Areas, which provide the focus for policies and actions to develop enterprise in deprived communities;
- a document *Tendering for Government Contracts*, which advises small businesses on finding and bidding for public sector work;
- a network of Local Business Partnerships around the country, which enables businesses and local authorities to work together to streamline regulations.

A government Small Firms Minister is responsible for promoting small business in Parliament. Government is also responsible for the provision of UK and EU funding to businesses. This is covered in the next section.

**Business Links** The DTI also manages the network of Business Links throughout the UK. Local Business Links in areas of the UK provide support, advice and guidance on a wide range of areas for businesses aiming to start up. These include advice on:
- how to set up a business and prepare a business plan;
- getting government funds and other finance;
- tax;
- employment requirements;
- legislation;
- managing the business, including sales, IT, importing and exporting, and financial control.

**Enterprise agencies** These were created by government specifically to help small and growing businesses. There is a network of local agencies throughout the UK. Most offer free advice on how to set up and run a business, training courses, contacts and information on potential investors.

**Chambers of Commerce** The British Chambers of Commerce are made up of local Chambers of Commerce. These are local, independent, non-profit making organisations funded by subscriptions from members which are businesses. Help given to small and growing businesses include training, information, networking with other businesses and help with suppliers of pensions, healthcare and legal protection.

**The Prince's Trust** The Prince's Trust offers support for 18-30 year olds who want to improve their career and prospects. It can provide training and advice or help in the form of a volunteer mentor to young people starting up in business. Sometimes it also provides funds, such as low interest loans or test marketing grants.

**Shell LiveWire** This is a scheme run by Shell to encourage people aged 16-30 to develop their business. It offers grants and advice. It also runs a competition, 'Young Business Start Up Awards', which gives £10,000 to the best business start up each year.

**Business clubs** The National Association of Business Clubs and Societies has clubs throughout the UK. They are made up from businesses in the local area, although there are many clubs that are not part of the Association which still offer help. Clubs can be based on one business area or a local area. Sometimes speakers, such as Inland Revenue inspectors, will be invited to talk at meetings about tax or grants. A list of members is available and businesses who are members provide help and advice to each other. A certain amount of inter-trading also takes place. This helps new businesses to make contacts and removes some of the risk when first trading.

**Federation of Small Businesses** This represents the interests of small businesses in the UK. It offers discounted schemes for insurance, medical care, financial services, Internet design and banking to its members.

**Trade Associations** Examples include The Wool Marketing Board, The Association of British Travel Agents and The Booksellers' Association. They provide information about certain types of business or industry.

**Internet websites** Many of the organisations mentioned above have websites which provide advice and guidance on starting a new business or running an existing business. Other organisations which provide help on the Internet include newbusiness.co.uk and virginbiz.net.

## Finance

Where do new businesses find the finance that is needed to buy materials, pay wages etc? Funds can come from a number of sources.

- Personal savings or past earnings. A person aiming to set up a business in the future may have saved for some years or a redundant employee can use payments made when they became unemployed.
- Funds from partners or investors. A partnership can obtain finance from all partners, even if some are not actively involved in the business. Limited companies can raise large amounts of finance. Investors buy a 'share' of the company by purchasing shares. This is then used to finance business activity and the shareholders are paid with a dividend as a reward.
- It is possible to buy machinery and equipment and pay for it at a later date or over a period of time. Businesses may allow components or materials to be bought on CREDIT SALE or HIRE PURCHASE, where the goods are used and the cost is paid over time, plus interest. Businesses often sell goods and are paid at a later date (30, 60 or 90 days). This is known as trade credit.
- A business may decide to lease or hire equipment from a hire company. A small construction firm, for example, may hire scaffolding for a large building rather than buy their own which they might not use all the time.
- Banks or other financial institutions. Banks offer loan and overdraft facilities and charge interest. Services such as business accounts, insurance and salary payments are also available. They may be free for a time if the business remains in credit. Banks often ask for security against a loan. This can be any assets owned by the business or perhaps the house of the owner. Banks also need convincing that the loan is secure. They will ask for a

business plan, references or proof of trading in the past. Loans can be in many forms. Some allow only the interest to be paid off in the first one or two years. It may also be possible to use a mortgage to buy premises.

- Help from organisations. Businesses starting up have been able to obtain funds from various organisations, as explained in the previous section.
- Government funds. Government funds are available for businesses locating in particular areas of the country (☞ unit 88). The government also runs a **small firms loan guarantee scheme**. This allows small firms starting up or which do not have a track record to borrow. Banks lend the money and government guarantees part of the loan. Loans guaranteed are from £5,000-£100,000 for new businesses and up to £250,000 for businesses over two years old. In 2002 the average loan was £60,000.
- EU funds. A variety of funds is available from the European Union, particularly for businesses setting up in areas with

---

Omar Samaha thought his experience in the restaurant trade as head waiter would be of great help when he set up his own business, Fresco. However, he underestimated the problems of obtaining finance. He scraped together some of his own money to take over the lease on a cafe in Westbourne Grove. But his bank would not offer him any money at first without any personal assets. So Omar put together a business plan and eventually the bank was persuaded to loan him £3,000. He was also able to obtain an overdraft of £3,000 when the bank turned down a further loan a short time after starting up.

A year later Fresco was doing well. Omar wanted to open a restaurant to capture evening trade in the way that Fresco did in the day. His partner put in £25,000, but banks were reluctant to lend him the other £25,000 he needed for the venture. They were unwilling to use the lease on Fresco as security because it was for less than 25 years. Omar pointed out that the banks seemed to focus only on his first six months when making a decision about loans, rather than the more impressive figures that the business achieved later. To secure the loan, Omar would have to remortgage his personal property with the bank. But changing lenders would cost him £5,000. The deal fell through and Omar had to pay £1,000 in solicitors' fees.

But this failed to dampen his enthusiasm for the idea of a new restaurant. The property boom meant that his flat had appreciated in value. Omar was able to remortgage and borrow on the strength of this. His latest venture is the Fresco Juice Bar in Whiteleys Shopping Centre, London. Having a successful business plan and years of profitable accounts is likely to make it far easier to obtain funds.

Source: adapted from startups.co.uk.

(a) Identify the sources of finance mentioned above.
(b) Explain the problems that the business faced with each source of finance.

 **Question 4**

problems. Grants are available in areas such as job creation, investment, energy conservation, new buildings, research into new markets and innovation.

● Business angels (☞ unit 44). The European Business Angels Network estimates there are around 125,000 investors in the UK, with an investment pool of around 3,000 million euros. Investment in businesses varies between 25,000 euros and 250,000 euros.

● Venture capitalists (☞ unit 44). These are organisations which provide funds for small and medium sized businesses with potential.

● Certain industries can sometimes offer funds for businesses. Examples have included British Coal Enterprise giving low-interest loans to firms thinking of locating in coal mining areas and similar offers from the British steel industry.

## How to set up

A business person must decide what form the new business will take. What alternatives are available?

**Setting up a new business alone** Perhaps the simplest way of starting a business is to set up alone. There are certain advantages and problems of being a sole trader (☞ unit 6). There are few legal requirements and trading can begin straight away. However, the owner will have to take all the responsibility and bear all costs.

**Setting up with others** One way of avoiding the problems of a sole trader is to set up with others. A partnership would allow the business person to share the load of running the business and to raise more finance, without the demands of becoming a limited company. It is, of course, possible to start business as a limited company. This may be likely if a business is to be run as a family concern (a private limited company), or if a great deal of finances was needed because of the scale of the operation (a public limited company). Limited companies are dealt with in unit 6.

**Buying a business** A potential business person may be able to buy an existing business. There are many examples of this. An electrician made redundant from a large public limited company may 'buy out' a local retailer selling electrical goods who wants to retire. Managers, shareholders or directors may wish to leave one company and buy out the interests of another. In some cases the managers of a company may try to buy the business from the shareholders because they feel the company can be run better. This is an example of a management buy-out (☞ unit 89). It is also possible for a worker buy out to take place, where workers buy out the shareholders of a business.

**Buying a franchise** A business could set up as part of a franchise (☞ unit 6). Franchises are designed to allow new businesses with little experience and limited finance to set up. The new business (the franchisee) buys the rights to use the name and sell the product of a well established business (the franchisor) for a fee. This reduces the risk for the new business. It also allows the new business to get help and guidance when it first operates.

**Licensing** This is similar to franchising. It is where a business sells the rights to use its copyright or patent on a product to another business. It may allow a business to produce its product. For example, Dyson earned 5 per cent for allowing USA producers to manufacture its vacuum cleaners under the names Fantom, Fury and Lightning. A business may also allow others to use its company name and logo. Coca-Cola does this in many countries worldwide, for example. This allows a business to earn revenue, without any any extra cost. A problem might be if the license is given to a poor producer or poor selling product which could affect the reputation of the business selling the licence.

## Running a business

When a business is set up, there are legal and operational tasks that must be carried out.

**Keeping records** All transactions which take place must be recorded. This includes all sales of goods or services, the purchase of all materials, equipment and the payment of all bills for heating, lighting, wages, transport etc. This information can be used to show how well the business is performing. There are also certain records that some businesses must keep by law. For example, a company must produce a profit and loss account (☞ unit 42).

**The use of documents** When goods and services are bought and sold, a number of documents are used. They provide evidence and records of the transactions that have taken place. Some documents that might be used include:

● an invoice - a document sent with goods sold on trade credit, informing the purchaser that payment is due on a certain date;

● a cash receipt - a proof of purchase given when something is paid for in cash;

● a credit note - a document issued to a purchaser when they have overpaid, allowing 'credit' on future payments;

● proof of delivery - proof that items have been delivered and received at a certain destination.

If a business person employs workers, they will be given a contract of employment (☞ unit 66). This shows the terms under which the employee is hired and with which they must conform. Employees also need to be provided with wages or salary slips, showing their total earnings and any deductions.

The larger the business becomes, the more documents it is likely to use. Examples of documents that may be used internally include memos from, say, the production manager to the marketing manager, or agendas for meetings to discuss a new promotional campaign.

**Tax and insurance** Part of any revenue earned by a business must be paid to the government.

- Taxation. Profits made by a business are liable for tax. Government policy (☞ units 97 and 105) has tried to reduce the corporation tax and income tax paid by businesses in the last decade to encourage growth and development. Businesses can claim allowances, which will reduce the amount of tax paid.

- Value Added Tax (VAT). Businesses must pay VAT on any goods they sell. Usually, they add this on to the price of a good or service. Some products in the UK are exempt from VAT, including children's clothing, food and books. A business will have VAT placed onto the cost of materials, components and other items they buy.

- National Insurance contributions. Employers must make NATIONAL INSURANCE CONTRIBUTIONS to the government and must also remove employees' contributions from their wages.

- Businesses will pay business rates to the local authority. This is a tax on the percentage value of any building owned by the business.

- Insurance. It is sensible for an entrepreneur to insure against damages and theft. If production ceases for any reason, this could be a major problem for a new business. Revenue will not be earned and there may be cash flow problems (☞ unit 46) or the business may not be able to afford the immediate cost of repairing or replacing a piece of machinery. Some insurance is required by law. All businesses must have public liability, in case a customer or visitor to the premises is injured and makes a claim.

## key terms

**Business plan** - a statement made by a business, outlining the way it will attempt to achieve its objectives.

**Copyright** - the ownership of material such as books and films which is protected by law from re-use without permission.

**Hire purchase/credit sale** - methods used to buy goods now and pay off the balance over a period of time. In the case of the former, the goods only belong to the buyer when the final payment is made.

**National Insurance contributions** - payments made by employees and employers to the government as a form of insurance premium.

**Patent** - a licence which prevents the copying of an idea.

## Knowledge ...Knowledge...Knowledge...Knowledge...Knowledge...Know

1. Give 6 reasons why people set up in business.
2. Briefly explain the likely changes an employee may find in their work if they become a business owner.
3. Where might a business idea come from?
4. What questions about:
   (a) the market;
   (b) finance;
   might a business person ask when starting a business?
5. How might a small business use a business plan?
6. List 6 aspects of a business plan.

7. What help and finance might:
   (a) Business Link;
   (b) The Department of Trade and Industry;
   (c) a commercial bank;
   provide for a small business?
8. Why might a business club be particularly useful for a small new business?
9. Why might a business need to use documents?

# Case study PhotoArtistry

Anne Herbert was asked by other artists so many times to print their work on her large format digital printer that she decided to set up a fine art printing business. She says fine art was 'more of a hobby at first that developed into a business'. The idea of flexibility and financial freedom, however, was appealing. Anne has been inspired by women of courage such as Anita Roddick. She is an avid reader of the business pages in Sunday magazines, particularly 'how people made it' stories. It wasn't Anne's first business idea. She had worked as a jewellery designer and wanted to design costume jewellery. But she did not have the money to start the business.

After taking a BA in fine art Anne bought a printer to print her own work costing £10,000. She was working for a computer security firm and decided to set up a website to see if other artists would be interested in having their own work printed. This would help her to pay for the printer. 95 per cent of orders were taken online. The website was also used to establish leads. A free print offer was given to attract customers to the service. The website cost £1,500 to set up. All the initial spending was self-funded. She has also bought other equipment, such as a machine to laminate prints, and computers to help the printing process as the business has grown and made profit.

So why does Anne think there is a market for her work? She argues that the 'market found her'. She initially only offered a large printing service. Then people asked her to print on canvas and stretch prints onto frames, so she added those services. But she still has to do the practical business stuff, such as registering the business and registering for VAT. She also has to work a 60-70 hour week, like many people starting and running their own business. Anne does a lot of the work herself. She has an accountant and a friend with marketing experience who works full time. Anne admits she knows little about things such as payroll, but is willing to learn.

Research has also been important. Anne says that she needed to know her market and her main competitors. She was looking to differentiate her products and give a unique USP. Computer packages are used to work out break-even points, costs and quantities required of the services offered. This helps to determine prices.

Anne spent time talking to friends before starting the business and to a person from Business Link, who has acted as a sort of mentor. Business Link was useful in helping her to write her business plan. It has never been used to apply for a bank loan, but has been used as a guide for the business. She took an MBA course at the Open University which gave her grounding in basic business principles. She is also aware of courses run by the Inland Revenue.

Apart from the website, other promotion is in the form of glossy brochures printed. A small stand was also taken at an NEC exhibition in Birmingham. But most of the promotion Anne suggests is by word of mouth.

Anne initially worked from home and ran the business as well as holding down a full time job. She was made redundant in May 2003. And she decided her home was getting too small to handle large canvas printing. She now works in an office/warehouse space of 1,500 square feet which is 10 minutes from where she lives.

Source: adapted from startups.co.uk.

(a) Using examples from the cases, explain what is meant by the terms:
  (i) Business Link;
  (ii) USP. (6 marks)
(b) Identify the ways in which PhotoArtistry has obtained:
  (i) finance;
  (ii) advice. (6 marks)
(c) Explain the reasons why Anne Herbert set up her business. (8 marks)
(d) Examine the factors that are likely to affect the success of the business. (10 marks)
(e) Evaluate how successful the business might be in the future. (10 marks)

# 3 Business Stakeholders

## Who is involved in business activity?

Various groups of people have an interest in business. Such groups are referred to as STAKEHOLDERS. The interest each stakeholder has in a business will vary according to the nature of their 'stake'. Figure 3.1 shows possible stakeholders that can be identified in business activity. They include:

- owners or shareholders;
- managers;
- employees;
- customers;
- government;
- suppliers;
- the community.

It could be argued that owners, managers and employees are internal stakeholders as members of the business organisation. The remainder could be seen as external stakeholders because they are not part of the business. However, there are likely to be exceptions to this. For example, some members of the community may be employees or shareholders.

Some stakeholders may have more than one interest in the business. An employee might also be a shareholder. Managers will be employees of the business. A customer might be a member of the local community.

Stakeholders in business will usually benefit from their involvement with the organisation. Employees will earn money which they can spend on goods and services. Customers will consume the goods and services supplied by the business and the government will collect tax from the organisation.

## Owners

A business is the property of its owner or owners. The owner of a van can use it to earn income by hiring it out. The owner of jewellery can wait for its value to increase and then sell it. It is possible for the owners of a business to do these things as well.

Not all owners are the same. The owner of a small business, such as a small retail outlet selling watches, may be the only person in the business. The owner would make all of the decisions, possibly use personal finance to start the firm and carry out all tasks, such as selling, ordering stock and recording transactions. In very large companies there can be thousands of joint owners. They all own **shares** (☞ units 6 and 44) in the company. This entitles them to a share in the profit, known as a DIVIDEND and a vote each year to elect the DIRECTORS of the company. Examples of shareholders might be David Whelan, the Chairman of JJB Sports plc, who it was reported owned nearly 40 per cent of its shares in 2003, or the people all over the UK who own shares in ICI or BT. The involvement of shareholders in the business will depend, perhaps, on their position in the business and the amount of money invested in it. Figure 3.2 shows a summary of the different types of business owner.

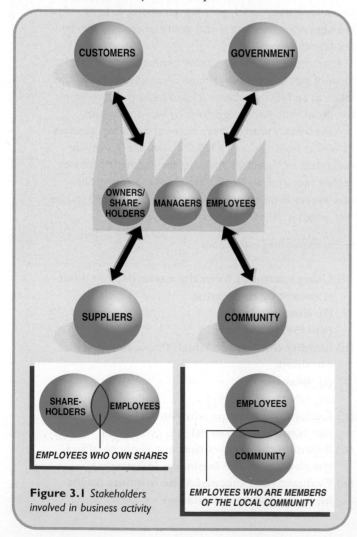

**Figure 3.1** *Stakeholders involved in business activity*

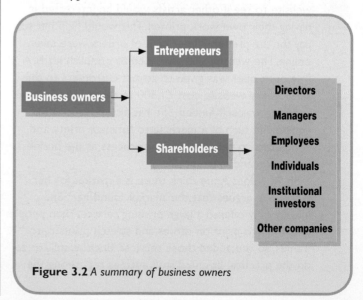

**Figure 3.2** *A summary of business owners*

# The entrepreneur

Unit 1 showed that **enterprise** was a **factor of production.** Arguably, it is the most important. Without an entrepreneur to organise the land, labour and capital, business activity would not take place. What is an entrepreneur? People who have this role usually perform three functions in business.

**Innovation** Business activity usually begins with the entrepreneur having a business idea. The entrepreneur could be said to be innovative. He or she is forming a new business where one did not exist before. When Anita Roddick opened the first Body Shop in March 1976 in Brighton, she created a new business idea of her own. This was to sell toiletries and cosmetics with conservation, the environment and animal rights in mind. Even when ideas are copied or adapted, it could be argued that the entrepreneur is being innovative. The creation of a business producing a vacuum cleaner which does not use dust bags by James Dyson may be said to be innovative. The British inventor Trevor Baylis was arguably innovative in creating a clockwork radio which could be wound up to work, rather than using electricity.

**Organisation** Land, labour and capital are hired by the entrepreneur and organised to produce goods or services. Decisions about the location of the premises, the method of production, product design, prices and wages are often made by the entrepreneur. If the business grows, it is likely that some of these tasks may be passed down to others.

**Risk taking** Setting up a business is risky. Money has to be paid out in advance to buy materials, business premises, equipment and pay wages. The entrepreneur may use some personal money to meet these costs. There is no guarantee that the final product or service will be sold. If goods are unsold then the entrepreneur will have to suffer this loss. It is not possible to insure against **unquantifiable** risks such as these, so the entrepreneur bears all the costs of failure.

The type of people who become entrepreneurs is extremely varied. Some, like Richard Branson, start businesses when they are young and help them to grow. Some people extend their hobbies to a business situation, some leave their jobs voluntarily to start a business, some use redundancy money to set up and some inherit businesses.

Entrepreneurs often tend to be associated with small firms. This is because the entrepreneur will face risk and will control all aspects of the business activity. Many small businesses do become large businesses and thus the role of the entrepreneur may well change. In large business organisations many people bear the risk, are innovative and are responsible for control. Someone such as Rupert Murdoch, the Chairman of BSkyB and News Corporation which owns *The Times* and *The Sun*, is arguably an example of an entrepreneur in a large company.

In November 2002, Stelios Haji-Ioannou stepped down as chairman of easyJet, the company that came from nowhere to become Europe's biggest discount airline in five years. Richard Branson paid tribute to him, saying 'Millions of people who could not afford to travel before are now travelling and he has done it with great style and panache'.

Mr Haji-Ioannou, son of a Greek millionaire, set up easyJet at Luton Airport in 1995. He leased two Boeing 737s and offered flights to Edinburgh for £29. In November 2002 easyJet was valued at more than £1 billion, reporting profits of £71.6 million for the year. Mr Haji-Ioannou said that he was standing down to devote more time to his other ventures. He announced plans to create new 'easy' companies, including a 'no-frills' cinema chain and a minibus service between London and other major cities in England. These new businesses are on top of the easy car-hire business and the Internet café business already up and running.

The new chairman at easyJet is Sir Colin Chandler, someone with a more traditional business background. Mr Haji-Ioannou reverted to his 'serial entrepreneur' roots. The qualities needed to run a big public company and get a company off the ground are very different.

The first easyCinema opened in Milton Keynes in May 2003. It replaces the first multiplex cinema, the Point, which opened with 10 screens in 1985. Mr Haji-Iaonnou was attracted to the industry by the 20 per cent occupancy rate. This means that only 1 in 5 seats are ever sold in cinemas. He planned to charge as little as 20p for some seats during the very quiet periods.

Source: adapted from *The Guardian* 26.11.2002 and 16.5.2003.

(a) Explain why Stelios Haji-Ioannou is an entrepreneur.
(b) Suggest why Stelios Haji-Ioannou stepped down as chairman from the successful easyJet company that he created.

# Type of shareholder

Certain types of business do not have shareholders, such as sole traders and partnerships. Limited companies can raise money by issuing shares (☞ unit 6). Shareholders become the 'joint owners' of the business. The shareholder or group of shareholders with the majority of shares, ie 51 per cent, will be the majority shareholder in the business. Examples of these shareholders are shown in Figure 3.2.

**Directors** Directors are elected by the shareholders each year and are responsible for running the business. They do not have to hold shares in the companies they run, but generally they do. Some directors have quite large shareholdings, sometimes large enough to exert control, such as in a family business. Some businesses have **worker directors**. In Germany and in some UK companies worker directors are workers that are co-opted onto the board of directors to represent the views of the workforce. The term can also sometimes be used to describe workers in a business owned largely by employees with shares, that also run the business.

**Managers** Managers are usually appointed by directors and are actively involved in running the business. Some managers own shares in their companies, but they do not have to. Sometimes they are allowed to buy shares or are given shares as a bonus. It is argued that if managers own shares in the company it might motivate them to perform well in their jobs. This is because if they perform well, profits may be higher and higher dividends can then be paid to shareholders like themselves.

**Employees** An increasing number of employees now own shares in companies. In the twenty years before 2000, shares in privatised industries (☞ unit 7) were made available to the workforce and the public as previously state owned industries became part of the private sector. In 2000, over 90 out of the FTSE 100 companies offered share as you earn schemes (☞ unit 60). Companies have also offered shares to employees as bonuses. Sainsbury's is an example of one company which has done this. It is unlikely that employees will own enough shares to have any control in the running of the business. However, it may motivate (☞ unit 59) workers to take an interest in the company.

**Individuals** It is possible for individuals to own shares in companies. Any member of the public is allowed to buy shares in any **public limited company** (☞ unit 6). One common way of buying them is through a **stockbroker.** Individuals may buy shares because they want to earn dividends. Buying shares is an alternative to other methods of saving, for example putting money in a building society account. Such people play no role in running the business. Also, they rarely have any control since they own only a small fraction of the total number of shares. If individuals are not happy with the performance of the company they may sell their shares. Or sometimes people buy shares, hoping to sell them at a higher price and make a profit.

**Institutional investors** These are financial institutions (☞ unit 44) such as insurance companies, pension funds and unit trusts who buy shares to earn income. They buy and sell very large numbers of shares, but rarely participate in the running of the companies. Their aim is to hold those shares which they think will generate the most return. In some cases they may exert control, since they own such large blocks of shares.

**Other companies** Some businesses hold shares to earn income, some to control other companies and some to build up stakes in other companies with a view to taking them over in the future.

## Managers

Businesses of all sizes employ managers. A MANAGER may be defined as an individual who is accountable for more work than he or she could undertake alone. In a small business the owner is likely to be responsible for all managerial tasks. When a business grows the responsibility for some decision making is often **delegated** (☞ unit 61) to others since it is not possible for one person to carry the whole burden.

There is a number of common functions of managers in business.

**Organising and decision making** Businesses are often divided into departments. A smaller business may have production, marketing, finance and administration departments. The owners may appoint one manager to control each department. Managers will have responsibility for all activities and employees in the department. For example, they may help to recruit employees, make decisions about how the department should be run and ensure that department objectives are met. Employees in the department will look to the manager for leadership, to solve problems, to communicate information to them, settle disputes, motivate them and represent the department at meetings.

**Planning and control** Managers are also likely to contribute to the overall planning of company activities along with the owner and other managers. They also have a controlling role in the business. This may involve control of finance, equipment, time and people, for example. In larger businesses, managers become more specialist and concentrate on a narrower aspect of management.

**Accountability** Managers are accountable to the owners. If the production department does not achieve a satisfactory level of output, the manager may have to 'shoulder the blame'. This might mean a loss of a bonus payment.

**Entrepreneurial role** Although managers may not risk their own money, they might risk their job. A manager might make a decision to install some revolutionary new machinery. This could be successful and the manager might be promoted. However, if the machinery is unsuccessful, leading to heavy losses, the manager may be sacked. In carrying out this task, the manager is innovating and risk taking.

## Employees

The role of employees in business tends to be to follow the instructions of employers. Employees are hired by businesses to help business activity. A business needs people with a range of skills and knowledge. Many provide a training programme for new employees to familiarise them with the firm's policies and working practices. Employees will be more productive if they are taught good working practices from the time they start at a new company. Note that managers of the business are usually employees.

Employees normally sign **contracts of employment** (☞ unit 66) agreeing to follow all reasonable instructions related to their job. In return for their time and effort they receive a payment, ie a **wage** or **salary**. The amount workers are paid depends on a wide range of factors such as age, experience, qualifications, the type of industry, the nature of the job (full time or part time) and the level of skill required.

The role of employees in business has begun to change in recent years.

- They have had to cope with the introduction of new technology.
- They have been encouraged by some companies to participate more in problem solving and decision making, perhaps in teams.
- They have become more flexible and have adapted to the introduction of new working practices. For example, many employees are trained in a number of tasks and are expected to be able to change from one job to another.
- Increased emphasis has been placed on training and learning new skills. For example, departmental managers have been encouraged to develop personnel skills.

## Customers

Customers are not 'members' of businesses, but they are vital to their survival. Customers buy the goods and services that businesses supply. Most customers are consumers who use or 'consume' products. Spending by customers generates income for businesses. Customers may be individuals, but could also be other businesses. For example, The Sage Group plc manufactures computer software for accounting systems. Most of its customers are other businesses.

It is important for businesses to understand the needs of their customers. Customers dictate the pattern of business activity, as firms will only produce goods and services which customers will buy. Businesses that produce unwanted goods or services may struggle and fail. The Concorde supersonic jets were taken out of service in 2003 because they were not commercially viable. There was insufficient demand for the service at the price needed to charge to cover the costs and make a profit.

Customers and consumers have many different relationships with businesses.

- Contact between businesses and customers takes place when goods or services are bought. This can vary. When services are bought there is usually a personal contact between the two groups, as there would be when a client makes an appointment to see a solicitor. In the case of water supply, the contact for many customers is limited, ie through the post when the quarterly bill arrives.
- Businesses need to communicate with consumers to find out what they want. **Market research** (☞ unit 19) helps a business to collect information about its potential customers.
- As well as collecting information from consumers, businesses also pass on information about the nature of products, the price charged, how products work and where they might be bought. **Advertising** (☞ unit 28) is often used to do this.
- Consumers are more aware today about products that are available, prices, channels of complaint and product performance. Consumers have more income than ever before, and much greater expectations of products. Businesses must take these expectations into account when

---

AStar Ltd is an insurance broker selling car, home, health and holiday insurance. Most of the policies are sold over the telephone, but a growing on-line business is beginning to contribute to the company's profit. Most of the company's shares are owned by the four directors. However, the company issues free shares to employees in relation to the amount of profit made each year. Last year the company made £2.5 million profit and 40 employees received 5,000 x 50p shares each.

(a) Explain one possible reason why AStar gives shares to its employees.
(b) To what extent can employees influence decision making at AStar?

Figure 3.2 *Shareholding at AStar Ltd*

- Employees 4%
- Ms Nicola Cuthbertson 16%
- Mrs Jenny Woodward 35%
- Mr Clay Samuels 29%
- Mr John Woodward 16%

**Question2**

designing, manufacturing and marketing products. For example, 35 years ago a radio in a new car would have been an 'extra'. Today, a complete 'sound system' in a car is virtually a necessity.

- Businesses operate in a world where consumers have increasing rights and protection. This is dealt with in unit 103.

Because of increased consumer expectations and awareness, improved consumer rights and fiercer competition in business, the vast majority of companies work hard at promoting good customer relations. Indeed, more and more businesses are happy to give consumers a lot more than their strict legal rights. Most stores will accept returned goods and reimburse customers without too much investigation. Free after sales service is common and sales staff receive a lot more 'customer care' training.

## Suppliers

Suppliers are businesses that provide resources which allow other businesses to produce goods and services. Resources might include raw materials, components, equipment, energy and services. It is important for good relations to exist between businesses and suppliers because they rely heavily on each other. Generally, businesses require suppliers to provide good quality resources at reasonable prices. They also need suppliers to be reliable and flexible. In return suppliers want businesses to provide a constant flow of profitable orders and to pay on time.

The relationship between suppliers and producers has become more important in recent years. The main reason for this is that modern production techniques often require businesses to cooperate. A business can only operate just-in-time manufacturing (☞ unit 80), for example, if suppliers are prepared to deliver quickly and at short notice.

## Government

The government can influence business in a number of ways. A certain amount of legislation is aimed at business in order to protect stakeholders. Health and safety regulations are designed to protect employees in the workplace. Environmental legislation aims to protect the community and the environment from business activity. For example, the landfill tax on the disposal of waste was intended to encourage greater recycling.

The government can also affect businesses through its economic policies (☞ unit 105). An increase in interest rates will raise the cost of borrowing for business. In addition, some government activity attempts to help business. The Private Finance Initiative encourages private businesses to build roads and hospitals, which they operate. More direct help may come from European Union (☞ unit 88) funds to set up in a particular area.

The government will want businesses to flourish because they provide jobs and generate wealth. If businesses are successful the government will also benefit. Tax revenues will rise, providing the government with extra funds.

## Community

Many communities have a major stake in local businesses. A business is likely to provide employment and training for local people. Certain businesses, particularly small ones, draw most of their customers from the local area. Indeed, in some remote areas residents may rely almost entirely upon the goods and services supplied by local firms such as shops. Some businesses even become involved in community life. They might sponsor local social or sporting events or help raise money for local charities.

Unfortunately the existence of business in local communities can also have drawbacks. Some businesses, particularly manufacturers located in residential areas, might create noise, congestion and air pollution. Their factories may be unsightly. As a result the local community might try to exert pressure on the owners to reduce the costs borne by the community or to relocate.

## Interdependence

There is a significant degree of interdependence within business. In large firms the owners are dependent upon the skill and ability of the management team. If managers perform well then the business is likely to make more profit which will benefit the owner. Managers rely on business owners for their jobs and to support their decisions.

Managers and other employees are also dependent upon each other. Employees rely on the **leadership** of management in order to do their jobs. Management depends on workers to produce output according to their instructions. Management will be accountable to the owners of the business if workers are inefficient.

Businesses are dependent on consumers. Business activity would not take place if consumers did not buy goods or services. However, consumers can only purchase these goods and services if they have income. They may earn this income from employment in business. Thus, business owners are dependent upon consumers for their income, and consumers, in their role as employees and managers, are dependent upon business owners for their income.

## Objectives and conflict

Conflict can occur in business when STAKEHOLDER OBJECTIVES are different. Each type of stakeholder is likely to have a set of goals which they want to achieve. It could be argued that:

- shareholders want regular, secure and high returns and a say in the goals of the business (☞ unit 4);
- managers want responsibility, high rewards and a lack of interference in their actions;
- employees want high earnings, an interesting job and secure employment;
- customers want quality products at low prices and a good service;
- suppliers want secure, regular and profitable orders;

- government wants to achieve a large number of goals including growth in the economy and low inflation;
- the local community wants thriving local businesses which do not cause problems.

Conflict can exist between many different groups of stakeholders.

**Employees and owners** What might lead to conflict between the employees and the owners of a business?

- Levels of pay. In most businesses, rates of pay are negotiated every year. Bargaining (☞ unit 74) takes place between employees and owners or managers. The two sides may disagree on new wage levels. This might be, for example, because workers want more than the owners or managers are prepared to pay.
- Working conditions. Conflict may arise if, for example, the working environment is too cold for employees to do their jobs.
- Changing practices. In recent years a number of new working practices have been introduced in business. Disputes may occur when employees are asked to perform new tasks or change the way they undertake existing tasks. Employees often feel that they are being asked to do more work when practices change.
- Redundancy. When employees are faced with the threat of losing their jobs, quite naturally they react. Workers are often angry when their jobs are lost due to reorganisation, for example.

**Owners and managers** In some businesses the management team may become powerful and influential. When this happens they may pursue their own interests rather than those of the owners. This might involve paying themselves high salaries or organising their time to suit their own needs, whilst achieving satisfactory levels of profit rather than high levels of profit. This would go against the interests of owners, who benefit more from higher profits. Such conflict may result in some owners selling their shares. This is often referred to as a **divorce of ownership and control** (☞ unit 6).

It is in everyone's interests to settle conflict as quickly as possible. Conflict can lead to lower levels of output and loss of profits for the owners. Managers and other employees may suffer from poor motivation, a lack of job security and loss of wages.

**Customers and business** What might lead to conflict between consumers and business?

- Price. Owners may wish to maximise their profit which might involve charging the highest possible price. However, consumers want to buy goods as cheaply as possible. If competition exists in the market (☞ unit 94) consumers will generally benefit. However, if there is a lack of competition, consumers may not have a choice except to go without.
- Quality. Consumers may be dissatisfied with the quality of the products they have bought. If consumers return goods

then businesses lose income, so disagreements often occur as to whether a firm should accept returned goods.

- Delivery time. Customers are often keen to receive the goods which they have ordered as quickly as possible. A dispute would occur if, for example, a business cannot deliver a wedding dress promised for the day of a wedding.
- After sales service. Consumers may be upset by poor after sales service. For example, if a person buys a hi-fi system and finds that it does not work, a dispute might emerge if the business refused to investigate the problem.

**Suppliers, managers and owners** 'New' production methods have led to a closer relationship between suppliers and managers. However, conflict does still exist. Some suppliers, particularly small firms supplying larger businesses, have criticised their customers' managers or owners for taking too long to pay for products. Late payment can cause severe hardship for smaller suppliers.

Similarly, late delivery by suppliers can cause problems for managers and owners of businesses which are customers. Late supply can delay production and may lead to lost orders and profit.

**Owners and the community** Conflict can arise between owners and the community when the quality of life enjoyed by local residents is threatened by business activity. The most likely causes of conflict are businesses disturbing the local community or polluting the nearby environment. An example of such conflict was the opposition of residents in South

---

In early 2003 Richard Lapthorne, former finance director of British Aerospace (now BAE Systems), was appointed chairman of Cable and Wireless (C & W). C & W is a global supplier of Internet data and voice solutions to businesses. The company which used to run the Mercury network in the UK, providing the only competition to BT in the 1980s, was once valued at £35 billion. On 21.9.2003 it was valued at just £2.961 billion. It has suffered the problems of other hi-tech companies - chronic overcapacity and falling prices for services that too many firms are offering to an insufficient number of customers.

In May 2003, the company announced plans to shed half the staff at the company's London headquarters. The cuts, to be accompanied by several hundred job losses across the group, were part of a plan to reduce overheads as the company struggled to reduce 'cash burn' across the group. One official involved in the plan said: 'It's part of the bigger overhaul. Terms of redundancy are being worked out — this will do nothing for morale'. Shares in C & W rose 4 $\frac{1}{2}$ p to 102 $\frac{3}{4}$ p after the job cuts were announced.

Source: adapted from the *Financial Times*, 30.5.2003.

(a) Explain the possible conflicts that might arise amongst the various C & W stakeholders as a result of the cost cutting exercise.

**Question 3**

Manchester to the construction of a new runway at Manchester Airport. They argued that noise pollution resulting from extra traffic would be intolerable.

An increasing amount of business activity is located away from residential areas. Popular sites on the edges of towns have developed. Industrial parks have been set up and some businesses have chosen to operate on greenfield sites (☞ unit 88). This trend would help to reduce conflict between business owners and local communities.

## Why might businesses take a stakeholder approach?

Traditionally, large business organisations have been run to further the interests of shareholders. This involves maximising shareholder value, which usually also involves raising the share price. This is called the SHAREHOLDER CONCEPT and often means that the interests of other stakeholders are ignored. In recent years some businesses have realised the benefits from meeting the needs of a wider range of

### key terms

**Directors** - people elected by shareholders to run companies.
**Dividend** - a proportion of a company's profits paid to owners of shares in that company.
**Manager** - an individual who is accountable for more work than he or she could undertake alone.
**Shareholder concept** – the traditional approach to running a business which involves focusing on the needs of the shareholders.
**Stakeholders** - groups who have an interest in business activity.
**Stakeholder concept** – an approach to running a business that involves taking into account the needs of all stakeholders.
**Stakeholder objectives** - the goals of people with interests in the business. What stakeholders want to achieve.

---

Companies like to be trusted. Enormous effort is made by businesses through public relations, reward schemes and other measures to boost public confidence. They want to persuade us that they are good 'corporate citizens.' It makes sense because it makes money. Trusting customers become loyal customers, who in turn are more likely to keep on buying as well as purchasing new products and services in the future. However, UK company law requires public limited companies (companies owned by shareholders) to prioritise the interests of shareholders. The owners must come first.

In 2003, a survey was carried out to explore the feelings of customers in the mortgage market. The survey was conducted by Jonathan Michie, the Sainsbury Professor of Management, Birkbeck, University of London. An extract from the findings is shown below.

'A sample of responses from first time buyers who had not yet chosen a mortgage provider.
● 78% agreed with the statement: "I like the fact that building societies have no shareholders".
● 55% agreed with the statement: "I am more likely to trust a building society than a bank".
● 66% agreed with: "In the future I am more likely to deal with a building society".

A sample of responses from customers of mutual and co-operative organisations (mutual and co-operative organisations do not have shareholders, they are owned by their members).
● Faced with the statement: "The Co-op is trustworthy", 37% agreed "slightly" and 58% agreed "strongly".
● 86% agreed with the statement: "The Co-operative acts more in members' interests because it is answerable to us and not to big City investors".
● 75% agreed with the statement: "As the Co-op board of directors is elected by local members, my interests will be more honestly represented".'

Source: adapted from *The Guardian*, 24.6.2003.

| Lender | Rate | Fixed period | Deposit | Fee | Redemption penalty |
|---|---|---|---|---|---|
| **FIXED RATES** | | | | | |
| Britannia | 3.64% | 2 years | 5% | £299 | Yes |
| Cheshire | 4.34% | 3 years | 20% | £295 | Yes |
| Coventry | 4.39% | 5 years | 5% | £299 | Yes |

| Lender | Rate | Discount period | Deposit | Fee | Redemption penalty |
|---|---|---|---|---|---|
| **DISCOUNT/ TRACKERS** | | | | | |
| Newcastle | 3.03% | 2 years | 10% | £345 | Yes |
| Abbey | 3.30% | 2 years | 5% | £299 | Yes |
| Nottingham | 3.28% | 3 years | 5% | £299 | Yes |
| Skipton | 2.99% | 5 years | 5% | £395 | Yes |

| Lender | Rate | Capped period | Deposit | Fee | Redemption penalty |
|---|---|---|---|---|---|
| **CAPPED RATES** | | | | | |
| Kent Reliance | 4.48% | 3 years | 5% | £295 | Yes |
| Marsden | 4.89% | 5 years | 25% | £345 | Yes |

**Table 3.1** *Mortgage deals*
Source: adapted from *London and Country Mortgages*.

Table 3.1 shows mortgage deals available on 28.9.2003. They were all offered by mutual organisations except for one, Abbey.

(a) Using information from the article, explain what is meant by the 'stakeholder concept'.
(b) What evidence is there in the article to suggest that companies which do not have shareholders look after their members better?

**Question 4**

stakeholders.

This has led to the rise of the STAKEHOLDER CONCEPT. Some businesses now take into account the needs of employees, customers, suppliers and the local community as well as shareholders when making important business decisions. The benefits of this approach might include the following.

- If the needs of employees are taken into account they may be better motivated, more productive, more loyal, more flexible and less likely to leave. Companies that focus too much on shareholder needs might find it difficult to recruit high quality staff.
- If businesses have a higher regard for the local community they might win their support. For example, if the local community is consulted when expansion plans are announced, there may be less resistance to the construction of new buildings. Having regard for the local community is also likely to improve the image of the company.
- Looking after suppliers can generate significant benefits. For example, if suppliers are paid more promptly they may become more flexible.
- If the needs of customers are satisfied more effectively there is likely to be an increase in business. For example, if firms deal with complaints in a friendly and supportive manner, customers are more likely to return and 'spread the good word'.

## Knowledge

1. Describe the interest that each internal stakeholder has in a business.
2. List 3 functions of an entrepreneur.
3. Why are entrepreneurs often associated with small businesses?
4. List 5 possible groups of shareholders.
5. Briefly explain 4 roles of management.
6. 'The role of employees in business is changing.' Explain this statement using an example.
7. Briefly explain 3 ways in which businesses and consumers are related.
8. Why are owners, managers and employees interdependent?
9. Explain one source of conflict between:
   (a) owners and managers; (b) managers and employees; (c) businesses and consumers.
10. Why might businesses adopt the stakeholder concept?

## Case study The Highland Bus Company

The Highland Bus Company provides bus services to a wide geographical area in the Scottish Highlands. It is owned by a small group of London-based shareholders and run by a management team from the company's headquarters in Inverness. The company was first formed in 1988 when James McGregor and his two brothers set up an express bus service between Inverness and Fort William. The company prospered and then began to grow quickly when the brothers started to acquire a number of other small bus companies throughout the Scottish Highlands.

Much of the McGregors' success was down to the control of costs. The brothers ran a very efficient operation. They ensured that every vehicle bought by the company was on the road earning fares. They also priced their services aggressively. For example, when competing for passengers on new routes they often charged half the fare of competitors. This resulted in a lot of the small operators either selling out to the McGregor brothers or just disappearing from the roads.

Once the competition was eliminated it was not uncommon to see prices rise by about 15-20 per cent above those charged by the original operators. However, since the services were reliable and more frequent than before, passengers didn't seem to complain very much. In addition, passenger traffic rose due to a sustained and effective marketing campaign. The Highland Bus Company, as it became named in 1992, used leaflets, local newspaper adverts and local radio stations to publicise its services. By 1999, the Highland Bus Company served 90 per cent of all bus routes north of Glasgow and Edinburgh.

In 2002 the brothers, who were all in their fifties, decided to step back from the company. They did consider selling out to a national passenger carrier such as Stagecoach. However, they felt that the price they would get in the current stock market climate would not reflect accurately the true value of the

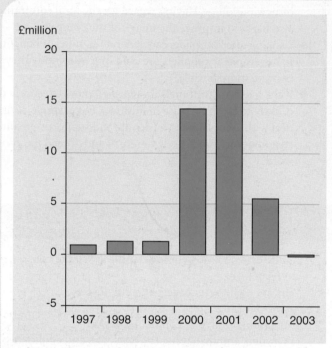

£million

**Figure 3.4** *Highland Bus Company, profit 1997-2003*

company. Instead they appointed Gillian French, from a national coach company. She was installed as chief executive and given an attractive salary package. In addition to her annual salary she was to get 5 per cent of the company's profit after tax. This was a huge incentive to grow the company and keep it profitable.

In pursuit of growth Gillian looked at the possibility of running special excursions from Glasgow and Edinburgh to all parts of the Highlands and Islands. This proved to be an unfortunate ploy. Such journeys were already subject to overcapacity. An investment in new buses, staff and marketing was a financial disaster. In an effort to recoup some of the losses Gillian embarked on a severe cost-cutting strategy throughout the organisation. She contracted out bus-cleaning, maintenance and payroll and cut administration staff to the bone. She also raised prices in the belief that customers would continue to use the services because they had no choice. Then, when passengers fell, she started to axe marginal routes. This led to more redundancies and attracted some unwanted media attention.

A group of people from Glen More, a small village in Sutherland, formed a protest group after their two-hourly bus service to Ullapool was reduced to a daily service. Further controversy arose when Gillian began delaying payments to suppliers in an effort to improve the company's cash flow. This led to one of the suppliers going out of business.

In early 2004 Gillian was sacked and James McGregor returned to the business to clear up the mess.

**(a)** Using examples from the case explain the terms:
   **(i)** shareholder;
   **(ii)** stakeholder. (6 marks)
**(b)** Describe Gillian's role as a manager in the business. (8 marks)
**(c)** Explain the effects of Gillian's appointment on stakeholders in the case. (12 marks)
**(d)** To what extent might the stakeholder approach to running a company be beneficial to shareholders? (14 marks)

HIGHLAND BUS COMPANY

# 4 Business Aims and Objectives

## Corporate aims

The CORPORATE AIMS of a business are its overall purpose. This is what the business is trying to achieve in the long term. It is likely that different types of businesses will have different aims. For example, a small plumbing business might have different aims from the Coca-Coca organisation. Aims are likely to be different at different times. A business might have a number of aims, not just the obvious one of making a profit, although not all organisations might suggest that they have this aim.

## Business objectives

All businesses have OBJECTIVES. These are the **goals** of the business. They are the outcomes or targets that the business wants to gain in order to achieve its aims. The objectives of a business can be derived from its aims. For example, a business supplying recycled wood for buildings might aim to be the most important supplier of the service in an area and the first name that everyone thinks of when buying these products. The objective might be to be supplying 40 per cent of all recycled wood in the area within the next three years.

It is important for a business to have well defined objectives. These will help the business to be clear about what it wants to achieve. The performance of the business could be assessed by how effectively it achieves its objectives. For example, a business might have the objective of increasing sales by 20 per cent over three years. If it had increased sales by only 5 per cent then it might conclude that it has been unsuccessful.

It is often argued that businesses must set objectives which are SMART. This means that they should be:
- specific - stating exactly what is trying to be achieved;
- measurable - able to be measured to decide if they have been achieved;
- agreed - have the approval and understanding of everyone involved;
- realistic - able to be achieved by the business taking into account its resources, competition, markets etc;
- time specific - state a time by which they should be achieved.

## Survival

From time to time all businesses, regardless of their size and status, will consider survival important.

**Early stages of trading** Most firms begin on a small scale, establish themselves and then grow. The owners of a new firm will probably be happy to see the firm survive in its first few months (or even years) of trading. Firms may encounter a number of problems when they first begin trading including:

- a lack of experience;
- a lack of resources;
- competition from established firms;
- unforeseen problems such as unexpected costs;
- limited recognition by customers.

Also, in the early stages decision makers might make mistakes. As a result of this uncertainty the most important business objective might be to survive in the initial stages of trading, such as the first three years.

**When trading becomes difficult** During a recession (☞ unit 96), for example, a business could face falling demand, bad debts and low confidence. In the UK recession of 1990-92 many well known companies ceased trading. In 1992 around 73,000 businesses collapsed. Improved trading conditions reduced this figure to around 40,000 in 1998. Individual businesses or industries may face difficulties due to competition from rivals, falling demand for their products or the effects of poor decisions. Arguably the objective of Apple, the computer manufacturer, in allowing Microsoft, a rival, to take a stake in its operation in 1997 was to protect the company during a difficult period.

**Threat of takeover** Firms sometimes become targets for other firms to take over. When this happens the survival of the firm in its existing form may be the main objective. One way to achieve this is to persuade the owners (the shareholders) not to sell shares to the person or company bidding for them.

In the long term it is unlikely that survival would remain the only objective, except perhaps for small businesses. Business owners tend to be ambitious and so pursue other objectives.

## Profit

It is often argued that the main objective of private sector businesses (☞ unit 6) is to make a profit. It is suggested that some businesses try to PROFIT MAXIMISE. This is achieved where the difference between the total revenue earned by the business from selling its products and the total costs of those products is the greatest. The manufacturer in Table 4.1 would produce 3,000 units as this is the output where its profit is

**Table 4.1** *Profit maximising position*

| | | | £000 |
|---|---|---|---|
| Output | Total costs | Total revenue | Profit |
| 2,000 | 10 | 20 | 10 |
| 3,000 | 15 | 30 | 15 |
| 4,000 | 30 | 35 | 5 |

highest.

It may be reasonable to assume that firms aim for as much profit as possible. In practice a business is more likely to have a satisfactory level of profit as an objective. This is known as SATISFICING. Why is this likely to be a more reasonable objective?

**Objectives of small firms** Owners of small firms may not want to expand their output to a point where their profits are maximised. This may be because:

- it involves employing more workers, making more decisions and working longer hours;
- they may want to keep their turnover below the VAT threshold, avoiding the need to charge their customers VAT and filling in VAT returns;
- they are happy with a satisfactory profit level and their current lifestyle.

**Information** In practice it may be difficult to identify precisely the level of output that will maximise profits. For a business to do this it must be able to measure all of its costs at every possible level of production. It must also be able to estimate accurately the prices it can charge and predict the likely demand at these prices.

**Other objectives** A business might sacrifice short term profit maximisation for long term profits. This might explain why a firm lowers its price initially to build a market share and then increases price when competitors have left the market. It might also account for firms operating in the short term at a loss. In this case, the owners may be optimistic that in the future sales will pick up.

## *Growth*

Many businesses pursue growth as their main objective. Business people argue that firms must grow in order to survive. Failure to grow might result in a loss of competitiveness, a

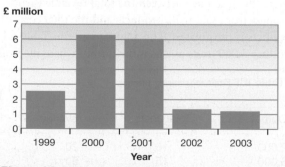

**Figure 4.1** *Profit/loss before tax*

**Figure 4.2** *Dividends per share*

**Figure 4.3** *Capial expenditure*
Source: adapted from Walker Greenbank plc, *Annual Report and Accounts, 2003.*

Walker Greenbank plc is an international group of companies which design, manufacture, market and distribute wallcoverings, furnishing fabrics and associated products for the consumer market.

**Part of quote from the Chairman**

'The decline in the market has been unprecedented and it is difficult to predict when it is going to stabilise. We believe the cost savings made this year will protect the group through this difficult period and if any upturn materialises the group will see a significant improvement in results. The focus will remain on cash generation, debt reduction and disposal of non-core assets ...'.

**Table 4.2** *Performance details 2003*

- Operating loss of £3.8m (£6.5m in 2002)
- Loss after taxation of £7.4m (£6.6m in 2002)
- Disposal of TWIL for £0.9m in January 2003
- £2.3 million cash generated from operating activities and debt reduced by £0.6m, the first net cash inflow since 1999
- Further cost savings in the year and headcount reduced by 10%

(a) What evidence is there to suggest that Walker Greenbank's main business objective in recent years may have been survival?

decline in demand and eventual closure. If a firm is able to grow and dominate the market, in the future it may be able to enjoy some monopoly power and raise its price. By growing, a firm can diversify and reduce the risk of business enterprise. It can sell to alternative markets and introduce new products. If one market or product fails it will have a range of others to fall back on. Firms can exploit economies of scale if they grow large enough. This will enable them to be more efficient and enjoy lower costs. Motives for growth are dealt with in unit 81.

A number of people involved in business activity might benefit from growth.

- Employees may find their jobs will be more secure (although this might not always be the case if growth involves purchasing more machinery).
- Managers and directors will tend to have more power and status. For example, a director of a large oul business is likely to enjoy more power and recognition than the director of a small manufacturer.
- The salaries of directors and the chairperson are often linked to the size of the firm.
- The owners of companies might have mixed feelings about growth. On the one hand, growth often means that current profits have to be invested to fund the expansion. However, growth might generate much higher profits in the future, which will benefit the owners.

## Increasing shareholder value

Many public limited companies (☞ unit 6) aim to increase SHAREHOLDER VALUE. This means they run the business in a way that will result in an increase in share price and an increase in dividends. Shareholders benefit when the share price goes up because when they sell their shares they may make a capital gain (a profit on the sale). However, shareholder value is closely linked to other business objectives. The share price will go up if there is an increase in demand for the shares, ie more investors want to buy them. An increase in demand will result if the company is expected to grow and become more profitable. Therefore, by growing the company and making more profit, shareholder value will increase.

Legislation requires companies to publish a measure of shareholder value in their annual reports. Figure 4.6 shows Silentnight Holdings total share holder return and the FTSE 350 index over the last five years. Silentnight plc is the market leader in two sectors of the domestic furniture market - beds and assembled cabinet furniture. TSR is total shareholder return, which represents share price growth and dividends reinvested. This is compared with the performance of the FTSE 350 which is an index of share prices for the top 350 companies in the UK. The graph shows that Silentnight has underperformed over the period.

**Figure 4.4** *Turnover, earnings per share and dividend per share*

**Figure 4.5** *Predicted market growth*

Geest produces and markets fresh prepared foods and market-fresh produce. It has a constantly changing product portfolio and at any point in time sells around 2,000 different products. Examples include ready meals, salads, pizzas, prepared vegetables and stir frys, prepared fruit, dips, pasta and bread products, pasta sauces, soups and desserts. In 2002 around 600 new products were launched.

Source: adapted from Geest, *Annual Reports and Accounts 2002*.

## Our vision
To become the best fresh prepared food and produce company wherever we operate.

We shall achieve this by excelling in service, quality, value and innovation to the delight of our customers.

We will grow in any geographical market where customer partnership and consumer demand can be developed.

(a) What evidence is there to suggest that growth is one of the objectives of Geest?
(b) Examine the possible effects of Geest's business objective on (i) shareholders and (ii) employees.

**Figure 4.6** *Silentnight's TSR vs the FTSE 350 index*
Source: adapted from Silentnight, *Annual Report and Accounts, 2003*.

## Managerial objectives

Sometimes the managers of a business are able to pursue their own objectives. For this to happen there must be some divorce of ownership and control. In other words the owners of the company do not necessarily control the day to day running of it. This may be possible when there is a very large number of joint owners as in a public limited company. Each owner has such a small part of the firm that he or she is able to exert little control over its running. As a result management take control and run the company according to their own objectives. These vary depending on individual managers. Some common examples might be to:

- maximise personal salary;
- maximise their departmental budgets;
- improve their status and recognition;
- maximise the number of employees in their charge;
- maximise their leisure time;
- delegate as much as work as possible;
- maximise fringe benefits, such as expense accounts for entertaining or company cars.

If managers are seen by owners to be abusing their power they are likely to be fired. To protect their positions managers often pacify owners by ensuring that the business generates enough profit to keep them satisfied. Profit may also be important to managers if their salaries are linked to profit levels.

## Sales revenue maximisation

SALES REVENUE MAXIMISATION is where businesses try to gain the highest possible sales revenue. This objective will be favoured by those employees whose salaries are linked to sales. Managers and sales staff are examples of staff paid according to the sales revenue which they generate. Sales revenue maximisation is not the same as profit maximisation. In Table 4.1, the business maximised profits at an output of 3,000 units. Producing 4,000 units would have maximised sales revenue (£35,000).

Geoffrey Horrocks is the chief executive of Arnold Carrington Associates, a family civil engineering business specialising in the construction of tower blocks. He has been with the company for 7 years and guided it from a position of insecurity in the late 1990s to one of growing prosperity. The company now employs 18 people and Geoffrey's role has changed significantly. Initially he was very much involved on the engineering side, but now he deals with clients and new business. Geoffrey has delegated a great deal of responsibility to his assistant and other members of the management team. He has seen his own salary rise from £12,500 in 1997 to £110,000 in 2004. Geoffrey is a valued member of the company, but the owners, who retired to Sardinia in 2000, have lost touch with the day to day running of the business. In addition, the Carrington family are extremely wealthy and the profit from this business represents less than 5 per cent of their annual income.

**Figure 4.7** *Arnold Carrington Associates, profit 1997 to 2004*

**Figure 4.8** *Geoffrey Horrocks, annual salary 1997 to 2004*

(a) Explain how it is possible for management to pursue its own objectives in this business.
(b) Examine the factors that might lead to a change in the objectives of this company.

# Image, reputation and social responsibility

In recent years businesses have started to appreciate how important their image is. Many have also seen the benefit of showing responsibility to a wider range of stakeholders, such as customers, employees and suppliers. Why has this happened?

● Legislation has been passed which favours consumers.
● There have been changes in social attitudes.
● Competitive pressure has forced businesses to take into account the needs of others.

**Customers** Companies with household names such as Heinz, Coca-Cola, Kellogg's, Ford, Cadbury's and Sainsbury's would not wish the general public to think badly of them. Some companies have made serious efforts in recent years to improve their image. For example, Skoda, the car manufacturer, has in the past had an image as a producer of 'budget', or 'unfashionable' cars. It has tried to shake off this image by exploiting its new owner's name, VW.

Faced with competition, firms are likely to lose sales if they don't take into account the needs of customers. Increasingly, firms are giving free after sales service, replacing unwanted goods without question and training their staff to deal with the public.

**Employees** Government and EU legislation and employee representative groups have influenced how businesses treat employees. A number of laws have been passed to protect workers (☞ units 69 and 70). An example of legislation which affects workers is the **Disability Discrimination Act, 1996.** This is designed to reduce discrimination by businesses against disabled workers.

One effect of legislation is that it protects companies with high standards of responsibility from those competitors who have little regard for health and safety at work. Unscrupulous firms will not be able to lower costs by neglecting health and safety because they will have to keep within the law.

Trade unions have argued for the rights of the workforce for many years. They have aimed to improve social facilities, wages and working conditions.

**Suppliers** Some firms have benefited from good relations with suppliers of raw materials and components. One example is in manufacturing, where companies are adopting **Just-in-time** manufacturing (☞ unit 80). This means that firms only produce when they have an order and stocks of raw materials and components are delivered to the factory only when they are needed. Reliable and efficient suppliers are needed by firms if they order stocks 'at the last minute'. Maintaining good relations with suppliers is likely to help this process. Examples of good relations might be prompt payment to suppliers or regular meetings to discuss each other's needs.

# Behavioural theories

BEHAVIOURAL THEORIES assume that business objectives are not determined by owners and managers alone. They suggest that other stakeholders, such as the government, consumers and pressure groups, may affect the firm's objectives. The objective a company has will depend on the power of these groups to influence decisions. It is argued that groups inside and outside the business have certain minimum goals.

● The owners will require a certain level of profit to retain their interest in the business.
● Workers will demand a minimum level of pay and acceptable working conditions if they are to be retained in employment.
● Suppliers will want regular contracts, reasonable lead times and prompt payment.
● Managers will insist on enough resources to carry out their tasks (this might include an appropriate expense allowance, for example).
● The government will require the company to obey laws and pay taxes.
● Customers will demand quality products at reasonable prices.
● Pressure groups, such as environmentalists, will try to protect their interests, eg avoiding pollution.

In practice, the group with the most influence will achieve its objectives. In the 1990s animal rights pressure groups, such as Lynx, persuaded customers to buy fewer fur products. Some businesses saw sales reduced as a result and others switched to the manufacture of synthetic fur clothing. Managers and owners of large businesses sometimes pursue a policy of delayering or downsizing - reducing the number of tiers in the business hierarchy (☞ unit 58). They are convinced that such measures will make their businesses more efficient and reduce costs. This results in many employees losing their jobs.

The influence of a group may change over time or if the organisation of a business changes. For example, increased legislation might give employees more influence over

**Figure 4.9** *Growth subject to a minimum profit constraint*

holidays and hours worked. A management buy out is likely to give managers more say in the business.

Sometimes groups will compromise. Figure 4.9 illustrates the total costs, total revenue and profit of a business. If it is dominated by the directors, they might have growth as an objective. This would be achieved at output level $Q_1$, where output is pushed to the limit before the firm makes a loss. However, the owners may prefer the business to produce a level of output $Q_2$ where profits are greatest. A compromise might be at $Q_3$, where a minimum level of profit is made for the owners, but output is high enough for some growth.

## Business operations

Businesses sometimes set objectives for the operation of the organisation. For example, a business might decide that it needs to **diversify** its product range. A company might be operating with a small, relatively specific type of products. If there was a decline in demand for these products, if there was a sudden increase in competition or if the products became out of date due to changes in technology, the business might fail. Diversification is one way in which a business can protect itself against declines in certain markets. This is sometimes the reason why businesses merge with others in different markets, known as lateral integration (☞ unit 89).

A business might also decide to change the **focus** of its organisation. It might, for example, decide to focus on its main areas rather than operating in a number of areas. This is often the reason why businesses divest themselves of, or sell parts of, their organisation to concentrate on their core activities.

## Objectives in the public sector

As a result of government policy in the last two decades of the twentieth century, public sector organisations (☞ unit 7) changed their objectives. Historically, the main objective of public sector businesses was to supply a public service. For example, previously state owned organisations, such as British Rail and British Gas, had to supply services in isolated regions which were unprofitable. Profit was not really a motive for public sector organisations. Many made losses.

In the 1990s public sector organisations aimed to offer their services in a more 'business like' way. The government expected them to operate efficiently and produce a cost effective and quality service. Some had fairly substantial 'surpluses', part of which are paid to the Treasury. Public sector organisations adopted many private sector business techniques, such as marketing, business planning, budgeting and investment appraisal. For example, many schools, colleges and hospital trusts actively marketed their services. Service providers were encouraged to compete for customers. Examples might be colleges trying to attract students to obtain government funds or NHS trusts competing to sell services to fund holding GPs.

For some public sector organisations performance targets

were set to ensure that a 'good' standard of service was supplied. For example, hospitals aimed to reduce waiting lists for beds and operations. Councils had their budgets cut to ensure that waste was minimised. Sixth form colleges were instructed to improve efficiency in the delivery of their education services. The performance rates of many public sector organisations are widely published. National league tables are compiled for crime and detection rates, exam results and truancy rates. Such tables are designed to introduce an element of competition in the public sector and inform the public of performance.

## What determines business objectives?

There is a number of factors that can influence the choice of objective.

**The size and status of the business** Many small businesses might be prepared to achieve only a satisfactory level of profit or survival in difficult times rather than expand or make a large profit. Large companies might be more concerned about growth and perhaps market domination. A business that is starting up is likely to be more concerned with survival. Later, when it has become established, other objectives such as growth may be more important.

**The power of stakeholders** As explained earlier, behavioural theorists argue that the stakeholder group which dominates the business is likely to have the most influence over objectives. Shareholders are likely to be more concerned about profit. Outside stakeholders might be more concerned with social objectives, such as the impact of production on the environment.

**Ownership** The ownership of the organisation can influence objectives. Sole traders might have different objectives from larger public limited companies or they could be the same. For example, a single owner might want to make as much profit as possible, just like the many owners of a plc. However, a plc might be very concerned about image, particularly before a share issue, whereas a sole trader may see this as a fairly unimportant objective. Whether the business is part of the public or private sector is also likely to be an influence. Public sector organisations, whilst increasingly becoming aware of the need to be efficient and make surpluses, might be more concerned about their impact on the public and society than some private organisations.

**Long and short term objectives** Long term and short term objectives might differ. In the long run business must make a profit to survive. In the short run, however, a business might be prepared simply to break-even, particularly if trading conditions are difficult. There are other reasons why firms might sacrifice profit in the short run. For example, firms entering a new and expanding market might take time to become established and might accept losses initially. Also, businesses seeking to invest in expensive projects that will lead to greater profit at a later date might sacrifice short term profit. For example, British Biotechnology plc, the pharmaceuticals company started in 1986, had still not made a profit by 2003. Many mobile phone companies accepted large initial expenses or losses to set up in the market, hoping to make profit only after a number of years.

**External and internal pressures** Pressures from outside business can affect objectives. **New legislation** may force a business to change its behaviour and take into account the effect of its activities on the environment or employees. The landfill tax, for example, might have encouraged greater recycling. Changes in employee legislation could increase costs and change profit objectives. **Changing market trends** can also influence objectives. Increasing demand for products may encourage a business to grow and expand into new areas of production.

Internal pressures might also play a part. For example, the appointment of a new chairperson might completely alter the goals of the organisation. A change in production techniques or a delayering (☞ unit 90) of management might also affect objectives.

**Risk** Pursuing some objectives might be more risky than others. For example, trying to achieve growth by entering new and unknown markets could be very risky for a business. Some businesses are happy to take risks because the potential rewards outweigh the costs involved. Others are risk averse. It might be argued by some that the move by Morrisons in 2003 to take over Safeway was risky because the company has little experience in integrating with such a large organisation.

**Corporate and business culture** The values and norms of behaviour developed by a business over time, its corporate culture (☞ unit 15), are likely to influence its objectives. For example, a business that has a caring corporate culture is likely to have different objectives from one with a competitive culture.

## Mission statements

Businesses are increasingly producing MISSION STATEMENTS. These include descriptions of the overall aims of the business. They tend to be aimed at stakeholders in the business. So they are often found printed in the Annual Report and Accounts of public limited companies. They include information for all stakeholders, including employees shareholders and also customers. They usually express the aims of the business in 'qualitative terms', such as emphasising the desire to be the 'best in the business' or to become the 'best in the field'. They also tend to include the values and principles of the business and perhaps its corporate culture (☞ unit 15).

Sometimes mission statements are brief. They might be a line or two stating the main priority of the business. This will help people to identify and remember the main purpose of the business. Or they might be a short statement or a page which can be displayed in places such as reception areas. They can then be viewed by staff, customers and suppliers, showing what the business is trying to achieve. They can also be placed on company websites. Sometimes businesses produce detailed mission statements. They might include a variety of features about the aims of the business, including its main purpose and how it might evaluate success. In some cases it might even include details of the objectives of the business as well, stating targets or outcomes.

An example of a mission statement is in Figure 4.10, which shows the mission statement of Reg Vardy plc, a distributor of new and used cars.

## How useful are mission statements?

It could be argued that it is important for all businesses to have a mission statement. They:
● help the business to focus;

**'Our purpose is to meet the needs of the motoring public'**

Enthusiasm and commitment are the distinctive characteristics of Reg Vardy, a company which has grown from one garage in a North Eastern mining town into one of the country's leading quoted motor groups.

Our company enjoys an extraordinary level of loyalty and dedication amongst its management and staff, now totalling almost 5,000. Together we are working to build Reg Vardy into a national force within the retail motor industry.

Whilst aiming to continue the Group's dramatic growth, we will all recognise the challenge of maintaining and improving standards of customer satisfaction. We are determined that, as we strive for commercial success, our Company motto 'In Pursuit of Excellence' will not be compromised.

**Figure 4.10** *Mission statement of Reg Vardy*
Source: adapted from Reg Vardy plc, *Annual Reports and Accounts, 2003.*

*Our mission*
to make a sustainable contribution to the progress of mobility for vehicles and people

*Our values*
respect customers, employees, shareholders, protect the environment and follow transparent corporate reporting practices

● *Leader on the world tyre market, Michelin is in pole position on all tyre mobility related service markets*
The Group's development is based on innovation and quality. It is acknowledged by professionals as the leader, ahead of the field in the most challenging technical segments. The Group is developing a portfolio of brands complementary to the Michelin brand, able to meet the requirements of all its customers: drivers, retailers, transport professionals and vehicle manufacturers.

● *To contribute to the progress of mobility is the essence of the Group's strategy*
In the future there will be many more vehicles but they will be safer, have greater driver/vehicle interaction and be more environmentally-friendly. This evolution in quality offers more opportunities for growth for Michelin, which intends to:

● remain a global player
● develop profitable, targeted, high added value growth
● optimise technology, innovation, marketing and service in all its areas of expertise.

● *The Group's objectives in the medium term*
Michelin is determined to constantly improve its ability to anticipate and react to any obstacles so that it can overcome them better. The Group's medium term objectives are to:

● balance its sales by increasing volumes in regions with high potential growth

● exceed the market's growth by at least 2% in volume terms on the segments and zones which are priority targets

● regularly achieve results that surpass the cost of capital employed by optimizing the allocation of assets, improving industrial flexibility, regularly achieving free cash-flow and aiming for an operating margin of 10% on average over the cycle from 2005 onwards.

Source: adapted from Michelin, *Annual Report and Accounts 2002.*

(a) Identify the objectives of the business from information included after its mission statement.

(b) Comment on the extent to which the objectives are SMART.

**Question4**

● provide a plan for the future for a business;
● make clear to all stakeholders what the business is trying to achieve.

However, it has been suggested that mission statements are little more than a publicity stunt. Indeed, there is evidence to suggest that many of the statements are predictable and bland. The vast majority of organisations have mission statements and most of them contain common themes such as:

● 'our aim is to maximise shareholder value';
● 'we will focus on customer needs';
● 'we aim to become the premier supplier of ...' ;
● 'in pursuit of excellence'.

Whether or not a mission statement actually affects the way a business operates is debatable. How many staff can remember the company's mission statement, for example? Even if a company is committed to its mission statement, it may have difficulties implementing the policies and measures needed to achieve its aims. This is particularly the case where companies operate in very diverse markets.

A further problem is that the aims and objectives of the business are not always easy to distinguish from the mission statement. Sometimes businesses state that their main aim is to expand the business through acquisition and organic growth. By placing outcomes in the statement it could be argued that these are then more specific and achievable goals or objectives. Also businesses may not make a distinction between aims and objectives deliberately in order to hide what they are trying to achieve. For example, a business

might state that its aim is to be more environmentally friendly and benefit the environment. But this might be a useful tool for increasing profit, which could be shown in its more measurable objectives. So the main aim of the business might be different from that stated.

## key terms

**Corporate aims** - the overall purpose of a business.
**Behavioural theories** - theories which state that business objectives are determined jointly by groups of interested parties.
**Mission statement** - a brief summary of a firm's aims and objectives.
**Objectives** - the goals or outcomes a business wants to achieve.
**Profit maximisation** - producing a level of output which generates the most profit for a business.
**Sales revenue maximisation** - producing a level of output where sales revenue is greatest.
**Satisficing** - generating sufficient profit to satisfy the owners, not necessarily at an output which gives greatest profit.
**Shareholder value** - the benefit to shareholders of a rising share price and rising dividends.
**SMART (objectives)** - goals which are specific, measurable, agreed, realistic and time specific.

## Knowledge

1. Under what circumstances might survival be an important objective?
2. Why might a successful business still not survive in its existing form?
3. What is the difference between short term and long term profit maximisation?
4. Why might a business pursue growth as an objective?
5. Which stakeholders involved in the business are likely to want business growth? Explain why.
6. List 5 examples of managerial objectives.
7. Who would favour sales revenue maximisation in an organisation?
8. Why has the importance of image and social responsibility as a business objective grown?
9. What factors determine business objectives?
10. What might be the objectives of public sector business organisations?
11. What is included in a mission statement?

# Case study Northern Foods

Northern Foods is a leading UK food producer. The company serves most of the leading retailers in the UK and operates in the eight core product areas.

1. Recipe dishes such as pasta meals and snacks, Indian, Chinese and other international dishes.
2. Chilled savoury products such as pies, pasties quiches and scotch eggs.
3. Speciality bread such as rolls, baps, muffins, scones, baguettes and croissants.
4. Bread-based snacks such as fresh chilled sandwiches, filed rolls and pizzas.
5. Cakes and puddings.
6. Fresh chilled dairy products such as desserts, yogurts, fromage frais and cottage cheese.
7. Biscuits under the name of Fox's, the UK's largest manufacturer of premium quality biscuits.
8. Frozen foods such as pizzas under the name of Goodfellas and Dalepack grillsteaks and burgers.

In addition to creating value for shareholders Northern also recognises the needs of other stakeholders such as employees, customers, suppliers, the community and the wider environment.

### Employees
Northern is committed to improving the welfare of its workforce. Many of its operations have received awards for health and safety performance. For example, Pennine Foods, Walter Hollands and Palethorpes each received a gold award from the Royal Society for the Prevention of Accidents. Northern is also committed to the development of its staff. For example, the company provides a flexible, modular training programme with business benefits accruing from work-related projects which form part of the curriculum. The Northern Foods Manufacturing Management Postgraduate Certificate is accredited by Sheffield Hallam University.

### Suppliers
In recent years Northern has consolidated its supply base. It claims to have a long history of trading fairly and responsibly throughout the supply chain. The company is currently working towards monitoring the ethical standards of its suppliers through a system of co-operation and collaboration.

### The community

Northern supports communities near to their operating units through donations, employee secondments and employee fundraising. Donations are made through the Northern Foods Social Responsibility Committee and site-based local charity committees. For example, £266,000 of cash donations were made in 2003. Beneficiaries included Oxfam, Samaritans, Sobriety Project Yorkshire, Farm Africa and the Citizen's Advice Bureau Grimsby. Northern also offers graduate trainee managers the chance to carry out a two week assignment with a local community organisation.

### The environment

Northern manages its impact on the environment by reducing emissions and making better use of resources. For example, the company met its target for energy efficiency improvement in line with the Climate Change Levy Agreement. Most of its sites beat the 2% reduction in energy consumption target and a computer programme to monitor energy consumption in their factories was developed. Also, the company's Gunstones Bakery won an award (Acorn Level 5) following an external audit for the development of an environmental management system.

### *Chief executive's statement*

*'Our aim remains the creation of shareholder value as the most effective added value food manufacturer addressing the UK retail market.'*

Source: adapted from Northern Foods, *Annual Report and Accounts, 2003.*

(a) What is meant by social responsibility as a business objective? (6 marks)

(b)(i) Calculate, as a percentage of turnover, the amount of money that Northern Foods donated to charities in 2003. (2 marks)

   (ii) To what extent, in your view, is Northern committed to the local community? (8 marks)

(c) Explain the factors which might affect the degree to which Northern Foods is socially responsible. (12 marks)

**Figure 4.11** *Turnover*

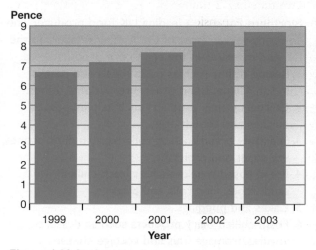

**Figure 4.12** *Dividend per share*

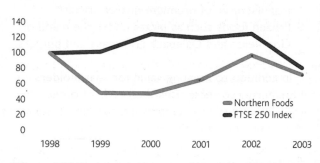

**Figure 4.13** *Total shareholder return (share price growth)*

(d)Which business objectives are the most important to Northern Foods in your view? (12 marks)

## What is strategy?

Unit 4 looked at the different objectives that businesses might have. Once a business has clarified its objectives it needs to plan how to achieve them and decide on the most suitable strategies to use. A company's STRATEGY is the pattern of decisions and actions that are taken to achieve its aims and objectives. For example, in August 2003 Telling Golden Miller Group plc floated on the Alternative Investment Market (AIM). The business is a London based bus and coach operator. The placing on the AIM raised £2 million for the business, which was to be used to fund acquisitions of businesses and new depots. Since the flotation, the company has bought Crystal Coaches in Dartford, which increased the bus routes operated by the Group from 13 to 17. In January 2004 Tesco raised £773 million by a share placing on the stock exchange to fund expansion.

## Planning and strategy

Most businesses will plan a strategy carefully. Business PLANNING involves deciding what is to be done, setting objectives and developing policies to achieve them. Some plans and strategies will be short term. These will focus on short term objectives such as surviving a recession. Others are long term and will be introduced to achieve long term objectives such as market domination.

There is a number of stages involved in the planning process. These include:
- identifying objectives;
- analysing the position of the business;
- deciding on a suitable strategy;
- implementing the strategy and evaluating its effectiveness.

## Identifying objectives

The first stage in the process is identifying the particular objectives the business wants to achieve. This is important because without clear objectives a business may begin to under-perform. At worst it could be taken over or collapse. It is possible to categorise the objectives of a business.

**Strategic objectives** These are objectives that concern the general direction and overall policy of the business. They are far reaching and can influence the performance of the organisation. They will also be long-term objectives and carry a degree of risk. An example might be the merger of two of the world's largest pharmaceutical companies, Glaxo Wellcome and SmithKline Beecham in 2000 to form GlaxoSmithKline.

**Tactical objectives** These are less far reaching than strategic objectives. They are tactical because they are calculated and the likelihood of achieving them is more predictable. Tactical

---

Bovis Homes, the house builder, which serves the lower/middle income market with average house prices of £190,800, announced it was in a position for another year of progress in January 2004. The improvement was put down to a wider spread of sites and the continued strength of the market. Previously Bovis had concentrated its sites in the South East, South West and the Midlands, but it had recently expanded into the North of England. It suggested that sales were ahead of average and prices 10 per cent higher than forecast. Analysts predicted profits of £118 million for the business, an improvement on the record £104.7 million in 2002.

De Vere Group is a Warrington based organisation with three core activities:
- 21 up market De Vere Hotels, including the flagship Belfry Hotel at the golf course;
- Village Leisure - a chain of mid-market hotels;
- Greens, a stand alone health and fitness club.

In January 2004 it announced plans to sell two of its mid-priced hotels and two of its De Vere hotels. It argued they 'no longer fitted the company profile'. The business had carried out a three month review aimed at improving returns.

In January 2004 Boots the Chemist was expected to announce plans to cut 1,000 of the 3,000 jobs at its head office as part of a shake up in the business. The move was part of a 'Getting in Shape' programme by the company. The Boots group hoped that this new strategy would make £100 million cost savings by 2005-2006.

Source: adapted from Manchester Online.

(a) Describe the changes in strategies at the three businesses.
(b) Explain possible objectives the businesses may have had in changing their strategies.

**Question 1**

objectives may be set in order to achieve strategic objectives. For example, if a business has set an objective to become a global operator in six years, establishing a foothold in Europe within one year may be a tactical objective.

**Operational objectives** These are lower level objectives and will be short term. They will carry little risk, require less planning and can be achieved fairly quickly. For example, completing a customer order by the end of the day might be an operational objective.

## Methods of analysis

Once a business has identified an objective, the next stage in planning its strategy is to consider its current position. A thorough analysis of its circumstances will provide the business with a variety of information that can be used to develop suitable strategies. Two methods that a business might use are SWOT analysis and PEST-G analysis.

## SWOT analysis

The purpose of SWOT ANALYSIS is to conduct a general and quick examination of a business's current position so that it can identify preferred and likely directions in future. SWOT analysis involves looking at the internal strengths and weaknesses of a business and the external opportunities and threats.

**Strengths** These are things that the business and its staff do which:
● they are effective at;
● they are well known for;
● make money;
● generate business and reputation;
● lead to confidence in the market;
● cause customers to come back for repeat business;
● cause other businesses to try to learn from them.

**Weaknesses** These are the things that the business does badly, that it is ineffective at or that it has a poor reputation for. It also includes the factors that cause losses, hardships, disputes, grievances and complaints for a business.

**Opportunities** These are the directions that the business could profitably take in future because of its strengths or because of the elimination of its weaknesses. This involves a consideration of the business environment from the widest and most creative possible standpoints.

**Threats** Threats to a business arise from the activities of competitors and from failing to take opportunities or to build on successes. Threats also come from complacency, a lack of rigour, and from falling profits, perhaps due to rising costs.

The analysis is often carried out as a discussion exercise. It is an effective way of gathering and categorising information, illustrating particular matters and generating interest in the

business and its activities quickly. The result of such an exercise may provide a basis on which a more detailed analysis can be conducted. SWOT analysis is often used as a method by which marketing departments can plan their marketing strategy (☞ unit 32).

## Pest-G analysis

PEST-G ANALYSIS examines the external environment and the global factors that may affect a business. It can provide a quick and visual representation of the external pressures facing a business, and their possible constraints on strategy. It is usually divided into five external influences on a business - political, economic, social, technological and green.

**Political** This is concerned with how political developments, regionally, nationally and internationally might affect a business's strategy. It might include a consideration of legislation, such as consumer laws, regulation, such as control of water companies, political pressures and the government's view of certain activities. In 2006 UK companies faced the prospect of having to comply with new UK legislation and EU regulations about age discrimination, for example.

**Economic** This might involve the analysis of a variety of economic factors and their effects on business. They might include:
● consumer activity - confidence, spending patterns, willingness to spend;
● economic variables - inflation, unemployment, trade, growth;
● government policy - fiscal, monetary, supply side, exchange rate;
● fixed and variable costs of the business;
● the effect of changes in product and labour markets.
For example, in a recession (☞ unit 96) demand for many products and services tends to fall. Businesses may also need to analyse the possible effects on their plans of government policy designed to lift the economy out of the recession.

**Social** What COMPETITVE ADVANTAGE might a business gain by social changes taking place outside of the business? For example, after the year 2000 the UK had a falling birth rate, an increase in life expectancy and an ageing population. This has led to the development of products, particularly private pensions, private medical schemes, sheltered housing developments and 'third age' holidays, aimed at the older age group. Pressure groups can also affect businesses (☞ unit 102). The anti-smoking lobby, for example, has led to smoke free areas in restaurants, in hotels, and on aircraft.

**Technological** Businesses operate in a world of rapid technological change (☞ unit 85). Organisations need to regularly review the impact of new technologies upon their activities. Products can become obsolete quickly. Production methods can become out of date. Communication may become inefficient as ICT develops. New markets may open.

For example, some music companies have considered sales via the Internet. The strategy towards R&D is vital in industries where technological change is rapid.

**Green** Environmental or 'green' factors can influence the decisions of a business. Environmental factors might include legislation to control pollution or consumers' views about the ingredients of products. Taking into account environmental considerations may raise costs, but might also generate greater sales.

## Types of business strategy

When a business has completed the analysis stage it must decide upon a suitable strategy to achieve its objectives. Strategies can take a number of forms.

**Functional strategies** Functional strategies are designed to improve the efficiency of a business. They focus on one area, such as production, marketing, product development or financial control. However, they should not be implemented in isolation. Cooperation between departments is essential if the strategy is to be effective. Examples of functional strategies might include:

- lean production (☞ unit 80) methods to reduce waste and lower production costs;
- improving staff skills with training;
- matching consumers' needs better, through improved market research techniques.

**Business level strategies** These are plans a company uses to gain a competitve advantage over its rivals. They are sometimes called **generic strategies** because all businesses can use them. They often involve exploiting a particular strength that a business has. Examples of generic strategies might include:

- cost leadership, where a business aims to be the lowest cost producer in the market so that its prices can be lower;
- consolidation in a market, perhaps by developing a more effective marketing strategy;
- diversification, where a business aims to produce a wider range of goods or services.

**Corporate strategies** These are aimed at the long term position of the business. They are designed to develop the overall shape and nature of the organisation. For example, they might involve:

- organic growth, where a business expands through internal development by opening 10 new stores per year;
- joining together formally with another company to form a larger organisation;
- buying other companies to grow quickly.

**Global strategies** These involve the development of a business outside national boundaries. For example:

- setting up production plants in countries where costs are lower;
- setting up operations in other countries to avoid tariffs;
- transferring skills or products to another country because competitors in those countries lack them.

## Implementation and evaluation

Once a business has identified its strategies they need to be implemented. The organisational and management systems needed to carry out the strategies have to be put into place. This might involve adapting existing systems or designing new ones. Businesses also need to maintain control while strategies are being implemented, ensuring that managers keep within their budgets, for example.

Finally, a business needs to assess whether the new strategies have been successful. To do this it must measure performance against targets that have been set. Information generated in the evaluation process may be used to adjust strategies if necessary.

## Corporate culture

CORPORATE CULTURE (☞ unit 15) is a set of values and beliefs that are shared by people and groups in the organisation. A simple way of explaining corporate culture might be to say that it is the 'way that things are done in business', eg the McDonald's way. For example, at Microsoft, the computer company, staff work long hours, dress casually and communicate by e-mail. These are the norms of behaviour.

Business leaders are able to create a corporate culture to help achieve the corporate objectives and strategy of the company. For example, some businesses encourage staff to solve their own problems and take risks. This will help the business to be more creative, which might make the company more innovative and give it a competitive advantage.

It is important to ensure that all staff working in an organisation understand its culture. If a positive corporate culture has been fostered by an organisation, new staff need to be trained when they are inducted (☞ unit 67). The culture must also be reinforced in everyday work situations.

There are certain benefits to a business of establishing a strong corporate culture.

- It provides a sense of identity for employees. They feel part of the business. This may allow workers to be flexible when the company needs to change or is having difficulties.
- Workers identify with other employees. This may help with aspects of the business such as team work.
- It increases the commitment of employees to the company. This may prevent problems such as high labour turnover or industrial relations problems.
- It motivates workers in their jobs. This may lead to increased productivity.
- It allows employees to understand what is going on around them. It also enables them to interpret the meaning of different organisational activities. This can

prevent misunderstanding in operations or instructions passed to them.

● It helps to reinforce the values of the organisation and senior management.

● It serves as a control device for management with which to shape employee behaviour. This can help when setting company strategy.

Marsden Wafers was in a bad way when it was bought by Alistair Marsden (no relation). The company is a wafer biscuit manufacturer in Wigan. It was purchased with help from five investors, including venture capitalists and the HSBC bank. The company had to change its name to Rivington Foods as creditors would not lend because of the previous bad reputation.

Marsden realised the value of an image to sell products. So he bought the rights to use the Pink Panther cartoon character in advertising. He needed to obtain a licence from owners MGM for this. Turnover grew from just under £1 million to £7.5 million in 2003 over an eight year period. The business sells to all the main supermarket chains, from Aldi to Tesco.

The business has perhaps found it difficult to sell into Europe. 'They are all chocolate and no biscuit' says Marsden. But this is perhaps being over critical, as the company has recently exported to markets in Kuwait and the Middle East. Not all products are winners. A wafer bar with pink chocolate did not sell because parents thought it contained 'nasties'.

The UK spends nearly £2 billion on biscuits each year and the total consumption of cakes and biscuits remains fairly constant. However, developments in production and packaging technology have meant that biscuit products now have a far longer shelf life. This makes them better for exporting overseas and selling on shelves in shops.

Rivington also has a range of gluten free wafers, endorsed by the Coeliac Society. They have taken advantage of the increased awareness of intolerance to gluten products and other ingredients which affect allergies and also a general trend in society for more health conscious products.

As a smaller manufacturer, Rivington will also be helped by product endorsement. For example, it has a range endorsed by celebrity chef Ainsley Harriot.

Source: adapted from *en*, February 2003.

(a) Analyse the situation of Rivington Foods using PEST-G factors.

**Question 2**

---

## Knowledge ...Knowledge...Knowledge

1. 'Strategy is designed to achieve business goals.' Explain this statement.
2. Outline the stages of planning strategies, placing them in order.
3. Explain the difference between strategic and operational objectives.
4. Identify the 4 areas of SWOT analysis, stating which are internal and which are external.
5. What is the purpose of PEST-G analysis?
6. Give 2 possible examples of (i) generic; (ii) corporate business strategies.
7. Why is strategy evaluation important?
8. State 3 advantages of a strong corporate culture.

## key terms

**Competitive advantage** - the advantage that a business has over rivals. It can be gained in a number of ways.
**Corporate culture** - the values, beliefs and norms that are shared by people and groups in an organisation.
**PEST-G analysis** - an analysis of the political, economic, social, technological and green factors affecting a business.
**Planning** - the process of deciding, in advance, what is to be done and how it is to be done.
**Strategy** - the pattern of decisions and actions that are taken by the business to achieve its objectives.
**SWOT analysis** - an analysis of the internal strengths and weaknesses and the external threats and opportunities facing a business.

# Case study Greene King

Beer drinking in the UK is in decline. Overall sales have fallen by 9 per cent over the last decade. Wine is more appealing to women in particular, and is predicted to overtake the beer maket within the next few years. Cask ale is in even more trouble, with a 7 per cent fall in 2002 alone.

But some companies are still in there and fighting. Greene King Brewing Company sees the decline in tastes for ales as a chance to push up its market share. Its brands include IPA, Abbot Ale, Ruddles County and Old Speckled Hen. It now has a 15.4 per cent market share.

Rooney Anand was appointed managing director in 2001. He found a traditional British brewing company - conservative, hierarchical, loyal to products and ingrained habits. 'We had good beer, good brands and strong customer relationships' he said and that 'what people lacked in external focus they made up for in passion: they'd bleed Greene King'. But the focus on production lacked urgency and looking at the outside world. Buying other companies was the way to grow, rather than internally. There was little communication across functions and no feel of 'one company'.

Anand changed it round by refocussing on underused assets rather than radical cuts in jobs and changes. The company was passionate about its beer, but then why was quality so variable? Improvements have been made in many areas including labs. Greene King upgraded and gained ISO 9001 quality status across the whole company. It also began training people to taste in every department. So far 500 have been trained. No batch leaves without tasting at every part in the process. Everyone is responsible for quality. People now understand what the product is and there is greater consistency. Publicans and their staff who sell the beer are also given training and advice on storage and handling - a revolutionary improvement.

Another effort is in strengthening the brands. Too often the brands have been left unchanged. Efforts therefore need to be made to open the brands up to wider audiences, without putting off core buyers. As the figures show, there is no inevitability to the

**Figure 5.1** *Greene King market share of cask ale*
Source: adapted from Greene King estimates.

**Figure 5.2** *Beer market sales*
Source: adapted from Industry estimates.

**Figure 5.3** *Cask ale sales*
Source: adapted from Greene King estimates.

**Figure 5.4** *Wine market sales*
Source: adapted from ACNielson.

decline in real-ale if it is handled correctly.

The company is keen to stress that not everything is perfect. It's a competitive world and keeping up is a marathon. However, Greene King argues that with honest products and good people there's little a firm can't do.

Source: adapted from *The Observer*, 26.10.2003.

(a) (i) **Describe the corporate culture at Greene King before the changes were made. (6 marks)**

   (ii) **Suggest two problems that this might have had for the business. (6 marks)**

(b) **'Greene King changed corporate strategy.' Explain this statement using examples from the article. (8 marks)**

(c) **Explain how social factors might affect the sales of beer and wine. (8 marks)**

(d) **Evaluate the operation of Greene King using SWOT analysis. (12 marks)**

# 6 Business Organisations in the Private Sector

## What is a business organisation?

Businesses are often referred to as organisations. An ORGANISATION is a body that is set up to meet needs. For example, the St. John's Ambulance organisation was originally set up by volunteers to train the public in life saving measures.

**Business organisations** satisfy needs by providing people with goods and services. All organisations will:

- try to achieve objectives (☞ unit 4);
- use resources;
- need to be directed;
- have to be accountable;
- have to meet legal requirements;
- have a formal structure (☞ unit 58).

## Private sector business organisations

Unit 1 showed the different methods of classifying business. One of these methods was by sector. The PRIVATE SECTOR includes all those businesses which are set up by individuals or groups of individuals. Most business activity is undertaken in the private sector. The types of business in the private sector can vary considerably. Some are small retailers with a single owner. Others are large multinational companies (☞ unit 109), such as Exxon Mobil and Cadbury Schweppes. Businesses will vary according to the legal form they take and their ownership.

- Unincorporated businesses. These are businesses where there is no legal difference between the owners and the business. Everything is carried out in the name of the owner or owners. These firms tend to be small, owned either by one person or a few partners.

- Incorporated businesses. An incorporated body is one which has a separate legal identity from its owners. In other words, the business can be sued, can be taken over and can be liquidated.

Figure 6.1 shows the different types of business organisation in the private sector, their legal status and their ownership. These are examined in the rest of this unit.

## The sole trader

The simplest and most common form of private sector business is a SOLE TRADER or SOLE PROPRIETOR. This type of business is owned by just one person. The owner runs the business and may employ any number of people to help.

Sole traders can be found in different types of production. In the primary sector many farmers and fishermen operate like this. In the secondary sector there are small scale manufacturers, builders and construction firms. The tertiary sector probably contains the largest number of sole traders. They supply a wide range of services, such as hairdressing, retailing, restaurants, gardening and other household services. Many sole traders exist in retailing and construction where a very large number of shops and small construction companies are each owned by one person. Although there are many more sole traders than any other type of business, the amount they contribute to total output in the UK is relatively small.

Setting up as a sole trader is straightforward. There are no legal formalities needed. However, sole traders or self-employed dealers do have some legal responsibilities once they become established. In addition, some types of business need to obtain special permission before trading.

- Once turnover reaches a certain level sole traders must register for VAT.
- They must pay income tax and National Insurance contributions.

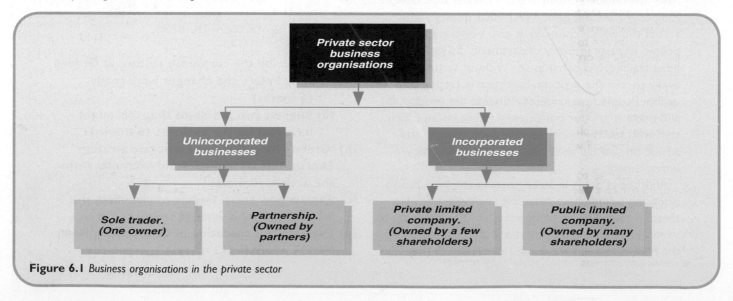

**Figure 6.1** *Business organisations in the private sector*

- Some types of business activity need a licence, such as the sale of alcohol or supplying a taxi service or public transport.
- Sometimes planning permission is needed in certain locations. For example, a person may have to apply to the local authority for planning permission to run a fish and chip shop in premises which had not been used for this activity before.
- Sole traders must comply with legislation aimed at business practice. For example, legally they must provide healthy and safe working conditions for their employees (☞ unit 69).

### Advantages of sole traders

- The lack of legal restrictions. The sole trader will not face a lengthy setting up period or incur expensive administration costs.
- Any profit made after tax is kept by the owner.
- The owner is in complete control and is free to make decisions without interference. For many sole traders independence is one of the main reasons why they choose to set up in business.
- The owner has flexibility to choose the hours of work he or she wants and to take holidays. Customers may also benefit. Sole traders can take individual customers' needs into account, stocking a particular brand of a good or making changes to a standard design, for example.

- Because of their small size, sole traders can offer a personal service to their customers. Some people prefer to deal directly with the owner and are prepared to pay a higher price for doing so.
- Such businesses may be entitled to government support.

### Disadvantages of sole traders

- Sole traders have UNLIMITED LIABILITY. This means that if the business has debts, the owner is personally liable. A sole trader may be forced to sell personal possessions or use personal savings to meet these debts.
- The money used to set up the business is often the owner's savings. It may also come from a bank loan. Sole traders may find it difficult to raise money. They tend to be small and lack sufficient **collateral**, such as property or land, on which to raise finance. This means money for expansion must come from profits or savings.
- Although independence is an advantage, it can also be a disadvantage. A sole trader might prefer to share decision making, for example. Many sole traders work very long hours, without holidays, and may have to learn new skills.
- In cases where the owner is the only person in the business, illness can stop business activity taking place. For example, if a sole trader is a mobile hairdresser, illness will lead to a loss of income in the short term, and even a loss of customers in the long term.
- Because sole traders are unincorporated businesses, the

---

Elaine Thomas took over the running of her parent's fish & chip shop in Newport in 1998 when they retired. She had always wanted to run the business herself because she had ideas on how it could grow. More than half of the current business was generated during lunch times. In the week customers came in from local businesses to buy their lunch. Summer lunch times were particularly busy. In the evenings her father had always closed the shop at 8.30 pm. He wasn't interested in the 11-12.00 pm 'drunks trade' as he called it. There were two pubs within 200 yards of the shop and it seemed like a missed opportunity to Elaine. Within two weeks of taking over the business she made the following changes.

- Opening hours were extended until 12.00 midnight.
- A delivery service to local businesses was offered if they placed telephone orders over £10 (this was intended to help boost winter lunchtime trade).
- The menu was extended, offering a much wider range of fast-foods such as pizzas, home-made pies and fresh sandwiches.
- A cheaper fish supplier was used.
- Two part-time staff were hired to help share the extra work load.

The changes seemed to pay off. Over the next four years sales grew by 15 per cent per annum. Elaine was delighted and as a result became even more ambitious. She decided to open a fish restaurant. She took out a £7,000 bank loan and refurbished an empty room at the back of the shop. This was when things started to go wrong. She did not get planning permission for the restaurant and was forced to borrow another £3,000 from

her parents to pay for legal costs. The opening of the restaurant was delayed and when it was finally opened the number of diners was disappointing. Elaine spent more money advertising the restaurant, but this didn't seem to make much difference. Then, the business had a number of other setbacks. One of the nearby pubs started to sell lunch time food and two local businesses that were customers relocated to Cardiff. Lunch time trade fell by two-thirds as a result. Also, one of Elaine's employees badly burned her hand in the chip fryer. Elaine was underinsured and had to pay the employee compensation from the business. Elaine started to lose enthusiasm and by 2003 she was forced into bankruptcy. She owed a total of £16,000 and after selling the assets of the business she was left with only £2,500.

Figure 6.2 *Business debts of Elaine Thomas*

(a) What features of a sole trader does this case show?
(b) Using this case as an example, explain what is meant by unlimited liability.

**Question** 1

owner can be sued by customers in the event of a dispute.
● The business may rely on the ability and drive of one person. If that person loses interest or dies then the business will cease.

## Partnerships

A PARTNERSHIP is defined in **The Partnership Act, 1890** as the 'relation which subsists between persons carrying on business with common view to profit'. Put simply, a partnership has more than one owner. The 'joint' owners will share responsibility for running the business and also share the profits. Partnerships are often found in the professions, such as accountants, doctors, estate agents, solicitors and veterinary surgeons. After sole traders, partnerships are the most common type of business organisation. It is usual for partners to specialise. A firm of chartered accountants with five partners might find that each partner specialises in one aspect of finance, such as tax law, investments or VAT returns.

There are no legal formalities to complete when a partnership is formed. However, partners may draw up a DEED OF PARTNERSHIP. This is a legal document which states partners' rights in the event of a dispute. It covers issues such as:
● how much capital each partner will contribute;
● how profits (and losses) will be shared amongst the partners;
● the procedure for ending the partnership;
● how much control each partner has;
● rules for taking on new partners.

If no deed of partnership is drawn up the arrangements between partners will be subject to the Partnership Act. For example, if there was a dispute regarding the share of profits, the Act states that profits are shared equally amongst the partners.

### Advantages of partnerships
● There are no legal formalities to complete when setting up the business.
● Each partner can specialise. This may improve the running of the business, as partners can carry out the tasks they do best.
● Since there is more than one owner, more finance can be raised than if the firm was a sole trader.
● Partners can share the workload. They will be able to cover each other for holidays and illness. They can also exchange ideas and opinions when making key decisions. Also, the success of the business will not depend upon the ability of one person, as is the case with a sole trader.
● Since this type of business tends to be larger than the sole trader, it is in a stronger position to raise more money from outside the business.

### Disadvantages of partnerships
● The individual partners have unlimited liability. Under the Partnership Act, each partner is equally liable for debts.

● Profits have to be shared amongst more owners.
● Partners may disagree. For example, they might differ in their views on whether to hire a new employee or about the amount of profit to retain for investment.
● The size of a partnership is limited to a maximum of 20 partners. This limits the amount of money that can be introduced from owners.
● The partnership ends when one of the partners dies. The partnership must be wound up so that the partner's family can retrieve money invested in the business. It is normal for the remaining partners to form a new partnership quickly afterwards.
● Any decision made by one partner on behalf of the company is legally binding on all other partners. For example, if one partner agreed to buy four new company cars for the business, all partners must honour this.
● Partnerships have unincorporated status, so partners can be sued by customers.

**Limited partnerships** The **Limited Partnerships Act 1907** allows a business to become a LIMITED PARTNERSHIP, although this is rare. This is where some partners provide capital but take no part in the management of the business. Such a partner will have LIMITED LIABILITY - the partner can only lose the original amount of money invested. She can not be made to sell personal possessions to meet any other

Doctors Wilkinson, Pritchard, Poonwalla and Sykes operate their medical centre as a partnership. The practice also employs three medical secretaries, three receptionists and two nurses. When the business was formed in 2001 it was decided that a Deed of Partnership was not needed. Each partner contributed £15,000 towards the setting up of the practice. Much of this money was spent converting an old Victorian house into a suitable practice.

Unfortunately, after two years, Dr Sykes decided to leave the practice. He did not share the same views as the other members of the partnership when it came to the prescribing of new drugs and treatments. This proved to be a problem. The business did not have enough money to pay off Dr Sykes and return the original capital contribution. The existing partnership had to be wound up and there was a difficult period when the partners couldn't agree how much profit Dr Sykes was entitled to as a result of leaving so suddenly.

(a) What are the advantages of drawing up a Deed of Partnership?
(b) In what way does the case illustrate the disadvantages of operating as a partnership?

Question 2

business debts. This type of partner is called a **sleeping partner**. Even with a limited partnership there must always be at least one partner with **unlimited liability**. The Act also allows this type of partnership to have more than 20 partners.

The **Limited Liability Partnership Act, 2000** allows the setting up of a LIMITED LIABILITY PARTNERSHIP. All partners in this type of partnership have limited liability. To set up as a limited liability partnership, the business has to agree to comply with a number of regulations, such as filing annual reports with the Registrar of Companies.

## Companies

There are many examples of LIMITED COMPANIES in the UK. They range from Garrick Engineering, a small family business, to British Airways which has many thousands of shareholders. One feature is that they all have a separate legal identity from their owners. This means that they can own assets, form contracts, employ people, sue and be sued in their own right. Another feature is that the owners all have **limited liability**. If a limited company has debts, the owners can only lose the money they have invested in the firm. They cannot be forced to use their own money, like sole traders and partners, to pay business debts.

The **capital** of a limited company is divided into **shares**. Each member or **shareholder** (☞ unit 3) owns a number of these shares. They are the joint owners of the company and can vote and take a share of the profit. Those with more shares will have more control and can take more profit.

Limited companies are run by **directors** who are appointed by the shareholders. The board of directors, headed by a **chairperson**, is accountable to shareholders and should run the company as the shareholders wish. If the company's performance does not to live up to shareholders' expectations, directors can be 'voted out' at an **Annual General Meeting (AGM)**.

Whereas sole traders and partnerships pay income tax on profits, companies pay corporation tax.

## Forming a limited company

How do shareholders set up a limited company? Limited companies must produce two documents - the **Memorandum of Association** and **Articles of Association**. The Memorandum sets out the constitution and gives details about the company. The **Companies Act 1985** states that the following details must be included.

● The name of the company.
● The name and address of the company's registered office.
● The objectives of the company, and the scope of its activities.
● The liability of its members.
● The amount of capital to be raised and the number of shares to be issued.

A limited company must have a minimum of two members, but there is no upper limit.

The Articles of Association deal with the internal running of the company. They include details such as:

● the rights of shareholders depending on the type of share they hold;
● the procedures for appointing directors and the scope of their powers;
● the length of time directors should serve before re-election;
● the timing and frequency of company meetings;
● the arrangements for auditing company accounts.

These two documents, along with a statement indicating the names of the directors, will be sent to the Registrar of Companies. If they are acceptable, the company's application will be successful. It will be awarded a **Certificate of Incorporation** which allows it to trade. The registrar keeps these documents on file and they can be inspected at any time by the general public for a fee. A limited company must also submit a copy of its annual accounts to the Registrar each year. Finally, the shareholders have a legal right to attend the AGM and should be told of the date and venue in writing well in advance.

## Private limited companies

**Private limited companies** are one type of limited company. They tend to be relatively smaller businesses, although certain well known companies, such as Reebok and Littlewoods, are private limited companies. Their business name ends in Limited or Ltd. Shares can only be transferred 'privately' and all shareholders must agree on the transfer. They cannot be advertised for general sale. Private limited companies are often family businesses owned by members of the family or close friends. The directors of these firms tend to be shareholders and are involved in the running of the business. Many manufacturing firms are private limited companies rather than sole traders or partnerships.

### Advantages

● Shareholders have limited liability. As a result more people are prepared to risk their money than in, say, a partnership.
● More capital can be raised as there is no limit on the number of shareholders.
● Control of the company cannot be lost to outsiders. Shares can only be sold to new members if all shareholders agree.
● The business will continue even if one of the owners dies. In this case shares will be transferred to another owner.

### Disadvantages

● Profits have to be shared out amongst a much larger number of members.
● There is a legal procedure to set up the business. This takes time and also costs money.
● Firms are not allowed to sell shares to the public. This restricts the amount of capital that can be raised.
● Financial information filed with the Registrar can be

inspected by any member of the public. Competitors could use this to their advantage.

● If one shareholder decides to sell shares it may take time to find a buyer.

---

Porterhouse Property Management Ltd was incorporated in November 2003 as a private limited company. The registered office of the company is 27 Market Street, Kendal, Cumbria. The main aim of Porterhouse Property, as set out in clause 4 of its Memorandum of Association, are to act as a property services company and enter into financial transactions of all kinds.

**Figure 6.3** *Porterhouse Property Management Ltd - shareholders*

The chairperson, Anita Dawson, hopes to expand the company rapidly. Porterhouse currently manage about 200 country cottages in the Lake District. However, Anita wants to start buying properties and expects to use bank loans and mortgages to fund the purchases. The company is owned by four shareholders and employs eight staff.

(a) Explain the main purpose of the Memorandum of Association for Porterhouse Property Management Ltd.
(b) Discuss the possible advantages to Porterhouse Property Management Ltd of forming a private limited company.

# Question 3

# Public limited companies

The second type of limited company tends to be larger and is called a **public limited company**. This company name ends in plc. There are around 1.2 million registered limited companies in the UK, but only around 1 per cent of them are public limited companies. However, they contribute far more to national output and employ far more people than private limited companies. The shares of these companies can be bought and sold by the public on the stock exchange (☞ unit 44).

To become a public limited company, a Memorandum of Association, Articles of Association and a **Statutory Declaration** must be provided. This is a document which states that the requirements of all the Company Acts have been met. When the company has been issued with a **Certificate of Incorporation**, it is common to publish a **Prospectus**. This is a document which advertises the company to potential investors and invites them to buy shares before a FLOTATION. An example of a company that has been floated on the stock exchange is Egg, the online bank. Egg was floated by Prudential in 2000. It was suggested that Tussauds, Europe's

biggest attractions business, responsible for the running of Madame Tussauds waxworks, the London Eye and Alton Towers, would be floated in early 2004. The majority owner, Charterhouse Development Capital, was aiming to sell it for around £900 million.

'Going public' is expensive. This is because:

● the company needs lawyers to ensure that the prospectus is 'legally' correct;
● a large number of 'glossy' publications have to be made available;
● the company may use a financial institution to process share applications;
● the share issue has to be **underwritten** (which means that the company must insure against the possibility of some shares remaining unsold) and a fee is paid to an underwriter who must buy any unsold shares;
● the company will have advertising and administrative expenses;
● it must have a minimum of £50,000 share capital.

A public limited company cannot begin trading until it has completed these tasks and has received at least a 25 per cent payment for the value of shares. It will then receive a Trading Certificate and can begin operating, and the shares will be quoted on the Stock Exchange or the Alternative Investment Market (AIM) (☞ unit 44).

The stock exchange is a market where second hand shares are bought and sold. A full stock exchange listing means that the company must comply with the rules and regulations laid down by the stock exchange. Many of these rules are to protect shareholders from fraud. The AIM is designed for companies which want to avoid some of the high costs of a full listing. However, shareholders with shares quoted on the AIM do not have the same protection as those with 'fully' quoted shares.

## Advantages

Some of the advantages are the same as those of private limited companies. For example, all members have limited liability, the firm continues to trade if one of the owners dies and more power is enjoyed due to their larger size. Others are as follows.

● Huge amounts of money can be raised from the sale of shares to the public.
● Production costs may be lower as firms may gain economies of scale (☞ unit 81).
● Because of their size, plcs can often dominate the market.
● It becomes easier to raise finance as financial institutions are more willing to lend to plcs.

## Disadvantages

● The setting up costs can be very expensive - running into millions of pounds in some cases.
● Since anyone can buy their shares, it is possible for an outside interest to take control of the company.
● All of the company's accounts can be inspected by members of the public. Competitors may be able to use some of this information to their advantage. They have to publish more information than private limited companies.

- Because of their size they are not able to deal with their customers at a personal level.
- The way they operate is controlled by various Company Acts which aim to protect shareholders.
- There may be a divorce of ownership and control (☞ unit 3) which might lead to the interests of the owners being ignored to some extent.
- It is argued that many of these companies are inflexible due to their size. For example, they find change difficult to cope with.

Some public limited companies are very large indeed. They have millions of shareholders and a wide variety of business interests situated all over the world. They are known as **multinationals** (☞ unit 109) which means that they have production plants in a number of different countries. For example, Kellogg's is an American based multinational company with a production plant and head office situated in Battle Creek, USA. Kellogg's has also had factories in Manchester, Wrexham, Bremen, Barcelona and Brescia near Milan.

## Exiting the stock market

Sometimes a business operating as a public limited company is taken back into private ownership. This may be called 'exiting the stock market'. Why does it happen?

- The people responsible for running the business might no longer be willing to tolerate interference from the external shareholders. For example, shareholders such as financial institutions may demand higher dividends when the senior managers would prefer to reinvest profits to generate more growth.
- Sometimes businesses lose favour with the stock market. This may happen when city analysts publish unhelpful or negative reports about companies failing to reach profit targets for example. Such publicity often has the effect of lowering the share price very sharply.
- A business currently operating as a plc may be bought outright by a private individual. For example, Philip Green, bought Bhs, the high street clothes retailer, from Storehouse in 2000. He also bought Arcadia in 2002 for a reported £770 million. Both of these companies were part of a plc organisation until purchased.

## Holding companies

Some public limited companies operate as HOLDING COMPANIES. This means that they are not only a company in their own right, but also have enough shares in numerous other public limited companies to exert control. This type of company tends to have a very diversified range of business activities. For example, in the UK the TTP Group plc is a holding company for a number of technology businesses. These include TTP LabTech, which supplies products to the healthcare and pharmaceutical sectors and Acumen Bioscience which develops and provides screening instruments for the drug discovery industry.

The main advantage of this type of company is that it tends to have a diverse range of business activities. This helps protect it when one of its markets fails. Also, because it is so large, it can often gain financial economies of scale. The main disadvantage is that the holding company may see the businesses it owns only as a financial asset. It may have no long term interest in the businesses or its development.

## Consumer co-operatives

The UK Co-operative Movement grew from the activities of 28 workers in Rochdale, Lancashire. In 1844 they set up a retail co-operative society - The Rochdale Equitable Pioneers Society. With capital of just £28 they bought food from wholesalers and opened a shop, selling 'wholesome food at reasonable prices'. The surplus (or profit) made was returned to members of the society in the form of a 'dividend'. The dividend was in proportion to how much each member had spent. The principles of the society were:

- voluntary and open membership;
- democratic ownership - one member, one vote;
- the surplus allocated according to spending (the dividend);
- educational facilities for members and workers.

The principles of the modern co-operative movement are similar. CONSUMER CO-OPERATIVES are usually organised on a regional basis, such as The West Midlands Co-op Society or the Southern Co-op. Co-operatives are owned and controlled by their members. Members can purchase shares which entitle them to a vote at Annual General Meetings. The members elect a board of directors to make overall business decisions and appoint managers to run day to day business. Co-operatives are run in the interests of their members. Members can put themselves forward to be elected to the board of directors and become involved in a range of different activities, such as help for local community groups. Any surplus made by the co-operative is distributed to members as a dividend. Shares are not sold on the stock exchange, which limits the amount of money that can be raised.

The world's largest consumer co-operative is The Co-operative Retail Group. This was set up in 2000 by the joining of two organisations:

- The Co-operative Retail Society (CRS) in Manchester, the largest co-operative retailer at the time;
- The Co-operative Wholesale Society (CWS), which acted as a manufacturer and wholesaler of 'own brand' products for co-operative retailers.

Consumer co-operatives often have a number of different activities.

- **Food retail activities.** Perhaps the most familiar activity of co-operatives is the co-operative retail food store. Co-operative retail stores have faced fierce competition from supermarkets in recent years. They have responded by offering convenience stores which stay open later and may be sited in rural locations, such as Chelmsford (Altogether Fresher and Food Centres shops run by Chelmsford Star Co-op) or Coventry, Warwickshire and Leicestershire (Lateshops run by the Heart of England Co-op). Some are now starting to offer on-line shopping.

- **Other retail activities.** These include department stores (such as Derrys run by The Plymouth and South West Co-op), furniture shops, electrical goods shops and off licences. Shoefayre is a consumer co-operative that specialises in selling footwear.
- **Financial services.** Co-operative Financial Services (CFS) is part of The Co-operative Retail Group. It owns and runs the Co-operative Bank, whose aim is to deal only in ethical transactions, and the Co-operative Insurance Society (CIS).
- **Travel.** The UK's largest independent travel agent is Travelcare, run by The Co-operative Retail Group. Many other consumer co-operatives also offer travel services.
- **Funeral.** Funeral services are offered by some co-operatives. Examples include the Lincoln Co-operative Funeral Services and The West Midlands Co-operative Funeral Services.
- **Farming.** The Co-operative Group runs Farmcare, a farm management business. It farms around 85,000 acres in 23 locations in the UK, mostly for landowners. It grows arable crops, fruit and vegetables and has 3,000 dairy cows.

## Worker co-operatives

Another form of co-operation in the UK with common ownership is a WORKER CO-OPERATIVE. This is where a business is jointly owned by its employees. A worker co-operative is an example of a producer co-operative - where people work together to produce a good or service. Examples might be a wine growing co-operative or a co-operative of farmers producing milk.

In a worker co-operative employees are likely to:
- contribute to production;
- be involved in decision making;
- share in the profit (usually on an equal basis);
- provide some capital when buying a share in the business.

In 2000 there were over 1,000 worker co-operatives in the UK. Examples ranged from Alpha Communications Ltd, a multimedia design company, to Edinburgh Bicycle Cooperative, a cycle retailer. One advantage of a worker co-operative is that all employees, as owners of the business, are likely to be motivated. Conflict will also tend to be reduced as the objectives of shareholders and employees will be the same. Worker co-operatives can involve the local community, either by giving donations to local bodies or even having them as members of the co-operative.

## Building and friendly societies

Most building societies and friendly societies in the UK are MUTUAL ORGANISATIONS. They are owned by their customers, or members as they are known, rather than shareholders. Profits go straight back to members in the form of better and cheaper products. Friendly societies began in the 18th and 19th centuries to support the working classes. Today friendly societies offer a wide range of 'affordable' financial services. These include savings schemes, insurance plans and protection against the loss of income or death. They also provide benefits such as free legal aid, sheltered housing or educational grants to help young people through university. These extra benefits are distributed free of charge, paid for by trading surpluses. The government gives friendly societies special tax treatment, which reduces the amount of tax that members pay.

Building societies used to specialise in mortgages and savings accounts. Savers and borrowers got better interest rates than those offered by banks. This was possible because building societies were non-profit making. In the 1980s building societies began to diversify and compete with banks. In the late 1990s a number of building societies, such as Halifax, Alliance and Leicester, and Northern Rock, became public limited companies. The main reason for this was because mutual organisations are restricted by law from raising large amounts of capital which might be used to invest in new business ventures. This **demutualisation** process involved societies giving members 'windfall' payments, usually in the form of shares, to compensate them for their loss of membership.

## Charities

Charities are organisations with very specialised aims. They exist to raise money for 'good' causes and draw attention to the needs of disadvantaged groups in society. For example, Age Concern is a charity which raises money on behalf of senior citizens. They also raise awareness and pass comment on issues, such as cold weather payments, which relate to the elderly. Other examples of national charities include Cancer Research Campaign, British Red Cross, Save the Children Fund and Mencap.

Charities rely on donations for their revenue. They also organise fund raising events such as fetes, jumble sales, sponsored activities and raffles. A number of charities run business ventures. For example, Oxfam has a chain of charity shops which sells second hand goods donated by the public.

Charities are generally run according to business principles. They aim to minimise costs, market themselves and employ staff. Most staff are volunteers, but some of the larger charities employ professionals. In the larger charities a lot of administration is necessary to deal with huge quantities of correspondence and handle charity funds. Provided charities are registered, they are not required to pay tax. In addition, businesses can offset any charitable donations they make against tax. This helps charities when raising funds.

## Franchises

If a person wants independence, but is better at carrying out or improving someone else's ideas than their own, franchising might be the ideal solution. Franchising has grown steadily. It was estimated that annual turnover of franchises in the UK was around £7 billion in 2000. There were around 550 business format franchises in 2000. Over 90 per cent of

Holly Watson is a sole trader. She runs a financial services business in London. She rented an office in Fulham and has enjoyed a great deal of success since setting up in 1991. In 1997 the Inland Revenue introduced self assessment for taxpayers. Holly believed that a lot of new business could be generated as a result. She initially wanted to attract new clients by offering a competitive self-assessment tax service. She then planned to develop further business with these clients by offering a wider range of financial services, such as personal investment plans and private pensions advice.

To carry out her plans Holly needed to:
- recruit staff experienced in income tax and self-assessment;
- go on a training course to improve her knowledge of the tax system;
- move into larger premises to accommodate the new staff and to build a reception area for clients. The reception area was a drafty corridor which was not in keeping with the image of a forward looking financial services company;
- invest in advertising and promotion to attract new clients.

After a meeting with her bank manager, Holly was faced with a problem. She needed to raise £75,000 to carry out her plans. The bank, however, would not lend her any of the money as Holly was unable to offer any collateral against a loan. The bank also felt that she may have difficulty repaying such a large amount given the current position of the business. It suggested that she invite new owners to contribute some capital to the business.

(a) Describe the possible alternative business organisations that may allow Holly to raise extra funds.
(b) Suggest one type of business organisation that may be suitable for Holly's business and explain the advantages and disadvantages of your recommendation.

franchisees reported that they were trading profitably.

There are many examples of franchises in the UK. They include names such as Wimpy, Dyno-rod, Body Shop and Holiday Inn. What types of FRANCHISE exist?
- Dealer franchises. These are used by petrol companies, breweries and vehicle and computer producers. The companies (the franchisors) agree that other businesses (the franchisees) can sell their products. A written agreement between the two will cover areas such as the back up service of the franchisor, maintaining the image of the franchisor, sales targets, stock levels and the 'territory' of the franchisee. For example, Ford Motor Company has not allowed dealers more than 5 dealerships or advertising outside the allocated 'area'. Ford does not charge a fee. It earns revenue by a mark up on sales to the dealer.
- Brand franchising. This is designed to allow an inexperienced franchisee to set up from scratch. It is used by businesses such as Wimpy and McDonald's. The franchisor will already have a reputation for a product or service. It 'sells' the rights of these branded products to the franchisee. The intention is that a consumer will know they are buying the same product whether in London or Edinburgh. It is important that franchisees are monitored to make sure that the standard is maintained. To buy the franchise a business will pay an initial fee, sometimes a deposit, and then an ongoing fee which is often a percentage of turnover (a royalty of, say, 10 per cent). Often publicity, marketing and support services are carried out by the franchisor.

The benefits to the franchisor might be:
- using the specialist skills of a franchisee (as in the case of Ford dealers' retailing skills);
- the market is increased without expanding the firm;
- a fairly reliable amount of revenue (because royalties are based on turnover not profits, money is guaranteed even if a loss is made by the franchisee);
- risks and uncertainty are shared.

The advantages to franchisees might be:
- the franchisor might advertise and promote the product nationally;
- they are selling a recognised product so the chance of failure is reduced;
- services such as training and administration may be carried out by the franchisor.

Franchising is not without its problems. The royalty must be paid even if a loss is made. Also franchisees may be simply 'branch managers', rather than running their own businesses, because of restrictions in the agreement. The franchisor has the power to withdraw the agreement and in some cases, prevent the franchisee from using the premises in future.

## Factors affecting the choice of organisation

**Age** Many businesses change their legal status as they become older. Most businesses when they start out are relatively small and operate as sole traders. Over time, as needs change, a sole trader may take on a partner and form a partnership. Alternatively, a sole trader may invite new owners to participate in the business, issue shares and form a private limited company. Public limited companies are often formed from established private limited companies that have been trading for many years.

**The need for finance** A change in legal status may be forced on a business. Often small businesses want to grow but do not have the funds. Additional finance can only be raised if the business changes status. Furthermore, many private limited companies 'go public' because they need to raise large amounts for expansion.

**Size** The size of a business operation is likely to affect its legal status. A great number of small businesses are usually sole traders or partnerships. Public limited companies tend to be large organisations with thousands of employees and a turnover of millions or billions of pounds. It could be argued that a very large business could only be run if it were a limited company. For example, certain types of business activity, such as oil processing and chemicals manufacture, require large scale production methods and could not be managed effectively as sole traders or partnerships.

**Limited liability** Owners can protect their own personal financial position if the business is a limited company. Sole traders and partners have unlimited liability. They may, therefore, be placed in a position where they have to use their own money to meet business debts. Some partnerships dealing with customers' money, such as solicitors, have to have unlimited liability in order to retain the confidence of their clients.

**Degree of control** Owners may consider retaining control of their business to be important. This is why many owners choose to remain as sole traders. Once new partners or shareholders become a part of the business the degree of control starts to diminish because it is shared with the new owners. It is possible to keep some control of a limited company by holding the majority of shares. However, even if one person holds 51 per cent of shares in a limited company, the wishes of the other 49 per cent cannot be ignored.

**The nature of the business** The type of business activity may influence the choice of legal status. For example, household services such as plumbing, decorating and gardening tend to be provided by sole traders. Professional services such as accountancy, legal advice and surveying are usually offered by partnerships. Relatively small manufacturing and family businesses tend to be private limited companies. Large manufacturers and producers of consumer durables, such as cookers, computers and cars, are usually plcs. The reason that these activities choose a particular type of legal status is because of the benefits they gain as a result. However, there are many exceptions to these general examples.

# key terms

**Consumer co-operative** - a business organisation which is run and owned jointly by the members, who have equal voting rights.

**Deed of Partnership** - a binding legal document which states the formal rights of partners.

**Flotation** - the process of a company 'going public'.

**Franchise -** an agreement where a business (the franchisor) sells the rights to other businesses (the franchisees) allowing them to sell products or use the company name.

**Holding company** - a public limited company which owns enough shares in a number of other companies to exert control over them.

**Limited company** - a business organisation which has a separate legal entity from those of its owners.

**Limited liability** - where a business owner is only liable for the original amount of money invested in the business.

**Limited Liability partnership** - a partnership where all partners have limited liability.

**Limited partnership** - a partnership where some members contribute capital and enjoy a share of profit, but do not participate in the running of the business. At least one partner must have unlimited liability.

**Mutual organisation** - businesses owned by members who are customers, rather than shareholders.

**Organisation** - a body set up to meet a need.

**Partnership** - a business organisation which is usually owned by between 2-20 people.

**Private sector** - businesses that are owned by individuals or groups of individuals.

**Sole trader or sole proprietor** - a business organisation which has a single owner.

**Unlimited liability** - where the owner of a business is personally liable for all business debts.

**Worker co-operative** - a business organisation owned by employees who contribute to production and share in profit.

Knowledge...Knowledge...Knowledge...Knowledge...Knowledge...Knowledge...Know

1. What is the difference between a corporate body and an unincorporated body?
2. State 3 advantages and 3 disadvantages of being a sole trader.
3. What is the advantage of a deed of partnership?
4. State 3 advantages and 3 disadvantages of partnerships.
5. What is meant by a sleeping partner?
6. What is the role of directors in limited companies?
7. What is the difference between the Memorandum of Association and the Articles of Association?
8. What is a Certificate of Incorporation?
9. Describe the advantages and disadvantages of private limited companies.
10. What are the main legal differences between private and public limited companies?
11. Describe the advantages and disadvantages of plcs.
12. How is a company prospectus used?
13. State an advantage and a disadvantage of a holding company.
14. State 3 features of a consumer co-operative.
15. State 3 benefits of a franchise for (a) the franchisor and the (b) the franchisee.

# Case study  James Hull Associates

James Hull owns Britain's largest private specialist dental business. His practice, which trades under the name of James Hull Associates, offers patients hi-tech clinical treatments, but also pampers them with soothing music and ceiling televisions in the dental surgery. James Hull has just appointed Numis Securities as a broker to look into floating the company, possibly before the end of 2003. The business is expected to be valued at between £55-£70 million and would result in Hull, who will retain 59 per cent of the business, becoming a multi-millionaire. Hull hopes to raise £20 million from the flotation.

The dental market is worth £3.25 billion a year and is said to be growing. Hull operates at the specialist end of the market. NHS dentist charges are around £80 per hour. This compares with up to £180 per hour in a private practice. However, specialists like James Hull, who may have spent a further five years training, can charge between £350 and £450 an hour. Mr Hull who started out doing mainly NHS work in 1988, currently runs 34 practices in which 85 per cent of the work is private with about 54 per cent specialist.

As part of his growth strategy James Hull bought the private practice element of the Eastman International Centre for Excellence in Dentistry, one of the most modern dentistry set-ups in the country it specialises in implants, gum and root canal work. Patients have been known to spend up to £95,000 on this type of treatment. He also announced the acquisition of two other specialist practices in October 2003. It is this specialist work that distinguishes James Hull's business from his quoted rivals, such as Oasis or Integrated Dental Holdings. The higher fees result in higher margins and faster growth for the company. Also, last year 500,000 implants were done in Germany compared to just 44,000 in the UK. Hull thinks the opportunities are huge. This will also make the flotation attractive to the City. However, dental groups have not performed that well on the stock market. The share price of Oasis is only $23^1/_4$ p. This is only about one third of its £73 million revenues. Another company, Integrated Dental Holdings (IDH), trading under the name of Whitecross, has seen its shares fall to 39p over the past year and trades at just over 10 per cent of forecast revenues of £70 million.

James Hull thinks his company will be more successful than his rivals. He says 'Although we're in the same sector, we're in a very different marketplace. People routinely pay between £5,000 and £100,000 for specialist dental treatment. We're not a "drill and fill" company'. Analysts in this sector also add that Oasis and IDH took on a lot of debt to fund their growth and are paying the price. Crucially, gross profit margins at James Hull Associates are 45 per cent compared with 39 per cent and 40 per cent of his rivals.

Source: adapted from *The Business*, 5/6.10.2003.

**(a) (i) James Hull is planning a flotation for his company. What does this mean? (6 marks)**
**(ii) Describe the procedure that the company will have to follow before it can operate as a plc. (6 marks)**
**(b) Explain the advantages and disadvantages to James Hull Associates of operating as a public limited company. (12 marks)**
**(c) Explain how much control James Hull will have over the business after the flotation. (8 marks)**
**(d) Using evidence from the article, discuss the extent to which the flotation of the company is likely to be successful. (18 marks)**

## Public sector organisations

The PUBLIC SECTOR is made up of organisations which are owned or controlled by central or local government or public corporations. They are funded by the government and in some cases from their own trading 'surplus' or profit. The amount of business activity in the public sector has decreased over the last 25 years as a result of government policy. Some public sector businesses have been transferred from the public to the private sector. However, the public sector still has an important role to play in certain areas of business activity.

## Which goods and services does the public sector provide?

It has been argued that certain PUBLIC GOODS and MERIT GOODS need to be provided by public sector organisations. Public goods have two features.

- **Non-rivalry** - consumption of the good by one individual does not reduce the amount available for others.
- **Non-excludability** - it is impossible to exclude others from benefiting from their use.

Take the example of street lighting. If one person uses the light to see her way across the street, this does not 'use up' light for someone who wants to look at his watch. Also, it is impossible to stop using the light shining across the street. This means that it would be unlikely that people would pay directly for street lighting. If you paid £1 for light to cross the street, someone else could use it for free! If people will not pay, then businesses cannot make a profit and would not provide the service. Other examples of public goods may include the judiciary, policing and defence, although in some countries private policing does exist. These public goods are provided free at the point of use. They are paid for from taxation and government borrowing.

Some argue that certain merit goods should be provided by the public sector. Examples include education, health and libraries. These are services which people think should be provided in greater quantities. It is argued that if the individual is left to decide whether or not to pay for these goods, some would choose not to or may not be able to. For example, people may choose not to take out insurance policies to cover for unexpected illness. If they became ill they would not be able to pay for treatment. As a result it is argued that the state should provide this service and pay for it from taxation. The provision of merit goods is said to raise society's standard of living.

## Government/publicly owned organisations

Government or publicly owned organisations may take a number of forms.

**Public corporations** PUBLIC CORPORATIONS are organisations set up by law to run services or industries on behalf of the government. Each corporation is run by a chairperson and board appointed by a government minister. The board is responsible for the day to day running of the corporation, but is accountable to the minister. The minister has the right to approve investment and to issue directions to the organisation in relation to matters which affect the public interest.

The **BBC** (**British Broadcasting Corporation**) is an example of a public corporation. It was given a royal charter to provide 'broadcasting services as public services'. It is run by a board of directors nominated by the Prime Minister, which is politically independent, although the government might try to influence its operations informally. The BBC is financed mainly though licence fees paid by television owners. However, as increasing amount of money is being raised from the sale and production of programmes for other TV companies, such as overseas businesses.

**The Post Office** Postal services in the UK have been provided by the public sector for many years. However, there has been a number of changes in the structure of the organisation during that time. In March 2001 the Post Office became a plc, but one wholly owned by the UK government. The change was brought about by the Postal Services Act 2000. It aimed to

(a) Is the example in the photograph above a public or a merit good? Explain your answer.
(b) Explain why either the private sector or the public sector may provide such a facility.

**Question** 1

create a commercially focused company with a more strategic relationship with the government. In November 2002 the name of the company was changed from Consignia to the Royal Mail Group plc. In the UK the business operates under three brands - Royal Mail, Post OfficeTM and Parcelforce Worldwide.

- **Royal Mail** provides postal services. The company has a statutory duty to provide a letter delivery service to every one of the 27 million addresses in the UK, at a uniform price, whatever the distance travelled. It must also carry out at least one daily collection from all letterboxes. Despite the increasing use of email and other electronic messaging and the continuing use of faxes, the volume of mail delivered by Royal Mail each day is 82 million items and growing.
- **Post OfficeTM** consists of a retail network with more than 14,400 branches, the combined UK total of the four major building societies and six banks. Only 500 branches are owned by Post Office Ltd, the operator of the branches. The rest are owned by the people who run the branches, including franchisees and subpostmasters and mistresses. The retail network offers more than 170 products, including financial services, travel services, government information and retail products such as greetings cards and stationery. Post OfficeTM claims that 94 per cent of people in the UK live within one mile of a post office branch, with 28 million people paying a visit at least once a week.
- **Parcelforce Worldwide** provides a time-guaranteed and next day parcel delivery service. It has the world's largest delivery network, covering more than 99.6 per cent of the world's population and reaching 239 different countries.

**Network Rail** In 1996 British Rail, the former nationalised rail industry, was broken up and sold off in parts. The largest part was Railtrack, the rail infrastructure which included the railway lines, stations, bridges, signals and property. Passenger transport services on the railway lines were provided by private train operators such as Virgin, Stagecoach and North Western. These businesses bid for operator's licenses from the government and paid Railtrack for using the network.

In 2002, after Railtrack was declared bankrupt, ownership was transferred to the not-for-profit company Network Rail. Network Rail is run by 100 'members' drawn from train operators, unions, passengers' groups and the public. There is perhaps some dispute about its legal status. The Office for National Statistics (ONS) classified Network Rail as a private corporation since its spending on track maintenance is not included on the national accounts. However, since the government is guaranteeing Network Rail's debt, the company cannot really 'go bust'. The strategic rail authority (SRA), the supervisory QUANGO accountable to the Department of Transport, controls Network Rail. In 2004 the government announced plans for a revamped organisation, with Network Rail running tracks and the SRA dealing with rail operations.

## The Bank of England

The Bank of England is a former privately owned business that was taken into public ownership in 1946. It has a special role in the monetary system. In 1997 it was given powers by the government to decide what the level of interest rates should be in the UK. It is headed by a governor, who is accountable to the Chancellor of the Exchequer.

One business organisation that remains in the public sector, for the time being, is the Tote, the state betting operation. However, the government plans to sell this soon for around £200 million. The Tote, which has a chain of 400 high street betting shops as well as on-course outlets, turned over £500 million in the last financial year. At the end of 2003 it was expected to announce record-breaking profits. Peter Jones, the Tote chairman, wants to double its outlets to over 1,000 to give proper national coverage and spread overheads over a wider base. Currently the Tote only has 5 per cent of the betting market. The growth is expected to be funded by partnering with private equity firms or rivals.

The new operator of the Tote will be offered a seven-year licence to run the business. This means that it is extremely likely that the pooled betting business will be sold to the racing industry. At the moment the Tote is not owned by any defined entity, so it would have to be renationalised before being sold. The legislation governing the sale is likely to prohibit the company being sold in its entirety after privatisation. Bookies such as Ladbrokes, Coral and William Hill are keen to bid separately for the shops. However, Labour MPs in particular would be outraged if the Tote went to the private sector as this would break a manifesto commitment. An industry alliance known as the Racecourse Trust is expected to take on the Tote, with profits being ploughed back into the industry. The government was under pressure from the Office of Fair Trading to scrap the Tote's monopoly on pooled betting, but will avoid out-and-out privatisation.

Source: adapted from *The Observer*, 23.11.03, *The Guardian*, 24.11.2003.

(a) Using this case as an example explain the difference between a public sector business and a private sector business.
(b) Why do you think the government does not want to transfer ownership of the Tote entirely to the private sector?

**Question 2**

## Local authority services

Some services in the UK are supplied by local authorities.
- Education. Local authorities are responsible for distributing most of the money allocated by the government to primary and secondary schools in the UK. However, some schools which have had problems have been taken out of local authority control and funded by central government.
- Recreation. Sports halls, libraries, swimming pools and parks are all examples of recreation services provided by local government.
- Housing. This includes the provision of council housing,

amenities for the homeless, sheltered accommodation and house renovation. The importance of this provision has diminished because of the purchase of council houses by tenants.

- Environment and conservation. Refuse collection, litter clearance, pest control, street cleaning and beach maintenance are examples of these services. However, an increasing number of councils is employing private sector businesses to carry out these services, such as Onyx Environmental Group plc.
- Communications. The provision of essential services to isolated towns and villages is one responsibility under this heading. Others include road maintenance and traffic control.
- Protection. This involves the provision of fire and police services, local justice, and consumer protection. Local authorities also employ trading standards officers and environmental health officers to investigate business practice and premises.
- Social services. Local government is also responsible for providing services such as community care, social workers and children's homes.

Most of the funding for the above services comes from central government grants. However, there is some scope for independent funding. For example, local authorities raise revenue from the council tax. Charges are also made for the supply of services like swimming pools and football pitches.

There are reasons why such services are provided by local rather than central government. First, it is argued that the local community is best served by those who are most sympathetic to its needs. Thus, local authorities should have the knowledge to evaluate those needs and supply the appropriate services. Second, central government is made up of large departments which often have communication problems. The decentralisation of many services should help to improve communication between the providers of services and the public. Finally, local councillors are accountable to the local electorate. If their policies are unpopular in the local community it is unlikely that they will be re-elected.

## Central government departments

Central government departments supply some important services. These departments are also used to implement government policy.

- **The Treasury** is responsible for the government's economic strategy. It has many aims, including maintaining a stable economy with low inflation and sound public finances, promoting UK economic prospects and a fair and efficient tax and benefit system, ensuring a fair, competitive and efficient market in financial services which is in the public interest, improving the quality and the cost effectiveness of public services and achieving regularity and accountability in public finance.
- **The Ministry of Defence** is responsible for the provision

and maintenance of the armed forces in the UK and in other parts of the world.

- **The Department for Work and Pensions** has a number of functions. It is responsible for providing benefits for those in need and other payments including child benefit, disability allowance, income support and housing benefit. It assesses benefit claims and allocates payments. It also provides help, support and benefits for people who are out of work, looking for work, returning to work or looking to start their own business.
- **The Department for Trade and Industry** aims to promote enterprise, innovation and increased productivity for business. It also provides information on all kinds of employment-related issues for employees. And it aims to develop a fairer and more prosperous economy for consumers, including consumer protection and market control.
- **The Department of Health** is responsible for the National Health Service (NHS) in the UK. It provides guidance and leadership for a variety of NHS organisations including regional health authorities, NHS trusts and Care Trusts. These organisations help to deliver local health care in the UK, such as hospitals, surgeries and health centres.
- **The Department for Education and Skills (DfES)** helps to shape government policies on education and learning and to implement these policies. These include policies designed to improve primary, secondary, tertiary, higher and adult education.
- **The Department for Environment, Food and Rural Affairs (Defra)** operates in a number of areas. For example, it seeks to limit global environmental threats, such as global warming, and safeguard people from the effects of poor air quality or toxic chemicals. It has the power to penalise those who break environmental legislation. It also aims to ensure animal health and welfare and clean and healthy water supplies, to help the food industry grow, and to protect the UK from harmful and illegal food imports.
- **The Department for Transport** implements the government's transport policy. It aims to oversee the delivery of a reliable and safe transport system which does not harm the environment. This includes areas such as road building, traffic safety and congestion, national railways, the operation of the London Underground, aviation, shipping and ports.
- **The Department for International Development (DFID)** works to promote sustainable development and eliminate world poverty.

Much of the work carried out by central and local government departments also benefits businesses in the private sector. For example, the Department for Transport gives contracts to large construction companies like Wimpey and Costain, to build roads and motorways.

## QUANGOs

Some activities carried out by the government are said to be politically non-controversial. These are controlled by QUANGOs (quasi autonomous non-governmental organisations). They tend to be specialised bodies providing services which central and local government does not have the resources or the expertise to carry out. QUANGOs receive funding from and are accountable to different government departments, depending on their area of specialism. Some examples include research councils, such as the Apple and Pear Research Council, forums, such as the Zoo Forum, advisory committees, such as the Advisory Committee for Business and the Environment, tribunals and funding councils. Well known QUANGOs in 2003 included Investors in People and the Higher Education Funding Council.

It has been suggested that there are over 5,000 QUANGOS in the UK. The government defines QUANGOs more narrowly only as non-departmental government bodies (NDGBs) and suggests that there are just over 1,000 in the UK, responsible for around £23 billion.

Some QUANGOs are quite powerful. For example the Millennium Commission had the responsibility for handling funds for projects designed to celebrate the new millennium. The National Rivers Authority is responsible for the upkeep of waterways in the UK and allocating funds to clean them up.

However, in recent years they have received a certain amount of criticism. It is argued that they are not entirely non-political and can be influenced by government to achieve its objectives. It has also been suggested that members appointed by government may be biased towards its stance on certain issues. The efficiency of their operations has also been criticised.

## Executive agencies

Executive agencies have become well established since their introduction in 1985. They are responsible for the supply of services previously provided by government departments. Examples include:

- the collection of government data - The Office for National Statistics;
- the processing of passport applications - The Passport and Records Agency;
- the administering of written driving tests - The Driver and Vehicle Licensing Agency;
- the operation of state pensions - The Pensions Service;
- the granting of patents - The Patents Office.

These have been separated from the policy making bodies which used to deliver them.

Executive agencies are headed by chief executives who are accountable to a government minister. Many of these leaders are recruited from the private sector. They are encouraged to introduce business principles when delivering services. The general policy of the government departments remains the responsibility of the permanent secretaries and senior civil servants.

Since the introduction of executive agencies the efficiency of services has improved considerably. For example, it now takes 7 days on average to process a passport application, compared with as much as 30 days at times in the past. Also, many benefit payments are now much cheaper to administer.

## Privatisation

PRIVATISATION is the transfer of public sector resources to the private sector. It was an important feature of government policy in the 1980s and 1990s, as shown in Table 7.1. It is still seen by some as a means of improving efficiency and further privatisation is always a possibility. Privatisation has taken a number of forms.

**The sale of nationalised industries** NATIONALISED INDUSTRIES played an important role in the UK before 1980. They included organisations such as British Rail, British Airways, British Steel and British Telecom. These were public sector organisations which, it was argued, should be owned and controlled by the state for a number of reasons.

- To supply services which were unprofitable, such as railways in isolated areas.
- To avoid the wasteful duplication of resources where a NATURAL MONOPOLY existed.
- To control strategic industries such as energy and transport.
- To prevent exploitation by monopoly suppliers.
- To save jobs when closure threatened.

These businesses were sold off to private buyers. They became private sector businesses, owned by private shareholders.

**The sale of parts of nationalised industries** Some nationalised industries were broken up by parts being sold off. The Jaguar car company, which was part of the then state-owned British Leyland, was sold for £297 million. Sealink, a part of British Rail, was sold for £40 million.

**Deregulation** This involves lifting restrictions that prevent private sector competition. The deregulation of the communications market has allowed Mercury and cable companies to compete with British Telecom. Deregulation has also allowed bus services to be run by private sector businesses.

**Contracting out** Many government and local authority services have been 'contracted out' to private sector businesses. This is where contractors are given a chance to bid for services previously supplied by the public sector. Examples include the provision of school meals, hospital cleaning and refuse collection. For example, Wolds Remand Centre, run by the Group 4 security company, was Britain's first privately run prison service. In the early 1990s local authorities were forced into compulsory competitive tendering (CCT). Private businesses **had** to be asked to quote on contracts for services, bidding against council services. The contract was awarded to the most efficient, least cost service. In 2000 the Labour government replaced this. Tendering would not be compulsory and contracts would be

**Table 7.1** *Sale of state owned companies to the private sector since 1979*

Date begun

| | | | |
|---|---|---|---|
| 1979 | British Petroleum | 1986 | British Gas |
| | ICL | 1987 | British Airways |
| | Ferranti | | Rolls Royce |
| | Fairey | | Leyland Bus |
| 1981 | British Aerospace | | Leyland Truck |
| | British Sugar | | Royal Ordnance |
| | Cable and Wireless | | British Airport |
| | Amersham International | | Authority |
| 1982 | National Freight Corporation | 1988 | British Steel |
| | Britoil | | British Leyland |
| 1983 | Associated British Ports | 1989 | British Water Authorities |
| | British Rail Hotels | 1990 | Electricity Area Boards |
| 1984 | British Gas Onshore Oil | 1991 | Electricity Generation |
| | Enterprise Oil | 1994 | British Coal |
| | Sealink Ferries | 1995 | British Rail |
| | Jaguar Cars | 1996 | British Energy |
| | British Telecom | | Railtrack |
| | British Technology Group | 2001 | Nats (air traffic control) |

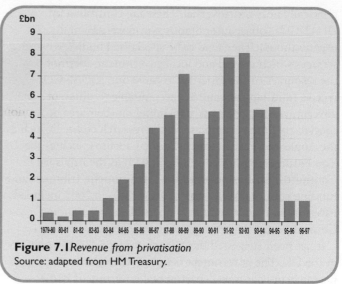

**Figure 7.1** *Revenue from privatisation*
Source: adapted from HM Treasury.

awarded for 'best value' - based also on effectiveness and quality as well as efficiency.

**The sale of land and property** Under the **1980 Housing Act**, tenants of local authorities and New Town Development Corporations were given the right to buy their own homes. Tenants were given generous discounts, up to 60 per cent of the market value of the house, if they agreed to buy. During the 1980s, for example, about 1.5 million houses were sold. The sale of land and properties has raised almost as much money as the sale of nationalised industries.

## The reasons for privatisation

During the 1980s and 1990s governments transferred a great deal of business activity from the public sector to the private sector. Different reasons have been put forward for this.

- The sale of state assets generates a great deal of income for the government. Figure 7.1 shows the revenue raised by privatisation between 1979 and 1997.
- Nationalised industries were inefficient. They lacked the incentive to make a profit, since their main aim was arguably to provide a public service. As a result their costs tended to be high and they often made losses. Also, many believed that they were overstaffed. Supporters of privatisation argued that if they were in the private sector, they would be forced to cut costs, improve their service and return a profit for the shareholders.
- As a result of deregulation, some organisations would be forced to improve their service and charge competitive prices. For example, in many areas, private firms began to compete for passengers on bus and train routes. Electricity and gas prices and telephone charges have also been reduced, arguably as a result of competition. Consumers would benefit from this and should also have greater choice. In addition, it is argued that there would be more

incentive to innovate in the private sector.
- Once these organisations had been sold to the private sector there would be little political interference. They would be free to determine their own investment levels, prices and growth rates. In the past government interference has affected the performance of nationalised industries.
- Privatisation would increase share ownership. It was argued that this would lead to a 'share owning democracy' in which more people would have a 'stake' in the success of the economy. For example, if you bought shares in BT, you would be a part owner of the company and get a dividend each year. Workers were encouraged to buy shares in their companies so that they would be rewarded for their own hard work and success.
- Privatisation should improve accountability. The losses made by many of these nationalised industries were put down to the fact that they were operating a public service. In the private sector these industries would be accountable to shareholders and consumers. Shareholders would expect a return on their investment and consumers would expect a quality service at a fair price. For example, if shareholders were not happy with the dividends paid, they could sell their shares.

## Impact of privatisation on business

How have businesses changed after transferring to the private sector?

- Achieving a surplus or profit has become a more important objective. For example, the profits of BT increased from around £1,000 million in 1984, when the company was first privatised, to around £3,000 million in 1996, to nearly £3,200 million in 1998. In recent years, however, profits have fallen due to competition and poor acquisitions.
- In some cases prices have changed. In a number of cases they have fallen. Most analysts would agree that charges

made for some telephone services, gas and electricity have fallen since privatisation, for example.

● Some of the newly privatised businesses have cut back on staffing levels. For example, the Rail, Maritime and Transport Union suggested that there were 20,000 to 30,000 job losses as a result of rail privatisation. British Energy shed a quarter of its workforce before privatisation.

● Many companies increased investment following privatisation. For example, BT increased investment between 1994 and 1998 from £2,171 million to £3,030 million. Many of the water companies raised investment levels to fund new sewerage systems and purification plants. Immediately after privatisation investment rose by about £1,000 million in the water industry. However, more recently some figures suggest that investment levels are falling.

● Some of the companies have begun to offer new services and diversify. For example, North West Water offers a Leakline service which promises to repair any leaks on a customer's property provided they are outside the house.

● There has been a number of mergers and takeovers involving newly privatised companies. For example, Hanson bought Eastern Electricity and an American railway company bought the British Rail freight service. North West Water and Norweb joined together to form United Utilities and Scottish Power bought Manweb.

## Arguments against privatisation

Arguments against privatisation have been put forward on both political and economic grounds. Most of the criticisms below are from the consumer's point of view.

● Privatisation has been expensive. In particular, the amount of money spent advertising each sale has been criticised. The money spent on expensive TV advertising was at the taxpayer's expense.

● It has been argued that privatisation has not led to greater competition. In some cases public monopolies with no competition have become private monopolies. These companies have been able to exploit their position. This has been a criticism levelled at gas and electricity companies. Also Railtrack managed to pay shareholders significant dividends, arguably at the expense of essential investment.

● Nationalised industries were sold off too cheaply. In nearly all cases the share issue has been over-subscribed. This shows that more people want to buy shares than there are shares available. When dealing begins on the stock market share prices have often risen sharply. This suggests that the government could have set the share prices much higher and raised more revenue. For example, there was an £11 billion rise in the value of electricity companies between privatisation in 1990 and 1996.

● Natural monopolies have been sold off. Some argue that they should remain under government control to prevent a duplication of resources.

● Once part of the private sector, any parts of the business which make a loss will be closed down. This appears to have happened in public transport. Some bus services or trains on non-profitable routes have been cut or stopped completely since deregulation.

---

In July 2001 Nats, the air traffic control system, was partly privatised. The organisation, which employs 5,200 people and has an annual turnover of over £500 million, is now owned by an Airline consortium (BA, Bmi, Virgin Atlantic, Britannia, Monarch, EasyJet and Airtours), the employees and the government. The main motive for the privatisation of Nats was to raise money. Air traffic is increasing by about 5 per cent a year and by 2010 traffic is expected to have risen by 43 per cent. When Nats was privatised it was working very close to its capacity. Investment was desperately needed to cope with the rise in traffic and the government felt that the private sector should fund this investment. The government also hoped to spend some of the sale proceeds on the development of public transport projects.

Unfortunately, just months after the part-privatisation, Nats began to experience financial difficulties. As a result of the terrorist attack on the New York World Trade Centre on September 11th 2001, Nats warned that revenue would fall by £230 million up to 2005 compared with previous forecasts. Transatlantic flights, which account for 44 per cent of revenues, fell by 14 per cent year-on-year in the final quarter of 2001. Overall, flights were 4 per cent lower and 11 per cent below Nats' own forecast of a year ago. The government was forced to put up to £30 million of taxpayers' money into an emergency package worked out with the banks who threatened to foreclose on loans to Nats. Banks also feared that if the government had not provided funds Nats would have gone bankrupt.

The part-privatisation of Nats was supposed to end the government's funding of the organisation. Before it went ahead the civil aviation authority (CAA), the industry regulator, warned that the part-privatisation of Nats could run into trouble in the event of a deep recession because of its suspect financial structure. Its fears have been well founded since the events of September 11th. Also many MPs, the unions and a significant number of the general public opposed the idea on safety grounds. A former transport spokesperson said part-privatisation was a crazy idea and the Liberal democrats said the government should have created a not-for-profits company that could have borrowed from the government through government-backed bonds.

(a) Using Nats as an example, argue the case for and against privatisation.

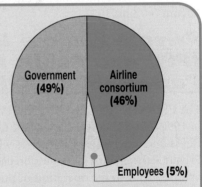

**Figure 7.2** *Ownership structure of Nats after part-privatisation* Source: adapted from *The Guardian*, 19.2.2002.

**Question 3**

- Share ownership arguably has not increased. Many who bought shares sold them very quickly after. In addition, a significant number of new shareowners only own very small shareholdings in just one company.
- Many of the nationalised industries are important for the development of the nation. To put them in private hands might jeopardise their existence. For example, one of the reasons why British Steel was nationalised was to save it from possible closure. If business conditions change for the worse a private company may not guarantee supply. Also, since the shares are widely available, it is possible for overseas buyers to take control of strategic UK firms.

# Regulation of privatised industries

One criticism of privatisation was that dominant industries, which were previously state owned, now operated as private sector businesses. They may be able to exploit their position by increasing their prices or reducing services. Because of this they must be controlled. Control of private sector firms is nothing new. The Competition Commission was set up to monitor firms which might act against the public's interest. It investigates cases where large dominant firms or firms merging might act to exploit their position.

Because privatisation created some private monopolies, the government set up specialist 'watchdog' agencies to protect the public. Regulatory bodies were set up to monitor and control the activities of public utilities such as gas and electricity, the organisation known as Ofgem, and the telecommunications industry, the organisation known as Ofcom (☞ unit 103).

# Private Finance Initiative (PFI) and Public Private Partnerships (PPP)

The PRIVATE FINANCE INITIATIVE (PFI) was introduced in 1992, but did not really take off until the end of the 1990s. PFI is one of a range of initiatives which fall under the Public Private Partnerships (PPP) umbrella. These involve the private sector in the operation of public services. The PFI is the most frequently used. Under a PFI scheme, a capital project such as a school, hospital or housing estate has to be designed, built, financed and managed by a private consortium, under contracts that typically last for 30 years. The private consortium will be paid regularly from government funds according to its performance during that time period. If the consortium misses performance targets it will be paid less. One example of an area where PFI has been used extensively by the government is in the construction of hospitals. The government had approved 15 acute hospital PFI schemes in England by 2003. Figure 7.3 shows the schemes and their capital value.

The main advantages of PFI include the following.

- The government does not have to fund expensive one-off

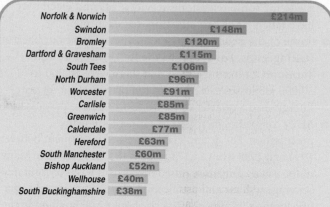

**Figure 7.3** *Planned PFI hospital schemes and their capital value*
Source: adapted from www.centre.public.org.uk.

payments to build large-scale projects that may involve unpopular tax increases.

- The risk involved in funding large-scale projects is transferred to the private sector. For example, if a construction company goes out of business before a project is completed the government does not have to meet any extra costs that might accrue, they are borne by the private consortium.
- Since the government is not funding the cost of projects the amount spent does not cause public borrowing to rise.

PFI does have its critics. For example, trade unions in the public sector often describe PFI as creeping privatisation of public services. Some possible disadvantages of PFI may include the following.

- As with any other forms of hire purchase the cost of the asset over a long period of time is greater than the capital cost. In particular the government can borrow money more cheaply than the private sector.
- There is a question mark over how much risk is genuinely transferred to the private sector given the government's record of bailing out private companies managing troubled public services.
- Concern has been expressed about the true cost of PFI. Public sector accountants claim that hospitals and schools would be cheaper to build using traditional methods of funding. The national audit office described the value for money test used to justify PFI projects as 'pseudo-scientific mumbo jumbo'.
- There is the worry that once private firms get involved in providing public services, the quality of provision falls as profit is pursued.
- Evidence suggests that PFI may be politically unpopular. In an election a government minister in the safe Labour seat of Wyre Forest was defeated by an independent candidate who stood as a protest against a new PFI hospital.

It may be another 20 years or more, when the first PFI contracts have been completed, before the real cost of PFI can be judged. However, the Institute of Public Policy Research, which argued that there should be no restriction on the private provision of public service, has since expressed its doubts.

Although John Prescott, the deputy Prime Minister, ruled out the wholesale privatisation of the London Underground in 1998, there has been private involvement in the provision of tube services. Under the controversial PPP, infrastructure companies maintain tracks, tunnels, stations and trains while London Underground (LU) still manages the day-to-day operation of the network and holds overall responsibility for safety. In April 2003, less than a week after the introduction of PPP, the controversy was fuelled by an incident at the Tottenham Court Road station on the Central Line.

The incident highlighted the critics' fears that safety could be at risk due to squabbles over the division of responsibilities. The network's two infrastructure maintenance companies and London Underground blamed each other for a fire alert which closed the Central Line one day in April. The problem arose when privately run Tube Lines carried out an overnight 'deep clean' of the station. This included cleaning the station's platform even though the line itself is maintained by rival infrastructure firm BCV, which was taken over by rival consortium Metronet a day later. While cleaning, dust was dislodged from the walls of the tunnel. The dust stuck to glue on the tracks which was left by contractors sticking up advertising posters on behalf of the PPP's third partner, publicly owned London Underground. The next day, when trains started running, the dust smouldered and set off fire alarms which forced the closure of a section of the Central Line for two hours during the morning rush.

Whoever was responsible for the delay could face big penalties. Under the PPP scheme, companies are fined if they exceed targets for delays. Fines can amount to £9 per passenger hour. More than 100,000 people were using the line during the morning rush meaning that a company could incur a six figure penalty for the two hour shutdown.

Tube Lines said that they clean the platform but had no responsibility for the track, BCV has responsibility for the track. However, BCV say it was LU's contractor's fault (a company called Viacom) for spilling the glue. A LU spokesman said that blame had not been attributed but also that Viacom had been spoken to. Insiders at LU said that BCV should have cleaned the glue from the line. However, BCV was still in public ownership the day of the incident. A spokesperson for RMT rail union said 'you'd better get used to it – this is the recipe for the future. The only people who are going to be kept happy by this arrangement is their lordships when it all spills into the courtroom'. 'This kind of thing was inevitable – we've been shouting it from the rooftops that this was going to happen'.

Source: adapted from *The Guardian*, 11.10.2003.

(a) Using this case as an example explain (i) what is meant by PPP (ii) how efficiency is guaranteed under PPP schemes.
(b) Analyse the possible disadvantages of PPP in this case.

**Question 4**

## key terms

**Merit goods** - goods which are underprovided by private sector businesses.
**Nationalised industries** - public corporations previously part of the private sector which were taken into state ownership.
**Natural monopoly** - a situation where production costs will be lower if one firm is allowed to exist on its own in the industry, due to the existence of huge economies of scale.
**Privatisation** - the transfer of public sector resources to the private sector.
**Private Finance Initiative (PFI)** - a scheme where private businesses build hospitals and schools, for example, funded by government.

**Public corporations** - organisations set up by law to run services on behalf of government.
**Public goods** - goods where consumption by one person does not reduce the amount available to others and, once provided, all individuals will benefit.
**Public sector** - business organisations which are owned or controlled by central or local government, or public corporations.
**QUANGOs** - Quasi Autonomous Non-Governmental Organisations.

## Knowledge

1. What is meant by a public corporation?
2. What is meant by non-rivalry and non-excludability when describing public goods?
3. Why are certain merit goods provided by the public sector?
4. Why do local authorities provide some public sector services?
5. How are local authority services funded?
6. Describe the responsibilities of 3 government departments.
7. Explain the difference between deregulation and contracting out as methods of privatisation.
8. What are the disadvantages of privatisation?
9. What is the function of Ofgem and Ofcom?
10. State 3 advantages and 3 disadvantages of PFI.

# Case study Network Rail

When Railtrack, the owner and keeper of Britain's rail network, went bust in 2002 travellers were probably glad to see the back of an organisation associated with delays, cancellations and accidents. One of the biggest criticisms of Railtrack was that, despite consistently missing operational targets, losing money and relying on subsidies, it still managed to find the cash needed to pay shareholders. Indeed, around £700 million was paid in dividends over its six-year stewardship of the network. Railtrack was criticised for a lack of investment and spending too much time talking up the share price. In October 2002 ownership of the company was transferred to the not-for-profit company Network Rail.

Despite being taken back into public ownership, the rail industry is still regulated by a government watchdog. Tom Winsor is the rail regulator. He was appointed by the government to investigate whether Network Rail really needs the £30 billion, over the next five years, it has asked for. Winsor says that his consultants have calculated that 30 per cent of the sum asked for is the cost of inefficiency. Some examples of this are explained below.

- A maintenance contract had included a clause saying workers would be paid from the moment they arrived at the site. This led to a situation where they used motorbikes to arrive quickly at work, while their tools followed behind in slower vans.
- Network Rail allows some contractors, who are paid on a cost-plus basis, to advise Network Rail on what work needs to be done. This is rather like asking builders what work needs doing on the house, letting them name the price and then paying a percentage profit on top.
- Some parts which should last for years are being replaced after only a few months. Allegedly, this is due to unscrupulous contractors or incompetence. For example, when ballast has to be renewed, contractors have renewed all the track and sleepers as well, even though they are a long way from being worn out.
- Poor planning when the network is shut down for maintenance work (known as 'possession' of the track) often results in wasted time. For example, during many six hour possessions productive work is only undertaken for two hours. It is also common for possessions to be cancelled at the last minute, sometimes after staff have arrived on site. Network Rail revealed that a quarter of possessions were badly managed with maintenance staff working only 30 per cent or 40 per cent of the allocated time.
- One of the main problems is the contracts that Network Rail have inherited from Railtrack. Nearly £5 billion of the company's £6 billion budget is spent through contractors. Around 2,000 contractors and subcontractors were involved in maintenance and

other work, each of them, and their suppliers, taking a slice of profit. It was also argued that £1 in every £8 spent went on the management of these contracts.
- A breakdown in trust has resulted in the employment of hundreds of people to check each other's work. This mistrust has also led to disagreements about who is to blame for delays and who should pay the fines.
- Problems have arisen because Network Rail does not have a complete record of all its assets. Originally, British Rail had a lot of information about its assets but it was not organised in a systematic way. When Railtrack took over the network in 1996, large numbers of staff left the industry. Unfortunately a great deal of knowledge went with them. On the one hand information contained in the heads of engineers was lost when they left, and on the other, huge quantities of written records were destroyed. Railtrack therefore lost a vital resources – asset knowledge.

Inefficiency was not the only problem detected. Teams went through all the spending plans for track, signals, bridges, tunnels, machinery, telecommunications and property. In one case less than half the work was considered fully justified. There is also a large body of work which is either exaggerated or which Winsor and his experts cannot assess due to a lack of information.

The potential cuts in the budget are enormous. Savings between £1.4 billion and £1.7 billion could be possible in the first two years. The West Coast Mainline upgrade could be further delayed, saving up to £1 billion. Winsor reckons that in five year's time cuts of up to £2 billion a year could be made. If his recommendations are accepted by the government, Network Rail will be forced to shave £7 billion off its spending plans for the period 2004-2009. However, the company would still need £22.5 billion, £1.5 billion more than the government has budgeted for.

Source: adapted from *The Observer*, 27.6.2003.

(a) **Suggest two possible reasons why the rail industry was privatised in 1996. (4 marks)**
(b) **Explain why Railtrack was taken back into public ownership. (6 marks)**
(c) **Analyse the reasons why a government watchdog is still needed to oversee the operations of a publicly owned business organisation. (12 marks)**
(d) **Evaluate the extent to which (i) passengers and (ii) taxpayers might benefit from the work of the rail industry regulator. (18 marks)**

# 8 Business Organisation

## How are businesses organised?

All businesses need to organise their activities. Running a business involves planning, decision making, co-ordination and communication. In order to simplify these complex tasks it is helpful to organise the business into a number of clearly defined sections. For example, a business selling books to customers by mail order from a warehouse may be organised into a number of departments.

- Buying and marketing. This department purchases books from publishers. It also deals with advertising and handles the production of the mail order catalogue.
- Warehousing/dispatch. This department stores books delivered to the warehouse and deals with requests for books from the orders department. It is then responsible for putting together customers' orders and checking, wrapping, addressing and transporting parcels.
- Orders. This department receives orders from customers and informs the warehouse. It also processes all the paperwork involved in the buying and selling of books.
- Administration and finance. This department deals with payments and receipts of cash. It also handles all the personnel work, including staff wages.

This type of STRUCTURE is simple but effective. Staff in each department will understand their role. They will also know what other departments are doing in relation to their own. Small businesses may feel that they do not need to organise themselves in this way. However, as businesses grow, so does the need for organisation (☞ unit 58). Without this, the efficiency of a business could suffer. Communications may break down, mistakes might be made and staff may become confused about their roles.

The mail order business described here is organised by **function**. This is explained in the next section. There are other methods of organising a business which may be more suitable in certain situations. Large businesses often combine different methods of organisation to gain the benefits of each.

## Organisation by function

One of the most common methods of organising a business is by function. This is where a business is divided into different sections or departments according to the operation undertaken. Typical functional departments in many larger businesses include production, marketing, finance and personnel. There is a number of advantages for a business in organising itself in this way.

- Specialisation. It allows each department to focus on just one business area. Specialist staff can be employed in each department. For example, the finance department may employ management and financial accountants and credit controllers. Specialisation should help to improve efficiency (☞ unit 84).

- Accountability. Each department is likely to have a manager who will be responsible for allocating departmental resources, employing staff and achieving departmental goals. The manager will be accountable to a senior executive and will be under pressure to perform. This method of organisation also allows a business to organise itself into cost or profit centres (☞ unit 39). For example, if a business decides to make one department into a cost centre, it may have to keep its costs within a limit. This will help accountability.
- Clarity. Organisation by function helps staff to understand their role and position in the business structure. For example, staff are likely to be trained in their department, will be familiar with their superiors and will know where to seek help and support.

This method of organisation will also have some drawbacks.

- Communication and co-ordination problems. When businesses are divided by function they often operate as self-contained units. Communication between departments may be limited, resulting in a lack of information sharing and some unnecessary duplication. Senior management may struggle with co-ordination if departments pursue their own objectives rather than those of the whole company. Individual departments may also be reluctant to work with other departments on projects.
- Inertia. Individual departments may become 'set in their ways' over time. They may try to resist change and prefer to

Wycombe Holdings designs and manufactures hand made furniture for retailers. However, it has recently developed an Internet shopping service where members of the public can buy furniture directly from the factory online. The company is organised into departments as shown in Figure 8.1.

Figure 8.1 *Wycombe Holdings, organisational structure*

(a) Analyse the advantages to Wycombe Holdings of using the above method of organisation.

continue their current practices.

- Bureaucracy. Organisations may become too bureaucratic. For example, there may be a large increase in paperwork if every communication from one department to another has to be made via memo or if transactions between departments require written confirmation. E-mail and company **intranets** (☞ unit 70) may solve this problem to some extent. However, time may still be wasted responding to requests.
- Suitability. Very large companies with a diversified product range could find this method of organisation unsuitable. For example, when an organisation grows there will be more departments and more layers of management. In this case senior management may find it increasingly difficult to influence what is happening lower down.

## Organisation by product or activity

When a business produces a wide range of different goods or services it could find that organisation by function is not effective. Different products may need different approaches to production and marketing. For example, a multinational group may operate a supermarket chain, a property company and a construction business. It is possible that each of these businesses may have different approaches to marketing which take into account the needs of their markets. It is also possible that different staff with different skills will be needed.

Large diversified companies often organise their business by grouping together different functional staff who are involved in the production of the same product lines or activities.

This method of organisation is often seen as 'a business within a business' and has a number of advantages.

- Each division is able to focus on the needs of a particular market segment. Thus, customers should find that their needs are satisfied more effectively.
- Each division is likely to operate as a profit centre. This will help to measure the performance of each division and allow comparisons in the business. Poor performing sections can be identified and action taken.
- Healthy competition may take place between each division. This could improve the overall performance of the organisation.
- There may be scope for reorganisation. Organisation by product provides some flexibility for the future. Loss making divisions can be closed down. Divisions supplying similar markets can be merged. Businesses that are bought by the company can be absorbed more easily. Divestment (selling) of parts of the business should also be easier.
- Co-operation may improve. Because each division is pursuing the same goal, eg profit, it is possible to share expertise and ancillary services. For example, the Burton Group, in the above illustration, might use the same

Arriva is a large public transport provider with a turnover that exceeded £2 billion in 2002. Its profit before tax for the year was £102.1 million. The company employs around 30,000 staff which is a 50 per cent increase since 1998. One of the company's main objectives is growth which it hopes to achieve through acquisitions, better service delivery, innovation and marketing. The organisation of Arriva is shown in Figure 8.2.

**Figure 8.2** *Arriva, organisational structure*

ARRIVA

| UK Bus | UK Trains | International | Vehicle Rental | Bus and Ccoach |

In the UK, Arriva is one of the largest bus operators with a fleet of over 6,000 vehicles serving customers in the North East, North West and South East of England, London, Yorkshire, the Midlands, Wales and Scotland.

Arriva operates two rail franchises in the UK. Arriva Trains Northern provides urban and inter-city passenger rail services across the North of England.

Arriva is one of the largest private sector providers of passenger transport in mainland Europe with some 5,000 vehicles operating in Denmark, Sweden, the Netherlands, Spain, Italy and Portugal. An extensive range of services includes trains, buses, commuter coaches and water buses.

Arriva Vehicle Rental has over 11,000 vehicles available for rent from 42 locations across the UK.

Arriva Bus and Coach distributes both new and good quality used buses and coaches for operations throughout the UK. It has the exclusive rights to import DAF bus and coach chassis and products.

Source: adapted from Arriva, *Annual Report and Accounts 2002*.

(a) Using information in Figure 8.2, explain how Arriva has organised its operations.
(b) Suggest reasons to explain why the business may be organised in this way.

transport fleet to serve all of its branches.

Disadvantages of organisation by product include the following.

- There may be a duplication of functions in different departments. For example, an accountant may be employed in each division. It may be more cost effective to employ a small team of specialist accountants for the whole organisation.
- Competition between divisions may become counter-productive. This is likely to occur when divisions compete for the organisation's resources. A division which fails to obtain resources may become poorly motivated.
- Senior management might lose control over each individual division. For example, a decision by a junior manager in one division to extend credit to customers for longer than company policy allows might go unnoticed.

## *Organisation by area*

Some businesses prefer to organise their activities on a geographical or regional basis. This is particularly the case if a business has a large number of very similar operations which are widely dispersed either nationally or globally. Many chainstores or multiples (☞ unit 30), for example, have this

method of organisation. They tend to have a large number of stores which operate in a very similar or sometimes identical way. For example, they might sell the same products, use the same procedures and look very similar. The stores are then grouped together in regions and will be accountable to a regional or area manager. Multinational businesses operating in many different countries may also organise themselves into regions of the world, such as Europe, North America and the Far East. The advantages of organising a business geographically include the following.

- Local needs. Sometimes the needs of customers, employees and the community vary in different geographical regions. If a business is organised regionally then it should be able to serve the needs of local people more easily. This is particularly the case for multinational companies. For example, the needs of Middle Eastern customers may be different from those of North American customers.
- Improved communications. Operating on a regional basis should improve communications. For example, a regional manager may be able to more easily inform local shops of a decision than all retail outlets. To some extent this benefit is not as important today as information and communication technology allows fast and easy

---

Hanson is a large multinational company with a turnover of over £4 billion. In 2002 the company made a pre-tax profit of £433.3 million and employed nearly 30,000 staff around the world. Its core products are summarised below. Figure 8.3 shows the organisation structure of the Hanson Group.

- **Aggregates** (crushed rock, sand and gravel). Hanson is the largest producer of aggregates in the world. It produces 215 million tonnes of aggregates every year from more than 400 quarries in the UK, North America, Australia and Asia Pacific.
- **Concrete products**, such as drainage pipes for water

systems and sewers and other precast concrete products such as manholes, box culverts, bridge components, retaining walls and concrete blocks and floors.

- **Bricks**. In 2002 the company made more than two billion bricks at over 35 plants in the UK, the USA and Canada.
- **Ready-mixed concrete**. Concrete is one of the world's most versatile and durable construction materials. Hanson is the third largest producer of ready-mixed concrete producing 30 million cubic metres every year from more than 800 sites in 13 different countries.

Source: adapted from Hanson, *Annual Report and Accounts*, 2002, 2003.

**Figure 8.3**
*The group structure of Hanson*

(a) Explain how Hanson is organised.
(b) Analyse the advantages of this type of organisation for the business.

**Question 3**

communication around the world.

- Competition. It may be possible to encourage healthy internal competition between different regions in the organisation. For example, prizes or bonuses are sometimes awarded to those regions with the highest sales or profits. In addition, regions are often used as training grounds for senior management.

Some disadvantages of regional organisation include the following.

- Duplication of resources. As with some other methods of organisation, it may not be cost effective for each region to provide certain specialist services, such as accountancy and research and development.
- Conflict. It is possible that local managers may begin to introduce their own policies. They might argue that their local situation requires a different approach from that of the business. This might lead to conflict with senior management as they see their authority being undermined.

## Organisation by customer

This method is similar to organising a business by product. It involves grouping together employees who deal with a specific customer or group. This method is particularly useful where the needs of distinct customer groups are different. For example, an advertising agency might organise itself according to customer. Senior staff may be given the accounts of the most important customers. This method of organisation has a number of advantages.

- Customer needs. The needs of different customers will be served more effectively by a department focused on one particular service. Also, customers might prefer to do business with a company that is sensitive to specific customer needs.
- Market segmentation. A business may divide its market into different market segments. The advantages of market segmentation are discussed in unit 20.

However, there may also be some difficulties.

- Customer definition. It is not always possible to clearly define a particular customer group. For example, students at university may be taking a modular course, which involves more than one faculty. This may cause problems for students if different faculties operate in different ways.
- Inefficiency. It is possible that some departments are too small because they do not have enough customers. In this case costs per customer could be high. This may affect the profitability of the whole organisation.
- Control and co-ordination. As with other methods of organisation where the company is split into discrete divisions, there may be problems of control and co-ordination. Communication between departments may be limited, individual departments may pursue their own goals and senior management may find it difficult to control the organisation.

Unilever is a multinational company, which manufactures food and home and personal care products. Some of its well known brands include Knorr soups and snacks, Magnum and Cornetto ice creams, Lipton teas, Findus frozen food meals, Dove soap and OMO washing detergent. Figure 8.4 provides two pieces of analysis of sales.

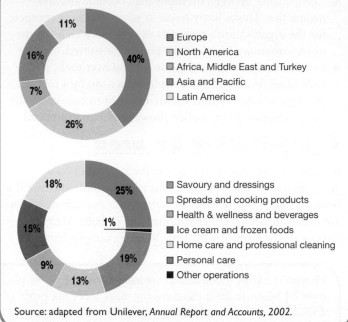

**Figure 8.4** *Turnover of Unilever by category, 2002*

Source: adapted from Unilever, *Annual Report and Accounts, 2002.*

(a) What two methods of organisation are suggested by Figure 8.4? Explain your answer.
(b) Analyse the possible reasons why the business might have organised itself using two methods.

**Question4**

## Organisation by process

The production of some products or services requires a series of processes. Departments could be established to take responsibility for each process. For example, a clothing company manufacturing children's clothes may be divided into departments. Each department operates in its own workshop in the factory.

- The first stage in the production process may be design. This department would be responsible for designing new clothes and producing computerised patterns for the cutting department.
- In the cutting department fabrics are cut to size by computer operated machines. The cut fabrics are then taken to the sewing department. Here the separate pieces of fabric are sewn together to form clothes.
- The finishing department is responsible for adding seams,

frills, buttons, zips and other accessories.
● The last process in the sequence is dispatch. This department is responsible for packing the clothes and preparing the products for distribution to retailers.

Organisation by process is very similar to organisation by function and has similar benefits. Teams of staff in each department may be more focused. The company may enjoy the advantages of specialisation. There is likely to be regular communication between each stage in the production process. Management will be able to monitor clearly the performance of each department. The main disadvantage of organisation by process is a lack of flexibility. It may be difficult to switch staff from one process to another. This may be because they are not trained to work in other departments or because they do not wish to transfer. In addition, departments will have to operate at the same pace. For example, if the cutting department slows down, resources in the sewing department may lay idle. Communications problems may also arise.

# key terms

**Structure of a business** - the way in which a business is organised.

## Knowledge...Knowledge...Knowle

1. What is meant by organisation by function?
2. Why might a business be organised in more than one way?
3. State 2 advantages and 2 disadvantages of a functional organisational structure.
4. Describe the advantages of a company organising itself by product.
5. When is regional organisation likely to be an appropriate method of organisation for a business?
6. Why might solicitors organise themselves according to customer group?
7. What is meant by organisation by process?
8. Suggest 2 types of business that may organise themselves by process.

# Case study StarCars

StarCars was formed in 1994 by Ernie Anderson. He started by purchasing a Porsche 911 and hiring it out in his home town of Oxford. Demand for the car was unbelievable. By 1996 he had bought another Porsche, a Ferrari and an Aston Martin and was beginning to develop a profitable business. By 1999 he had five car hire centres - a head office and centre in Oxford, centres in Reading and Watford, and two others in London. The business was organised as shown in Figure 8.5.

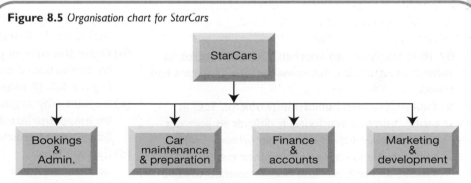

**Figure 8.5** *Organisation chart for StarCars*

● **Bookings & Admin**. Each centre had one full time and two part-time staff handling bookings and administration. They dealt with customers when they booked cars, picked them up and dropped them off.
● **Car maintenance and preparation**. A 'mobile' mechanic was based at Oxford, but dealt with maintenance work on all of the cars. In each centre one person cleaned the cars and prepared them for customers before they were picked up.
● **Finance and accounts**. Two people were employed at Oxford to process wages, deal with staff problems, record business transactions, produce accounts and carry out purchasing.
● **Marketing and business development**. This section was set up in 1998 when the business started to expand. Ernie played an important role, but also hired two other staff to help him. This part of the business bought the cars. It was time consuming because the cars were expensive and required research, comprehensive knowledge, sound negotiation skills and careful judgment. The role of one of the staff was to advertise the business and find suitable sites for new centres.

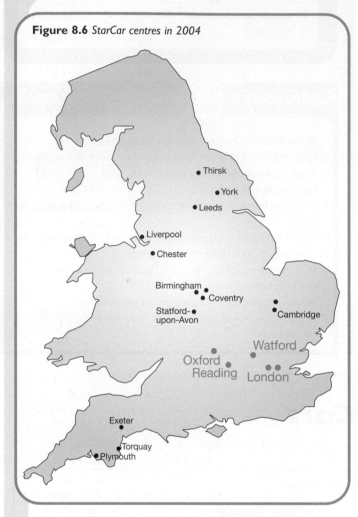

**Figure 8.6** *StarCar centres in 2004*

Thirsk
York
Leeds
Liverpool
Chester
Birmingham
Coventry
Statford-upon-Avon
Cambridge
Watford
Oxford
Reading
London
Exeter
Torquay
Plymouth

By 2004 StarCars had another fourteen centres, as shown on Figure 8.6. But some serious problems had arisen.

● There were communication problems. Staff in other centres often found it difficult to sort out wage queries with Oxford. Also, when a centre had a problem, such as a customer dispute, it was difficult to settle because noone seemed to have any authority. Ernie, who made all the key decisions, was often unavailable.

● Because of the distances involved, the mobile mechanic found it impossible to maintain cars all over the country. The mechanic was overworked, even though eventually an assistant was employed.

● Ernie worried about the accountability of each centre. Although he trusted the majority of his staff, he felt that there was not enough incentive for each centre to maximise performance.

● Because of the geographical distance between centres, staff felt isolated. There was often a lack of

leadership and some staff became demotivated. Staff turnover had also risen, particularly in the centres away from the South East.

Ernie felt that the solution was to organise the company geographically. Looking at Figure 8.6, he thought that the company could be divided into six areas. It would be necessary to appoint a manager responsible for each region and delegate a lot more responsibility. Regional managers would make daily visits to each centre in the region, recruit staff, and attend a management meeting with Ernie every two weeks in Birmingham. Managers could take decisions on behalf of their region without consulting Ernie.

Ernie decided to outsource all car maintenance to another business and to allow managers to buy cars for their region based on regional demand. However, managers would have to be carefully trained in this task. Ernie also decided to pay managers a low basic salary, but offer an incentive package based on the amount of time cars were hired out. If cars were hired out 80 per cent of the time an annual bonus of £10,000 would be paid. If this rose to 95 per cent a further £17,000 would be paid. Ernie expected all managers to reach the first target and the company would make a reasonable profit based on this performance. However, the second target was likely to be more of a challenge.

(a) **Explain why you think Ernie organised StarCars by function initially. (6 marks)**

(b) **Draw the new organisational chart suggested by Ernie, based on geographical location in Figure 8.6. (8 marks)**

(c) **Explain why organisation by product might be inappropriate for StarCars. (6 marks)**

(d) **Explain why accountability is likely to improve after the reorganisation. (12 marks)**

(e) **To what extent will the new organisation structure help overcome the problems StarCars is experiencing? (18 marks)**

# 9 Business and the Economic System

## The basic economic problem

Unit 1 showed that business activity involved satisfying consumers' **needs** and **wants**. Businesses aim to satisfy these wants and needs by producing goods and services. When food is produced or a bus service is provided **resources** (land, labour, capital and enterprise) are used up. These resources are scarce relative to needs and wants. In other words, there are not enough resources to satisfy all consumers' needs and wants. This is known as the BASIC ECONOMIC PROBLEM. This means businesses, individuals and the government must make **choices** when allocating scarce resources between different uses. For example, a printer may have to choose whether to buy a new printing press to improve quality or some new computer

software to improve administrative efficiency.

Economics is the study of how resources are allocated in situations where they have different uses. The choices faced by decision makers can be placed in order of preference. For example, a business may be considering three investment options but can only afford one. The decision makers might decide that the order is:

1. a new computer system;
2. a fleet of cars for the sales force;
3. a warehouse extension.

The business will allocate resources to the purchase of the new computer system. The other two options are **foregone** or given up. The benefit lost from the next best alternative is called the OPPORTUNITY COST of the choice. In this example it would be the benefit lost by not having a fleet of new cars.

## The function of an economy

What is an economy? An ECONOMY is a system which attempts to solve the basic economic problem. In the national economy the resources in a country are changed by business activity into goods and services which are bought by individuals. In a household economy the family budget is spent on a range of goods and services. Local and international economies also act in the same way, but at different levels. The function of an economy is to allocate scarce resources amongst unlimited wants. The basic economic problem is often broken down into three questions.

- **What should be produced?** In developed economies the number of goods and services produced from resources is immense. The economic system must decide which resources will be used to produce which products. For example, what proportion of resources should be used to produce food, housing, cars, cigarettes, cosmetics or computers? Should resources be used for military purposes? Should resources be used to generate wealth for the future? In less developed countries the decision about what to produce may be simpler. This is because the choices available are limited. For example, a very poor African village might be faced with the decision whether to produce wheat or maize. However, this is still a question about resource allocation and what to produce.

- **How should it be produced?** The way in which goods and services are produced can vary. Decisions have to be made about such things as where production will take place, the method of production and the materials and labour that will be used.

- **For whom should it be produced?** An economy has to determine how the final goods and services will be allocated amongst competing groups. For example, how much should go to students, should the unemployed receive a share of output, should Ethiopia receive a proportion of total UK output, should managers get more

---

Michael Shears runs a restaurant in London. It has only been open six months and although it has made a good start, the business is experiencing cash flow problems. Michael incurred some unexpected costs when converting the building into an attractive restaurant location. Consequently all the start-up capital was used up. However, he has managed to borrow a further £2,000 to continue the development of the business, but she cannot afford to fund all of the anticipated expenditure. Michael has identified four urgent items of expenditure:

- invest in a local radio advert to boost 'off-peak' business;
- develop and furnish a bar area where diners can wait comfortably for a table;
- completely upgrade the restaurant crockery. Michael bought the first set second hand and it does not reflect the quality of the food;
- invest in some top quality wine. The current stock does not compliment the quality of the food.

Ideally Michael would like to meet all of the above expenditure. However, he can only afford one in the list.

(a) Explain how the above example illustrates the concept of opportunity cost.
(b) Michael places the above list in the following order of preference.
   1. Develop and furnish a bar area.
   2. Invest in a local radio advert.
   3. Invest in some top quality wine,
   4. Completely upgrade the restaurant crockery.
   What is the opportunity cost in this example?

## Question 1

than workers?

How the above questions are answered will depend on the type of **economic system**. It is usual to explain how resources are allocated in three types of economy - the free market economy, the planned economy and the mixed economy. The way business activity is organised will be different in each of these systems.

The organisation of production in different economic systems is also influenced by the **political system**. For example, in countries where there are free democracies, a significant proportion of goods and services are produced by independent businesses. On the other hand, in those few remaining countries which are dominated by the state, usually **communist** systems, the government plays the most important role in the production of goods and services.

## Market economies

In MARKET ECONOMIES (also known as CAPITALIST ECONOMIES or FREE ENTERPRISE ECONOMIES) resources are allocated through markets (☞ unit 1).

The role of government in a free market system is limited. Its main functions are:

- to pass laws which protect the rights of businesses and consumers and punish offenders;
- to issue money and make sure that the monetary system (☞ unit 1) operates so that markets work efficiently;
- to provide certain essential products and services that would not be provided for everyone by firms, such as policing, national defence and the judiciary;
- to prevent firms from dominating the market and to restrict the power of trade unions. These activities would restrict competition and affect the workings of the market.

**What to produce** This decision is often made by consumers. Businesses will only produce goods if consumers will buy them and so firms must identify consumers' needs and respond to them. Firms which produce unwanted products are likely to fail.

Resources will be used to produce those goods and services which are profitable for businesses. If consumers buy more of a particular product, prices will tend to rise (☞ unit 93). Rising prices will attract firms into that industry as they see the chance of profit. For example, in recent years, new firms have set up supplying accommodation for the elderly, to exploit rising demand as the population ages in the UK.

As demand for out of date and unwanted products falls their prices will also fall. Firms will leave these industries due to a fall in profit. They will sell unwanted resources like land, buildings and equipment and make labour redundant. These resources will be used by other businesses. For example, many textile mills have closed down due to a lack of demand. Some of the buildings have been bought by other businesses and converted into furniture stores or health centres.

**How to produce** In market economies businesses decide this.

Businesses aim to make a profit. They will choose production methods which reduce their costs. Competition in business forces firms to keep costs and prices low. Consumers will prefer to buy their goods from firms which offer lower prices, although other things such as quality will also influence them.

**How are goods and services allocated?** Firms produce goods and services which consumers purchase with money. The amount of money consumers have to spend depends on their income and wealth. In market economies individuals own the factors of production. For example, workers earn wages from selling their labour. Owners of capital receive interest, owners of businesses receive profits and the owners of land receive rent. All of these can be spent on goods and services. Those individuals with the most money can buy the most products.

In practice there are no pure market economies in the world. However, some countries such as the USA and Japan have economies which possess many of the characteristics of market economies.

## Implications of market economies

The working of a free market economy can affect business and consumers in many ways.

- Resources are allocated automatically by the forces of demand and supply (☞ unit 93). For example, if more people decide to buy a product, the business will expand output, hire more factors of production and earn more revenue.
- Resources are not wasted in the production of unwanted goods.
- There should be a wider choice of goods and services.
- Individuals are free to set up in business and to choose how to spend their income.
- Competition should lead to lower costs and improve quality as firms try to impress consumers. Innovation might also be more widespread as firms try to develop new products to offer more choice and new production techniques to lower costs.
- There is often an unequal DISTRIBUTION OF INCOME. Groups that cannot be involved in economic activity, such as the old or the ill, may have little or no income. Owners of profitable businesses can build up great wealth.
- MARKET IMPERFECTIONS often occur. For example, a large firm may dominate an industry by driving out competition. The large company can then force up prices and exploit consumers.
- Some goods are not provided by private firms. These include defence, but also services where they may not make a profit.
- A lot of time and money is wasted when businesses collapse. For example, a failed construction company may own partly completed buildings which can become derelict if buyers cannot be found.

In March 2002 ITV Digital went into administration. The demise of the company was bad news for the parent companies, Carlton and Granada, the Football League, subscribers, suppliers and the government. The ambition of Carlton and Granada was to build a pay TV operation capable of competing with BSkyB. They hoped that the purchase of the rights to broadcast live Nationwide football would be the kingpin of the operation.

ITV Digital disintegrated after two years of false starts, poor management and £800 million investment. After one of the worst recessions in advertising spending in memory, Carlton and Granada decided it could not tolerate the venture's massive losses. However, the cost of cutting loose from ITV Digital would be expensive, with long term repercussions. In the short term, bills of £50-£120 million could be incurred, even before any potential legal action from the Football League.

The body that represents lower league teams threatened to sue Carlton and Granada for up to £500 million in lost broadcasting and sponsorship revenues if they reneged on the three-year broadcasting deal. It was the league's refusal to renegotiate the deal that finally tipped ITV Digital over the edge. However, it was unlikely that the 72 clubs relying on the income from the deal will get anything like the money they were owed. Indeed, around 30 clubs could themselves have been on the brink of collapse. Suppliers, such as BT, set top box manufacturers and content providers could also be in trouble. They could also threaten multimillion pound law suits to recover money owed. ITV Digital's 1.3 million subscribers felt confused and angry.

The biggest losers in all of this could be the government. It was hoping to switch off the analogue television signal between 2006-2010. It would then be free to auction off the spare analogue spectrum to raise money for public expenditure. This is similar to the sale of third generation mobile phone licences. With the collapse of ITV Digital, it appeared that the government would have problems meeting the 2006-2010 target, especially taking into account the fact that Britain's cable companies, NTL and Telewest which have 1.8 million subscribers between them, were also having financial problems.

Sources: adapted from *The Guardian*, 28.3.2002 and *The Observer*, 31.3.2002.

(a) In what ways does this case illustrate some of the problems associated with market economies?
(b) How is BSkyB and the BBC likely be affected by the demise of ITV Digital?

Question 2

---

- Resources are often very slow to move from one use to another. For example, some workers may refuse to move from one area to another if a firm closes down, resulting in underused resources and unemployment.
- Consumers may lack the information to make choices when buying products. The range of products, their quality and their prices change so frequently that consumers find it difficult to keep up to date. Also, some firms use marketing techniques to influence consumer choice.
- In order to keep costs low, firms may choose to pollute the environment. For example, they might discharge poisonous substances into rivers.

## Planned economies

In PLANNED or COMMAND ECONOMIES, government has a vital role. It plans, organises and co-ordinates the whole production process. This is unlike a market economy, where planning and organising is carried out by firms. Another difference is that resources in planned economies belong to the state. Individuals are not permitted to own property, land and other non-labour means of production.

**What to produce** This decision is made by government planners. They decide the type and mix of goods and services to be produced. Planners make assumptions about consumers' needs. For example, they decide how many cars, how much milk, how many shirts and how much meat should be produced. Planners then tell producers, such as farms and factories, exactly what to produce.

**How to produce** Government also tells producers how to produce. **Input-output analysis** is often used to make plans. For example, with a given level of technology, the state may know the land, labour, tractors and fertiliser (inputs) needed to make 1 million tonnes of wheat (the output). If an area needs 20 million tonnes, it is possible to work out the inputs needed. A complex table is drawn up which helps planners calculate the resources needed to meet the various output targets. Plans are often for 5, 10 or 15 years.

**How are goods and services allocated?** Goods and services are distributed to consumers through state outlets. People purchase goods and services with money they earn. Prices are set by the planners and cannot change without state instruction. Sometimes there are restrictions on the amount of particular goods and services which can be bought by any one individual, cars for example. Some goods and services, like education and health care, are provided free by the state.

## Implications of planned economies

How does a planned economy affect the businesses and consumers that operate in it?
- There tends to be a more equal distribution of wealth and income. The state provides a minimum level of payment to all individuals. In addition, people are not allowed to own property, so wealth cannot be accumulated through private ownership.
- Resources are not duplicated. There is no competition in

the supply of a service like public transport, whereas in a market economy several buses might drive along the same road competing for the same passengers.

● Production is for need rather than profit. Planners decide what is needed and what is produced. Resources are not wasted through businesses producing unwanted goods.

● Long term plans can be made taking into account a range of future needs, such as population changes and the environment.

● Many resources are used up in the planning process. Vast bureaucracies, employing large numbers of people, are needed to supervise, co-ordinate and carry out plans.

● People tend to be poorly motivated. As there is no profit, there is no incentive to motivate entrepreneurs.

● Planners encourage the production of standardised goods with little variety and choice for consumers.

● Planners often get things wrong. This can lead to shortages of some goods and services and surpluses of others. Also, planners' choices are not necessarily those of individuals. For example, many command economies produce large quantities of military goods.

● Shortages of goods often result in long queues outside state shops. This often leads to black markets. Goods and services are sold unofficially by individuals well above the state imposed prices. It is argued that this leads to bribery and corruption.

● The standard of living is often poor compared with countries which use other types of economic system.

Many of the former communist countries, such as Russia, Poland and the Czech Republic, reformed their economic and political systems after 1989. They changed from planned economies to mixed economies, with a greater freedom of markets. This led to problems, as described later in this unit. In 2004 examples of planned economies might include North Korea, Cuba and Vietnam. They have many of the characteristics listed here. However, some have introduced limited private ownership and free markets to help solve some of the problems of state run systems.

## Mixed economies

In reality, no country has an economy which is entirely planned or free market. Most economic systems in the world have elements of each system.

They are known as MIXED ECONOMIES. In mixed economies some resources are allocated by the government and the rest by the market system. All Western European countries have mixed economies. The public sector (☞ unit 7) in mixed economies is responsible for the supply of some public goods and merit goods. Decisions regarding resource allocation in the public sector are made by central or local government. In the private sector production decisions

---

North Korea is one of the world's most centrally planned and isolated economies. More than 90 per cent of the economy is socialised, agricultural land is collectivised, and the state-owned industry produces 95 per cent of manufactured goods. State control of economic affairs is unusually tight because of the small size of the population, its homogeneity and the strict rule of the leadership.

Output of the extractive industries includes coal, iron ore, magnesite, graphite, copper, zinc, lead and precious metals. Manufacturing is centred on heavy industry, including military industry, with light industry lagging far behind. Despite the use of improved seed varieties, expansion of irrigation, and the heavy use of fertilisers, North Korea has not yet become self-sufficient in food production. A shortage of arable lands, several years of poor harvests, and a cumbersome distribution system have resulted in chronic food shortages. Huge international food aid has prevented mass starvation since 1995-96, but the population remains a victim of prolonged malnutrition and deteriorating living conditions. Large amounts of military spending eat up resources needed for investment and private consumption.

The collapse of communism in the former Soviet Union and Eastern Europe in 1989-91 has disrupted important technological links. North Korea remains far behind South Korea in economic development and living standards. In November 2003, the international credit ratings agency Standard & Poor's (S&P) warned that it was simply a matter of time before the North Korean economy totally

**Table 9.1** *Data for North Korea*

| | |
|---|---|
| **Population:** | 22.5m (est. 2003) |
| **Climate:** | Temperate with rainfall concentrated in the summer |
| **Land use:** | Arable 14%, permanent crops 2.5%, other 83.5% |
| **Natural resources:** | Coal, lead, tungsten, zinc, graphite, magnesite, iron ore, copper, gold, pyrit, salt, fluorspur and hydropower |
| **Birth rate:** | 17.6 per 1,000 (est. 2003) |
| **Death rate:** | 6.93 per 1,000 (est. 2003) |
| **Literacy rate:** | 99% |

disintegrates. A spokesperson for S&P said 'The economic model of North Korea is not sustainable'. 'We think the political leadership in North Korea does not have the capacity to undertake reforms that, say, China, began in 1979 or Vietnam began in 1986.'

Source: adapted from www.theodora.comnomy.

(a) What evidence is there in the case to suggest that North Korea is a planned economy?

(b) Analyse the drawbacks of planned economies using examples from the case.

**Question3**

are made by firms in response to the demands of consumers.

In the public sector, public goods and merit goods are usually provided free when used and are paid for by taxes. Examples might be roads and street lighting. In mixed economies the state usually provides a minimum standard of living for those unable to work. In the UK the state provides benefits as workers look for work and certain sickness benefits. In the public sector the state will own a significant proportion of production factors and service provision.

In the private sector individuals are allowed to own the means of production. Businesses are set up by individuals to supply a wide variety of goods and services. Competition exists between these firms. As a result, there will tend to be choice and variety. One of the roles of the government is to ensure that there is fair competition in the private sector. All private sector goods and services are allocated as in the market system described earlier.

What should be the 'degree of mixing' in this type of economy? The government will decide how much business activity there will be in the private sector and how much in the public sector. Some countries, like Sweden, allow the government to play a greater role in the supply of goods and services than others, like the UK. For example, in Sweden the government spends around 60 per cent of national income, whilst in the UK the government spends around 40 per cent. In countries where the government plays an important economic role, social provision will tend to be greater, taxes higher and the distribution of wealth and income more equal. In countries where the private sector plays the most important economic role, social provision will tend to be lower with fewer free goods and services at the point of sale. Also, taxes will be lower and the distribution of wealth and income less equal. For example, in the last two decades, income tax rates have fallen in the UK and fewer services have been supplied by the state. The distribution of income has changed in favour of the 'wealthy' during this time.

# Problems of changing systems

In the late 1980s and the 1990s major changes took place in a number of Eastern European countries. The former communist regimes were overthrown and replaced by some form of democracy. In most cases, the new governments wished to introduce market economies to replace the older planned systems which were thought to be inefficient. Although each country has had different experiences, there are some common features which all countries changing to a market system have faced. Many problems have arisen as a result of these changes. Businesses in these countries have had to change how they operate to cope with new demands.

**Inflation** Most countries have experienced inflation - a rise in the general price level. Under a planned system prices were set by the state and, in theory, inflation did not exist. However, following liberalisation of their markets former planned economies experienced high inflation rates. In countries such as Armenia, Russia and Georgia inflation rates were more than 1,000 per cent in the early 1990s. In 2003 Hungary has forecast to have an inflation rate of only 5 per cent. Inflation affects the functions of money (☞ unit 98). In some countries businesses have reverted to bartering for resources, exchanging their products for other goods or services. Alternatively, they have exchanged their goods for currencies with stable values, such as the dollar.

**Establishing the system** A change to a market economy will not take place overnight. The institutions in Western economies which help the market system to work will take time to develop and operate in the former planned economies. Businesses may have problems raising finance due to a lack of institutions able to loan money. In many countries there is no stock market where shares in a company can be sold to raise finance. Other problems may result from the previous inefficiencies of planned systems. Transport, communications and markets for buying and selling goods are not yet ready for the level of business activity that will take place under a market system. This can result in late deliveries, a lack of information and a restriction in selling opportunities.

**Competition** Businesses in former planned economies now face competition from both within the country and from abroad. Some countries have suffered from cheap foreign goods being sold in their economy. Prices of home produced goods and services are likely to be higher than before. Previously the state had kept the prices of resources low so that the prices of final goods were also low. Removal of these controls would mean having to increase prices to make a profit.

**Unemployment** In a planned system unemployment should not exist. The state provides work for all individuals and makes sure that they have minimum living standards. In 2003 unemployment in Estonia, for example, was forecast to be greater than 10 per cent.

**Running the business** The new entrepreneurs in former planned economies will be the managers and employees of ex-state run firms. These people have no experience of how to operate in a market system. They face the prospect of making a profit or going out of business, unheard of under a planned system. Also, businesses are not used to operating under a system where profit and earnings motivate people to work. Many would still suffer from the lack of initiative associated with the planned system. Finally, the ability to organise, run and motivate business activity in these countries may not exist, and many people require training, often from Western firms or training agencies.

It has been argued that those countries with the most recent history of a market system have adjusted best to the transition. Before the Second World War, Hungary, Poland,

Slovenia and the Czech and Slovak Republics all had market systems. Countries that were part of the former USSR, with communist systems, have not performed as well. In 1996, for example, economic growth in the Slovak Republic was 7 per cent compared to -4.9 per cent in Russia. Growth did achieve positive figures by 2000, although Russia experienced further problems in the years that followed.

**Transfer of ownership** One major problem facing all economies changing from a planned to a market system is the transfer of ownership. Previously all resources and businesses were state owned. Farms, factories and shops now have to be passed on to employees and managers. In the former East Germany all state firms were placed in the hands of an agency (the Treuhand) which sold them off. In the former USSR, people were given vouchers which entitled them to a share of a company.

Many Eastern European countries are undertaking a huge privatisation process. In some cases privatisation experts from the UK and other western economies are recruited to advise on the transfer of assets from the public to the private sector.

---

After regaining independence in 1991, Lithuania attempted to recover from the command economy of the former Soviet Union. The country faced major problems, such as huge inflation (mainly due to considerably increased costs of raw materials and other resources from Russia) and falling GDP caused by the change in economic style and loss of previous economic relations. Domestic and foreign investment also fell in line with economic performance in the early 1990s. It was hard for the Lithuanian government to subsidise the big inefficient manufacturers without the involvement of the Soviet Union. Thus, drastic measures of privatisation had to be taken, changing the balance between government investment and private sector investment.

Almost 50 per cent of state property has been privatised and trade is diversifying, with a gradual shift away from the former Soviet Union to Western markets. Lithuania implemented the privatisation process more rapidly than any other Central or Eastern European country. The programme was introduced in 1991 and by 1995 eighty five per cent of a total of 8,214 companies had been privatised. Investment vouchers were chosen as the basis for privatisation. These were issued by the government and could be used for the purchase of property. 24 per cent of the vouchers have been used by Lithuanians to purchase their own apartments or houses and 66 per cent for the privatisation of state enterprises.

The process of privatisation is the backbone of the Lithuanian transformation process. It has had a significant impact on the general economic development of the country, the creation of a competitive business environment, and the development of a system of corporate governance and securities market. The privatisation of Lithuania's electricity distribution and generation companies, the state alcohol monopoly, and Lithuanian Airlines and Railways are all pencilled in for the next few years.

Source: adapted from www.nationmaster.com and www2.omnitel.net.

(a) Explain the role played by privatisation in Lithuania when changing from a planned to a more market orientated economy.
(b) Examine the problems faced by Lithuania when changing from a planned to a more market orientated economy.

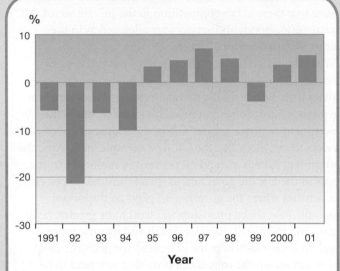

**Figure 9.1** Growth in GDP (%), Lithuania

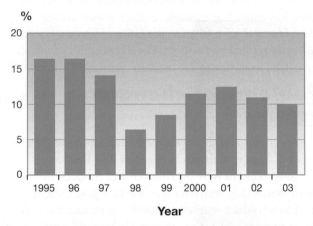

**Figure 9.2** Lithuania unemployment rate (average annual)

# key terms

**Basic economic problem** - how scarce resources with different uses are allocated to satisfy wants.

**Distribution of income** - the amount of income and wealth different groups have in a particular country.

**Economy** - a system which attempts to solve the basic economic problem.

**Market economy or capitalist economy or free enterprise economy** - an economic system which allows the market mechanism to allocate resources.

**Market imperfection** - any factor which hinders the free operation of markets, such as where one firm dominates resulting in exploitation.

**Mixed economy** - an economic system which allows both the state and the market mechanism to allocate resources.

**Opportunity cost** - the benefit of the next best option foregone when making a choice between a number of alternatives.

**Planned economy or command economy** - an economic system in which the state is responsible for resource allocation.

## Knowledge...Knowledge...Knowledge...Knowledge...Knowledge...Know

1. Why do businesses, individuals and government need to make choices about the resources they use?
2. Give 2 examples of opportunity cost.
3. What is the function of an economy?
4. What are the 3 questions an economy aims to answer?
5. Describe the benefits of market economies for:
   (a) businesses; (b) consumers.

6. Describe the problems of planned economies for:
   (a) firms; (b) consumers.
7. What determines the degree of 'mix' in a mixed economy?
8. 'A free market system in former planned economies will take time to work.' Give 3 examples which support this statement.

# Case study China

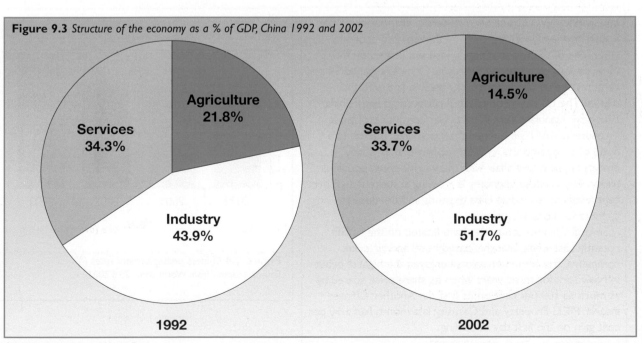

**Figure 9.3** *Structure of the economy as a % of GDP, China 1992 and 2002*

1992
- Agriculture 21.8%
- Services 34.3%
- Industry 43.9%

2002
- Agriculture 14.5%
- Services 33.7%
- Industry 51.7%

Source: adapted from World Bank.

China, the world's fastest growing economy, is on course to overtake Britain in two years or so. National output is moving forward so fast that the country is in danger of overheating. The economy surged 9.1 per cent in the July-September period as domestic firms increased investment and foreign manufacturers such as Ford and Sony once again poured money into a country that has become the workshop of the world. According to government officials, the amount of economic activity in China soared to £570 billion in the first nine months of the year. This put China on course to achieve a growth rate of 8.5 per cent for 2003, the fastest in more than five years. If the country can maintain this pace it will overtake Britain and France to become the world's fourth biggest economy well before the end of 2005.

Business leaders are already hailing China as the powerhouse for growth in Asia, a role once held by Japan. With neighbouring nations increasing sales of raw materials to factories in China, imports jumped by 40.5 per cent in the first nine months of the year.

Many of those factories are foreign-owned as multinational firms rush to exploit China's abundant cheap labour. The latest is Ford, which announced plans yesterday for a new $1.5 billion (£900 million) plant in Chongching. 'China is really the engine that drives the entire region' Ford's chief executive officer, William Clay Ford, told reporters. 'We do expect to expand aggressively in China.' Japanese manufacturers are also pumping cash into their neighbour's economy. Sony, the world's second-biggest consumer electronics maker, revealed it has invested $8 billion in China and forecast that the country would become its second biggest market, behind only the US, within five years.

Although tens of millions of rural Chinese people scratch out a living well below the poverty line, the average disposable income in towns and cities which are home to two-fifths of China's 1.3 billion people rose 9 per cent to (£460) in the first nine months of this year. The government boasted that its measures had created 6.25 million jobs in the first nine months of the year, leaving an urban unemployment rate of 4.2 per cent. Much of the new work was created through construction projects in cities including Shanghai, as well as huge public infrastructure undertakings such as the Three Gorges dam, the world's biggest engineering project.

However, the risks for the Chinese economy are growing along with its size. A flood of spending on property and construction has raised fears of overheating and highlighted the problems of overlending by Chinese banks. With credit easy to acquire, fixed-asset investment rose 30.5 per cent in the first nine months of this year. Such is the risk of overheating that economists now believe the government is downplaying the pace of growth. GDP figures have long been criticised as unreliable, though usually for being exaggerated rather than too modest.

Source: adapted from *The Guardian*, 18.10.2003.

Investors on Wall Street were yesterday clamouring to take a stake in the explosive growth of the Chinese economy when one of the nation's biggest insurers floated on the New York stock exchange. Shares in China Life gained 34 per cent in value to $25 before falling back in line with the market. The US has a complicated relationship with China. American manufacturers in particular are critical of trade agreements that have opened their domestic market to a flood of cheap imports. Wall Street, however, is clearly embarking on a love affair with the world's most populous nation. The Chinese economy is growing at more than 8 per cent a year as its middle class expands and develops an appetite for consumer goods.

Several Chinese companies have floated on the NYSE recently. Last week, Shanghai-based hotel and air ticket company Ctrip.com International enjoyed the highest debut in New York for three years when its share price soared by as much as 108 per cent on its first day. Another Chinese insurer, PICC Property and Casualty, last month had a 50 per cent gain on the first day of trading.

Source: adapted from *The Guardian*, 18.12.2003

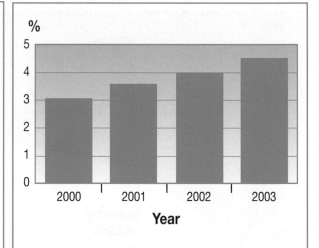

**Figure 9.4** *Chinese unemployment rates (%)*
Source: adapted from World Bank, 29.8.2003.

Figure 9.5 *Growth of investment and GDP in China*

Figure 9.6 *Export and import levels in China (US$m)*

Figure 9.7 *Inflation in China (%)*

Source: adapted from World Bank, 29.8.2003.

(a) **Using examples from the case outline two problems that countries face when changing their economic system.**
**(4 marks)**

(b) **What sort of businesses would you expect to develop in the future in China? Explain your answer. (6 marks)**

(c) **What evidence is there in the case to suggest that the Chinese economy has become more open? (12 marks)**

(d) **Evaluate the advantages and disadvantages to a UK manufacturer of locating a plant in China. (18 marks)**

# 10 Collecting, Presenting and Interpreting Data

## Why do businesses collect data?

Information is a valuable resource in business. Businesses collect large amounts of information or DATA about their own organisations. They may also employ companies, such as Reuters, which specialises in the collection and sale of information. Examples of data that a business might collect include:

● costs of production;
● share prices and exchange rates;
● company reports;
● weekly or monthly sales figures;
● business news, for example about a potential takeover;
● market research findings.

Data are collected by businesses for a number of reasons. Most importantly perhaps, data are required in the decision making process (☞ unit 11). Managers, employees and others involved in business activity need up to date and accurate data to help them make effective decisions. For example, a business choosing from a number of investment opportunities would require the latest information on the costs and expected return of each project.

Data are required to monitor the progress of a business. Business performance could be gauged by looking at the growth or decline in turnover or profit. Changes in productivity rates can be calculated if a business has data on its inputs and output.

All businesses keep records which contain a wide range of **qualitative** (about nature or characteristics) and **quantitative** (involving measurement) data. These records contain information that is important to the business. Such records might include monthly sales figures, staff files, customer files and market reports. It is important that records are regularly

updated so that they are correct when required by the business. Businesses make use of **backdata,** such as sales in previous years, to forecast what might happen in future (☞ unit 36).

Data are also used to help control a business. Financial data on payments and receipts are used to control cash flow (☞ unit 46). A financial controller, for example, might delay payment to a supplier until money is received from customers in order to avoid a cash flow problem.

## Why do businesses present data?

Once data has been collected it can be stored, retrieved and presented. The volume of data collected by businesses is enormous and it is important to avoid making mistakes. The development of information and communication technology (☞ units 70 and 85) in recent years has made the handling of data far easier and less prone to error. Data can be stored on computer memory or a disk, 'called up' on a computer screen, manipulated and presented in a variety of styles. Businesses may make use of graphs, charts, tables and other pictorial methods of communicating data. Presenting data in this way:

● can be more concise and easier to understand than written information;
● can take less time to interpret;
● can identify trends clearly;
● may be effective in creating an impact or an image;
● can be used to impress a potential client.

The method of presentation a business chooses will depend on the type of data collected, who and what it is required for and how it is likely to be used. Data can be presented 'internally' and 'externally'. Examples of data presented to those inside a business might be:

● the sales department presenting a breakdown of regional sales

**Figure 10.1** *Share price, pre-tax profits and sales by division for Tate & Lyle, 2002*

Source: adapted from Thomson Datastream, company.

figures to senior management to illustrate the popularity of products in an area or the effectiveness of promotion;
- the production manager presenting the accounts department with weekly time sheets to allow the calculation of wages and costs;
- the research and development department providing an analysis of monthly expenditure to enable budgets to be calculated;
- the personnel manager providing an analysis of staff turnover to illustrate possible problems or improvements in human resource management;
- the market research department providing research data to allow products to be designed to fit consumers' needs.

Examples of data presented to those outside the business could be:
- the accounts department providing Customs and Excise with VAT details to claim back tax on sales which are exempt from VAT;
- the publication of an Annual Report and Accounts to illustrate a company's progress over the last year to stakeholders;
- the presentation of a new market range by the marketing department to a potential customer.

Figure 10.1 shows some business data for Tate & Lyle, the sweeteners and starches producer. The data shows that the share price has fluctuated but risen over the period. Pre-tax profits have fallen between 1998 and 2002, with a huge loss being made in 2001. In 2002, the largest sales were those in the Americas division, £1.7 billion, and total sales for the year were £3.9 billion.

## Bar charts

A BAR CHART is one of the simplest and most common means of presenting data. Numerical information is represented by 'bars' or 'blocks' which can be drawn horizontally or vertically. The length of the bars shows the relative importance of the data. Table 10.1 shows data on the profit made by Ragwear plc, a manufacturer, over the last six years. They are presented as a bar graph in Figure 10.2.

**Table 10.1** Profit for Ragwear plc over a six year period

|  | Yr1 | Yr2 | Yr3 | Yr4 | Yr5 | Yr6 | £m |
|---|---|---|---|---|---|---|---|
| Profit | 2.1 | 2.9 | 3.8 | 4.1 | 3.2 | 4.9 | |

The main advantage of using a bar chart is that it shows results very clearly. At a glance the reader can get a general feel of the information and identify any trends or changes over the time period. Figure 10.2 shows that profit has continued to increase over the period apart from a 'dip' in year 5. This might indicate to the firm that trading conditions in year 5 were unfavourable or that the firm's performance was

**Figure 10.2** Profit levels for Ragwear plc over a six year period

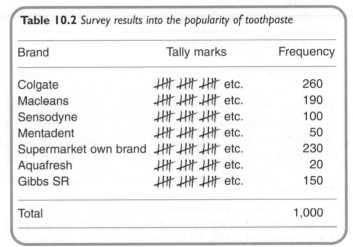

**Table 10.2** Survey results into the popularity of toothpaste

| Brand | Tally marks | Frequency |
|---|---|---|
| Colgate | ╫╫ ╫╫ ╫╫ etc. | 260 |
| Macleans | ╫╫ ╫╫ ╫╫ etc. | 190 |
| Sensodyne | ╫╫ ╫╫ ╫╫ etc. | 100 |
| Mentadent | ╫╫ ╫╫ ╫╫ etc. | 50 |
| Supermarket own brand | ╫╫ ╫╫ ╫╫ etc. | 230 |
| Aquafresh | ╫╫ ╫╫ ╫╫ etc. | 20 |
| Gibbs SR | ╫╫ ╫╫ ╫╫ etc. | 150 |
| Total | | 1,000 |

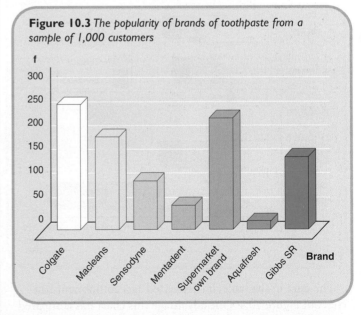

**Figure 10.3** The popularity of brands of toothpaste from a sample of 1,000 customers

relatively poor. Bar charts are more attractive than tables and may allow the reader to interpret the data more quickly.

The bars in Figure 10.2 are drawn vertically. They could also, however, be drawn horizontally. They are also three dimensional, but they could have been two dimensional.

It is possible to produce a bar chart from collected data, such as from market research. This data may be collected in a

**tally chart** as in Table 10.2, which shows the results of research into the brands of toothpaste bought by a sample of supermarket customers. The total number of times each item occurs is known as the **frequency** (f). So, for example, the most popular from the survey is Colgate and the least popular is Aquafresh. Figure 10.3 shows the data from Table 10.2 as a bar chart.

## Component bar charts

A COMPONENT BAR CHART allows more information to be presented to the reader. Each bar is divided into a number of components. For example, the data in Table 10.3 shows the cost structures of five furniture manufacturers in a particular year. The total cost is broken down into labour, materials and overheads.

**Table 10.3** *Cost structures of five furniture manufacturers and overheads*

£000

|  | Oakwell | Stretton | Bradford | Jones | Campsfield |
|---|---|---|---|---|---|
| Labour | 50 | 36 | 70 | 45 | 90 |
| Materials | 18 | 25 | 48 | 23 | 50 |
| Overheads | 10 | 10 | 19 | 9 | 25 |

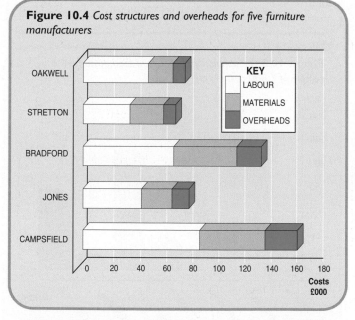

**Figure 10.4** *Cost structures and overheads for five furniture manufacturers*

The data in the table are presented as a component bar chart in Figure 10.4. One advantage this chart has compared to the simple bar chart is that total costs can be seen easily. There is no need to add up the individual costs. It is also easier to make instant comparisons. For example, labour costs are the greatest proportion of total cost at Oakwell. This might suggest to a firm that Oakwell uses a more labour intensive production technique than the others. Also, labour costs at Oakwell are higher than at Stretton, but not as high as

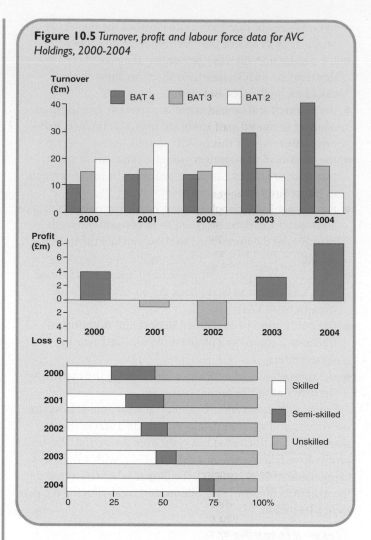

**Figure 10.5** *Turnover, profit and labour force data for AVC Holdings, 2000-2004*

at Campsfield. This might indicate that Oakwell is less efficient than Stretton and a much smaller business than Campsfield.

Figure 10.5 shows three other styles of bar chart, illustrating data for AVC Holdings. This is a company that produces three types of machine tool, code named BAT 4, BAT 3 and BAT 2.

- The top chart is a **parallel** bar chart. It shows the turnover contributed by each of the company's three products. Over the time period the turnover for BAT 4 has increased from £10 million to £40 million. Sales of BAT 3 have remained fairly steady at around £15 million each year. The turnover from BAT 2 has declined from £20 million to £7 million. This type of graph is similar to a component bar chart. The advantage is that it is easier to compare changes between the components, although it is more difficult to compare totals.

- The middle chart is a **gain and loss** bar chart. It shows the profitability of the company over the time period. The performance of AVC Holdings worsened in the first three years and then improved. The profit in 2004 was £8 million. This type of chart distinguishes very clearly between positive and negative values.

- The bottom chart is a **percentage component** bar chart. It shows the breakdown of the workforce in terms of their skill with each section represented as a percentage of the workforce. In 2000 nearly 25 per cent of the workforce were skilled. In 2004 this had risen to around 70 per cent. The chart also shows that the numbers of semi-skilled workers had fallen as a percentage of the total. This might indicate that the firm had introduced new technology, leading to unskilled staff being replaced with skilled staff. One disadvantage of this presentation is that changes in the total size of the workforce are not shown.

UK Coal is Britain's largest producer of coal. The group employs over 7,000 people and has more than 20 deep and surface mine sites that produce around 20 million tonnes of coal a year. Table 10.4 shows the profit before tax, dividend per share and cash flow before financing and dividends between 1999 and 2002.

**Table 10.4** *Profit before tax, dividend per share and cash flow before financing and dividends between 1999 and 2002 for UK Coal*

|  | 1999 | 2000 | 2001 | 2002 |
|---|---|---|---|---|
| Profit/loss before tax (£000) | (130,029) | 17,761 | (26,484) | (83,111) |
| Dividend per share (p) | 7.5 | 10 | 10 | 10 |
| Cash flow before financing and dividends (£000) | 25,203 | 52,758 | 75,895 | (25,183) |

Source: adapted from UK Coal, *Annual Report and Accounts, 2002.*

(a) (i) Construct appropriate bar charts to present the data in the table.
 (ii) Explain briefly what the bar charts show.
(b) Discuss whether you think the use of bar charts in (a) is an effective way of presenting the data.

# Question 1

**Figure 10.6** *A pictograph for GPA Group showing orders for aircraft in March 1999 for each year to 2007*

Number of aircraft

# A pictograph or pictogram

A PICTOGRAPH or PICTOGRAM is another form of chart. It presents data in a similar way to bar charts. The difference is that data are represented by pictorial symbols rather than bars. Figure 10.6 shows an example of the orders which GPA Group has received for its aircraft over a nine year time period. The pictograph shows a general decline in orders. This might indicate that there is a general decline in the market or that customers are delaying future orders. One problem with a pictograph is that it is not always easy to 'divide' the symbols exactly. This makes it difficult to read precise quantities from the graph. For example, in Figure 10.6, in 2001 the number of orders is more than 60, but the last symbol is a fraction of an aircraft which makes it difficult to determine the exact size of orders placed in that year. The main advantage of this method is that the graphs tend to be more eyecatching. Such a method might be used in business presentations to attract clients or in reports to the public.

# Pie charts

In a PIE CHART, the total amount of data collected is represented by a circle. This is divided into a number of segments. Each segment represents the size of a particular part relative to the total. To draw a pie chart it is necessary to perform some simple calculations. Table 10.5 shows the details of monthly output at five European plants for a multinational brick producer. The 360 degrees in a circle have to be divided between the various parts which make up the total output of 50,000 tonnes. To calculate the number of degrees each segment will contain, a business would use the following formula:

$$\frac{\text{Value of the part}}{\text{Total}} \times 360°$$

**Table 10.5** *Monthly brick output at five European plants*

|  | Bedford | Brescia | Lyon | Bonn | Gijon | Total |
|---|---|---|---|---|---|---|
| Output (tonnes) | 10,000 | 8,000 | 5,000 | 15,000 | 12,000 | 50,000 |

Thus, the size of the segment which represents the monthly brick output in Bedford is:

$$= \frac{10,000}{50,000} \times 360°$$

$$= 0.2 \times 360°$$

$$= 72°$$

Using the same method it can be shown that the size of the other segments representing output at the other plants will be: Brescia 58°; Lyon 36°; Bonn 108°; Gijon 86°. The number of degrees in each segment added together make 360°. A pie chart can now be drawn using a protractor or a spreadsheet or DTP software package on a computer. The pie chart is shown in Figure 10.7. Bonn makes the largest contribution to monthly output with Gijon second. The company might use this information to compare with monthly production targets.

Pie charts are useful because readers get an immediate impression of the relative importance of the various parts. They can also be used to make comparisons over different time periods. There are however, drawbacks with pie charts.

● They do not always allow precise comparisons to be made between the segments.
● If a total consists of a very large number of components, it may be difficult to identify the relative importance of each segment.
● It is difficult to show changes in the size of the total pie. For example, if the total rises over time it is possible to make the 'pie' bigger. However, the exact size of the increase is often difficult to determine because it involves comparing the areas of circles.

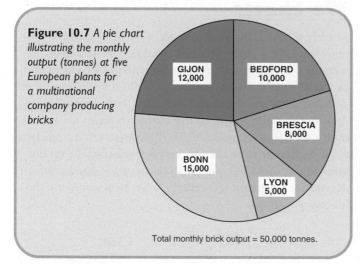

**Figure 10.7** *A pie chart illustrating the monthly output (tonnes) at five European plants for a multinational company producing bricks*

GIJON 12,000
BEDFORD 10,000
BRESCIA 8,000
BONN 15,000
LYON 5,000

Total monthly brick output = 50,000 tonnes.

## Histograms

Table 10.7 illustrates some data collected by market researchers on behalf of a cinema chain. It concerns the age profile of a sample of cinema goers on a Saturday. The chart shows the number of viewers in the sample that falls into various age ranges (known as **classes**). The total number of times each item occurs in each class is known as the frequency (f). So the total number of viewers in the 10-19 age range is 290. This type of data is usually shown as a HISTOGRAM as in Figure 10.8. A histogram looks similar to a bar chart, but there are some differences.

● In a histogram it is the **area** of the bars which represents the frequency. In a bar chart it is the length or height of the bars. For example, in Figure 10.8, all the columns have the same width except for the last one where the age range covers two decades and not one. This means that the frequency in the figure is not 200 as shown in the table, but 100 (200÷2 = 100). This is because in the table 200 viewers fall into the age range 60 - 79, whereas the histogram shows

Aston Villa FC is a Premier League football club. In the last financial year, 2003, its turnover was £45.4 million. Aston Villa's revenue is generated from six main sources. Table 10.6 shows the revenue from each source for 2002 and 2003.

**Table 10.6** *Aston Villa revenue and its sources for 2002 and 2003*

| | £ million | |
|---|---|---|
| | **2003** | **2002** |
| Match receipts | 9.7 | 10.2 |
| Broadcasting | 17.0 | 15.5 |
| Merit awards | 2.5 | 5.7 |
| Merchandising | 3.7 | 3.8 |
| Catering | 4.4 | 4.1 |
| Other commercial income | 8.1 | 7.4 |

Source: adapted from Aston Villa, *Annual Report and Accounts, 2003.*

(a) Construct two pie charts to show the sources of revenue for Aston Villa FC in 2002 and 2003.
(b) Discuss the advantages and disadvantages to the business of presenting the data in this way.

**Question 2**

**Table 10.7** *The age profile of cinema goers on a Saturday*

| Age range | Frequency |
|---|---|
| 0-9 | 180 |
| 10-19 | 290 |
| 20-29 | 500 |
| 30-39 | 400 |
| 40-49 | 350 |
| 50-59 | 280 |
| 60-79 | 200 |
| Total | 2,200 |

100 viewers in the age range 60 - 69 and 100 in the range 70 - 79. However, the area of the last bar coincides with the data in the table, ie it is equal to 200. The total area represented by all columns is equal to the sample size of 2,200.

● Bar charts and histograms can be used for **discrete data** - data which only occur as whole numbers, such as the number of people employed in a store. Histograms are most useful when recording **continuous data** - data which occur over a range of values, such as weight or age.
● Histograms tend to be used for grouped data, for example the number of people between the ages of 0 and 9.

The histogram in Figure 10.8 shows that the most frequently occurring age range of viewers is 20 - 29. The information might be used by the cinema chain to help plan a marketing strategy. It is possible to show the information in Table 10.7 by plotting a curve called a frequency polygon. It is drawn using the histogram and involves joining all the mid-points at the top of the 'bars' with straight lines. The frequency polygon for the data in Table 10.7 is shown in Figure 10.8. Arguably, the visual pattern of the data is shown more clearly by the frequency polygon.

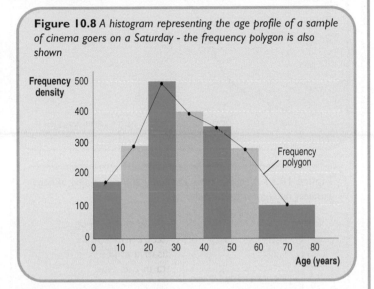

**Figure 10.8** *A histogram representing the age profile of a sample of cinema goers on a Saturday - the frequency polygon is also shown*

## Tables

Tables are used to present many forms of data. They may be used:

- if data are qualitative rather than quantitative;
- where a wide range of variables needs to be expressed at the same time;
- where the numbers themselves are at the centre of attention;
- when it is necessary to perform calculations on the basis of the information.

Some would argue that the use of tables should be avoided if possible. However, a poorly or inaccurately drawn graph would be less effective than a neatly presented table. Table 10.8 provides a list of the world's most powerful computers. It shows clearly where the world's largest computers are located

in order of size. It also shows the name of the company that manufactures the computer, the power of each computer and the country of location. This is a good example of a table being used to show a variety of qualitative and quantitative data (☞ unit 19).

## Line graphs

LINE GRAPHS are probably the most common type of graph used by a business. A line graph shows the relationship between two variables. The values of one variable are shown on the vertical axis and the values of the other variable are placed on the horizontal axis. The two variables must be related in some way. The values of the variables can be joined by straight lines or a smooth curve. If **time** is one of the variables being analysed it should always be plotted on the horizontal axis. Output is usually plotted on the horizontal axis. The main advantage of this type of graph is the way in which a reader can get an immediate picture of the relationship between the two variables. Also, it is possible to take measurements from a line graph when analysing data. It is much more difficult to do this when reading figures from a table. Quite often more than one line is shown on a line graph so that comparisons can be made. **Economic data** is often presented on a line graph. A line graph showing interest rates over the recent period may influence a business's decision to invest, for example.

## Cumulative frequency curves

When collecting data and recording it in a table, it is possible to show CUMULATIVE FREQUENCY. This is the total frequency up to a particular item or class boundary. It is calculated by adding the number of entries in a class to the total in the next class - a 'running total'. Table 10.9 shows the weights of cereal packages coming off a production line in a particular time period.

The cumulative frequencies in the table can be plotted on a graph. The graph is called an **ogive** and is shown in Figure 10.10. It can be seen, for example, that 270 packages weigh below 201.5 grams.

**Table 10.8** *The World's top 10 most powerful computers*

| Position | Company | Location | Country | Year | Rmax (Gigaflops)* |
|----------|---------|----------|---------|------|-------------------|
| 1 | NEC | Earth Simulator Center | Japan | 2002 | 35860 |
| 2 | HP | Los Alamos National Laboratory | USA | 2002 | 7727 |
| 3 | HP | Los Alamos National Laboratory | USA | 2002 | 7727 |
| 4 | IBM | Lawrence Livermore National Laboratory | USA | 2000 | 7226 |
| 5 | Linux | Network Lawrence Livermore National Laboratory | USA | 2002 | 5694 |
| 6 | HP | Pittsburgh Supercomputing Center | USA | 2001 | 4463 |
| 7 | HP | Commissariat a l'Energie Atomique | France | 2001 | 3980 |
| 8 | HPTi | Forecast Systems Laboratory | USA | 2002 | 3337 |
| 9 | IBM | HPCx | UK | 2002 | 3241 |
| 10 | IBM | National Center for Atmospheric Research | USA | 2002 | 3164 |

\* Floating point operations per second

Source: adapted from Top 500 Supercomputers website.

**Table 10.9** Cumulative frequency of package weights

| Weights falling within these ranges (grams) | Frequency | Cumulative frequency |
|---|---|---|
| 198-199 | 30 | 30 |
| 199-200 | 50 | 80 (30 + 50) |
| 200-201 | 150 | 230 (30 + 50 + 150) |
| 201-202 | 70 | 300 (30 + 50 + 150 + 70) |
| 202-203 | 40 | 340 (30 + 50 + 150 + 70 + 40) |
| 203-204 | 5 | 345 (30 + 50 + 150 + 70 + 40 + 5) |

Kingfisher, which owns B&Q, Brico Depot, Castorama and Screwfix, operates around 550 stores in seven countries across Europe and Asia. In September 2003 the group suggested that hot weather across Europe would impact on sales for the year. However, Kingfisher reported that its total sales in the 13 weeks up to November 1 grew 8.2 per cent, including a rise of 2.7 per cent on a like-for-like basis. Following the news release in November the share price rallied 2 per cent.

**Figure 10.9** Kingfisher share price and FTSE All Share index for 2003

Source: adapted from Thomson Datastream.

(a) What information does Figure 10.9 show?
(b) What are the advantages of presenting data in this way?

## A Lorenz curve

A LORENZ CURVE is a special type of line graph. It is a cumulative frequency curve which can be used to show the difference between actual distribution and an equal distribution. Figure 10.11 is a Lorenz curve which illustrates the way in which business is distributed between different hotels in a town. What does the curve show? If business was shared equally between all hotels then the line would be a straight 45° line. So, for example, 30 per cent of the town's hotels would get 30 per cent of all business, measured here as

**Figure 10.10** A cumulative frequency distribution (ogive) showing the weights of 345 cereal packages

**Figure 10.11** A Lorenz curve illustrating the distribution of hotel business amongst a town's hotels

the number of rooms occupied. The Lorenz curve shows the actual distribution of business amongst the town's hotels. For example, 50 per cent of the town's hotels have only 10 per cent of the total hotel business. This obviously indicates a very unequal distribution of business amongst the town's hotels. The further the Lorenz curve is drawn away from the 45° line the more unequal the actual distribution will be. A business might use this to analyse market share. The Lorenz curve is often used to show the distribution of wealth in a particular country.

## Bias in presentation

Just as bias can affect the collection of data it can also affect its presentation. When presenting profit figures to shareholders or sales figures to customers, managers will want to show the business in the best light. There is a danger that figures may be distorted in the way they are presented, in order to make performance look better than it was.

There are two main ways in which bias can occur.

- The method of presentation could exaggerate the actual rate of change shown by the data. This can be done by cutting and expanding one axis of a graph. Darrel Huff, an American statistician, called this a 'Gee-Whiz' graph. Figure 10.12 shows the same data presented in two different ways. In graph (b) the profit axis has been cut and extended. This gives a far better impression of the growth in profit than in graph (a). Similar bias can be introduced into bar charts, pie charts and pictographs.

- A business could leave out figures that do not fit into the 'picture' it wants to portray. For example, in a presentation to customers a firm may show its sales figures have been rising over the past five years, but omit to show that the total market has been increasing at a faster rate. This, in fact, means that the market share of the business has been falling.

**Figure 10.12** *The same profit figures for a business presented to show two different pictures*

## Spreadsheets

Some types of numerical data can be presented effectively using a SPREADSHEET. A spreadsheet allows the user to enter, store and present data in a grid on a computer screen. Just as a word processor is able to manipulate text, spreadsheets can do the same with numerical data. Table 10.10 shows that the grid is made up of a number of 'cells' or blank boxes. These cells are arranged in rows (information across the spreadsheet) and columns (information down the spreadsheet). Each blank cell is able to carry information which will fall into one of three categories.

- Numerical data - these are the numbers entered by the user which will be manipulated by the program.
- Text - this refers to the words used in the spreadsheet, often headings.
- Formulae - these are the instructions given by the user which tell the computer to manipulate the numerical data, for example, add a column of entries to give a total.

An example of a spreadsheet is illustrated in Table 10.10. It contains data relating to a firm's production costs. Each column (from B to G) shows the costs of various items each month. Each row shows particular costs over the entire period. For example, row 2 shows the labour costs each

**Figure 10.13** *Rolls Royce share price*

Source: adapted from *The Financial Times*.

Rolls Royce produces jet engines for the aircraft industry. In 2003 the company's profits halved and the share price fell below the level of privatisation in 1987.

(a) How might you redraw the graph in Figure 10.13 so that the fall in the share price looks much less obvious?

(b) Why might rolls Royce wish to present the data in the way described in (a)?

## Question 4

**Table 10.10** *An example of a spreadsheet which contains cost data*

| | A | B | C | D | E | F | G |
|---|---|---|---|---|---|---|---|
| 1 | | Jan | Feb | March | April | May | June |
| 2 | Labour | 200 | 210 | 230 | 210 | 200 | 230 |
| 3 | Materials | 100 | 100 | 110 | 130 | 100 | 110 |
| 4 | Fuel | 35 | 35 | 35 | 30 | 30 | 20 |
| 5 | Overheads | 25 | 25 | 30 | 30 | 35 | 35 |
| 6 | Total costs | 360 | 370 | 405 | 400 | 365 | 395 |

*The formulae for total costs in row 6 is shown below.*

| 6 | Total costs | =SUM(B2..B5) | =SUM(C2..C5) | =SUM(D2..D5) | =SUM(E2..E5) | =SUM(F2..F5) | =SUM(G2..G5) |
|---|---|---|---|---|---|---|---|

month. Row 6 shows the total cost each month. The total cost is automatically calculated by the program.

In this case the formula for cell B6 would be B2 + B3 + B4 + B5 or = SUM (B2..B5). If the business changed any of the entries, the totals in row 6 would change automatically.

Some spreadsheets are much larger than the screen itself with up to 250 columns and 8,000 rows. The screen can only show part of the spreadsheet. Scrolling is used to solve this problem. This enables the user to scan over the entire spreadsheet until the section they need is shown on the screen. The advantages of spreadsheets are listed below.

- Numerical data is recorded and shown in a clear and ordered way.
- Editing allows figures, text and formulae to be changed easily to correct mistakes or make changes in the data.
- It is easy to copy an entry or series of entries from one part of the spreadsheet to another. This is particularly useful when one figure has to be entered at the same point in every

column.

- The user can add, subtract, multiply and divide the figures entered on the spreadsheet.
- A spreadsheet can calculate the effect of entry changes easily. This is sometimes referred to as the 'what if' facility, eg what would happen to cell X (total costs) if the entry in cell A (labour costs) increased by 10 per cent? The answer can be found very quickly.
- Some spreadsheet programs allow graphs and diagrams to be drawn from figures in the spreadsheet.

One problem with spreadsheets is in printing the results. Some simple spreadsheets will tend to print everything being used. This can be time consuming and wasteful. Other programs allow the user to print specific rows, columns or cells. Some spreadsheets permit the sheet to be printed sideways to allow for a wide sheet to be printed. A further complication is what should be printed out for some of the cells, eg for a particular cell, should it be the result of a formula or the formula itself?

## Databases

A DATABASE is really an electronic filing system. It allows a great deal of data to be stored. Every business which uses computers will compile and use databases. The information is set up so that it can be updated and recalled when needed. Table 10.11 shows part of a database of a finance company which gives details about their clients. The collection of common data is called a file. A file consists of a set of related records. In the database pictured in Table 10.11 all the information on Jane Brown, for example, is a record. The information on each record is listed under headings known as fields, eg name, address, age, occupation, income each year. A good database will have the the following facilities.

- 'User-definable' record format, allowing the user to enter any chosen field on the record.
- File searching facility for finding specified information from a file, eg identifying all clients with an income over £24,000 in the above file. It is usually possible to search on more than one criterion, eg all females with an income over £24,000.
- File sorting facility for rearranging data in another order, eg arranging the file in Table 10.11 in ascending order of income.
- Calculations on fields within records for inclusion in reports.

In the world of business and commerce there is actually a market for information held on databases. It is possible to buy banks of information from market researchers who have compiled databases over the years. Names and addresses of potential customers would be information well worth purchasing if it were legally available. The storage of personal data on computer is subject to the **Data Protection Act** (☞ unit 69). Any company or institution wishing to store personal data on a computer system must register with the Data Protection Office. Individuals have a right under the Act to request details of information held on them.

---

**Table 10.11** *An extract from a simple database*

| Surname | First name | Address | Town | Age | Occupation | Income p.a. |
|---------|-----------|---------|------|-----|-----------|-------------|
| Adams | John | 14 Stanley St | Bristol | 39 | Bricklayer | £15,000 |
| Appaswamy | Krishen | 2 Virginia St | Cardiff | 23 | Welder | £25,000 |
| Atkins | Robert | 25 Liverpool Rd | Cardiff | 42 | Teacher | £21,000 |
| Biddle | Ron | 34 Bedford Rd | Bath | 58 | Civil servant | £40,000 |
| Brown | Jane | 111 Bold St | Newport | 25 | Solicitor | £22,000 |

---

# key terms

**Bar chart** - a chart where numerical information is represented by blocks or bars.

**Component bar chart** - a chart where each bar is divided into a number of sections to illustrate the components of a total.

**Cumulative frequency** - the total frequency up to a particular item or class boundary.

**Data** - a collection of information.

**Database** - an organised collection of data stored electronically with instant access, searching and sorting facilities.

**Histogram** - a chart which measures continuous data on the horizontal axis and class frequencies on the vertical axis.

**Line graph** - a line which shows the relationship between two variables.

**Lorenz curve** - a type of cumulative frequency curve which shows the disparity between equal distribution and actual distribution.

**Pictograph or pictogram** - a chart where numerical data is represented by pictorial symbols.

**Pie chart** - a chart which consists of a circle where the data components are represented by the segments.

**Spreadsheet** - a method of storing data in cells in such a way that a change in one of the entries will automatically change any appropriate totals.

Knowledge...nowledge...Knowledge...Knowledge...Knowledge...Knowledge...Kno

1. Why is it important for a business to present data clearly, accurately and attractively?
2. What are the main advantages of using bar charts?
3. What is the main disadvantage of using pictographs?
4. State 3 types of data that component bar charts can be used to illustrate.
5. What is the difference between a histogram and a bar chart?
6. Why are pie charts a popular method of data presentation?

7. What is the main disadvantage of using tables to present data?
8. State 2 ways in which bias may be shown when presenting data.
9. State the 3 types of information which a cell in a spreadsheet can carry.
10. What are the main advantages of spreadsheets?
11. What are the advantages of databases for firms?

# Case study Euro Disney

Euro Disney operates two theme parks with over forty attractions, seven hotels, two conference centres, a Disney Village and a golf course. The complex is located near Paris in France and has a number of attractions.

● Adventureland aims to create an atmosphere able to fulfil the dreams of archaeologists or explorers. It contains scenes of impenetrable African jungles to an exotic South Seas island, to the magical trails and treasures of the Orient. Adventureland brings to life the universe of ancient legends, action movies and Disney adventure films.

● Main Street USA is the reconstruction of a typical small town in America in the last century, such as Missouri where Walt Disney grew up. In this historic setting guests can enjoy a meal and shop in an atmosphere reminiscent of America's golden age between 1890 and 1910.

● Discoveryland is where visitors can catch a glimpse of tomorrow as imagined by European visionaries of the past. This starts with a trip through time in the company of Jules Verne, Leonardo de Vinci and HG Wells.

● Spectacular rides include Space Mountain, Peter Pan's flight, Indiana Jones and the Temple of Peril, Star Tours and Big Thunder.

Euro Disney has become a very popular tourist attraction since it was opened. Indeed, according to the company, 89 per cent of guests intend to recommend the destination.

Source: all information adapted from Euro Disney, *Financial Report*, 2002.

**1**

## Financial overview 2002

In 2002 the company opened a second theme park, Walt Disney's Studios Park. Since this attraction opened record attendances, occupancies and per guest selling were achieved, despite the weak tourism environment. Annual revenue from all sections of the business rose by 7 per cent. However, a loss of 33.1 million euros was made. This was due to the exceptional pre-opening expenditure associated with Walt Disney's Studio Park, such as staff training and advertising.

**2**

| Theme Parks attendance (millions of guests) | Theme Parks average spending per guest (in euros excluding VAT) | Hotel occupancy (in %) | Average spending per room (in euros, including VAT) |
|---|---|---|---|
| 12  12.2  13.1 | 42.2  43.1  44.4 | 82.9  86.0  88.2 | 183  186.3  193.3 |
| 00  01  02 | 00  01  02 | 00  01  02 | 00  01  02 |

**3**

Breakdown of visitors by transportation

| | |
|---|---|
| 56.1% | Car |
| 14.6% | Coach |
| 12.6% | Plane |
| 12.5% | Train |
| 4.2% | Railway |

**4**

Breakdown of revenues by activities in 2002

- **49%** Theme Parks
- **38%** Hotels and Disney Village
- **10%** Other revenues
- **3%** Real Estate

**5**

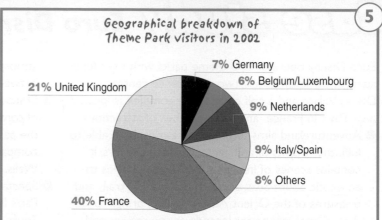

Geographical breakdown of Theme Park visitors in 2002

- **7%** Germany
- **6%** Belgium/Luxembourg
- **9%** Netherlands
- **9%** Italy/Spain
- **8%** Others
- **40%** France
- **21%** United Kingdom

**6**

**Revenues of the Group were generated from the following sources:**

| (Euros in millions) | Year ended September 30 2002 | Year ended September 30 2001 | Variation Amount | Variation Percent |
|---|---|---|---|---|
| Theme Parks | 526.0 | 476.4 | 49.6 | 10.4% |
| Hotels and Disney Village | 411.7 | 386.5 | 25.2 | 6.5% |
| Other | 111.0 | 105.1 | 5.9 | 5.6% |
| *Resort segment* | *1 048.7* | *968.0* | *80.7* | *8.3%* |
| Real Estate Development Segment | 27.3 | 37.2 | (9.9) | (26.6)% |
| **Total revenues** | **1 076.0** | **1 005.2** | **70.8** | **7.0%** |

**7**

**Evolution of the share price**
(Base 100 as of October 2001)

— Euro Disney
— SBF 120*

* Index of top 120 French shares

(a) Describe the geographical breakdown of theme park visitors. **(4 marks)**

(b) Present the information contained in Box 3 using an alternative method. Explain why the method you have selected may be more effective. **(8 marks)**

(c) The information in Box 4 and Box 6 is similar. Explain which you think is more informative. **(8 marks)**

(d) (i) Explain what the data in Box 7 shows.

   (ii) How might the graph in Box 7 be presented to show the information in a better light? **(8 marks)**

(e) Evaluate the performance of Euro Disney in 2002. **(12 marks)**

## Why do businesses make decisions?

Businesses are DECISION MAKING units. Making the 'right' decisions help a business to achieve its aims and objectives (☞ unit 4). Some of the decisions faced by a business might include:

- how much output to produce of different products in a week or a month;
- who should be promoted from the shop floor to a supervisory level;
- whether the price of a product should be raised;
- how the construction of a new warehouse should be financed;
- what should be the design a of a new company logo;
- which supplier should be used to provide components;
- whether a product should be withdrawn from the market; and many others.

Businesses are forced to make decisions because choices nearly always exist. A business often has to decide which course of action to take from many different possible alternatives. For example, a company that needs to hire a van for a week might have to choose between 10-15 local companies, all of which are able to supply the van to the required specifications. The person responsible for vehicle hire in the company will need to make this decision. A more important decision may have to be made by a business that is rationalising production. The directors and management may need to choose which factory to close from all of those owned by the business.

Decision making is also necessary to solve problems in a business. For example, if the workforce goes on strike the management may have to decide on an appropriate course of action. A business may also have to take decisions to solve problems such as lengthy queues which develop when consumers are buying goods or possible delays which may take place in the construction of a new factory.

All decisions involve some risk. Decisions where the outcome is unpredictable, where many factors can affect success or which affect a large part of a firm's operations for a long period are most risky. A business may be able to minimise the risk by collecting accurate and comprehensive data and by using decision making models. These are dealt with later in this unit.

## Types of decision

It is possible to classify the decisions made by businesses in different ways.

**Programmed decisions** This idea was put forward by H.A.Simon in his 1965 book *The New Science of Management Decisions*. These are repetitive decisions. A set routine for making the decisions will have been established. For example, a supermarket branch manager may have to prepare a rota every week. This will involve decisions about which staff should be on duty during various shifts. The decisions are repetitive (carried out weekly). Also, a procedure is likely to have been developed which specifies exactly how decisions should be made. There may be formal rules which control decisions, such as the minimum number of staff stacking shelves at any one time. The rules will have been developed and improved over time. The decisions may even be carried out on a computer. For these reasons the decisions have been programmed.

**Non-programmed decisions** Simon argued that these are novel or unstructured decisions. For example, a business may be forced to move its premises because its current location is subject to a compulsory purchase order by a local authority. This is an unusual problem and it is unlikely that a decision making procedure will have been developed to resolve the problem. A decision like this will also have a long lasting effect on the organisation.

In practice decisions will not fall neatly into the two categories above. Many decisions will be partly programmed and partly non-programmed. For example, managers may develop a decision making structure to apply to unforeseen events. Decisions in a business are also likely to be either strategic, tactical or operational.

**Strategic decisions** STRATEGIC DECISIONS concern the general direction and overall policy of a business. They are far reaching and can influence the performance of the organisation. They will also be **long term** decisions, which means that they will affect the business for a period of more than one year. Strategic decisions tend to have a high risk because the outcome of the decision is likely to be unknown.

Examples of strategic decisions might include:

- the planned sale by Northern Rock of its credit card business to the Cooperative Bank in 2003;
- the proposed £3 billion takeover of Safeway by Morrisons in 2003.

These decisions are all likely to have long term effects on the businesses concerned. They often involve moving into new areas which will require new resources, new procedures and retraining. Whether or not the decisions were the 'right' ones may not be known for several years because it will take time to evaluate their effects on the businesses involved.

**Tactical decisions** TACTICAL DECISIONS tend to be medium term decisions which are less far reaching than strategic decisions. They are tactical because they are calculated and because their outcome is more predictable. In a business, tactical decisions may be used to implement strategic decisions. For example, as a result of Morrison's strategic decision to take over Safeway, some tactical decisions might have been:

● if any staff will be made redundant or if any staff need to be recruited;
● where duplication occurs, if stores should be closed;
● what should happen to any stores that are closed;
● what retraining of staff might be required and which staff would be retrained;
● what methods of promotion should be used for the new business.

Operational decisions OPERATIONAL DECISIONS are lower level decisions, sometimes called administrative decisions. They will be short term and carry little risk. Such decisions can normally be taken fairly quickly. They require much less thought and evaluation than strategic and tactical

decisions. Every day a business makes a large number of operational decisions.

Examples might include:
● how many checkouts to have open in a retail outlet at a particular time of day;
● how much time should allocated to a task in a factory;
● how to stagger breaks for sales staff in a department store so that a minimum number are always on the shop floor;
● when to order new invoices for an office and what quantity to order.

## Who makes decisions?

Decisions are made by all staff in a business. However, responsibility for the decision will vary according to the employee's position in the hierarchical structure. A senior manager can delegate decision making powers to a junior manager, but will retain ultimate responsibility for decision

Sony, the consumer electronics and entertainment group, has recently completed a four year restructuring programme. In light of the company's performance during that time critics suggest that it has lost its way. Sony responded to this criticism with a new restructuring plan and a preview of two products it hopes will convince sceptics it has a viable strategy for growth. Sony plans to spend a further ¥300 billion (£1.4 billion) mainly to restructure its electronic business in the next three years. It will allocate resources to strategic areas such as semi-conductors, while non-core assets and non-profitable activities will be sold off.

In its critical product strategy, Sony unveiled two prototypes it hopes will convince critics that its plan to integrate audio-video (AV) products and games can be effected and become profitable. One is the PSX, which incorporates the functions of a games machine, TV tuner, hard-disk and DVD recorder and will be released in Japan first later this year. A portable personal digital assistant, in the Clie series, will also be launched this year as a model for the integration of AV and mobile communications. Figures 11.1 and 11.2 and Table 11.1 show some financial information for Sony.

Source: adapted from *The Financial Times*, 29.5.2003.

**Table 11.1** *Sales by business, 2003*

| Year to Mar 31 | ¥bn | Year-on-year change(%) |
|---|---|---|
| **Electronics** | | |
| Information & communications | 959 | -17.9 |
| TV | 846 | 0.4 |
| Video | 823 | 2.1 |
| Audio | 683 | -8.7 |
| Components | 537 | 2.2 |
| Semiconductors | 205 | 12.3 |
| Total | 4,543 | -4.8 |
| | | |
| **Other businesses** | | |
| Games | 936 | -5.1 |
| Pictures | 803 | 26.3 |
| Music | 559 | -5.0 |
| Financial services | 513 | 6.1 |
| | | |
| Total sales | 7,474 | -1.4 |

Source: adapted from Thomson Datastream, company information.

**Figure 11.1** *Sony share price*

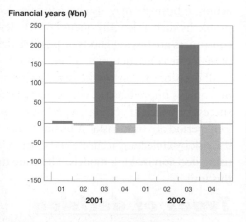

**Figure 11.2** *Operating profit/loss*

(a) Describe the strategic decisions made by Sony and explain why you think they are strategic.
(b) What evidence is there to support the critics' view that Sony may have lost its way?

**Question 1**

making. Also, the size of the company will influence who makes decisions. For example, a sole trader with no employees will make all the decisions. As businesses grow and more staff are employed, decision making is likely to be delegated.

**Strategic decisions** These are likely to be made by the owners of the business. Such decisions are so important and far reaching that only the owners can be responsible for their outcome. However, in some public limited companies these decisions will be made by the board of directors. Directors are appointed to run plcs in the interests of the owners, the shareholders, who can number thousands. Some important strategic decisions may require the shareholder's consent. For example, shareholders at Hanson, the conglomerate business, were consulted before the group was demerged into four smaller companies in 1996.

**Tactical decisions** Business managers are likely to make tactical decisions. Such decisions are often required to implement the strategic decisions made by the owners or the senior management team. Important tactical decisions, such as the promotion campaign for a new product, tend to be made by those near the top of the business hierarchy. Less important tactical decisions will often be made by middle or junior managers.

**Operational decisions** Nearly all employees will be involved in operational decisions. Lower level decisions, such as what task should office staff at an NHS trust hospital perform, are constantly taken by all staff in the business. Sometimes managers may be consulted by their subordinates if they need guidance or approval for a decision.

It is argued that delegating decisions to those further down the hierarchy can help motivation. This empowerment (☞ unit 61) of employees can also help to solve problems quickly without the need to consult managers. In the last decade a number of UK business have handed decision making to factory, team or group workers, giving them the authority to identify and solve problems before or as they occur. This has led to improvements in both efficiency and quality (☞ unit 84). The removal of layers of management has also improved decision making in some cases by reducing the number of levels in the chain of command, although this can lead to problems if not supported by retraining and changes in organisational culture (☞ unit 15).

## *The decision making process*

A business makes decisions in order to achieve objectives (☞ unit 4). For example, it might decide to launch a new product in order to diversify. Decisions are made at all levels in a business and it is useful to have a flexible and logical process which can be followed by all involved. Figure 11.3 shows the stages in the decision making process.

**Identifying objectives** The first stage in the process is to identify the objective a business wants to achieve. The objective might be a corporate objective, such as growth or survival in a poor trading period. These decisions are likely to be complex and might be taken by the board of directors. For lower level objectives, such as filling a part time vacancy, decisions may be taken by junior managers. A business's objectives might be different at different stages in its growth. Business activities controlled by local government may have different objectives from public limited companies. The business also needs to develop criteria to measure whether it has achieved its objectives. Quite often the objective is to solve a problem. This might be planning for an uncertain future or dealing with a low level of profitability.

**Collecting information and ideas** People need information and ideas to make decisions. The amount and nature of the information needed will depend on the decision. For example, the decision whether or not to launch a new product might require some information about possible sales levels and consumer reactions, costs of production and reactions of competitors. It could take several months to collect all this

---

Conduit, the Dublin-based call centre business, is to cut 250 jobs at its new 11 88 88 directory inquiries service after only twelve days' operation. The new 118 directory service was launched in August 2003 after BT's 192 service was scrapped by phone regulator, Oftel. The measure was designed to end BT's monopoly over the directory enquiries market, worth over £280 million.

Conduit said the losses would be confined to temporary jobs only. The jobs were created to deal with the expected rush of calls in the immediate period after the withdrawal of the 192 service. Some of the jobs will be cut from Conduit's call centre in Cardiff, 110 from its Welwyn Garden City centre in Hertfordshire and 30 from its Gloucester call centre. Its Swansea centre will escape cuts.

Conduit, which also provides directory services in Ireland, Switzerland and Austria, said that the extra staff had been taken on in the knowledge that they may not be needed for very long. 'It was not possible to predict the level of calls made to various 118 services once 192 was switched off,' a spokesperson said. 'Conduit put in place the capacity to handle more calls than it expected to receive through a mixture of its own staff and short-term agency staff. It was a strategic decision to have over capacity which could be quickly scaled back, rather than face the criticism other 118 services have had, struggling with increased demand'.

Source: adapted from *The Guardian*, 5.9.2003.

(a) Using examples from the case distinguish between strategic and tactical decisions.
(b) Who might have made the decisions described in (a)? Explain your answer.

**Question2**

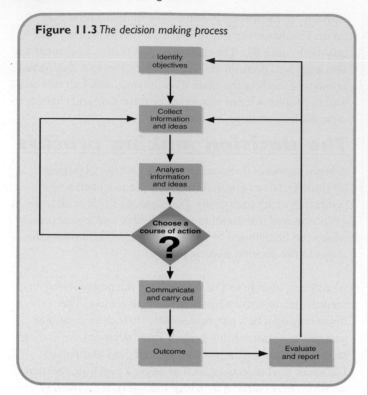

**Figure 11.3** *The decision making process*

information. Other decisions could perhaps be made from information which the business already has. A decision whether or not to dismiss an employee might be made on the basis of information from the personnel department.

Where does the business get its ideas? It might set up a working party to collect information and ideas from within the firm. The working party would then produce a report or make a presentation to the decision makers. Alternatively, individuals or departments might submit ideas and information. Another way of obtaining information and ideas is to hold discussions amongst staff in the firm.

Analysing information and ideas The next stage in the process is to analyse information to look for alternative courses of action. Possible courses of action may be based on previous ideas or completely new ideas. The aim is to identify which course of action will best achieve the business's objective or solve the problem. It may be possible to test the alternatives before the one that is chosen is carried out.

Making a decision Next the decision has to be made. This is the most important stage in the process. Decision makers have to commit themselves to one course of action. It is difficult to change the decision, so getting it right is vital. For example, once production begins following the decision to launch a new product, it is difficult for the firm to change its mind. If the product does not sell, this can lead to a loss of money. Some decisions can be reversed. For example, if the owner of a shop decides to close on Tuesday afternoons, but then finds the loss of sales is intolerable, the owner can easily reopen again.

Sometimes the decision makers feel that they cannot reach a

decision. They may have to obtain more information and complete the previous two stages in the process again.

Communication Once a decision has been made, personnel are informed and the decision is carried out. Quite often the people making the decisions are not those that carry them out. Instructions may be passed by the decision makers to someone else, probably a manager, explaining what action should be taken. For example, if the directors decide to begin selling their products in a new country, instructions must be sent to the marketing manager. In smaller firms decision makers are more likely to carry out their own decisions.

Outcome Once a decision has been carried out it will take time before the results are known. Sometimes this can be quite a long time. For example, the companies which decided to build the Channel Tunnel will not know for several decades whether or not it will be a commercial success.

Evaluate the results Finally, decision makers need to evaluate the outcome of their decisions. This is often presented as a report. It may be necessary to modify the course of action on the basis of the report. For example, it might be necessary to revise the objectives or collect some more information, as shown in Figure 11.3. There may be problems in following such an approach. Objectives may be difficult to identify or unrealistic. Information may be limited, incorrect or misleading. People making decisions in the process may have different views and this may lead to differences of opinion about what is the best course of action, for example.

## Decision making models

The use of MODELS or SIMULATIONS is widespread in business. Models are replicas or copies of problem areas in business. They are theories, laws or equations, stating things about a problem and helping in our understanding of it. There is a number of common features to models.

● They reflect the key characteristics or behaviour of an area of concern.
● They tend to be simplified versions of areas of concern.
● They simulate the actions and processes that operate in the problem area.
● They provide an aid to problem solving or decision making.
● Models often make use of formulae to express concepts. Some models can be carried out using computer software. This allows decisions to be made quickly and many variables affecting decisions to be included.

Management science and operations research are areas which often make use of decision making models. For example, linear programming (☞ unit 91) provides a model which allows decision makers to determine optimal solutions to a wide range of business problems. It has been used to make decisions such as:
● how to minimise waste in production;

**Figure II.4** *Interest rates, inflation rates and unemployment in the UK*
Source: adapted from Thomson Datastream.

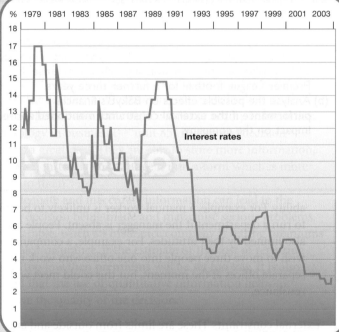

Wilson Hotels plc owns 18 country hotels in the UK. The company specialises in rural locations offering residents short breaks in peaceful surroundings with a strong emphasis on high quality cuisine. Wilson Hotels is profitable but wants to expand. It is considering raising £5 million to build 5 hotels in the Scottish Highlands. The company has already invested heavily in feasibility studies and seeking planning permission. It has got the go ahead to build 3 hotels and is waiting on permission for the other two.

Funding for the projects will have to be external. The company's reserves are modest because of its policy of paying shareholders relatively high dividends. It will also be necessary to recruit quite large numbers of staff. Each hotel will require up to 110 staff (a mixture of full-time and part-time).

The company is keen to go ahead with the investment programme but is worried about the size of the borrowing. A number of institutions have expressed an interest in providing funds and a decision must be made within the next month whether to go ahead with the investment or not. One or two people involved in the decision making process wonder whether the future economic conditions will suit such a large investment. Some economic data is shown in Figure 11.4.

(a) (i) Explain how the information in Figure 11.4 might help make the decision faced by Wilson Hotels.
  (ii) What other information might be useful to the decision makers?
(b) Assuming that Wilson Hotels decides to go ahead with the investment project, how might it evaluate the outcome of the decision?

## Question 3

---

● how to allocate resources between two competing tasks;
● how to find the least cost mix of ingredients for a product.
Another example in the area of marketing is the use of Ansoff's Matrix (☞ unit 32). This model is used to help consider the relationship between the strategic direction of the business and its marketing strategy.

A simulation involves trying to mimic what might happen in reality. It allows a business to test ideas and make decisions without bearing the consequences of 'real action' if things go wrong. Imagine a business has a problem. A simulation can be carried out several times, quickly and cheaply, in order to test alternative decisions. There is no risk and resources are not used up. Simulations are often used to deal with problems such as queues in business (☞ unit 92).

## *Constraints on decision making*

Businesses cannot make decisions with complete freedom. In many situations there are factors which hinder, limit or restrict particular courses of action. These CONSTRAINTS may make the decision easier because they eliminate some

# 12 Decision Trees

## Making decisions

Every day, businesses make decisions (☞ unit 11). Most, if not all, involve some risk. This could be because the business has limited information on which to base the decision. Furthermore, the outcome of the decision may be uncertain. Launching a new product in a market abroad can be risky because a firm may not have experience of selling in that market. It may also be unsure about how consumers will react.

When faced with a number of different decisions a business will want to choose the course of action which gives the most return. What if a printing company had to decide whether to invest £750,000 in a new printing press now or wait a few years? If it bought now and a more efficient machine became available next year then it might have been more profitable to wait. Alternatively, if it waits it may find the old machine has problems and costs increase.

When the outcome is uncertain, decision trees can be used to help a business reach a decision which could minimise risk and gain the greatest return.

## What are decision trees?

A DECISION TREE is a method of tracing the alternative outcomes of any decision. The likely results can then be compared so that the business can find the most profitable alternative. For example, a business may be faced with two alternatives - to launch a new product in Europe or in the USA. A decision tree may show that launching a new product in Europe would give £5 million profit, whereas launching in the USA would only give a profit of £1 million.

It is argued by some that decision making is more effective if a **quantitative approach** is taken. This is where information on which decisions are based, and the outcomes of decisions, are expressed as numbers. In a decision tree, numerical values are given to such information. The decision tree also provides a pictorial approach to decision making because a diagram is used which resembles the branches of a tree. The diagram maps out different courses of action, possible outcomes of decisions and points where decisions have to be made. Calculations based on the decision tree can be used to determine the 'best' likely outcome for the business and hence the most suitable decision.

## Features of decision trees

Decision trees have a number of features. These can be seen in Figure 12.1 which shows the decision tree for a business that has to decide whether to launch a new advertising campaign or retain an old one.

**Decision points** Points where decisions have to be made in a decision tree are represented by squares and are called decision points. The decision maker has to choose between certain

courses of action. In this example, the decision is whether to launch a new campaign or retain the old one.

**Outcomes** Points where there are different possible outcomes in a decision tree are represented by circles and are called **chance nodes**. At these chance nodes it can be shown that a particular course of action might result in a number of outcomes. In this example, at 'B' there is a chance of failure or success of the new campaign.

**Probability or chance** The **likelihood** of possible outcomes happening is represented by probabilities in decision trees. The chance of a particular outcome occurring is given a value. If the outcome is certain then the probability is 1. Alternatively, if there is no chance at all of a particular outcome occurring, the probability will be 0. In practice the value will lie between 0 and 1. In Figure 12.1, at 'B' the chance of success for the new campaign is 0.2 and the chance of failure is 0.8.

It is possible to estimate the probability of events occurring provided information about these events can be found. There are two sources of information which can be used to help estimate probabilities. One source is **backdata** (☞ unit 10). For example, if a business has opened 10 new stores in recent years, and 9 of them have been successful, it might be reasonable to assume that the chances of another new store being successful are $^9/_{10}$ or 0.9. Another source is research data. For example, a business might carry out marketing research to find out how customers would react to a new product design. 80 per cent of people surveyed may like the product and 20 per cent may dislike it.

**Expected values** This is the financial outcome of a decision. It is based on the predicted profit or loss of an outcome and the probability of that outcome occurring. The profit or loss of

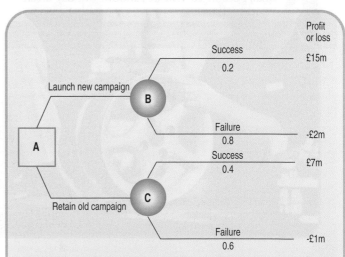

**Figure 12.1** *A simple decision tree based on a decision whether to retain an existing advertising campaign or begin a new one*

any decision is shown on the right hand side of Figure 12.1. For example, if the launch of a new campaign is a success, a £15 million profit is expected. If it fails a loss of £2 million is expected.

## Calculating expected values

What should the firm decide? It has to work out the expected values of each decision, taking into account the expected profit or loss and the probabilities. So, for example, the expected value of a new campaign is:

Success      Failure

Expected value =   0.2   x   £15m   +   0.8   x   (-£2m)
            (probability) (expected profit)(probability) (expected loss)

=   £3m   -   £1.6m

=   1.4m

The expected value of retaining the current campaign is:

Success      Failure

Expected value =   0.4   x   £7m   +   0.6   x   (-£1m)

=   £2.8m   -   £0.6m

=   2.2m

BGS Holdings owns a chain of 32 pubs and bars in the north of England. Due to intense competition, revenue has fallen in the last couple of years. As a means of boosting revenue it has been suggested that the chain, in line with many other competitors, should use 'happy hours' to attract more customers. Traditionally a 'happy hour' is a period of time (not always an hour) where drinks are sold at reduced prices. The problem though is choosing the right 'hour' when prices should be reduced. It is thought not to be a good idea to choose a period of time which is already popular. This is because sales of drinks would already be very high and to cut prices during this time would reduce margins significantly. In order to help make the decision an investigation was carried out in a sample of 4 pubs. The data gathered during the investigation is shown in Table 12.1.

**Table 12.1** Happy Hour data gathered by BGS Holdings

| Happy Hour period | Probability of success | Estimated effect on profit | Probability of failure | Estimated effect on profit | Expected value |
|---|---|---|---|---|---|
| 3-4pm | 0.5 | +£1,300 | ? | -£200 | ? |
| 4-5pm | 0.5 | +£1,700 | ? | -£400 | ? |
| 5-6pm | 0.7 | +£400 | ? | -£1,200 | ? |
| 6-7pm | 0.6 | +£1,000 | ? | -£800 | ? |
| 7-8pm | 0.6 | +£1,100 | ? | -£400 | ? |

(a) Complete Table 12.1.
(b) On financial grounds, when should the 'happy hour' be arranged?

**Question 1**

From these figures the firm should continue with the existing campaign because the expected value is higher.

## Numerous outcomes

It is possible to have more than two outcomes at a chance node. For example, at point 'B' in Figure 12.1 there might have been 3 outcomes:

- the probability of great success may be 0.2 with a profit of £15 million;
- the probability of average success may be 0.4 with a profit of £6 million;
- the probability of failure may be 0.4 with a loss of -£2 million.

The expected value is now:

= (0.2 x £15 m) + (0.4 x £6 m) + (0.4 x -£2 m)
= £3 m + £ 2.4 m - £0.8 m
= £4.6 m

## Decisions, outcomes and costs

In practice businesses face many alternative decisions and possible outcomes. Take a farmer who has inherited some land, but does not wish to use it with his existing farming business. There are three possible decisions that the farmer could make.

- Sell the land. The market is depressed and this will earn £0.6 million.
- Wait for one year and hope that the market price improves. A land agent has told the farmer that the chance of an upturn in the market is 0.3, while the probabilities of it staying the same or worsening are 0.5 and 0.2 respectively. The likely proceeds from a sale in each of the circumstances are £1 million, £0.6 million and £0.5 million.
- Seek planning permission to develop the land. The legal and administration fees would be £0.5 million and the probability of being refused permission would be 0.8, which means the likelihood of obtaining permission is 0.2. If refused, the farmer would be left with the same set of circumstances described in the second option.

If planning permission is granted the farmer has to make a decision (at node E). If the farmer decides to sell, the probability of getting a good price, ie £10 million, is estimated to be 0.4, while the probability of getting a low price, ie £6 million, is 0.6. The farmer could also develop the land himself at a cost of £5 million. The probability of selling the developed land at a good price, ie £25 million, is estimated to be 0.3 while the likelihood of getting a low price, ie £10 million, is 0.7.

The information about probability and earnings is shown in Figure 12.2. What decision should the farmer make? The sale of the land immediately will earn £0.6 million.

The expected value of the second option, waiting a year, is:

Expected value = 0.3 x £1m + 0.5 x £0.6m + 0.2 x £0.5m
= £0.3m + £0.3m + £0.1m
= £0.7m

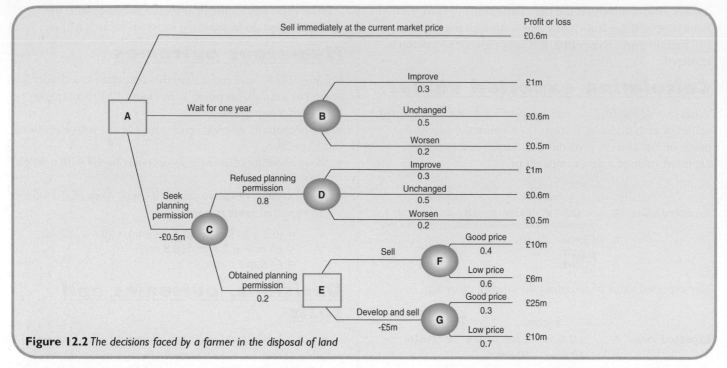

**Figure 12.2** *The decisions faced by a farmer in the disposal of land*

Since this earns more than the first option, it would be a better choice. We could show this in Figure 12.4 (over the page) by crossing the 'selling immediately' path with a //, indicating that the first option will not be taken up. The expected value of the second option (£0.7 million) is shown in the diagram at node B.

A **rollback technique** can then be used to work out the expected value of the third option, seeking planning permission. This means working from right to left, calculating the expected values at each node in the diagram. The expected value at node D is:

Expected value = 0.3 × £1m + 0.5 × £0.6m + 0.2 × £0.5m
= £0.7m

The expected value at node F is:

Expected value = 0.4 × £10m + 0.6 × £6m
= £4m + £3.6m
= £7.6m

The expected value at node G is:

Expected value = 0.3 × £25m + 0.7 × £10m
= £7.5m + £7m
= £14.5m

Colin Andrews is the owner of Slade farm near Spalding. He specialises in vegetable crops and allocates about 400 acres of land each year to the production of potatoes and swedes. He decides what crops to plant in October each year.

If Colin plants potatoes he estimates that the probability of a good crop is 0.3, which will generate £50,000 profit. The probability of an average crop is 0.3, which would result in £30,000 profit. The probability of a poor crop is 0.4, which would result in only £10,000 profit.

If swedes are planted, either a good crop or a bad crop will result. He estimates that the probability in each case is 0.5. A good crop will generate a profit of £40,000 and a poor crop only £10,000. Figure 12.3 is a decision tree which shows this information.

(a) What is happening at points B and C in the decision tree?
(b) Calculate the expected values of each course of action and decide, on financial grounds, which course Colin should take.

**Figure 12.3** *The alternative courses of action faced by Colin Andrews*

| | Profit |
|---|---|
| Plant potatoes — B — Good crop 0.3 | £50,000 |
| Average crop 0.3 | £30,000 |
| Poor crop 0.4 | £10,000 |
| Plant swedes — C — Good crop 0.5 | £40,000 |
| Poor crop 0.5 | £10,000 |

**Question 2**

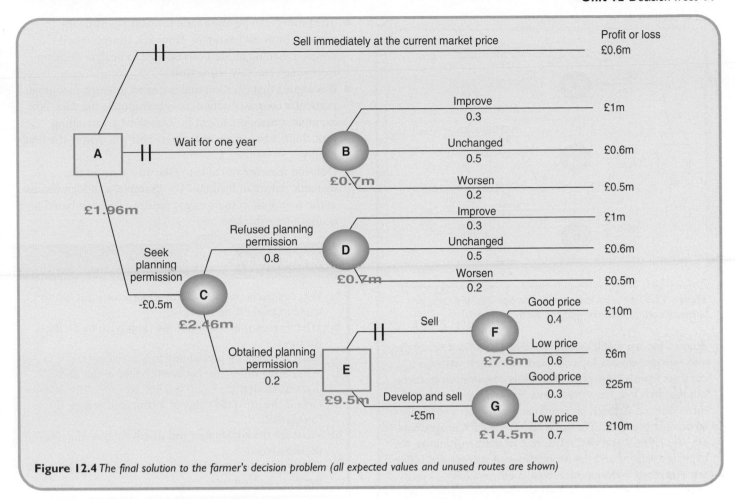

**Figure 12.4** *The final solution to the farmer's decision problem (all expected values and unused routes are shown)*

At node E, a decision node, the farmer would choose to develop the land before selling it. This would yield an expected return of £9.5 million (£14.5 million - £5 million) which is higher than £7.6 million, ie the expected return from selling the land undeveloped. Thus, in Figure 12.4 the path representing this option can be crossed. The expected value at node C is now:

Expected value = 0.2 x £9.5m + 0.8 x £0.7m
= £1.9m + £0.56m
= £2.46m

Finally, by subtracting the extra cost of seeking planning permission (£0.5 million), the expected value of the final option can be found. It is £1.96 million. Since this is the highest value, this would be the best option for the farmer. This means a // can be placed on the line to node B as £0.7 million is lower than £1.96 million. All of the expected values are shown in Figure 12.4.

Figure 12.4 shows profit or loss (taking into account costs) and then the **extra** costs of planning permission are subtracted in the calculation. However, a decision tree may show revenue on the right side instead of profit and **all** costs indicated on the diagram must be subtracted. Whichever is shown, the method of calculation is the same.

## Advantages and disadvantages of decision trees

Decision trees can be applied to much more complicated problems. They have some major advantages.
- Constructing the tree diagram may show possible courses of action not previously considered.
- They involve placing numerical values on decisions. This tends to improve results.
- They force management to take account of the risks involved in decisions and help to separate important from unimportant risks.

The technique also has some limitations.
- The information which the technique 'throws out' is not exact. Much of it is based on probabilities which are often estimated.
- Decisions are not always concerned with quantities and probabilities. They often involve people and are influenced by legal constraints or people's opinions, for example. These factors cannot always be shown by numerical values. Qualitatitive data may also be important.
- Time lags often occur in decision making. By the time a decision is finally made, some of the numerical information may be out of date.

**Figure 12.5** *The costs, revenues and probabilities of success and failure of each research programme for Trumed plc*

Trumed plc is a medical company that carries out research into new treatments for colds and influenza. It has won a contract from a large pharmaceuticals corporation to carry out research into new treatments. Trumed has identified three distinct research programmes to develop a vaccination to combat the strain. The code names for each programme are VAC1, VAC2 and VAC3. The cost of the programmes, the expected returns and the probabilities of success and failure are illustrated in the decision tree in Figure 12.5.

(a) Calculate the expected values of each research programme and advise Trumed which is the best option.

## Question 3

- The process can be quite time consuming, using up valuable business resources. However, computerised decision making models can be used to analyse decision trees which can save some time.
- It is argued that decision makers, in an attempt encourage a particular course of action, may manipulate the data. For example, a manager might be 'biased' when attaching probabilities to certain outcomes. This will distort the final results.
- Decision trees are not able to take into account the dynamic nature of business. For example, a sudden change in the economic climate might render a decision based on a decision tree obsolete.

1. Why are decision trees useful when a business has to make important decisions?
2. What is meant by a quantitative approach to decision making?
3. What is meant by probability in a decision tree?
4. What is the difference between chance nodes and decision nodes?
5. How is the expected value of a course of action calculated?
6. What are the advantages and disadvantages of using decision trees?
7. State 3 possible situations where a business might make use of a decision tree.

## key terms

**Decision trees** - a technique which shows all possible outcomes of a decision. The name comes from the similarity of the diagrams to the branches of trees.

# Case study The DVD Shop

The DVD Shop is a small chain store that sells a very wide range of DVDs. It claims to be able to supply any listed DVD within 24 hours. It owns 23 branches, mainly in the West Midlands, and is under pressure from shareholders to expand quickly. The company was floated on the stock exchange seven years ago and has pursued a strategy of organic growth. This has been a little slow, but at the same time dividend payments to shareholders have been stable. A decision has to be made to take the company through its next phase of development. Three

alternative strategies have been identified. The revenue from each option is expected to be generated over a three year period.

**Continue to grow organically** This has proved to be a reliable strategy in the past for The DVD Shop, opening about 3 new stores a year without having to raise large amounts of capital. If this strategy is continued the expected cost will be £20 million. If organic growth is successful an additional £80 million in revenue will be generated. However, if the strategy begins to fail only £20 million will be generated. The probability of success is estimated to be 0.9. Therefore the probability of failure will be 0.1.

**Buy another small chain of DVD shops** This is the most expensive strategy. Two chains have been identified – Sound&Vision in London with 12 branches and JustDVDs in Greater Manchester with 9 branches. Before any acquisition is made £4 million fees would have to be paid to consultants to check out the viability of an acquisition. Assuming that both options are acceptable Sound&Vision will cost £50 million to buy and JustDVDs £38 million.

If the purchase of Sound&Vision is successful £120 million in revenue is expected to be generated. If it fails £80 million will be generated. The chances of success are 0.6. If the purchase of JustDVDs is successful £100 million is expected to be earned. If it fails the revenue generated will fall to £70 million. The probability that the purchase of JustDVDs will be successful is estimated to be 0.7.

**Figure 12.6** *The costs, revenues and probabilities of success and failure of the expansion strategies of The DVD Shop*

**Set up a franchising operation** It is thought that a franchising operation might speed up growth. Another advantage is that the setting up costs are very minimal, only £1 million. If this option were successful revenue would rise by £80 million. Even if the project was only moderately successful £40 million would be generated. If the franchising operation failed only £20 million would be generated. The chances of success were estimated to be 0.5, moderate success at 0.3 and the chances of failure are 0.2.

**(a)** **If The DVD Shop decides to grow organically the probability of success is estimated to be 0.9. Explain what the** probability of failure would be in this case. **(4 marks)**

**(b)** **Calculate the expected values for each option and determine on financial grounds which option The DVD Shop should select. (14 marks)**

**(c)** **After the consultants had researched into the acquisition options it was found that Sound&Vision could be purchased for £45 million and that the expected revenue from a successful purchase would be £140 million. How might this affect your answer in (b)? (10 marks)**

**(d)** **Evaluate the disadvantages to The DVD Shop of using decision trees to make the decision about its strategy. (12 marks)**

## Why analyse data?

A business can make great use of the data which it has collected about such things as costs, sales, markets and profits. Presenting the data will allow a firm to find out important information, such as the proportion of total costs accounted for by employees' wages. However, when looking at more complex problems, the data may need to be analysed in more detail. This can involve:

● finding out the most likely outcome, such as the most likely purchaser of a new product;
● forecasting what may happen in the future, such as the need for extra employees;
● finding out variations, such as by how much output changes at different times of the week, day or year;
● finding out whether the quality of a product is being maintained.

Sometimes businesses can use data which has been analysed for them. Government departments produce information on factors which might influence businesses, such as the rate of inflation. Industry bodies may provide data. For example, ABTA gives information on the market for tourism.

There is a variety of techniques which can be used to analyse data. This unit looks at measures of central tendency and dispersion, and the next looks at forecasting and predicting from data. While these methods can help a business to make better decisions, they must also take into account the nature of the data they are using. A certain amount of data is unreliable. It may be out of date, collected in less than a thorough way, or incomplete. Analysing this data, and making decisions based on incorrect figures, may cause problems. A firm that decides to increase its stocks because data show they are running low each week may have large quantities of unwanted goods if the data proves to be incorrect.

## Central tendency

Much of the information that a business collects will be too detailed to be useful. It is necessary for this raw data to be organised into a form that decision makers can use more effectively. One method allows the business to discover the most **likely** or **common** outcome from the data. This involves calculating the CENTRAL TENDENCY from the data - usually known as the **average**.

Knowing the most likely outcome will be useful in a number of situations. A business may be interested in:

● the level of stock ordered most often;
● the production level a department achieves most often;
● the average sales each month;
● the average number of days lost through injury.

Table 13.1 shows the amount of stock ordered by a small business over a period of time. How can the business find the average quantity of stock ordered each week? There are three ways of doing this - finding the **mean**, **median** or **mode**.

**Table 13.1** *Amount of stock ordered by a business over a 40 week period*

| 6 | 8 | 10 | 12 | 8 | 10 | 8 | 10 | 14 | 10 |
|---|---|----|----|---|----|---|----|----|----|
| 10 | 8 | 10 | 12 | 10 | 12 | 12 | 14 | 12 | 12 |
| 8 | 14 | 10 | 12 | 12 | 12 | 10 | 10 | 12 | 12 |
| 6 | 10 | 14 | 12 | 8 | 12 | 8 | 12 | 10 | 8 |

**Arithmetic mean** The arithmetic MEAN is the figure that most think of as an average. Simply, it can be calculated by adding the value of all items and dividing by the number of items. The formula for calculating the arithmetic mean ($\bar{x}$) is:

$$\bar{x} = \frac{\text{sum of items}}{\text{number of items}}$$

The mean for the first four orders in Table 13.1 would be:

$$\bar{x} = \frac{6 + 8 + 10 + 12}{4} = \frac{36}{4} = 9$$

Working out the mean in this way for all figures is time consuming. Imagine a multinational adding up the stock needed by every department for a year!

One method used to save time and improve accuracy is to work out the frequency (f) from the figures. The frequency is the number of times an item occurs. The **frequency distribution** for the figures in Table 13.1 is shown in Table 13.2.

**Table 13.2** *Frequency distribution for stock ordered by a business over a 40 week period*

| Quantity of stock ordered (x) | Frequency (f) | Quantity (x) x frequency (f) |
|---|---|---|
| 6 | 2 | 12 |
| 8 | 8 | 64 |
| 10 | 12 | 120 |
| 12 | 14 | 168 |
| 14 | 4 | 56 |
| | $\sum f = 40$ | $\sum fx = 420$ |

where $\sum$ = the sum of (adding up all the values).

The mean can be calculated by:
● multiplying the quantity of stocks ordered (x) by the frequency (f);
● then adding up all these values and dividing by the total frequency.

The formula for calculating the mean of a frequency distribution is:

$$x = \frac{\Sigma fx}{\Sigma} = \frac{420}{40} = 10.5$$

Therefore, when the business orders stock, on average it orders 10.5 units. The company might use 10.5 as its average order quantity for stock control.

The advantage of using the mean as a measure of average value is that it takes into account all data. It is also a figure which is generally accepted as representing the average. However, it can be distorted by extreme values, resulting in a figure which is untypical and which may be misleading. For example, if the order in the ninth week had been 94 instead of 14 as in Table 13.1, the $\Sigma fx$ in Table 13.2 would have been 500 and the mean would have been $500 \div 40 = 12.5$.

**The median** The MEDIAN is the **middle** number in a set of data. When figures are placed in order, the median would be half way. For example, the median of the figures 3, 6, 8, 10 and 12 would be 8. The median for 1, 2, 3, 4, 5, 6 would be 3.5, the half way point. If a business had production figures of 200, 220, 240 and 260 units, the median would be half way between 220 and 240. In this case the median is found by an average of 220 and 240:

$$\frac{240 + 220}{2} = \frac{460}{2} = 230$$

Again, these are simple figures. Businesses, however, have large amounts of data and finding the median may require the use of a formula:

$$\frac{n + 1}{2} \text{ (for odd numbers) or } \frac{n}{2} \text{ (for even numbers)}$$

where n is the number of values or total frequency. In practice, with large numbers of figures, the latter formula is used.

In Table 13.1 there are 40 values. The median value would be $40 \div 2 =$ the 20th item if they were placed in order from smallest to largest, ie 6, 6, 8, 8, 8 etc. This is orders of 10 units. You can see from the cumulative frequency in Table 13.3. The 20th item in the cumulative frequency column must have been for an order of 10 units.

**Table 13.3** *Cumulative frequency of stock ordered by a business over a 40 week period*

| Quantity of stock ordered (x) | Frequency (f) | Cumulative frequency |
|---|---|---|
| 6 | 2 | 2 |
| 8 | 8 | 10 |
| 10 | 12 | 22 |
| 12 | 14 | 36 |
| 14 | 4 | 40 |

The median is a useful measure of the average because, unlike the mean, it is not distorted by extreme values. However, the problem with the median is that it ignores all data other than the middle value.

**The mode** This is the value that occurs most frequently. From the figures in Table 13.1, the MODE would be 12 units, as this is the order quantity which occurs most often (14 times). As with the median, the mode is unaffected by mean values and has the added attraction of being easy to calculate. The main problem with the mode value is that it does not take account of all values and might, therefore, prove misleading when taken as a measure of the average. There might also be several modes within a set of data, which will make the measure less useful.

Ashwear is a company that manufactures a variety of clothing. Table 13.4 shows information about the cost of its various products.

**Table 13.4**

| Cost of production | Number of products |
|---|---|
| £2 | 4 |
| £4 | 10 |
| £6 | 18 |
| £8 | 8 |
| | 40 |

(a) Calculate:
   (i) the arithmetic mean;
   (ii) the median;
   (iii) the modal;
   cost of production.
(b) The firm is considering launching 10 new products and has estimated that they will all have a production cost of £10. Calculate the likely effect that this will have on your answers to question (a).

## Question 1

## Grouped data

Data is often put into convenient groups, called **classes**. Table 13.5 shows the results of marketing research into the ages of people buying a particular firm's products. The quantity purchased by each age group (the frequency) is shown in the second column.

How does a business find the average? It is not possible to find the mode, but it is possible to find the **modal group**. This is the group with the highest frequency, in this case consumers between the ages of 30-39 (25).

To find the mean, take points at the centre of each age group, such as 24.5, which is the central point between the ages of 20 and 29. This is shown in column 3. Multiplying the frequency (f) by the central point (x) allows column 4 to be calculated. The **mean** can be found using the formula:

$$x = \frac{\sum fx}{\sum f} = \frac{3,600}{100} = 36$$

where $\sum$ is the sum of all values.

**Table 13.5** *Marketing research results showing the ages of people buying a firm's products*

| Ages of consumers | Quantity purchased (f) | Centre of interval (x) | fx |
|---|---|---|---|
| 0 - 9 | 3 | 4.5 | 13.5 |
| 10 - 19 | 10 | 14.5 | 145.0 |
| 20 - 29 | 21 | 24.5 | 514.5 |
| 30 - 39 | 25 | 34.5 | 862.5 |
| 40 - 49 | 22 | 44.5 | 979.0 |
| 50 - 59 | 14 | 54.5 | 763.0 |
| 60 - 69 | 5 | 64.5 | 322.5 |
| $\sum f = 100$ | | $\sum fx = 3,600.0$ | |

The figure of 36 is an estimate because it has been assumed that the average age of the 10 people in the age group 10-19 is 14.5. In fact, it could have been more or less. This is true of all age groups.

The **median** can also only be estimated. To find the median a business would need to calculate a cumulative frequency table. The information in Table 13.5 has been used to do this in Table 13.6. Part (a) shows the original table. Part (b) shows how a cumulative frequency table can be calculated. 3 goods were bought by consumers under the age of 9. 10 goods were bought by consumers aged 10-19, so 13 goods in all were bought by consumers under the age of 20. The last point is 100, showing the 100 goods bought altogether by all consumers. It is possible to draw this as a cumulative frequency polygon or **ogive** as in Figure 13.1.

What is the median age of consumers buying the products? If there are 100 goods, the median value can be found by drawing a line at 50 to the cumulative frequency curve. This gives a median of 35.

**Table 13.6** *Frequency and cumulative frequency tables*

| (a) | | (b) | |
|---|---|---|---|
| Ages of consumers | Quantity purchased | Ages of consumers | Cumulative frequency |
| 0 - 9 | 3 | 10 or less | 3 |
| 10 - 19 | 10 | 20 or less | 13 |
| 20 - 29 | 21 | 30 or less | 34 |
| 30 - 39 | 25 | 40 or less | 59 |
| 40 - 49 | 22 | 50 or less | 81 |
| 50 - 59 | 14 | 60 or less | 95 |
| 60 - 69 | 5 | 70 or less | 100 |
| = 100 | | | |

**Figure 13.1** *A cumulative frequency polygon showing the ages of consumers purchasing a firm's product.*

Table 13.7 shows the salary ranges of employees in a business.

**Table 13.7**

| Salary range (£) | Number of employees |
|---|---|
| 8,001 - 9,000 | 6 |
| 9,001 - 10,000 | 15 |
| 10,001 - 11,000 | 40 |
| 11,001 - 12,000 | 25 |
| 12,001 - 13,000 | 10 |
| 13,001 - 14,000 | 4 |
| | 100 |

(a) What is the modal salary group?
(b) Estimate the mean salary. Use approximate mid class values of 8,500, 9,500 etc.
(c) Estimate the median by drawing a cumulative frequency graph on graph paper.

**Question 2**

## Dispersion

The previous section explained how a business can calculate an average. The business may also be interested in how wide the data are spread - the DISPERSION. It may be that information is widely spread or there is a narrow dispersion. If the data are widely spread, the average is likely to be distant from the rest of the data. If, however, there is a narrow spread, the average will be close to the rest of the data and more typical.

**Table 13.8** *Monthly production figures*

| Month | Jan | Feb | Mar | Apr | May | Jun | Jul | Aug | Sep | Oct | Nov | Dec |
|-------|-----|-----|-----|-----|-----|-----|-----|-----|-----|-----|-----|-----|
| Sales | 40 | 46 | 52 | 54 | 54 | 52 | 58 | 56 | 54 | 56 | 42 | 36 |

Units

Table 13.8 shows the monthly output figures for a production plant. In order, the figures will be:

36   40   42   46   52   52   54   54   54   56   56   58

It is possible to calculate the spread in a number of ways.

**Range** The RANGE is the most simple method. It is the difference between the highest and lowest value. In Table 13.8 this would be 58 - 36 = 22. The main problem with the range is that it can be distorted by extreme values. Just one rogue figure can vastly increase the value of the range out of all proportion to its size.

**Interquartile range** The INTERQUARTILE RANGE considers the range within the central 50 per cent of a set of data. It therefore ignores the bottom and top 25 per cent (quarter). This gives it the advantage of being far less prone to distortion by extreme values than the range.

In order to calculate the interquartile range it is necessary to arrange data with the lowest item first and the highest item last. The first quartile, which is a quarter of the way along, must then be found, followed by the third quartile, which is three-quarters of the way along. The difference between the first and the third quartiles provides the interquartile range.

Using the data in Table 13.8 it is possible to calculate the first quartile using the formula:

$$\text{First quartile (Q1)} = \frac{n}{4}$$

where n equals the number of values. The first quartile shows the value below which 25 per cent of all figures fall. So:

$$\text{Q1} = \frac{12}{4} = 3$$

The third quartile can be calculated using the formula:

$$\text{Third quartile (Q3)} = \frac{3(n)}{4} = \frac{3 \times 12}{4} = \frac{36}{4} = 9$$

In the data the third item is 42 and the ninth is 54. So the interquartile range is 54 - 42=12. The interquartile range for these production figures is therefore narrower than the range. When dealing with large amounts of data **deciles** or **percentiles** may have to be used as they give more exact

figures. Deciles are the 10, 20 etc. per cent values. In the production figures, the 50th per cent of the values will be 50 per cent of 12 (6), or the sixth value of 52 units of production.

**Mean deviation** The range and the interquartile range only take into account the spread between two figures in a set of data. However, there are many figures and each will **deviate** from the mean. In business this could be for reasons such as:
- the results from market surveys varying between regions;
- sales varying on a monthly or weekly basis;
- the output from a machine varying in quality as parts begin to wear out;
- the quality of products received from different suppliers varying according to the specifications they have used.

In Table 13.8 the arithmetic mean of the production figure is:

$$\frac{600}{12} = \frac{\text{(total production over the period)}}{\text{(the number of months)}} = 50 \text{ units}$$

The deviation of each production total from the mean is shown in Table 13.9.

**Table 13.9**

| Months | Production (x) | Deviation (x-x̄) |
|--------|----------------|------------------|
| Jan | 40 | -10 |
| Feb | 46 | - 4 |
| Mar | 52 | +2 |
| Apr | 54 | +4 |
| May | 54 | +4 |
| Jun | 52 | +2 |
| Jul | 58 | +8 |
| Aug | 56 | +6 |
| Sep | 54 | +4 |
| Oct | 56 | +6 |
| Nov | 42 | - 8 |
| Dec | 36 | -14 |
| | $\Sigma$ (x) = 600 | $\Sigma$ (x-x̄) = 72 (ignoring signs) |

units

The MEAN DEVIATION provides one figure, by averaging the differences of all values from the mean. It is usual to ignore the plus and minus signs and use the formula:

$$\text{Mean deviation} = \frac{\Sigma (x-\bar{x})}{n}$$

where $\Sigma$ = the total of all values
(x- x̄) = the difference between the mean and the value ignoring the sign
n = the number of values.

The mean deviation for the monthly production figures in Table 13.9 would be:

$$\frac{72}{12} = 6$$

This is the average deviation of all values from the mean. The larger the mean deviation, the wider the spread or dispersion. As a method of calculating dispersion, mean deviation has problems, notably the removal of the plus and minus signs. The next section shows two other measures of dispersion, the **variance** and the **standard deviation**, which attempt to deal with this.

Table 13.10 shows the petrol consumption per annum for area sales representatives working for Quantex plc, a producer of office equipment.

**Table 13.10** *Monthly figures*

Gallons per annum

| Region | North West | North East | South West | South East | West Midlands | East Midlands | Wales | Scotland |
|--------|-----------|-----------|-----------|-----------|---------------|---------------|-------|----------|
| Number of gallons used | 1,200 | 1,360 | 1,140 | 1,000 | 1,150 | 1,300 | 1,250 | 2,000 |

(a) Calculate the mean deviation from the figures.
(b) Calculate the;
  (i) range;
  (ii) interquartile range;
  from the figures.
(c) Which of your answers to (b) do you think is of more use to the business?

Question 3

# The variance and the standard deviation

Both the range and the interquartile range are basic measures of dispersion. They only take into account the spread between two figures in a set of data. The mean deviation is also of limited use because of cancelling out of positive and negative deviations. A more sophisticated measure of dispersion is needed if businesses are going to be able to gain accurate and useful conclusions from a set of raw data.

By using the VARIANCE a business can look at the average of the spread of all data from the mean. Table 13.11 shows the figures for production from Table 13.9. To remove the plus and minus figures the deviations have to be squared, rather than ignoring the signs as in the mean deviation calculation. This is shown in the fourth column of Table 13.11.

**Table 13.11**

| Months | Production figures | Deviations from mean $(x-\bar{x})$ | Deviations squared $(x-\bar{x})^2$ |
|--------|-------------------|-----------------------------------|-----------------------------------|
| Jan | 40 | -10 | 100 |
| Feb | 46 | - 4 | 16 |
| Mar | 52 | +2 | 4 |
| Apr | 54 | +4 | 16 |
| May | 54 | +4 | 16 |
| Jun | 52 | +2 | 4 |
| Jul | 58 | +8 | 64 |
| Aug | 56 | +6 | 36 |
| Sep | 54 | +4 | 16 |
| Oct | 56 | +6 | 36 |
| Nov | 42 | - 8 | 64 |
| Dec | 36 | -14 | 196 |
| | | | $\Sigma\,(x-\bar{x})^2 = 568$ |

The variance can be calculated by:

$$\frac{\Sigma\,(x-\bar{x})^2}{n} = \frac{568}{12} = 47.333$$

The original figures were expressed in units of production, but the variance figures are expressed in units 'squared'. To return to the original units it is necessary to find the **square root** of the variance. This is known as the STANDARD DEVIATION, ie:

$$\sqrt{\frac{\Sigma\,(x-\bar{x})^2}{n}} = \sqrt{47.333} = 6.88$$

# Using the variance and the standard deviation

It is possible to use the variance and standard deviation with far more detailed data. Say that a local council is interested in the age profile of its employees because it is considering the introduction of an early retirement policy, and it wants to calculate the likely costs of such a policy over the next few years. Table 13.12 shows how it might use the mean and the standard deviation.

● As group data are shown in the table, the total frequency is found by multiplying the mid-point of each age class (column 2) by the frequency (column 3) and then adding these values (bottom of column 4). The mean age is then found by:

$$\frac{\Sigma\,f(x)}{\Sigma f} = \frac{8,365}{230} = 36.4 \text{ years}$$

● The variance is found first by calculating how much each mid-point deviates from the mean (column 5). Next each of these values must be squared to cancel out the plus and minus signs (column 6). Finally, the frequency of these squared values can be found by multiplying column 6 by column 3 to give column 7.

- The variance is the sum of column 7 divided by the total frequency so:

$$\frac{\Sigma f(x-\bar{x})^2}{\Sigma f} = \frac{37,673}{230} = 164$$

- The standard deviation is:

$$\sqrt{\frac{\Sigma f(x-\bar{x})^2}{\Sigma f}} = \sqrt{164} = 12.8$$

The standard deviation is a measure of the average deviation from the arithmetic mean of a set of values. It is calculated by using the formula:

$$1 \text{ standard deviation equals } \sqrt{\frac{\Sigma f(x-\bar{x})^2}{\Sigma f}}$$

**Table 13.12**

| 1 Age class | 2 Age class mid-point (x) | 3 Frequency (f) | 4 Mid-point x frequency (fx) | 5 Deviation from mean $(x-\bar{x})^2$ mean = 36.4 | 6 Deviations squared $(x-\bar{x})^2$ | 7 Frequency of deviations squared $f(x-\bar{x})^2$ |
|---|---|---|---|---|---|---|
| 16-20 | 18 | 25 | 450 | -18.4 | 338.6 | 8,456 |
| 21-25 | 23 | 29 | 667 | -13.4 | 179.6 | 5,208 |
| 26-30 | 28 | 32 | 896 | -8.4 | 70.6 | 2,259 |
| 31-35 | 33 | 36 | 1,188 | -3.4 | 11.6 | 418 |
| 36-40 | 38 | 27 | 1,026 | 1.6 | 2.6 | 70 |
| 41-45 | 43 | 23 | 989 | 6.6 | 43.6 | 1,003 |
| 46-50 | 48 | 18 | 864 | 11.6 | 134.6 | 2,423 |
| 51-55 | 53 | 17 | 901 | 16.6 | 275.6 | 4,685 |
| 56-60 | 58 | 13 | 754 | 21.6 | 466.6 | 6,066 |
| 61-65 | 63 | 10 | 630 | 26.6 | 707.6 | 7,076 |
| | | $\Sigma f = 230$ | $\Sigma fx = 8,365$ | | | $\Sigma f(x-\bar{x})^2 = 37,673$ |

Unlike the interquartile range it takes into account all items in a set of data. It is thus much less likely to be distorted by a 'rogue' piece of data within a range. In the example above of the local council, the data had a mean of 36.4 years with a standard deviation of 12.8 years. This would tell the organisation information about both the average age of its employees and the spread of ages.

The standard deviation can be used in a number of ways by a business.

- To establish whether the results of a market research survey are significant and show variations from what was expected (☞ unit 36).
- To find out the quality of batches of products being bought (eg grain being bought by a flour mill) where it would be impossible to check all the batches.
- To check on the standards of output of a production line.
- To identify the likely range of productivity in a workforce

where it would be impossible to carry out a work study of all those employed.

# Index numbers

When faced with large amounts of data, it may be difficult for firms to see exactly what is happening. Also figures are often for very large amounts and are measured in different values. This makes interpretation and comparison a problem.

One method to help a business analyse and interpret data is the use of INDEX NUMBERS. Table 13.13 shows the production figures and unit costs for a company manufacturing small components. It is not easy to immediately see the changes in production or costs from the data. Changing these figures into index numbers will make them easier to interpret.

The first stage in working out an index is to decide on a BASE YEAR. This is given a value of 100 and acts as the base from which all other figures in the index can be compared. In the example, 2000 is taken as the base year and has a value of 100 in the index. Next, all other figures must be changed into index figures based upon the base year.

**Table 13.13** *Production levels and unit costs of a small component manufacturer*

| Year | 2000 | 2001 | 2002 | 2003 | 2004 | 2005 |
|---|---|---|---|---|---|---|
| Production levels (units) | 25,000 | 24,350 | 25,500 | 26,300 | 26,950 | 25,950 |
| Unit Costs (£) | 1.23 | 1.25 | 1.24 | 1.27 | 1.30 | 1.31 |

For production levels in 2001, this is:

$$\frac{\text{Number produced in 2001}}{\text{Number produced in 2000}} \times 100 = \frac{24,350}{25,000} \times 100 = 97.4$$

In 2002, it would be:

$$\frac{\text{Number produced in 2002}}{\text{Number produced in 2000}} \times 100 = \frac{25,500}{25,000} \times 100 = 102$$

A similar process would be carried out for the material costs. The results are shown in Table 13.14 and Figure 13.2.

**Table 13.14** *Index numbers for production levels and unit costs of a small component manufacturer*

| Year | 2000 | 2001 | 2002 | 2003 | 2004 | 2005 |
|---|---|---|---|---|---|---|
| Production levels | 100 | 97.4 | 102.0 | 105.2 | 107.8 | 103.8 |
| Unit costs | 100 | 101.6 | 100.8 | 103.3 | 105.7 | 106.5 |

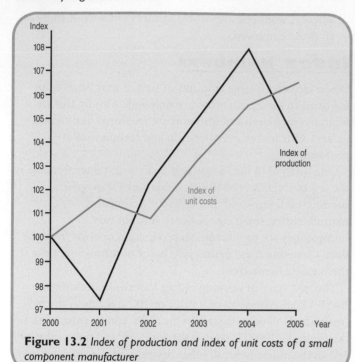

**Figure 13.2** *Index of production and index of unit costs of a small component manufacturer*

It is now easier for the business to analyse this data. It could use the results in a number of ways.

● To identify trends and forecasts.
● The percentage increase in production or costs can be calculated. For example, between 2000 and 2005, the index of unit costs rose from 100 to 106.5 or 6.5 per cent.
● To compare figures that are measured in different values. The production levels of the business are measured in units and costs are expressed in money values. It is possible to compare the trends in both on the same graph. This is particularly useful for the business. Between 2004 and 2005, for example, production had started to fall whereas material costs were continuing to rise, although not at as great a rate.
● Presenting the data in a clear and easy way for shareholders or managers.

## Problems of index numbers

A business will need to take care when producing its index.
● Updating the base year. From time to time a business will need to change its base year which will affect index figures in the years that follow. After a number of years the firm will no longer be interested in comparing this year's figures with those of, say, 10 years ago (the base year). It will want to compare this year's figures with a more recent base year. So for example, in Table 13.13 if the base year was 2003 instead of 2000, the index of production in 2004 and 2005 would be:

2004     $\dfrac{26,950}{26,300} \times 100 = 102.5$

A manufacturing company in the South East employs 100 workers. It has become concerned at the level of pay increases over recent years. Table 13.15 shows the average level of wages for some groups in the business.

**Table 13.15**

|  |  |  |  | £ |
| --- | --- | --- | --- | --- |
|  | 2000 | 2001 | 2002 | 2003 |
| Managers | 25,000 | 30,000 | 32,000 | 35,000 |
| Administration | 10,000 | 10,500 | 11,000 | 12,000 |
| Production | 12,000 | 15,000 | 16,800 | 18,000 |

(a) Using 2000 as a base year, calculate the index for each category.
(b) If 5 per cent of workers are employed as managers, 25 per cent in administration, 55 per cent in production (the other 15 per cent being cleaners etc.), calculate the total cost in 2003 of each category.
(c) How could the business use the index in future pay bargaining?

**Question 4**

and 2005     $\dfrac{25,950}{26,300} \times 100 = 98.7$

● Choice of base year. A firm must be careful to choose a base year which is representative. If a year is chosen where costs, prices or output are high, then index figures in later years will be lower than if a more appropriate year was picked. A base year where figures were low will inflate index numbers in following years.
● Nothing has been said so far about the importance of different items that make up an index. A firm's unit costs would be made up of many different items. This is dealt with in the next section.

## A weighted index

A more accurate index would take into account that changes in some items are more important than others. The costs of a business may be made up of labour, capital, electricity, etc. The firm might be able to construct an index showing how costs change over a period. However, if it spends more on, say, machinery than labour, then the figures for spending on capital must be WEIGHTED.

Table 13.16 shows a business which spends different amounts on various costs of production over a period. Using year X as the base year, the index of the total cost is calculated by:

$$\frac{\text{Year Y index}}{\text{n items}} = \frac{424}{4} = 106 \text{ or 6 per cent}$$

where n = total amount.

**Table 13.16**

£ per annum

| | Year X | Year Y | Year X index | Year Y index ([Costs in year X ÷ costs in year Y] x 100) |
|---|---|---|---|---|
| Wage costs | 100,000 | 103,000 | 100 | 103 |
| Rent/rates | 50,000 | 55,000 | 100 | 110 |
| Materials | 250,000 | 260,000 | 100 | 104 |
| Production costs | 100,000 | 107,000 | 100 | 107 |
| | | | 400 ÷ 4 =100 | 424 ÷ 4 =106 |
| Total costs | 500,000 | 525,000 | | |

This says nothing, however, about the weightings of the different costs. Looking at Table 13.16, it is possible to work out the proportion of spending on each item in year X.

| | | |
|---|---|---|
| Total wage cost | = 20 per cent | (100,000 ÷ 500,000) x 100 |
| Rent/Rates | = 10 per cent | |
| Materials | = 50 per cent | |
| Production costs | = 20 per cent | |

A business can now calculate a weighted index using these figures. This is shown in Table 13.17. The index in year Y is multiplied by the weighting, so the weighted index of, say, total wage costs is 103 x 20 per cent = 20.6

**Table 13.17**

| | Weighting | Year Y index | Weighted Year Y index (weighting x Year Y index) |
|---|---|---|---|
| Total wage costs | 20% | 103 | 20.6 |
| Rates/rents | 10% | 110 | 11.0 |
| Materials | 50% | 104 | 52.0 |
| Production costs | 20% | 107 | 21.4 |
| | | | 105.0 |

The weighted index is now 105. When the percentage spent on each item is taken into account the increase in prices is 5 per cent rather than 6 per cent, as shown in Table 13.16.

# A weighted index over time

The example so far has only dealt with an index over two years. Table 13.18 shows calculations for another 2 years based on changes in the index numbers. The proportion spent on each item is assumed to remain the same. This is known as the **base year** or **Laspeyre** method of calculation.

It is also possible to recalculate the index each year based on the weightings in the current year. This is known as the **Paasche** method and can be useful if weightings change frequently. In Table 13.18 the weighting in year A (the most

**Table 13.18**

| | Year X Index | Year Y Index | Year Z Index | Year A Index |
|---|---|---|---|---|
| Total wage costs | 100 | 103x20% = 20.6 | 105x20% = 21 | 106x20% = 21.2 |
| Rent/rates | 100 | 110x10% = 11 | 110x10% = 11 | 108x10% = 10.8 |
| Materials | 100 | 104x50% = 52 | 106x50% = 53 | 110x50% = 55 |
| Production costs | 100 | 107x20% = 21.4 | 110x20% = 22 | 115x20% = 23 |
| Weighted index | 100 | 105.0 | 107.0 | 110.0 |

recent year) may have been:

| | | |
|---|---|---|
| Total wage cost | = | 15 per cent |
| Rents/rates | = | 10 per cent |
| Materials | = | 45 per cent |
| Production costs | = | 30 per cent |

The index numbers for each year would have been multiplied by current percentages and not the weightings for the base year. So in year A the weighted index using the Paasche method would be:

| | | | | | |
|---|---|---|---|---|---|
| Total wage cost | 106 | x | 15% | = | 15.9 |
| Rents/rates | 108 | x | 10% | = | 10.8 |
| Materials | 110 | x | 45% | = | 49.5 |
| Production costs | 115 | x | 30% | = | 34.5 |
| | | | | | 110.7 |

Businesses can use weighted indexes in a number of ways, especially where there is a number of items which they wish to include in an index. For example, a business which sells five products and wishes to construct a single index to show its changes in sales over the last ten years may consider using one. Products with high sales levels could be given a higher weighting than those with low sales levels. In this way, a weighted index would more accurately reflect overall changes in sales.

A well known index in the UK is the Retail Price Index (RPI). This measures the rate of inflation by finding out how the average household spends its money and monitoring any falls or rises in the prices of those goods and services. The RPI is an example of a **weighted index** as it gives greater importance to some items than to others. For example, a rise in the price of petrol might be given a higher weighting than a rise in the price of soap. A change in the price of a product with a high weighting will consequently have a relatively greater impact upon the index than a similar change in the price of a product with a low weighting.

In 2004 the government announced that inflation would now be measured by the Consumer Price Index (CPI). This is calculated using a similar method to the RPI, but with different features (☞ unit 98).

# key terms

**Base year** - a period, such as a year, a month or a quarter, which other figures are compared to, It is given a value of 100 in the index.

**Central tendency** - a measure of the most likely or common result from a set of data (the average).

**Dispersion** - a measure of the spread of data.

**Index number** - an indicator of a change in a series of figures where one figure is given a value of 100 and others are adjusted in proportion to it. It is often used as an average of a number of figures.

**Interquartile range** - the range between the central 50 per cent of a set of data.

**Mean** - the value in a set of data around which all other values cluster; commonly used in business as the average of a set of data.

**Mean deviation** - the average deviation of all figures from the mean, which ignores plus and minus signs in its calculation.

**Median** - the value which occurs in the middle of a set of data when the data is placed in rank order.

**Mode** - the most commonly occurring item in a set of data.

**Range** - the difference between the highest and the lowest values in a set of data.

**Standard deviation** - the average deviation from the arithmetic mean of a set of data (accounting for plus and minus signs in the calculation) found by the square root of the variance.

**Variance** - the average deviation of all figures from the mean, which removes plus and minus signs by 'squaring' the deviation figures.

**Weighting** - a process which adjusts an index number to take into account the relative importance of a variable.

## Knowledge...Knowledge...Knowledge...Knowledge...Knowledge...Know

1. Why might businesses need to analyse data?
2. What are the differences between the mean, median and mode as measures of central tendency?
3. How is the mean of grouped data calculated?
4. List 5 measures of dispersion that might be used in analysing data.
5. Explain 2 possible uses in business of the standard deviation.
6. Why might a business use index numbers rather than actual figures?
7. State 3 uses that a business might have for index numbers.
8. Why might weighted index numbers be more useful than a simple index?
9. Explain the difference between the Laspeyre and Paasche methods of calculating a weighted index.

# Case study EcoFibre Ltd

EcoFibre Ltd is a manufacturer of cereal products. Four years ago it launched a range of cereal bars after research indicated a growing trend towards more healthy 'snack eating' amongst its potential customers. One of its products, Nutrafibre, is a low sugar grain bar. The product was well received in tests. But it has not been selling as well as the business would like. So EcoFibre has developed a marketing campaign to inform customers of the possible benefits of reduced sugar intake.

**Table 13.19** Market research results

| Quantity of Nutrafibre purchased in a year | Before the campaign | After the campaign |
|---|---|---|
| 1-10 | 16 | 36 |
| 11-20 | 44 | 44 |
| 21-30 | 84 | 112 |
| 31-40 | 142 | 162 |
| 41-50 | 204 | 182 |
| 51-60 | 160 | 184 |
| 61-70 | 138 | 136 |
| 71-80 | 114 | 92 |
| 81-90 | 62 | 30 |
| 91-100 | 36 | 22 |
| | 1,000 | 1,000 |

**Table 13.20** Expenditure on products in the cereal bar range

£000

| Product | Year 1 | Year 2 | Year 3 | Year 4 |
|---|---|---|---|---|
| A | 30 | 45 | 45 | 60 |
| B | 10 | 22 | 24 | 22 |
| C | 60 | 60 | 45 | 42 |
| D | 10 | 12 | 14 | 16 |
| E | 50 | 55 | 50 | 40 |
| F | 40 | 48 | 50 | 44 |
| | 200 | | | |

Table 13.19 shows the results of a market research survey of 1,000 customers into the amount of this product they would buy in a period of time, before and after the promotion campaign.

The business will now analyse the information. It is particularly interested in the average or mean quantity purchased per year and the standard deviation before and after the campaign.

The business is also concerned generally about customer spending on the range of cereal bars. It has collected the information in Table 13.20. It aims to calculate a weighted index of expenditure to examine how overall spending on the range has changed. It will use the Year 1 as the base year.

(a) What is meant by:
   (i)   the mean quantity purchased; (2 marks)
   (ii)  the standard deviation; (2 marks)
   (iii) a weighted index of expenditure? (2 marks)
(b) Using the information in Table 13.19, calculate:
   (i)  the modal group before and after the promotion campaign; (2 marks)
   (ii) the mean quantity of Nutrafibre purchased before and after the promotion campaign (use the central points as 5, 15, 25, 35, etc.) (8 marks)
(c) (i)  Calculate the standard deviation of Nutrafibre purchased before and after the promotion campaign. (8 marks)
   (ii) Using your calculation of the mean and standard deviation values, evaluate the success of the promotion campaign. (8 marks)
(d) (i)  Calculate a weighted index of expenditure for years 1-4 using the information in Table 13.20. (8 marks).
   (ii) Using your calculations discuss whether the business has cause for concern. (10 marks)

## Expanding the business

Many businesses start up each year in the UK and many fail. Table 14.1 shows that in 2002, 175,800 businesses started up based on VAT registrations. Those that do survive will expect to grow, expand production and increase sales and profits.

**Table 14.1** *Business start-ups and failures (based on VAT registrations and de-registrations), UK*

|      | Registrations | De-registrations |
|------|--------------|-----------------|
| 1997 | 187,700      | 151,900         |
| 1998 | 187,500      | 153,500         |
| 1999 | 181,400      | 160,400         |
| 2000 | 184,000      | 165,500         |
| 2001 | 174,600      | 167,200         |
| 2002 | 175,800      | 176,000         |

Source: adapted from Small Business Service.

Growth can take place by producing and selling larger numbers of existing products or services, launching new products or services or by finding new markets. For example, a taxi firm setting up in a town area may gain more customers and increase sales as a result of its prompt timekeeping and helpful drivers. It may then decide to offer a limousine service, to drive people to theatre shows or functions, which charges a higher price and raises more revenue.

Growth can also take place when businesses join together. A business may decide to buy another. The turnover of the combined businesses will be higher. For example, in December 2000 GlaxoSmithKline plc was created from the merger of two London based pharmaceutical companies, Glaxo Wellcome and SmithKline Beecham. In 2001 the combined company had a turnover of 33.4 billion euros.

Some businesses grow by franchising their operations or licensing. For example, a large car manufacturer might give businesses the franchise to sell its products or a multinational manufacturer of drinks may give a foreign business a licence to use the company name abroad for a fee.

As a business grows it is likely to face issues and challenges that may not exist in a smaller organisation. Even if they do, they are likely to be less complex and relatively less important.

## Raising finance

Different methods of finance are available for a business that is starting up. Some of these methods will also be suited to a business seeking to expand. The method that a business chooses is likely to depend on how much is required, the position of the business and the use of the funds.

**Private funds** Small business entrepreneurs may be willing to put their savings into a business to expand. Unless they have built up a large amount of savings, have had a windfall gain or have been given a large sum of money, this is only likely to provide limited funds. There are some examples, such as multi millionaires ploughing large amounts of their own money into football clubs in order to finance transfers which they hope will bring success and benefit the club in future.

**Partners'/shareholders' funds** The owner of a small business may decide to bring in a partner to finance expansion. However, the partner is likely to want some control of the business and some reward for the investment. Private limited companies can raise funds by selling shares to existing or new shareholders. They also have the option of 'going public' and becoming a public limited company (plc). The shares of plcs may be traded 'second hand' on stock exchanges, such as the London Stock Exchange. The Alternative Investment Market (AIM) and OFEX were set up in the 1990s to give smaller, young growing companies the opportunity to raise capital by selling their shares. All of these methods reduce the control and ownership of existing shareholders.

**Bank loans** A business can apply to a bank for a loan, for example to buy more equipment or new technology. The bank may want some **collateral** against the loan in case of failure to pay. It would also consider the current position of the business, perhaps by examining its accounts. The business may also need to write a business plan to explain its strategy to the bank.

**Asset leasing and hire purchase** These provide useful sources of finance for the funding of new investment when a business lacks sufficient funds, for example to purchase new technology.

**Venture capital/business angels** These are organisations or individuals that are prepared to invest in growing businesses, hoping to see rewards in future. They often provide funds for businesses that are considered too risky by other investors. The problem is that they often take a certain share in the business as reward for their investment.

**Government and EU funds** Examples of funds available for expansion include Regional Selective Assistance for projects that would create or safeguard jobs in EU countries or loans from the European Investment Bank for capital projects (☞ unit 88).

**Merger capital** A merger or joint venture with another business may provide capital for growth. For example, one company may have a potentially profitable area into which it can expand, but not have the liquid funds to do so. Another business may have stockpiled money over a period. A merger or joint venture would give the combined business the funds to take advantage of the opportunity for growth.

Retained profit As a business grows, it would hope eventually to make a profit. It will be able to use retained profit to fund further expansion. The amount of money available for expansion will depend on the amount of profit from previous years. Large plcs often have huge retained profits in any year.

The **cash flow** of a business is affected by growth. A growing business is likely to have increased production and sales, which it hopes will lead to greater profits. However, often the business will have to pay out for raw materials, wages and perhaps machinery before it produces and se... products. This can lead to cash flow problems (☞ unit 4...) the business does not have enough money to pay for its inputs. Possible solutions to a lack of cash might be delaying payments or taking out a short term loan, although these are likely to be temporary measures. Improving credit control (☞ unit 48) might be a better option. A situation where a business has grown so rapidly that it has put a strain on its financial resources is known as **overtrading** (☞ unit 48).

## Accounting

Keeping records As a business expands, the records it keeps become larger and more complicated. A supplier of pine furniture may increase its sales from 20 to 100 retailers over a period of time. The amount of materials it buys from suppliers will also increase. Records of these transactions must be kept. Invoices must be sent out with the products sold. The business may decide that it needs to buy or improve its computers or computer software in order to keep efficient records of these transactions.

Keeping accounts The accounts of a small business may be fairly straightforward. Sole traders can produce their own accounts and provide information to the Inland Revenue on a self assessment form. As a business grows it may employ an accounting firm to produce its accounts to comply with legal requirements. The annual accounts of sole traders and limited companies have slightly different categories, although all transactions are recorded. Very large companies employ their own accountants, not only to produce the accounts, but to provide help and guidance to the company when making decisions.

Payments As the number of customers increases, so do problems in getting payments from them. Credit control becomes more complex the larger a business becomes. Computer software may be used to maintain lists of age debtors, people who have been owing money for certain periods. Credit controllers may be employed by the business. Alternatively, a factor may be employed to chase outstanding debt.

## Changing legal status

As a business grows it is possible that it will change its legal organisation (☞ unit 6).

A **sole trader** wishing to expand by bringing in others who will invest and help to run the business may be forced to change to a **partnership**. Partners may want some say in the business. Partnership legislation or a partnership deed of agreement will set out the responsibilities and the rewards to each partner.

Some people willing to put money into a business would not be prepared to accept the unlimited liability of certain types of partnership. This is because they would be personally responsible for the debts of the business. Changing to a

---

Jayney de Nordwall started life as a producer of television commercials. But she left to make her own films. Her plan was to make three short films and build up relationships with film makers. Initially, everything went smoothly. She found out about Techinvest, an organisation that would put her in touch with business angels to raise the finance needed. Her first two films were a success. 'Jump' starred Cold Feet's John Thompson and 'About a Girl' was entered for the Sundance Film Festival. She then moved on to feature films. But her first film had to be scrapped after seven months of work when a similar film appeared. She is now looking to produce a new film, but realises that bills still need to be paid so she does a lot of freelancing. Alice Morrison, chief executive of North West Vision which offers grants and loans to budding directors and producers says 'It's important to keep your day job'.

North Star productions was set up by Neil Fitzmaurice, co-writer of Phoenix Nights, and his brother Tony. Their first film was low budget, with money raised from family and friends. Their second film will cost around £1.7 million, but this time the company is trying to attract 17 private investors.

Red Productions in Manchester creates drama for television, including 'Clocking Off' on BBC and 'The Second Coming ' drama on ITV. A ten series project can cost around £3 million. But one issue is payment. Different broadcasters pay in different ways. Channel 4, for example, pays in tranches, with some upfront for development. ITV pays on delivery.

Source: adapted from *en*, December, January 2004.

(a) Identify the sources of finance used by the businesses in the article to fund expansion.
(b) Explain why these sources of finance may have been chosen.
(c) Suggest why the businesses might experience cash flow difficulties.

**Question 1**

limited company would give them the security of limited liability.

Setting up a **private limited company** has certain implications for a business. For example, the owners of the business, the shareholders, must sign a Memorandum of Association and Articles of Association. These provide details about the company, such as its name, objectives and capital, as well as the rights of shareholders and the role of directors.

A private limited company may decide to become a **public limited company**. This also has implications for the business. The company name must change, from Ltd to plc. Shares in a public limited company are available to outside investors and traded second hand on stock exchanges. This means that plcs have larger numbers of investors and can raise large amounts of finance. Controlling a plc may require owners to buy larger numbers of shares. Investors are willing to buy shares hoping to receive a dividend or to sell them for a higher price than they paid and make a profit.

## *Planning*

Planning is vital to all businesses, no matter what size. Even a small retailer must plan what to buy, what to sell, how large

the business will be in the next few years and when to employ more staff. The larger a business, however, the more complicated planning becomes. Larger businesses have more resources. They have more sales, more stocks, more employees etc. This makes accurate marketing, human resource and production plans essential.

- Without careful and co-ordinated planning, individual departments may make decisions which conflict with each other. Poor communication can raise the costs of the business. This is an example of a **diseconomy of scale**.
- Inaccurate forecasts and predictions will lead to greater problems in larger businesses and could increase costs.
- Without planning, the most efficient method of working may not be used. For example, too many workers may be working on a project or workers without suitable skills may be doing a job.
- The plans must be appropriate. Sometimes managers are accused of **short-termism**. This is where they set plans which they know can be achieved in the short term. Setting short term, achievable plans allows managers to achieve the results required by shareholders or lenders of money. However, taking a short term view is not always

The Carphone Warehouse is a well known success story. It provides a one stop shop for mobile phones and accessories. It was started in 1989 by Charles Dunstone with just £6,000. By 2002 it had 470 stores in the UK and 647 in the rest of Europe, and had appeared in fast track 100 league tables as one of the UK's fastest growing companies. The business initially expanded rapidly by targeting smaller customers, including small businesses and private individuals, when existing mobile phone companies were ignoring these groups.

The business was floated in July 2000 on the London Stock Exchange. Shares were sold at 200p and the business raised £185 million, mainly for expansion in Europe. 11,500 people applied to buy shares. By 2003 it had become one of only a handful of dotcom companies to pay dividends on its shares to shareholders. Its founder and major shareholder Mr Dunstone, with over third of shares, would receive just over £3 million in dividends.

The company has been branching out into related telecom product areas. In February 2003 it launched a cheap rate fixed line telephone service called Talk Talk, for example.

Figure 14.1 shows the results of a survey by City lawyers Eversheds into the reasons why businesses float. It shows, for example, that very few (3 per cent) said that they would float to start up a new company.

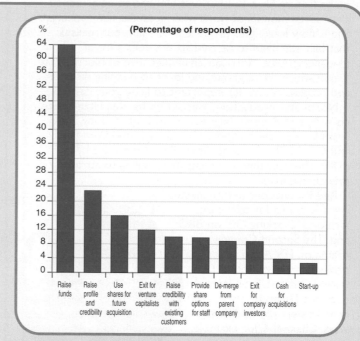

Source: adapted from www.fastrack.co.uk, news.zdnet.co.uk, www.guardian.co.uk.

**Figure 14.1** *Reasons for seeking a stock market flotation*

(a) Explain the implications of the flotation of the company on the business.
(b) Discuss whether the flotation was necessary for further growth of the business.

the best strategy. For example, a business might decide that it does not want to invest in machinery that uses new technology now because of the cost. Although this might leads to short term profit, in the long run it could be a disaster if the machine is needed to produce new products. The business might fail because it has not planned for long term changes.

Some companies make use of theories or models to help understand the markets in which they operate (☞ unit 11). A business may even try to develop a corporate culture (☞ unit 15) so that everyone in the organisation works towards the same business goals.

## Marketing

An expanding market, increasing output and an increase in sales can have a number of implications for the marketing of a business.

**Marketing research** A small business such as a window cleaner is likely to know his market. The revenue of the business may be determined by the buildings in the area, how often people want their windows cleaning and the competition faced. A UK retailer selling imported American comics may know most of his customers personally. As businesses get larger it becomes more difficult to keep and find out information about the consumers of the product. The importer of a new comic may know that 100 people will buy it each month. Estimating the sales of a new car is more difficult. This is why large businesses spend great sums on researching the market. They also look for new ways to find out about customers, such as finding out the products bought by holders of loyalty cards in supermarkets. Larger businesses also make use of databases to collect information about the buying patterns of customers.

**Distribution** As a business and its markets grow, the difficulties of getting the product to consumers increase. The producer of a local newspaper perhaps needs to send its current issue to an area such as Yorkshire or an even smaller local region such as Stafford. A multinational company, such as Coca Cola, has to get its products to customers in many countries around the world. As a business grows the total costs of distribution will increase. The total costs of distributing newspapers nationally will be larger than the costs of circulating a local newspaper. However, the cost for a textile manufacturer transporting 1,000 products to a retailer in a large van instead of a fleet of smaller vans is likely, on average, to be less. This is an example of an economy of scale. Some businesses continue to own and distribute their own products as they grow. Others employ specialist businesses to deliver their products.

**Marketing methods** A small business may be able to advertise its products by a leaflet or an advert in the local paper. As a business grows it may have to consider other methods of

advertising and promotion. Large businesses make use of relatively expensive television and cinema advertisements. They also make use of other forms of promotion such as free products, display material and exhibitions. As a business grows its name itself may become a marketing tactic. Well known company names become a corporate brand. People will buy products and services of the business because of the reputation. In some cases, certain specialist small firms also have a company brand.

**Target markets** Business that start may sell into local markets or niche markets. One of Richard Branson's earliest business ventures was selling second hand records. As a business expands it may either sell into wider markets or produce other products to sell. It is then said to have a product portfolio (☞ unit 24). Large businesses have many different products selling into a variety of markets.

## Production

As a business grows, this is likely to affect the way in which it produces goods or provides services.

**Changing production methods** As a company grows so might its production methods. A small company making hand made furniture may employ a worker to produce the goods from start to finish. This is likely to be time consuming and costly for a business expecting to produce 1,000 kitchen units a day. It may therefore be necessary to buy new machinery, retrain employees and change methods of production as a business grows. Many large companies use large scale machinery and assembly lines to mass produce products. This large scale production of similar products reduces the average costs of each product. Some large businesses are recognising the benefits of combining the advantages of large scale output with producing a product from start to finish. They are organising production into teamwork, known as cell production.

**Relocation and land** As a business grows it may become 'too big' for its premises. It then has a decision to make. Should it expand in its current location or should it relocate? This decision is likely to be based on a number of factors, including available land and employees, the need for related businesses, the market and government and EU aid (☞ unit 88).

**Reorganisation** As output increases and production methods change, it may be necessary to reorganise production. For example, some businesses have found that time can be saved and efficiency improved if related operations are carried out in a cell, with machines near to each other.

**Purchasing** A larger business will tend to order more supplies than a smaller business. This will increase total costs, although buying in bulk may be able to reduce the average costs. It is vital for all orders to be on time, but perhaps even more so for a larger business. Large amounts of supply will require storage space, as will stocks of finished goods for distribution. Some businesses have reduced this cost by asking for supplies just before production begins.

## Human resources

Business growth can have a major impact on human resource management.

**Reorganisation** The organisation of the business may need to change as it grows. A sole trader making candle holders may be the manager of the business, might make the products and may even deliver them to the retailer. As a business grows the owners may delegate some work to other employees and give them responsibilities. The larger the business grows, the greater may be the need to delegate. A limited company will have a hierarchy. The overall responsibility for company-wide policy will be taken by the directors. Departmental managers may be responsible for employees in their area. Some large business have recognised the problems caused by too many layers in the hierarchy, such as poor communication or task duplication. This has led to delayering (☞ unit 90), for example removing one layer of managers. Businesses that grow by means of a merger sometimes find that jobs are duplicated. This may lead to reduction in the workforce or redundancies in certain types of jobs and expansion in other areas.

**Recruitment** As a business grows it will need to recruit more workers. It must make sure that the workers it recruits have the appropriate skills required. It may employ staff from outside the business or from within (☞ unit 64).

**Industrial relations** A larger business may find that more conflicts of interest develop between different stake holders. Workers in smaller businesses may feel that they and the owners all have the same interests. In large organisations disagreements can take place over many things. Workers may push for higher wages just at the time that the company needs to control costs. Workers may feel aggrieved at large dividends paid to shareholders. Individual workers may disagree with the decisions of managers.

**Motivation** It has been suggested that one problem with larger businesses is the motivation of workers. Some workers feel isolated in large operations. They may feel that they are just a 'cog in the machine' and their work is not valued. Workers on assembly lines have often complained of monotonous and boring operations. Businesses use a variety of motivational techniques to deal with this problem. These range from:

- financial incentives such as bonuses;
- reorganising work so that the employee does not carry out the same task all the time;
- other non financial incentives, such as company health schemes or company cars;
- ideas to develop company loyalty, such as group activities.

## Is business growth desirable?

One argument put forward for the growth of businesses is that they can reduce average costs. A small business may buy a computer for £1,200. If it is used by a part time worker for 15 hours a week, the average cost per hour each week is £80. If a larger business makes use of the computer for a full working week of 40 hours, the average cost falls to £40.

There are other benefits of large size. A large business is more likely to obtain sizeable finance than a small firm. A large business may also have a stronger marketing image than a smaller business and be able to buy in bulk.

In some cases a business might decide to reduce the size of its operations. This is known as RETRENCHMENT. There is a number of reasons why a business might do this.

- If a business grows too large it may experience rising average costs or diseconomies of scale (☞ unit 81). For example, a large factory might find that it has to spend

---

New Heights is a furniture retailer in London. The business started in 1999 with £740,000 from family and friends and in 2001 it had a turnover of £5.5 million. It offers an alternative to the humdrum world of flatpack and veneer. The business idea is that people will pay more for well crafted solid wood furniture. Wood such as cherry and maple is imported from suppliers in the USA, where supplies are abundant and the price is right.

The first store was set up in Cricklewood, away from the furniture mecca of central London but on a good high street position and in a good catchment area. This strategy paid off and the business now has five stores in London. Continued growth is the aim, with two new stores planned for Nottingham and West London.

Staff are vital. Each new member receives 2-3 weeks' training in product knowledge and IT. They are trained to be socially confident and not just sit behind a till. The aim is for staff to be multi-tasking and the business argues that this is 80-90 per cent complete.

New Heights has loftier ambitions for the future. Chief executive Gareth Williams argues 'We are totally driven by the idea of building a natural furniture brand.' The company has its eye on taking this wider part of the furnishings market, although this aim is limited by its cash flow as the founders are loathe to give anything away to new investors.

Source: adapted from *Growing Business*, September 2002.

(a) Examine the effects on:
  (i) marketing;
  (ii) production;
  (iii) human resources;
  of the growth plans of New Heights.

large amounts on pollution control. A smaller factory may not generate as much pollution, and may not have to spend as much.

- The business might decide that a smaller operation might be more efficient and better able to compete with other businesses in the market. For example, a printing business might decide that it is better able to meet the needs of its customers with smaller presses that can be changed quickly than with large presses that require long print runs.
- Companies realise the mistakes they have made in the past. For example, they might have expanded into markets which were not profitable or produced products which did not make a profit.
- Changes in the market may have taken place. For example, many businesses that grew rapidly as a result of the Internet boom found that they later had to operate as smaller organisations as the nature of the market changed.
- Economic and social changes. Recessions (☞ unit 96) in the economy often lead to organisations going out of business. Some attempt to survive by reducing the size of their operations, hoping that demand will increase at a later time.
- Business strategy. Examples might be the sale of unprofitable parts of a business not related to its core activities or a reduction in the number of branches in order to concentrate on increasing sales in those that are retained.

Retrenchment has a number of implications for business. Investment is likely to be put back and objectives could be changed. There may be a high turnover of staff, particularly senior staff. New managers may be needed who are more suited to cost control, for example.

Knowledge...owledge...Knowle

1. How might a business be able to grow?
2. State 5 ways in which a business might obtain funds for expansion.
3. Why might obtaining funds from partners or shareholders be a problem?
4. Why might a investor in a business wish a partnership to become a limited company?
5. Suggest 2 reasons why planning in a larger company is important.
6. Explain 3 effects that the expansion of a business might have on its marketing.
7. Explain 3 effects that the expansion of a business might have on its production.
8. Explain 3 effects that the expansion of a business might have on its human resource planning.
9. Explain 3 reasons why retrenchment might take place.

## key terms

**Retrenchment** - a decision by a business to reduce its size of its operations in an attempt to improve them.

---

BT is now in better shape than at any time since the telecommunications bubble burst in 2001. Debt has been cut from £30 billion to £9 billion. BT's finances were in a terrible state after it overpaid for third generation mobile licences and over-expanded abroad. One of the consequences of support by investors for the business was that Cellnet, BT's mobile phone arm, was demerged and separately listed on the stock exchange.

The business has increased profits as a result of effective cost cutting. The management system has been streamlined and old bureaucratic methods of working have been done away with. Thousands of jobs have been axed and call centre work has been shifted to low cost countries such as India.

Some City analysts are worried that even a slimmed down, leaner and fitter BT might find it difficult to compete. They suggest its massive fixed line system is in long term decline. But the company argues that 'BT owns the only fixed network' which is a 'cash cow that minimises downsize risk'. The company plans to enter other markets in future. These include the pay-per-view TV market with the launch of a new BT branded digital TV and Internet service.

Source: adapted from *The Observer*, 26.10.2003.

(a) Using examples from the article, explain why the strategy of BT after 2001 might be an example of retrenchment.
(b) To what extent might the 'leaner and fitter BT' be able to compete in new markets?

Question4

# Case study Kidstuff

Kidstuff is a business run by James and Judith Johnson in the North West, Merseyside and the Wirral. The business provides specialised, originally designed and unusual children's clothing. Fabrics are bought in bulk from wholesalers, the clothes are made up and then sold in local markets in the area. The average price of a stall per day was £15. The business operated 4 out of 7 days a week. James and Judith charged between £7 and £18 for the clothes although the average price was around £12. They felt that they could charge a slightly higher price than other clothing stalls because of the uniqueness of their service. Sometimes customers will suggest their own designs and these can be made up at an extra cost.

The business was set up as a partnership. It was started with the £11,000 that Judith and James received when they were made redundant. They were keen not to borrow from a bank. Judith's mother also put in £5,000 of her own savings. Part time machine operators were employed to make the clothes in their own homes. When they were finished, they would be stored at Judith's and James' house, ready to be taken to markets in the area.

Figure 14.2 shows the change in revenue, profit and costs of the business in the first three years. Costs include the materials, the wages of the operators, the hiring of stalls and some leaflets to advertise the business. The market for their product was likely to be limited in the areas in which the business operated and they decided that they had to expand. They have had a meeting with an independent adviser. A number of alternatives were suggested.

If the method chosen was a success and resulted in expansion, this would have a number of implications for the business.

**Markets further afield** Markets in Salford and North Wales had not been considered initially because of the distance and greater costs. This might involve leaving earlier in the morning and arriving home later. Costs might include vehicle maintenance, petrol, other costs such as staying overnight at a hotel if they worked late. One problem was that the markets would have to take place on days that they did not work already. It would also mean an increase in the number of days a week they worked. James and Judith had considered employing someone from another area to sell their products in these markets.

**Other markets** Craft fairs, village fairs and other related sales opportunities could be one way of expanding. Again this would mean working extra days, with increased costs, but nor further afield. The size of these markets was likely to be fairly limited and people were not likely to spend a great deal. It was suggested that they would only provide a small increase in turnover.

**Changing production** The success of the business so far had been based on the uniqueness of the product and the chance to charge a relatively high price. Now that it was successful, the business could perhaps offer more standardised clothing at a slightly cheaper price. It may also offer related products, such as hand made table mats or chair backs. They could be sold at existing markets on the same days they were operating. James and Judith were concerned that the new products would appear the same as those of others and the price reduction would not make them as profitable.

**Opening a shop** The business had considered opening its own shop. Premises in Formby, an area of relatively high income earners, had recently become available to rent at £6,000 a year. The shop would then give them an established base from which to build up regular clients. They could also use the shop to store stock. The shop could be opened 6 days a week, or even 7 perhaps, by employing a part time sales assistant.

**Remain the same size** The business could operate exactly as it is at present, without any major changes in markets, production or premises.

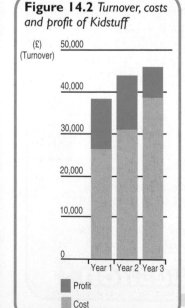

**Figure 14.2** *Turnover, costs and profit of Kidstuff*

(£) (Turnover)

50,000
40,000
30,000
20,000
10,000
0

Year 1 | Year 2 | Year 3

■ Profit
■ Cost

**(a) Describe the main changes in:**
**(i) turnover;**
**(ii) costs;**
**(iii) profit;**
**of the business in the first three years.**
**(12 marks)**
**(b) Identify the effects that** the changes in sales in the last three years might have had on the business. **(10 marks)**
**(c) Examine the possible effects of each of the five alternative strategies on the business in future. (14 marks)**
**(d) Discuss the most suitable alternative strategy for the business. (14 marks)**

# 15 Corporate Culture

## What is corporate culture?

Corporate or organisation culture (☞ unit 5) is a set of values and beliefs that are shared by people and groups in an organisation. A simple way of explaining corporate culture might be to say that it is the 'way that things are done in a business', eg the McDonald's way. For example, at Microsoft, the computer company staff work long hours, dress casually and communicate by e-mail. These are the **norms** of behaviour.

The corporate culture of a business will often be reflected in its **mission statement** (☞ unit 4). So, for example, if the mission statement of a business includes that it aims to protect the environment, then parts of its culture could involve recycling where possible, using renewable resources and buying the most efficient energy saving equipment. Staff might be expected to be vigilant about turning off lights and reusing paper.

The corporate culture of a business can influence decision making. For example, General Electric in the USA stresses that employees should feel ownership for the company. It also encourages low level managers to behave like entrepreneurs. This means that managers tend to make their own decisions and often take risks. Insurance companies may encourage caution and conservative attitudes in employees as they do not want risky decisions to be made.

Business leaders are able to create a corporate culture as part of the **strategy** of the company (☞ units 5, 16 and 17). Computer companies often encourage employees to perform tasks in a creative way. This is because they believe that it will lead to innovation, which is the source of their **competitive advantage** (☞ unit 5).

It is important that the corporate culture of a business is understood by all the people that work in the organisation. It is usually transmitted to new members and reinforced informally, by stories, symbols and socialisation, and more formally through training.

## The growth of corporate culture

The idea of corporate culture became popular in the 1980s. Tom Peters and Robert Waterman (1982), in their book *In Search of Excellence*, highlighted the potential impact that company values could have on the success of a business. Terrence Deal and Allan Kennedy's (1982) book, *Corporate Cultures*, suggested that the culture of any organisation could be managed to improve the effectiveness of the business. There was a certain amount of evidence to support these ideas.

- The success of Japanese organisations. Japanese businesses appeared able to establish and maintain cooperative, team-based organisational cultures.
- A growing awareness that successful leadership was not only concerned with profits, costs and sales, but also with the ability to motivate and to gain the commitment of employees.
- The belief that there was a relationship between a strong corporate culture and improved business performance. It was suggested that a company's corporate culture could be made stronger by the actions of managers.

Management theorists have therefore stressed the importance of developing a strong corporate culture. To help with this, the idea of a '**culture gap**' has been used. This is the difference between the culture that a company possesses and the kind that senior management would like to have. Businesses can fill this gap by techniques that change the corporate culture.

## Developing a strong corporate culture

All organisations have cultures to some extent. However, only a minority have a 'strong' culture that is highly visible and which affects the behaviour of employees and other stakeholders. It has been suggested that firms with a strong culture and little or no 'culture gap' are the ones that are likely to perform effectively. How might a business develop a strong corporate culture? Buchanan and Huczyenski (1991) argued that four areas can be examined.

**Core elements of corporate culture** The corporate culture of a business is its shared values, beliefs and norms. For a corporate culture to form, a stable collection of people needs to have shared a significant history, involving dealing with problems. This allows a social learning process to take place. Top managers are often viewed as 'culture carriers'. They are the people that set the firm's standards and its values and beliefs. The way that a culture develops is often influenced by the founders of the business. For example, Anita Roddick, the founder of The Body Shop, created a strong corporate culture of fair trade, fair employment practices and ethical standards for products.

**Packaging corporate culture** The values, beliefs and norms must be effectively 'packaged'. The corporate culture must be embedded into the everyday 'fabric' of the business. It must inform individuals how things are done. Packaging can come in different forms. Each helps to strengthen the company values, beliefs and norms.

- Stories. They are based on original events, but can include a mix of truth and fiction. Stories help to explain current practices. For example, an employee at Procter & Gamble noticed that the labels on a product at his local supermarket were mounted off centre. He bought the whole stock, assuming that P&G would reimburse him, which it did. This story helps to communicate the importance of quality in the business.

● Heroes. These may be living or dead people. Through their deeds and words they represent the culture of the organisation and can be role models for others to follow. They might be company founders, leaders or successful employees. For example, the thoughts of Ray Kroc, who bought the hamburger restaurants from the McDonald brothers, are played to staff who attend the company's training courses.

● Sagas and Legends. These are historical accounts of actual events, which may have become embellished over time. An example is the 3M worker who tried to find a use for rejected sandpaper minerals. He was fired for spending time on this. However, he kept coming back and eventually succeeded. He went on to become vice-president of the company's Roofing Granules Division, which he helped to create.

● Symbols, slogans and mottoes. Examples of symbols include the Coca-Cola, Nike and IBM logos. Slogans such as Caterpillar's 'Forty-eight hours part service anywhere in the world' are well known. The Hard Rock Café's staff motto has been 'Love All, Serve All'.

**Communicating corporate culture** The corporate culture of the business must be communicated to employees and other stakeholders. Formal and informal methods can be used to do this. Formal methods are highly visible, consciously designed, regular events and activities. They provide opportunities for employees to acquire the company values and beliefs. Examples include:

● rites and occasions - planned, often dramatic, activities that show different aspects of culture. Examples may be the unveiling of a product, the honouring of employees' work and a lecture from an inspirational leader about future company prospects;

● rituals - a sequence of activities which express and reinforce the ideas, values, beliefs and norms of the company. Many American companies arrange regular Friday afternoon 'beer busts' at which employees can get together and relax.

● courses - induction, orientation and training courses which have the values, beliefs and norms of the organisation communicated within them.

Informal cultural transmission refers to the informal way in which culture is passed on. For example, the ways in which employees typically communicate and express themselves represent their company's culture.

**Cultural networks** The strength of a business's corporate culture depends on the homogeneity (similar beliefs and ideas) of group members. It also depends on the length and intensity of shared experiences by members of cultural networks. Cultural networks are groups of individuals that are socialised into the values, norms and beliefs of the business through working together over time.

---

Virgin is a brand that is familiar to millions of people. It was founded by Richard Branson and the Virgin Group has operated in many areas including music, holidays and airlines, cola, radio, rail travel and financial services. It is suggested that Branson looks for business opportunities where large organisations have become 'lazy'. He prefers to build his own corporate culture and embody learning and fun into his aggressive plans. Staff of the Virgin Atlantic Airways, for example, reflect the ideals of Branson. It is argued that 'Mr. Branson's presence is felt through the enthusiasm evident in his employees, most of whom seem to be having a better time at their jobs than their counterparts on other airlines.'

Richard Branson's best selling books and his autobiography contain stories of his early business ventures. He began entrepreneurial life growing Christmas trees as a youngster. At 16 Branson started the youth magazine, *Student*. At 21 he set up Virgin Records, signing the Rolling Stones, Peter Gabriel, and Janet Jackson. In 1991 Virgin was sold for close to $1 billion.

New projects are launched with extensive media coverage. The Virgin train's launch party also marked the opening of ticket sales via the Virgin website in February 1999. In November 2003, over 1,000 gold members of Virgin Atlantic's Flying Club attended a party in central London to celebrate the launch of Virgin's Upper Class Suite.

The Management Centre of Europe says 'Virgin is one of many companies that fits the prototype of a business which can benefit from empowerment strategies. Employees work closely with customers, innovation is critical, the environment and processes are changing rapidly, and employees need motivation'. It also argues 'Giving employees more input, personal accountability and responsibility can directly turn into reduced labour costs. Many companies have found enlightened work practices result in less safety problems, less turnover, and better efficiency through improved interdepartmental coordinate. A good example here is the low-fare airline Virgin Express which has a fun and flashy public relations image, but also tries to be equally cutting edge in its approach to employees.'

Source: adapted from www.ltbn.com, www.vnunet.com, www.crash.net, www.mce.be.

(a) Using examples, explain the methods used at Virgin to establish a corporate culture.
(b) Explain how the corporate culture at Virgin might affect:
  (i) the business;
  (ii) employees;
  (iii) customers.

# Types of corporate culture

Studies have shown that there are different ways of categorising corporate cultures. John Kotter and James Heskett (1992) suggested that there are two types of culture.

**Adaptive cultures** In businesses with adaptive cultures, managers are able to introduce a culture that allows a business to adapt to changes in its external environment. Such businesses are more likely to survive in a changing environment. Features of businesses with an adaptive culture include:

- a bias for action - employees are encouraged to be entrepreneurial and take risks and managers have a 'hands on' approach;
- the company sticks to 'what it knows best'. It also emphasises close relations with customers;
- the organisation should be lean (☞ unit 80) and decision making should be decentralised.

**Inert cultures** These are businesses where managers all accept the values and norms of the business, which never change. Such cultures promote inertia. Decision making is often centralised. The problems with such structures is that managers can not see problems if the environment changes.

Another way of describing cultures is to look at the solidarity and sociability in businesses. This was proposed by Gareth Jones and Rob Goffee (1998) in *The Character of a Corporation*. **Sociability** is the relations between individuals who see each other as friends. **Solidarity** describes cooperation between individuals which takes place when the need arises or when there is a shared interest.

**Networked organisations** These have high sociability and low solidarity. Examples might be Heineken and Phillips. Such a culture encourages teamwork, creativity and openness. Workers enjoy working. However, discipline may be difficult because of friendships and productivity may suffer. There may also be too much concern with compromise, rather than the best solution.

**Mercenary organisations** These have low sociability and high solidarity. Examples may be PepsiCo and Mars. The culture is about getting things done, now. Targets are set. Roles are clearly defined. People consider: 'What's in it for me' when working. The advantages of this are that a business has a focus. It can respond to threats and does not tolerate poor performance. However, workers only work together if they have to. Also, because roles are clearly defined, there may be conflict over 'grey' areas of work.

**Fragmented organisation** These have low sociability and low solidarity. Examples might be law firms, consultancies or newspapers. This form of culture is best suited to businesses where individuals do not need to work with each other.

**Communal organisations** These have high solidarity and high sociability. Examples might be Hewlett Packard and Johnson & Johnson. They are like networked businesses, but more cohesive and goal orientated, and less mercenary than mercenary organisations. They are concerned with shared values and seek to find ways to support and maintain such values. They are careful to recruit, induct and train employees that have similar values to the business. Leaders are important as they guide the business. One problem despite the advantages of shared goals is that they may stifle individual creativity. There is also a need to recruit those who fit in with the culture of the business.

---

In 2002 BP, the oil giant, had to cut production targets for the third time in a year. Year on year net income had also fallen 13 per cent. It was suggested that at the heart of the problem was BP's corporate culture. The company was accused of entrenched arrogance and of ignoring internal warnings that its goals were unrealisable, and that the businesses had a 'culture of fear'.

Mike Phillips, oil analyst at Datamonitor said 'BP has long been considered the cream of oil stocks, with a decade-long reputation for hitting ambitious growth targets, but a third cut to production targets in eight weeks has injured its reputation'. He suggested that pressure may have been put on business managers at BP and 'some of them seem to have thought it would be a good idea to promise targets that were difficult to achieve'. The company argued that a number of factors had led to it not meeting its production targets, such as project delays and hurricanes in Mexico. It did have contingency plans in place to deal with such occurrences, but did not envisage so many problems. A further criticism was that the company felt that it could 'buck the trend' of declining gas production, whereas others had cut back.

There was a suggestion that targets could be replaced as a measure of performance in future by profitability. This could affect middle managers. They were likely to be the first to feel any wide-ranging shake-up in an attempt to trim costs out of a business that had grown through the acquisitions of Burmah Castrol, Arco and Amoco in the 1990s. There might also be sales of non-core assets, chiefly in Europe.

Source: adapted from *The Observer*, 3.11.2002.

(a) Identify the type of culture (networked, mercenary, fragmented or communal) that might have existed at BP using examples from the article.
(b) Discuss the (i) benefits and (ii) problems to the business of this type of culture.

**Question 2**

# Resistance to change

At times senior management may decide that the corporate culture of a business is not appropriate for the new corporate strategies (☞ units 5, 16 and 17) that it is trying to introduce. One indication of this might be a CULTURE GAP - a difference between the current culture and the culture that managers want.

To what extent can a business change its culture? Some argue that if the culture of a business can be sustained by the strength of management, company stories and socialisation, it should be possible for these to be changed. A new culture can then be introduced. On the other hand, the longer a culture is allowed to develop, the stronger it will become. Beliefs and practices become more widely shared and deeply held. This makes them harder to change. A corporate culture learned over many years can not be altered overnight.

There might be certain **constraints** on a business's ability to change corporate culture.

- Structural and technological issues. A company's culture is affected by factors such as businesses procedures, the way buildings and plant are organised, the type of technology used, and the responsibilities of employees in the organisational hierarchy. It may be possible to change these over time. In the short term, changing technology, for example, may be difficult and costly.
- Cultural change brought about by managers is often resisted by employees. There is often a limit to the amount of change to values and norms that they will accept. Mergers are a particularly difficult time for staff. Familiar symbols, beliefs, values and shared meanings are often disrupted.
- Managers may be an obstacle to change. They may have an interest in keeping things the same. A change in corporate culture may threaten these interests.
- The effects of external factors. The operation of pressure groups or competitors may constrain how a business can change its culture. For example, it might be difficult for the police force to develop a culture which promotes norms of casual dress, rewards risk takers and encourages radical ideas, such as the legalisation of soft drugs.
- Corporate culture and national cultures. Attempts to establish a corporate culture in a multinational firm can be undermined by the strength of national cultures. Geert Hofstede (1984) examined the attitudes of 116,000 employees in the same multinational company located in 40 different countries. He found, for example, that in countries such as Argentina and Spain, inequality was accepted. Managers were expected to make decisions. There was a lack of trust between superiors and subordinates. Workers wanted to be directed by the boss. In Australia and Canada, however, the relationships between individuals at different levels in the organisation were close and there was mutual trust. Employees expected to be involved in decision making.

Corus was created from the merger of British Steel and Dutch business Koninkliike Hoogvens in 1999. After the merger it became the fourth biggest steel company in the world, with market value of £4.1 billion. In 2003 it was worth only 3 per cent of that. The problem was the differences in the two companies, particularly the way that business was done in the Netherlands and in the UK. Under Dutch law, large companies are required to have works councils and supervisory boards. Supervisory boards are independent and oversee the activities of management boards. These are made up of executives who are forbidden to be employees or hold stocks. The un-elected nature of the supervisory board may seem strange to UK businesses. UK management is largely ignorant about the strength of works councils and supervisory boards which can make or break mergers and deals.

The Netherlands also works on consensus. There is continuous consultation and cooperation between government, employers associations and trade unions. It was suggested that it was naive to think that this would sit easily with the UK style of 'Anglo Saxon' decision making from management at the top. A criticism of Corus by UK trade unions was that decisions were not put forward to a supervisory board, as they are in Holland. Instead they were just announced by management. However, the company argued that it is a very decentralised organisation. Allan Johnson, the executive director for HR said 'We don't beam down too much from the head office to out there.' He argued that external factors such as the exchange rate and a loss of customers abroad led to problems, not the internal organisation culture of the business.

Source: adapted from *People Management*, 3.4.2003.

(a) Identify the different corporate cultures mentioned in the article.
(b) Explain why corporate culture at Corus became a problem.

**Question 3**

# Advantages of a strong corporate culture

It is argued that there are certain advantages to a business of establishing a strong corporate culture.

- It provides a sense of identity for employees. They feel part of the business. This may allow workers to be flexible when the company needs to change or is having difficulties.
- Workers identify with other employees. This may help with aspects of the business such as team work.
- It increases the commitment of employees to the company. This may prevent problems such as high labour turnover or industrial relations problems.
- It motivates workers in their jobs. This may lead to increased productivity.

- It allows employees to understand what is going on around them. This can prevent misunderstanding in operations or instructions passed to them.
- It helps to reinforce the values of the organisation and senior management.
- It acts as a control device for management. This can help when setting company strategy.

## Criticisms of corporate culture

It has been suggested that a business will benefit if management ensures that:

- there is a strong corporate culture:
- the 'culture gap' is kept to a minimum and there is a single corporate culture that all people in the business work towards.

Certain criticisms of this view have been put forward.

**Corporate culture and economic performance** John Kotter and James Heskett (1992) researched the relationship between corporate culture and economic performance. They tested the idea that a strong culture improves performance by measuring the strength of the culture of 207 large firms from a variety of industries. A questionnaire was used to calculate a 'culture index' for each firm. They then looked for any correlation between a strong culture and the firm's economic performance over an eleven year period. The research did show a positive correlation, but weaker than most management theorists would have expected. Strong culture firms seemed almost as likely to perform poorly as their weak-culture rivals.

**Different perspectives on corporate culture** There are other views on the nature of corporate culture.

- A business is made up of sub-cultures which coexist. Sometimes these are in harmony, but sometimes in conflict. There may be differences of interests and opinions among different groups. As a result, cultural practices in companies are interpreted in different ways by employees. These may not always be those intended by management. For example, a profit-sharing scheme may be seen as a sign of equality by one group. Everyone gets a share in the profits, not just management and shareholders. Another group, however, may see it as a bribe for employees to conform with the company.
- The main feature of business life is ambiguity. Companies lack clear centres due to decentralisation, delegation and the employment of temporary and part-time workers. Also, new working practices often leave employees physically separated and socially distant. As a result, employees share some viewpoints, disagree on others and are indifferent to yet others.

These approaches are seen as positive, to meet the requirements of the complexity of business life. The way businesses do things can be interpreted in a variety of ways. Values, beliefs, and norms may not be shared between individual employees or between employees and management. The reason why someone does something in the way they do may not be just because management has created a culture that everyone follows. It may be because of other factors, such as outside influences, internal politics, self-interest, the sub-culture of a group, or different individual personalities.

---

Royal Dutch/Shell group, the oil group, believes that managing talent is a matter of 'tugging at the heartstrings' of employees. It argues that young recruits choose companies because of the values, beliefs and the culture of the organisation. As a result, Shell has developed a set of business principles which places honesty, integrity and respect for people at the core of its corporate culture. Shell organises a worldwide survey of all employees to find out how they feel about the company. Michael Osbaldeston, head of Shell Global Learning, says 'The result gives us a clearer picture of how attractive a company Shell is to work for and how we could do better in the future'.

Retaining innovative workers is crucial for the Pentland Group, which designs and produces sportswear such as Speedo and Ellesse. It changed the working environment by incorporating lots of natural light, communal space, coffee bars and a gym into its new building. But it found that this, in itself, was not enough without good management practice. It has just completed a company-wide assessment of its management behaviour. It found that the immediate supervisor is massively influential in terms of people's productivity. 'Good management is fundamental to releasing talented workers to do what they do best and when you do that you retain them' says Chris Matcham, group human resources director.

Source: adapted from Guardian Unlimited.

(a) Explain the features of successful corporate cultures of the businesses in the article.
(b) Suggest possible benefits to these businesses of the corporate cultures they have adopted.

**Question 4**

---

## key terms

**Culture gap** - a difference between the culture that a business has and what it would like it to be.

1. How can corporate culture affect decision making?
2. Suggest 3 reasons for the growth in corporate culture.
3. State 4 ways in which a business might develop a strong culture.
4. Suggest 4 different types of culture.
5. How might corporate culture be packaged?
6. How might corporate culture be communicated?

7. What are the constraints on the ability of a business to change culture?
8. How might national culture affect the introduction of a corporate culture?
9. State 5 advantages of a strong corporate culture.
10. Explain 2 criticisms of the idea of a corporate culture.

# Case study AXA

How does a global insurance company create an effective corporate culture? Deciding on a name might not seem vital. AXA's original suggestion 'Elan' meaning 'leap forward' in French seemed well suited. However, it was then suggested that it referred to a moose in Canada and was dropped.

Cultural and linguistic barriers were just some issues facing the French company Mutuelle Unis (now AXA) when creating a global culture. Today AXA employs 140,000 people across 50 countries after a series of acquisitions of other business, including Guardian Royal Exchange in the UK and Nippon Nantai in Japan. The culture needs to cross language, social, cultural and ethnic barriers. Senior executive vice president Francoise Colloc'h said 'It has been more about taking the best part of each company to try to make that part of the AXA culture, rather than destroying the past of those companies and saying there is only one way - the Unis way'.

The company originally set about putting in place values representing how to treat clients, shareholders and employees. Seven values were identified, as shown in Table 15.1. However, the business found that, because they were devised by the French company, they reflected French rather than global culture. For example, the word loyalty in Japan could be interpreted as committing ritualistic suicide - hari-kiri. So in 2001 employees from seven countries reworked the values. Five new values were identified.

Was this enough to create a global culture? To make it work, staff had to 'live' the values. So staff were recruited against behaviour linked to values. These values were explained at interviews and induction. Appraisal is also based on behaviour of staff and whether they fit in with the values. Staff that do not meet the values are helped with a development plan and performance is reviewed

regularly. Those that can not adapt are asked to leave. Its a slightly 'big brother' approach, underlined by the fact that people have been let go over behaviour and replaced by others with the same values as the company.

Some analysts believe that AXA has done a great job in creating a uniform culture across all businesses. However, others point out that there may still be problems if businesses are acquired in non-western countries. For example, China has largely removed the idea of professionalism after its cultural revolution. So AXA has tried to let individual countries interpret the values. It has also tried to use graphic representations rather than words to show values, such as pictograms.

Source: adapted from *People Management*, 6.2.2003.

**Table 15.1** *AXA's old and new values*

| Old | New |
| --- | --- |
| • loyalty | • professionalism |
| • courage | • integrity |
| • pride | • team spirit |
| • ambition | • innovation |
| • realism | • pragmatism |
| •• imagination | |
| • integrity | |

(a) **Why might the business have needed to change its corporate culture? (6 marks)**
(b) **What type of culture now exists at AXA? Explain your answer. (8 marks)**
(c) **Examine the barriers that may have prevented the new corporate culture being introduced. (12 marks)**
(d) **Explain the benefits of the approach to corporate culture used at AXA for the business. (12 marks)**
(e) **As the business grows in future, discuss the extent to which it will be able to keep its corporate culture in the same form or whether and how it might need to be changed. (12 marks)**

## What is strategy

In 2004 the UK's largest car dealer Pendragon announced a £230 million takeover of smaller rival CD Bramall. Pendragon would double its nationwide chain of franchises to 250 as a result. In the same year Greeting Card Group Ltd, the UK's largest 'value' greeting card retailer, bought a warehouse, office building and 2.7 acres of expansion land in Peterborough to set up a new head office with 100 staff.

These are examples of strategies used by businesses. A business's strategy is the pattern of decisions and actions that are taken by the business to achieve its objectives (☞ units 4 and 5). A business is likely to have a variety of objectives. For many businesses, the major goal is to improve performance so that profits increase. For example, in 2003 *The Times* followed *The Independent* to launch a tabloid version of the newspaper. Official circulation figures reported that this boosted sales of *The Times* by 14,000 copies a day, although others reported it as closer to 35,000. It was the only broadsheet, apart from *The Financial Times*, to increase its readers in December, usually a poor month because of a lack of interest in news over Christmas. The increase in sales was so encouraging that the paper doubled its print run to 150,000.

Changes in the external environment of the business

have led many businesses to rethink their strategy. The success of businesses from Japan and other Asian countries in global markets has led Western companies to rethink their approach to quality, delivery, price and satisfying employees' and consumers' needs. Changes such as the opening up of markets in eastern Europe, the introduction of the euro in 1999 and growing EU regulations are all likely to affect the strategy of UK businesses.

## Planning and strategy

It is likely that the strategy of a business will, to some extent, be a planned strategy. Business planning involves deciding what is to be done, setting objectives and developing policies to achieve them (☞ unit 5). The planning process that a business might carry out is shown in Figure 16.1. It could be argued that businesses go through a number of stages when planning their strategies.

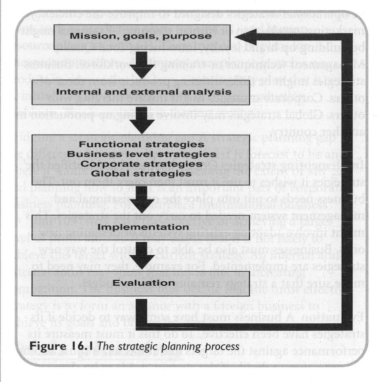

**Figure 16.1** *The strategic planning process*

Identifying missions and goals Businesses have many objectives and goals, the things they want to achieve. A company may want to increase its market share over a period of time or have more specific goals such as achieving a 10 per cent market share over the next 5 years. Companies also have missions. These are the reasons why the company exists and what it is trying to do. They are often found in **mission** or **corporate statements** (☞ unit 4). For example, the mission of EasyJet, the low cost airline service in 2004 was:

'To provide our customers with safe, good value, point to point air services. To effect and to offer a consistent and

---

In 2003 it was announced that British Airways (BA) would install 190 IBM self service kiosks at Heathrow Airport and all British Airways destination airports across Europe. The kiosks are designed to make check in faster and more convenient, whilst optimising space at airports. Customers can use the touch sensitive screens to check in, select seats and ask for upgrades without having to queue at desks. The new system was expected to reduce check in queues, providing a major boost to the volume of passengers that BA could handle at peak times.

The move was part of BA's ceBA business transformation strategy, which will change how customers do business with the airline. BA expected to achieve 50 per cent self service check in by 2005. BA's CIO, Paul Coby, said 'Effective use of IT is fundamental in simplifying the way in which British Airways does business' and that the new machines would improve customer service and achieve greater levels of efficiency. He also argued that it takes less than a minute to check in 'so the benefits for both passengers and British Airways are significant in an industry being driven to increase lead factors while reducing costs.'

Source: adapted from www.ibm.com/news/uk.

(a) Explain the objectives that BA may have had in its transformation strategy.

## Market segments

Unit 19 showed the different market research methods that a business might use. Market research provides a wide variety of information about the people who may be interested in buying a business's products. For example, it might tell a business that a new chocolate bar will mainly be bought by people aged 16-25. It might indicate that older people have bought more of a magazine than younger people in the last year.

Producers may use this information to identify people with similar needs. Breaking down a market into sub-groups with similar characteristics is known as MARKET SEGMENTATION. A business can then target these groups and develop products and services for each of them.

Threshers, the off-licence chain, has in the past made use of such information. Each branch stocked goods which were suitable to the population of the area that they were serving. Branches in towns such as Eastbourne or Cheltenham, for example, had products geared towards the 'older' customer. They were, therefore, more likely to promote whisky and sherry than lager and vodka.

## Segmentation by age

Many businesses pay attention to the age of their customers. Of particular interest is the segment that includes the over 60s as this segment is growing as a proportion of the total population. The marketing of financial services for older people has become popular in recent years. So has a number of other products and service areas, ranging from specialist holidays to the development of retirement housing.

---

Camelot is going to take the National Lottery into nightclubs and bars to encourage more under 25s to participate. In an attempt to inject some interest for younger players, Camelot is to introduce a game in clubs and bars where anyone with a lottery ticket will have their name put into a hat. A draw will take place at midnight and the lucky winner gets a free limousine ride home. Diane Thompson, Chief Executive of Camelot, said 'We know that a key customer group who we traditionally fail to engage with are the under 25s - the 'night owl' crowd. So we intend to take the brand right into their bars and clubs.'

Source: adapted from *The Guardian*, 20.9.2001.

(a) What evidence is there in the article that Camelot is breaking the market down into segments?
(b) Explain why targeting this market might be successful for Camelot.

**Question 1**

## Segmentation by gender

Manufacturers may target either males or females. Some car producers, for example, have targeted women in their promotional campaigns for smaller hatchbacks. Manufacturers of perfumes and related products have realised the growing market for personal care products amongst men. Major brand names such as Armani and Yves Saint Laurent, as well as sports companies, have produced a range of products geared towards males. Mobile phone manufacturers target a growing number of females buying the latest 'technological gadgets', by designing accessories to suit their requirements.

## Segmentation by level of education or occupation

Sometimes a business can segment its market based on how far the consumer has progressed through the education system. The market is usually divided into those who have or have not studied at higher education level. An example might be a magazine aimed at those with certain qualifications. Magazines are also sometimes geared towards particular occupations such as farming. Others are geared towards a type of employee, such as a manager or outworker.

## Segmentation by social class

Markets are often divided by social class. Table 20.1 shows two measures of social class used in the UK. For the 2001 population census, the Registrar General divided social class into eight areas. Classes are based on employment status and conditions. This division is usually used in government reports and surveys. The Institute of Practitioners in Advertising (IPA) divides social class into six categories. These are used to decide which group to target for promoting a product. Because of regular changes in the pay and status of different occupations, these categories are revised from time to time. For example, the Registrar General's classification previously had only five classes.

Research often breaks these categories down even further. For example, AB, C1, C2, D and E are sometimes used to highlight the difference between levels of management, and skilled and unskilled manual workers. The media often refers to ABC1s. It is suggested that some businesses are particularly interested in people who might fall into this category as they tend to have higher incomes and levels of spending. Table 20.2 shows information from a study about the attitudes of people in the ABC1 group to financial services. This could be used by banks, insurance or pension companies to decide which customers to target.

## Segmentation by income

Although linked to some extent to 'social classes' described

**Table 20.1** *Segmentation by social class*

**Registrar General's classification**

**Class 1** Higher managerial and professional occupations
  1.1 Employers in large organisations
      (eg corporate managers)
  1.2 Higher professionals (eg doctors or
      barristers)
**Class 2** Lower managerial and professional occupations
      (eg journalists, actors, nurses).
**Class 3** Intermediate occupations
      (eg secretary, driving instructor).
**Class 4** Small employers and own account workers
      (eg publican, taxi driver).
**Class 5** Lower supervisory, craft and related occupations
      (eg plumber, butcher, train driver).
**Class 6** Semi-routine occupations
      (eg shop assistant, traffic warden).
**Class 7** Routine occupations
      (eg waiter, road sweeper).
**Class 8** Never worked/long-term unemployed.

**IPA classification**

A - Higher managerial, administrative or professional.
B - Middle management, administrative or professional.
C1 - Supervisory or clerical, junior management.
C2 - Skilled manual workers.
D - Semi and unskilled manual workers.
E - State pensioners, casual or lowest paid workers,
    unemployed.

**Table 20.2** *Financial Services and ABC1s*

- More than one-third of ABs and more than three in ten C1s borrow more than they save. Those with children are nearly twice as likely as those without to owe more than they have saved.
- ABs and C2s find saving easier than C1s, Ds and Es.
- Just over two-thirds of ABs, and almost two-thirds of C1s, expect to fund their children out of savings and investments.
- Around one-third of ABs and one-fifth of C1s have bought savings plans, investments or insurance over the telephone. Only three ABs and two C1s in 100 have bought them over the Internet.
- Only one AB in eight, and one C1 in 16, sets aside more than £200 a month to save for a retirement pension, in addition to National Insurance contributions.
- Almost one in five ABs, and nearly one in four C1s, puts less than £50 a month into a pension.
- ABs are less worried than other social groups about the accessibility of bank or building society branches, and so are less worried about branch closures.

Source: adapted from www.researchmarkets.com.

above, income groups can be different. For example, a self-employed skilled manual worker, such as an electrician, may receive the same income as a middle manager. However, because of his or her occupations the two people will be in different social classes.

## Segmentation by religion

Businesses may divide markets by religious groups. Food producers, for example, may specialise in producing Kosher food for Jewish people. Digital television has seen the growth of American style Christian television channels in the UK.

## Segmentation by ethnic grouping

Markets can sometimes be segmented by country of origin or ethnic grouping. Radio stations have been geared towards African-Caribbean groups. Some products, such as clothing or hair accessories, are also geared towards this grouping.

## Segmentation by family characteristics

The features of entire families may be used to segment the market. Examples of these segments include 'young singles, married with no children' (if both partners have jobs they are sometimes referred to as 'DINKIES' - double income, no kids) and 'older singles'.

## Segmentation by political voting preference

Newspapers are an example of a product that is geared towards people who are likely to vote for a particular political party. *The Guardian*, for example, is arguably aimed at Labour or Liberal Democrat voters, whereas *The Daily Telegraph* has traditionally been geared towards Conservative voters.

## Segmentation by geographical region

This might include considering the region of a country that consumers live in and the nature of the region, eg rural, urban, semi-rural or suburban. It may also consider the type of house, road or area of a city that people live in. This method can be especially useful in large or highly culturally diverse markets, where buying patterns are influenced by region. Businesses selling into the EU are likely to break this area down into more manageable segments. Many large businesses selling into global markets have different products for different countries or areas. For example, Nestlé has sold refrigerated profiteroles in France and a fortified drink called Milo with a malted taste in Japan. The Maggi and Crosse & Blackwell soups are adapted to suit different tastes, by varying the ingredients from one country to another.

# Segmentation by personality and lifestyle

Consumers are sometimes classified according to their psychological characteristics. So, for example, sports products may be aimed at those who are interested in 'extreme' sports such as skiboarding. Chocolate manufacturers have identified two categories of chocolate eaters. 'Depressive' chocolate lovers eat chocolate to unwind predominantly during the evening. 'Energetic' chocolate eaters eat chocolate as a fast food and live life at a fast pace. People's attitude to life may also be used to segment the market. Some pension funds are geared towards those who only want investments in 'ethical' businesses. Clothes may be geared at those who are interested in 'retro' fashions from earlier decades.

# Segmentation by purchases

This segments consumers according to their behaviour when purchasing a product. So, for example, consumers may be categorised according to the quantity and frequency of their purchases. One example of this is British Airways, which established an 'Executive Club' to encourage and develop the custom of regular business travellers.

# Uses of market segmentation

Why might a business attempt to identify different market segments?

● The main reason is that it would hope that the information would allow it to sell more products overall and perhaps increase its profit.
● It would hope to be able to gain greater knowledge about its customers so that it could vary its products to suit their needs better.
● It might be able to target particular groups with particular products.
● It would hope to prevent products being promoted to the wrong people which would waste resources and possibly lead to losses.

---

One of the most commonly targeted groups for advertisers are ABC1s. In the past commercial radio was not seen as a useful way of reaching such audiences. However, recently there has been a growth in the number of 'medium' ABC1s which are part of the listenership. During a typical week, 65 per cent of ABC1s tune in or listen to commercial radio. Over a month its reach rises to 83 per cent. ABC1s tend to listen for extended periods of time, around 12 hours a week. They also have high loyalty levels to their favourite stations. On average they tune in to 2.6 different stations a week. Even younger ABC1s, who might be more experimental, tend to stay loyal to one or two stations. This information is particularly useful for advertisers using a mixed media to promote products. ABC1s often avoid TV advertising.

Main listening periods tend to take place in the morning. On a typical week 61 per cent of ABC1 adults tune into commercial radio. 19 per cent listen on Saturdays and 15 per cent on Sundays. Around a fifth of time listened to commercial radio by ABC1s is in the car. Most is at breakfast and when going home.

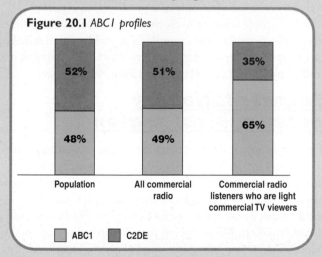

**Figure 20.1** ABC1 profiles

Source: adapted from www.rab.co.uk.

(a) Examine the reasons why commercial radio might be a useful promotional medium for businesses aiming at ABC1s.
(b) Suggest how a business might appeal to ABC1s most effectively using this medium.

**Question 2**

---

Like Coca-Cola, Vimto has a secret recipe based on blackcurrant, raspberry and grape extracts. To generations of northerners it's the taste of their sweet youth. For those who are from the South of England or older than eight, the name Vimto might sound rather like an industrial kitchen cleaner. But it is, in fact, a sweet, fruit cordial that's big with kids and even bigger in the North.

Nichols, the Merseyside based family business that makes Vimto, is launching a campaign with the aim of making it as widely drunk in the South as it is in the North, and as popular in pubs and clubs as it is in playgroups and creches. Vimto is a strong brand selling £210 million in 30 countries. In the North West, men between 17 and 34 are 30 per cent more likely to drink Vimto than any other soft drink. Their aim is to make it more cosmopolitan, appealing, amongst others, to 17 to 34 year old women.

Source: adapted from The Guardian, 29.8.2003.

(a) In what two ways has the market for Vimto been segmented?
(b) How might market segmentation assist Nichols in efforts to increase sales of Vimto?

**Question 3**

● It might hope to market a wider range of differentiated products.

In many cases a business might employ a variety of the segmentation methods explained above. So, for example, a manufacturer of luxury apartments may be interested in segments that included single men or women with no children, in the 30-40 age range, with high incomes that fall into social class AB.

Research into why businesses are successful has shown why market segmentation is so important. One survey, for example, revealed that Japanese businesses paid far more attention to market segmentation than British businesses. A number of the UK businesses surveyed did not see their markets as made up of segments. They felt that anyone in the market could be a customer and that there was little real purpose in 'breaking down the market'. As a result, such businesses were pushed into low quality, low price segments. The Japanese businesses, however, had been able to successfully target more up-market segments.

## key terms

**Market segmentation** - breaking down a market into sub-groups which share similar characteristics.

## Knowledge ...Knowledge...Knowledge...

1 What is meant by a market segment?
2 Explain the difference between segmenting by age and by gender.
3 What are meant by social classes when discussing market segments?
4 Explain how markets can be segmented by types of purchase.
5 What might be the advantages to a business of segmenting the market?

---

**Table 20.3** *Participation in selected sports by young people (aged 6-16) outside lessons by gender, 2002, per cent*

|  | Males | Females |
|---|---|---|
|  |  | **%** |
| Football | 57 | 18 |
| Cycling | 53 | 45 |
| Swimming, diving, lifesaving | 48 | 55 |
| Tennis | 25 | 20 |
| Roller skating and blading, skateboarding | 25 | 22 |
| Cricket | 22 | 5 |
| Walking lasting more than 1 hour, hiking | 21 | 23 |
| Athletics | 13 | 13 |
| Cross country, jogging, road running | 12 | 10 |
| Aerobics, keep fit | 5 | 19 |

Source: adapted from *Social Trends*, Office for National Statistics.

**Figure 20.2** *Participation in sport or physical activity by age, 2000-01, per cent*

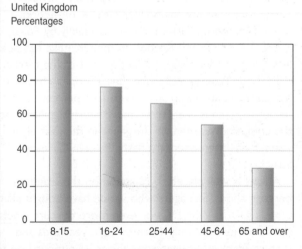

Source: adapted from *Social Trends*, Office for National Statistics.

(a) Using information from the data above, advise a manufacturer of sports leisurewear on the market segments it might target and the type of clothing it might produce.

**Question4**

# Case study The market for trainers

When your trainers wear out what should you buy? Or should you just change them because they look wrong? What are people in the street wearing?

Richard Wharton is buying director of Offspring, a trainer shop where you don't have to pretend that trainers are about sport. He can tell what someone will buy as soon as they walk in. A woman who looks like she would rather be in Prada might be steered towards a pair of white Converse Jack Purcells or Puma Mostros. If she's 'more of a council house girl' perhaps some Adidas Superstars or Puma Sprints. The customer wearing the new parka and split denims will head for Nike Dunks, Converse or Dunlop Green Flash. At JD Sport the Nike Air Max 90 are attractive to 'gangsta rap kind of people, though actually most of them live at home with their parents'.

Nike, started in 1972, has built its business on the assumption that hi-tech trainers would always be 'cool'. The strategy has helped it become a company that does $10 billion of business every year worldwide. It sells almost half of all the sneakers in the USA. However, current fashions are for simpler, cleaner, old-school looks. This trend is driven in the UK mainly by Puma, Adidas, Converse and Reebok. In the UK Nike has been less dominant, with about 18.5 per cent of the market. Adidas and Reebok, reflecting their European heritage, have been relatively stronger with 13.5 per cent and 13 per cent. Puma is likely to be much more significant now the company has seen a resurgence in the past eight years. It has even opened a flashy shop in Carnaby Street.

Adidas is well placed to capitalise on the trend for heritage shoes. Teenagers who would have bought skater brands such as Vans, DCs or even more obscure labels now say these are only worn by eight year olds and skaters. Teens and twentysomethings have moved on to retro shoes with slim soles and simple lines.

Nike, which benefited from a very twentieth-century love of sport, fashion and technology, finds itself associated with the hi-tech trainer at the moment it may have become unfashionable. Nike is fighting back though. The Nike Rift, a split-toed shoe developed for the African Rift Valley runners who ran barefoot but needed shoes for the Olympics, was very fashionable last year. In 2003 Nike launched the Shox XT. Its foam cylinders are supposed to work like shock absorbers, pushing your foot forwards every time your heel hits the ground.

Source: adapted from *The Guardian*, 10.1.2003.

**Table 20.4** *Who wears what?*

| Age | What they are wearing |
|---|---|
| Aged 14-18 | ● Hard-wearing Vans Maverick - come in bold designs.<br>● Prada Sport - eye-catching silver and blue.<br>● Gola Harriers - popular with teenage girls because they come in bright colours. |
| Aged 19-25 | ● Nike Dunks - hi-tech skate shoes based on an Eighties design.<br>● Converse John Varvatos - a designer update to the classic Converse high top trainer.<br>● DKNY Leanores - an elegant brown and cream shoe for young women. |
| Aged 26-35 | ● Adidas Yohji Y3 - achingly hip footwear.<br>● Paul Smith's Target - red retro design.<br>● Puma Sprint - white and pale blue running shoes for women that are too smart for the gym. |
| Aged 36+ | ● Reebok Classic - functional trainers for ageing lads who now value comfort over style.<br>● New Balance Novo - the cute, colourful range originally marketed to US. |

(a) **Using examples, identify the different market segmentation methods in the market for trainers. (6 marks)**

(b) **Choose one method of segmentation and describe the characteristics of trainers that might appeal to different market segments. (6 marks)**

(c) **Explain why trainer manufacturers might want to sell to different market segments. (8 marks)**

(d) **Examine how methods of market segmentation for trainers might be used successfully by manufacturers of sports clothing. (10 marks)**

(e) **Discuss the extent to which selling to different market segments is likely to be a successful marketing strategy for trainers manufacturers. (10 marks)**

## What is a market?

A market is anywhere that buyers and sellers communicate to exchange goods or services (☞ unit 1). They can range from street markets, to markets for cars in many countries around the world, to goods and services bought over the Internet. Markets might be classified in a number of ways depending on their characteristics.

**Geographically** Markets might be **local, national** or **international**. A market held every Saturday in a small town is an example of a local market, as products are sold in the local area. National markets in the UK might be newspapers sold around the UK such as *The Guardian* or *The Financial Times*. Some products are sold in many countries in international markets, such as Coca-Cola and Pepsi, whereas some are sold just in areas such as Europe or Asia.

**Buyer** Goods such as ice cream and services such as DVD rental are bought by consumers in **consumer** markets. But sometimes products, such as machinery, are bought from a business by another business in **industrial** or **producer** markets.

**Industry** Markets might be classified according to whether they involve **primary industry**, such as oil extraction or fishing, **secondary industry** involving manufacturing, or **tertiary industry** involving services. Sometimes markets are classified according to individual industries or products. So, for example, the motor car industry and the computer industry make up different markets within the manufacturing sector.

**Size** Markets might be mass markets, where products are sold to many people in many countries who have similar needs, such as washing up liquid. Or they might be niche markets for specialist products sold to consumers with particular tastes and needs, such as the market for vegan food products.

Products are likely to fit into different categories. For example, a computer business such as Apple is a manufacturer in secondary industry, selling computer products in international markets, to both businesses and consumers. A tanning salon might sell niche market sunbed and beautician tertiary services, in local markets to consumers.

## Market size

The size of a market can be estimated or calculated by the total sales of all businesses in the market. Market size is usually estimated in a number of ways.

- **Value.** This is the total amount spent by customers buying products. For example, it was estimated that fast food products in the UK accounted for sales worth £7.8 billion

in 2002. This included branded fast food chains and independent outlets selling hot or cold eat-in food without table service, or takeaway food.

- **Volume.** This is the physical quantity of products which are produced and sold. For example, global crude steel production was nearly one billion tonnes in 2003, the highest ever. The UK produced around 12 million tonnes. Some estimates of volume are based on the number or percentage of users, subscribers or viewers. This is often the case in markets for services, such as the number of mobile phone users, the number of television viewers or the percentage of households with digital television.

Different markets are likely to differ in size. For example, recreational product markets can have different sizes. Sales of fitness equipment totalled £250 million in 2002 in the UK. In comparison, in the UK computer and video games market, sales of leisure software products in 2003 were £1.26 billion.

The market for all types of drinks in the UK was £41.39 billion in 1999. This accounted for 7.4 per cent of all consumer spending in the UK. Spending on drinks used to be around 10 per cent of all consumer spending. The fall indicated the downward pressure on prices in the drinks market even though the UK consumed a wider range of drinks products than before. The total drinks market was predicted to grow by 11 per cent over the next five years, around half the level of the period.

Source: adapted from www.theaccountants.co.uk.

(a) What was the estimated size of the UK drinks market (i) in 1999 and (ii) five years later?
(b) What might the information for the period up to 1999 indicate about changes in:
   (i) the size of the UK drinks market by volume;
   (ii) the size of the UK drinks market by value?

Question 1

## Market growth

Markets can grow either rapidly or slowly, or they might contract and get smaller. Take the example of the market for recreational products. Sales of fitness equipment totalled £250 million in 2002. There had been high rates of growth for the previous two years. But it was suggested that sales growth would slow down as the market reached maturity (☞ unit 24).

However, sales of computer and video games in the UK had risen to £1.26 billion in 2003, an increase of 7.1 per cent over the previous year. In fact, sales of these products had been rising steadily for 20 years. It was predicted that this trend would continue.

On the other hand the market for handheld organisers was predicted to decline for the second straight year in 2003. Sales were predicted to fall from 12.4 million units worldwide to 11.35 million units in 2003, an 8.4 per cent decline. It was suggested that the fall was due to the rise in ownership of 'converged' mobile phones which combine organisers with phone call facilities.

What factors are likely to influence whether a market gets bigger or becomes smaller and the rate of growth or decline?

- Economic changes. An increase in income, for example, can affect different markets. Rising incomes might help the growth of the luxury car market or the market for high class restaurants. Rising incomes in countries in eastern Europe might increase the growth of products exported to these countries.
- Social changes. Changes in society can lead to a growth or decline in markets. The decline in the number of marriages and the growth in the number of lone parent families has perhaps led to a growth in the market for child care and other child support services, and for housing.
- Technological changes. Changes in technology can cause a rapid growth in certain markets and decline in others. The DVD market has expanded rapidly in recent years, perhaps at the expense of the video market. It has been suggested that MP3 players and downloading technology have led to a decline in the CD market.
- Demographic changes. Changes in the age structure of the population can affect markets. The ageing of the UK population has led to a growth in products aimed at people aged over 50, such as holidays and mobility aids.
- Changes in legislation. The privatisation of the telecommunications market, for example, has led to a growth in a variety of communication markets, including mobile phones.

## Market share

MARKET SHARE or market penetration is the term used to describe the proportion of a particular market that is held by a business, a product, a brand (☞ unit 27) or a number of businesses or products. Market share is shown as a percentage. The market share of a business can be calculated as:

$$\frac{\text{Sales of the business}}{\text{Total sales in the market}} \times 100$$

Why might the measurement of market share be important? It might indicate a business that is a **market leader**. This could influence other companies to follow the

ELSPA, the Entertainment and Leisure Software Publishers Association, announced on 8 January 2004 that the UK computer games market was still buoyant and growing. UK sales of leisure software products reached an all time high in 2003 of £1.26 billion. This was an increase of 7.1 per cent over the previous year. Roger Bennett, ELSPA director general, said 'The UK video games industry sales have been on the rise for the last 20 years' and that 2004 would see the 'dynamic trend continue'.

He commented that 2003 'had provided substantial evidence of the way video games have been integrated into mainstream entertainment culture' and that the industry would 'garner new audiences from every demographic and age group.' Christmas was a particularly strong selling period, with a record 15 titles achieving platinum status of 300,000 units sold. FIFA 2004, produced by Electronic Arts, achieved double platinum status.

The presence of three 'next generation consoles' - PS2, Xbox and GameCube - helped to increase software sales. Sales of older generation consoles and games were still strong as well.

Source: adapted from www.planetgamecube.com.

(a) Describe the changes in the size of the market for video games over the period in the article.
(b) Explain the factors which may have influenced changes in the size of the market.

leader or influence the leader to maintain its position. It might influence the strategy (☞ unit 5) or objectives (☞ unit 4) of a business. A business that has a small market share may set a target of increasing its share by 5 per cent over a period of time. It may also be an indication of the success or failure of a business or its strategy.

Figure 21.1 shows the market shares of supermarkets in the UK in September 2003. It shows for example, that the market leader was Tesco and that three quarters of the market sales were accounted for by the 'big five' supermarket chains. However, care must be taken when interpreting the market share of businesses.

- The share of the market can be measured in different ways. Market share is calculated as the sales of a business as a percentage of total market sales. Sales can be calculated in a number of ways. They might be the **value** of sales, such as £100 million a year. Or they might be calculated by the **number** or **volume** of sales, for example, 6 million products sold each year or 10 million visitors to attractions owned by a theme park company.

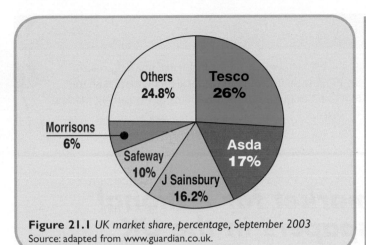

**Figure 21.1** *UK market share, percentage, September 2003*
Source: adapted from www.guardian.co.uk.

- The market and the time period chosen can affect the results. Figure 21.2 shows the market shares of mobile phone handset producers in the UK. In 2002 Nokia clearly had the majority of sales in this market. However, Figure 21.3 suggests that in 2000 in the world market Nokia's dominance was not as great. In 2004 Safeway was taken over by Morrisons, giving the new business a market share similar to J Sainsbury in Figure 21.1.
- The type of product and business included might also affect the results. The results in Figure 21.2 might be different if the market had included all telephones and not just hand held telephones. This would then have included land line telephone businesses. Take another example. In 2000 it was reported that Scottish and Newcastle plc had

over 50 per cent of the beer market. However, in the UK drinks market, beer made up only 40 per cent of drinks spending. So the market share of the UK drinks market of Scottish and Newcastle plc would be less than 50 per cent because the drinks market would include the sales of other drinks manufacturers such as Coca-Cola (carbonated soft drinks) and Tetley GB Ltd (tea).

The Internet broadband market in the UK is shown in Tables 21.1 and 21.2. Broadband services can be provided by cables or Asymmetric Digital Subscriber Line (ADSL), which uses existing copper telephone lines. Internet Service Providers (ISPs) are companies that provide broadband Internet services using one of these methods.

Source: adapted from www.endersanalysis.com.

**Table 21.1** *Broadband connections, December 2001 and August 2002*

|  | Total 2001 | Market share 2001 | Total 2002 | Market share 2002 |
| --- | --- | --- | --- | --- |
| Cable | 196,000 | 59% | 352,000 | 52% |
| ADSL | 136,000 | 41% | 330,000 | 48% |
| Total | 332,000 | 100% | 682,000 | 100% |

**Table 21.2** *ISP broadband connections, August 2002*

|  | Total | Market share |
| --- | --- | --- |
| **Cable** | **352,000** | **52%** |
| NTL | 160,000 | 23% |
| Telewest | 192,000 | 28% |
| **ADSL** | **330,000** | **48%** |
| BT | 190,000 | 28% |
| Freeserve | 7,500 | 1% |
| Others | 135,000 | 20% |

Source: adapted from company reports, oftel.

(a) Describe the changes in market share that took place between 2001 and 2002.
(b) Analyse the market share of BT in the provision of Internet services in August 2002.

**Question ③**

**Figure 21.2** *UK mobile phone market shares, 2002*
Source: adapted from GFK.

- Nokia 55.3%
- Siemens 12.7%
- Samsung 6.6%
- Sony Ericson 6.1%
- Motorola 5.7%
- Others 13.6%

**Figure 21.3** *Worldwide mobile phone market shares, 2000*
Source: adapted from news,bbc.co.uk

- Nokia 30.6%
- Motorola 13.3%
- Ericson 9.7%
- Siemens 8.6%
- Alcatel 5.6%
- Panasonic 5.4%
- Others 26.8%

**key terms**

**Market share** - the proportion of total sales in a particular market for which one or more businesses or brands are responsible. It is expressed as a percentage and can be calculated by value or volume.

Knowledge...Knowledge...Knowledge...Knowledge...Knowledge...Knowledge...Know

1. State 4 ways in which markets can be classified.
2. Explain 2 ways in which the size of a market can be calculated.
3. What is meant by a market that is (a) growing and (b) declining?
4. Give 4 factors that might influence market growth.
5. What is the formula used to calculate market share?
6. Give 3 examples of the problems of measuring market share.

# Case study — The market for national newspapers in the UK

Table 21.3 shows the market for national newspapers in the UK in December 2003. The 'circulation ice age' as it has been called threatens the existence of many British newspapers. Advertising revenue is down in many businesses and sales of newspapers continue to fall. There seems to be no loyalty left amongst audiences who drift from one free CD offer here to a royal exclusive there. And people also have other things to read, not just newspapers. Where are the newspaper readers of tomorrow? They are probably playing the latest computer game on PS2.

But two newspapers are trying to buck these trends. *The Independent* launched a 'tabloid' edition on 30 September 2003. Initially this worked and readers responded. But it now faces stiffer competition after the launch of a similar tabloid by *The Times* on 26 November 2003. Sales of *The Times* were believed to have risen by 20,000 copies a day as a result.

Some commentators on *The Independent* say that its appearance and design is much cleaner than existing tabloids. There are no double page spreads and the use of pictures is more visually appealing. Where are the buyers for this new version coming from? Probably not from other newspapers in any great numbers. But there might be an audience among the young commuter classes who have yet to settle into the habit of reading a particular paper, or in fact any paper, on a regular basis. If this is the case then the rise might be short lived rather than continuous and difficult to sustain over a long period.

What if every newspaper launched a tabloid alternative? Would the retail trade have enough space to stock them? Would it increase the cost to stock them, as *The Independent* now faces, adding greatly to distribution costs?

Source: adapted from *The Guardian*, 10.10.2003, 5.12.2003.

**(a)** Describe the features of the market for daily newspapers in the UK. **(6 marks)**
**(b) (i)** Calculate the size of the market in December 2002 and December 2003. **(4 marks)**
    **(ii)** Calculate and describe the change in the size of the market between December 2002 and December 2003. **(4 marks)**
**(c)** From Table 21.3, assess the changes in the market share of *The Sun* and *The Independent* over the period December 2002 to December 2003. **(8 marks)**
**(d)** Examine the factors that may affect:
    **(i)** the size of the market in future; **(8 marks)**
    **(ii)** the market share of *The Times*. **(8 marks)**

**Table 21.3** *National daily newspaper circulation, December 2003*

| Title | Dec 2003 | Dec 2002 |
|---|---|---|
| The Sun | 3,276,454 | 3,447,108 |
| Daily Mirror | 1,900,155 | 2,031,596 |
| Daily Star | 828,825 | 819,203 |
| Daily Record | 484,894 | 522,388 |
| Daily Mail | 2,299,043 | 2,327,732 |
| Daily Express | 851,199 | 916,055 |
| Daily Telegraph | 888,613 | 923,815 |
| Times | 594,134 | 619,682 |
| Financial Times | 425,387 | 440,036 |
| Guardian | 359,273 | 378,516 |
| Independent | 205,303 | 181,933 |

Source: adapted from Audit Bureau of Circulations.

## Marketing objectives and tactics

MARKETING OBJECTIVES are the **goals** that a business is trying to achieve through its marketing. A business might have a number of marketing objectives.

**Growth** A business might want to increase sales, revenue, profit and market share (☞ unit 21) through marketing. It might be able to increase its revenue by selling more products. Or it might be able to charge a higher price. Both should lead to higher profits. So might launching new products. Businesses aiming to grow often attempt to create a **competitive advantage** over their rivals (☞ unit 5). Marketing can help a business to do this. Examples of businesses that have grown rapidly as a result of marketing include the low cost flight companies EasyJet and Ryanair.

**Maintaining sales and market share** A business may attempt to prevent losses and declining sales, and maintain market share, through its marketing. There are reasons why a business might do this.

● When a new product is launched. New products often require marketing and promotion to break into the market and for sales to take off.
● To develop over the long term. Some products have very long life cycles (☞ unit 24) such as the Mini motor car and Heinz Beans. They have sold continuously over many years as a result of marketing extension strategies designed to maintain sales. Extension strategies are often used in the mature stage of the product life cycle to prevent a decline in sales.

**Product differentiation** It is possible to **differentiate** products from those of competitors by changing the marketing mix (☞ unit 23), such as charging a lower or higher price, changing the packaging, design and ingredients of the product, advertising and other forms of promotion, or selling the product in different types of retailer. Examples might be the change in the name and advertising of the sweets Opal Fruits to Starburst or the setting up of a website by BA to sell flights through the Internet.

**Product introduction and innovation** The marketing objective of a business might be to launch new products onto the market. Market research could have indicated that this product would be successful. Some businesses introduce products regularly, such as new versions of computer software and games. Car producers regularly introduce newer versions of cars to replace older models. For example, the Ford Mondeo replaced the Sierra and the Ford Focus replaced the Escort. Some products, however, are genuinely new and innovative. It might be that new technology has created a new product or research has found a new medicine, for example.

**Consumer knowledge and satisfaction** Consumers need to know what products are available from businesses. They also need to be happy about the products they buy. Businesses which have satisfied consumers are more likely to gain brand loyalty (☞ unit 27).

A company's marketing objectives will be influenced by the corporate aims and objectives of the business (☞ unit 4). For example, the aim of a DVD and video rental chain might be to become the most well known name in the UK. Its objective might be to increase sales turnover by 20 per cent over 2 years to achieve this. So its marketing objectives could be to spend an extra £1 million on promotion to teenagers in magazines and product 'tie-ins' to make them more aware of the service.

There is a relationship between the different marketing objectives. For example, in the early 1990s Adidas found its market share under threat in the European sports shoe market. This was a partly as a result of a successful

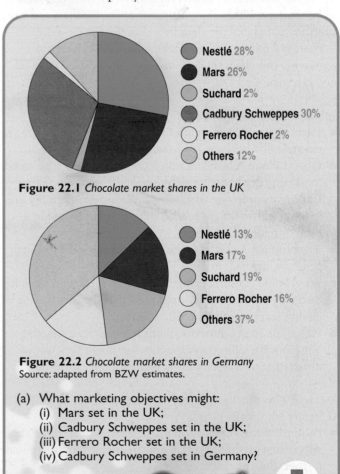

**Figure 22.1** *Chocolate market shares in the UK*

- Nestlé 28%
- Mars 26%
- Suchard 2%
- Cadbury Schweppes 30%
- Ferrero Rocher 2%
- Others 12%

**Figure 22.2** *Chocolate market shares in Germany*
Source: adapted from BZW estimates.

- Nestlé 13%
- Mars 17%
- Suchard 19%
- Ferrero Rocher 16%
- Others 37%

(a) What marketing objectives might:
   (i) Mars set in the UK;
   (ii) Cadbury Schweppes set in the UK;
   (iii) Ferrero Rocher set in the UK;
   (iv) Cadbury Schweppes set in Germany?

**Question 1**

promotional campaign by Nike. Adidas attempted to regain market share by its own marketing campaign, with the objective of differentiating its product. It promoted its trainers as having 'street credibility'. After the year 2000, Adidas launched a number of product ranges with a 'retro' 1970s look in an attempt to increase sales and win market share.

There is also a relationship between the marketing objectives of a business and its MARKETING TACTICS. Marketing tactics are short term, small scale methods a business might use to achieve its marketing objectives. For example, a furniture business with the objective of increasing sales revenue after Christmas might have a 30 day offer where customers can choose a free chair with any three seater sofa they buy.

## Constraints on marketing objectives

It is argued that the marketing objectives a business sets should be SMART in the same way as the overall objectives of the business (☞ unit 4). They should be **specific**, stating exactly what is trying to be achieved, able to be **measured** to decide if they have been achieved, which usually involves setting **targets**, **agreed** by everyone involved, **realistic** and able to be achieved within the constraints of the business and **time specific**, stating exactly when they should be achieved.

There is a number of constraints that could affect the marketing objectives set by a business. They can be internal and external.

**Internal** These include the following.
● Finance. It may be difficult to launch new products, for example, if a business lacks funds.
● Organisation. A business which does not have a specialised marketing department might have a different marketing strategy from to one which does. A business operating in many countries might market differently from one in a local or national market.
● The product. A product with a poor image is unlikely to generate increases in sales.
● Price. Some consumers might expect to see a high price for 'luxury' products or they might feel that they are lacking in quality and buy other products instead.
● Place. The channels of distribution can affect marketing. For example, selling over the Internet might be a way of differentiating a service or increasing sales.

**External** These include the following, sometimes called PEST-G factors (☞ unit 31).
● Political factors. Legislation might restrict the type of advertising used for a product in an attempt to differentiate it from those of rivals.
● The economy. Increases in consumer spending, falls in interest rates (☞ unit 97) and low inflation (☞ unit 98) can all improve the chances of a business increasing its

sales and profit. An increase in the number of new businesses may reduce the market share of a company that is dominant.
● Social factors. Changes in tastes can affect spending by consumers. Fashionable products can often increase sales rapidly.
● Technology. New products may be created as technology develops. The Internet has also helped to increase consumer awareness of products.
● Green or environmental factors. These can often restrict the type of product that a business produces, such as the development of businesses selling managed wood as an alternative to other wood or plastic products.
These factors are often found by carrying out a

---

In 2004 Kodak announced it would cease production of traditional 35 mm cameras in the US and Europe at the end of the year. Sales in America fell below 8 million in 2003, a 20 per cent fall since 2002. The decision was based largely on the runaway success of digital cameras. Sales of film for traditional cameras had fallen by £2 billion in two years.

Kodak was betting its future on digital photography, printing and health imaging. The President of Kodak's digital and film imaging systems said 'We will focus our film investments on opportunities that provide faster and attractive returns'. But Kodak did not intend to halt production of traditional cameras totally. There were plans to expand manufacturing in Asia, Latin America and Eastern Europe where demand was still growing. It would also continue to produce disposable 35 mm cameras.

Kodak also announced plans to cease production of its Advanced Photo System cameras, launched in 1996, which gave wide shot capability. Demand had failed to live up to expectations.

Digital cameras are now outselling traditional cameras. Previously they had been more expensive, produced poorer quality pictures and needed large amounts of battery power. However, the quality of digital cameras sold for less than £200 has now improved greatly. Statistics show that only 14 per cent of pictures taken on digital cameras are printed. The rest are downloaded, emailed or deleted.

Supporters of traditional cameras argue that their photographs are still superior to those of digital cameras, particularly in the depth of colour.

Source: adapted from the *Daily Mail*, 14.1.2004.

(a) Carry out a marketing audit of Kodak to identify the (i) internal factors and (b) external factors affecting its marketing objectives.

Question 2

MARKETING AUDIT. This is an analysis of the internal organisation and procedures of the business and the external factors which affect its marketing decisions. It will also help to identify the strengths, weaknesses, opportunities and threats faced by the business, called SWOT analysis (☞ unit 31).

## Changing objectives into strategy

Figure 22.3 shows the stages involved in developing marketing strategies from marketing objectives.

- The first three stages involved in the process help the business to set its **marketing objectives**. It is important that the marketing objectives fit in with the overall corporate aims and objectives of the organisation to prevent conflict. A marketing audit and SWOT analysis will help to decide achievable and feasible marketing objectives.
- The business can then decide what **marketing strategies** to use to achieve its marketing objectives. Some of the marketing strategies that a business might use are explained in the rest of this unit.
- The business will then carry out it marketing strategies.
- Having carried out its marketing strategies, a business must evaluate how effective they have been. This review will affect future corporate aims and objectives, marketing objectives and marketing strategies set by the business.

The process of using marketing planning, marketing strategies and marketing budgets is explained in detail in units 31-33.

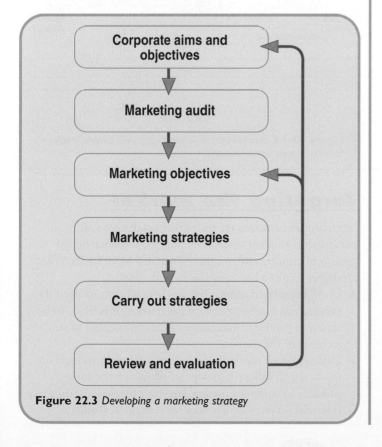

**Figure 22.3** *Developing a marketing strategy*

Corporate aims and objectives

Marketing audit

Marketing objectives

Marketing strategies

Carry out strategies

Review and evaluation

## Marketing strategies

MARKETING STRATEGIES are the approaches taken by a business to help it achieve its objectives. A business can have a number of different strategies.

**Competitive strategies** These are strategies which allow a business to compete more effectively with competitors. A business might try to differentiate its products from those of rivals. Or it might attempt to target a particular market segment. Or it might try to be the lowest cost organisation in the market.

**Growth strategies** These are strategies which try to increase sales. The Ansoff Matrix is a useful model to analyse these strategies (☞ unit 32). There are four strategies a business might use.

- **Market penetration or expansion** involves expanding sales of existing products in existing markets. A business would hope to increase the brand loyalty of its existing customers and persuade people buying other products to change. Examples of penetration might be the growth of Nokia phones or Tesco supermarket becoming the market leaders in the UK in their markets.
- **Product development** is the introduction of new products to existing markets. An example might be the introduction of a tabloid version of *The Times* and *The Independent* newspapers.
- **Market development** is where a business markets existing products in new markets. A business might decide to market a product to a new **segment** of the market (☞ unit 20), such as a different age group, type of user or country. An example might be the introduction in the UK of the Spanish retail clothes chain Zara.
- **Entry into new markets** involves new products developed for new markets. A business might decide to market a new product aimed specifically at a new market. They are likely to be genuinely new products, such as the introduction of MP3 players or DVD machines.

**Market positioning** MARKETING POSITIONING takes into account the views and perceptions that consumers have about products. To make a choice from a vast number of products, consumers categorise products according to a range of factors, such as quality, status or value for money. These categories define the products' position.

Businesses know that consumers position products in relation to those of competitors. There can be a 'pecking order' or 'product ladder'. Products might be **market leaders**. They are usually the main selling product and decisions on prices and promotion are often followed by other products, known as **market followers**.

Businesses use various methods to place their products in the desired position in consumers' eyes. For example, in the food and drinks market a business might stress products':

- benefits, such as the warmth of 'Ready Break' breakfast cereal or the low fat and low calories of 'Special K';
- UNIQUE SELLING POINT or PROPOSITION, such as the minerals and herbs in Purdey's drinks which are designed to give energy;
- attributes, such as Flora Pro-active and Benecol which emphasise reductions in cholesterol. Attributes are also important for technical products, such as mobile phones or computers, where consumers need information about such factors as memory to make a decision;
- origin, for example in the beer market Castlemaine emphasises it is from Australia while Boddingtons stresses it is from Manchester;
- luxury, such as Thorntons chocolates.

As markets and consumers' tastes change a business may try to REPOSITION its product. This can involve changing the image of the product, its features or its target market. For example, Lucozade was changed from a drink which people took when they were ill to one used by sports people.

In January 2004 Wall's announced it was to launch 'diet' versions of its top selling ice cream brands, such as Magnum and Carte d'Or. This was in response to the decision by many parents to ban their children from eating ice cream, following a number of recent surveys showing the relationship between eating fatty foods and obesity. It was argued that over a third of youngsters aged 2-15 were overweight and one in six were clinically obese.

Ice cream was facing an image crisis and in danger of being placed in the same category as other perceived junk foods such as burgers, fries and crisps. The diet versions of Magnum would cut the fat content from 17 per cent to 11.7 per cent and Carte d'Or from 5 per cent to less than 2.5 per cent.

The chairman of Unilever Ice Cream and Frozen Food, the makers of Wall's Magnums and Carte d'Or said 'One of the great myths is that you can't sell diet ice cream. We are going to debunk that. About 20 per cent of our total ice cream portfolio will be changed in a significant way.' He also added 'We will get a competitive advantage' and that 'We are moving to a higher unsaturated fat profile. We want to be beyond reproach.'

Source: adapted from *The Daily Mail*, 22.1 2004.

(a) Explain Wall's strategy using (a) the Ansoff Matrix and (b) market positioning.
(b) Examine the reasons why the business might be following these marketing strategies.

## Market mapping

A useful method for analysing the position of a product in relation to other products in the market is market mapping. PERCEPTUAL or MARKET MAPS show the position of a variety of products in a market based on the **perceptions of customers** rather than businesses. The information used to position products within a map may be found by market research.

Perceptual maps show two attributes of products. Figure 22.4 shows a perceptual map of men's clothes shops drawn from a survey of customers in Merseyside and Lancashire. It shows shops which people perceive have large numbers of younger customers and charge lower prices, such as Top Shop, shops which customers feel have more highly priced adult men's clothes, such as Ted Baker, and shops with moderately priced clothes aimed at older customers, such as Greenwoods.

The business can then use this to decide where to position its own products. For example, a new business might decide to aim at younger customers. Or a business might reposition itself, for example, charging higher prices and changing its products to appeal to more older customers.

**Figure 22.4** *A possible perception map of men's clothes retailers* Source: independent survey.

## Targeting the market

Sometimes businesses try to market products to all consumers. At other times they might choose particular groups to concentrate on, their TARGET MARKETS. What strategies might a business use in each case?

- **Undifferentiated marketing** is where a business aims its products at most sections of the market. It is likely to be suited to products that cannot be differentiated to suit sections of the market.
- **Differentiated marketing** is where different products are marketed to different groups of people or the same product by different means. For example, some banks have financial services which vary for teenagers, students,

businesses and retired couples or online, telephone and branch banking.

● **Concentrated marketing** is where a business focuses on a certain section of the market. An example might be a product that is available only to certain people, such as an under 26 European student rail pass.

Some businesses are trying to move away from undifferentiated marketing strategies to better target consumer needs. Milk, for example, has in the past been mainly marketed in an undifferentiated way. There was little choice other than pasteurised or sterilised. Today milk is differentiated according to fat level, such as full fat, semi-skimmed or skimmed, or by source, such as cows milk, goats milk or soya.

A business might make use of CONSUMER PROFILES to target the market. This is information which tells a business about consumers of a particular product and their characteristics. It might include where they live, how old they are, whether they are male or female, how much they earn or their lifestyle. For example, in the UK 50 per cent of cinema goers are age 15-24. Cinemas might target this age group when deciding which films to show.

Identifying the target market can be more complicated. Sometimes the buyer might not be the main influence on the choice of product. An increasing example of this is the effect of PESTER POWER. This is where children constantly 'nag' to persuade their parents to purchase products. They might be the latest brand of clothing that is worn by their friends at school, buying Sky television and its many channels or a fast food burger meal when shopping. It has been suggested by some researchers in the UK that pester power results in a

---

Kids are a major driving force in decisions to buy. And it's not just toys. They voice demanding opinions in everything including computers, television sets, vehicles and holiday destinations. More than 30 per cent of parents surveyed by Cartoon Network and global research body NFO among 3,218 kids aged aged 7-14 said that their children would accompany them to go and buy electronic and non-electronic durables. The survey also showed that pester power had increased in areas like toothpaste, toothbrushes and hair shampoo. Important features that influence children include appealing advertisements and free gifts. Musical adverts and star studded adverts have had a heavy influence on them too. Their main television favourites are cartoons, sports programmes and movies.

Source: adapted from www.chenaibest.com.

(a) Explain how consumer profiles might be useful to businesses selling computers and television sets using examples from the article.
(b) How might the information in the article affect the choice of target market of these businesses?

---

purchase in around two-thirds of cases.

## Mass vs niche marketing

MASS MARKETING is similar to undifferentiated marketing. A business will offer almost the same products to all consumers and promote them in almost the same way. Examples of products that might be mass marketed include Coca-Cola and Microsoft computer software.

Mass marketing has a number of features and benefits. Products are usually sold to large number of consumers. They may also be marketed in many different countries, known as **global marketing**. This means that businesses can manufacture large quantities and the average costs can be reduced as the business gains economies of scale (☞ unit 81).

However, there can be problems. It is often expensive to set up production facilities to provide mass marketed products. Such products also face competition in parts of the market from producers who might be more effective by targeting market segments. So mass marketing does not necessarily guarantee profitable products.

NICHE MARKETING involves a business aiming a product at a particular, often tiny, segment of a market. It is the opposite of mass marketing, which involves products being aimed at whole markets rather than particular parts of them. Tie Rack and Classic FM are both examples of attempts to exploit niche markets.

Why do firms attempt this type of marketing?

● Small firms are often able to sell to niche markets which have been either overlooked or ignored by other firms. In this way, they are able to avoid competition in the short run at least.
● By targeting specific market segments, firms can focus on the needs of consumers in these segments. This can allow them to gain an advantage over firms targeting a wider market.

There is, however, a number of problems with niche marketing. These include the following.

● Firms which manage successfully to exploit a niche market often attract competition. Niche markets, by their very nature, are small and are often unable to sustain two or more competing firms. Large businesses joining the market may benefit from economies of scale which small firms are unable to achieve.
● Many small firms involved in niche marketing have just one product aimed at one small market. This does not allow a business to spread its risks in the way that a business producing many goods might be able to.
● Because niche markets contain small numbers of consumers, they tend to be faced by bigger and more frequent swings in consumer spending than larger markets. This may mean a rapid decline in sales following an equally rapid growth in sales.

# key terms

**Consumer profiles** - statistical information about consumers of a particular product and their characteristics

**Marketing audit** - an analysis of the internal organisation and procedures of the business and the external factors which affect its marketing decisions.

**Marketing objectives** - goals that a business attempts to achieve through its marketing.

**Marketing positioning** - the view consumers have about factors such as the quality, value for money and image of the product relative to those of competitors.

**Marketing strategies** - the goals that a business is trying to achieve through its marketing.

**Marketing tactics** - the short term, small scale methods a business can use to achieve its marketing objectives.

**Mass marketing** - the marketing of a product to all possible consumers in the same way.

**Niche marketing** - the marketing of products to a particular, small segment of the market.

**Unique selling point or proposition** - the aspects of a product that make it unique to others.

**Repositioning** - an attempt to change the views of consumers about a product relative to its competitors.

**Perceptual or market maps** - diagrams showing two characteristics of a product in relation to those of other products in the market.

**Pester power** - the constant requesting by one group of another to buy products. It often applies to children 'nagging' parents to make purchases.

**Target market** - the consumers which businesses choose to concentrate their selling efforts on.

## Knowledge...Knowledge...Knowledge...Knowledge...Knowledge...Knowledge...Know

1. Identify 5 marketing objectives.
2. What else must marketing objectives fit in with?
3. Explain the difference between an internal and external marketing audit.
4. State 3 types of marketing strategy.
5. What is meant by (a) PEST-G factors and (b) SMART marketing objectives?
6. Identify the 4 types of strategy used in the Ansoff Matrix.
7. What does a perception map tell a business about its products?
8. Explain the difference between differentiated and undifferentiated marketing.
9. Explain the difference between mass and niche marketing.
10. Why might a business concentrate on a niche market?

# Case study Recovery Kitchens Ltd

Recovery Kitchens Ltd is owned and run by Elle Jeffers and Arturo Vasques. The business manufactures kitchens using recycled and reclaimed wood. It sells mainly to two types of customer - those who are concerned about the environment and want to see wood recycled rather than destroyed, and those who want a genuinely 'old' looking and aged kitchen to fit in with the style of their house. The business operates from a workshop in the North West of England which has enough space for its current needs but little room for expansion.

The kitchens do not come cheap. There is a tremendous amount of work involved in reclaiming old wood and making it suitable for production. Sources of wood have to be found. The wood has to be sanded, prepared and recut. Sometimes wood that has been bought turns out not to be suitable.

The business has been operating for about three years and now has a strong loyalty from customers who want this type of product. They tell their friends, who also buy kitchens. And sales have started to pick up in other areas of the country, particularly East Anglia, where the style of kitchen suits a great deal of older housing which is relatively cheaper than nearer to London.

Recovery Kitchens Ltd has been thinking of making some changes. It is concerned about its long term position. It is facing competition from some local businesses that offer cheaper pine products which can look very similar to reclaimed wood kitchens or more customers wanting kitchens for older properties. It is also considering whether it should reduce its price a little. It has asked local people for their views on the prices charged by some kitchen manufacturers and their knowledge of the company name. This produced the perceptual map in Figure 22.5.

The business is concerned about whether it will have the finance to buy the managed wood. It might have to borrow, and interest rates look set to rise.

Source: adapted from independent research.

expensive 'Shaker - type' kitchens which have a simple style and traditional feel.. And it feels that it can take the idea of the environmental image of the business further by making kitchens from managed wood. This is wood where the supplier guarantees to replant trees for all those cut down. Recovery Kitchens Ltd can then use this in its promotion to further enhance its green image and offer something a little different to

**(a) What are the target markets of the business? (4 marks)**

**(b) Explain the internal and external factors that might affect the business. (12 marks)**

**(c) Explain why the business might be said to be operating in a niche market. (8 marks)**

**(d) Examine the possible objectives of the business in moving to managed wood kitchens. (12 marks)**

**(e) Discuss whether the business should follow its new strategy and sell managed wood kitchens. (14 marks)**

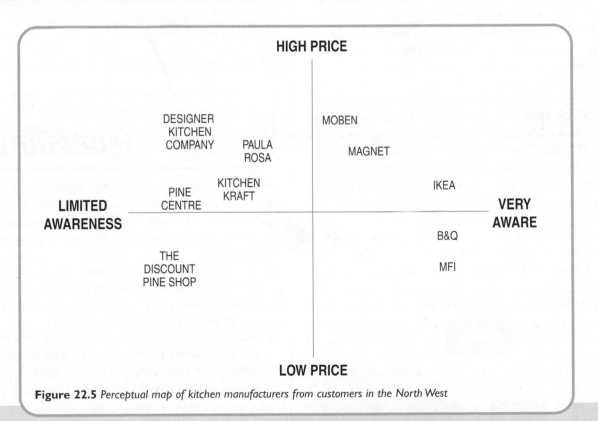

**Figure 22.5** *Perceptual map of kitchen manufacturers from customers in the North West*

## The Marketing Mix

In order to achieve its marketing objectives (☞ unit 22), as well as the overall objectives of the company, a business must consider its MARKETING MIX. The marketing mix refers to those elements of a firm's marketing strategy which are designed to meet the needs of its customers. There are four parts to the marketing mix - product, price, promotion and place. These are often known as the four 'Ps', as illustrated in Figure 23.1. To meet consumers' needs, businesses must produce the right product, at the right price, make it available at the right place, and let consumers know about it through promotion.

Product Businesses must make sure that their products are meeting the needs of their customers. This means paying close attention to a number of the features of the product.

● How consumers will use the product. A furniture manufacturer, for example, would market different products for home use than it would for office use. Products created for the office would need to be sturdy, able to withstand regular use and be long lasting. Products created for the home would need to stress features such as the quality of the fabric, design and the level of comfort.

● The appearance of the product. This is likely to involve a consideration of such things as colour. Food manufacturers, for example, go to great lengths to ensure that their products have an appealing colour. In some cases this means adding artificial colourings to alter the appearance. There are many other factors to be taken into account during the product's design. These include shape, taste and size. Deodorant manufacturers and toilet cleaning fluid producers amongst others might also consider aroma.

● Financial factors. There is little point in a firm producing a product which meets the needs of consumers if it cannot be produced at the right cost. All things being equal, a good produced at high cost is likely to be sold for a high price. Unless consumers are convinced that a product is value for money, they are unlikely to purchase it. They might take into consideration factors such as the quality of the product or **after sales service**.

**Figure 23.1** *Elements of the marketing mix*

```
                    MARKETING
                       MIX
        ┌──────────┬───────────┬──────────┐
    PRODUCT      PRICE       PLACE     PROMOTION
  Appearance   Cost based   Retailers  Advertising
  Function     Competitor   Wholesalers Sales promotion
  Cost         based        Distribution Personal selling
               Consumer based
```

In 2001 JJB, the sports and fitness wear retailer was pumping up sales. David Whelan, the Chairman of JJB, said sales had been supported by special, selective offers and advertising campaigns. JJB's product policy is to stock the main brands such as Nike, Reebok and Adidas alongside a selection of secondary brands like Patrick and Lotto. Mr Whelan said 'JJB believes that it will maintain its current market leading position by this product policy and by regular, selective promotions.' The company is also closing small high street stores in favour of large out-of-town stores. In 2001 it had 232 superstores.

In 2003 it sold its TJ Hughes department stores which sold discounted clothing. The business aimed to concentrate on its core activities, selling sports clothing and equipment. It also aimed to further open large superstores. A spokesperson said 'Our two-storey sites which have a health club on the ground floor and a superstore above it have been very successful. We will look to expand this concept in the future. We have about 13 of these stores across the M62 corridor from Hull to Southport and there is a lot of scope for growth'.

Source: adapted from *The Guardian*, 6.7.2001 and www.manchesteronline.co.uk.

(a) Identify elements of the marketing mix from the article.
(b) Explain how these elements might help JJB to gain a competitive advantage over its rivals.

**Question 1**

● The product's life cycle (☞ unit 24). After a period of time the sales of all products rise and then later start to fall. A business must decide whether to allow the product to decline and cease its production or to try to revive it in some way.

● A product's unique selling proposition (☞ unit 22). This is the aspect or feature of the product that may differentiate it from its rivals. It may help a business to gain a **competitive advantage** (☞ unit 5) over competitors.

● Market position (☞ unit 22). This is the view that consumers have of a product compared to that of its competitors. For example, a product might be seen as 'up market' or alternatively 'low cost' by buyers.

Price The pricing policy that a business chooses is often a reflection of the market at which it is aiming. Prices will not always be set at the level which will maximise sales or short run profits. For example, a business may charge a high price because it is aiming to sell to consumers who regard the product as exclusive rather than because production costs are high. The way in which the customers influence the pricing policy of a business is dealt with in unit 26. However, factors such as production costs can also influence pricing (☞ unit 38).

Promotion There is a number of promotional methods a business can use including above the line promotions, such as TV advertising, and below the line promotions such as personal selling (☞ units 28 and 29). A business will choose a promotion method it feels is likely to be most effective in the market in which it operates. For example, methods such as '10 per cent off your next purchase' are used with 'fast moving consumer goods', such as canned food and packets of biscuits. National television advertising will only be used for products with a high sales turnover and a wide appeal.

Place This refers to the means by which the product will be distributed to the consumer (☞ unit 30). The product must get to the right place, at the right time. This means making decisions about the way in which the product will be physically distributed, ie by air, sea, rail or road. It also means taking into account how the product is sold. This may be by direct mail from the manufacturer or through retail outlets such as supermarkets.

When considering the marketing mix of services, the 4Ps are sometimes argued to be 7Ps. The importance of the following is also stressed.

- The **people** involved in providing the service.
- The **process** - the mechanisms, activities and procedures involved in delivering the service, such as delivery time of a meal.
- **Physical evidence**, such as the appearance of the environment in which the service is provided.

# Choice of marketing mix

Each business must decide upon its own marketing mix. It is important that the right **balance** between price, product, promotion and place is achieved. It could be argued that as businesses become more market orientated all elements are important. However, at times businesses may stress one or more elements of the mix. The mix a business chooses will depend upon certain factors.

- The type of product it is selling. For example, a business marketing highly technical products is likely to emphasise its products' qualities rather than giving a free good as a promotion. However, a business marketing a product very similar to that of its competitors may wish to emphasise a lower price or use some method of promotion.
- The market they are selling to. Businesses selling consumer goods aimed at the mass market are likely to emphasise the promotional and price aspects of their marketing mix. Firms selling machinery or industrial goods are likely to stress the product itself.
- The degree of competition it faces. A business operating in a competitive market, with many close rivals, is likely to

stress the importance of price in its marketing mix. In less competitive markets price might not be seen as being so important.

- The marketing mix of competitors. Businesses cannot afford to ignore the mix chosen by competitors. For example, confectionery manufacturers lay particular emphasis upon the availability of their products in a wide range of retail outlets. These include petrol stations, newsagents, off-licences and DIY stores. The emphasis here is on place. Any business wishing to compete in this market would, therefore, be unable to overlook the importance of place in this marketing mix.
- The position of a business within an industry. Businesses that are leaders within their industries tend to have a greater degree of freedom over the particular marketing mix which they choose. Such businesses include Nike and Coca-Cola. Other businesses are in less strong positions, but may operate in industries with strong market leaders. Where this occurs the relatively weaker businesses often choose to 'mimic' the marketing mix of the dominant business.

---

Three decades after the launch of the VW Golf it was given the 'nerd treatment' in adverts in an attempt to revive sales. The message is keep buying the iconic car that changed the world. Analysts pointed to a range of problems that led to a near 60 per cent fall in fourth quarter profit of the business. But the major worry seemed to be the prospect of its core model flopping. One expert said 'I think the advertising has backfired. What they are saying is really "we don't need to change". In today's market that is going to cause problems'. Another argues 'the seeds were planted a few years back, around 1999/2000' and suggested that the problem was the poor products launched at the time. All models apart from two showed falling sales in January. These included the Beetle (down 6.4 per cent), the Passat (down 19 per cent) and the Polo (down 40 per cent).

Another problem seems to stems from the price. In the past VW may have had the brand loyalty to charge a higher Mercedes-like premium price in its market segment. But no more. Given the weak market in Europe and the cut-throat competition, particularly from the USA, the Golf was too expensive. You could get a car for 15,220 euros. But there was no radio, air conditioning or other features now considered as standard. If added, the price came to 17,100 euros, compared to 15,200 for the GM Astra. On the first of February 2004 VW threw in air conditioning free and sales rose from 350 to 650 a day. The market has also been more innovative with the development of small people movers. VW in contrast has been conservative, with few innovations.

Source: adapted from *The Observer*, 22.2.2004.

(a) Using examples from the article, suggest the factors that might influence the marketing mix of the VW Golf.
(b) Examine changes that VW might need to make to its marketing mix given the difficulties it faces.

**Question2**

# The marketing mix and the scope of business activity

A wide range of organisations is engaged in marketing activities. Marketing is not confined to well known businesses, such as BMW and PepsiCo, operating in a national and international environment. It is also used by smaller firms operating in local markets. However, the size of a business and the extent to which it operates in the private or public sector can affect its marketing mix.

**Non-profit making organisations** There has been a huge increase in the marketing activities in which non-profit organisations such as schools and colleges, charities and hospitals engage. One of the reasons for this is that non-profit organisations in the public sector (☞ unit 7) increasingly need to compete with other similar businesses for their customers (who are still usually called patients, students, clients or other appropriate terms by these organisations). The funding of such organisations is now usually linked to their ability to attract 'customers'. For example, if a college student chooses to attend College A to study for a course, rather than College B, College A will receive funding for this student and College B will not. This provides an incentive for public sector organisations to attract students. Not surprisingly they have employed marketing strategies and techniques to help them meet consumer needs and gain an advantage over rival organisations.

For many non-profit organisations, particularly those in the public sector, price may be less important as a component of the marketing mix than for other businesses. There are two reasons for this. First, such organisations often do not receive any money directly from their customers. For example, colleges and hospitals receive their money through funding organisations set up by the government. Second, the price which their customers are charged is often set by the government and is, therefore, out of the control of individual organisations.

For charities, pricing is also likely to be a less important element of the marketing mix. This is because they do not have a priced product in the sense that many other businesses do. Instead they rely on donations from individuals and groups.

**Small businesses** For many small businesses, particularly sole proprietors, sophisticated marketing strategies are beyond their means. They often have so much work keeping their businesses ticking over on a day to day basis, they do not get the chance to think strategically about their marketing. Certain elements of the marketing mix may be out of the control of small business owners. For example, a survey by Barclays Bank found that 60 per cent of small businesses depend upon word of mouth to promote themselves. In addition, many small businesses do not have the opportunity to alter the way in which their goods or services are distributed. Thus, the importance of place in the marketing mix may be less.

**Businesses operating in industrial markets** Such firms have other businesses as their consumers. For example, the manufacturers of fork lift trucks do not market their products for use in consumers' homes. Instead, they are aimed at businesses who are interested in buying these products, such as warehouses. The differences between consumer and industrial markets mean that the marketing mix for businesses operating in these two areas may vary a great deal. Whereas the marketing mix for many mass market consumer goods often places emphasis upon advertising campaigns in the media, industrial marketing tends to rely upon personal contacts and the role of personal selling (☞ unit 29). International shows or fairs are important events, where producers can make contact with industrial customers.

**Consumer markets** Many marketing theories and concepts have been developed to explain the behaviour of consumer markets, especially those for high sales, mass market goods.

---

In 2003 Jenny Bodey set up the smallest of small businesses in a single shop. It was a wedding shop in Bootle, Liverpool, called The Bridal Lounge. By Christmas 2003 and January 2004 she had experienced record days of sales. Perhaps this was her choice of business. The profit margins on products in this market are very high. Dresses that are bought for £119 can be sold for £449 and still remain competitive. In the first year sales were predicted to be £56,000 but turned out to be nearer £80,000. She could now easily look at opening a second shop within a couple of years, although she needs to be careful because the area where her current shop is sited has very low overheads.

Jenny also has some advice for others looking to start up. She says budding entrepreneurs should not be too keen to offer discounts and promotions. 'I was giving people £100 of accessories with certain deals, but I've halved that. People don't expect a deal to be so generous. She also says 'I did quite a lot of advertising from regional based wedding magazines to wedding brochures and the local press. If I had a stall at a wedding fair I would take an advert in the brochure as everyone who visited my stall would take the brochure away with them.'

Source: adapted from *en*, February, 2004.

(a) Suggest reasons why the marketing mix of this business has been successful.

**Question 3**

---

## key terms

**Marketing mix** - the elements of a business's marketing that are designed to meet the needs of its customers. The four elements are often called the 4 'Ps' - price, product, promotion and place.

Most businesses operating within such markets tend to focus upon all aspects of the marketing mix, paying a great deal of attention to every element.

**International marketing** Businesses engaged in international marketing (☞ unit 34) will often vary their marketing mix from one country or region of the world to another. Product names, product specifications, prices, distribution networks and promotional campaigns may all be different. For example, car and paper prices are often lower in Europe than in the UK.

Knowledge...nowledge...Knowledge...Knowledge...Knowledge...Knowledge...Kno

1. Identify the 4 elements of the marketing mix.
2. What features of a business's product are important in the marketing mix?
3. Explain the difference between price and place in the marketing mix.
4. State 4 factors that influence a business's choice of marketing mix.
5. 'The size of a business is likely to affect its marketing mix.' Explain this statement.
6. Why might advertising be less important to a supplier of industrial equipment than personal contact with customers?

# Case study Cinemas and the Internet

UK cinema chains are dramatically stepping up their efforts to reach movie goers. They are building up highly sophisticated databases so that they can immediately alert customers when their favourite film actor is next going to appear on the screen. Targeting specific movie audiences is one of the chief preoccupations of the major cinema chains, who are desperate to foster customer loyalty. Recognising the surge of interest in Bollywood movies, Warner Village Cinemas has created a dedicated Bollywood mini website. 'Bollywood is quite a thing at the moment and the Asian market needs to be catered for,' says Sarah Kelly, director of marketing and sales for Warner Village.

Online ticket sales are booming. In 2001 Warner Village Cinemas sold 1.5 million tickets on the net in the UK and the figures are continuing to climb in line with the current boom in cinema attendances. 'It's 200 per cent up. Consumers want convenience and it's our role to make it as convenient as possible for them to book tickets with us' Kelly says.

New media is increasingly becoming a crucial part of the marketing mix. For the release of Spider Man, Warner Village Cinemas offered a free downloadable superhero screen saver and a competition to win tickets to the premiere. For another summer smash, Stuart Little 2, kids were encouraged to download vouchers that they could take to the cinema to claim a model of the plane flown by the mouse star.

Like Warner Village Cinemas, the Odeon chain has seen a huge surge in online cinema bookings and is equally enthusiastic about the potential of new media

and its ability to personalise communications. 'The web is a great source of information and it allows us to speak very effectively to different audience segments' says Luke Vetere, head of marketing for Odeon UK.

Some commentators argue that mobile technology will become increasingly important. This could mean film trailers being sent direct to mobiles with a link to a ticket buying service. This might involve, for example, receiving a picture of Tom Cruise and the times when you can **see** his latest film.

Regular movie goers should prepare themselves for a virtual avalanche of Tinseltown and Bollywood new media marketing. It will be coming soon, as they say, to a computer, mobile phone and TV screen near you.

Source: adapted from *The Guardian*, 12.8.2002.

(a) **Identify elements of Warner Village Cinemas' marketing mix using examples from the article. (8 marks)**
(b) **Explain the factors that may have influenced Warner Village Cinemas' marketing mix. (10 marks)**
(c) **Explain why cinema chains might be placing so much emphasis upon new media as part of their marketing mix. (10 marks)**
(d) **To what extent do you think new media marketing techniques as described in the article would be useful to:**
(i) **small businesses;**
(ii) **colleges seeking to target school leavers? (12 marks)**

## The product life cycle

A business aiming to achieve its marketing objectives
(☞ unit 22) must be aware of the PRODUCT LIFE CYCLE.
The product life cycle shows the different stages that a
product passes through and the sales that can be expected at
each stage. Most products pass through six stages -
development, introduction, growth, maturity, saturation and
decline. These are illustrated in Figure 24.1.

**Development** During the development stage the product is
being designed. Suitable ideas must be investigated,
developed and tested. If an idea is considered worth
pursuing then a **prototype** or model of the product might be
produced. A decision will then be made whether or not to
launch the product. A large number of new products never
progress beyond this stage. This is because management is
often reluctant to take risks associated with new products.

During the development stage it is likely that the business
will spend to develop the product. As there will be no sales at
this stage the business will initially be making a 'loss' on the
product.

**Introduction** This stage is when the product is new on the
market and sales are often slow. Costs are incurred when the
product is launched. It may be necessary to build a new
production line or plant, and the firm will have to meet
promotion and distribution costs. Therefore, it is likely that
the product will still not be profitable.

The length of this stage will vary according to the product.
With brand new technical products, eg washing machines,
compact disc players and personal computers, the
introduction stage can be quite long. It takes time for
consumers to become confident that such products 'work'. At
first the price of such products may be quite high. On the
other hand, a product can be an instant hit resulting in very
rapid sales growth. Fashion products and some FAST

MOVING CONSUMER GOODS may enjoy this type of
start to their life.

**Growth** Once the product is established and consumers are
aware of it, sales begin to grow rapidly. The product then
becomes profitable. If it is a new product and there is a rapid
growth in sales, competitors may launch their own version.
This can lead to a slowdown of the rise in sales.

**Maturity** At some stage the growth in sales will level off. The
product has become established with a stable market share at
this point. Sales will have peaked and competitors will have
entered the market to take advantage of profits.

**Saturation** As more firms enter the market it will become
saturated. Some businesses will be forced out of the market,
as there are too many firms competing for consumers.
During the maturity and saturation stages of the product life
cycle many businesses use extension strategies to extend the
life of their products. These are discussed below.

**Decline** For the majority of products, sales will eventually
decline. This is usually due to changing consumer tastes, new
technology or the introduction of new products.

## Different product life cycles

Many products have a limited life span. Their product life
cycles will look similar to that shown in Figure 24.1. For
some products there is a very short period between
introduction and decline. They are sometimes called 'fads'.
The slope of the product life cycle in the introduction and
growth period will be very steep and the decline very sharp.
Examples of such products might be Rubik cubes in the
1980s and children's toys, such as the Micropets in 2003.
Once consumers lose interest in a product and sales fall, a
business may withdraw it from the market. It may be
replaced with another new product. Sometimes poor selling
products are withdrawn in case they damage the image of the
company.

However, businesses must take care not to withdraw a
product too early. Over time certain products have become
popular again. For example skateboards which were popular
in the 1980s regained popularity in the mid-1990s and the
early twenty first century.

Some businesses still enjoy profits from products which
were launched many years ago. The Oxo cube was launched
in 1910, Kellogg's Cornflakes were launched in 1906 and
Theakston's Old Peculier, a strong ale, was launched in the
eighteenth century. These products still sell well today in a
form fairly similar to their original.

Because of the high cost of investment, car producers often
set product life cycles of 10 years for their models. For many

**Figure 24.1** *The various stages of the product life cycle*

Sales

Development Introduction Growth Maturity Saturation Decline

products life cycles are getting shorter, especially in areas like electronics. In the computer industry, some models and software have become obsolete within a very short period as new versions appear which are more technically advanced. For example, in 1995 Microsoft launched its operating software Windows 95. It was later replaced by Windows 98, Windows 2000 and Windows XP.

## Extension strategies

It is clear from the product life cycle that the sales of products decline, although at different rates. Firms can attempt to extend the life of a product by using EXTENSION STRATEGIES. They may decide to use one or more of the following techniques.

● Finding new uses for the product. Video tape which had previously been used for video recorders attached to televisions was adapted to be used with portable camcorders.

● Finding new markets for existing products. During the last ten years there has been a boom in the sales of sports clothing. This was largely due to a significant increase in the use of sports clothing as fashionwear.

● Developing a wider product range. Lucozade was originally sold as a product to those recovering from an illness. By extending the product range to include a 'Sports' version, a huge increase in sales has been achieved. Lego constantly develops new versions of a product that started out as a plastic set of building blocks.

● Gearing the product towards specific target markets. Mobile phone companies have packages geared to the needs of 18-21 year olds. Banks have accounts for teenagers under 17 which provide cheque books and cash dispenser cards but not cheque guarantee cards.

● Changing the appearance, format or packaging. Coca-Cola is available in traditional sized cans, in glass or plastic bottles, or in mini sized cans. Swatch constantly redesigns its entire range of watches as a means of stimulating consumer interest.

● Encouraging people to use the product more frequently. Manufacturers of what were previously known as 'breakfast cereals' have used promotional campaigns to encourage the use of their products at different times throughout the day.

● Changing the ingredients or components. Many microwave food products are available as 'weight watchers' or 'low fat' meals, as well as more traditional meals. Many cars are now equipped with CD players and air conditioning as standard.

The effect that an extension strategy can have on the product life cycle is shown in Figure 24.4. As the market becomes saturated and sales begin to fall, the decline in sales is delayed by the use of an extension strategy.

It would be sensible for a business to try to extend the life of a mature product **before** sales start to decline. Firms that can predict falling sales from **market forecasts** (☞ unit 36)

may attempt to use extension strategies before the decline takes place, ie in the maturity stage.

## The product life cycle and capacity

Capacity utilisation is the extent to which a business uses the

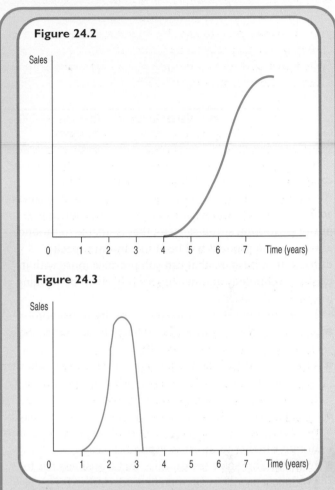

**Figure 24.2**

**Figure 24.3**

(a) Examine Figures 24.2 and 24.3. For each of these, name a product which you think might have a similar product life cycle.

(b) Why do some products have a very long life cycle (greater than 50 years)?

(c) Sketch the current product life cycle of three of the following products:
  (i)   A compact disc by a leading performance artist/group (you will need to specify the name of the CD);
  (ii)  ice cream Mars Bars;
  (iii) Coca-Cola;
  (iv)  Hovis bread;
  (v)   Rice Krispie bars;
  (vi)  Finding Nemo DVD;
  (vii) the Ford Focus;
  (viii) a football strip of a Premier League team (you will need to specify the team).

**Question 1**

**Figure 24.4** *The effect of extension strategies on the product life cycle*

capacity that it has to produce a particular product (☞ unit 84). It is the relationship between what a business actually produces and what it is capable of producing. A business working at full capacity that is unable to produce any more of a product will be at maximum capacity utilisation. A business that can still produce more with its existing technology and machinery is likely to be working at less than full capacity.

The product life cycle is linked to capacity utilisation.

● At launch sales of a product are likely to be limited. So a business will have spare capacity.
● When a product is at its growth stage a business will often be expanding its production and using up spare capacity to meet the rising demand for the product.
● When a product is in its maturity stage a business may be operating at full capacity. If sales continue to grow it must decide whether to invest to expand capacity.
● In the decline stage the capacity that a business has to produce a product will often be underutilised. This is because sales and therefore production may be cut back.

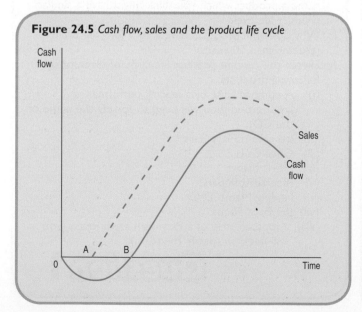

**Figure 24.5** *Cash flow, sales and the product life cycle*

One of the main reasons why businesses seek to extend the life cycles of products is so that they can continue to operate at nearer to full capacity. Products with long maturity stages allow businesses to operate at or near full capacity for a number of years and can be highly profitable.

## The product life cycle and cash flow

Figure 24.5 shows the cash flow of a business over a product life cycle.

● Before product launch a business will spend to develop the product and yet no money is coming into the business from sales. So cash flow is likely to be negative.

Breaking up is hard to do. Has the UK fallen out of love with the KitKat? It was launched as Rowntree's Chocolate Crisp in 1935 and renamed KitKat in 1937. The following year it was the company's most popular product. It first became a national favourite in the war years of the 1940s when the government endorsed it as a healthy, cheap food.

Ever since it has been the most popular chocolate bar in the UK. It was one of the main reasons behind the takeover of Rowntree by Nestlé in 1989. It maintained its supremacy even faced with competition from Nestlé's own Smarties and Black Magic. According to the KitKat website, 47 bars are eaten every second in the UK.

However, in 2003 sales fell by 5 per cent from nearly £123 million in 2002 to £116 million by the end of 2003. 'Saying the business is in crisis is extreme' argued a consumer brands analyst. 'But maintaining its position in the UK confectionery market is going to be a challenge. It's a cut-throat market.' UK consumers eat £4 billion worth of chocolate a year. But analysts believe that saturation point has almost been reached.

Information resources statistics now suggest that KitKat has been overtaken by its rivals Dairy Milk and the Mars Bar. Consumers may also be looking to healthier brands in future. So how will the company react. To some extent it already has with the launch of KitKat Chunky in 1999 and KitKat Orange. And in future it is considering launching lemon cheesecake KitKat, already a hit in Japan and Germany, as well as a curry flavoured version.

Source: adapted from *The Independent*, 15.2.2004.

(a) Using information from the article, draw and label the product life cycle for KitKat.
(b) Identify significant periods in the product life cycle of KitKat using examples from the article.
(c) Discuss how changes made in the future might affect the product life cycle of KitKat.

**Question 2**

- At launch, at point A, a product begins to sell. Cash flowing out of a business is still likely to be greater than cash flowing in, so cash flow will be negative. Sales have yet to take off and a business might be spending on promoting the product.
- In the growth period, eventually revenue from the product will be greater than spending (point B) and so cash flow becomes positive. This is because sales will be increasing and average costs may be falling as output increases (☞ unit 81).
- In the maturity stage cash flow will be at its highest. The product will be earning its greatest revenue.
- In the decline stage, sales will fall and so cash flow will decline.

## Uses of the product life cycle

Why might a business be interested in analysing the product life cycle of its existing products or anticipating the life cycle of new products?

- It will illustrate the broad trends in revenue that a product might earn for the business.
- It will identify points at which businesses may need to consider launching new products, as older ones are in decline.
- It will identify points at which extension strategies may need to be introduced.
- It may help a business to identify when and where spending is required, eg on research and development at the start, on marketing at the introduction and when extension strategies are required.
- It may help to identify points at which a business should no longer sell a product.
- It will help a business to manage its product portfolio - its mix of products. This is discussed in the next section.
- It will give an indication of the profitability of products at each stage in its cycle.
- It will allow a business to plan different styles of marketing that a product might need over its life cycle.

## The product mix

Product life cycle analysis shows businesses that sales of products eventually decline. It is possible to delay this decline using extension strategies.

A well organised business will attempt to phase out old products and introduce new ones. This is known as managing the PRODUCT MIX (or PRODUCT PORTFOLIO). With a constant launch of new products, a business can make sure a 'vacuum' is not created as products reach the end of their life.

Figure 24.6 shows how a business can manage its product mix. Say that a business over a particular time period aims to launch three products. By organising their launch at regular intervals, there is never a gap in the market. As one

**Figure 24.6** *Launching products successively (as older products decline, new products are launched onto the market)*

product is declining, another is growing and further launches are planned. At point (i), as sales of product X are growing, product Y has just been launched. This means that at point (ii), when sales of product X have started to decline, sales of product Y are growing and product Z has just been launched.

This simple example shows a 'snapshot' of three products only. In practice, a business may have many products. It would hope that existing products remain in 'maturity' for a long period. The profit from these mature products would be used to 'subsidise' the launch of new products. New products would be costly at first, and would make no profit for the business.

Examples of businesses that have successfully managed their product mix are sweet manufacturers. Companies such as Nestle produce a wide range of products, including KitKat, Milky Bar and Yorkie, and constantly look to launch new products.

The product mix includes **product lines**. These are groups of products which are closely related to each other. One example is the launch of a range of products associated with a new film. Product lines in this area include anything from T-shirts and mugs to books and CDs for films such as Shrek, Finding Nemo and Lord of the Rings. One of the most successful product lines of all time has been the Mickey Mouse merchandise of the Walt Disney Company.

## Managing the product mix

One problem for firms in planning their product mix is that it is very difficult in practice to tell what stage of the life cycle a product is at. Also, there is no standard lifetime for products. For example, young people's fashion clothing has life cycles which can be predicted with some certainty. Others are less reliable. Who, for example, could have predicted the lengthy life cycles of products such as Heinz baked beans and the VW Beetle, or the short life of products such as the Sinclair C5 - a sort of 'mini-car' introduced in the 1980s.

A useful technique for allowing firms to analyse their product mix is the **Product Portfolio Matrix** developed by the Boston Consulting Group. It is sometimes called the

**Table 24.1** *The Product Portfolio Mix (Boston Matrix)*

|  |  | MARKET GROWTH | |
|---|---|---|---|
|  |  | High | Low |
| MARKET SHARE | High | STAR | CASH COW |
|  | Low | PROBLEM CHILD | DOG |

**Boston Matrix**. This matrix places products into four categories.

- 'Star' products are those with a large share of a high growth market.
- 'Problem children' might have future potential as they are in growth markets, but their sales are not particularly good.
- 'Cash cows' are those which are able to generate funds, possibly to support other products. They are mature products with a stable market share.
- 'Dogs' are products that may be in decline.

These are shown in Table 24.1.

Businesses must ensure that their product mix does not contain too many items within each category. Naturally, firms do not want lots of 'Dogs', but they should also avoid having too many 'Stars' and 'Problem children'. Products on the left hand side of the table are in the early stages of the product life cycle and are in growing markets, but the cost of developing and promoting them will not yet have been recovered. This will drain the firm's resources. Balancing these with 'Cash cows' will mean the revenue from the 'Cash cows' can be used to support products in a growing market. The development cost of 'Cash cows' is likely to have already been recovered and promotional costs should be low relative to sales.

This does not mean though that firms would want lots of 'Cash cows' and few 'Problem children' and 'Stars'. This is because many of the 'Stars' and perhaps some 'Problem children' might become the 'Cash cows' of the future.

The Boston Matrix has not been without its critics. They argue that the matrix can cause businesses to focus too much upon pursuing increases in market share as opposed to, for example, attempting to consolidate market share or improve other aspects of the performance of a product. It is also suggested that the model fails to take account of the way in which products within a business can support one another.

## *New product development*

Planning the product mix requires the continual development and launch of new products. New products are needed to replace products coming to the end of their life cycle and to keep up with changes in the market. This is called **new product development**.

In some industries the need to plan ahead is very important. In the chemical industry, development work is

Lokotronics is a company producing a range of electrical goods. Table 24.2 shows the sales from just four of its products over the period 1996 to 2004.

**Table 24.2**

Sales (000)

| Year | Product A | Product B | Product C | Product D | All products |
|---|---|---|---|---|---|
| 1996 | 2 | 8 | - | - | |
| 1997 | 4 | 10 | - | - | |
| 1998 | 8 | 6 | 9 | - | |
| 1999 | 12 | 3 | 15 | - | |
| 2000 | 18 | 1 | 18 | 2 | |
| 2001 | 20 | - | 16 | 6 | |
| 2002 | 22 | - | 11 | 15 | |
| 2003 | 22 | - | 10 | 20 | |
| 2004 | 21 | - | 8 | 25 | |

(a) From the sales figures, describe the product life cycles of:
  (i) Product A;
  (ii) Product B.
(b) Calculate the total sales of all products in each year.
(c) Comment on the management of the product mix over the period.

**Question 3**

done on products which might not reach the market for over ten years. In the motor industry many cars take over five years to develop.

New products normally pass through five stages when they are being developed.

**Generating ideas** The first stage is when firms generate ideas. Ideas for new products come from a variety of sources.

- Identifying gaps in the market, perhaps through market research. An example of this has been the development of vegetarian microwave dishes by food producers.
- Scientific research. Firms such as ICI devote huge amounts to research and development expenditure. As a result they have developed products ranging from 'non-drip paint' to bio-degradable plastics.
- Creative ideas or 'brainstorming'. Products such as the jet engine have come about as a result of this.
- Analysing other products. When developing new products many businesses will analyse products manufactured by competitors. They aim to include, adapt or improve upon the best features of these products in their own designs. Some businesses adapt their own successful products to make new products.

**Analysis** The second stage is the analysis of those ideas generated in the first stage. There are a number of questions a firm might ask. Most importantly, it must find out if the

**Table 24.3**

| Stage | Number of ideas | Pass rate |
|---|---|---|
| Generation of ideas | 40 | 1 in 5 |
| Business analysis | 8 | 1 in 2 |
| Development | 4 | 1 in 2 |
| Test marketing | 2 | 1 in 2 |
| Commercialisation and launch | 1 | 1 in 1 |

product is marketable - if enough consumers wish to buy it to allow the firm to make a profit. Businesses must also decide if the product fits in with the company's objectives, if it is legal and if the technology is available to produce it.

**Development** The third stage is the actual development of the product. This may involve technical development in the laboratory or the production of a prototype. Such work will be carried out by the **research and development** department. An important part of this process is the actual design of the product. Some preliminary testing may be carried out to find out whether or not the product actually meets consumers' needs.

**Test marketing** Stage four involves the TEST MARKETING of a product. Test marketing occurs when a new product is tested on a small, representative section of the total market. The test market area should share characteristics which are similar to those found in the market as a whole. The benefit of test marketing is the high degree of reliability of results gained. It is carried out because of the high cost and risk of launching a product in a large, usually national, market. Test marketing can itself be costly, but not as expensive as a national launch which fails. One problem is that it allows competitors to see the new product and gives them the chance to take counter-action before a national launch.

**Commercialisation and launch** The final stage is the launch and commercialisation. Here any problems found during test marketing must be solved. The firm will then decide on the 'marketing package' it will use to give the product launch

the greatest chance of success.

At each of the five stages, many ideas are rejected. This means that very few ideas generated in the first stage will actually end up as a product launched onto the market. In Figure 24.7 and Table 24.3, an example is shown where 40 ideas were put forward for a new product. In this company the majority of ideas do not get beyond the first stage. The pass rate at this stage is only 1 in 5, with 4 out of 5 ideas being rejected. After that, the number of ideas which survive from one stage to the next increases as the pass rate falls from 1 in 5 ideas to 1 in 2. At the end of the process, only 1 out of a total of 40 ideas has survived to be launched onto the market.

## Constraints on new product development

There is a wide range of **constraints** on businesses. These will restrict the number of new products developed.

**Availability of finance and resources** In highly competitive markets businesses find that their profit margins are squeezed. This means that financial and human resources are often not available to develop new products. An example of this is in the market for budget fashion clothing. Businesses in this market tend to copy products developed for designer labels.

**Cost** Even when businesses have resources, the cost of developing new products may be prohibitive. The development of products in the electronics market can cost millions of pounds. As technological boundaries have been

In 2000 LG Electronics introduced its famous Internet fridge. For £8,000 owners could check their email, surf the web and watch TV all on the LCD screen on the front of their fridge. LG is still very proud of the product. 'We are constantly looking at ways of developing products in this area,' said Andrew Mullen, LG's New Product Development Manager.

Mr Mullen promises that in future the fridge will be able to connect to a security camera so owners can see who is knocking at their door. LG is also working on variations of the fridge, though it could be some time before they come to market. Mr Mullen does believe, though, that within a decade Internet access and entertainment facilities will be a staple on all fridges other than really cheap models.

Source: adapted from *The Guardian*, 26.7.2003.

(a) To what extent is this product a result of new product development?
(b) Identify the constraints which may have restricted the development of the LG Internet fridge.

**Figure 24.7** *New product development*

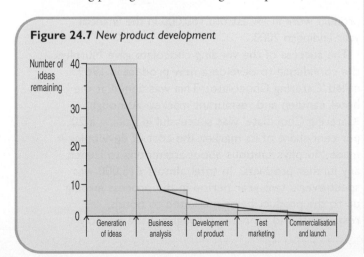

pushed forward, the cost of even modest new product development has risen sharply. Also, in many markets products have increasingly shorter life spans. This means that less time is available to recover development costs.

**Market constraints** There is little point in a business developing a new product unless consumers are prepared to purchase it at a price which can cover development and production costs. Many so-called 'tremendous ideas' for new products have been abandoned. This is because firms believe they cannot find a profitable market for the product. In addition, consumers can be resistant to change. This is often because of the time and effort consumers need to spend in getting to know how new products 'work'. There is also evidence that consumers are resistant to new products which represent a radical departure from existing products. New versions of existing products are sometimes more popular with consumers than totally new ideas for this reason.

**Legal constraints** Firms cannot develop whatever new products they wish. Legislation must be taken into account. For example, a pharmaceutical company wishing to develop a new product must be sure that it adheres to health legislation.

**Technology** The development of technology can affect the type of product or service provided. 100 years ago computers did not exist. Today they are sold in a variety of ways to different businesses. Internet cafes have also been set up which allow consumers to pay for time on the Internet. Technology may also affect manufacturing processes. Developing a new material for use in clothing which it is not possible to produce in the quantities required is unlikely to be successful.

## key terms

**Extension strategies** - methods used to extend the life of a product.
**Fast moving consumer goods** - products with high levels of sales which are sold within a short period of time, such as soap powder or tinned foods.
**Product life cycle** - this shows the different stages in the life of a product and the sales that can be expected at each stage.
**Product mix (product portfolio)** - the particular mix of products which a firm is marketing.
**Test marketing** - testing a product out on a small section of a market prior to its full launch.

## Knowledge

1. Briefly describe the various stages in the product life cycle.
2. Why might a product have a 'steep' life cycle?
3. How can a firm extend the life of its products?
4. Explain how a business can prevent a 'vacuum' in its product mix.
5. What is meant by a product line?
6. What is meant by the Product Portfolio Matrix?
7. How can the Product Portfolio Matrix help a business to manage its product mix?
8. What is meant by new product development?
9. State 2 ways in which a business can generate new product ideas.
10. What is meant by the 'pass rate' of new products?

# Case study Murphy Drinks Ltd

Murphy Drinks Ltd had been producing powdered chocolate drinks for over thirty years. The company was set up as the market for vending machines producing hot drinks had just begun to mushroom in the 1960s. Its first product, 'Murphy's Vending Chocolate', came onto the market in 1963.

Its success in gaining a 35 per cent share of the market for vended chocolate drinks in under five years acted as the foundation stone for the future actions of the company. Ever since 1968, the percentage market share held by Murphy's vending chocolate had never fallen below this 35 per cent mark and, at times, had risen as high as 42 per cent. Sales generated by this product were in excess of £160,000 in the financial year ending in 2003.

The success of the vending chocolate gave Murphys the confidence to develop a new product in 1969 called 'Catering Chocolate'. This was aimed at the hotel, canteen and restaurant market. Although 'Catering Chocolate' was successful in gaining a 20 per cent share of its market, the cost of developing it made Murphys cautious about attempting to launch any further products. In total, almost £15,000 was spent over a two year period in the process leading up to the product being marketed to hotels, restaurants and canteens throughout the country.

It wasn't for another eighteen years that Murphys attempted to launch a new product. This time, in response to changing tastes in the hot drinks market, it developed a low calorie chocolate drink called 'Lifestyle'. This low calorie drink was sold in sachets and distributed mainly through the larger supermarket chains. Despite its past successes, Murphys initially found it difficult to establish a firm footing for this product. However, the last two years, 2002 and 2003, had witnessed a substantial growth in the sales of 'Lifestyle' as consumer and retailer resistance to it was broken down by a series of promotional campaigns. Sales revenue in 2003 amounted to over £100,000.

Encouraged by the success of 'Lifestyle' in the retail sector, Murphys had made the decision in 2003 to launch a product line which it had been developing for a number of years. This was a range of flavoured chocolate drinks called 'Hi-lifes'. There was a high degree of initial interest from consumers in this product range, but it was too early - only six months after the launch - to evaluate its likely success.

Murphys also wanted to develop a new chocolate drink (called Bliss) and had a number of ideas which needed to be considered. However, members of the board of directors were split on this issue. Some were keen to go ahead with the new product development programme for two main reasons: first, out of concern about the falling sales of 'Catering Chocolate' and second, because they felt that now was the time to capitalise upon their recent success with 'Lifestyle'. Other members of the Board were much more cautious. Not only were they concerned about

**Table 24.4** *Cost of developing a new chocolate drink (Bliss)*

|  | Cost per idea | No. of ideas | Pass rate |
| --- | --- | --- | --- |
| Generation of ideas | £50 | 40 | 1 in 5 |
| Analysis of ideas | £500 | 8 | 1 in 2 |
| Development | £8,000 | 4 | 1 in 2 |
| Test marketing | £13,000 | 2 | 1 in 2 |
| Launch and commercialisation | £35,000 | 1 | 1 in 1 |

upsetting their present product mix, but there were worries about the cost of developing this product.

Table 24.4 shows the different stages involved in the development of this new product and the cost at each stage.

**(a) At what stage of the life cycle were each of Murphy's products in 2003? Explain your answer. (6 marks)**

**(b) From the figures given in the table, calculate the total cost to Murphys of developing the new chocolate drink, Bliss. (6 marks)**

**(c) Other than cost, what might prevent Murphys from developing a new product? (8 marks)**

**(d) Examine the possible extension strategies that Murphys might use for Catering Chocolate. (10 marks)**

**(e) Evaluate the extent to which Murphy's existing product mix is well managed. (10 marks)**

## Price and demand

Businesses operate in markets where they produce and sell, or **supply**, products that consumers want and are able to buy, or DEMAND. The interaction of supply and demand can determine the price of a product (☞ unit 93). This unit considers the factors affecting the demand for an individual business's products and the way in which these factors can influence the price that the business might charge.

## The demand curve of a business

Businesses need to understand how the demand for a product can affect the price that they can charge for it. This relationship can be shown by a demand schedule and a demand curve. For most products the relationship between demand and price is inverse. As the price goes up, the quantity demanded goes down. As the price goes down, the quantity demanded goes up. So, for product A shown in Figure 25.1, a rise in price from OP to $OP_1$ (£20 to £40) will lead to a fall in the quantity demanded from OQ to $OQ_1$ (£5,000 to £3,000).

Some products have a demand curve which looks different to that shown in Figure 25.1. 'Prestige' perfumes are designed to appeal to wealthy consumers. A low price might put off

**Table 25.1** *The demand schedule for Product A*

| Price (£) | Quantity demanded |
|---|---|
| 10 | 6,000 |
| 20 | 5,000 |
| 30 | 4,000 |
| 40 | 3,000 |
| 50 | 2,000 |

Table 25.2 shows the demand schedules for three products manufactured by different businesses.

**Table 25.2** *The demand schedule for products A, B and C*

| Price (£) | Quantity demanded(A) | Quantity demanded(B) | Quantity demanded(C) |
|---|---|---|---|
| 5 | 50,000 | 10,000 | 40,000 |
| 10 | 30,000 | 15,000 | 30,000 |
| 15 | 20,000 | 25,000 | 25,000 |
| 30 | 10,000 | 16,000 | 20,000 |

(a) Draw the demand curve for each product.
(b) Identify the types of product which might have a demand curve like product B.

## Question 1

consumers of such a product, given the association made between a higher price and high quality. This means that the quantity demanded over lower price ranges may increase as price rises for such a product. This would create an entirely different demand curve. Figure 25.2 shows the demand curve for such a product. An increase in price from OP to $OP_1$ causes the quantity demanded for this perfume to increase from OQ to $OQ_2$. However, an increase in price from $OP_1$ to $OP_2$ causes the quantity demanded to fall from $OQ_2$ to $OQ_1$. In this part of the curve a more normal relationship between demand and price exists. An increase in price leads to a fall in the quantity demanded. Speculative goods are also said to have upward sloping demand curves. As prices rise people buy more of them, hoping to sell them for a profit at a later date.

**Figure 25.1** *The demand curve for Product A*

**Figure 25.2** *The demand curve for a prestige perfume*

## Other factors influencing the demand for a business's products

Other than price there is a range of factors affecting the demand for an individual business's products. A change in any of these factors can cause a shift in the whole demand curve (as opposed to a change in price which causes a movement along the demand curve). Figure 25.3 shows an increase in the demand for a product by the demand curve moving outwards from D to $D_1$. A decrease in the demand for the product is shown by the demand curve shifting inwards, from D to $D_2$. What factors might lead to a change in demand and how will this affect a particular business?

● The consumers at which the product is aimed may experience an increase in income. The business may be able to sell more of the product at a given price (OQ -$OQ_1$) or charge a higher price (OP - $OP_1$). If incomes fall, the demand curve shifts inwards and the quantity demanded may fall (OQ - $OQ_2$) or the price may fall (OP - $OP_2$). An example may be increased demand for Bosch dishwashers as incomes increase.

● The price of a rival's goods may change. If a rival's price goes up, customers may be more willing to buy more of this product. If a rival's prices fall customers may reduce demand for this product. An example may be a fall in demand for one newspaper as another cuts its price.

● The price of a complementary product may fall. For example, if the price of DVD players falls, people may buy more of these and so the demand for DVDs themselves could increase. A rise in the price of a complementary product may lead to a fall in demand for the related product.

● Changes in tastes and fashion. There has been a change in the type of food products that have become popular in recent years. Examples include organic foods bought from supermarkets, flavoured and specialist coffees from shops such as Starbucks, and cholesterol reducing spreads such as Flora Proactive and Benecol.

● Marketing campaigns. Asda, for example, has pursued a low pricing marketing campaign and is often found to have the lowest supermarket prices in studies. It has supported this with the 'Asda price' adverts on television showing people saving money.

● Changes in population. A large shopping mall such as the Trafford Centre in Manchester is likely to find an increase in demand if offices and housing are drawn close to its location.

● Government legislation and regulation can affect demand. Local pubs and breweries, for example, may find a fall in demand as a result of a reduction in the legal alcohol limit for drinking and driving.

## How businesses use demand curves

Demand curves are useful tools to businesses in terms of analysing and planning their marketing activities. In particular they enable businesses to:

● calculate revenue to be earned for any given price change;
● predict the likely reaction of consumers to price changes;
● predict the likely impact upon revenue of price changes.

## Calculating revenue

One of the reasons why businesses are interested in their demand curve is because it enables them to calculate revenue that may be earned for a particular price that is charged. Revenue can be calculated using using a simple formula:

**Price x quantity demanded = total revenue**

Table 25.3 reproduces Table 25.1 showing the revenue that a business will earn for product A at different prices, given its demand schedule.

**Table 25.3** *The demand schedule for Product A*

| Price (£) | Quantity demanded (Q) | Total revenue (P x Q) |
|---|---|---|
| 10 | 6,000 | 60,000 |
| 20 | 5,000 | 100,000 |
| 30 | 4,000 | 120,000 |
| 40 | 3,000 | 120,000 |
| 50 | 2,000 | 100,000 |

So, for example, the revenue of the business at a price of £30 would be £30 x 4,000 = £120,000. If the price were to change to £20 the revenue would be £20 x 5,000 = £100,000. Thus we can see that a change in price from £30 to £20 has led to a fall in revenue from £120,000 to £100,000, a fall of £20,000.

This process can help a business to identify the point on

**Figure 25.3** *An increase and a decrease in demand*

**Table 25.4** *The demand schedule for Product A*

| Price | Quantity demanded | Total revenue | Quantity demanded (+2,000) | Total revenue |
|---|---|---|---|---|
| (£) | (Q) | (P x Q) | (Q) | (P x Q) |
| 10 | 6,000 | 60,000 | 8,000 | 80,000 |
| 20 | 5,000 | 100,000 | 7,000 | 140,000 |
| 30 | 4,000 | 120,000 | 6,000 | 180,000 |
| 40 | 3,000 | 120,000 | 5,000 | 200,000 |
| 50 | 2,000 | 100,000 | 4,000 | 200,000 |

the demand curve and the price at which revenue is maximised. This can be seen from Table 25.3. At prices below £30 the business actually increases the revenue by raising its price. At prices above £40 revenue falls as prices are increased. The business earns most revenue between £30 and £40.

It is also possible to show the effect of changes in demand on revenue. Table 25.4 shows the effect on Product A's revenue of an increase in demand of 2,000 at each price level.

## *Price sensitivity*

All businesses are likely to be concerned about the sensitivity of the demand for their products to price changes. In other words, they will want to predict what will happen to the quantity demanded of their product if there is a change in price. The sensitivity of quantity demanded to changes in price is known as the PRICE ELASTICITY OF DEMAND (PED). It can be calculated using the following formula:

$$PED = \frac{\text{Percentage change in quantity demanded}}{\text{Percentage change in price}}$$

or

$$\frac{\text{Change in quantity demanded}}{\text{Original quantity demanded}} \div \frac{\text{change in price}}{\text{original price}}$$

**Inelastic demand** A business selling its product in a particular market may face the demand schedule and demand curve in Table 25.6 and Figure 25.4. If the price is raised from £5 to £6 (a 20 per cent change), the quantity demanded falls from 10,000 to 9,000 units (a 10 per cent change). This is shown in Figure 25.5. The price elasticity of demand is:

$$PED = \frac{-10\%}{20\%} = (-)0.5$$

or $$PED = \frac{-1,000}{10,000} \div \frac{1}{5} = \frac{-1}{10} \times \frac{5}{1} = \frac{-1}{2} \text{ or } (-)0.5$$

It is usual to ignore the minus sign, so that a figure that is less than 1 but greater than 0 tells the business that demand for the product is **price inelastic**. This means that the percentage change in quantity demanded is less than the

A stationery shop selling fibre tipped pens has estimated the following demand schedule for its products.

**Table 25.5** *The demand schedule for fibre tipped pens*

| Price (£) | Quantity demanded |
|---|---|
| 2 | 800 |
| 3 | 600 |
| 4 | 500 |
| 5 | 400 |
| 6 | 350 |
| 7 | 300 |
| 8 | 260 |
| 9 | 225 |
| 10 | 200 |

(a) Calculate the change in total revenue for fibre tipped pens of:
  (i) an increase in price from £2 to £3;
  (ii) an increase in price from £7 to £10;
  (iii) a decrease in price from £5 to £3.
(b) Explain why the business might be reluctant to raise prices above £7 per pen.

*Question 2*

**Table 25.6** *A demand schedule*

| Price £ | Quantity demanded (units) | Total revenue £ |
|---|---|---|
| 4 | 11,000 | 44,000 |
| 5 | 10,000 | 50,000 |
| 6 | 9,000 | 54,000 |

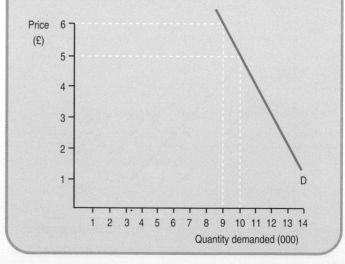

**Figure 25.4** *The effect of a change in price on quantity demanded*

percentage change in price. In other words, consumers do not change the quantity of a good they demand proportionally more than any change in price.

What effect will a change in price have on a business's total revenue? Table 25.6 and Figure 25.4 show that a rise in price from £5 to £6 will increase revenue from £50,000 to £54,000. This is because the rise in price is proportionally greater than the fall in the quantity demanded. A business which raises its price will hope that demand for the product is price inelastic.

A reduction in price from £5 to £4 will result in a fall in revenue from £50,000 to £44,000, even though the quantity demanded has increased from 10,000 to 11,000 units.

Elastic demand A business operating in a different market may face the demand schedule in Table 25.7. An increase in price from £20 to £24 (a 20 per cent change) results in a fall in quantity demanded from 10,000 units to 6,000 units (a 40 per cent change). Price elasticity of demand is therefore:

$$PED = \frac{-40\%}{20\%} = (-)2$$

or $$PED = \frac{-4,000}{10,000} \div \frac{4}{20} = \frac{-1}{10} \times \frac{5}{4} = \frac{-1}{10} \text{ or } (-)2$$

As this figure is greater than 1, the business can conclude

**Table 25.7** *A demand schedule*

| Price £ | Quantity demanded (units) | Total revenue £ |
|---|---|---|
| 16 | 14,000 | 224,000 |
| 20 | 10,000 | 200,000 |
| 24 | 6,000 | 144,000 |

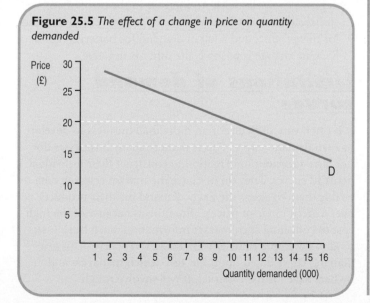

**Figure 25.5** *The effect of a change in price on quantity demanded*

Kaldor Ltd manufactures reproduction juke boxes which play CDs. Jukeboxes that play old 45 records can cost around £1,000 or a great deal more. Large jukeboxes in pubs can cost thousands of pounds as well. But Kaldor had seen other 'reproduction' jukeboxes that did not cost as much and were far smaller. It decided to manufacture smaller jukeboxes that stand on a table. They sold for £200 and hold three CDs at a time. The jukeboxes have been selling well and so the business raised the price to £240. As a result sales fell from 800 to 600 per month. Kaldor is now questioning the decision to raise the price.

(a) Calculate the price elasticity of demand for Kaldor's jukeboxes.
(b) Explain whether or not the decision to raise the price was a good choice by the business.

**Question 3**

that demand for its product is relatively **price elastic**. This means that the percentage change in quantity demanded is greater than the percentage change in price. When demand is price elastic, consumers react to changes in price by changing the quantity they demand by a greater proportion.

Table 25.7 and Figure 25.5 show that if the business reduces its price from £20 to £16, quantity demanded will increase from 10,000 to 14,000 and total revenue will increase from £200,000 to £224,000. This is because the increase in quantity demanded is proportionally greater than the fall in price. If a business is aiming to cut its price, it will hope demand for the product will be price elastic. An increase in price from £20 to £24 will lead to a fall in revenue from £200,000 to £144,000.

# Factors affecting price elasticity of demand

There are two main factors which are thought to affect the price elasticity of demand.

- The number of substitutes for a product. A product with a wide range of substitutes is likely to be highly sensitive to price changes and relatively price elastic. This is because the more substitutes there are for a particular product, the more easy it is for consumers to purchase another product when price changes occur. For example, most types of fish are likely to be relatively price elastic. This is because if the price of one type of fish goes up, consumers can easily swap to another type of fish.
- Time. The longer the period of time, the more price elastic the demand for a product is likely to be. The more time consumers are given, the more able and willing they are to adjust their buying habits. Take, for example, a rise in the price of gas. Over a short period of time, it would be difficult for consumers to buy less gas. Ownership of a gas cooker and gas central heating systems means in the short term that it is difficult to use other types of power. However, over a longer period of time it may be possible for consumers to switch to oil or electricity.

# Income elasticity of demand

INCOME ELASTICITY OF DEMAND is a measure of the sensitivity of demand to changes in income. It can be calculated using the formula:

$$\frac{\text{Percentage change in quantity demanded}}{\text{Percentage change in income}}$$

Businesses will want to know the income elasticity of demand for their products. This will help them to judge the effect of a change in their consumers' income on the demand for their products.

- If a rise in income leads to a relatively greater rise in quantity demanded then income elasticity of demand is positive and greater than one.
- If a rise in income leads to a relatively smaller rise in quantity demanded then income elasticity is positive but less than one.
- If a rise in income leads to no change in quantity demanded then income elasticity of demand is zero.
- If a rise in income leads to a fall in quantity demanded then income elasticity of demand is negative.

# Advertising elasticity of demand

ADVERTISING ELASTICITY OF DEMAND is a measure of the responsiveness of demand to changes in advertising expenditure. It is measured by the following formula:

$$\frac{\text{Percentage change in quantity demanded}}{\text{Percentage change in advertising expenditure}}$$

Businesses need to be able to measure the effectiveness of their advertising campaigns. One way of doing this is to consider the impact on consumer demand of spending on advertising. This can provide businesses with valuable data which can enable them to judge how far consumers are influenced by advertising campaigns. It also allows businesses to evaluate the relative success of advertising campaigns. If the percentage increase in quantity demanded is a great deal larger than the percentage increase in advertising spending, then advertising elasticity of demand is strong and positive. This may tell a business that advertising is effective in influencing consumers.

# Cross elasticity of demand

The CROSS ELASTICITY OF DEMAND shows the response of quantity demanded of one good to a change in the price of another. It allows a business to gauge how demand for its products will react if the price of either rival's products or complementary goods change. It can be calculated using the formula:

$$\frac{\text{Percentage change in quantity demanded of good X}}{\text{Percentage change in price of good Y}}$$

- Goods which are substitutes and compete with each other have a positive cross elasticity. An increase in the price of one newspaper (good Y) should lead to a fall in demand for this product and an increase in demand for another newspaper (good X). Both changes are positive. A fall in the price of good Y will lead to a fall in the demand for good X. Two negatives cancel out to make a positive.
- Goods which are complements to each other have a negative cross elasticity. An increase in the price of an electrical product (good Y) should lead to a fall in demand for this product and a fall in demand for batteries (good X). One change is positive, the other is negative.

# Limitations of demand curves

It is often very difficult for an individual business to develop its own demand curve. This is because many businesses do not have sufficient information to construct their individual demand curves. They do not have the market research data to enable them to assess the likely demand for their products over a given range of prices. Often this is because of the high cost of collecting such market information. Such businesses tend to develop a PERCEIVED DEMAND curve. This is a demand curve based upon the 'feel' which managers and owners have for their market. It will involve rough estimations of the likely impact upon demand of upwards or downwards changes in prices.

Some larger businesses with access to detailed market information are in a much better position to develop demand curves which can assist them in making more informed decisions about their prices. However, even for such businesses the demand curve may be of limited value. This is because the demand curve can only provide information about the likely response of consumers to a change in the price of a particular product at a given point in time. In fast changing markets such information may quickly go out of date and will be of limited value unless it is regularly updated.

## key terms

**Advertising elasticity of demand** - the responsiveness of demand to a change in advertising expenditure.
**Cross elasticity of demand** - the responsiveness of the demand of one product to a change in the price of another.
**Demand** - the quantity of a product purchased at any price.
**Income elasticity of demand** - the responsiveness of demand to a change in income.
**Price elasticity of demand** - the responsiveness of demand to a change in price.
**Perceived demand** - the demand which the managers and owners of a business believe exists for their products in a particular market.

## Knowledge...Knowledge...Knowle

1. What does the demand curve of a business show?
2. What might the demand curve for a product judged on quality rather than price look like?
3. What are the factors affecting the demand for a product?
4. How is price elasticity of demand calculated?
5. What is the difference between inelastic and elastic demand?
6. What effect will a change in price have on the revenue of a firm facing inelastic demand for its product?
7. State 2 factors affecting the price elasticity of demand for a product.
8. Why might a business be interested in its advertising elasticity of demand?
9. Suggest a limitation when using a demand curve for a business.

IceStyle is a manufacturer of skiing products, including skis, snowboards and skiboards, outdoor clothing and skiing accessories. Recently it has found that the price of skiing holidays for its customers has risen by 4 per cent due to the level of the exchange rate. This resulted in a 6 per cent fall in sales last year. In an attempt to battle against the fall in demand, the business launched a high profile marketing campaign designed to promote skiwear as leisure clothing. It particularly targeted the 'youth' market, attempting to stress a link between extreme sports and fashion. So far a 10 per cent increase in advertising expenditure has resulted in a 2 per cent increase in sales.

(a) Using the figures above calculate the:
    (i)  cross elasticity of demand;
    (ii) advertising elasticity of demand.
(b) In each case, what do the results tell IceStyle about the demand for its product?

Question**4**

# Case study *Bodyline*

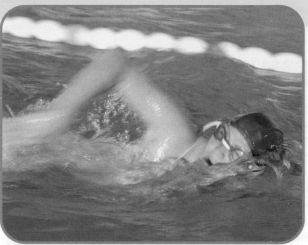

Bodyline is a small firm based in the West Midlands which manufactures womens' swimwear. Its products are distributed through four main types of outlet - mail-order catalogues, department stores, womens' clothing chains and independent retailers.

The business was set up in early 2003. The two women, Elaine and Penny, who started up the firm had originally been friends at University. One had studied for a degree in Art and Design, the other in Business Studies.

Their main product was to be a swimsuit, the Californian, which had been designed in a wide range of dazzling colours. Their marketing strategy had been to aim for the bottom end of the market, offering a cheap, but fashionable garment which would be within the reach of a wide number of consumers' pockets. Marketing research into the demand for the Californian showed that sales at different prices were likely to be as in Table 25.8.

Elaine and Penny found that they were able to sell all of their production at a price of £18. They sold Californians at this price for six months and made a fair profit. The market was fairly stable at this time and few sudden changes were expected in the near future. Penny felt that by reducing the price a little they would be able to capture more of the market. Elaine was not so sure and the two debated the decision over the next six months without taking any action.

By early 2004 a number of rival businesses developed similar product lines using bright colours, having seen the initial success of Bodyline in the market. As Elaine had commented, one of the worst things about the new products was that 'the Californian designs no longer stood out in the shops and are the same as other products now available'. In what had seemed like a short period of time to these two entrepreneurs, their niche in the market had all but disappeared.

After their initial success many of the new businesses had attempted to undercut Bodyline's prices. The effect on the demand curve for the Californian is shown in Table 25.9.

**(a)** What is the relationship between price and demand for Californians shown in Table 25.8? Use examples in your answer. (6 marks)

**(b)** Calculate the elasticity of demand for Californians for a reduction in price from:
   **(i)** £18 to £16;
   **(ii)** £16 to £14.
   (6 marks)

**(c)** Explain whether demand for Californians is elastic or inelastic and how this would affect price and demand. (6 marks)

**(d)** Using Table 25.9, explain the idea of cross elasticity of demand for Californians. (10 marks)

**(e)** Assess whether you think Penny was right to suggest a reduction in price using your answer to (b) and total revenue calculations. (12 marks)

**Table 25.8** *Demand curve for Californians*

| Price | Quantity of Californians |
|-------|--------------------------|
| £14 | 18,000 |
| £16 | 14,000 |
| £18 | 10,000 |
| £20 | 6,000 |

**Table 25.9** *Effect of a change in competitors' prices on the demand for Californians*

| Price of other products | Quantity of Californians |
|-------------------------|--------------------------|
| £14 | 16,200 |
| £12 | 12,600 |
| £10 | 9,000 |
| £8 | 5,400 |

## Pricing strategies

The extent to which a business can influence its price will depend upon the degree of competition that it faces. A fruit and vegetable stall on a local market could be faced with several other stalls close by, as well as local supermarkets. It will need to set prices that are in line with its immediate competitors. Otherwise the consumers can easily choose to buy elsewhere. In contrast Virgin and GNER are the only train operators on many of the mainline routes in the UK and face much less direct competition than the market stall. The effects of the degree of competition that a business faces is explained in unit 94.

When a business does have the scope to set its price there is a number of PRICING STRATEGIES it might choose. When launching **new products** it might choose one of the following strategies.

- Penetrating the market. A business may set its price deliberately low in order to gain a footing in the market. This could also be used when a business is launching an existing product into a new market, for example.
- Skimming or creaming. If a business realises that its product has a unique selling point (☞ unit 22) it may be in a position to charge a high price for a limited time in order to take advantage of the newness of the product. This is known a skimming or creaming the market. New generation mobile phones which can take and send pictures are priced much higher than 'traditional' phones as mobile phone companies skim this new market.

When a business is looking at pricing strategies for **existing products** it might choose from the following strategies.

- Price taking. In very competitive markets a business might decide to follow closely another firm's price increases or reductions. The retail market for 'white goods' such as fridges and freezers is an example.
- Price leadership. In some markets, often controlled by a small number of large companies, there is an accepted price leader. They will decide first to increase or lower prices, knowing that other companies will soon follow. The pricing of petrol is an example.
- Destroying competition or capturing the market. Some firms may seek to capture the market through aggressive price cutting. EasyJet and Ryanair have pursued this policy to gain increased market shares of the air travel market.
- Price discrimination. A business may be in a position to discriminate by charging different prices for the same product to different groups of consumers. For example renting a caravan on a holiday park for two weeks in the school holidays will often cost twice as much as renting the same caravan in June or September.

## Pricing tactics

Once a company has decided upon its overall pricing strategy, it can also use price as a tactical promotional tool. This will usually involve temporary changes in prices to attract customers to specific products for a period. These PRICING TACTICS may include the following.

- Special promotional offers, such as buy one, get one free. Waterstone's has offered three paperback books for the price of two and Morrisons two pizzas for £5.
- Loss leaders. A business may deliberately lower the price of a popular product in order to attract customers into the store to buy the product and hopefully other products.
- Discounts on normal prices. This might be for a period of time, such as just before Christmas, for regular customers, such as special offers for loyalty card holders, or for people who buy larger quantities, for example schools getting discounts on supplies of pens, paper and stationery.
- Introductory offers. This is where the price a customer pays for the first purchase is lower than for subsequent purchases. For example, Broadband has been offered by service providers at £5.50 per month for the first three months and then £15.50 per month after three months.

## Factors affecting pricing decisions

What factors influence the price a business sets for its product?

**Objectives** The pricing strategy chosen by a business is likely to reflect the extent to which it wants to maximise profits or sales. A business seeking to maximise short term profits may use more aggressive and perhaps risky pricing strategies.

**The marketing mix** The price chosen by a business must complement the other aspects of the marketing mix (☞ unit 23). This means that the price must fit in with the nature of the product itself and the way in which it is being promoted and distributed to consumers. For example, a low quality product being sold in retail outlets at the bottom end of the market is likely to be sold at a fairly low price.

**Costs** A business which cannot generate enough revenue over time to cover its costs will not survive. In the long run, a business must charge a price which earns enough revenue to cover its total cost of production (fixed and variable) at any level of output. This means that businesses must take account all of their costs when setting price. In the short run, however, it is unlikely that a business would expect to cover the fixed costs of its factory or machinery (☞ unit 38). Providing its price is high enough to generate revenue that covers its variable costs, the firm will stay in business.

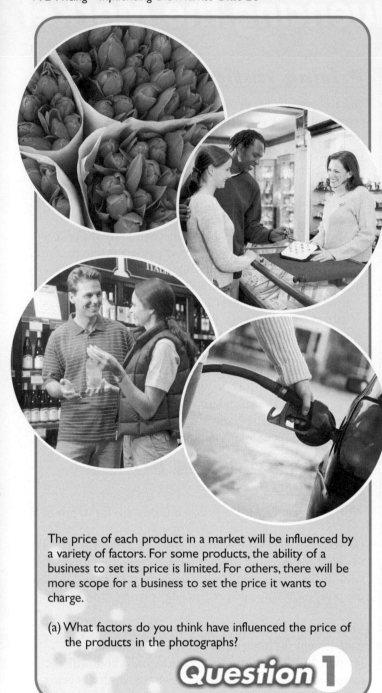

The price of each product in a market will be influenced by a variety of factors. For some products, the ability of a business to set its price is limited. For others, there will be more scope for a business to set the price it wants to charge.

(a) What factors do you think have influenced the price of the products in the photographs?

**Question 1**

may generate low sales because of doubts about its **value for money**. A product priced too low may also generate low sales. This is because consumers often suspect that such products have something wrong with them or that they are of inferior quality. For example, a business marketing high fashion clothing would be careful to ensure that its products were priced higher than those offered to the mass market.

Businesses have the opportunity to influence consumer perceptions through aspects of the marketing mix, such as advertising. By improving the view consumers have of the product, businesses can give themselves more scope when setting prices. In some cases firms actually encourage consumers to think of their products as expensive. For example, Thorntons Chocolates have been marketed as a quality confectionery item.

**Market segment** Businesses that produce a range of products are likely to have some aimed at particular market segments (☞ unit 20). This is true, for example, of all major car manufacturers. They are, therefore, likely to charge different prices for each segment. However, the price which they charge to one segment of the market will affect the prices charged to other segments. A product competing in the top end of the market will need to have a different price from one aimed at the middle or bottom end of the market.

**Legal constraints** The price of a number of products is affected by **taxation**. This raises the price above the level that might have been set by manufacturers. Products affected greatly by taxation include cigarettes, alcoholic drinks and petrol. There is also a number of products which are offered to consumers below the price that producers would normally charge. Such products are **subsidised** by the government. An example might be low priced travel on public transport for young people and pensioners. The price of products such as water and gas are determined by regulatory bodies (☞ unit 103).

## Cost based pricing

All businesses are influenced by their costs when determining prices with costs acting as a 'bottom line' when choosing a price. But some use COST-BASED PRICING as their strategy for price setting. Businesses using cost-based pricing are those where the influence of cost is more important than other factors such as market conditions or competitors' pricing. The local garage repair business or domestic repair services like electricians and plumbers are likely to take a cost-based approach.

There is a number of methods that businesses use to set their prices which are based upon particular costs.

**Cost plus pricing** This involves setting a price by calculating the average cost (☞ unit 38) of producing goods and adding a MARK-UP for profit. If a business produces 10,000 goods costing £50,000, the average cost would be £5.00. A mark up of 20 per cent would mean goods would cost an extra £1.00 and the price would be £6.00 per product. Retailers often use

Revenue below this will cause the firm to cease production. As a result businesses may have greater flexibility in the short term when making pricing decisions.

**Competition** Competition can affect pricing decisions (☞ unit 94). For a market trader, the price of her goods is largely determined by prices on nearby stalls selling similar goods. Such a trader will have little room for manoeuvre compared to a business which faces less competition.

**Consumer perceptions and expectations** Businesses must pay attention to what consumers think a product is worth. A product priced above what consumers consider its value to be

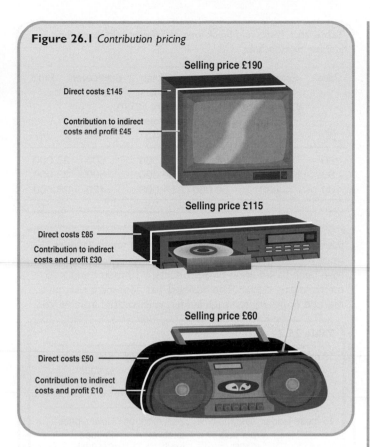

**Figure 26.1** *Contribution pricing*

Selling price £190

Direct costs £145

Contribution to indirect costs and profit £45

Selling price £115

Direct costs £85

Contribution to indirect costs and profit £30

Selling price £60

Direct costs £50

Contribution to indirect costs and profit £10

**Figure 26.2** *Absorption/full cost pricing*

Selling price £220

Direct costs £145

Allocation of indirect/ overhead costs £55

10% mark-up for profit £20

Selling price £104.50

Direct costs £85

Allocation of indirect/ overhead costs £10

10% mark-up for profit £9.50

Selling price £71.50

Direct costs £50

Allocation of indirect/ overhead costs £15

10% mark-up for profit £6.50

this method of pricing. Say that a department store buys a colour TV from wholesalers for £200 and its mark-up to allow for a profit is 100 per cent. The retail price to consumers will be £400.

The attractiveness of cost plus pricing is that it is a quick and simple way of setting a selling price. It also ensures that sales revenue will cover total costs and generate profit. A criticism, however, is that a fixed mark-up does not allow a business to take market needs into account when setting prices. In addition, no attempt is made to allocate indirect costs to particular products. This means they do not reflect the resources being allocated by the business to that particular product or product range.

**Contribution pricing** This method takes into account that different products within a company might need to be priced using different criteria. For each product, a price is set in relation to the **direct costs** of producing that product and any **contribution** (☞ units 40 and 52) that the business wants that product to make towards covering its **indirect cost** and towards profit. Thus for a manufacturer of electrical goods, some prices might be as set out as in Figure 26.1.

No one product will be **expected** to account for all the indirect costs of the business. Each product's selling price would make some contribution to meeting indirect costs. If the producer expected to sell 100 items of each product and had to cover indirect costs of £6,500 and generate profit of £2,000 (£8,500) then:

Product A  £45x100 = £4,500  contribution
Product B  £30x100 = £3,000  contribution
Product C  £10x100 = £1,000  contribution

£8,500

This allows businesses more flexibility than the cost plus approach. Successful products can be priced to make a large contribution. Less successful products or new products can be priced more competitively, as they need only to make a lower contribution to overheads and profits. Indeed, new products might even be making a negative contribution, ie their price does not even cover the **marginal cost** of production. Demand factors as well as cost factors are now being taken into account.

**Absorption cost/full cost pricing** A business may attempt to take into account the indirect costs that can be attributable to a particular product in deciding on a price. This is known as **absorption** or **full cost pricing** (☞ unit 52). In its simplest form an arbitrary method is used to allocate indirect costs to each product, for example, a percentage of total sales or total direct costs. The electrical goods manufacturer might charge the prices in Figure 26.2. A mark-up is then added for profit.

A more sophisticated method of allocation can also be used. Using this method to allocate indirect costs, each element of the cost will be treated separately. This means the

**Figure 26.3**

Selling price £214.50

Direct costs £145

Allocation of admin costs £15

Allocation of marketing costs £10

Allocation of factory costs £25

10% mark-up £19.50

Indirect/ overhead costs £50

**Table 26.1** *Profits and break-even at different price levels for a briefcase manufacturer*

| Price | Estimated demand at given price | Total revenue | Total costs (Fixed costs = £30,000 variable costs = £30) | Break-even point | Profit |
|---|---|---|---|---|---|
| (£) | | (£) | (£) | | (£) |
| 80 | 1,100 | 88,000 | 63,000 | 600 | 25,000 |
| 90 | 1,000 | 90,000 | 60,000 | 500 | 30,000 |
| 100 | 800 | 80,000 | 54,000 | 429 | 26,000 |

selling price of a product will absorb elements of each overhead cost.

As we can see from Figures 26.2 and 26.3 the price of the TV is different according to the method used. A different costing formula will lead to a different final price. Under the arbitrary method a larger allocation of indirect/overhead costs was made to the television's final price.

**Target pricing** This is sometimes known as **target profit pricing**. It involves businesses setting prices that will earn them a particular level of profit, which has been clearly targeted. When setting a target price (or profit) businesses make use of break-even analysis (☞ unit 41). Figure 26.4 shows the break-even chart for a small business producing leather briefcases. It is based upon a selling price of £90, fixed costs of £30,000 and variable costs of £30 per briefcase. In order to break-even the business must produce and sell 500 briefcases. If, however, it wishes to target a profit of £30,000 then it must produce and sell 1,000 briefcases. Using break-even analysis in this way businesses can target a particular level of profit for their product.

We know from unit 25 that the price which is charged for a product affects the demand for a product. The precise relationship between demand and price is measured by price

**Figure 26.4** *A break-even chart for a briefcase manufacturer*

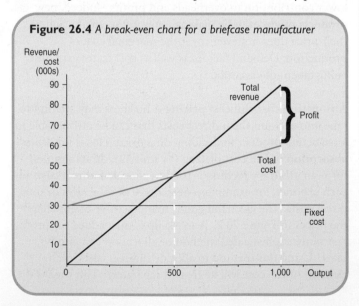

Patel and Co has been manufacturing aluminium ladders since the business was set up in 2000. Its sales up to now have been based upon two products, a 10 metre and a 15 metre folding ladder. The business has adopted a cost plus method of pricing for each ladder, as illustrated in Table 26.2.

**Table 26.2**

| 10 metre ladder | Average cost per unit £92 | 20% mark-up to cover profit £18.40 | Selling price to trade £110.40 |
|---|---|---|---|
| 15 metre ladder | Average cost per unit £125 | 20% mark-up to cover profit £25.00 | Selling price to trade £150.00 |

Because of the success of these two products and pressure from competition, the company has developed a new product, a ladder which would allow people to gain constant access to their lofts, but which will be permanently attached to the loft entrance. With a third product, the company's accountant felt that a contribution pricing approach should now be used to price each of their products. He set out some initial calculations of their likely prices, as in Table 26.3.

**Table 26.3**

| | Direct costs per unit | Contribution to indirect cost and profit | Price |
|---|---|---|---|
| 10 metre ladder | £80 | £35 | £115 |
| 15 metre ladder | £105 | £40 | £145 |
| Loft ladder | £185 | £5 | £190 |

The pricing for the loft ladder was set at a level which was in line with the price of competitors, which was £190.00.

(a) Identify the benefits to the company of using a contribution pricing approach compared to a cost plus approach for their ladders.

(b) Is the loft ladder a viable product for the company to produce given the figures produced by the accountant? Explain your answer.

elasticity of demand. Thus the briefcase manufacturer may wish to estimate the demand for its briefcases at various price levels. It can then choose a price and associated sales which will enable it to make the profit that it wants. This is shown in Table 26.1. Table 26.1 shows that the business would not benefit at present from either lowering or raising its price from £90.

## Problems of cost based pricing

Cost based pricing does have a number of problems. It is a product and cost orientated approach which does not refer to consumers' wishes or flexibility. Contribution pricing does, however, allow more flexibility than cost plus pricing for a particular marketing strategy. Full or absorption cost pricing may result in prices being set too high or too low in relation to consumers' wishes or competitors' prices. They are also inflexible in response to market changes, as these would not necessarily be reflected in the costs of a company. The more sophisticated the costing method used when pricing, the more accurate is the allocation of costs to a product, but the further the price might be from what the market will bear.

## Market orientated pricing

MARKET ORIENTATED PRICING methods are those which are based upon an analysis of the conditions in the market at which a product is aimed. As such, they are much better suited to market orientated businesses.

**Penetration pricing** This is used by businesses seeking to gain a foothold in a market, either with new products or with established products being placed in new markets. It involves pricing a product at a low level so that retailers and consumers are encouraged to purchase the product in large quantities.

There are two main reasons why businesses use penetration pricing.

● Consumers are encouraged to develop the habit of buying the product, so that when prices eventually begin to rise they will continue to purchase it.

● Retailers and wholesalers are likely to purchase large quantities of the product. This should mean that they will not buy from other suppliers until they have sold most of their stock. Businesses can thus gain a significant slice of the market.

Penetration pricing, because of its high cost, is often used by large firms operating in mass markets, such as those selling biscuits, sweets, washing powder and canned drinks. It is also a policy used by new businesses or established businesses in other areas to break into a new market. It is not a policy that is suitable for products with short life cycles. There is usually not enough time to recover the cost of lost revenue from the initially low price. One exception to this is new CD singles. They are sometimes launched at a lower price in the first few weeks of release before being raised to their full price.

**Market skimming** Market skimming involves charging a high price for a new product for a limited period. The aim is to gain as much profit as possible for a new product while it remains unique in the market. It usually means selling a product to the most profitable segment of the market before it is sold to a wider market at a lower price.

There are two reasons why businesses adopt market skimming. They may try to maximise revenue before competitors come into the market with a similar product. Often new techniques or designs mean that entirely new products, or new versions of a product can be offered. Examples include new fashions in clothes, new childrens' toys and new inventions. When first launched, a basic digital watch could cost as much as £50 or £60. Now they often sell for as little as a few pounds. Market skimming can also be used to generate revenue in a short period of time so that further investment in the product can be made. Companies in the electronics and pharmaceutical industries often use skimming for this reason.

**Customer value pricing** This involves charging the price that consumers are prepared to pay. Products which have prestige names attached to them, such as Rolex, may be able to command a higher price because of the status of these names. Products for one-off events, such as music festivals or sports finals, may be given a high price because they are unique.

**Loss leaders** LOSS LEADERS are products priced at very low levels in order to attract customers. The price of a loss leader is set lower than the average total cost of producing the product. The company selling the product makes a 'loss' on each product sold. Businesses use this pricing technique because they expect the losses made on the loss leader to be more than compensated for by extra profits on other products. It is often used by larger supermarkets which sell everyday products such as baked-beans, bananas and corn flakes for very low prices. They aim to attract more customers into their stores, drawn in by the low prices. The 'captive' customers will then buy more highly priced and profitable items.

**Psychological pricing** Many businesses seek to take account of the psychological effect of their prices upon consumers. This is known as psychological pricing. A common example is the use of prices just a little lower than a round figure, such as £199.99 rather than £200, or £29.99 rather than £30. Businesses using these slightly lower prices believe that they will influence the consumers' decision as to whether or not to purchase. Such slightly lower prices also suggest that consumers will be looking for value for money. For this reason, the producers of high status products such as prestige cars or designer clothing tend to avoid such prices. Instead, they often choose prices which psychologically match their consumers expectations of higher quality. So, for example, a price of £100 may be charged for a designer shirt rather than £99.99.

Table 26.4 shows the range of prices being offered by various retailers for a FujiFine Pix Digital Camera.

(a) Describe the type of pricing strategies in this market.

(b) Compare strategies that may be being adopted by Simple Computers with Cameras2U.com.

**Table 26.4**

| Retailer | Price |
|---|---|
| Cameras2U.com | £84.99 |
| Simply Computers | £149.00 |
| Digital Camera Company | £109.00 |
| CPixMania | £86.00 |
| Ebuyer | £82.24 |
| Argos | £99.99 |

Source: adapted from kelkoo.co.uk.

**Question 3**

**Price discrimination** Price discrimination occurs when a firm offers the same product at different prices when consumers can be kept separate. An example is BT's policy of charging different prices to business and residential users at different times of the day and the weekend. This allows BT to take into account the differences in cost which exists at peak and off peak times. So, for example, calls may be charged at a higher rate on Monday to Friday, 8am-6pm, than at weekends.

This price discrimination is **time based**. The price you pay for a phone call is based upon the time of day or the day of the week when you use the service. Other businesses which use this policy are rail companies (cheaper off peak travel), and holiday firms which charge higher prices for their product during school holidays.

Price discrimination can also be **market based**. This involves offering different market segments the same product at different prices. An example of this is students being given discounts on coach and bus travel.

**Discounts and sales** These tend to support the pricing strategies used by businesses. They often mean a reduction in the standard price for particular groups of consumers. A very common form of discount is the seasonal 'sales' of retailers. The aim is to encourage purchasers at times when sales might otherwise be low and to clear out of date and out of fashion stock. Discounts may also be given to those customers who buy in bulk or in large quantities.

## Competition based pricing

With COMPETITION BASED PRICING it is the prices charged by competitors which are the major influence on a producer's price. It is used mostly by businesses which face fierce and direct competition. As a rule, the more competitive the market and the more homogeneous the products competing in that market, the greater the pressure for competition based pricing. Markets similar to the model of oligopoly (☞ unit 94) will often use this form of pricing. For example, soap powder producers tend to be influenced by the price of competitors' products.

**Going rate pricing** This occurs in markets where businesses are reluctant to set off a price war by lowering their prices and are concerned about a fall off in revenue if prices are raised. They examine competitors' prices and choose a price broadly in line with them. It also occurs when one dominant business establishes a position of **price leadership** within a market. Other firms will follow suit when the price leader changes its prices. This type of policy can be seen when a petrol company changes the price of a gallon of petrol or when banks and building societies change interest rates.

Companies which operate in markets where going rate pricing occurs will often be frustrated by their inability to control their prices more closely. A strategy often used in such circumstances is to establish a strong **brand** identity for your product and to differentiate it from others on the market (☞ unit 27). This would be through unique design features or quality of service. An oil company's decision to upgrade all of its service stations is an example of an attempt to achieve this. A strong brand identity and unique product features allow firms much greater scope for choosing their own price levels.

**Destroyer pricing** The aim of destroyer pricing is to eliminate opposition. It involves cutting prices, sometimes greatly, for a period of time long enough for your rivals to go out of business. It could be argued that the offering of low price airline tickets by Ryanair and EasyJet in the 1990s was designed to drive out competition from the national European airline carriers and force some of them out of business. Some, like BA and KLM, responded by setting up their own low-price carriers and cutting prices. Others, like Sabena and SwissAir, did go out of business.

**Closed bid pricing** This method of pricing occurs when firms have to TENDER a bid for work which they are going to carry out. This is common practice for firms dealing with the government or local authorities. For example, if a new road is to be built firms will be invited to put in a bid to win a contract for the work. Firms will clearly need to pay very close attention to the price at which they expect their competitors to bid. Sometimes, when a number of firms bid for a contract, those with the highest prices are likely to be rejected. Another example of this type of pricing are the bids that the government organises for the National Lottery. In 2004 Camelot had won both the rounds of bidding against rival companies, including Richard Branson's Virgin group.

## Knowledge...Knowledge...Knowle

1. State 5 pricing strategies a business might use.
2. Identify 4 different pricing tactics that a business might use.
3. What are the main factors affecting a firm's pricing decisions?
4. Explain the difference between cost plus pricing and contribution pricing.
5. State one advantage and one disadvantage of cost plus and contribution pricing for a firm.
6. What is meant by absorption cost pricing?
7. Why might a firm use penetration pricing?
8. What is market skimming?
9. What types of firm might use market skimming as a pricing strategy?
10. Why might a business sell a product as a loss leader?
11. What is meant by psychological pricing?
12. What is meant by price discrimination?
13. Under what circumstances might a firm use competition based pricing?
14. Explain the terms:
    (a) going rate pricing;
    (b) destroyer pricing;
    (c) closed bid pricing.
15. Give 2 examples of tendering.

## key terms

**Competition based pricing** - methods of pricing based upon the prices charged by competitors.
**Cost based pricing** - methods of pricing products which are based upon costs.
**Loss leaders** - products with prices set deliberately below average total cost to attract customers who will then buy other, more profitable, products.
**Market orientated pricing** - methods of pricing based upon the pricing conditions in the market at which a product is aimed.
**Mark-up** - that part of a price which seeks to provide a business with profit as opposed to covering its costs. It is used in cost plus pricing.
**Pricing strategies** - the pricing policies or methods of pricing adopted by businesses.
**Tender** - a bid to secure a contract for work.
**Pricing tactics** – ways of using price as a promotional tool usually over a short period of time.

## Case study Anatomy of a Budget Flight

On today's 10.45 EasyJet Flight from Luton to Nice, a popular route in August, some people will have paid only £20 for their seats. A flight of nearly 700 miles for less than the price of 2 CDs. Yet the airline still makes a profit. How does it do it?

Others on the flight, the late bookers, may have paid closer to £140 for the same flight. But this still represents a revolution in travel. The average price for all EasyJet flights is £48.70. In the days before no-frills airlines, a passenger would pay over £200 for a seat to Nice, however early they booked.

Low fares still equate to very healthy profits

**Table 26.5** *The cost of a single EasyJet flight*

| | |
|---|---|
| Ground handling charges (baggage, check-ins etc ) | £542 |
| Airport charges | £817 |
| Credit card charges (for on-line bookings) | £101 |
| Administration (contribution to head office costs) | £728 |
| Fuel | £614 |
| Navigation (for air traffic control) | £420 |
| Advertising | £215 |
| Cost of the aircraft | £676 |
| Tax on profits | £251 |
| Crew salaries and training | £643 |
| Maintenance and servicing | £584 |
| **Total outgoings** | **£5,591** |
| **Ticket sales** | **£6,136** |
| **Profit** | **£545** |

for the low-cost airlines. Ryanair is the only European carrier to make profits in each of the past 13 years. For EasyJet, every time a flight takes off the company receives on average £6,136 in fares and makes £545 in profit. This represents good business when it caries twenty million passengers on 156,000 flights in a year. Its profit margin of 8.9 per cent is well above that of Tesco, which makes just 3.6p in the pound profit.

Table 26.5 shows how the £6,136 and £545 are accounted for.

There is a broad philosophy behind behind the low-cost airline game which was set out 30 years ago by Herb Kelleher who founded SouthWest Airlines in Texas, the world's first budget airline. His philosophy had 4 rules.

- Rule 1 – Only fly one type of plane. This makes maintenance and repairs easier. Southwest, EasyJet and Ryanair all uses the Boeing 737.
- Rule 2 – Drive down cost every year. EasyJet seek to reduce costs by 8 -10 per cent each year by reaping economies of scale. It demands better terms from suppliers and uses the Internet to cut out travel agent fees.
- Rule 3 – Turn around your aircraft as quickly as possible. A sit anywhere policy for passengers makes loading quicker. A single plane should make 8 flights a day and only spends 30 minutes standing still on the tarmac at each end.
- Rule 4 – Don't try to sell anything except seats. Price is the best form of loyalty. Avoid loyalty schemes, AirMiles or duty frees.

Source: adapted from *The Guardian*, 20.8.2003.

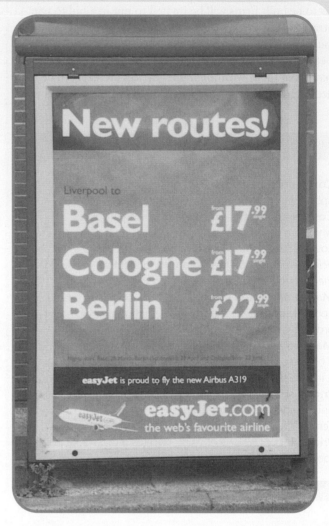

(a) Using examples from the article, explain what is meant by:
  (i) price discrimination;
  (ii) full cost pricing. (6 marks)
(b) Using Table 26.5, explain the method of costing that might be used by EasyJet to determine the price of its flights. (6 marks)
(c) Explain, using examples, how Herb Kelleher's 4 rules might influence the pricing strategy of low-cost airlines. (8 marks)
(d) Examine how a business such as **BA** might respond to the strategies used by competitors such as Ryanair and EasyJet. (10 marks)
(e) Evaluate the effectiveness of EasyJet's pricing strategies. (10 marks)

## What is a brand?

A BRAND is a name, term, sign, symbol, design or any other **feature** that allows consumers to identify the goods and services of a business and to differentiate them from those of competitors. So a recognised brand might be:

- the use of the 'Mc' **name** by McDonald's in its products such as the Egg McMuffin or Chicken McNugget;
- the Nike 'swoosh' **logo**;
- the three stripes **design** on Adidas sports products;
- the use of the **colour** orange in promotions by the Orange communications company or B&Q;
- the **slogan** 'You've been Tangoed' with the Tango drink;
- the '**tune**' which accompanies references to the Intel Pentium Processor fitted into computers in radio and television adverts.

A brand might be one product, a family or range of products or the actual business itself. So, for example, a Nestlé KitKat is an individual product produced by Nestlé. KitKat Chunky and KitKat Kubes are also part of the KitKat family. Nestlé is the name of the company which produces KitKats, other confectionery products such as Milky Bar and Smarties, and foods such as breakfast cereals.

BRAND NAMES are the parts of the brand that can be spoken, such as the name of the product, ie Heinz Baked Beans or a Barbie doll. A BRAND MARK is the design or symbol used in the brand, such as the apple used on Apple Macintosh computers. It is possible to protect the use of a

TRADEMARK by copyright (☞ unit 87). A company might use its TRADE NAME as a brand, such as Virgin, Disney or Starbucks. In some cases the company name might be as well known as its products or even more well known. Sony would be known to many people, as might its Sony Walkman, but many other products in its organisation might not.

Table 27.1 shows the most valuable brands in 2002.

**Figure 27.1** *World's leading brands, 1997*

Source: adapted from *Financial World*.

Compare Figure 27.1 to Table 27.1.
(a) Describe the main changes that took place.
(b) Suggest reasons to account for these changes.

## Question 1

## Brand equity

Well known brands are important to a business. It is argued that brands **add value** to a product. A business will hope that its products:

- will be known by large amounts of consumers - they will have **brand awareness or recognition**;
- will be bought rather than those of others - they will have **brand preference**;
- will be bought by customers over and over again - they will have **brand loyalty**.

Products that have these compared to other products are likely to have BRAND EQUITY. They are important assets that are worth something to businesses which have them (☞ unit 45). They will generate high revenue, promotion and repeat purchases. Sometimes they can be sold for a high value. For example, when Nestlé bought Rowntree for $2.5

| Table 27.1 *Most valuable brands by value, 2002* | | | |
|---|---|---|---|
| Rank | Brand name | Brand value ($ million) | Parent company |
| 1 | COCA-COLA | 69,637 | Coca-Cola Company |
| 2 | MICROSOFT | 64,091 | Microsoft Corp. |
| 3 | IBM | 51,188 | IBM Corp. |
| 4 | GE | 41,311 | General Electric Company |
| 5 | INTEL | 30,861 | Intel Corp. |
| 6 | NOKIA | 29,970 | Nokia Corp. |
| 7 | DISNEY | 29,256 | Walt Disney Company |
| 8 | MCDONALD'S | 26,375 | McDonald's Corp. |
| 9 | MARLBORO | 24,151 | Philip Morris Companies |
| 10 | MERCEDES | 21,010 | DaimlerChrysler AG |
| 11 | FORD | 20,403 | Ford Motor Company |
| 12 | TOYOTA | 19,448 | Toyota Motor Corp. |
| 13 | CITIBANK | 18,066 | Citigroup Inc. |
| 14 | HEWLETT-PACKARD | 16,776 | Hewlett Packard |
| 15 | AMERICAN EXPRESS | 16,287 | American Express |
| 16 | CISCO SYSTEMS | 16,222 | Cisco Systems Inc. |
| 17 | AT&T | 16,059 | AT&T Corp. |
| 18 | HONDA | 15,064 | Honda Motor Company |
| 19 | GILLETTE COMPANY | 14,959 | Gillette Company |
| 20 | BMW | 14,425 | Bayerische Motoren Werke |

Source: adapted from *Business Week*, Interbrand.

## What is promotion?

PROMOTION is the attempt to draw attention to a product or business in order to gain new customers or to retain existing ones. Different methods of promotion are shown in Figure 28.1.

Businesses often refer to promotion **above the line** and **below the line**. Above the line promotion is through independent media, such as television or newspapers. These allow a business to reach a wide audience easily. Most advertising is carried out 'above the line'. Some advertising, however, is carried out by methods over which a firm has direct control, such as direct mailing. These and other direct methods of promotion (known as below the line promotion) are dealt with in unit 29. This unit looks at how businesses advertise their products through different media.

## The objectives of promotion

A business must be clear about exactly what it is trying to achieve through its promotion. The main aim of any promotion is to obtain and retain customers. However, there is a number of other objectives, some or all of which any successful campaign must fulfil.

- To make consumers aware or increase awareness of a product.
- To reach a target audience which might be geographically dispersed.
- To remind consumers about the product. This can encourage existing consumers to re-purchase the product and may attract new consumers.
- To show a product is better than that of a competitor. This may encourage consumers to switch purchases from another product.
- To develop or improve the image of a business rather than a product. Much **corporate advertising** is carried out with this in mind, and is dealt with later in this unit.
- To reassure consumers after the product has been purchased. This builds up confidence in the product and may encourage more to be bought at a later date.
- To support an existing product. Such promotions may be used to remind consumers that a reliable and well thought of product is still available.

Businesses sometimes consider their promotion using **models**. For example, AIDA is a method used to consider advertising. It suggests that effective advertising will raise **A**wareness (A) and encourage **I**nterest (I), **D**esire (D) and **A**ction (A), so that consumers buy the products. The DAGMAR (**D**efining **A**dvertising **G**oals for **M**easured **A**dvertising **R**esults) model is also used to measure the effect of advertising. A business can measure how far the group that is targeted has progressed along the scale below.

Unawareness...Awareness...Comprehension...Conviction...Action

## Types of advertising

Advertising has achieved a central place in business activity across the world as firms have begun to face global as well as national competition. In the UK it has been estimated that between 1 and 2 per cent of national income is spent on advertising.

Advertising is often placed into different categories. INFORMATIVE ADVERTISING is designed to increase consumer awareness of a product. Examples include the classified advertisements in local newspapers, new share offers, grants available to small firms and entries in the *Yellow Pages*. New products may be launched with informative advertising campaigns to make consumers aware of their presence. It is usually argued that this type of advertising helps consumers to make a rational choice as to what to buy.

PERSUASIVE ADVERTISING tries to convince consumers to purchase a product, often by stressing that it is more desirable than others. It is argued that this type of advertising distorts consumer buying, pushing them to buy products which they would otherwise not have bought. In reality, almost all advertising is persuasive to some extent. Very few major campaigns aim to be entirely informative.

REASSURING ADVERTISING is aimed at existing customers. It tries to persuade them that their purchase was correct and that they should continue to buy the product. Banks and building societies often use this method to assure customers that their investments are safe.

## Types of advertising media

There is a wide range of ADVERTISING MEDIA that firms can choose from in order to make consumers aware of their products.

**Television** Because of its many advantages, television

**Figure 28.1** *Methods of promotion*

Advertising

Sales promotions

Exhibitions and trade fairs

Personal selling

**PROMOTION**

Direct mailing

Merchandising

Public relations

Branding

advertising is often used by businesses marketing consumer goods to a mass market. The fast changing trends in television were likely to provide opportunities for television advertising after the year 2000. 99 per cent of males and females watch television in the UK. The growth of cable, satellite and digital television may attract companies to advertise on television. By 2004 half of UK households had access to some form of digital television. Businesses may be particularly attracted to advertise on digital television as packages on Sky, for example, may be subscribed to by higher earning and spending groups.

Newspapers and magazines Newspapers and magazines are an important medium for the advertising of mass market products. It has been estimated that there were 39 million readers of a national newspaper each week in 2002 and that four out of five adults read a national newspaper. Newspapers and magazines can also be useful for targeting a particular audience or market segment (☞ unit 20). For example, businesses selling riding equipment might advertise in *Horse and Hound* or a business selling musical equipment might advertise in *Total Guitar*. Newspaper advertising can also be useful for smaller businesses. It was estimated in 2004 that 40 million adults weekly read a local newspaper.

Cinema Cinema attendances fell from a high of around 1.4 billion in 1951 to reach a low of 53 million in 1984. The 1990s, however, saw a revival in attendances, partly as a result of the better facilities offered by large multiplex cinemas. By 2003 attendances had improved to 167 million. As a result, advertisers began to pay greater attention to this medium. Firms such as Wrangler have even produced advertisements principally designed for use on large cinema screens. Of all the advertising media available to a business, the cinema has the greatest potential for having a strong impact on its audience.

Radio In recent years there has been a growth in the number of independent radio stations in the UK. These include local stations, such as Capital in London and Key 103 in Manchester, national stations such as Virgin and Talk Radio and specialist stations such as Smooth FM and Classic FM. For advertisers this has meant an increase in both the number and type of radio stations on which they can advertise.

There has been an increase in the number of people listening to radio. This trend may be likely to continue with the development of digital radio and Internet radio stations. Both large companies such as Cunard and Kleenex Tissues, as well as smaller businesses, have found radio effective in reaching target customers.

Posters or billboards Posters appear in a variety of locations and tend to carry short messages. This is because motorists and pedestrians usually only have a few seconds to consider them. An effective poster is likely to be large, attention grabbing and placed in a site where it is highly visible to large numbers of

people. The development of electronic screens containing 'posters' with rotating advertisements is a development in this area which may attract businesses.

The Internet  Figure 28.1 shows the dramatic increase in the importance of the Internet as an advertising medium in the UK. By 2003, 48 per cent of households (11.9 million) could

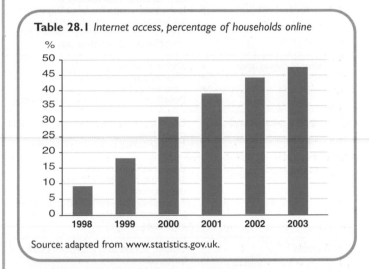

**Table 28.1** *Internet access, percentage of households online*

Source: adapted from www.statistics.gov.uk.

Online supermarket shopping was slammed by customers for being slow and frustrating in a survey by *The Grocer* magazine in 2004. The survey asked supermarkets to deliver 33 items. Not one store was able to deliver all thirty three and one store even sent out-of-date sausages.

Net users, particularly first timers, criticised supermarket websites as being difficult to navigate. Some take too far too long to log on and there were often problems working out exactly where products which customers were looking for were located on the site.

Of the six supermarkets tested, Sainsbury's and Asda were amongst the most efficient, delivering 32 of the 33 items requested. One customer argued 'I was so disappointed by online shopping ... it could be a lot clearer', another that ' I spent too long trying to guess which department items would be in' and one even said 'I would not consider using the service again'. Logging on time varied from ten seconds in one case to ten minutes in another.

The deputy editor of *The Grocer* said 'Time and again we hear that navigating a supermarket Internet site is an issue, even for those with fast Internet connections'. Some good news was that there was said to be improved choice on websites. Tesco is the market leader for online shopping with nearly a nationwide coverage and products of £12.2 million. Asda plans to cover 40 per cent of the UK from August.

Source: adapted from *The Daily Mirror*, 20.4.2004.

(a) Examine the advantages and disadvantages to supermarkets of using the Internet to advertise to customers.

**Question 1**

**Table 28.1** *Advertising media*

| Medium | Advantages | Disadvantages |
|---|---|---|
| Television | • Creative advertisements can attract attention and have a great impact.<br>• Advertisements can demonstrate the product in use.<br>• Can reach a vast audience.<br>• Increased scope for targeting the audience, eg digital television.<br>• The message can be reinforced by continuous advertisements. | • Relatively expensive initial cost.<br>• The message is short lived.<br>• Consumers may not watch commercials.<br>• Technical information is difficult to explain.<br>• There may be a delay between seeing the advert and visiting the shops. |
| National newspaper | • National coverage.<br>• Reader can refer back.<br>• Relatively cheap.<br>• Detail of the product can be provided. | • No movement or sound.<br>• Usually limited to black and white.<br>• Individual adverts may be lost amongst large quantities of other advertisements. |
| Regional newspaper | • Good for regional campaigns and test marketing.<br>• Can be linked to local conditions. | • Cost per reader higher than national newspapers.<br>• Reproduction, layout etc. may be poor. |
| Magazines | • Colour advertisements possible.<br>• Targeting possible with specialist magazines.<br>• Advertising can be linked to features.<br>• Magazines may be referred to at a later date. | • A long time exists between advertisements being placed and magazine being printed.<br>• Competitors' products are also being advertised.<br>• No movement or sound. |
| Cinema | • Colour, sound and movement can be used.<br>• Advertisements can be highly localised.<br>• A 'captive' audience for advertisements.<br>• Great impact on the consumer.<br>• Age groups can be targeted. | • Limited audience.<br>• Message is short lived.<br>• Message may only be seen once. |
| Radio | • Enables use of sound.<br>• Most consumer groups covered.<br>• Minority programmes can target audiences.<br>• Produced cheaply.<br>• Younger audience targeted. | • Not visual.<br>• No copy of material.<br>• Interruptions to music may prove irritating.<br>• May not capture the audience's attention. |
| Posters and billboards | • National campaigns possible.<br>• Most groups covered.<br>• May encourage impulse buying through location close to shops.<br>• Seen repeatedly.<br>• Excellent for short, sharp messages, eg, election 'promises'. | • Limited amount of information.<br>• Difficult to measure effectiveness.<br>• Weather and graffiti can ruin the poster. |
| Internet | • Relatively cheap and easy to set up.<br>• Number of 'hits' can be monitored.<br>• Can be targeted.<br>• Can be easily changed. | • Limited audience.<br>• Possible technical problems of connection, viewing, ordering, maintaining. |

access the Internet from home, an increase from just 9 per cent in 1998. As a result, businesses have shown a growing interest in advertising via websites on the Internet. One major advantage is that websites can be accessed by consumers all over the world, giving companies a worldwide market. Many companies now have their own websites to advertise products and some even allow customers to purchase online using credit cards. By 2003 over half of UK Internet users were using websites to buy goods and services.

The advantages and disadvantages of different advertising media are shown in Table 28.1.

## Choice of advertising media

How do firms decide which medium will be most suitable for their product? There is a number of factors that advertisers may take into account.

Cost  Small firms will be mainly concerned with what media they can afford. Larger firms will need to consider the cost effectiveness of each of the different media. For example, although television is the most expensive medium, it reaches huge numbers of consumers. This means the cost per sale from a television advertisement may be relatively low. The Internet is a relatively low cost method of advertising.

**The audience reached** Given that many products are aimed at certain segments, it makes sense for firms to place their advertisement in a medium which the target audience is likely to see or hear. Firms must aim to reduce **wastage** in their advertising. 'Wastage' means advertising to those other than the target audience. Clearly a certain amount of wastage will occur with most TV advertising, whilst very little will occur when advertising in, say, specialist magazines. Advertising on the Internet can be targeted, but the audience may be limited.

**The advertising of competitors** A major TV advertising campaign by one firm may, for example, be followed by a counter campaign from its competitors.

**The impact** Firms will aim to make the greatest impact when advertising. Different products will require different media to do this. For example, some products such as sports equipment will benefit from being shown in action to have the most impact on an audience. Television and cinema are the obvious choice of media in such cases.

**The law** There are legal restrictions in the UK which mean that some products cannot be advertised in particular media. This is discussed in detail later in this unit. One example of this is the ban on advertising tobacco on TV in the UK.

**The marketing mix** The advertising campaign should be integrated with other types of below the line promotion (☞ unit 29). For example, sponsorship of a sports event and an advertisement for the product on the sports pages of a newspaper may be effective.

**The presentation and recording of information** If an advertisement is designed to be visual, with little written information, then posters on billboards or magazine articles can be effective. Magazine advertisements can also include a lot of text, usually in small print. Advertising on television will also be useful for visual images and has the advantage that words can be spoken at the same time. A short radio advert can provide a certain amount of spoken information, although it will be difficult for the listener to remember everything. Advertising on the Internet allows large amounts of information to be downloaded free of charge.

## *Controls on advertising*

Consumers sometimes complain that advertisements either mislead or exploit. For this reason, there is regulation, legislation and codes of practice to protect the consumer.

**Legislation and regulation** The **Trades Descriptions Act, 1968** states that products must correspond to the claims made for them in advertisements. It is, therefore, illegal to include ingredients on a label which are not present or make unproven claims about the effects of, say, weight loss products. Descriptions of services provided by firms must

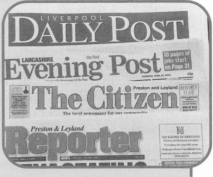

In 2004 it was reported that readership of regional newspapers rose to 40 million adults every week. This was a year-on-year increase for the industry as a whole of 1.8 per cent. Readership of paid-for weekly newspapers grew by 15 per cent over the past 10 years. The weekly paid-for sector represented 80 per cent of all regional titles.

Kevin Beatty, managing director of Northcliffe Newspapers and chairman of the Newspaper Society's Marketing Committee, said 'Local and regional newspapers are in excellent health: readership is on the increase and major new advertisers are coming into the medium because of its closeness to communities and its proven effectiveness. All mainstream media are battling to maintain audience share; the fact that once again nearly half of all local and regional titles have grown circulation reflects the strong and enduring affinity this industry retains with its customers.'

Source: adapted from www.newspapersoc.org.uk, 26.2.2004.

(a) Examine the factors which may influence businesses to advertise in regional and local newspapers.
(b) Assess which types of business are most likely to use this form of media.

**Question 2**

also be accurate. The Act prevents businesses from misleading the consumer about 'sales'.

The **Competition Commission** has powers to investigate anti-competitive behaviour by firms (☞ unit 103). Such anti-competitive behaviour may be in the form of high levels of spending on advertising, for example. This raises costs within an industry and could act as a barrier to prevent other firms from entering the market.

The **Office of Communications** (Ofcom) regulates the communications industry (☞ unit 103). It took over the roles of the Broadcasting Standards Commission, the Independent Television Commission, the Radio Authority and the Radiocommunications Agency which monitored advertising on radio and television.

**Independent bodies** The main independent body which regulates and controls advertising in the UK is the **Advertising Standards Authority** (ASA). It is an independent body responsible for making sure that advertisements conform to the **British Code of Advertising, Sales Promotion and Direct Marketing** (The CAP Code). This states that advertisements should be:
● legal, decent, honest and truthful;

- prepared with a sense of responsibility to consumers and to society;
- in line with the principles of fair competition generally accepted in business.

Over 10,000 advertisements are referred to the ASA each year. In 2002, 13 per cent of advertisements complained about were found to breach the Code. In 2004 the ASA upheld a claim against an advertisement which stated 'Complete Brush Wash System from Alpine Cleaning Services ... The only mobile brush wash machine available with built in pressure washer!' The complainants, who possessed a similar machine, challenged the claim.

If the ASA finds that an advertisement breaches the Code, it may ask the business involved to withdraw the advertisement. Although it has no legal power to force a business to withdraw an advertisement, the ASA can put pressure on a business to do so by:

- publishing its findings;
- withdrawing privileges associated with ASA membership;
- asking media to refuse to carry future advertisements.

In the example of the car wash system above, the ASA worked with the company to amend the wording on the advertisement.

The ASA can also refer the business to the Office of Fair Trading (☞ unit 103), which has the power to seek an injunction to prevent further advertisements. Businesses often make use of the ASA's service which allows advertisements to be checked before they are shown, to make sure they comply with the Code.

Around 30 million press advertisements are published in the UK each year. ASA research shows that the majority are legal, decent, honest and truthful. Compliance with the CAP Code achieves levels of 96 per cent for press advertisements, 99 per cent for posters and 91 per cent for direct marketing.

**Pressure groups** Certain pressure groups (☞ unit 102) seek to influence advertising. FOREST, for example, is a pressure group which aims to defend the rights of tobacco firms to advertise. The British Medical Association (BMA) and Action on Smoking and Health (ASH) take the opposite view. Women's groups have sought to influence firms to produce advertisements which are not sexist. Pressure groups campaigning for better safety on roads have sought to persuade car and tyre manufacturers to produce advertisements showing less aggressive driving.

## *Advertising and society*

Advertising has the potential to affect the lives of many people. This is because, for most, regular exposure to advertising is almost unavoidable. How might advertising affect individuals?

- It adds to the cost of marketing products. This money could have been spent on improving products or price reductions. It is likely that consumers will pay more of any advertising costs than firms.

It is argued that advertising encourages people to buy products which they might not otherwise have purchased. This may, perhaps, lead to a society where people are judged according to how much they consume rather than their value as human beings.

---

In 2001 the ASA ruled on an objection to a poster for a computer company. It contained a picture of an iBook laptop computer with an image of a skateboarder. The objection was that the image shown on the iBook screen in the poster misrepresented and exaggerated the quality of the screen images on the iBook.

The advertisers argued that the poster did not misrepresent the images on an iBook screen. They demonstrated still and moving images on an iBook and explained that the screen image had to be converted before being placed onto the poster to be printed. Because the poster image had been enlarged, the printed image on the poster was not as well-defined as the iBook screen image. The ASA acknowledged that, for technical reasons, it was impossible to transfer the screen image directly onto a poster. It ruled that the image shown on the iBook screen in the poster did not misrepresent the screen images available on the iBook and that the poster was not misleading.

---

In 2002 the ASA ruled on a poster and leaflet for an Internet car trader. It stated 'Would you buy a used car from this man?' and claimed 'Now you can. AA Buyacar ...'. A footnote stated 'Please note that the AA will act as an appointed intermediary for the purchase of your vehicle from our reputable supplier. Your contract for the purchase of the vehicle will be with the supplier.' The objections were that the advertisements misleadingly implied customers could buy from the AA and that the footnote on the poster was illegible at normal viewing distance.

In both cases the complaints were upheld. In the first case, the ASA ruled that the advertisement implied that cars could be bought direct from the AA. It concluded that the headline claim was misleading and advised the advertisers not to repeat the claim and to reword it with help from the Committee of Advertising Practice (CAP) Copy Advice team.

In the second case the ASA considered that the footnote in the leaflet was legible, but it was too small on the poster to be read by a sighted person, with normal vision, viewing for a reasonable length of time, at a reasonable distance. It asked the advertisers to ensure that footnotes on posters were legible in future and advised them to seek help from the CAP Copy Advice team.

Source: adapted from www.asa.org.uk.

(a) Explain why the advertising in the above cases might have been investigated by the ASA.
(b) Suggest how the decisions by the ASA might affect how the businesses approach advertising in future.

**Question 3**

- Environmentalists are concerned about high levels of consumption and the role of advertising in encouraging this. They doubt whether the earth's resources can sustain current levels. There is a growing trend amongst consumers to look at the type of goods they buy and also how much they consume, as they become more aware of long term problems.
- Advertising can encourage people to buy products which are regarded as being damaging to society.
- Advertisements often encourage behaviour which might be to the detriment of society as a whole. An example is the fast 'macho' driving often seen in advertisements for cars and related products.

In its defence, the advertising industry would point to a number of arguments to justify its role.

- Advertisements offer a choice to consumers which allows them to make more informed consumption decisions.
- Advertisements give valuable information to consumers which might otherwise be difficult to come by.
- Advertisers respond to and reflect the needs, wishes and attitudes of consumers; they do not 'create' them.
- Advertising earns revenue for television and radio and allows newspapers and magazines to be sold at lower prices.
- The advertising industry employs large numbers of people. They are employed directly, through advertising agencies, and indirectly through jobs that may result from a successfully advertised product.

## Corporate advertising

CORPORATE ADVERTISING is concerned with promoting a company as a whole, rather than individual products. An example of corporate advertising can be seen in the detergent market. Companies such as Unilever and Nestlé have their name on branded packcts. The amount spent on corporate advertising has doubled in recent years and this trend is expected to continue.

Companies ranging from ICI to Benetton to BP have jumped on this bandwagon.

There are two reasons why companies need to sell themselves now more than ever. First, companies must now be seen to be responsible good 'citizens' (☞ unit 111). This means communicating. Second, there is growing pressure for the company to become a **brand** (☞ unit 27). Companies need to ensure that their corporate image is positive.

Corporate advertising often makes use of **slogans**, **brand names** or **catchlines**. Nestlé, for example, identifies its name on products. So, for example, all KitKats have the name Nestlé clearly marked on their covers. Even more dramatically, the Chambourcy brand of yoghurt was renamed Nestlé. Nestlé uses the corporate slogan 'Good food, Good life' to build up its reputation as a company which can be trusted to provide quality food and improve life. In a similar way, Vodafone, by sponsoring Ferrari's Formula 1 racing team, is attempting to build a successful brand image by encouraging customers to associate its product with another successful product.

Corporate advertising allows a company to advertise its whole philosophy. Corporate messages are aimed at a variety of different, yet connected, audiences. These include employees, local groups, the trade, government, the media, financial institutions and the 'general public', as well as consumers themselves. There are problems, however. The corporate values of one company may not be different to those of another, so that target audiences may not be able to distinguish between the messages of different firms. Also, less may be spent on advertising individual brands, as a business uses resources to promote the whole company.

---

BASF Corporation is the world's leading chemical company, producing high-performance products, such as chemicals, plastics, performance products and agricultural products. In 2002 it had sales of $34 billion and more than 89,000 employees throughout the world. 'Helping make products better' is its slogan and 'We don't make a lot of the products you buy. We make a lot of the products you buy better' is its corporate statement. This has made the BASF corporate advertising campaign the most recognised of any corporate campaign from the North American chemical industry. The business does not make many finished products. Virtually all of the 6,000-plus products made by the company are ingredients that enhance the finished products consumers buy. Its television advertising campaign features many of these products with comments. They include:

- a picture of a tennis player, focussed in on the shoe, with the phrase 'we don't make the tennis shoe we make it grip **better**';
- a picture of a band in a recording studio with the phrase 'we don't make the studio, we make it quieter';
- a picture of a man on a beach with the phrase 'we don't make sun screen, we make it stronger'.
- a picture of a car being filled with petrol with the phrase 'we don't make the fuel, we make it burn cleaner'.

In 2004 the company introduced a new innovative ultraviolet light (UV) absorber that will help sunscreen and cosmetic manufacturers. ' ... Uvinul A Plus offers reliable protection against UVA rays that penetrate deeper into the skin over long periods without the need for additional stabilisation' said Alyson Emanuel, Director, Cosmetic Ingredients for BASF in North America.

Source: adapted from www.basf.com.

(a) Identify features of corporate advertising by the company.
(b) Explain why such a business might use corporate advertising.

# key terms

**Advertising media** - the various means by which advertisements can be communicated to the public.
**Corporate advertising** - advertising which is meant to promote a whole company rather than a particular product or product line.
**Informative advertising** - advertising which primarily seeks to provide consumers with information about a product.

**Persuasive advertising** - advertising which seeks to influence and persuade consumers to buy a product.
**Promotion** - an attempt to retain and obtain customers by drawing attention to a firm or its products.
**Reassuring advertising** - a method used to assure consumers about their purchases and encourage them to make repeat purchases.

## Knowledge...Knowledge...Knowledge...Knowledge...Knowledge...Know

1. What is above the line promotion?
2. Why might advertising be both above and below the line promotion?
3. What are the objectives of promotion?
4. What choices of advertising media do firms have?
5. What criteria might firms use in order to decide upon their choice of advertising media?

6. What is the role of an advertising agency?
7. What is the role of the ASA?
8. Why might an advertisement be banned under the Trades Descriptions Act?
9. State 3 arguments for and 3 arguments against advertising.
10. What is the objective of corporate advertising?

# Case study Conrack and Eco-Store

## Conrack

Conrack Ltd is a private limited company which specialises in manufacturing products from 'managed' wood. Managed wood is wood which when cut down for timber is replaced by planting a new tree. Its policy is only to purchase wood from suppliers that guarantee to conform with these requirements.

The business has been successful in selling to customers who are interested in preserving the environment. They are attracted by the idea that the products they buy do not use up the earth's resources, which are preserved for future generations. Conrack's slogan is 'What we use, we replace'. Products include kitchen and dining tables. It also manufactures housing 'parts', such as window ledges and doors, from managed wood, as well as conservatories and garden outhouses.

In 2004 the business had a manufacturing factory just outside Manchester and two retail outlets in the area north of Manchester. Its turnover was £800,000 and it had a promotion budget of around £15,000 per annum. It had concentrated mainly on local

advertising in the region. The managing director, Kim Barnett, argued that small scale but thought provoking advertisements might be particularly influential in attracting interest in the company's products.

# Eco-Store

The Eco-Store is a company with a national chain of stores in the UK. The shops are based on 'old style' American stores. Food is sold loose from barrels and sacks to remove the need for packaging and waste. Liquids and drinks are filled into bottles or containers rather than being sold in plastic or glass bottles. Environmentally friendly goods are also sold. These include products made from recycled plastic and wood and recycled paper. The company has seen rapid growth in the 1990s and early twenty first century. By 2004 it had a turnover of £200 million. It had decided to review its marketing strategy. It particularly wished to develop a caring image for the company. It hoped in its advertisements to stress the 'homely nature' of the stores and products. It felt that this would attract families to shop at its stores.

**Table 28.2**

**Advertisement in local newspaper per week** -
£51 per issue (based on a business card sized advertisement of 5 cm x 2 cm)

**Advertisement on local radio**
Fixed costs - £500-£1,000
Cost per minute - £100-£200

**Leaflets**
Single colour
Fixed costs - £125
Cost per thousand - £50
Full colour
Fixed costs - £200
Cost per thousand - £200

**Internet website**
£1,000 per year

**Poster on a fleet of buses for a month** - £300

**Insert into *Yellow Pages* per annum**
1.5 cm box - £154
3 cm box - £272
4.5 cm box - £367

**Advertising in a specialist magazine (per issue)**
1/4 page black and white £400
Full page 2 colour £1,300
Full page full colour £1,700

**Advertising in a national newspaper** -
£20,000 per quarter page advert

**Television advertising** - £50,000 per 30 seconds, plus fixed costs.

(a) **Identify the possible objectives of the two businesses. (6 marks)**
(b) **How might Eco-Store be able to make use of corporate advertising? (6 marks)**
(c) **Explain, using examples, how the methods of promotion might be made:**
   (i) **persuasive;**
   (ii) **informative;**
   (iii) **reassuring;**
   **for customers of the businesses. (6 marks)**
(d) **Examine the factors which might affect the choice of medium of each business. (10 marks)**
(e) **Select appropriate media which the business might use. Justify your choices for each business. (12 marks)**

## What is promotion?

Promotion below the line refers to those promotional methods which do not depend upon media such as newspapers and TV. Instead, it takes place by methods over which firms have some degree of control. These include direct mail advertising, exhibitions and trade fairs, sales promotions, merchandising, packaging, personal selling and public relations. A business, such as Hilton Hotels, might promote its hotels by using a combination of promotions, for example public relations and sales promotions.

Below the line promotion allows a business to aim its marketing at consumers it knows are interested in the product. Above the line advertising in newspapers means that the promotion is seen by most of the readers, even though some will not be interested. With below the line promotions, firms are usually aiming their message at consumers who are either known to them or who have been chosen in advance. For example, direct mail advertisers will pick exactly which consumers they wish to send their mail to, rather than going for blanket coverage. Businesses promoting through exhibitions, such as the Boat Show, can be certain that the majority of those attending will be interested in the products on show.

There may be problems that result from below the line promotions.
- As with advertising, they are expensive and their outcome is difficult to predict.
- They are often 'one off' events, which have an impact for a limited period.
- Some types of promotion, such as direct mail and personal selling, are disliked by consumers.

## Direct mailing

Direct mailing involves sending information about a product or product range through the post. The consumer can usually buy the product by placing an order by post or telephone. Although sometimes unpopular with the public, direct mail is a fast growing area of promotion. It has proved very effective for firms trying to reach a target audience. Some companies use direct e-mailing, where consumers or businesses receive product information through their e-mail inbox. Systems, however, exist for unwanted e-mails to be blocked as this method of selling has proved unpopular for some people.

Direct mail is one means of **direct marketing** (☞ unit 30), which is often seen as part of a firm's distribution network.

## Exhibitions and trade fairs

Exhibitions and trade fairs are used by firms to promote their products. They are visited by both industrial and ordinary consumers. Examples of better known fairs and exhibitions include the Motor Show, the Boat Show and the Ideal Homes

Anna Lever runs a shop which sells imported comics from the USA and Europe. She stocks well known comics by Marvel and DC, such as X-men and Batman, and also a small line of European comics. Anna also sells comics by independent publishers in the UK. The market for comic sales in the UK tends to be a niche market, selling to specialist collectors, teenagers, students and children, and older people who Anna argues 'want to recapture their youth, by reading the stories they read when they were children and teenagers.'

There is a small number of chains selling comics in the UK, such as Forbidden Planet, but many other independent shops. The nearest competitor for Anna's shop is over 50 miles away. Anna often tries local mailing in the area. General mailing to all people tends to be waste of time, so she must carefully target her audience. She also keeps clients regularly updated via e-mails. Most regular customers are happy to receive information about the latest issues although some newer customers have objected to this 'spam'.

Every month Anna makes the trip to the nearest city and puts up a stall in the comic mart on Sundays. She tends to see the same faces there all the time, and can build up contacts. There may also be people coming to 'have a look' on their day off and some have become regular clients. She has also occasionally taken a stand at the large fair held at the NEC in Birmingham a few times a year. She finds the trip is tiring, takes a lot of time out of her week and does not always pay for itself.

Source: adapted from company information.

(a) Why might it be important for Anna's business to use a trade fair as part of its promotional mix?
(b) Assess whether a trade fair might be more successful than direct mail advertising in promoting and selling comics.

Exhibition. Why do businesses find them useful?

- They give the chance to show how a product actually works. This is important in the case of bulky or complex technical products. The marketing of industrial and agricultural machinery is often done through trade fairs.
- Consumer reaction to a product can be tested before it is released onto the market.
- Some trade fairs and exhibitions are held overseas. They can form a part of a firm's international marketing strategy.
- A fair or exhibition may attract press coverage. New products may be launched to take advantage of this. The Motor Show is widely used for this purpose.
- They allow customers to discuss a product with members of the management team. It is not unusual for the managing directors of a business to attend a trade fair. For industrial consumers, in particular, this can be a valuable point of contact.
- Technical and sales staff are available to answer questions and discuss the product.

## Sales promotions

Sales promotions are the incentives offered to consumers to encourage them to buy goods and services. They are used to give a short term 'boost' to the sales of a product. This is different to building up brand recognition and loyalty, which may be a longer term aim. There is a variety of sales promotions that a business can use.

- Coupons and loyalty cards. These involve either providing money off or refunds on specific purchases or allowing savings to be made over time for being a loyal customer. The Boots Advantage loyalty card, first launched in 1997, had 15 million customers by 2004.
- Competitions. Prizes are sometimes offered for competitions. To enter, consumers must first buy the product. Tabloid newspapers often use this type of promotion. They try to attract customers through large cash prizes in their 'bingo' competitions.
- Product endorsements. These are widely used by a range of manufacturers, where well known personalities are paid to use products. For example, sports products companies will sign up teams and successful sports personalities to promote their products. The competition between sports companies has often been reflected by the teams they supply - Real Madrid has worn Adidas while Manchester United and Barcelona have worn Nike.
- Product placing. This involves a firm paying for product brands to be placed on the sets of films and TV programmes. Car manufacturers are often eager to see their vehicles driven by Hollywood stars in popular movies.
- Free offers. A free 'gift' may be given with the product. An example of might be music magazines, which regularly offer readers free CDs of featured artists.
- Special credit terms. This has been increasingly used by firms. It includes offers such as interest free credit and 'buy now pay later' schemes.

Why have these methods become popular?

- Sales promotions can be used as a method to break into a new market or introduce a new product into an existing market. They can also be used as a means of extending the **product life cycle** of an existing product (☞ unit 24).
- They are a means of encouraging consumers to sample a good or service which they might not have bought otherwise. Once the initial good has been purchased it is likely that further goods will be bought. Many magazines offer free gifts ranging from CD Roms to make-up in their first issues hoping that their consumers will continue to buy.
- Customers feel 'rewarded' for their custom. They may, as a result, develop a loyalty to a particular product or business.
- Customers identify products or businesses with things that they like or are attracted to. A customer is therefore more likely to purchase a product.
- Sales promotions provide businesses with feedback on the impact of their marketing expenditure, for example, through the number of coupons returned or the amount spent on loyalty cards.

Sales promotions are not without problems. The free flight offer of Hoover in 1992 is one example. It offered two free flights to the US with the purchase of products worth over £200. The company misjudged the number of people taking advantage of the offer. This meant extreme pressure on the company to produce the goods consumers were demanding. Also many consumers did not receive the holidays on dates or at times they wished. By 1993 there were so many complaints that Maytag, Hoover's US parent company, had to intervene

---

Evidence of product placement abounds in Hollywood movies. In Charlie's Angels a mobile handset rings and the action cuts to a shot of a Nokia phone. In Mission Impossible 2 Tom Cruise can be seen donning a well known brand of sunglasses. In the last Austin Powers movie Mike Myers said 'Hey!Hey!Hey! Get your hands off my Hiney baby!' seconds before a bottle of Heineken beer appeared in the shot. The marketing agency involved in the Heineken placement estimated a sales increase of 15 per cent and greatly increased product recognition amongst 21 to 29 year olds.

Nearly all Hollywood studios today have a department devoted to product placement and it is part of the everyday business of making movies. In many cases cash does not change hands. Often a company such as mobile phone maker or an airline will agree to provide their good or service free in exchange for a prominent placement.

Source: adapted from news.bbc.co.uk/1/hi/entertainment.

(a) Identify the benefits of using product placement as a method of sales promotion from the article.
(b) What might be the disadvantages of this method of promotion?

to make sure flights or compensation were provided. It was estimated that the cost of dealing with these problems was £21.1 million.

## Branding

A brand is a name, term, sign, symbol, design or any other feature that allows consumers to identify the goods and services of a business and to differentiate them from those of competitors. So a recognised brand might be a brand name such as Tesco or Virgin, a logo such as the Ellesse logo on sports wear or another feature such as the use of the colour orange in B&Q stores. The use of brands as a means of promotion is covered in detail in unit 27.

## Merchandising

MERCHANDISING is an attempt to influence consumers at the POINT OF SALE. The point of sale is anywhere that a consumer buys a product. It may be, for example, a supermarket, a department store, a bank or a petrol station. Consumers are intended to buy based on 'what they see' rather than from a sales assistant. The aim of merchandising is to encourage sales of a product and therefore to speed up the rate at which stocks are turned over (☞ unit 82).

There is a number of different features of merchandising.

● Display material. A good display should attract attention, enhance certain aspects of a product and encourage the 'right frame of mind' to make a purchase. Department stores lay great stress on window displays. Banks make sure that the services which they offer, such as insurance and loan facilities, are well displayed in their branches.

● The layout of products at the point of sale. Many retail outlets, such as supermarkets, design the layout of their stores very carefully. Their aim is to encourage consumers to follow particular routes around a store. Retail outlets often place popular items at the back or sides of a store. Consumers, on their way to these, are encouraged to walk past other items which they might buy. Another tactic is to place related products next to each other, so consumers buy both.

● Stocks. A firm must make sure that stock levels are maintained and shelves are quickly restocked. Shelf space is usually allocated according to the amount of a product which a business expects to sell. For example, a supermarket will give more space to products on special offer.

● Appropriate lighting and the creation of desirable 'smells'. Generally lighting is kept soft where browsing is encouraged and bright where there is a need to suggest cleanliness as, for example, at a cosmetics counter. Smells are used to encourage the right atmosphere. Bread smells are often wafted into supermarkets and food retailers.

## Packaging

A product's packaging is important in its overall marketing. This is because consumers often link the quality and design of a product's packaging with the quality of the product itself. Unsuitable packaging may affect sales.

What factors should firms consider when deciding upon how to package their product?

● Weight and shape. These can affect the cost of distributing a product. For example, bulky packaging may mean high distribution costs.

● Protection. Products must not be damaged in transit or in storage. They must also be protected against light, dust and heat.

● Convenience. The packaging must be easy to handle by the consumer and distributors.

● Design. The design of the packaging should be eye catching and help the consumer to distinguish it from others. It should also fit in with the overall marketing of the product and project the brand image. Colour is likely to be important here.

● Information. It is likely that the package will contain information required by the consumer. For technical products, the packaging will need to include information about how the product should be used. For food products, there are legal requirements about the information that must be on the package, such as details of the ingredients contained.

● Environmental factors. Manufacturers are facing increasing pressure to cut down on the amount and type of packaging placed around products. Consumers and pressure groups (☞ unit 102) stress the wastefulness of this and its impact upon the environment. The response of some manufacturers to this pressure has been to use recyclable materials.

## Personal selling

Personal selling occurs when a company's sales team promotes a product through personal contact. This can be done over the

---

Domino's Pizza has 230 stores across the UK and Ireland and over 7,000 stores worldwide. It was the first pizza delivery company in the world to offer online pizza ordering. Dominoes is estimated to have a 20 per cent share of the UK pizza and delivery market.

Domino's heat wave delivery bags are specially designed to keep the pizzas oven-hot during delivery. They contain a patented disc that is preheated as well as being specially lined. The inner material of the bag is made of Thinsulate insulation, which eliminates unwanted moisture and keeps the pizza hot and crisp.

The pizza is contained in a corrugated pizza box. This design keeps moisture from weakening the box, while preventing cheese from sticking to the top during delivery. The packaging also shows the company's logo. It has been suggested that more than 80 per cent of the pizza's box is made from recycled paper.

Source: adapted from www.dominos.com and www.dominos.co.uk.

(a) What factors might be important to the business in deciding the packaging for its take-away pizzas?

Question 3

telephone, by setting up meetings, in retail outlets, or by 'knocking on doors'. In general, the more highly priced, technically complex or individual the product, the greater the need for personal selling. Most firms supplying industrial markets rely upon personal selling in the form of **sales representatives**.

The main advantage of personal selling over other methods is that individuals can be given personal attention. Most forms of promotion tend to deliver a 'standard message' to a 'typical' consumer. With personal selling the individual consumer's needs can be dealt with and the product shaped to meet these needs.

There are certain purposes which personal selling can serve.
● Creating awareness of and interest in a product.
● Explaining the functions and technical aspects of a product.
● Obtaining orders and, in some cases, making deliveries.
● Encouraging product trials and test marketing.
● Providing rapid and detailed feedback from the consumer to the producer via the sales representative.

One disadvantage with personal selling is that it can be expensive. The cost of maintaining a team of sales representatives can be very high. Another problem is the dislike of 'callers' by consumers. There are also legal and ethical issues about the way products are sold that need to be considered.

## Public relations

PUBLIC RELATIONS is an organisation's attempt to communicate with groups that form its 'public'. Such groups may include the government, shareholders, employees and customers. The aim of such communications is to increase sales by improving the image of the firm and its products. This can be done directly by the business itself through a public relations activity. On the other hand a television programme or a newspaper could be used.

Consumers appear to attach great importance to messages conveyed through public relations. Take the example of a new restaurant which has just opened. It would expect to promote a positive image of itself through its own promotional materials. Such communications may, therefore, be taken 'with a pinch of salt' by consumers. However, a good write-up in a newspaper or restaurant guide is likely to be taken much more seriously by consumers.

Businesses often use **press conferences** to attract publicity. These might involve inviting journalists to a company presentation, where they are given information. The business may take the opportunity to launch a new or updated product. Sometimes, businesses provide free products for conference members to try out. Conferences may also be used for presentations to trade customers.

Businesses also make use of **press releases**. These are written accounts of events or activities which may be considered newsworthy. For example, new multi-million pound contracts gained by firms such as British Aerospace are announced on

TV news bulletins. Such news stories usually originate from press releases issued by businesses themselves.

Because of the importance of maintaining good relations with the media, a business may appoint a **publicity manager**. As well as promoting favourable press stories, publicity managers must respond to criticisms and try to ensure that there are no unfavourable press notices.

Other than conferences what other public relations activities may firms use?
● Donations to charities etc. These can range from a small contribution to a college mini bus appeal to a large

Virgin is a company noted for its effective marketing. In November 2003, Virgin Blue, the group's budget airline announced the details of its share flotation. Sir Richard Branson said at a press conference in Brisbane 'We believe the future is bright for Virgin Blue and, as such, we plan to maintain a significant stake in Virgin Blue as part of our global airline strategy'.

In 2004 the Virgin website contained the following press release.

**'VIRGIN MOBILE BACKS YOUNG DRIVING TALENT WITH SPONSORSHIP OF BRITISH FORMULA BMW TEAM'**
Virgin Mobile, the UK's fastest growing mobile network, is delighted to confirm its sponsorship of the British Formula BMW team set up by Barwell Motorsport, in a bid to establish one of the most high-profile young driver support schemes in British motorsport – The Virgin Mobile Scholarship.'

Source: adapted from www.virgin.com and www.smh.com.au.

(a) Identify the promotional methods used by the Virgin Group in the article.
(b) Explain how such methods might benefit the business.

**Question 4**

donation to Comic Relief's 'Red Nose Day' or the 'Children in Need' appeal . Whilst some make payments anonymously, others take advantage of the opportunity for a good public relations event. The approach of a firm to such an event is likely to be determined by its particular ethical stance (☞ unit 110).

- Sponsorship. This is popular in the sporting world. Examples have included the links between Coca-Cola and the Olympic Games, McDonald's and the World Cup, and Nike and Tiger Woods. Other types of sponsorship take place in the arts world with ballet, opera and theatre being sponsored by businesses. Firms such as ICI and BP choose to sponsor educational programmes.

- Company visits. Jaguar Cars and Warburtons Bakeries have allowed members of the public to visit their manufacturing and research plants as part of their public relations activities.

## key terms

**Merchandising** – a promotion specifically at the point of sale of a product.

**Point of sale promotion** - a promotion at any point where a consumer buys a product.

**Public relations** - an organisation's attempts to communicate with interested parties.

## Knowledge

1. What is below the line promotion?
2. What is direct mailing?
3. Why do businesses promote their products at trade fairs and exhibitions?
4. Identify 4 different types of sales promotions.
5. Where is merchandising likely to take place?
6. Which aspects of their merchandising should businesses pay attention to?
7. What factors do businesses need to consider when packaging their products?
8. What is the main advantage of personal selling?
9. What is public relations?
10. Under what circumstances might public relations activities be most effective?

# Case study The Card Up Their Sleeve

According to market researchers, around 85 per cent of households have at least one loyalty card. The use of loyalty cards began in the British supermarket retail market, one of the most competitive in the world. Merlin Stone, business researcher for IBM, states 'Grocery retailing in the UK is a classic oligopoly with the top three or four firms accounting for 60 per cent of the market'. In such a fierce climate there's a constant search for smart weapons to gain an edge.

The loyalty scheme began with the Tesco Clubcard in 1995. One year later Clubcard holders were spending 28 per cent more at Tesco and 16 per cent less at Sainsbury's. Sainsbury's retaliated with the Reward card and other retailers including Boots and WH Smiths developed similar schemes. In September 2002 a new 'consortium' loyalty card - Nectar - was introduced, with members including Sainsbury's, BP, Debenhams and Barclaycard. By February 2004, with the help of a £50 million advertising campaign, Nectar had 11 million UK households signed up.

There is no catch or con to loyalty reward schemes. Tesco gives customers a point worth a penny for every pound spent. Card holders receive Clubcard vouchers which they can spend instore or redeem against special offers such as hotel tokens or free bowling or cinema tickets. Boots gives the most generous rates - 4 points (worth 4p) per pound spent and the Boots Advantage card now has 15 million members. Running such schemes will cost the companies substantial sums. So where is their return?

Retailers who launch loyalty schemes experience between 1 and 4 per cent increase in sales. But in addition to the increased sales, the cards have given retailers ways of analysing their shoppers. Every swipe of the card sends customer spending information into a databank profile of their purchase history, along with the information customers give when they sign up for the card. This allows retailers to find out about the customers' habits, lifestyle and preferences. For example a mother or father of teenage children may spend up to £150 per week in a supermarket. The retailer will analyse this expenditure for a period of months and identify those areas where the family could be tempted to increase their purchases. The family may only buy one type of cereal and so the retailer might give an incentive of extra loyalty points on a different, but high-profit, cereal. Tesco, for example, sends loyalty letters with special offers to 10 million Clubcard homes four times a year.

A proportion of shoppers do not want to play the loyalty game. For them, a more important consideration in deciding where to shop is price. Asda, which does not run a loyalty scheme, has just come top of the *Grocer* magazine's Lowest Priced Shopping Basket for the sixth year running. In 2003 the store's market share rose from 15.5 per cent to 16.3 per cent and was challenging hard for the number two slot in the supermarket pecking order.

Source: adapted from *The Guardian*, 19.7.2003.

(a) **Why were loyalty cards were first introduced into the grocery retail sector in the UK? (6 marks)**

(c) **Explain why Sainsbury's, BP, Debenhams and Barclaycard might have launched a 'consortium' loyalty card. (6 marks)**

(d) **Analyse how loyalty cards would help retailers like Tesco to improve the impact of their other sales promotion methods. (8 marks)**

(d) **Assess the benefits and costs of loyalty card schemes for:**
   (i) **consumers:**
   (ii) **retailers. (10 marks)**

(e) **Evaluate Asda's decision not to introduce a loyalty card. (10 marks)**

## Channels of distribution

Distribution is about one of the 4 'Ps' of the marketing mix (☞ unit 23) - place. A business must get the product to the right place, at the right time. A product which is effectively priced and promoted may not be a success unless the consumer is able to purchase it easily.

A CHANNEL OF DISTRIBUTION is the route taken by a product as it passes from the producer to the consumer. Figure 30.1 shows some of the most popular channels of distribution that are open to a business. A producer can sell its products:

- directly to the consumer (channel 1);
- through a retail outlet (channels 2, 4, 6, 7);
- through a wholesaler (channels 3, 4, 7);
- using an agent (channels 5, 6, 7).

Sometimes the channel of distribution can be straightforward. Take the example of a village bakery. The bread and cakes are baked in the same place as they are sold. Consumers buy direct from the producer (channel 1 in Figure 30.1). Other examples include the sale of 'home' produced local computer software, the sale of farm products 'on site', or the sale of music or data which is downloaded from the Internet.

However, some businesses manufacture their goods and provide their services from large, central units in order to benefit from **economies of scale** (☞ unit 81). Their consumers may be located over a wide geographical area. Having a distribution channel similar to that of the village baker could mean disaster. It is likely, in this case, that more complex methods of distributing the product are needed. This may involve the use of INTERMEDIARIES - wholesalers, retailers or agents.

## Intermediaries

What intermediaries are involved in the distribution of products?

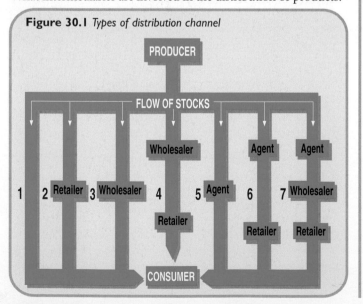

**Figure 30.1** *Types of distribution channel*

**Wholesalers** These often act as links between producers and retailers. Their main task is to buy in bulk from manufacturers and to break this down into smaller quantities which can then be handled by retailers. Examples in the UK include Makro and Costco. Channel 4 in Figure 30.1 has traditionally been the most common method of distribution because of the benefits for the businesses involved. Wholesalers can benefit **manufacturers** in a number of ways.

- They have well established distribution networks and are likely to have strong links with retailers.
- By breaking the manufacturers' products down into smaller batches and taking care of distribution problems, they free the manufacturer to concentrate upon production.
- For multi-product firms, they can help to solve distribution problems, especially when wide geographical areas are involved. Figure 30.2 shows how wholesalers are able to help a firm producing six products distributed over a wide area. By using a wholesaler, the manufacturer is able to deliver all six products to one site. Imagine the difficulties if the manufacturer had to deliver every one of the products to each of the retailers.
- They can bear the cost of storage or warehousing.
- They provide a source of market research information, for example, by asking retailers how their stock is selling in different areas.

Wholesalers also help **retailers**. They offer a choice of products from a variety of manufacturers and provide a 'local' service, often delivering products. Wholesalers sometimes sell direct to the public (channel 3). An example might be a kitchenware wholesaler holding a one week sale for members of the public in order to clear out old stock.

Despite the benefits wholesalers offer, they are not without their problems. Some wholesalers may not promote the products as a business might want, which might harm the firm's marketing efforts. By using a wholesaler the business is passing on the responsibility for marketing - possibly a risky venture. The wholesaler is also likely to take some of the profit.

**Retailers** Because of the problems of wholesalers, a number of manufacturers prefer to deal with retailers directly, by setting up their own distribution networks. Many of the larger retail outlets, such as Sainsbury's and Marks & Spencer, have dealt directly with the manufacturer. This is shown as channel 2 in Figure 30.1. Retailers are an important part of distribution, particularly to manufacturers selling to consumer markets. Retailing is dealt with in more detail later in this unit.

**Agents and brokers** The usual role of agents is to negotiate sales on behalf of a seller. A ticket agency, for example, will sell tickets to consumers for a range of events, such as concerts and plays. The ticket agency does not usually take

**Figure 30.2** *Wholesalers and multi-product firms*

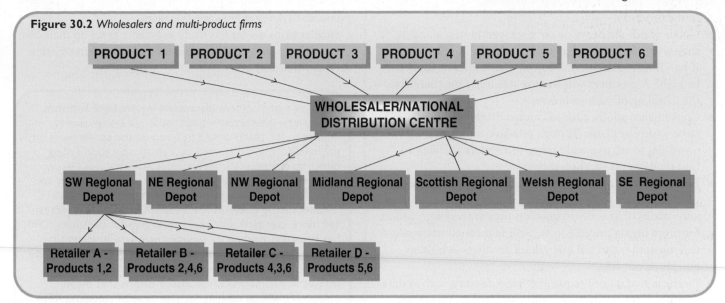

ownership of the tickets it offers. Instead it takes a **commission** (☞ unit 60) on those which it does sell and returns the rest.

Most travel agencies operate in this way. They earn commission on those holidays which they sell, but never actually buy 'blocks' of holidays. The agents are the link between those providing a good or service and those wishing to buy them (channel 5 in Figure 30.1).

Agents are often used by firms wishing to break into a foreign market. They are helpful to businesses which are unsure about the trading practices and legal requirements in foreign countries. They help to take the risk out of trading abroad. People and organisations which are involved in the buying and selling of commodities, such as copper, tin, coffee or sugar, in international markets are known as brokers. After being bought these commodities are broken down and sold on to firms for processing or to be used in manufacturing.

## The choice of distribution channel

How does a producer decide which channel of distribution will get the product to the right place at the right time? An efficient channel of distribution will allow a business to make products available to consumers quickly, when required, and at a minimum distribution cost to the firm itself. Large firms often choose different channels for different products.

There are many factors that can influence a business's decision.

**The product** The nature of the product itself will influence the type of distribution channel chosen.
- Perishable or fragile goods, such as fresh fruit, require direct channels of distribution, so that the time spent handling the product is reduced.
- Technically complex goods also need a direct link between the producer and the consumer. This is so that any problems which arise from installation or use can be

quickly dealt with, without the need to go through an intermediary. Firms installing computers operate in this way to maintain close links with consumers.
- Goods or services which are tailor made tend to have more direct channels, so that the consumer's needs can be passed

Many supermarkets now sell organic and wholefood products grown by farmers. Such competition has made it increasingly difficult for independent health food shops. But rather than simply stoking up at the next supermarket visit, consumers are now clubbing together, forming buying groups to make even bigger savings buying direct from wholefood wholesalers. Priya Hallam, a member of a buying group in Ashbourne, Derbyshire, said 'Some friends told us how much they were saving each year. By cross referencing the items we always brought with the equivalent from our local wholesaler, we worked out we would save over a thousand pounds a year. That's before the cost of petrol to travel to our local Sainsbury's.'

Forming a buying group, for those living in remote rural areas, may be the only way to get products to the door. Highland Wholefoods in Scotland, for example, serves many groups who live miles from a suitable wholefood retailer.

The motivation for setting up buying groups varies. Saving time and money is the main reason, with wholesale prices being around 25 per cent cheaper on organic items. But Tess Rigby who runs the Ashbourne buying group says 'It's helped me to become vegan, because I no longer have to drive round lots of different shops to get what I want.'

Source: adapted from *The Observer*, 10.8.2003.

(a) Describe how the channels of distribution have changed in the article.
(b) Explain the possible (i) benefits and (ii) problems for customers of the new channel of distribution.

**Question 1**

to the producer.
- Goods which are heavy or are packaged in non-standard shapes are likely to require a direct channel of distribution. If handling is difficult, the cost of distribution is likely to be high. A producer will want to minimise the charges for the handling of such products.
- Convenience goods, such as canned drinks and food, need to be widely available through retailers. Firms that are unwilling to sell to a wide range of retailers are likely to find rival brands on shop shelves.
- Producers wishing to sell large quantities of low valued goods are likely to use a wholesaler. They will not want to keep stocks of low valued goods if they are receiving orders for more highly priced goods. Selling through wholesalers will mean they can sell low valued products in bulk, as quickly as possible.
- Products that do not require physical delivery, such as data or other forms of computer file, can use direct methods. However, they might also be available through intermediaries such as retailers for those without the technology to use the Internet in this way.

**The market**
- Large and dispersed markets may require intermediaries. Smaller, local markets can often use a system where consumers buy directly. This is also true of the size of an order, where smaller orders can be sent by a more direct channel of distribution.
- The market segment (☞ unit 20) at which the product is aimed may influence the retail outlet at which the product is made available. For example, products aimed at travelling business people may be sold near to railway stations. Consumer goods are often sold via a retailer or directly to the consumer, whereas industrial products may pass through an agent or wholesaler. International sales may also need to be made through an agent.
- The time period within which consumers expect a response to orders is sometimes an influence. A business may be forced to find the most direct means of distribution or lose an urgent order to a rival.

**Legal restrictions** Legislation may influence the channel that can be used for particular products. Certain drugs, for example, can only be sold by pharmacists through a prescription. Only those with special gaming licences are able to operate casinos.

**The company** Larger companies are often able to set up their own distribution networks. They have the resources to set up warehouses, build and operate distribution sites and purchase transport. They are also often able to take advantage of **economies of scale** (☞ unit 81). For example, a large firm may be able to purchase a fleet of lorries. Manufacturers may open up their own retail outlets, but this will only be effective if the value of the product is high, a wide range of goods or services are sold or large quantities are sold. An alternative is for a

producer to develop links with retailers.

Smaller firms are far less likely to be able to set up their own distribution system. They would tend to use intermediaries, such as wholesalers.

KFM Ltd manufactures interactive whiteboard software. Increasingly, interactive whiteboards are being used in education for teaching and in business for conferences and presentations. KFM started as a small operation selling direct to customers from an industrial estate in Milton Keynes. It would place adverts in specialist magazines and often tailor products to the specific needs of customers.

Recently the business has expanded and now wants to sell more standardised products in greater quantities. KFM has been approached by a retail chain which wants to stock its product range in stores under the 'business and education' section. The retailer feels that the growing market in interactive whiteboards means that more customers will be looking for this type of software. KFM has also been looking to expand in the USA. It is interested in adapting its products for the US market. However, it is aware that legislation might affect its product specification and also that it lacks knowledge about the US market. It has considered a number of alternatives - using an agent to find a retail chain to stock the products, selling to a warehouse business or licensing the product to a US manufacturer.

(a) Examine the factors that might affect KFM's channel of distribution:
   (i)   as a small operation;
   (ii)  as it expands in the UK;
   (iii) as it expands abroad.
(b) Which channel of distribution would you advise KFM to use? Explain your answer.

**Question2**

## Physical distribution

Physical distribution is the movement of products from one place to another. It is an important part of the marketing process for two main reasons.
- Failure to deliver a product in the right quantities, at the right place and at the right time can damage an effective marketing effort.
- The cost of physical distribution can be high - in some cases higher than the cost of actually producing the product.

Two aspects of physical distribution are important to a business - holding stocks and transporting products.

**Holding stocks** Ideally a business would be able to guarantee every customer the product they wanted, whenever they wanted it. To do this a firm would have to hold huge amounts of stock. Holding excessive amounts of stock is very costly. Holding very low stock levels, however, could mean turning down orders.

The solution is for a business to assess the level of stocks needed to maintain an agreed level of customer service. This often means holding enough stock to satisfy regular orders, but not enough to deal with sudden changes in demand. This will depend on the market in which the product is selling.

**Transporting products** This is concerned with how goods can be physically delivered to markets. Firms need to consider the relative costs and speed of transporting their goods by road, rail, sea or air. For example, aeroplanes are faster than ships when transporting exports from the UK. However, firms must decide whether this advantage outweighs the costs which result from using this mode of transport. There are times when the nature of a product dictates the transport. For example, an Orkney Islands based firm which sells freshly caught lobsters to Paris restaurants has little choice but to fly this product to France.

When transporting goods, firms must also consider possible damage to or deterioration of goods. Packaging may help to reduce damage and deterioration, for example, if vacuum packs are used.

## Retailing

Retailers are responsible for the sale of products to the final consumer. It is unlikely that products bought by a consumer from a retailer will be sold again, in the way that wholesalers distribute to many different retailers. Second hand exchanges are perhaps the only exception to this.

Retailers have a major role to play in the distribution of most products. This is because they have the ability to reach huge numbers of consumers, in different markets, over a wide area. Retailers, therefore, can influence manufacturers, insisting on high standards of product quality and delivery times.

Marks & Spencer, for example, is particularly concerned about the quality of products supplied to it. It has an advantage over some retailers because the products which it stocks are OWN BRANDS (☞ unit 27) and because of its size and influence in the retail sector. Smaller retailers may have little influence over manufacturers. This is because the success of such retailers in attracting customers is often dependent upon whether or not they stock brands which are currently in demand.

Retailers can be grouped according to their characteristics.

**Multiple shop organisations** These are businesses with perhaps ten or more establishments, or a group of specialist shops dealing in a particular group of products. Examples include Oddbins, the wine merchants, and Carphone Warehouse, the mobile phone retailer. For consumers, multiple shops have two benefits. They usually offer a wide choice of products in their specialist area. Also, they have often developed an established image, so consumers will be familiar with the level of service, value for money and quality which they can expect.

**Supermarkets** These sell mainly foodstuffs in premises with a minimum of 400 square metres of floor space. Many buy direct from manufacturers rather than through wholesalers and sell products which are fast moving, ie with a short SHELF LIFE, in large volumes. The majority of supermarkets are part of chains, such as Sainsbury's, Tesco, and Asda. There is an growing trend for supermarkets to provide 'own-brand' goods. There has also been a growth of supermarkets stressing lower prices and selling less well known brands. Examples include Aldi and Netto.

**Superstores or hypermarkets** These are huge stores which tend to be found on the outskirts of towns and cities. Their advantage is the ability to offer a range of products under one roof. Many of the multiple organisations mentioned above now have superstores in out of town locations. Examples include PC World, Comet and Marks & Spencer.

**Department stores** Large department stores are found in some city centres, selling a vast variety of different goods on many floors. Famous department stores include Harrods in London and Macy's in New York. Business such as Debenhams and Selfridges also run department stores. They tend to sell more highly priced and luxury goods. However, the high cost of running such stores has forced their closure some cases. Increasingly there is a trend for some stores to towards lease or rent space within the store to businesses selling branded goods (☞ unit 27), such as clothing.

**Retail co-operatives** Retail co-operatives (☞ unit 6) differ from other types of retail organisation in terms of their ownership and the way in which profits are distributed. They are owned by 'members' rather than shareholders and profits are distributed to customers in the form of a dividend rather than being given to shareholders. Retail co-operatives have faced extreme competition from large superstores and hypermarkets. They have attempted to compete by setting up their own superstores and concentrating on convenience stores with late night opening hours, geared to the needs of the local community. Parts of the Co-operative organisation, such as the travel business and the funeral service operation, continue to thrive.

**Independent retailers** The smaller local shop, often owned by a sole trader, is still important for selling many types of products, eg newspapers and tobacco. These rely heavily on the supply of nationally known or branded goods through a wholesaler or a manufacturer's agent. Groups of independent retailers might also join together in order to benefit from the bulk purchasing of stock or joint advertising. These are sometimes known as **voluntary chains**. They are an attempt by independent retailers to match the strengths of large chains.

## Direct marketing

DIRECT MARKETING is sometimes thought to be the same

as direct mailing (☞ unit 29). In fact, direct mailing is just one type of direct marketing. Direct marketing occurs when sales are made without intermediaries being involved. For consumers, this means being able to make purchases from their own homes.

Direct marketing is perhaps the fastest growing means of distribution and is expected to continue into the future. There is a number of reasons for this. Changing work patterns and technology mean that many now find it easier to shop from home. The increased range of products available, and their specialised nature, mean that certain products cannot be purchased from 'usual' outlets such as shops. Also, the increased use of credit cards makes buying in this way easy and direct.

Direct marketing also has advantages for firms. There are no intermediaries to take part of the profits. The producer is able to control its own marketing and also has a chance to reach consumers, who might not otherwise have bought from shops.

Direct marketing can be achieved through a variety of methods.

**The Internet** Shopping via the Internet is rapidly increasing in popularity as more people have a computer at home and make use of fast broadband connection. Customers are often able to search for company websites, browse the products available and their prices, and then place the order online. They are often able to pay with their credit card by entering financial details onto a website order form, which is then processed. Depending on the products for sale, the customer will either:

● have products delivered to their home after the order is processed;
● be allowed to download products such as information or music to their computer;
● be allowed access to information on screen on a website.

Using the Internet for shopping has major advantages for both customers and businesses.

● Orders can be placed at any time that customers have access to the computer, at any time of day or night.
● Customers do not have to travel. They can view a large range of products from their computer and pay for them online.
● It is possible to buy products from other countries and use services such as 'PayPal' to pay in other currencies.

However, not all people have access to, or knowledge about, the Internet. Orders might experience technical problems and people can not test or handle the products in a similar way to viewing in a catalogue. Also, people may resent the spam (junk mail on computer) that often results from buying online.

**Direct mail** This involves posting promotional materials to homes and workplaces. Consumers then place an order and products are sent to the buyer's address. At present, the average British adult receives five items of direct mail each month. This is just half the average in Europe, and one-tenth of what floods through the average US letterbox.

There is a number of benefits of direct mail for businesses and consumers.

● Personalised communications with the potential purchaser's name on a letter can improve sales.
● Groups of consumers or **market segments** can be targeted.
● Detailed information can be provided.
● Groups of consumers who are widely dispersed can easily be reached.

Despite its benefits, it is unpopular in some quarters and also suffers from a number of disadvantages.

● Consumers do not like the personalised nature of direct mail and the amount sent to their home address.
● The databases with potential consumers' names and addresses on them quickly go out of date, so that a large amount of mail goes to the wrong people.
● It is felt to be a 'waste of paper' which uses up a valuable resource - wood.

For many businesses, such as Readers Digest, direct mailing has been very successful. In addition, many charities such as Oxfam and Greenpeace are able to raise large sums in this way.

**Direct response advertisements** These are advertisements placed in newspapers and magazines, and on the TV and

---

In 2000 Great Universal Stores (GUS), the UK's biggest home shopping group, cut 800 jobs when it merged its struggling mail order business with the Argos catalogue shop to try to reverse falling profits. GUS faced a 5.7 per cent drop in annual pre-tax profit to £379.6 million. The biggest fall occurred in the British mail order business, where pre-tax profit fell by £85 million to £21 million.

The company argued that a substantial fall in clothing sales at its mail order business, with catalogues such as Kays and Great Universal, was caused by competition from discount retailers. The merged business was expected to save costs of £80 million over a three year period, partly by combining buying and delivery systems. GUS's chief executive said 'We think we can lower the risk by combining it with Argos.'

Argos's pre-tax profits rose from £117 million to £137.4 million. In the present financial year the company said Argos reported sales growth of 18 per cent in April and May. UK mail order sales dropped 7 per cent in the same months because of a continued lack of demand for clothing. The company announced a rollout of its Argos Additions catalogue at all its stores by 2001 and believed it could become a business worth £300 million.

Source: adapted from *The Guardian*, 9.6.2000.

(a) What examples of direct marketing and retailing are suggested in the article?
(b) Contrast the advantages of these types of distribution from the consumers point of view.

Question **3**

The music industry faces a huge task in combating illegal downloading of music from the Internet. Record companies have long argued that 'free' downloading or sharing music, which the customer does not pay for, has reduced record sales. However, a study by Harvard and the University of North Carolina suggests that file-sharing may help music sales. It concluded that file-sharing had no effect on the sale of popular CDs in the second half of 2002. It even suggested that for the top 25 albums, with sales of more than 600,000 copies, there was a positive effect - 150 downloads were said to increase sales by one copy.

People are prepared to pay for downloading music. Napster is the former illegal online download site which now sells legal downloads paid for by customers. Its figures show that the biggest purchasers of downloads to burn on to CDs via its on-demand service are the same people who pay $10 a month to listen to as much music as they like via its streaming service.

Some feel that the music industry should turn the current challenges facing it to its advantage. Paul Myers, CEO at Wippit which has signed deals to distribute music from EMI, believes the music business should be thinking long term and says 'This message would be much more powerful if it was also backed up by a campaign encouraging legal downloads. A TV commercial for the new Outkast CD or a personal message to a P2P user could contain the message "If you're going to download it, download it legally from Wippit".'

People outside the US are also showing interest in legal downloads. This is backed by figures from Peter Gabriel's OD2, Europe's largest digital music distribution service. It showed that over a million digital downloads were bought via its retail partners across Europe. This bodes well for the arrival of Apple's iTunes and the new Napster in the UK.

How long will the music industry still be about selling CDs? 'Five years from now we'll still be selling CDs, but I think a substantial part of our business will be digital sales' said one commentator.

Source: adapted from *The Guardian*, 5.4. 2004.

(a) Describe how music is sold to customers using examples from the article.
(b) Examine the factors that might affect the distribution and sales of music.
(c) Discuss whether 'Five years from now we'll still be selling CDs, but a substantial part of the business will be digital sales'.

**Question 4**

radio. Consumers are encouraged to fill in a coupon or make a telephone call in order to purchase a product. There should be enough information in the advertisement to allow people to make a decision.

Direct response broadcasting is the selling of products through TV commercials, often in late night slots. Records, CDs and telephones have been sold in this way. There are now TV channels devoted entirely to direct response advertising, such as QVC on Sky Television. The introduction of digital television has increased this type of marketing. Consumers with digital television are linked to a telephone line which allows interactive television and the direct ordering of products.

**Personal selling** This can be a useful form of direct marketing. It is dealt with in unit 29.

**Telephone selling** This involves ringing people up at their home or workplace and trying to sell a good or service. The advantage is that the seller can deal personally with a consumer. However, it is felt to be intrusive by many consumers. It has often been used as a means of marketing financial services, such as insurance, and advertising space on products such as calendars.

**Mail order catalogues** This involves a range of products being included in a catalogue which people can read through at home. Orders can usually be placed by telephone or in writing. It has been seen recently as an outdated means of marketing, but innovations such as the Next Directory with 24 hour delivery have breathed new life into it.

## Trends in retailing and direct marketing

Retailing is a fast changing sector of the UK economy. Today's retail scene is very different from that which existed 30 years ago. Changes in direct marketing have also greatly affected the way in which goods and services are purchased by customers. What are the changes that have taken place?

**Shopping centres** A number of American-type shopping 'malls' have been built in the UK. These include the MetroCentre in Gateshead, The Mall near Bristol and the Trafford Centre in Manchester. They contain a wide range of retail outlets, cafes and restaurants and other services, such as theatre booking. They are designed to provide all the shopping facilities that customers need in one place. They promote shopping as a leisure activity and a 'day out for the family'. They are often found away from city areas because of their size.

**Retail parks** There has been a growth of out-of-town retail 'parks', such as Kinnaird Park near Edinburgh and Fosse Park South near Leicester. They are usually sited on the edges of urban developments as a result of a lack of building land and relatively high rents in city and town areas. Retail parks often contain superstores of high street chains, supermarkets or hypermarkets and restaurant chains. The extent to which they will benefit customers depends on a variety of factors. Those able to travel may benefit from a wider choice of products in a particular superstore. Another benefit is the ease of parking. However, if there is a limited number of retailers, customers may be unable to compare prices as they might in the 'high street' or city centre. Those without transport may face increased prices at local shops as retailers attempt to cover their costs. Retail parks are sometimes criticised for leading to traffic congestion and also for a decline in town centre retailing.

**Call centres** These are usually large offices with staff sitting at telephones who deal with customers. They are mainly used to sell insurance, airline tickets and hotel rooms. They also act as information centres for providers of rail or telephone services. In 1998 there were 3,500 call centres in the UK employing 400,000 people. However, after the year 2000 there was an increasing trend for businesses, such as BT, to site their call centres in low labour cost countries such as India.

**Changes in technology** Many developments in retailing have resulted from new technology. For example, bar codes on products are a common feature in most retail outlets. They recognise the cost of products, allowing them to be quickly totalled. Some supermarkets have facilities for customers to 'read' prices as they shop around the supermarket, which saves time at checkouts. Increasingly electronic point of sale (Epos) data is used to gauge consumer tastes, so that trends can be identified and particular groups targeted. Tesco, for example, has used the information from loyalty cards to select wine buyers for 'cheese and wine tasting evenings'. Bar codes can also be used to update stock levels. Many retailers use in-store cameras to record when and where consumers are tempted to pause and consider whether to buy a product. Cameras are also used for in-store security.

**The growth of 'online shopping'** As explained earlier, there is an increasing trend for online shopping via websites on the Internet. Many businesses, including supermarkets such as Tesco, have their own sites. Barnes and Noble has fought with Amazon to be the world's largest bookseller by expanding its sales online.

**Discount stores** Discount stores are chains of shops under one name which specialise in selling cheaper products. They

are often aimed at customers looking for value for money. However, many customers may find a particular product sold cheaper than in other retail chains. They also encourage impulse buying, as people are motivated to buy a product at a low price which otherwise they might not have bought. Examples of discount chains include The Works, which specialises in stationery and books, and Poundland, which sells products for £1.

**Variable opening hours** There has been a growing trend for longer opening hours to fit in with patterns of work and leisure. Some 'convenience stores' attract customers by staying open until 11pm at night. Flexible opening hours were previously an advantage of small businesses. However, some supermarkets also remain open until late on certain days and others have all night shopping. Increasingly, city centre retailers are opening on Sunday.

**Diversifying** Increasingly retailers are offering a wider variety of products and services. The traditional products for sale at one type of retailer are changing as they are faced with growing competition. Many garages, for example, now sell food and magazines. Some even offer microwave cooking facilities. Financial services are also becoming available in places where they were unlikely to be sold previously. Pensions are available from Marks & Spencer and some supermarkets offer banking facilities and pharmacies. Supermarkets are also diversifying by selling non-food products such as clothing and electrical goods.

**The relative decline of independents** In the last 50 years the number of independent grocers in the UK has been cut by over two-thirds. This has largely been due to the increasing growth of supermarket and hypermarket chains selling food.

**Reductions in costs** Businesses have increasingly been looking for ways to reduce distribution costs. This has led to businesses wishing to supply in larger quantities to retailers in order to achieve economies of scale (☞ unit 81). Retailers can also benefit from lower costs by buying in bulk. The larger retail chains are in a stronger position to do this. This has, to some extent, accounted for the decline in the independent retailer. Remaining open for longer hours may also reduce a business's average total costs (☞ unit 38). This is because the fixed costs of the business, such as the retail outlet, are being spread over a greater output. Even though variable costs may increase, average total costs may fall.

**Second hand shops** There have been second hand shops in the UK for many years, including second hand car dealerships. Charity shop chains, such as Age Concern and Scope, have gained a high profile in town centres in certain parts of the UK. It is likely, however, that this will always be a small part of the total retail market.

**Knowledge** owledge...Knowled

1. Why is distribution so important to a firm's marketing mix?
2. What is a channel of distribution?
3. List the 5 types of organisation which can be involved in a channel of distribution.
4. What is the main role of an intermediary?
5. Explain the difference between a wholesaler and a retailer.
6. Why do manufacturers use wholesalers?
7. What is the difference between an agent and a broker?
8. What factors might influence the choice of distribution channel?
9. What is the difference between direct mailing and direct marketing?
10. Why might a business be reluctant to use direct mailing?
11. Explain 4 trends in retailing and their effect on business.

## key terms

**Channel of distribution** - the route taken by a product as it passes from producer to consumer.

**Direct marketing** - a method of distributing products directly to consumers, without the use of intermediaries such as wholesalers and retailers.

**Intermediaries** - firms which act as a link between producers and consumers in a channel of distribution.

**Own brands** - products which have the brand name of their retailer on them.

**Shelf life** - the average length of time it takes for a product to be sold, once it has been displayed by a retailer.

# Case study Tesco

When it comes to shopping, Tesco is one of the most well know names in the UK. In 2003 it had group sales of £28,613 million, an 11.5 per cent increase over the previous year. Its pre-tax profits were £1,361 million, up by 13.3 per cent. Table 30.1 shows the number of stores the business has in a variety of countries and its potential new stores in future.

**Table 30.1** *Tesco stores*

| Number of stores | Sales area | New stores opened inc. acquisitions in 2002/03 | Planned openings in 2003/04 | Country |
|---|---|---|---|---|
| 1,982 | 21.8m sq ft | 1,265 | 59 | United Kingdom |
| 77 | 1.7m sq ft | 1 | 6 | Republic of Ireland |
| 53 | 2.5m sq ft | 5 | 5 | Hungary |
| 66 | 3.4m sq ft | 20 | 5 | Poland |
| 17 | 1.6m sq ft | 2 | 4 | Czech Republic |
| 17 | 1.4m sq ft | 4 | 4 | Slovakia |
| 52 | 4.8m sq ft | 17 | 6 | Thailand |
| 21 | 2.1m sq ft | 7 | 8 | South Korea |
| 3 | 0.3m sq ft | 1 | 1 | Taiwan |
| 3 | 0.3m sq ft | 3 | 1 | Malaysia |
| 2,291 | 39.9m sq ft | 1,325 | 99 | |

'Our strategy of building a profitable international business of scale, both in Europe and Asia continues to make excellent progress. In a six-year period we have built up a substantial chain of hypermarkets. Our overseas operation now accounts for almost half of Group space.'

Source: adapted from Tesco plc, *Annual Review and Summary Financial Statement, 2003*, Financial highlights, Our markets, Chief Executive's review.

Innovation is part of our every day job for customers. This year we have introduced over 5,000 new food products, increased our Finest brand to nearly 1,100 products and introduced 500 Grab & Go counters in our stores.

Source: adapted from Tesco PLC, *Annual Review and Summary Financial Statement, 2003*, Chief Executive's review.

Tesco.com is the largest e-grocer and most profitable e-retail business in the world. This year our turnover reached £447 million. Each week in the UK we deliver over 110,000 orders. We have 65 per cent share of the UK internet grocery market.

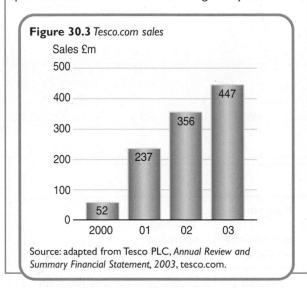

**Figure 30.3** *Tesco.com sales*

Sales £m

- 2000: 52
- 01: 237
- 02: 356
- 03: 447

Source: adapted from Tesco PLC, *Annual Review and Summary Financial Statement, 2003*, tesco.com.

We acquired T&S Stores, a leading convenience retailer. This acquisition increases our share of the convenience market from one to five per cent. We will convert 450 T&S stores to our Express format over the next three to four years bringing the Tesco range and offer to many more customers in neighbourhood locations.

Source: adapted from Tesco PLC, *Annual Review and Summary Financial Statement, 2003*, Chief Executive's review.

Half our new space in the UK this year has been for non-food. This, along with improved capability has seen our non-food market share grow to 5 per cent. This year we have achieved a 16 per cent share of chart music sales, introduced our Finest brand to non-food, and extended the Value brand. We have gained share on Health and Beauty extending our volume market leading position. Cherokee, our exclusive clothing range is available in over 300 stores. Cherokee, Florence & Fred and the Value clothing brands have gone from strength to strength.

Source: adapted from Tesco PLC, *Annual Review and Summary Financial Statement, 2003*, Chief Executive's review.

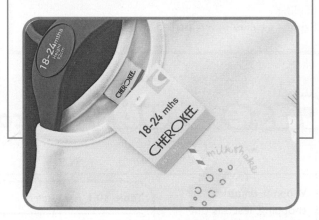

In April 1997, Tesco and GXS developed the Trading Information Exchange (TIE). Via a web, suppliers can view daily electronic point-of-sale (EPOS) data. This allows them to respond more quickly to variations in customer demand and to ensure that optimum stock is available on Tesco shelves at all times. A spokesperson for Procter & Gamble, for example, reported that the system allowed it to spot that a product had sold 8,000 units in two days instead of the expected 10,000 a week. The stock of the product was instantly replenished, which avoided disappointing customers.

Source: adapted from www.gxs.com/downloads/cs_tesco2.

(a) **Describe the channel of distribution at Tesco using an example. (4 marks)**

(b) **What retail category might Tesco fall into? Explain your answer. (4 marks)**

(c) **Explain how Tesco is making use of:**
   (i) **new technology;**
   (ii) **direct marketing. (8 marks)**

(d) **Examine how the use of technology might affect:**
   (i) **Tesco;**
   (ii) **its suppliers**
   (iii) **customers. (12 marks)**

(e) **Assess the factors which may influence how Tesco operates in future. (12 marks)**

# 31 Marketing Planning

## Marketing planning

To help make marketing decisions a business must plan effectively. MARKETING PLANNING is the process by which future marketing activities are systematically planned. Not all businesses have a marketing plan. Some smaller businesses, for example, may make marketing decisions on a short term basis or in response to changing conditions. However, we will see later that planning has a number of benefits for all businesses.

A business's MARKETING PLAN is influenced by the **strategic plans** of the business (☞ units 16 and 17) and the overall corporate aims. A large public limited company such as Unilever, Nestlé, Unigate or the Rank Group will have an overall plan for the business and the aims and objectives that it wishes to achieve. Companies within the business will then develop marketing plans for their businesses and for individual products which fit in with the overall strategic plan. For example, the Rank Group will have an overall corporate strategy. This will influence the plans of its divisions. Detailed marketing plans may be drawn up for Mecca Bingo outlets in its gaming division and its Hard Rock Cafe operations. A manufacturer such as Unilever will have corporate objectives, but detailed marketing plans will be drawn up by Lipton Teas, which is part of Unilever, and even for individual products such as Flora.

## The marketing plan

The marketing plan is concerned with a number of questions.

**Where is the business at present?** A business can only plan where it is going if it knows where it is starting from. Finding out where a business is at the moment involves a **marketing audit**. This analyses the **internal** and **external** factors which affect a business's performance. Most businesses analyse their current position by using SWOT analysis (☞ units 5 and 16), which identifies the business's strengths, weaknesses, opportunities and threats. Table 31.1 shows a possible SWOT analysis for a manufacturer of soft drinks. The business will have some control over internal factors. External factors are out of the control of a business. These include political, economic, social, technological and green (PEST-G) factors outlined later in this unit (☞ unit 16).

**Where does the business wish to be in future?** This involves the business setting **objectives** to be achieved. The objectives provide goals and targets for the business to aim at. They may include such goals as a growth in sales or gaining a certain market share in future.

**Table 31.1** *SWOT analysis of a soft drinks manufacturer*

*STRENGTHS (the strong points of the business)*

- Current products are market leaders in some countries in terms of sales and market share.
- Brand loyalty to products and to the corporate identity.
- Effective promotion.
- Flexibility in production methods.
- Excellent distribution network.
- Constant R&D leading to new ideas.

*WEAKNESSES (the problems it has at present)*

- Age of the life cycle of certain products.
- Restricted product range could cause problems if sales suddenly fall.

*OPPORTUNITIES (that may arise in future)*

- Expansion into newer markets such as sports drinks, low calorie drinks and drinks with new flavours.
- Expansion into new geographical areas such as Eastern Europe.
- Development of a global brand and possible global marketing.
- Possible growing demand for soft beverages.
- Legislation on drink driving may encourage growth of soft drink sales.

*THREATS (that may arise and should be avoided/prevented if possible)*

- Growing competition from supermarket own brands.
- Increasing competition from competitors bringing out new products.
- Competition from alcoholic beverages and non-alcoholic beers and lagers.
- Legislation on ingredients could force changes in production.

**How will a business achieve its objectives?** A business must decide how to get where it wants to go. It will have **marketing strategies** (☞ unit 32) which it will use to achieve its objectives. For example, if it wishes to increase its market share at the expense of a market leader then it may use market challenger strategies. Marketing strategies can be expressed in terms of the marketing mix (☞ unit 23). So a company wishing to gain a 10 per cent increase in market share must make sure that it has the the right product, at the right price, with an effective promotion and distribution policy.

# Factors influencing the market plan

A marketing audit should identify the internal and external factors which affect a business. There is a number of possible factors that may fall into each category.

## Internal factors

- The marketing mix. Of great importance to the internal audit will be an examination of the effectiveness of the marketing mix. This will include an analysis of each element of the marketing mix. For example, projections regarding the life span and future profitability of each of the firm's products may be carried out. It should also include an analysis of how well the elements of the marketing mix fit together, for example, the extent to which distribution channels are compatible with the promotions may be considered.
- People. A huge range of people will be involved in devising and implementing marketing plans. The objectives of these people will determine the targets set in the plan. Also the skills and abilities of those people working for a firm will determine whether targets can be met.
- Finance. Firms can set themselves ambitious marketing goals. However, unless finance is available to fund plans, such goals are unlikely to be achieved. This is discussed in unit 33 under 'Marketing Budgeting'.
- Production processes. Any marketing plan must take into account whether the firm can produce the product. There is little point in planning to increase market share unless enough of the product can be produced to achieve this. Similarly, a firm cannot plan to launch a new product if it cannot manufacture it.

**External factors** An analysis of the external influences on a business usually involves a consideration of PEST-G factors. These are the political, economic, social, technological and environmental factors which affect a business's performance.

- Political. There is an increasing amount of legislation and regulation that may affect the marketing plans of a business. It can vary from controls on the ingredients of products to restrictions on price changes of the privatised utilities, such as water and gas. Much of the new legislation affecting the UK is from the European Union.
- Economic. A wide range of economic factors may affect a business's marketing plans. A buoyant economy, for example, may lead to increased demand for products, higher incomes and the possibility of price increases. Growing unemployment may lead to a fall in future levels of demand. Marketing plans should also take into account the pricing, promotion, distribution and product policies of rival businesses.
- Social. Changes in society can have consequences for marketing planning. The decline of the so-called nuclear family and the changing role of women may influence how

a business promotes its products. The ageing of the population may influence the types of products which are developed and the channels of distribution used to deliver products to customers.

- Technological. Changes in technology can affect marketing plans in a variety of ways. It may make it possible for

---

Knightsbridge is perhaps the last place you would expect a food fight. But in 2003 America's hottest fast food brand, Krispy Kreme, arrived in Britain. Dubbed the 'fast food of the future', the company opened its first fast food shop in Harrods' food hall. It might sound like an unlikely competitor for Britain's afternoon tea brigade, especially in the Atkins society of today. But the company can't make enough of its calorie-laden snacks in the US. Profits have doubled every year for the past three years. Competition to run franchised stores in the US is so strong that rights to new sites are traded like shares. In 2003 *Fortune* magazine branded Krispy Kreme as the hottest food business in America.

The British may never have tried a Krispy Kreme doughnut. But most people have seen the red, green and white logo on US programmes shown in the UK. The doughnut is Homer Simpson's favourite. Sex and the City has an over-eating boyfriend who loves them. And snacks feature in major films, such as Bruce Almighty. They are also the thing to be seen eating at weddings and parties. Even Madonna has been photographed eating them.

There's more to the product than a sweet taste. Marketing plays an important role. Doughnuts are baked freshly every minute in glass ovens in the front of shops. Customers can see them as they walk past a store. Harrods is having a hole cut in the window to encourage customers to walk through and buy. And sales staff play a part as well. They give any customer not buying a doughnut a free one within sixty seconds.

This is also the right time to move into Europe. When things are bad people comfort themselves with sugar. During the recent economic downturn the only fast food firms that have grown are doughnut chains. These include Krispy Kreme and its competitor Dunkin Doughnuts, owned by British drinks business Allied Domecq.

But can Britain be tempted away from biscuits and cakes? Thirty new stores will be opened in the UK in the next year. Don Henshall, head of the UK operation, says 'In Britain the doughnut is a market without a market brand. Krispy Kreme wants to be that brand. It's a big shift to get your head around, but look what has happened in the coffee market. Ten years ago Britons all drank awful instant coffee - now look how the choice has grown.'

Source: adapted from *The Observer*, 28.9.2003.

(a) Identify:
  (i) where Krispy Kreme is in the UK market at present;
  (ii) where the business wants to be in future.
(b) Explain any strengths, weaknesses, opportunities and threats for Krispy Kreme in the UK market.

**Question** 1

businesses to manufacture products that were previously thought to be too costly. It may also lead to greater obsolescence and shorter product life cycles. New technological developments such as interactive television and the Internet may change the promotional methods that a business uses.

● Green factors. Environmental factors are playing an increasing role in the operation of businesses (☞ unit 112). Legislation on pollution and emissions might influence production. The expectations of consumers about packaging and ingredients might affect marketing. Pressure groups (☞ unit 102) can affect decisions. Taking into account the effects of operations on the environment can increase business costs, but may also increase sales.

Businesses should be careful to consider how each of the above factors affects consumers and their buying behaviour. Changes in external factors can cause changes in the wants and needs of consumers. An effective plan should anticipate these changes as well as any other issues affecting consumers' needs.

## The benefits of marketing planning

● The main benefit of marketing planning is that it ensures a business takes time to reflect upon its marketing activities. In today's competitive environment it is not enough for businesses to carry on doing what they have done successfully in the past. They must constantly evaluate and develop their marketing policies. The marketing plan allows them to do this and can be seen as a means of ensuring the survival of the business.

● The marketing plan **co-ordinates** the various aspects of marketing. It takes a holistic view of a business's marketing activities. This should lead to better co-ordination and integration of the different elements of marketing. It should also allow all employees and all areas of the business to be aware of marketing objectives, helping to ensure that they 'pull in the same direction'.

● The marketing plan makes sure that human and financial resources are used where they are most needed. It will also make sure resources will not be wasted on unprofitable activities.

● Businesses will set marketing objectives and targets in their marketing plan. Management, as a result, will have a clear set of criteria against which they can evaluate the success of products.

● Marketing plans may encourage greater employee motivation. Employees are likely to be more prepared for changes in company policy and in the climate of trading. They should therefore be able to act in a more confident and informed manner. They are also likely to feel more secure in the knowledge that the business has planned for the future.

● A marketing plan should make banks feel more confident about offering loans to a firm. Shareholders may also be more confident about buying shares in a business.

## Problems with marketing planning

For many businesses the main problem with marketing plans lies in their confusion as to what marketing actually is. Marketing plans often concentrate upon issues such as product development or increasing sales, but ignore customers' needs. Satisfying consumers' needs should be at the forefront of any marketing plan. A plan which centres around the expected success of a new advertising campaign, for example, is unlikely to be successful unless consumers' needs are satisfied. British Airways, Dunlop, and Woolworths are all businesses which have won awards for advertising campaigns in the past. It is arguable whether these campaigns

Paul Rossington had just been appointed Marketing Manager of SBC plc, a firm which had forty years' experience of supplying a range of instrumentation and components to the aircraft industry.

Paul had decided that his first act would be to involve a range of managers in drawing up a marketing plan. To this end, he called a meeting requesting the presence of all senior managers within the firm.

At the meeting, he began with a short presentation outlining the advantages to SBC plc of marketing planning. He then invited comments from all those assembled. The sales manager chipped in with the first comment; 'It's about time we started advertising more heavily in trade journals and stopped turning out products with the wrong specifications'. The production manager came next; 'I don't know why you dragged me up here to this meeting. You concentrate on the marketing and I'll get on with the production side. So long as you keep me informed of developments we'll be happy down in production.'

Paul was beginning to feel uncomfortable, but it wasn't until the senior accountant's remark that he really felt worried about having accepted this new post. 'I suggest you go away and write this plan and then call another meeting when you're in a position to discuss it with us', she had said.

(a) What advantages of marketing planning would you have advised Paul to mention in his brief presentation?
(b) From the comments made at the meeting, explain any problems which you think SBC plc will have with marketing planning.

**Question 2**

directly led to any improvement in sales.

Many businesses in the UK are organised into personnel, finance, production, and marketing departments. The success of the marketing plan will depend upon each of these areas being prepared to put aside their own goals to satisfy consumers' needs. This can be difficult, especially in a large business, where loyalty to the department can override more important goals. One suggested way of solving this problem is for businesses to be organised around customer groups rather than 'functions'.

Marketing plans often include too much information for them to be useful to managers. In order to overcome this problem, plans should be brief and concentrate upon key factors.

There is a danger that a business may embrace the planning ethos too eagerly. This may lead to the establishment of planning departments which become isolated from those responsible for carrying the plans out. This can have the effect of further divorcing marketing plans from the needs of customers.

Marketing plans often fail to **prioritise** objectives. Plans may include as many as 100 objectives. This means that it becomes difficult to decide whether objectives are being met.

Overall, it is important that a business's marketing plan is geared up to the particular set of circumstances in which it operates. This means a marketing plan which is sensitive to prevailing market conditions, the nature of the markets in which the business is operating and the customers at which the business's products are aimed.

## Evaluating marketing plans

It is essential that businesses evaluate the success of their marketing plans. This will provide them with information on which to base future plans. Businesses also need to know whether or not planned activities were carried out in the manner which was planned.

The evaluation of marketing plans can take place both during the period of time in which the plan is being carried out and at the end of the time period (often one year) that the plan covers. Evaluation which takes place during the period of implementation may allow managers and directors to better control marketing activities.

It is important that marketing plans are evaluated against clear, measurable criteria. To do this, clear performance targets must be agreed and set during the process of marketing planning. Such performance targets are often time specific. This means that they are expected to be achieved by a certain date during the implementation of the plan. For example, a plan may require a 5 per cent growth in market share by the end of the first six months. A business may use a number of methods to evaluate a marketing plan.

**Sales analysis** This is an analysis of either the volume or the value of sales. If a business achieves a sales target then it may consider its marketing plan to be successful. This method is

Figure 31.1 shows the results of research by Tim Ambler and Flora Kokkinaki of the London Business School. They carried out a survey of 531 finance officers and marketers who were asked: 'What measures does your company use to track marketing ... performance?' From the results 5 main categories, shown in Figure 31.1, were identified. The figure indicates how frequently senior management used these measures according to marketers and finance officers.

**Figure 31.1** *Importance of measures of marketing effectiveness for senior management (average)*

531 senior marketers and finance officers were asked to rate the importance that senior management attaches to different measures of market effectiveness in a 7 point scale.

Source: adapted from LBS.

(a) Explain what is likely to be included in 'Financial' measures of marketing effectiveness.
(b) Why are senior managers likely to regard this as the most important measure of marketing effectiveness?
(c) Suggest reasons why other measures of marketing effectiveness may be more important in certain instances.

**Question 3**

the most commonly used to evaluate marketing plans. Sales analysis is especially valuable to a business as it can be linked to a whole range of variables such as:

● sales by region;
● sales by product;
● sales by customer types;
● sales via different distribution channels.

The problem with using sales analysis in isolation is that it may not be related to what is taking place in the wider market. For example, a business may be experiencing high sales growth and so consider its marketing plan successful. However, it may be operating in a growing market in which competitors are experiencing even higher sales growth.

**Market share analysis** This method examines a business's sales in terms of market share. It enables performance in relation to competitors to be more accurately guaged. For example, if a business meets its target of an increase in market share of 5 per cent over a year then it may consider its marketing planning to be successful. Together, sales analysis and market share analysis are a powerful tool for evaluating marketing planning.

**Marketing profitability analysis** Profitability is concerned with the relationship between profits and costs. In the context of marketing planning, profitability analysis is calculated by subtracting the marketing costs of a product from the revenue gained from the product:

MARKETING PROFIT = sales revenue of a product
(quantity sold x price) - marketing costs (marketing research, advertising, distribution, promotion etc.)

Thus a product with high revenue and relatively low marketing costs will be highly profitable. In contrast a product with low sales revenue and relatively high marketing costs will be less profitable.

The main benefit of calculating marketing profitability is that it can highlight some of the most and least profitable markets. Take the example of a business seeking to increase sales of a particular product by moving into two new markets A and B. In market A, an increase in sales of 10 per cent can be achieved with additional marketing costs of 5 per cent. In market B an increase in sales of 45 per cent can be achieved with additional marketing costs of 5 per cent. This business may wish to focus upon the more profitable market B.

The problem with calculating marketing profitability is that it is often difficult to calculate the marketing costs of particular products. For example, many promotional activities, such as trade fairs and corporate advertising, cannot be easily apportioned to individual products in businesses with a range of products.

**Satisfaction surveys** Many businesses undertake analysis of their customer satisfaction surveys. These are detailed surveys designed to identify the reactions of customers to their products. They use this data to assess the extent to which marketing plans are leading to increases or decreases in customer satisfaction.

**Number of enquiries generated** Many businesses pay very careful attention to the numbers of enquiries generated in particular aspects of their business. For example, financial service businesses monitor and evaluate the enquiries generated by direct mailshots as a means of evaluating the success of such promotions.

## key terms

**Marketing planning** - the process by which marketing activities are identified and decided upon.
**Marketing plan** - a detailed account of the company's marketing at present, what it wants it to be in future and how it intends to change it.

Knowledge...Knowledge...Knowled

1. How is a marketing plan affected by a business's strategic plan?
2. State 3 aspects of the marketing plan.
3. What does SWOT analysis show?
4. State 3 internal and 3 external factors that may be taken into account when carrying out a SWOT analysis.
5. State 3 benefits of marketing planning.
6. State 3 problems of marketing planning.
7. Suggest 4 ways in which a business might evaluate its marketing plan.

## Case study The XBox, 2001-2004

### 2001

Microsoft launched its XBox video game console in 2001. It planned to spend $500 million on the launch of the new product, including spending on marketing, advertising and support to retailers and software makers. Prior to the launch, the senior vice president of the company's games division said 'We have to build demand for this to be successful.' The new product, which would include DVD drive and Internet access, was part of the plans of the business to move beyond the PC market. Microsoft also planned to tap into the market for devices that combine television and the Internet, and to offer online gaming.

Microsoft was developing 30 video games inhouse and approving many games from other software developers. It was suggested that the XBox would have three times the performance of Sony's PlayStation 2 (PS2). By the time the XBox was released Sony's PS2 and Sega's Dreamcast would already have been on the market for a year.

Source: adapted from news.com.

## 2002

One down three to go. In February 2002 Sega announced that it would cease production of the Sega Dreamcast games console and quit the hardware business. Instead it decided to produce games for other games consoles. The three left remaining were Sony's PS2, Microsoft's XBox and Nintendo's GameCube. In 2002 there were 30 million PS2 consoles worldwide (as well as 90 million old PS1 consoles). Contrast that to the 4 million XBoxes worldwide.

The Internet gaming market is growing. It has been estimated that it would be a $20 billion industry by 2005. In 2002 Sony's PS2 and Microsoft's XBox were planned to be linked to the Internet for interactive gaming. However, unlike the XBox the PS2 would require additional equipment to be bought. Previously people could play games through their PCs on the Internet. But now they could take advantage of the stunning graphics of games consoles.

Source: adapted from www.ciol.com, abcnews.go.com.

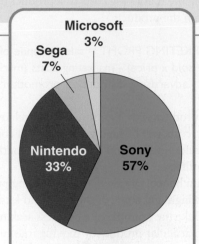

**Figure 31.2** *Games consoles market share estimates, February 2002*
Source: adapted from market research firm, NPD.

## 2003

Between August 2002-03 Microsoft's XBox was the only gaming console to show positive market share growth in the US. It was suggested that sales increased 6 per cent in the US, giving it a 27 per cent market share. In comparison sales of Sony's PS2 fell to 36 per cent and Nintendo's GameCube fell to 22 per cent. In May 2003 the price of the XBox was cut in the US from $199 to $179 in response to a similar cut in the price of Sony's PS2. XBox sales have been fuelled by the success of its almost 400

software games, including Star Wars games. XBox Live, Microsoft's online gaming service, had over half a million subscribers.

In October 2003 Nintendo reduced the price of its GameCube to $99 in the US. Within 35 days it was suggested that it had doubled its market share in the US from 19 to 37 per cent as a result, becoming a strong second in the market.

Source: adapted from xcox.the maingroup.com and www.forbes.com.www.lawrence.com.

## 2004

In 2004 Sony announced that it had shipped over 50 million consoles since the launch of PS2 in 2000. This compared to nine million sales worldwide of Microsoft's XBox. This gave XBox 15 per cent of the global market, a long way from Sony's estimated 70 per cent global market share. The majority of XBoxes are in the US (6 million), with 2.2 million in Europe. Microsoft admits it is weak in Asia, where it has struggled to make an impact in Japan in particular.

Analysts suggested that Microsoft loses $100 on every XBox it sells. Yet the company has strong relationships with retailers and it has acquired game developers RARE and Bungie to produce games exclusive to XBox.

Microsoft is pinning many of its hopes on the broadband market. It is particularly concentrating its marketing on areas of the world where broadband

penetration is high, such as South Korea. This gives great possibilities when XBox live is launched in these countries.

Source: asia.cnet.com,and www.forbes.com.

## Trends and forecasts

It is suggested that the video games console market has a cyclical trend in its pattern of sales. Levels in 2003 were expected to fall worldwide compared to 2002 by more than 2 million units. Although shipments of Microsoft XBox and Nintendo GameCube were expected to rise, this was not enough to offset the expected fall in Sony PS2. Price cutting was also likely to reduce revenues by

£2 billion. However, the three companies were expected to introduce new versions of their games consoles by 2005, generating an upward trend. It was estimated that by the end of 2003 the Sony PS2 was the market leader, followed by the Microsoft XBox and then the Nintendo GameCube.

Source: adapted from www.instat.com.

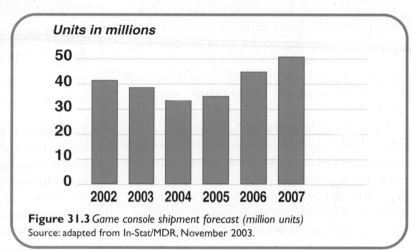

**Figure 31.3** *Game console shipment forecast (million units)*
Source: adapted from In-Stat/MDR, November 2003.

(a) Using examples from the information, describe the benefits of marketing planning for businesses in the game consoles market. (6 marks).

(b) Explain the external and internal factors affecting businesses in the game consoles market. (10 marks)

(c) Carry out a SWOT analysis of X-Box's position in the market. (12 marks)

(d) Evaluate the success of marketing planning by Microsoft for X-Box. (12 marks)

## Marketing analysis and strategy

It is important for a business to understand the needs of its customers. An understanding of customers' needs helps a business to determine how to price, promote and place a product. For example, information gained from market research by a company may indicate that the most likely buyers of a new product will be females, over the age of 25, who are professionals. Finding out about the needs of this group should allow the company to decide how to target the market and the best marketing mix for those consumers being targeted. The business may decide to promote the product in colour supplements of quality newspapers, to use high quality paper in the product and to charge a relatively high price.

Such strategies tend to be operational (☞ unit 17). However, many businesses have to make marketing decisions which include wider and longer term marketing issues. These include matters such as how a business can gain a competitive advantage (☞ unit 5), in which markets a business should operate and where a business wishes to be in future years. These **marketing strategies** can affect the entire business.

## Marketing decision making

The decisions taken by businesses about their marketing strategy can be based on a number of factors. Sometimes the strategy a business chooses might be based on 'hunches'. These may be qualitative factors that are not quantifiable. This is often the case in smaller businesses, where one person or just a few people make the decisions. For example, a partner in a design business might decide to promote the design of websites at the expense of its film service because she 'feels' that the business will gain more customers this way and increase turnover and profit. Or a sole trader manufacturing specialist fashion clothes might have a 'gut feeling' that a certain style will be making a comeback.

A more rigourous approach, often used by larger businesses, is where:
● assumptions are made and objectives are set;
● information is gathered;
● a hypothesis or theory is put forward;
● this is tested using quantifiable data;
● then it is reviewed.
This approach is similar to the testing of theories used in subjects like science. In business, a multinational company aiming for growth, based on market research information could hypothesise that the market for sales in China will grow greatly during the next five years. It could test market products in China to verify its ideas. The business might then decide to target its products and marketing at the Chinese market as a

result. This approach is sometimes referred to as the **marketing model**.

It is often suggested that such an approach reduces the risk that decision will be incorrect and strategies will fail. However, this does not mean that gut feeling decisions cannot be effective, but they may be more risky. Large businesses might not be prepared to take this type of risk. Small businesses might not want to either. But the may have no choice if they do not have the time or resources to carry out detailed decision making techniques.

## Factors influencing a business's marketing strategy

There is a number of factors that may influence a business's marketing strategy.

**The objectives of the business** The marketing strategy that a business uses must reflect the objectives of the business as a whole. Marketing strategies must therefore be consistent with the wider corporate objectives of the organisation (☞ unit 4). For example, a business which is aiming to reduce the number of countries into which it operates should not develop international marketing strategies which go against this wider, corporate strategy (☞ units 16 and 17). However, marketing strategies are not always secondary to corporate objectives. In some businesses, marketing information and strategies often have a strong influence upon corporate objectives and strategy. A growing market amongst ethical customers, for example, may persuade the business to deal only with those businesses that conform to certain ethical principles.

**The strategies of competitor businesses** As shall be seen later in this unit, many businesses take account of the strategies of their competitors when setting their own marketing strategies. For example, if a competitor promotes all of its company products on the internet successfully, other businesses may follow.

**The structure of the market** Marketing strategies will be influenced by the level of competition and the degree of change within different markets. In less competitive markets, with relatively little change, for example, businesses may find that their strategies require only minor adjustments from one period to another. In more competitive and dynamic markets businesses may find that marketing strategies require far reaching changes on an annual basis. For example, a manufacturer of active wear clothing aimed at 16-24 year olds may need to constantly monitor changes in tastes.

**The attitudes of key decision makers within businesses** Marketing strategies are likely to be influenced by the attitudes of decision makers towards matters such as the desirability of risk and change. Such attitudes are influenced by the environment within which a business operates, but also by the views of managers and directors and the culture of the business itself (☞ unit 15). For example, new managers aiming to alter the 'direction' of a business may decide to change the entire distribution network to mail order and sell off its retail outlets because this has worked successfully in other businesses.

**The size of the business** Larger businesses are likely to be strongly influenced by one or more of the above factors when making decisions about their marketing strategies. Smaller and medium sized businesses, however, often find strategic decision making more challenging. This is because the owners and managers of such businesses are often so immersed in the operational side of their work that they take few opportunities to adopt a strategic outlook. As a result, marketing strategy may be influenced by 'intuition' and responses to daily pressures.

**The strengths of the business Asset-based or asset-led marketing** (☞ unit 18) is where a business develops those products that make the best use of its 'core competences'. These are the major strengths of the firm. It produces goods or services that make the best use of its resources. Many businesses see brand loyalty or goodwill as a major **intangible asset**.

The marketing strategy adopted by such businesses will therefore attempt to develop products that can be associated with the brand names of its successful products. Many food manufacturers have followed this marketing strategy in recent years. Examples have included ice cream Mars Bars and Kit Kat Chunky. One of the most successful companies in the world, the Walt Disney Company, has perhaps followed this strategy into a number of areas. The launch by IKEA of a new range of furniture or a construction company moving into house renovation might be other examples. Examples in the service industry might include travel companies buying cottages to let for holidays or buying ships to sell cruise holidays.

## Competitive marketing strategies

Many businesses are finding that the markets in which they operate are increasingly competitive. Two factors might explain this. First, the increasing internationalisation of trade means that many markets that were dominated by domestic business are now open to foreign competition. Businesses operating within the EU experienced increases in competition after the creation of the single European market (☞ unit 107). Second, government attempts throughout the world to release market forces have led to many markets being privatised and liberalised. This has often led to greater competition.

These changes have led businesses to pay careful attention to their competitors when creating marketing strategies. Businesses often carry out COMPETITOR ANALYSIS. This provides businesses with a variety of information about their rivals. Businesses can then use this information to develop suitable COMPETITIVE MARKETING STRATEGIES. Competitive strategies allow businesses to compete most effectively with their rivals and to maximise their competitive advantage.

## Competitor analysis

Competitor analysis allows a business to develop a knowledge and understanding of its competitors' behaviour before deciding on a suitable strategy. There is a number of aspects to competitor analysis.

In 2004 Levi went back to the drawing board with its classic Levi 501 jeans. They were recut in a bid to attract a new generation of wearers. Too many young people were put off by 'middle aged men' such as Top Gear presenter Jeremy Clarkson, who continued to wear jeans. The company planned to spend £10 million on the new jeans aimed at the under 25s rather than over 40s. The jeans would retail at £50 a pair and would resemble the original denim work trousers designed and marketed by Levi Strauss in 1873. A TV campaign would support the launch. The company suggested that the 501s on general sale in the UK were very eighties and nineties and had begun to look dated. Levi had faced competition from a wide variety of jeans manufacturers. These included own brand jeans from shops such as Gap, 'designer' jeans from Firetrap, Armani and Ted Baker, as well as traditional jeans manufacturers such as Wrangler.

In the USA everybody's heard of Levi jeans, but not enough people were buying them. Instant brand recognition is not enough. It had some success in wooing women, particularly its new low waist jeans for young women. People knew that Levis made good quality jeans, but wanted more than a box fit. Research has shown that its image perception is improving, but it needs to react more quickly to fast changing trends in the fashion scene.

Source: adapted from *The Daily Mail*, 30.1.2004 and www.mercurynews.com.

(a) Identify the factors that may have contributed to the changes in marketing strategy by Levis.
(b) To what extent do you think that Levis might make use of its assets in its new strategy?

**Question 1**

**Identifying competitors** This would appear to be a straightforward task for a business. For example, a cinema complex in Bristol may consider that its competitors are other cinemas in the same city. However, this would be based upon the assumption that the Bristol cinema defines its competitors as other businesses offering the same or similar products. Further analysis of a cinema's competitors might reveal that cinema complexes are competing not only with other such complexes, but also with a range of other leisure based businesses, such as bowling alleys, football clubs and sports centres. Businesses can define their competitors in three main ways.

● Other businesses providing the same or a similar product. For example, P&O, the business which operates cross Channel ferries, might identify Brittany Ferries and Sea France as its competitors. This is because all these competitor companies also offer cross Channel ferries. Some businesses may wish to take this aspect of competitor analysis further by identifying those businesses providing the same or a similar product to the same market segment. Here P&O would analyse the market segments using Brittany Ferries and Sea France.

● Other businesses with products which provide the same service. In this case P&O might regard its competitors as Hoverspeed, which operates Seacats and hovercrafts across the Channel and Le Shuttle which, like cross Channel ferries transports passengers and vehicles between Folkestone and Calais. A wider interpretation of this category would include Eurostar, the train service which uses the Channel Tunnel to transport passengers from Britain to continental Europe and airline companies offering flights from London to cities such as Paris and Brussels.

● Other businesses seeking to satisfy the same or a similar customer need. Here P&O may see themselves as competing with other travel businesses competing for holiday spending money.

Michael Porter developed a model which identified five 'forces' of competition which affect a business (☞ unit 94). These include new market entrants competing with established businesses, competition from substitute products, competition from the rivalry of established firms, the bargaining power of consumers and the bargaining power of suppliers. Porter supports the view suggested above, that an analysis of competition should not be restricted to businesses producing the same or a similar product. He extends his view of competition not only to businesses competing for the same customers, but also to businesses competing for suppliers and to future competitors entering markets.

---

On October 23 2003 Capital Radio was knocked off its perch as the No.1 London radio station for the first time in 30 years. It was replaced by Chrysalis-owned Heart. Other stations in the Capital group fared better. London alternative music station Xfm, for example, added listeners and market share. Outside London, Century FM recorded its best ever listening figures.

(a) Using the methods of identifying competitors in the text above, describe the possible competitors to Capital Radio.
(b) Using the data in the tables, examine the possible objectives of:
(i) Capital Radio;  (ii) Heart;  (iii) Xfm.

**Table 32.1** *London commercial radio stations' share of listeners, three months to September 14, 2003*

| Position | Station | Share |
|---|---|---|
| 1 | Heart | 7.2% |
| 2 | Capital 95.8 | 7.0% |
| 3 | Classic | 5.2% |
| 4 | Magic | 5.0% |
| 5 | Kiss | 4.1% |
| 6 | Virgin | 3.4% |
| 7 | LBC | 2.4% |
| 8 | Capital Gold | 2.3% |
| 9 | Xfm | 2.1% |

Source: adapted from Rajar.

**Table 32.2** *All London radio stations' share of listeners, three months to September 14, 2003*

| Position | Station | Share |
|---|---|---|
| 1 | BBC Radio 4 | 15.8% |
| 2 | BBC Radio 2 | 10.0% |
| 3 | Heart | 7.2% |
| 4 | Capital | 7.0% |
| 5 | Classic | 5.2% |
| 6 | Magic | 5.0% |
| 7 | BBC Radio 1 | 4.5% |
| 8 | BBC Radio 5 | 4.4% |
| 9 | Kiss | 4.1% |
| 10 | Virgin | 3.4% |
| 11 | LBC | 2.4% |
| 12 | Capital Gold | 2.3% |
| 13 | Xfm | 2.1% |
| 14 | Jazz | 2.0% |
| 15 | BBC Radio 3 | 1.7% |
| 16 | BBC London | 1.1% |

Source: adapted from Guardian Unlimited, 23.9.2003.

**Table 32.3** *Time spent on selected free time activities, 2001-02*

| | Hours and minutes per day | |
| | Males (weekday) | Females (weekday) |
|---|---|---|
| TV, video and radio | 2;02 | 1:39 |
| Socialising | 0:32 | 0:44 |
| Games and hobbies | 0:18 | 0:09 |
| Reading | 0:15 | 0:16 |
| Sports and exercise | 0:11 | 0:09 |
| Attending entertainment and cultural events | 0:03 | 0:05 |

Source: adapted from *Social Trends, 2004*, Office for National Statistics.

**Question 2**

**Examining competitors' strengths and weaknesses** Here a business will wish to examine a whole range of elements of competitors' businesses, from the specifications and technical aspects of competitors' products, through to relationships with suppliers and customers. Especially important in this type of competitor analysis is the identification of **critical success factors**. These are the factors which may give a competitor an edge in the market and allow it stand out from others. For example, the critical success of a business could be identified as the quality of its product or the after sales service provided to customers.

The main problem associated with examining customers' strengths and weaknesses is the difficulty of obtaining data. In general there is a need to rely upon secondary data and the experiences of customers, suppliers and others associated with the competitor business.

**Identifying competitors' objectives and strategies** It is important that not too much emphasis is placed upon the assumption that competitors will be attempting to maximise their profits. Some businesses attempt to satisfice rather than to maximise profits. Other businesses have objectives which do not directly relate to increased profits even if, in the longer term, the aim is to create additional profits. Such objectives include entering new markets, improving cash flow and leading a market technologically. Again, businesses will need to rely heavily upon secondary data when undertaking competitor analysis in this area.

## Competitive strategies - cost leadership, differentiation and focus

It is suggested that there are three main competitive marketing strategies.

**Cost leadership** The aim of following a cost leadership strategy is to gain a cost advantage over competitors. This cost advantage can then be passed on to consumers in the form of lower prices. Businesses can gain a cost advantage by having higher levels of productivity and more efficient supplier and distribution networks. Amstrad is an example of a business which has pursued this strategy. It provides electrical goods cheaper than those of competitors. The main problem with cost leadership is that it focuses upon costs of production and lower prices rather than the needs of customers. This may create certain problems. For example, consumers might not always wish to purchase the lowest price product as it may have been perceived as being of lower quality.

**Differentiation** This strategy is where a business offers consumers something different from that which is offered by its competitors, in order to gain an 'edge' over them. The difference can be in terms of something real, such as a technical difference in the product itself, or perceived, such as a strong brand identity developed through a promotional campaign. In the latter case, consumers must actually believe the perceived difference. Guinness, for example, has been differentiated both in terms of its smooth consistency and taste, and through a campaign which promotes it as an 'intelligent' drink.

**Focus** Businesses adopting focus strategies concentrate upon particular market segments rather than the market as a whole. They attempt to meet effectively the needs of a clearly defined group of consumers. By following this strategy, a business seeks to gain a competitive advantage over other businesses which spread their efforts over a wider range of consumers. For example, there is a small but thriving market for hand made, made to measure suits.

## Competitive strategies - market positioning

Another set of alternative competitive marketing strategies is based upon the 'position' which a business wishes to occupy in relation to other businesses operating in the same market.

**Market leader strategies** In many markets there is one business which is generally recognised as the MARKET LEADER. Market leaders tend to have the largest share of a particular market. Market leaders may also be businesses which lead the market in terms of price changes and promotional spending. An example of a market leader might be Microsoft in the software market. There is a number of strategies which market leaders can adopt to improve or maintain their market leadership.

● Expanding the total market. As holders of the largest market share, market leaders stand most to gain by expanding the market. Expanding the market can be achieved by attracting new product users, promoting new uses for the product or encouraging greater product usage. For example, breakfast cereal manufacturers have tried to get consumers to eat cereal at different times of the day.

● Expanding market share. Market leaders may use the range of elements in the marketing mix to expand their current market share at the expense of competitors'. For example, Microsoft increased its share of the computer software market by establishing its product as the standard PC operating system.

● Defending current market share. The aim here is to prevent competitors from increasing their market share at the expense of the market leader. Most market leaders take the view that defending market share can best be achieved by continually improving the way in which they meet consumer needs. Often this is achieved with the use of complex and sophisticated marketing strategies. For example, some commentators have seen the development by Nestlé of a range of brands in the instant coffee market not only as an example of meeting new needs, but also as a sophisticated form of defence. The development of the Alta Rica, Cap Colombie and Blend 37 brands can be seen as a defence of Nescafé and Gold Blend from competitors seeking to damage Nestlé's share of this market by gaining a foothold in smaller segments.

**Market challenger strategies** MARKET CHALLENGERS are those businesses with a substantial share of the market. However, they hold second, third or lower positions in the market in relation to the market leader. Not all businesses with lower market shares than the leader are market challengers. To be defined as market challengers businesses must be in a strong enough position to challenge the leader and be willing to adopt strategies to win more market share. There are three main types of strategies which market challengers can adopt.

- Direct attacks on the market leader. Here the market challenger must be prepared to directly compete in terms of the market leaders' strengths and also to match its marketing mix. To do this the market challenger must be able to match the resources of the market leader and to respond to retaliatory actions by the market leader. Such retaliatory action often takes the form of price cutting and aggressive promotion and distribution campaigns.
- Indirect attacks on the market leader. Because of the problems involved in mounting a direct attack upon a market leader, many market followers choose to adopt less confrontational strategies. One of the most common is to identify areas in which the market leader is less strong and to develop products designed to address these weaknesses. For example, businesses have attempted to compete with crisp manufacturers Walkers by offering exotic snack foods such as popadums and Chinese rice crackers.
- Attacking firms other than the market leader. This allows a business to increase its market share by attacking relatively weaker businesses. For example, many of the larger brewing businesses have increased their market share in this way in the UK by taking over smaller breweries.

**Market follower strategies** Many businesses occupying lower positions in a market do not wish to challenge the market leader. Challenges on a market leader often lead to retaliatory action and cause expensive battles which often hurt challengers more than they do leaders. For this reason many businesses choose to follow the strategy of market leaders. There are three main types of MARKET FOLLOWERS.

- Those who imitate market leaders. Own brand products in supermarkets fall into this category, as do canned drinks such as Virgin Cola. In more extreme cases imitation may lead to cloning. This occurs when one business seeks to copy the market leaders' products without originating anything itself.
- Innovative businesses. Such businesses lack the resources to challenge market leaders. They tend to willingly follow

moves made by market leaders so that they do not change the structure of the market.

- Businesses not capable of challenging market leaders which are content to satisfice. It is not unusual to find such businesses in the take away food market. These businesses have little competitive advantage. They tend to be vulnerable to changes in the market and may fail as a consequence.

**Market niche strategies** Market niches are very small segments of the market. They are sometimes described as segments within segments. The majority of businesses which operate in niche markets tend to be small and medium sized. However, some larger businesses have divisions specialising in market niches. Niches can be based upon geographical location, specific product differentiation, customer group or product type. Examples of businesses adopting market niche strategies include Tie Rack, Reuters and TVR, the sports car manufacturers.

Travel giants, such as Thomas Cook and JMC, slashed their prices of Spanish holidays by an average £150 in 2004. This was almost unheard of. But it was in response to the growing impact made by cut price airlines. It was seen as a deliberate attempt to win back custom from the low cost airlines.

It was the first time that the major companies felt that they had to cut the cost of ordinary family holidays to popular destinations. Two adults travelling to Majorca with Thomas Cook would save £120. Five adults going to Gran Canaria with JMC would save £210. Cosmos introduced a 'two kids free' deal to seven family resorts.

Bookings for holidays in popular resorts such as Spain had been sluggish. However, resorts outside the eurozone, such as in the eastern Mediterranean, were doing well.

Source: adapted from *The Daily Mail*, 26.1.2004.

(a) Analyse the competitive strategies and market positions of the businesses in the travel industry using examples from the data.

# Marketing strategies for growth

Many businesses operate in or intend to move into markets where business growth is both desirable and possible. Businesses operating in such markets will tend to emphasise growth in their corporate and marketing objectives. Growth may be in the form of increased sales revenue or turnover, greater profits, increased capital or more land and employees. There is a range of marketing strategies that growth orientated businesses can adopt. Growth orientated marketing strategies are not suited to all businesses, however. In shrinking markets, for example, a business may wish to maintain previous sales levels or just survive rather than aim for growth.

The ANSOFF MATRIX is a useful tool for businesses aiming for growth. The Ansoff Matrix shown in Figure 32.1 illustrates both existing and new products within existing and new markets. Four possible marketing strategies to achieve growth are revealed by the Matrix.

|  |  | PRODUCT | |
|---|---|---|---|
|  |  | **Existing** | **New** |
| **MARKET** | **Existing** | Market penetration | Product development |
|  | **New** | Market development | Diversification |

**Figure 32.1** *The Ansoff Matrix*

**Market penetration** As suggested by the Ansoff Matrix, the purpose of market penetration is to achieve growth in existing markets with existing products. There is a number of ways in which businesses can achieve this.

- Increasing the brand loyalty of customers so that they use substitute brands less frequently. Well known brands such as Kellogg's Corn Flakes make use of this strategy.
- Encouraging consumers to use the product more regularly. An example might be encouraging people to drink canned drinks at breakfast.
- Encouraging consumers to use more of the product. An example might be a crisp manufacturer producing maxi sized crisp packets rather than standard sized crisp packets.

**Product development** This is concerned with marketing new or modified products in existing markets. The development of the Ford Focus, intended to act as a replacement for the Ford Escort, is an example of product development. Confectionery manufacturers such as Cadbury and Nestlé regularly use this strategy in order to stimulate sales growth.

**Market development** This involves the marketing of existing products in new markets. For example, the Halifax has extended its banking activities to the Spanish market and Harvey Nichols, a retail outlet previously limited to London, has opened a branch in Leeds and Manchester.

**Diversification** This occurs when new products are developed for new markets. Diversification allows a business to move away from reliance upon existing markets and products. This allows a business to spread risk and increase safety. If one product faces difficulties or fails, a successful product in another market may prevent the business overall facing problems. However, diversification will take a business outside its area of expertise. This might mean that its performance in new markets is relatively poor compared to more experienced operators. The move by Mercedes Benz into the market for small, high volume cars and the move by Virgin into financial services and the air passenger business are perhaps examples of this marketing strategy.

# Marketing strategy issues

**Social marketing** SOCIAL MARKETING was first analysed by Kotler and Zaman in 1971. It was defined as 'the design, implantation and control of programs to influence the acceptability of social ideas involving considerations of product planning, pricing. Communication, distribution and market research'. In the late 1990s it was agreed by many researchers that it involved the use of marketing techniques to bring about changes in behaviour that benefit society. So social marketing makes use of the tools of commercial marketing, such as market research, segmentation, branding and the use of the marketing mix.

Examples of social marketing might include a reduction in tooth decay by improved dental hygiene, an improvement in people's health by changing their diet, a reduction in disease by improved medication or an improvement in the water system by the use of fluoride.

Social marketing is not the same as businesses being socially responsible (☞ unit 111). This tends to be businesses that consider the effect on the environment etc, but are ultimately judged on profit for shareholders. Social marketing is different because its success is judged on the benefit to society rather than commercial goals. Nor is it the same as ethical businesses that are concerned about fair and socially acceptable business practices (☞ unit 110).

However, some profit orientated businesses do engage in social marketing. Procter & Gamble, for example, contributed to a major social marketing drugs prevention initiative in the North East of England.

**Green marketing** Today the world faces a 'green' problem - the need to make the environment sustainable and yet still develop. This provides a number of challenges for marketing. GREEN MARKETING has been defined as 'the management process responsible for identifying, anticipating and satisfying customers and society in a profitable and sustainable way'. It involves using resources in a way that is sustainable, so they can be replenished or replaced in future. It also involves producing pollution and waste which can be absorbed into the environmental system.

The adoption of green marketing policies can have implications for marketing strategy. Businesses must try to identify 'green consumers' through market research. Businesses will only be able to satisfy their needs if they can find out the concerns of these consumers. Products and packaging must be environmentally friendly. They must be designed for re-use or recycling. Promotion may need to change. Advertising must be chosen to present a green image. Discounts may need to be given to persuade people to change to more environmentally friendly products. Sponsorship must be carefully chosen. Pricing might also be affected. Sometimes consumers might pay a slightly higher prices for free range products, for example. Distribution channels must be chosen which reduce pollution and congestion.

It has been suggested that effective green marketing will be successful if businesses have marketing strategies which follow the 7 Cs.

- Customer orientated, taking into account the views of customers about the environment.
- Commercially viable, so that products will meet consumer needs but still make a profit.
- Credible to customers, but also to other stakeholders, such as shareholders or government.
- Consistent with marketing and other business aims and objectives.
- Clear and not hidden in technical jargon.
- Co-ordinated with other business strategies.
- Communicated effectively, both internally to employees and others in the business and externally, to consumers and other stakeholders outside the business.

The impact on businesses of adapting more environmentally policies is explained in unit 112.

Internet marketing The growth of the Internet (☞ unit 70) has led many businesses to consider the use of INTERNET MARKETING STRATEGIES. These are the marketing approaches used by a business selling products over the Internet. They may be similar to those used by businesses using other methods of distribution (☞ unit 30). However, there are some specific factors relating to marketing via the Internet that a business might need to consider when deciding on an Internet marketing strategy.

- Targeting the market. The target market might be regarded as restricted or larger. For example, the target market might be only people using the Internet. So a business selling an online magazine to older people in a particular area of the country might have a smaller target market than usual. However, a magazine about a topic that appeals to all people, no matter what age, region or country they come from might gain a larger market from the Internet because it is a worldwide web.
- Market research. It may be possible to gain research

information about the market from the Internet. For example, some businesses download cookies and spyware onto computers to find out information about users of websites. There is software available to prevent this, so information may be restricted.

- The website. The main point of contact with the company on the Internet is the website. Image management is important. A well designed website that operates efficiently will present a good image. People like pictures, but text is more important. Users must be able to find their way around the website easily.
- Promotion. There is a variety of forms of promotion that businesses can use for their website on the Internet. They can buy advertising on other sites. They can make sure their site is included on search engines. They can also use bulletin board systems (BBSs). A BBS is like a storage facility that allows people to send and receive messages through their computers, as well as send and receive files. They can be used to gather information about a topic or to buy and sell products. Many businesses use BBSs to send electronic mail to distributors and to talk to business prospects. Mail order business, banks and travel agents often make use of BBSs.
- The nature of the product for sale can influence the website. Some products are sold online or can be downloaded, such as subscriptions to sites or written information. Others sell products which are sent to customers.
- Methods of payment. Businesses must decide how customer will pay for products. Some allow purchasers of products to pay online using credit cards. Businesses must be aware and comply with legislation about privacy of financial information. And they must comply with data protection legislation (☞ unit 69) regarding information they keep about customers.
- Coordination. Internet marketing must be coordinated with other forms of marketing. For example, it is often useful to include the website address with other forms of publicity such as leaflets or advertisements.

Buzz marketing BUZZ MARKETING is where businesses attempt to generate a positive image or 'buzz' about products through non-traditional marketing methods. It is a form of 'stealth' strategy. It usually involves businesses using word of mouth to promote a product. A business might employ groups to talk about products in appropriate places, for example software games in Internet cafes. People who are thought to be 'trend setters' might be employed to ride around in vehicles, eat food in public or wear clothing. For example, DaimlerChrysler generated pre-launch promotion for its PT Cruiser in the USA by placing cars in rental fleets around the trendy Miami Beach area.

The advantage of this type of marketing is that it can be a cheap and effective method for a narrow range of products, which have a target market and which people care about. It may also be useful for younger target audiences who have yet to develop brand loyalties. However, it is argued that it might be less effective for products that people have less interest in, such as washing powder. It might also lose its effectiveness if all businesses are attempting to generate a buzz for their products.

## key terms

**The Ansoff Matrix** - a model which identifies growth strategies for businesses based on an analysis of their products and their markets.

**Buzz marketing** - a strategy which uses word of mouth and peer group approval to market products.

**Competitor analysis** - identifying the strengths and weaknesses of competitors and their products.

**Competitive marketing strategies** - marketing strategies directly based upon particular approaches to dealing with competitors.

**Green marketing** - a strategy which takes into account the effects of marketing on the environment.

**Internet marketing strategies** - the use of the worldwide web to market and sell products.

**Market challengers** - businesses which are in a position to threaten the market leader.

**Market follower** - a business which mimics or copies the strategies of the dominant businesses or businesses in the market.

**Market leader** - a business which makes decisions which tend to be followed by other businesses in the market.

**Social marketing** - a strategy where the success of marketing is evaluated on the extent to which society benefits.

A successful buzz campaign hinges on finding the right messages carriers. Ford was aware of the importance of this to its strategy when replacing the well loved Escort with the Ford Focus. The idea was to position the Focus as a hip, young person's car and help it win the war against competitors such as the market leading Honda Civic.

Ford looked for its style gurus in the New York youth marketing boutique Fusion Five. It was able to identify 120 influential buyers in five markets - New York, Miami, Los Angeles, Chicago and San Francisco. Each of the 120 people were given a Focus to drive for 6 months. They kept a record of where they went and what they did.

So did it work? Well certainly for Joe Regner, a 21 year old operations manager in Miami. He spotted a yellow Focus parked near the hip hop station WEDR and stopped to check it out. The Focus had been loaned to a DJ at the station, Jill Tracey. Joe ordered his and persuaded his girlfriend to switch from buying a Honda Civic. Ford sold over 200,000 cars in its first full year.

The person who ignites the buzz depends on the product. ConAgra Foods' Hebrew National Unit searched 12 US cities for 250 PTA presidents, Hispanic community leaders and Jewish mothers to serve on 'mom squads'. They drive around in yellow vehicles with a Hebrew National logo, hosting backyard hot dog barbecues and passing out discount coupons. The company vice chair of marketing said that even a loved American food like hot dogs can benefit from 'viral marketing'.

Source: adapted from www.businessweek.com.

(a) Explain why this strategy might be known as viral marketing.
(b) Examine the factors that might lead to the success of this type of marketing.

**Question 4**

Knowledge...Knowledge...Knowledge...Knowledge...Knowledge...Knowledge...Know

1. What is meant by a strategic marketing decision?
2. What factors will affect a business's marketing strategy?
3. State the 3 aspects of competitor analysis.
4. How might a business define its competitors?
5. What are the 5 forces of competition according to Porter?
6. What is meant by a critical success factor?
7. Explain the difference between a cost leadership and a differentiation strategy.
8. Suggest 3 ways in which a market leader might protect its market position.
9. Suggest 3 ways in which a market challenger might improve its market position.
10. What 4 methods of growth strategy are suggested by the Ansoff Matrix?
11. How might a business gain greater penetration in an existing market with an existing product?
12. State 5 ways in which Internet marketing might affect the marketing strategy of a business.

# Case study *Coca-Cola*

**Table 32.4** *Coca-Cola Company, key financial information, 2002*

| | |
|---|---|
| Sales | $19,564m |
| One year growth in sales | 2.6% |
| Net income | $3,050m |
| One year growth in net income | 23.2% |
| Employees | 56,000 |
| One year employee growth | 47.4% |

Source: adapted from www.hoovers.com.

## Sales and net income

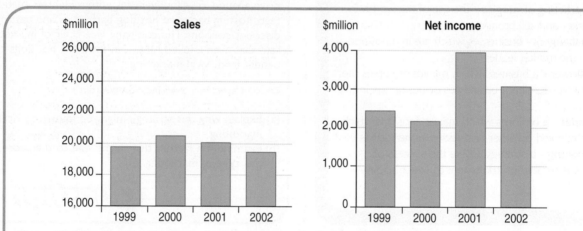

**Figure 32.2** *The Coca-Cola Company, sales and net income ($million)*
Source: adapted from www.hoovers.com.

## Problems or not?

Coca-Cola is the world's leading soft drinks company and regarded by many as the best known brand in the world. So why in 2000 did observers suggest there may be problems? Between 1997 and 2000 it had three different chief executives and it slipped from 3rd to 15th in the US ranking of most admired companies published by business magazine *Fortune*. In 1999, despite no evidence of contamination, the product was banned in France, Luxembourg, Belgium and the Netherlands. It was also investigated by the European Commission for acting as a monopolist and the share price fell from £50 in 1998 to £30. It faced growing competition from many sources, including cappuccino chains and energy drinks. A UK agent for drinks manufacturers suggested that parents in the UK preferred children to drink Sunny Delight. It may also have suffered from its own dominance. Some people regarded large conglomerates with suspicion. And their large centralised structure made it difficult to respond quickly to marketing challenges.

Source: adapted from *The Guardian*, 2.10.2000.

## Diversification

Coca-Cola has been diversifying. In Japan it sells tea for example. In 2001 it planned to launch five new brands in the UK. These included Fanta Icy lemon, a still drink for teenagers called Alive and a sport energy drink called PowerAde.

In the UK Coca-Cola owns Malvern Water. In 2004 it planned to increase its presence in the bottled water market by launching the Dasani brand backed by a £7 million advertising campaign. It believed this would double its share of the UK bottled water market worth £800 million. The perceived benefits of drinking bottled water instead of tap water had led to a surge in this market. It is largely dominated in Europe by Danone and Nestlé which together account for around a third of all sales. However, the product was withdrawn quickly after chemicals were detected and plans to relaunch it were postponed.

In 2002 the company launched Vanilla Coke. The product followed on from a DIY trend in the USA where people would add a shot of vanilla to their coke drink to make it sweeter. It was predicted that the product would be as successful as previous versions such as the lemon flavoured diet coke launched in 2001 and cherry coke launched in the 1980s, but avoid the problems of New Coke which changed the taste of coke original in 1985 but was hastily withdrawn due to poor response.

Source: adapted from *The Guardian*, 2.10.2000 and 18.4.2004,enjoyment.independent.co.uk and www.euromonitor.com.

## Marketing

Coca-Cola has changed its marketing to take advantage of new advertising initiatives. In Britain it used the Coke Auction. People collect tokens from coke bottles and cans and then use them to bid on the Internet for goods and services. A student won £6,000 towards fees and living expenses. Another winner had lunch with Kevin Keegan.

In 2001 it planned to spend £25 million on viral or buzz advertising. This was used for the Energy drink Burn launched by the company in October 2000. There is no large advertising campaign behind Burn. It was just stocked in trendy London bars and customers talked it up by word of mouth. Coca-Cola argued that customers in this niche market would have rejected a large advertising campaign.

The company also planned to involve trendy advertising agencies such as Soul and Mother in its promotion in the UK. And in 2002 it doubled its advertising expenditure to over £50 million in the UK, including sponsoring Team England in the World Cup.

Source: adapted from *The Guardian*, 8.2.2001 and www.euromonitor.com.

## UK market share

In 2001 Coca-Cola maintained its share of the UK soft drinks market at 19.7 per cent. Fruit and vegetable juice showed strong growth. One hundred per cent juice grew by 6.5 per cent in 2002. Britains were increasingly prepared to pay a premium for concentrated juice, including smoothies.

Source: adapted from *The Guardian*, 8.2.2001 and www.euromonitor.com.

**(a) Identify the competitors of Coca-Cola. (6 marks)**

**(b) Explain the position of Coca-Cola in relation to its competitors. (6 marks)**

**(c) Explain the different marketing strategies used by (i) Coca-Cola and (ii) other businesses in the soft drinks market. (14 marks)**

**(d) Examine reasons why these businesses may have used such strategies. (12 marks)**

**(e) Discuss the extent to which Coca-Cola's marketing strategies have been successful. (12 marks)**

## US market share

In the USA Coca-Cola had 44.3 per cent of the US soft drinks market in 2002. It saw its market share drop in 2001 by 0.5 per cent, but gain 0.6 per cent in 2002. Pepsi, its nearest rival, had 31.4 per cent market share.

**Figure 32.3** *Market share of the US soft drinks market*

Source: adapted from *The Guardian*, 10.1.2003 and www.findarticles.com.

The MARKETING BUDGET specifies and sets out clearly the financial elements of the marketing plan. Like budgets for other aspects of business activity (☞ unit 47), the marketing budget is a **plan** of what the business hopes to achieve in the forthcoming period. So, for example, a business may plan to achieve an increase in sales or profits next year. The marketing plan will then outline the spending the business intends to make on marketing next year in order to achieve this increase. It will show the planned sales and the planned costs of marketing to generate these sales.

When setting marketing budgets a balance must be maintained. On the one hand businesses must set precise financial plans associated with marketing activities. It is important that plans are precise if managers are to use the budget to control spending and to set **targets** for sales. However, changes in the internal and external marketing environment mean that some flexibility may be built into the budget.

Businesses that have planned well are more likely to remain within their budget and achieve the sales levels targeted. However, sometimes the actual marketing spending and sales are different from the budget. A business must identify why these **variances** (☞ unit 54) have taken place. If sales are lower than planned or marketing expenditure higher, a business can identify the reasons and make sure that any problems are corrected in future budgets.

Marketing budgets are often planned for a year and may be broken down into monthly amounts. They may also be broken down into more detailed categories. For example, a business might plan how much it is spending on different forms of promotion and advertising.

## Types of marketing budget

There is a number of ways in which a business might construct a budget.

**The affordable budget** This is where the budget for marketing expenditure is based upon what is expected to be left over after more important expenses have been met. So a business might decide, for example, that once it has paid for its raw materials, labour costs and overheads, it has £10,000 left over to spend on marketing. The problem with this method is that it takes no account of market requirements and conditions. It could be that the business actually needs to spend £30,000 for its marketing to be effective.

**Historical budgeting** This is where the budget for marketing expenditure is based upon what has been spent on marketing activities in previous years. Sometimes an extra amount is added to allow for the effects of inflation. As with affordable budgets, it takes no account of market factors. It is also based upon the sometimes mistaken assumption that previous years' expenditures have been appropriate.

**As a percentage of past sales** This is where the budget for marketing expenditure is based upon previous sales of a product. Products are allocated a marketing budget in line with their sales records. So, for example, a product that has sold particularly well in the past may have a higher amount spent on its advertising than a product with poor sales.

The benefit of this method is that successful products are rewarded with high promotional budgets. This should help their future success. Businesses using this method sometimes refer to their **advertising: sales ratio**. This is the means by which businesses decide on the proportion of sales revenue to allocate to future advertising. Businesses in the cosmetics industry, for example, generally have a ratio of 20 per cent or more. Businesses operating in industrial markets may have ratios as low as one per cent or even less. For example, scrap metal dealers may have advertising expenses per annum of less than 0.1 per cent of their sales revenue.

The problem with this budgeting method is that it can lead to particular products being sent on a downward spiral. Falling sales lead to lower marketing expenditure, which leads to lower sales and so on. Sometimes, however, it may be in the strategic interest of a business to increase marketing expenditure on a product with falling sales.

**Competitor based budgeting** This involves setting marketing budgets in relation to competitors' spending. It may mean spending amounts similar to that of competitors, matching competitors' spending exactly, or exceeding competitors' spending. The problem with this method is that marketing expenditure may not be set in relation to the marketing objectives of a business itself. Instead such expenditure may be set in relation to the marketing objectives of the competitor.

**Objective and task budgeting** This method involves setting marketing expenditure in relation to marketing objectives and the tasks or actions which must be completed to achieve these objectives. To do this a business must cost all of the marketing activities in which it expects to be engaged over a particular period of time. Many regard this as the most desirable method of marketing budgeting. This is because it is based upon the needs of particular businesses and products operating in particular market conditions.

## Factors influencing the marketing budget

A number of factors might influence the marketing budget set by a business.

**Business aims and objectives** The marketing budget must be planned with the corporate aims of the business in mind and its business objectives (☞ unit 4). For example, if the business aims to grow in future, it is likely that the marketing budget will plan for an increase in sales, perhaps brought about by an increase in promotion expenditure. The marketing budget is also constrained by other budgets. A business might want to spend an extra £50,000 on promotion. However, if there is a need to employ more specialist workers, then funds might be diverted to the budget of the human resources department.

Rewards The level of reward is likely to affect the marketing budget. For example, a business might be faced with a choice when expanding. It might have the alternative of spending more on marketing or alternatively on reorganisation of production. If the rewards gained by the reorganisation are likely to be greater then the business might decide not to increase promotion. Similarly, if a business might decide to spend more on marketing a new product because it predicts that it will be very profitable.

Behaviour of competitors The actions of rival businesses can affect marketing. Large increases in spending on marketing by competitors might have to be matched if a business wants to remain competitive. Some businesses could not compete with others if they did not have enormous marketing budgets, such as in the motor car industry.

Nature of the market and customers Some markets do not require large amounts of promotion. For example, a wholesale business selling imported cycle parts to cycle shops might simply need to send out regular price lists and product descriptions or use a website. Businesses selling to customers around the world, such as Coca-Cola or McDonald's, are likely to spend vast amounts on marketing. Businesses also sometimes spend large amounts to launch new products on the market (☞ unit 24). They might reduce marketing spending later in the product life cycle as sales decline to gain greater profit.

## Benefits and problems of marketing budgeting

There are certain benefits of marketing budgets for a business.
- They provide a business with a means of controlling marketing costs.
- They can be used to identify where costs have been too high or where marketing has been ineffective in raising sales.
- They can be used to plan the future of the business with some certainty, so other decisions can be made.
- They can be used by other departments to coordinate strategies to make the business more efficient.
- They set targets for the marketing department, which can be used to motivate employees and identify improvements in productivity.
  However, there may also be problems.
- They might be too much of a straightjacket on decision

making. This is particularly important if there are sudden and unexpected changes in the market.
- They might be seen by employees as a means by which a business can judge them if targets are not met, and so could be demotivating.
- They might lead to poor decision making if they are inaccurate.
- They might conflict with other objectives of the business. Different stakeholders often have different objectives (☞ unit 3). Managers, for example, might attempt to 'empire build' by trying to obtain large budgets.
- They can be constraining on other business decisions. For example, managers might over or understate budget requirements, fearing they will lose their budget or may be given too great a target next year.

---

Holland & Knight is a large law firm. It has more than 1,200 attorneys in 333 offices and over 100 practice areas. The marketing budget is derived from the annual strategic plans drawn up by business. Each year there is a clean plan and a new budget. Expenditure is evaluated on the return on investment (ROI). A high ROI signals a good marketing investment. Marketing expenditures are constantly evaluated by both the attorney and marketing staff during the year.

Holland & Knight is a very client-orientated business. It relies heavily on relationship marketing, including client events, sponsorship, newsletters and seminars. It also spends on web development but not a great deal on advertising. During the past several years around 2.5-3 per cent of turnover has been allocated to marketing budgets.

There is an emphasis on 'cross marketing' within the business. Clients are 'owned' by the whole business rather than one member of the business. So the whole business is accountable for each client. This helps it to identify other services which might be useful for the client.

Source: adapted from www.firmmarketingcentre.com.

(a) Explain reasons why marketing budgeting is likely to be important for this business.
(b) Examine the factors that are likely to affect the marketing budget of the business.

Question 1

---

## Trends in marketing expenditure

What trends are taking place in marketing expenditure in the UK? Figure 33.1 shows that the UK experienced a slowdown between 2002-03, but expected to see an increase between 2003-04. However, the overall picture between 2001 and 2004 was an increase in expenditure. Some reasons given for increases in expenditure by businesses included:
- to drive forward the growth of the company;
- to help with the launch of new products;

- in response to competition - either to match others' increases or to take advantage when others cut their budgets;
- in response to external factors, ie fears by US holidaymakers about flights, agricultural disease such as foot and mouth or economic slowdown.

A breakdown of the types of marketing spending shows

**Figure 33.1** *Change in total marketing expenditure, UK, 2001-04*

Source: adapted from *Marketing Expenditure Trends, 2003*, P.Barwise and A.Styler, London Business School.

some interesting trends. Figure 33.2 shows that advertising in the media accounted for by far the largest proportion of marketing expenditure in 2003. But of greater interest to businesses for the future might be the trends taking place in Figure 33.3. They show that the greatest changes in expenditure over the period 2001-04 have been on 'interactive

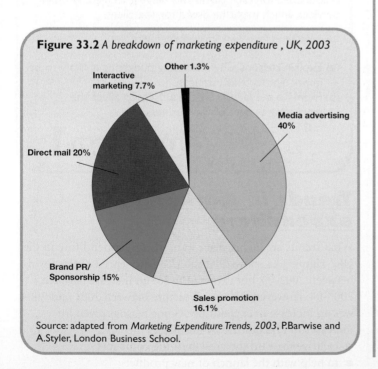

**Figure 33.2** *A breakdown of marketing expenditure , UK, 2003*

Source: adapted from *Marketing Expenditure Trends, 2003*, P.Barwise and A.Styler, London Business School.

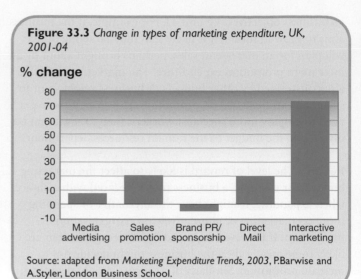

**Figure 33.3** *Change in types of marketing expenditure, UK, 2001-04*

Source: adapted from *Marketing Expenditure Trends, 2003*, P.Barwise and A.Styler, London Business School.

marketing' or the use of the Internet for marketing purposes. these include a number of marketing methods, such as:

- online promotions and incentives;
- advertising on other websites;
- the use of password protected websites;
- online sales;
- the use of permission based emails.

Another feature has been the long term growth of direct marketing and the use on inhouse marketing rather than advertising agencies. Businesses were increasingly carrying out their own marketing rather than employing specialist outside organisations. The growth in the use of the Internet would have helped businesses to do this.

## key terms

**Marketing budget** - a plan, agreed in advance, showing the funds to be used for marketing and how they will be allocated. The budget shows expected sales and marketing expenditure.

Knowledge...nowledge...Knowled

1. What does a marketing budget show?
2. What will a variance in a marketing budget show?
3. What is the difference between historical budgeting and task based budgeting?
4. State 4 factors that might influence a marketing budget.
5. State 4 benefits of marketing budgets.
6. State 4 problems of marketing budgets.
7. 'There has been a growth in emphasis on interactive marketing.' Explain what this means.

# Case study *Jenson Ltd*

Increasingly manufacturing businesses are making use of computer aided technology. Computer aided design (CAD) is the use of computers and computer software in the design of products. Computer aided manufacture (CAM) is the use of the use of computers to aid the manufacture of products, such as in computer numerically controlled (CNC) milling machines and lathes. Many computer aided products and services are sold to other businesses by manufacturers and software providers.

In 2002 a survey was carried out on the marketing expenditure of businesses in the computer aided technology industry. Figures 33.4 - 33.7 show some of the results of the survey.

Jenson Ltd is a designer of computer software for the industry. It is setting its marketing budget for next year. It is concerned that budgets in recent years have been inaccurate. In particular marketing expenditure seems to have been planned poorly and costs have often been higher than expected. One of the reasons is that they were always based on figures in previous years, but circumstances changed. It also tended to budget carefully, without any real consideration of what might be happening to marketing in the industry generally.

The business wants to expand rapidly next year. So it is looking to market its products more aggressively. It has decided to launch a number of new software products and feels that they will be well received by users of computer software in the industry. But it must make sure that it is targeting its market correctly, with the right type of promotion. It has decided to use some of the information in the survey to set the components of its marketing budget. It plans to spend around 5 per cent of its turnover on marketing this year. It has targeted direct mail to businesses as its main expenditure. However, it is also considering spending a lot more of its marketing budget on media advertising, such as trade magazines, as it feels this could reach an untapped market.

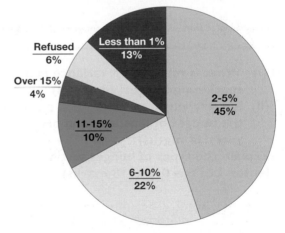

**Figure 33.4** *Survey results on marketing budgets - What proportion of your turnover is spent on marketing?*

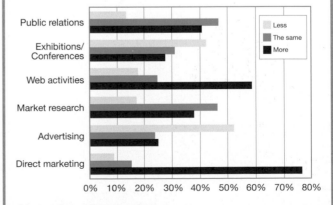

**Figure 33.5** *Survey results on marketing budgets - Has the proportion of the marketing budget spent on the following activities increased, decreased or stayed the same?*

Source: adapted from www.business advantage.co.uk/Spaghetti/cam.htm.

**Figure 33.6** *Survey results on marketing budgets - What proportion of your turnover is allocated to direct marketing?*

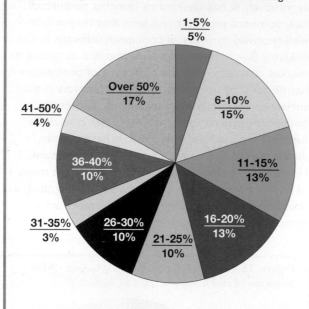

**Figure 33.7** *Survey results on marketing budgets - What proportion of your turnover is allocated to advertising?*

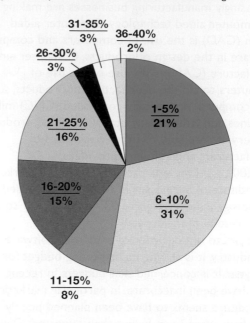

Source: adapted from www.business advantage.co.uk/Spaghetti/cam.htm.

(a) (i) **What is meant by a variance in a marketing budget? (4 marks)**

(ii) **Identify why a variance took place in the budget of Jenson Ltd in previous years. (4 marks)**

(b) **Explain the types of budget setting that Jenson Ltd has used. (10 marks)**

(c) **Examine the factors that might influence the setting of Jenson Ltd's budget next year. (10 marks)**

(d) **Evaluate the choices that Jenson intends to make about the allocation of its marketing budget. (12 marks)**

## The importance of international marketing

At one time businesses may have thought that marketing products overseas was an adventurous act. It was generally undertaken by large businesses which had grown too big for domestic markets. Today, however, the world has 'shrunk' due to, amongst other things, rapid changes in international transport and telecommunications. One effect of this is that a business now needs to consider the threat from foreign competition and the opportunities which might be gained from marketing internationally.

For many firms international marketing is no longer an option. It is necessary if a business is to survive in a competitive business environment. For British firms this was the case after trade barriers between European Union nations were lifted in 1992 (☞ unit 107) and perhaps with the expansion of the EU in 2004. The increase in the size and number of multinationals has contributed to the increase in international trading. The globalisation of business activity (☞ unit 109) has also affected business marketing strategy.

Why might businesses market their products internationally?

- Profits. By selling in overseas markets, a business might have the potential to increase its profits through an increase in sales. Overseas markets may be more lucrative than domestic ones. Manufacturing and distribution costs may be lower abroad. The product might also sell at a higher price on foreign markets than in the home market.
- Spreading the risk. If a business only produces in one country then it may face problems caused by downturns in demand due to recession (☞ unit 96). The more countries a firm operates in, the less vulnerable it is to changes in the business climate of any single country.
- Unfavourable trading conditions in the domestic market. Businesses often find that the market for a product is saturated or in decline. One option for a firm is to try and breathe new life into the product by introducing it into an overseas market. This is an example of an **extension strategy** (☞ unit 24). British American Tobacco industries, for example, have started to sell in developing countries as domestic market sales have declined.
- Legal differences. Legal restrictions on the sale of products vary from one country to another. For example, developing countries have fewer restrictions on which drugs can be offered for sale. Some pharmaceutical companies (in what many regard as unethical practice) have sold drugs banned on health grounds in the UK to these nations.

## Why the overseas market is different

There can be many rewards for a business entering an overseas market.

One problem that it will face, however, is that market conditions will be different to those in the domestic market. This makes selling abroad very risky. What are the differences that are likely to affect the success of foreign sales?

**Political differences** A firm must take into account the political stability of the country in which it plans to sell. Political instability can make trading almost impossible. Also, a change of government can bring about a change in attitude towards foreign companies. A firm thinking of investing a large sum in its operations abroad will need to weigh up the political situation carefully. A number of businesses, for example, were affected by the change in government in Hong Kong in 1997 as ownership of the area was transferred from the UK to China.

**Cultural differences** One difference which often causes problems for British businesses is that English is not the main or even the second language in many countries. In Eastern

---

Philips is a manufacturer of a wide range of television, video, audio, computer and communications products. Its website contained the following information in 2003.

**Achievements per region**
Global market share growth 2002, 10.5% to 2003. Year to date 10.8%.

**Europe**
- Continued prominence in Western and Central Europe.
- Making inroads in developing and emerging markets.

**North America**
- Repositioned brand and established credibility with leading retailers.
- Expanded placements significantly.
- Major progress with Wal Mart, DirecTV and other key channel partners.

**Asia Pacific/Middle East/Africa**
- Regained growth momentum in Monitors, GSM and TV.

**Latin America**
- Derisked business model implemented.
- Continued leadership in Brazil.

Source: adapted from www.philips.com.

(a) Using examples from the data, explain why the business might want to operate in different markets.

Question 1

Europe for example, German and Russian may be more widely spoken than English.

Other cultural differences may influence the way a product is marketed. For example, a product name suitable in one country may have a totally different meaning in another - the French lemonade Pssschit would require a new name were it to be sold in the UK. Colours have different meanings throughout the world. In the Far East, white rather than black is associated with mourning. In India fashion models of the sort used to promote products in the West are considered too thin. In some countries, what may be regarded as a 'bribe' in the UK is common business practice. Payments to government or industry officials may be required to get things done, from electricity connection to securing contracts.

**Differences in legislation** Such differences can affect the way in which a business produces and markets its products.
- Product labelling. US laws are far more stringent than UK laws about the amount of information which should be included on food labels.
- Product safety. Some countries have very strict legislation governing safety standards on childrens' toys. Others are less strict.

- Environmental impact. All cars sold in California, for example, must be fitted with a catalytic convertor.
- Advertising. Cigarette advertising on television is outlawed within EU countries.

**Economic and social differences** Some of the economic factors which businesses must consider include levels of income, levels of sales and corporation tax, how income is distributed, the use of tariffs or other import barriers and the level and growth of population. For example, many foreign businesses took advatage of investment opportunities in China in 2004 after the country 'opened up' its economy and its trading arrangements.

Social factors which firms may need to consider include literacy levels, the role of women, religious attitudes, readiness to accept new ideas, and the habits and attitudes of social groups.

**Differences in business practice** The usual amount of time it takes to receive payment may vary in different countries. Other differences include accounting techniques, company ownership (most British companies are relatively independent whereas those in other EU nations are often controlled by families or banks) and distribution (in many EU countries greater use is made of rail transport than in the UK).

---

Whirlpool, a US based company, is one of the world's biggest manufacturers of 'white goods', household appliances such as fridges, dishwashers and cookers. In 2002 it had a turnover of more than $11 billion.

In the case of dishwashers, the products for the main markets in North America and Europe are quite different. Because in many US homes the machines double as garbage disposers, US-style dishwashers have mechanisms for chopping up bits of food. They also use more energy and water and tend to be noisier.

Consumers' tastes for fridges vary even more. US consumers prefer 'larder-size' cabinets which nearly all contain air-blowing systems to make them frost-free. The Germans want lots of space for meat, while the Italians are keen on special vegetable compartments. To cater for the large number of vegetarians in India, often within families that contain meat eaters, the fridges often require internal sealing systems to stop smells of different foods intermingling.

The company also received a bronze award for the Supermatic Tapa Lava-Lava scrubber lid, a scrubbing and drying attachment to manual washing machines used by customers in Mexico.

The Whirlpool *Annual Report and Accounts, 2002* contained the following statements.

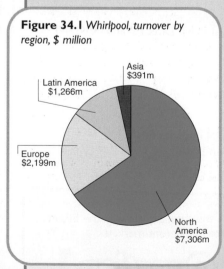

**Figure 34.1** *Whirlpool, turnover by region, $ million*

- Asia $391m
- Latin America $1,266m
- Europe $2,199m
- North America $7,306m

**Europe**
'With the 2002 acquisition of Polar S.A., Whirlpool Europe gained a strategic, low cost manufacturing position in Poland that will help serve the entire region. The company expects its ... strategy ... to result in improved contributions and productivity... .'

**Latin America**
'Whirlpool's Brazil-based compressor business, Embraco, remained a strong performer for the company. In 2002 exports from the regional operations, which include compressors and major appliances, reached a record high, rising more than 50 per cent. The company expects exports in the region will be an increasingly positive factor in the operation's ongoing performance.'

**Asia**
'Among the significant introductions in Whirlpool China was the launch of a new Whirlpool sixth sense clothes washer with sensor washing technology suited to the Chinese market. We also acquired the remaining 20 per cent of the shares from our former partner in a washing machine joint venture in Shanghai.'

Source: adapted from *The Financial Times* and Whirlpool, *Annual Report and Accounts, 2002.*

(a) Identify the ways in which the business enters foreign markets.
(b) Examine the potential implications for the business of using these methods.

Question2

Adapting products to fit in with local, national and regional needs can be costly. It is cheaper to have one product with one brand name and a promotional package which fits all markets. Businesses must attempt to cater for national consumer tastes, whilst trying to gain economies of scale from operating in international markets.

# Methods of entering overseas markets

Once a business has made the decision to enter an overseas market, it must decide the best way to do this.

**Exporting** This is often the first step for a business wishing to enter an overseas market. It involves manufacturing products at home but selling them abroad. The great advantage of exporting is that it minimises the risk of operating abroad. It can also be used as a means of testing out the ground.

Sometimes, the business may have little or no control over how the product is actually marketed in the countries to which it is sent. For this reason many firms exporting abroad make use of overseas agents (☞ unit 30). These agents are able to play an active role in the marketing of the product.

**Franchising** (☞ unit 6) This involves one business selling a licence to others. The licence allows one firm to use another's name, product or service in return for an initial payment and further commission or royalties.

This is a quick and relatively easy way into foreign markets and it allows the franchiser a high degree of control over the marketing of its product. However, a share of the profit does go to the franchisee. Firms such as PizzaExpress, Budget Rent-a-Car and Kentucky Fried Chicken have used this as a way of entering overseas markets.

**Licensing** This is similar to franchising. Franchising is used in service industries, such as fast foods and car hire. Licensing, however, involves one firm producing another's product and using its brand name, designs, patents and expertise under licence. This means that goods do not have to be physically moved abroad. Instead they are produced abroad by the foreign licensee. Also, it means that firms can avoid operating overseas. The main disadvantage is that the success or failure of the venture is largely in the hands of the licensee.

**Joint ventures** (☞ unit 89) This involves two companies from separate countries combining their resources. One new enlarged company is formed to launch a product onto one market. An example of this is the Royal Bank of Scotland's alliance with Banco Santander of Spain to provide banking and financial services throughout Europe. Joint ventures are increasingly being used by businesses wishing to enter Eastern European markets.

One advantage of this form of venture is that the risks are shared between two firms. Also, each business can draw on the strengths of the other. One business may have research and development strengths, for example, while others may have strengths in manufacturing. However, many joint ventures have broken down due to conflicts which occur.

**Direct investment** Direct investment requires the setting up of production and distribution facilities abroad. They can be obtained by merger or takeover, or they may be built for this specific purpose. It is an increasingly common way for firms to reach overseas markets. For example, many Japanese manufacturers such as Nissan and Toyota set up plants in the UK in the 1990s. It was argued that there were a number of advantages to these businesses of direct investment.

● They could avoid paying import duties (☞ unit 100) that were placed on foreign products entering the EU.
● They could take advantage of the relatively low costs and availability of relatively cheap labour in the UK.
● They could take advantage of government and EU incentives to invest in the area (☞ unit 88).
● There would be lower distribution costs.
● They could take advantage of local knowledge.

**Mergers or takeovers** Buying a business in another country may allow a company to produce and sell its products more easily. This method of entering foreign markets has similar advantages to direct investment and is most often used by **multinationals** (☞ unit 109).

# The ethics of international marketing

The behaviour of some businesses in their international marketing activities has been questioned. Concerns have been raised about businesses from wealthier countries operating in areas such as Africa, Asia and South America. For example, some tobacco companies have focussed their marketing efforts on countries with lower incomes. With health concerns about smoking and laws being passed to reduce smoking there has been a decline in the number of cigarettes purchased in western Europe and North America. One response of tobacco companies has been to focus their efforts upon poorer countries where attitudes to smoking are less negative. Also, some food companies have engaged in selling what many regard as unnecessary products to poorer consumers. Examples include sales of baby milk to mothers when breast feeding babies would be a cheaper and healthier option.

1. Give 5 reasons why international marketing can be so important to firms.
2. How does entering an overseas market allow a firm to spread its risks?
3. State 3 differences between overseas and domestic markets.
4. How can an agent help a business to export its products?
5. In what ways can a business enter an overseas market?
6. What is meant by licensing?
7. What is the difference between direct investment and joint ventures?
8. List 2 concerns about businesses marketing their products overseas.

# Case study McDonald's

McDonald's is the world's leading food service retailer with more than 300,000 local McDonald's restaurants serving 47 million customers each day in more than 100 countries. More than 70 per cent of McDonald's restaurants around the world are owned and operated by independent, local businessmen and women.

In 2002 McDonald's warned that it was on track to post its first ever loss. It suggested that it might make a loss in the final three months of the year. Intense competition from rivals offering alternative fast food, such as pizzas, sandwiches and tacos, had put the business under pressure. In a retrenchment exercise, the business pulled out of three countries in Latin America and the Middle East.

Source: adapted from news.bbc.co.uk.

**Table 34.1** *McDonald's total revenues, nine months ended 30 September, $ million*

| Country | 2003 | 2002 |
|---|---|---|
| US | 4,460.6 | 4,076.3 |
| Europe | 4,291.2 | 3,789.1 |
| APMEA* | 1,811.8 | 1,788.0 |
| Latin America | 620.4 | 619.4 |
| Canada | 561.6 | 473.7 |
| Partner brands | 839.5 | 760.0 |
| **Total** | **12,585.1** | **11,506.5** |

\* Asia Pacific/Middle East/Africa.
Source: adapted from www.mcdonalds.com/corp/news.

In 2004 McDonald's Japan, which is 50 per cent owned by US giant McDonald's, said sales increased 2 per cent in November 2003 compared with a year earlier. This broke a two year slump in the country which had been affected by mad cow disease, competition from local rivals, such as beef bowl restaurant chain Yoshinoya D&C, and weak consumer spending. McDonald's was likely to benefit from the remodelling of its stores and menu changes. To revive fortunes, McDonald's aimed to offer promotional products such as 'Gratin Croquette Burgers' which appealed to local tastes.

Source: adapted from www.ccfa.org.cn.

In December 2003 McDonald's announced another step in its revitalisation plan. Part of this included:
● discontinuing its development of non-McDonald's brands outside the US, including Donatos Pizzeria in Germany and Boston Market in Canada and Australia;

● retaining a minority investment in Pret a Manger in the UK, but closing its Pret operations in Japan.

Source: adapted from www.mcdonalds.com/corp/news.

**Figure 34.2** *McDonald's operating margins, company operated and franchised restaurants, nine months ended 30 September, $ million, 2003*

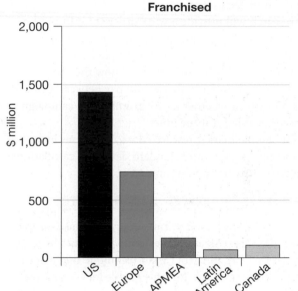

Source: adapted from www.mcdonalds.com/corp/news.

In 2003 McDonald's announced positive results for the nine months to end September 2003. It reported 'Europe delivered its highest quarterly sales increase this year. We've had solid performance in many European markets ...' and 'To strengthen the business we are working to increase relevance ... by enhancing our value positioning and adding more menu choice.' It also added that around the world it recently launched its first ever global marketing initiative, 'I'm lovin' it'. This initiative was designed to reaffirm McDonald's marketing leadership.

**(a)** Describe how McDonald's has differentiated its marketing in different countries. **(6 marks)**
**(b)** Explain how McDonald's has entered overseas markets. **(10 marks)**
**(c)** Examine the factors that are likely to affect McDonald's marketing success in overseas markets. **(12 marks)**
**(d)** Assess the extent to which McDonald's international marketing marketing **(i)** has been a success in the past and **(ii)** might be a success in future. **(12 marks)**

## Sample results

Businesses carry out market research to find out what their customers want. It is highly unlikely that a business will be able to carry out market research on everyone in the population. So businesses tend to choose a **sample** of people to survey. There is a variety of sampling techniques that can be used. These vary from completely random samples, where everyone has an equal chance of being chosen, to quota sampling, where the population is segmented into groups with similar characteristics and a certain number of people are selected out of each segment.

Market research will provide a wide variety of information about the people in the sample. Businesses then analyse this data to find out the significance of the sample results. For example, a business may be interested to know the likely proportion of the population that would pay between £10 and £20 for its product or whether a new promotional campaign has increased the sales of its product.

To analyse sample market research data, businesses make use of probability, average and standard deviation calculations and the normal distribution (☞ unit 13).

## Probability and sampling

The reason why businesses carry out surveys and take samples is to try to reduce the risk and uncertainty that exists in every business decision. PROBABILITY is a technique that helps a business to quantify risk and it forms a basis for the analysis of sampling data.

A probability is a simple ratio between the event the business is interested in and the total number of events that could occur, ie:

$$\text{Probability (P)} = \frac{\text{Required event}}{\text{Total events}}$$

Take an example of a card drawn from a pack of 52 playing cards. The probability of drawing a 'Heart' would be:

$$\text{P(a Heart)} = \frac{13}{52} = \frac{1}{4} = 0.25$$

Similarly, for drawing a card that is from one of the other suits:

$$\text{P(a Club)} = \frac{13}{52} = \frac{1}{4} = 0.25$$

$$\text{P(a Diamond)} = \frac{13}{52} = \frac{1}{4} = 0.25$$

$$\text{P(a Spade)} = \frac{13}{52} = \frac{1}{4} = 0.25$$

There are three important laws of probability:

- The sum of the probabilities of all the possible events will equal 1. Thus the probability of drawing a Heart, a Club, a Diamond or a Spade will equal 1 (0.25 + 0.25 + 0.25 + 0.25 = 1).
- To obtain the probability of one event or another event occurring, **add** the probabilities (the addition rule). Thus the probability of drawing a Diamond or a Spade = 0.25 + 0.25 = 0.5.
- To obtain the probability of one event and another occurring, **multiply** the probabilities (the multiplication rule). Thus the probability of drawing a Diamond and a Spade on two successive draws = 0.25 x 0.25 = 0.0625.

Two examples can be used to illustrate how probability might affect a business. The first example considers its use in marketing. However, it is possible to use probability in other areas of the business, such as production or stock control. The second example shows how the business might evaluate problems arising in its administration department.

**To quantify the risk associated with making a decision** Say that a business has the following information about the launch of a new product.

- Probability of gaining a high demand = 0.6, expected return £6 million.
- Probability of gaining a medium demand = 0.2, expected return £3million.
- Probability of gaining a low demand = 0.2, expected return £1 million.

This information about the likelihood of high, medium or low demand would have been derived from market research. The likely outcome from the decision to launch the new product will be:

- 0.6 probability of a return of £6m = 0.6 x £6m = £3.6m;
- 0.2 probability of a return of £3m = 0.2 x £3m = £0.6m;
- 0.2 probability of a return of £1m = 0.2 x £1m = £0.2m.

Given that these are the only three outcomes possible (the sum of the three probabilities = 1), then the average return the company can expect from the launch of such a product = £3.6m + £0.6m + £0.2m = £4.4m. If, for example, the cost to the business of launching such a product is £3m, then by the laws of probability, such a launch would be worth the risk. This use of probability is found in decision trees (☞ unit 12).

**To establish the possible range of events that might occur in business situations** Say an estate agency has three photocopiers in operation. The photocopiers are known to break down one day in every ten. What is the chance that all three are out of operation at once? There is a number of alternative combinations to consider.

- All 3 copiers are working.
- 2 copiers are working and 1 is faulty.

- 1 copier is working and 2 are faulty.
- All 3 copiers are faulty.

If a working copier is (w) and a faulty copier is (f), the possible combinations amongst the three machines are:

| Machine | 1 | 2 | 3 | |
|---|---|---|---|---|
| | w | w | w | All 3 machines are working |
| | w | w | f | |
| | w | f | w | 2 are working and 1 is faulty |
| | f | w | w | |
| | w | f | f | |
| | f | w | f | 1 is working and 2 are faulty |
| | f | f | w | |
| | f | f | f | All 3 machines are faulty |

If the probability of a working machine (p) is 0.9 then the probability of a faulty machine (q) is 0.1. It is possible to work out the probability of all these combinations.

- All 3 machines working = 1 x 0.9 x 0.9 x 0.9 = 0.73 (or 73%).
- 2 machines working and 1 faulty = 3 x 0.9 x 0.9 x 0.1 = 0.24 (or 24%).
- 1 machine working and 2 faulty = 3 x 0.9 x 0.1 x 0.1 = 0.027 (or 2.7%).
- All 3 machines are faulty = 1 x 0.1 x 0.1 x 0.1 = 0.001 (or 0.1%).

In algebraic terms the probabilities are worked out using the binomial expansion:

$$p^3 + 3p^2q + 3pq^2 + q^3 = 1$$

Thus for this business there is only a 0.001 chance (0.1 per cent) of all three machines being out of action at once. But there is a 0.24 (24 per cent) chance of at least one machine being out of action, which might be a problem for the company. Although 3 machines have been used in this example, a business might need to look at combinations involving 2, 4 or more machines. Probabilities would then be worked out using, for example:

$$p^2 + 2pq + q^2 = 1 \text{ (for 2 machines)}$$

$$p^4 + 4p^3q + 6p^2q^2 + 4pq^3 + q^4 = 1 \text{ (for 4 machines)}$$

## The normal distribution

The NORMAL DISTRIBUTION is a statistical model that will tell a business what the expected range of outcomes from a particular population will be. It is used where businesses have been carrying out large scale sampling, for example in market research or in quality control, where they want to find out what range of results to expect.

The normal distribution occurs in many different contexts. For example, if a large group of sixth form students, representing the full ability range, took a Business Studies examination, then the frequency distribution of their marks may resemble a normal distribution, as shown in Figure 35.1.

Littlehurst is a manufaturer of electronic sensor equipment. Its most popular product is a sensor device that is used to test corrosion in metal on equipment. It has tested two new hand held sensor devices with a sample of its customers and has found the following information.

Test product A  Probability of success - 0.3 Expected revenue - £200,000
Probability of failure - 0.7 Expected revenue - £50,000
Cost of launch - £90,000

Test product B  Probability of success - 0.5 Expected revenue - £120,000
Probability of failure - 0.5 Expected revenue - £30,000
Cost of launch - £80,000

(a) Calculate:
   (i) the returns that the company can expect from each product;
   (ii) the profit or loss that the company can expect from each product.
(b) Suggest which product the company should launch based on the above information alone.
(c) If the cost of the launch of product B fell to £65,000, how might this affect your answer to (a)?

**Question 1**

Some students will do very well, some students will do very badly, but the majority of students will fall close to and either side of the average (mean) score.

The resulting NORMAL DISTRIBUTION CURVE shows all the possible outcomes (range of marks) and the frequency at which they occurred (number of students at each mark). It is 'bell-shaped' and symmetrical about the mean value.

Normal distributions will differ in their shallowness or steepness. The weights of people in a population are likely to be quite evenly spread as in Figure 35.2(a), whilst IQ scores in a population are likely to be more closely bunched around the average, with few high or low scores as in Figure 35.2(b). It is the spread of the data that determines the curves' steepness or shallowness. This spread can be measured by the use of **standard deviations** (☞ unit 13).

Whatever the spread of the normal distribution curves,

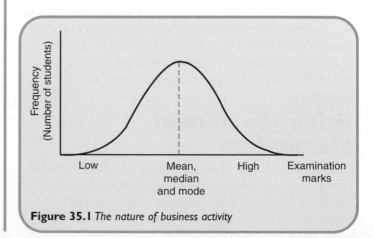

**Figure 35.1** *The nature of business activity*

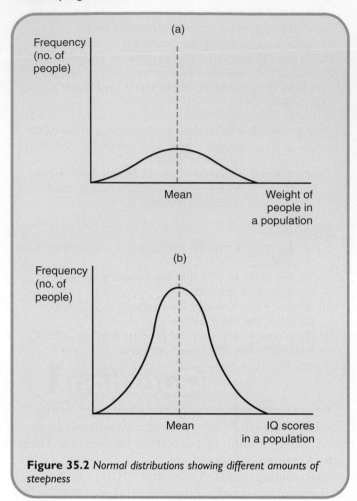

**Figure 35.2** *Normal distributions showing different amounts of steepness*

**Figure 35.3** *A normal distribution showing standard deviations*

they have particular features in common.
- The curve is symmetrical about the mean.
- The mean, mode and median of the distribution is equal.
- 50 per cent of all values lie either side of the mean value.
- The curve can be divided into 3 standard deviations (SDs) either side of the mean.
    68 per cent of the population will lie between + or - 1 SD.
    96 per cent of the population will lie between + or - 2 SDs.
    99.8 per cent of the population will lie between + or - 3 SDs.

Thus nearly all results will lie within + or - 3 SDs of the mean. A small proportion (0.2 per cent) will lie outside this range, but this is so small businesses are not concerned about it in practice. The exact distribution of the range of results possible is shown in Figure 35.3. The normal distribution has a certain predictability. Therefore any results that lie outside the expected range become significant and unexpected.

## Using the normal distribution

One business context where the normal distribution can be used is in the analysis of market research data. A business might ask, 'was the result of a survey possible purely by chance or was there a significant difference between the actual result and the expected one?'

Say that a company which manufactures potato crisps has used a market research company to discover whether their new 'Sweet and Sour' flavour, which has been heavily promoted since its launch, is well known by the public. On average, the company would expect 50 per cent of those asked to recognise a flavour, but following the promotion they would expect a higher recognition. If the market research company asks 900 consumers, what results might the company expect to get to measure whether the promotion was successful?

The first stage in the use of normal distribution to answer this question involves the calculation of the expected RANGE OF RESULTS from such surveys. To do this it is necessary to calculate the mean and the standard deviation for this particular distribution.

The mean for a normal distribution can be calculated using the formula:

$$\text{mean} = n \times p$$

where n = the sample size
and p = the probability of an event occurring.

The standard deviation for a normal distribution can be calculated using the formula:

$$1 \text{ standard deviation (1SD)} = \sqrt{npq}$$

where n = the sample size;
p = the probability of an event occurring;
and q = the probability of an event not occurring.
For the market research on the 'Sweet and Sour' crisps:
n = 900
p = 0.5
q = 0.5

Therefore, for such surveys as this:

$$\text{mean} = 900 \times 0.5 = 450$$

$$1SD = \sqrt{900 \times 0.5 \times 0.5} = \sqrt{225} = 15$$

The full range of results can be + or - 3SD from the mean where:

2SD = 30
3SD = 45

Therefore, the range for this normal curve will be:

450 + or - 45 = 405 to 495.

The normal curve can now be drawn based on this information as in Figure 35.4. For the company, this normal curve provides a tool to help it analyse any market research results.

● 68 per cent of all results will show that between 435 and 465 people recognise the flavour (given a mean of 450).

● 96 per cent of all results will show that between 420 and 480 people recognise the flavour.

● 99.8 per cent of all results will show that between 405 and 495 people recognise the flavour.

These percentages are usually referred to as **confidence levels** (☞ unit 19).

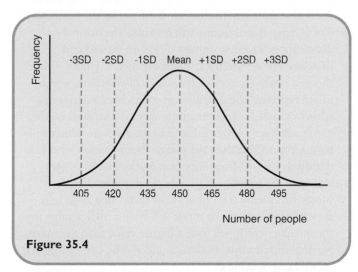

**Figure 35.4**

A manufacturer of dental products is particularly interested in the hygiene habits of its customers. The business expects that the average length of time people take before changing their toothbrush is 90 days and the standard deviation is 20 days.

(a) Draw a normal distribution. Assuming that the information is normally distributed, calculate and plot onto the graph:
   (i) the expected average length of time people take to change their toothbrush;
   (ii) the range of results between minus 3 and plus 3 standard deviations (in days).
(b) What percentage of its customers might the business expect to change their toothbrush:
   (i) after 70 days;
   (ii) after 130 days?

# Confidence levels

Look again at the previous example about sweet and sour flavoured crisps. Only if marketing research results showed more than 495 people recognised the flavour could the company be totally confident that its promotion has been effective in increasing recognition above the 50 per cent level. Suppose the actual result was 486 people recognising the product? How significant would this be? We can find this in terms of standard deviations (z) by using the formula:

$$z = \frac{x - m}{s} \quad \begin{array}{l} \text{where } x = \text{the value} \\ m = \text{the mean} \\ s = \text{the standard deviation} \end{array}$$

so:

$$z = \frac{486 - 450}{15} = \frac{36}{15} = 2.4 \text{ SDs from the mean}$$

To find out what percentage of the population lies between the mean and +2.4SDs, a normal distribution table, as in Table 35.1, can be used. This shows the areas under the standard normal distribution from the mean. Because this is a frequency distribution, the area represents the number in the population between each value.

Reading from the left hand column of the table, 49.18 per cent (or 0.4918) of the population will lie between the mean and +2.4SDs. To include all values up to and including 486 it is necessary to add this to the 0.5 or 50 per cent on the other side of the mean. This gives a total of:

$$0.5 + 0.4918 = 0.9918 \text{ or } 99 \text{ per cent}$$

This is shown as a shaded area on Figure 35.5. The company can therefore be 99 per cent certain that a result of 486 represents an improvement over the 50 per cent average. If it wanted to be even more certain, it would need to take 3 standard deviations (rather than 2.4) into account.

**Figure 34.5** *A normal distribution showing standard deviations*

**Table 35.1** *Table of standard normal curve areas*

| (z) | .00 | .01 | .02 | .03 | .04 | .05 | .06 | .07 | .08 | .09 |
|-----|-----|-----|-----|-----|-----|-----|-----|-----|-----|-----|
| 0.0 | .0000 | .0040 | .0080 | .0120 | .0160 | .0199 | .0239 | .0279 | .0319 | .0359 |
| 0.1 | .0398 | .0438 | .0478 | .0517 | .0557 | .0596 | .0636 | .0675 | .0714 | .0753 |
| 0.2 | .0793 | .0832 | .0871 | .0910 | .0948 | .0987 | .1026 | .1064 | .1103 | .1141 |
| 0.3 | .1179 | .1217 | .1255 | .1293 | .1331 | .1368 | .1406 | .1443 | .1480 | .1517 |
| 0.4 | .1554 | .1591 | .1628 | .1664 | .1700 | .1736 | .1772 | .1808 | .1844 | .1879 |
| 0.5 | .1915 | .1950 | .1985 | .2019 | .2054 | .2088 | .2123 | .2157 | .2190 | .2224 |
| 0.6 | .2257 | .2291 | .2324 | .2357 | .2389 | .2422 | .2454 | .2486 | .2517 | .2549 |
| 0.7 | .2580 | .2611 | .2642 | .2673 | .2704 | .2734 | .2764 | .2794 | .2823 | .2852 |
| 0.8 | .2881 | .2910 | .2939 | .2967 | .2995 | .3023 | .3051 | .3078 | .3106 | .3133 |
| 0.9 | .3159 | .3186 | .3212 | .3238 | .3264 | .3289 | .3315 | .3340 | .3365 | .3389 |
| 1.0 | .3413 | .3438 | .3461 | .3485 | .3508 | .3531 | .3554 | .3577 | .3599 | .3621 |
| 1.1 | .3643 | .3665 | .3686 | .3708 | .3729 | .3749 | .3770 | .3790 | .3810 | .3830 |
| 1.2 | .3849 | .3869 | .3888 | .3907 | .3925 | .3944 | .3962 | .3980 | .3997 | .4015 |
| 1.3 | .4032 | .4049 | .4066 | .4082 | .4099 | .4115 | .4131 | .4147 | .4162 | .4177 |
| 1.4 | .4192 | .4207 | .4222 | .4236 | .4251 | .4265 | .4279 | .4292 | .4306 | .4319 |
| 1.5 | .4332 | .4345 | .4357 | .4370 | .4382 | .4394 | .4406 | .4418 | .4429 | .4441 |
| 1.6 | .4452 | .4463 | .4474 | .4484 | .4495 | .4505 | .4515 | .4525 | .4535 | .4545 |
| 1.7 | .4554 | .4564 | .4573 | .4582 | .4591 | .4599 | .4608 | .4616 | .4625 | .4633 |
| 1.8 | .4641 | .4649 | .4656 | .4664 | .4671 | .4678 | .4686 | .4693 | .4699 | .4706 |
| 1.9 | .4713 | .4719 | .4726 | .4732 | .4738 | .4744 | .4750 | .4756 | .4761 | .4767 |
| 2.0 | .4772 | .4778 | .4783 | .4788 | .4793 | .4798 | .4803 | .4808 | .4812 | .4817 |
| 2.1 | .4821 | .4826 | .4830 | .4834 | .4838 | .4842 | .4846 | .4850 | .4854 | .4857 |
| 2.2 | .4861 | .4864 | .4868 | .4871 | .4875 | .4878 | .4881 | .4884 | .4887 | .4890 |
| 2.3 | .4893 | .4896 | .4898 | .4901 | .4904 | .4906 | .4909 | .4911 | .4913 | .4916 |
| 2.4 | .4918 | .4920 | .4922 | .4925 | .4927 | .4929 | .4931 | .4932 | .4934 | .4936 |
| 2.5 | .4938 | .4940 | .4941 | .4943 | .4945 | .4946 | .4948 | .4949 | .4951 | .4952 |
| 2.6 | .4953 | .4955 | .4956 | .4957 | .4959 | .4960 | .4961 | .4962 | .4963 | .4964 |
| 2.7 | .4965 | .4966 | .4967 | .4968 | .4969 | .4970 | .4971 | .4972 | .4973 | .4974 |
| 2.8 | .4974 | .4975 | .4976 | .4977 | .4977 | .4978 | .4979 | .4979 | .4980 | .4981 |
| 2.9 | .4981 | .4982 | .4982 | .4983 | .4984 | .4984 | .4985 | .4985 | .4986 | .4986 |
| 3.0 | .4987 | .4987 | .4987 | .4988 | .4988 | .4989 | .4989 | .4989 | .4990 | .4990 |

High Style is a manufacturer of clothing for tall people. It provides a bespoke leg length service. It will turn up trousers to suit the leg length specified on an order. On average, it expects the people buying its trousers to have an inside leg length of 35 inches with a standard deviation of 0.5 inches.

(a) Assuming the leg lengths of its customers are normally distributed, what range of lengths would the business expect its customers to have? Plot these figures onto a normal distribution.
(b) If the business tested a sample of 100 people, what percentage would expect it to be:
   (i) above 36.5 inches;
   (ii) between 35 inches and 36 inches;
   (iii) between 35 inches and 35.8 inches;
   (iv) below 34.2 inches?
   Use Table 35.1 to answer this question.

# Limitations of the normal distribution

As with all models used in business decision making, there are possible problems with its use.

- The sample size has to be large otherwise it is unlikely that the distribution will be normally distributed. A large sample size helps to smooth out the peaks and troughs in smaller frequency distributions.

- The calculation of the mean and the standard deviation are based on probability figures that themselves might be based upon estimates rather than exact figures. In the example of market research, the 0.5 probability used to calculate the likely response to the market research on crisps was an estimate based upon previous experience.

- Especially in the area of quality control, a 'one-off' reading which is a long way from the expected mean may not be sufficient to reject a batch or shut down a machine. Further sampling would be important to confirm the evidence of the first sample before costs are incurred by the business.

- Not all large distributions will resemble the normal distribution. The distribution might be skewed and therefore not symmetrical about the mean. Figure 35.6(a) shows a positively skewed frequency distribution, which might represent the distribution of teachers' salaries in a school or college. In a positively skewed distribution, the mode will have a lower value than the median, which will have a lower value than the mean. Figure 35.6(b) shows a negatively skewed frequency distribution, which might represent the number of people per day attending a successful cinema over a period of time. In a negatively skewed distribution, the mode will have a higher value than the median, which will have a higher value than the mean. Normal distribution analysis could not be used with such skewed distributions.

**Figure 35.6** *Skewed distributions*

## Knowledge...Knowledge...Knowledge

1. What statistical concepts are used to analyse market research data?
2. What does probability measure?
3. Why is the normal distribution a useful tool for businesses to use in analysing data?
4. What are the distinguishing features of a normal curve?
5. What is the difference between a normal distribution and a skewed distribution?

# Case study Heritage Cottages Ltd

Heritage Cottages Ltd is a company which hires out cottages and bungalows in various areas of England. Most customers book directly with the business via the telephone and view properties in the company brochure which shows the cottages that are available. The brochure is produced each November and Heritage has traditionally advertised the availability of the brochure in a range of weekly magazines between December and April. The management was always careful to analyse the responses that resulted from these advertisements each week. Over a five year period it calculated that the mean number of responses was 1,500 each week with a standard deviation of 125.

For the 2003-04 season Heritage decided to shift its advertising over the December to April period to the Sunday papers, such as *The Sunday Times* and *The Observer*. It wanted to see if this resulted in a significant increase in the number of customer enquiries. It carried out a survey of the responses over the twenty week period that it ran the advertisements. Heritage found that the mean level of response had risen to 1,800 for the 2003-04 season. The company was pleased with the outcome and decided, on the basis of these figures, to continue advertising in the Sunday papers for the following season.

**(a)** What is meant by the terms (i) mean number of responses and (ii) significant increase in customer enquiries? Use examples from Heritage Cottages in your explanation. (6 marks)

**(b)** Explain why the results from the 5 year analysis by Heritage Cottages of responses to a magazine advertisement might be normally distributed. (8 marks)

**(c)** (i) Draw a normal distribution curve which shows the full range of responses that the company achieved. (6 marks)

(ii) How many standard deviations from the mean did the 1,800 responses from the Sunday newspaper advertisements represent? (6 marks)

**(d)** Was the business right to be pleased with the outcome from the switch to newspaper advertisements? Consider the normal distribution diagram from your answer to **(c)** and other factors that Heritage Cottages might need to take into account in evaluating the move from magazine to newspaper advertising. (14 marks)

## Forecasting

Businesses are keen to know about what might happen in the future. Anything they can predict accurately will reduce their uncertainty and will allow them to plan. Predictions may be based on a variety of data. They could be based on current information provided by managers. Most forecasts are based on **backdata** gathered from a variety of marketing research techniques. The accuracy of forecasts will depend on the reliability of the data.

What might a business like to predict with accuracy? Some examples might include:

● future sales of products;
● the effect of promotion on sales;
● possible changes in the size of the market in future;
● the way sales fluctuate at different times of the year.

A variety of techniques can be used to predict future trends. One of the most popular is **time series analysis**, which is discussed in the next section.

## Time series analysis

TIME SERIES ANALYSIS involves predicting future levels from past data. The data used are known as **time series data** - a set of figures arranged in order, based on the time they occurred. So, for example, a business may predict future sales by analysing sales data over the last 10 years. The business, of course, is assuming that past figures are a useful indicator of what will happen in the future. This is likely to be the case if trading conditions are **stable** or if the business needs to forecast trends in the short term. Time series analysis does not try to explain data, only to describe what is happening to it or predict what will happen to it.

There are likely to be four components that a business wants to identify in time series data.

● **The trend**. 'Raw' data can have many different figures. It may not be easy to see exactly what is happening from these figures and so a business often tries to identify a trend. The trend shows the pattern that is indicated from the figures. For example, there may be a trend for sales of a new product to rise sharply in a short period as it becomes very popular.
● **Cyclical fluctuations**. For many businesses there may be a cycle of 'highs and lows' in their sales figures, which rise over a number of years and then fall again. It is argued that these are a result of the recession-boom-recession of the trade cycle in the economy. In a recession, for example, people have less money to spend and so the turnover of a business may fall in that period.
● **Seasonal fluctuations**. Over a year a business is unlikely to have a constant level of sales. The seasonal variations are very important to a business such as a travel agent or a 'greetings card' producer, where there may be large sales at

some times but not at others.
● **Random fluctuations**. At times there will be 'freak' figures which stand out from any trend that is taking place. An example may be the sudden boost in sales of umbrellas in unusually wet summer months or the impact on consumers' spending of a one-off event such as a summer music festival.

## Identifying the trend

An analysis of figures will tell a business whether there is an upward, downward or constant trend. Identifying the trend allows the business to predict what is likely to happen in future. The first step is to smooth out the raw data. Take an example of a toy manufacturer, whose yearly sales over 10 years are shown in Table 36.1.

**Table 36.1** *Yearly sales of a toy manufacturer (£000)*

| 1995 | 1996 | 1997 | 1998 | 1999 | 2000 | 2001 | 2002 | 2003 | 2004 |
|------|------|------|------|------|------|------|------|------|------|
| 300 | 500 | 600 | 550 | 600 | 750 | 850 | 1,100 | 800 | 1,100 |

It is possible to calculate a trend by using a MOVING AVERAGE. The average can be taken for any period the business wants, such as a year, a month or a quarter. For now we will assume the toy manufacturer uses a 3 year average.

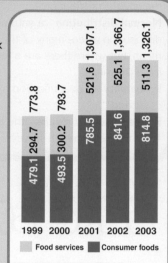

Dairy Crest is the UK's leading chilled food company. It operates in six major areas - spreads, cheeses, liquid products, fresh dairy products, household products and ingredients. Its consumer foods division sells to retailers and its food services division includes the household milk business and dairy ingredients operation. Figure 36.1 shows the annual turnover over the last five years.

(a) Identify the trends shown in the data.
(b) Explain the factors that might lead to a rising trend of sales in future.

**Figure 36.1** *Turnover, £m*
Source: adapted from Dairy Crest, *Annual Report and Accounts*, 2003.

**Question 1**

The average of sales in the first 3 years was:

$$\frac{300 + 500 + 600}{3} = \frac{1,400}{3} = 466.7$$

The first year's sales 'drop out' and the next year's sales are added to give a moving average. The average for the next three years was:

$$\frac{500 + 600 + 550}{3} = \frac{1,650}{3} = 550$$

If the business continues to do this, the results will be as shown in Table 36.2. Notice that the moving average is placed at the centre of the 3 years (ie the average for 1995-97 is plotted next to 1996).

**Table 36.2** *3 year moving average for sales of a toy manufacturer (£000)*

| 1995 | 1996 | 1997 | 1998 | 1999 | 2000 | 2001 | 2002 | 2003 | 2004 |
|------|------|------|------|------|------|------|------|------|------|
| 300 | 500 | 600 | 550 | 600 | 750 | 850 | 1,100 | 800 | 1,100 |
| | 466.7 | 550 | 583.3 | 633.3 | 733.3 | 900 | 916.7 | 1,000 | |

What if the firm had used a 4 year period instead of 3 years? No one year is the centre point and simply placing the figure in between two years may result in misleading predictions in future. The solution is to use CENTRING. This uses a 4 and 8 year moving **total** to find a mid point. So, for example, in Table 36.2:

| Year | 1995 | 1996 | 1997 | 1998 | 1999 |
|------|------|------|------|------|------|
| (£000) | 300 | 500 | 600 | 550 | 600 |

1,950 + 2,250    =    4,200
(4 year moving totals)    (8 year moving total)

This can then be used to find the mid-point, which is 1997. The **trend** or **four period centred moving average** can be found by dividing the 8 year moving total by 8, the number of years, as shown in Table 36.3.

Plotting the four period centred moving average figures onto a graph (as shown in Figure 36.2) shows the trends in the figures. It is clear to see that sales appear to be rising over the period. The trend line is 'smoother' than the line showing the actual sales figures. It eliminates any fluctuations in sales each year and gives a more obvious picture of the trend that has been taking place.

# Predicting from the trend

Having identified a trend that is taking place the business can now predict what may happen in future. Figure 36.3 shows the trend data from Figure 36.2, but with a line drawn to

**Table 36.3** *Calculating a 4 year moving average for a toy manufacturer*

£000

| Year | Sales | 4 year moving total | 8 year moving total | Trend (4 year centred moving average = 8 year moving total ÷ 8) |
|------|-------|---------------------|---------------------|------------------------------------------------------------------|
| 1995 | 300 | | | |
| 1996 | 500 | | | |
| 1997 | 600 | 1,950 | 4,200 | 525.00 |
| 1998 | 550 | 2,250 | 4,750 | 593.75 |
| 1999 | 600 | 2,500 | 5,250 | 656.25 |
| 2000 | 750 | 2,750 | 6,050 | 756.25 |
| 2001 | 850 | 3,300 | 6,800 | 850.00 |
| 2002 | 1,100 | 3,500 | 7,350 | 918.75 |
| 2003 | 800 | 3,850 | | |
| 2004 | 1,100 | | | |

**Figure 36.2** *Annual sales of a toy manufacturer*

A business has recently gathered data on its sales revenue as shown in Table 36.4, and wants to calculate a 3 and 4 period moving average.

**Table 36.4** *Sales revenue*

(£000)

| Period | 1 | 2 | 3 | 4 | 5 | 6 | 7 | 8 | 9 | 10 |
|--------|---|---|---|---|---|---|---|---|---|----|
| Sales revenue | 100 | 130 | 160 | 175 | 180 | 190 | 190 | 180 | 220 | 250 |
| 3 period moving average | | 130 | 155 | | | | | | | |
| 4 period moving average | | | 151.3 | | | | | | | |

(a) Calculate the 3 and 4 period moving averages for as many years as you can to complete the table.
(b) Plot the sales figures and both trend lines onto a graph on graph paper and explain the relationship between the trend and the actual sales revenue figures.

**Question 2**

predict the likely sales in 2005. The graph shows that sales of the toy manufacturer's goods may reach about £1,160,000.

The business has made certain assumptions when predicting this figure. First, no other factors were likely to have changed to affect the trend. If other factors changed, resulting in different sales figures, then the prediction is likely to be inaccurate.

Second, the sales figures are predicted by drawing a line through the trend figures and extending it to the year 2001. The broken line through the trend in Figure 36.3 is called the LINE OF BEST FIT. It is the best line that can be drawn which matches the general slope of all points in the trend. The line is an average, where points in the trend on one side of the line are balanced with those on the other. In other words, it is a line which 'best fits' **all** points in the trend.

It is possible to draw the line of best fit by plotting the trend figures on graph paper accurately and then adding the line of best fit 'by eye', so that points fit equally either side of the line. Extending the line carefully should give a reasonable prediction.

To help draw the line, it should pass through the coordinates $(\overline{X}, \overline{Y})$ where $\overline{X}$ is the average of the years and $\overline{Y}$ is the average sales. These coordinates can be calculated using the figures in Table 36.3.

$$\overline{X} = \frac{\Sigma X \text{ (the total years)}}{N \text{ (the number of years)}} = \frac{1997+1998+1999+2000+2001+2002}{6} = \frac{11,997}{6} = 1999.5$$

$$\overline{Y} = \frac{\Sigma Y \text{ (the total sales in the trend)}}{N \text{ (the number of years)}}$$

$$= \frac{£525,000 + £593,750 + £656,250 + £756,250 + £850,000 + £918,750}{6} = \frac{£4,300,000}{6}$$

$$= £716,667$$

This point is shown on Figure 36.3. The actual predicted figure for the year 2005 is £1,162,550. This can be found by a method known as 'the sum of least squares'. Computer software can be used by businesses to calculate the line of best fit and to predict from the trend.

# Variations from the trend

How accurate is the prediction of **around** £1,160,000 sales of toys by the year 2005? Even allowing for the assumptions above, the prediction may not be accurate because it is taken from the trend, and the trend 'smoothed out' variations in sales figures. To make an accurate prediction, the business will have to find the average variation over the period and take this into account.

We can find how much **variation** there is from the trend by calculating:

Actual sales - trend.

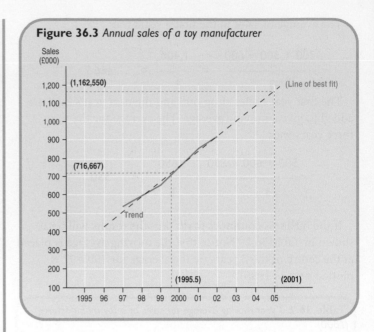

**Figure 36.3** *Annual sales of a toy manufacturer*

**Table 35.5**

(£000)

| Year | Sales | Trend (4 year centred moving average) | Variation in each year |
|------|-------|----------------------------------------|------------------------|
| 1995 | 300 | | |
| 1996 | 500 | | |
| 1997 | 600 | 525.00 | +75.00 |
| 1998 | 550 | 593.75 | -43.75 |
| 1999 | 600 | 656.25 | -56.25 |
| 2000 | 750 | 756.25 | - 6.25 |
| 2001 | 850 | 850.00 | +/- 0 |
| 2002 | 1,100 | 918.75 | +181.25 |
| 2003 | 800 | | |
| 2004 | 1,100 | | |

So, for example, the **cyclical** variation in Table 36.3 would be as shown in Table 36.5. The average of the variations over the period 1995-2004 is (in £000):

$$\frac{+75 - 43.75 - 56.25 -6.25 +/-0 +181.25}{6} = \frac{+150}{6} = +25 \text{ (or +£25,000)}$$

If the predicted value based on the trend was £1,160,000, then adding £25,000 may give a more accurate predicted figure of £1,185,000.

# Seasonal variations

Earlier it was stated that a business may be interested in variations in any one year. It is possible to predict from a trend and use **seasonal** variations to make a more accurate prediction. Table 36.7 shows sales of a business over a 3 year period, including sales in each quarter. A 4 quarter moving

Table 36.6 shows the yearly sales figures of a furniture manufacturer over a period of 10 years.

**Table 36.6**

units

| Period | 1 | 2 | 3 | 4 | 5 | 6 | 7 | 8 | 9 | 10 |
|--------|---|---|---|---|---|---|---|---|---|----|
| Sales | 5,000 | 5,200 | 5,800 | 6,000 | 5,800 | 7,000 | 8,200 | 7,400 | 7,600 | 8,400 |

(a) Calculate a four yearly moving average from the figures to show the trend taking place.
(b) Plot the trend onto a graph on graph paper and predict the likely output in year 11.
(c) Calculate:
  (i) the cyclical variation for each year;
  (ii) the average cyclical variation over the period.

*Question* 3

average has been calculated and also the variation in each quarter.

Carrying on the trend to predict the sales for the fourth quarter of the year 2003 might give a figure of £470,000. (It would be possible to find this by drawing and extending a line of best fit through the trend.) As we know, this is a 'smoothed out' figure. A more accurate prediction might be to calculate the **average seasonal variation** in the fourth quarter, for example (in £000):

$$\frac{-97.125 - 117.5}{2} = \frac{-214.625}{2} = -107.313$$

By subtracting £107,313 from the total of £470,000, this gives a more accurate prediction of £362,687.

**Table 36.7**

(£000)

| Year | Quarter | Sales | 4 quarter moving average | Variation |
|------|---------|-------|--------------------------|-----------|
| 2000 | 3 | 460 | | |
|      | 4 | 218 | | |
| 2001 | 1 | 205 | 328.5 | -123.5 |
|      | 2 | 388 | 346.0 | +42.0 |
|      | 3 | 546 | 358.25 | +187.75 |
|      | 4 | 272 | 369.125 | - 97.125 |
| 2002 | 1 | 249 | 383.625 | -134.625 |
|      | 2 | 431 | 396.625 | +34.375 |
|      | 3 | 619 | 404.0 | +215.0 |
|      | 4 | 303 | 420.5 | -117.5 |
| 2003 | 1 | 277 | | |
|      | 2 | 535 | | |

## *Causal modelling*

Time series analysis only describes what is happening to information. Causal modelling tries to explain data, usually by finding a link between one set of data and another. For example, a business may want to find whether there is a link between the amount that it spends on advertising and its sales.

Table 36.8 shows data that have been collected about advertising and sales by a business at different times. The data in the table are plotted onto a SCATTER GRAPH in Figure 36.4. Advertising (the **independent** variable) is shown on the horizontal (X) axis. Sales (the **dependent** variable) are shown on the vertical (Y) axis. The figure shows, for example, that in one period (E) the business had advertising spending of £1,500 and sales of 1,800 units. In another period (G) the business had advertising spending of £3,500 and sales of 5,800 units.

**Table 36.8**

| Period | Advertising expenditure (£000) | Sales (000) | (£million) | (million) | (£million) |
|--------|-------------------------------|-------------|------------|-----------|------------|
| | X | Y | X² | Y² | XY |
| A | 1.0 | 3.2 | 1.0 | 10.24 | 3.2 |
| B | 2.0 | 4.5 | 4.0 | 20.25 | 9.0 |
| C | 3.0 | 1.8 | 9.0 | 3.24 | 5.4 |
| D | 4.0 | 3.0 | 16 | 9.0 | 12.0 |
| E | 1.5 | 1.8 | 2.25 | 3.24 | 2.7 |
| F | 2.5 | 1.6 | 6.25 | 2.56 | 4.0 |
| G | 3.5 | 5.8 | 12.25 | 33.64 | 20.3 |
| H | 1.2 | 4.7 | 1.44 | 22.09 | 5.64 |
| I | 2.7 | 5.9 | 7.29 | 34.81 | 15.93 |
| J | 3.0 | 3.5 | 9.0 | 12.25 | 10.5 |
| K | 3.6 | 3.1 | 12.96 | 9.61 | 11.16 |
| L | 7.0 | 3.5 | 0.49 | 12.25 | 2.45 |
| | | | $\Sigma X^2$ =81.93 | $\Sigma Y^2$=173.18 | $\Sigma XY$=102.28 |

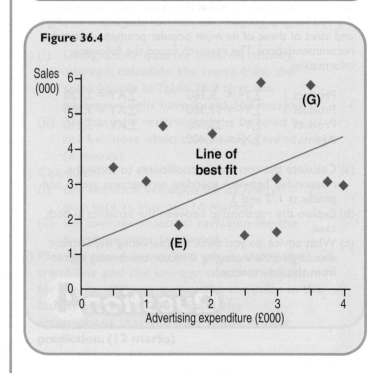

**Figure 36.4**

- Capacity. Some businesses conduct billions of transactions each year. If records of these transactions were stored in manual systems a huge quantity of resources would be required. In addition, access to information stored in a computer is very easy. From the billions of transactions that might be recorded, an operator can instantly call up details of one single transaction.
- Efficiency. Because large volumes of data can be processed quickly, computer systems require a smaller workforce than manual systems. Therefore the cost of collecting and recording transactions can be reduced.
- Data handling. Information can be input and accessed from different locations around the country or the world. For example, a supermarket chain might have several hundred branches in the UK, each with twenty or more checkouts. The sales information from all of these sources eventually goes to one central processing unit where it is sorted and stored in the appropriate accounts. Information from every store can be retrieved and monitored from head office. **Electronic data exchange** may be used to transmit information in this way.
- User friendly. The design of accounting programmes means that staff do not need a detailed knowledge of bookkeeping and accounts to be able to input and retrieve data. Consequently, training costs could be lower and a business might employ non-specialist staff in the accounts department to keep labour costs down.
- Accuracy. Computerised systems are more accurate than manual systems when processing data. Partly this is because computers do not become distracted or tired when performing large numbers of routine operations.
- Security. By using a system of passwords, it is possible to restrict access. This prevents the unauthorised use of sensitive information. **Intranets** (☞ unit 70), which allow one computer to communicate with another like the larger Internet, may be also used by larger businesses. However, with intranets the communication is confined to computers within a business, therefore, outsiders are prevented access.

## Disadvantages of computerised systems

The widespread use of computerised accounting systems suggest that the benefits outweigh the drawbacks. However, there are certain disadvantages.

- Cost. The cost of purchasing and then upgrading computer hardware and software can be expensive. Staff training costs can also be high. It is sometimes necessary to employ specialist IT staff to monitor the system. This adds to the cost.
- Technical problems. There is a wide range of computer systems and it is not always easy for a business to choose the most appropriate package. If an incorrect choice is made the mistake may be costly. Problems often arise when a new computer system is installed. It might not run

smoothly because of 'bugs' in the system. Other difficulties arise if a 'virus' is downloaded from the Internet or via an email, or if inexperienced staff cause the system to crash. When this occurs, it can lead to problems and delays to staff, customers and suppliers.
- Industrial relations. The use of computerised systems may cause industrial relations problems. If staff see technology as a threat to their jobs or status, they might not cooperate with management when systems are installed This can result in delays and friction between managers and employees.
- Security. Although security can be increased by the use of passwords, employees or outsiders might be able to 'hack' into the system. This unauthorised access might be used by a disgruntled employee to sabotage the business, or by a competitor who hopes to gain an advantage.
- Operator error. Computer systems are only effective if data is inputted correctly. If inaccurate data is entered, the reports that are generated will also be inaccurate, misleading and of little use. This problem is sometimes described as 'GIGO', ie garbage in, garbage out.

## Social auditing

Unit 111 discusses the growing importance of social responsibility in business. In an effort to become better corporate citizens some businesses carry out a SOCIAL AUDIT. This is a way of measuring and reporting on an company's social and ethical performance. It is a move away from the traditional method of evaluating performance which measures accounting information such as revenue, profit or dividends. Businesses that undertake social audits are accountable to a wider range of stakeholders and are also committed to following the audits recommendations. Social accounting may look at the firm's impact on the environment, the workforce, suppliers or the wider community.

Social accounting might use the following process.

- Identify the stakeholders (☞ unit 3) who are affected by its activities. These could be employees, suppliers, customers or local communities.
- Select a range of indicators that can be used to measure social performance. For example, to assess the impact a firm has on the environment it might measure factory emissions, water usage, fuel usage, waste generation or the use of recycled materials. Some businesses set targets which they hope to achieve.
- Gather information and report on the company's performance. This is an ongoing process and involves monitoring the indicators selected in the previous stage. Both quantitative and qualitative data may be gathered.
- Arrange for a social audit to be carried out. This might be done internally by assessing whether performance targets have been met from the previous year. Alternatively a business might employ an independent social auditing consultant. This acts as a safeguard against misleading information and can protect the interests of stakeholders.

Critics argue that social accounting is just a public relations exercise and a means of improving its corporate image. However, companies that have adopted social accounting, such as BP, Shell, the Coop and Body Shop, would probably say that it helps them to satisfy the needs of a wider range of stakeholders. It makes them aware of the impact the business has on society.

## Knowledge...Knowledge...Knowledge...Knowledge...Knowledge...Know

1. Why is it important for managers to have access to information?
2. Which users have a legal right of access to accounts?
3. State the internal users of accounts.
4. How might the media use accounts?
5. Explain the importance of accounts to shareholders and potential investors.
6. What might be the role of a management accountant in business?
7. State 5 advantages and 5 disadvantages of using IT in accounts.
8. Explain the significance of the term GIGO when using computers in accounts?
9. Explain how a business might undertake a social audit.
10. List the financial statements that might appear in the Annual Report and Accounts of a public limited company.

---

Balfour Beatty's business is in the creation and care of essential assets. It serves the international markets for rail, road and utility systems, buildings and complex structures. Over recent years the company has recognised that its social and ethical performance has come under increasing scrutiny. In response to this Balfour Beatty now publishes a comprehensive Safety, Environment and Social report. It covers four key areas - sustainable development, safety and health, environment and social. The report is audited by csr network Ltd, an independent specialist in the field of corporate social reporting. Figure 37.4 shows environmental data about various businesses that make up the Balfour Beatty group, such as Heery.

(a) Explain how the data shown in Figure 37.4 might be used by Balfour Beatty.
(b) Why is it important that Balfour Beatty's social report is audited?

**Figure 37.4** *Balfour Beatty environmental data*

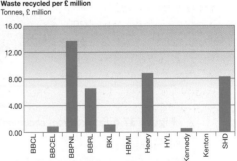

Source: adapted from Balfour Beatty, *Safety, Environment and Social Report*, 2002.

**Question 3**

## key terms

**Accounts** – financial statements that provide information about a firm's financial circumstances.
**Accounting** – the process of recording, classifying, and summarising business transactions with the aim of providing useful financial information for a range of users.
**Auditing** – an accounting procedure which checks thoroughly the authenticity of a company's accounts.
**Bookkeepers** – people involved in the recording and classifying of business transactions.
**Financial accounting** – the preparation of company accounts from business records.
**Management accounting** – the preparation of financial statements, reports and data for use by managers.
**Social auditing** – collecting information and reporting back on the impact of the business on society and the environment.

# Case study Scottish & Newcastle

Scottish & Newcastle is a major international brewing group. Some of its famous brands include Fosters, John Smith's, Kronenbourg, Youngers Tartan and Newcastle Brown Ale. It operates breweries in at least fourteen different countries in Europe and Asia and exports to more than sixty countries worldwide.

**Figure 37.5** *Turnover, operating profit, profit before tax and dividend per share*

**Turnover**
£m

| | |
|---|---|
| 2002 | 4,199.2 |
| **2003** | **4,985.6** |

**Operating profit**
£m

| | |
|---|---|
| 2002 | 538.9 |
| **2003** | **657.9** |

**Profit before tax**
£m

| | |
|---|---|
| 2002 | 442.3 |
| **2003** | **507.3** |

**Dividend per share**
£m

| | |
|---|---|
| 2002 | 29.29 |
| **2003** | **30.18** |

**Figure 37.6** *Extracts from chairman's statement*

**Performance**

"Our businesses continued to focus on developing strong market positions and S&N's key brands continued to gain value and share across their markets.

Group turnover increased by 18.7% to £4,985.6m and operating profit rose to £657.9m including the first time contributions from Hartwall, BBH and Mythos Breweries. Operating profit also benefitted from a reduction in royalty payments to Danone following the acquisition of Danone's remaining interests in Brasseries Kronenbourg and Alken Maes, but has been impacted by incremental costs in the UK supply chain.

Our Managed Retail business continued to outperform its competitors in like for like sales, cost efficiency and return on investment with operating profits up 6.5% in a very competitive market.

Your directors are pleased to recommend a final dividend of 20.0p, an increase of 3.0%."

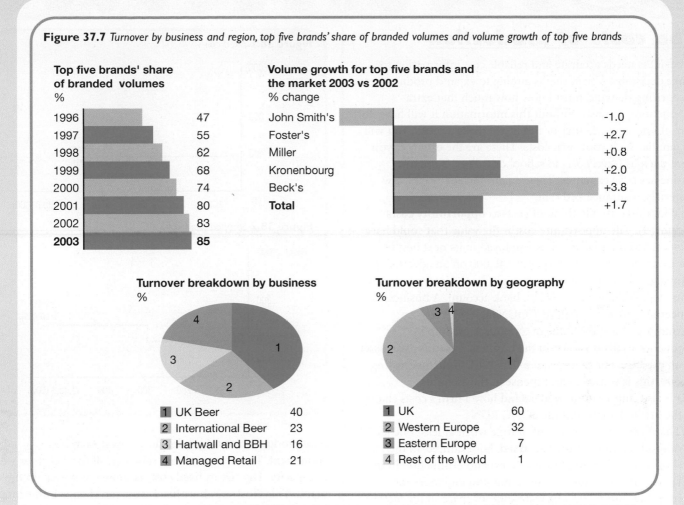

**Figure 37.7** *Turnover by business and region, top five brands' share of branded volumes and volume growth of top five brands*

Top five brands' share of branded volumes %

| Year | | Value |
|---|---|---|
| 1996 | | 47 |
| 1997 | | 55 |
| 1998 | | 62 |
| 1999 | | 68 |
| 2000 | | 74 |
| 2001 | | 80 |
| 2002 | | 83 |
| **2003** | | **85** |

Volume growth for top five brands and the market 2003 vs 2002 % change

| Brand | | Value |
|---|---|---|
| John Smith's | | -1.0 |
| Foster's | | +2.7 |
| Miller | | +0.8 |
| Kronenbourg | | +2.0 |
| Beck's | | +3.8 |
| **Total** | | +1.7 |

Turnover breakdown by business %

| | Segment | Value |
|---|---|---|
| 1 | UK Beer | 40 |
| 2 | International Beer | 23 |
| 3 | Hartwall and BBH | 16 |
| 4 | Managed Retail | 21 |

Turnover breakdown by geography %

| | Segment | Value |
|---|---|---|
| 1 | UK | 60 |
| 2 | Western Europe | 32 |
| 3 | Eastern Europe | 7 |
| 4 | Rest of the World | 1 |

**Figure 37.8** *Extract from Corporate Social Responsibility Report*

Being a good neighbour

We are very aware of our responsibilities to the communities in which we operate, especially in countries whose cultures and infrastructures are very different to our own.

The CSR report contains several examples of work we have undertaken within the supply chain in order to influence the social and environmental performance of our suppliers, to share our knowledge and to support the development of their businesses.

We also undertake many activities to support our local communities. These range from funding the building of a new fire station in Portugal to a mentoring scheme for small businesses in Belgium.

Source: adapted from Scottish & Newcastle, *Annual Report and Accounts, 2003.*

(a) (i) **Identify four users that might be particularly interested in the financial information in Figure 37.5. (4 marks)**

(ii) **Explain what their interest might be. (8 marks)**

(b) **Describe the function of the chairman's statement in Figure 37.6. (6 marks)**

(c) **Analyse the reasons why competitors might be interested in the information in Figure 37.7. (10 marks)**

(d) **On the basis of the evidence provided, discuss which stakeholders are the most influential in the business. (12 marks)**

## The costs of production

A business needs accurate and reliable cost information to make decisions. A firm that is aiming to expand production to meet rising demand must know how much that extra production will cost. Without this information it will have no way of knowing whether or not it will make a profit. You will be familiar with your own costs. These are the expenses you have, such as travel costs to school or college. Similarly, businesses have expenses. These might include wages, raw materials, insurance and rent.

Economists usually think of costs as **opportunity costs** (☞ unit 9). The opportunity cost is the value that could have been earned if a resource was employed in its next best use. For example, if a business spends £40,000 on an advertising campaign, the opportunity cost might be the interest earned from depositing the money in a bank account. A business is concerned, however, with ACCOUNTING COSTS. An accounting cost is the value of a resource used up in production. This is shown in the business accounts as an asset or an expense. For example, if a firm buys some fuel costing £5,500, this is shown as an expense in the accounts.

It is also important to understand how a firm's costs change in the SHORT RUN and the LONG RUN.

- The short run is the period of time when at least one factor of production (☞ unit 1) is **fixed**. For example, in the short run, a firm might want to expand production in its factory. It can acquire more labour and buy more raw materials, but it has a fixed amount of space in the factory and a limited number of machines.
- In the long run, all factors can vary. The firm can buy another factory and add to the number of machines. This will increase **capacity** (the maximum amount that can be produced ☞ unit 84) and begin another short run period.

## Fixed costs

Costs which stay the same at all levels of output in the short run are called FIXED COSTS. Examples might be rent, insurance, heating bills, depreciation (☞ unit 49) and business rates, as well as **capital costs** such as factories and machinery. These costs remain the same whether a business produces nothing or is working at full capacity. For example, rent must still be paid even if a factory is shut for a two week holiday period when nothing is produced. It is worth noting that 'fixed' here means costs do not change as a result of a change in **output** in the short run. But they may increase due to, say, inflation. Figure 38.1 shows what happens to fixed costs as a firm increases production. The line on the graph is horizontal which shows that fixed costs are £400,000 no matter how much is produced.

What happens over a longer period? Figure 38.2 illustrates 'stepped' fixed costs. If a firm is at full capacity, but needs to

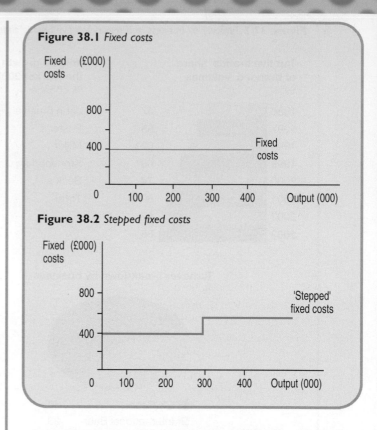

**Figure 38.1** *Fixed costs*

**Figure 38.2** *Stepped fixed costs*

raise production, it might decide to invest in more equipment. The new machines raise overall fixed costs as well as capacity. The rise in fixed costs is shown by a 'step' in the graph. This illustrates how fixed costs can change in the long run.

## Variable and semi variable costs

Costs of production which increase directly as output rises are called VARIABLE COSTS. For example, a baker will require more flour if more loaves are to be produced. Raw materials are just one example of variable costs. Others might include fuel, packaging and wages. If the firm does not produce anything then variable costs will be zero.

Figure 38.3 shows a firm's variable costs. Assume that the firm buying new machinery in Figure 38.1 produces dolls and that variable costs are £2 per doll. If the firm produces 100,000 dolls it will have variable costs of £200,000 (£2 x 100,000). Producing 500,000 dolls it will incur variable costs of £1,000,000 (£2 x 500,000). Joining these points together shows the firm's variable costs at any level of output. As output increases, so do variable costs. Notice that the graph is **linear**. This means that it is a straight line.

Some production costs do not fit neatly into our definitions of fixed and variable costs. This is because they are not entirely fixed or variable costs. Labour is a good example. If a firm employs a member of staff on a permanent basis, no

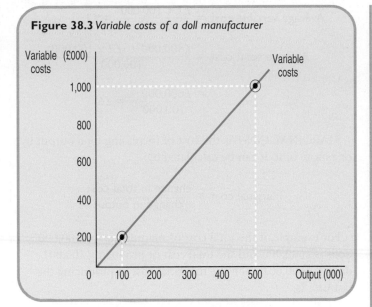

**Figure 38.3** *Variable costs of a doll manufacturer*

matter what level of output, then this is a fixed cost. If this member of staff is asked to work overtime at nights and weekends to cope with extra production levels, then the extra cost is variable. Such labour costs are said to be SEMI-VARIABLE COSTS. Another example could be the cost of telephone charges. This often consists of a fixed or 'standing charge' plus an extra rate which varies according to the number of calls made.

## Total costs

If fixed and variable costs are added together they show the TOTAL COST of a business. The total cost of production is the cost of producing any given level of output. As output increases total costs will rise. This is shown in Figure 38.4, which again shows the production of dolls. We can say:

Total cost (TC) = fixed cost (FC) + variable cost (VC)

The business has fixed costs of £400,000 and variable costs of £2 per doll. When output is 0 total costs are £400,000. When output has risen to 300,000 dolls, total costs are £1,000,000, made up of fixed costs of £400,000 and variable costs of £600,000 (£2 x 300,000). This information is summarised in Table 38.1. Figure 38.4 shows the way that total costs increase as output increases. Notice that as output increases fixed costs become a smaller proportion of total costs.

**Table 38.1** *Summary of cost information for the doll manufacturer*

| | | | £000 |
|---|---|---|---|
| Output (units) | Fixed cost | Variable cost | Total cost |
| 0 | 400 | 0 | 400 |
| 300 | 400 | 600 | 1,000 |

Jimmy Draper has run his own building firm for 25 years in Worcester. When he first set up he concentrated on repair and maintenance work and employed just one other person. However, he became more ambitious and eventually took on extensions and loft conversions. Seven years ago he built his first complete house. He made a handsome profit on the construction and also benefited from rapidly rising house prices. He now employs 12 staff and keeps 15 sub-contractors busy.

(a) Look at the photograph. State two examples of
(ii) fixed costs and (ii) variable costs.
(b) Jimmy owns a builder's yard and office on a local industrial estate. What semi-variable costs might be incurred in the office? Explain your answer.

**Question 1**

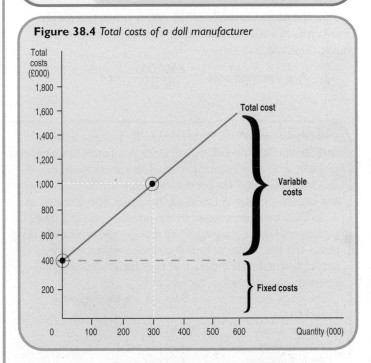

**Figure 38.4** *Total costs of a doll manufacturer*

## Direct and indirect costs

Costs can also be divided into direct and indirect costs. DIRECT COSTS are costs which can be identified with a particular product or process. Examples of direct costs are raw materials, packaging, and direct labour. INDIRECT

COSTS or OVERHEADS result from the whole business. It is not possible to associate these costs directly with particular products or processes. Examples are rent, insurance, the salaries of office staff and audit fees. Indirect costs are usually fixed costs and direct costs variable costs, although in theory both direct and indirect costs can be fixed or variable.

## Average and marginal costs

The AVERAGE COST is the cost per unit of production, also known as the UNIT COST. To calculate average cost the total cost of production should be divided by the number of units produced.

$$\text{Average cost} = \frac{\text{Total cost}}{\text{output}} \text{ or } \frac{\text{Fixed cost} + \text{variable cost}}{\text{output}}$$

It is also possible to calculate **average fixed costs**:

$$\text{Average fixed cost} = \frac{\text{Total fixed cost}}{\text{output}}$$

and **average variable costs**:

$$\text{Average variable cost} = \frac{\text{Total variable cost}}{\text{output}}$$

Take the earlier example of the doll manufacturer with fixed costs of £400,000 and variable costs of £2 per unit. If output was 100,000 units:

$$\text{Average fixed cost} = \frac{£400,000}{100,000} = £4$$

$$\text{Average variable cost} = \frac{£2 \times 100,000}{100,000} = £2$$

$$\text{Average total cost} = \frac{£400,000 + (£2 \times 100,000)}{100,000}$$

$$= \frac{£600,000}{100,000} = £6$$

MARGINAL COST is the cost of increasing total output by one more unit. It can be calculated by:

$$\text{Marginal cost} = \frac{\text{change in total cost}}{\text{change in output}}$$

For example, if the total cost of manufacturing 100,000 dolls is £600,000 and the total cost of producing 100,001 dolls is £600,002, then the marginal cost of producing the last unit is:

$$\text{Marginal cost} = \frac{£600,002 - £600,000}{100,001 - 100,000} = \frac{£2}{1} = £2$$

The relationship between average and marginal cost and their uses for the businesses are discussed in unit 52.

## The problems of classifying costs

There is a number of possible ways in which costs can be classified.

- By type. This involves analysing business costs and deciding whether they are **direct or indirect**.
- By behaviour. Economists favour this method. They classify costs according to the effect that a change in the level of output has on a particular cost. **Fixed, variable,**

---

Stella Parker and Fiona Dobson recently set up a business partnership. They rented a small kiosk in a Luton shopping mall to make and sell mini-pizzas to shoppers, shop workers and nearby office staff. They got the idea from similar kiosks they had seen on holiday in Lloret de Mar, Spain. They decided to make their own pizza bases on the premises and use fresh ingredients for the toppings. They thought the aroma of baking pizzas and the display of freshly chopped vegetables would attract customers. The oven that they leased allowed mini-pizzas to be produced in batches of 10.

The costs incurred by the business are shown below.

**Fixed costs**

| | |
|---|---|
| Rent for kiosk | £140 per week |
| Lease on oven | £50 per week |
| Other fixed costs | £10 per week |

**Variable costs**

| | |
|---|---|
| Bases | £5.50 per batch |
| Toppings | £3.50 per batch |
| Other variable costs | £1.00 per batch |

**Table 38.2** *Cost schedule for Stella's and Fiona's mini-pizza business*

| Batches | 0 | 10 | 20 | 30 | 40 | 50 | 60 | 70 | 80 | 90 | 100 |
|---|---|---|---|---|---|---|---|---|---|---|---|
| Total fixed costs | 200 | 200 | 200 | 200 | 200 | 200 | 200 | 200 | 200 | 200 | 200 |
| Bases | 0 | 55 | | | | | | | | | |
| Toppings | 0 | 35 | | | | | | | | | |
| Other variable costs | 0 | 10 | | | | | | | | | |
| Total variable costs | | | | | | | | | | | |
| Total costs | | | | | | | | | | | |

(a) Complete Table 38.2 and plot the graphs for fixed costs, variable costs and total costs (use a range of output from 0 to 100 batches).

(b) Show the effect on your graph of an increase in fixed costs to £300.

(c) Explain why the oven lease and pizza toppings are both examples of direct costs.

**Question 2**

**semi-variable, average and marginal costs** all fall into this category.

- By function. It is possible to classify costs according to the business function they are associated with. For example, costs could be listed as **production, selling, administrative or personnel**.
- By nature of resource. This involves classifying costs according to the resources which were acquired by a business, for example, **materials, labour or expenses**.
- By **product, job, customer or contract** A multi-product manufacturer, such as Heinz for example, might classify costs according to the product line (beans, soups, puddings) they are associated with. Solicitors might classify costs by identifying them with particular clients.

The classification of costs is not always straightforward. In some cases the same business cost can be classified in several ways. For example, the earnings of a full time administrative assistant may be classified as a fixed cost, if they do not vary with output, and an indirect cost, if they are not associated with a particular product. The costs of a worker earning piece rates might be a direct cost if they can be associated with a particular product and a variable cost if they rise as the output of the worker increases.

Another problem relating to costs concerns the allocation of indirect costs. When calculating the cost of producing particular products it is necessary to allocate indirect costs to each of the different products a business manufactures. In practice this may be difficult. The methods of allocation are discussed in unit 52.

The way in which costs are classified will depend on the purposes for which the classification is being undertaken and the views of the management team.

## Long run costs

Most of the costs discussed so far in this unit have been short run costs, ie the time period where at least one factor of production is fixed. In the long run, all factors of production are likely to be variable.

## Total revenue

The amount of money which a firm receives from selling its product can be referred to as TOTAL REVENUE. Total revenue is calculated by multiplying the number of units sold by the price of each unit:

Total revenue = quantity sold x price

For example, if the doll producer mentioned earlier sells 300,000 dolls at a price of £5 each:

Total revenue = 300,000 x £5 = £1,500,000

Figure 38.5 shows what happens to total revenue as output rises. Notice that the graph is **linear**.

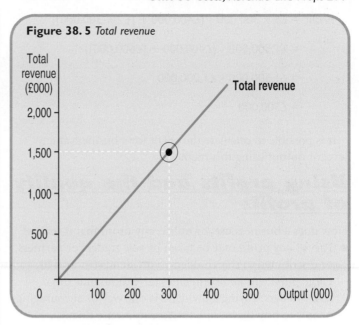

**Figure 38.5** *Total revenue*

## Profit and loss

One of the main reasons why firms calculate their costs and revenue is to enable them to work out their **profit** or **loss**. Profit is the difference between revenue and costs.

Profit = total revenue - total costs

For example, if the doll manufacturer in the earlier example produces and sells 300,000 dolls, they sell for £5, fixed costs are £400,000 and variable costs are £2 per unit, then:

Thompson & Son makes standard golf trolleys which it sells to pro-shops at golf clubs. The trolleys are hired out by the pro-shops to players. Last year Thompson & Son made and sold 5,000 trolleys. Figure 38.6 shows the costs and profit made by the business last year.

(a) What was the value of total revenue for Thompson & Son last year ? Explain your answer.
(b) Calculate (i) the price charged for the trolleys and (ii) the average cost per trolley.

**Figure 38.6** *The uses of total revenue of Thompson & Son*

**Question 3**

Profit = £5 × 300,000 - (£400,000 + [£2 × 300,000])

= £1,500,000 - (£400,000 + [£600,000])

= £1,500,000 - £1,000,000

= £500,000

It is possible to calculate the profit for a business at any level of output using this method.

# Using profits and the quality of profits

How does a business use, or utilise, any profit that it makes?

● Part of any profit may be taken by sole traders or partners, or distributed to shareholders as dividends (☞ unit 6). Large public limited companies have thousands of shareholders. Paying a dividend is one way of encouraging people to buy shares so businesses can raise finance.

● The remaining, undistributed, profit is retained within the business. Retained profit can then be used for investment and future growth. For example, a business might invest in new machinery or produce innovative new products. It is unlikely that all profit will be invested. So some will be retained in case of emergencies or to safeguard the business in future if trading conditions get worse.

On the other hand, losses will result in the reduction of any retained profit for previous years. It is also likely that a business making losses would not pay a dividend.

The **quality** of the profit made by a business is sometimes said to be important. It may be possible for a business to make a short term profit by raising its price or cutting its costs. Or a business can sell machinery to raise revenue. These one-off activities may increase revenue or reduce costs. However, higher prices might reduce sales. Selling machinery might reduce output. So profit might not recur. It is argued, therefore, that profits that are earned earned year after year are likely to be of higher quality for a business then one-off profits.

Knowledge...Knowledge...Knowled

1. What is the difference between opportunity costs and accounting costs?
2. How do you account for a 'stepped' fixed cost function?
3. Why are some costs said to be semi-variable?
4. What happens to variable costs as a proportion of total costs when output rises?
5. Explain the difference between direct and indirect costs.
6. How is:
   (a) average fixed cost;
   (b) average variable cost;
   calculated?
7. How is total revenue calculated?
8. What information is required to calculate a firm's profit?
9. What problems might there be when clarifying costs?

# key terms

**Accounting cost** - the value of an economic resource used up in production.

**Average cost or unit cost** - the cost of producing one unit, calculated by dividing the total cost by output.

**Direct cost** - a cost which can be clearly identified with a particular unit of output.

**Fixed cost** - a cost which does not change as a result of a change in output in the short run.

**Indirect cost or overhead** - a cost which cannot be identified with a particular unit of output. It is incurred by the whole organisation or department.

**Long run** - the time period where all factors of production are variable.

**Marginal cost** - the cost of increasing output by one more unit.

**Semi-variable cost** - a cost which consists of both fixed and variable elements.

**Short run** - the time period where at least one factor of production is fixed.

**Total cost** - the entire cost of producing a given level of output.

**Total revenue** - the amount of money the business receives from selling output.

**Variable cost** - a cost which rises as output rises.

# Case study Customer Services Training (CST)

Handa Bakila left her job as head of customer services for an international airline to set up Customer Services Training. She is based in Dorchester and provides specialised training courses for staff in the retail sector. Her courses usually last for one day and tend to focus on dealing with face-to-face customer complaints. However, Handa is flexible and happy to tailor the subject of courses to the needs of clients. In 2002 she charged £600 for a day's course which she set up in a local hotel near to the client's premises. She takes a maximum of 40 trainees and includes refreshments and lunch time meals in the price.

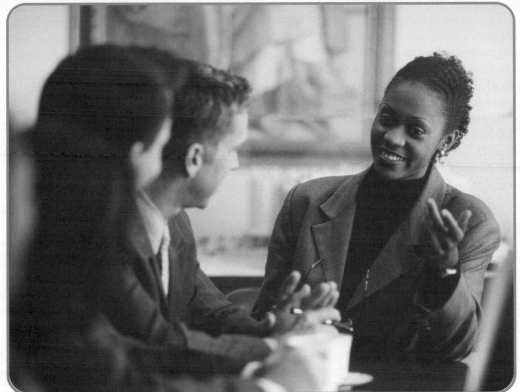

In 2002 CST put on 200 courses and made a reasonable profit. However, Handa felt that her effort was worth a greater financial reward. In 2003 she decided to advertise her services more aggressively in London. Handa would be able to charge more and the amount of time spent travelling would be reduced. She spent £3,000 on a special promotion and decided to raise the price of the training courses from £600 per day to £800 per day. Handa felt that this was justified because of the higher variable costs associated with arranging courses in London. In 2003 the number of courses arranged by CST fell to 150.

(a) **Using examples from the case explain the difference between fixed and variable costs. (8 marks)**

(b) **In 2002, what was the marginal cost of the 200th course? Explain your answer. (4 marks)**

(c) **Calculate the profit made by CST in (i) 2002 and (ii) 2003. (14 marks)**

(d) **To what extent did Handa's decision to raise price from £600 to £800 achieve her objective? (14 marks)**

Table 38.3 *Financial information for CST 2002 and 2003*

|  | 2002 | 2003 |
|---|---|---|
| Car lease per annum | 5,000 | 5,000 |
| Insurance per annum | 1,000 | 1,200 |
| Other fixed costs per annum | 2,000 | 2,800 |
| Special promotion | 0 | 3,000 |
|  |  |  |
| Room hire fees per course | 150 | 200 |
| Refreshment costs per course | 150 | 180 |
| Training materials per course | 50 | 50 |
| Other variable costs per course | 50 | 70 |
|  |  |  |
| Price per course | 600 | 800 |

(Units: £)

## Collecting cost data

A business incurs costs at all stages of production. It will have to pay for resources bought from outside the business, such as raw materials or components. It will have labour, electricity and other costs involved in producing products from these materials. Cost data can be used in a variety of ways. For example, a builder might gather cost data to determine how much it has cost to build an extension for a customer. Unless the builder knows exactly how much the extension has cost to build, it will be very difficult to set a price that will make enough profit. Cost data might also be used to evaluate the performance of different departments in the business. Departments that keep costs low are likely to have performed well.

## Cost centres

One way of collecting and using cost data effectively is to divide the business into COST CENTRES. A cost centre is an individual part of the business where costs are incurred and can be recorded easily. For example, Canning Insurance has four types of insurance which it offers customers - Car Insurance, House Insurance, Holiday Insurance and Life Assurance. Each of these operates as a cost centre. The total costs incurred by the business during 2003 was £5.6 million. The costs incurred by each cost centre were:

- Car Insurance £1.2 million;
- House Insurance £2.0 million;
- Holiday Insurance £0.9 million;
- Life Assurance £1.5 million.

Canning Insurance might conclude from this information that the Holiday Insurance has the best control over its costs. However, other factors will have to be taken into account, such as the size of each department.

How can a business be divided into cost centres? There is a number of ways and the method chosen by a business will depend on its circumstances.

- **By product.** Canning Insurance, in the example above, uses this method. It means that costs are measured for each of the products of a business. So each product is a cost centre.
- **By department.** Many businesses are divided into departments such as marketing, production, accounts and human resources. Each department can be treated as a cost centre.
- **By geographical location.** A business which has operations all over the country or world might use this method. For example, a supermarket chain with stores all over the UK may treat each one as a cost centre.
- **By employee.** In some businesses it is appropriate to measure the costs incurred by individual members of staff. For example, a salesperson could be treated as a cost centre and examples of costs might be wages, National Insurance

contributions, motor expenses, overnight accommodation expenses and entertaining expenses.
- **By machine.** It is possible to use a machine, such as a vehicle, as a cost centre by recording all its costs. These might be leasing charges and payments for fuel, motor tax, insurance and maintenance.

## Profit centres

A PROFIT CENTRE is very similar to a cost centre. The difference is that in addition to recording costs at each centre, revenues are also recorded. This allows a business to calculate how much profit each centre makes. The use of profit centres makes it much easier to compare the performance of each different part of the business. For example, a supermarket chain can identify the most profitable stores in the country by comparing the profit each centre makes. Profit centres can only be used effectively if an activity generates revenue. For example, since a research and development department does not generate any revenue directly, it is unlikely to be used as a profit centre. A business can be divided into profit centres in the same way as it would be into cost centres, provided the centre generates revenue.

## Advantages of using cost and profit centres

There are certain advantages to a business of using cost and profit centres.

**Improving accountability** Although it is important to measure the performance of the whole business, it is also helpful to monitor the progress of different products, regions or departments, for example. Cost and profit centres can be used to hold individual parts of the business accountable. Without cost and profit centres an inefficient department might not be identified and held accountable for its poor performance.

**Helping decision making** To make decisions about different parts of the business managers need financial information about those different parts. Cost and profit centres help provide this information. For example, if managers are trying to decide which product to discontinue, to make way for a new product, it can use information gathered from profit centres. Managers are likely to stop supplying the least profitable product.

**Improving motivation** The performance of cost and profit centres is likely to depend on the quality of work done by the people employed in them. It is possible to motivate staff in centres by offering them incentives to achieve goals or targets. For example, a clothes chain might give bonus payments to staff working in stores if they achieve monthly profit targets. This should help to motivate them to produce their best work. It is also common to delegate control of cost and profit centres to middle managers. Managers may be better motivated if they are offered promotion, for example, when targets are met.

**Tracing problems** If part of the business is suffering it may be possible to trace a specific problem if cost or profit centres are used. For example, if one of the stores in a supermarket chain is suffering from a high labour turnover, its recruitment and training costs will be high. Labour productivity may also be lower. This will restrict the performance of the store and will show up as higher costs if it were operating as a cost centre. This may not come to light so easily if the costs of the entire business were recorded together.

# Problems of cost and profit centres

Dividing a business into cost and profit centres might also lead to problems.

**Conflict** If a business is divided into individual parts, conflict between those parts may arise. Staff are likely to be more interested in the performance of their own centre than the performance of the whole business. This might lead to competition for resources and a reluctance to share valuable information. The performance of the whole business might suffer as a result.

**Cost allocation** Not all costs are incurred directly by a particular cost centre. Some costs are incurred by the business as a whole. For example, a chain store might spend £2 million on a national advertising campaign. How should this cost be allocated between cost or profit centres? One way might be to divide the cost equally between all the stores. But this might not be fair because a very large store may get more benefit from the campaign than a smaller store. This suggests that the larger store should bear more of the campaign's cost. In practice, the allocation of such costs between centres is difficult. When costs are not allocated fairly the performance of a particular centre can be distorted.

**Factors outside the business** It is common for the performance of a business to be affected by external factors such as the state of the economy, competition, the weather or pressure groups. However, it is possible that the performance of each individual cost or profit centre is not affected to the same extent. For example, a UK fast food chain might

experience intense competition in the south west, therefore the performance of centres operating in that region will be hit. This might have a demotivating effect on staff in those centres.

**Wasting resources** Operating cost or profit centres may result in the business as a whole wasting money. If all centres are responsible for performing the same tasks there may be some duplication of resources. For example, it may be more cost effective if the purchasing of resources for each department in a business is done centrally. Resources may also be wasted gathering financial information from each centre. It is possible that the costs of operating cost or profit centres may not be outweighed by the benefits.

**Staff pressure** Some of the staff given the responsibility of running a cost or profit centre may not have the skills to do so. This might create pressure and demotivate staff. This is more likely to happen if responsibility is delegated too far down the hierarchical structure.

## Knowledge...Knowledge...Knowledge

1. State 2 reasons why it might be important to gather cost information.
2. Explain how it is possible to use a product as a cost centre.
3. State 3 other ways of choosing a cost centre.
4. Explain the difference between a cost centre and a profit centre.
5. Explain why it might not be possible to operate a maintenance department in a business as a profit centre.
6. Explain 4 advantages of using cost and profit centres.
7. What problems might be encountered when using cost and profit centres?

## key terms

**Cost centre** - an individual part of a business where costs can be identified and recorded easily.
**Profit centre** - an individual part of the business where costs and revenue can be identified and recorded easily.

# Case study MacSports

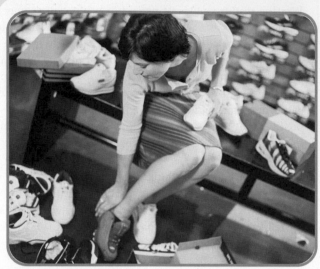

Irene MacDonald owns MacSports, a small chain of sports shops in Scotland. The business consists of six stores located around some of the larger Scottish towns and cities. They sell sports equipment, sportswear and an increasing amount of sports energy products.

Irene divided the business into profit centres when she opened the third shop. She wanted to know exactly how each shop performed so that she could monitor the performance of the individual parts of the business and reward the staff in the best performing shops. Each shop had a manager and was paid a bonus of 5 per cent of profit each year. Also, staff in the best performing shop each year were given a free weekend holiday in New York or Paris. In 2003 the best performing shop was Glasgow East. This is shown in Table 39.1, which includes Irene's directors salary.

After analysing the data, Irene was concerned about the performance of the Inverness shop, managed by Andy. Shortly after the publication of the data she made a special visit to the store. She made a few brief notes which are shown in the memo below.

(a) Using examples from the case explain the term profit centre. (6 marks)
(b) Describe the allocation of the director's salary between profit centres. (6 marks)
(c) Explain how MacSports uses profit centres to motivate its staff. (8 marks)
(d) Examine the reasons why conflict might arise between MacSports' profit centres. (10 marks)
(e) To what extent can Andy be blamed for the poor performance of the Inverness shop? (10 marks)

- Too much sports equipment, not enough sportswear
- Scruffy part-time staff
- Poorly displayed stock — especially in the window

But Andy, the manager, says:
- Road works in the high street have disrupted pedestrian traffic for 7 months
- Part-time staff have been very unreliable

**Table 39.1** *MacSports, revenues, costs and profit 2003*

|  | Glasgow East | Glasgow West | Aberdeen | Edinburgh | Inverness | Dundee |
|---|---|---|---|---|---|---|
| **Revenue** | 165,001 | 128,990 | 99,210 | 111,999 | 54,008 | 83,000 |
| **Costs** |  |  |  |  |  |  |
| Wages | 46,000 | 36,000 | 30,000 | 32,000 | 27,000 | 28,000 |
| Stock | 61,009 | 49,330 | 37,009 | 54,000 | 26,000 | 21,000 |
| Heat & light | 3,000 | 3,540 | 2,100 | 2,900 | 1,990 | 2,001 |
| Director's salary | 10,000 | 10,000 | 10,000 | 10,000 | 10,000 | 10,000 |
| Other costs | 8,600 | 6,003 | 5,400 | 6,500 | 4,500 | 3,000 |
| Total costs | 128,609 | 104,873 | 84,509 | 105,400 | 69,490 | 64,001 |
| **Profit/loss** | **36,392** | **24,117** | **14,701** | **6,599** | **-15,482** | **18,999** |

## What is contribution?

Craig Eckert sells second hand cars. His last sale was £400 for a Golf GTI. He bought the Golf at a car auction for £220. The difference between what he paid for the car and the price he sold it for is £180 (£400 - £220). This difference is called the CONTRIBUTION. It is not profit because Craig has fixed costs to pay such as rent, insurance and administration expenses.

Contribution is the difference between selling price and variable costs. In this case the selling price was £400 and the variable cost was £220. The £180 will contribute to the **total fixed costs** of the business and the **profit**.

## Contribution per unit and total contribution

A business might calculate the contribution on the sale of a single unit, or the sale of a larger quantity, such as a whole year's output.

Unit contribution In the above example the unit contribution was calculated. It was the contribution on the sale of one unit, a single car. The formula for calculating the unit contribution is:

Contribution per unit = selling price - variable cost

Total contribution When more than one unit is sold the total contribution can be calculated. For example, a textile company receives an order for 1,000 pairs of trousers. The variable costs are £7.50 a pair and they will be sold for £9.00 a pair. The total contribution made by the order is:

Total contribution = total revenue - total variable cost
= (£9.00 × 1,000) - (£7.50 × 1,000)
= £9,000 - £7,500
= £1,500

The £1,500 in this example will contribute to the textile company's fixed costs and profit. The total contribution can also be calculated by multiplying the unit contribution by the number of units sold.

Total contribution = unit contribution × number of units sold
= (£9.00 - £7.50) × 1,000
= £1.50 × 1,000
= £1,500

## Contribution and profit

Contribution can be used to calculate profit. Take the example again of Craig Eckert the car salesperson. He wants to

calculate the profit his business makes in January. Table 40.1 shows the variable cost and selling price of cars in January 2004. The fixed costs of the business in the same month are also shown in Table 40.2

**Table 40.1** *Variable costs and price of cars sold by Craig Eckert - January 2004*

(£)

| Description | Variable cost | Selling price | Contribution |
|---|---|---|---|
| Nissan Micra | 410 | 490 | 80 |
| VW Polo | 900 | 1,200 | 300 |
| Fiat Tipo | 560 | 620 | 60 |
| Volvo 740 SE | 460 | 580 | 120 |
| Seat Ibiza | 320 | 370 | 50 |
| Astra Auto | 1,100 | 1,350 | 250 |
| Nissan Primera | 1,250 | 1,520 | 270 |
| BMW 318i | 1,900 | 2,500 | 600 |
| Escort Estate | 200 | 250 | 50 |
| Golf GTI | 220 | 400 | 180 |
| **Total** | **7,320** | **9,280** | **1,960** |

**Table 40.2** *Monthly fixed costs of the business*

| Description | £ |
|---|---|
| Office rent | 300 |
| Insurance | 20 |
| Telephone | 50 |
| Administration expenses | 50 |
| **Total** | **420** |

The total contribution from car sales in January was £1,960. This is calculated by subtracting the total variable costs, ie the cost of purchasing the cars, from the total revenue (£9,280 -

£7,320). Total revenue is the amount of money received from the sale of the 10 cars during January. The profit for January 2004 is:

> Profit = total contribution - fixed costs
>     = £1,960 - £420
>     = £1,540

So the business made £1,540 profit in January 2004.

In unit 38 profit was calculated by subtracting total costs from total revenue. If this method is used here, the profit made by Craig Eckert's business in January is:

> Profit = total revenue - total cost
>     = total revenue - (fixed cost + variable cost)
>     = £9,280 - (£420 + £7,320)
>     = £9,280 - £7,740
>     = £1,540

The answer is the same as before, £1,540. However, the contribution method can often be quicker than the method explained in unit 38 because there is slightly less calculation.

## Fixed costs, variable costs, contribution and profit

The relationship between fixed costs, variable costs, profit and contribution is shown in Figure 40.1. The pie charts show information from Craig Eckert's business in January 2004. Figure 40.1 shows how the total revenue of £9,280 is divided between the variable cost (£7,320) and contribution (£1,960). The second chart shows how total revenue is divided between variable cost (£7,320), fixed costs (£420) and profit (£1,540). Note that the value of contribution (£1,960) is equal to the value of fixed cost (£420) and profit (£1,540) added together.

## Contribution costing

How can a business make use of contribution calculations? Calculating the contribution to fixed costs and profit that a product makes might help a business in decision making. This is known as contribution costing (☞ unit 52). For example, say that a design business has limited time and resources. It has been approached by two clients who want a new corporate logo and image designing this week. The prices and variable costs and contribution are shown below.

● Design 1 - Price £3,000, variable costs £2,500, contribution per unit £500 (£3,000 - £2,500)
● Design 2 - Price £3,000, variable costs £800, contribution per unit £2,200 (£3,000 - £800)

So the business might choose the second design as it contributes more to fixed costs and profit.

## Other uses of contribution

A business might use contribution in a number of other ways.

● Contribution can be used to calculate the **break-even point**. This is the level of output where total cost and total

Mandy Weston runs an automatic car wash near Junction 1 on the M27 in Hampshire. She charges £4 for each wash. In the last week of February the business washed 480 cars.
   Mandy rents a giant washing machine for £600 per week and pays students a total of £300 per week to help run the business. Other fixed costs, such as insurance and advertising, amount to £100 per week. Variable costs, such as water, detergent and electricity, are £1.50 a wash.

(a) Calculate the total contribution for the last week in February.
(b) Calculate the profit made by Mandy's business in the last week of February using two methods.

**Question 2**

**Figure 40.1** *The relationship between variable costs, contribution, fixed costs and profit for Craig Eckert's business - January 2004*

revenue are exactly the same. This is explained in unit 41.

● Some businesses price their products in relation to the variable costs incurred. This is called **contribution pricing** and is explained in unit 26.

● Sometimes a business has to make a **special order decision**. Contribution is used to help a business decide whether to accept an order from a customer below the normal listed price. This is explained in unit 52.

## key terms

**Contribution** – the amount of money left over after variable costs have been subtracted from revenue. The money contributes towards fixed costs and profit.

## Knowledge ...Knowledge...Knowledge...Knowledge...Knowledge...Know

1. A product sells for £10 and the variable costs are £8.50. What is the contribution per unit?

2. A clothes retailer buys 240 jumpers for £27. The jumpers are sold for £39 each. What is the total contribution made by the jumpers?

3. What is the formula for calculating profit using contribution?

4. If total contribution is £120,000 and fixed costs are £96,000, what is profit?

5. If total variable costs are £450,000 and contribution is £225,000, what is total revenue?

6. State 3 ways in which contribution can be used by a business to help make decisions.

## Case study Kumas Kitchens

Stanley and Nita Kumas run a food business in Oxford. They rent a mobile kitchen unit for £300 a month and sell kebabs to late night revellers in Oxford City centre. They sell four different kebab products and a selection of fizzy drinks. Details of costs, prices and sales for June 2004 are shown in Tables 40.3 and 40.4.

In July 2004 Nita suggested that they try to sell oven ready fries. The mobile kitchen unit had an oven which was rarely used and it wouldn't be too much trouble to sell another product. They both agreed and fries were introduced in August. They sold for £1.00 per portion and the variable costs were 60p. In that month 130 portions were sold. Unfortunately the quality of the fries was unstable because the oven could not retain a constant heat. Also people were often kept waiting for

the fries. This resulted in complaints from customers and some suggested that they might take their business away.

**Table 40.4** *Monthly fixed costs (£)*

| | |
|---|---|
| Rental charges | 300 |
| Insurance | 65 |
| Fuel | 30 |
| Charitable donation | 25 |
| Other fixed costs | 20 |

(a) **State three possible examples of variable costs incurred by Stanley and Nita's business. (3 marks)**

(b) **Using the Lamb Kebab as an example, explain the difference between unit contribution and total contribution. (6 marks)**

(c) **Calculate the total contribution made by each of the products sold in June 2004. (10 marks)**

(d) **Calculate the profit made by the business in June 2004. (6 marks)**

(e) **Calculate the total contribution made by the oven ready fries in August and discuss whether Stanley and Nita should continue to sell them. (10 marks)**

**Table 40.3** *Costs, price and sales of products sold by Stanley and Nita's business in June 2004*

(£)

| | Lamb Kebab | Chicken Kebab | Special Kebab | Felafel Kebab | Fizzy Drinks |
|---|---|---|---|---|---|
| Price | 2.20 | 2.00 | 2.50 | 1.70 | 1.00 |
| Variable costs | 1.20 | 0.90 | 1.30 | 0.40 | 0.30 |
| June sales | 550 | 620 | 290 | 160 | 280 |

## Breaking even

Businesses often like to know how much they need to produce or sell to BREAK-EVEN. If a business has information about fixed costs and variable costs and knows what price it is going to charge, it can calculate how many units it needs to sell to cover all of its costs. The level of sales or output where **total costs** are exactly the same as **total revenue** is called the BREAK-EVEN POINT. For example, if a business produces 100 units at a total cost of £5,000, and sells them for £50 each, total revenue will also be £5,000 (£50 x 100). The business will break-even at this level of output. It makes neither a profit nor a loss. Firms may use break-even analysis to:

- calculate in advance the level of sales needed to break-even;
- see how changes in output affect profit;
- see how changes in price affect the break-even point and profit;
- see how changes in costs affect the break-even point and profit.

Other applications of break-even analysis are discussed in unit 53.

## Calculating the break-even point using contribution

It is possible to calculate the break-even point if a firm knows the value of its fixed costs, variable costs and the price it will charge. Take an example of a small producer, Joseph Cadwallader, who makes wrought iron park benches in his foundry. His fixed costs (FC) are £60,000 and variable costs (VC) £40 per bench. He sells the benches to local authorities across the country for £100 each.

The simplest way to calculate the break-even point is to use **contribution** (☞ unit 40). Contribution is the amount of money left over after the variable cost per unit is taken away from the selling price. For Joseph's park benches, the contribution is:

$$\text{Contribution} = \text{selling price} - \text{variable cost}$$
$$\text{Contribution} = £100 - £40$$
$$\text{Contribution} = £60$$

To calculate the number of benches Joseph needs to sell to break-even, the following formula can be used:

$$\text{Break-even point} = \frac{\text{Fixed costs}}{\text{Contribution}}$$

$$= \frac{£60,000}{£60}$$

$$= 1,000 \text{ benches}$$

Eric Wiggens supplies and fits alarm systems to motor cars. He supplies and fits the alarms for £99. The variable costs of each alarm fitted are the cost of the alarm, £45, plus other variable costs of £14. Annual fixed costs, which include a leasing charge on his van, other motor expenses, insurance and administration costs, are £9,800.

(a) How many alarms must be sold and fitted by Eric to break-even during the year?
(b) Eric has been considering a price reduction to generate more business. If he charges £84, how many alarms must be sold and fitted to break-even?

**Question 1**

Joseph Cadwallader's business will break-even when 1,000 park benches are sold.

## Calculating the break-even point using total revenue and total cost

Another way of calculating the break-even point is to use the total cost and total revenue equations. In the case of Joseph Cadwallader:

$$\text{Total cost} = \text{fixed cost} + \text{variable cost}$$
$$\text{or TC} = £60,000 + £40Q$$
$$\text{and Total revenue} = \text{price} \times \text{quantity sold}$$
$$\text{or TR} = £100Q$$

where Q is the quantity produced and sold, ie the number of park benches. A firm will break-even where total cost is equal to total revenue. Therefore we can write:

$$\text{TC} = \text{TR}$$
$$£60,000 + £40Q = £100Q$$

To find Q we can calculate:

$$60,000 = 100Q - 40Q$$
$$60,000 = 60Q$$
$$\frac{60,000}{60} = Q$$
$$1,000 = Q$$

It is possible to check whether this answer is correct by calculating total cost and total revenue when 1,000 benches are produced. If the answers are the same, the break-even quantity is correct.

TC = £60,000 + (£40 x 1,000) = £60,000 + £40,000 = £100,000

TR = £100 x 1,000 = £100,000

Both TC and TR are equal to £100,000, so the break-even quantity is 1,000 benches. This also confirms that the answer using the contribution method was correct.

## Profit and loss

Total cost and total revenue equations can be used to calculate the amount of profit or loss the firm will make at particular levels of output. At any level of output below the break-even point the firm will make a loss. Output produced above the break-even level will make a profit. Thus, if the bench manufacturer were to produce 1,200 benches, profit would be:

$$
\begin{aligned}
\text{Profit} &= \text{TR - TC} \\
&= (£100 \times 1,200) - (£60,000 + [£40 \times 1,200]) \\
&= £120,000 - (£60,000 + £48,000) \\
&= £120,000 - £108,000 \\
\text{Profit} &= £12,000
\end{aligned}
$$

## Break-even charts

The use of graphs is often helpful in break-even analysis. It is possible to identify the break-even point by plotting the total cost and total revenue equations on a graph (☞ unit 38). This graph is called a BREAK-EVEN CHART. Figure 41.1 shows the break-even chart for Joseph Cadwallader's business. Output is measured on the horizontal axis and revenue, costs and profit are measured on the vertical axis. What does the break-even chart show?

- The value of total cost over a range of output. For example, when Joseph produces 1,500 benches total costs are £120,000.

**Figure 41.1** *Break-even chart for Joseph Cadwallader*

---

Graham Jones produces beer trays which he sells to cafés and local authorities. He has recently secured two new contracts and is about to step up production in his small factory. This has increased his fixed costs quite significantly. In order to see the effect the increase in costs would have on the profitability of his business over a range of output he drew up a break-even chart.

**Figure 41.3** *Break-even chart for Graham Jones*

(a) Using the break-even chart shown in Figure 41.3 state:
    (i) the number of beer trays needed to break-even;
    (ii) total revenue and total cost at this level of output;
    (iii) the price charged for the beer trays;
    (iv) the value of fixed cost per month;
    (v) the value of variable cost per tray.
(b) Graham expects to produce and sell 800 beer trays per month. State:
    (i) the amount of profit made at this level of output;
    (ii) total variable cost.

**Question3**

---

AutoCafe Ltd manufactures automatic coffee machines in a small factory based in Swansea. They are sold directly to offices, factories and other employers for £500 each. AutoCafe's annual fixed costs are £250,000. The variable costs incurred when making a single machine are shown in Figure 41.2.

**Figure 41.2** *The variable costs incurred by AutoCafe Ltd when making one coffee machine*

(a) Show the formulae for (i) total cost and (ii) total revenue.
(b) Calculate how many coffee machines AutoCafe Ltd needs to produce in a year to break-even.
(c) Calculate how much profit would be made if AutoCafe Ltd produced 4,000 coffee machines in a year.

**Question2**

- The value of total revenue over a range of output. For example, when Joseph produces 1,500 benches total revenue is £150,000.
- Some break-even charts show the level of fixed costs over a range of output. For example, the fixed costs for Joseph's business are £60,000.
- The level of output needed to break-even. The break-even point is where total costs equal total revenue of £100,000. This is when 1,000 benches are produced.
- At levels of output below the break-even point, losses are made. This is because total costs exceed total revenue.
- At levels of output above the break-even point, a profit is made. This profit gets larger as output rises.
- The relationship between fixed costs and variable costs as output rises. At low levels of output fixed costs represent a large proportion of total costs. As output rises, fixed costs become a smaller proportion of total costs.
- The profit at a particular level of output. If Joseph produces 1,500 benches, profit is shown by the vertical gap between the total cost and total revenue equations. It is £30,000.

# The margin of safety

What if a business is producing a level of output above the break-even point? It might be useful to know by how much sales could fall before a loss is made. This is called the MARGIN OF SAFETY. It refers to the range of output over which a profit can be made. The margin of safety can be identified on the break-even chart by measuring the distance between the break-even level of output and the current (profitable) level output. For example, Figure 41.4 shows the break-even chart for Joseph Cadwallader. If Joseph produces 1,200 benches the margin of safety is 200 benches. This means that output can fall by 200 before a loss is made. If Joseph sells 1,200 benches the chart shows that total revenue is £120,000, total cost is £108,000 and profit is £12,000.

Businesses prefer to operate with a large margin of safety. This means that if sales drop they still might make some profit. With a small margin of safety there is a risk that the business is more likely to make losses if sales fall.

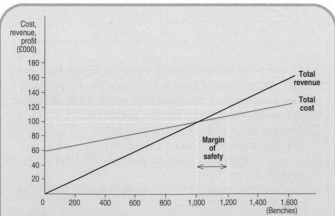

**Figure 41.4** *Break-even chart showing the margin of safety for Joseph Cadwallader's business*

# Advantage of break-even analysis

The break-even chart is an easy visual means of analysing the firm's financial position at different levels of output. Business decision makers can see at a glance the amount of profit or loss that will be made at different levels of production. The chart can also be used to show the effect on the break-even point, the level of profit and the margin of safety of changes in costs or price.

**Changes in price** Figure 41.5 shows the effect of a 10 per cent increase in price for Joseph Cadwallader. This causes the total revenue function to shift from $TR_1$ to $TR_2$ indicating that total sales revenue has increased at all levels of output. The higher price means that the business will break-even at a lower level of output, ie 857 benches. It will also mean higher levels of profit (or lower losses) at every level of output. The margin of safety will also increase assuming an output of 1,200 benches is produced. (This is not shown in Figure 41.5.)

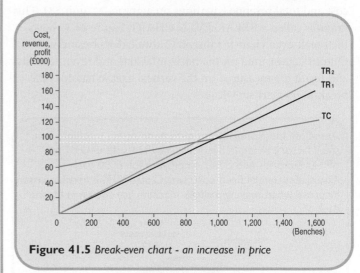

**Figure 41.5** *Break-even chart - an increase in price*

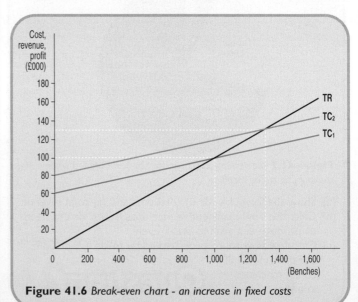

**Figure 41.6** *Break-even chart - an increase in fixed costs*

**Increases in fixed costs** Figure 41.6 shows the effect of an increase in fixed costs of £20,000 for Joseph Cadwallader. The total cost function makes a parallel shift upwards from $TC_1$ to $TC_2$. This occurs because a rise in fixed costs causes total cost to increase by the same amount at every level of output. As a result the break-even level of output rises to 1,333 benches. At all levels of output profit falls (or losses rise). There is no longer a margin of safety if 1,200 benches are produced. Joseph's business will make a loss at this output.

**Increase in variable costs** An increase in variable costs will increase the gradient of the total cost function. This is illustrated in Figure 41.7 by a shift from $TC_1$ to $TC_2$. The break-even level of output for Joseph Cadwallader rises to 1,200 benches when variable costs rise by £10. At an output of 1,200 there is no margin of safety as the firm breaks-even.

# Limitations to break-even analysis

Break-even analysis as an aid to business decision making does have some limitations. It is often regarded as too simplistic, and many of its assumptions are unrealistic.

- It assumes that all output is sold and no stocks are held. Many businesses hold stocks of finished goods to cope with changes in demand. There are also times when firms cannot sell what they produce and choose to stockpile their output to avoid laying off staff.
- The break-even chart is drawn for a given set of conditions. It cannot cope with a sudden increase in wages and prices or changes in technology.
- The effectiveness of break-even analysis depends on the quality and accuracy of the data used to construct cost and revenue functions. If the data is poor and inaccurate, the conclusions drawn on the basis of the data are flawed. For example, if fixed costs are underestimated, the level of

output required to break-even will be higher than suggested by the break-even chart.
- Throughout the analysis it has been assumed that the total cost and total revenue functions are linear. This may not always be the case (☞ unit 53).
- Many businesses produce more than one single product. It is likely that each product will have different variable costs and different prices. The problem is how to allocate the fixed costs of the multi-product business to each individual product. There is a number of ways, but none is perfect. Therefore, if the fixed costs incurred by each product is inaccurate, break-even analysis is less useful.
- Some fixed costs are stepped. For example, a manufacturer, in order to increase output, may need to acquire more capacity. This may result in rent increases and thus fixed costs will rise sharply. Under these circumstances it is difficult to use break-even analysis.

**Figure 41.7** *Break-even chart - an increase in variable costs*

## key terms

**Break-even** - where a business sells just enough to cover its costs.
**Break-even chart** - a graph containing the total cost and total revenue functions, illustrating the break-even point.
**Break-even point** - the level of output where total revenue and total cost are the same.
**Margin of safety** - the range of output between the break-even level and the current level of output, over which a profit is made.

## Knowledge

1. How can break-even analysis be used?
2. How can the contribution be used to calculate the break-even level of output?
3. How can the break-even level of output calculation be checked?
4. State 5 things which a break-even chart can show.
5. What effect will a price increase have on the margin of safety?
6. What effect will a fall in fixed costs have on the margin of safety?
7. What effect will a fall in variable costs have on the break-even level of output?
8. State 3 limitations of break-even analysis.

# Case study Jeffers Garden Designs

During a long hot summer Marion Jeffers noticed that the garden furniture she bought the last year had faded badly. She decided she could do better. So she set up in business making her own furniture designs and selling them to garden centres and retailers in Wiltshire. She drew up a business plan, which included a schedule of her costs and a break-even chart. These are shown in Table 41.1 and Figure 41.8. Marion aimed to break-even in the first year. She knew that covering her fixed and variable costs would be a challenge. However, Marion felt she could charge £200 for a furniture set which included folding wooden chairs, a table and umbrella. She could also avoid renting or buying premises by converting an unused barn on her land into a workshop.

**Table 41.1** *Marion Jeffers' fixed and variable costs*

| Fixed costs | £ |
| --- | --- |
| Machinery | 2,600 |
| Tools & equipment | 2,200 |
| Van | 2,100 |
| Barn conversion costs | 2,300 |
| Other fixed costs | 800 |
| **Total** | **10,000** |

| Variable costs | £ |
| --- | --- |
| Labour | 60 |
| Wood | 20 |
| Canvass | 10 |
| Metal fittings and screws | 5 |
| Other variable costs | 5 |
| **Total** | **100** |

**(a)** Using the example in the case explain what is meant by break-even. **(5 marks)**

**(b)** Marion's business plan also included a table to show how much profit/loss she would make at different levels of output. This is shown in Table 41.2, but it is incomplete. Using the break-even chart in Figure 41.8 complete Table 41.2. **(7 marks)**

**Table 41.2**

| No. of sets | 40 | 80 | 100 | 120 | 160 |
| --- | --- | --- | --- | --- | --- |
| Total revenue | | | | | |
| Total cost | | | | | |
| Profit/loss | | | | | |

**(c) (i)** In the first year of trading Marion produced and sold 140 garden sets. State the margin of safety and explain what it means. **(6 marks)**

   **(ii)** Calculate the profit at this level of output. **(2 marks)**

**(d)** In the second year the fixed costs for the business fell to £6,000.

   **(i)** Calculate how many garden sets the business would need to produce and sell to break-even in the second year of trading (assume that price and variable costs remain the same). **(8 marks)**

   **(ii)** In the second year Marion's business produced and sold 120 garden sets. Calculate the profit made by the business. **(6 marks)**

**(e)** Discuss the problems Marion may have encountered when using break-even analysis. **(8 marks)**

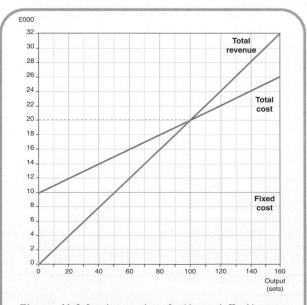

**Figure 41.8** *Break-even chart for Marion Jeffers' business*

## The nature of profit

Profit is the driving force in most businesses. There are few, if any, which attach no importance to making profit, the exceptions perhaps being charities. Even state run industries, whose major objective has been to provide a comprehensive service (☞ unit 7), have pursued profits in recent years.

Profit has a number of functions. The prospect of making profit motivates people to set up in business. Without profit there would be little incentive for individuals to commit their time and personal resources to business activity. Economists often refer to **normal profit**. This is the minimum reward an entrepreneur must receive in order to maintain interest in the business. If the business does not earn this amount of profit the owner will pull out and pursue other opportunities.

Profit also helps resource allocation in market economies (☞ unit 9). Businesses that make profits are able to purchase more raw materials and labour in order to expand production. Investors are attracted to those businesses that are likely to give the greatest financial reward. Economists call this abnormal profit - the amount by which total profit is greater than normal profit.

The amount of profit that a business makes is a measure of how well it is performing. Those firms that supply quality products which are efficiently produced and sold at prices which are attractive to consumers will tend to be more profitable. However, there are other factors which affect the performance of a business, such as the competition a business faces (☞ unit 94). From an accountant's point of view, profit is the amount of money left over in a particular trading period when all business expenses have been met. Profit can then be:

● retained;
● used to pay tax;
● distributed to the owners of the company.

Gabrielle Fisher terminated her contract with a large fabric manufacturer and set off on a tour of Malaysia and the Phillipines. On return, and inspired by her trip to the Far East, Gabrielle set up in business designing fabrics based on Oriental patterns. She had given the venture a great deal of thought. Gabrielle was highly regarded in the industry and could command a £30,000+ salary as a fabric designer. She felt that unless she could clear £25,000 after all business expenses had been met, the venture would not be worth her while.

(a) What is the value of normal profit for Gabrielle?
(b) Why might she accept a lower return than her previous salary?
(c) If Gabrielle cleared £40,000 in her first trading year what would be the value of abnormal profit?

**Question 1**

If expenses exceed sales revenue in a trading period then there will be a loss. It is the accountant's definition of profit which we will be referring to in this unit.

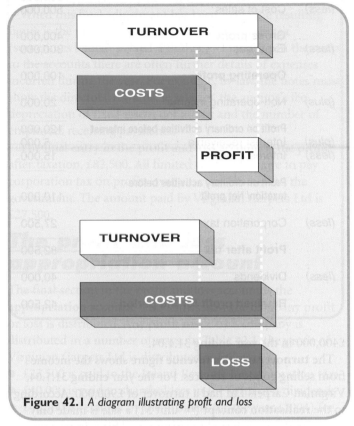

**Figure 42.1** *A diagram illustrating profit and loss*

## Measuring profit

At the end of the trading year most owners like to see how well their company has performed. One initial indication of performance is the amount of profit (or loss) that the business has made during that year. Figure 42.1 illustrates how profit (and loss) is measured. It is the difference between turnover and business costs. Businesses measure their profit by compiling a **profit and loss account**. This is a summary of all business transactions and shows the flow of expenditure and income in a trading period. A profit and loss account for the year ending 31 January 2004 is shown in Table 42.1 (over the page). It shows the business transactions for Virginian Carpets Ltd, a carpet wholesaler which specialises in Moroccan carpets. It is divided into three sections: the TRADING ACCOUNT; the PROFIT AND LOSS ACCOUNT; the PROFIT AND LOSS APPROPRIATION ACCOUNT.

## The trading account

The trading account shows the revenue earned from selling products (the turnover) and the cost of those sales. Subtracting one from the other gives GROSS PROFIT. In Table 42.1, Virginian Carpets Ltd made a gross profit of

Matalan made a name for itself as a discount retailer, selling clothes to lower income consumers from fairly basic retail stores. However, since 2001 Matalan has adopted a new marketing strategy. It has been changing its image, partly due to greater competition from other discount stores such as Primark. The company is improving the appearance of its stores and extending its product line with the aim of attracting more middle-class shoppers. The 2003 profit and loss account for Matalan is shown in Table 42.5.

(a) What is the value of:
  (i) operating profit in 2003;
  (ii) turnover in 2002;
  (iii) dividends in 2003;

**Table 42.5** *Profit and loss account for Matalan plc, 2003*

|  | 2003 £m | 2002 £m |
|---|---|---|
| **Turnover** | 1,021.5 | ? |
| Cost of sales | 855.3 | 710.4 |
| **Gross profit** | 166.2 | 137.0 |
| Administrative expenses | 47.9 | 29.1 |
| **Operating profit** | ? | 107.9 |
| Net interest payable | 0.9 | 0.3 |
| **Profit on ordinary activities before taxation** | 117.4 | 107.6 |
| Taxation | 30.7 | 33.5 |
| **Profit on ordinary activities after taxation** | 86.7 | 74.1 |
| Dividends | ? | 29.3 |
| **Profit retained for the period** | 53.4 | 44.8 |

Source: adapted from Matalan plc, *Annual Report and Financial Statements*, 2003.

(b) (i) Calculate the percentage change in turnover and profit after tax between 2002 and 2003.
  (ii) Briefly explain to what extent Matalan's new marketing strategy is proving to be a success.

**Question 3**

- The **taxation** payable and the **proposed** dividend are shown in the **current liabilities**. Tax is owed to the Inland Revenue and dividends are eventually paid to the shareholders.
- The **depreciation** figure from operating expenses has an effect on the **fixed assets** section of the balance sheet. The value of fixed assets is reduced each year by the amount shown as depreciation in the profit and loss account.

## Public limited company accounts

Public limited companies have similar accounts to those of private limited companies, such as Virginian Carpets. They must also publish their accounts by law. This allows the public to see the financial position and performance of the company and decide if buying its shares is worthwhile. Existing shareholders can also gauge the company's performance.

It is likely that the published profit and loss account of a large public limited company will be slightly different from that of a private company.

- Accounts often show the **earnings per share** (☞ unit 56) in the appropriation account. This is calculated by dividing the profit after tax by the total number of issued shares. For example, if a company's net profit after tax is £1.6

million and 5 million shares have been issued:

$$\text{Earnings per share} = \frac{\text{Net profit after tax}}{\text{No. of shares issued}}$$

$$= \frac{\text{£1.6m}}{\text{5m}}$$

$$= 32p$$

The earnings per share gives an indication of a company's performance.

- Plcs usually pay dividends twice a year. About half way through the financial year a company might pay an **interim dividend**, usually less than half the total dividend. At the end of the financial year the **final dividend** is paid.
- From time to time business may make a 'one-off' transaction. An example of an **exceptional item** might be a very large bad debt which is deducted as normal in the profit and loss account, but disclosed separately in the notes. In recent years some of the commercial banks have had to make such entries after incurring bad debts from

**Table 42.6** *The profit and loss account of Joanna Cullen, a sole trader*

**JOANNA CULLEN**
**Trading and profit and loss account for the year ended 31.5.04**

| 2003 £ | | 2004 £ | £ |
|---|---|---|---|
| 130,000 | Turnover | | 150,000 |
| | | | |
| 25,000 | Opening stock | 30,000 | |
| 65,000 | Purchases | 70,000 | |
| | | | |
| 90,000 | | 100,000 | |
| 30,000 | *less* Closing stock at selling price | 35,000 | |
| | | | |
| 60,000 | | | 65,000 |
| | | | |
| 70,000 | Gross profit | | 85,000 |
| | *less:* | | |
| 1,000 | Casual labour | 2,000 | |
| 2,500 | Motor expenses | 3,000 | |
| 800 | Telephone | 1,000 | |
| 2,500 | Printing, stationery and advertising | 3,000 | |
| 1,300 | Electricity | 1,500 | |
| 8,000 | Rent and rates | 9,000 | |
| 400 | Insurance | 500 | |
| 2,500 | Bank interest and charges | 2,500 | |
| 2,000 | Depreciation - car | 2,000 | |
| 900 | Depreciation - fixtures and fittings | 900 | |
| 21,900 | | | |
| | | | 25,400 |
| | | | |
| 48,100 | Net profit | | 59,600 |

Third World countries. An example of an **extraordinary item** might be the cost of management restructuring. Generally they arise from events outside the normal business activities and are not expected to occur again. The expenditure would normally be listed in the profit and loss account, below the line showing profit after tax.

- In the profit and loss appropriation account of a public limited company, the retained profit figure is sometimes called **transfer to reserves**.
- **Net interest** may sometimes be shown. This is difference between interest paid and any interest received. For example, if a business paid £2.6 million interest during the year and also received £0.2 million interest, **net interest payable** would be £2.4 million (£2.6 million - £0.2 million). If a business paid £2.6 million interest and received £3.0 million interest, **net interest receivable** would be £0.4 million.
- Limited companies often produce **consolidated accounts**. This happens when a business group is made up of several different companies or divisions. Each company is likely to retain a separate legal identity and produce its own accounts. However, the group is also obliged to produce accounts for the whole organisation. These consolidated

accounts are produced by adding together the results of all the individual companies.

## Sole trader accounts

Table 42.6 shows the trading and profit and loss account for Joanna Cullen, a retailer selling computers. The differences and similarities between the profit and loss account of a sole trader and a limited company can be illustrated from Table 42.6. The profit and loss account of a sole trader normally shows how the year's purchases are adjusted for stock by including opening and closing stocks. In addition, a more detailed list of expenses is included. This allows a comparison with the previous year. A profit and loss appropriation account is not included since there is only one owner and all profit is transferred to the capital account in the balance sheet.

## The uses of profit and loss accounts

- Business owners are keen to see how much profit they have made at the end of the trading year. The size of the profit may be a guide to the performance of the business. A comparison is also possible because a profit and loss

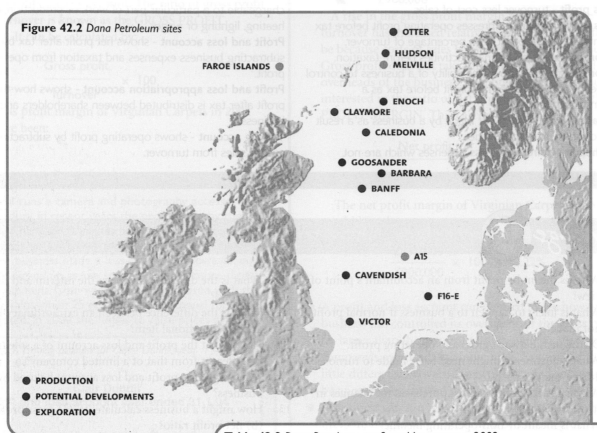

**Figure 42.2** Dana Petroleum sites

- OTTER
- HUDSON
- MELVILLE
- ENOCH
- CLAYMORE
- CALEDONIA
- GOOSANDER
- BARBARA
- BANFF
- A15
- CAVENDISH
- F16-E
- VICTOR

FAROE ISLANDS

● PRODUCTION
● POTENTIAL DEVELOPMENTS
● EXPLORATION

(a) **Identify four possible examples of administration costs for Dana Petroleum. (4 marks)**

(b) **In 2002, according to the profit and loss account, earnings per share were 0.62p. Explain what this means and how it could have been calculated. (8 marks)**

(c) **Using the case as an example, explain whether the business had net interest payable or receivable. (8 marks)**

(d) **Calculate the (i) gross profit and (ii) net profit margins for 2001 and 2002. (8 marks)**

(e) **Using the answers in (d), and any other information in the case, evaluate the company's performance in 2002. (12 marks)**

**Table 42.8** Dana Petroleum, profit and loss account, 2002

### Dana Petroleum plc
### Profit and loss account year ended 31.12.02

| | 2002 £000 | 2001 £000 |
|---|---|---|
| **Turnover** | **38,588** | 26,639 |
| Cost of sales - continuing operations | 26,606 | 16,839 |
| **Gross profit** | **11,982** | 9,800 |
| Administrative expenses | 2,663 | 1,596 |
| **Operating profit** | **9,319** | 8,204 |
| Group share of loss of associated company | 54 | 58 |
| **Profit on ordinary activities before Interest** | **9,265** | 8,146 |
| Interest receivable | 677 | 866 |
| Interest payable and similar charges | 1,711 | 1,345 |
| **Profit on ordinary activities before taxation** | **8,231** | 7,667 |
| Taxation | 1,266 | 1,234 |
| **Profit on ordinary activities after taxation** | **6,965** | 6,433 |
| Minority interest | 155 | 850 |
| **Profit for the financial year** | **6,810** | 5,583 |
| **Earnings per share** | **0.62p** | 0.59p |

Source: adapted from Dana Petroleum plc, *Annual Report and Accounts, 2002.*

# 43 The Balance Sheet

## Introduction to the balance sheet

What does a BALANCE SHEET show? It is like a photograph of the financial position of a business at a particular point in time. The balance sheet contains information about the **assets** of a business, its **liabilities** and its **capital**.

- ASSETS are the resources that a business owns and uses. Assets are usually divided into current assets and fixed assets. Current assets are used up in production, such as stocks of raw materials. They can also be money owed to a business by debtors. Fixed assets, such as machinery, are used again and again over a period of time.
- LIABILITIES are the debts of the business, ie what it **owes** to other businesses, individuals and institutions. Liabilities are a **source** of funds for a business. They might be short term, such as an overdraft, or long term, such as a mortgage or a long term bank loan.
- CAPITAL is the money introduced by the owners of the business, for example when they buy shares. It is another source of funds and can be used to purchase assets.

In all balance sheets the value of assets (what a business uses or owns) will equal the value of liabilities and capital (what the business owes). Why? Any increase in total assets must be funded by an equal increase in capital or liabilities. A business wanting to buy extra machinery (an asset) may need to obtain a bank loan (a liability), for example. Alternatively, a reduction in credit from suppliers (a liability) may mean a reduction in stocks that can be bought (an asset). So:

Assets = capital + liabilities

| Sources of funds | | Uses of funds | |
|---|---|---|---|
| **Liabilities** | £000 | **Assets** | £000 |
| **Current liabilities** | | **Fixed assets** | |
| Trade creditors | 120 | Premises | 200 |
| Taxation | 70 | Plant and equipment | 100 |
| Dividend | 80 | Financial investments | 120 |
| **Long term liabilities** | | | |
| Mortgage | 150 | **Current assets** | |
| **Capital and reserves** | | Stocks of goods | 180 |
| Shareholders' capital | 400 | Debtors | 200 |
| Retained profit | 170 | Cash at bank | 190 |
| | 990 | | 990 |

**Figure 43.1** *The assets, liabilities and capital of a private limited company*

This is shown in Figure 43.1. The diagram shows the types of asset and liability that might appear on the balance sheet of a private limited company. There are differences in the assets and liabilities shown in the balance sheets of sole traders and limited companies. This is explained later in this unit.

In March 2003 Kathy Smith, a qualified and experienced nurse, set up HomeCare. The business provides care services to elderly patients who live on their own. Most of her clients are private but she also does some work for the health service. Kathy used £10,000 of her own money to set up the business. The following information is also known about the business.

- It has a long term bank loan of £5,000.
- HomeCare owns a specialised vehicle with a wheelchair lift valued at £13,200.
- There is £1,670 cash in the business bank account.
- HomeCare owes £300 to a local newspaper for an advert it placed.
- HomeCare is owed £250 by one of its clients.
- Kathy has some cash in hand that belongs to the business.

(a) Which of the above items are HomeCare's assets?
(b) Use the equation 'Assets = capital + liabilities' to calculate the value of cash in hand.

**Question**

**Table 43.1**

### BREAKOUT LTD
### Balance sheet as at 31 August 2004

| | £000 | £000 |
|---|---|---|
| **Fixed assets** | | |
| Premises | 1,200 | |
| Fixtures and fittings | 1,100 | |
| Equipment | 700 | |
| | | 3,000 |
| **Current assets** | | |
| Stocks | 800 | |
| Debtors | 500 | |
| Cash at bank | 400 | |
| | 1,700 | |
| **Current liabilities** | | |
| Trade creditors | 200 | |
| Other liabilities | 300 | |
| Dividends | 200 | |
| | 700 | |
| **Net current assets** | | |
| (working capital) | | 1,000 |
| **Total assets less** | | |
| **current liabilities** | | 4,000 |
| **Creditors: amounts** | | |
| **falling due after one year** | | |
| Mortgage | 1,100 | |
| Bank loan | 200 | |
| | | 1,300 |
| **Net assets** | | **2,700** |
| **Capital and reserves** | | |
| Ordinary share capital | | |
| (2,000,000 shares at £1) | 2,000 | |
| Retained profit | 700 | |
| | | **2,700** |

FIXED ASSETS are assets with a life span of more than one year. They might include the buildings, musical and lighting equipment, drinks equipment behind the bar, tables and seats.

CURRENT ASSETS are assets that are likely to be changed into cash within one year. They might include cash deposited at the bank and stocks of goods, such as cigarettes and drinks. They might also include customers or businesses that owe money to Breakout Ltd - the debtors of the business.

CURRENT LIABILITIES are debts that have to be repaid within 12 months. They might include money owed to suppliers of drinks or food, telephone and electricity bills - the creditors of Breakout Ltd. They may also include corporation tax payable to the Inland Revenue for profit earned in the past or dividends owing to shareholders. Bank overdrafts are also a current liability.

The value of NET CURRENT ASSETS or **working capital** can be found by:
Current assets - current liabilities
Calculating working capital is important for a business. The working capital a firm has indicates whether or not it can afford to pay its day to day bills.

The value of **total assets less current liabilities** can be found by:
(Fixed assets + current assets) - current liabilities

The debts that a business owes which are payable to creditors after 12 months are LONG TERM LIABILITIES. They might include a mortgage which has been taken out to purchase buildings. They could also include any long term loans used to buy equipment, for example.

The value of NET ASSETS can be found by:
(Total assets less current liabilities) - long term liabilities

The **capital and reserves** figure is equal to the value of net assets. The total of capital and reserves is sometimes called **capital employed** or **shareholders' funds**. Capital and reserves are a liability for the business - money that it owes. Shareholders' funds include the money that is put into the business by people purchasing shares. It is the value of shares when first sold rather than the current market value. Retained profit is profit that the business has made in previous years. It is money which is owed to the owners. However, it has been retained in the business to buy equipment or to help cash flow rather than distributing it as a dividend.

**Table 43.2** *Information from a balance sheet for Barden Ltd as at 30.4.04*

| | £000 | £000 |
|---|---|---|
| **Fixed assets** | | |
| Factory | 11,000 | |
| Plant and machinery | 5,000 | |
| Equipment | 2,500 | |
| Financial assets | 1,000 | |
| | | 19,500 |
| **Current assets** | | |
| Stocks | 3,000 | |
| Work-in-progress | 2,500 | |
| Debtors | 3,500 | |
| | 9,000 | |
| **Current liabilities** | | |
| Trade creditors | 3,500 | |
| Other liabilities | 2,500 | |
| | 6,000 | |
| **Net current assets** | | **** |
| **Total assets less current liabilities** | | **** |
| **Creditors falling due after more than one year** | 6,000 | |
| **Net assets** | | **** |
| **Capital and reserves** | | |
| Share capital | 9,000 | |
| Other reserves | 2,000 | |
| Retained profit | 5,500 | |
| | | **** |

Barden Ltd manufactures components for forklift trucks. It is located in Bristol and serves a major manufacturer of forklift trucks in Cardiff. Table 43.2 shows information that may be contained in the balance sheet for Barden Ltd as at 30.4.04.

(a) Suggest two examples of:
  (i) other current liabilities;
  (ii) creditors falling due after more than one year;
  that the business might have.
(b) Explain why:
  (i) the value of debtors is shown as an asset;
  (ii) the value of trade creditors is shown as a liability.
(c) From the information in Table 43.2, calculate the value of:
  (i) net current assets;
  (ii) total assets less current liabilities;
  (iii) net assets;
  (iv) capital and reserves.

**Question 2**

## Presenting the balance sheet

Table 43.1 shows the balance sheet of Breakout Ltd. It is a business that owns a small chain of nightclubs. It is presented here in a vertical format. Businesses now use this method when presenting their accounts, although in the past they were shown in a horizontal format similar to Figure 43.1. The balance sheet is a record of the company's assets, liabilities and capital.

One advantage of presenting the balance sheet in this format is that it is easy to see the amount of **working capital** (current assets - current liabilities) that a business has. This is important because the working capital shows whether a business is able to pay its day to day bills (☞ unit 48). The net assets (total assets - current liabilities - long term liabilities) of a business are also clearly shown.

## The balance sheets of public limited companies

Table 43.3 shows the balance sheet of a public limited company, Crestfell plc. It is a major manufacturer of food products. A number of new balance sheet items are included compared to those of a private limited company. They reflect the type of transactions of a public limited company.

- **Investments** might be shares held by Crestfell in another company. Investments can be fixed or current assets.
- **Tangible fixed assets** could be factories and equipment.
- **Intangible assets** might be the value of the company's good name with customers (goodwill, ☞ unit 45).
- The value of **provision for liabilities and charges** would include a variety of charges such as reorganisation costs, post retirement benefit payments and deferred taxation.
- **Called up share capital** might include different types of shareholders' funds, including ordinary and preference share capital.
- **Revaluation** sometimes appears under capital and reserves to balance an increase in the value of fixed assets. A business may buy a building for £100,000. Later it may be worth £160,000. This £160,000 would be included in the tangible assets figure. However only £100,000 would appear under capital and reserves as this was the original amount spent. Capital and reserves have to be revalued by £60,000 so that assets still equal liabilities plus capital and reserves.

**Table 43.3** *The balance sheet of Crestfell plc, 31 August 2004*

### Crestfell plc
### Balance sheet as at 31 August 2004

| | 2004 (£m) | 2003 (£m) |
|---|---|---|
| **Fixed assets** | | |
| Tangible assets | 920 | 780 |
| Intangible assets | 150 | 140 |
| Investments | 20 | 10 |
| | 1,090 | 930 |
| **Current assets** | | |
| Stocks | 220 | 210 |
| Debtors | 410 | 390 |
| Cash at bank | 70 | 40 |
| | 700 | 640 |
| **Creditors** (amounts falling due in one year) | (550) | (500) |
| **Net current assets** (working capital) | 150 | 140 |
| **Total assets less current liabilities** | 1,240 | 1,070 |
| **Creditors** (amounts falling due after more than one year) | (350) | (240) |
| Provision for liabilities and charges | (70) | (70) |
| **Net assets** | **820** | **760** |
| **Capital and reserves** | | |
| Called up share capital | 110 | 100 |
| Revaluation | 130 | 130 |
| Retained profit | 580 | 530 |
| | **820** | **760** |

Figures in brackets show values to be subtracted.

Company law requires both **private and public** limited companies to show both this year's and last year's figures in published accounts. This allows comparisons to be made. When the balance sheets for Crestfell plc as at 31 August 2003 and 2004 are compared, most of the figures have changed.

## Depreciation and the balance sheet

In accounting, it is recognised that the cost of a fixed asset is gradually consumed as it wears out. The measure of **consumption** or any other reduction in the useful economic life of a fixed asset is known as DEPRECIATION.

**Table 43.4** *Notes to the accounts of Crestfell plc showing depreciation of tangible fixed assets, 2004*

**Tangible assets**

| | Land & buildings £m | Plant, machinery & vehicles £m | Fixtures & fittings £m | Total £m |
|---|---|---|---|---|
| Cost | 380 | 950 | 70 | 1,400 |
| Depreciation & amortisation | 50 | 400 | 30 | 480 |
| Net book value | 330 | 550 | 40 | 920 |

Accountants must make an allowance for this when showing the value of assets. They estimate the amount by which asset values depreciate. They then deduct depreciation from the value of assets before placing the value on the balance sheet. The term AMORTISATION is used for the changing value of fixed assets with a limited life, such as a lease or an intangible asset. For example, a business may pay to lease a building. The lease has a value. When the lease runs out after, say, 10 years, it has no value.

Details about depreciation are shown in the **notes to the accounts**. An example of these notes is shown in Table 43.4. Unit 49 shows how depreciation can be calculated.

## Sole trader balance sheets

Earlier it was mentioned that sole trader balance sheets will be different to those of limited companies. Take the example of Joanna Cullen, a sole trader running a retail outlet that sells computers. Her balance sheet is shown in Table 43.5. There is a number of differences between a sole trader and a limited company balance sheet.

- The sole trader has a capital account rather than a 'capital and reserves' section. Sole traders are set up with the personal capital introduced into the business by the owner. Joanna Cullen introduced a further £4,500 into the business during 2004, according to the balance sheet in Table 43.5.
- It is likely that a sole trader will need to withdraw money from the business for personal reasons during the year. This is subtracted from the capital account and is shown as DRAWINGS in the balance sheet. The balance on the capital account is the amount owed to the owner. This is equal to the assets of the company.
- A limited company has many sources of capital and reserves. However, all companies will show shareholders' funds (often listed as capital and reserves), which will not be in a sole trader's balance sheet.
- The shareholders of a limited company are paid a dividend. This appears in the figure for current liabilities. As sole traders do not have shareholders no such figure will be included in their accounts.

**Table 43.5** *Balance sheet for Joanna Cullen as at 31 May 2004*

**JOANNA CULLEN**
**Balance sheet as at 31 May 2004**

| 2003 £ | | 2004 £ | £ |
|---|---|---|---|
| | **Fixed assets** | | |
| 10,000 | Car | | 8,000 |
| 7,900 | Fixtures and fittings | | 7,000 |
| 17,900 | | | 15,000 |
| | **Current assets** | | |
| 30,000 | Stocks | 35,000 | |
| 4,000 | Debtors and prepayments | 5,000 | |
| 3,000 | Bank account | 4,000 | |
| 1,000 | Cash in hand | 1,000 | |
| 38,000 | | 45,000 | |
| | **(*less*) Current liabilities** | | |
| 20,000 | Creditors and accrued charges | 25,000 | |
| 18,000 | Working capital | | 20,000 |
| 35,900 | **NET ASSETS** | | 35,000 |
| | (FINANCED BY) | | |
| 30,000 | **Opening capital** | | 35,900 |
| - | Capital introduced | | 4,500 |
| 48,100 | (*add*) Net profit | | 59,600 |
| 78,100 | | | 100,000 |
| 42,200 | (*less*) Drawings | | 65,000 |
| 35,900 | | | 35,000 |

# The use of balance sheets

The balance sheet has a number of uses for a business.

- In general, it provides a summary and valuation of all business assets, capital and liabilities.
- The balance sheet can be used to analyse the **asset structure** of a business. It can show how the money raised by the business has been spent on different types of asset. The balance sheet for Crestfell plc in Table 43.3 shows that £1,090 million was spent on fixed assets in 2004. Current assets, however, accounted for only £700 million.
- The balance sheet can also be used to analyse the **capital structure** of a business. A business can raise funds from many different sources, such as shareholders' capital, retained profit and long term and short term sources.
- Looking at the value of **working capital** (☞ unit 48) can

Seafood City is cash and carry, owned by Malcolm Partridge a sole trader. It sells a wide range of fresh and frozen fish and seafood. It serves retailers, hotels, restaurants, and increasingly members of the public who are prepared to exceed the £50 minimum spending limit. The balance sheet for Seafood City is shown in Table 43.6.

**Table 43.6** *Balance sheet for Seafood City, 2003*

**Seafood City**
**Balance sheet as at 31.12.03**

| | £ | £ |
|---|---|---|
| **Fixed assets** | | |
| Fixtures and fittings | | 129,300 |
| Vehicle | | 23,100 |
| | | 152,400 |
| **Current assets** | | |
| Stocks | 131,210 | |
| Debtors | 31,390 | |
| Cash at bank and in hand | 10,070 | |
| | 172,670 | |
| **Less Current liabilities** | | |
| Trade creditors | 45,790 | |
| Loan | 12,000 | |
| | 57,790 | |
| **Working capital** | | *** |
| **NET ASSETS** | | 267,280 |
| FINANCED BY: | | |
| **Opening capital** | | *** |
| Add Net profit | | 110,010 |
| | | 300,030 |
| Less Drawings | | 32,750 |
| **CAPITAL EMPLOYED** | | 267,280 |

(a) (i) Calculate the value of working capital for Seafood City.
   (ii) Explain why the working capital is an important item in the balance sheet.
(b) (i) What is the value of opening capital for Seafood City?
   (ii) What will be the value of opening capital for Seafood City in the next financial year?

**Question 3**

indicate whether a firm is able to pay its everyday expenses or is likely to have problems. The value of working capital is the difference between current assets and current liabilities. It shows the money left over after all current liabilities have been paid that can be used to settle the day to day debts of the business. In the 2004 balance sheet for

Crestfell plc the value of working capital was £150 million.

● A balance sheet may provide a guide to a firm's value. Generally, the value of the business is represented by the value of all assets less any money owed to outside agents such as banks or suppliers. The value of Crestfell plc in 2004 was £820 million.

## Limitations of balance sheets

There are also limitations to balance sheets.

● The value of many assets listed in the balance sheet may not reflect the amount of money the business would receive if it were sold. For example, fixed assets are listed at cost less an allowance for depreciation (☞ unit 49). However, the depreciation allowance is estimated by accountants. If estimates are inaccurate, the value of assets will also be inaccurate .

● Many balance sheets do not include intangible assets (☞ unit 45). Assets such as goodwill, brand names and the skills of the workforce may be excluded because they are difficult to value or could change suddenly. If such assets are excluded, the value of the business may be understated.

● A balance sheet is a static statement. Many of the values for assets, capital and liabilities listed in the statement are only valid for the day the balance sheet was published. After another day's trading, many of the figures will have changed. This can restrict its usefulness.

● It could be argued that a balance sheet lacks detail. Many of the figures are totals and are not broken down. For example, the value of tangible assets for Crestfell plc in 2004 was £920 million. This figure gives no information about the nature of these assets.

# key terms

**Amortisation** – used to refer to depreciation in the context of leases and intangible assets. In the USA amortisation is taken to mean the same as depreciation.
**Assets** - resources used or owned by the business in production.
**Balance sheet** - a summary at a point in time of business assets, liabilities and capital.
**Capital** -  a source of funds provided by the owners of the business used to buy assets.
**Current assets** - assets likely to be changed into cash within a year.
**Current liabilities** - debts that have to be repaid within a year.
**Depreciation** – the measure of wearing out, consumption or other reduction in the useful economic life of a fixed asset.
**Drawings** - money withdrawn by a sole trader from the business for personal use.
**Fixed assets** - assets with a life span of more than one  year.
**Liabilities** - the debts of the business which provide a source of funds.
**Long term liabilities** - debts that are payable after 12 months.
**Net assets** - the value of total assets minus current liabilities minus long term liabilities. The value is equal to capital and reserves on the balance sheet.
**Net current assets** - current assets minus current liabilities. Also known as working capital.

# Knowledge...Knowledge...Knowledge...Knowledge...Knowledge...Know

1. What is a balance sheet?
2. Why is a balance sheet a static business document?
3. Why must the value of assets on a balance sheet be equal to the value of liabilities plus capital?
4. What is the difference between fixed and current   assets?
5. State 3 examples of the fixed assets that a business  might have.
6. State 3 examples of the current assets that a business might have.
7. Why is the balance sheet shown in a vertical format?
8. What is the difference between tangible and intangible fixed assets?
9. What is the difference between current and long term liabilities?
10. State 3 current liabilities that a business might have.
11. Why is revaluation of assets sometimes included under capital and reserves?
12. How does depreciation affect the balance sheet?
13. State 3 items that might appear on the balance sheet of  a public limited company but not a sole trader.
14. Suggest 3 uses of balance sheets for a business.
15. Suggest 3 limitations of balance sheets.

# Case study  Pubs 'n' Bars plc

Pubs 'n' Bars plc owns and operates a group of community pubs located mostly in the south of England. The company was listed on the alternative investment market (AIM) in 1999 and since then it has grown from owing 51 to 64 public houses. 43 of the pubs are run by managers with the remainder being operated by tenants on three year leases. The tenants are tied to the company's nominated beer supplier. Most of the pubs are 'locals', each with its own character and attracting customers from the immediate area. Managers are encouraged to take an entrepreneurial approach to running the pubs by introducing new sources of income, such as food and accommodation.

A strategic change was also made to the running of the company. This involved switching those pubs where the provision of food was an important source of income from managed houses to tenancies. This change affected six of the group's pubs. It was felt that such businesses were run more effectively when run by 'owner operators'. This did prove to be the case. Table 43.7 shows the balance sheet for Pubs 'n' Bars plc for 2002. Table 43.8 shows an analysis of current liabilities.

Source: adapted from Pubs'n'Bars, *Annual Report and Accounts, 2002*.

(a) Describe the main tangible assets that Pubs 'n' Bars is likely to own. (4 marks)

(b) Describe what has happened to working capital over the two years. (4 marks)

**Table 43.8** *An analysis of current liabilities for Pubs 'n' Bars, 2002*

**Creditors: Amounts falling due within one year**

| | 2002 £ | 2001 £ |
|---|---|---|
| Bank loans and overdrafts | 642,597 | 3,262,282 |
| Trade creditors | 760,433 | 642,075 |
| Amounts owed to group undertakings | - | - |
| Corporation tax | 338,812 | 273,086 |
| Social security and other taxes | 301,092 | 341,480 |
| Other creditors | 228,991 | 68,256 |
| Obligations under finance leases | 337,110 | 285,860 |
| Accurals and deferred income | 246,130 | 215,577 |
| Proposed dividends | 235,809 | 214,372 |
| | 3,090,974 | 5,302,988 |

**Table 43.7** *Pubs 'n' Bars plc balance sheet as at 31st December*

| | 2002 £ | 2001 £ |
|---|---|---|
| **Fixed assets** | | |
| Tangible assets | 23,515,713 | 21,413,377 |
| Intangible assets | 1,666,483 | 1,731,267 |
| | 25,182,196 | 23,144,644 |
| **Current Assets** | | |
| Stocks | 552,299 | 623,517 |
| Debtors | 2,609,391 | 1,456,145 |
| Cash at bank and in hand | 39,833 | 52,112 |
| | 3,201,523 | 2,131,774 |
| **Creditors: Amounts falling due within one year** | (3,090,974) | (5,302,988) |
| **Net Current Assets/ (Liabilities)** | 110,549 | (3,171,214) |
| **Total Assets less Current Liabilities** | 25,292,745 | 19,973,430 |
| **Creditors: Amounts falling due after more than one year** | (11,569,149) | (9,290,099) |
| **Provisions for Liabilities and Charges** | (227,426) | (230,411) |
| **Net Assets** | 13,496,170 | 10,452,920 |
| **Capital and Reserves** | | |
| Called up share capital - equity interests | 4,287,442 | 4,287,442 |
| Share premium account | 4,522,209 | 4,522,209 |
| Revaluation reserve | 2,866,802 | 559,712 |
| Profit and loss account | 1,819,717 | 1,083,557 |
| **Shareholders' Funds** | 13,496,170 | 10,452,920 |

(c) (i) Explain, using examples from the case, what is meant by 'Creditors: Amounts falling due within one year'. (6 marks)

(ii) How might Pubs 'n' Bars be affected by the change in this amount? Explain your answer. (6 marks)

(d) Analyse what has happened to the value of Pubs 'n' Bars over the two years. (10 marks)

(e) Discuss how useful the balance sheet is to Pubs 'n' Bars plc. (10 marks)

## The need for funds

Firms need money to get started, ie to buy equipment, raw materials and obtain premises. Once this initial expenditure has been met, the business can get under way. If successful, it will earn money from sales. However, business is a continuous activity and money flowing in will be used to buy more raw materials and settle other trading debts.

If the owner wants to expand, extra money will be needed over and above that from sales. Expansion may mean larger premises, more equipment and extra workers. Throughout the life of a business there will almost certainly be times when money has to be raised from outside.

The items of expenditure above fall into two categories - CAPITAL EXPENDITURE or REVENUE EXPENDITURE. Capital expenditure is spending on items which may be used over and over again. A company vehicle, a cutting machine and a new factory all fall into this category. Capital expenditure will be shown in a firm's balance sheet because it includes the purchase of fixed assets (☞ unit 43). It also includes the maintenance and repair of buildings and machines.

Revenue expenditure refers to payments for goods and services which have either already been consumed or will be very soon. Wages, raw materials and fuel are all examples. It also includes the maintenance and repair of buildings and machines. Revenue expenditure will be shown in a firm's profit and loss account (☞ unit 42) because it represents business costs or expenses.

## Internal sources of finance

Figure 44.1 shows how sources of finance are either internal or external. Internal sources can only be used when a business is established because money cannot be taken out of a business until revenue has been generated by trading activities. Although most of this unit focuses on external sources of finance, internal sources are very important. This is because internal sources are cheap. A business does not have to pay interest, for example, if it uses its own money to fund activities. There are three important internal sources of finance.

● **Profit**. Retained profit (☞ unit 42) is profit after tax that has not been returned to the owners. It is the single most important source of finance for a business. Around 65 per cent of all business funding comes from retained profit. It is the cheapest source of finance, with no financial charges such as interest, dividends and administration. However, there is an opportunity cost. If retained profit is used by the business it cannot be returned to the owners. This may lead to conflict if the shareholders of a public limited company, for example, see that dividend payments have been frozen because the directors have used the profit in

the business.

● **Working capital**. It may be possible to 'squeeze' working capital to provide extra finance for the business. One way of doing this is to operate a 'tighter' credit policy. For example, a business might reduce the trade credit period, so that money is received from customers more quickly. Or a business might collect long-standing debts by applying more pressure to customers. Both these options might result in a loss of orders and damage customer relations. Another approach is to reduce stock holding. Money tied up in stocks is unproductive. If a business can reduce stock, money is released and can be used for more productive activities. But having too little stock can be a problem. For

(a) Look at the photographs. State which transactions to buy these items are revenue expenditure and which are capital expenditure.
(b) Why might expenditure on equipment need to be repeated?
(c) Explain why it might be easier to cut capital expenditure rather than revenue expenditure.

Building materials

Equipment

Petrol

## Question 1

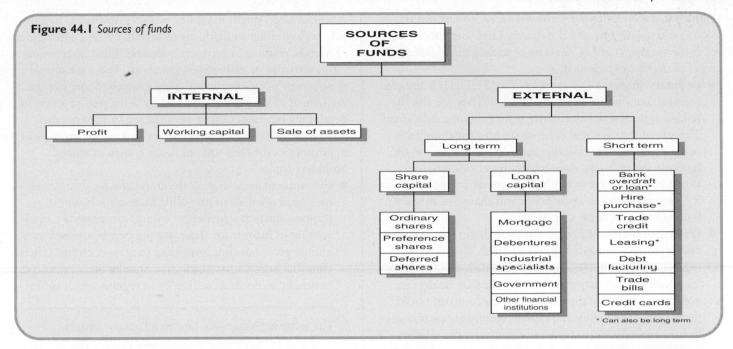

**Figure 44.1** *Sources of funds*

example, a business might find it difficult to cope with a surge in demand if stocks are too low.

● **Sale of assets.** An established business may be able to sell some unwanted assets to raise finance. For example, machinery, land and buildings that are no longer required could be sold off. Large companies can sell parts of their organisation to raise finance. For example, in 2003 Scottish & Newcastle put its £2.4 billion pub estate up for sale. It wanted to sell the 1,540 pub estate to focus on brewing. Another option is to raise money through a SALE AND LEASEBACK. This involves selling an asset, such as property or machinery, that the business still wants to use. The sale is made to a specialist company that leases the asset back to the seller. This is an increasingly popular source of finance.

## External long term sources of finance

External long term capital can be in the form of share capital or loan capital.

**Share capital** For a limited company SHARE CAPITAL is likely to be the most important source of finance. The sale of shares can raise very large amounts of money. ISSUED SHARE CAPITAL is the money raised from the sale of shares. AUTHORISED SHARE CAPITAL is the maximum amount shareholders want to raise. Share capital is often referred to as PERMANENT CAPITAL. This is because it is not normally **redeemed**, ie it is not repaid by the business. Once the share has been sold, the buyer is entitled to a share in the profit of the company, ie a **dividend** (☞ unit 3). Dividends are not always declared. Sometimes a business makes a loss or needs to retain profit to help fund future business activities. A shareholder can make a CAPITAL GAIN by selling the share at a higher price

**Table 44.1** *Summary and explanation of the ways in which new shares can be made available to investors on the stock exchange*

| | |
|---|---|
| **INITIAL PUBLIC OFFERING (IPO)** | |
| **Public issue** | Potential investors might apply to an ISSUING HOUSE, such as a merchant bank, after reading the company prospectus. This is an expensive method, but suits big issues. |
| **Offer for sale** | Shares are issued to an issuing house, which then sells them at a fixed price. This is also expensive but suits small issues. |
| **Sale by tender** | The company states a minimum price which it will accept from investors and then allocates shares to the highest bidders. |
| **PLACING** | |
| **Private placing** | Unquoted companies (who do not sell on the Stock Exchange) or those with small share sales approach issuing houses to place the shares privately with investors. |
| **Stock exchange placing** | Less popular issues can be placed by the stock exchange with institutional investors, for example. This is relatively inexpensive. |
| **AN INTRODUCTION** | Existing shareholders get permission from the Stock Exchange to sell shares by attracting new shareholders to the firm. No new capital is raised. |
| **RIGHTS ISSUE** | Existing shareholders are given the 'right' to buy new shares at a discounted price. This is cheap and simple, and creates free publicity. Issues can be based on current holdings. A 1 for 5 issue means that 1 new share is issued for every 5 currently held. |
| **BONUS ISSUE** | New shares are issued to existing shareholders to capitalise on reserves which have built up over the years. No new capital is raised and shareholders end up with more shares, but at lower prices. |

than it was originally bought for. Shares are not normally sold back to the business. The shares of public limited companies are sold in a special share market called the STOCK MARKET or STOCK EXCHANGE, dealt with later in this unit. Shares in private limited companies are transferred privately (☞ unit 6). Shareholders, because they are part owners of the business, are entitled to a vote. One vote is allowed for each share owned. Voting takes place annually and shareholders vote either to re-elect the existing board of directors or replace them. Different types of shares can be issued.

● **Ordinary shares**. These are also called EQUITIES and are the most common type of share issued. They are also the riskiest type of share since there is no guaranteed dividend. The size of the dividend depends on how much profit is made and how much the directors decide to retain in the business. All ordinary shareholders have voting rights. When a share is first sold it has a nominal value shown on it - its original value. Share prices will change as they are bought and sold again and again.

● **Preference shares**. The owners of these shares receive a fixed rate of return when a dividend is declared. They carry less risk because shareholders are entitled to their dividend before the holders of ordinary shares. Preference shareholders are not strictly owners of the company. If the company is sold, their rights to dividends and capital repayments are limited to fixed amounts. Some preference shares are **cumulative**, entitling the holder to dividend arrears from years when dividends were not declared. Some are also **redeemable**, which means that they can be bought back by the company.

● **Deferred shares**. These are not used often. They are usually held by the founders of the company. Deferred shareholders only receive a dividend after the ordinary shareholders have been paid a minimum amount.

When a company issues shares there is a variety of ways in which they can be made available to potential investors as shown in Table 44.1.

**Loan capital**  Loan capital may come from a number of sources.

● Debentures. The holder of a debenture is a creditor of the company, not an owner. This means that holders are entitled to an agreed fixed rate of return, but have no voting rights. The amount borrowed must be repaid by the expiry date.

● Mortgage. Only limited companies can raise money from the sale of shares and debentures (☞ unit 6). Smaller enterprises often need long term funding, to buy premises for example. They may choose to take out a mortgage. A mortgage is usually a long term loan, from, say, a bank or other financial institution. The lender must use land or property as security on the loan.

● Industrial loan specialists. A number of organisations provide funds especially for business and commercial uses. These specialists tend to cater for businesses which have difficulty in raising funds from conventional sources. In recent years there has been a significant growth in the number of VENTURE CAPITALISTS. These provide funds for small and medium sized companies that appear to have some potential, but are considered too risky by other investors. Venture capitalists often use their own funds, but also attract money from financial institutions and '**Business Angels**'.
Business Angels are individuals who invest between £10,000 and £100,000, often in exchange for an equity stake.

A typical Angel might make one or two investments in a three year period, either individually or together with a small group of friends, relatives or business associates. Most investments are in start-ups or early stage expansions. There are several reasons why people become Business Angels. Many like the excitement of the gamble involved, or being part of a new or developing business. Others are attracted by the tax relief offered by the government. Some are looking for investment opportunities for their unused income, such as retired business people.

● Government assistance. Both central and local government have been involved in providing finance for business. Business start up schemes (☞ unit 2) can provide a small amount of income for those starting new businesses for a limited period of time, providing they meet certain criteria. Financial help is usually selective. Smaller businesses tend to benefit, as do those setting up in regions which suffer

The following letter was sent to a financial advisor.

Dear Sir

I want to start my own business. I believe there is a niche in the bar market on the south coast of England. What is the best way of raising £60,000? This would allow me to rent premises. But I would prefer to buy because I think renting is wasted money. It is likely that this would cost nearer £200,000.

Advisor's reply

Buying freehold will not only save the 'wasted' rent but also provide an asset which the financier can use as security. You may therefore find more success going for this option.
    You should speak to your local banks and get them to look at your proposal and business plan. The government's Small Firm Loan Guarantee Scheme is aimed at people like you – those looking for start-up capital but with little security. The government acts as guarantor of 75 per cent of the loan up to a limit of £100,000 for start-ups. But the lending is done by banks and they must like the project and believe that it will succeed.
    You will therefore need to raise additional capital to get the £200,000 required. One idea is to use a business angel. To find such a backer you could speak to the National Business Angels Network. It may also be worth checking your local Business Link to see if you are eligible for any grants.

(a) Why might the Small Firm Loan Guarantee Scheme be suitable for the entrepreneur in the above example?
(b) Discuss the advantages to the entrepreneur of raising money from a business angel.

**Question 2**

**Figure 44.2** *A hire purchase agreement and the parties involved in the three way transaction*

from heavy unemployment.

● Other financial institutions. Banks, for example might under certain conditions give a business a long term loan which will be repaid over a number of years. The bank may require some form of collateral on the loan, and a business may need to present a business plan (☞ unit 2) to secure the loan.

# External short term sources of finance

**Bank overdraft** This is probably the most important source of finance for a very large number of businesses. Bank overdrafts are flexible. The amount by which a business goes overdrawn depends on its needs at the time. Interest is only paid by the business when its account is overdrawn.

**Bank loan** A loan requires a rigid agreement between the borrower and the bank. The amount borrowed must be repaid over a clearly stated time period, in regular instalments. Most bank loans are short or medium term. Banks dislike long term lending because of their need for security and liquidity. Sometimes, banks change persistent overdrafts into loans, so that firms are forced to repay at regular intervals.

**Hire purchase** This is often used by small businesses to buy plant and machinery. Sometimes, a hire purchase agreement requires a down payment by the borrower, who agrees to repay the remainder in instalments over a period of time. FINANCE HOUSES specialise in providing funds for such agreements. Figure 44.2 illustrates the working of an agreement and the parties involved. The buyer may place a down payment on a machine with the supplier and receives delivery. The finance house pays the supplier the amount outstanding and collects instalments (including interest) from the buyer. The goods bought do not legally belong to the buyer until the very last instalment has been paid to the finance house.

If the buyer falls behind with the repayments the finance

house can legally repossess the item. Finance houses are less selective than banks when granting loans. Hence their interest rates are higher. They add a servicing charge for paying in instalments which also leads to higher rates. Hire purchase agreements can sometimes be for longer periods.

**Trade credit** It is common for businesses to buy raw materials, components and fuel and pay for them at a later date, usually within 30-90 days. Paying for goods and services using trade credit seems to be an interest free way of raising finance. It is particularly profitable during periods of inflation. However, many companies encourage early payment by offering discounts. The cost of goods is often higher if the firm does not pay early. Delaying the payment of bills can also result in poor business relations with suppliers.

**Leasing** A LEASE is a contract in which a business acquires the use of resources such as, property, machinery or equipment, in return for regular payments. In this type of finance, the ownership never passes to the business that is using the resource. With a **finance lease**, the arrangement is often for three years or longer and, at the end of the period, the business is given the option of then buying the resource. In accounting, the payments are treated as capital expenditure. With an **operating lease**, the arrangement is generally for a shorter period of time, and the payments are treated as revenue expenditure.

There are some advantages of leasing.
● No large sums of money are needed to buy the use of equipment.
● Maintenance and repair costs are not the responsibility of the user.
● Hire companies can offer the most up to date equipment.
● Leasing is useful when equipment is only required occasionally.

Jo Li runs a mini-market in Gloucester. He sells a wide range of groceries, confectionery, newspapers, greetings cards, stationery and a small range of hardware products. He also rents out videos and allows his daughter space in the store to sell freshly made pizzas. The business is successful but Jo Li works very hard. The store is open from 7.00 am to 10.30 pm seven days a week. He has recently obtained a licence to sell alcohol. He spent £6,000 of retained profit extending the premises so that extra shelving could be fitted to develop the sale of beers, wines and spirits. Jo Li now needs to stock the new section at an estimated cost of £3,000.

(a) What are the advantages to Jo Li of using retained profit to extend the premises?
(b) Discuss whether Jo Li should use a bank overdraft or trade credit to buy the stock for the new section of the mini-market.

**Question 3**

- A leasing agreement is generally easier for a new company to obtain than other forms of loan finance. This is because the assets remain the property of the leasing company.

However:
- over a long period of time leasing is more expensive than the outright purchase of plant and machinery;
- loans cannot be secured on assets which are leased.

**Debt factoring** When companies sell their products they send invoices stating the amount due. The invoice provides evidence of the sale and the money owed to the company. Debt factoring involves a specialist company (the factor) providing finance against these unpaid invoices. A common arrangement is for a factor to pay 80 per cent of the value of invoices when they are issued. The balance of 20 per cent is paid by the factor when the customer settles the bill. An administrative and service fee will be charged.

**Trade bills** This is not a common source of finance, but can play an important role, particularly in overseas trade and commodity markets. The purchaser of traded goods may sign a **bill of exchange** agreeing to pay for the goods at a specified later date. Ninety days is a common period. The seller of the

goods will hold the bill until payment is due. However, the holder can sell it at a discount before the maturity date to a specialist financial institution. There is a well developed market for these bills and all holders will receive payment at the end of the period from the debtor.

**Credit cards** Businesses of all sizes have uses for cards. They can be used by executives to meet expenses such as hotel bills, petrol and meals when travelling on company business. They might also be used to purchase materials from suppliers who accept credit cards. Credit cards are popular because they are convenient, flexible, secure and avoid interest charges if monthly accounts are settled within the credit period. However, they tend to have a credit limit. This may make them unsuitable for certain purchases.

## Capital and money markets

Businesses have to look to external sources for their finance. **Financial intermediaries** are the institutions responsible for matching the needs of **savers**, who want to loan funds, with those of **investors**, who need funds. These groups do not naturally communicate with each other. Intermediaries provide the link between them.

A number of financial institutions hold funds for savers, paying them interest. In addition, they make finance available to investors who, in turn, are charged interest. Some deal in capital, ie permanent and long term finance, while others deal in money, ie short term loans and bills of exchange. They offer a variety of commercial and financially related services.

**The stock market** The capital market is dominated by the London Stock Exchange, which deals in second hand shares. The main function of a stock exchange is to provide a market where the owners of shares can sell them. If this market did not exist, selling shares would be difficult because buyers and sellers could not easily communicate with each other. Savers would be less inclined to buy shares and so companies would find it more difficult to raise finance by the issue of shares.

A stock exchange enables mergers and takeovers to take place smoothly (☞ unit 89). If the price of a company's shares begins to fall due to poor profitability, a predator may enter the market and begin to build up a stake in that company. Once the stake is large enough a predator can exert control over the company.

A stock exchange also provides a means of protection for shareholders. Companies which have a stock exchange listing have to obey a number of Stock Exchange rules and regulations, which are designed to safeguard shareholders from fraud.

Finally, it is also argued that the general movement in share prices reflects the health of the economy. However, there are times when share price movements could be very misleading. For example, they fell very sharply in 2003 just before the Iraq war when the UK economy was quite stable.

Insurance companies, pension funds, investment trusts,

Winters, a small building contractor, has just won a contract to build an extension to a local factory. The contract is worth £78,000 and is expected to take two months. Colin Winter, the owner, employs two other staff and operates from a small builder's yard in Leamington Spa. The contract, Winters' second big job this year, requires the use of an excavator. The business does not own an excavator, but has found that it is having to lease one from a Warwick-based plant hire company more and more often. The hire charges for a JCB are £19 per hour, including the driver. Colin expects to need the excavator for six full working days. Not for the first time he felt frustrated at the high cost of acquiring specialised equipment. Before going ahead with the lease he enquired about the cost of a brand new JCB. A local dealer quoted a price of £39,000. At the moment, he could not raise the finance to buy a JCB outright.

(a) Explain the advantages to the business of using a lease to fund the acquisition of the excavator.
(b) Calculate the cost of leasing the excavator. State any assumptions you feel are necessary.
(c) Suggest how Colin might fund the purchase of a new excavator.
(d) What factors might encourage the business to buy an excavator outright?

**Question 4**
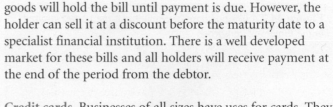

unit trusts and issuing houses (merchant banks) are some of the institutions which trade in shares.

**Banks and other financial institutions**  The money market is dominated by the major commercial banks, such as the NatWest or the HSBC. They allow payments to be made through the cheque system and deal in short term loans. Savings banks and finance corporations also deal in short term funds. Building societies also provide a source of finance. They have tended to specialise in long term loans for the purchase of land and property.

At the heart of this highly complex market system is the **Bank of England**. This plays a role in controlling the amount of money loaned and interest rates (☞ unit 97).

In recent years many of the above institutions have changed in nature. Due to competition, changes in legislation and mergers there has been a great deal of diversification. In particular, there is now little real difference between the role of a building society and that of a bank.

**The Alternative Investment Market and OFEX**  In June 1995 the Alternative Investment Market was established. Its purpose was to give small, young and growing companies the chance to raise capital and trade their shares more widely, without the cost of a full stock market listing. In order to join the market, a nominated adviser must be appointed, such as a stockbroker, banker or lawyer. The adviser must supervise the admission procedure and be responsible for ensuring that the company complies with AIM regulations. The admission procedure takes three months. The cost of a listing is about £100,000.  Another market called OFEX was set up by J.P. Jenkins, the specialist market-maker in small company shares. It is not regulated by the stock exchange, but only stock exchange member firms can deal directly on OFEX. OFEX offers a market place in the shares of unlisted companies that have no interest in joining AIM. Two of Britain's biggest private companies, Weetabix and National Parking Corporation, both feature on OFEX. Also, OFEX acts as a 'feeder' to AIM because flotation and other costs are less at the initial stages.

# *The choice of the source of finance*

A number of factors are important when choosing between alternative sources of finance.

**Cost**  Businesses obviously prefer sources which are less expensive, both in terms of interest payments and administration costs. For example, share issues can carry high administration costs while the interest payments on bank overdrafts tend to be relatively low.

**Use of funds**  When a company undertakes heavy capital expenditure, it is usually funded by a long term source of finance. For example, the building of a new plant may be financed by a share issue or a mortgage. Revenue expenditure

tends to be financed by short term sources. For example, the purchase of a large amount of raw materials may be funded by trade credit or a bank overdraft.

**Status and size**  Sole traders, which tend to be small, are limited in their choices of finance. For example, long term sources may be mortgages and perhaps the introduction of some personal capital. Public and private limited companies can usually obtain finance from many different sources. In addition, due to their size and added security, they can often demand lower interest rates from lenders. There are significant economies of scale (☞ unit 81) in raising finance.

**Financial situation**  The financial situation of businesses is constantly changing. When a business is in a poor financial situation, it finds that lenders are more reluctant to offer finance. At the same time, the cost of borrowing rises. Financial institutions are more willing to lend to secure businesses which have **collateral** (assets which provide security for loans). Third World Countries which are desperate to borrow money to fund development are forced to pay very high rates indeed.

**Gearing**  GEARING is the relationship between the loan capital and share capital of a business (☞ unit 56). A company is said to be **high geared** if it has a large proportion of loan capital to share capital. A **low geared** company has a relatively small amount of loan capital. For example, two companies may each have total capital of £45 million. If the first has loan capital of £40 million and share capital of only £5 million it is high geared. The other company may have share capital of £30 million and loan capital of £15 million. It is relatively low geared.

The gearing of a company might influence its finance. If a business is high geared, it may be reluctant to raise even more finance by borrowing. It may choose to issue more shares instead, rather than increasing the interest to be paid on loans.

There are several ways of measuring gearing. One way is to look at the relationship between loans and equity.

$$\text{Gearing ratio} = \frac{\text{Loans}}{\text{Equity}} \times 100$$

**Table 44.2** *Advantages and disadvantages of being high geared and low geared*

| | Advantages | Disadvantages |
|---|---|---|
| Low geared | The burden of loan repayments is reduced. The need for regular interest payments is reduced. Volatile interest rates are less of a threat. | Dividend payments have to be met indefinitely. Ownership of the company will be diluted. Dividends are paid after tax. |
| High geared | The interest on loans can be offset against tax. Ownership is not diluted. Once loans have been repaid the company's debt is much reduced. | Interest payments must be met. Interest rates can change, which causes uncertainty. Loans must be repaid and may be a burden, increasing the risk of insolvency. |

If the ratio is less than 50 per cent the company is said to be low geared. This means that the majority of a business capital is likely to be raised from shareholders. Table 44.2 shows the advantages and disadvantages of being low or high geared.

## Capital structure

The CAPITAL STRUCTURE of a business refers to the different sources of funds a business has used. Capital structures can vary considerably depending on the type of business. For example:

- sole traders will not have any share capital in their capital structure;
- firms which have funded expansion by reinvesting profits may not show any long term loan capital in their capital structure;
- debt laden companies may have large amounts of loan capital in their capital structure.

## Sources of finance and the balance sheet

Unit 43 showed how a balance sheet is produced. The liabilities 'side' shows the debts of the company, ie the money owed to others. It is made up of:

- capital – money introduced by the owners of the company;
- other liabilities – money owed to people and institutions other than the owners, such as a bank.

It was also stated that these are the sources of funds used by the business, for example to buy assets. The liabilities side is divided into three sections – capital and reserves, long term liabilities and current liabilities.

**Capital and reserves** Capital is the amount of money owed by the business to the owners. If all the company's assets were sold and the liabilities paid off, any money remaining would belong to the owners. Initially, capital represents the amount of money used to start a business.

During the life of a business the amount of capital changes. It will increase if the owners introduce money or if profits are retained. If the owners withdraw money from the firm or a loss is made then the capital of the business will fall. Because of this, capital is known as an **accumulated fund**. Capital is not physical in nature, and the term is used differently by business personnel and economists. To the accountant, capital is the difference between assets and liabilities.

$$\text{Capital} = \text{total assets} - \text{total liabilities}$$

If there is negative capital, where liabilities are greater than assets, then the firm is said to be INSOLVENT. In this situation it is illegal for the firm to continue trading. **Working capital** or circulating capital, is the amount of money a business needs to fund day to day trading. This could be payment of wages and energy costs or the purchase of components. Unit 48 shows how a business calculates it

working capital. Here we can say:

$$\text{Working capital} = \text{current assets} - \text{current liabilities}$$

In the case of sole trader or a partnership, capital might be introduced from personal savings or a loan. For a public limited company, the main source of capital is from the sale of **ordinary shares**, ie share capital. The total value of **issued share capital** is shown in the **shareholders' funds**. This is the money raised from the sale of shares. It is calculated by multiplying the number of shares sold by the price at which they were originally sold, ie the nominal value. In the notes to the accounts the **authorised share capital** will be stated. This is the maximum amount of share capital that shareholders want the company to raise. The authorised share capital is often larger than the issued share capital, but never smaller, as companies keep their options open to issue more shares later. For tax reasons preference shares are much less popular in today's business.

Reserves are shareholders' funds which have been built up over the life of the company. Three kinds are shown in the balance sheet.

- Share premiums. If a company issues shares, and the price they charge is higher than the nominal value, the share premium will be the difference. For example, if a 25p share is issued at 40p, the share premium is 15p. Dividends cannot be declared by the business as a result of such premiums.
- Revaluations. At times, particularly during periods of high inflation, some of the company's assets increase in value. If the values are updated on the asset side of the balance sheet then it is necessary to make an equal adjustment on the liabilities side. The entry is recorded under the heading of revaluation. It is a reserve because the benefit of any increase in asset values will be enjoyed by the owners of the company.
- Retained profits. The directors always retain a part of the company's profits as a precaution or to finance new business activities. When profits are not paid as dividends they are retained in reserve.

**Long term liabilities** Long term loans over a year must be repaid by the company and are called long term liabilities. The most common listed in company balance sheets are debentures and mortgages.

**Current liabilities** Current liabilities are those short term financial debts which must be repaid within one year.

- Trade creditors. This is when goods are purchased from suppliers and paid for at a later date. Another current liability which is very similar is an accrued charge. Certain expenses occur from day to day, but are only invoiced periodically. For example, most firms use electricity every day but are billed only four times a year. If at the end of a trading year a bill has not been received, accountants will estimate the charge for the electricity used and record it in

the balance sheet as an accrued charge.
- Bank loans and overdrafts. Loans which are repayable within twelve months are classed as current liabilities. In addition, even if bank overdrafts last for more than a year, because they are repayable 'on demand' they are shown as current liabilities.
- Taxation. Most firms pay tax at the latest possible date. When a company has been notified by the Inland Revenue,

the amount owed to them is shown in the balance sheet as a current liability.
- Dividends payable. Once a dividend has been declared it has to be approved at the Annual General Meeting by the shareholders. It is assumed that the proposed dividend will be approved and because it will be paid shortly after it is listed as a current liability.

## Knowledge

1. Why do businesses need to raise finance?
2. State the internal sources of finance.
3. What is the difference between ordinary, preference and deferred shares?
4. State the advantages to a business of a bank overdraft compared with a bank loan.
5. What is the difference between a finance lease and an operating lease?
6. What is the function of financial intermediaries?
7. Describe the functions of a stock exchange.
8. What factors affect the choice of source of finance?
9. 'Capital structures can vary depending on the type of business.' Explain this statement with an example.

## key terms

**Authorised share capital** - the maximum amount which can be legally raised.
**Capital expenditure** - spending on business resources which can be used repeatedly over a period of time.
**Capital structure** - the way in which funds are raised by a business.
**Capital gain** - the profit made by selling a share for more than it was bought for.
**Equities** - another name for an ordinary share.
**Finance houses** - a specialist institutions which provide funds for hire purchase agreements.
**Gearing** - the relationship between funds raised from loans and from issuing shares.
**Insolvency** - where a company does not have enough assets to meet its liabilities. An inability to meet debts.
**Issuing house** - any institution which deals with the sale of new shares.
**Issued share capital** - amount of current share capital

arising from the sale of shares.
**Lease** - a contract to acquire the use of resources such as property or equipment.
**Permanent capital** - share capital which is never repaid by the company.
**Revenue expenditure** - spending on business resources which have already been consumed or will be very shortly.
**Sale and leaseback** - the practice of selling assets, such as property or machinery, and leasing them back from the buyer.
**Share capital** - money introduced into the business through the sale of shares.
**Stock market** - a special share market, usually where second hand shares can be traded.
**Venture capitalists** - providers of funds for small or medium sized companies that may be considered too risky by other investors.

# Case study Karr Associates

Karr Associates organises trips, visits and events for companies that want to entertain clients. Clients would be taken to see high profile sporting events, such as race meetings and international cricket, football and rugby matches. Karr Associates was also getting an increasing number of inquiries for hospitality at Premier League football stadiums. By 2004 the business was well established. But Seth Karr, the founder, felt that he needed a website and brochures to promote the business to more lucrative clients. Seth estimated that the total cost would be £15,000, mainly because he would have to outsource the jobs to specialists. He would need to meet the cost of:

● someone to write the brochure;
● an IT expert to design and run the website;
● a photographer to take high quality photographs at some of the events that he organised;
● a printer to produce the brochure;
● a mailing company to distribute the brochure to potential clients.

In addition to this promotion, Seth felt that the company's office should reflect the quality shown in the brochure. He could hardly negotiate deals for glamorous corporate hospitality in his current office above a carpet shop. Seth found a number of possible new offices, but they were far more expensive than he anticipated. Also, most landlords wanted tenants to sign fairly long term lease agreements with a six month payment up front. To meet this payment and furnish the office would cost £20,000.

Seth knew that the finance for this new approach would have to come from outside the business. All the retained profits had been used up. Karr Associates didn't really own anything to sell. Seth had accounts to show that the business was profitable, but had very little collateral. After a meeting with his accountant Seth looked again at his finance options.

1. A mortgage, using his own apartment as security.
2. An unsecured bank loan.
3. Set up a limited company and sell shares to members of the family.
4. Attract a business angel to invest in the company.

Apart from the unsecured bank loan, which Seth favoured, all the options had their disadvantages. He decided to go for an unsecured bank loan on the grounds that the business was very profitable, very

Figure 44.3 *Karr Associates, profit 1998-2003*

low geared and was capable of repayment within four years. He spent two weeks writing a detailed business plan, arranged a meeting with the bank manager, and hoped that his powers of persuasion would do the trick. Figure 43.3 shows the profit made by Karr Associates in the last five years.

(a) Explain what is meant by an unsecured bank loan. (4 marks)

(b) Calculate the monthly payments Karr Associates would have to make to the bank if the unsecured loan was granted at a rate of 8 per cent a year, over 4 years. Include both the interest and the capital sum of £35,000. (6 marks)

(c) Discuss the factors that might have led Seth and his accountant to arrive at the finance options listed above. (10 marks)

(d) Analyse the disadvantages of using (i) a mortgage secured on the apartment (ii) a business angel to raise the £35,000. (10 marks)

(e) Discuss whether or not the bank manager is likely to grant Karr Associates an unsecured loan. (10 marks)

## Assets and the balance sheet

Assets are the **resources** used by business. A company will **use** the funds it earns to purchase assets which add value to a company. Most assets are physical in nature and are used in production. However, there are some, such as goodwill, which do not fall into this category, although they still add value. They are called intangible assets because they are non-physical. One of the functions of a balance sheet (☞ unit 43) is to provide a summary of all business assets and their values. Assets are usually valued at their original cost, less a deduction for depreciation. This is to take into account that they wear out over a period of time and are worth less (☞ unit 49).

## Fixed assets

Resources with a life span of more than one year are called **fixed assets** (☞ unit 45). Fixed assets, such as machinery, can be used again and again until they wear out. Some fixed assets like land and property do not depreciate, although they have to be repaired. In the balance sheet, fixed assets are divided into **tangible**, **intangible** and **financial** assets. Each of these are dealt with in detail in the following sections.

## Tangible assets

TANGIBLE ASSETS are physical assets that can be touched. The most long term or the least **liquid** of these assets (the most difficult to turn into cash) appear at the top of the list of fixed assets on the balance sheet. For a farmer or a small manufacturing company these are likely to be the most important and largest fixed assets, if owned.

Land and property can either be **freehold** or **leasehold**. Freehold property is owned outright by the business. It is valued on the balance sheet at its original cost, less depreciation. In the past, inflation has resulted in soaring property prices. Accountants have advised many companies to revalue their land and property so that the accounts reflect more accurately a 'true and fair view' of the company. When assets are revalued in this way on the assets side of the balance sheet, an equivalent entry must be made on the liabilities side in reserves to balance the accounts.

Leasehold land and property is rented from an owner and is a company asset. Any capital amount paid for the lease appears separately as 'leasehold property'. This amount is **written off** (☞ unit 49) over the period of the lease. This means the value of the lease is reduced by an amount each year as it depreciates.

Fixed assets which are not land or property are referred to as plant, machinery and equipment. Again, they are valued at cost less depreciation. Large companies often have vast amounts of these assets. The balance sheet will, in this case, not list separate assets, but give only a total.

## Intangible assets

Some fixed assets are not tangible, but are still valuable, income-generating resources. These are INTANGIBLE ASSETS.

**Goodwill** Over many years of trading companies build up goodwill. They may have gained a good reputation, which means that customers will use their services or purchase their products. If the company is to be sold in the future, some value needs to be placed on this goodwill and included in the purchase price. From an accountant's point of view, goodwill is equal to the amount by which the purchase price of a business exceeds the **net assets** (total assets - total liabilities).

Take the example of Amanda Storey, a young, newly qualified accountant, who decides to set up in business. She considers renting an office, advertising her services in the local press and distributing business cards. However, she is approached by Geoff Horrocks, an accountant who is considering retirement. Clearly it would pay Amanda to buy Geoff's list of established clients. The agreed price would represent goodwill.

According to accounting convention (☞ unit 51) the value of **purchased** goodwill should be shown on the balance sheet and then depreciated (or amortised) over its expected useful economic life. The reason for this is that goodwill eventually wears off unless there is new investment to maintain or improve customer relations. In the case of businesses that have not been sold, the value of goodwill is omitted from the balance sheet. Therefore any goodwill, or other intangible assets shown on the balance sheet, means that they have been purchased.

**Patents, copyrights and trademarks** If a company or an individual invents and develops a unique product, a patent (☞ unit 87) can be obtained from the patent office. This is a licence which prevents other firms from copying the product. Patents have been granted in the past for products as diverse as cats eyes in 1935 and Polaroid cameras in 1946.

Copyright prevents the re-use of published works, such as books, plays, films and music without the author's consent. Michael Jackson allegedly paid £48 million for a back catalogue of 250 Beatles' songs, out-bidding former Beatle Paul McCartney. Substantial fees are paid to copyright owners of music used in TV advertisements. Occasionally, certain magazines will allow a part of their publication to be used free of charge. Trademarks generally signify a manufacturer's name. The right to sell another company's products may have to be registered if they carry a trademark and a fee may be charged.

**Research and development** Normally research and development (R&D) costs are classified as revenue expenditure (☞ unit 44). However, if a project is expected to earn a substantial income in the future, its costs may be recorded as capital expenditure and included as an intangible asset in the balance sheet. The costs are written off over the period when income is generated.

**Brand names** Many companies enjoy successful brand names. Recently, some of these companies have debated the inclusion of these intangible assets in the balance sheet because they generate income for a lengthy period of time in some cases. This means that the amount a successful brand name is estimated to be worth should be included as an intangible asset on the balance sheet, so that the true value of a company's assets is made clear.

When an intangible asset is written off it is described as **amortisation** rather than depreciation.

## Financial assets

These are often called **investments** in the balance sheet. They usually refer to shares held in other companies. If the shareholding in a particular company is more than 50 per cent then that company is classified as a **subsidiary**. If the holding is between 20 per cent and 50 per cent then the company is described as an **associated company**. Finally, any holdings of less than 20 per cent are called **trade investments**.

There is a number of motives for holding shares in other companies. These are shown in Figure 45.1. Some companies hold shares to earn income. **Holding companies** (☞ unit 6) such as Kingfisher, for example, specialise in buying and controlling other companies. In some cases, businesses are bought, broken up, and parts sold at a profit. This activity has

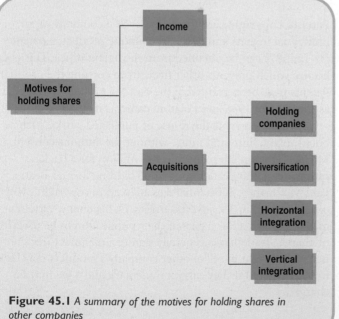

**Figure 45.1** *A summary of the motives for holding shares in other companies*

been described as **asset stripping**.

Another motive for holding shares is to diversify in order to reduce risk. Companies also buy firms in the same line of business to exploit economies of scale, ie horizontal integration (☞ unit 81). They may also seek to buy out their suppliers or distribution networks, ie vertical integration.

Finally, other financial investments might include government bonds or deposits of foreign currency. All financial assets are listed at cost in the balance sheet.

## Current assets

Short term assets which can be changed into cash within one year are called **current assets** (☞ unit 43). There is a number of common current assets.

**Stocks** Most businesses hold stocks of finished goods. Stocks are classed as current assets because the business would hope to sell them within twelve months. The quantity of stocks held by a company will depend on the nature of the company.

**Work-in-progress** is also classified as stock. It represents

---

Reg Vardy operates 78 new car dealerships of which 17 represent specialist makes and models. The remaining dealerships operate as franchises. The company also has a contract hire business, Vardy Contract Motoring. In 2003 Reg Vardy's profit before tax rose 19 per cent to £38.8 million. Of this, £3.95 million was achieved from the sale of property and receipts of goodwill on the disposal of businesses. During 2003 the total market for new cars in the UK was expected to be 2.45 million, possibly the largest on record. However, due to over-supply in the market, prices have been depressed. Nevertheless Reg Vardy has performed well and expected to do even better in 2004.

Source: adapted from Reg Vardy, *Annual Report & Accounts, 2003*.

**Table 45.1** *An extract from Reg Vardy balance sheet, 2003*

|  | 2003 | 2002 |
|---|---|---|
|  | £000 | £000 |
| **Fixed assets** |  |  |
| Intangible assets (goodwill) | 1,324 | 1,278 |
| Tangible assets | 154,788 | 162,024 |
| Investments | 3,155 | 3,155 |
|  | 159,267 | 166,457 |

(a) Give four possible examples of tangible assets that Reg Vardy might own.
(b) Some of Reg Vardy's profit has been generated from goodwill. Explain what is meant by goodwill and how this has arisen.

partly finished goods, eg half built properties. We also include stocks of raw materials and components in current assets. The business would expect to change them into finished goods which would then be sold, hopefully within a year.

**Debtors** In some lines of business, when a sale is made, it is common to receive payment at a later date. Any amounts owing by these customers at the end of the financial year are listed as **debtors** in the balance sheet. In order to speed up the payment of bills some firms offer cash discounts. In addition, debt factors offer a debt collecting service.

Related to debtors is another current asset - **prepayments**. A prepayment is a sum, such as insurance, rent or uniform business rate, which is paid in advance. At the end of the financial year any service which has been paid for but not fully consumed is listed in the balance sheet as a prepayment.

**Cash at bank** Most businesses deposit their takings in a bank. From the bank account various business expenses are paid for. If the bank balance is positive at the end of the trading year the amount will be shown as a current asset in the balance sheet.

**Cash in hand** Many businesses have cash on their premises. This is often called **petty cash**. Cash is used to pay for small or unexpected transactions, eg the purchase of toilet paper.

Together, cash at bank and cash in hand represent the firm's most **liquid resources**. Businesses need to hold just the right amount of cash. Too much cash means business opportunities are being wasted as the money could be invested in other assets. Too little cash may prevent the business from making urgent purchases. Cash management is dealt with in more detail in unit 46.

**Investments** Some investments held by businesses may be short term. They may include shares in other companies, bonds or deposit accounts. If it is possible to convert these investments into cash within 12 months they are listed as investments under current assets.

## Liquidity

**Liquidity** (☞ unit 48) refers to the speed or ease with which assets can be converted into cash without suffering any capital loss. For example, a house is an illiquid asset. It could be sold for cash for, say, £100, but the owner would be likely to lose money. In the balance sheet the least liquid assets (fixed assets) are listed at the top and the most liquid (current assets) are placed at the bottom.

Fixed assets like land and buildings tend to be very illiquid. It can sometimes take a long time to sell such assets. Possibly the most illiquid of all assets is a highly specialised item of machinery, ie a machine which has been especially made for a company. This type of capital good will prove very difficult to sell since demand will be limited.

Some fixed assets may be much easier to sell and are

therefore more liquid. Vehicles, non-specialised machinery like a cement mixer or a JCB, and standard tools and equipment, which have a variety of uses, are all examples.

The least liquid of the current assets is stock. Stocks of finished goods are expected to be sold, but business fortunes change and sales can never be guaranteed. The liquidity of raw material stocks can vary. Non-specialised materials like coal will be more liquid than specialised components since they are easier to sell. Debtors are more liquid than stocks because goods have been sold and the business is legally entitled to payment. However, money has not yet been

Bellway plc is a construction company with 14 regional house building divisions. In 2002 the company sold 6,044 homes across all 14 divisions. Despite the total home production in the UK falling to its lowest level for 54 years, Bellway has, since 1992, trebled the number of homes sold and quadrupled its market share. It was one of the first companies to embrace the trend towards inner city living. This has resulted in apartment schemes being developed in every division, representing 35 per cent of the total homes sold. Profit before tax rose from £101.5 million to £125.3 million in 2002.

Source: adapted from Bellway, *Annual Report & Accounts, 2002.*

**Table 45.2** *Current assets and an analysis of stocks for Bellway, 2002*

|  | 2002 £000 | 2001 £000 |
| --- | --- | --- |
| **Current assets** | | |
| Stocks | 737,262 | 644,421 |
| Debtors | 21,522 | 21,491 |
| Cash at bank and in hand | 73,381 | 4,059 |

|  | 2002 £000 | 2001 £000 |
| --- | --- | --- |
| Work in progress and stocks | 736,009 | 639,572 |
| Grants | (3,348) | (8,483) |
| Payments on account | (19,548) | (9,387) |
|  | 713,113 | 621,702 |
| Showhomes | 17,723 | 14,483 |
| Part exchange properties | 6,426 | 8,236 |
|  | 737,262 | 644,421 |

(a) Using this case as an example, explain what is meant by work-in-progress and why it is classified as a current asset.

(b) Calculate the percentage change in the value of stocks between 2001 and 2002 and suggest a reason for the change.

**Question2**

Aled Thomas owns a sheep farm in Gwent. The farm has been in the family for 112 years. It consists of 2,000 acres of hill farmland, a large five bedroomed farmhouse, some outbuildings, one tractor and other tools and equipment. The farm has struggled to generate cash in recent years so Aled started to run a bed and breakfast operation in 2001. This has helped to improve the liquidity of the business.

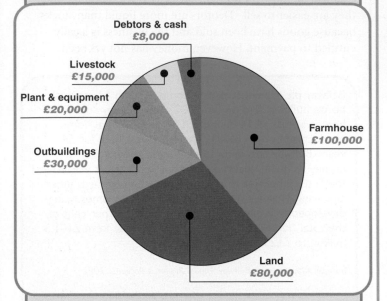

**Debtors & cash £8,000**

**Livestock £15,000**

**Plant & equipment £20,000**

**Outbuildings £30,000**

**Farmhouse £100,000**

**Land £80,000**

**Figure 45.2** *Asset structure of Aled Thomas's farm*

(a) Farmers are sometimes described as 'asset rich and cash poor'. Using examples from the case, explain what you think this means.
(b) How do you think the bed and breakfast operation improved the liquidity of the business?

# Question3

received so it cannot be spent. In addition, there are times when firms cannot pay and so the debt has to be written off (known as bad debts).

Cash at the bank and cash in hand are obviously the most liquid assets of all.

## Asset structure

The ASSET STRUCTURE of a business refers to the amount of capital employed in each category of asset. Asset structures will vary according to the nature of the industry in which a business is competing. Manufacturing companies will tend to have a large amount of capital tied up in plant, machinery and equipment. Construction firms will have a significant amount of work-in-progress. Businesses which face seasonal demand may hold large stocks of finished goods at particular times of the year. In the retail trade, public houses and restaurants will have very few debtors, or even none.

A profit maximising company will want to purchase those assets which yield the greatest return. Fixed assets are the productive assets of a business, so firms will want to invest as much of their capital as possible in these. However, some capital must be kept in current assets to fund day to day expenditure. It is not possible to conduct business activity without current assets. Some firms may exist with very little capital employed in fixed assets. Retailers often have a large proportion of current assets if they rent premises (stock in particular).

## Company law and the balance sheet

According to the **1948** and the **1967 Companies Acts** the following information should be included in the balance sheet.
- The authorised and issued share capital.
- The amount of share premium.
- The amount of reserves.
- Details of debentures, mortgages, long term loans, short term loans, overdrafts, trade creditors, proposed dividends, taxation due and amounts due to subsidiaries.
- The separation of fixed and current assets.
- The method of valuation of fixed assets.
- The aggregate amounts provided for depreciation of fixed assets.
- Values of trade investments and shares in subsidiaries and any amounts due from subsidiaries.
- Details of current assets.
- The corresponding figures for the end of the previous year should be given.

These legal requirements are attempts to make company accounts standard and help protect the interests of shareholders. Much of the legislation is designed to clarify certain financial information so that the readers of accounts are not misled. The legislation does not place any unnecessary financial or administrative burden on the company and does not affect its decision making.

**Table 45.3** *Assets and liabilities of Westwood Frozen Foods plc*

| | (£000) |
|---|---|
| Cash at bank and in hand | 40 |
| Share capital | 4,400 |
| Warehouse | 2,500 |
| Taxation | 2,410 |
| Other reserves | 1,250 |
| Debentures | 2,000 |
| Debtors | 9,480 |
| Stock | 6,410 |
| Trade creditors | 8,120 |
| Bank overdraft | 6,480 |
| Retained profit | 5,920 |
| Equipment | 5,810 |
| Vehicles | 3,240 |
| Investments | 3,100 |

Westwood Frozen Foods plc is a frozen food wholesaler. It has a large depot just outside London and distributes frozen food to small and medium sized retailers, hotels and other businesses in the catering industry. The company also owns Seafood Ltd, a subsidiary which supplies a wide range of frozen sea food. Table 45.3 shows some financial information about the assets and liabilities which would be included in the company's balance sheet for the year ending 31.5.2003.

(a) Identify the (i) fixed assets and (ii) current assets.
(b) Draw pie charts to show: (i) the relative values of fixed assets; (ii) the relative values of current assets; (iii) the relative values of fixed to current assets; (iv) the relative values of assets to each other.
(c) Explain why this type of business may have such an asset structure.

**Question 4**

# key terms

## Knowledge ...Knowledge...Knowledge...Knowledge...Knowledge...Know

1. What is the difference between tangible and intangible assets?
2. How is it possible to calculate the value of goodwill?
3. Distinguish between a subsidiary, an associated company and a trade investment.
4. What is meant by asset stripping?
5. What is the difference between debtors and prepayments?
6. What is the difference between a liquid and an illiquid asset?
7. Why is a specialised machine an illiquid asset?
8. What is the main determinant of a firm's asset structure?

# Case study Oxford Biomedica and Air

## Oxford BioMedica

Oxford BioMedica specialises in the development of novel therapeutics for the treatment of cancer, neurodegenerative diseases and other disorders. During 2002 the company progressed from being a research-orientated company to a mid-stage product development company, with successful trials being completed for its products TroVax and MetXia.

In 2002 the biotechnology industry continued to suffer from the general downturn in the market, with many companies running short of liquid resources. Oxford BioMedica saw its share price fall along with many others in the industry.

However, through careful management the company was able to extend the cash life of the business by almost a year and bring its products closer to the market. Oxford BioMedica plans to use partners in the pharmaceuticals industry to produce and market its products.

In 2002 the company's turnover was just £173,000. It made a loss for the year of £11.66 million. This is typical of companies in this industry which research for long periods and may not sell products until they are trialled and developed. Figure 45.3 shows the asset structure of the business.

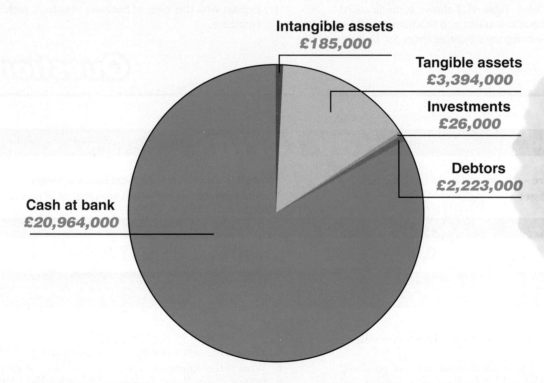

**Figure 45.3** *Asset structure, 2002*
Source: adapted from Oxford BioMedica, *Annual Report and Accounts*, 2002.

### Air music & media group plc

Air music & media group plc was founded in 1995, when Air music & media began trading with USA and European customers. The group set up two record labels through its subsidiary, Going For A Song Ltd, between 1997 and 2000 and has access to around 100,000 music tracks.

Air's core activities are the development and acquisition of music copyrights, the licensing of third party music copyrights and the exploitation of those rights through the production and sale of budget priced audio compact discs and cassettes. In 2002, sales were mainly to music wholesalers or distributors.

Air's products cover a broad spectrum of music genres. Collectively the products could be referred to as middle of the road or easy listening. Most of the products comprise music by well known artists or compilations such as 50s, 60s, 70s and 80s music and rock 'n' roll, country, jazz, blues, ambient, new age and world music. The products retail at below £5 in the UK. This is significantly different to chart or fashion-led music products, which typically retail at £15. In 2002 Air turned over £4.374 million and made a profit after tax of £522,859. Figure 45.4 shows the asset structure of the group in 2002.

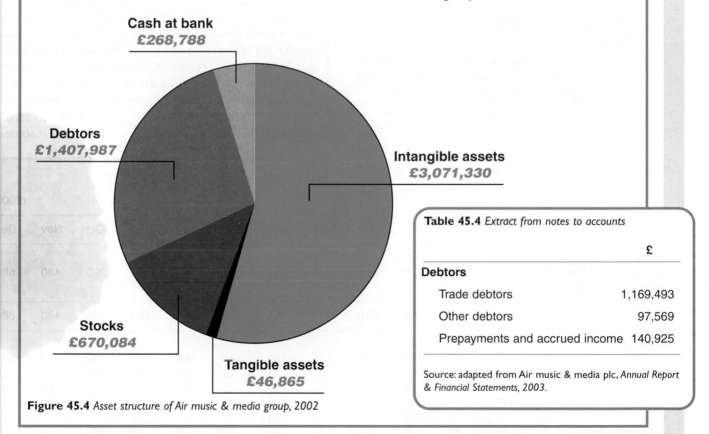

Cash at bank
£268,788

Debtors
£1,407,987

Intangible assets
£3,071,330

Stocks
£670,084

Tangible assets
£46,865

**Table 45.4** *Extract from notes to accounts*

|  | £ |
| --- | --- |
| **Debtors** | |
| Trade debtors | 1,169,493 |
| Other debtors | 97,569 |
| Prepayments and accrued income | 140,925 |

Source: adapted from Air music & media plc, *Annual Report & Financial Statements, 2003.*

**Figure 45.4** *Asset structure of Air music & media group, 2002*

(a) An analysis of Air's debtors is shown in Table 45.4. Explain the difference between trade debtors and prepayments for the company. (6 marks)

(b) The investments for Oxford BioMedica are shares in subsidiaries. Explain what this means. (6 marks)

(c) Calculate the proportion of total assets which are current assets for each company. (8 marks)

(d) Assess the liquidity of each company. (8 marks)

(e) Account for the differences in the asset structures of Air and Oxford BioMedica. (12 marks)

## The importance of cash

Cash is the most LIQUID of all business assets. A business's cash is the notes and coins it keeps on the premises and any money it has in the bank, for example. Cash is part of, but not the same as, working capital (☞ unit 48). Working capital contains other assets, such as money owed by debtors, which are not immediately available if a business needs to pay bills, for example.

Why is cash so important to a business? Without cash, it would cease to exist. There is a number of reasons why firms fail. The most common tend to be:

- lack of sales;
- inadequate profit margins;
- poor choice of location;
- reliance on too small a customer base;
- poor management of working capital;
- poor cash flow.

According to a Confederation of British Industry (CBI) survey, 21 per cent of business failures are due to poor cash flow or a lack of working capital. Even when trading conditions are good, businesses can fail. Many of these businesses may offer good products for which there was

**Figure 46.1** *Continuous cash flow into and out of a business organisation*

some demand. They have the potential to be profitable and yet still went into RECEIVERSHIP (☞ unit 106). Probably the most likely cause of this is that they ran out of cash.

The role of cash in a business is shown in Figure 46.1 which shows a simple CASH FLOW CYCLE. This is the continuous movement of cash into and out of a business. Initially, cash is used to buy or hire resources. These resources are converted into goods or services which are then sold to customers in exchange for cash. Some of the money from sales will be used to finance further production. In a successful business, this flow of cash is endless. If this flow of cash ceases at some stage

**Table 46.1** *Cash flow forecast statement for Fishman's Ltd*

(£000s)

| | Jan | Feb | Mar | Apr | May | Jun | Jul | Aug | Sep | Oct | Nov | Dec |
|---|---|---|---|---|---|---|---|---|---|---|---|---|
| **Receipts** | | | | | | | | | | | | |
| Cash sales | 451 | 360 | 399 | 410 | 490 | 464 | 452 | 340 | 450 | 390 | 480 | 680 |
| Capital introduced | | | | | | | | | 300 | | | |
| **Total receipts** | 451 | 360 | 399 | 410 | 490 | 464 | 452 | 340 | 750 | 390 | 480 | 680 |
| **Payments** | | | | | | | | | | | | |
| Goods for resale | 150 | 180 | 150 | 180 | 150 | 180 | 150 | 180 | 150 | 180 | 220 | 250 |
| Leasing charges | 20 | 20 | 20 | 20 | 20 | 20 | 20 | 20 | 20 | 20 | 20 | 20 |
| Motor expenses | 40 | 40 | 40 | 40 | 40 | 40 | 40 | 40 | 40 | 40 | 40 | 40 |
| Wages | 100 | 100 | 100 | 100 | 100 | 100 | 100 | 105 | 105 | 105 | 125 | 125 |
| VAT | | | 126 | | | 189 | | | 187 | | | 198 |
| Loan repayments | 35 | 35 | 35 | 35 | 35 | 35 | 35 | 35 | 35 | 35 | 35 | 35 |
| Telephone | | 11 | | | 12 | | | 12 | | | 14 | |
| Miscellaneous | 20 | 20 | 20 | 20 | 20 | 20 | 20 | 20 | 20 | 20 | 20 | 20 |
| **Total payments** | 365 | 406 | 491 | 395 | 377 | 584 | 365 | 412 | 557 | 400 | 474 | 688 |
| **Net cash flow** | 86 | (46) | (92) | 15 | 113 | (120) | 87 | (72) | 193 | (10) | 6 | (8) |
| **Opening balance** | 11 | 97 | 51 | (41) | (26) | 87 | (33) | 54 | (18) | 175 | 165 | 171 |
| **Closing balance** | 97 | 51 | (41) | (26) | 87 | (33) | 54 | (18) | 175 | 165 | 171 | 163 |

Brackets show minus figures.

then the business will be unlikely to continue.

## Controlling cash flow

It is important that a business continually monitors and controls its cash flow. It must ensure that it has enough cash for its immediate spending. However, it should avoid holding too much cash because cash is an unproductive asset. Holding cash means that the business might lose out on the profit from investing the cash. A business will have more effective control over its cash flow if it:

● keeps up to date business records;
● always plans ahead, for example by producing accurate cash flow forecasts;
● operates an efficient credit control system which prevents slow or late payment.

The need to keep up to date records of business transactions is very important. The quality of decision making is better if accurate information is available when choosing between different courses of action. Problems can arise if decisions are based on inadequate or inaccurate information. For example, say a business fails to record that a £20,000 payment has been made to a supplier. A manager may go ahead with the purchase of a new machine costing £30,000 believing that the firm's cash position is better than it actually is. The business may not have enough money in the bank to cover a cheque given in payment.

Advances in information technology have enabled businesses to keep more up to date records and access information very quickly. However, mistakes can still occur if computer operators fail to input information correctly. Methods of improving cash flow are dealt with in unit 48, which considers how a business might improve its liquidity.

## Cash flow forecasting

Most businesses produce a regular CASH FLOW FORECAST. This lists all the likely receipts (**cash inflows**) and payments (**cash outflows**) over a future period of time. All the entries in the forecast are estimated because they have not occurred yet. The forecast shows the planned cash flow of the business month by month. Table 46.1 shows a twelve month cash flow forecast statement for Fishman's Ltd, a grocery wholesaler located in Ipswich.

What is predicted to happen to cash flow at Fishman's over the twelve month period?

**January** The company will have an opening cash balance of £11,000 in January. In January receipts are expected to be £451,000 and payments £365,000. This means that an extra £86,000 (£451,000 - £365,000) will be added in this month - a positive net cash flow. The closing balance should be £97,000 (£11,000 +£86,000).

**February** In February expected payments (£406,000) are

The **receipts** of the business are the monthly inflows of cash. For Fishman's, cash sales result from the sale of groceries to local retailers and other customers. The sales figures are probably based on the previous year's. In September the owners have introduced £300,000 of fresh capital to the business. The total amount of cash a business expects to receive each month is shown as total receipts. Some businesses sell goods on credit. If this is the case, the figures in the statement should show cash actually received in that month and not the value of goods sold.

**Payments** are the outflows from the business. Some payments are for the same regular amounts, such as leasing charges (£20,000) and loan repayments (£35,000). Other payments vary, such as purchases of goods for resale. Some payments such as telephone charges are made on a quarterly basis. It is also possible for payments to be annual such as accountancy fees. These do not appear for Fishman's, perhaps because they employ their own accountant. The total amount of cash a business expects to pay out each month is shown as total payments. If a business buys goods on credit, cash payments made to suppliers are included when they occur and not the value of goods received in a particular month.

**Net cash flow** for a month is found by subtracting total payments from total receipts. If receipts are greater than payments, net cash flow is positive. If payments are greater than receipts, net cash flow is negative - shown by brackets around a figure.

● The **opening balance** in January will be the value of December's closing balance in the previous year.
● The **closing balance** for a month is found by adding or subtracting the net cash flow for the month from the opening balance.
● The closing balance of one month becomes the opening balance of the next month. It can be positive or negative figure.

greater than expected receipts (£360,000). This means that there will be a negative net cash flow of £46,000 in February. However, the opening balance of £97,000 will cover this and the business will not have a cash flow problem. It ends the month with a positive closing balance of £51,000 (£97,000 - £46,000).

**March** In March payments again will be greater than receipts, giving a negative net cash flow of £92,000. However, this is now greater than the opening balance of £51,000. This means that the business faces a negative closing balance of £41,000 and will have a cash flow problem. It would have to find some way to finance this, perhaps by borrowing from a bank.

**March to May** The business will have cash flow problems in March and April, when it faces negative closing balances, even though in April receipts are greater than payments (a positive net cash flow). In May, however, the negative opening balance of £26,000 is outweighed by the positive net cash flow of £113,000. The business will have a positive closing balance of £87,000 and no cash flow problem.

**June to December** In June and August, but not July, the business would have cash flow problems. From September onwards, when there will be positive closing balances every month, there appear to be no cash flow problems. This is because the owners plan to introduce £300,000 into the business in September.

## Why do businesses prepare cash flow forecasts?

Businesses draw up cash flow forecast statements to help control and monitor cash flow in the business. There are certain advantages in using statements to control cash flow.

**Identifying the timing of cash shortages and surpluses** A forecast can help to identify in advance when a business might wish to borrow cash. At the bottom of the statement the monthly closing balances are shown clearly. This will help the reader to identify when a bank overdraft will be needed. For example, Table 46.1 showed that Fishman's would need to borrow money in March, April, June and August. In addition, if a large cash surplus is identified in a particular month, this might provide an opportunity to buy some new equipment, for example. A business should try to avoid being overdrawn at the bank because interest is charged. If certain payments can be delayed until cash is available, this will avoid unnecessary borrowing.

**Supporting applications for funding** When trying to raise finance, lenders often insist that businesses support their applications with documents showing business performance, outlook and solvency. A cash flow forecast will help to indicate the future outlook for the business. It is also common practice to produce a cash flow forecast statement in the planning stages of setting up a business.

---

Ella Sankey owns a launderette business in London. She leases premises and employs two local people on part time contracts. There are 14 washing machines, 6 dryers and 2 computers offering Internet services. The launderette is open from 7.00 am to 11.00 pm, but is only staffed between 10.00 am and 5.00 pm. Ella manages the business from home and can be contacted by mobile phone if there are problems. Her main task is to empty the machines each day and bank the cash. Revenue has fallen by 25 per cent in the last 18 months. The business lost student trade when washing machines were installed in the halls of residence. Ella has produced a six monthly cash flow forecast to monitor the cash position of the business, as shown in Table 46.2.

(a) Explain how Ella Sankey would calculate:
   (i)  total payments in July;
   (ii) net cash flow in July;
   (iii) the closing balance in July;
   (iv) the opening balance in August.
(b) Explain what is happening to the cash position of Ella's launderette business and suggest reasons why she might be worried about the future.

**Table 46.2** *Cash flow forecast for Ella Sankey's business, July-December 2003*

|  | July | Aug | Sept | Oct | Nov | Dec |
|---|---|---|---|---|---|---|
| **Receipts** | | | | | | |
| Cash | 3,464 | 3,556 | 3,647 | 3,588 | 3,612 | 3,541 |
| Sale of old machines | | | 450 | | | |
| Capital introduced | | | 2,500 | | | |
| Total receipts | 3,464 | 3,556 | 6,597 | 3,588 | 3,612 | 3,541 |
| **Payments** | | | | | | |
| Lease on premises | 1,000 | 1,000 | 1,000 | 1,000 | 1,000 | 1,000 |
| Wages | 1,200 | 1,200 | 1,200 | 1,200 | 1,200 | 2,000 |
| Electricity | | 986 | | | 1,098 | |
| New machines | | | 3,000 | | | |
| Water | | | 430 | | | 510 |
| Other expenses | 150 | 150 | 150 | 150 | 150 | 150 |
| Drawings | 1,000 | 1,000 | 1,000 | 1,000 | 1,000 | 1,000 |
| Total payments | 3,350 | 4,336 | 6,780 | 3,350 | 4,448 | 4,660 |
| **Net cash flow** | 114 | (780) | (183) | 238 | (836) | (1,119) |
| **Opening balance** | 1,004 | 1,118 | 338 | 155 | 393 | (443) |
| **Closing balance** | 1,118 | 338 | 155 | 393 | (443) | (1,562) |

(£)

**Question 1**

**Enhancing the planning process** Careful planning in business has become more important in recent years. This helps to clarify aims and improve performance. Producing a cash flow forecast is a key part of the planning process because it is a document concerned with the future.

**Monitoring cash flow** During and at the end of the financial year a business should make comparisons between the predicted figures in the cash flow forecast and those which actually occur. By doing this it can find out where problems have occurred. It could then try to identify possible reasons for any significant differences between the two sets of figures. For example, it might be that an overpayment was made. Constant monitoring in this way should allow a business to control its cash flow effectively.

## Improving forecasts

Cash flow forecasts may not be helpful if they are inaccurate. Very inaccurate forecasts could lead to businesses getting into trouble and running out of cash. How can a business improve the accuracy of its cash flow forecasts?

**Accurate data** A cash flow forecast is based on anticipated flows of cash into and out of the business. Some of these flows will be known for certain. For example, a business usually knows what some of its overheads will be next year,

such as rent, rates and insurance. Other costs such as wages may have been negotiated for the next year. Variable costs such as raw materials are may be more difficult to predict. This is because output might fluctuate unexpectedly or suppliers may change their prices.

Generally, cash outflows are easier to predict than cash inflows. Most of the cash coming into the business is from sales. It can sometimes be difficult to estimate what sales will be exactly in future. Some businesses have advanced orders, such firms in the holiday industry, which will help to improve accuracy. Others do market research, whilst many rely on projections based on the previous year's figures. When cash inflows and outflows are unknown it is better to overestimate costs and underestimate revenues. New businesses have particular problems when producing forecasts. This is because they have no past data on which to base projections. They also tend to underestimate costs and over estimate revenues.

**Biased forecasts** Businesses sometimes manipulate cash flow forecasts. For example, a business may overestimate cash inflows to improve the strength of the business on paper. It might do this if it was borrowing money from a bank. A manager may overestimate costs and underestimate sales so that credit can be taken when the real figures are better. If forecasts are biased they are not likely to be accurate.

---

Kieran Venkat runs an off-licence in the Manchester suburb of Rusholme. He has recently extended his premises into the property next door and is looking to acquire a wider range of stock. The cost of the extension has completely exhausted the business of its cash reserves and Kieran needs to borrow some money to buy stock. He needs to borrow £5,000 for nine months. In order to support his application for a bank loan he drew up the nine month cash flow forecast shown in Table 46.3. The forecast assumes that the loan has been granted and repayments are included.

(a) Calculate the following figures for Kieran's cash flow forecast.
　(i)　Cash sales and total receipts for October.
　(ii)　Total payments for August.
　(iii)　Closing balance for November.
　(iv)　Opening balance for January.
(b) As well as supporting his application for a bank loan, how else might this cash flow forecast help Kieran in running his business?

**Table 46.3** *Cash flow forecast statement for Kieran Venkat*

(£)

| | Jul | Aug | Sep | Oct | Nov | Dec | Jan | Feb | Mar |
|---|---|---|---|---|---|---|---|---|---|
| **Receipts** | | | | | | | | | |
| Cash sales | 3,800 | 4,000 | 5,000 | ? | 6,000 | 9,000 | 7,000 | 3,000 | 3,500 |
| Bank loan | 5,000 | | | | | | | | |
| Total receipts | 8,800 | 4,000 | 5,000 | ? | 6,000 | 9,000 | 7,000 | 3,000 | 3,500 |
| **Payments** | | | | | | | | | |
| Stock | 7,000 | 3,000 | 3,400 | 3,400 | 4,000 | 6,100 | 4,800 | 2,000 | 2,400 |
| Loan repayments | 620 | 620 | 620 | 620 | 620 | 620 | 620 | 620 | 620 |
| Casual labour | 200 | 200 | 200 | 200 | 200 | 400 | 200 | 200 | 200 |
| Miscellaneous costs | 100 | 100 | 100 | 100 | 100 | 100 | 100 | 100 | 100 |
| Drawings | 500 | 500 | 500 | 500 | 500 | 500 | 500 | 500 | 500 |
| Insurance | | | | 450 | | | | | |
| Advertising | 370 | | | | | | | | |
| Telephone | | | 170 | | | 200 | | | 210 |
| Total payments | 8,790 | ? | 4,990 | 5,270 | 5,420 | 7,920 | 6,220 | 3,420 | 4,030 |
| **Net cash flow** | 10 | (420) | 10 | (270) | 580 | 1,080 | 780 | (420) | (530) |
| **Opening balance** | (90) | (80) | (500) | (490) | (760) | (180) | ? | 1,680 | 1,260 |
| **Closing balance** | (80) | (500) | (490) | (760) | ? | 900 | 1,680 | 1,260 | 730 |

(c) On the basis of this cash flow forecast alone, discuss whether a bank would grant Kieran a loan.

**Table 46.4** *Thorntons, cash flow statement*

|  | 2002 £000 | 2001 £000 |
|---|---|---|
| **Cash inflow from operating activities** | 21,160 | 21,117 |
| Returns on investments and servicing of finance | (3,489) | (4,155) |
| Taxation | 507 | 902 |
| Capital expenditure and financial investment | (2,754) | (1,587) |
| Equity dividends paid | (4,486) | (4,492) |
| **Cash inflow before use of liquid resources and financing** | 10,938 | 11,785 |
| Management of liquid resources | (2,292) | 264 |
| Financing  - issue of shares | 1 | - |
|  - decrease in debt | (10,752) | (10,716) |
| **(Decrease)/increase in cash in the period** | (2,105) | 1,333 |

Source: adapted from Thorntons plc, *Annual Report and Accounts*.

**Table 46.5** *Thorntons, net cash inflow from operating activities*

|  | 2002 £000 | 2001 £000 |
|---|---|---|
| **Operating profit** | 10,410 | 10,148 |
| Loss on disposal of fixed assets | 405 | 73 |
| Depreciation charges | 13,373 | 13,117 |
| Amortisation charges | 113 | - |
| Non-cash movements in provisions | (443) | (584) |
| **Operating cash flows before working capital improvements** | 23,858 | 22,754 |
| Cash flow relating to previous years provisions | (33) | (107) |
| (Increase)/decrease in stocks | (853) | 3,781 |
| Increase in debtors | (1,674) | (1,413) |
| Decrease in creditors | (138) | (3,898) |
| **Net cash flow from operating activities** | 21,160 | 21,117 |

Source: adapted from Thorntons plc, *Annual Report and Accounts*.

**Coping with external factors** Cash flow forecasts could be improved if business managers could predict future events such as changes in interest rates, the weather and the behaviour of competitors. One way to allow for unforeseen events is to have **contingency funds** built into the cash flow forecast. For example, a business may make a monthly allowance for unexpected costs, including it as a cash outflow. Another approach could be to make regular adjustments to cash flow forecasts during the trading period. If forecasts are updated regularly, predictions may be more accurate. It is also possible to produce a series of forecasts. For example, a business might produce three, a 'worst case', a 'best case' and one in the 'middle'. This could show the business what is likely to happen to its cash position in different situations.

# Cash flow statements

The management of funds is easier if there is documented information on business performance. The balance sheet (☞ unit 43) shows the assets and liabilities of a business at a point in time. The profit and loss account shows how the year's profit is distributed. In 1991, the Accounting Standards Board (ASB) published its first Financial Report Standard, FRS 1 'Cash flow Statements'. The new standard required companies to publish a CASH FLOW STATEMENT in the annual accounts. Note that this is **not** the same as a cash flow forecast. Cash flow statements may include receipts and payments from the previous two years. These may not be disclosed elsewhere in published financial statements. Another advantage is that a cash flow statement must be shown in a standardised presentation. This allows a comparison between different companies.

FRS 1 requires cash flows to be disclosed under standard headings. These are:
● operating activities;
● returns on investments and servicing of finance;
● taxation;
● investing activities;
● financing;
in that order.

Table 46.4 shows a cash flow statement for Thorntons plc, the confectionery company. The entries in the cash flow statement are explained as follows.
● In 2002 the net cash inflow from operating activities was £21.16 million. The way in which the business generated this profit is shown in Table 46.5.
● From this £3.489 million is subtracted. This is the difference between interest received from money invested and interest paid on loans. In 2002 Thorntons made a net payment of interest.
● During the year Thorntons received a corporation tax repayment from the Inland Revenue equal to £507,000.
● In 2002 Thorntons spent £2.754 million on capital expenditure, such as tangible assets.
● £4.486 million was paid to shareholders in the form of dividends.
● The net cash inflow before the use of liquid resources and financing was £10.938 million.
● In 2002 £2.292 million cash was placed in a deposit account.
● A very small amount of capital was raised through the issue of shares, just £1,000.

Look at Table 46.4 and 46.5.
(a) What happened to Thorntons' net cash position in 2001?
(b) Explain why these statements might be useful to Thorntons.

**Question 3**

- £10.752 million was used to repay much of Thorntons debt.
- The total net cash outflow for Thorntons in 2002 was £2.105 million.

## Criticisms of cash flow statements

The inclusion of cash flow statements helps to clarify the cash position of a business. However, there are some criticisms of cash flow statements.

- In practice, little new information is shown in the statements. The law encourages disclosure but does not enforce it.
- Small limited companies are not bound to publish a cash flow statement because they are owner managed. However, medium sized firms are. This seems to lack a little logic since most medium sized firms are also owner managed.
- Cash flow statements are based on historical information. It is argued that cash flow statements based on future predictions are more useful.

## The difference between cash and profit

It is important for businesses to recognise the difference between cash and profit. At the end of a trading year it is unlikely that the value of profit will be the same as the cash balance. Differences between cash and profit can arise for a number of reasons.

- During the trading year a business might sell £200,000 worth of goods with total costs of £160,000. Its profit would be £40,000. However, if some goods had been sold on credit, payment by certain customers may not yet have been received. If £12,000 was still owing, the amount of cash the business had would be £28,000 (£40,000-£12,000). Thus, profit is greater than cash.
- A business may receive cash at the beginning of the trading year from sales made in the previous year. This would increase the cash balance, but not affect profit. In addition, the business may buy resources from suppliers and not pay for them until the next trading year. As a result its trading costs will not be the same as cash paid out.
- Sometimes the owners might introduce more cash into the business. This will increase the cash balance, but have no effect on the profit made. This is because the introduction of capital is not treated as business revenue in the profit and loss account. The effect will be the same if a business borrows money from a bank.
- Purchases of fixed assets will reduce cash balances, but have no effect on the profit a company makes. This is because the purchase of assets is not treated as a business cost in the profit and loss account.
- Sales of fixed assets will increase cash balances but have no effect on profit unless a profit or loss is made on disposal

**Table 46.6** *Cash flow forecast statement for Jeanwear Ltd, July to December*

(£)

| | Jul | Aug | Sep | Oct | Nov | Dec |
|---|---|---|---|---|---|---|
| **Receipts** | | | | | | |
| Cash sales | 40,000 | 50,000 | 50,000 | 70,000 | 90,000 | 90,000 |
| Bank loan | | | | | | 30,000 |
| Total cash receipts | 40,000 | 50,000 | 50,000 | 70,000 | 90,000 | 120,000 |
| **Payments** | | | | | | |
| Cost of sales | 18,000 | 30,000 | 30,000 | 40,000 | 60,000 | 60,000 |
| Wages | 8,000 | 8,000 | 8,000 | 10,000 | 10,000 | 8,000 |
| Overheads | 10,000 | 18,000 | 10,000 | 15,000 | 20,000 | 15,000 |
| Computer system | | | | | | 50,000 |
| Total payments | 36,000 | 56,000 | 48,000 | 65,000 | 90,000 | 133,000 |
| **Net cash flow** | 4,000 | (6,000) | 2,000 | 5,000 | - | (13,000) |
| **Opening balance** | 12,000 | 16,000 | 10,000 | 12,000 | 17,000 | 17,000 |
| **Closing balance** | 16,000 | 10,000 | 12,000 | 17,000 | 17,000 | 4,000 |

**Table 46.7** *Profit per month Jeanwear Ltd*

| | Jul | Aug | Sep | Oct | Nov | Dec |
|---|---|---|---|---|---|---|
| Profit* | 4,000 | (6,000) | 2,000 | 5,000 | 0 | 7,000 |

* Cash sales - operating costs (cost of sales + wages + overheads)

Jeanwear Ltd produces denim products for the mail order market. It advertises products in weekend newspaper supplements. It has enjoyed some success in recent years. However, the directors believe that profits could be raised if it could cut costs. At the beginning of 2004 it was decided that a new computer system would be installed. This was expected to reduce administrative overheads and the monthly wage bill. Table 46.6 shows a cash flow forecast statement and profits for the six month trading period starting in July 2004. It was anticipated that the computer system will be bought and installed in December. Part of the cost would be met by a bank loan.

(a) What is the difference between the profit made by the business over the period and the closing cash balance?
(b) Suggest two reasons why there may have been this difference.
(c) Explain the effects on the (i) cash flow and (ii) profit of the business if the computer system had not been bought.

**Question 4**

of the asset. This is because the cash from the sale of a fixed asset is not included in business turnover.

- The amount of cash at the end of the year will be different from profit because at the beginning of the year the cash balance is unlikely to be zero. If, at the beginning of the year, the cash balance for a business is £23,000, then the amount of cash a business has at the end of the year will exceed profit by £23,000.

It is possible for a business to trade for many years without making a profit. For example, British Biotech, a pharmaceuticals company, traded between 1985-98 without ever making a profit. The company survived because it was able to generate cash. Extra cash was introduced by shareholders on several occasions since 1985. In 1998 the company lost £44.8 million. However, the cash in the bank was £132.8 million. Shareholders may be happy to contribute more capital if they think that a company has a lot of potential. However, it is possible for a profitable business to collapse if it runs out of cash. This is likely to happen if a business has to meet some substantial unexpected expenditure or if a bad debt occurs.

## Knowledge ...Knowledge...Knowledge...Knowledge...Knowledge...Knowledge...Know

1. Explain the operation of the cash flow cycle.
2. Why is it important that a business:
   (i) does not hold too much cash;
   (ii) holds sufficient cash?
3. Briefly explain what a cash flow forecast includes.
4. How does a cash flow forecast indicate whether a business faces cash flow problems in future?
5. Explain why a business prepares a cash flow forecast.
6. What are the advantages of businesses preparing cash flow statements?
7. How is it possible for a profitable business to collapse?

## key terms

**Cash flow cycle** - the continuous movement of cash in and out of a business.
**Cash flow forecast** - a prediction of all expected receipts and expenses of a business over a future time period which shows the expected cash balance at the end of each month.

**Cash flow statement** - a financial statement which shows sources and uses of cash in a trading period.
**Liquid asset** - an asset which is easily changed into cash.
**Receivership** - the liquidation (selling) of a firm's assets by an independent body following its collapse.

# Case study Westview Caravans

Betty and Bob Hawkins own a small caravan site in Devon. They bought the business in 2000 when they retired. They preferred to spend their £200,000 life savings on a small business rather than invest it in other ways. They felt that running the business would not only generate a steady annual income but also occupy their time. The business consisted of a dwelling house on a cliff top and eight four-berth caravans.

In the first two years the business did well, as projected by the previous owners. However, in 2002 a storm during Autumn damaged four of the eight caravans. About the same time Bob was ill for a few weeks and wasn't able to carry out repairs. The couple had little spare cash and couldn't really afford to pay a contractor to carry out the necessary work.

Betty and Bob sit down to think about their cash flow for 2003. The site is closed from November to March, so there is no revenue in these months. They decide to repair two of the caravans in March. However, they will have to replace the other two in July using a bank loan. They are reluctant to take out a loan, but they are worried that operating with only six caravans will reduce their revenue.

Before approaching the bank, Betty and Bob draw up a cash flow forecast. They look at the bank statements of the business from previous years and produce Table 46.8 showing the expected revenue from letting the caravans and expected overheads for 2003. The following financial information is also available.

● £250 interest is expected to be received in April.
● Betty and Bob include the £8,000 bank loan in July which they hope the bank will give them.
● Betty and Bob take £1,100 every month from the business for their own use.
● £500 ground rent and £400 rates are payable each month.
● Water rates are expected to be £560 in April and £680 in October.
● Repairs are expected to be £450 in March.
● The new caravans will cost £10,000 in July.
● The opening balance is £5,200 in January.

**Table 46.8** *Estimated letting revenue and other overhead costs, 2003*

|  |  |  |  |  |  |  |  |  |  |  |  | (£) |
| --- | --- | --- | --- | --- | --- | --- | --- | --- | --- | --- | --- | --- |
|  | JAN | FEB | MAR | APR | MAY | JUN | JUL | AUG | SEP | OCT | NOV | DEC |
| Letting revenue | 0 | 0 | 0 | 1,200 | 1,800 | 2,000 | 4,100 | 5,400 | 3,200 | 1,000 | 0 | 0 |
| Other overheads | 0 | 0 | 0 | 200 | 200 | 300 | 300 | 300 | 200 | 100 | 0 | 0 |

**(a)** Explain why a cash flow forecast might be helpful to Betty and Bob when applying for a bank loan. **(4 marks)**

**(b)** Produce a cash flow forecast for Betty and Bob's caravan business for 2003. **(12 marks)**

**(c) (i)** Calculate the expected profit for 2003. **(6 marks)**

**(ii)** Using examples, explain why the expected cash position at the end of the trading year is different to the expected profit. **(8 marks)**

**(d)** Discuss whether you think the bank will give Betty and Bob a loan for the new caravans. **(10 marks)**

## What is budgeting?

As businesses expand the need for control grows and becomes more difficult. A small business can be run informally. The owner is the manager, who will know everyone, be aware of what is going on and will make all decisions. In larger firms work and responsibility are delegated, which makes informal control impractical. To improve control, budgeting has been developed. This forces managers to be accountable for their decisions.

A BUDGET is a plan which is agreed in advance. It must be a plan and not a forecast - a forecast is a prediction of what might happen in the future, whereas a budget is a planned outcome which the firm hopes to achieve. A budget will show the money needed for spending and how this might be financed. Budgets are based on the objectives of businesses. They force managers to think ahead and improve co-ordination. Most budgets are set for twelve months to coincide with the accounting period, but there are exceptions. Research and Development budgets, for example, may cover several years.

Information contained in a budget may include revenue, sales, expenses, profit, personnel, cash and capital expenditure. In fact, budgets can include any business variable (known as a budget factor) which can be given a value.

One very well known budget is 'The Budget'. The Chancellor of the Exchequer prepares a budget for a particular period. It will take into account the government's spending plans and how these plans will be financed by taxes and other sources of funds.

## Approaches to budgeting

Budgets can be divided into different categories. Objectives budgets and flexible budgets take different approaches to planning.

- **Objectives budgets** are based on finding the best way of achieving particular objectives (☞ unit 4). They contain information on how a business will achieve these objectives. For example, a sales budget might show how a sales target will be met.
- **Flexible budgets** are designed to change as business changes. Changes in business conditions may result in very different outcomes than those budgeted for. A flexible budget takes these into account. For example, the sales budget may be altered if there is sudden increase in demand resulting in much higher sales levels.

A business will also set budgets over the long term and short term.

- **Capital budgets** plan the capital structure and the liquidity of a business over a long period of time. They are concerned with equity, liabilities, fixed and current assets and year-end cash balances.

- **Operating budgets** plan the day to day use of resources. They are concerned with materials, labour, overheads, sales and cash. There are three important operating budgets. The **profit budget** estimates the annual business costs, the year's turnover and the expected profit for the year. The **cash budget** simply plans the receipts and payments. It shows a firm its cash balance at specified times in the budget period. The **budgeted balance sheet** incorporates the budgeted profit and loss account and the closing balance in the cash budget. It also takes into account planned changes in assets and liabilities.

## The preparation of budgets

The way in which a budget might be prepared is shown in Figure 47.1. It is a step by step process. The first step is to decide upon a budget period and state the objectives which are to be achieved. The budget period may vary according to the type of budget, but one month or one year is usual. Often the objectives will be set at board level. Targets for performance, market share, quality (provided it can be quantified) and productivity are all examples.

John Chandler is marketing manager at Wicksons, a chain of 54 shoe shops. Most of the marketing budget is used for adverts in magazines and promotions in stores. The business also has a stand at the Milan Shoe Exhibition, where it has the chance to develop contacts and research future styles. One of John's responsibilities is to produce cost budgets for his department. The cost budget for the second six months of 2003 is shown in Table 47.1.

**Table 47.1** *Cost budget for Wicksons marketing department, 2003*

| | | | | | | (£) |
|---|---|---|---|---|---|---|
| | JUL | AUG | SEP | OCT | NOV | DEC |
| Wages & salaries | 4,300 | 4,300 | 4,300 | 4,300 | 4,300 | 4,300 |
| Office expenses | 500 | 500 | 450 | 450 | 450 | 400 |
| Advertising expenses | 2,000 | 10,000 | 2,000 | 2,000 | 10,000 | 2,000 |
| Promotion expenses | 2,500 | 2,200 | 3,800 | 1,700 | 1,600 | 2,500 |
| Milan Shoe Exhibition | | | | | 12,000 | |
| Other overheads | 500 | 500 | 500 | 500 | 700 | 500 |

(a) How much does the Wicksons' marketing department plan to spend in the second half of 2003?
(b) Explain how the preparation of this budget might help Wicksons.

 **Question 1**

The next stage involves obtaining information upon which the budget can be based. Some information can be obtained from previous results. Historic information can be useful, although some budgetary techniques ignore the past and make a fresh start. Forecasts are another source of information. These are estimates of likely future outcomes. Some business variables are easier to forecast than others. It is fairly easy to predict future costs, but difficult to estimate future sales. This is because sales levels are subject to so many external factors.

It is then possible to prepare two important budgets - the sales budget and the production budget. These budgets are related and affect all other budgets. For example, sales targets can only be met if there is productive capacity. Also, a firm would be unlikely to continue production if it could not sell its products. The sales budget will contain monthly sales estimates, expressed in terms of quantities per product, perhaps, and the price charged. From the sales budget, and with knowledge of stock levels, the production budget can be determined. This will show the required raw materials, labour hours and machine hours. At this stage the business should know whether or not it has the capacity to meet the sales targets. If it is not possible, then it may be necessary to adjust the sales budget.

Subsidiary operating budgets can be drawn up next. These will be detailed budgets prepared by various departments. Budgets are often broken down, so that each person in the hierarchy (☞ unit 58) can be given some responsibility for a section of the budget.

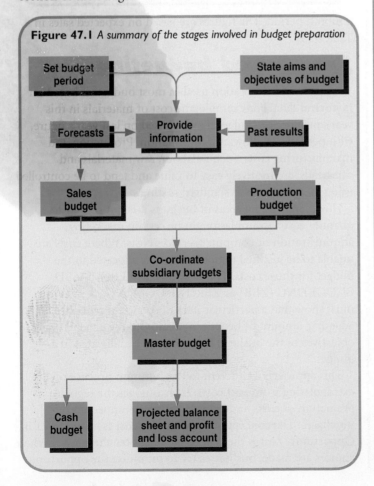

**Figure 47.1** A summary of the stages involved in budget preparation

- Set budget period
- State aims and objectives of budget
- Forecasts
- Provide information
- Past results
- Sales budget
- Production budget
- Co-ordinate subsidiary budgets
- Master budget
- Cash budget
- Projected balance sheet and profit and loss account

The master budget is a summary statement. It shows the estimated income, anticipated expenditure, and, thus, the budgeted profit for the period. The cash budget can also be prepared when all other budgets are complete. This budget is particularly useful since it shows the monthly flows of cash into and out of the business. It will help to show whether future cash flow problems might occur.

The final step is to prepare the projected balance sheet. This shows the financial position that will result from the firm's budgets.

## Problems of preparing budgets

Business may sometimes find that there are problems when preparing budgets.

**Using planned figures** Problems tend to arise because figures in budgets are not actual figures. The figures are plans, which could be based on historical data, forecasts or human judgment. A business might simply take historic data and add an arbitrary percentage to arrive at the budgeted value. The most important data in the preparation of nearly all budgets is sales data. If sales data are inaccurate, many of the firm's budgets will be inexact. The accuracy of sales data might be improved if market research is used (☞ unit 19). However, it may be difficult to estimate sales of new products for a future period.

**Collecting information** The preparation of budgets is a managerial process. It requires a great deal of co-ordination. This is because different parts of the organisation provide information for budgets. Some businesses appoint a budget officer. This person is responsible for collecting data and opinions, keeping managers to the budget timetable and carrying out budgetary administration.

**Time** Preparing budgets can be time consuming and use up resources. The whole process can also be held up. This is because many of the major budgets, such as the master budget, cannot be prepared until other smaller budgets have been produced. A delay in approving budgets is also likely to cause problems. If budgets are prepared after the start of the time period in which they will be used, their value is reduced. To avoid delay, a business must prepare a careful timetable for their approval and stick to it.

**Conflict** The preparation of budgets may lead to conflict between departments or members of staff. For example, a business may only have limited funds. The marketing department may want to promote a product but new machinery may be needed in the R&D department.

## Preparing a sales revenue budget

A sales revenue budget will show the planned revenue for a period of time. Emerald Artwork produces four products,

AD23, AD24, AE12 and AE13. They sell for £12, £20, £25 and £30 respectively. The planned sales levels for a four month period in 2004 are shown in Table 47.2.

**Table 47.2** *Planned sales figures for Emerald Artwork*

|       | FEB | MAR | APR | MAY |
|-------|-----|-----|-----|-----|
| AD23  | 100 | 100 | 100 | 100 |
| AD24  | 50  | 80  | 80  | 100 |
| AE12  | 40  | 50  | 40  | 50  |
| AE13  | 30  | 30  | 50  | 50  |

The sales revenue budget is prepared by showing the planned revenue in each month. This is calculated by multiplying the predicted sales levels by the prices. The sales revenue budget is shown in Table 47.3.

**Table 47.3** *A sales revenue budget for Emerald Artwork*

|       | FEB | MAR | APR | MAY |
|-------|-----|-----|-----|-----|
| AD23  | £1,200 (£12x100) | £1,200 (£12x100) | £1,200 (£12x100) | £1,200 (£12x100) |
| AD24  | £1,000 (£20x50) | £1,600 (£20x80) | £1,600 (£20x80) | £2,000 (£20x100) |
| AE12  | £1,000 (£25x40) | £1,250 (£25x50) | £1,000 (£25x40) | £1,250 (£25x50) |
| AE13  | £900 (£30x30) | £900 (£30x30) | £1,500 (£30x50) | £1,500 (£30x50) |
| Total | £4,100 | £4,950 | £5,300 | £5,950 |

# A production budget

Once Emerald Artwork has produced a sales budget, it is possible to calculate its production budget. The example in Table 47.4 assumes stock levels stay the same throughout the

**Table 47.4** *A production budget for Emerald Artwork covering production of all 4 products*

|       | FEB | MAR | APR | MAY |
|-------|-----|-----|-----|-----|
| Cost of materials (£3 per unit) | £660 (£3x220) | £780 (£3x260) | £810 (£3x270) | £900 (£3x300) |
| Direct labour costs (£4 per unit) | £880 (£4x220) | £1,040 (£4x260) | £1,080 (£4x270) | £1,200 (£4x300) |
| Indirect labour costs (£2 per unit) | £440 (£2x220) | £520 (£2x260) | £540 (£2x270) | £600 (£2x300) |
| Overheads (10% of direct & indirect costs) | £1,320x10% = £132 | £1,560x10% = £156 | £1,620x10% = £162 | £1,800x10% = £180 |
| Total | £2,112 | £2,496 | £2,592 | £2,880 |

The Mansfield Motor Centre is a large motor business based on the outskirts of Mansfield. The business employs 32 staff and made a profit of £5.8 million in 2002. Table 47.5 shows a six month sales revenue budget for 2003.

**Table 47.5** *Six month sales revenue budget for the Mansfield Motor Centre, 2003*

(£000)

|       | JAN | FEB | MAR | APR | MAY | JUN | TOTAL |
|-------|-----|-----|-----|-----|-----|-----|-------|
| Repairs and servicing | 458 | 456 | 786 | 876 | 776 | 765 | 4,117 |
| MOTs | 110 | 98 | 97 | 89 | 103 | 130 | 627 |
| Motor car sales | 1,445 | 1,256 | 1,329 | 1,876 | 2,228 | 2,667 | 10,801 |
| Parts and accessories sales | 786 | 978 | 678 | 834 | 1,021 | 1,200 | 5,497 |
| **Total** | **2,799** | **2,788** | **2,890** | **3,675** | **4,128** | **4,762** | **21,042** |

(a) Explain how the sales revenue budget for Mansfield Motor Centre has been calculated.
(b) Suggest where the information in the above budget might have come from.

**Question 2**

4 month period. The figures are based on expected sales in Table 47.2.

# Zero-based budgeting

The financial information used in most budgets is based on **historical** data. For example, the cost of materials in this year's production budget may be based on last year's figure, with perhaps an allowance for inflation. Production and manufacturing costs, such as labour, raw materials and overheads, are relatively easy to value and tend to be controlled using methods such as standard costing.

However, in some areas of business it is not so easy to quantify costs. Examples might be certain marketing, administration or computer services costs. Where costs are unable to be justified then no money is allocated in the budget for those costs. This is known as ZERO-BASED BUDGETING (ZBB) or ZERO BUDGETING. A manager must show that a particular item of spending generates an adequate amount of benefit in relation to the general objectives of the business for money to be allocated in a budget.

This approach is different to the common practice of extrapolating from past costs. It encourages the regular evaluation of costs and helps to minimise unnecessary purchases. The concept of **opportunity cost** is linked to ZBB. Opportunity cost is the cost of the next best alternative. When choices are made, businesses try to minimise the opportunity

Questcorp plc is a large provider of security systems in the UK. It specialises in systems which protect business premises in rural locations. The financial controller of Questcorp has suggested that expenditure in some departments could be better controlled if the company used zero-based budgeting. The expenditure for four departments is shown in Table 47.6.

**Table 36.6** *Expenditure in four key departments for Questcorp plc*

|  | | | | | £ |
| --- | --- | --- | --- | --- | --- |
|  | **2000** | **2001** | **2002** | **2003** | **2004** |
| Marketing | 120,000 | 140,000 | 178,000 | 219,000 | 270,000 |
| R&D | 250,000 | 321,000 | 377,000 | 679,000 | 900,000 |
| Production | 300,000 | 400,000 | 560,000 | 780,000 | 980,000 |
| Admin. | 45,000 | 50,000 | 54,000 | 79,000 | 93,000 |

(a) How might the R&D budget holder justify spending in the department?
(b) Why might zero-based budgeting be a problem for the marketing department launching a new product?
(c) To what extent might Questcorp benefit from zero-based budgeting?

# Question 3

cost. ZBB also involves a cautious approach to spending, so that costs are minimised. Both include an element of 'value for money'.

The main advantages of ZBB are that:
- the allocation of resources should be improved;
- a questioning attitude is developed which will help to reduce unnecessary costs and eliminate inefficient practices;
- staff motivation might improve because evaluation skills are practised and a greater knowledge of the firm's operations might develop;
- it encourages managers to look for alternatives.
ZBB also has some disadvantages.
- It is time consuming because the budgeting process involves the collection and analysis of quite detailed information so that spending decisions can be made.
- Skilful decision making is required. Such skills may not be available in the organisation. In addition, decisions may be influenced by subjective opinions.
- It threatens the status quo. This might adversely affect motivation.
- Managers may not be prepared to justify spending on certain costs. Money, therefore, may not be allocated to spending which could benefit the business.
To deal with these possible problems, a business might give each department a 'base' budget of, say, 50 per cent. Departments could then be invited to bid for increased expenditure on a ZBB basis.

# The benefits of budgets

- Budgets provide a means of controlling income and expenditure. They regulate the spending of money and draw attention to losses, waste and inefficiency.
- They act as a 'review' for a business, allowing time for corrective action.
- Budgets can emphasise and clarify the responsibilities of executives.
- They enable management to delegate responsibility without losing control, because subordinates are expected to meet budget targets which are known in advance by senior management.
- Budgets help ensure that capital is usefully employed by checking that the capital employed is consistent with the planned level of activity.
- They help the co-ordination of the business and improve communication between departments.
- Budgets provide clear targets which can be understood by personnel lower down in the organisational structure (☞ unit 58). They should also help to focus on costs.

# The drawbacks of budgets

- Budgets might lead to resentment from some of the firm's personnel, particularly if they are not involved in the preparation. This could result in poor motivation and targets being missed.
- If budgets are too inflexible then it is possible that the business could suffer. For example, a member of the sales team may be prevented from finalising an overseas contract because the overseas travel budget is spent.
- If the actual business results are very different from the budgeted ones then the budget can lose its importance.

# Variances

A VARIANCE in budgeting is the difference between the figure that the business has budgeted for and the actual figure. Variances are usually calculated at the end of the budget period, as that is when the actual figure will be known. They can be **favourable** (F) or **adverse** (A).

Favourable variances occur when the actual figures are 'better' than the budgeted figures.
- If the sales revenue for a month was budgeted at £25,000, but turned out to be £29,000, there would be a £4,000 favourable variance (£29,000-£25,000).
- If cost were planned to be £20,000 and turned out to be £18,000, this would also be a favourable variance of £2,000, as actual costs are lower than planned.
Adverse variances are when the actual figures are worse than the budgeted figures. Actual sales revenues may be lower than planned, or actual costs may be higher than planned.

Managers will examine variances and try to identify reasons why they have occurred. By doing this they might be able to improve the performance of the business in the future. The determination and use of variances is discussed in more detail in unit 54.

## key terms

**Budget** - a quantitative economic plan prepared and agreed in advance.
**Variance** - the difference between the actual value and the planned value in a budget.
**Zero based budgeting or zero budgeting** - a system of budgeting where no money is allocated for costs or spending unless they can be justified by the fund holder (they are given a zero value).

Knowledge...Knowledge...Knowle

1. How might a budget improve managerial accountability?
2. What is the difference between objectives budgets and flexible budgets?
3. State examples of 3 types of budget.
4. Suggest 3 problems when preparing a budget.
5. Describe the benefits of budgets.
6. Describe the drawbacks of budgets.
7. What does an adverse variance tell a business?
8. What might cause a sales variance?
9. Why might a business use zero-based budgeting?

Hammond Gardening Services Ltd is owned by Mike Hammond. He employs one other person and provides garden maintenance services in Surrey. He has two main sources of revenue - maintenance contracts with schools and hospitals and work from private households. Mike advertises his services regularly in local newspapers and enjoyed an increase in business in 2003 due to the warm summer. Table 47.7 shows revenues and costs for Hammond Gardening Services in 2003.

**Table 47.7** *Hammond Gardening Services, costs and revenue, 2003*

|  | Budget | Actual | Variance |
|---|---|---|---|
| **Revenue** | | | |
| Maintenance contracts | 35,600 | 36,100 | 500F |
| Private households | 36,400 | 38,980 | 2,580F |
| **Total revenue** | **72,000** | **75,080** | **3,080F** |
| | | | |
| **Costs** | | | |
| Wages | 12,000 | 13,050 | 1,050A |
| Motor expenses | 2,400 | 2,800 | 400A |
| Materials | 1,200 | 1,450 | 250A |
| Advertising | 650 | 350 | 300F |
| Other overheads | 1,800 | 1,970 | 170A |
| **Total costs** | **18,050** | **19,620** | **1,570A** |
| | | | |
| **Profit** | **53,950** | **55,460** | ******* |

(a) Using information in the case, explain what is meant by (i) a favourable and (ii) an adverse variance.
(b) Calculate the profits variance for the business in 2003 and explain reasons why it is favourable.

**Question 4**

# Case study Maison JP et Chateau JP

Jean Paul Delmoureaux owns two restaurants in London. The business is well established and under strict financial control. Jean Paul, who trained as a chef in some of the world's top hotels, set up the business in 1996 when he opened Maison JP in Hampstead. Serving high quality French cuisine, the restaurant quickly grew in popularity, attracting diners from all over London. In 1999 he opened Chateau JP in Notting Hill. Both restaurants are aimed at diners who are willing to pay a little more for meals and the prices

reflect this. However, costs are high due to the expensive locations, highly paid staff and the high quality fresh ingredients. To keep the high costs under control Jean Paul has always used budgets. Every six months Jean Paul meets with each restaurant manager to agree a budget. Annual budgets were used, but Jean Paul found that they lacked accuracy. Tables 47.8 and 47.9 show the costs and revenue for the restaurants in the first six months of 2004.

Managers used to complain about preparing the

budgets. They argued that it was too time-consuming when they would be better employed running the restaurants. Jean Paul responded by offering managers financial rewards related to the budgets. Managers are now given 30 per cent of any favourable variance on the six-monthly budgets.

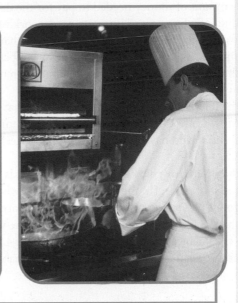

**Table 47.8** *Maison JP, costs and revenues*

(£)

| | JAN | FEB | MAR | APR | MAY | JUN | TOTAL |
|---|---|---|---|---|---|---|---|
| Budgeted revenue | 51,000 | 53,000 | 56,000 | 62,000 | 65,000 | 70,000 | 357,000 |
| Budgeted costs | 41,900 | 42,900 | 45,200 | 47,100 | 48,500 | 50,500 | 276,100 |
| Budgeted profit | 9,100 | 10,100 | 10,800 | 14,900 | 16,500 | 19,500 | 80,900 |

(£)

| | JAN | FEB | MAR | APR | MAY | JUN | TOTAL |
|---|---|---|---|---|---|---|---|
| Actual revenue | 50,230 | 53,700 | 56,400 | 62,500 | 71,000 | 72,100 | 365,930 |
| Actual costs | 42,150 | 42,650 | 45,200 | 47,300 | 50,750 | 49,200 | 277,250 |
| Actual profit | 8,080 | 11,050 | 11,200 | 15,200 | 20,250 | 22,900 | 88,680 |

**Table 47.9** *Chateau JP, costs and revenues*

(£)

| | JAN | FEB | MAR | APR | MAY | JUN | TOTAL |
|---|---|---|---|---|---|---|---|
| Budgeted revenue | 55,000 | 56,000 | 61,000 | 68,000 | 73,000 | 76,000 | 389,000 |
| Budgeted costs | 44,800 | 44,700 | 45,200 | 48,100 | 50,300 | 53,800 | 286,900 |
| Budgeted profit | 10,200 | 11,300 | 15,800 | 19,900 | 22,700 | 22,200 | 102,100 |

(£)

| | JAN | FEB | MAR | APR | MAY | JUN | TOTAL |
|---|---|---|---|---|---|---|---|
| Actual revenue | 56,400 | 59,300 | 64,200 | 71,300 | 71,000 | 77,100 | 399,300 |
| Actual costs | 43,350 | 43,150 | 44,600 | 47,100 | 50,800 | 52,200 | 281,200 |
| Actual profit | 13,050 | 16,150 | 19,600 | 24,200 | 20,200 | 24,900 | 118,100 |

(a) **Where might the information contained in the budgets have come from? (6 marks)**

(b) **Calculate the following variances for both restaurants for the six month period: (i) total revenue; (ii) total costs; (iii) profit. (6 marks)**

(c) **Which restaurant manager has produced the most accurate budget? Explain your answer. (6 marks)**

(d) **Analyse the advantages to Jean Paul Delmoureaux of using budgets in his business. (10 marks)**

(e) **Jean Paul Delmoureaux is suspicious about the variance for Chateau JP. He suspects that the manager might have deliberately overestimated costs in the budget so that the bonus will be larger. To what extent might this be true? (12 marks)**

## What is working capital?

WORKING CAPITAL (sometimes called circulating capital) is the amount of money needed to pay for the day to day trading of a business. A business needs working capital to pay expenses such as wages, electricity and gas charges, and to buy components to make products. The working capital of a business is the amount left over after all current debts have been paid. It is:

- the relatively liquid assets of a business that can easily be turned into cash (cash itself, stocks, the money owing from debtors who have bought goods or services);

*minus*

- the money owed by a business which needs to be paid in the short term (to the bank, to creditors who have supplied goods or services, to government in the form of tax or shareholders' dividends payable within the year).

In the balance sheet of a company (☞ unit 43) working capital is calculated by subtracting current liabilities from current assets:

Working capital = current assets - current liabilities

## Working capital problems

Provided that current assets are twice the size of current liabilities, working capital is usually large enough for most businesses to avoid problems. However, if the value of current assets is less than one and a half times the size of current liabilities, a business may be short of working capital. It might then have problems meeting its immediate debts. Some businesses, such as supermarkets and retailers, can operate if their working capital is smaller than this. These businesses have a very quick turnover of goods and sales are usually for cash which prevents possible problems developing.

Cash is only part of working capital. It is possible for a business to have adequate working capital because its current assets are three times the size of its current liabilities. However, over a very short period of time it may have insufficient cash to pay its bills. It will therefore have a cash flow problem (☞ unit 46).

## The working capital cycle

Managing working capital in a business is crucial. In many types of business, particularly manufacturing, delays or **time lags** exist between different stages of business activity. For example, there is a lag between buying materials and components and changing them into finished goods ready for sale. Similarly, there may be a delay between finishing the goods and the goods being sold to a customer. The WORKING CAPITAL CYCLE, shown in Figure 48.1, helps to illustrate the intervals between payments made by a business and the receipt of cash. The cycle shows the movement of cash and other liquid resources into and out of a business. Time lags can occur at a number of stages in the working capital cycle.

**Lag 1** Businesses usually purchase resources such as raw materials, components, fuel and other services from suppliers on credit. This means that a business can obtain resources without having to pay for them immediately. There might be a lag of up to 90 days before payment to suppliers has to be

---

**Table 48.1** *Merchant Retail Group's current assets and current liabilities, 2002 and 2003*

|  | 2003 £000s | 2002 £000s |
|---|---|---|
| **Current assets** | | |
| Stocks | 16,949 | 15,107 |
| Debtors | 8,142 | 8,479 |
| Investments | 426 | 0 |
| Cash at bank and in hand | 952 | 541 |
|  | **26,469** | **24,127** |
| **Current liabilities** | | |
| Loans and overdrafts | 10,939 | 18,414 |
| Trade creditors | 8,561 | 6,290 |
| Corporation tax | 3,853 | 3,326 |
| Other taxes and social security | 1,514 | 1,548 |
| Other creditors | 1,059 | 846 |
| Accruals and deferred income | 2,782 | 2,983 |
| Proposed dividends | 2,178 | 1,638 |
|  | **30,886** | **35,045** |

Source: adapted from Merchant Retail Group, *Annual Report and Accounts, 2003.*

Merchant Retail Group is a specialist perfumery retailer and department stores group. The Group has three main businesses The Perfume Shop, Joplings and A. de Gruchy.

- The Perfume Shop has 86 branches situated in prime shopping locations. It sells a wide range of branded perfumes at value for money prices.
- Joplings is a department store division located in the north east of England. It operates four stores including the landmark department store in Sunderland and a ten acre retail park at Hexham.
- A. de Gruchy, located in St Helier, is the leading department store on Jersey.

(a) Calculate the working capital for the Merchant Retail Group in 2003 and 2002.

(b) Comment on:
  (i) the amount of working capital in 2003;
  (ii) the change in working capital from 2002 to 2003.

Question 1

**Figure 48.1** *The working capital cycle*

made. The length of the lag depends on suppliers' conditions. When a business is first set up, trade credit may not be granted until that business has proved to be creditworthy.

**Lag 2** The next lag may occur as resources are turned into products using fixed assets, such as equipment. Work-in-progress (partially finished goods) is created and other costs are incurred, such as wages. The production process can take a long time depending on the nature of business activity. For example, for a cereal farmer this time lag could be about nine months. This would be the time it takes for corn seeds to be planted, grow into plants and eventually ripen so that the corn can be harvested. Alternatively, a furniture manufacturer might take about four to six weeks to make two armchairs and a settee for a customer.

**Lag 3** Even when production is complete, a time lag can exist. Businesses may store their finished goods before they are sold to customers. This can be expensive. There may be warehousing costs and opportunity costs. However, storage enables a business to cope with unexpected increases in demand and allows continuous production. In recent years many businesses have adopted just-in-time (☞ unit 80) manufacturing methods. Goods are only produced to order. This minimises stock holdings and reduces this time lag. When goods are distributed to customers further costs result, such as transport and handling costs.

**Lag 4** A fourth time lag occurs when goods have finally been sold to customers. It is common business practice to allow customers to pay their bills over 30-90 days. However, depending on the nature of the business activity, this time lag can vary. For example, in many areas of retailing, goods are sold for cash only and this time lag is eliminated. Once cash has been collected from customers much of it is used to keep the process going, for example buying more materials and paying wages.

**Williams & Son**

Williams & Son is a small property development company in Bradford. It buys plots of land or derelict properties and then builds houses or small apartment blocks. The business aims to complete one or two developments each year. Williams & Son incurs legal costs and pays architects fees before any building can begin. Most of the materials used by Williams & Son are bought on 60 days' credit from local builder's suppliers. Sometimes the new properties are not sold until after they have been completed. The business employs two other workers.

**Tina's Taxi Service**

Tina McKenna leases two minibuses and operates an airport taxi service in Gloucester and Cheltenham. She employs two drivers and also drives herself. The 24 hour service is successful, but competition is tightening in the area. Drivers are paid 25 per cent of their fares and get to keep their tips. They are paid weekly. All journeys are booked through Tina and drivers are instructed to accept only cash when collecting fares. In addition to the drivers' wages the main variable cost is diesel. Tina has an account with a local garage and is given 30 days credit.

(a) Analyse the differences in the working capital cycles of the two businesses above.

**Question 2**

Figure 48.1 also shows that a business can enjoy injections of cash from sources other than the sale of products. Loans, the sale of assets and new capital are common examples. However, at the same time there will be cash drains from the business. Cash will leak from the cycle to pay dividends or drawings, to pay tax, to repay loans and to purchase new fixed assets.

## Managing working capital

The length of time lags can be crucial when managing the working capital cycle. Business managers must attempt to prolong the first time lag by delaying payments to suppliers. However, this requires careful judgment because a business would not want to damage relations with valuable suppliers. Also, if payments are delayed for too long this could cause hardship for suppliers and eventually contribute to their downfall. Managers would ideally want to reduce:

● production time;
● the storage time of finished goods before they are dispatched to customers, by reducing stock holdings or encouraging just-in-time manufacturing, for example;
● the time it takes for customers to settle their bills, by monitoring and checking late payments or offering discount for early settlement, for example.

## Liquidity and profibility

Businesses that have difficulty controlling their cash flow and working capital are often said to have LIQUIDITY PROBLEMS. Liquid assets (☞ unit 45) are those assets that

Oldbury Metal Fittings Ltd makes a wide range of metal brackets, hinges, handles and other small metal products for manufacturers in the West Midlands area. All of its products are made to order and are sold on 120 day credit terms. Most of its suppliers offer 60 day credit terms. Products are manufactured in batches of around 500 - 1,000. An order takes no more than two days to complete. On the 12.6.2004 the managing director of the company received a memo from the company accountant.

## OLDBURY METAL FITTINGS LTD MEMO

**To:** MD    **From:** Patricia    **Date:** 12.6.2004.

I think we should meet urgently to discuss the company's working capital. Once again the timing of payments and receipts is causing problems.

(a) Describe the nature and length of the four time lags in the working capital cycle for Oldbury Metal Fittings.
(b) Suggest why the problem in the memo has probably arisen.
(c) Explain two possible measures which might help to overcome the problem.

## Question 3

are easily changed into cash. They either do not have enough cash to pay immediate debts or cannot convert their liquid assets into cash quickly enough. It is possible for businesses to calculate whether they have sufficient working capital using a ratio such as the **current ratio** (☞ unit 56) . This is calculated by:

$$\text{Current ratio} = \frac{\text{Current assets}}{\text{Current liabilities}}$$

If a typical business has a current ratio of between 1.5:1 and 2:1 then it should not experience these problems.

A business could use the **acid test ratio** (☞ unit 56) as a measure of liquidity. This method excludes stock from current assets as stock is not a very liquid asset.

$$\text{Acid test ratio} = \frac{\text{Current assets - stocks}}{\text{Current liabilities}}$$

If the acid test ratio is equal to 1, or very close to 1, this would suggest that the business has sufficient working capital.

## Sources of liquidity problems

LIQUIDITY crises in a business often result from a number of errors in the control of working capital.

**Overtrading** Young and rapidly growing businesses are particularly prone to OVERTRADING. Overtrading occurs when a business is attempting to fund a large volume of production with inadequate working capital. Established companies trying to expand can also face this problem.

**Investing too much in fixed assets** In the initial stages of a business, funds are limited. Spending large amounts quickly on equipment, vehicles and other capital items drains resources. It may be better to lease some of these fixed assets, leaving sufficient cash funds.

**Stockpiling** Holding stocks of raw materials and finished goods is expensive. Money tied up in stocks is unproductive. Stocks may become obsolete. In addition, stocks of raw materials in particular cannot be easily changed into cash without making a loss. Stock control is an important feature of managing working capital. Firms should not buy in bulk if discounts are not enough to compensate for the extra cost of holding stocks.

**Allowing too much credit** A great deal of business is done on credit. One of the dangers is that firms allow their customers too long for payment. This means that the firm is waiting for money and may actually be forced to borrow during this period. Failure to control debtors may also lead to bad debts. Taking early action is the key to the effective control of debtors. At the same time businesses must maintain good relations with customers. Small firms are particularly vulnerable if they are owed money by much larger companies. Powerful businesses are often accused of endangering smaller companies by delaying payments to them.

**Taking too much credit** Taking more credit might appear to help a firm's cash position since payments are delayed. However there are some drawbacks. Taking too much credit might result in higher prices, lost discounts, difficulties in obtaining future supplies and a bad name in the trade. At worst, credit might be withdrawn.

**Overborrowing** Businesses may borrow to finance growth. As more loans are taken out interest costs rise. Overborrowing not only threatens a firm's cash position, but also the overall control of the business. It is important to fund growth in a balanced way, by raising some capital from share issues. A well publicised example was the overborrowing by Robert Maxwell from the employees' pension fund of Maxwell Communications.

**Underestimating inflation** Businesses often fail to take inflation into account. Inflation raises costs, which can cause cash shortages. This is often the case if higher costs, such as wages or raw materials, cannot be passed on in higher prices. Inflationary periods are often accompanied by higher interest rates which place further pressure on liquid resources.

Inflation is also a problem because it is difficult to predict future rates. Although it can be built into plans, firms often underestimate it.

**Unforeseen expenditure** Businesses are subject to unpredictable external forces. They must make a financial provision for any unforeseen expenditure. Equipment breakdowns, tax demands, strikes and bad debts are common examples of this type of emergency expense.

**Unexpected changes in demand** Although most businesses try to sustain demand for their products, there may be times when it falls unexpectedly. Unpredicted changes in fashion could lead to a fall in demand. This could lead to a lack of sales and cash flowing into a company. Travel companies in the UK have faced this problem in the past. Companies have to 'buy' holidays before they are sold. External factors, including a recession, may have led to many of these holidays remaining unsold as consumers changed their holiday buying patterns. Firms may also have lost revenue if holidays were discounted in an attempt to sell them.

**Seasonal factors** Sometimes trade fluctuates for seasonal reasons. In the agriculture industry, cereal farmers have a large cash inflow when their harvest is sold. For much of the year, though, they have to pay expenses without any cash flowing in. This situation requires careful management indeed, although it is possible to predict these changes.

**Poor financial management** Inexperience in managing cash or a poor understanding of the working capital cycle may lead to liquidity problems for a business.

## Resolving a liquidity crisis

Liquidity problems can be prevented by keeping a tight control on working capital. Inevitably though, there will be occasions when firms run short of liquid resources. When this does happen the firm's main aim will be survival rather than profit. The following measures might be used to obtain liquid resources.

● Stimulate sales for cash, offering large discounts if necessary.
● Sell off stocks of raw materials - below cost if necessary.
● Sell off any fixed assets which may not be vital for operations.
● Sell off fixed assets and lease them back.
● Mount a rigorous drive on overdue accounts.
● Sell debts to a factoring company.
● Only make essential purchases.
● Extend credit with selected suppliers.
● Reduce personal drawings from the business.
● Negotiate additional short term loans.

In all cases, action must be taken quickly. If the firm survives the liquidity crisis, it is important to identify the causes and make sure it does not happen again.

Newsplayer, the online broadcaster is facing a cash crisis after revealing it has just over £100,000 left in the bank, and its directors are not being paid while new funds are raised. The company, which owns 1,000 hours of ITN and Reuters news material, made pre-tax losses of £2.4 million for the six months to April 30. Turnover from its range of video-on-demand services, including Newsplayer.com, and its licensing agreements with other sites has also slumped to £113,505 compared with £350,526 for the previous six months. With just £100,252 left in the bank, the directors of the company said they would take payment in the form of shares until new funds could be raised.

Having recently signed agreements with NTL to provide two channels to its broadband service and with EMI to provide digital download services, the company's chief executive remained confident that Newsplayer would pull through its current cash flow problems.

It is attempting a £700,000 share placement to pay for the acquisition of US partner Global Media Services and fund ongoing operations. Having transferred all its technology resources to the US, the company said it would save more than £500,000 a year and had reduced its costs to less than £900,000 a year. 'In addition to the content and distribution deals we have signed during the period, the first half of the year has seen a focus on increasing efficiency and reducing costs,' the chief executive added.

The company said it remained confident it would break even before the end of the year, but the group's forecast relies on increasing the number of deals to boost revenues. It has suffered from the slow roll-out of the high speed broadband connections required to view video footage over the Internet and last year said it was switching its focus to the more developed markets in the US and Asia.

Source: adapted from *The Guardian*, 30.7.2003

(a) Explain why Newsplayer may have experienced cash flow and liquidity problems.
(b) Explain how the business may overcome these problems.

**Question 4**

## Credit control

Most businesses have some sort of CREDIT CONTROL system, so that money owing can be collected quickly and easily. A 'tight' or 'easy' credit policy may be adopted. Tight credit terms may be used to improve liquidity, reduce the risk of bad debts, exploit a sellers market, or maintain slender profit margins. Easy credit terms may be designed to clear old stocks, enter a new market or perhaps help a regular customer with financial difficulties.

The company accountant and the sales manager often work closely with the credit controller, since credit policy

**Figure 48.2** *A summary of a typical credit control procedure*

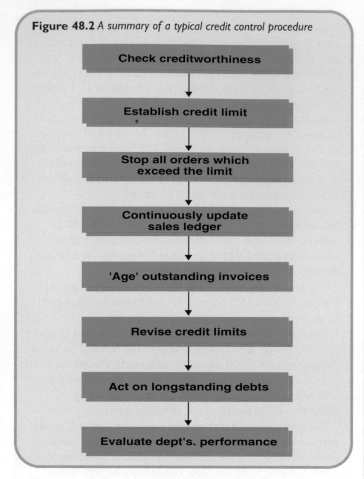

will affect the financial position of the firm and sales. Between them they set targets for the credit control department such as the value of bad debts or the length of time it takes to collect debts.

Firms have procedures to help credit control. Figure 48.2 shows an example. Many firms will not do business with a new customer until their creditworthiness has been checked. This can be done by asking for references from a supplier, a banker's reference, or a credit rating agency's report. From this information the credit controller can set a credit limit based on the risk involved.

When an order exceeds the credit limit, the credit controller should investigate. The result may be a stop being placed on the order, a request to the customer to pay any outstanding debt, or simply allowing the order to go ahead.

Credit control records, which show customer orders and payments, must be up to date. Every month outstanding invoices must be 'aged', to identify customers who owe money over 30, 60 and 90 days.

If there are persistent debts, the credit controller must take action. A statement of the account should be sent, followed by a second one with a letter. Next a telephone call to the debtor should be followed by a personal visit. Finally, as a last resort, it may be necessary to take legal action to recover the debt.

Some firms use an independent **debt factor** (☞ unit 44) to assist in credit control. There has been quite a growth in this type of business in recent years. A factor is a business that will provide finance to a business against its debts for a fee. It often pays a certain amount to the business 'up front' and the remainder as debts are collected.

# Late Payment of Commercial Debts

Small businesses complain that larger organisations use their power to exploit smaller firms by making them wait before payment is made. This can create severe cash flow problems for small businesses, particularly when the large firm is the only customer of the small firm. The government recognised the problem and introduced the **Late Payment of Commercial Debts (Interest) Act 1998** to give small firms help. The Act financially penalises late payers. It gives businesses a right to charge interest on unpaid commercial debts. Interest can run from three points, depending on how a contract is drafted.

● An agreed date.
● A fixed occurrence (ie delivery of the goods).
● Thirty days from (i) the day after the supplier has performed its duties, eg delivery, or (ii) 30 days after the buyer has received notice the supplier is claiming a sum due (for example receipt of an invoice).

Interest can be claimed at the rate of 8 per cent above the official dealing rate of the Bank of England. So if this was 4 per cent, interest on the debt can be lawfully charged at 12 per cent. Compensation can also be claimed. This is claimed as a fixed sum as well as accruing interest as follows:

● if the debt is less than £1,000 - £40;
● if the debt is £1,000 but less than £10,000 - £70;
● if the debt is more than £10,000 - £100.

Only time will tell whether this Act will be effective. Its critics say that the worst thing a business can do when a customer can't or won't pay is ask for even more money.

Knowledge...Knowledge...Knowle

1. How is the value of working capital calculated?
2. At what point does a business have sufficient working capital to avoid a problem?
3. State 4 time lags that exist in the working capital cycle.
4. State 2 ways in which time lags can be reduced.
5. What is meant by a liquidity problem?
6. What does the current ratio show?
7. State 5 causes of a liquidity crisis.
8. What could a business do with its stocks of raw materials to help in a liquidity crisis?
9. What steps should a credit controller take to deal with persistent debts?
10. How might a business prevent a debt problem before it gives credit to a customer?

# key terms

**Credit control** - the process of monitoring and collecting the money owed to a business.
**Liquidity** - the ease with which an asset can be changed into cash.
**Liquidity problems -** difficulties that arise because of the lack of assets that can easily be converted into cash to make immediate payments.

**Overtrading** - a situation where a business attempts to raise production without increasing the size of its working capital.
**Working capital** - the funds left over to meet day to day expenses after current debts have been paid. It is calculated by current assets minus current liabilities.
**Working capital cycle** - the flow of liquid resources into and out of a business.

# Case study Emerson Engineering Ltd

Emerson Engineering Ltd makes a range of components in a modern factory in Sheffield. It employs 43 staff. About 80 per cent of its output is sold to two manufacturers in the UK. The company is efficient, ambitious and reasonably profitable. In recent years it has grown by taking over some smaller competitors in the north.

In 2003 Emerson's sales director gave a presentation at an industrial exhibition in Munich. As a result the company received a number of inquiries from foreign producers. Eventually one of the larger companies placed a sizeable order. To meet these orders Emerson had to step up production. This involved recruiting 4 more staff, purchasing a new machine, buying more materials and components and paying overtime to employees.

However, the expansion began to escalate following a visit to the factory by some French delegates. Two days after their visit another large order was received. Emerson was now beginning to feel stretched. It needed to recruit more staff and buy even more resources. Emerson's cash had run out and the company was dangerously close to exceeding its overdraft limit. Indeed, it would have to exceed this limit at the end of the month to pay wages, which again included large overtime payments.

One of the problems was the credit terms agreed with the foreign customers. They were offered 90 days credit and so far none of the work for these orders had been delivered. The credit period did not start until the goods had been delivered. To add to this was the usual problem of exacting payment from its regular two customers. Whilst they provided Emerson with a reliable stream of profitable orders, they nearly always seemed to delay payment to well

beyond the agreed credit period.

Two days before the foreign orders were due to be delivered on 23.5.2003, an emergency board meeting was held to discuss the cash flow problem. During the meeting three possible solutions were discussed.

- Sale and lease back of machinery to Henderson Associates, a specialist sale and lease back company.
- Sell debts to a debt factoring company.
- An unsecured short term bank loan.

Table 48.2 shows the value Emerson's current assets and current liabilities the day of the emergency board meeting and 12 months ago. Figure 48.3 shows the company's monthly cash position in the previous trading period.

**Table 48.2** *Current assets and current liabilities for Emerson Engineering Ltd, 23.5.2003*

|  | 2003 £000s | 2002 £000s |
|---|---|---|
| **Current assets** | | |
| Stocks of raw materials and components | 1,229 | 1,001 |
| Work-in-progress | 3,445 | 1,765 |
| Debtors | 2,189 | 1,778 |
| Cash at bank | 0 | 1,239 |
| | **6,863** | **5,783** |
| **Current liabilities** | | |
| Trade creditors | 3,112 | 2,311 |
| Taxation | 1,299 | 1,365 |
| Other creditors | 2,100 | 1,765 |
| Bank overdraft | 2,460 | 0 |
| | **8,971** | **5,441** |

**Figure 48.3** *Emerson Engineering Ltd end of month cash position, 2002*

(a) **What evidence is there in the case to suggest that Emerson is overtrading? (6 marks)**

(b) (i) **Calculate the value of working capital for Emerson in 2002 and 2003. (6 marks)**

    (ii) **Do the answers in (i) confirm that Emerson has a cash flow problem? Explain your answer. (6 marks)**

(c) **Explain the disadvantages to Emerson of using (i) sale and lease back (ii) debt factoring to resolve the cash crisis. (10 marks)**

(d) **Discuss whether you think Emerson is in danger of going out of business. (12 marks)**

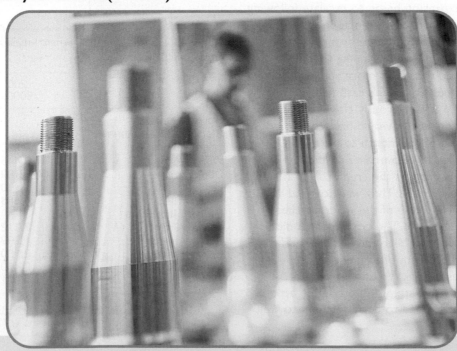

## How are assets valued?

One of the problems in financial accounting is how to place a value on assets. Accountants value assets at **historical cost**, ie the cost of the asset when it is first purchased (☞ unit 51).

There are reasons why assets should be valued in this way. Business transactions are entered into records as they occur. For example, if a firm buys a vehicle for £15,000 and pays cash, two entries will be made in the records. Also, accountants would argue that historical cost can be checked. It is based on actual costs and is better than methods which involve estimates. Other methods of valuation, such as those which take into account inflation, are also used. As yet, though, a suitable replacement has not been found.

One problem with historical cost accounting is how to put a value on fixed assets like property. In recent years there have been times when the values of land and buildings have risen sharply - as much as 30 or 40 per cent in one year. Unless the accounts are amended, they will not reflect the true value of the business. It is common now to revalue assets such as property every few years. Inflation distorts the value of assets and any other value which is measured in money terms.

This unit considers the valuation of two sets of assets - fixed assets, such as machinery, and current assets, such as stock. The valuation of these assets causes particular problems for accountants.

## Valuing fixed assets - the use of depreciation

Fixed assets are used again and again over a long period of time. For example, a milling machine might be used for many years to produce metal components. A motor business would expect automated production lines to run for many years.

During their operation fixed assets are consumed and its value is 'used up'. This measure of consumption or any other reduction in the useful economic life of a fixed asset is known as depreciation (☞ unit 43).

Why might fixed assets depreciate?

● Machinery, tools and equipment all suffer wear and tear when they are used. They deteriorate, which can sometimes affect their operation or effectiveness. Eventually they will have to be replaced.

● Changing technology can often make assets OBSOLETE. Although a machine may still work, it may not be used because a new machine is more efficient.

● Capital goods which are hardly used or poorly maintained may depreciate quickly. The life of machinery can be prolonged if it is 'looked after'.

● The passing of time can also lead to depreciation. For example, if an asset is leased, the 'buyer' can use the asset for a period of time. As the expiry date gets close, the lease becomes worth less and less.

## Depreciation and the accounts

Each year accountants must work out how much depreciation to allow for each fixed asset. This can then be used in the balance sheet and the profit and loss account.

The balance sheet (☞ unit 43) will show the NET BOOK VALUE of assets. This is their original value minus depreciation. So if a piece of machinery is bought for £10,000 and depreciates by £3,000 in the first year, its book value would be £7,000. The book value falls each year as more depreciation is deducted.

Depreciation is shown in the profit and loss account under expenses (☞ unit 42). This indicates that part of the original value is 'used up' each year (known as revenue expenditure (☞ unit 44). Eventually the entire value of the asset will appear as expenses, when the asset depreciates fully. This process of reducing the original value by the amount of depreciation is known as WRITING OFF.

There are good reasons why a firm should allow for depreciation each year in its accounts.

● If it does not, the accounts will be inaccurate. If the original value of assets was placed on the balance sheet this would overstate the value. The value of assets falls each year as they depreciate.

● Fixed assets generate profit for many years. It seems logical to write off the value of the asset over this whole period, rather than when it is first bought. This matches the benefit from the asset more closely with its cost.

● A sensible firm will know that assets must be replaced in future and allow for this. Even though depreciation appears as an expense on the profit and loss account, it is actually a

**Figure 49.1** *A summary of the factors which might cause depreciation*

- Wear and tear
- Passing of time
- **CAUSES OF DEPRECIATION**
- Obsolescence
- Lack of maintenance

PROVISION. Expenses involve paying out money. In the case of depreciation, no money is paid out. A business simply recognises that assets have to be replaced and 'provides' for this by placing a value in the accounts.

# Calculating depreciation - the straight line method

The STRAIGHT LINE METHOD is the most common method used by business to work out depreciation. It assumes that the net cost of an asset should be written off in equal amounts over its life. The accountant needs to know the cost of the asset, its estimated residual value, ie its 'scrap' value after the business has finished with it, and its expected life in years. The formula used is:

$$\text{Depreciation allowance (each time period)} = \frac{\text{Original cost - residual value}}{\text{Expected life (years)}}$$

Assume a delivery van costs £28,000 to buy and has an expected life of 4 years. The residual value is estimated at £4,000.

**Table 49.1** *A summary of the annual depreciation allowance and book value of the delivery van using the straight line method*

| Year | Depreciation allowance (each year) £ | Net book value £ |
|------|------|------|
| 1 | 6,000 | 22,000 |
| 2 | 6,000 | 16,000 |
| 3 | 6,000 | 10,000 |
| 4 | 6,000 | 4,000 |

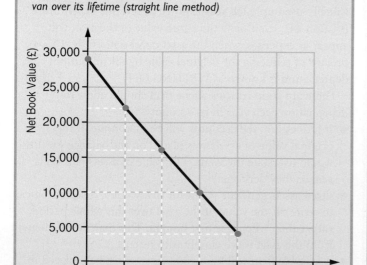

**Figure 49.2** *A graph illustrating the book value of the delivery van over its lifetime (straight line method)*

$$\text{Depreciation allowance} = \frac{£28,000 - £4,000}{4 \text{ years}}$$

$$= \frac{£24,000}{4}$$

$$= £6,000$$

When calculating depreciation it is helpful to draw up a table to show how an asset is written off over its lifetime. Table 49.1 shows the depreciation allowance charged to the profit and loss account each year, and the net book value which is listed in the balance sheet. We can illustrate this on a graph as shown in Figure 49.2. These are some advantages to using this method.

● It is simple. Little calculation is needed and the same amount is subtracted from the book value each year.
● It is useful for assets like a lease, where the life of the asset and the residual value is known precisely.

# Calculating depreciation - the reducing balance method

The REDUCING or DECLINING BALANCE METHOD assumes that the depreciation charge in the early years of an

Edwards Ltd produces plank and strip boards for wooden flooring and skirting boards for the building industry. The business operates from a small factory in Nottingham. In 2003 a new computerised sawing machine was bought for £39,000. Kerry Edwards, the owner of the business, expects the new machine to last for 6 years when it will have a residual value of £3,000.

(a) Calculate the annual depreciation allowance using the straight line method.
(b) (i) Draw up a table to show how the machine is written of over its life.
 (ii) What is the net book value at the end of year 4?

**Question 1**

**Table 49.2** *A summary of the annual depreciation allowance and book value of the vehicle using the reducing balance method*

| Year | Depreciation allowance (each year) £ | Net book value £ |
|---|---|---|
| 1 | 11,200 (28,000 x 40%) | 16,800 |
| 2 | 6,720 (16,800 x 40%) | 10,080 |
| 3 | 4,032 (10,080 x 40%) | 6,048 |
| 4 | 2,419 (6,048 x 40%) | 3,629 |

asset's life should be higher than in the later years. To do this, the asset must be written off by the same percentage rate each year. This means the annual charge falls.

Assume a vehicle is bought for £28,000 and has a life of four years. Table 49.2 shows how the vehicle can be written off using the reducing balance method. A 40 per cent charge will be made each year and the firm expects a **residual value** of £3,629.

Table 49.2 shows the depreciation allowance in the profit and loss account in each of the four years. It also shows the book value which would be listed in the balance sheet. Notice that the depreciation allowance falls every year. This is shown in Figure 49.3. What if the business expected the residual value to be £4,000? The depreciation charge for this can be calculated using the formula:

$$\text{Depreciation rate} = \left[1 - \sqrt[n]{\frac{\text{Residual value}}{\text{Cost}}}\right] \times 100$$

Where n = estimated life of the asset, ie 4 years, so:

$$\text{Depreciation rate} = \left[1 - \sqrt[4]{\frac{4,000}{28,000}}\right] \times 100 = 38.52\%$$

**Figure 49.3** *A graph illustrating the book value of the vehicle over its lifetime (reducing balance method)*

There are some advantages to using the reducing balance method.

● It takes into account that some assets, machinery for example, lose far more value in the first year than they do in the fifth year, say. So the book value reflects more accurately the real value of the asset in the balance sheet.

● For many assets, maintenance and repair costs grow as the asset ages. Using the declining balance method results in a more equal total expense each year for fixed assets related costs. For example, at the end of year 1 the depreciation charge for a machine might be £4,500 with only a £500 maintenance charge. In year 5 the depreciation charge might have been £1,500 and repairs and maintenance may have been £3,000. Although the two totals are not the same (£5,000 and £4,500), as the depreciation charges fall the maintenance and repair costs rise.

William Marshall owns an arable farm in Suffolk. He farms 6,000 acres and employs 4 staff. In the summer of 2004 William decided that he was no longer prepared to lease a combine harvester to harvest his cereal crops. He purchased a brand new combine harvester for £75,000. With good care and maintenance he hoped to keep the machine for 5 years. (After five years a residual value of £5,832 was estimated.)

(a) Draw up a table to show the annual depreciation allowance and the book value at the end of each year. Use the reducing balance method and write off 40 per cent each year.

(b) Draw a line graph to show the annual book value at the end of each year.

(c) Explain why the reducing balance method of depreciation might be more suitable for an asset like a combine harvester.

**Question 2**

## Other methods of calculating depreciation

The **sum-of-the-years' digits method** assumes that fixed assets depreciate quicker in the early years. The calculation is based on the sum-of-the-years' digits, given the expected life of an asset, less the residual value. For an asset which has an expected life of 4 years the sum-of-the-years' is 10, ie 4+3+2+1 = 10. The depreciation charge for the first year will be $^4/_{10}$ of the original cost, the second year it will be $^3/_{10}$ of the original cost and so on.

Assuming a cost of £28,000, a life span of 4 years and a residual value of £4,000, the **net value** of the asset is £24,000 (£28,000 - £4,000). We can draw up a table to show the annual depreciation charge and the book value each year (Table 49.3).

Table 49.3 shows that the depreciation allowance falls in a similar way to the reducing balance method.

**Table 49.3** *A summary of the annual depreciation allowance and book value of the asset above, using the sum-of-the-years' digits method*

| Year | Depreciation allowance (each year) | Net book value |
|------|-----------------------------------|----------------|
| | £ | £ |
| 1 | 9,600 (24,000 x 4/10) | 18,400 |
| 2 | 7,200 (24,000 x 3/10) | 11,200 |
| 3 | 4,800 (24,000 x 2/10) | 6,400 |
| 4 | 2,400 (24,000 x 1/10) | 4,000 |

Another method called the **usage method** (or **machine hour method**) takes into account that some assets wear out more rapidly the more they are used. Thus, depreciation is based on the number of hours a machine, for example, is used during the accounting period. It is not a method that is often used by firms.

# The disposal of assets

The book value of assets rarely reflects their precise value. So if an asset is sold, a business usually makes a profit or a loss. This is likely if the asset is sold before the end of its expected life. For example, if a machine is bought for £100,000 with an expected life of 10 years and residual value of £15,000, the depreciation allowance each year will be £8,500 (using the straight line method). If the firm decides to sell the machine at the end of year 7 and receives £44,000, it earns a profit of £3,500 because the book value at the end of year 7 is £40,500. A firm must show this in the accounts. It is common practice to deal with profit or loss on disposal by adjusting that year's depreciation charge. If a profit is made, the depreciation charge will be reduced by the amount of the profit. If a loss is made, the depreciation charge will be increased by the amount of the loss. If the profit or loss is very large then it will be treated as an exceptional item in the accounts (☞ unit 42).

---

Venetta Gains runs a design business in Cheltenham. Due to the rapid growth in her business in areas such as fabric design, she has decided to buy a new computer. She spent £5,000 on a system which would include a software design package. Venetta planned to use the computer for 8 years, by which time it would have a scrap value of £200.
(a) Calculate the annual depreciation allowance using the straight line method and draw up a table to show the book value at the end of each year.
(b) At the end of the third year Venetta was forced to upgrade her system because it had become outdated. Venetta sold her old system for £1,000. Calculate the profit or loss on disposal.
(c) Comment on the size of the profit/loss.

# Valuing current assets - stock valuation

When accounts are produced, a firm must calculate the quantity and value of the stocks which it is holding. The value of **stocks** at the beginning and the end of the trading year, ie the **opening stock** and the **closing stock**, will affect the gross profit for the year. This is because the cost of sales in the trading account is adjusted for changes in stock. If, for example, the closing stock is overvalued, then the cost of sales will be lower and the gross profit higher. This is shown in Tables 49.4 and 49.5. In Table 49.4 the closing stock is £11,300, the cost of sales (adjusted for stock) is £57,400 and gross profit is £40,500.

In Table 49.5 the closing stock is now valued at £14,100 instead of £11,300, so the cost of sales (adjusted for stock) is lower at £54,600 and the gross profit higher at £43,300.

A **stock take** can be used to find out how much stock is held. This involves making a list of all raw materials, finished goods and work-in-progress. Stock valuation is more difficult. The 'prudence' concept in accounting (☞ unit 51) does not allow selling prices to be used because profit is only recognised when a sale has been made. So stocks are valued at historic cost or net realisable value, whichever is the lowest. Normally stocks would be valued at cost. But there are circumstances when net realisable value is lower. If goods are

**Table 49.4**

| | £ | £ |
|---|---|---|
| Turnover | | 97,900 |
| Opening stock | 12,300 | |
| Cost of sales | 56,400 | |
| | 68,700 | |
| *Less* closing stock | 11,300 | |
| | | 57,400 |
| Gross profit | | 40,500 |

**Table 49.5**

| | £ | £ |
|---|---|---|
| Turnover | | 97,900 |
| Opening stock | 12,300 | |
| Cost of sales | 56 400 | |
| | 68,700 | |
| *Less* closing stock | 14,100 | |
| | | 54,600 |
| Gross profit | | 43,300 |

**Table 49.6** *A record of stock transactions showing how a closing stock figure is calculated using the FIFO method of stock valuation*

| Date | Stock received and price | Stock issued and price | Stock valuation | |
|---|---|---|---|---|
| | | | Goods in stock | Total £ |
| 01.6.04 | 100 @ £5 | | (100 @ £5 = £500) | 500 |
| 04.6.04 | 200 @ £6 | | (100 @ £5 = £500) (200 @ £6 = £1,200) | 1,700 |
| 25.6.04 | | 100 @ £5 | (200 @ £6 = £1,200) | 1,200 |
| 02.7.04 | | 100 @ £6 | (100 @ £6 = £600) | 600 |
| 12.7.04 | 200 @ £6.50 | | (100 @ £6 = £600) (200 @ £6.50 = £1,300) | 1,900 |
| 23.7.04 | | 100 @ £6 | (200 @ £6.50 = £1,300) | 1,300 |
| 24.7.04 | | 100 @ £6.50 | (100 @ £6.50 = £650) | 650 |

damaged in stock, they may sell for a lot less than they cost to produce. Also, some products face severe changes in market conditions. Clothes tend to fall in value when fashions change, and may need discounts to sell them.

What happens to stock valuation when the cost of stock changes over time? Say a business buys some goods at the start of the year, but finds that half way through their cost of replacement has gone up. How are they valued? Three methods can be used.

● FIFO (first in first out).
● LIFO (last in first out).
● Average cost.

# First in first out

The FIRST IN FIRST OUT method assumes that stock for production is issued in the order in which it was delivered. Thus, stocks that are bought first are used up first. Any unused stocks at the end of the trading year will be those most recently bought. This ensures that stocks issued for production are priced at the cost of earlier stocks, while any remaining stock is

valued much closer to the replacement cost. Assuming that the opening stock is zero, consider the following stock transactions in Table 49.6.

On 1.6.04 a business receives 100 units of stock at £5, which means it has £500 of goods in stock. On 4.6.04, an extra 200 units at £6 (£1,200) are added, making a total of £1,700. On 25.6.04, 100 units are issued from stock for production. As it is first in first out, the goods are taken from the 1.6.04 stock, priced at £5 - the first stock to be received. This means £500 is removed from stock leaving 200 units valued at £6 (£1,200) left in stock.

By using the FIFO method, the value of stocks after all the transactions is £650.

# Last in first out

The LAST IN FIRST OUT method assumes that the most recent deliveries are issued before existing stock. In this case, any unused stocks are valued at the older and probably lower purchase price. Table 49.7 shows how the previous transactions are adjusted for a LIFO stock valuation. On

**Table 49.7** *A record of stock transactions showing how the closing stock figure is calculated using the LIFO method of stock valuation*

| Date | Stock received and price | Stock issued and price | Stock valuation | |
|---|---|---|---|---|
| | | | Goods in stock | Total £ |
| 01.6.04 | 100 @ £5 | | (100 @ £5 = £500) | 500 |
| 04.6.04 | 200 @ £6 | | (100 @ £5 = £500) (200 @ £6 = £1,200) | 1,700 |
| 25.6.04 | | 100 @ £6 | (100 @ £5 = £500) (100 @ £6 = £600) | 1,100 |
| 02.7.04 | | 100 @ £6 | (100 @ £5 = £500) | 500 |
| 12.7.04 | 200 @ £6.50 | | (100 @ £5 = £500) (200 @ £6.50 = £1,300) | 1,800 |
| 23.7.04 | | 100 @ £6.50 | (100 @ £5 = £500) (100 @ £6.50 = £650) | 1,150 |
| 24.7.04 | | 100 @ £6.50 | (100 @ £5 = £500) | 500 |

## The nature of investment

Investment refers to the purchase of capital goods. Capital goods are used in the production of other goods, directly or indirectly. For example, a building contractor who buys a cement mixer, some scaffolding, a lorry and five shovels has invested. These goods will be used directly in production. If the contractor buys a computer, a filing cabinet and a photocopier for the firm's office, this is indirect investment. Although these items will not be used in production the business would not run as efficiently without them.

Investment might also refer to expenditure by a business which is likely to yield a return in the future. For example, a business might spend £20 million on research and development into a new product or invest £10 million in a promotion campaign. In each case, money is being spent on projects now in the hope that a greater amount of money will be generated in the future as a result of that expenditure.

Investment can be **autonomous** or **induced**. Autonomous investment is when a firm buys capital goods to replace ones which have worn out. Any new investment by the firm resulting from rising sales or expansion is induced investment.

## Types of investment

Investment can be placed into various categories.

- Capital goods. This includes the purchase of a whole variety of mechanical and technical equipment. Vans, lathes, computers, robots, tools, vehicles and information technology are examples.
- Construction. This includes spending on new buildings that are bought or constructed by the firm. Factories, shops, warehouses, workshops and offices are examples.
- Stocks. This is a less obvious item of investment, since it does not fit neatly into the earlier definition. However, because stocks of finished goods and work-in-progress (☞ unit 82) will earn income in the future when they are sold, they are classed as investment.
- Public sector investment. Central and local government fund about twenty five per cent of all investment in the economy. Examples of public sector investment include the building of schools, motorways, hospitals and expenditure on goods like buses, dustcarts and equipment for the civil service. The factors which influence the level of public sector investment are often very different from those which affect private sector investment. This is dealt with later in this unit.

## Risk in investment

The decision to invest by business is the most difficult it has to make because of the risk involved. There is often a number of alternative choices. A firm buying a new fleet of cars for its sales staff has to decide which model of car will suit the

company best of all. There may also be a considerable choice of projects. For example, a firm may need to choose whether investment in a new packaging machine which increases efficiency would be more profitable than a new computer system.

If all cost and revenue data upon which a decision would be based was accurate, there would not be a problem. However, revenue information in particular comes from predictions. It may be based on forecasts of future demand and conditions in the economy. Even costs, which are perhaps easier to predict, can vary.

Most investment decisions are uncertain because they are

---

In March 2002, ITV Digital, the world's most expensive digital terrestrial TV company, went into administration. It was hoped that the purchase of the rights to broadcast live Nationwide football would be the kingpin of the operation. However, after an investment of £800 million and one of the worst recessions in advertising spending in memory, Carlton and Granada decided they could not tolerate the massive losses. The cost of cutting loose from ITV Digital would be expensive and could have long term repercussions. In the short term, bills of £50-£120 million could be incurred. This was before any potential legal action from the Football League.

The body that represents lower league teams threatened to sue Carlton and Granada for up to £500 million in lost broadcasting and sponsorship revenues if they reneged on a three-year broadcasting deal. It was the league's refusal to renegotiate the deal that finally tipped ITV Digital over the edge. However, it was unlikely that the 72 clubs relying on income from the deal would get anything like the money they were owed. Indeed, around 30 clubs could themselves be on the brink of collapse. Suppliers such as BT, set top box manufacturers and content providers could be left in the lurch. They could also threaten multimillion pound law suits to recover money owed. Meanwhile ITV Digital's 1.3 million subscribers were left feeling betrayed, confused and angry.

The biggest losers in all of this could be the government. It was hoping to switch off the analogue television signal between 2006-10. The government is keen to drive forward the population's commitment to digital TV. It would then be free to auction off the spare analogue spectrum to raise money for public expenditure. This is similar to the sale of third generation mobile phone licences.

Sources: adapted from *The Guardian*, 28.3.2002 and *The Observer*, 31.3.2002.

(a) Using this case as an example, explain why investment is risky.
(b) Describe briefly the effects of the failed investment on the (i) private sector and (ii) public sector.

## Question 1

long term decisions, where resources are committed for a period of time. Investment projects have failed both in the private sector and the public sector. For example, in the private sector, independent TV production company, the Television Corporation, had to write off £13 million on Californian subsidiary Pacifica in 2003. The company was still reeling from a failed bid to set up a Formula One version of power boating. The company had already written off £2.6 million, including £400,000 in the previous year. In the public sector, the government spent a lot of money on equipment which was used in the development of the Concorde aircraft. This also proved to be commercially unsuccessful. Concorde services were stopped in 2004.

Investment is also said to be risky because it is often funded with borrowed money. This means that the return on any investment project must also cover the cost of borrowing. Also, if the investment project fails the company may be left with a heavy debt burden and possibly without the means to repay it. The Channel Tunnel project experienced such problems in the late 1990s. Around £5 billion was owed to several hundred banks following the construction of the tunnel link. Although the company was covering its operating costs, it has ceased interest payments to the banks. It was suggested that it was unlikely ever to be able to repay the original £5 billion borrowed. This was still the case in 2004.

## The factors affecting private sector investment

Figure 50.1 shows the factors which might affect private sector investment decisions.

**Motives** To begin with, firms must have a reason to invest.
- All firms have to replace worn out equipment.

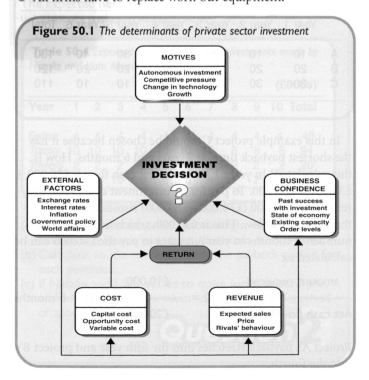

**Figure 50.1** *The determinants of private sector investment*

- To be competitive on costs, price and quality, firms may have to invest or risk losing customers to their rivals. For example, most building societies invested in the refurbishment of their branches in the 1990s. Once one society improved its branch most others copied.
- The availability of new technology (☞ unit 85) may persuade firms to invest. When technology becomes available, firms are often keen to use it if they can afford to.
- Firms may wish to grow, to be more profitable or to increase their market influence. Growth involves investment in more plant, equipment and other productive assets.

**Return** If firms have a reason to invest, they must then decide whether it is worthwhile. One influence on this is the return on the investment. The return on an investment project can be found by subtracting the cost of the project from the expected revenue. There are three major costs. Capital costs might be the cost of a new factory. Opportunity costs (☞ unit 9) are the foregone alternatives the investment funds might have been used for, eg higher dividends to shareholders. Direct variable costs include the running costs of the project, eg labour or fuel costs.

Calculating the expected revenue is not easy. Expected sales are hard to predict with accuracy because many factors affect them. Market research (☞ unit 19) can only predict sales to some extent. Sales can also be influenced by the price set by the business in the future and by rivals' behaviour. Both of these factors are unpredictable.

**Business confidence** Entrepreneurs and managers will be either optimistic or pessimistic about the future of their businesses. Confidence may be influenced by a range of factors. These include whether or not previous investment has been a success, the state of the economy, the existing level of capacity and future order levels. A pessimistic business person may be less likely to invest than an optimistic one.

**External factors** External influences can be direct or indirect. For example, high interest rates may directly affect the cost of investment. If money is borrowed the business will pay back more. This can indirectly affect confidence. Inflation could affect costs, revenue and confidence. World affairs, such as problems in the Middle East in 2003, or rising exchange rates, may make investment abroad seem less attractive.

## The factors affecting public sector investment

What factors influence investment by central government and local authorities?
- Investment in new schools, roads and hospitals, for example, will be influenced by national and local needs. As the demands of the population grow, more of these facilities will be needed.
- Political factors may also influence the quantity and type of

# Case study Parkinson & Co

Parkinson & Co is a food processing company. It has a large factory in Reading and produces a range of canned food products such as soups, vegetables, fruits, processed meats and beans. The business is keen to expand but is unable to increase capacity at its current site. It is considering the construction of a new factory and operating from twin sites. Since an increasing amount of its produce is sold in Europe, sites are being considered in Lyon, France and Valencia, Spain.

## The Lyon Site

The main advantage of this site is that distribution costs and delivery times would be minimised. Parkinson & Co has customers in Germany, Belgium, Italy and Austria, and Lyon is more central than Valencia. However, labour costs are likely to be higher and French workers are represented by strong trade unions. Working practices in Lyon are much less flexible than those in the UK and any effort by Parkinson & Co to introduce untraditional working practices might be met with some resistance. Another problem is that planning permission may be more difficult to obtain in Lyon.

## The Valencia Site

Although the Valencia site is further away from most customers than the proposed Lyon site, it is a much cheaper option. The cost of land is lower in this part of Spain and planning permission is more readily granted for commercial developments. Wage rates are lower and there is a more plentiful supply of labour since unemployment is higher here. It is thought that industrial relations might be better as well. However, another problem is the level of congestion on the roads around this part of Spain. This could affect delivery times.

The capital costs and estimated net cash flows from the two factories over a six year period are shown in Table 50.12.

(a) **Using this case as an example, explain the difference between induced and autonomous investment. (4 marks)**

(b) **For each of the two sites calculate the:**
  (i) **payback period (to the nearest month); (4 marks)**
  (ii) **average rate of return; (6 marks)**
  (iii) **net present value. (8 marks)**

(c) **On purely financial grounds, which site is the most financially viable? Explain your answer. (4 marks)**

(d) **Discuss the advantages and disadvantages to Parkinson & Co of using the methods of investment appraisal in (b). (10 marks)**

(e) **Using all the available information, discuss which site you think Parkinson & Co should select. (14 marks)**

**Table 50.12** *Capital cost and estimated net cash flows from the two factories*

|  | Year 0 | Year 1 | Year 2 | Year 3 | Year 4 | Year 5 | Year 6 |
|---|---|---|---|---|---|---|---|
| **The Lyon site** | | | | | | | |
| Capital cost | 8.2m | | | | | | |
| Estimated net cash flow | | 2.3m | 2.6m | 2.7m | 3.0m | 3.3m | 3.4m |
| **The Valencia site** | | | | | | | |
| Capital cost | 6.1m | | | | | | |
| Estimated net cash flow | | 2.2m | 2.5m | 2.7m | 2.9m | 3.2m | 3.2m |

**Table 50.13** *Present value of £1 receivable at the end of 6 years at 5%*

| After | Year 0 | Year 1 | Year 2 | Year 3 | Year 4 | Year 5 | Year 6 |
|---|---|---|---|---|---|---|---|
| Present value of £1 | £1.00 | £0.95 | £0.90 | £0.86 | £0.82 | £0.78 | £0.75 |

## Business transactions

Business activity involves purchasing resources, such as raw materials, labour and machinery, and selling goods or services that have been produced using these resources. The purchase of resources from suppliers and the sale of products to customers are examples of BUSINESS TRANSACTIONS. Other examples include borrowing money from a bank and the payment of taxes. For a small business, such as Robinson's fish and chip shop, examples of business transactions might include:

- the purchase of potatoes from a wholesaler for £250;
- the sale of fish and chips to a customer for £4.30;
- the payment of £140 interest to a bank;
- the sale of a portion of chips and curry sauce to a customer for £2.90;
- a payment of £120 to an employee.

It is important for a business to keep accurate records of these transactions. Every single transaction should be recorded. In this example the sales made by the fish and chip shop are likely to be recorded on a till roll. The value of purchases may be written in a book. During the year such a business may be involved in possibly thousands of individual transactions.

In contrast, for a very large business such as BT, the number of transactions that take place in a year is immense. Every telephone call made using the BT network is recorded as a separate transaction. Such transactions are recorded electronically and their value is calculated by computer. BT's customers receive quarterly statements summarising these transactions. BT must also record details of its expenditure, such as payments to its employees and purchases of telecommunications equipment.

## Recording business transactions and the accounting process

Bookkeepers are responsible for recording business transactions. They play an important role in the **accounting process**. This involves recording, classifying and summarising business transactions. The aim of the process is to generate useful financial information that can be communicated to a range of business stakeholders, such as shareholders, managers and the media, for example (☞ unit 3). Many sole traders keep their own records because they cannot afford bookkeepers. As a firm grows, it may become cost effective to take on a bookkeeper, part-time perhaps. In large businesses, with their own finance departments, bookkeepers will work under the supervision of accountants. It is also likely that most of their work will be done on a computer.

Jules Germaine runs a music business and is also a professional musician. He makes part of his income from hiring his services to touring bands who want a musician to play on a few songs, but not to be a permanent band member. Sometimes he is paid in a lump sum after a gig. Other times he is paid regularly over a period of time.

Another part of his business involves, selling instruments to collectors. He is a regular visitor the USA and he has a number of contacts there who can find him old instruments from people's houses. They try to hunt down 'finds' in attics or garages that might be worth something. Jules can fix these up and then sell them to shops or to specialist collectors.

A final part of his services is the teaching of music. He will often buy in music notation paper for this students, reeds for instruments and DVDs and videos to show playing techniques.

(a) Identify the business transactions that take place in the Jules Germaine's music business.
(b) Explain why the business might find it difficult to keep accurate records of transactions.

## Question 1

Figure 51.1 illustrates the stages in the accounting process. When a transaction takes place, it should be verified by a **document** - an invoice, receipt or cheque stub perhaps. From these documents entries are made in the company's books. The first entries are likely to be made in the books of **prime entry**, where details of all transactions may be recorded almost as they happen. The **day books** will contain records of purchases and sales, while the **cash book** lists the flows of money into and out of the business. At the end of the month, entries in these books will be totalled and recorded in **ledgers**. The main purpose of these subsidiary books is to avoid overloading the ledgers.

Ledgers form the basis of any book-keeping system. A ledger contains details of individual business accounts. The **sales ledger** records transactions with customers and the **purchase ledger** records those with suppliers. The accounts of customers and suppliers are called personal accounts. All others are impersonal and are recorded in the nominal ledger. The headings in the nominal ledger might include:

- the wages account, which records the wages paid to

employees;
- the purchase account, which records all business purchases from suppliers;
- the sales account, which records all business sales.

From time to time a company may wish to check that all previous entries were made correctly. This can be done by producing a TRIAL BALANCE. Finally, various accounts can be produced using the information gathered from book-keeping. They include the profit and loss account (☞ unit 42), the balance sheet (☞ unit 43) and cash flow statements(☞ unit 46).

**Figure 51.1** *Stages in the accounting process*

# The need for accounting concepts

The accounts of a business should reflect a 'true and fair' view of its financial position. To achieve this accountants apply a series of 'rules' or ACCOUNTING CONCEPTS. These are also known as **conventions** or **principles**. In the USA, and increasingly in the UK, the expression GAAP is used to refer to 'generally accepted accounting principles'.

By using agreed concepts when analysing and presenting financial information, accountants can avoid confusion and inconsistency. There is also less scope for presenting misleading financial information and the accounts of different businesses can be compared more easily.

The concepts or principles have developed over time as a framework within which accountants operate. In the UK, the Accounting Standards Committee (ASC) was established in the 1970s. This committee issued a number of **Statements of Standard Accounting Practice (SSAPs)**. The ASC described four 'fundamental accounting concepts' in its Statements of Standard Accounting Practice (SSAP 2). These are the:
- going concern concept;
- consistency concept;
- prudence concept;
- accruals or matching concept.

Since 1990, the regulation of accounting in the UK has passed over to the Accounting Standards Board (ASB). SSAPs still exist, but any new standards are now called **Financial Reporting Standards (FRSs)**. During 2001, the Financial Reporting Standard *Accounting Policies (FRS 18)* was introduced to replace SSAP 2. These are:
- relevance;
- reliability;
- compatibility;
- understandability.

FRS 18 states that a business should regularly review its accounting policies to ensure they remain the most appropriate to the business's circumstances. Specific disclosure about the policies used, and any changes to the policies, must be made.

In addition to the fundamental concepts listed above, a number of others are generally accepted. These include objectivity, business entity, money measurement, historical cost, dual aspect, realisation and materiality.

# Accounting concepts

**Objectivity** As far as possible accounts should be based on verifiable evidence rather than on personal opinion. In other words they should be objective rather than subjective. So, for example, an accountant should value a transaction on the basis of an invoice rather than his or her own personal opinion. This avoids bias. Consider what might happen if two accountants were asked their opinion on the value of a particular transaction, for example the purchase of new premises. They might disagree because value can be measured in many different ways. However, if they were asked to value the transaction according to the invoice, they would likely record exactly the same value.

**Going concern** Accountants assume that the business will continue for an indefinite period of time. Assets are valued as if they will continue in their present use, rather than at NET REALISABLE VALUE - the value the asset would raise if it were sold. Assets are therefore valued at the cost when they are bought, known as HISTORICAL COST. This holds even if the asset is bought at a bargain, eg half the manufacturer's recommended price. If things change, and it is necessary for the business to cease trading, assets may be valued according to what they 'might realise'. In some cases this might be less than their cost. Special accounting techniques will then be used to deal with the situation.

**Accruals or matching** This means that costs and revenue should be matched with the period in which they occur. For example, at the end of the trading year a company may have an outstanding electricity bill for power used in that trading period. According to this principle, the cost should be included even though the bill is unpaid. Related to this is the **realisation** concept. This states that profit occurs when goods or services change hands and not when payment is made.

**Consistency** Once a decision has been made about the allocation of costs or the valuation of assets it should not be changed. This will make comparisons more meaningful and reduce the chance of figures being distorted.

**Prudence and caution** If an asset is bought at a bargain price, rather than the recommended price, the lower value is always recorded. This conforms with the concept of **prudence** and **caution**. Accountants undervalue future revenue or profit until it is realised. In contrast, they make provision for costs or losses immediately they occur, even if they are only forecast.

**Materiality** Accountants should avoid wasting time trying to accurately record items of expenditure which are trivial. For example, a business might purchase a waste paper bin for the office for £1.50. This bin might last for 15 years or more, however, the bin is not a 'material' item. Even though it is expected to be used for many years the purchase should be recorded once and treated as an expense in the year it was bought. No attempt should be made to 'write off' the expenditure over the period of time the bin is in use. There is no law which governs materiality. Different firms may use a variety of arbitrary methods to determine which items of expenditure are material and which are not. For example, a business may decide that all items of expenditure under £50 should be treated as expenses in the period for which they were bought, even if some items are actually used for many years. The method of assessing materiality will be selected by accountants using their judgment.

**Separate entity** A business is a 'legal' person in its own right and has a separate identity from that of the owners. Where a sole trader, for example, uses a van for personal reasons and business, it is important to divide the running costs between the owner and the business.

**Money terms** When recording business transactions, it has long been common practice to record them in money terms.

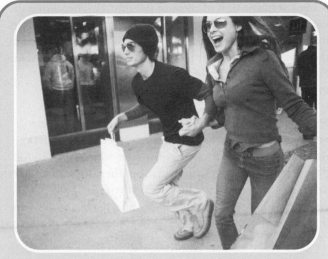

Chris and Amy Phillips opened up a modern boutique in a fashionable part of London in September 2003. They took out a lease, transformed the premises with very stylish fittings and purchased some exclusive stock from French and Italian clothes suppliers. They invested £25,000 of their own money in the venture. The business started well, but after Christmas trade fell away. In March 2004 it was running out of cash. Chris and Amy were overdrawn at the bank and losing heart very rapidly. They felt that the business might have to close down and wondered how much money they would be left with. The balance sheet for the boutique is shown in Table 51.1.

**Table 51.1** *Balance sheet for Chris and Amy's business*

|  | £ | £ |
|---|---|---|
| **Assets** | | |
| Fixtures and fittings | | 9,800 |
| Stock | | 12,200 |
| Debtors | | 2,400 |
| | | 24,400 |
| **Less Liabilities** | | |
| Trade creditors | 7,500 | |
| Lease | 2,000 | |
| Bank overdraft | 1,300 | |
| | | 10,800 |
| | | 13,600 |
| **Financed by:** | | |
| Capital | | 13,600 |
| | | **13,600** |

(a) Explain how an accountant might have valued Chris and Amy's fixed assets if the business was a going concern.
(b) If Chris and Amy did close down the business, what factors might have affected the value of the assets?

Question 2

Money acts as a unit of account (☞ unit 1). This allows the values of goods and services to be expressed accurately and makes comparison easier. Financial statements only include those matters which can be easily expressed in money terms. For example, the skills of the workforce would not be included.

**Historical cost** All assets are valued according to their original cost rather than what they are currently worth. Accountants prefer to deal with values which have, in the past, been confirmed with evidence. They do not like to rely on estimates, even if the historical entries are dated.  This convention has been subject to change, particularly when, due to inflation, the historical cost values become inaccurate and do not provide a true and fair view of the company's financial position.

**Dual aspect** The DUAL ASPECT concept states that every transaction has two effects on the business's accounts. Suppose, for example, that a business buys some goods on credit. Assets, increase, because stocks increase, and liabilities also increase because money is owed to a creditor. Similarly, if the business repays a loan of £1,000 to a bank, there is a dual aspect. Liabilities decrease, because the loan is repaid, and assets decrease because the business has less money. In accordance with the dual aspect concept, each transaction is recorded twice by bookkeepers.

# key terms

**Accounting concepts, principles or conventions** – rules or guidelines that accountants follow when drawing up accounts.
**Business transactions** – an event that affects the finances of the business, for example, the purchase of resources from suppliers and the sale of products to customers.
**Dual aspect** – the idea that every transaction has two effects on the accounts.

**Historical cost** - the value of an asset when purchased, ie the amount paid.
**Net realisable value** - the value of an asset when sold, ie the amount received.
**Trial balance** - a statement that lists all the balances on all accounts in the accounting system.

# Knowledge Knowledge...Knowledge...Knowledge...Knowledge...Know

1. Describe the stages in the accounting process.
2. What is the role of the bookkeeper in the accounting process?
3. What is the difference between day books and ledgers?
4. What is the function of the trial balance?
5. State 3 final accounts of a business that are produced from the accounting process.
6. What is the role of the Accounting Standards Board?
7. What is an FRS?
8. What are the fundamental concepts which aim to make the accounts a 'true and fair' view of the firm's financial position?
9. What is meant by the concept prudence and caution?
10. Explain the difference between objectivity and subjectivity in accounting.

# Case study Healthcare Staffing Services

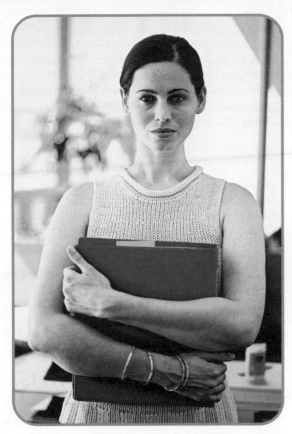

Christine Thompson runs Healthcare Staffing Services, an employment agency in Ealing, London. The business specialises in the provision of staff for local hospitals, nursing homes and retirement homes. She has a total of 450 staff registered with her agency and is developing a very profitable business at a time when there are staff shortages in the industry and the rates paid for supply staff are very high.

She enjoys most aspects of the business, particularly interviewing prospective recruits and dealing with health care managers. However, she is not so keen on recording the business's transactions. Like many sole traders she records business transactions herself. In one respect she is quite diligent. Christine keeps all receipts and invoices. However, the only written records that she makes are the payments and receipts in a cash book. She does this on the last Sunday in every month. At the end of the financial year Christine pays a local

accountant to produce her accounts. At the end of 2003 five transactions were giving Christine some concern.

- One month before the end of the trading year Christine paid her annual office rent of £12,000. However, Christine decided not to include the payment in her records because nearly all of the amount related to next year.

- During the year Christine purchased the following items - a calculator for £12, an office kettle for £9 and a painting for £8.50. These items are expected to be used by the business for many years to come and Christine wonders whether the expenditure should be 'written off' over their life, just like the office computer.

- Christine uses her car for business purposes throughout the week. However, at weekends she uses it for personal travel. Total motor expenses for the whole year are £6,700. She is not sure how to divide the motor expenses between business and personal use.

- During the year Christine purchased a new printer for her computer which cost £400. However, she noticed that the supplier had reduced the price of the printer three months later to £199. She is not sure which value to record.

- Christine has been supplying relief nursing staff to a small private hospital in West London for 3 months, but has not yet received payment for their wages from the hospital, a total of £24,000.

**(a)** Describe three possible business transactions that might be undertaken by Healthcare Staffing Services. **(6 marks)**

**(b)** Explain why Christine keeps all the receipts and invoices for the business. **(6 marks)**

**(c)** Christine keeps records in a cash book. Explain what this means. **(6 marks)**

**(d)** Explain why accounting concepts are necessary when producing the accounts of Healthcare Staffing Services. **(8 marks)**

**(e)** Explain how Christine should treat each of the above transactions according to the appropriate accounting concepts. **(14 marks)**

# 52 Costing Methods

## What is costing?

The process of measuring the likely consequences of a business activity is called COSTING. Costing systems benefit a business in a number of ways. They provide managers with financial information on which to base decisions. They help to identify the profitable activities, avoid waste and provide information for cost cutting strategies. Costing can also assist the marketing department in setting the price of products. Examples of costing exercises include:

- measuring the cost of manufacturing individual products;
- calculating whether or not it would be more economical to contract out a particular business operation, eg security;
- determining the cost of moving to a new business location;
- estimating the cost of decorating the office.

What costing methods might be used by firms? Methods include absorption, standard and marginal costing.

## Absorption costing

ABSORPTION COSTING is also known as FULL COSTING or TOTAL COSTING. The main principle of absorption costing is that all the overheads or indirect costs are 'absorbed' by cost centres. In other words, all overheads are included when calculating the cost of producing particular items. The main problem is how to allocate a firm's overheads between different cost centres (☞ unit 39). One simple approach is to use an arbitrary method. For example, a manufacturer which makes two metal components code named ZX 1 and ZX 2 may have the direct costs of producing 100,000 of each component shown in Table 52.1.

Assume that total indirect costs are £300,000. We need to calculate the percentage each component contributes to total direct cost.

$$\text{For ZX 1} = \frac{200}{500} \times 100 = 40\%$$

$$\text{For ZX 2} = \frac{300}{500} \times 100 = 60\%$$

The £300,000 indirect costs can now be allocated to each component.

For ZX 1 indirect costs = 40% x £300,000 = £120,000
For ZX 2 indirect costs = 60% x £300,000 = £180,000

**Table 52.1** Direct costs of two components

| | | | £000 |
|---|---|---|---|
| Component | ZX 1 | ZX 2 | Total |
| Direct cost | 200 | 300 | 500 |

---

Bantom Ltd manufactures motorbikes in its Bristol factory. It makes three models:
- the Fury - a racing bike with a 1000 cc engine;
- the Trialmaster - a popular trials bike;
- the XL10 - a standard 500 cc road bike.

Details of the direct production costs are shown in Table 52.2. Bantom also incurs indirect costs of £600,000 per month. The company manufactures 100 of each bike per month.

**Table 52.2** Direct costs for Bantom Ltd

| | | | (£ per bike) |
|---|---|---|---|
| | Fury | Trialmaster | XL10 |
| Direct labour | 250 | 150 | 200 |
| Raw materials | 150 | 120 | 100 |
| Components | 400 | 300 | 340 |
| Other direct costs | 200 | 130 | 160 |

(a) Calculate the direct costs of producing 100 of each motorcycle.
(b) Allocate the indirect costs of production to each product as a percentage of direct costs.
(c) Calculate the full cost of producing 100 of each bike.

## Question 1

The total cost or full cost of producing 100,000 of each component can now be calculated. This is done by adding the allocated indirect costs to the direct costs.

For ZX 1 full cost = £120,000 + £200,000 = £320,000
For ZX 2 full cost = £180,000 + £300,000 = £480,000

This approach is often criticised for the arbitrary way it allocates indirect costs. It could result in misleading costings because the allocation of indirect costs is not based on any

**Table 52.3** Bases for apportioning overheads

| Indirect costs | Basis |
|---|---|
| Rent and rates | Floor area of cost centres |
| Heating and lighting | Floor area, the volume or size of cost centres |
| Personnel costs (ie health & welfare) | Number of staff employed by each centre |
| Buildings insurance | Floor area or book value of buildings in each centre |
| Machinery & equipment insurance | Book value of machinery used by each centre |
| Depreciation (plant, machinery & tools) | Book value of assets used by each centre |
| Maintenance | Book value of assets used by each centre |
| Supervisory costs | Number of staff, or hours worked by supervisor in each centre |
| Staff canteen | Number of staff employed by each centre |
| Administration | Number of staff employed by each centre |

actual indirect costs incurred.

To improve the accuracy of absorption costing a business may prefer to **apportion** overheads or indirect costs. This involves allocating a certain percentage or proportion of indirect costs to each cost centre. A business must decide on what basis to apportion indirect costs. The basis depends on the nature of the indirect cost. Table 52.3 shows how a selection of overheads might be apportioned.

To illustrate absorption costing take the example of Dudley Car Exhausts which manufactures three types of exhaust systems, the E1, E2, and E3. Factory time and direct cost details (per system) are shown in Table 52.4. Annual indirect costs include rent, selling costs, overheads and administration. These are £12,000, £18,000, £24,000 and £4,000 respectively. Rent is apportioned according to the factory time used by each system. Selling costs and overheads are apportioned equally between all systems. Administration is apportioned according to the labour input of each system (most administration costs in this case are labour related, eg wages). Dudley Car Exhausts produces 1,000 of each system every year.

**Table 52.4** *Factory time and direct costs for Dudley Car Exhausts*

| System | Labour (£) | Materials (£) | Fuel (£) | Factory time(hrs) |
|--------|-----------|---------------|----------|-------------------|
| E1 | 2 | 3 | 1 | 1 |
| E2 | 2 | 4 | 2 | 3 |
| E3 | 4 | 4 | 2 | 2 |
| Total | 8 | 11 | 5 | 6 |

Using the absorption costing method it is necessary to allocate every single business cost to the production of the three systems. For E1 the total direct cost is calculated by adding labour, materials and fuel, ie $(2 + 3 + 1 = £6)$. To apportion rent to the production of one E1 system it is necessary to take into account the amount of factory time one E1 system uses, ie $^1/_6$ of the total time and also the number of E1 systems produced, ie 1,000 during the year. The following calculation must now be performed:

$$\text{Rent apportioned to one E1 system} = £12,000 \times \frac{1}{6} \times \frac{1}{1,000}$$

$$= \frac{£12,000}{6,000}$$

$$= £2$$

Selling costs and overheads are split equally between each system, so that selling costs are £6 and overheads £8 for each system. Administration costs are apportioned according to the amount of labour used to make each system. For the E1 system the allocation can be calculated as follows.

Administration costs apportioned to one E1 system

$$= £4,000 \times \frac{£2}{£8} \times \frac{1}{1,000}$$

$$= £4,000 \times \frac{1}{4} \times \frac{1}{1,000}$$

$$= \frac{£4,000}{4,000}$$

$$= £1$$

The complete cost schedule for all three systems is shown in Table 52.5.

**Table 52.5** *The cost of producing the three exhaust systems using the absorption method of costing*

(£)

| System | Direct | Rent | Selling | Overheads | Admin. | Total |
|--------|--------|------|---------|-----------|--------|-------|
| E1 | 6 | 2 | 6 | 8 | 1 | 23 |
| E2 | 8 | 6 | 6 | 8 | 1 | 29 |
| E3 | 10 | 4 | 6 | 8 | 2 | 30 |
| Total | 24 | 12 | 18 | 24 | 4 | 82 |

Some businesses use the absorption method to set the price of their products. Once the cost of each unit has been calculated a profit percentage is added to determine the selling price.

# Advantages and disadvantages of absorption costing

There are certain advantages to a business in using the absorption cost method of apportioning indirect costs.

● It ensures that all costs are fully recovered. This means that businesses will cover their costs as long as the actual costs and level of activity are similar to the budgeted figures. Therefore if a business uses a cost-plus pricing policy, it knows that the prices charged will generate a profit.

● It is fair provided overheads are not allocated in an arbitrary way. This is because costs are apportioned to those activities that actually incur them.

● The method conforms to the accounting standard SSAP 9 *Stocks and work-in-progress* (☞ unit 57). This states that absorption costing should be used when valuing stocks in the final accounts. This is because absorption costing includes a share of the fixed costs. It therefore recognises these fixed costs in the same period as revenues, and so conforms to the 'matching' principle.

However, the method does have some limitations.

● Cost information used might be inaccurate. This is because the figures are generally based on historical data which may not reflect future costs or activity levels. As a result, businesses might **underabsorb** or **overabsorb** their overheads and could set prices that are too low or too high.

● In practice, absorption costing can be complex, time consuming and expensive to gather detailed information from different cost centres. This is particularly the case for small firms that do not employ specialist cost accountants.

● Some costs are difficult to apportion exactly to a particular cost centre. For example, how can a business apportion electricity costs to different cost centres accurately if there is only one meter?

---

Renfrews is a small department store in Leeds. It has five departments and each one is operated as a cost centre. This helps to monitor the costs of running the business. A newly appointed cost accountant has suggested that the current method of apportioning overheads is inappropriate and should be reviewed. Table 52.6 shows the direct costs and some other details relating to the various cost centres. An analysis of overheads is also given. The value of overheads in 2003 was £500,000.

**Table 52.6** *Information for each cost centre operated by Renfrews, 2003*

|  | Food Hall | Women's wear | Men's wear | Electrical goods | Toys | Total |
|---|---|---|---|---|---|---|
| Direct costs | £400,000 | £200,000 | £100,000 | £200,000 | £100,000 | £1,000,000 |
| Staff employed | 12 | 8 | 4 | 6 | 6 | 36 |
| Floor space | 800m² | 600m² | 600m² | 400m² | 200m² | 2,600m² |

**Overheads**
| Rent & electricity | = £300,000 |
|---|---|
| Administration | = £200,000 |
| **Total** | **= £500,000** |

(a) Suggest suitable bases for apportionment for the overheads. Explain your answer.
(b) Using the bases of apportionment shown in (a), calculate the full or total cost of operating each department at Renfrews in 2003.

## Standard costing

Some businesses focus on standard costs. A standard cost is a planned or 'target' cost. It is normally associated with a specific activity or a particular unit of production. For example, a business manufacturing cans of fizzy drink may say that the standard cost per can is 17p. This means that the **usual** cost per can is 17p. STANDARD COSTING involves calculating the usual or planned costs of an activity and then comparing these with the actual costs incurred. The difference between the standard cost and the actual cost is called a

variance (☞ unit 47). Standard costing helps businesses to monitor and control costs. For example, the standard cost and actual cost of making a circuit board for an electronics company is shown in Table 52.7. In this example the actual cost is 50p more than the standard cost.

**Table 52.7** *The standard cost and actual cost of producing a circuit board*

| Description | Standard cost | Actual cost |
|---|---|---|
| Materials | 90p | 90p |
| Components | 120p | 120p |
| Labour | 350p | 400p |
| Indirect costs | 140p | 140p |
| Total | 700p | 750p |

This means that there is a variance of 50p. Such a variance is likely to result in the business carrying out an investigation to determine why the actual cost of manufacturing the circuit board was higher than expected, ie higher than the standard cost. In this case the actual cost is higher because the labour cost was £4 compared with an expected labour cost of £3.50. This may have been caused by, say, a new recruit working a little more slowly than a fully experienced operative.

## Advantages and disadvantages of standard costing

There are certain advantages to a business in using standard costing.

● By comparing standard costs with actual costs a business can identify areas of weakness and inefficient practice. For example, large adverse variances on materials costs might suggest that materials are being wasted in production.

● Staff can be motivated if they achieve cost targets which they are involved in setting. In some cases staff might be rewarded financially if they reach or exceed targets.

● Standard costs may represent the best estimate of what a product should cost to make. So, by using standard costs, estimates of costs for products and price quotations for orders are likely to be more reliable.

However, there may also be disadvantages.

● Like absorption costing, standard costing requires a business to gather a large amount of information. This process can be time consuming and expensive. Also, since standard costs are updated regularly, this cost is ongoing.

● The method may be inappropriate if certain management methods are used. For example, if kaizen (☞ unit 80) is adopted, where workers are expected to strive for continuous improvement, standards might become a barrier to innovation. Employees might regard standards as 'ceilings' and therefore the incentive to improve further is

removed.
- Standard costing may encourage staff to strive for favourable variances, even if this harms the firm's overall objectives. For example, staff may take short cuts to reduce costs. This might reduce the quality of the product and lead to a fall in sales.

# Contribution or marginal costing

CONTRIBUTION or MARGINAL COSTING ignores fixed costs and focuses on variable costs. The method involves looking at the amount of **contribution** a product or order makes (☞ unit 40). Contribution can be calculated as selling price minus variable cost for a unit. Total contribution is the revenue from units sold (price x quantity) minus the total variable costs. Generally, if the revenue from products or orders exceeds the variable costs, ie the contribution is positive, then managers are likely to consider them for production.

A situation where contribution costing might be helpful is when choosing which orders to accept from customers. For example, Thompson Engineering has received two late orders and only has the resources to accept one. One is for 1,000 metal panels and the other for 800 metal brackets. Details of the revenue, variable costs and contribution are shown in Table 52.8.

**Table 52.8** *Sales revenue, variable costs and contribution for two orders received by Thompson Engineering*

(£)

|  | Metal panels | Metal brackets |
|---|---|---|
| **Revenue** | **12,000** | **17,000** |
| **Variable costs** |  |  |
| Materials | 3,000 | 5,500 |
| Direct labour | 4,200 | 6,900 |
| Other variable costs | 1,700 | 3,000 |
| **Total variable costs** | **8,900** | **15,400** |
| **Contribution** | **3,100** | **1,600** |

In this example, where only one order can be accepted, Thompson Engineering is likely to accept the order for the metal panels. This is because the panels make the largest contribution out of the two orders. Even though the metal brackets generates more revenue, the panels' contribution is £1,500 higher (£3,100 - £1,600). Note that the marginal costs of the orders are £8,900 for the panels and £15,400 for the brackets. In each case they are the same as the total variable costs.

In this case fixed costs have been ignored. This is because accepting either of the orders had no effect on Thompson Engineering's fixed costs. However, in circumstances where accepting orders results in additional fixed costs, they must be taken into account.

Coates manufactures biscuits in its Derby factory. The company has a reputation for innovative product development. It generally introduces at least one new product each year. Sometimes the new products are added to the product range, other times they replace existing products. A new product, 'Coates Krunchie', is ready for launch which the company plans to use as a replacement for one of its existing products. Two products are being considered for withdrawal, both nearing the end of their life cycle. Table 52.9 shows the 2003 revenue and variable costs for the two products facing withdrawal.

**Table 52.9** *Sales revenue and variable costs for the two products that Coates is considering for withdrawal*

(£)

|  | Dairy Krunchie | Coates Shortcake |
|---|---|---|
| **Revenue** | **129,000** | **112,000** |
| **Variable costs** |  |  |
| Materials | 67,500 | 56,400 |
| Direct labour | 36,400 | 32,100 |
| Other variable costs | 16,900 | 19,200 |

(a) Calculate the contribution made by each of the existing products in 2003.
(b) Which of the two products should be withdrawn to make way for 'Coates Krunchie'? Explain your answer.

# Question 3

# Special order decisions

Sometimes businesses receive orders which are unexpected, from a new customer or for a new product perhaps. On these occasions a business has to decide whether or not to accept the order. The business will consider whether or not the order is profitable. However, even if the order is not profitable it may still be accepted. This may be because the business is considering the size of the **contribution** when making the decision to accept the order.

For example, Powerfire Ltd makes high speed powerboats for the luxury boat market.
- Its **fixed costs** are £500,000 per annum and **variable costs** £18,000 per boat.
- The **price** of the boats is £23,000 each and last year the business **produced and sold** 120 boats.
- The **total costs** of the business are £500,000 + (£18,000 x 120) = £2,660,000.
- The **total revenue** of the business is £23,000 x 120 = £2,760,000.
- This generated a **profit** of £2,760,000 - £2,660,000 = £100,000.

What if, unexpectedly, the business received an order from a new customer for 10 boats, for which the customer was only willing to pay £19,000 each? The contribution that this order would make is:

**revenue** of 10 x £19,000 (£190,000) *minus*
**variable costs** only of 10 x £18,000 (£180,000)
= £10,000.

Note that only the variable costs are taken into account for the order of 10 extra boats because the fixed costs have been covered by production of the original 120 boats. Sale of the extra 10 boats at £19,000 would help to raise profit to £110,000 assuming last year's figures (£100,000 plus £10,000). If Powerfire sold all 130 boats for £19,000 it would make a **loss** of £370,000. This is found by revenue of £2,470,000 (£19,000 x 130) minus costs of £2,840,000 (£500,000 + [130 x £18,000]).

The single unexpected order is worth accepting on financial grounds because the contribution is positive and annual profit rises. However, it would only be accepted if the price of all other boats is unchanged. A number of non-financial factors might also be considered before accepting the order:

● Capacity. A business must ensure that it has enough resources to complete the order. For example, are workers prepared to work extra hours? Is there enough space in the factory? Will it replace other, more profitable, production?

● Customer response. If existing customers find out that products have been sold to others for lower prices this might cause resentment. It might damage the image of the company and lead to lost sales in the future.

● Future orders. Sometimes unprofitable orders are accepted in anticipation of future, more profitable orders, from the new customer.

● Current utilisation. An unprofitable order may be accepted to keep staff occupied. It may be better to have permanent staff employed completing orders with small contributions rather than doing nothing.

● Retaining customer loyalty. A business may accept an unprofitable order from a regular customer as a favour in order to retain their loyalty.

## Advantages and disadvantages of contribution costing

There are advantages to a business in using the contribution costing method.

● It is simple to operate. Unlike absorption costing, the difficulty in sharing fixed costs between different products or cost centres is avoided. There is the advantage that under or overabsorption of overheads does not occur.

● It is a useful decision making tool. It can be used when ranking products or choosing between orders. It is also useful when deciding whether to make or buy-in a particular product or component.

However, there are some disadvantages.

● In some industries contribution costing is inappropriate, particularly when fixed costs represent the majority of a firm's costs. For example, the cost to a train or bus operator of carrying one more passenger is almost zero. Most of the operator's costs are fixed and the variable cost of transporting one more passenger is perhaps just the cost of issuing the ticket. If most customers only pay fares that cover the low variable costs, a business will make a loss because it will not cover the huge fixed costs. However, this does explain the benefit of filling empty seats at discount fares, as long as fixed costs are already covered. The money earned from these passengers adds a lot more to revenue than it does costs.

● When valuing stocks in final accounts, SSAP 9 *Stocks and work-in-progress*, states that the absorption method should be used and not the marginal costing method.

● It can lead to bias in costing calculations. For example, a cost centre that uses a high proportion of overheads may be making a positive contribution. However, when the amount of overheads are taken into account that same centre may be making a loss for the business.

## The relationship between marginal and average cost

Average total cost and marginal cost were defined in unit 38. These two curves are shown in Figure 52.1. Notice that the marginal cost curve cuts the average cost curve at its lowest

---

Phillip Partington manufactures golfing umbrellas. He sells them to a wide range of wholesalers and golfing organisations for a price of £4. He is not operating at full capacity and has just been approached by a Swedish company to see if he could supply 20,000 umbrellas for £3.50. Phillip's cost structure is shown in Table 52.10. He currently produces 100,000 umbrellas a year, but has the capacity to produce 130,000.

**Table 52.10** *Phillip Partington's cost structure*

| Materials and components | per unit | £0.70 |
|---|---|---|
| Direct labour | per unit | £1.60 |
| Other variable costs | per unit | £0.50 |
| Fixed costs | | £80,000 |

If the Swedish order was accepted, a further £13,000 in fixed costs would be incurred to cover exporting expenses.

(a) Calculate (i) the annual contribution and (ii) the amount of profit made; without the Swedish order.
(b) On financial grounds alone, advise Phillip whether or not to accept the Swedish order. Show all calculations.
(c) Discuss two non-financial considerations which might influence the final decision.

**Question 4**

point. Why? Consider a business building houses with an average cost of £50,000.

● If another house is built (the marginal house) with a higher than average cost, the average cost will rise;
● if the marginal house cost less than the average cost, the average cost would fall;
● if the marginal house cost £50,000 (the same as average cost) then the average cost would remain the same.

So the marginal and average costs are equal when average costs are constant. On a U-shaped average cost curve this is only at the one point, the lowest point. At all other points the average cost curve in Figure 52.1 is either rising or falling.

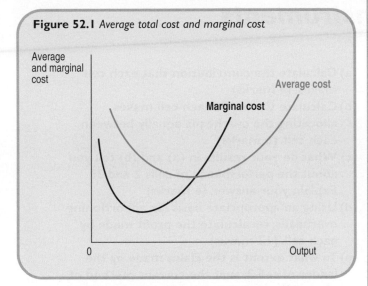

**Figure 52.1** *Average total cost and marginal cost*

## The closing-down point

In the short run it may be worth continuing production of a product even when a loss is being made. This can be shown for a whole company as well. Consider the case of a shop whose present cost and revenue conditions are shown in Table 52.11. If the shop remains open it incurs total costs of £1,500 and generates £700 in sales revenue. This results in a loss of £800. However, if the shop closes this loss is increased to £1,000. Although total costs fall to £1,000 because there are no variable costs to pay, total revenue falls to zero because there are no sales. Thus, in the short run it pays the shop to remain open because losses are lower. However, when revenue is incapable of covering variable costs the firm should close down.

Diagrammatically, the CLOSING-DOWN POINT can be shown by combining the average total cost, average variable cost and marginal cost curves (☞ unit 38), as in Figure 52.2. The closing-down point is where marginal cost is equal to average variable cost. When the price falls below $P_1$ on the diagram, the firm can no longer cover its variable costs. At this point the firm may decide to close down.

**Table 52.11** *Cost and revenue information for a shop*
£

|  | Open | Closed |
|---|---|---|
| Fixed cost | 1,000 | 1,000 |
| Variable cost | 500 | - |
| Total cost | 1,500 | 1,000 |
| Total revenue | 700 | - |
| Loss | 800 | 1,000 |

**Figure 52.2** *The firm's short run closing-down point*

## key terms

**Absorption costing or full costing or total costing** - a method of costing which involves charging all the costs of a particular operation to a unit of output.
**Closing-down point** - the level of output in the short run where a firm should cease its operations, ie where marginal cost is equal to average variable cost.
**Costing** - the process of measuring the likely economic consequences of a particular business activity or operation.
**Contribution or marginal costing** - the process of costing the production of one more unit of output.
**Standard costing** - the process of calculating the costs of a specific activity and then comparing them with the actual costs incurred.

1. Describe the benefits of costing.
2. How might the following indirect costs be apportioned: (a) office wages; (b) corporate advertising; (c) factory insurance?
3. What is the main advantage of the absorption costing?
4. In what way is the absorption method limited?

5. How are fixed costs treated in contribution costing?
6. What is meant by standard costing?
7. What are the advantages and disadvantages of contribution costing?
8. When might a loss making contract be accepted?
9. Explain when a firm should close down in the short run.

# Case study AK Instruments

AK Instruments makes machines for the food processing industry. The company leases a factory and employs 228 staff. To deal with the wide variety of designs and customers the business uses a system called 'cell production'. There are four cells and each is responsible for its own design, purchasing, production and maintenance of a specific 'family' of products. Each 'family' of products has its own similarities and features. Two hundred of the staff are split between the various cells and most of the remainder are employed in the office, dealing with administrative work.

The business has been under pressure recently from foreign competition. As a result profits have been modest. It has also been suggested that cells 2 and 3 are 'holding the company back' because in some years they make a loss. However, the team leader of cell 3 says that the way overheads are currently allocated favours cells 1 and 4. At the moment the overheads are divided equally between the four cells. This is an arbitrary method of allocation.

Following a formal request from the leaders of cells 2 and 3 the financial director is to investigate the claim that the allocation of overheads is currently unfair.

(a) **Calculate the contribution that each cell makes. (4 marks)**
(b) **Calculate the profit each cell makes, allocating the overheads equally between each cell. (6 marks)**
(c) **What do your results in (a) and (b) tell you about the performance of cells 2 and 3? Explain your answer. (6 marks)**
(d) **Using an appropriate basis for apportioning overheads, recalculate the profit made by each cell. (12 marks)**
(e) **To what extent is the claim made by the leader of cell 3, that the current method of allocating overheads (dividing them equally between each cell) is unfair, true? (12 marks)**

**Table 52.13** *Overheads*

|  | £000s |
| --- | --- |
| Leasing charges | 1,200 |
| Factory canteen | 2,000 |
| Administration | 2,000 |
| Depreciation | 3,000 |
| **Total** | **8,200** |

**Table 52.12** *Financial and other information relating to AK Instruments*

|  |  |  |  |  | (£000) |
| --- | --- | --- | --- | --- | --- |
|  | Cell 1 | Cell 2 | Cell 3 | Cell 4 | Total |
| **Revenue** | **9,900** | **5,100** | **6,200** | **10,400** | 31,600 |
| **Variable costs** |  |  |  |  |  |
| Materials & components | 1,900 | 1,200 | 1,300 | 2,000 | 6,400 |
| Direct labour | 2,800 | 1,500 | 2,100 | 2,400 | 8,800 |
| Other variable costs | 1,800 | 900 | 800 | 2,800 | 6,300 |
|  | Cell 1 | Cell 2 | Cell 3 | Cell 4 | Total |
| Staff employed | 75 | 25 | 50 | 50 | 200 |
| Floor space | 1,000m² | 1,000m² | 1,000m² | 3,000m² | 6,000m² |
| Book value of machinery | £8m | £4m | £4m | £8m | £24m |

## Constructing break-even charts

**Break-even charts** (☞ unit 41) provide a visual means of analysing the effect of changes in output on total cost, total revenue, profit and the margin of safety. The effects of changes in fixed costs, variable cost and price on profit and the margin of safety can also be shown. A break-even chart can be constructed by plotting the total cost and total revenue equations on a graph. The graph should measure output on the horizontal axis and costs, revenue and profit on the vertical axis.

Consider Reidle Bros, a small canoe manufacturer. It incurs fixed costs of £20,000 per annum and variable costs of £75 per canoe. The canoes are sold for £125 to agents and wholesalers. The following steps can be used to construct a break-even chart.

**Calculating the break-even point** It is helpful to calculate the break-even point before constructing the graph. For Reidle Bros the total costs (TC) and total revenue (TR) equations are:

$$TC = £20,000 + £75Q \text{ (fixed costs + variable costs)}$$

$$TR = £125Q \text{ (price} \times \text{quantity)}$$

Reidle Bros will break-even when total revenue equals total costs. This is where:

$$
\begin{aligned}
£20,000 + £75Q &= £125Q \\
£20,000 &= £125Q - £75Q \\
£20,000 &= £50Q \\
\frac{£20,000}{£50} &= Q \\
400 &= Q
\end{aligned}
$$

Therefore, Reidle Bros will break-even when it manufactures 400 canoes.

**Calculating points on the total revenue and total cost functions** Both the total cost and total revenue functions are **linear** or straight. Therefore the lines can be drawn by joining two points which lie on each function. To plot the total revenue function we need to choose two levels of output and calculate the total revenue at each level. Any two levels of

output could be chosen. However, construction will be simpler if 0 is chosen as one of the points. It is also helpful to choose a second value which is twice that of the break-even point. This would be 800 (2 x 400) in the case of the canoe manufacturers. This will ensure that the break-even point is in the centre of the chart. This improves presentation. The value of total revenue at each of these output levels is shown in Table 53.1.

**Plotting the total revenue (TR) function** The TR function can now be plotted on the graph. The output axis should run from 0 to 800 canoes and the other axis from 0 to £100,000. Using the information in Table 53.1, the two points, or coordinates, on the TR function are (0, 0) and (800, £100,000). If these are plotted on the graph and joined up the TR function will appear as shown in Figure 53.1.

**Plotting the total costs (TC) function** To plot the TC function we need to calculate the total cost at two levels of output. It is useful to use the same values as those used for the TR function, ie 0 and 800. The TC function can now be plotted on the graph. From Table 53.1 the two points which lie on the TC function are (0, £20,000) and (800, £80,000). If these are plotted on the graph and joined up the TC function will appear as shown in Figure 53.1. Note that the total cost function does not start at coordinates 0,0. At an output of zero, the business still has fixed costs of £20,000.

**Analysis from the diagram** The break-even chart is now complete. An analysis of certain points on the diagram can be made.

● The break even point can be identified and plotted. It is usual to draw lines to show the number of canoes Reidle Bros must sell to break-even (400), and the value of TR and TC at this level of output (£50,000). The break-even point should coincide with the calculation made in the first

**Table 53.1** *Values of TR and TC at two levels of output for Reidle Bros*

| Q | TR | TC |
|---|---|---|
| 0 | 0 | £20,000 |
| 800 | £100,000 (125 x 800) | £80,000 (20,000 + [75 x 800]) |

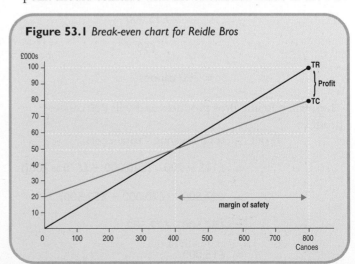

**Figure 53.1** *Break-even chart for Reidle Bros*

step, ie 400 canoes.

- The profit at certain levels of output may be indicated. For example, at an output of 800 canoes, the profit is £100,000 - £80,000 = £20,000.
- The margin of safety can be indicated. This is the difference between the output of the business and the break-even point. At an output of 800 canoes it is 800 -400 = 400 canoes.

Joanne Williams, a student, believed she could make some money during the summer holidays by operating as a mobile ice-cream vendor. She hired a purpose built van from one of the national ice-cream producers. This cost £200 per week. The variable costs per ice-cream cone were 30p. Joanne was under contract to sell ice-cream cones for 80p each. In order to analyse the profit potential at different sales levels she drew up a break-even chart.

(a) Draw a break-even chart for Joanne Williams.
(b) Using your chart state: (i) the number of cones needed to break-even; (ii) the profit she would make if she sold 700 cones.
(c) On your chart show the margin of safety if 700 cones were sold.

## Question 1

## Target rate of profit

Break-even analysis can be used to calculate the amount of output needed to generate a certain level of profit. For example, if Reidle Bros wanted to make £15,000 profit, the level of output required to do this would be:

$$\frac{\text{Fixed cost + profit target}}{\text{Contribution}}$$

$$= \frac{£20,000 + £15,000}{£50 \ (£125 - £75)}$$

$$= \frac{£35,000}{£50}$$

$$= 700 \text{ canoes}$$

Thus, when Reidle Bros produces and sells 700 canoes profit is:

Profit = total revenue - total costs

= £125 × 700 - (£20,000 + [£75 × 700])

= £87,500 - (£20,000 + £52,500)

= £87,500 - £72,500

= £15,000

Palmer and Minton manufacture lawn tractors in their Hereford factory. They are sold through mail order for £900 each. Their fixed costs are £50,000 p.a. and variable costs £700 per tractor. Palmer and Minton established their partnership in 1998 and for the first two trading years they broke-even. In the next financial year they set a profit target of £150,000.

(a) Calculate how many lawn tractors Palmer and Minton need to produce and sell to reach their profit target.
(b) Calculate the margin of safety if the profit target is reached.

## Question 2

## Break-even price

Sometimes a business may want to know how much to charge for its product to break-even. In these circumstances a business must know how much it is going to produce and sell. For example, assume Reidle Bros aimed to sell 500 canoes and its objective was to break-even at that level of output. The price it should charge to break even would be:

$$\text{Break-even price} = \frac{\text{Total cost}}{\text{Output}}$$

$$= \frac{£20,000 + (500 \times £75)}{500}$$

$$= \frac{£20,000 + £37,500}{500}$$

$$= \frac{£57,500}{500}$$

$$= £115$$

Thus, if output was 500, Reidle Bros must charge £115 per canoe to break-even.

## Price needed to reach a target rate of profit

A business may want to determine the price it needs to charge in order to reach a target rate of profit. For example, if Reidle Bros wanted to make a profit of £40,000, and its production capacity was 1,000 canoes, the price it would need to charge to reach this target rate of profit would be:

$$\text{Price} = \frac{\text{Profit target + total cost}}{\text{Output}}$$

$$= \frac{£40,000 + (£20,000 + 1,000 \times £75)}{1,000}$$

$$= \frac{£40,000 + £95,000}{1,000}$$

$$= \frac{£135,000}{1,000}$$

$$= £135$$

Thus, Reidle Bros would have to charge £135 for each canoe in order to make £40,000 profit if it produced and sold 1,000.

# Accounting for changes in costs and revenues

One of the weaknesses of break-even analysis discussed in unit 41, is the assumption that the total cost and total revenue functions are **linear.** This indicates that as output increases, total cost and total revenue rise by the same proportion. What actually happens to total costs and total revenue as output increases can affect the decisions a business makes based on its break-even analysis, given a fixed amount of capital.

**Total cost** Assume a factory is built for 1,000 workers. As more workers are employed they can specialise in different tasks (☞ unit 1). 500 workers are likely to be more productive than one, for example. At some point, however, the opportunity to take advantage of specialisation may be used up and although total output will continue to rise, each extra worker will be less

**Table 53.2** *The effect on output and total cost as a firm employs more workers given a fixed amount of capital*

| Capital (machines) costing £100 each | Labour (workers) costing £200 per week | £ Fixed costs (machinery) | £ Variable costs (labour) | Total cost (£) | Output (units) |
|---|---|---|---|---|---|
| 10 | 0 | 1,000 | 0 | 1,000 | 0 |
| 10 | 1 | 1,000 | 200 | 1,200 | 20 |
| 10 | 2 | 1,000 | 400 | 1,400 | 54 |
| 10 | 3 | 1,000 | 600 | 1,600 | 105 |
| 10 | 4 | 1,000 | 800 | 1,800 | 152 |
| 10 | 5 | 1,000 | 1,000 | 2,000 | 180 |
| 10 | 6 | 1,000 | 1,200 | 2,200 | 192 |

productive. For example, if 2,000 workers were employed in the above factory, there would not be enough machinery available for all workers to be usefully employed.

This is called the law of DIMINISHING RETURNS. It states that as more of a variable factor (labour here) is added to a fixed factor (say capital) the output of the extra workers will rise and then fall. In other words output will rise but at a diminishing rate. In extreme cases output may even fall. This is called negative returns.

How does this affect the costs of a business? Table 53.2 shows the effect on output and total cost of hiring labour at £200 per week with fixed capital costs of £100 per machine. The output per worker always rises, but eventually at a diminishing rate. For example, when the fourth worker is employed output rises by 47 units, but the fifth worker adds only 28 units. Total costs rise as the firm employs more labour. The effect of diminishing returns on the firm's total cost function is shown in Figure 53.2. Notice that it is non-linear.

**Total revenue** The total revenue function drawn earlier in this unit assumed that each unit would be sold for the same price. In reality, it is unlikely that a firm can continually sell

Julia Robinson owns a large farm and supplies apples to cider producers. Apple production is only part of the farm's output. Most of the profit is generated from milk production. Julia is happy if apple production breaks even each year. The orchard was inherited from her grandfather and Julia does not wish to cease apple production for sentimental reasons, even though it is generally unprofitable. Whether she achieves her aim depends on how many apples she harvests and the going market price. At the end of the season Julia had picked 60,000 kilos. The fixed costs associated with apple production were £6,000 for the year. Variable costs were 40p per kilo.

(a) Calculate the price per kilo Julia would need to receive in order for apple production to break-even.
(b) Calculate the profit Julia would make from apple production if the market price was: (i) 48p per kilo; (ii) 51p per kilo.

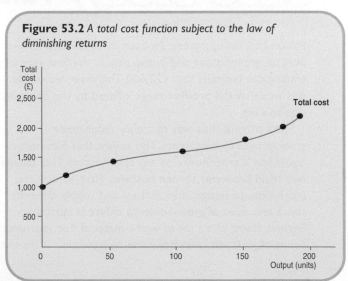

**Figure 53.2** *A total cost function subject to the law of diminishing returns*

its output for the same price. There comes a point where additional sales can only be made if the price is lowered, for example a business may offer lower prices to customers who buy larger quantities. Figure 53.3 shows that as the price is lowered to encourage more sales the total revenue earned by the business falls.

---

Aimsley House is a private nursing home located in Bournemouth. It is well established and has served the local council for many years. Aimsley House generally operates at full capacity. It can accommodate up to 25 patients. Up until 1998 Aimsley House and the local council had negotiated financial terms upon which patients would be accepted. However, in 1999 the council informed the management of Aimsley House that, in the future, terms would not be negotiable. The council would state how much they are prepared to pay per patient and local homes would have to tender for the business at the 'going price'. This announcement was a cause of concern for the management of Aimsley House. They wondered whether the business would continue to make a healthy profit. The fixed costs at Aimsley House are £150,000 per annum and variable costs are £5,000 per resident.

(a) Assuming that Aimsley House continues to operate at full capacity, calculate the price that would enable the management to make £50,000 profit per annum.
(b) Assume that the council offers a price of £12,500 per patient every year.
  (i) Calculate the amount of profit Aimsley House would make.
  (ii) Discuss whether the management of Aimsley House should accept this offer.

**Question 4**

---

The graph also shows a total cost function subject to diminishing returns. Notice that there are now two break-even points, $Q_1$ and $Q_2$. When linear functions are used on a break-even chart, as output is increased beyond the break-even level of output, profit continues to increase indefinitely. When non-linear functions are used profit can only be made over a particular range of output, ie between $Q_1$ and $Q_2$. If production is pushed beyond $Q_2$ losses are made.

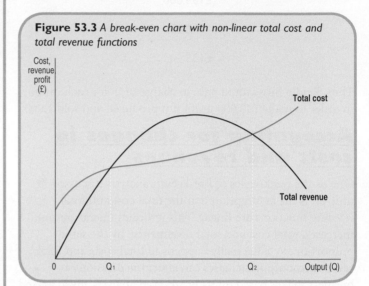

**Figure 53.3** *A break-even chart with non-linear total cost and total revenue functions*

**key terms**

**Diminishing returns** - the eventual decline in output each extra worker adds to total output when the opportunity to specialise is used up.

---

## Case study Falcon Ltd

Falcon Ltd, set up by Eric Hobson in 2002, supplies and puts up greenhouses and outhouses. In the first year of trading the business lost £23,600. The main reason for this was that the product range offered by the company was too big.

Eric's original idea was to supply tailor-made greenhouses to customers. This meant that a customer could buy a greenhouse to any specification. This caused two main problems for the business. First, it took too much time to design, manufacture and supply different styles and sizes of greenhouse to different customers. Second, there was a lot of waste material. For example, panes of glass left over from one construction were not

reused in the next because the design was different. Eric also had staffing problems. He only employs two staff but during the first year he recruited and lost 11 employees. It seemed that the problem was low pay. All 11 workers left for higher paid jobs. The disruption caused by the high labour turnover compounded what turned out to be a very frustrating year for Eric.

During the winter Eric attended a seminar for new business people organised by his local Chamber of Commerce. This was a valuable experience. He learnt a lot and decided to rethink his business strategy for the next year. One key decision was to supply standard greenhouses only which he would sell for £800. He also

**Figure 53.4** *Fixed costs for Falcon Ltd*

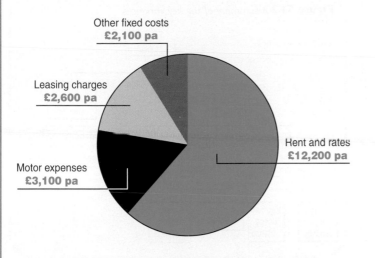

Other fixed costs
£2,100 pa

Leasing charges
£2,600 pa

Motor expenses
£3,100 pa

Rent and rates
£12,200 pa

**Figure 53.5** *Variable costs for Falcon Ltd*

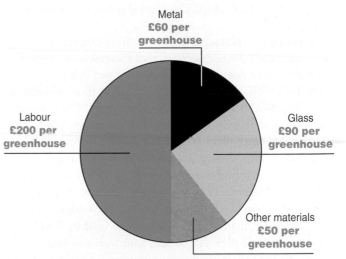

Metal
£60 per
greenhouse

Labour
£200 per
greenhouse

Glass
£90 per
greenhouse

Other materials
£50 per
greenhouse

set a financial target. He wanted the business to break-even next year. However, in order to do this Eric had to gather some information on costs. This information is shown in Figures 53.4 and 53.5.

**(a) Show the equations for total cost and total revenue and calculate the number of greenhouses that Falcon Ltd needs to sell to break-even in 2003. (6 marks)**

**(b) (i) By the end of the year Eric had sold 60 greenhouses. Construct the break-even chart and show the profit made by Falcon Ltd at this level of output. (12 marks)**

**(ii) Label the margin of safety on the graph and explain what it means for Falcon Ltd. (8 marks)**

**(c) In 2004, Eric decided to outsource the production of the greenhouse frames to reduce construction time. It would also reduce fixed costs since he can now operate from much smaller premises. Assuming that fixed costs fell by £4,000, make the necessary adjustments to the break-even chart and show the new level of break-even output. (8 marks)**

**(d) In 2004, Eric decided to set a profit target of £26,000 for the business. Calculate how many greenhouses Falcon Ltd would need to sell to meet this target. (6 marks)**

**(e) To what extent might Falcon Ltd be affected by the law of diminishing returns in the future? (10 marks)**

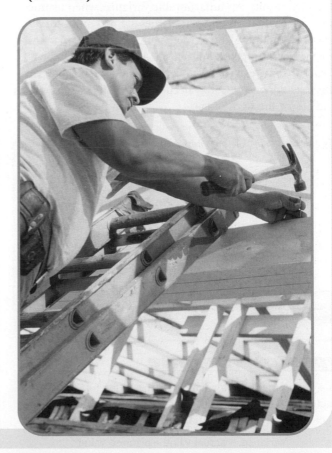

## What is budgetary control?

BUDGETARY CONTROL involves a business looking into the future, stating what it wants to happen, and then deciding how to achieve these aims. The control process is shown in Figure 54.1.

- Preparation of plans. All businesses have objectives (☞ unit 4). If the sales department increases sales by ten per cent, how does it know whether or not this is satisfactory? Targets are usually set which allow a business to determine if its objectives have been met. The results it achieves can then be compared with the targets it sets.
- Comparisons of plans with actual results. Control will be effective if information is available as quickly as possible. Managers need budgetary data as soon as it is available. Recent developments in information technology have helped to speed up the supply of data. For budgeting purposes the financial year has been divided up into smaller control periods - usually four weeks or one calendar month. It is common to prepare a budget for each control period. At the end of the period the actual results can then be compared with targets set in the budget.
- Analysis of variances. This is the most important stage in the control process. VARIANCE ANALYSIS involves trying to find reasons for the differences between actual and expected results. An unfavourable variance, when planned sales are 1,000 units and actual sales are 800 units, for example, might be due to inefficiency. It is then up to the management to take some action. A variance might be the result of some external factor influencing the business. In this case the business may need to change its business plans and adjust the next budget.

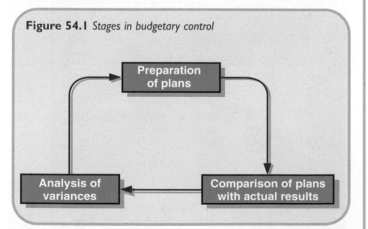

**Figure 54.1** *Stages in budgetary control*

Preparation of plans → Comparison of plans with actual results → Analysis of variances →

## Types of variance

Unit 47 explained that a **variance** is the difference between the actual and the planned figure that the business had budgeted for. It can be calculated by:

Variance = actual value - planned value

A favourable variance is where, for example, actual sales revenues are greater than planned revenues or actual costs are

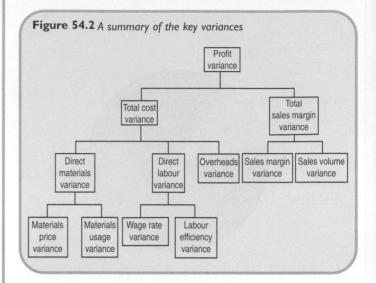

**Figure 54.2** *A summary of the key variances*

Llantrisant Holdings design and manufacture dials, instruments and sensor equipment for the electronics industry. The company relocated when it won a substantial contract to supply a large South Korean electronics company. The South Korean company set up a factory in Cardiff and was keen for its suppliers to be located in close proximity. Llantrisant Holdings delivers just-in-time to its Korean customer. Llantrisant has begun to enjoy substantial efficiency gains in the last 18 months. Representatives from its South Korean customer visited the Llantrisant factory before awarding the contract. During their visit they made helpful recommendations about alternative working practices.

**Table 54.1** *Budgeted profit and loss account and actual figures for Llantrisant Holdings (1999)*

|  | Budgeted | Actual | Variances |
|---|---|---|---|
| Sales revenue | 7,435 | 7,546 |  |
| Cost of sales | 4,950 | 4,100 |  |
| Gross profit | 2,485 | 3,446 |  |
| Overheads | 1,250 | 1,280 |  |
| Operating profit | 1,235 | 2,166 |  |

(a) (i) Complete Table 54.1 by calculating the variances.
   (ii) Explain whether the operating profit variance is adverse or favourable.
(b) Analyse the variance which has had the most influence on the operating profit variance.

**Question 1**

lower than planned. An adverse variance may be where actual sales revenues are less than planned or actual costs are higher than planned.

Figure 54.2 shows examples of variances that a business might decide to calculate and analyse. The profit variance is influenced by all other variances. A change in any one of the variances will affect profit. Most variances are linked to the costs incurred by a business. This suggests that variance analysis provides a very good way of monitoring business costs. There may be other variances which are not shown in the diagram. The number of possible variances is equal to the number of factors which can influence business costs and revenue.

## Profit variances

The most important of all variances is the **profit variance**. Differences between actual profit and planned profit will be of particular interest to business owners, managers and other stakeholders. The performance of most businesses is often measured by profit. All other variances will affect the profit variance, though not by the same magnitude. For example, if planned sales in January are £45,000 and actual sales are £48,500, there is a favourable sales variance of £3,500 (£48,500 - £45,000). This does not necessarily mean that the profit variance will improve by £3,500. This is because the extra sales are likely to generate a cost variance. This will offset some of the benefit.

## Direct materials variance

Figure 54.2 shows that the **total cost variance** can be influenced by several cost variances. One of these is the **direct materials variance**. This is the difference between budgeted direct materials costs and actual direct materials costs. Direct materials include raw materials, components and any other resources used directly in production. For example, a biscuit manufacturer may use flour as one of its raw materials. Table 54.2 shows the budgeted and actual price of flour and the budgeted and actual usage of flour in a particular budget period. According to the table, the budgeted direct materials cost of the flour is £3,000. However, the actual direct materials cost is £2,860. This gives a favourable direct materials variance of £140 in this budget period.

**Table 54.2** Cost and usage of flour for a biscuit manufacturer

| | Price (per kilo) | Usage (kilos) | Direct materials cost |
|---|---|---|---|
| Budgeted | £1.50 | 2,000 | £3,000 |
| Actual | £1.30 | 2,200 | £2,860 |
| Direct materials variance | | | £140 (F) |

The favourable variance in Table 54.2 is influenced by two other variances.

**Materials price variance** This will result when the actual price of direct materials is different from the budgeted or standard price. In Table 54.2 this is calculated by:

Materials price variance = (budgeted price - actual price) x actual usage
= (£1.50 - £1.30) x 2,200
= £0.20 x 2,200
= £440 (F)

The materials price variance is favourable because the actual cost is lower than the budgeted cost. This variance may be the responsibility of the purchasing department. Materials price variances could arise for a number of reasons, for example:
- materials may be obtained at a special discount;
- a new supplier might have been found;
- unexpected inflation may raise prices;
- a price war may have broken out in the market.

**Materials usage variance** A materials usage variance is found by comparing the actual usage of materials and the budgeted usage. The difference is valued at the budgeted price. For the biscuit manufacturer above the variance is:

Materials usage variance = (budgeted usage - actual usage) x budgeted price
= (2,000 - 2,200) x £1.50
= -200 x £1.50
= £300 (A)

The materials usage variance is adverse because the actual usage is greater than the budgeted usage. The effect will lead to lower profit. This variance might be the responsibility of the production manager. Materials usage variances might arise

Simpson's potato chips are produced by Simpson Ltd. It supplies the retail trade in Yorkshire and a few other outlets in the north. Its factory is located in Dewsbury and it employs 24 staff. The most important raw material is potatoes which it purchases from a large potato farmer in Lincolnshire. Table 54.3 shows the budgeted and actual prices paid for potatoes and the budgeted and actual usage of potatoes in a particular budget period.

**Table 54.3** Budgeted and actual prices and usage of potatoes for Simpson Ltd

| | Price (per kilo) | Usage (kilos) | Direct material cost |
|---|---|---|---|
| Budgeted | 10p | 20,000 | £2,000 |
| Actual | 12p | 24,000 | £2,880 |

(a) For the budget period calculate:
  (i) the materials price variance;
  (ii) the materials usage variance;
  (iii) the direct materials variance.
(b) Explain how the results in
  (a) might affect the business.

**Question 2**

because materials are:
- wasted in production due to sloppy or careless work;
- wasted because they are inferior;
- used more efficiently because staff take more care in their work;
- wasted due to a machine malfunction.

The direct materials variance for the biscuit manufacturer is £140 (F). It is influenced by both the materials price variance which is favourable, £440, and the materials usage variance which is adverse, £300. Notice that the adverse usage variance is outweighed by the favourable price variance.

## Direct labour variances

The direct wage bill is the amount of money paid to workers involved in production. A direct labour variance will occur when the budgeted direct wage bill is different to the actual direct wage bill. In the case of the biscuit manufacturer, the budgeted wage rates and actual wage rates, and the budgeted number of labour hours and the actual number of labour hours used in a particular budget period, are shown in Table 54.4. The planned direct wage bill is £7,500. However, the actual wage bill is £8,320. This results in a £820 adverse variance. The direct labour variance is influenced by two other variances.

**Table 54.4** *Budgeted and actual wage rates and labour hours for the biscuit manufacturer*

|  | Wage rate | No. of labour hours | Direct wage bill |
|---|---|---|---|
| Budgeted | £5.00 | 1,500 | £7,500 |
| Actual | £5.20 | 1,600 | £8,320 |
| Direct labour variance |  |  | £820 (A) |

**Wage rate variances** A wage rate variance will result if there is difference between the budgeted wage rate paid to workers and the actual wage rate paid. In the case of the biscuit manufacturer the wage rate variance is :

Wage rate variance = (budgeted wage rate - actual wage rate) x actual hours
$$= (£5.00 - £5.20) \times 1,600$$
$$= -£0.20 \times 1,600$$
$$= £320 \text{ (A)}$$

The wage rate variance is adverse because the actual wage rate is higher than the budgeted wage rate. The personnel manager may be responsible for this variance. The factors which might influence wage rates could include:
- trade union pressure;
- shortages of skilled labour;
- using a different type of labour;
- government legislation, such as raising the minimum wage.

**Labour efficiency variances** There will be a labour efficiency variance if there is a difference between the budgeted number of labour hours required in a budget period and the actual number of labour hours used. In the case of the biscuit manufacturer, the labour efficiency variance is:

Labour efficiency variance = (budgeted hours - actual hours) x budgeted wage
$$= (1,500 - 1,600) \times £5.00$$
$$= -100 \times £5.00$$
$$= £500 \text{ (A)}$$

The labour efficiency variance is adverse because the actual number of hours worked is greater than the budgeted number. The production manager may be responsible for this variance. The factors which might influence the number of labour hours used might include:
- the productivity of workers;
- the reliability of machinery used by workers;
- how well trained workers are.

---

Wallace & Co. makes a range of swimwear which it sells to retailers in the UK. It operates six monthly budget periods. The direct labour budget is shown in Table 54.5. The actual figures for 2004 are also shown. Although swimwear is subject to seasonal demand, Wallace & Co. prefers to keep production fairly constant and build up stocks during the winter. This has helped to maintain good industrial relations in the past.
(a) For the six month budget period calculate:
  (i) the wage rate variance;
  (ii) the labour efficiency variance;
  (iii) the direct labour variance.
(b) Explain what is likely to have caused the direct labour variance.

**Table 54.5** *Direct labour budget and actual figures for Wallace & Co, 2004*

|  | Jan | Feb | Mar | Apr | May | Jun |
|---|---|---|---|---|---|---|
|  | Btd. Act. | Btd. Act. | Btd. Act. | Btd. Act. | Btd. Act. | Btd. Act. |
| Labour (hrs) | 800 810 | 800 820 | 800 810 | 800 200 | 800 800 | 800 810 |
| Wage rate | £5 £5 | £5 £5 | £5 £5 | £5 £5 | £5 £5 | £5 £5 |
| Direct lab. costs (£) | 4,000 4,050 | 4,000 4,100 | 4,000 4,050 | 4,000 1,000 | 4,000 4,000 | 4,000 4,050 |

Btd. = budgeted   Act. = actual

**Question3**

The direct labour variance for the biscuit manufacturer is £820 (A). It is influenced by the wage rate variance, £320(A), and the labour efficiency variance, £500 (A).

# Overheads variances

Overheads variances arise when planned overhead costs are different from the actual overhead costs. Overheads are the general expenses incurred by a business (☞ unit 42). Table 54.6 shows the annual budgeted and actual overheads for the biscuit manufacturer. The overhead variances are also shown. The total overheads variance is adverse (£4,200). The main reason for this is the adverse distribution variance of £7,000. Some of the overheads in Table 54.6 do not have any variances. This is because the budgeted figures are exactly the same as the actual figures. This may happen when a business pays some of its bills in advance. For example, a business will normally know what rent is going to be charged in the next twelve months. This helps businesses to produce more accurate budgets.

Sometimes a business might separate overheads into fixed and variable costs (☞ unit 38). A business could then calculate the fixed overhead variance and the variable overhead variance. Overhead variances might be caused by:
- excessive or under utilisation of a service, such as wasteful or uneconomic use of a service;
- price changes for a service, such as an increase in accountancy fees;
- a change in the nature of a service, such as using oil for heating instead of electricity.

**Table 54.6** *Annual budgeted and actual overheads for the biscuit manufacturer*

| Description | Budgeted | Actual | Variance |
|---|---|---|---|
| Rent | £60,000 | £60,000 | 0 |
| Rates | £5,500 | £5,500 | 0 |
| Insurance | £1,200 | £1,300 | £100 (A) |
| Maintenance | £16,000 | £15,000 | £1,000 (F) |
| Distribution | £78,000 | £85,000 | £7,000 (A) |
| Telephone | £1,700 | £1,600 | £100 (F) |
| Administration | £64,000 | £62,000 | £2,000 (F) |
| Accountancy fees | £4,500 | £4,700 | £200 (A) |
| Depreciation | £20,000 | £20,000 | 0 |
| Total | £250,900 | £255,100 | £4,200 (A) |

# Sales margin variances

A sales margin variance will arise if there is either a change in the price charged by the business or a change from the budgeted volume of sales. Table 54.7 shows budgeted and actual prices and budgeted and actual sales volumes for cases of biscuits in a particular budget period. The budgeted value of sales is £20,000. However, the actual sales value is £21,320. This generates a favourable sales margin variance of £1,320 in this budget period.

**Table 54.7** *Budgeted and actual prices and sales volumes for cases of biscuits*

| | Price (per case) | Sales (cases) | Sales value |
|---|---|---|---|
| Budgeted | £2.50 | 8,000 | £20,000 |
| Actual | £2.60 | 8,200 | £21,320 |
| Sales margin variance | | | £1,320 (F) |

The favourable variance shown in Table 54.7 is influenced by two other variances.

**Sales margin price variance** This will occur if the actual price charged by a business is different from the budgeted price. For the example above this is:

Sales margin price variance = (actual price - budgeted price) x actual sales
= (£2.60 - £2.50) x 8,200
= £0.10 x 8,200
= £820 (F)

The sales margin price variance is favourable because the actual price charged is higher than the budgeted price. This variance may be the responsibility of the sales or marketing department. Such variances might arise due to:
- the chance to charge premium prices;
- sales in non-planned markets with different prices;
- changes in market conditions, such as a rival leaving the market.

**Sales volume variance** This will occur if the actual level of sales is different from the budgeted sales. For the biscuit manufacturer this is:

Sales volume variance = (actual sales - budgeted sales) x budgeted price
= (8,200 - 8,000) x £2.50
= 200 x £2.50
= £500 (F)

The sales volume variance is favourable because the actual number of sales is greater than the budgeted number. This variance is likely to be the responsibility of the marketing department or the sales manager. Sales volume variances may arise due to:
- changes in the state of the economy;
- competitors' actions;
- changes in consumer tastes;
- government action, such as a cut in income tax;
- changes in the quality of the product;
- changes in marketing techniques.

The sales margin variance for the biscuit manufacturer is £1,320 (F). It is influenced by both the sales price margin variance, £820 (F), and sales volume variance, £500 (F).

Bromford Motors is a large car dealership based in Wimbledon, London. It sells cars for a Japanese car manufacturer. The company operates a very strict budget regime. The five sales staff have a fraction of their pay linked to budget performance. Table 54.8 shows the budgeted and actual prices and volume of cars sold for a particular budget period.

**Table 54.8** *Budgeted and actual prices and sales of cars for Bromford Motors*

|  | Average price | Volume | Sales value |
|---|---|---|---|
| Budgeted | £9,500 | 250 | £2,375,000 |
| Actual | £9,325 | 269 | £2,508,425 |

(a) For the budget period calculate the:
   (i) the sales margin price variance;
   (ii) the sales volume variance;
   (iii) sales margin variance.
(b) Explain the possible causes of the variances in (a).

## Cash variances

One variance not shown in Figure 54.2 is the cash variance. This is because cash and profit are not the same (☞ unit 46). Cash budgets are concerned with liquidity, not profitability. A cash variance will show the difference between budgeted cash flows and actual cash flows. Table 54.9 shows the budgeted and actual cash flows for a carpet retailer in a three month budget period. The cash variances are also shown. A favourable cash variance arises when more cash flows in than was planned and if cash outflows are lower than planned. An adverse cash variance is caused by more cash flowing out than budgeted or less cash flowing in. In Table 54.9 all the closing balance cash variances are adverse. This means that the amount of cash actually left at the end of each month was lower than budgeted. For example, in January it was planned to have £5,500 at the end of the month. However,

the actual closing balance was £3,900 giving an adverse variance of £1,600.
Cash variances can be caused by many factors. Some examples include:
- lower or higher than expected cash sales;
- customers not settling their accounts on time;
- unexpected costs;
- unexpected inflation.

## Benefits of variance analysis

- It allows senior managers to monitor the performance of the organisation as a whole, as well as different sections of the organisation. For example, analysing departmental cost variances may allow a business to find out why certain costs are too high. Alternatively, it allows businesses to identify good practice and discover why some costs are lower.
- Prompt variance analysis allows managers to assess whether variances are caused by internal or external factors. Once causes have been traced, they can be corrected.
- By identifying variances and their causes managers may be able to produce more accurate budgets in future. This will aid planning and perhaps improve the performance of the business.
- Budgetary control in general helps to improve accountability in businesses. It can also be linked to performance related pay. For example, budget holders may receive a bonus payment at the end of the budget period if they can show favourable variances.

## key terms

**Budgetary control** - a business system which involves making future plans, comparing the actual results with the planned results and then investigating causes of any differences.
**Variance analysis** - the process of calculating variances and attempting to identify their causes.

**Table 54.9** *Budgeted and actual cash flows for a carpet retailer*

(£)

|  | JANUARY | | | FEBRUARY | | | MARCH | | |
|---|---|---|---|---|---|---|---|---|---|
|  | Budgeted | Actual | Variance | Budgeted | Actual | Variance | Budgeted | Actual | Variance |
| Cash receipts | 25,000 | 25,600 | 600F | 26,000 | 27,100 | 1,100F | 30,000 | 29,800 | 200A |
| Cash inflow | 25,000 | 25,600 | 600F | 26,000 | 27,100 | 1,100F | 30,000 | 29,800 | 200A |
| Purchases | 15,000 | 17,000 | 2,000A | 15,000 | 16,000 | 1,000A | 20,000 | 22,000 | 2,000A |
| Wages | 6,500 | 6,600 | 100A | 6,500 | 6,700 | 200A | 8,000 | 7,600 | 400F |
| Overheads | 2,000 | 2,100 | 100A | 2,000 | 1,800 | 200F | 2,500 | 2,000 | 500F |
| Cash outflow | 23,500 | 25,700 | 2,200A | 23,500 | 24,500 | 1,000A | 30,500 | 31,600 | 1,100A |
| Net cash flow | 1,500 | (100) | 1,600A | 2,500 | 2,600 | 100F | (500) | (1,800) | 1,300A |
| Opening balance | 4,000 | 4,000 | 0 | 5,500 | 3,900 | 1,600A | 8,000 | 6,500 | 1,500A |
| Closing balance | 5,500 | 3,900 | 1,600A | 8,000 | 6,500 | 1,500A | 7,500 | 4,700 | 2,800A |

## Knowledge ...Knowledge...Knowledge...Knowledge...Knowledge...Knowledge...Know

1. Describe the 3 steps in budgetary control.
2. Why is the profit variance probably the most important of all?
3. What is the difference between the materials price variance and the materials usage variance?
4. What might cause a direct materials variance?
5. What is the difference between the wage rate variance

and the labour efficiency variance?
6. What might cause a direct labour variance?
7. Why might some overhead variances be 0?
8. Explain the difference between the sales margin price variance and the sales volume variance.
9. What is a cash variance?
10. State 4 benefits of variance analysis.

# Case study Windrush Training Services

Windrush Training Services is a small company quoted on AIM. When it was floated in 1994 it offered a range of training services to businesses in London. However, it got into difficulties and its shares were suspended in 2000. A new management team was appointed and the company became more focused by specialising in training courses for the financial services sector. The new managing director identified a market niche. There was a need for employees in the financial services sector to be kept in touch with a growing body of regulatory

guidelines. Windrush used direct marketing to sell its short update courses to financial analysts, stockbrokers, equity houses and financial advisers.

The company raised some fresh capital through a rights issue and trading in its shares began again in January 2002. The new management team recognised a greater need for financial direction. It produced a twelve month cash budget for 2003 and used variance analysis to aid cash control.

**Table 54.10** *Cash budget for Windrush Training Services, 2003*

(£000)

| | JAN | FEB | MAR | APR | MAY | JUN | JUL | AUG | SEP | OCT | NOV | DEC |
|---|---|---|---|---|---|---|---|---|---|---|---|---|
| Fresh capital | 800 | | | | | | | | | | | |
| Course fees | 200 | 200 | 220 | 220 | 250 | 250 | 300 | 300 | 350 | 350 | 300 | 300 |
| Total inflow | 1,000 | 200 | 220 | 220 | 250 | 250 | 300 | 300 | 350 | 350 | 300 | 300 |
| Wages | 100 | 100 | 100 | 100 | 100 | 110 | 110 | 110 | 110 | 110 | 110 | 220 |
| Rent | 10 | 10 | 10 | 10 | 10 | 10 | 10 | 10 | 10 | 10 | 10 | 10 |
| Marketing | 20 | 20 | 15 | 15 | 10 | 10 | 10 | 5 | 5 | 5 | 5 | 5 |
| Heat & light | | | 5 | | | 5 | | | 5 | | | 5 |
| VAT | | | 92 | | | 108 | | | 142 | | | 142 |
| Other expenses | 25 | 25 | 25 | 25 | 25 | 25 | 25 | 25 | 25 | 25 | 25 | 25 |
| Total outflow | 155 | 155 | 247 | 150 | 145 | 268 | 155 | 150 | 297 | 150 | 150 | 407 |
| Net cash flow | 845 | 45 | (27) | 70 | 105 | (18) | 145 | 150 | 53 | 200 | 150 | (107) |
| Opening balance | (990) | (145) | (100) | (127) | (57) | 48 | 30 | 175 | 325 | 378 | 578 | 728 |
| Closing balance | (145) | (100) | (127) | (57) | 48 | 30 | 175 | 325 | 378 | 578 | 728 | 621 |

**Table 54.11** *Actual cash movements for Windrush Training Services, 2003*

(£000)

| | JAN | FEB | MAR | APR | MAY | JUN | JUL | AUG | SEP | OCT | NOV | DEC |
|---|---|---|---|---|---|---|---|---|---|---|---|---|
| Fresh capital | 800 | | | | | | | | | | | |
| Course fees | 160 | 180 | 170 | 160 | 190 | 240 | 300 | 310 | 390 | 590 | 530 | 200 |
| Total inflow | 960 | 180 | 170 | 160 | 190 | 240 | 300 | 310 | 390 | 590 | 530 | 200 |
| Wages | 100 | 100 | 100 | 100 | 100 | 110 | 110 | 110 | 110 | 110 | 110 | 300 |
| Rent | 10 | 10 | 10 | 10 | 10 | 10 | 10 | 10 | 10 | 10 | 10 | 10 |
| Marketing | 20 | 20 | 15 | 15 | 20 | 20 | 25 | 25 | 25 | 30 | 30 | 30 |
| Heat & light | | | 5 | | | 5 | | | 5 | | | 5 |
| VAT | | | 76 | | | 88 | | | 150 | | | 196 |
| Other expenses | 20 | 19 | 21 | 10 | 23 | 19 | 15 | 5 | 21 | 17 | 19 | 32 |
| Total outflow | 150 | 149 | 227 | 135 | 153 | 252 | 160 | 150 | 321 | 167 | 169 | 573 |
| Net cash flow | 810 | 31 | (57) | 25 | 37 | (12) | 140 | 160 | 69 | 423 | 361 | (373) |
| Opening balance | (990) | (180) | (149) | (206) | (181) | (144) | (156) | (16) | 144 | 213 | 636 | 997 |
| Closing balance | (180) | (149) | (206) | (181) | (144) | (156) | (16) | 144 | 213 | 636 | 997 | 624 |

(a) Explain, using an example from the case, what is meant by a cash variance. (6 marks)
(b) Calculate the annual variances for each item of receipts and expenditure and show whether they are favourable or adverse. (10 marks)
(c) Explain a possible link between the course fee variance and the marketing expenditure variance. (6 marks)
(d) What might account for the 'other expenses' variances? (8 marks)
(e) Discuss the possible benefits of budgetary control to Windrush Training Services. (10 marks)

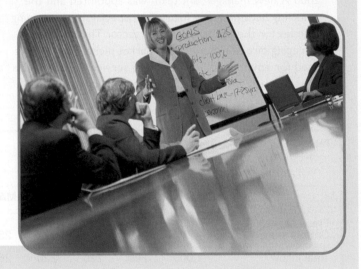

## When are accounts compiled?

The compilation of accounts involves using the information generated by recording business transactions to produce a balance sheet, profit and loss account and cash flow statement (☞ units 42, 43 and 46). Some businesses use computer software to compile accounts on a regular basis.

Final accounts are compiled at the end of the trading year. Small businesses such as sole traders, partnerships and small limited companies may employ chartered or certified accountants to compile their accounts. Business owners provide records of transactions and supporting documents. Most large companies and many medium-sized companies employ their own accountants who compile accounts for the business. However, companies which produce their own accounts must get them audited by an independent firm of accountants.

Once the accounts have been compiled they can be used by the various stakeholders. Public limited companies distribute their annual reports and accounts to all their shareholders.

## Compiling the balance sheet

Figure 55.1 shows a summary of the balance sheet structure (☞ unit 43). Accountants produce balance sheets according to accounting convention set out by the Accounting Standards Board (ASB) and the **Companies Act, 1985**.

A balance sheet can be compiled by inserting the appropriate information in the correct positions in the structure. Consider the financial information in Table 55.1 for Corporate Signs Ltd, a business which makes neon signs for companies. All the information relates to the assets, liabilities

**Table 55.1** *Financial information for Corporate Signs Ltd, 31.1.04 (£)*

| | |
|---|---|
| Mortgage | 100,000 |
| Share capital | 100,000 |
| Other reserves | 71,000 |
| Premises | 231,000 |
| Debtors | 75,000 |
| Vehicles | 87,000 |
| Stocks and work in progress | 98,000 |
| Plant and equipment | 199,000 |
| Current liabilities | 201,000 |
| Retained profit | 290,000 |
| Cash at bank | 112,000 |
| Unsecured bank loan | 60,000 |
| Intangible assets | 20,000 |

and capital of the company on 31.1.2004.

To compile the balance sheet for Corporate Signs Ltd, the following step-by-step approach might be used.

- Identify which of the items are assets, which are liabilities and which are capital and reserves.
- Write the title and date at the top of the account.
- List the fixed assets and add them up. Fixed assets are premises (£231,000), plant and equipment (£199,000) and vehicles (£87,000). All these are tangible assets (a total of £517,000). Intangible assets are £20,000. Fixed assets are therefore tangible plus intangible assets, a total of £537,000.
- List the current assets and add them up. Current assets are stocks and work in progress (£98,000), debtors (£75,000) and cash at bank (£112,000) which total £285,000.
- List the current liabilities and add them up. Current liabilities are stated as £201,000. These are the amounts falling due within one year.
- Enter the value for net current assets by subtracting current liabilities from current assets (£285,000 - £201,000 = £84,000).
- Enter the value for total assets less current liabilities by adding fixed assets to net current assets (£537,000 + £84,000 = £621,000).
- List the creditors: amounts falling due after one year and add them up. These are the mortgage (£100,000) and the unsecured bank loan (£60,000) which total £160,000.
- Enter the value for net assets by subtracting creditors: amounts falling due after one year from total assets less current liabilities (£621,000 - £160,000 = £461,000).
- List the capital and reserves and add them up. Capital and reserves are share capital (£100,000), other reserves (£71,000) and retained profit (£290,000) which total £461,000.
- Check that the value of capital and reserves (also shown as shareholders' funds or capital employed on some balance

**Figure 55.1** *Balance sheet summary diagram*

| | £ | |
|---|---|---|
| Fixed assets | A | |
| Current assets | B | |
| Current liabilities | C | |
| Net current assets (working capital) | D | B-C |
| Total assets less current liabilities | E | (A+B)-C *or* A+D |
| Creditors: amounts due after one year (Long term liabilities) | F | |
| Net assets | G | E-F *or* (A+D)-F |
| Capital and reserves (Capital employed or shareholders' funds) | H | G=H |

sheets) are the same as net assets. If the balance sheet has been compiled accurately, the value of net assets should be exactly the same as capital employed.

If the above steps are followed the result should be the same as the balance sheet shown in Table 55.2. Remember that normally both the current trading figures, and the previous year's figures, are shown in the accounts.

---

**Table 55.2** *Balance sheet for Corporate Signs Ltd, 31.1.2004*

### CORPORATE SIGNS LTD - BALANCE SHEET AS AT 31 JANUARY 2004

| | £ |
|---|---|
| **Fixed assets** | |
| Tangible assets | |
| Premises | 231,000 |
| Plant and equipment | 199,000 |
| Vehicles | 87,000 |
| | 517,000 |
| Intangible assets | 20,000 |
| | 537,000 |
| **Current assets** | |
| Stocks and work in progress | 98,000 |
| Debtors | 75,000 |
| Cash at bank | 112,000 |
| | 285,000 |
| **Current liabilities** | 201,000 |
| **Net current assets** | 84,000 |
| **Total assets less current liabilities** | 621,000 |
| **Creditors:** amounts falling due after one year | |
| Mortgage | (100,000) |
| Unsecured bank loan | (60,000) |
| **Net assets** | 461,000 |
| **Capital and reserves** | |
| Share capital | 100,000 |
| Other reserves | 71,000 |
| Retained profit | 290,000 |
| **Capital employed** | 461,000 |

---

## Transactions and the balance sheet

How might a transaction affect the balance sheet? There are two sides to every transaction and transactions can affect both assets and liabilities. For example, when a business makes a sale it will receive cash (an increase in assets) but reduce its stock of finished goods (a decrease in assets). Table 55.4 shows the balance sheet of Gregory Issacs plc, a construction

---

Superscape Group plc develops 3D technology and applications for mobile devices. The company's Swerve technology has been developed specifically for wireless environments. Swerve is being used by many of the mobile industry's leading businesses. Table 55.3 shows some financial information about the assets, liabilities and capital of the company in 2002 and 2003.

**Table 55.3** *Financial information for Superscape plc, 2002-03*

| | (£000) | |
|---|---|---|
| | **2003** | **2002** |
| Retained profit | -46,673 | -37,993 |
| Intangible assets | 110 | 324 |
| Share premium | 47,679 | 46,172 |
| Tangible assets | 359 | 636 |
| Share capital | 8,954 | 3,775 |
| Current liabilities | 957 | 1,257 |
| Other fixed assets* | 0 | 90 |
| Debtors | 1,105 | 868 |
| Cash at bank | 9,343 | 11,293 |

\* Long term investments.

Source: adapted from Superscape Group plc, *Annual Report and Accounts, 2003.*

(a) Compile the balance sheet for Superscape plc using the information in Table 55.3.
(b) What might account for the change in the value of tangible assets over the two years?

**Question 1**

company, as at 31 August 2004. How might four transactions affect the balance sheet?

- **Transaction 1.** The company buys a range of new equipment for one division of the business for £1 million. It arranges to pay by credit. This will increase fixed assets (equipment) by £1 million and current liabilities (trade creditors) by £1 million.
- **Transaction 2.** A consignment of stocks is ordered costing £500,000 on credit. This will increase current assets (stocks) by £500,000 and current liabilities (trade creditors) by £500,000.
- **Transaction 3.** The company makes an interim dividend payment to shareholders of £1.8 million. This will decrease current assets (cash at bank) by £1.8 million and creditors: amounts due within one year (dividend) by £1.8 million.
- **Transaction 4.** A debtor repays £200,000 to the company. This will only affect current assets. Debtors will fall by £200,000 and cash at bank will increase by £200,000.

It is assumed here that all these transactions are carried out on 1 September 2004. The effects of these transactions are shown in Table 55.4.

**Table 55.4**

| GREGORY ISSACS PLC BALANCE SHEET AS AT 31 AUGUST 2004 | | GREGORY ISSACS PLC BALANCE SHEET AS AT 1 SEPTEMBER 2004 | |
|---|---|---|---|
| | £m | | £m |
| **Fixed assets** | | **Fixed assets** | |
| Tangible assets | 84.8 | Tangible assets | 85.8 |
| Investments | 0.8 | Investments | 0.8 |
| | 85.6 | | 86.6 |
| **Current assets** | | **Current assets** | |
| Work in progress and stocks | 802.4 | Work in progress and stocks | 802.9 |
| Debtors | 84.4 | Debtors | 84.2 |
| Cash at bank | 10.8 | Cash at bank | 9.2 |
| | 897.6 | | 896.3 |
| **Creditors: amounts falling due within one year** (current liabilities) | | **Creditors: amounts falling due within one year** (current liabilities) | |
| Trade creditors | 246.6 | Trade creditors | 248.1 |
| Taxation | 12.8 | Taxation | 12.8 |
| Dividend | 20.8 | Dividend | 19.0 |
| | 280.2 | | 279.9 |
| **Net current assets** (working capital) | 617.4 | **Net current assets** (working capital) | 616.4 |
| **Total assets less current liabilities** | 703.0 | **Total assets less current liabilities** | 703.0 |
| **Creditors: amounts falling due after one year** | (199.8) | **Creditors: amounts falling due after one year** | (199.8) |
| **Net assets** | **503.2** | **Net assets** | **503.2** |
| **Capital and reserves** | | **Capital and reserves** | |
| Called up share capital | 91.2 | Called up share capital | 91.2 |
| Revaluation reserve | 91.5 | Revaluation reserve | 91.5 |
| Profit and loss account | 320.5 | Profit and loss account | 320.5 |
| | **503.2** | | **503.2** |

> Equipment is a tangible asset. The value of tangible assets rises by £1m, from £84.8m to £85.8m

> The value of fixed assets has also increased by £1m from £85.6m to £86.6m

> The value of stocks has increased by £500,000, from £802.4m to £802.9m

> The value of debtors has fallen by £200,000, from £84.4m to £84.2m

> The value of cash at bank has fallen by £1.8m and then risen by £200,000, an overall fall of £1.6m from £10.8m to £9.2m

> The value of current assets has fallen by £1.3m, from £897.6m to £896.3m

> The value of trade creditors has increased by £1m and £500,000 (£1.5m) from £246.6m to £248.1m

> The value of dividends has fallen by £1.8m, from £20.8m to £19m

> The value of current liabilities has fallen by £300,000 from £280.2m to £279.9m

> The value of net current assets has fallen by £1m from £617.4m to £616.4m

> The value of total assets less current liabilities, creditors due after one year, net assets and capital and reserves have not changed. This is because transactions on that particular day have not affected either long term liabilities or capital and reserves

# Compiling the profit and loss account

The structure of a profit and loss account was explained in unit 42. Accountants produce profit and loss accounts according to accounting convention set out by the ASB and the Companies Act. There is, however, some variation when looking at the profit and loss accounts of limited companies.

The profit and loss account will contain three key sections.

- The trading account, where gross profit is calculated.
- The profit and loss account, where net profit is calculated.

- The profit and loss appropriation account, which shows how the net profit is distributed.

Consider the financial information in Table 55.6, which shows the revenue and expenses incurred by a supermarket chain. The following steps could be used when compiling a profit and loss account from a set of figures:

**For the trading account**

- Write the title and date at the top of the account.
- Enter the value for turnover (£3,000m).
- Enter the value for cost of sales (remember that the cost of

Look at Table 55.5 showing information that may be contained in the balance sheet of Barden Ltd. On 1.5.2004 the following transactions were undertaken by Barden.
● Debtors repaid £1,000,000, deposited into the bank.
● £2,500,000 of materials were bought on trade credit.
● A machine was sold off for £500,000 and money paid into the bank.
(a) Produce a new balance sheet for Barden Ltd which takes these transactions into account.
(b) A year later the balance sheet for Barden Ltd showed the following values:
● fixed assets of £20,000,000;
● current assets of £12,000,000;
● current liabilities of £8,000,000;
● long term liabilities of £4,000,000.
Calculate the value of:
(i) net current assets;
(ii) total assets less current liabilities;
(iii) capital and reserves.

**Table 55.5** *Information from a balance sheet for Barden Ltd, as at 30.4.2004*

|  | £000 | £000 |
|---|---|---|
| **Fixed assets** | | |
| Factory | 11,000 | |
| Plant and machinery | 5,000 | |
| Equipment | 2,500 | |
| Financial assets | 1,000 | |
| | | 19,500 |
| **Current assets** | | |
| Stocks | 3,000 | |
| Work-in-progress | 2,500 | |
| Debtors | 3,500 | |
| | 9,000 | |
| **Current liabilities** | | |
| Trade creditors | 3,500 | |
| Other liabilities | 2,500 | |
| | 6,000 | |
| **Net current assets** | | 3,000 |
| **Total assets less current liabilities** | | 22,500 |
| **Creditors falling due after more than one year** | 6,000 | |
| **Net assets** | | 16,500 |
| **Capital and reserves** | | |
| Share capital | 9,000 | |
| Other reserves | 2,000 | |
| Retained profit | 5,500 | |
| | | 16,500 |

**Table 55.6** *Financial information for a supermarket chain 2004*

|  | £m |
|---|---|
| Turnover | 3,000 |
| Administrative expenses and distribution costs | 400 |
| Taxation | 45 |
| Cost of sales | 2,500 |
| Interest paid (net) | 5 |
| Dividends | 30 |
| Non-operating income | 30 |

sales must be adjusted for stock (☞ unit 42). The value of cost of sales has already been adjusted in Table 55.6 and is £2,500m.
● Enter the value for gross profit by subtracting cost of sales from turnover (£3,000m - £2,500m = £500m).

**For the profit and loss account**
● Enter the administrative/operating expenses underneath the gross profit (£400m).
● Enter the value for operating profit by subtracting operating expenses from gross profit (£500m - £400m = £100m).
● Enter the value of other income below operating profit (£30m).
● Enter the value for profit before interest and tax by adding non-operating income to operating profit (£100m + £30m = £130m).
● Enter the value for (net) interest payable underneath the value of profit before interest and tax (£5m).

**Table 55.7** *Profit and loss account for a supermarket chain*

**PROFIT AND LOSS ACCOUNT
YEAR ENDED 31.1.2004**

|  | £m |
|---|---|
| **Turnover** | 3,000 |
| Cost of sales | 2,500 |
| **Gross profit** | 500 |
| Administrative expenses and distribution costs | 400 |
| **Operating profit** | 100 |
| Non-operating income | 30 |
| **Profit before interest and tax** | 130 |
| Interest paid (net) | 5 |
| **Profit on ordinary activities before tax** | 125 |
| Taxation | 45 |
| **Profit on ordinary activities after tax** | 80 |
| Dividends | 30 |
| **Retained profit** | 50 |

- Enter the profit on ordinary activities before tax by subtracting (net) interest paid from profit before interest and tax (£130m - £5m). This gives a total of £125m.

**For the profit and loss appropriation account**
- Enter taxation underneath profit on ordinary activities before tax (£45m).
- Enter the value for profit on ordinary activities after tax by subtracting taxation from profit on ordinary activities before tax (£125m - £45m) which gives £80m.
- Enter dividends underneath profit on ordinary activities after tax (£30m).
- Enter the value for retained profit (or loss) for the financial year by subtracting dividends from profit on ordinary activities after tax (£80m - £30m = £50m).

The retained profit for the financial year figure is the last entry in the accounts (although the earnings per share is usually listed in public limited company accounts underneath retained profit). If the above steps are followed then the result should be the same as the profit and loss account shown in Table 55.7.

# Additional entries for inclusion in the profit and loss account

The profit and loss account shown here is fairly simple. Profit and loss accounts for other businesses may appear slightly different. This is because they contain additional information. Whether they do or not depends on the nature of their business and what has happened during the trading year. Some possible differences are described below.
- Exceptional items, if they occur, should be included after operating profit in the account. If the exceptional item is a cost, such as a bad debt, then it should be subtracted from operating profit. If it is revenue, it should be added.
- Sometimes the operating expenses are split into specific expenses. For example, they might be divided between distribution costs and administration expenses. It is quite normal to show these items separately and then subtract them from gross profit.
- The figure for interest paid shown here is a net figure (net interest = interest paid - interest received). The actual breakdown of interest paid and received would be shown in the notes to the accounts. Net interest can be positive or negative. Some businesses receive no interest, so the figure would simply be for interest paid. In other accounts both the figures for interest paid and received will be shown.
- Some businesses do not calculate gross profit in the account. This might be because they provide services rather than make goods. If this is the case all costs and expenses are added together and subtracted from turnover to calculate operating profit.

The list above is not definitive. In reality it is rare to find two companies with identical entries in their profit and loss accounts.

# The trial balance

In practice accountants use the **trial balance** (☞ unit 51) to compile final accounts. The trial balance is an account which lists all the debit balances and all the credit balances in the entire book-keeping system. In the trial balance:
- **debit entries** represent assets and expenses. They show where money has gone, for example, expenditure on assets such as plant, equipment and vehicles or expenses such as wages, advertising and materials.
- **credit balances** represent liabilities and revenue. They show inflows of money from sales, loans, capital and other sources.

In the trial balance the debit total should equal the credit total. This is because all transactions have been entered twice using the double entry system of recording. This helps to check that transactions have been entered accurately. However, it is still possible for the trial balance to balance even if errors have been made. This is because some errors will not be traced, for example, if a transaction is not recorded at all.

Table 55.8 shows the trial balance for Kingsmead Leisure Park. The debit side shows all balances relating to expenses, such as marketing expenses, and assets such as cash. The credit side shows all balances relating to revenue, such as turnover, and liabilities, such as creditors. Note that the total value of debits £4,901,000 is equal to the total value of credits £4,901,000.

**Table 55.8** *Trial balance for Kingsmead Leisure Park as at 31.7.04*

(£000)

|  | Debit | Credit |
|---|---|---|
| Turnover |  | 2,413 |
| Purchases | 380 |  |
| Marketing expenses | 920 |  |
| Operating expenses | 712 |  |
| Non-operating income |  | 100 |
| Interest paid | 200 |  |
| Taxation | 80 |  |
| Debtors | 71 |  |
| Stock as at 31.7.03 (opening stock) | 34 |  |
| Bank account | 804 |  |
| Tangible assets | 1,700 |  |
| Creditors |  | 901 |
| Long term loan |  | 1,000 |
| Share capital |  | 200 |
| Profit and loss account |  | 287 |
|  | 4,901 | 4,901 |

MSB International is a business that offers recruitment services. It has tended to specialise in the recruitment of IT and telecommunications staff for businesses. However, in August 2003, to reduce its dependency on these sectors, MSB Finance was launched to recruit qualified accountants across a range of sectors. Table 55.9 shows some financial information for MSB International.

**Table 55.9** *Financial information for MSB International, 2002-03*

| | (£000) | |
| --- | --- | --- |
| | **2003** | **2002** |
| Turnover | 84,062 | 145,987 |
| Cost of sales | 71,252 | 121,698 |
| Administration expenses | 12,667 | 21,866 |
| Exceptional item | -422 | 0 |
| Net interest paid | 142 | 534 |
| Taxation | 32 | 646 |
| Dividends | 410 | 546 |

Source: adapted from MSB International, *Annual Report and Accounts, 2003*.

(a) Using the information in Table 55.9, compile a profit and loss account for MSB International by calculating (i) gross profit, (ii) operating profit, (ii) profit before interest and tax, (iv) profit on ordinary activities before tax, (v) profit on ordinary activities after tax and (vi) retained profit.

(b) Describe the main changes over the two years.

## Question 3

## Compiling the profit and loss account from the trial balance

By following the steps described earlier it is possible to compile a profit and loss account for Kingsmead Leisure Park, from the information in the trial balance. However, there are some additional factors which need to be taken into account.

● Only the revenue and expense entries in the trial balance are needed to compile the profit and loss account.

● The cost of sales figure needs to be adjusted for stock. In the case of Kingsmead Leisure Park the opening stock is given in the trial balance (£34,000). If the closing stock is £40,000, cost of sales can be calculated by:

| | |
| --- | --- |
| Opening stock | £34,000 |
| Add purchases | £380,000 |
| | £414,000 |
| Less closing stock | £40,000 |
| Cost of sales | £374,000 |

● In the case of Kingsmead Leisure Park there is no dividend payment for the year. As a result retained profit will be the same as profit after tax.

The completed profit and loss account for Kingsmead is shown in Table 55.10.

**Table 55.10** *Profit and loss account for Kingsmead Leisure Park*

**KINGSMEAD LEISURE PARK - PROFIT AND LOSS ACCOUNT YEAR ENDED 31.7.04**

| | (£000) |
| --- | --- |
| **Turnover** | 2,413 |
| Cost of sales | 374 |
| **Gross profit** | 2,039 |
| Marketing expenses | 920 |
| Operating expenses | 712 |
| **Operating profit** | 407 |
| Non-operating income | 100 |
| | 507 |
| Interest paid | 200 |
| **Profit on ordinary activities before tax** | 307 |
| Taxation | 80 |
| **Profit on ordinary activities after tax** | 227 |
| Dividends | - |
| **Retained profit** | 227 |

## Compiling the balance sheet from the trial balance

By following the steps listed earlier it is possible to compile a balance sheet from the trial balance. The asset and liability entries in the trial balance are transferred into the normal balance sheet structure. However, when preparing a balance sheet in this way a number of factors must be taken into account.

● The stock figure in the current assets section of the balance sheet will be the closing stock figure (£40,000) not the opening stock figure in the trial balance.

● The retained profit in the profit and loss account (£227,000) is added to the profit and loss account entry in the trial balance (£287,000). This gives a new profit and loss account balance of £514,000.

The completed balance sheet for Kingsmead Leisure Park is shown in Table 55.11.

## Compiling accounts for sole traders

The examples used so far in the unit have involved the accounts of limited companies. When compiling the accounts of sole traders the same principles for account construction still apply. However, there are some important differences to be recognised.

● The bottom of the balance sheet for a limited company shows capital and reserves. For a sole trader the bottom of the balance sheet shows the capital owed to the owner. It is made up of the opening balance plus the net profit for the year.

● Drawings will usually appear on the trial balance for a sole trader. Drawings are usually transferred to the capital account in the balance sheet. They are subtracted at the end of the capital account to determine the closing capital balance. For example, the closing capital for G.M. Smith, a market trader, is:

| | |
|---|---|
| Opening capital | £56,811 |
| Add net profit | £21,006 |
| | £77,817 |
| Less drawings | £15,000 |
| Closing capital | £62,817 |

**Table 55.11** *Balance sheet for Kingsmead Leisure Park*

### KINGSMEAD LEISURE PARK - BALANCE SHEET AS AT 31.7.04

| | (£000) |
|---|---|
| **Fixed assets** | |
| Tangible assets | 1,700 |
| **Current assets** | |
| Stock | 40 |
| Debtors | 71 |
| Cash at bank | 804 |
| | 915 |
| **Current liabilities** | 901 |
| **Net current assets** | 14 |
| **Total assets less current liabilities** | 1,714 |
| **Long term liabilities** | (1,000) |
| **NET ASSETS** | 714 |
| **Capital and reserves** | |
| Share capital | 200 |
| Profit and loss account | 514 |
| **CAPITAL EMPLOYED** | 714 |

**Table 55.12** *Trial balance for Paulo Campolucci*

### PAULO CAMPOLUCCI - TRIAL BALANCE AS AT 31.1.2004

| | Debit £ | Credit £ |
|---|---|---|
| Turnover | | 121,001 |
| Purchases | 52,009 | |
| Stock at 31.1.03 | 5,991 | |
| Operating expenses | 36,002 | |
| Non-operating income | | 567 |
| Interest paid | 21,000 | |
| Tools and equipment | 13,532 | |
| Vehicle | 12,500 | |
| Debtors | 4,399 | |
| Cash at bank | 10,000 | |
| Current liabilities | | 16,001 |
| Long term bank loan | | 14,000 |
| Drawings | 12,000 | |
| Capital account | | 15,864 |
| | 167,433 | 167,433 |

Paulo Campolucci runs a small shoe manufacturing business in Bath. At the end of each trading year his daughter, Ellen, compiles his business accounts. Ellen handles her father's tax affairs and the first task before completing his self-assessment tax form is to compile the business accounts. The trial balance for the business is shown in Table 55.12.

(a) What is the advantage to Paulo Campolucci of producing a trial balance?

(b) Compile the profit and loss account for Paulo Campolucci from the trial balance and show that net profit is equal to £12,897. Note that the closing stock is £6,331.

(c) Compile the balance sheet for Paulo Campolucci from the trial balance and show that the value of closing capital is £16,761.

1. When do businesses normally compile their accounts?
2. Which assets are listed first in the balance sheet?
3. How is net current assets calculated in the balance sheet?
4. How is the net assets figure calculated in the balance sheet?
5. How is gross profit calculated in the trading account?
6. What entries will appear in the profit and loss appropriation account?
7. How are exceptional items dealt with in the profit and loss account?
8. Under what circumstances might gross profit not appear in a profit and loss account?
9. What do: (a) debit entries; (b) credit entries; represent in the trial balance?
10. Why should the value of debit entries equal the value of credit entries?
11. Does the trial balance include closing stock or opening stock for a business?
12. State 2 differences between a sole trader balance sheet and a limited company balance sheet.

# Case study Somerfield

Somerfield, a UK supermarket chain, operates 589 stores under the Somerfield brand and 680 under the Kwik Save brand. Somerfield merged with Kwik Save in 1998 after concerns that, on their own, the two companies might find it difficult to survive in the market. The company employs 54,000 staff and has over 6,000 own label products.

During the year 2002-03 Somerfield continued the development of a new format for the Kwik Save stores. This involved a new concept with brighter, fresher and more colourful stores. Layouts are more logical and easier to shop, with new shelving and refrigerator units. Somerfield also invested in new business ideas.

- **Somerfield forecourts**. This was a joint venture with Elf to open Somerfield convenience stores on petrol forecourts. A sharpening-up exercise was undertaken on its existing 18 sites during the year and sales grew by 9 per cent.
- **Somerfield franchises**. A number of partnerships were being developed. For example, under a pilot scheme six stores were being converted into convenience outlets trading under a joint Somerfield/Martin's name.

Table 55.13 shows some financial information for Somerfield.

(a) **Compile the 2003 profit and loss account for Somerfield (include the 2002 figures). (12 marks)**

(b) **Compile the 2003 balance sheet for Somerfield (include the 2002 figures). (14 marks)**

(c) **To what extent has the performance of the business improved over the two years? (14 marks)**

**Table 55.13** *Financial information for Somerfield, 2002-03*

| | | £ million |
| --- | --- | --- |
| | 2003 | 2002 |
| Turnover | 4,668.3 | 4,640.5 |
| Cost of sales | 4,544.3 | 4,514.5 |
| Administration expenses | 101.9 | 96.6 |
| Non-operating income* | 17.0 | 6.1 |
| Net interest paid | 4.3 | 13.3 |
| Taxation** | 5.0 | 6.0 |
| Dividends | 8.0 | 4.9 |
| Tangible assets | 1,013.9 | 941.7 |
| Other fixed assets*** | 7.6 | 7.0 |
| Stocks | 290.4 | 324.8 |
| Debtors | 117.8 | 115.2 |
| Cash at bank and in hand | 127.7 | 86.2 |
| Other current assets**** | 0.5 | 2.6 |
| Current liabilities | 766.8 | 669.7 |
| Long term liabilities | 25.2 | 74.7 |
| Share capital | 49.6 | 49.4 |
| Share premium | 34.2 | 33.4 |
| Revaluation | 69.6 | 76.2 |
| Other reserves | 335.3 | 335.3 |
| Retained profit | 277.2 | 238.8 |

* Profit on disposal of fixed assets.
** In both years Somerfield received tax credits from the Inland Revenue. These amounts should be added to profit.
*** Investments.
**** Short term investments.

Source: adapted from Somerfield plc, *Annual Report and Accounts, 2003*.

## The investigation process

Unit 3 showed stakeholders who may be interested in a company's accounts. Different users are interested for different reasons. For example, shareholders may want information to assess the rewards for holding shares. Managers may try to gauge performance. This unit explains how the information in the final accounts can be interpreted. It is possible to base investigation on some of these figures alone. Also, information can be obtained by combining some of these figures and carrying out a RATIO ANALYSIS. The chairperson's report, the directors' report and the notes to the accounts provide extra material as well.

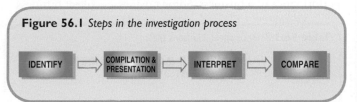

**Figure 56.1** *Steps in the investigation process*

IDENTIFY ⟹ COMPILATION & PRESENTATION ⟹ INTERPRET ⟹ COMPARE

The investigation process is shown in Figure 56.1. The first step is to **identify** the figures that are relevant from the final amounts. Suitable data must be used. For example, an accountant might need information on current assets and current liabilities, rather than total assets and total liabilities, in order to assess the solvency (☞ unit 44) of the business.

Once the correct figures have been chosen they can be **compiled** and **presented** into a useful form, such as percentages.

To **interpret** ratios an understanding of their significance is needed. Ratios can be used to find out the firm's financial position, assess performance, analyse capital structure and help shareholders when deciding whether to invest.

Finally, ratios may be used to make a variety of **comparisons**. For example, it is common to compare this year's figures with those of last year.

## What are ratios?

Financial ratios can be calculated by comparing two figures in the accounts which are related in some way. It may be one number expressed as a percentage of another or simply one number divided by another. For an accounting ratio to be useful the two figures must be connected, eg profit is arguably related to the amount of capital a firm uses.

Ratios on their own are not particularly useful. They need to be compared with other ratios. For example, knowing that a firm has a net profit to sales ratio of 11 per cent may not be helpful. However, if it was 9 per cent the year before, this can be compared with the present figure. There is a number of ways in which ratios can be compared.

**Over time** The same ratio can be compared in two time periods, eg the current financial year and the previous one. Comparisons over time also show trends. This allows a business to decide whether or not certain aspects are improving.

**Interfirm comparisons** It is possible for a business to compare its results with others in the same industry. This could highlight particular strengths or weaknesses. For example, a handbag manufacturer with a turnover of £120,000 might think its £30,000 profit satisfactory. Another manufacturer may have a profit of £50,000 on a turnover of £130,000. Assuming that the two firms are very similar, the relative profit of the first business is not as good. It is important that firms compare 'like with like'.

**Interfirm comparisons over time** Using the two standards above we can make interfirm comparisons over time. This shows trends that may exist. Such comparisons are quite popular and could help analyse the behaviour of a whole industry, over a lengthy time period.

**Results and forecasts** Management, for example, may want to compare actual results with predicted results. Management prepare budgets and make forecasts about the future. Decision makers will also try to account for differences which exist between the actual results and their estimates. This is called variance analysis (☞ units 47 and 54).

## Types of ratio and their users

Ratios fall into one of four general categories.

**Performance ratios or profitability ratios** Performance ratios help to show how well a business is doing. They tend to focus on profit, capital employed and turnover. Stakeholders such as owners, managers, employees and potential investors are all likely to be interested in the profitability and efficiency of a business. However, when measuring performance a business must take into account its objectives. For example, a performance ratio using profit may not be appropriate if the business is pursuing another objective, such as survival. Competitors might also use performance ratios to make comparisons of performance. Activity ratios are likely to be used internally by managers. This is because they focus on how well a business uses its resources. For example, the performance of the credit control department could be assessed by looking at how quickly debts are collected.

**Liquidity ratios** Liquidity ratios illustrate the solvency of a business - whether it is in a position to repay its debts. They focus on short term assets and liabilities. Creditors are likely to be interested in liquidity ratios to assess whether they will receive money that they are owed. Money lenders and suppliers, for example, will be interested in how easily a business can repay its debts. Potential investors might also have an interest in liquidity ratios for the same reason. In addition, managers might use them to aid financial control, ie to ensure that they have enough liquid resources to meet debts.

**Gearing ratios** Gearing ratios show the long term financial position of the business. They can be used to show the relationship between loans, on which interest is paid, and shareholders' funds, on which dividends might be paid. Creditors are likely to be concerned about a firm's gearing. Loans, for example, have interest charges which must be paid. Dividends do not have to be paid to ordinary shareholders. As a business becomes more highly geared (loans are high relative to share capital) it is considered more risky by creditors. The owners of a business might prefer to raise extra funds by borrowing rather than from shareholders, so they retain control of the business. Gearing ratios can also show the relationship between fixed interest bearing debt and the long

term capital of a business. This is discussed later in this unit.

**Shareholders' ratios** The owners of limited companies will take an interest in ratios which help measure the return on their shareholding. Such ratios focus on factors such as the earnings and dividends from shares in relation to their price. Potential investors will also show an interest in shareholders' ratios.

There may be other bodies or institutions which might use the above ratios. The media produce reports about businesses which they publish. They might use a range of ratios when reporting on particular businesses. In some newspapers the dividend yield and price/earnings ratio are actually published every day for a range of public limited companies. The Inland Revenue might also use ratio analysis when investigating the performance of a business. Some businesses collect business

**Table 56.1** *Profit and loss account, Hudsons plc*

### HUDSONS PLC PROFIT AND LOSS ACCOUNT
### Y/E 31.7.04

|  | 2004 £000 | 2003 £000 |
|---|---|---|
| **Turnover** | 70,000 | 63,000 |
| Cost of sales | 55,000 | 50,000 |
| **Gross profit** | 15,000 | 13,000 |
| Operating expenses | 9,500 | 9,000 |
| **Operating profit** | 5,500 | 4,000 |
| Income from investments | 100 | 80 |
| **Profit on ordinary activities before tax and interest** | 5,600 | 4,080 |
| Net interest paid | 1,100 | 600 |
| **Profit on ordinary activities before tax (net profit)** | 4,500 | 3,480 |
| Taxation | 1,100 | 680 |
| **Profit on ordinary activities after tax** | 3,400 | 2,800 |
| Dividends | 900 | 700 |
| Retained profit | 2,500 | 2,100 |

**Table 56.2** *Additional financial information, Hudsons plc*

|  | 2004 | 2003 |
|---|---|---|
| Number of ordinary shares | 40,000,000 | 40,000,000 |
| Share price 31st July | 135p | 94p |

**Table 56.3** *Balance sheet, Hudsons plc*

### HUDSONS PLC BALANCE SHEET
### AS AT 31.7.04

|  | 2004 £000s | 2003 £000s |
|---|---|---|
| **Fixed assets** |  |  |
| Tangible assets | 21,000 | 19,800 |
| Investments | 500 | 400 |
|  | 21,500 | 20,200 |
| **Current assets** |  |  |
| Stocks | 8,500 | 7,100 |
| Debtors | 500 | 400 |
| Cash at bank and in hand | 3,000 | 2,100 |
|  | 12,000 | 9,600 |
| **Creditors:** |  |  |
| amounts falling due within one year (current liabilities) | 8,100 | 7,000 |
| **Net current assets** (working capital) | 3,900 | 2,600 |
| **Total assets less current liabilities** | 25,400 | 22,800 |
| **Creditors:** |  |  |
| amounts falling due after one year (long term liabilities) | (8,000) | (6,500) |
| **Net assets** | 17,400 | 16,300 |
| **Capital and reserves** |  |  |
| Called up share capital | 2,000 | 2,000 |
| Other reserves | 1,400 | 2,800 |
| Profit and loss account | 14,000 | 11,500 |
| Shareholders' funds | 17,400 | 16,300 |

data and sell it to other users. For example, an agency might write a financial report on a business and part of it might consist of comments about particular ratios.

## Ratio Analysis

Tables 56.1-56.3 show the profit and loss account and balance sheet for Hudsons plc, and some additional information from the notes to the accounts. Hudsons sells electrical goods such as TVs, videos, DVD players, music systems and computers. The figures shown in the accounts will be used in this unit to illustrate how ratios can be calculated and interpreted.

## Performance ratios or profitability ratios

Assuming that a company's aim is to make a profit, performance ratios will focus on the year's profit. The profit figure alone is not a useful performance indicator. It is necessary to look at the value of profit in relation to the value of turnover, for example, or the amount of money that has been invested in the business.

**Return on capital employed (ROCE)** One of the most important ratios which is used to measure the performance of a business is the RETURN ON CAPITAL EMPLOYED (ROCE). This is sometimes referred to as the **primary ratio**. It compares the profit, ie return, made by the business with the amount of money invested, ie its capital. The advantage of this ratio is that it relates profit to the size of the business. When calculating ROCE, it is standard practice to define profit as net profit (or operating profit) before tax and interest. This is sometimes described as **earnings before interest and tax** (EBIT). Tax is ignored because it is determined by the government and is therefore outside the control of the company. Interest is excluded because it does not relate to the business's ordinary trading activities. ROCE can be calculated using the formula:

$$\text{ROCE} = \frac{\text{Profit before tax and interest}}{\text{Long term capital employed}} \times 100$$

For Hudsons the profit before tax and interest in 2004 was £5,600,000. Long term capital employed was £25,400,000. Long term capital employed is shareholders' funds plus any long term loans, ie £17,400,000 + £8,000,000.

$$\text{For 2004 ROCE} = \frac{£5,600,000}{£25,400,000} \times 100 = 22.0\%$$

$$\text{For 2003 ROCE} = \frac{£4,080,000}{£22,800,000} \times 100 = 17.9\%$$

The return on capital employed will vary between industries, however, the higher the ratio, the better. Over the

---

**Table 56.4** *Calculating ROCE using other measures of capital*

**ROCE (Total capital employed)** Total capital may be used to calculate the ROCE. Total capital employed can be found by:
- adding together the fixed assets and the current assets. For Hudsons in 2004, fixed assets were £21,500,000 and current assets were £12,000,000, so total capital employed was £33,500,000;
- adding capital and reserves (£17,400,000), long term liabilities (£8,000,000) and current liabilities (£8,100,000) together to give £33,500,000.

For Hudsons, the profit before tax and interest in 2004 was £5,600,000. The ROCE for 2004 can be calculated as:

$$\text{ROCE} = \frac{\text{Profit before tax and interest}}{\text{Total capital employed}} \times 100 = \frac{£5,600,000}{£33,500,000} \times 100 = 16.7\%$$

This measure of ROCE gives a lower percentage than ROCE using long term capital because the figure for capital is higher.

**ROCE (Shareholders' capital or net assets)** This looks at the return on the shareholders' capital, which is total share capital plus reserves. However, it is conventional to use the term net assets rather than shareholders' capital. Hudsons' balance sheet shows that shareholders' capital/funds is £17,400,000 in 2004. This is the same as net assets. The RETURN ON NET ASSETS for Hudsons in 2004 can be calculated using the formula:

$$\text{Return on net assets} = \frac{\text{Profit before tax and interest}}{\text{Net assets}} \times 100 = \frac{£5,600,000}{£17,400,000} \times 100 = 32.2\%$$

The return on net assets gives a higher percentage than other measures of ROCE because the figure for capital is lower.

---

two years Hudsons has seen its ROCE increase from 17.9 per cent to 22.0 per cent. To decide whether Hudsons has performed well, this would have to be compared with another business in the same industry. An investor might also compare the ROCE with the possible return if the capital was invested elsewhere. For example, if £25,400,000 was placed in a bank account in 2004 it might have earned a 4 per cent return. So the 22 per cent ROCE in 2004 seems impressive. However, an investor in the company will also want to be rewarded for the risk involved. The £25,400,000 invested by shareholders in Hudsons is at risk if the business fails. So, for the investment to be worthwhile, the ROCE must be far greater than the return that could be earned in a 'safe' investment. Increasing profit with the existing capital employed will improve the ROCE ratio for a business.

It is possible to use other measures of capital when calculating the ROCE. These are explained in Table 56.4.

**Gross profit margin** The GROSS PROFIT MARGIN is also known as the **mark-up**. This shows the gross profit made on sales turnover. It is calculated using the formula:.

$$\text{Gross profit margin} = \frac{\text{Gross profit}}{\text{Turnover}} \times 100$$

For Hudsons in 2004 gross profit was £15,000,000 and turnover was £70,000,000.

$$\text{For 2004 Gross profit margin} = \frac{£15,000,000}{£70,000,000} \times 100 = 21.4\%$$

$$\text{For 2003 Gross profit margin} = \frac{£13,000,000}{£63,000,000} \times 100 = 20.6\%$$

Higher gross margins are usually preferable to lower ones. It may be possible to increase the gross profit margin by raising turnover relative to cost of sales, for example by increasing price. Or cost of sales could be reduced relative to turnover. However, the gross profit margin required will tend to be different for different industries. As a rule, the quicker the turnover of stock, the lower the gross margin that is needed. So, for example, a supermarket with a fast stock turnover is likely to have a lower gross margin than a car retailer with a much slower stock turnover. Some supermarkets are therefore very successful with relatively low gross profit margins because of the regular and fast turnover of stock.

The gross margin for Hudsons has improved slightly over the two years. Interfirm comparisons would help to confirm whether this was a satisfactory performance.

Net profit margin The NET PROFIT MARGIN helps to measure how well a business controls its overheads. If the difference between the gross margin and the net margin is small, this suggests that overheads are low. This is because net profit equals gross profit less overheads. The net profit margin can be calculated by:

$$\text{Net profit margin} = \frac{\text{Net profit before tax and interest}}{\text{Turnover}} \times 100$$

For Hudsons in 2004 net profit before tax and interest was £5,600,000 and turnover was £70,000,000.

$$\text{For 2004 Net profit margin} = \frac{£5,600,000}{£70,000,000} \times 100 = 8.0\%$$

$$\text{For 2003 Net profit margin} = \frac{£4,080,000}{£63,000,000} \times 100 = 6.5\%$$

Again, higher margins are usually better than lower ones. The net profit margin for Hudsons has improved over the two years. This suggests that the business was able to restrict overhead spending as a proportion of turnover more effectively in 2004 than in 2003.

Tony Parker owns two thriving businesses in London. The first, managed by his eldest daughter, is a fish and chip shop in Greenford. It is located just round the corner from Greenford tube station. The second, managed by his son, is a gift and souvenir shop located by the Tower of London. He monitors the performance of both businesses very carefully and likes to compare the two at the end of the year. Tony uses the gross and net profit margins to make comparisons. Table 56.5 shows some financial information for both businesses.

**Table 56.5** *Turnover, gross profit and net profit for Tony Parker's businesses*

| | Fish & chip shop | Gift & souvenir shop (£) |
|---|---|---|
| Turnover | 252,600 | 365,900 |
| Gross profit | 75,400 | 154,900 |
| Net profit | 32,000 | 38,700 |

(a) (i) Calculate the gross and net profit margins for the two businesses.
(ii) Based on the results in (i), which business has the best performance? Explain your answer.
(b) To what extent are the comparisons useful?

**Question 1**

## Activity ratios

Activity ratios or 'asset usage ratios' are used to measure how effectively a business employs its resources.

Asset turnover The ASSET TURNOVER ratio measures the productivity of assets. It looks at how much turnover is generated by the assets employed in the business. The formula is:

$$\text{Asset turnover} = \frac{\text{Turnover}}{\text{Net assets}}$$

The turnover for Hudsons in 2004 was £70,000,000 and the net assets were £17,400,000.

$$\text{For 2004 Asset turnover} = \frac{£70,000,000}{£17,400,000} = 4.02$$

$$\text{For 2003 Asset turnover} = \frac{£63,000,000}{£16,300,000} = 3.87$$

The ratio shows that, in 2004, for every £1 invested in net

assets by Hudsons, £4.02 of turnover was generated. Over the two years the asset turnover improved by a few pence. The asset turnover varies in different industries. In retailing, where turnover is high and the value of fixed assets is relatively low, like Hudsons, the asset turnover can be 3 or more. In contrast, in manufacturing, where there is often heavier investment in fixed assets, the ratio is generally lower. For example, it can be 1 or less. Increasing turnover using the same assets, so that assets work more effectively, is a method of improving the ratio.

Stock turnover The STOCK TURNOVER ratio measures how quickly a business uses or sells its stock. It is generally considered desirable to sell, or 'shift', stock as quickly as possible. One approach to stock turnover is to calculate how many times during the year a business sells its stock. The formula is:

$$\text{Stock turnover} = \frac{\text{Cost of sales}}{\text{Stocks}}$$

The cost of sales for Hudsons in 2004 was £55,000,000. The value of closing stocks as shown in the balance sheet was £8,500,000.

$$\text{For 2004 Stock turnover} = \frac{£55,000,000}{£8,500,000} = 6.5 \text{ times}$$

$$\text{For 2003 Stock turnover} = \frac{£50,000,000}{£7,100,000} = 7.0 \text{ times}$$

Another approach to stock turnover is to calculate the number of days it takes to sell the stock. This is found by:

$$\text{Stock turnover} = \frac{\text{Stocks}}{\text{Cost of sales}} \times 365$$

$$\text{For 2004 Stock turnover} = \frac{£8,500,000}{£55,000,000} \times 365 = 56 \text{ days}$$

$$\text{For 2003 Stock turnover} = \frac{£7,100,000}{£50,000,000} \times 365 = 52 \text{ days}$$

High stock turnovers are preferred (or lower figures in days). A higher stock turnover means that profit on the sale of stock is earned more quickly. Thus, businesses with high stock turnovers can operate on lower profit margins. A declining stock turnover ratio might indicate:

● higher stock levels;
● a large amount of slow moving or obsolete stock ;
● a wider range of products being stocked;
● a lack of control over purchasing.

So improvements to purchasing methods or better control of stock levels, for example, should improve the stock turnover ratio of a business.

Stock turnover differs considerably between different industries. Supermarkets often have a relatively quick stock turnover of around 14 to 28 days. This means that they sell the value of their average stock every two to four weeks. Manufacturers generally have much slower stock turnover because of the time spent processing raw materials. However, in recent years, many manufacturers have adopted **just-in-time production** techniques (☞ unit 80). This involves ordering stocks only when they are required in the production process and, therefore, stock levels tend to be lower. As a result stock turnover is faster. Businesses which supply services, such as banks, travel agents and transport operators, are not likely to hold very much stock. Therefore this ratio is not likely to be used by service industry analysts.

Over the two years, Hudsons' stock turnover has worsened very slightly. However, to determine whether a stock turnover of 56 days is good, comparisons with other electrical goods retailers would have to be made.

Debt collection period This ratio measures the efficiency of a business's credit control system. The DEBT COLLECTION PERIOD is the average number of days it takes to collect debts from customers. It can be calculated using the formula:

$$\text{Debt collection period} = \frac{\text{Debtors}}{\text{Turnover}} \times 365$$

According to the balance sheet the value of debtors for Hudsons in 2004 was £500,000. Turnover was £70,000,000.

$$\text{For 2004 Debt collection period} = \frac{£500,000}{£70,000,000} \times 365 = 2.6 \text{ days}$$

$$\text{For 2003 Debt collection period} = \frac{£400,000}{£63,000,000} \times 365 = 2.3 \text{ days}$$

Businesses often vary the amount of time they give customers to pay for products they have bought on credit. Credit periods may be 30, 60, 90 or even 120 days. Businesses prefer a short debt collection period because their cash flow will be improved. Retailers will have a very low debt collection period, perhaps just a few days. This is because most of their sales are for cash. This appears to be the case for Hudsons. Although the debt collection period has risen from 2.3 days to 2.6 days over the two years, there is unlikely to be a problem. Hudsons' sales will be for cash and the debtors value on the balance sheet is likely to be for prepayments (☞ unit 43) not customer debts. Improving turnover relative to debtors will improve the ratio. However, businesses often try to improve this ratio by reducing debtors relative to turnover using credit control (☞ unit 48).

# *Liquidity ratios*

A business must make sure that it has enough liquid assets to pay any immediate bills that arise (☞ unit 48). Liquid assets include cash and assets that can be quickly switched into cash such as stocks, debtors and short-term investments. Two widely used ratios to monitor liquid assets are the current ratio and the acid test ratio.

**Current ratio** The CURRENT RATIO focuses on current assets and current liabilities. It is also known as the **working capital ratio** and is calculated using the formula:

$$\text{Current ratio} = \frac{\text{Current assets}}{\text{Current liabilities}}$$

For Hudsons, current assets were £12,000,000 in 2004 and current liabilities were £8,100,000. Both of these figures are shown in the balance sheet.

$$\text{For 2004 Current ratio} = \frac{£12,000,000}{£8,100,000} = 1.48 \text{ or } 1.48:1$$

$$\text{For 2003 Current ratio} = \frac{£9,600,000}{£7,000,000} = 1.37 \text{ or } 1.37:1$$

It is suggested that a business will have sufficient liquid resources if the current ratio is between 1.5:1 and 2:1. If the ratio is below 1.5 it might be argued that a business does not have enough working capital. This might mean that a business is **overborrowing** or **overtrading** (☞ unit 48). Operating above a ratio of 2:1 may suggest that too much money is tied up unproductively. Money tied up in stocks does not earn any return.

The current ratio for Hudsons has hardly changed over the two years, rising slightly from 1.37:1 to 1.48:1. As with other ratios, judgement on what is satisfactory depends to a large extent on comparisons within the industry. For example, retailers often have very low current ratios, perhaps 1:1 or below. This is because they hold fast selling stocks and generate cash from sales. Since Hudsons is a retailer, it might be well satisfied with a current ratio of 1.48:1 in 2004.

Hudsons may be able to improve its current ratio by increasing its current assets relative to current liabilities, or reducing its current liabilities relative to its current assets. For example, current assets might be improved by better stock or credit control. Current liabilities might be reduced by reducing short term creditors.

**Acid test ratio** The ACID TEST RATIO or QUICK RATIO is a more severe test of liquidity. This is because stocks are not treated as liquid resources. Stocks are not guaranteed to be sold and they may become obsolete or deteriorate. They are therefore excluded from current assets when calculating the ratio.

$$\text{Acid test ratio} = \frac{\text{Current assets} - \text{stocks}}{\text{Current liabilities}}$$

The information required to calculate the acid test ratio are found in Hudsons' balance sheet.

$$\text{For 2004 Acid test ratio} = \frac{£12,000,000 - £8,500,000}{£8,100,000} = 0.43 \text{ or } 0.43:1$$

$$\text{For 2003 Acid test ratio} = \frac{£9,600,000 - £7,100,000}{£7,000,000} = 0.36 \text{ or } 0.36:1$$

If a business has an acid test ratio of less than 1:1 it means that its current assets less stocks do not cover its current

Baxter & Son supplies local shops, hotels, restaurants and pubs in the Lincolnshire area with poultry and game. The business has been in the family for 132 years and makes good returns on the capital employed. However, it had started to suffer from liquidity problems. Baxter & Son paid its suppliers cash, but gave its customers 30 day credit terms. In 2004 Phil Baxter, the managing director, decided to offer customers a 5 per cent discount if they paid cash on delivery. Some financial information is shown in Table 56.6.

**Table 56.6** *Turnover, current assets and current liabilities for Baxter & Son, 2001–2004*

(£)

|  | 2004 | 2003 | 2002 | 2001 |
|---|---|---|---|---|
| Turnover | 138,100 | 141,800 | 136,200 | 121,000 |
| **Current assets** | | | | |
| Stocks | 2,500 | 2,600 | 2,300 | 2,200 |
| Debtors | 6,400 | 12,100 | 11,200 | 9,800 |
| Cash & bank | 1,800 | 0 | 0 | 700 |
| **Current liabilities** | | | | |
| Bank loan | 7,000 | 7,000 | 8,000 | 8,000 |
| Other creditors | 3,100 | 4,600 | 4,300 | 5,100 |
| Bank overdraft | 0 | 4,600 | 2,200 | 0 |

(a) (i) Calculate the current ratios for Baxter & Son between 2001 and 2004.
   (ii) What evidence is there to suggest that the business was beginning to experience liquidity problems?
(b) (i) Calculate the debt collection period for Baxter & Son between 2001 and 2004.
   (ii) Discuss whether the 5 per cent cash discount offered to customers has worked.

Question 2

liabilities. This could indicate a potential problem. However, as with the current ratio, there is considerable variation between the typical acid test ratios of businesses in different industries. Again, retailers with their strong cash flows, may operate comfortably with acid test ratios of less than 1. Since Hudsons is a retailer and its stock is likely to be sold quite quickly, an acid test ratio of 0.43:1 may be acceptable to the business. The methods of improving the current ratio can all be used here, although changing stock levels are not an option as stocks are excluded from the calculation.

# Gearing ratios

Gearing ratios can be used to analyse the **capital structure** of a business. They compare the amount of capital raised from ordinary shareholders with that raised in loans and, in some cases, from preference shareholders and debentures. This is important because the interest on loans and dividends for preference shareholders are fixed commitments, whereas the dividends for ordinary shareholders are not. Gearing ratios can assess whether or not a business is burdened by its loans. This is because highly geared companies must still pay their interest even when trading becomes difficult.

Gearing ratio There are several different versions of the GEARING RATIO. One widely used relates the total long term loans and other fixed cost capital to long term capital employed. The formula is:

$$\text{Gearing ratio} = \frac{\text{Fixed cost capital}}{\text{Long term capital}} \times 100$$

Fixed cost capital includes long term loans from banks, certain preference shares and debentures. Long term capital includes shareholders' funds, any reserves and long term loans. For Hudsons in 2004 the fixed cost or interest/dividend bearing debt, according to the balance sheet, is loans of £8,000,000 (creditors: amounts falling due after one year). The value of shareholders' funds, including reserves, was £17,400,000.

$$\text{For 2004 Gearing ratio} = \frac{£8,000,000}{£17,400,000 + £8,000,000} \times 100 = 31.5\%$$

$$\text{For 2003 Gearing ratio} = \frac{£6,500,000}{£16,300,000 + £6,500,000} \times 100 = 28.5\%$$

If the gearing ratio is less than 50 per cent the company is said to be low geared. This means that the majority of the capital is provided by the owners. If the ratio is greater than 50 per cent the company is high geared. This means that a much higher proportion of total capital is borrowed. With a gearing ratio of around 30 per cent in both years, Hudsons is low geared. Although gearing rose slightly over the two years,

the increase is not significant.

Another version of the gearing ratio looks at the relationship between borrowing and equity. In this context borrowing is defined as long term loans. For Hudsons in 2004 it was the creditors: amounts falling due after one year of £8,000,000. Equity is defined as ordinary share capital plus reserves which for Hudsons in 2004 was £17,400,000. The ratio is calculated using the formula:

$$\text{Gearing ratio} = \frac{\text{Borrowing}}{\text{Equity}} \times 100$$

$$\text{For 2004 Gearing ratio} = \frac{£8,000,000}{£17,400,000} \times 100 = 46.0\%$$

When this definition of gearing is used, a ratio that is greater than 100 per cent means that debt is greater than equity. In most industries, this would be regarded as high geared and could prove to be an unacceptable risk for potential lenders. This is because, if there was a downturn in trading, a company might struggle to meet interest payments. However, this is not the case for Hudsons since the ratio is below 100 per cent. A business can improve its gearing ratio by reducing its long term borrowing relative to its capital.

Interest cover The gearing ratio is a balance sheet measure of financial risk. INTEREST COVER is a profit and loss account measure. The ratio assesses the burden of interest payments by comparing profit and interest payments. It is calculated using the formula:

$$\text{Interest cover} = \frac{\text{Profit before interest and tax}}{\text{Interest}}$$

The profit before tax and interest for Hudsons in 2004 was £5,600,000 as shown in the profit and loss account. The amount of interest paid during the year was £1,100,000.

$$\text{For 2004 Interest cover} = \frac{£5,600,000}{£1,100,000} = 5.1 \text{ times}$$

$$\text{For 2003 Interest cover} = \frac{£4,080,000}{£600,000} = 6.8 \text{ times}$$

If interest cover is 1, this means that all of the firm's profit would be used to pay interest. This is obviously not sustainable in the long term. In the case of Hudsons, the cover has fallen over the two years. However, for a low geared company like Hudsons, this is still likely to be satisfactory. A figure of between 1 and 2 is likely to cause problems for a business, suggesting that it is becoming difficult for a company to meet its debt payments.

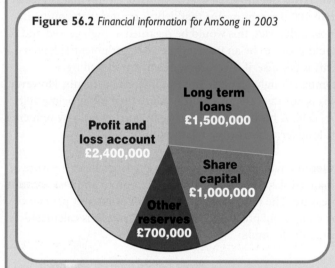

AmSong plc manufactures electronic equipment for the music and media industries, including mixing desks, digital recording equipment and monitor speakers. Its factory is in Leicester and it employs 143 staff. The company has done very well in recent years and is beginning to receive orders from Europe. However, AmSong is running short of capacity and needs to extend its premises and buy more plant and machinery. To do this it must raise some fresh capital, about £500,000. The directors are hoping that a bank loan might be granted. In 2003, AmSong made a profit before tax and interest of £750,000. The net interest paid during the year was £90,000. Some financial information is shown in Figure 56.2.

**Figure 56.2** *Financial information for AmSong in 2003*

- Long term loans £1,500,000
- Profit and loss account £2,400,000
- Share capital £1,000,000
- Other reserves £700,000

(a) Calculate (i) the gearing ratio and (ii) the interest cover for AmSong.

(b) Based on the results in (a), do you think a bank is likely to grant AmSong a £500,000 loan?

Question 3

## Shareholders' ratios

Shareholders' ratios provide information to help investors to make decisions about buying or selling shares. They are often used to analyse the performance of public limited companies. However, they can also be helpful to the owners of private limited companies.

**Earnings per share** The EARNINGS PER SHARE (EPS) is a measure of how much profit each ordinary share earns after tax. It does not, however, show how much money is actually paid to ordinary shareholders. This is because companies usually retain some profit in reserve. The EPS is generally shown at the bottom of the profit and loss account in the published accounts of plcs. EPS can be calculated by:

$$\text{Earnings per share} = \frac{\text{Profit after tax}}{\text{Number of ordinary shares}}$$

For Hudsons in 2004 the net profit after tax was £3,400,000 as shown in the profit and loss account. Note that if the company had any preference shareholders, any dividends paid to these would have to be subtracted from profit. According to the additional information shown in Table 56.2, the number of ordinary shares issued in 2004 was 40,000,000.

$$\text{For 2004 Earnings per share} = \frac{£3,400,000}{40,000,000} = 8.5\text{p}$$

$$\text{For 2003 Earnings per share} = \frac{£2,800,000}{40,000,000} = 7.0\text{p}$$

Over the two years the EPS for Hudsons has improved. However, on its own, this does not necessarily indicate a satisfactory performance. Only when the EPS is compared with the company's share price and with the EPS of comparable companies is it possible to make a judgment. Improvements in profits relative to the number of shares will improve this ratio.

**Price/earnings ratio** The PRICE/EARNINGS (P/E) RATIO is one of the main indicators used by investors in deciding whether to buy or sell particular shares. The P/E ratio relates the current share price to the EPS. It is calculated using the formula below. The ratio is often expressed as the number of times by which the share price can be divided by the EPS.

$$\text{Price/earnings ratio} = \frac{\text{Share price}}{\text{EPS}}$$

In the case of plcs which are listed on the Stock Market, their share price is published daily in *The Financial Times*, other newspapers and on the Internet. The share prices for Hudsons on 31st July are shown as additional information in Table 56.2. In 2004 the share price was 135p. The EPS was 8.5p as calculated above.

$$\text{For 2004 Price/earnings ratio} = \frac{135\text{p}}{8.5} = 15.9 \text{ times}$$

$$\text{For 2003 Price/earnings ratio} = \frac{94\text{p}}{7.0\text{p}} = 13.4 \text{ times}$$

The P/E ratio of 15.9 means that the market price of the share is 15.9 times higher than its current level of earnings. Assuming that nothing changes, it would take 15.9 years for these shares to earn their current market value. The P/E ratio for Hudsons rose over the two years from 13.4 to 15.9, indicating that investors had increased confidence in the future profitability of the company. As a result, demand for the shares rose, causing the price to jump from 94p to 135p. Rising investor confidence in this case may have been justified since Hudson's EPS rose from 7.0p to 8.5p.

Price/earnings ratios provide a useful guide to market confidence and can be helpful in comparing companies. However, a general rise or fall in share prices will affect P/E ratios, so care must be taken when interpreting changes.

**Dividend per share** The DIVIDEND PER SHARE is the ratio that shows how much money ordinary shareholders receive per share.

$$\text{Dividend per share} = \frac{\text{Dividend (ordinary shares)}}{\text{Number of shares}}$$

For Hudsons the dividend paid to shareholders in 2004 was £900,000. This is shown in the profit and loss account. The number of shares issued by Hudsons in 2004 is shown as additional information and was 40,000,000.

$$\text{For 2004 Dividend per share} = \frac{£900,000}{40,000,000} = 2.25\text{p per share}$$

$$\text{For 2003 Dividend per share} = \frac{£700,000}{40,000,000} = 1.75\text{p per share}$$

The dividend per share paid to Hudsons' shareholders increased from 1.75p per share to 2.25p over the two years. This is quite a significant improvement. However, to determine whether or not it is satisfactory the dividend per share must be compared with the share price. This involves calculating the dividend yield.

**Dividend yield** The DIVIDEND YIELD is the dividend per ordinary share expressed as a percentage of the current share price.

$$\text{Dividend yield} = \frac{\text{Dividend per share}}{\text{Share price}} \times 100$$

For Hudsons the share price is shown in Table 56.2 under additional information. On 31.7.04 it was 135p. The dividend per share was calculated above and was 2.25p in 2004.

$$\text{For 2004 Dividend yield} = \frac{2.25\text{p}}{135\text{p}} \times 100 = 1.7\%$$

$$\text{For 2003 Dividend yield} = \frac{1.75\text{p}}{94\text{p}} \times 100 = 1.9\%$$

Over the two years the dividend yield has fallen for Hudsons, even though the dividend per share rose significantly. The reason for this is that the share price also rose sharply. Whether a dividend yield of 1.7 per cent is adequate depends on what might be earned in other companies and other forms of investment. However, when making this judgment, it must be remembered that dividends are not the only reward for holding shares. Investors may make a capital gain if the shares are sold for a higher price than when they were bought.

**Return on equity** The RETURN ON EQUITY looks at the return on the money contributed by, and belonging to, ordinary shareholders. It defines equity as the ordinary shareholders' capital plus reserves. Profit after tax is used in this calculation. Note also that any payments made to preference shareholders should also be subtracted from this profit. The formula to calculate return on equity is:

$$\text{Return on equity} = \frac{\text{Profit after tax}}{\text{Equity}} \times 100$$

For Hudsons the net profit after tax in 2004 was £3,400,000. The value of ordinary share capital and reserves or shareholders' equity was £17,400,000.

$$\text{For 2004 Return on equity} = \frac{£3,400,000}{£17,400,000} \times 100 = 19.5\%$$

$$\text{For 2003 Return on equity} = \frac{£2,800,000}{£16,300,000} \times 100 = 17.2\%$$

Hudsons' return on equity improved slightly over the two years from 17.2% to 19.5%. As with all ratio analysis, judgment on whether this was satisfactory depends to a large extent on comparisons with similar companies in the same industry.

**Dividend cover** The DIVIDEND COVER measures how many times a company's dividends to ordinary shareholders could be paid from net profit.

$$\text{Dividend cover} = \frac{\text{Profit after tax}}{\text{Dividends (ordinary shares)}}$$

For Hudsons the profit after tax in 2004 was £3,400,000. The dividend paid to ordinary shareholders is shown in the profit and loss account and was £900,000 in 2004.

$$\text{For 2004 Dividend cover} = \frac{£3,400,000}{£900,000} = 3.8\text{ times}$$

$$\text{For 2003} \quad \text{Dividend cover} = \frac{£2,800,000}{£700,000} = 4.0 \text{ times}$$

For Hudsons the dividend cover has fallen slightly over the two years. A cover of 3.8 means that the dividends could have been paid 3.8 times over in 2004. If the cover is too high, shareholders might argue that higher dividends should be paid. If it is too low, it may mean that profits are low or that the company is not retaining enough profit for new investment.

It is possible for a business to pay dividends even when there is not sufficient profit in the current year to cover the payment. A company might do this to help retain the loyalty of shareholders. The money to cover the payment would have to come from reserves.

Lorraine Day has around £50,000 of her savings invested in QuantiFact, an online business information provider. She has seen reports in the media suggesting that the company is struggling, due to growing competition in the market. Lorraine gathered some up to date financial information about the company which is shown in Table 56.7.

**Table 56.7** *Financial information for QuantiFact*

|                         | 2004  | 2003  |
|-------------------------|-------|-------|
| Earnings per share      | 41p   | 39p   |
| End of year share price | 480p  | 515p  |
| Dividends               | £10.5m | £12m  |
| Number of shares issued | 105m  | 100m  |

(a) Calculate (i) the price earnings ratio, (ii) the dividend per share and (iii) the dividend yield for QuantiFact for 2004 and 2003.
(b) On the basis of the results in (a), explain whether you would advise Lorraine to sell the shares or not.

# Limitations to ratio analysis

Although ratios offer a useful method of analysing business performance, they do have several limitations. The following factors all affect their usefulness.

**The basis for comparison** It is important when analysing differences between businesses to compare 'like with like'. This means that valid comparisons can often only be made between businesses in the same industry. Even then,

differences in the size of the business, in their accounting policies, product ranges and in their financial year-ends can make comparisons difficult.

**The quality of final accounts** Ratios are usually based on published financial statements and therefore depend on the quality of these statements. One factor that can affect the quality of accounting information is the change in monetary values caused by inflation. Rising prices distort comparisons made between different time periods. For example, in times of high inflation, asset values and turnover might rise rapidly in monetary terms. However, when the figures are adjusted for inflation, there might be no increase in **real terms**. There is also the possibility that accounts have been **window dressed** (☞ unit 57). This would result in distorted ratios.

**Limitations of the balance sheet** Because the balance sheet is a 'snapshot' of a business at the end of the financial year, it might not be representative of the business's circumstances throughout the year. If, for example, a business experiences its peak trading activity in the summer, and has its year end at a time when trade is slow, in the New Year, balance sheet figures for stock and debtors will be unrepresentative.

**Qualitative information is ignored** Ratios only use quantitative information. Some important qualitative information may affect the performance of a business. For example, in the service industry the quality of customer service may be an important indicator. Ratio analysis cannot take this into account very easily.

1. Briefly describe the steps involved in the investigation process when analysing a set of accounts.
2. Why might interfirm comparisons be useful?
3. What is the difference between performance and activity ratios?
4. What is the difference between liquidity ratios and gearing ratios?
5. How do gross and net profit margins differ?
6. What do stock turnover and debt collection period measure?
7. Describe the difference between the current ratio and the acid test ratio.
8. What is meant by a high geared company?
9. Why is interest cover a profit and loss account measure of financial risk?
10. Which of the shareholders' ratios measures the actual financial return shareholders receive ?
11. Which ratio reflects the prospect of capital growth?
12. Describe the limitations of ratio analysis.

# key terms

**Acid test ratio** - similar to the current ratio but excludes stocks from current assets. Sometimes called the quick ratio.

**Asset turnover** - a measure of the productivity of assets.

**Current ratio** - assesses the firm's liquidity by dividing current liabilities into current assets.

**Debt collection period** - the number of days it takes to collect the average debt.

**Dividend cover** - how many times the dividend could have been paid from the year's earnings.

**Dividend per share** - the amount of money a shareholder will actually receive for each share owned.

**Dividend yield** - the amount received by the shareholder as a percentage of the share price.

**Earnings per share** - the amount each ordinary share earns.

**Gearing ratios** - explore the capital structure of a business by comparing the proportions of capital raised by debt and equity.

**Gross profit margin** - expresses operating profit before tax and interest, ie gross profit, as a percentage of turnover.

**Interest cover** - assesses a firm's ability to meet interest payments by comparing profit and interest payable .

**Net profit margin** - shows the firm's ability to control overheads and expresses net profit before tax as a percentage of turnover.

**Price/earnings ratio** - relates the earnings per share to its market price and reflects the return from buying shares.

**Ratio analysis** - a numerical approach to investigating accounts by comparing two related figures.

**Return on equity** - measures the return on shareholders' investment by expressing the profit earned by ordinary shareholders as a percentage of total equity.

**Return on net assets** - expresses profit as a percentage of long term assets only.

**Return on capital employed** - the profit of a business as a percentage of the total amount of money used to generate it.

**Stock turnover** - the number of times in a trading year a firm sells the value of its stocks.

# Case study Glyme Valley Farm and Cold Aston Farm

Patrick and Gillian O'Rourke have always wanted to own a farm. Patrick has worked on farms all his life and has a great deal of experience in mixed farming. Gillian, on the other hand, has been in publishing and recently sold her Gloucester-based publishing business for £350,000. They are now in a position to buy a small farm, although they expect to have to borrow some money to help fund the purchase. After several months of searching they have identified two possible targets. Both farms are private limited companies and both owners are keen for a quick sale.

## Glyme Valley Farm - Price £400,000

Glyme Valley Farm is located in Glympton, Oxfordshire. It consists of 1,200 acres of arable land owned by a local educational establishment, farm buildings, agricultural machinery and a flock of 400 sheep. The current owner, 72 year old Reginald Enser, has recently been taken into care and the farm is up for sale so that the sale proceeds can be used to meet the cost of caring. The profit and loss account and balance sheet are shown in Tables 56.8 and 56.9.

**Table 56.8** Glyme Valley Farm profit and loss account, 2004

GLYME VALLEY FARM -
PROFIT AND LOSS ACCOUNT Y/E 31.1.04

|  | £ |
|---|---|
| **Turnover** | 1,532,000 |
| Cost of sales | 451,000 |
| **Gross profit** | 1,081,000 |
| Overheads | 900,000 |
| **Operating profit** | 181,000 |
| Non-operating income | 2,000 |
| **Profit before interest** | 183,000 |
| Interest (net) | 152,000 |
| **Profit on ordinary activities before tax** | 31,000 |
| Taxation | 11,000 |
| **Profit for the year after tax** | 20,000 |
| Dividends | 8,000 |
| **Retained profit for the period** | 12,000 |

**Table 56.9** *Glyme Valley Farm Balance sheet, 2004*

GLYME VALLEY FARM - BALANCE SHEET
AS AT 31.1.04

|  | £ |
|---|---|
| **Fixed assets** | |
| Buildings | 610,000 |
| Machinery | 567,000 |
| | 1,177,000 |
| **Current assets** | |
| Stocks | 13,000 |
| Debtors | 15,000 |
| Cash at bank | 1,500 |
| | 29,500 |
| **Creditors:** amounts falling due in one year | 28,000 |
| **Net current assets** | 1,500 |
| **Total assets less current liabilities** | 1,178,500 |
| **Creditors:** amounts falling due after one year | (800,000) |
| **Net assets** | 378,500 |
| **Capital and reserves** | |
| Share capital | 200,000 |
| Retained profit | 178,500 |
| | 378,500 |

**Table 56.10** *Cold Aston Farm profit and loss account, 2004*

COLD ASTON FARM -
PROFIT AND LOSS ACCOUNT  Y/E 31.3.04

|  | £ |
|---|---|
| **Turnover** | 1,141,000 |
| Cost of sales | 322,000 |
| **Gross profit** | 819,000 |
| Overheads | 761,000 |
| **Operating profit** | 58,000 |
| Non-operating income | 2,000 |
| **Profit before interest** | 60,000 |
| Interest (net) | 15,000 |
| **Profit on ordinary activities before tax** | 45,000 |
| Taxation | 18,000 |
| **Profit for the year after tax** | 27,000 |
| Dividends | 9,000 |
| **Retained profit for the period** | 18,000 |

**Table 56.11** *Cold Aston Farm Balance sheet, 2004*

COLD ASTON FARM -
BALANCE SHEET AS AT 31.3.04

|  | £ |
|---|---|
| **Fixed assets** | |
| Buildings | 210,000 |
| Machinery | 167,000 |
| | 377,000 |
| **Current assets** | |
| Stocks | 36,000 |
| Debtors | 27,000 |
| Cash at bank | 5,000 |
| | 68,000 |
| **Creditors:** amounts falling due in one year | 36,000 |
| **Net current assets** | 32,000 |
| **Total assets less current liabilities** | 409,000 |
| **Creditors:** amounts falling due after one year | (56,000) |
| **Net assets** | 353,000 |
| **Capital and reserves** | |
| Share capital | 100,000 |
| Retained profit | 218,000 |
| Other reserves | 35,000 |
| | 353,000 |

## Cold Aston Farm - Price £450,000

Cold Aston Farm is situated in Cold Aston, Gloucestershire, near to where Patrick and Gillian currently live. The farm has more land, 1,700 acres, but some of it is prone to flooding. As a result, yields from the land can be quite variable. The land is owned by a wealthy landowner. The farm is also quite run down. For example, the cattle sheds are derelict and the barn roof has been blown off. The agricultural machinery is also old and much of it needs replacing. The farm is owned by Roger and Davina Bartlett who inherited it from their father two years ago. Roger and Davina have lost interest in farming and want to sell up. The profit and loss account and balance sheets are shown in Tables 56.10 and 56.11.

(a) Calculate the (i) gross profit margin; (ii) net profit margin; (iii) ROCE for both farms. (6 marks)

(b) Using the answers from (a), analyse the profitability of both farms. (8 marks)

(c) Use ratio analysis to assess the liquidity and gearing of both farms. (16 marks)

(d) Based on your calculations and information in the case, which farm would you advise Gillian and Patrick to buy. (10 marks)

(e) What other factors might be taken into account before a final decision about the purchase is made? (10 marks)

## The valuation of a business

Unit 56 showed that financial ratios can be used to investigate a company's accounts. A relatively high net profit margin might show that one business has performed better than another. It might also show that its own performance has improved over time. A relatively low gearing ratio might indicate that a business has raised most of its finance from its shareholders, rather than through loans.

To some extent, calculating financial ratios can help place a VALUE on a business. For example, businesses which have adequate working capital and high profit margins and returns on capital employed will tend to have more value than those which do not. The value of a business is how much it is worth to a **stakeholder** (☞ unit 3) or any other interested party, such as a potential buyer. For example, in May 2003, a management team bought Holmes Place, the health group. The purchase price was £25.4 million. This was the agreed value of the business at the time of the sale.

Different people might place different values on the same business. A seller is likely to place a higher value on a company than a buyer. This is sometimes called the **expectation gap**. Differences in value might also occur because a business might be worth more to one particular buyer. For example, Asda might place a higher value on an independent supermarket located in a town where it was not represented than Tesco might if they already had a store in that town. The difference in value occurs due to strategic considerations.

## Reasons for valuation

There may be times when it is necessary to have some idea how much a business is worth.

Planning a sale If the owners are considering the sale of a business, it will be necessary to know its value before putting it 'on the market'. Homeowners will normally ask an estate agent to value their house before putting it up for sale. Similarly, business owners might consult an accountant to help place a value on their business. Such valuations normally provide a starting point for negotiations between buyers and sellers. In many cases the agreed sale price will be different from the original valuation.

A takeover One company may be thinking about taking over another. In this case it will need to know the value of the company it is buying in order to decide whether it has enough funds to go through with the acquisition. Sometimes a takeover can work out more expensive than anticipated. This is often the case in a hostile takeover (☞ unit 89). The current owners might resist the takeover by refusing to sell their shares. This could drive up the price. Also, another company

might want to take over the same firm. This could result in a bidding war, where the price is inflated until the business is eventually sold to the highest bidder.

Merging When two companies merge, they need to know the value of each business. This is because the conditions of the merger have to be determined so that both companies can agree. For example, if one firm is twice the value of the other, it might mean that the new board of directors is made up of

---

In May 2003, Chiron, the US biotechnology company, agreed to buy PowderJect, the UK vaccines group. The agreed cash price for PowderJect was £542 million, the equivalent of 550p per share. This was at the higher end of analysts' expectations and about 30 per cent higher than the share price three months before, when the approach by Chiron was first made.

Analysts were concerned about PowderJect's dependence on sales of Fluvirin, its influenza vaccine, which was about to be subjected to competition from the US. Paul Drayson, chief executive, suggested that the sale of the company to Chiron was a better alternative than trying to broaden the base of the business through acquisitions. Last year PowderJect became only the second biotech company in the UK to report a profit. Chiron had been stalking PowderJect for sometime. They even made an informal offer of 450p per share about 12 months ago. Figure 57.1 shows the PowderJect share price and the global market shares of vaccines.

Source: adapted from *The Financial Times*, 20.5.2003.

**Figure 57.1** *PowderJect Pharmaceuticals' share price and global vaccines market share 2001*

Global vaccines market share 2001

1. Aventis Pasteur 29%
2. Glaxo-SmithKline 25%
3. Wyeth 16%
4. Merck 14%
5. Chiron 7%
6. PowderJect 3%
7. Others 6%

Total $5.4bn

Source: adapted from Thomson Datastream, Merrill Lynch.

(a) What was the value of PowderJect in May 2003?
(b) Why was it necessary to value the company at that time?
(c) Who will benefit from the sale of PowderJect?

## Question 1

six representatives from the highest valued company and three from the other. It is also necessary to know the value of the merging companies so that accountants can merge their financial affairs.

**Demerger or management buy-out** This is very similar to the sale of a business. In the case of a demerger it is necessary to calculate the value of the company before it is divided into smaller units. This then helps to calculate the value of the new, smaller companies when demerger takes place. Valuation of the new companies is required so that the number of new shares being issued, and their price, can be determined. In the case of a management buy-out or buy-in, valuation of the business or part of the business being sold is necessary to help set the sale price.

**Flotation** If a business, or part of a business, is being floated on the stock exchange (☞ unit 44) it is necessary to know the value. Again, this is required so that the number of shares being issued and their price can be determined. During the privatisation era of the 1980s it was suggested that many companies, such as BT and Powergen, were sold off by the government way below their true value. The government argued that it was necessary to price the share issues attractively in order for the flotation to be a success.

**Securing loans** When a business wants a loan the bank may require some collateral for security. If this is the case, the business, or part of the business, may be used. The bank may need to know the value of the business in order to clarify the value of the collateral.

**Other reasons** It may be necessary to calculate the value of the business if:
- the owner is involved in a divorce settlement, where the business is being shared out between husband and wife;
- a business has been inherited and inheritance tax is being calculated by the Inland Revenue;
- business owners or shareholders are curious about how much their business would be worth if sold;
- a business person is considering the sale of the business to retire;
- to make financial comparisons between businesses in an industry, for example, in an industrial survey.

# *Methods of valuation*

There is a number of techniques which could be used to value a business.

**Market capitalisation** This can be calculated using the formula:

## MARKET CAPITALISATION
= the current share price x the number of shares issued

For example, on 14 February 2004, the share price for British Airways was 311p and the number of shares issued in the company was 1,082,636,656. The value of the company could have been £3.367 billion using this measure. This method of valuation may be distorted because external factors can cause the share price to change, such as interest rates and the actions of speculators. If the share price falls by 10 per cent due to one of these factors, this does not necessarily mean that the value of the company has fallen by 10 per cent.

**Capitalised earnings** This method is often used to value the holdings of the majority shareholders in a business. When shareholders buy shares, they buy the right to a future stream of profits that the business will make, known as **maintainable earnings**. Multiplying these maintainable earnings by the price/earnings ratio of a company gives the capitalised earnings. So:

## CAPITALISED EARNINGS
= price/earnings ratio (P/E) x maintainable earnings

Unit 56 explained that the price earnings ratio shows the relationship between the amount each share earns for the investor and the current market price of the share. The P/E ratios of plcs are published each day in newspapers such as *The Financial Times*. A discount is often applied to the P/E ratios of private limited companies as their shares are not sold openly.

Maintainable earnings are the sustainable profits, after tax, that a business is capable of generating on a recurring basis. How can a value for maintainable earnings be estimated? It is necessary to consider all factors affecting a company's ability to maintain its current level of profit. This usually means starting with profits after tax for the current financial year. Then the figure is adjusted for one-off items of income or expenditure and directors' payments in excess of the market rate. So the estimate of maintainable earnings requires some human judgment. A subjective decision needs to be made about what non-recurring income and spending to take into account.

**Discounted cash flow (DCF)** This method may be used to value an entire company. It may also be used as a benchmark to compare the capitalised earnings value. To calculate the DCF a business needs to forecast annual cash flows and a discount factor. The discount factor will be the purchaser's cost of capital, such as the interest rate. Unit 49 explained how it is possible, using the DCF method, to calculate the net present value of a future stream of income. This will tell a business what the value of any future income streams is worth now.

Financial institutions, such as banks and venture capitalists, tend to prefer this method. It focuses on future cash flows rather than historic profit. They argue that valuations based on forecasts of future cash flows provide a better guide to the firm's ability to repay capital than a valuation based on past profits.

**Net assets** This method is most suitable when assets make up a major part of the value of the business. This might be the case with property or investment companies, for example. It might also be used if the company is a loss maker and the buyer of the business intends to sell the assets and then reinvest the cash. It might be used if a business has had difficulties and is being purchased from a receiver (☞ unit 106) for example. In this case the business may be bought at a discount to the value of net assets. The net assets of a business are:

Net assets = (fixed assets + current assets)
- (current and long term liabilities)

This is quite a simple method of valuation because the value of net assets is shown clearly on all business balance sheets.

**Return on investment (ROI)** This method might be used, for example, when a choice has to be made about which business to buy from two alternatives. This method uses similar techniques to the calculation of capitalised earnings. However, rather than maintainable earnings after tax it uses **maintainable operating profits** (profit before interest and tax). ROI can be found by:

$$ROI = \frac{\text{Maintainable operating profit}}{\text{Purchase price}}$$

When using this method to choose between different businesses for acquisition, the business with the highest ROI will be selected. Again, a subjective judgment is required regarding non-recurring income and spending when estimating maintainable operating profits.

**The pricing curve** Accountants have developed a rule-of-thumb measure to determine the value of a business. The pricing curve shown in Figure 57.2 can be used to give some idea of a company's value. The curve is based on aggregate sales values of private companies. To use the curve it is necessary to determine the operating profits of the company before tax and interest. However, the profit figure must be adjusted to take into account factors specific to the company. For example, if the current owners are paying themselves too much money, the profit figure should be raised accordingly. Once profits have been adjusted the curve can be used to obtain a value. For example, if earnings (profits) before interest and tax were £3 million, reading from the curve, the business would be worth £35 million.

Oasis Healthcare plc, through its wholly owned subsidiary, Oasis Dental Care Ltd, is the leading owner/operator of dental practices in England and Wales. The company has over 120 dental practices, predominantly under the 'Oasis' brand.

The UK dental market is worth about £3.5 billion and is currently growing at 10 per cent a year. However, the market is highly fragmented and underdeveloped. Individual practice partnerships, of which there are over 3,000 with three or more surgeries, represent the typical business unit. Oasis Healthcare's strategy is growth through acquisition. The company believes there are significant cost savings to be made through volume buying and centralisation of administration. Since flotation on AIM in July 2000, Oasis has raised £50 million to fund its acquisitions. It has purchased 67 practices and is becoming a national provider of dental care services.

Table 57.1 shows some financial information for Oasis Healthcare. Note that the fixed assets value includes £44.155 million of intangible assets. Most of this is accounted for by goodwill resulting from the acquisition of dental practices.

**Table 57.1** *Financial information for Oasis Healthcare as at 31.3.2003*

| | |
|---|---|
| Fixed assets | £56,285,000 |
| Current assets | £8,003,000 |
| Creditors: amounts falling due within one year | £13,048,000 |
| Long term liabilities | £36,101,000 |
| Share price | 16.5p |
| Number of issued shares | 63,939,466 |

Source: adapted from Oasis Healthcare, *Annual Report and Accounts, 2003*.

(a) Calculate the value of Oasis Healthcare plc using the
   (i) market capitalisation method and the (ii) net assets method.
(b) Explain how this case illustrates some of the problems of valuation.

**Question 2**

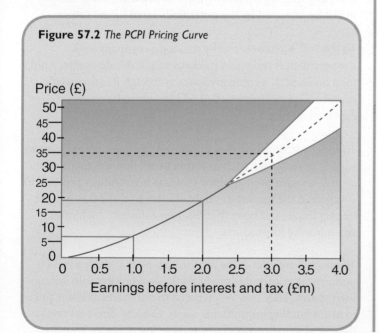

**Figure 57.2** *The PCPI Pricing Curve*

Price (£) vs Earnings before interest and tax (£m)

# Problems of valuation

The valuation of a business is often difficult. A company's value may not be known until it is placed on the market and sold. Certain problems exist when calculating the value of the business using the methods in the last section.

- When calculating the market capitalisation of a business the current share price is used. Sometimes the share price does not reflect accurately the performance of the business. Share prices can be influenced by external factors, such as interest rates and the actions of speculators. Also, the share price of a particular company may be a lot lower than one would expect because the company is 'out of favour' with the City. If share prices do not reflect the performance of the business the valuation will be inaccurate.
- The determination of maintainable earnings and maintainable operating profit require some human judgment. They are both concerned with the sustainable profits that a business is capable of generating on a **recurring** basis. The profit figures in the current accounts therefore need to be adjusted for non-recurring income and spending. This decision about what is non-recurring is likely to vary depending on who is making it.
- The DCF method also requires some human judgment. It is necessary to predict future cash inflows. This is difficult to do because a wide range of external factors, such as competitor's actions and the state of the economy, might influence future cash inflows.
- When using net assets to value a company, the true value of some assets may not appear on the balance sheet. These are intangible assets such as goodwill, brand names and copyrights. Therefore, if excluded, the value of the company would be understated. Many accountants choose not to include the value of intangible of assets because they are difficult to value. Also, the value of intangible assets can change quite sharply and suddenly.

To overcome some of the problems, businesses might use more than one method of valuation.

# The regulation and manipulation of accounts

The preparation of financial accounts in the UK is subject to a regulation. This is necessary to establish some uniformity in accounting. Before the regulatory framework existed it was difficult to make comparisons between company accounts. There were serious differences in the way accountants calculated profits due to the different methods they used. To overcome this problem the Accounting Standards Committee (ASC) was formed. Over a period of about 20 years this committee issued 25 statements of standard accounting practice (SSAPs). The statements provided uniform methods for practice, such as dealing with VAT (SSAP 5) and accounting for depreciation (SSAP 12). These SSAPs did help to reduce the variations in profit reporting. However, during the 1980s the ASC was subject to criticism because it had no legal power to enforce its standards, the standards were often too general and they were slow.

The regulatory framework is now the responsibility of the **Accounting Standards Board**. The board took over SSAPs. Any new standards are now called Financial Reporting Standards (FRSs). By 1998 the ASB had issued 8 FRSs. For example, FRS1 deals with the preparation of cash flow statements. In addition, Company Acts have certain requirements regarding accounting procedures. For example, businesses should adopt the accounting conventions discussed in unit 51, such as prudence, caution and going concern. Company accounts should also be presented in certain formats. Generally, the law requires that accounts should give a 'true and fair view' of a company's financial position.

Despite the existence of a regulatory framework, it is still possible to disguise the true financial position of a business. Information may be presented so that the financial position appears to be different than it really is. This is called MANIPULATING or WINDOW DRESSING the accounts.

# Why might accounts be manipulated?

There is a number of reasons why accounts might be manipulated.

**To appease shareholders** Stakeholders may not be satisfied with the performance of the business. Shareholders might also be concerned that poor performance might affect the size of the dividend. The accounts might exaggerate the performance of the company to pacify these groups.

**To attract investment** A business might be trying to raise funds externally. Overstating the financial position of the company might persuade lenders to provide funds. They might be attracted by the potentially large future returns.

**To fend off a takeover bid** By making a company look stronger than it really is, a predator might decide against a bid for a business. If a company looks as though it is financially sound and performing well, it will appear to be more expensive to buy.

**To show a stronger market position** A company might want to suggest to outsiders, such as competitors, that it is financially sound. It might hope to show that it is in a stronger position to compete in the market. It might also try to show that it is the market leader and hope that this may influence customers when buying its products.

**To affect share sales** If the accounts show that the business is performing poorly, this might panic shareholders into selling their shares. They may be prepared to sell shares at lower prices to avoid holding unprofitable assets. Current directors might then be able to buy up shares at these lower prices, knowing

Caldy plc is a company which operates a chain of 'themed' public houses. The company, which is listed on AIM, has seen its market capitalisation fall recently since it published its annual accounts. This is illustrated by movements in the share price shown in Figure 57.3. However, this has not discouraged the three executive directors in the company from purchasing substantial blocks of shares.

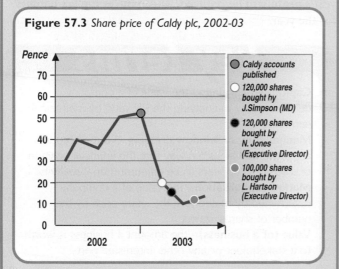

**Figure 57.3** *Share price of Caldy plc, 2002-03*

Legend:
- Caldy accounts published
- 120,000 shares bought by J.Simpson (MD)
- 120,000 shares bought by N. Jones (Executive Director)
- 100,000 shares bought by L. Hartson (Executive Director)

(a) What evidence is there to suggest that the accounts of Caldy plc may have been window dressed?
(b) State two reasons, apart from window dressing, why share prices may not reflect the value of the business.
(c) (i) What stakeholders may be interested in the information in the accounts suggested by Figure 57.3 and the article?
   (ii) Evaluate how they may react to this information.

**Question 3**

that the business is actually in a stronger position than is indicated. On the other hand, this may have the adverse effect of allowing outsiders to buy shares in a plc.

**To reduce taxation** The accounts may disguise the true financial strength of the business to reduce tax liability. Reducing the profit of a business should reduce the amount of corporation tax paid.

## *Methods of manipulation*

There is a number of ways in which accounts can be manipulated.

**Depreciation** It is possible for assets to be depreciated at a slower or faster rate. This will affect both the balance sheet and the profit and loss account. A change in the depreciation charge can be achieved by changing the method of calculating depreciation. For example, if a company buys a new machine for £100,000 (with a 6 year estimated life and residual value of £10,000), the depreciation allowance in the first year could be

£15,000 using the straight line method (SLM) or £40,000 using the reducing balance method (RBM) (☞ unit 49). If the RBM is used rather than the SLM, the higher depreciation charge would reduce the company's profit by £25,000 (£40,000 - £15,000). The choice of method would also mean that the book value of the machine would be lower in the balance sheet. Therefore the value of tangible assets and net assets would be lower.

**Creditors and debtors** By changing the value of creditors or debtors the solvency of a company can be manipulated. For example, if a business makes a serious effort to collect outstanding debts before the end of the trading year then the value of liquid assets will increase. The company will therefore appear to be in a healthier position. Similarly, if the value of creditors can be reduced on the balance sheet by repaying outstanding debts, the company will appear to be financially stronger.

**Stock valuation** By changing the method of stock valuation (☞ unit 49) the book value of stock might be increased or decreased. This will affect the profit and loss account and the balance sheet. For example, by using the FIFO method of stock valuation, a firm's closing stock might be £2,400,000. By using the AVCO method it might be reduced to £1,900,000 (if stock prices have risen during the year). By switching from FIFO to AVCO the value of cost of sales will be increased by £500,000 and therefore the value of profit will fall by £500,000. In the balance sheet, if the value of stocks is £500,000 lower the value of current assets will also be lower by the same amount. This will also reduce working capital and net assets.

**Writing off** A business can reduce its profits by 'writing off' investments or debt. This means, for example, if a debt of £40,000 is 'written off', it is called a bad debt and included as an expense in the profit and loss account. It is subtracted from gross profit and as a result net profit would fall by £40,000. The same would happen if an investment was written off.

**Profits** By suppressing costs, accountants can show greater profits. For example, a business might decide to pay month 12 salaries to staff in month 1 of the next trading year. This will reduce the salary bill in the current year, which is part of the operating expenses on the profit and loss account. Reducing the value of perating expenses will increase the value of net profit. The amount of retained profit can be manipulated by raising or lowering the dividend payment for the current trading year. If the dividend payment is reduced than retained profit for the year will be higher.

**Asset manipulation** A company can improve its gearing (☞ unit 56) by selling fixed assets and leasing them back. By selling fixed assets the business can use the proceeds to repay debt, such as loans. Reducing the amount of money raised from loans relative to the amount raised from shareholders will improve the gearing of the business. For example, a company's gearing may be:

$$\text{Gearing} = \frac{\text{Debt}}{\text{Equity}} \times 100 = \frac{£12m}{£24m} \times 100 = 50\%$$

If fixed assets of £4 million are sold and then leased back, with the money being used to repay loans, gearing is now:

$$\text{Gearing} = \frac{£8m}{£24m} \times 100 = 33.3\%$$

As a result of this the company has become more low geared. However, it will have to meet the cost of leasing assets in the future. This will reduce profit.

Any manipulation made to the accounts in the current trading year will usually show up in the next trading year. For example, an effort to suppress costs this year by postponing certain payments will mean that profit this year will be higher. However, assuming that the payments are made in the next trading year, the profit for that year will be lower.

**Earnings management** In some industries it is possible for a business to choose when to 'recognise' business income. For example, a TV production company can choose to recognise the income from a new programme when the programme contract is signed, when the programme is delivered, or when the invoice is issued. By choosing to recognise income in the next financial year, the current year's profit will be reduced. This reduces the tax liability for the year.

## key terms

**Capitalised earnings** - the value of a company determined by multiplying the P/E ratio by maintainable earnings.

**Manipulating or window dressing** - where accounts are presented in such a way that the financial position of a business appears to be different than it really is.

**Market capitalisation** - the value of a company determined by multiplying the share price by the number of shares issued.

**Value (of a business)** - the amount a business is worth to a stakeholder or any other interested party.

## Knowledge ...Knowledge...Knowledge...Knowledge...Knowledge...Know

1. What is meant by the expectation gap in relation to the value of a business?
2. Explain 2 reasons why a hostile takeover might lead to a rise in the value of a business.
3. State 5 reasons for valuing a business, other than for a takeover.
4. What information is needed to calculate (i) market capitalisation and (ii) maintainable earnings?
5. How does DCF allow a business to be valued?
6. State 4 problems which might occur when valuing a business.

7. Why is it necessary to regulate the presentation of accounts?
8. State 4 reasons why the accounts might be manipulated.
9. Briefly explain 2 ways in which accounts could be manipulated to exaggerate the value of a company.
10. Briefly explain 2 ways in which accounts could be manipulated to show a company in a poorer light.
11. How can the gearing of a company be affected by window dressing?

# Case study JMC

JMC is a quoted construction company that undertakes large scale construction work such as roads, bridges and other infrastructure projects. Jane Marsh owns 51 per cent of the company and is the chief executive. The company has doubled in size in the last three years due to a programme of acquisitions. This growth has pleased shareholders since both profits and dividends have grown as well. The company's share price has also risen from 162p in 2002 to 325p in 2004. JMC is currently looking at another acquisition. It wants to break into the Scottish market and two companies have emerged as possible targets, although only one will eventually be bought. The two companies, Thistle Holdings and Glasgow Construction, have both heard on the 'grapevine' that they may be subject to takeover bids. However, no official announcement has yet been made.

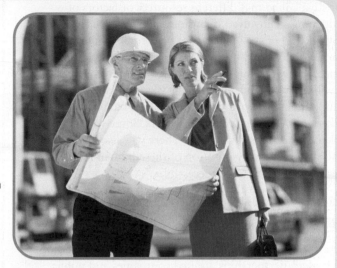

**Thistle Holdings** This appears to be a soundly run company. It has a lot of road maintenance contracts with various Scottish councils. It will not take kindly to a takeover bid, but if the price is right the shareholders may be happy to sell. Jane thinks this would be a good company to buy, but the price could be high.

**Glasgow Construction** Much less is known about this company. Its main area of business is the construction of hydroelectric power stations in the Scottish Highlands. It is felt that a bid by JMC would be regarded as entirely hostile and unwelcome. However, the company could be bought cheaply and there is a suspicion that the accounts have been boosted artificially. For example, JMC's accountant thinks that some assets may have been sold and leased back. It is also thought that the year's profit may have been inflated by the management of earnings. It is thought that some of the income (about £2 million) for a project due to start next year, has been included in this year's profit and loss account. The contracts for the project were signed this year.

(a) **Why will it be necessary to value Thistle Holdings and Glasgow Construction? (6 marks)**
(b) **Use two methods of valuation to determine the value of Thistle Holdings and Glasgow Construction. (12 marks)**
(c) **Explain the effects on the accounts of Glasgow Construction if the alleged manipulations have taken place. (10 marks)**
(d) **Explain why Glasgow Construction might have manipulated its accounts. (10 marks)**
(e) **Assuming that the alleged manipulations have taken place, evaluate which company would be best for JMC to take over. (12 marks)**

**Table 57.2** *Financial information for Thistle Holdings and Glasgow Construction*

|  | Thistle Holdings | Glasgow Construction |
|---|---|---|
| Fixed assets | £104m | £71m |
| Current assets | £32m | £20m |
| Creditors: amounts falling due within one year | £28m | £12m |
| Long term liabilities | £50m | £25m |
| Share price | £3.25 | £1.10 |
| No. of shares issued | 20m | 50m |
| Profit after tax | £4.6m | £4.9m |

## Human resources

Unit 1 explained that different resources or factors of production are involved in business activity. The HUMAN RESOURCES of the business are the people employed by the business. In a small business, such as a window cleaning service, the owner might be the only human resource. He or she will carry out most, if not all, tasks. In a large multinational company there are likely to be thousands of workers. Some will be manual workers. Some will be skilled workers or administration staff. There will also be managers and directors. The organisation of these human resources is vital if a business is to be successful.

## The formal organisation of a business

There are several types of business organisation, including sole traders, partnerships, limited companies and public sector organisations (☞ units 6 and 7). However, each will have its own internal structure - the way in which human resources are organised. This is known as the FORMAL ORGANISATION of the business. It takes into account such things as:

● the relationships between individuals;
● who is in charge;
● who has authority to make decisions;
● who carries out decisions;
● how information is communicated.

Different businesses tend to have different objectives (☞ unit 4). There will also be differences in relationships, how they are managed and how decisions are made. Because these activities can be arranged in various ways, businesses tend to have different BUSINESS STRUCTURES. There are, however, likely to be some similarities. For example, many large companies are controlled by a few directors, are divided into departments with managers, section heads and have many workers in each department.

One method of organising a business is where managers put people together to work effectively based on their skills and abilities. The structure is 'built up' or it '**develops**' as a result of the employees of the business. In contrast a structure could be **created** first, with all appropriate job positions outlined, and then people employed to fill them. It has been suggested that the entrepreneur Richard Branson worked out a complete organisation structure for his Virgin Atlantic airline before setting up the company and then recruited the 102 people needed to fill all the positions.

## Organisation charts

Many firms produce ORGANISATION CHARTS. These illustrate the structure of the business. Figure 58.1 shows a 'traditional' type of chart. It is a chart for an engineering firm, Able Engineering. Different types of businesses are likely to have different charts. The chart in Figure 58.1 may be simpler than one drawn for a large public limited company, although the style will be similar. It may be more involved, however, than a chart for a partnership.

Why do businesses draw such charts?

● To spot communication problems. An organisation chart indicates how employees are linked to other employees in the business. If information is not received, the business can find where the communication breakdown has occurred by tracing the communication chain along the chart.

● Organisation charts help individuals see their position in a

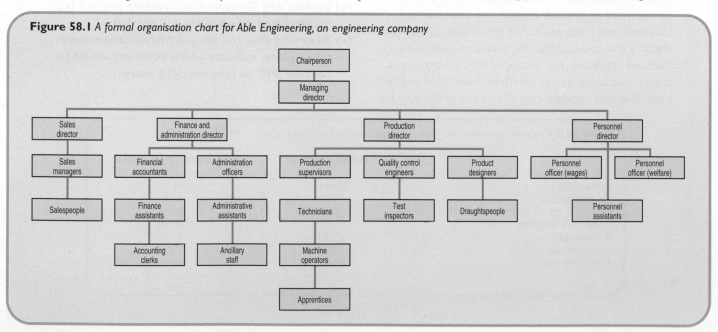

**Figure 58.1** *A formal organisation chart for Able Engineering, an engineering company*

business. This can help them appreciate their responsibilities, who has authority over them and who they are accountable to.

● Organisation charts allow firms to pinpoint areas where specialists are needed. For example, in Figure 58.1 Able Engineering recognises it needs designers and draughtspeople as part of the production 'team'.

● Organisation charts show how different sections of the firm relate to each other. For example, the chart for Able Engineering shows the relationship between salespeople and technicians. They are both at the same level in the hierarchy, but work in different departments and are responsible to different managers.

Simply producing an organisation chart is of limited use to a business. The business will only achieve its objectives if it understands the relationships between employees and other parts of the business.

---

Ainscough Engineering Ltd produces ground support equipment for the aviation industry. The company has a traditional organisational structure. The managing director is responsible to the chairperson and has a sales director, finance director, personnel director and production director accountable to her. On the production side of the business, there are a works manager, technicians, test engineers and machine operators. In addition, the company employs a number of personnel assistants, financial and administrative staff, and salespeople.

(a) Draw an organisation chart from the information about Ainscough Engineering Ltd.
(b) Briefly explain two ways in which the business might use the chart.

## Question 1

## *Chain of command and span of control*

When deciding on its organisation structure, a business must take into account two important factors - the management **hierarchy** and the **span of control**.

The HIERARCHY in a business is the order or levels of management in a firm, from the lowest to the highest rank. It shows the CHAIN OF COMMAND within the organisation - the way authority is organised. Orders pass down the levels and information passes up. Businesses must also consider the number of links or levels in the chain of command. R. Townsend, in his book *Up the Organisation*, estimated that each extra level of management in the hierarchy reduced the effectiveness of communication by about 25 per cent. No rules are laid down on the most effective number of links in the chain. However, businesses generally try to keep chains as short as possible.

Another factor to be taken into account is the SPAN OF CONTROL. This refers to the number of subordinates

working under a superior or manager. In other words, if one production manager has ten subordinates his span of control is ten. Henri Fayol (☞ unit 62) argued that the span of control should be between three and six because:

● there should be tight managerial control from the top of the business;

● there are physical and mental limitations to any single manager's ability to control people and activities.

A narrow span of control has the advantage for a firm of tight control and close supervision. It also allows better co-ordination of subordinates' activities. In addition, it gives managers time to think and plan without having to be burdened with too many day to day problems. A narrow span also ensures better communication with subordinates, who are sufficiently small in number to allow this to occur.

A wide span of control, however, offers greater decision making authority for subordinates and may improve job satisfaction (☞ unit 59). In addition, there are likely to be lower costs involved in supervision. Figure 58.2 shows two organisation charts. In the first (a), there is a long chain of command, but a narrow span of control. The second (b) shows a wide span, but a short chain.

## *Authority and responsibility*

Employees in the hierarchy will have responsibility and

**Figure 58.2**

(a) A long chain of command and a narrow span of control. A production department may look like this. One manager is helped by a few assistant managers, each responsible for supervisors. These supervisors are responsible for skilled workers, who are in charge of a group of semi-skilled workers. Close supervision is needed to make sure quality is maintained. This is sometimes referred to as a tall organisational structure.

(b) A short chain of command and a wide span of control. A higher or further education department may look like this, with a 'head' of department, a few senior staff and many lecturing staff. Staff will want a degree of independence. This is sometimes referred to as a flat organisational structure.

authority. However, these terms do not mean the same thing.

RESPONSIBILITY involves being accountable or being required to justify an action. So, for example, managers who are responsible for a department may be asked to justify poor performance to the board of directors. The personnel department may be responsible for employing workers. If a new worker was unable to do a particular job, they would be asked to explain why.

AUTHORITY, on the other hand, is the ability to carry out the task. For example, it would make no sense asking an office worker to pay company debts if she did not have the authority to sign cheques. Employees at lower levels of the hierarchy have less responsibility and authority than those further up. However, it may be possible for a superior to **delegate** (pass down) authority to a subordinate, eg a manager to an office worker, but retain responsibility. Increasingly, businesses are realising the benefits of delegating both authority and responsibility.

## Line, staff and functional authority

Line, staff and functional authority are terms used to describe the type of relationship that managers may have with others in the hierarchy.

**Line authority** Line authority is usual in a hierarchy. It shows the authority that a manager has over a subordinate. In Figure 58.1, the production director would have line authority over the designers. Communication will flow down from the superior to the subordinate in the chain of command. The advantage of this is that a manager can allocate work and control subordinates, who have a clear understanding of who is giving them instructions. The manager can also delegate authority to others if they feel this will make decision making more effective.

In large organisations, the chain of command can be very long. This means that instructions given by those at the top of the chain of command may take time before they are carried out at a lower level.

**Staff authority** Many larger organisations now have staff authority. Staff authority might be when a manager or department in a business has a function within another department, for example, giving specialist advice. A marketing manager may give advice to the production department based on market research into a new product. Personnel managers have responsibilities for personnel matters in all departments. Although the specialist can give advice, they have no authority to make decisions in the other department.

**Functional authority** Functional authority is when a specialist has the authority to make a line manager accept his or her advice. It is different from staff authority, where the specialist can only advise. For example, the finance manager may have overall authority over the budget holder in the marketing department.

Problems may occur in a business if people do not

understand where authority and responsibility rest. This means that managers must know whether their authority is line, staff or functional. Unfortunately, this can lead to friction. Line managers are sometimes thought of as 'first class citizens' and staff managers are thought of as costly 'overheads' who are not contributing anything of worth to the organisation. Also, the authority of functional managers is not accepted by line managers at times.

## Delegation

Managers are increasingly being asked to carry out strategic activities that affect the whole business. This has resulted in the need to DELEGATE authority and responsibility for certain tasks to employees further down the hierarchy. Delegation can provide benefits to a business, as explained in the next section. When is delegation likely to be effective?

- Researchers such as Spetzer (1992) have suggested that employees need to be **empowered** (☞ unit 61) in order to make effective decisions. They need to be given self-confidence and control of what they do.
- If managers only delegate when they are overloaded, subordinates may be resentful.

---

The Manchester Film Association is an SME in the centre of the city's 'cultural quarter'. Its main activities are video, film and multimedia production. It employs 9 full time staff. Mike joined the company 6 months ago. He recently graduated, but has little work experience. However, he has proven so far in the work that he has done for clients to be innovative. He often has ideas that no-one else has considered. Shoaib has worked for the business for 15 years. He has built up considerable production and post-production skills. Lisa had previously set up her own website design and consultancy operation. She has experience in managing projects, working to deadlines and taking responsibility for clients' requests.

The managing director of the business, Paula, has been approached by a fast growing leisure company to produce an innovative multi-media training programme on CD Rom for newly recruited employees. The company wants the programme to be interactive, but it must be ready within two months. Paula decided to ask Mike to look after the project. However, almost from the start he seemed to have problems. He did not ask for help when it would have been useful. He found it difficult to organise others and often missed deadlines he had set. After four weeks, Paula was concerned that the project would not be completed.

Source: adapted from company information.

(a) Explain why delegation may not have been effective in this case.
(b) Examine what action Paula should now take.

**Question 2**

- Delegation requires planning. Managers must be clear about what needs to be done. Instead of freeing time, poor delegation may take up managers' time as they try to correct problems.
- Managers must take time to explain delegated tasks clearly. Employees may waste time or make mistakes because of lack of information. Telling subordinates why the work is important helps to create shared values.
- Allow participation. It is useful to discuss the task with those to whom it has been delegated. Subordinates will then know from the start what the task will include. It also helps managers to decide if delegation is appropriate. A person may feel they do not have the skills to carry out the task.
- The employee given a delegated task should also be given the authority and responsibility to carry it out. Managers must tell others in the business that the delegated person is acting on his or her behalf. This will avoid difficulties, such as the questioning of authority.
- Managers must avoid interfering with delegated tasks.
- Delegated tasks should be given to suitable employees. It would be inappropriate to delegate a marketing task to an employee in personnel. Employees must also have the training to carry out the task.
- Provide support and resources. If an employee is delegated a task without suitable support and resources this could lead to anxiety, frustration and the task being badly done.

Research has shown that when factors like these are taken into account, delegation was four times as likely to be successful.

# Centralisation and decentralisation

Centralisation and decentralisation refer to the extent to which authority is delegated in a business. If there was complete centralisation, then subordinates would have no authority at all. Complete decentralisation would mean subordinates would have all the authority to take decisions. It is unlikely that any business operates in either of these ways. Even if authority is delegated to a subordinate, it is usual for the manager to retain responsibility.

Certain functions within a business will always be centralised, because of their importance. For example, decisions about budget allocation are likely to be centralised as they affect the whole company. The decision to distribute profits is also taken only by a few.

**Advantages of centralisation** Why might a business centralise authority?

- Senior management have more control of the business, eg budgets.
- Procedures, such as ordering and purchasing, can be standardised throughout the organisation, leading to economies of scale and lower costs.
- Senior managers can make decisions from the point of view of the business as a whole. Subordinates would tend

to make decisions from the point of view of their department or section. This allows senior managers to maintain a balance between departments or sections. For example, if a company has only a limited amount of funds available to spend over the next few years, centralised management would be able to share the funds out between production, marketing, research and development, and fixed asset purchases in different departments etc.

- Senior managers should be more experienced and skilful in making decisions. In theory, centralised decisions by senior people should be of better quality than decentralised decisions made by others less experienced.
- In times of crisis, a business may need strong leadership by a central group of senior managers.
- Communication may improve if there are fewer decision makers.

**Advantages of decentralisation or delegation** Some delegation is necessary in all firms because of the limits to the amount of work senior managers can carry out. Tasks that might be delegated include staff selection, quality control, customer relations and purchasing and stock control. A greater degree of decentralisation - over and above the

---

In 2003 The Future Network plc, the international specialist magazine publisher, announced the final stages of the restructuring of its UK business, which began in February 2001. Under the reorganisation plan, Future divided its UK business into three operating divisions – games, computing and entertainment. This was to be accompanied by a reduction in fixed operating costs in the UK by approximately £4 million, through cuts in staffing levels and property overheads.

The changes to the business involved reductions in centralised support services, and in Internet and magazine teams and rationalisation of the company's property portfolio. There was also to be an important change in the way the UK business was managed, by devolving operational responsibility to the individual divisions as profit centres.

Colin Morrison, Chief Operating Officer of The Future Network, said 'This plan is important because of the substantial reduction in our fixed operating costs against a broadly unchanged magazine portfolio. But much more than that, this restructuring and decentralisation plan simplifies our business, and will improve our focus, agility and control. We will now be more streamlined and much better placed to take advantage of our market-leading positions in the important UK market.

Source: adapted from www.thefuturenetwork.plc.uk.

(a) Describe the organisational changes at The Future Network plc.
(b) Examine the possible benefits and disadvantages for the business of these changes.

**Question 3**

minimum which is essential - has a number of advantages.

- It empowers and motivates workers (☞ unit 61).
- It reduces the stress and burdens of senior management. It also frees time for managers to concentrate on more important tasks.
- It provides subordinates with greater job satisfaction by giving them more say in decision-making, which affects their work (☞ unit 59 on McGregor's Theory Y).
- Subordinates may have a better knowledge of 'local' conditions affecting their area of work. This should allow them to make more informed, well-judged choices. For example, salespeople may have more detailed knowledge of their customers and be able to advise them on purchases.
- Delegation should allow greater flexibility and a quicker response to changes.  If problems do not have to be referred to senior managers, decision-making will be quicker.  Since decisions are quicker, they are easier to change in the light of unforeseen circumstances which may arise.
- By allowing delegated authority, management at middle and junior levels are groomed to take over higher positions. They are given the experience of decision making when carrying out delegated tasks. Delegation is therefore important for management development.

# Different forms of business structure

Despite the variety of formal business organisation that exists, there are four main types of structure most often found.

**The entrepreneurial structure** In this type of business structure, all decisions are made centrally. There are few collective decisions and a great reliance on 'key' workers. It is often found in businesses where decisions have to be made quickly, such as newspaper editing.

Most small businesses also have this type of structure, as illustrated in Figure 58.3(a). These businesses rely on the expertise of one or two people to make decisions. Decision making is efficient up to a point because:
- decisions can be made quickly;
- subordinates understand to whom they are accountable;
- little consultation is required.
However, as the business grows, this structure can cause inefficiency as too much of a load is placed on those making decisions.

**The bureaucratic, pyramid or hierachical structure** This is the traditional hierachical structure for most medium sized and large businesses and perhaps the most well known. It is illustrated in Figure 58.3(b). Decision making is shared throughout the business. Employees are each given a role and procedures are laid down which determine their behaviour at work.

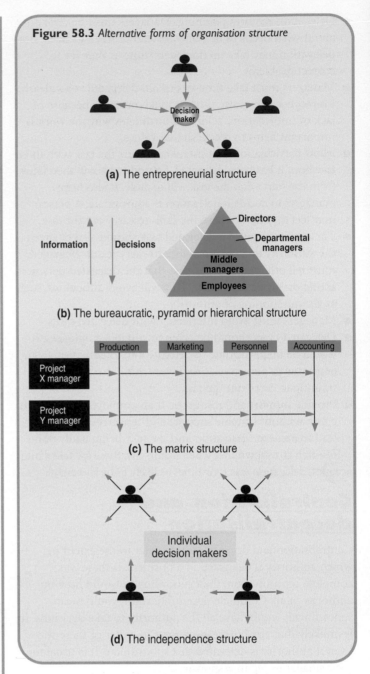

**Figure 58.3** *Alternative forms of organisation structure*

**(a)** The entrepreneurial structure

Information    Decisions

Directors
Departmental managers
Middle managers
Employees

**(b)** The bureaucratic, pyramid or hierarchical structure

Production    Marketing    Personnel    Accounting

Project X manager

Project Y manager

**(c)** The matrix structure

Individual decision makers

**(d)** The independence structure

Specialisation of tasks (☞ unit 1) is possible. This means that a departmental structure, with finance, personnel, production and marketing employees, can be set up. Specialisation may allow the business to enjoy economies of scale. Recently, this type of structure has been criticised for its inability to change and meet new demands.

**The matrix structure** This emphasises getting people with particular specialist skills together into project teams, as illustrated in Figure 58.3(c). Individuals within the team have their own responsibility. The matrix structure was developed to overcome some of the problems with the entrepreneurial and bureaucratic structures. **Matrix management** involves the co-ordinating and support of specialist teams within a matrix structure.

Managers often argue that this is the best way of organising people, because it is based on the expertise and skills of employees and gives scope for people lower down the organisation to use their talents effectively. For example, a project manager looking into the possibility of developing a new product may draw on the expertise of employees with skills in design, research and development, marketing, costing etc. A college running a course for unemployed people may draw on the skills of a number of lecturers in different departments. In this way, a matrix structure can also operate within a business that has a bureaucratic structure. The matrix model fits in with managers who have a Theory Y view of employees (☞ unit 59). It is suggested that this structure improves flexibility and motivation of employees. It has recently lost favour because it often needs expensive support systems, such as extra secretarial and office staff. There may also be problems with co-odinating a team drawn from different departments and the speed of decision making.

**The independence structure** This emphasises the individual and is almost a 'non-organisation'. The other three methods put together the contributions of a number of people so that the sum of their efforts is greater than the parts. All efforts are co-ordinated so that the business benefits. The independence structure is a method of providing a support system. Barristers' chambers and doctor's clinics have worked in this way. It is attractive to independent people who are confident of their ability to be successful. This form of organisation tends to be unsuitable for most types of business because of the lack of control and co-ordination.

# Informal business structure

Organisation charts show the formal organisation of a business. However many relationships between employees in business are informal. The INFORMAL BUSINESS STRUCTURE is the network of relationships that develop between members on the basis of their common interests and friendships. These relationships can affect the way a business operates. Krackhardt and Hanson (1993) in a study of informal networks in the banking industry found three types of relationship.

- Advice networks - who depends on who to solve problems and provide information.
- Trust networks - which employees share potential information and back each other up in times of crisis.
- Communication networks - which employees regularly talk to each other on work related matters.

They recommended that businesses use informal structures to solve problems. For example, a study showed that a bank's task force group was unable to find ways of improving the bank's performance. The leader of the task force held a central position in the 'advice network'. Employees relied on her for technical advice. However, she only had one 'trust link' with a colleague. Management did not want to label the group as a failure or embarrass a valued employee by dismissing her as team leader. Instead, it redesigned the task force in line with the informal organisation of the business by adding a person in the trust network to share responsibility for group leadership.

# Factors influencing organisational structures

There is a number of factors which might influence the organisation and the structure of a business.

- Size. As a business grows, it is likely to move away from an entrepreneurial structure towards one where authority is passed to other employees. A large firm will also tend to have a longer chain of command, with more levels in the hierarchy.
- Views of the owners or leadership styles. If owners wish to retain control in the business, they will want a narrow span of control. Owners or managers who wish to motivate or encourage employees may delegate decision making.
- Business objectives. If the business decides to expand rapidly, perhaps by merger, it is likely to find that its span of control gets wider. An example might be a business setting up an operation in a foreign country or deciding to sell into a foreign market.
- External factors. Changes in external factors can often influence business organisation. In periods of recession or rising costs, a business may be forced to reduce its chain of command to cut costs. Similarly, in a period of economic growth (☞ unit 101), a firm may employ extra managers as specialists to gain economies of scale.
- Changes in technology. The introduction of new technology can change the structure of a business. For example, a new system of production may remove the need for quality controllers, or an information technology system could reduce the role of administration.
- The informal structure. If the informal structure does not complement and support the formal structure, this may lead to problems.
- Corporate culture (☞ unit 15). The norms of behaviour in a business might influence its organisational structure. For example, a business that has developed with a team based approach to decision making, a casual dress code and a management that are very approachable might find it difficult to change suddenly to a structure with layers of hierarchy and formal decision making processes. Charles Handy in *Understanding Organisations* (1976) identified four cultures which reflect the organisation structures in Figure 58.3. The **power** culture is structure (a) with one powerful decision maker. The **role** culture is structure (b) where everyone in the hierarchy has a clear role. The **task** culture is structure (c) based on a team approach. The **person** culture is structure (d).

# Recent trends

Some businesses over the last ten years have changed their organisations to make them into flatter structures. This is process is called **delayering** (☞ unit 90). It has often meant taking out layers of middle management, which will affect the hierarchy, span of control and chain of command. Businesses have also changed their organisation in other ways.

● A study by Cressey and Jones suggested that banks have moved from traditional, bureaucratic, stratified structures, with narrow job tasks, into profit centred, performance orientated businesses that empower employees to take responsibility.

● According to Paul Iles there is a much greater emphasis on multi-skilled teams and delayered organisations in manufacturing. This has led to greater financial flexibility,

employee autonomy, self-monitoring and devolved decision making.

● Du Gay suggested that a number of factors have led to changes in the retail sector. Increased globalisation and competition have meant businesses must be able to respond more quickly. As a result they have reduced the number of layers in their hierarchy. Also businesses need to be more aware of consumers' needs. As a result they have restructured into flatter, team based organisations to allow employees to see that the way they work should be more helpful for the way they would consume.

---

**Figure 58.4** *Wesley Hains' organisational structure*

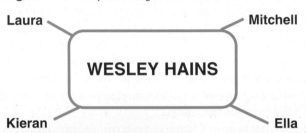

Wesley Hains runs a card design business in Cardiff. He employs four staff - Laura, Mitchell, Kieran and Ella. Laura manages the office in Cardiff dealing with telephone and e-mail enquiries, visitors, administration and a small amount of marketing. Mitchell, Kieran and Ella are

card designers and all work from home in various parts of the country. Mitchell lives and works in a small croft in Glen Cona in North West Scotland. The designers are all linked by computer to the main Cardiff office. This ensures good communications. For example, design briefs are sent direct by Wesley using e-mail and design copy is transmitted direct to Wesley's terminal when designs are completed. Some specialisation takes place amongst the designers. Mitchell designs birthday cards, Kieran designs postcards and Ella works on specialist projects. Wesley is occupied with customers, ensuring that design briefs are satisfied by his designers and looking for new business. He spends three days a week out of the office.

(a) What type of organisational structure does the business have at present?
(b) In September, Wesley secured a contract with an American card manufacturer. Wesley had to recruit four more designers as a result. He decided to employ a full-time salesperson to sell designs in the US. He also bought a small printing business in Newport to print and supply cards as well as designing them. Explain why Wesley might decide to change the organisational structure of his business.

**Question 4**

---

# key terms

**Authority** - the right to command a situation, a task or an activity.
**Business structure** - the way in which a business is organised.
**Chain of command** - the way authority and power are passed down in a business.
**Delegation** - authority (and sometimes responsibility) passed down from superior to subordinate.
**Formal organisation** - the relationships between employees and the organisational structure determined by the business, as shown in an organisation chart.

**Hierarchy** - the order or levels of management of a business, from the lowest to the highest.
**Human resources** - the employees of a business.
**Informal business structure** - the relationships between employees that are based on the common interests of employees.
**Organisation chart** - a diagram which illustrates the structure of an organisation.
**Responsibility** - the duty to complete a task.
**Span of control** - the number of subordinates working under a superior.

Knowledge...owledge...Knowledge...Knowledge...Knowledge...Knowledge...Kno

1. What are the features of the internal structure of a business?
2. How might an organisation chart be used in a firm's induction programme?
3. Draw a simple organisation chart showing:
   (a) a partnership with two partners and 6 employees;
   (b) a large company with a board of directors, six departments, and two more levels in the hierarchy.
4. What is meant by a 'wide span of control'?
5. What problems might a 'wide span of control' have for a business?
6. Explain the difference between line, staff and functional authority.
7. Why might businesses have line, staff and functional authority?
8. Give three situations where centralised decision making may be useful for a business.
9. What factors influence effective delegation?
10. Why is empowerment important when tasks are delegated?
11. State 4 advantages of delegation.
12. What problems might a matrix structure cause for a business?
13. What type of business might be organised with:
    (a) an entrepreneurial structure;
    (b) an independence structure?
14. Why is it important for businesses to understand their informal business structures?

# Case study AGF Irish Life and Granada

### AGF Irish Life

AGF Irish Life is the largest commercial general insurer in Ireland. It has an income of over £250 million and 800 staff. In 2000 it faced a volatile domestic market for insurance. And there was an added threat from European insurers interested in international business. So it turned a threat into an opportunity under the banner Project 2000.

The company delayered and it changed its traditional if somewhat static departmental structure (including sales, underwriting, claims etc.) into dynamic teams, each responsible for the total needs of a targeted group of brokers. The customer benefited by having the same people dealing with all their needs. Employees were also empowered and became mulitskilled in the process. A 30 per cent improvement in turnaround time for enquiries was found as a result of the new system. Another feature was that tasks could be carried out concurrently.

Source: adapted from www.topcall.com.

### Granada

In 2001 Granada made 100 staff redundant as part of a sweeping reorganisation involving a delayering of the management structure. The company argued 'We do not need a second layer of people to second guess the management at ITV.' It was also suggested that the organisation would be streamlined. The old complicated structure would be replaced by a simpler, two-pronged organisation. One part, Granada Content, would deal with production while the other, Granada Platforms, would deal with broadcasting. Granada Content would also handle the company's online and broadband activities.

Source: adapted from *The Guardian*, 13.6.2001.

(a) **Identify the changes in the organisational structures at the two businesses. (6 marks)**
(b) **What factors have influenced the changes in organisational structures? (10 marks)**
(c) **Explain how the changes might affect:**
   (i) **employees at the businesses;**
   (ii) **management at the businesses;**
   (iii) **clients of the business. (12 marks)**
(d) **Assess to what extent the changes will benefit the businesses. (12 marks)**

## The satisfaction of needs

If asked, most people who work would probably say they do so to earn money to buy goods and services. However, this is not the only **need** that is satisfied by working.

A list of people's needs that may be satisfied from work might be very long indeed. It could include, for example, the need for variety in the workplace, which may be satisfied by an interesting job. Employees may also need to feel appreciated for the work they do, which could be reflected in the prestige attached to their job.

Individuals are not the same. Therefore, it is likely that lists made by any two people of their needs and how they can be satisfied will be very different. There are some reasons for working that could apply to everyone, such as the need to earn money. However, some reasons have more importance for particular individuals than others. One employee may need to work with friendly colleagues, whereas another might be happy working on his own.

Why is it important for a business to find out what satisfies the needs of its employees? It is argued that if an individual's needs are not satisfied, then that worker will not be MOTIVATED to work. Businesses have found that even if employees are satisfied with pay and conditions at work, they also complain that their employer does not do a good job in motivating them. This applies to all levels, from the shopfloor to the boardroom. It appears in many companies that employers are not getting the full potential from their employees because they are not satisfying all of their employees' needs. Figure 59.1 shows one example of how a business might make decisions, having first identified an employee's needs.

It is important for a business to motivate its employees. In the short run a lack of motivation may lead to reduced effort and lack of commitment. If employees are watched closely, fear of wage cuts or redundancy may force them to maintain their effort even though they are not motivated. This is **negative motivation**. In the long term, a lack of motivation

may result in high levels of absenteeism, industrial disputes and falling productivity and profit for a business. So it is argued that well motivated employees will be productive which should lead to greater efficiency and profits for a business.

## Maslow's hierarchy of needs

The first comprehensive attempt to classify needs was by **Abraham Maslow** in 1954. Maslow's theory consisted of two parts. The first concerned classification of needs. The second concerned how these classes are related to each other.

Maslow suggested that 'classes' of needs could be placed into a **hierarchy**. The hierarchy is normally presented as a 'pyramid', with each level consisting of a certain class of needs. This is shown in Figure 59.2.

The classes of needs were:
- physiological needs, eg wages high enough to meet weekly bills, good working conditions;
- safety needs, eg job security, safe working conditions;
- love and belonging, eg working with colleagues that support you at work, teamwork, communicating;
- esteem needs, eg being given recognition for doing a job well;
- self-actualisation, eg being promoted and given more responsibility, scope to develop and introduce new ideas and take on challenging new job assignments.

Figure 59.2 can also be used to show the relationship between the different classes. Maslow argued that needs at the bottom of the pyramid are basic needs. They are concerned with survival. These needs must be satisfied before a person can move to the next level. For example, people are likely to be more concerned with basic needs, such as food, than anything else. At work an employee is unlikely to be concerned about acceptance from colleagues if he has not eaten for six hours.

Once each level is satisfied, the needs at this level become less important. The exception is the top level of SELF-ACTUALISATION. This is the need to fulfil your potential.

**Figure 59.1** *Satisfying an individual's needs*

REVISE — If need is not satisfied

IDENTIFY THE NEED/MOTIVATION → INCENTIVE → SATISFACTION → RESULT/OUTCOME

The employee may need to be involved in decisions to feel wanted and recognised as important to the company.

Set up discussions with management about goals and working practices.

The employee feels as if their opinion and contribution is valuable.

The employee may be willing to work longer hours or take more responsibility.

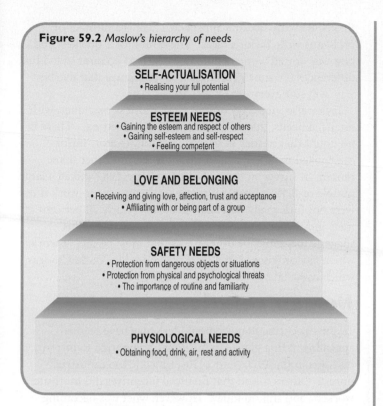

**Figure 59.2** *Maslow's hierarchy of needs*

**SELF-ACTUALISATION**
• Realising your full potential

**ESTEEM NEEDS**
• Gaining the esteem and respect of others
• Gaining self-esteem and self-respect
• Feeling competent

**LOVE AND BELONGING**
• Receiving and giving love, affection, trust and acceptance
• Affiliating with or being part of a group

**SAFETY NEEDS**
• Protection from dangerous objects or situations
• Protection from physical and psychological threats
• The importance of routine and familiarity

**PHYSIOLOGICAL NEEDS**
• Obtaining food, drink, air, rest and activity

Maslow argued that although everyone is capable of this, in practice very few reach this level.

Each level of needs is dependent on the levels below. Say an employee has been motivated at work by the opportunity to take responsibility, but finds he may lose his job. The whole system collapses, as the need to feed and provide for himself and his dependants again becomes the most important need.

Maslow's ideas have great appeal for business. The message is clear - find out which level each individual is at and decide on suitable rewards.

Unfortunately the theory has problems when used in practice. Some levels do not appear to exist for certain individuals, while some rewards appear to fit into more than one class. Money, for example, needs to be used to purchase 'essentials' such as food, but it can also be seen as a status symbol or an indicator of personal worth.

There is also a problem in deciding when a level has actually been 'satisfied'. There will always be exceptions to the rules Maslow outlined. A well motivated designer may spend many hours on a creative design despite lack of sleep or food.

## Taylor's Scientific Management

Research into the factors that motivate individuals had been carried out long before Maslow's 'hierarchy' of needs. **Frederick W. Taylor** set out a theory of SCIENTIFIC MANAGEMENT in his book *The Principles of Scientific Management* in 1911. Many of the ideas of today's 'scientific management school' come from the work of Taylor.

The turn of the century in the USA was a time of rapid expansion. Compared to today, the organisation of work on

the shop floor was left much more in the hands of workers and foremen. Workers often brought their own tools and decisions about the speed of machines were left to operators. There were few training programmes to teach workers their jobs and skills were gained simply by watching more experienced colleagues. Decisions about selection, rest periods and layoffs were frequently made by foremen.

Taylor suggested that such arrangements were haphazard and inefficient. Management did not understand the shop floor and allowed wasteful work practices to continue. Workers, on the other hand, left to their own devices, would

---

In 2003 an administrative, secretarial and support staff survey from London recruitment consultant Gordon Yates examined what has the greatest impact on job satisfaction. 70 per cent gave 'a good boss' the highest rating with 'interesting work' also highly placed. Only 35 per cent put 'salary level' in the top position. Despite being paid more money, PAs were more dissatisfied than ever. In 2003, 41 per cent were less satisfied with their work and 20 per cent were undecided whether to remain in their current career. Much of this dissatisfaction is rooted in the uncertain economic climate and the resultant redundancies, budget cutbacks and higher workloads. But the greatest impact on job satisfaction comes from human elements of the job - a good boss, interesting work, pleasant colleagues and a positive working atmosphere. Secretarial and support staff still appear to be valued lowly, despite having pivotal roles in offices. 'I'm not recognised as a valued member of the team,' said one secretary. Other comments included 'I'm not challenged enough', 'It's boring work' and 'I don't get enough variety'

A survey by Lloyds TSB and campaign group Working Families found one in five employees think they work for 'the boss from hell'. Another concern was finding sufficiently stimulating work. Working for many people seems to make the job less interesting. 'Because I work for so many people, I cannot really do PA things and am rather turning into a glorified typist,' said one secretary. A quarter of today's support staff are graduates who tend to seek increasing challenges, responsibility and advancement in the role.

When asked 'What do you like best about working as a secretary or in a support role?' responses included 'Being the lynchpin, being and feeling productive.' There is a particularly strong impression that this group takes pleasure in the fact that they are encouraged to utilise their skills of organising and supporting others. 'I can organise people well and find it rewarding when I have made their job/day easier' says one.

Source: adapted from *The Guardian*, 19.1 2004.

(a) Using Maslow's hierarchy of needs, explain the factors that are likely to influence the motivation of secretarial and support staff in the surveys.
(b) Using Maslow's hierarchy of needs, explain why being paid more money may not necessarily motivate such staff.

**Question 1**

**Table 59.1** *Taylor's method, designed to find the 'best way' to carry out a task at work*

- Pick a dozen skilled workers.
- Observe them at work and note down the elements and sequences adopted in their tasks.
- Time each element with a stop watch.
- Eliminate any factors which appear to add nothing to the completion of the task.
- Choose the quickest method discovered and fit them in their sequence.
- Teach the worker this sequence; do not allow any change from the set procedure.
- Include time for rest and the result will be the 'quickest and best' method for the task. Because it is the best way, all workers selected to perform the task must adopt it and meet the time allowed.
- Supervise workers to ensure that these methods are carried out during the working day.

do as little as possible. 'Soldiering' would also take place (working more slowly together so that management did not realise workers' potential) and workers would carry out tasks in ways they were used to rather than the most efficient way. Taylor's scientific principles were designed to reduce inefficiency of workers and managers. This was to be achieved by 'objective laws' that management and workers could agree on, reducing conflict between them. Neither party could argue against a system of work that was based on 'science'. Taylor believed his principles would create a partnership between manager and worker, based on an understanding of how jobs should be done and how workers are motivated.

**Taylor's approach** How did Taylor discover what the 'best way' was of carrying out a task? Table 59.1 shows an illustration of Taylor's method.

Taylor had a very simple view of what motivated people at work - money. He felt that workers should receive a 'fair day's pay for a fair day's work', and pay should be linked to output through piece rates (☞ unit 60). A worker who did not produce a 'fair day's work' would face a loss of earnings; exceeding the target would lead to a bonus.

In 1899 Taylor's methods were used at the Bethlehem Steel Works in the USA, where they were responsible for raising pig-iron production by almost 400 per cent per man per day. Taylor found the 'best way to do each job' and designed incentives to motivate workers.

Taylor's message for business is simple - allow workers to work and managers to manage based on scientific principles of work study. Many firms today still attempt to use Taylor's principles. In the 1990s the Bishop of Salford, when shown around a Littlewoods store, was told by the store manager that what he was looking for from potential Littlewoods workers was 'strong backs and nimble fingers'. This may not have been the official approach from Littlewoods, but it was seen locally as the use of Taylor's ideas.

**Problems with Taylor's approach** There is a number of problems with Taylor's ideas. The notion of a 'quickest and best way' for all workers does not take into account individual differences (☞ unit 71). There is no guarantee that the 'best way' will suit everyone.

Taylor also viewed people at work more as machines, with financial needs, than as humans in a social setting. There is no doubt that money is an important motivator. Taylor overlooked that people also work for reasons other than money. A survey in the early 1980s (Warr, 1982) asked a large sample of British people if they would continue to work if it were not financially necessary to do so. Nearly 70 per cent of men and 65 per cent of women said they would. This suggests there may be other needs that must be met at work, which Taylor ignored, but were recognised in Maslow's ideas which came later.

## Human relations

Taylor's scientific management ideas may have seemed appealing at first glance to business. Some tried to introduce his ideas in the 1920s and 1930s, which led to industrial unrest. Others found that financial incentives did motivate workers, and still do today. However, what was becoming clear was that there were other factors which may affect workers' motivation.

**The Hawthorne studies** Many of the ideas which are today known as the 'human relations school' grew out of experiments between 1927 and 1932 at the Hawthorne Plant of the Western Electric company in Chicago. Initially these were based on 'scientific management' - the belief that

---

Anmac Ltd is a small expanding high-tech company. It employs approximately 25 workers in two factories, one at Chester and one at Stafford. The employers organise work on a fairly informal basis. Workers work at their own pace, which often results in a variable level of output. Recently orders for their advanced micro-electronic circuit boards have increased rapidly. The firm has decided that, to cope with the orders, increased production is needed. Two suggestions have been put forward.
- Encourage the workers to work overtime at the Chester plant.
- Redeploy some of the workers from Chester to Stafford where there is a shortfall of workers.
The workers at the Chester plant are mainly married women in their twenties, many with young, school aged children and husbands who also work.

(a) Explain how Taylor's scientific management principles might be used to solve the problems faced by Anmac Ltd.
(b) What problems might Anmac Ltd find in using such principles?

**Question2**

workers' productivity was affected by work conditions, the skills of workers and financial incentives. Over the five year period, changes were made in incentive schemes, rest periods, hours of work, lighting and heating and the effect on workers' productivity was measured. One example was a group of six women assembling telephone relays. It was found that whatever changes were made, including a return to the original conditions, output rose. This came to be known as the HAWTHORNE EFFECT.

The study concluded that changes in conditions and financial rewards had little or no effect on productivity. Increases in output were mainly due to the greater cohesion and communication which workers in groups developed as they interacted and were motivated to work together. Workers were also motivated by the interest shown in their work by the researchers. This result was confirmed by further investigations in the Bank Wiring Observation where fourteen men with different tasks were studied.

The work of **Elton Mayo** (and Roethlisberger and Dickson) in the 1930s, who reported on the Hawthorne Studies, has led to what is known today as the human relations school. A business aiming to maximise productivity must make sure that the 'personal satisfactions' of workers are met for workers to be motivated. Management must also work and communicate with informal work groups, making sure that their goals fit in with the goals of the business. One way to do this is to allow such groups to be part of decision making. Workers are likely to be more committed to tasks that they have had some say in.

There are examples of these ideas being used in business today. The Volvo plant in Uddevalla, opened in 1989, was designed to allow workers to work in teams of 8-10. Each team built a complete car and made decisions about production. Volvo found that absenteeism rates at Uddevalla averaged 8 per cent, compared to 25 per cent in their Gothenburg plant which used a production line system. Other examples have been:

- Honda's plant in Swindon where 'teamwork' has been emphasised - there were no workers or directors, only 'associates';
- McDonald's picnics, parties and McBingo for their employees where they were made to feel part of the company;
- Mary Kay's seminars in the USA, which were presented like the American Academy awards for company employees.

**Problems** There is a number of criticisms of the human relations school.

- It assumes workers and management share the same goals. This idea of workplace 'consensus' may not always exist. For example, in the 1980s Rover tried to introduce a programme called 'Working with Pride'. It was an attempt to raise quality by gaining employee commitment. This would be achieved by greater communication with

employees. The programme was not accepted throughout the company. As one manager stated: 'We've tried the face-to-face communications approach. It works to a degree, but we are not too good at the supervisory level ... enthusiasm for the Working with Pride programme is proportionate to the level in the hierarchy. For supervisors it's often just seen as a gimmick ...'.

- It is assumed that communication between workers and management will break down 'barriers'. It could be argued, however, that the knowledge of directors' salaries or redundancies may lead to even more 'barriers' and unrest.
- It is biased towards management. Workers are manipulated into being productive by managers. It may also be seen as a way of reducing trade union power.

**Table 59.2** *The effect of introducing a piece rate system into clothes manufacture*

| Group | Number in group | Action taken to introduce system | Resignations within 40 days of introduction | Change in output |
|-------|-----------------|----------------------------------|---------------------------------------------|------------------|
| A | 100 | Group told the changes will take place next week | 17% | -2% |
| B | 150 | Management introduces changes with the help of group to suit their needs | 0% | +10% |
| C | 200 | Group told the changes will take place next week | 7% | 0% |
| D | 50 | Management explains the need for change to group | 2% | +2% |
| E | 100 | Management explains the need for change and discusses this with the group | 0% | +5% |

Table 59.2 shows the results of a survey carried out in Bryant and Gillie, a manufacturer of children's clothing. The company introduced a piece rate system of work - a system where employees are paid according to the number or quantity of items they produce. Five groups were involved in the new system. Different actions were taken to introduce the system to each group. The table shows the effect on labour turnover and output of these actions.

(a) To what extent do the results support the human relations explanation of workers' motivation?
(b) Using the results of the survey in Table 59.2, advise the management on the likely action needed to motivate workers when changing work practices.

Question 3

# Theory X and Theory Y

In 1960 **Douglas McGregor** published *The Human Side of Enterprise*. It was an attempt to apply the implications of Maslow and the work of Taylor and Mayo to business. In it, he gives different reasons why people work. He coined the terms Theory X and Theory Y to describe these differences. Table 59.3 shows the main ideas of the two theories.

Theory X assumes that people are lazy. If this is accepted, then the only way to get people to work is by using strict control. This control can take one of two forms. One method is to use coercion - the threat of punishment if rules are broken or targets not achieved. This is often known as the 'stick' approach. The problem with threats is that they are only effective if the person being threatened believes that they will be carried out. Modern employment laws and company wide agreements, have made this difficult for managers. For this reason, a 'carrot' approach may be more suitable. People have to be persuaded to carry out tasks by promises or rewards. In many ways this theory is similar to Taylor's view of people at work as shown earlier in this unit.

Theory Y, on the other hand, assumes that most people are motivated by those things at the top of Maslow's hierarchy. In other words, people are responsible, committed and enjoy having control over work. Most people, given the opportunity, will get involved in work, and contribute towards the solution of a problem that may arise. This theory is similar in some ways to the **human relations school**.

Business managers tend to say that their own assumptions are closer to Theory Y than to Theory X. But tests on management training courses tend to show that their attitudes are closer to Theory X than they might like to admit. In addition, many managers suggest that, while they

## Table 59.3 *Theory X and Theory Y*

| Theory X | Theory Y |
|---|---|
| • Workers are motivated by money | • Workers have many different needs which motivate them |
| • Workers are lazy and dislike work | • Workers can enjoy work |
| • Workers are selfish, ignore the needs of organisations, avoid responsibility and lack ambition | • If motivated, workers can organise themselves and take responsibility |
| • Workers need to be controlled and directed by management | • Management should create a situation where workers can show creativity and apply their job knowledge |

In the heatwave of 2003, 510 staff at Volkswagen were invited to cool down with ice cream or watermelon by the business. This casual treat reflects the approach of the business and its total reward package. The head of HR says 'We are a service business ... so all our value added has to be through our people. This means that they have to be as motivated as possible.' This is not to suggest that the formal stuff is not important. The company is in the top 25 per cent of payers, offering good earnings, pension schemes and maternity benefits. So although people are driven by cash benefits, the business suggests that this is not enough. 'Younger recruits in particular now ask about sabbatical, flexible working and green policies. We have to be able to provide them with a genuine and credible answer.'

The change in attitude to the workforce began about 5 years ago. Ideas about bundling cash and non-cash motivator together came from the USA. Their introduction has been driven by a number of factors. Shortages of skilled staff have led to employers' attempts to maximise their attractiveness. Economic downturns also led employers to stress the benefits of flexible working, training and career progression.

Source: adapted from *People Management*, 29.1.2004.

(a) Using examples from the article, explain whether Volkswagen is taking a Theory X or Theory Y approach to motivation.
(b) Explain how taking such an approach might affect Volkswagen.

**Question 4**

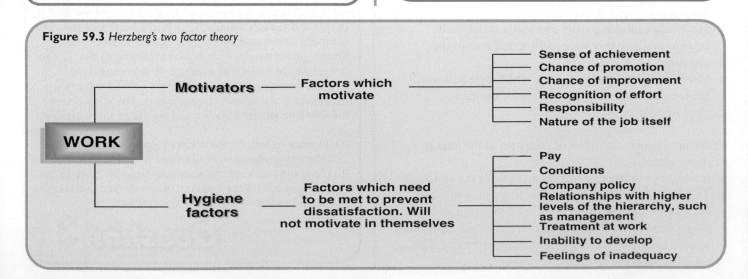

Figure 59.3 *Herzberg's two factor theory*

**WORK**

**Motivators** — Factors which motivate
- Sense of achievement
- Chance of promotion
- Chance of improvement
- Recognition of effort
- Responsibility
- Nature of the job itself

**Hygiene factors** — Factors which need to be met to prevent dissatisfaction. Will not motivate in themselves
- Pay
- Conditions
- Company policy
- Relationships with higher levels of the hierarchy, such as management
- Treatment at work
- Inability to develop
- Feelings of inadequacy

themselves are like Theory Y, workers are closer to Theory X. This theory has been used by managers to organise employees in business.

In practice, it could be argued that most firms behave according to Theory X, especially where shopfloor workers are concerned. The emphasis is on the use of money and control to encourage workers to behave in the 'correct way'. The same organisations might behave according to the assumptions of Theory Y when dealing with management. A representative of a banker's union wrote in the *Independent on Sunday*, 'The lower down the ladder you are, the less control you have over your work environment. Managers can do as they please, stretch their legs whenever they want. Clerical workers, if they are working in a data-processing centre, for example doing entries for cheques or credit cards, are disciplined if they don't complete a given number of key strokes in an hour or a day. Half the time they don't know what they are doing. They don't see any end product. More and more work has been downgraded.'

## Herzberg's two-factor theory

In 1966 **Fredrick Herzberg** attempted to find out what motivated people at work. He asked a group of professional engineers and accountants to describe incidents in their jobs which gave them strong feelings of satisfaction or dissatisfaction. He then asked them to describe the causes in each case.

**Results** Herzberg divided the causes into two **categories** or **factors**. These are shown in Figure 59.3.

- MOTIVATORS. These are the factors which give workers **job satisfaction**, such as recognition for their effort. Increasing these motivators is needed to give job satisfaction. This, it could be argued, will make workers more productive. A business that rewards its workforce for, say, achieving a target is likely to motivate them to be more productive. However, this is not guaranteed, as other factors can also affect productivity.
- HYGIENE FACTORS. These are factors that can lead to workers being **dissatisfied**, such as pay or conditions. Improving hygiene factors should remove dissatisfaction. For example, better canteen facilities may make workers less dissatisfied about their environment. An improvement in hygiene factors alone is not likely to **motivate** an individual. But if they are not met, there could be a fall in productivity.

There is some similarity between Herzberg's and Maslow's ideas. They both point to needs that have to be satisfied for the employee to be motivated. Herzberg argues that only the higher levels of Maslow's hierarchy motivate workers.

Herzberg's ideas are often linked with **job enrichment** (☞ unit 61). This is where workers have their jobs 'expanded', so that they can experience more of the production process. This allows the workers to be more involved and motivated, and have a greater sense of

achievement. Herzberg used his ideas in the development of clerical work. He selected a group of workers in a large corporation. Performance and job attitudes were low. Herzberg redesigned these jobs so that they were given more responsibility and recognition.

**Problems** Herzberg's theory does seem to have some merits. Improving pay or conditions, for example, may remove dissatisfaction at first. Often, however, these things become taken for granted. It is likely that better conditions will be asked for in following years. Evidence of this can be seen in wage claims which aim to be above the rate of inflation in some businesses every year. Job enrichment may also be expensive for many firms. In addition, it is likely that any benefits from job improvements will not be seen for a long time and that businesses will not be able to continue with

'To have a really happy workforce, you've got to do more than pass out party hats and serve birthday cake.' Over the years, I've tried a lot of things to make work fun, such as playing rock music, group lunches and sports after work. But after a while people get tired of it. Beyond the money, people expect more and more out of their work today. They want to contribute, learn, grow and feel that they are part of a successful enterprise that is making a difference in the world. Try to take into account the following.

- Today's workers at all levels want to know why they are doing something. Don't just say, 'Drop everything you're doing and rush this shipment out. Take time to explain why.
- Today's workers want to work hard and have pride in their work, but they need appreciation and recognition for their contribution. Be generous with compliments.
- Today's workers want input and accessibility to their managers, but many shy away from giving input unless you make it easy for them. Small group meetings where you ask for suggestions are a good way to get people involved.
- Today's workers want to feel that their work is making a difference. Explain why their work matters. Tell them success stories about people who use your products and post press clippings on the bulletin board.

Recently the person who runs our website left for another job. The manager of this area wanted to get a qualified candidate from the outside. But I want our company to go out of our way to retain people. So we divided the job among several people, giving them all a great chance to grow and learn something new. Another manager told me that when I'm in a good mood it helps boost up everyone else, but when I'm not, it darkens people's days.

Source: adapted from Streetwise Small Business Start-Up.

(a) Explain the (i) factors which motivate employees (ii) hygiene factors which are needed to prevent dissatisfaction using examples from the business in the article.

**Question 5**

such a policy in periods of recession.

Surveys that have tried to reproduce Herzberg's results have often failed. This may have been because different groups of workers have been examined and different techniques used. Also, there is a problem in relying too much on what people say they find satisfying or dissatisfying at work as this is subjective. For example, if things go wrong at work individuals have a tendency to blame it on others or factors outside of their control. On the other hand if individuals feel happy and satisfied when they are at work then they tend to see it as their own doing.

## McClelland's managerial needs

**David McClelland** suggested that what motivates people is that they learn in early childhood that certain types of behaviour lead to 'gratification'. They develop needs based on this behaviour. For example, a girl may have a great need to achieve, encouraged by parents who help her to be successful at school. When she becomes employed, she will behave in a similar way. There are, McClelland argues, three basic needs - achievement, affiliation, power.

- The need for achievement. This is one of the keys to a company's success. People who have high achievement needs often become successful entrepreneurs (☞ unit 2). Such people like to take responsibility and risks, and want quick feedback on how they have performed. They like to set their own goals and standards and achieve these on their own. However, it is also likely that people with a need to achieve will not work well in groups.
- The need for affiliation. McClelland found that some successful people in business did not, as he expected, score high on the need to achieve. In large firms, managers' goals can often by achieved by working with others, rather than by their own efforts. Such managers have a need to relate to others and will try to gain the acceptance of their superiors and work colleagues.
- The need for power. Some individuals with high achievement and affiliation needs still had problems in influencing or controlling others, McClelland found. To be successful there was often a need to get people to work together. McClelland called this the power motive. He recognised that although the need for power is often seen as undesirable (where one person dominated others) it can also be seen in a positive light. It might reflect the ability of an individual to persuade, influence or lead people. Research suggests that people with a need for power tend to be in higher and more influential positions in business.

According to McClelland, a business needs to know how these three needs affect an individual. For example, a person that has high affiliation needs may not make a good marketing manager. Such a person would, based on the theory, constantly look for acceptance and support for all decisions. It is likely that this job would need someone who was far more self-motivated.

## Vroom/Lawler and Porter

The theories of motivation that have been dealt with so far assume that people try to meet goals and so satisfy their needs. Vroom's and Lawler and Porter's theories state that this relationship is not so simple. First, each individual will have different goals. Second, people only act to achieve their goals if they feel there is a chance of success. Third, the value of the goal to the individual will also affect that person's motivation.

These theories might affect the way a business designs its pay and benefit systems and also the design of tasks and jobs to enable people to satisfy their needs. They take into account that people have different needs, and that some may want autonomy and responsibility at work, whereas others may not.

## Criticisms of motivation theories

At first sight it would appear that a business interested in increasing its employees' motivation at work has a fairly simple task. The theories in this unit are divided into two groups. The scientific management/Theory X group argues that workers are lazy, need controlling and are only interested in monetary rewards. The human relations school/Theory Y/Vroom group argues workers have many needs that might be achieved if they have more control and responsibility. A business, it seems, only needs to identify which view is effective and use the findings to motivate its workforce.

In practice it is difficult to conclude whether either one of these broad perspectives is 'right or wrong'. Any one view may be right or wrong depending on the circumstances. If the business is geared towards hierarchy and authority, and work is routine and monotonous, people may choose to do such work in return for cash. For example, in 1969 Goldthorpe and Lockwood in their famous study, The Affluent Worker, found that workers on a Vauxhall car assembly line saw work as a means to earn high wages. This would allow workers to enjoy life outside work more. Wedderburn and Crompton's study in 1972 of a large chemical plant in North East England found much the same thing. Their results showed that the level of pay, job security and good welfare benefits were far more important to workers than job interest. In such cases, individuals regard monetary rewards as being more important than such factors as responsibility.

However, at other times, job interest and involvement may outweigh financial rewards. This may be true, for instance, in worker buyouts, when employees are prepared to accept lower financial rewards to maintain job security and have a say in the running of the business.

It is also argued that many motivation theories were developed in earlier times, when work conditions were different. Work methods did not need the advanced levels of technological knowledge and problem solving skills that they do today. These skills now require higher levels of education and a change in the relationship between management and the shop floor.

Maccoby (1988) suggested that motivation theories which are too concerned with giving promotion and control to the individual employee may be misdirected. He argued that individuals can be given extra responsibilities in a variety of ways, such as dealing with more customers, teaching other employees, solving problems and making deals. This type of employee does not need as much management, since she is more likely to manage herself or to work as part of a team with shared management. The word **empowerment** (☞ unit 61) is often used to describe this view of motivation. Team empowerment is used to describe teams that are given discretion to make unsupervised decisions.

What conclusion can be drawn from these points?

● Employees are likely to have different priorities at different times and in different circumstances.

● Employees aiming to increase their wage or salary are not likely to show much interest in job satisfaction (at that time).

● When employees are not involved in pay bargaining then they are likely to be interested in the quality of working life and job satisfaction.

● A business cannot generalise about what motivates people.

It must try to understand the views workers may have at any one time, before deciding how best to motivate them.

● Employees in modern organisations are likely to be more skilled in team working, problem solving and the use of information technology. Motivation theories have to take this into account to be useful to a business.

## key terms

**Hawthorne effect** - the idea that workers are motivated by recognition given to them as a group.

**Hygiene factors** - those things that can lead to workers being dissatisfied.

**Motivated** - being encouraged to do something.

**Motivators** - those things that can lead to workers being satisfied.

**Self-actualisation** - a level on Maslow's hierarchy where an employee realises his or her full potential.

**Scientific management** - a theory that suggests that there is a 'best' way to perform work tasks.

## Knowledge

1. Why is it important for business to satisfy workers?
2. Name 5 needs in Maslow's hierarchy that an individual might have at work.
3. What are the aims of Taylor's scientific management theory?
4. According to Taylor, how are people motivated?
5. What is meant by the human relations school of thought?
6. What, according to the human relations school, is the main motivator at work?
7. Explain the difference between Theory X and Theory Y.
8. How is Theory X like Taylor's view of scientific management?
9. According to Herzberg's theory, what factors are likely to:
   (a) increase job satisfaction;
   (b) reduce dissatisfaction at work?
10. What general conclusions can a business draw from the criticisms of motivation theory?

# Case study Mendelsons

Lee Worsnip has worked as an assistant in the financial analysis department of Mendelsons Insurance for two years. He is 24 years of age and joined Mendelsons from college with good exam results. Lee also obtained some extra qualifications by taking night school courses. He started as junior clerk, and quickly moved to a more senior post, which paid a better salary. However, he has been in this post for a while now.

Lee's aim was to use the job as a stepping stone to one of the sales teams. The business was pleased that Lee looked on the job in this way, as it is in favour of encouraging people to get on. However, it is difficult to get onto one of the sales teams, particularly when the company has placed so much emphasis on its graduate recruitment. This may be one of the things that seems to be bothering Lee. Recently the Unit Trust team hired a graduate trainee instead of Lee, although he did accept that the new recruit had an advantage as she was a qualified actuary.

Until a few months ago, Lee had been an above average employee. He was always cheerful, enthusiastic and willing, and picked things up quickly. Lee used to make an excellent contribution to regular weekly meetings. And he was prepared to do one-off projects, always seeming to be able to squeeze in the extra work. He was also quite prepared to work late.

Lately, however, he seems to lack motivation. He has missed some meetings and taken days off. He complained that other members of the meetings had more senior posts and felt they did not listen to his views. He said 'I shouldn't be treated simply as some Theory X worker who gets their pay and goes home.'

The other day, Lee refused to take on a low level task. He suggested that he was fed up doing routine work and not leaving the office every day until 8 o'clock. Lee also argued that he was never allowed to make decisions and his work was always checked, as if he wasn't trusted. In the end some of these tasks had to be given to other members of staff, increasing their work load. Lee's absences has put additional pressure on the team.

Lee has also started being offhand. He was

overheard several times being rude to people who asked him for information or help. Last week, at a team meeting about new procedures, Lee suggested that they had been drawn up in secret behind his back.

**(a)** What is meant by the terms:
   **(i)** lack of motivation;
   **(ii)** Theory X worker? **(6 marks)**
**(b)** Explain the problems that **(i)** Lee and **(ii)** the business might have as a result of a lack of motivation. **(10 marks)**
**(c)** Using a motivation theory, examine reasons why Lee may lack motivation. **(12 marks)**
**(d)** Suggest ways in which the business might improve Lee's motivation. **(12 marks)**

## Financial and non-financial rewards

Unit 59 outlined theories which have tried to explain the factors that motivate people at work. Some of these theories stress that money is the most important factor. The scientific/Theory X approach, in particular, argues that workers respond to **financial rewards**. It is argued that such rewards are necessary to motivate a reluctant workforce. Employees see work as a means to an end. As a result they are far more likely to be interested in monetary rewards.

In contrast, the human relations/Theory Y view argues that workers are motivated by a variety of factors. An employee working in a car assembly plant, for example, may be highly motivated by working as part of a team. Poor pay may lead to employees being dissatisfied, which can make other **non-financial rewards** less effective in motivating them.

The next two units examine how these theories can be used. This unit looks at how a business might use financial rewards and incentives.

## Payment schemes

How are employees rewarded for the work they do? There is a number of methods that may be used.

**Time rates**  TIME RATES are used when workers are rewarded for the amount of time they spend at work. Employees are paid in the form of weekly **wages** or monthly **salaries**. For many workers in the UK, pay is fixed in relation to a standard working week. Workers who work longer than this may be paid **overtime**, perhaps at a higher rate.  In addition, holidays with pay are included for most British industries. Examples of time rates are the £22,000 a year paid to a teacher or the £5.00 per hour paid to a cleaner in, say, Newcastle.

Time rates are a simple way of calculating pay for a business. They are useful when a business wants to employ workers to do specialist or difficult tasks that should not be rushed.  Employees can ensure that work is of a high quality without worrying about the time they take.

Time rates are also useful when working out the pay of service sector employees or people working in groups. In these cases it is very difficult for a business to work out the exact value of the employee's output.  An example might be doctors, where it is virtually impossible to calculate the value of work. From an employee's point of view, time rates guarantee income.

**Annualised hours**  Many employers have found that payment based on a fixed working week can be inflexible. For example, half the year employees may be idle after 3pm every day, but are still paid for a 'full day's' work. The other half of the year they may work into the evening and be paid overtime. To cater for fluctuations in demand some employers pay staff on the basis of a certain number of hours to be worked in a year. These are known as ANNUALISED HOURS CONTRACTS.

For annualised hours contracts, the number of hours to be worked each year is fixed. However, the daily, weekly or monthly hours are flexible. So employees may have a longer working day at peak times and work less when demand is slack. An employee's pay is calculated on the basis of an average working week, for example 35 hours, which is paid regardless of the actual number of hours the employee works.

There are certain advantages. An employee has a guaranteed income each week. Employers often see this as a way of avoiding overtime, reducing costs, increasing flexibility and improving efficiency. One water company found that its service engineers would leave a job part completed in order to get back to their depot by 5pm, even if the job only required a further hour's work. When the company introduced annualised hours contracts the engineers had to complete any job they had started, even if it meant working beyond 5pm. The advantage for the water company was much greater customer satisfaction and efficiency, as service engineers did not have to make two round trips to a job. The engineers were able to negotiate a higher basic pay. They also benefited from a more flexible shift system, which meant they could increase their number of rest days.

**Piece rates**  A system of PIECE RATES is the easiest way for a business to make sure that employees are paid for the amount of work they do. Employees are paid an agreed rate for every item produced. For this reason it is known as a PAYMENT BY RESULTS system. It is often used in the textile industry. Piece rates are arguably an INCENTIVE to workers. The more they produce, the more they earn.

From a business's point of view, this system links pay to output.  However, there is a number of problems.  Employees have no basic pay to fall back on if machinery fails or if the quality of the goods produced is unacceptable. Trade unions, in particular, have campaigned against this method of payment as it often results in low pay and low living standards. There have also been disputes in the past about what 'rate' should be paid. Some firms may feel that the method encourages workers to sacrifice quality in favour of higher rewards.

Because of the problems of lack of basic pay, most firms use a system where pay is made up of two elements. There is a fixed or basic pay, calculated on the time worked and a variable element, often when a **target** has been reached. It is argued that this extra element motivates workers to increase productivity, while the time element gives security.  Incentive schemes are dealt with later in this unit.

**Commission** In some businesses COMMISSION makes up the total earnings of the workers. This is true of some insurance salespeople and some telesales employees. Commission, like piece rates, is a reward for the quantity (or value) of work. Employees are paid a percentage of the value of each good or service that is sold. It could be argued that it suffers from the same problems and gives the same incentive as a piece rate system. The benefit to the employer is that it can indicate the level of business 'won' rather than just output achieved. Earnings surveys have shown that the numbers of people receiving commission is falling. The proportion of people's total earnings made up of commission is also declining.

**Fees** Fees are payments made to people for 'one-off' tasks. Tasks tend to be geared towards the needs of the client, rather than a standard service or product. The amount paid will depend on a variety of factors. These might include the time taken to finish the task or the difficulty of the task. Often fees are paid to people providing services, such as solicitors, performers etc.

**Fringe benefits** FRINGE BENEFITS are payments other than wages or salaries. They include things like private medical insurance, profit-related bonus schemes, a company car, subsidised meals, transport allowances, loan or mortgage facilities etc. Fringe benefits have grown in importance. This is especially the case in the executive, management and professional area. From an employer's view, providing benefits rather than pay may actually be cheaper as they do not need to pay National Insurance contributions. An employee might also prefer to receive benefits such as private medical insurance, that avoids waiting for treatment, rather than pay. Despite their attraction, fringe benefits can cause status problems. Also, benefits such as a company car may be liable for tax, although some benefits avoid tax such as certain company pension schemes.

Table 60.1 shows some of the fringe benefits that have been offered by companies in the UK.

## Employer objectives for pay

There is a number of objectives employers will have when paying their workforce.

**Motivation** It has been argued that workers are motivated by money (☞ unit 59). This may be a rather simple view of workers' behaviour. Yet it is clear from the way that employers use money incentives that they believe employees react to the prospect of increasing their earnings. For example, many firms are attempting to link pay with performance because they believe that employees care about pay.

Employers must give consideration to any system they use. For example, if payments are made when targets are achieved, these targets must be realistic. Payment systems are often negotiated between **groups**, such as company representatives and trade unions.

---

The Directors Remuneration Report Regulations, introduced in 2002, were an attempt to increase the transparency of perks given to executives in plcs. This would be particularly useful for shareholders reading annual reports, concerned about their investment and the relationship between the earnings of executives and their rewards. Several firms had already reported perks given to executives before the regulations came into force, including a free monthly ration of 400 cigarettes given to British American Tobacco directors and various benefits to company chief executives such as:
- a £20,000 relocation allowance paid by BT;
- free dental benefits for life paid by HSBC;
- £230,000 annual rent paid by Reuters.

The value of such perks are unlikely to eat too much into the bottom line profits of companies at the moment. But it was suggested that they should be ignored by shareholders at their peril, as UK perks were modest compared to those of US executives.

Source: adapted from *The Observer*, 27.4.2003.

(a) Explain the effects that the legislation might have on the different stakeholders mentioned in the article.

---

| Table 60.1 *Fringe benefits* | | |
|---|---|---|
| **Company** | **Function** | **Fringe benefit** |
| Dyson Appliances | Vacuum cleaner manufacturer | Dyson cleaner at reduced rate for new employees |
| Text 100 | PR Agency | 2 'Duvet days' (unscheduled holidays) a year |
| Air Products | Industrial gas supplier | Free exercise classes and subsidised gym and yoga classes, free annual medical checks |
| Saatchi & Saatchi | Advertising agency | Company pub - 'The Pregnant Man' |
| Virgin Group | Travel, entertainment, media, retail and financial services | 24 hour parties |
| Body Shop | Cosmetics manufacturer and retailer | £100 a year to 'buy' a training course in new skill of their choice |
| Tesco | Food retailer | SAYE tax free share option scheme |

**Cost** Employers are interested in the profitability or cost-effectiveness of their business. Any system that is used by the business must, therefore, attempt to keep the cost of labour as low as possible in relation to the market wage in that industry. This should enable the firm to increase its profits.

**Prestige** Managers often argue that it is a 'good thing' to be a good payer. Whether high pay rates earn an employer the reputation of being a good employer is arguable. What seems much more likely is that the low-paying employer will have the reputation of being a poor one in the eyes of employees.

**Recruitment and labour turnover** Payment rates must be competitive enough to ensure the right number of qualified and experienced employees stay within the business. This will prevent a high level of **labour turnover** (☞ unit 63). This is also true of vacant posts. A business must pay rates which encourage the right quality and quantity of applicants.

**Control** Certain methods of payment will reduce costs and make the control of labour easier. These are examined later in this unit.

# Employee objectives for pay

Employees will have their own objectives for the payment they receive.

**Purchasing power** A worker's standard of living is determined by the level of weekly or monthly earnings. The **purchasing power** of those earnings is affected by the rate of inflation (☞ unit 98). Obviously, in periods of high inflation workers are likely to seek higher wages as the purchasing power of their earnings falls. Those whose earnings fall behind the rate of inflation will face a decline in their purchasing power.

**Fair pay** Employees often have strong feelings about the level of payment that is 'fair' for a job. The employee who feels underpaid may be dissatisfied and might look for another job, be careless, or be absent a great deal. Those who feel overpaid may simply feel dishonest, or may try to justify their pay by looking busy.

**Relativities** Employees may be concerned about how their earnings compare with those of others. 'How much do I get relative to ...' is an important factor for a worker. Workers with a high level of skill, or who have trained for a long period, will want to maintain high wages relative to less 'skilled' groups. **Flat rate** pay increases, such as £10 a week for the whole workforce, would erode differences. A 5 per cent increase would maintain the differences.

**Recognition** Most people like their contribution to be recognised. Their pay gives them reassurance that what they are doing is valued.

**Composition** Employees often take into account the way their earnings are made up. It is argued that younger employees tend to be more interested in high direct earnings rather than indirect benefits like pensions. Incentive payments are likely to interest employees who want to increase their pay. Married women and men are generally less interested in overtime payments, for example, and regard other factors more highly.

# Incentive schemes

The pay that employees receive often reflects the nature of the job. However, some payment systems try to relate pay to the performance or commitment that an employee makes to the business, known as **incentive schemes**. Businesses attempt to induce high commitment and performance from employees with high pay in order to gain the maximum output.

**Incentive schemes for manual and non-manual employees**
Incentive payments have been widely used in the management of manual workers in the past. Increasingly, incentives are being paid to workers not directly involved in production. Schemes are now being used for administrative workers and in service industries. For example, a business may set sales targets for its departments. Employees in those departments can then be rewarded with a BONUS once targets are reached. Sales representatives in many companies are set targets each month and are paid bonuses if they reach them.
Bonus payments come in many forms. One method is a bonus paid per extra output above a target as in the piece rate system. However, one-off payments are often used by businesses to motivate workers. Bonuses can be paid at certain times of the year in a lump sum (often at Christmas). They can also be built into the monthly salary of some workers, such as staff working in certain hospitals.

Although the bonus may be paid for reaching a target, it may also be for other things. Rewards for punctuality or attendance are sometimes used. Some businesses reward their 'best' salesperson with a bonus. One unusual example of this is Richer Sounds, the hi-fi retail outlet, where workers in a retail outlet that performed best over a period were rewarded with the use of a Rolls Royce for a month!

The problem with regular bonuses is that they are often seen as part of the employee's basic pay. As a result, they may no longer act as a motivator.

**Productivity agreements** are also a form of bonus payment, where rewards are paid providing workers achieve a certain level of 'productivity'. They are usually agreed between employees' groups and management to 'smooth over' the introduction of new machinery or new techniques that workers need to learn.

Incentive schemes fall into three categories.
- Individual schemes. Individual employees may be rewarded for exceeding a target. The benefit of this scheme is that it rewards individual effort and hence employees are more likely to be motivated by this approach.
- Group incentives. In some situations, like assembly lines,

the need is to increase group output rather than individual output. Where one worker relies on the output of others, group incentives may also have benefits. They can, however, put great pressure on all group members to be productive. It can also be difficult for a new recruit to become part of the group, as existing members may feel they will have to compensate for his inexperience.

● Factory-wide schemes. Employees are given a share of a 'pool' bonus provided the plant has reached certain output targets. The benefit to management is that incentives are related to the final output rather than sections of the plant. Furthermore, in theory at least, employees are more likely to identify with the company as a whole.

The difficulty with this type of scheme is that there is no incentive to work harder, as there is no direct link between individual effort and reward. Some employees that work hard may have their rewards reduced by others who do not - the same problem as group incentives.

**Incentive schemes for managers and directors** In the 1990s there has been a large increase in the use of incentive schemes for managers and directors. These have usually been linked to how well the company has performed, often following restructuring, delayering (☞ unit 90) or the privatisation of companies such as the public utilities (☞ unit 7). Share ownership schemes are often used to motivate managers.

There is evidence to suggest that management perform better if they 'own' part of a business, for example after an internal buyout. However, other research indicates that incentive schemes may not necessarily be the most important motivator at work for many managers. The Ashridge Management Index is a indicator of managers' attitudes based on a survey of 500 middle and senior managers. When asked what motivates them, 61 per cent of managers placed challenging work first. Other high-scoring motivators included 'letting people run their own show' and 'seeing the impact of decisions on the business'. These factors, along with high basic salary (35 per cent), topped the motivation league table.

## Types of incentive scheme

Incentive schemes can take many forms. **Individual output schemes** relate pay to the performance of individual employees.

**Piece rate schemes** We have already seen that piece rates can be an incentive. Producing more will earn the worker more. Each unit, over and above a target, is rewarded with a bonus or commission payment. In the past there have often been disputes about the rate that should be paid for each unit produced. Businesses have tried to solve this by using individual time-saving schemes - the incentive is paid for time saved when carrying out a task. Using Taylor's work study methods (☞ unit 59) a work study engineer calculates the **standard time** that an employee should take to complete a task. The employee then receives incentive payments if the task is completed in a shorter time. If it is not possible to work due to shortage of materials or some other reason, the time involved is not counted. Such schemes, however, mean employees still suffer from variable payments. Despite these problems this type of incentive can be used when carrying out short, manual tasks where output can vary.

**Performance related pay** PERFORMANCE RELATED PAY (PRP) schemes link the annual salary of an employee to their performance in the job. PRP schemes have spread rapidly in recent years and now form an important part of white collar pay in the public and private sector. Nearly all the major banks, building societies and insurance companies now use performance systems. A number of large manufacturers, such as Cadbury's and Nissan, have introduced schemes (at times extending them to the shop floor) as well as public sector industries, such as the civil service, NHS and local government.

The shift towards PRP can be seen as part of a more general movement towards 'pay flexibility' in British industry.

● Organisations have sought to tie pay increases to measures of business performance, not just through PRP schemes

One of the biggest changes that took place at Marks & Spencer after the year 2000 was in rewards. 'We've had a performance element and a cost of living increase for around five years. Last year we abandoned the cost of living increase for managers. We put all the 2.5 per cent available in 2001 into a performance based review' said a spokesperson. A senior bonus scheme which used to apply to the top 50 or 60 executives was extended to around 1,000 managers. This is partly based on profit.

Staff are also eligible to a sales related bonus. This has been a major influence on performance now that local managers have been given greater discretion over awarding bonuses. For example, six staff at Purdsey who were short of their target with a day left set up a gift shop in Yorkshire Water's head office to make up the difference and meet the target. This is indicative of the improvement in motivation and morale. A new bonus scheme based on attendance has reduced absenteeism significantly. For example, the absenteeism rate fell from 4.5 per cent to 1 per cent in the M&S food hall at the MetroCentre in Gateshead.

Source: adapted from *People Management*, 10.1.2002.

(a) Describe the (i) employee incentives and
(ii) management incentives mentioned in the article.
(b) Examine the possible objectives of the incentive schemes.

**Question 2**

but through other mechanisms, such as profit sharing.

- There has been a move away from national, industry- wide pay agreements to local, plant-wide agreements. This has given managers greater discretion in the way they match rewards to particular business units.
- There is a new focus on the individual employee and rewards which reflect her performance and circumstances, which has meant that collective methods of pay determination have become less important.

PRP schemes come in many forms, but the majority have some common features.

- Individual performance is reviewed, usually over a year. This may take the form of comparing performance against agreed objectives.
- At the end of the review the worker will be placed in a 'performance category'. The 'excellent' performer, for instance, may have exceeded all his agreed targets and produced work of a high standard. The category the worker falls into will determine the size of payment or whether payment is made at all.
- The performance payment can vary. Sometimes there may be a small cash bonus or the award of increments on a pay scale. In others, the entire salary and progression through scales can depend on the results of the performance review. This kind of 'merit only' scheme means a 'poor' performer will be punished, as they will not receive extra pay.

There are problems with PRP. It is based on individual achievement, so the better a person does the more that person is paid. However, there may be disputes about how performance is to be measured and whether a person has achieved enough to be rewarded. Also, the system is not likely to work if people do not react to the possibility of rewards by working harder.

The following example of two sales consultants highlights some practical problems. Jane and Ruth are sales consultants for an insurance company and both had set targets for a six month period. Ruth met her target comfortably and received the agreed bonus of £5,500 for reaching on-target earnings. Jane failed to reach her agreed target because her sales manager left the company and poached three of Jane's best customers just before they signed agreements with Jane. Jane's bonus was therefore reduced to only £2,500 for a lower level of sales. Jane had no control over this, but felt she had worked just as hard as Ruth and therefore deserved a similar bonus.

Research also shows that many organisations may be out of tune with their employees, placing too much emphasis on incentives. The effectiveness of performance related pay, in particular, is called into question. Ashridge researchers describe it as 'the biggest mismatch between what organisations are seen to be relying on to motivate managers and what actually motivates them'. Research by ACAS also suggests that PRP schemes tend to demotivate rather than motivate staff.

**Commission** As explained earlier, commission is where employees are often rewarded for the amount of orders they bring in to a business, for example salespeople. The more business they gain, the more they are paid.

**Collective output schemes** relate pay to the performance of a group or other unit of the business.

**Measured daywork** The idea of measured daywork may provide the answer to the problems of piece rate schemes. Instead of employees receiving a variable extra amount of pay depending on their output, they are paid a fixed sum as long as an agreed level of output is maintained. This should provide stable earnings and a stable output, instead of 'as much as you can, when you can, if you can'.

The first major agreement based on the principles of measured daywork was the National Power Loading Agreement in coal mining in 1966. London Docks and British Leyland both reverted to more traditional 'payment by result' methods in the late 70s. Although productivity gains may not have been great, most surveys found that measured daywork improved industrial relations and that less expenditure was spent on dealing with grievances. Furthermore, measured daywork seemed to give management a greater control over such payment schemes. In practice, the need for flexibility in reward schemes has meant that measured daywork is rarely used as an incentive scheme today.

**Profit sharing** Profit sharing takes place in business organisations such as partnerships (☞ unit 6). Profits are either shared equally or as agreed in any partnership deed of agreement drawn up by the business. Partners or employees of business have an incentive to be as productive as possible. The more profit the business makes, the more they earn.

**Profit related pay** Profit related pay involves employees being paid a cash 'bonus' as a proportion of the annual profits of the company. In previous years a certain amount of profit related pay has been exempt from taxation. However, this was no longer to be the case after the year 2000. Profit related pay has a number of problems for employees. It is not linked to individual performance and rewards can fluctuate from year to year depending on the performance of the business.

**Share ownership** Businesses may offer the possibility of purchasing shares in the company as an incentive. This is sometimes reserved for managers. In large businesses wider share ownership amongst all employees may be encouraged. There is a number of different employee share schemes. **Savings-related** share option schemes, for example, allow an employee to save each month over, say, five years. They can then take up an option to purchase a number of shares at a value stated when the shares are offered - the option price. The advantage of buying shares to employees is that they feel part of the company and are rewarded with **dividends**

(☞ unit 3) if the company performs well.

In the 1990s evidence suggested that share ownership was slowly spreading among growing businesses. Out of 63 companies floated on the Stock Exchange in 1996, 39 operated all employee share schemes. However, 52 companies had Inland Revenue approved executive share schemes. Even more had non-approved schemes for top executives. A UK index of quoted employee-owned companies showed that share prices had outperformed those of conventionally owned rivals over the past few years. The index tracked 30 companies where more than 10 per cent of shares were held by or for employees. The index rose threefold since January 1992, outstripping the FT-SE All Share index by 89 per cent. A survey of EU companies suggested there was a growing trend towards share ownership schemes in the twenty first century.

Incentive schemes can also relate to the **input of employees**.

Merit pay This bases pay upon the behaviour of employees, such as flexibility, co-operation and punctuality. Employees demonstrating these traits may be rewarded more highly than others.

Skills-based pay Here employees are rewarded according to the physical and mental capabilities. So, for example, an employee demonstrating a wider range of skills may earn higher rewards.

---

**Table 60.2** *Extent of incentive schemes (% of organisations offering incentives)*

| Scheme | Management employees | Non-management employees |
|---|---|---|
| | | % |
| IPRP* | 40 | 25 |
| Team-based pay | 8 | 8 |
| Skill/competency pay | 6 | 11 |
| Profit-related pay | 35 | 34 |
| Employee share ownership | 17 | 15 |

\* Individual performance related pay.

Source: adapted from Institute of Personnel Development (IPD).

A survey of 5,000 businesses by the IPD suggested that a variety of different incentive schemes were used by UK businesses. Some were more popular than others. Also, some were used more for manual than non-manual employees.

(a) Suggest reasons to account for the use of incentive schemes shown in Table 60.2.

Question 3

---

## Problems with incentive schemes

There is a number of problems that financial incentives schemes have.

- Operating problems. For incentives to work, production needs to have a smooth flow of raw materials, equipment and storage space, and consumer demand must also be fairly stable. These conditions cannot be guaranteed for long. If raw materials did not arrive or ran out, for example, the worker may not achieve a target and receive no bonus for reasons beyond his control. If this happens the employee is unlikely to be motivated by the scheme, and may negotiate for a larger proportion of earnings to be paid as guaranteed 'basic' pay.

- Fluctuating earnings. A scheme that is linked to output must result in fluctuating earnings. This might be due to changes in demand, the output of the worker or machinery problems. As in the case above, the worker is likely to press for the guaranteed part of pay to be increased, or store output in the 'good times' to prevent problems in the 'bad'. Alternatively, workers may try to 'slow down' productive workers so that benefits are shared out as equally as possible.

- Quality. The need to increase output to gain rewards can affect quality. There is an incentive for workers to do things as quickly as possible and this can lead to mistakes. Workers filling jars with marmalade may break the jars if they work too quickly. This means the jar is lost and the marmalade as well, for fear of splinters. For some businesses, such as food processing, chemicals or drug production, errors could be disastrous.

- Changes in payment. Because of the difficulties above, employers constantly modify their incentive schemes. Improved schemes should stop workers manipulating the system and may give renewed motivation to some workers. However, constant changes mean that employees do not always understand exactly how to gain rewards.

- Quality of working life. Incentive schemes which use payment by results require a certain type of job design (☞ unit 61). This often means tight control by management, routine and repetition. Theory X (☞ unit 59) argues that production will only be efficient if workers know exactly what to do in any situation and their activities are tightly controlled by management. The result of this is that boredom and staleness may set in and the worker's 'standard of life' at work may be low.

- Jealousy. Individual workers may be jealous of the rewards earned by their colleagues. This can lead to problems in relationships and a possible lack of motivation. Increasingly, businesses are using group or plant-wide incentives to solve this.

- For incentives to work effectively it must be possible to measure performance. For example, a business must be

able to measure the number of components made by a worker if she is paid a bonus after 20,000 are made a month.
● Problems may take place if the rewards are based on the performance of a team, but some workers are more productive then others in the team.

Given these problems, why are financial incentive schemes still used by many firms? Managers may find a use for a certain incentive scheme. For example, a scheme can be used to overcome resistance to change. A business introducing new technology, such as computers, may offer an incentive for staff to retrain or spend extra time becoming familiar with the new system. Employees often see benefits in such systems of payment. They may feel that they are gaining some control over their own actions in the workplace, being able to work at their own pace if they so wish. Furthermore, many businesses believe that incentive schemes ought to work as it is logical to assume that employees work harder if they are offered financial rewards.

## Are incentives effective?

How effective are incentive schemes according to research?
● Pearce and others (1985) research into merit pay amongst managers in US Social Security Administration found little effect on organisational performance. The Institute of Personnel Development (1999) suggested that managers view merit pay as having only a modest effect on employee commitment. In a study, 53 per cent said that there had been 'no change' in such commitment.
● Gerhard and Milkovich (1992) found the use of bonuses for managers had a positive effect on the rate of return on capital employed in business.
● Kruse and Weitzman (1990) found that profit sharing had a positive effect on productivity and company performance, although whether schemes led to improved performance or whether such performance allows business run such schemes is debatable.

The Department for Education insisted that teachers' pay must be linked to performance as part of its plans to modernise public sector services and that teachers could not expect an above-inflation pay increase in 2004. The department was also considering giving individual schools more power to set pay rates for their staff. A spokesperson said 'The government is strongly of the view that the priority for this year is not a general increase in pay above the rate of inflation, but instead action to promote workforce reform and tackle workload issues.'

In 2002, the government introduced a performance-related bonus scheme to boost teachers' pay and help retain staff. Experienced teachers, who had taught for six years, could apply for a one-off bonus of £2,000. Almost all teachers who applied for the performance pay got it. But a study by the Institute of Education in London found little evidence that payments had improved results or attracted more people into teaching. It suggested that it was difficult to determine the impact of any one teacher on a pupil's progress. 'A pupil may have private tuition, help at home, or any number of external influences. So we may never know objectively whether performance-related pay has positive effects on pupil learning outcomes' said Professor Dalton, co-author. He argued that 'market theories do not necessarily work in the public sector. A bricklayer may lay more bricks if paid a bonus, but this does not apply to teachers, who are highly motivated professionals already working to maximum capacity.' The research even suggested that bonus payments could be counterproductive because teachers were used to working together instead of competing with each other.

The researchers said it is a 'difficult if not impossible task' to devise a performance related pay system for teachers that makes them work harder and more productively, does not need expensive monitoring, encourages teamwork and discourages teaching to the test.

Source: adapted from the *Daily Telegraph, The Independent*, 2002.

(a) Evaluate the possible effectiveness of performance related pay for teachers.

**Question 4**

# key terms

**Annualised hours contracts -** a payment system based on a fixed number of hours to be worked each year, but a flexible number of hours each day, week or month.

**Bonus -** usually an extra payment made in recognition of the contribution a worker has made to the company.

**Commission -** a payment system where employees are paid a percentage of the value of each good or service that is sold.

**Fringe benefits -** payments made to employees instead of salaries or wages.

**Incentive -** a reward given to employees to encourage them to work harder.

**Payment by results -** payment methods that reward workers for the quantity and quality of work they produce .

**Performance related pay -** management's attempts to increase worker productivity by linking pay with performance.

**Piece rates -** a payment system where employees are paid an agreed rate for every item produced.

**Time rates -** a payment system that rewards workers for the amount of time they spend at work.

Knowledge...Knowledge...Knowledge...Knowledge...Knowledge...Know

1. What is the difference between financial and non-financial rewards?
2. What are the problems for employees of using a piece rate system?
3. Why might a piece rate system be used as an incentive?
4. Give 3 examples of the use of commission.
5. State 4 objectives that employees may have for pay.
6. State 4 objectives a business might have for a system of payment.
7. What is the difference between an individual and a factory-wide incentive scheme?
8. Why might a group incentive scheme discourage some workers rather than encourage them?
9. Describe how a measured daywork system operates.
10. What is meant by profit sharing?
11. Briefly explain 4 problems with incentive schemes.

# Case study  Incentives for Value Added Resellers

Value Added Resellers (VARs) are businesses which take a manufacturer's product and add their own value before selling it. For example, a VAR might take an operating system, add its own specialist software for, say, architects, and then sell the bundle to architect businesses. Manufacturers offer VARs a number of incentives to sell their products.

'The best incentive is money in the pocket' said one VAR. Most incentive schemes are based on money and commissions. Other means are used, but do they work? 'Freebies' such as day trips and air miles are commonly on offer. But in the day-to-day slog of running a business, motivation to take advantage of such benefits can be hard to muster. 'We don't really bother with these schemes' said one VAR. 'They create more administration than they're worth. 'Luxury rewards are still available as part of wider packages. For example, the top performing VAR for SolidWorks, was invited to Hawaii.

Opinions on whether rewards for individuals are effective will depend on to whom you speak. There will always be salespeople who thrive on beating the competition and who want to gain recognition for doing so. Peter Dickin, marketing manager at Delcam, feels that a more inclusive approach is required. 'Incentives targeted just at salespeople neglect the contribution of others, which can be demotivating. We tend to favour schemes that foster team building.'

Incentive schemes that reward a group of high-performing VARs have to be carefully structured to create a level playing field to give companies of different sizes and locations a chance. Clearly this is not always being achieved. One disgruntled VAR said 'I have never, ever been incentivised by any scheme I have worked with in the past. Overpaid VAR managers justify their own existence, even so far as coming up with jollies that they had no prior interest in, such as driving racing cars and sailing around the Leeward Isles.'

Schemes based mainly on the volume of sales can have negative implications for all parties. 'The aims of the incentives that we work to are not those that suit our long-term business goals, nor the needs of our customers,' said one VAR. 'They are generally incentives to motivate short-term business.'

The opportunity to gain marketing funds is another regular element of incentive schemes, particularly where a business wants to make inroads into a particular market. IBM, for example, offers a special marketing fund to companies who join its Top Contributor Programme and commit themselves to selling $100,000 of software to the SME (small and medium sized business) market.

As free trips and luxury gifts are used less, terms such as 'active business management' have crept into the language of incentives. 'We don't incentivise on volume' explains John Mitchell, Manager of Indirect Channels, Europe, PLM Solutions. 'We incentivise VARs to invest in their business and improve the quality of their service to our customers.'

Many VARs are dubious about whether the incentives on offer actually made them do anything differently. Not offering incentives doesn't go down well either. One VAR said "Our own main vendor doesn't offer any incentive schemes (or even buy drinks at the bar at sales events). So we will have to do our best focusing upon making money for ourselves.'

Source: adapted from retailsystemseller.com.

(a) **What is meant by the terms:**
    **(i)   luxury rewards;**
    **(ii)  incentivise on volume? (6 marks)**
(b) **Describe the different payment and incentive schemes in the article. (10 marks)**
(c) **Examine the advantages and disadvantages to such schemes for VARs. (12 marks)**
(d) **Assess which incentives are likely to be most motivating to VARs selling products such as computers for manufacturers to small businesses. (12 marks)**

## The need for non-financial rewards

Financial rewards have often been used in the past by firms in an attempt to motivate employees to improve productivity. However, increasingly businesses have realised that:

- the chance to earn more money may not be an effective motivator;
- financial incentive schemes are difficult to operate;
- individual reward schemes may no longer be effective as production has become organised into group tasks;
- other factors may be more important in motivating employees.

If other factors are more important than pay in motivating workers, it is important for firms to identify them. Only then can a business make sure its workforce is motivated. Figure 61.1 shows some of the factors that employees might consider important in their work environment. Many of these have been identified by the theories of Mayo and McGregor (☞ unit 59). A business may consider introducing non-financial incentives to help employees satisfy these needs.

## Job design and redesign

The dissatisfaction with financial incentive schemes reached its peak in the 1960s and 1970s. In response the 'Quality of Working Life Movement' began to develop ideas which were based around the 'human relations school', as first outlined by the Hawthorne studies (☞ unit 59). It was argued that workers were likely to be motivated by non-monetary factors and that jobs needed to be DESIGNED or REDESIGNED to take these factors into account. Five principles were put

Investing in the skills of people makes smart business sense according to Ben Reed of IPBartenders. If you don't the good people leave and the poor ones stay. 'On the Continent barpeople are regarded as professionals' says Reed. 'They are held in high esteem' and that is not always the case in the UK. Work is often treated as casual and staff are treated accordingly. Staff should be encouraged to develop skills and take pride in their work. Recognition of a job well done is a key factor in developing satisfaction.

Happy, successful staff need to be empowered and inspired. This goes beyond telling staff what to do and how to do it. They need to know why and they need to have the skills to make informed customer decisions. Many skills are required to serve the customer what they want, including a knowledge of customer choice, how to mix drinks and the popularity of certain brands. Staff with a knowledge of wines are far more able to influence customer choice. They also need to be aware of legislation regarding drinking age and how to cope with tricky situations.

It is also important for them to have the right equipment and materials. Making sure that the work areas is sensibly organised and uncluttered will help. And workers will also respond to co-operation and team work. Team incentives can be very useful. Remember, if staff don't enjoy working in the bar, customers won't enjoy drinking in it.

Source: adapted from *The Publican*, 27.10.2003.

(a) Suggest ways in which a business might motivate its bar staff other then paying higher wages.
(b) Explain how this will affect:
   (i) employees;
   (ii) customers;
   (iii) the business.

**Question 1**

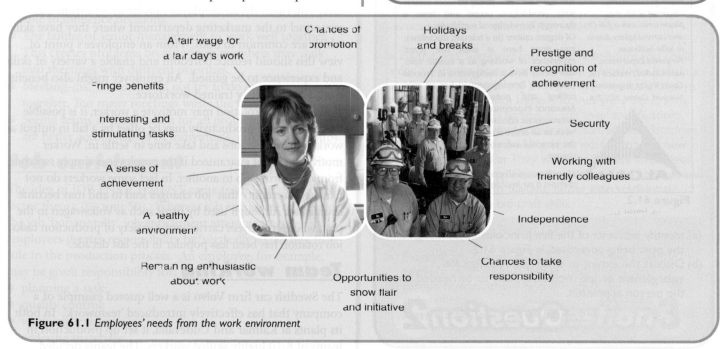

A fair wage for a fair day's work
Chances of promotion
Holidays and breaks
Prestige and recognition of achievement
Fringe benefits
Interesting and stimulating tasks
Security
A sense of achievement
Working with friendly colleagues
A healthy environment
Independence
Remaining enthusiastic about work
Opportunities to show flair and initiative
Chances to take responsibility

**Figure 61.1** *Employees' needs from the work environment* individuals the skills and responsibilities to deal with a greater variety of issues will allow a business to respond more quickly and effectively to problems. So for example, a receptionist might have been trained to pass on calls to other people in a business. Multiskilling this job could mean that the receptionist now deals with more straightforward enquiries himself. This would result in a quicker response to the customer's enquiry. It would also free up time for other people to work on more demanding activities.

Certain motivation theories suggest that giving individuals more skills and responsibilities can improve their work performance (☞ unit 59). A criticism of multiskilling is that individuals are only given more skills so that they are expected to work harder without any extra pay. Problems may also result if workers are not trained adequately for their new roles.

# Quality control circles

QUALITY CONTROL CIRCLES are small groups of workers (about 5-20) in the same area of production who meet regularly to study and solve production problems. In addition, such groups are intended to motivate and involve workers on the shopfloor. Unlike job enlargement and job enrichment, they allow the workforce directly to improve the nature of the work they are doing.

Quality control circles are becoming popular in Britain. They started in America, where it was felt workers could be motivated by being involved in decision making. The idea gained in popularity in Japan and was taken up by Western businesses. Examples of their use can be found in Japanese companies setting up plants in the UK in the 1990s. Honda at Swindon has had 52 teams of six people looking at improvements that can be made in areas allocated to the groups, for example, safety.

Quality control circles are only likely to work if they have the support of both management and employees. Businesses have to want worker participation and involvement in decision making, and set up a structure that supports this. Workers and their representatives also need to support the scheme. Employees must feel that their views within the circle are valued and must make a contribution to decisions.

# Empowerment

Unit 58 explained that decisions that were delegated would be more successful if employees were empowered. EMPOWERMENT of employees involves a number of aspects.

● Recognising that employees are capable of doing more than they have in the past.
● Making employees feel trusted, so that they can carry out their jobs without constant checking.
● Giving employees control of decision making.
● Giving employees self confidence.
● Recognising employees' achievements.
● Developing a work environment where employees are

motivated and interested in their work.

Many businesses now recognise the need to empower employees. There is a number of advantages of this for a business and for employees.

● Employees may feel more motivated. This should improve productivity and benefit the business in the long term, for example by reducing absenteeism.
● Employees may find less stress in their work, which could reduce illness and absenteeism.
● Decisions may be made by those most suited to make them.
● There may be greater employee skills and personal development.
● Businesses may be able to streamline their organisations and delegate decision making.

However, empowerment is sometimes criticised as simply a means of cutting costs and removing layers from the business. Passing decision making down the hierarchy might allow a company to make managers redundant. Employees are given more work to do, but for the same pay. Some businesses argue that they want to empower workers, but in practice they are unable or unwilling to do this. For example, a manager may feel insecure about subordinates making decisions that might affect his position in the business. Feeling that they may 'make the wrong decision' might lead to constant interruptions which are counter-productive. A further problem is the cost involved to the business, such as the cost of training employees or changing the workplace.

# The problems of job redesign

A business may decide to redesign jobs to increase workers' motivation. The actual process of redesigning existing jobs is often difficult to carry out in practice for a number of reasons.

● Employees' reactions. Employees may be familiar with the old approach to doing a job and may resent new changes. They might not want the extra duties that result from job redesign.
● Employers' views and costs. Job redesign may be expensive. New methods often require extra training. In addition, redesigned jobs might lead employees to claim extra pay for new responsibilities. There is no guarantee that the redesign of jobs will increase productivity in the long term.
● Technology. The introduction of new machinery can make job redesign more difficult. Certain jobs have had to be redesigned almost totally as new technology has changed production processes. In some cases employees have had to learn totally new skills, such as when newspaper page design on computer screens replaced old methods of cutting and pasting type onto pages. At other times skills may be made redundant. When Morgan cars produced their front panels in the late 1980s with machinery instead of their usual 'handmade' techniques, workers were arguably turned from skilled panel makers to non-skilled machine operators.

- Effects on output and productivity. Redesigned jobs need to be evaluated to gauge whether they have actually motivated the workforce to increase output.

# Employee involvement schemes in practice

The non-financial methods so far in this unit are examples of EMPLOYEE INVOLVEMENT SCHEMES. They can be categorised according to how involved employees are. For example, in teamworking employees are encouraged to extend the range and type of tasks undertaken at work. Employees are less involved perhaps through quality circles. This is an example of an upward problem solving scheme, designed to tap into employee knowledge and opinion. However, studies seem to indicate that downward communication schemes are more popular. They are designed to inform and educate employees and include informal and formal communication (☞ unit 70). The level of active employee involvement here tends to be minimal.

Surveys have shown that employee involvement schemes have been increasingly used by UK businesses over the last 20 years. But they have had problems. Sometimes they contradict each other and they are rarely part of a human resource strategy. Managers often lack the enthusiasm and commitment and many employers have not given enough time and resources to training supervisors to run them.

# Goal setting and management by objectives

Goal setting is part of a more general theory of **management by objectives** (MBO). MBO was put forward by Peter Drucker in 1954 and is covered in unit 62. It suggests that a business should define objectives or targets for an individual to achieve and revise those targets after assessing the performance of the worker.

In 1984 Ed Locke wrote *Goal Setting: A motivational technique that works*. According to Locke, the idea that in order to improve job performance you need to motivate workers by making jobs more satisfying is wrong. He argued that satisfaction comes from achieving specific **goals**. In addition, the harder these goals are, the greater the effort and satisfaction. His message was for businesses to set specific goals that people can achieve and that have been negotiated. 'Do your best', he argued, is not specific. Employees must also have feedback on the progress they are making and then they will perform. The assumption behind the theory is that people will do what they say they will do, and then will strive hard to do it.

# Organisation behaviour modification

Businesses have used the theory of organisation behaviour modification (OBMod) with management by objectives when motivating employees. OBMod assumes that workers'

behaviour is determined by the consequences of their actions. For example, a worker who receives a reward as a result of increasing productivity is likely to work harder. Similarly, workers try to avoid behaving in ways that produce no reward or lead to punishment.

OBMod is based on the work of psychologists such as Thorndike and Skinner, who argue that since we cannot observe people's attitudes we should observe their behaviour. Managers should therefore observe how employees' behaviour is affected by the consequences of their actions. These consequences can be broken down into four categories.

- The employee receives something he likes.
- Something the employee dislikes is taken away.
- Something the employee likes is taken away.
- Something the employee dislikes is given.

The first two categories are known as **reinforcers**, as they lead to an increase in the behaviour that precedes them. If a junior manager gives a good presentation and receives praise (something he likes), then the behaviour that resulted in praise (the good presentation) will be reinforced. This is an example of **positive reinforcement**. If something the employee dislikes is taken away, this is called **negative reinforcement**.

The other two categories are kinds of **punishment**. They tend to reduce the behaviour that precedes them. For example, if a worker is constantly late and is fined (something he dislikes), he may try to reduce the number of times he is late.

Examples of positive reinforcement include:

- employees in Xerox's personnel department being given 'X certificates' to pass to others in the company that they felt deserved reward. Each certificate was redeemable for $25;
- passengers being given coupons on American Airlines which they can pass on to staff who they feel deserve recognition;
- an American factory in Mexico where 15 per cent of the workforce arrived late. Management decided to reward good timekeeping by paying workers two pesos (16 cents at the time) a day extra if they started work early. Lateness fell from 15 per cent to 2 per cent, at little extra cost to the company.

# Employee Assistance programmes

Employee Assistance Programmes (EAPs) started in America in the 1940s. They began to appear in the UK in the 1990s. These schemes have been developed to help staff cope with difficulties, such as the loss of someone close or the effects of unemployment on the household. In addition, they are sometimes used to help with dealing with personal internal conflicts inside a business. An EAP usually consists of confidential telephone counselling on an issue for employees and their families, paid for by employers. Employers are aware that life for individual employees is becoming more demanding. They recognise that if they want to motivate employees, they need to provide support services that cater for their more general needs. Sometimes such services are provided directly by employers, but it is more common to use a third-party supplier. Staff can then be assured of privacy and neutrality. Some two million employees in Britain are covered by these schemes. 75 per cent of them

receive the service from a consultancy.

## Achieving a work-life balance

Recently there has been a stress on the need for employers to deal with the work-life balance of employees. Life is becoming faster and more complex, but without the support of communities or extended families. It is suggested that unless employers are sympathetic and supportive of employees' external needs, there could be an increase in health related absences such as stress. This could affect the operation and efficiency of the business.

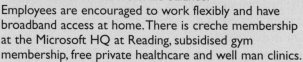

Is Microsoft the best business to work for in the world? Its employees seem to think so. The IT sector is very competitive. So giving financial rewards such as stock options have had to be redesigned. How do you keep the best and brightest when they feel that they have had a pay cut? Microsoft has won accolades for its work-life balance. Employees are encouraged to work flexibly and have broadband access at home. There is creche membership at the Microsoft HQ at Reading, subsidised gym membership, free private healthcare and well man clinics.

But how does a company that asks employees to work such long hours win awards for work-life balance? It's more than just about balancing day to day life. It's about choice. Workers are empowered to make choices about when they work and what they do, and they are listened to. An attempt to take away fuel cards from employees and get them to pay on their own cards was scrapped within half an hour after negative feedback. Openness is a recurrent theme, as is trust. Employees can work where and when they want to as long as they keep the schedule up to date.

Source: adapted from *People Management*, 12.6.2003.

(a) Explain why employees might be motivated at Microsoft.
(b) Examine the possible problems of such an approach for the business.

**Question 4**

## key terms

**Employee involvement schemes** - systems used to motivate employees through their participation in decision making of the business.
**Empowerment** - to give official authority to employees to make decisions and control their own activities.
**Job design (redesign)** - changing the tasks and activities of a job, perhaps in an attempt to motivate workers.
**Job enlargement** - giving an employee more work to do of a similar nature.
**Job enrichment** - an attempt to give employees greater responsibility and recognition by 'vertically' extending their role in the production process.
**Job rotation** - the changing of jobs or tasks from time to time.
**Multiskilling** - the processes of enhancing the skills of employees.
**Teamworking** - Employees working in small groups with a common aim.
**Quality control circles** - small groups of workers in the same area of production which meet regularly to study and solve all types of production problems.

## Knowledge

1. State 5 possible non-financial rewards that may be an incentive for individuals.
2. What principles would a 'good' job have according to the 'Quality of Working Life Movement'?
3. State 4 methods of job redesign.
4. 'Job enlargement is simply a method of horizontal loading.' Explain this statement.
5. Under what circumstances might job rotation not lead to an increase in productivity?
6. Suggest 4 problems of working in teams.
7. Why is job enrichment said to extend an employee's role in the firm vertically?
8. What are the advantages to an employee of quality control circles?
9. State 3 features of empowerment.
10. Show, using an example, how positive reinforcement can motivate a worker.
11. Why might a business have an Employee Assistance Programme?
12. What is meant by achieving a work-life balance?

# Case study BMW's New Oxford Way

each shift has a 45 minute team talk so that workers can discuss problems and air suggestions and ideas. These ideas have led to changes in practices. For example, a worker in one area of production suggested recycling screws that were being thrown out further down the production line. This led to an increase in supply of 1 million screws. Another suggestion to use rubber instead of foam strips saved thousands of pounds.

The scheme also lets managers and directors work on the production line. So workers and employers work side by side, which has reduced the gulf between them. A manager said 'Wings is saying "here is the empowerment to go and do things".'

Three years on workers appear to have seized the opportunities. 'There is more enthusiasm ... the conversations are no longer negative ... people are better informed and more open ...' said a manager. And the business itself has seen tangible benefits. BMW has implemented over 8,000 staff ideas and production targets in 2002 were exceeded by more than 60 per cent. Changes contributed to savings of more than £6.3 million over a 12 month period.

Source: adapted from *People Management*, 6.11.2003.

BMW is known by many car buyers for its high quality products. When it sold The Rover Group in 2000 it retained the Mini brand. But it knew that the overhaul of the Mini would also require changing practices at its production plant at Cowley in Oxford. The £230 million refit of its Oxford plant by BMW corresponded with the launch of a major change programme - The New Oxford Way.

The central element of the programme was Wings (Working in Groups). It involves hundreds of self-steered teams of between 8 -15 people across manufacturing areas. They were given the power to tackle production problems themselves, when before they would have had to call in other departments. Tasks are also rotated within groups to prevent boredom on the production line.

The focus in the groups is on initiative and self-management rather than being management led. Employees receive external training and coaching in working as part of a team. Heike Schneeweis, HR Director at BMW, said that the setting up of Wings created a turnaround in working practice and behaviour. She argued that the teams 'diminished the power of the traditional hierarchical structure and gave more responsibility to working teams.'

The day to day duties of one member in each team has been halved so that they can concentrate on developing team members and the way teams operate. Every fortnight,

(a) **Suggest examples of:**
  (i) **job rotation;**
  (ii) **job redesign;**
  (iii) **multiskilling;**
  (iv) **job enrichment;**
  **which have taken place at BMW. (8 marks)**
(b) **What view of motivation is management likely to take about workers at BMW? (8 marks)**
(c) **Explain the benefits of team working at BMW for:**
  (i) **employees;**
  (ii) **the business itself. (12 marks)**
(d) **Discuss to what extent empowerment is necessary for the success of the Wings system. (12 marks)**

## What is management?

Unit 3 explained that managers are an important group involved in business activity. It is difficult to define exactly what is meant by 'management'. However, many agree that managers are responsible for 'getting things done' - usually through other people. The term manager may refer to a number of different people within a business. Some job titles include the word manager, such as personnel manager or managing director. Other job holders may also be managers, even though their titles do not say it.

It could be argued that managers:

● act on behalf of the owners - in a company, senior management are accountable to the shareholders;

● set objectives for the organisation, for example, they may decide that a long term objective is to have a greater market share than all of the company's competitors;

● make sure that a business achieves its objectives, by managing others;

● ensure that corporate values (the values of the organisation) are maintained in dealings with other businesses, customers, employees and the general public.

## The functions of management

**Henri Fayol**, the French management theorist, listed a number of **functions** or **elements** of management.

**Planning** This involves setting objectives and also the strategies, policies, programmes and procedures for achieving them. Planning might be done by line managers who will be responsible for performance. However, advice on planning may also come from staff management who might have expertise in that area, even if they have no line authority. For example, a production manager may carry out workforce planning (☞ unit 63) in the production department, but use the skills of the personnel manager in planning recruitment for vacancies that may arise.

**Organising** Managers set tasks which need to be performed if the business is to achieve its objectives. Jobs need to be organised within sections or departments and authority needs to be **delegated** so that jobs are carried out. For example, the goal of a manufacturing company may be to produce quality goods that will be delivered to customers on time. The tasks, such as manufacturing, packaging, administration, etc. that are part of producing and distributing the goods, need to be organised to achieve this goal.

**Commanding** This involves giving instructions to subordinates to carry out tasks. The manager has the authority to make decisions and the responsibility to see tasks are carried out.

Sibelius produces the number one selling system for writing music on computers. It was started by two brothers - Ben and Jonathan Finn. In 2001 Jeremy Silver joined and spent his first three months developing a three year plan. Perhaps as a result, in 2002 he was appointed chief executive and amalgamated the London and Cambridge offices of the business in London. He realised he had to tread carefully, saying 'You have to be sensitive because you can't come into a business that has been in operation for nine years and make radical transformations overnight.' Having gained the confidence of the owners, Jeremy had to win over the staff. He felt that he needed to be seen to make changes which would benefit both staff and the owners.

The relocation he had pushed for went a long way to solving the communication problems that existed between the two sites, along with changes in internal communication systems. He said 'When I started here I spent time with everybody individually. I did that very systematically, fixing slots with every member of staff. There is an all company meeting every Monday at 10am and we have an open door policy which ensures that people can just walk into your office and talk to you.' Bringing the US office in line has been a little more tricky. The staff there are not used to communicating so much with head office. But he hopes to solve this problem by spending more time in the US. The business has also started pension and health care schemes to tell employees 'We believe in you'.

Source: adapted from *People Management*, 7.8.2003.

(a) Explain the functions of management that Jeremy Silver might have carried out at Sibelius.

(b) Examine the possible benefits for the business.

**Co-ordinating** This is the bringing together of the activities of people within the business. Individuals and groups will have their own goals, which may be different to those of the business and each other. Management must make sure that there is a common approach, so that the company's goals are achieved.

**Controlling** Managers measure and correct the activities of individuals and groups, to make sure that their performance fits in with plans.

## Management by objectives

**Peter Drucker** worked in the 1940s and 1950s as a business adviser to a number of US firms. He is credited with the idea of MANAGEMENT BY OBJECTIVES (MBO) from his book *The Practice of Management* (1955). Drucker grouped the operations of management into five categories.

● Setting objectives (☞ unit 4) for the organisation. Managers decide what the objectives of the business should be. These objectives are then organised into targets.

Managers inform others of these targets.

- Organising the work. The work to be done in the organisation must be divided into manageable activities and jobs. The jobs must be integrated into the formal organisational structure (☞ unit 58) and people must be selected to do the jobs (☞ unit 65).
- Motivating employees (☞ unit 59) and communicating information (☞ unit 70) to enable employees to carry out their tasks.
- Job measurement. It is the task of management to establish objectives or yardsticks of performance for every person in the organisation. They must also analyse actual performance and compare it with the yardstick that has been set. Finally, they should communicate the findings and explain their significance to others in the business.
- Developing people. The manager should bring out the talent in people.

Drucker's MBO approach suggests that employees and employers need to work to shared objectives based on the **mission statement** and corporate aims of the business (☞ unit 4). If they didn't, different sections of a business might work differently. For example, the marketing department may want to develop and launch a new product that might need additional production capability. At the same time the production department may be looking to save costs by closing down parts of the manufacturing plant.

Drucker argued that businesses need to:

- set out their clear objectives;
- make plans that would enable those objectives to be realised;
- implement those plans;
- monitor and evaluate whether the objectives had been achieved.

Objectives must be SMART - specific, measurable, agreed, realistic and time specific (☞ unit 4).

Businesses that make use of MBO must take into account that employees can be involved in many different functions and levels. Once corporate objectives have been set by senior managers, managers within functional areas must plan exactly how they can be achieved. This will mean setting objectives for groups and individuals further down the hierarchy. This process can be used by a business to appraise the performance of employees against objectives (☞ unit 4). A business can then reward employees with bonuses or other methods for achieving objectives. This should help to motivate workers, as long as the objectives to be achieved are clear and understood by employees.

## Advantages and disadvantages of MBO

There are some advantages with management by objectives.

- Employees can be motivated to perform at improved levels once clear objectives have agreed between them and their line managers.
- Because employees and managers know their objectives

they will work to a single purpose.

- Objectives and plans can be co-ordinated throughout the organisation. This means that different business functions should not pull in different directions and frustrate each others' work
- MBO helps senior managers to have a much clearer system of controlling the direction and performance of the business.

Although there a many potential advantages to MBO, there may be problems.

- MBO may be unresponsive to changing conditions. The time involved in setting the mission statement, corporate objectives and other objectives might result in a dated plan and implementation process. As a result managers may not be responding to new challenges because they are following a plan developed some time ago.
- MBO assumes that all people in a business have the same goals and concerns. However, there is evidence that people have different approaches to work. A young enthusiastic manager developed through a company's graduate training programme may have an optimistic and go getting approach to work. A long standing employee who sees work as being a means to enjoying other things in life and who has been passed over for promotion may be more cynical about the objectives set by management.
- In the 1990s Drucker himself suggested that MBO only works if you know the objectives clearly. But he also suggested that many businesses may not.

Kaplin Price is a furniture manufacturer. It is increasingly facing stiff competition from abroad, but is not certain how best to react to this. Should it expand rapidly? Or should it rationalise to some extent? What would happen if it differentiated its products in some way from those of its competitors? Unless it makes a decision soon, it might find that its costs have escalated and it may be forced to shut down.

It has also experienced difficulties with its internal organisation. Last year it attempted to launch a new range of products with the intention of expanding its market share. It was not clear exactly what share it wanted to achieve, just that it wanted sales to grow. It set in place an incentive system for its sales representatives. Those that reached a certain target of sales would receive a bonus. However, it did not explain to the reps exactly what the target would be. This meant that they lacked motivation and whether they should be paid the bonus or not was decided by managers with a 'gut feeling' about individuals if there had been improved sales from the whole team.

(a) Using examples, examine ways in which adopting an MBO approach might solve the difficulties faced by Kaplin Price.

Question 2

# Being a manager

In contrast with Fayol or Drucker, **Charles Handy** argued that any definition of a manager is likely to be so broad it will have little or no meaning. Instead he outlined what is likely to be involved in 'being a manager'.

**The manager as a general practitioner** Handy made an analogy between managing and staying 'healthy'. If there are 'health problems' in business, the manager needs to identify the symptoms. These could include low productivity, high labour turnover or industrial relations problems. Once the symptoms have been identified, the manager needs to find the cause of trouble and develop a strategy for 'better health'. Strategies for health might include changing people, through hiring and firing, reassignments, training, pay increases or counselling. A manager might also restructure work through job redesign, job enrichment (☞ unit 61) and a redefinition of roles. Systems can also be improved. These can include communication systems, reward systems, information and reporting systems budgets and other decision making systems, eg stock control.

**Managerial dilemmas** Handy argued that managers face dilemmas. One of the reasons sometimes given for why managers are paid more than workers is because of the dilemmas they face.

- The dilemma of cultures. When managers are promoted or move to other parts of the business, they have to behave in ways which are suitable for the new position. For example, at the senior management level, managers may deal more with long term strategy and delegate lower level tasks to middle management more often. If a promoted manager maintains a 'culture' that she is used to, which may mean taking responsibility for all tasks, she may not be effective in her new position.
- The trust-control dilemma. Managers may want to control the work for which they are responsible. However, they may have to delegate work to subordinates, trusting them to do the work properly. The greater the trust a manager has in subordinates, the less control she retains for herself. Retaining control could mean a lack of trust.
- The commando leader's dilemma. In many firms, junior managers often want to work in project teams, with a clear task or objective. This can mean working 'outside' the normal bureaucratic structure of a larger organisation. Unfortunately, there can be too many project groups (or 'commando groups') for the good of the business. The manager must decide how many project groups she should create to satisfy the needs of her subordinates and how much bureaucratic structure to retain.

**The manager as a person** Management has developed into a profession and managers expect to be rewarded for their professional skills. Managers must, therefore, continue to develop these skills and sell them to the highest bidder.

# Managerial roles

**Henry Mintzberg** suggested that, as well as carrying out certain functions, the manager also fulfils certain roles in a firm. He identified three types of role which a manager must play.

- Interpersonal roles. These arise from the manager's formal authority. Managers have a **figurehead** role. For example, a large part of a chief executive's time is spent representing the company at dinners, conferences etc. They also have a **leader** role. This involves hiring, firing and training staff, motivating employees etc. Thirdly, they have a **liaison** role. Some managers spend up to half their time meeting with other managers. They do this because they need to know what is happening in other departments. Senior managers spend a great deal of time with people outside the business. Mintzberg says that these contacts build up an informal information system, and are a means of extending influence both within and outside the business.
- Information roles. Managers act as channels of information from one department to another. They are in a position to do this because of their contacts.
- Decision making roles. The manager's formal authority and access to information means that no one else is in a better position to take decisions about a department's work.

Through extensive research and observation of what managers actually do, Mintzberg drew certain conclusions about the work of managers.

- The idea that a manager is a 'systematic' planner is a myth. Planning is often carried out on a day-to-day basis, in between more urgent tasks.
- Another myth is that a manager has no regular or routine duties, as these have been delegated to others. Mintzberg found that managers perform a number of routine duties, particularly 'ceremonial' tasks.
- Mintzberg's research showed that managers prefer verbal communication rather than a formal system of communication (☞ unit 70). Information passed by word of mouth in an informal way is likely to be more up to date and easier to grasp.

# Leadership

The ability to lead within organisations is of growing interest to businesses. This has resulted from the need to lead companies through change, brought about by an increase in competition and changes in technology and economic conditions.

Earlier in this unit it was shown that a manager might have a leadership **role**. To be a good leader in business it has been suggested that a manager must know what direction needs to be taken by the business and plan how to achieve this. Leaders will also be able to persuade others that the decisions that they have taken are the correct ones.

Leaders are often thought to be charismatic people who have 'something about them' that makes them stand out from others. It has been argued that there are certain personality traits (☞ unit 71) that are common to leaders. However, studies have failed to prove this is the case.

In order to identify 'leadership', studies have shifted to examine what leaders, and in particular managers, do - that is, what behaviour is associated with leadership. This is dealt with in the next sections.

# The qualities of leadership

One approach to finding out what makes good leaders is to identify the qualities that they should have. A number of **characteristics** have been suggested.

- Effective leaders have a positive self image, backed up with a genuine ability and realistic aspirations. This is shown in the confidence they have. An example in UK industry might be Richard Branson, in his various pioneering business activities. Leaders also appreciate their own strengths and weaknesses. It is argued that many managers fail to lead because they often get bogged down in short term activity.
- Leaders need to be able to get to the 'core' of a problem and have the vision and commitment to suggest radical solutions. Sir John Harvey-Jones took ICI to £1 billion profit by stirring up what had become a 'sleeping giant'. Many awkward questions were raised about the validity of the way things were done, and the changes led to new and more profitable businesses on a worldwide scale for the firm.
- Studies of leaders in business suggest that they are expert in a particular field and well read in everything else. They tend to be 'out of the ordinary', intelligent, and articulate. Examples might be Anita Roddick, the founder of Body Shop or Bill Gates, the founder of Microsoft.
- Leaders are often creative and innovative. They tend to seek new ideas to problems, make sure that important things are done and try to improve standards. One example might have been the restructuring of BHS by David Dworkin. He reorganised the business so that stock did not remain on the shelves until it sold at full price. The price of slow selling stock was cut immediately to get rid of it and new stock brought in.
- Leaders often have the ability to sense change and can respond to it. A leader, for example, may be able to predict a decline of sales in an important product or the likelihood of a new production technique being available in the future.

One of the key leadership issues after the year 2000 is likely to be how to deal with international markets and globalisation (☞ unit 109). Leaders may face challenges such as:

- international recruitment to overcome domestic staff shortages (☞ unit 76);
- cross-border mergers, acquisitions and joint ventures (☞ unit 89);
- the opening of new markets in Eastern Europe, South East Asia and China (☞ unit 108);
- European social policy directives, affecting business in member countries; (☞ unit 107);
- developments in information and communications technology (☞ unit 85).

Chris Mallard is business unit manager for one of Timkin Desford's two steel businesses which make components for the automotive industry. He inherited a business in pain, with a lack of investment, worried owners and an industry with problems. The workforce seemed to have been living in the shadow of closure forever.

Mallard had to achieve a 40 per cent reduction in costs in 18 months for the business to survive. One solution was to change the manufacturing process. It would involve redesigning processes, setting tasks and using appropriate controls. But he felt that this was just the traditional way of doing things. So forced himself to look at the problems of the business though fresh eyes. 'The real task was gaining trust and changing people's mindsets' he said. As a result he developed a plan called 'constant communication'. It relied on people talking, arguing, questioning and reflecting, and then talking some more. It was uncomfortable and not what people expected. He also took a higher profile and had to keep reminding himself that disagreement doesn't have to mean conflict.

Eventually people got used to the system. They developed faith in the proposals and the results were that targets were met ahead of schedule and there was a rejuvenated workforce. He said 'It was tough and I felt I was constantly going against the flow' but that it could not have been done any other way.

Source: adapted from *People Management*, 28.6.2001.

(a) Examine the leadership characteristics shown at Timkin Desford.

**Question 3**

# Leadership styles

Another approach is to examine different styles of leadership. There is a number of styles that managers might adopt in the work setting.

**Autocratic** An AUTOCRATIC leadership style is one where the manager sets objectives, allocates tasks, and insists on obedience. Therefore the group become dependent on him or her. The result of this style is that members of the group are often dissatisfied with the leader. This results in little cohesion, the need for high levels of supervision, and poor levels of motivation amongst employees.

Autocratic leadership may be needed in certain circumstances. For example, in the armed forces there may be a need to move troops quickly and for orders to be obeyed instantly.

**Democratic** A DEMOCRATIC leadership style encourages participation in decision making. Democratic leadership styles can be persuasive or consultative.

● Persuasive.  This is where a leader has already made a decision, but takes the time to persuade others that it is a good idea. For example, the owner of a business may decide to employ outside staff for certain jobs and persuade existing staff that this may ease their work load.

● Consultative. This is where a leader consults others about their views before making a decision. The decision will take into account these views. For example, the views of the marketing department about whether to launch a new range of products may be considered.

Democratic leadership styles need good communication skills. The leaders must be able to explain ideas clearly to employees and understand feedback they receive (☞ unit 70). It may mean, however, that decisions take a long time to be reached as lengthy consultation can take place.

It has been suggested that a democratic style of leadership may be more effective in business for a number of reasons.

● There has been increased public participation in social and political life. Democratic management reflects this trend.

● Increasing income and educational standards means that people now expect greater freedom and a better quality of working life.

● Research suggests that this style is generally more effective. Managers are able to 'tap into' the ideas of people with knowledge and experience. This can lead to better decisions being made.

● People involved in the decision making process are likely to be more committed and motivated, to accept decisions reached with their help, to trust managers who make the decisions and to volunteer new and creative ideas.

**Paternalistic** PATERNALISTIC leaders are similar to autocratic leaders. They make all the decisions and expect subordinates to obey these decisions. However, whereas an autocratic leader may be uninterested in the well being of subordinates, a paternalistic leader places a great deal of importance on their welfare. In the past there have been number of paternalistic leaders, such as Joseph Rowntree and George Cadbury. Examples of their concern for employees included the building of new houses which they could rent at low rates. As with autocratic leaders, paternalistic leaders do not give subordinates control over decision making.

**Laissez- faire** A LAISSEZ-FAIRE type of leadership style allows employees to carry out activities freely within broad limits. The result is a relaxed atmosphere, but one where there are few guidelines and directions. This can sometimes result in poor productivity and lack of motivation as employees have little incentive to work hard.

## *Team-based leadership*

The growth of flatter and matrix style structures,

empowerment, job redesign and team working has affected the type of leadership that managers might use in a business. Managers are more likely today to organise and co-ordinate the workings of a variety of employees at different levels, in different functions and with different skills. In a sense they have become **team-based leaders**.

Traditional approaches to leadership and management that are linked to authority, status and power are likely to be of limited use to team based leaders. Team leaders are less likely to be individuals who give orders and have a clear understanding of exactly how a task is to be done than people who:

● have the the ability to bring together the right blend of workers to allow business problems to be solved and action implemented;

● can motivate staff in the team to problem solve and accomplish a task;

● know and understand corporate objectives;

● know what resources are available to implement actions to achieve objectives;

● evaluate a team and decide if the task has been carried out.

Team-based leadership often happens in businesses where the idea and use of a hierarchy is less relevant. This may happen, for example, in a SINGLE STATUS organisation where every worker is treated the same. They have the same

---

John Timpson is chief executive of the 320 strong chain of key cutting and shoe repair outlets. The business has doubled its sales to £48 million and tripled profits to £3.5 million over the past six years.  He believes the business he runs now is on far better shape than ever.

This might in part be due to his somewhat unconventional management style. He is a keen advocate of upside-down management. He works hard to make sure that stores remain the focus of the business, constantly visiting and encouraging staff to take responsibility for their own outlets. 'It's the only way you can run this business,' he says. 'Don't you get fed up when you go into a shop and they say 'I can't do that or I'll have to check with the area manager.'

Timpson states 'I've put a notice up in the shops which says that the staff have got my authority to do whatever they want to give you amazing service. They can spend up to £500 without authorisation to settle complaints. There's not much I can do to help customers walking into our Dumfries or Plymouth shop right now.'

The relationship is based on trust. Despite the stores dealing primarily in cash, theft isn't an issue. Employees can write to complain without fear of reprisals. Branch staff are also consulted about any major policy changes.

Source: adapted from *en*, June 2001.

(a) Using information from the article, explain the leadership approaches at Timpson.
(b) Suggest implications for the business of these approaches.

**Question4**

facilities, same dress codes and same terms and conditions of employment. Every worker is made to feel as if they are an important part of the organisation.

## Factors affecting leadership styles and approaches

The type of leadership style adopted by managers will depend on various factors.

- The task. A certain task may be the result of an emergency, which might need immediate response from a person in authority. The speed of decision needed and action taken may require an authoritarian or autocratic style of leadership.
- The tradition of the organisation. A business may develop its own culture which is the result of the interactions of all employees at different levels. This can result in one type of leadership style, because of a pattern of behaviour that has developed in the organisation. For example, in the public sector (☞ unit 7) leadership is often democratic because of the need to consult with politicians etc.
- The type of labour force. A more highly skilled workforce might be most productive when their opinions are sought. Democratic leadership styles may be more appropriate in this case.
- The group size. Democratic leadership styles can lead to confusion the greater the size of the group.
- The leader's personality. The personality of one manager may be different to another manager and certain leadership styles might suit one but not the other. For example, an aggressive, competitive personality may be more suited to an authoritarian leadership style.
- Group personality. Some people prefer to be directed rather than contribute, either because of lack of interest, previous experience, or because they believe that the manager is paid to take decisions and shoulder responsibility. If this is the case, then an autocratic leadership style is more likely to lead to effective decision making.
- Time. The time available to complete a task might influence the leadership style adopted. For example, if a project has to be finished quickly, there may be no time for discussion and an autocratic style may be adopted.

## Why do leaders adopt different styles?

A number of theories have been put forward to explain the most appropriate leadership style when dealing with certain situations or groups at work.

**Fiedler** In 1976, F. Fiedler argued that 'it is easier to change someone's role or power, or to modify the job he has to do, than to change his leadership style'. From his 800 studies he found that it is difficult for people to change leadership styles - an 'autocrat' will always lead in autocratic style whereas a leader that encourages involvement will tend to be 'democratic'. Different leadership styles may also be effective depending on the situation. He concluded that, as leaders are unable to adapt their style to a situation, effectiveness can only be achieved by changing the manager to 'fit' the situation or by altering the situation to fit the manager.

In business it is often difficult to change the situation. Fiedler suggested that a business should attempt what he called **leadership match** - to choose a leader to fit the situation. Leaders can be either **task orientated** or **relationship orientated**. So, for example, a business that faced declining sales might need a very task orientated manager to pull the business around, even if the tradition of the firm might be for a more democratic style of leadership.

**Hersey and Blanchard** P. Hersey and K.H. Blanchard argued that a leader's strategy should not only take account of the situation, but also the maturity of those who are led. They defined maturity as the ability of people to set targets which can be achieved and yet are demanding.

A leader will have **task behaviour or relationship behaviour**. Task behaviour is the extent to which the leader has to organise what a subordinate should do. Relationship behaviour describes how much support is needed and how close personal contact is. Together these will decide which of the following leadership styles will be used.

- **Delegating** leadership is where a leader allows subordinates to solve a problem. For this type of leadership style to work, subordinates need to be mature and require little support at work.
- **Participating** leadership is where a leader and subordinates work on a problem together, supporting each other. In this situation subordinates are slightly less mature than when a leader delegates and so need more support.
- **Selling** leadership is where a leader persuades others of the benefits of an idea. Workers are likely to be only moderately mature and require a great deal of support.
- **Telling** leadership is where a leader tells others what to do. Workers are fairly immature. They are told exactly what to do and little contact or support is needed.

**Wright and Taylor** In 1984, P. Wright and D. Taylor argued that theories which concentrate on the situation or maturity of those led ignore how skillfully leadership is carried out. They produced a checklist designed to help leaders improve the performance of subordinates. It included the following.

- What is the problem? An employee may, for example, be carrying out a task inefficiently.
- Is it serious enough to spend time on? This could depend on the cost to the business.
- What reasons may there be for the problem? How can it be solved? These are shown in Table 62.1.
- Choosing a solution and evaluating if it is the most effective one.
- Evaluation of the leader's performance.

## The work of the personnel department

Many large and medium sized businesses today have a personnel department. Its main role will be to manage the firm's HUMAN RESOURCES. These are the employees or personnel in a business that help it to achieve its objectives. They might include production workers, office staff, members of the marketing team, accountants or cleaners.

The personnel department will deal with many factors associated with employees. These include:
- human resources or workforce planning;
- recruitment and selection;
- induction and training;
- promotion and transfers;
- appraisal and termination of employment;
- discipline;
- rewards and conditions of employment;
- working conditions;
- career development and welfare;
- wage bargaining.

## What is human resources planning?

HUMAN RESOURCES PLANNING or WORKFORCE PLANNING is the method by which a business forecasts how many and what type of employees it needs now and in future. It also involves matching up the right type of employees to the needs of the business. A business will work out its labour requirements, its **demand**, and make sure that an appropriate **supply** is planned. For example, a growing business, such as a call centre, might find that it needs an extra 20 telephone operators over the next year. It may, therefore, plan to recruit an extra 20 operators over the period. An engineering business that loses a large order for parts may plan to make 50 workers redundant.

The HUMAN RESOURCES or WORKFORCE PLAN is usually one of the responsibilities of the personnel or human resources department and is one part of **human resources management**. It is also linked to the plans of the organisation. For example, when two accounting businesses, Cooper & Lybrand and Price Waterhouse, planned to merge they anticipated a growing demand for accounting skills, particularly in areas such as Eastern Europe, Latin America and China, and felt that the combined firm would be better able to cope. The companies planned to take on an extra 1,000 employees a week worldwide as a result. If staff were not used in one country, they would be deployed elsewhere.

The steps that a business takes when planning its workforce are shown in Figure 63.1. So:

Change in demand for workers = workers from within the business + workers from outside the business

Planning can be **short term** or **long term**. Short term planning is aimed at the immediate needs of the business, such as filling vacancies left, say, as a result of maternity leave. Long term planning will try to plan for the future. For example, if a company was aiming to change its production techniques in the next few years, it would need to plan the number of employees, training needed and perhaps the incentives and motivation that workers would require.

## Forecasting employee demand

In the future a business may need more workers, less workers

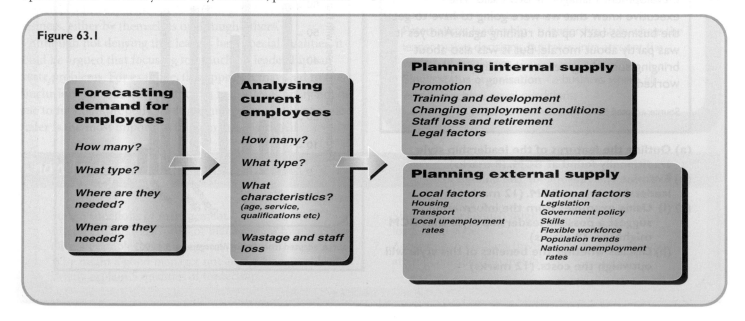

**Figure 63.1**

**Forecasting demand for employees**

How many?

What type?

Where are they needed?

When are they needed?

**Analysing current employees**

How many?

What type?

What characteristics? (age, service, qualifications etc)

Wastage and staff loss

**Planning internal supply**

Promotion
Training and development
Changing employment conditions
Staff loss and retirement
Legal factors

**Planning external supply**

Local factors
Housing
Transport
Local unemployment rates

National factors
Legislation
Government policy
Skills
Flexible workforce
Population trends
National unemployment rates

or workers with different skills. How might a business predict the workers it needs in future?

**Using past information** Forecasting techniques allow a business to predict what will happen in future from past figures. Figures collected from years in the past are referred to as **time series** data or **backdata** (☞ unit 13). So, for example, if a business has had a steady increase in staff of 2 per cent a year over the last five years, it might expect this to continue. However, this method is not very sophisticated. It does not take into account the development of the business that may be outlined in a business plan. It predicts the number of employees required based on previous growth or reduction figures, without considering future plans. A business, for example, may decide to install new machinery, which might reduce the number of employees it needs.

**Workers' productivity** A manufacturer may employ a total of 50 staff and produce 550 products a week. This means that it has an output per worker of 11 products (550÷50). If it wanted to produce an extra 55 products, it would need to employ an extra 5 staff (55÷11). If output had to be cut to 495 products, only 45 workers would be needed (495÷11). This is a rather simple way of predicting demand. It does not take into account **economies** and **diseconomies** of scale (☞ unit 81). As demand for products increases, a business may be able to raise output by using equipment more efficiently rather than hiring more workers. In addition, an increase in output will have a smaller effect on non-production workers. For example, if the amount of work doubled, support services may only need to increase by 30-50 per cent. Although more technical and production staff may be employed, this may not be matched by an increase in management and office staff.

**Work study** This allows a business to find the numbers of staff needed to carry out a task efficiently. For example, a business may decide to change its production methods so that all of a product was manufactured in a 'cell' rather than as parts in batches (☞ unit 79). This would mean that workers would work in teams, take responsibility for decisions and have to be multi-skilled. Careful consideration would need to be made of exactly what extra work staff would be doing and whether more or less staff would be needed. Without suitable work studies, a business may over or underestimate the actual number of staff needed to carry out future business plans.

**Using business and management knowledge** A business may ask experienced managers at all levels for their views on the employees needed in the future. For example, the manager of a large firm of solicitors may know that more part time staff are likely to be needed in the near future as there is a growing number of clients suing others for personal accident compensation. The manager of an advertising agency may predict that staff may be needed for the growing market in

internet advertising. The manager of a hotel chain may predict that fewer staff are needed for catering as the demand for conference meals has fallen off.

**Calculating staff loss** Workers leave their jobs from time to time. They may retire, be promoted, be dismissed, join other businesses, leave to have children or simply resign. If a worker leaves a job then a **vacancy** exists which the business has to fill. One useful indicator of people leaving a business is the **percentage wastage rate** or the **labour turnover index.** This shows the number of employees leaving as a percentage of those who could have left. For example, if a business employing 70 staff finds that 18 left the previous year, the wastage rate or LABOUR TURNOVER is:

$$\frac{\text{Number of staff leaving per period}}{\text{Average number of staff in post during the period}} \times 100 = \frac{18}{70} = 25.7\%$$

This could be used to predict the numbers of employees that may leave in future and the need to employ new workers. Similar predictions may be made about the numbers of employees that are likely to be promoted or to retire.

Many factors might influence the demand by a business for

Ancillary staff working in public services include cleaners, laundry staff and caterers. In the late 1980s research on labour turnover in the NHS revealed an average rate of 45 per cent a year among ancillary staff. In one health authority it was 111 per cent. Privatisation has had a great effect on ancillary workers. In the early 1990s, 98 per cent of care provided by social services in England, such as meals on wheels and personal care, came from local authority in-house workforces. In 2000 just under half did.

The introduction of compulsory competitive tendering (CCT), where local authority services were bid for by private suppliers, saw a great reduction in the number of workers employed. Competition meant the cutting of labour costs and workloads had to be increased.

In 2001 the government announced a near 50 per cent increase in hospital consultants in England over the next decade. Rises in nurses, midwives, GPs and physiotherapists were also promised to help restore the credibility of the service at a time of complaints about waiting lists for consultations and treatment, ward hygiene and quality of life in hospitals. A Department of Health source said 'Increasing the number of staff in training is vital if we are to increase the capacity of the NHS and its ability to deliver faster, better care for patients when and where they need it.'

Source: adapted from *The Guardian*, 9.1.2001 and 15.2.2001.

(a) Examine how demand for staff in the NHS might be estimated.

 **Question 1**

workers. If more products are sold, more workers may need to be employed to increase output. New equipment may require workers with different skills. Labour saving equipment might reduce the need for workers. Businesses that have a high labour turnover might need to employ new workers on a regular basis. Promotion or retirement will also create vacancies. A change in the goals of the business may increase or decrease demand for staff. A business aiming to reduce the layers in its hierarchy may demand fewer workers in future. Changes in production techniques, such as a move from assembly line production to team work or cell production, might mean that fewer or different types of workers are demanded by a business. The latest business theories can also affect demand. The move to teamwork in the 1990s in some businesses may have increased demand for 'team leaders'.

## Analysing current employee supply

Once a business has decided on the number and type of employees it needs in future, its next step is to ask: 'how do we ensure that we have the right people at the right time to meet the workforce planning requirements?'

A starting point is for a business to analyse the current position of its employees. This is likely to involve calculating the number of employees working in particular jobs and identifying their category and function. It may also mean gathering information on their age, length of service, qualifications and performance results. For example, a business that wants to employ managers may look at the number of graduates on its staff. A business trying to reduce its workforce by retirement may examine the ages of its employees. Data relating to employee 'flows' through the business, staff loss and how the nature of the present staff is changing are also important. For example, a business that wants to introduce flexible work practices may take into account the number of part time staff it has or the percentage of the business that is made up of teleworkers (☞ unit 76).

From the analysis of future demand and the current workforce, a business can decide on the number and type of employees that it may plan to recruit **internally** and **externally** in future to achieve its targets (☞ unit 64). It can also decide how it might reduce its existing workforce if necessary. These are discussed in the next sections.

## Planning internal employee supply

A business may plan to meet future changes in demand with workers from inside the organisation. It may also plan to reduce its workforce. Whether a business can meet its future workforce requirements from existing employees may depend on a number of factors.

**Promotion** A business may decide to promote employees from inside the organisation. Some businesses encourage internal promotion (☞ unit 64). The advantage of promoting existing workers is that they already know about the business's practices and culture. They may also be able to adapt more easily to a new job than an outsider. Some workers may also have been 'filling in' temporarily and have experience of the job. Promoting internally would leave a vacancy further down the hierarchy which would need to be filled. This would add costs and time to filling the vacancy.

**Staff development and training** A business is more likely to be able to find a suitable employee from inside the organisation if it has training and development programmes (☞ unit 67). Training may provide the skills needed to allow an employee to move to a new position. For example, many larger businesses have graduate training programmes which train employees with degrees for management positions. Businesses that have development programmes which identify how workers can improve, appraise workers' abilities and view the development of employees as important, are more likely to employ an internal candidate. If a business needs to reduce its workforce in a particular department it may consider retraining its employees and **redeploying** them to another part of the organisation.

**Staff loss and retirement** A workforce supply plan should also take into account staff loss and rates of retirement. High rates of labour turnover, as explained earlier, create vacancies. However, they may also lead to large numbers of skilled workers leaving a business which can affect the number of suitable internal candidates for a job. If large numbers of employees are retiring, this may lead to problems when trying to fill senior management posts which require experienced employees. A business may make use of retirement as a means of reducing the workforce if necessary. People can sometimes be encouraged to take 'early retirement', if they are given a financial incentive (☞ unit 66).

**Flexibility** A business may be able to change its workforce practices and conditions in order to meet its labour supply requirements. For example, a business may change the number of hours that people work in a period. Employees may be asked to work 1,950 hours in a year rather than 37.5 hours a week. This means that a business can have employees in work for longer than 37.5 hours when they are needed at peak times. If a business wants to add extra responsibility to the role of workers it may encourage teamwork or the multiskilling of workers. It may also decide to make new jobs part time or jobs that can be shared by two people in order to increase the flexibility of the business.

**Legal factors** If a business finds that its demand for workers is likely to fall in future it may decide to make workers redundant. There are legal conditions which affect how and when workers can be made redundant (☞ unit 66). They may also be entitled to redundancy or **severance** payments.

T Hodgson is a shop that specialises in painting and decorating materials. It employs seven full time staff. It also hires three part time staff, usually at weekends. Recently two of its older staff have retired, including its main buyer of specialist paints. It now has to appoint someone with the knowledge to buy in the latest painting materials. It has decided to promote one member of staff who has shown initiative in taking courses at night school. But it is concerned that more training may be necessary. As it has lost a 'shop floor' employee, it must also consider whether to hire more part time workers or make one of its part time workers into a full time employee.

In 2003 Sainsbury's confirmed plans to cut jobs as part of a two-year review of the company's operations. It aimed to cut over 1,000 positions in total, mainly through normal staff turnover, by March 2005. The reduction was expected to generate annual savings of about £20 million, but added 'The process is not about saving money, it is about streamlining the organisation.' Most of the redundancies were to come from the company's supply chain operation and not staff in stores. 350 jobs had already been axed, including 50 in marketing. A spokesperson said that redeployment and natural staff turnover had accounted for another 300 posts, leaving 500 jobs still to be cut. The review is part of a three-year recovery programme launched last year which was designed to make overall savings of £250 million a year.

Source: adapted from *The Guardian*, 13.6.2003.

(a) Explain the ways in which these businesses have met their human resource requirements from their current employees.
(b) Discuss the effects of these methods on:
  (i) the businesses;
  (ii) their employees.

## Planning external employee supply

A business may plan to employ workers from outside the organisation. There are local and national factors that have to be taken into account by a business when planning its external employee requirements.

- The availability and price of housing in an area. Some employees may not be able to afford housing in a highly priced area such as London, for example. The availability of new housing on a nearby estate may encourage young families with children to move to an area.
- The ease and availability of public transport. Working at a factory in a remote area may prove difficult for an employee without a car. Areas with efficient rail or bus links may prove popular for some workers. Possible restrictions or charges on cars in city areas may influence external employee supply in future.

- Competition. The closing or opening of other businesses in an area may either help or hinder external supply of labour. If businesses close there may be more skilled labour from which to choose. New businesses may reduce the availability of skilled workers. However, they are also likely to train workers, so that it may be possible to 'headhunt' required employees more easily (☞ unit 64).
- Unemployment. High rates of unemployment in an area lead to a large supply of workers who are available for work. This increases choice for a business looking to recruit from outside the organisation. High rates of national unemployment may make workers more willing to travel.
- Availability of skills. Specialist skills may be found in particular areas. For example, the area around Stafford, known as the Potteries, traditionally had skilled pottery workers. Some workers made unemployed in shipyard areas such as Tyneside were able to transfer their skills to other related industries when shipyards closed.
- The availability of flexible workers. Many businesses are taking advantage of the use of teleworkers (☞ unit 76). These are people who are employed to work at home and make use of technology such as the fax and computer to communicate with the business. They work from home which reduces business costs. Some workers are 'employed' by the business, but are not guaranteed work. They are brought in only when required, such as when demand is high. An example might be a delivery firm asking drivers to be 'on call' in case of busy periods. The availability of these workers increases the flexibility of businesses.
- Government training and subsidies. Government funded training and employment schemes subsidise businesses for taking on young workers for a period of time (☞ unit 67). This reduces their cost to a business and allows a 'trial run' of a possible employee.
- Population and demographic trends. Changes in the structure of the population can affect external recruitment (☞ unit 64). In the UK there is a growing number of older workers who are available for work. The increase in the number of women joining or returning to the workforce is also likely to affect the supply plans from outside the organisation.
- Government legislation. There are restrictions on the nature and type of advertisements that can be used when recruiting from outside the business. There are also laws which protect the pay and conditions of workers when they are employed (☞ units 68 and 69).
- Costs. The earnings of workers from outside the business might affect recruitment. Hiring workers on lower wages can reduce costs. The cost of setting up factories or offices to employ workers must also be taken into account and businesses must assess the relative costs of employees in different areas and with different skills.

Seasonal workers employed by Asda at Christmas 2003 would have benefits and job security equivalent to those of full-time colleagues. The new 'seasonal squad' would have the same status as permanent staff, but with a contract to work an annual, rather than weekly, number of hours. The new recruits would be allowed to work for as little as ten weeks of the year. The contracts would cover Christmas, Easter and the school summer holidays. Positions included greeters, porters, checkout operatives and warehouse workers. 'We recognise that people are looking for flexibility across the working year, not just the working week' said Caroline Massingham, Asda retail people director. 'If you're one of the many people that want to balance long periods of leave with a fulfilling job, the options are limited,' she also added.

Asda hoped that more over 50s would be encouraged to join its 22,357 workers in this age group. The supermarket's flexible working package includes one week's leave for new grandparents and up to two years for a career break. It said that since recruiting older workers, it has seen absence levels drop, customer service improve and labour turnover fall.

Source: adapted from *The Guardian*, 24.10.2003.

BT confirmed plans to open two new call centres in India in 2003 that would create more than 2,000 jobs. The centres would be in Delhi and Bangalore. The cost of opening call centres in India is up to 30 per cent cheaper than in the UK. The two new call centres, which will cost around £3 million to set up, will deal with operations such as telephoning people in the UK to remind them to pay their bills. Last summer, HSBC's Indian call centre employees were praised by the company for being more efficient, polite and enthusiastic than their British counterparts.

Research by recruitment business Adecco suggested British companies will create up to 100,000 call centre jobs in India by 2008. This would slash their wage costs and take advantage of a pool of skilled workers, many of them graduates. Once a call centre is set up, the wage bill makes up two-thirds of its operation costs. Indian call centre workers earn about £1,200 a year, less than a tenth of the £12,000 starting salary of an employee in Britain. But there can be problems. Businesses can have difficulties keeping a grip on everyday operations in a centre so far away from their base and there may be quality control issues.

Source: adapted from *The Guardian*, 7.3.2003.

(a) Explain why these situations are examples of planning employee supply from outside the organisation.
(b) Examine the factors that might affect the recruitment of workers from outside the organisation in these situations.

**Question 3**

## key terms

**Labour turnover** - the number of people that leave a business over a period of time as a percentage of the number of people employed.

**Human resources** - the employees or personnel in a business which help it to achieve its goals.

**Human resources plan or the workforce plan** - the suggested quantity, quality and type of employees a business will require in future and how this demand is to be met.

**Workforce planning or human resources planning** - the process of calculating the number of employees a business needs in the short term and the long term and matching employees to the business's requirements.

## Knowledge Knowledge...Knowledge

1. State 5 tasks that the personnel department may carry out.
2. What are the steps a business takes when planning its workforce?
3. Explain 3 ways that a business might forecast its demand for employees.
4. Suggest 3 reasons why a business may demand more employees.
5. State 3 features of a business's current workforce that it may be interested in analysing.
6. Suggest 5 factors that might affect the possibility of recruiting employees from within the business.
7. Why is labour turnover important to a business?
8. Explain 2 ways in which a business might make itself more flexible.
9. Explain the difference between redeploying workers and retirement as a means of reducing the workforce.
10. Suggest 5 factors that might affect the external supply of workers.

# Case study *Stewart and Mathers*

Stewart and Mathers is a solicitor, with offices in Lancashire and London. Its head office is situated in Skelmersdale, a 'new town' created to rehouse the overspill of people moving out of Liverpool in the 1960s as inner city housing was knocked down. Skelmersdale is situated next to the M58 and is a half an hour's drive from the cities of Manchester and Liverpool. The planners decided that:

- high private car usage must be catered for, while still encouraging public transport;
- pedestrians and traffic should be separated in the town centre and residential areas;
- industry should be concentrated in separate, but easily accessible, areas;
- open spaces should be provided, but the housing should be designed to foster a close community atmosphere;
- there must be no urban sprawl, and a clear boundary between town and country;
- the town must try and attract a balanced population structure;
- housing in Skelmersdale was to be high density, but without high rise flats;
- residential areas were to be close to the town centre where most facilities were concentrated.

After the year 2000 the business saw a steady growth in its sales of services. Table 63.1 shows figures relating to the workforce over the period. Stewart and Mathers realised that more cases were being taken out against individuals and companies for accidents which led to personal injury. This mirrored the situation in the USA. Large sums were often paid to employees injured at work, to people who had been hurt in 'road rage' attacks and for complaints against the State for injuries as a result of badly maintained roads or pavements. Most of

| Table 63.1 | Sales revenue (£m) | Total employees | Employees leaving |
|---|---|---|---|
| 2000 | 1.1 | 70 | 3 |
| 2001 | 1.2 | 72 | 4 |
| 2002 | 1.4 | 75 | 5 |
| 2003 | 1.6 | 80 | 5 |
| 2004 | 2.0 | 100 | 6 |

the decisions in the business were taken by the three partners, two of whom had previous experience of working in other countries. There were 10 people in the business who were 'fee earners'.

The organisation decided that it wanted to expand rapidly to take advantage of growing business in this area. It encouraged its administrative staff lower in the hierarchy to train in law qualifications or take the Institute of Law examination. This would allow them to progress to become a solicitor's assistant. It advertised widely in the local area to fill vacancies and 'headhunted' graduates of the ILEX (Institute of Legal Secretaries) courses at local colleges who had been trained in basic law skills. It would also be able to take advantage of the government's New Deal by employing young workers for a small number of posts.

However, some of its senior management positions needed to be filled quickly and so the business advertised in national magazines and quality newspapers. If necessary it was prepared to subsidise managers for a short time if they were prepared to move to the area immediately. This might mean that they have to leave property unsold in a different part of the country or leave family and work away from home for a period.

(a) **What factors could have affected the promotion of internal employees within the business to higher posts? (6 marks)**
(b) **Explain how the business may have forecast the increased need for employees after the year 2000. (10 marks)**
(c) (i) **Calculate the labour turnover of the business over the period. (4 marks)**
   (ii) **Examine the possible effects of changes in labour turnover on the business. (10 marks)**
(d) **To what extent might the business be able to recruit workers from outside the organisation for:**
   (i) **jobs at the base of the hierarchy;**
   (ii) **managerial jobs? (10 marks)**

# 64 Recruitment

## The need for effective recruitment

This unit concentrates on the first stage in the management of human resources - recruitment. The personnel department will aim to attract the 'best' candidates for the job and then to choose the most suitable. If the wrong person is recruited, this can cause problems for a business. The person appointed may find the job boring or too difficult, which could lead to a lack of motivation and poor productivity. If the person leaves, there will be administration costs for the personnel department. The business will face the extra costs of advertising, interviewing and training. There will also be a settling in period until the new employee has learned the job.

Employing a suitable person should allow the business to get the most out of its human resoources. In addition, recruiting the best employees may give a business a competitive edge over rivals (☞ unit 5). To make sure the 'best' person is chosen, businesses must be clear about:

- what the job entails;
- what qualities are required to do the job;
- what rewards are needed to retain and motivate employees.

Recruitment is becoming more and more important in business. This is especially the case where employees need to be flexible or work autonomously, or where direct control over workers is difficult.

## Job analysis

Before a business recruits new employees, the personnel department usually carries out some form of JOB ANALYSIS. Job analysis is a study of what a job entails. It contains the skills, training and tasks that are needed to carry out the job.

Job analysis can be used by firms in many ways. These include selecting employees, setting pay, disciplinary interviews, promotion and job appraisal (dealt with later in this unit). For example, if a firm was trying to choose an applicant for the post of systems analyst, it may use job analysis to find out exactly what a systems analyst does in that firm.

In order to find out about what is involved in a job, the personnel department must gather data about all the different elements in that job. It is likely that people associated with the job will have different views about what is involved.

- The occupant of the job. She will have the most detailed knowledge of what the job requires. However, she might change the information to exaggerate her own status, or leave parts of the job out because they are taken for granted.
- The job holder's superior. She will have her own view of what the job involves, but is unlikely to be fully aware of all job details.
- Subordinates and others with whom the job holder is in regular contact. They are likely to have observed the

behaviour of the job holder over a period of time. Once again, any bias or error which the observer may have must be taken into account.
- Specialist observers, such as job analysts. These can provide an independent view of the work being carried out. The major problem is that the job holder, knowing she is being observed, may adjust her behaviour.

Having collected this information, it must then be analysed. This is often done by using five categories.

**Task analysis** This involves the study of those tasks an employee carries out when doing their job. Any job will be made up of a variety of tasks. A task is seen as a collection of activities that result in an objective being achieved. For example, an employee may have the task of reporting on stock levels in the company.

**Activity analysis** This is a study of the activities which make up a task. These will include physical activities and the intellectual demands of the job. So an employee whose task is to do a stock check might need to understand how to use the computerised stock control program and understand the concept of lead time (☞ unit 82).

**Skills analysis** This involves a study of the skills that are needed to do the job. These could be the ability to use a computer program or the ability to work with others, for example.

**Role analysis** This is the information gathered from the job holder, superiors and colleagues. The duties, responsibilities and behaviour expected from the job holder are discussed to produce a role description which all involved agree upon.

**Performance analysis** This attempts to set the criteria that will be used when evaluating how well a job holder carries out the job. It involves identifying standards and expectations. For example, an employee may need to ensure that stock wastage is kept to a certain level. This will give a target to aim at while carrying out stock control.

## Job description

Once a business has analysed what a job entails, it is important to draw up a description of the job. The JOB DESCRIPTION is a simple 'word picture' of the job. It will often contain some of the elements in Table 64.1.

The job description has a number of uses. It allows the firm to tell candidates for a job what is expected of them. It also helps personnel officers to decide on the qualities that successful candidates must have.

When candidates are appointed, the job description can be used to gauge whether the employee is doing the job

**Table 64.1** *Possible job description of a design artist*

| | |
|---|---|
| General information | Job title, such as 'designer'.<br>Place of job within the business.<br>Job summary, eg main tasks. |
| Job content information | Tasks involved, eg details of tasks.<br>Purpose of tasks, eg develop designs for products.<br>Methods involved, eg drawing, CAD etc.<br>Other duties, eg part of design team.<br>Responsibility, eg control of other staff. |
| Working conditions | Physical environment, eg work area.<br>Social environment, eg holidays.<br>Economic conditions, eg length of working day. |
| Performance information | Criteria for measuring performance, eg quality of designs. |

'properly', by comparing their activities with the description. Disputes about the work an employee has to do can also be settled by looking at the job description.

A good example of 'tight' job descriptions are those for McDonald's employees. They are given because employees are

**Table 64.2** *A possible person specification of a draughtsperson*

| | |
|---|---|
| Attainments | Essential to have evidence of application and capacity for detailed work.<br><br>Desirable to have some knowledge of technical drawing and of engineering terms.<br><br>Must have at least 4 GCSEs grade C or above, or vocational qualification in engineering or manufacturing at equivalent level.<br><br>Previous experience of record keeping in technical office or library is essential.<br><br>Experience of working with engineering drawings is desirable. |
| General intelligence | Brisk reactions and accurate memory are needed. |
| Specialised aptitudes | Neat, quick and accurate at clerical work. |
| Interests | Practical and social. |
| Disposition | Self-reliant, helpful, friendly. |
| Circumstances | Likely to stay for at least 3 years. |

expected to be very flexible and interchangeable in their jobs (☞ unit 76) - so that when a worker comes to a job or task, they know exactly what to do. McDonald's employees have in the past been given a 385 page operations manual. It was full of details on how each task should be performed. It included instructions such as 'Cooks must turn, never flip, hamburgers... once, never two at a time ... Cashiers must make eye contact and smile at every customer'.

The job description is a means of communication (☞ unit 70). It suffers from the usual problems of misunderstanding and distortion. It is also a simplification, as it is rarely possible to include every feature of a particular job.

## Person specification

Once the skills and knowledge needed to perform a particular job have been outlined in the job description, they are often reworded into a PERSON SPECIFICATION (sometimes referred to as the human specification or the job specification). This shows a profile of the type of person needed to do the job.

Such a description can then form the basis for the selection of the most suitable person to fill the job. Table 64.2 shows a possible example.

It is important that the person specification fits the 'culture' of a business (☞ unit 15). Goffee (London Business School) and Jones (Henley Management College) suggest that there are two cultures in the workplace - sociability and solidarity.

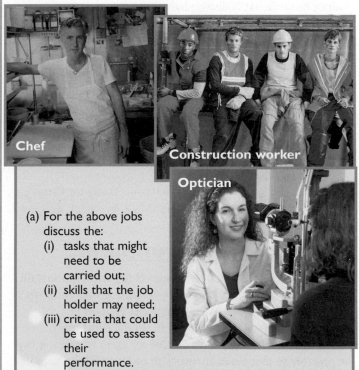

Chef

Construction worker

Optician

(a) For the above jobs discuss the:
  (i) tasks that might need to be carried out;
  (ii) skills that the job holder may need;
  (iii) criteria that could be used to assess their performance.

(b) Suggest problems that a business might have if it did not carry out a job analysis for the jobs in the photographs.

**Question 1**

The sociable workplace has a friendly atmosphere, openness and a sharing of ideas. A workplace with solidarity has mutual interests and shared goals. A business must ensure that individuals who are recruited fit the culture of the organisation or they may be an unsuitable appointment.

## Job evaluation

A business can use JOB EVALUATION to compare the value of different jobs. Any job can be broken down into a number of factors. These are the skills, effort, responsibility, knowledge and tasks that the job entails. This allows the business to decide on the wages or salary for that job. If another job has greater skill or responsibility, then the business may award it a higher rate of pay.

Job evaluation has become more popular over the last decade. It has been seen by businesses as a rational way of working out why some jobs are paid more than others. It has also been used in equal pay cases (☞ unit 68). For example, if there is a dispute about equal pay, the job evaluation will help to show if employees are doing work of equal value. When using job evaluation, a business must remember certain points.

● Job evaluation is about the job and not the performance of the employee in the job.
● Experienced people decide on the value of a job. Whilst this is likely to give useful results, they are not 'perfect'.
● It allows firms to set differential rewards for jobs. This does not rule out collective bargaining (☞ unit 74) to raise these rates.
● Only pay is determined, not other earnings, such as incentives.

The most popular method of job evaluation is a points scheme. A number of factors (skill, problem solving etc.) are found which are common to all jobs. Each factor is given a weighting according to its importance. A job description is then prepared and points are allocated to each factor. The total number of points determines the value of the job, and the wages or salary to be paid.

Whilst it can be useful, job evaluation is costly for firms. Also, some jobs will still be 'underpaid' or 'overpaid', as it is a matter of human judgment.

## Methods of recruitment

If vacancies do exist then the personnel department must fill them. Often firms fill vacancies by recruiting new employees - **external** recruitment. An alternative is to appoint **internally** from within the business. In the short term, particularly if funds are not available for extra workers, it may be possible to reorganise the work in order to fill the 'gaps' left by vacant positions. For example, the work could be shared out between the remaining employees.

This option might be used if the workload was felt to be too light in the department before the vacancy existed, or if the section is very 'tightly knit'. A further option is to pay existing workers overtime rates to cover the output lost by the

employee who has left. Internal reorganisation is not without its problems. These include how the work should be divided and what rewards employees should receive for 'extra' work.

External recruitment to fill vacancies is likely to become increasingly difficult given the population trends in some Western developed countries. In the UK, skills shortages and demographic changes (☞ unit 95) will make recruitment from outside more difficult. Employers will either need to change their strategies to take into account the falling number of potential recruits in competitive markets, or be faced with vacant positions. This may require the use of innovative forms of recruitment, employing previously inactive workers, flexible working (☞ unit 76) or job sharing. In addition, with many jobs now requiring high levels of skill, some businesses may find a shortage of appropriately qualified and experienced people.

## Internal recruitment

It is argued that internal recruitment strengthens employees' commitment to the company. The personnel department of Kellogg's, for example, has stated the following courses of action in its recruitment policy handbook.

'(a) Offer the job to an existing employee, as a promotion or transfer.
(b) Advertise internally, if a suitable candidate is likely to be available internally.
(c) Advertise externally if no suitable candidate is likely to exist internally (and display notice internally to the effect that the advertisement is appearing).

Except in special cases, all vacancies should be advertised internally before external recruitment methods are used.'

There is a number of advantages to advertising jobs 'inside' the business.
● It gives employees within the company a chance to develop their career.
● There may be a shorter induction period as the employee is likely to be familiar with the company.
● Employers will know more about internal candidates' abilities. This should reduce the risk of employing the 'wrong' person.
● Internal recruitment may be quicker and less expensive than recruiting from outside the business.
However, there are also disadvantages.
● Internal advertising limits the number of applicants.
● External candidates might have been of better quality.
● Another vacancy will be created which might have to be filled.
● If, having investigated ways of filling the vacancy internally the business still does not appoint, then it must find ways to obtain candidates externally.

## External recruitment

There are many ways of attracting candidates from outside the company. The choice of method often depends on the type of vacancy and the type of employee a business wants. Each method has its own benefits and problems, although it could be argued that the overall advantages of external advertising are the opposite of the disadvantages of internal advertising, for example, there is a wider number of applicants.

**Commercial employment agencies** These are companies that specialise in recruiting and selection. They usually provide a shortlist of candidates for a company to interview, but can also provide temporary workers. Examples include Alfred Marks and Hays Accountancy Personnel.

The advantage of commercial agencies is that they are experienced in providing certain types of worker, such as secretaries and clerical staff. They also minimise the administration for the employer involved in recruiting staff. Their main drawback is that they tend to produce staff who only stay in a job for a short time. Another problem for the business is the cost of paying fees to the agency.

**Job centres and professional recruitment agencies** These are government run and private organisations which try to help people obtain work. Their main advantage is that they can find applicants easily and can quickly draw from local or national databases.

**Headhunting** 'Headhunting' involves executive agencies approaching individuals, who have a reputation in a field of work, with employment offers. The main advantage is that a business can directly approach someone with a known specialism. This is of particular use to employers not experienced in a specialist field. The main disadvantages are the cost, the fact that the recruit may remain on the consultant's list even after they have changed jobs, and that

candidates outside the 'network' are excluded.

**The Careers Service** As well as providing career guidance to young people and adults, the Careers Service also collects local job vacancies and distributes them to their clients in schools and in the local area. Their main advantage is that they can produce regular enquiries from young people who are likely to be looking no further than the local area for employment and who would be able to take up a post quickly. Their disadvantage is that they work on a local rather than a regional or national basis.

**Government funded training schemes** Government funded training schemes (☞ unit 67) provide training for the young, long term unemployed, lone parents and disabled in order to improve their job prospects. They include for example:

● the New Deal, which allows people to have subsidised employment and training with a business or work experience with a voluntary organisation or environmental task force;

● Modern Apprenticeships, run by businesses and training providers, where employees and apprentices sign a 'training agreement' for the period of the apprenticeship. Employees are usually given employed status and train towards a vocational qualification.

The advantage to a business of offering such a scheme is that the costs of employing workers will be reduced because of the funding from government. The business will also have a 'free trial' of a potential employee.

**Visiting universities - 'the milkround'** This involves companies visiting universities around the country with the aim of recruiting employees. Its main advantage is that it

---

The Ceramic Company is a business based just outside Stafford. It is owned by Geoff and Janet Kelsey. It employs 10 staff, some of which are part time. Its main products are clay pots manufactured for earthenware and household goods retailers. Larger pots are manufactured for garden centres in the area. The business also manufactures hand painted tiles. This is a time consuming and fairly labour intensive process, but has been a growing proportion of total sales over the last year.

As sales have expanded, particularly to areas outside the locality, Janet is spending more time away from the workshop. Janet feels that she needs to appoint one of the staff to be the manager in her absence. The person would handle the ordering of materials, coordinate work to meet deadlines and deal with full time and part time staff as well as outworkers. Both Geoff and Janet feel that it would be easier to promote someone from within the business as there may not be enough work to justify the appointment of a full time manager.

However, they are both concerned that although two possible candidates have worked for the business for eight

years, they do not have the experience of organisation. In particular, when a large order comes in, there is often a need to quickly order materials and perhaps organise part time workers to work extra hours. Of the other two possible candidates, one is part time, but has had experience of managing a garden centre in the area. The other is the youngest worker in the business, although she is keen to develop with the company. She has seen the possibility of moving into other craft areas. Recently she was interviewed for a business that specialised in interior design, but she turned down the job.

Source: adapted from company information.

(a) Explain why this is an example of an internal recruitment method.
(b) Suggest benefits to the business of recruiting in this way.
(c) Discuss which candidate the business should recruit for the new post.

provides easy access to candidates of graduate standard. It is also fairly inexpensive and convenient through using the university appointments service. The main drawbacks are that often the interviewees are simply enquiring about a job and that interview schedules can be very time consuming and tiring. These problems have become worse as student numbers have increased in recent years.

**Advertising** Apart from using the above methods, employers will often advertise their jobs to a wider audience. They may place their own adverts in the media or they may deal with an advertising agency to get help with drafting advertisements and placing them in suitable media. The agency will usually book the space in the chosen media, prepare the layout, read and correct proofs, and check that the right advertisement has appeared in the right publication, at the right time. The agency will usually be aware of the following methods of job advertising.

- Vacancy lists outside premises. This is an economical method, but it will only be seen by a few people and little information can be included.
- Advertising in the national press. This has the advantage of wider coverage. However, it can be costly and may reach people who are not interested.
- Advertising in the local press. This will be read by local people seeking employment. Evidence suggests, however, that the local press is not read by professionals.
- Advertising in the technical press. This reaches the appropriate people, but may be published infrequently.
- Television advertising. This reaches large numbers, but can be expensive.

**Internet recruitment** Businesses can advertise jobs on their own Internet website or they can hire space on other sites. A company website is used to provide a great deal of information and adding a section advertising jobs might be relatively low cost method of advertising, especially if many jobs are advertised. The business would also not need to pay an agency to advertise the jobs. Some sites are set up to advertise jobs in particular specialist areas, such as teaching or the NHS. However, a possible problem with this form of advertising is that it only reaches those who have access to and can use the Internet, and who can find the required website.

## Producing a job advertisement

As important as choosing the most appropriate media through which to advertise a vacancy is the drafting of the advertisement. The decision on what to include in a recruitment advertisement is important because of the high cost of space and the need to attract attention. Both factors will encourage the use of the fewest number of words. Some of the information that might be included is:
- the job title;
- the name and address of the employer;
- the salary and any other remuneration;
- details of the vacancy;

**Recruiting new staff?**

**It pays to find the experts, but where are they?**

Agency Central is an independent on-line Directory of Recruitment Agencies, where you can search for agencies that specialise in placing the types of staff that you need.

You can search for recruitment agencies (we list over 1,000) in a number of different ways (specialist skills, geographic location, etc) and review details about your selected agencies before choosing to go ahead and make contact. There's even a pre-defined template where you can e-Mail information about the vacancy you need to fill.

So no matter what role your looking to fill, make sure you've chosen the best agencies to work on your behalf.

www.AgencyCentral.co.uk
**The right direction in recruitment.**

Carlotta Del Santo runs a travel business in Kent which specialises in sports holidays in Spain and the Balearic Islands. She has recently found a great increase in demand for corporate and club golfing holidays and club trips to see Spanish football matches. The business now needs to recruit two new employees. An employee who speaks fluent English and Spanish is needed to liaise with operators abroad. Another employee with experience in organising travel holidays is also required.

(a) Identify the methods of recruitment suggested in the advertisement.
(b) Examine the advantages of these methods to Carlotta's business when recruiting employees.

**Question 3**

- the skills and experience required for the successful candidate;
- any other benefits;
- what the applicant needs to do to apply;
- where to apply and to whom.

# Employee segmentation

The standard of service is increasingly important to customers buying products. Providing an excellent service means matching employees' actions to the needs of customers. So businesses are trying to answer the question 'What behaviour by employees creates greater customer satisfaction?'

One way of doing this is to segment employees into groups depending on the profile of customers. This is known as EMPLOYEE SEGMENTATION. It means that businesses must organise and recruit specific types of employees to match the profiles of their customers. So, for example, B&Q knows that its customers often want advice about products. Therefore it recruits staff with experience of DIY who can talk sympathetically to customers about its products. In call centres it has meant a change of approach to one based on relationships with customers. Employees now tailor responses to customers' needs, based on information about the customer which is shown on a computer screen. Productivity is measured not by how many calls are taken but by how many problems are resolved first time. It is argued that such an approach leads to greater customer loyalty and repeat sales for businesses.

# Factors affecting recruitment

A study by Illes and Robertson (1997) of recruitment strategies identified factors which can affect recruitment and make it successful.

- The recruitment literature sent out to candidates can influence their decision about whether to apply or not. Informal sources of information, such as word of mouth and referrals, are seen as more accurate sources of information than formal advertisements. Applicants who come through such informal routes are more likely to stay with the business, reducing levels of labour turnover (☞ unit 63). This is because they have more realistic expectations when appointed.
- Businesses that want to recruit from under-represented groups, such as ethnic groups, the disabled or women, must ensure that their recruitment strategies are targeted, rather than using general recruitment procedures.
- The recruitment message affects applicants. Glossy, positive images may attract applicants, but can cause problems later if the job does not meet expectations. Job previews and work samples can lead to self-selection. Once experienced, a candidate may decide not to continue with the application. Site visits and opportunities to talk to colleagues can also help. Different messages may affect different groups. For example, flexible schedules can attract retired people.
- The behaviour of recruiters can affect applicants. For example, the presence of women recruiters and managers on site visits and interviews can create a positive impression.
- Applicants appear to respond well to recruiters who are seen as competent, informed and credible, and have interpersonal skills.
- Delays in response put off applicants as they may indicate how they will be treated if appointed.
- Applicants seem to respond more positively towards recruiters of the same gender, ethnicity, age and location.

# key terms

**Employee segmentation** - when a business recruits types of employees who match the profiles of its customers.
**Job analysis** - a study of what the job entails, such as the skills, tasks and performance expected.
**Job description** - a simple word picture of what the job entails.
**Job evaluation** - a method used by businesses to compare the value of different jobs and perhaps set wages or salaries.
**Person specification** - a profile of the type of person needed to do a job.

The Halifax is working to recruit older professionals who have technical expertise and might be looking to wind down. Martin Freeth, a lawyer in the Halifax legal department is an example. He was recruited shortly before he turned sixty. He says 'I deal with mortgage queries from the branch network, but occasionally I speak directly to borrowers when they are upset. It's useful to have a weight of experience to calm them down because there are few situations I haven't come across'. The products that Halifax sells do appeal to older customers, but the sales operation has been wrongly seen as a 'young environment'. So the business is holding open days aimed at customers aged 45-60.

The Halifax is also looking to train school leavers. It suggests that such groups face even more prejudice, that a real plan is needed and that work experience needs to be improved as it has often missed its mark.

Another important part of recruitment is the advertising. Past adverts were seen as too dull, with people simply shown in staff uniforms. They did not portray a fun, dynamic environment in which to work. Now when a branch has a vacancy it uses a recruitment guide to select appropriate pictures with approved images. The recruitment advertisements will now include staff and models of different age, sex and race. Research has shown that 90 per cent of staff now recognise the responsibility to equal opportunities. This was only 25 per cent in 1998.

Source: adapted from *People Management*, 22.2.2001.

(a) Explain the features of recruitment at Halifax which might make it effective using examples the article.

(b) To what extent is the business using employee segmentation methods?

## Knowledge ...Knowledge...Knowledge...Knowledge...Knowledge...Know

1. Why do businesses need to recruit effectively?
2. Give 2 reasons why companies carry out job analysis.
3. How is a job description useful to the personnel department?
4. What is the difference between a job description and a person specification?
5. Give 5 factors that might be on a person specification.
6. How might job evaluation be used by a business?
7. State two ways in which a business could reorganise instead of appointing internally or externally to cover a vacancy.

8. What is meant by:
   (a) internal recruitment;
   (b) external recruitment?
9. Give 3 reasons why a business might recruit internally.
10. State 5 methods of external recruitment.
11. Why might a business recruit using an advertising agency rather than a job centre?
12. What factors are important to show in a job recruitment advertisement?

# Case study Online recruitment

Many retailers are going online to find extra staff at peak sales times. At Harrods the January sales staff had been carefully recruited to deal with the rush. Harrods used the Internet to attract the staff it needed. Other sites such as Monster.co.uk and inretail.co.uk have set aside special sections for seasonal staff. Richard Jenkins, recruitment manager at New Look, said the Internet was an obvious choice to find people willing to handle the tills at this time of year. He suggested that Internet recruitment represents a significant part of overall recruiting at the business and was likely to expand.

The trend is not just limited to retailers. The Tussaud's Group, which operates Alton Towers and Thorpe Park, also uses the Internet for seasonal rushes. An obvious advantage is speed. People can be recruited quickly as jobs can be posted that day. Asking the applicant to answer 'screening questions' can save time sorting through applications. But perhaps the greatest advantage is targeting. Group advertising manager at Tussaud's, Matthew Mee, says 'You can pinpoint niche populations more accurately' and that 'Internet advertising has benefits because 'an advertisement in a newspaper is hit or miss because it relies on people buying the paper that day.' Jobs are placed on websites for a month rather than just a day. Another major advantage is cost savings, particularly the savings from commission to recruitment agencies. These can sometimes be 15-30 per cent of the salary of the job.

It is possible to place one-off adverts on sites. But the real savings come from running the whole recruitment process online. This means everything from posting the job on the website or on sites run by other companies, receiving CVs by e-mail, and sending offers of jobs. The optician chain, Vision Express, is a business which has opted for an integrated online recruitment system. Heidi Farrell, resourcing manager at the company, realised that it did not have a 'standard advertising approach' and that recruitment was rather piecemeal, using a variety of different methods in an ad-hoc way. Another problem was that the company recruited from four main groups - optical professionals, managers, sales assistants and lab technicians. These groups have different interests and concerns. Finding the right way to recruit them can be difficult. The Internet approach allowed a standardised recruitment process to be set up.

Like many other businesses, Vision Express does not just use the Internet. The initial recruitment strategy uses press advertising to get things rolling. This is an effective way of launching the campaign. A recruitment advert placed in a trade paper in November had several people in the advanced stages of recruitment just two weeks later.

Some businesses have even taken things further. They are becoming so concerned about reducing time and cutting costs that they are texting applicants on mobile phones. Often the recruitment process starts with a telephone interview, so texting is a natural extension process given the new technology available. It is easy for an applicant to return a message and the loss of several days can be prevented.

However, this does not mean that the days of the recruitment advertisers are numbered. The Chairman of the Association of Online Recruiters says that traditional advertisements still have a place. But he thinks that they may become corporate branding exercises. They will set out the organisation's values and direct job seekers to the website of the business. He predicts that the website will become more like the 'hub' of recruitment activity. Others are more cautious. Many businesses are using websites simply as shop windows for jobs. But recruitment is not done online. This is because there can be technical problems with online systems. People also sometimes have difficulty understanding the process online. One suggested 'nothing substitutes for a well planned recruitment campaign and selection process by businesses who know what they are doing'.

Source: adapted from *People Management*, 26.12.2002.

(a) **Identify alternative methods to Internet recruitment suggested in the article. (4 marks)**

(b) **Explain why recruitment using the Internet is an example of an 'external' source of recruitment. (6 marks)**

(c) **Examine the (i) benefits and (ii) problems of using Internet recruitment for retail businesses looking to hire employees in rush periods such as Christmas. (10 marks)**

(d) **Compare Internet recruitment and headhunting as methods of hiring managers for retailers such as Vision Express. (10 marks)**

(e) **Discuss the extent to which Internet advertising will be the most popular method of recruitment in future and whether all businesses are likely to use Internet advertising. (10 marks)**

## Effective selection - making the right choice

Selection is growing in importance for firms. As explained in unit 64, businesses need to recruit and then select the 'right' person for the job. If the candidate chosen is unsuitable, the business may be faced with the cost of poor performance by the employee. There will also be extra costs in selecting and training a replacement when that employee leaves.

Businesses have also realised the need for a fair and valid choice of candidate. The most suitable applicant will only be chosen if selection is based on ability, skills and knowledge, rather than race or gender, for example. **Equal opportunities** legislation has helped to make impartial selection more likely, although there are still arguments about the 'fairness' involved in selection (☞ unit 68).

Effective selection should lead to the most suitable candidate being employed, in terms of their skills and motivation, as well as reducing the cost of selection. Personnel managers play an important part in this. They help to prepare the job analysis, job description, and person specification, and decide exactly how to recruit. They also advise on the nature of application forms, how to SHORT LIST or LONG LIST from them, and how to conduct tests and interviews. Finally, they will influence how the information is evaluated and what decisions should be made about candidates.

## Application

The first time that a business receives information about candidates for a job it is advertising is when they apply for the job. Applicants may have collected details about the job from the business itself or from a job centre, for example. Some jobs ask for a letter of application from the applicants in which they explain why they want the job. This is often accompanied by a CURRICULUM VITAE (CV). The CV is a list of the applicant's:

- personal details (name, address, nationality etc.);
- educational qualifications;
- hobbies and interests;
- past job experience;
- reasons why the candidate is suitable for the job (strengths);
- references or names and addresses of referees who will provide references. **References** are a confirmation of the abilities, skills and experience of the candidate.

Growing use is being made of application forms by businesses. They have a number of benefits. All applicants give details in a standard way, rather than the different approaches of letters of application. This makes sorting applications and short listing far easier. This task is often called 'pre-selection'. It involves the 'sifting out' of applicants who least fit the requirements of the person specification and job description. The application form is often used as the basis of the interview and can be a starting point for personnel records.

The application form covers the information contained in a CV above, such as personal details, education and job experience. Certain forms leave out some of the above, while others include much more. Whatever the format, the form helps applicants 'present' their case. Also, by gaining biographical information, the personnel department has a simple way of matching the applicant's qualifications, interests, past experience etc. to their person specification (☞ unit 64). This allows the firm to decide quickly which of the applicants is suitable for a job. Table 65.1 shows a checklist

**Table 65.1**

- Handwriting is often larger than type. Do the boxes/areas on the form give enough room for the applicant to complete the information?
- Forms that take too long to complete may be completed haphazardly or not at all. Is the time the form takes to complete appropriate to the information the employer needs?
- Some questions may be illegal, offensive, or not essential. Does the form ask only for information appropriate to the job?
- Word processing software makes it possible to produce separate application forms for each post advertised and to make them user friendly. One way of doing this is to use introductory paragraphs explaining why the information in each section is being sought.

Frost Frame is a small company producing double glazed windows. It has decided to expand production. In particular, it is looking for someone with skills in working with stained glass. Having placed an advertisement in the local newspaper, the company sent out application forms. The standard application form was used which had been devised for all general workshop employees. It did not ask any questions related to the applicant's specific skills. After four weeks it has received three applications and only one candidate looks worth interviewing. However, it is unclear from his answers whether he will be entirely suitable.

(a) Identify problems that Frost Frame may have had with its application form.
(b) Analyse the possible implications for the company if it decides not to interview the candidate?

**Question 1**

of points which can be used to help a business design an application form.

# Interviews

Most people have at least one experience of being interviewed prior to employment. Few people enjoy interviews. Often this is because the interviewer appears to be more interested in finding fault than being helpful.

The personnel department is usually involved in interviewing, both in carrying them out and helping managers to adopt good interview practice. By following certain guidelines, the business hopes to employ the 'right' person for the job. It also aims to carry out the interview in a way that is fair to all candidates and well structured. These guidelines might include the following.

- The interview should allow information to be collected from candidates which can be used to predict whether they can perform the job. This can be done by comparing replies with the criteria that successful applicants should have.
- The business should give candidates full details about the job and the organisation. This will help them decide whether the job would suit them.
- The interview should be conducted so that candidates can say that they have had a fair hearing.

The interview has, however, been criticised as not always being an effective 'tool'. Some of the main criticisms are:

- interviewers often decide to accept or reject a candidate within the first three or four minutes of the interview, and then spend the rest of the time finding evidence to confirm their decision;
- interviews seldom change the initial opinion formed by the interviewer seeing the application form and the appearance of the candidate;
- interviewers place more stress on evidence that is unfavourable than on the evidence that is favourable;
- when interviewers have made up their minds very early in the interview, their behaviour betrays their decision to the candidate.

The problem with these criticisms is that they do not solve the problems, only identify them. No matter what other means of selection there may be, the interview is crucial. If it is thought to be unreliable, it should not be discarded. Businesses must simply make sure they carry it out properly.

# Conducting an interview

There is a number of factors which could be taken into account when carrying out interviews. The interview should be conducted around a simple plan and be based on a number of questions against which all candidates will be assessed. It is also considered good practice to prepare a suitable place for the interview, such as a warm, quiet, ventilated room. The interviewer should also ensure that the candidates have a friendly reception and are informed of what is expected of them.

An average interview may take around 30 minutes. An interview plan organises the time to cover the important areas in assessing applicants. The plan must be flexible enough to allow the interviewer to explore areas that may come up during the interview. An example is shown in Table 65.2.

Many recruitment handbooks spell out the 'dos and don'ts' of interviewing. Some of the 'dos' that the interviewer may take into account include the following.

- Introduce yourself to the candidate.
- Adopt a suitable manner, show respect and be friendly.
- Make sure the interview is not interrupted.
- Conduct the interview at an unhurried pace.
- Have a list of questions that need to be asked.
- Encourage the candidate to talk by using 'open' questions such as:

  'Tell me about your present/last job ...'

  'What is your opinion on ...?'

  'What do you find interesting in ...?'

- Concentrate on those areas not fully covered by the application form.
- Be alert for clues in the candidate's answer, probe where necessary, and be more specific in the questioning if you are not satisfied.
- When the interview has ended, make sure the candidate has no further questions and let the candidate know when the decision will be made, eg within seven days.
- Write up your assessment notes immediately.
- Prepare for the next interview.

The interviewer will have gained a great deal of information from the interview. It will help the interviewer to have a

**Table 65.2** *Organising an interview*

| Organisation | Tasks | Time (minutes) |
|---|---|---|
| Introduction | Who are they? | 2 |
| | Who are you? | 3 |
| Body of interview | Begin questioning. Ask questions which probe what they have learnt from their experiences/qualifications /interests and how they would apply this to their new position. | 10 |
| | Let the candidate ask questions. Explain about the organisation. | 5 |
| | If any questions are left, clear them up. | 5 |
| | Tell the candidate what happens next, eg 'We will let you know in 10 days'. | 3 |
| Close of interview | Finish tidily. | |
| After the interview | Assess the candidate. | 10/15 |
| | Prepare for next interview. | 10/15 |

checklist of the criteria used when assessing candidates. Table 65.3 shows two possible lists. The interviewer can make notes about candidates next to each criterion and compare the information with the person specification after the interview, to decide if the person is suitable.

---

**Table 65.3** *Criteria used in assesing candidates*

| Rodgers' 7 point plan | Munro-Fraser 5 point plan |
| --- | --- |
| Physical make-up | Impact on others |
| Attainments | Qualifications |
| General intelligence | Innate abilities |
| Specialised aptitude | Motivation |
| Interests | Emotional adjustment |
| Disposition | |
| Circumstances | |

---

## Testing

Businesses appear to be taking a greater interest in testing. There are strong arguments for and against the use of tests in selection. Those in favour argue that many interviews in business are unstructured and do not really allow a business to predict performance. They also point to the greater accuracy and objectivity of test data. Those against dispute this objectivity. They also argue that predictions from test results can mislead. For example, does a high test score mean high job performance and a low score mean low job performance?

There is a number of tests that are used in selection. These are often associated with different levels of staff.

- Aptitude tests measure how well a candidate can cope when faced with a business situation or problem.
- Attainment tests measure an individual's ability using skills they have already acquired. For example, a candidate for an administration post may take a word processing test.
- Intelligence tests aim to give an indication of overall 'mental' ability. A variety of questions are asked in such tests covering numeracy and literacy skills, as well as general knowledge. It is assumed that a person who scores highly will be able to retain new knowledge and to succeed at work.
- Personality tests, also known as psychometric tests, examine the **traits** or **characteristics** of employees. For example, they might indicate that a manager does not change her mind once her decision is made or that an employee is willing to experiment and adapt to change. Personality tests may allow a business to predict how hard working or motivated a employee will be or how suited she is to a job. The usefulness of such tests depends on whether the business feels that they are a suitable way of selecting employees. The business must also have qualified personnel to carry out the tests. Such tests do have problems. There is unlikely to be a standard personality profile of the 'ideal employee' to compare tests results against. The tests also rely on the individual being honest. Often, however, candidates try to pick the answer that they feel is wanted. In addition, some traits measured in the tests may not be relevant to job performance.

## Selection exercises

As well as interviews and tests, more and more companies are using a variety of:
- role play exercises;
- group presentations;
- PSYCHOMETRIC TESTS, which attempt to assess a candidate's personality;

---

- One of eight applicants applying for a trainee position was put forward largely due to the level of maturity shown. Most candidates, all university graduates, acted their age. He got the edge by being positively different. He was calm, relaxed and self assured.
- A candidate was not put forward due to the number of times he laughed during interview. Even allowing for nerves, he did not appear serious enough.
- A candidate was too rehearsed. Each question was given the same answer, which at times was not appropriate to the question being asked.
- A candidate was rejected because of her attitude towards an aptitude test. Another candidate was rejected on his attitude towards a female interviewer, when he tried to flirt.
- A candidate was rejected when his mobile phone went off during the interview. This may not be a problem in itself, but the candidate then had a lengthy telephone call.
- A candidate was recommended for second interview and offered a job. The main attribute was the candidate's honesty. She had suffered some illness with her previous employer. The candidate gave a complete and honest account of her illness and current prognosis.
- A candidate's CV was average in presentation and detail, but the enthusiasm and spirit in the covering letter encouraged the business to interview the candidate.
- A candidate gave only a satisfactory interview. However, what stood out was his approach having received a call for interview. He contacted the interviewer thanking him for the opportunity of the interview and confirming he would be attending. He then independently approached the interviewer's secretary to make sure he had the right directions and was polite to the secretary on attending the interview.

Source: adapted from www.sfrecruitment.co.uk.

(a) Using examples from the case, advise candidates of features of a successful interview.
(b) Using examples, explain how interviews might be useful for helping a business to select the most suitable candidate for a job.

**Question 2**

- simulations;
- assessment centres, which attempt to evaluate a wider range of skills using a variety of techniques to help a business analyse the capabilities of candidates.

These allow candidates to demonstrate social skills and problem solving skills which they may need to use in the job. For example, a salesperson may show persuasive communication skills in a role play situation. The use of exercises has a number of benefits for a business.

- They allow more information to be gathered about a candidate than other methods of selection.
- They show how well candidates react to situations such as team working, responding to customers or meeting deadlines.
- They allow large numbers to be assessed and may save on costs.

---

The Skipton Building Society's Accelerate to Management Programme (ATM) is aimed at people in lower level management and supervisory jobs. In 2003, five candidates were picked out of sixteen who applied with the backing of their line manager. The selection process starts with a verbal and numerical reasoning test. Candidates are also given a OPQ 32 personality profile which assesses their drive and self-perception. Candidates who 'pass through' are then invited to a competency based interview with a panel of senior managers and HR specialists. Shortlisted candidates are then asked to give a brief verbal presentation on a specific subject. The business argues that a crucial factor in the whole selection process is a high level of motivation. The ATM programme manager says 'We look for signs of enthusiasm and understanding about what they would be taking on'.

Source: adapted from *People Management*, 24.7.2003.

(a) What evidence is there that the business short lists and long lists candidates?
(b) Identify the selection methods used by The Skipton Building Society.
(c) Suggest advantages to the business of using these methods for the selection of candidates for management jobs.

**Question 3**

---

## Interviewing and technology

Businesses are increasingly making use of technology in selection.

Videoconferencing Some businesses use videoconferencing as an interviewing tool (☞ unit 70). For example, it can cost less than £1,000 for a recruiter in the UK to interview six candidates in the US by video link. Videoconferencing is not likely to replace the face-to-face interview because people still need the 'human touch'. However, it will help to save time and money. Glaxo-SmithKline, the pharmaceuticals company,

has used video-interviewing in the initial screening of candidates. It has found this to be a way of saving on travel expenses, particularly when an interview would have involved international air travel.

Telephone interviews There is a growing trend among companies to select candidates by using the telephone. Phone interviews have a number of advantages. Savings can be made on costs and managers need to spend less time away from their desks. They can also prevent discrimination due to visual appearance. However, telephone interviews are not always suited to all types of interview situation and certain candidates may not interview well over the telephone.

The Internet The use of online questionnaires on company, websites can help in the short or long listing process. For example, it may be possible to assess a candidates CV from answers given to a standard questionnaire. This will reduce costs greatly in the application stage. It might even be possible to given candidates an online tests to assess their abilities.

The future In future, businesses might even consider using technology such as webcams and the Internet for interviews. This might be used, for example, if a candidate had to be interviewed from another country.

## Evaluating selection

How can a business tell if selection has been effective? It could simply decide that if it has appointed the 'right' candidate, then its aim has been achieved. However, selection will involve costs to a business. There will be expenses in sending out application forms and perhaps travelling expenses for candidates. Staff will also have to give up time to carry out the interviews.

So, for example, if ten people were interviewed for three posts, but only one applicant was suitable, selection may not have been effective. In this case the firm would have to readvertise and interview other candidates as two posts would be unfilled. The personnel department's role would be to check all stages of selection to find out where problems had arisen. For example, when short listing, a suitable candidate may have been 'left out'. At an interview a possible candidate may have been rushed, so he was not given the chance to do his best.

Research in the 1990s and after the year 2000 suggests certain factors that lead to successful selection.

- Ability tests, job knowledge tests and situational judgement tests, where candidates are tested on how they would respond to a real business problem, have been found to be very effective in predicting future job performance.
- Personality measures and employment interviews, especially when they are structured, have emerged as stronger predictors of job performance than was previously believed.

EasyJet has 80 per cent of ticket sales via the Internet. So it makes sense for it to use this in its selection process. Pilots, for example, are asked to fill in a customised, online application form. All correspondence between applicants and EasyJet is then carried out online. Successful applicants are invited to a pilot workshop or assessment centre. Unsuccessful ones are filed away to be contacted later when they may have more experience.

CVs and applications are picked up from the website and sent to the relevant manager. But they are also logged on to the HR system where they can be electronically screened to see how they match up to existing jobs and vacancies. This allows personnel to build up a database of potential recruits for the future.

The business can be very effective in screening out applicants that have little chance of selection. Pilots, for example, must have a number of flying hours. It is immediately obvious from the application form if a candidate does not have this experience. It also filters out speculative applications from 16-year olds wanting to be pilots.

The business is less convinced about the value of online testing. EasyJet uses psychometric tests for recruiting pilots, but these are still pen and paper tests. One of the problems is the lack of feedback form candidates with online testing.

Source: adapted from recruiter.totaljobs.com.

(a) Identify the methods of selection used at EasyJet.
(b) Discuss to what extent online selection methods are useful for the business in the selection of pilots.

**Question 4**

# key terms

**Curriculum Vitae** - a list of the applicant's personal details, experience and qualifications.
**Long listing** - reducing the number of total candidates to a manageable list, that might be reduced further.

**Psychometric tests** - methods of selection designed to assess a candidate's personality.
**Short listing** - reducing the original number of candidates to a small number to be interviewed.

# Knowledge ...owledge...Knowledge...Knowledge...Knowledge...Know

1. Why has selection become increasingly important to businesses?
2. State 5 features covered in an application form.
3. What criteria might a personnel department take into account when designing an application form?
4. Name 4 types of tests that a personnel department might carry out when selecting applicants for a job.
5. What are the main problems with personality tests as a method of selection?

6. Explain the main problems with interviews.
7. State 5 'dos' when conducting an interview.
8. How might a business evaluate its selection procedure?
9. How might a business make use of technology when conducting an interview?
10. What is meant by a selection exercise?

# Case study Breaking with tradition

Looking smart and smiling at an interview may be a thing of the past. At Inkfish Call Centre anyone given an initial interview won't even have to leave home. Why? Because they are carried out by telephone. 'It's popular with candidates who often find it a lot less daunting and more relaxing than being thrown straight into a face-to-face interview' says Ruth Ebbern-Robinson, head of HR. Telephone interviews resulted from a policy to employ a wider age group. Many of the recruiters at the business were young and so 'Telephone interviewing soon proved a good way of avoiding any kind of discrimination by young folk who can think people are over the hill at 40. It worked perfectly because if you can't see someone, you don't know how old he or she is. People who are successful in the phone interview are then invited to a selection day run by company personnel representing a wide range of ages' according to Ruth Ebbern-Robinson.

Telephone interviews also avoid discrimination on ethnic grounds and disability. There are no visual clues and research has found that there's no bias towards accent. A company spokesperson at B&Q says about telephone interviews, 'We introduced it a few years ago to provide a consistent means of recruitment and one in which we couldn't, even subliminally, prejudice certain groups such as people with disabilities'. She also says 'Candidates benefit because telephone interviews can be arranged at a mutually convenient time, and time and money is saved by cutting out travel. You don't have to think about what you're going to wear and there's a good chance you won't even need to take time off from your current job'.

Businesses may also benefit. If a job involves communicating by phone, it gives employers an insight into the employee's telephone skills. Not having to find a location also means that more candidates can be interviewed, leading to a fairer recruitment process.

However, telephone interviews do have problems.

- Research shows that interviews with multiple interviewers are most fair and valid, which is not possible over the phone.
- If the job does not require any telephone communication, there is a chance that the candidate might not be comfortable with this kind of medium.
- Not everyone can find somewhere quiet in their home or at work for a phone interview.
- Interviewees may find that telephone interviews are structured, with questions which are less open ended than those asked in a face-to-face interview.
- Interviews may be through an automated system. This

is rare, although it is becoming popular for secretarial, receptionist and other customer-facing positions.
- Interviewees may answer questions too quickly. Silences are more prominent over the phone and can seem longer than they really are.

Shell uses telephone interviews for graduates. Candidates may not live near a Shell recruitment centre or simply prefer to be interviewed by phone. Shell then invites successful candidates along to a follow-up interview in person. Angela Baron, employee resourcing adviser for the CIPD, believes this is essential. 'Telephone interviews are no substitute for more detailed interviewing' she says. 'Telephone interviews are particularly beneficial for applicants who switch careers.' 'Many companies would see from this person's CV that they have no direct experience for this role and bin it. Those that use telephone interviews, on the other hand, would have the chance to check out their generic skills and may wind up with a more suitable recruit.'

Source: adapted from *The Guardian*, 13.8.2003.

(a) **Explain what is meant by (i) a CV and (ii) face-to-face interview. (4 marks)**

(b) **Explain why employers might use telephone interviews for employees in sales or call centres. (6 marks)**

(c) **Examine the ways in which a business might short list candidates for telephone interviews. (6 marks)**

(d) **Explain the advantages of telephone interviewing for:**
   **(i) employees;**
   **(ii) businesses. (8 marks)**

(e) **Suggest the factors that a business like B&Q might need to take into account to carry out a successful telephone interview. (8 marks)**

(f) **Discuss whether telephone interviews on their own are likely to lead to a successful appointment. (8 marks)**

## The contract of employment

Once a business has selected an employee (☞ unit 65), the successful candidate must be **appointed**. Once appointed, employees are entitled to a CONTRACT OF EMPLOYMENT. This is an agreement between the employer and the employee under which each has certain obligations. It is 'binding' to both parties in the agreement, the employer and the employee. This means that it is unlawful to break the terms and conditions in the contract without the other party agreeing.

As soon as an employee starts work, and therefore demonstrates that she accepts the terms offered by the employer, the contract comes into existence. It is sometimes a written contract, although a verbal agreement or an 'implied' agreement are also contracts of employment. The **Employment Rights Act, 1996** requires employers to give employees taken on for one month or more a **written statement** within two months of appointment. This written statement sets out the terms and conditions in the contract. Some common features shown in the written statement are:
● the names of the employer and the name of the employee;
● the date on which the employment is to begin;
● the job title;
● the terms and conditions of employment.

## The duties and rights of employees and employers

Employees that are appointed by a business are covered by certain employment protection rights. Government legislation makes it a duty of employers to safeguard the rights of individuals at work. These are **individual labour laws**, as opposed to collective labour laws which affect all employees (☞ units 73-75). They fall into a number of areas.

Discrimination Employees can not be discriminated against on grounds of gender, race or disability (☞ unit 68). So, for example, a business can not refuse to appoint a candidate for a job only because that person is female.

Pay Employees must be paid the same rate as other employees doing the same job, a similar job or a job with equal demands (☞ unit 68). They also have the right to itemised pay statements and not to have pay deducted for unlawful reasons.

Absences Employees have a right to maternity leave, time off for union or public duties and time off to look for training or work at times of redundancy. They also have a right to guaranteed payments during a period of lay off or medical suspension. Employees have a right to return to work after maternity leave. **The Employment Act, 2002** extended the rights of parents who worked. It gave working mothers and working adoptive parents 26 weeks paid maternity leave and a further 26 week unpaid maternity leave. It increased maternity pay as well. Two weeks paid leave were also given to working fathers.

Dismissal Employees have the right not to be dismissed or face disciplinary action for trade union activity or on health and safety grounds. They also have a right to notice of dismissal. Employers have the right to terminate contracts of employment under certain circumstances, such as misconduct. These are discussed later in this unit.

Health and safety Employers have duties to provide a safe and healthy environment in which employees can work (☞ unit 69). In the UK the **Health and Safety at Work Act, 1974** is the main legislation protecting employees. However, many other UK and EU regulations exist and are being constantly introduced to raise standards of safety at work.

The duties of employees may be set out in the written statement of the contract of employment. For example, employees may be expected to conform to standards of behaviour and conduct at work. These may include standards of attendance, punctuality, dealings with colleagues and dress. Standards of quality and accuracy of work, speed of work and safety are also likely to be expected of employees.

## Vicarious liability

In certain circumstance legislation forces business to have VICARIOUS LIABILITY. This is where a business must accept responsibility for the actions of its employees. Employers are

---

In 2003 a partner in a firm of solicitors drew up documents that were then used to commit fraud. Neither the fraudulent partner nor the firm benefited from the crime. However, the House of Lords judged that the firm was liable for the actions of its employees. This judgment was based not on the benefit to the employer because there was none, other than usual solicitors' fees, but on the wrongful act committed in the course of employment. This is what made the partnership liable. Even if the employee had acted entirely for his own benefit, the employer would still be liable. The employer would have made a decision that the employee was fit to do the job and so the risk that the employee would commit a wrongful act would lie with the employer.

Source: adapted from *People Management*, 9.10.2003.

(a) Explain why the solicitors partnership was vicariously liable in this case.
(b) Explain how this might affect (i) the business and (ii) the employee.

**Question 1**

liable for the wrongful acts of employees providing these happen during the course of their employment and are connected with it. So, for example, a construction business may be liable if its workers cause damage to an adjoining building whilst carrying out repairs to a client's building. Businesses found to be vicariously liable might incur fines or other penalties.

# Conditions of work and service

The written statement of the contract of employment will contain information about the conditions of work and service agreed by the employer and employee. Conditions may include the following.

**The number of hours to be worked** The statement will show the hours to be worked per week or over a period such as a year in the case of annualised hours (☞ unit 60). The number of hours must conform to legislation. For example, in 1998 the **European Union Working Time Directive** allowed workers to limit their working hours to a maximum of 48 hours per week, although workers such as junior doctors and senior executives were excluded. Details of the start and finish times may also be included, along with any meal or rest breaks. If an employee is expected to work 'shifts', this should be stated. Shift work is where an employee may work, for example, from 9am-5pm in the day for a week and then from 9pm-5am at night the following week.

The **Employment Act, 2002** introduced, for the first time, rights regarding flexible working. Mothers and fathers of children under 6 or disabled children under 18 have the right to request flexible working arrangements. Employers can only refuse the request if there is a clear business reason.

**The designation of the job** Workers may be employed in **full time** jobs or **part time** jobs. They may also be given a **permanent job** or a **temporary job** that only lasts for a period of time. The period of employment would usually be stated in the case of a temporary job. If a worker is expected to be based in a factory or office, this place of employment should also be mentioned. Some employees may be expected to work from home or to travel. If this is the case then arrangements that cover this such as support from the employer or travel expenses should be mentioned. These are discussed in the next section.

**Pay** The method of payment used to reward the employee is usually included in the written statement. She might be paid a wage or a salary. Payment may be by cheque or directly into a bank account. The rate of pay would be specified, such as £5 per hour or an annual salary of £20,000 a year. There may also be an indication of any bonuses, commission or overtime, incentive schemes and deductions from wages. Pay must conform to legislation. For example, employers are bound by the **Equal Pay Act 1970** (☞ unit 68). This states that an employee must be paid the same rate as another employee doing the same job, a similar job or a job with equal

demands.

**Benefits** Benefits that the employer is offering to the employee are usually included.

● The annual number of days paid **holiday** is often stated and any restrictions on when they can be taken. Statutory holidays are often stated as being taken.

● If the business runs its own **pension scheme** or offers to contribute to an individual or stakeholder pension, this may be stated along with contribution rates.

● There may be information on the length of time and the rate at which **sick pay** is available over and above any statutory rate.

● Any other benefits given by the business might also be included. Benefits can be wide ranging, from subsidised holidays to membership of leisure facilities to company cars.

**Disciplinary procedures** The written statement may indicate the immediate superior of the employee, who might be responsible for induction, training, supervision and discipline. In a larger business these are likely to be carried out by the personnel department. The **Employment Rights Act, 1996** states that employers must explain their disciplinary procedures. These are the rules that set standards of conduct at work. Employees must also be clearly informed of the consequences of breaking these rules, how this will be investigated and the rights of appeal against a decision. Employees that break rules could be liable for disciplinary action. This may be in the form of a verbal or written warning, suspension or even dismissal in some cases.

**Notice** Employees may leave a business to change jobs, to stop work totally or to have children. When employees do not intend to return they have to 'hand in their notice'. In other words they have to inform (or notify) the employer before they leave. The length of time that notice must be given by employees before they leave may be indicated in the written statement and must comply with legislation. This may be 'one week's notice' or 'one month's notice' for example. Similarly, the contract may state the length of 'notice' to be given by employers to employees before making them redundant or dismissing them. The length of notice will vary depending on the length of service.

**Grievance procedures** If an employee has a complaint against other staff or against their treatment at work then a business may have its own internal grievance procedure. Details of these procedures and who to contact in case of complaints may be included in the written statement. Employees should also be aware of how to contact an industrial tribunal, ACAS (the arbitration service) or a trade union in the case of a complaint. The **Employment Act, 2002** introduced minimum internal grievance procedures that businesses must have. They are designed to improve communication, so that employees can raise grievances, and to reduce the number of unfair dismissal claims.

**Employee rights** The rights of employees to union

Source: Equal Opportunities Commission.

(a) Describe the duties of employers suggested in the posters.
(b) Explain how these duties might affect the conditions of service of employees.

**Question 2**

representation, time off and equality of treatment as explained above may be outlined in the written statement of the contract of employment. The **Employment Act, 2002** gave trade union representatives the right to time off for training so that they can carry our their duties.

## Types of employment

A number of different definitions can be used to classify the way in which people are employed.

**Employees and self-employment** If an employer provides and controls work, supplies equipment and pays tax and National Insurance contributions for the worker, then the worker is an EMPLOYEE. An employee will work under the conditions of the contract of employment agreed with the employer. If the worker makes her own decisions about accepting work and conditions of work, and pays her own tax and National Insurance contributions, the worker is likely to be SELF-EMPLOYED. Working at home does not necessarily mean a worker is self-employed, as discussed in the section on homeworkers later in this unit. To be self-employed, a worker must be in business on her own account. Businesses sometimes 'contract out' work to self-employed people to save on the costs of extra employees. For example, buildings in city centres which are mainly glass may hire window cleaners rather than employing staff, even though regular cleaning may be needed.

**Permanent and temporary employment** PERMANENT

workers are employed by a business for an indefinite period of time. For example, a flour mill may employ a full time quality controller to check wheat as it arrives. He will work for the business until he leaves, either by choice, because he is forced to by the business or when he retires. TEMPORARY workers are employed for a limited period. For example, the mill may employ temporary workers for a period of six months to operate machines that 'mill' the wheat into flour.

In the UK, around 10 per cent of all workers are temporary workers. Businesses needing casual work at busy times employ temporary workers. So do farms, which employ seasonal workers as 'pickers' during the harvesting period. Shops employ retail assistants at Christmas for a fixed period. One advantage of temporary workers is that they no longer have to be employed once demand falls off. They can also be hired when required, for example to cover staff on maternity leave or for 'one-off' tasks. Costs may be lower because temporary workers do not receive the benefits of permanent workers. Some businesses use temporary jobs to try out workers who may later become permanent. One problem with temporary workers, businesses argue, is that they are less reliable than permanent staff.

The **Employment Act, 2002** introduced the right for fixed term employees not to be treated less favourably than similar permanent staff.

**Full and part time employment** Workers may be employed full time or part time by a business. Part time workers are defined in *Labour Market Trends* published by The Office for

National Statistics as 'people normally working for not more than 30 hours a week except where otherwise stated'. An advantage of part time workers is the flexibility they provide for a business. For example, part time workers may be employed at times of peak trade, such as in public houses at the weekend. They may be employed to allow supermarkets to stay open later in the evening.

Part time work can also benefit employees. It allows workers such as lone parents who have difficulty working full time to be employed. Students or others with low incomes can supplement their wages. The long term unemployed or people who are retraining may find it a way to 'get back to work'.

The **Part-time Workers (Prevention of Less Favourable Treatment) Directive 2000** and the **Employment Relations Act, 1999** ensure that part time workers are treated no less favourably in their terms and conditions of employment than full time colleagues. For example, the Directive states that part timers working under 30 hours a week must receive the same hourly, overtime, sickness and maternity pay, and leave and holiday entitlements as a 'comparable' full-time employee of the same employer. Equal treatment also applies to redundancies, training and access to pensions schemes. Exceptions are allowed to meet 'legitimate objectives' of employers.

**Homeworkers and teleworkers** A wide range of different people working in the UK might be classed as **homeworkers**. It may include for instance farmers, shop owners, representatives, telesales people, hotel owners and some computer operators. They may be employed by a business to work at home or they may be self-employed. They may be full time or part time. **Teleworker homeworkers** are people who work from their own home, or use it as base, and who could not do so without a telephone or computer. There were 2.2 million teleworkers in the UK, around 7.4 per cent of the workforce, in 2004.

For an employer, the use of homeworkers has a number of advantages. As these workers are not based at the place of employment, the cost of equipment is reduced and less space is needed. There are also fewer problems with absenteeism and transport delays, such as people arriving late to work or who are unable to get to work because of bad weather. People with children are able to work more easily, at times when they want. However, there may be communication problems if staff can not be contacted. Also, it is far more difficult to monitor and control the work of employees.

**Flexible working arrangements** Different types of workers can have flexible working arrangements. There are many different types of flexibility. Workers might have flexible working hours, having to work a number of hours in the day or week, but able to choose what hours to work. Or they might work a reduced number of days but longer hours each day. **Job sharing** is becoming more popular as people seek

part time work. This is where the tasks involved in a job description are divided between two people, for example. They often work at different times. Examples could be a legal secretary's job, part of which is carried out by one person from 9am to 12am and another person from 12am to 5pm, or two GPs in a doctors practice working on different days or weeks.

A growing number of businesses are taking advantage of the use of flexible arrangements. Legislation in the UK allows certain employees to request flexibility. Flexible arrangements can be beneficial for both employees and employers. Employees can choose the times they want to work to fit in with circumstances. Employers have the chance to change work patterns to fit in with production and demand.

**Table 67.1** *The growth in temporary work by occupation, 1992-2000, per cent of total net increase*

**Standard Occupational Classification**

| | | | |
|---|---|---|---|
| 1. Managerial and administrative | 5 | | |
| 2. Professional | 26 | *Including:* | |
| | | Engineers | 5 |
| | | Health | 3 |
| | | Teaching | 14 |
| 3. Associate professional | 10 | *Including:* | |
| | | Computer programmer | 2 |
| | | Welfare worker | 2 |
| 4. Clerical and secretarial | 23 | | |
| 5. Craft and related | -1 | | |
| 6. Personal and protective | 23 | *Including:* | |
| | | Health related | 4 |
| | | Childcare related | 17 |
| 7. Sales | 7 | | |
| 8. Operatives | 7 | | |
| 9. Routine manual | 0 | | |

(a) Describe the changes taking place in the table.
(b) Explain why these changes might have taken place.

**Question 3**

## Termination of contracts

Why might a contract of employment come to end? The contract may be terminated either by the employee or the employer for a number of reasons.

**Changing jobs and promotion** Employees may leave a business to change jobs. Their existing contract would end and they would be given a contract for their new job. As stated earlier, employees can not usually leave immediately. They often have to work out a period of 'notice', such as one week or one month. Employees who are promoted internally (☞ unit 63) are also likely to be given a new contract of employment as their terms and conditions may have changed. For example, a machine operator who was appointed to be supervisor may have different wages, benefits, deductions and leave entitlements.

**Dismissal** Employees may be dismissed for a number of reasons. These may be for unfair reasons, such as joining a trade union. If an employment tribunal finds that a person has been dismissed unfairly, it has the power to reinstate the employee. There are lawful reasons, however, for dismissing an employee. These may include misconduct or because an employee is incapable of doing a job. A period of notice is required, but the length will vary depending on how long the employee has worked for the business. The **Employment Relations Act, 1999** reduced the qualifying period for protection against unfair dismissal to one year.

**Redundancy** Another lawful method of dismissing an employee is on grounds of redundancy. This is where there is no work or insufficient work for the employee to do. The **Employment Rights Act, 1996** states that employees are entitled to redundancy or SEVERANCE payments. They also need to meet other criteria. For example, they must have a contract of employment (ie not be self-employed). Some people, such as members of the armed forces, The House of Commons and the House of Lords are not covered by the Act. Neither are people who are retiring over the age of 60/65 or who are coming to the end of a contract or an apprenticeship.

**Retirement and early retirement** Some people decide to leave work when they are entitled to this state pension. However, many take 'early retirement' and finish work before. They will then live on state benefits or a private pension which they can draw upon at an earlier age. Some employers that want to get rid of older workers or reduce staff numbers offer attractive 'early retirement' packages to encourage people to leave work. People do not have to leave work at these ages. Some employees are now seeing the benefit of employing older workers (☞ unit 68).

**Illness** Employers can dismiss employees if they are no longer able to do a job. However, employees may chose to leave a job themselves if they are too ill to continue. Some businesses provide private health cover for employees who need to finish work. Other employees would need to live on state benefits or private insurance benefits.

**End of duration of contract** Some temporary employees are only given a contract to work for a limited period of time. For example, contractors may hire construction workers to work on a large project, such as a shopping centre, for a period of two years. After the project finished the employees' contract would end.

## Breach of contract

If either the employee or employer suffers a financial loss as a result of a BREACH OF CONTRACT by the other party, they may claim damages. For example, an employee on a fixed term contract who is asked to work an extra two weeks to finish the job, but is not paid, may claim as a result. Claims by employees and employers are normally taken to either the the county court or another civil court. An employee can take a claim to an industrial tribunal if an amount is outstanding when the contract is terminated and if it is not related to certain categories, such as patents. Industrial tribunals often settle claims quicker than courts but there is a limit to the amount they can award.

---

Rue du Paris is a chain of restaurants specialising in French cuisine. It expanded rapidly in the 1990s and employed increasing numbers of employees. However, the setting up of many celebrity chef restaurants and the growing number of restaurants aimed at clients wishing to spend large amounts on meals meant that by 2003 it was facing problems. Its main aim was to change its staffing levels to suit a slimmed down organisation.

The business faced a number of staffing problems. Chefs at Rue de Paris had been moving to work for competitors at higher rates of pay. After training its employees for a number of years, they took their skills elsewhere. Some of its least experienced chefs had been 'moonlighting' at other restaurants. They had hurried their cooking, leaving early to work in other establishments and in many cases they had broken the terms of their employment contracts. A few chefs were over the age of 60. They had a great deal of experience, but perhaps the company was looking to younger people with new ideas that could really move the business forward.

Some of the newer restaurants had been set up with flexible staff because the business was unsure how they would perform. Some staff had been employed on fixed term contracts, for example. Other staff had part time contracts, with flexible hours. Two restaurants in particular had been doing very poorly and the company had to decide whether to close them.

(a) Examine the ways in which the business might terminate the contracts of its employees which may help solve the problems it faces.

Question 4

# key terms

**Breach of contract** - breaking of terms agreed in the contract of employment by the employers and the employees.

**Contract of employment** - an agreement between an employer and an employee in which each has certain obligations.

**Employee** - a worker for whom an employer provides and controls work, supplies equipment and pays tax and National Insurance contributions.

**Permanent employment** - employment for an indefinite period of time.

**Self-employed** - a worker who makes his or her own decisions about accepting work and conditions of work, and pays his or her own tax and National Insurance contributions.

**Severance pay** - an amount payable to an employee on termination of contract.

**Temporary employment** - employment for a limited or finite period of time.

**Vicarious liability** - when employers are liable for the wrongful actions of their employees.

## Knowledge ...Knowledge...Knowledge...Knowledge...Knowledge...Know

1. 'A contract of employment is an agreement that is binding to both parties.' Explain this statement.
2. What is a written statement of the contract of employment?
3. State 3 rights of employees of a business.
4. State 3 duties of employees of a business.
5. Suggest 5 conditions of work that may appear on the written statement.
6. Explain 3 differences between an employee and a person who is self-employed.
7. Why might a business employ temporary workers?
8. What is meant by job sharing?
9. What are the advantages of job sharing for an employee?
10. What is meant by a homeworker?
11. Suggest 3 advantages of homeworkers for a business.
12. State 5 reasons why a contract of employment may be terminated.

# Case study The growth of teleworkers

Teleworking is becoming popular for both employers and employees. The Labour Force Survey (LFS) and other market research estimates suggest that the number of teleworkers in the UK is around 2.2 - 2.4 million. This is about 7.4 - 8.6 per cent of the UK working population. The LFS defines teleworkers as 'people who do some paid or unpaid work in their own home who could not do so without using both a telephone and a computer'. This includes:

● people who work in their own home (teleworker homeworkers);
● teleworkers who work elsewhere but use home as a base;
● occasional teleworkers who spend at least one day a week working in their own home or using home as a base.

Lloyds TSB has recognised the benefits of teleworkers. A spokesperson stated 'Under the company's new Work Options scheme, employees can ask to work a variety of ways - job sharing, variable hours, teleworking, reduced hours and term-time working.' These provide staff with a means to 'balance home and work life effectively in a win-win initiative which aims to meet the aims of the business and individuals'. The initiative has been introduced not only to allow staff to work differently but to enable the business to retain skilled workers and attract new employees. The option was not just available to women, men or carers with children, but all staff, whether for study, sport or other commitments.

Source: adapted from www.royaldeaf.org.uk.

Footballfangs.com is a London based business that offers football kits, fashion clothing and fancy dress outfits for dogs. The business was set up by Tracey Davis and is run by her and her friend from home. They do not employ other full time or part time staff. The products are sold online via a website. The business also sells wholesale football shirts for dogs to Premiership and League clubs. All products are imported and sold globally. The website is updated every day and designed and managed in-house.

The business hopes to expand in future. It aims to be the market leader in the UK and Europe and take a sizeable chunk of the US market. It has thought about the possibility of using teleworkers in future to increase sales.

Source: adapted from www.the-bag-lady.co.uk.

In 2002 an agreement was signed in Brussels between major European multinational employers and trade unions on the protection of teleworkers. It was hoped that this would form the basis of future legislation. The deal covered data protection, privacy, equipment, health and safety, organisation of work, training and collective rights issues. The aim was to give teleworkers the same protection as premises-based employees. Several companies currently adopt similar proposals, including British Gas and IBM.

Source: adapted from news.zdnet.co.uk.

**Table 67.2** *Teleworkers: employees and self-employed, part time and full time*

**Per cent**

### Teleworker homeworkers

|  | All | Men | Women |
|---|---|---|---|
| Employees | 44 | 43 | 45 |
| Self-employed | 56 | 57 | 55 |
| Full-time | 52 | 74 | 34 |
| Part-time | 47 | 26 | 66 |

### Home-based teleworkers

|  | All | Men | Women |
|---|---|---|---|
| Employees | 41 | 40 | 46 |
| Self-employed | 59 | 60 | 54 |
| Full-time | 81 | 88 | 57 |
| Part-time | 19 | 12 | 43 |

### Occasional teleworkers

|  | All | Men | Women |
|---|---|---|---|
| Employees | 84 | 82 | 88 |
| Self-employed | 16 | 18 | 12 |
| Full-time | 90 | 96 | 78 |
| Part-time | 10 | 4 | 22 |

Source: adapted from *Labour Force Survey*.

**Table 67.3** *Teleworkers by occupation*

**Per cent**

### Teleworker homeworkers

|  | All | Men | Women |
|---|---|---|---|
| Managers & senior officials | 22 | 28 | 16 |
| Professional | 19 | 30 | 10 |
| Associate professional & technical | 27 | 31 | 23 |
| Administrative & secretarial | 24 | 5 | 40 |
| Skilled trades | 3 | * | * |
| Sales and customer service | * | * | * |
| Other | 5 | * | 7 |

### Home-based teleworkers

|  | All | Men | Women |
|---|---|---|---|
| Managers & senior officials | 21 | 22 | 20 |
| Professional | 20 | 19 | 24 |
| Associate professional & technical | 24 | 21 | 34 |
| Administrative & secretarial | 3 | * | 9 |
| Skilled trades | 23 | 29 | * |
| Sales and customer service | 3 | 2 | 5 |
| Other | 6 | 6 | 6 |

### Occasional teleworkers

|  | All | Men | Women |
|---|---|---|---|
| Managers & senior officials | 37 | 42 | 28 |
| Professional | 33 | 31 | 35 |
| Associate professional & technical | 17 | 15 | 20 |
| Administrative & secretarial | 5 | * | 11 |
| Skilled trades | 5 | 7 | * |
| Sales and customer service | * | * | * |
| Other | 3 | 3 | * |

Source: adapted from *Labour Force Survey*.

**(a)** Identify the different types of employment using examples from the data. **(4 marks)**

**(b) (i)** What types of workers are most suited to telework? **(4 marks)**

    **(ii)** Explain why these occupations are suited to telework. **(6 marks)**

**(c)** Outline the benefits to staff and employers at Lloyds TSB of using teleworkers. **(8 marks)**

**(d)** Examine how the introduction of legislation to protect teleworkers might affect teleworkers. **(8 marks)**

**(e)** Discuss whether Footballfangs.com should employ teleworkers in its business in future. **(10 marks)**

## Induction

Newly appointed employees are most likely to leave the business in the early weeks of employment. This is called the **induction crisis**. How can employers prevent this? One approach is to help the new employee settle in quickly and feel comfortable in the new job by using an INDUCTION programme. Induction programmes are not usually about a specific job the employee will be doing, but the way in which the business works. They may contain information about some or all of the following.

- The organisation - history, development, management and activity.
- Personnel policies.
- Terms of employment - including disciplinary rules and union arrangements.
- Employee benefits and services.
- Physical facilities.
- General nature of the work to be done.
- The role and work of the supervisor.
- Departmental rules and safety measures.
- The relationship of new jobs to others.

They may also contain:

- a detailed description of the employee's job;
- introduction to fellow workers;
- an explanation of the values that the business feels are important, such as good attendance;
- follow up after several weeks.

Even with these, induction is unlikely to work without careful timing and without making sure that the employee adjusts to the new social and work environment. Experiments have shown that it is possible for the time taken for induction to be halved and costs reduced by two-thirds if it is well planned. To do this, the programme must focus on the anxieties of the new employees, instead of on what it is thought they should be told.

## The aims of training

Training involves employees being taught new skills or improving skills they already have. Why might a business train its employees? It is argued that a well trained workforce has certain benefits for the business.

- Well trained workers should be more productive. This will help the business to achieve its overall objectives, such as increasing profit.
- It should help to create a more flexible workforce (☞ unit 76). If a business needs to reorganise production, workers may have to be trained in new tasks.
- It will help the introduction of new technology. New machinery or production processes can be introduced more quickly if workers are trained to use them effectively.
- It should lead to increased job satisfaction for employees. Well motivated workers are more likely to be more productive.
- It should reduce accidents and injuries if employees are trained in health and safety procedures.
- It may improve the image of the company. Customers are more likely to have confidence in personnel who are confident, competent and have knowledge of products or processes. Good applicants are also more likely to be attracted if a training programme is part of the job.
- It can improve employees' chances of promotion. The business, as a result, should have qualified people in important posts.
- Training can give a business a competitive advantage over rivals (☞ unit 5). This is increasingly important in competitive markets.
- Globalisation means that businesses are increasingly

**Figure 67.1** *National learning targets, England, 2004*

**Targets for 11-year-olds**
- 85% of **11-year-olds** reaching the expected standard for their age in literacy
- 85% reaching the standard in numeracy

**Targets for 14-year-olds**
- 75% of **14-year-olds** reaching the expected standard for their age in English
- 75% reaching the standard in Maths
- 70% reaching the standard in Science

**Targets for 16-year-olds**
- 54% of **16-year-olds** getting 5 higher grade GCSEs
- 95% getting at least 1 GCSE
- 92% getting 5 or more GCSEs (including Maths and English)

**Targets for young people**
- 85% of **19-year-olds** with a 'level 2' qualification
- 60% of **21-year-olds** with a 'level 3' qualification

**Targets for adults**
- 52% of **adults** with a 'level 3' qualification
- 28% with a 'level 4' qualification

**Learning & skills council targets**
- 55% of **19-year-olds** with a 'level 3' qualification
- 80% of **16-18-year-olds** in structured learning

**Targets for organisations (2002)**
- 45% of medium-sized or large organisations recognised as Investors in People
- 10,000 small organisations recognised as Investors in People

Source: adapted from Department for Education and Skills and www.northumberlandinfonet.org.uk.

competing in international markets. Training is important if a business wants to be able to operate in these markets.

# The need for training

It could be argued that, if left to themselves, businesses would not spend enough on training. They may feel that the costs of training are too high or that they will not see enough benefits. In this case there is said to be LABOUR MARKET FAILURE. The market, in this case the labour market (☞ unit 104), is not working at its most efficient. When market failure takes place, the government often attempts to solve the problems. It could do this either by:

● providing government training courses;
● providing incentives for individuals to train or for businesses to encourage their employees to take courses.

The government sets education, training and learning targets in the UK. Figure 67.1 shows the targets in England for 2004.

A major problem with the UK supply of labour is SKILLS SHORTAGES amongst workers. This is where there is a large number of vacancies because individuals do not have the abilities, skills, experience or qualifications necessary to do the jobs which employers require. In March 2004 the Office for National Statistics published figures suggesting that the five highest ranked occupations with skills shortages were science and technology professionals and associate professionals, skilled construction and building trades, business and public service

---

Park Royal in west London is Europe's biggest industrial estate. There are 1,800 firms employing 40,000 people. But it demonstrates a lot that is wrong with the UK workforce. Manufacturing grew here by 11 per cent in 2002, the only place in London it expanded. But workers earn on average less than £12,000 a year. Most have only basic skills and some have none at all. A large number of recent immigrants work on the site. Many have English only as their second language. The older businesses which used to employ apprentices or train workers in a 'paternalistic way' have all moved, leaving a mass of smaller, often struggling, companies to fill the gaps.

People in the building industry also face problems. They can go to college to learn the basics of carpentry. But they can only qualify with work experience. However, many small firms won't take on unqualified workers to give them the experience they need.

Attempts to upgrade skills through training mean that people could earn more and the area might be regenerated. There is also a high degree of staff turnover. Reducing this would leave more money to pay higher wages.

Source: adapted from *People Management*, 12.6.2003.

(a) Examine the reasons why skills shortages might exist at Park Royal.
(b) Suggest how improving skills shortages might benefit businesses.

**Question 1**

---

professionals and skilled metal and electrical trades. Occupations which seemed less likely to have skills shortages included administration, sales and customer services.

# Identifying the need for training

How does a business know if training is required? One method might be to use the job description (☞ unit 64) to find the skills and knowledge needed to do the job. If there is a difference between the knowledge and skills of the employee and those actually required, this may indicate a need for training.

Employees can also be asked about areas where they feel their performance is inadequate, areas where they have problems, and any 'gaps' in their knowledge and skills. This should make them more committed to training. Training needs are found at different levels within a business.

● The organisational level. A business may need to train workers if there have been changes in a company's goals or objectives, or an introduction of new processes. For example, a move to 'Just-in-time' methods of stock control (☞ unit 82) may mean that workers must be able to constantly monitor stock. Training may also be needed as a result of company surveys or changes in the law. Sometimes workers find that their jobs no longer exist, due to changes in technology or reorganisation of the business for example. As a result, it may be necessary to **retrain** these workers in the knowledge and skills needed for completely new jobs.
● The departmental level. An indication of the need for training may come from personnel statistics, such as absence levels, turnover levels, production levels and customer complaints. Any differences between departments could show that training is needed.
● The individual level. At this level information from appraisal may be useful. Managers may also request that employees receive extra training. Increasingly, however, workers are identifying their own needs and designing their own personal development plans.

Once a need for training has been identified, a business must decide what skills and approaches should be achieved at the end of the training period. They may be something as simple as 'be able to replace a tyre'. There may also be some criteria to measure how well the trainee has learnt the skill, such as 'type a letter with no more than one mistake', and details on how to perform a task, such as 'always be polite and helpful when taking telephone calls'.

Training needs may be put together as a training or staff development plan. However, the business must take into account whether it has the financial resources to carry out the plan. This will depend on its **training budget**.

# The cost of training

Businesses faced with problems may see spending on training as a luxury which has to be cut. This is often the case in times of recession (☞ unit 96). For example, in the recession of 1991 in the UK the number of people receiving job-related training fell by 177,000 from the 1990 figure. Businesses often argue that training leads to increased costs, disruption, wasted time and more effort on their part. Financial costs might include the wage allowance paid to the employee, supervision costs, fees for training at a local college and equipment and travel allowances. To some extent these costs are offset by government payments for training schemes paid to the employer.

At one end of Park Royal in west London is a success story. Hazelwood Breadwinner employs 650 people making sandwiches for supermarkets, airlines and other retail outlets. Darrin Sinclair, the training manager, says 'The company does a fair amount of training' with help from the European Social Fund. But a tight budget prevents him doing as much as he would like. For instance, at £600 a head, the cost of putting people through the supervisor's exams is too much. So his 20 trainees will just get a certificate of participation.

Park Royal Partnership is a body set up by local employers to regenerate the area through improving transport, the environment, business advice and training. It has recently got together with local colleges and other umbrella organisations to break through the minefield of government funding, the shape it takes, the strings attached and the poor communication to providers.

In particular, training for adults has taken a back seat to training the unemployed and young people in the past. Furthermore, at the other end of the spectrum training and development has tended to focus on managers and professionals. Those who had skills tended to get even more. This left the low skilled in a twilight zone with few career prospects.

Source: adapted from *People Management*, 12.6.2003.

(a) Identify the barriers to training that exist using examples in the article.

## On-the-job and off-the-job training

The Spring 1998 Labour Force Survey showed that nearly 3.4 million employees of working age said that they had received job-related training in the four weeks before the survey. The figure for Spring 2002 was 3.9 million. Training is sometimes divided into two types. **On-the-job training** takes place when employees are trained while they are carrying out an activity, often at their place of work. **Off-the-job training** takes place away from the job at a different location. It may, for example, involve release from the job for periods of time to attend a course at a college. Table 67.1 shows information on the relative importance of on-the-job and off-the-job training.

**Table 67.1** *Employees of working age (16-64 males, 16-59 females) receiving job related training four weeks before before survey, Spring 2001, percentages of all employees of working age*

| | Percentages and hours | | |
|---|---|---|---|
| | Males | Females | All persons |
| Any job related training | 14.4% | 18.5% | 16.4% |
| On-the-job only | 4.7% | 5.5% | 5.1% |
| Off-the-job only | 6.8% | 9.5% | 8.1% |
| Both on- and off-the-job training | 2.9% | 3.6% | 3.2% |
| Average number of hours of training in the last week | 14.6hrs | 11.9hrs | 13.1hrs |

Source: adapted from *Labour Force Survey*, Office for National Statistics.

## Methods of training

Business may use a variety of training methods. Some might be carried out as the job is being done. Others might take place away from the job. Sometimes training may be a combination of training whilst doing the job and away from the place of work.

**Working next to another employee** This is a traditional type of on-the-job training sometimes referred to as 'sitting next to Nellie'. 'Nellie', the experienced worker, shows the trainee exactly what to do. It can vary from working next to a machine operator to travelling with a salesperson. One-to-one training like this has complications for a business. Where one employee is training another, the quality of the training will depend on the ability, willingness and time available to the tutor. Such training may mean that one employee does not 'produce' themselves, while they are training the other employee. In cases where a specialist is employed to train others, this can be costly for the business.

**Coaching** This is where a coach will guide the trainee through the use of the equipment or a process in the same way that swimmers are trained. An example might be a technician being trained how to operate a heart monitor whilst working in a hospital.

**Mentoring** This involves the trainee being 'paired' with a more experienced employee. The trainee carries out the job but uses the 'tutor' to discuss problems that may occur and how best to solve them

**Job rotation** In some large companies this has been used for the training of 'high fliers'. The employee works in different departments for short periods - picking up skills from each. The aim is that when the person is promoted and reaches the 'top' of the business, she will have a range of experiences which can be used.

**In-house courses** Businesses may put on courses for their achieve the standard can display a plaque, which is valid for a certain period.

# Evaluation of training

As businesses have demanded greater value for money, it has become important to evaluate training. Evaluation is simple when the result of the training is clear to see, such as when training workers to use new technology. Where training is designed to give a certain result, such as:

- a health and safety course;
- a word processing course;
- a design course;

evaluation can be based on observed results. This may be a reduction in accidents, increased typing speed or designs with greater impact.

It is more difficult to evaluate the success of a management training course or a programme of social skills development. It is usual to use end of course questionnaires, where course members answer a number of questions. The problem is that the course will have been a break for most employees from the normal work routine. This can make the participants' view of training appear of more value than it is. Also questionnaires tend to evaluate the course and not the learning. This often means that the person attending the course is assessing the quality of the tutors and visual aids, instead of what has been learnt.

To overcome these problems a business might:

- ask participants and managers to complete a short questionnaire at the start of the course to focus their minds on what they hope to get from it;
- give out another questionnaire at the end of the course focusing on learning and what could be applied back at the job;
- give further questionnaires to review the effects of the course on performance.

This helps employees to concentrate on what has been learnt. This process may, however, be costly for the business.

# Appraisal

After a period of time working in a job (and regularly after), a firm may APPRAISE the employee. This is an attempt by the business to find out the qualities, usefulness or worth of its employees.

Appraisal can be used by a business to:

- improve performance;
- provide feedback;
- increase motivation;
- identify training needs;
- identify potential for promotion;
- award salary increases;
- set out job objectives;
- provide information for human resource planning;
- assess the effectiveness of the selection process.

The problem with having all of these aims is that the person carrying out the appraisal may have conflicting roles. If

appraisal is designed to help performance and to act as a basis for salary awards, the appraiser would have to be both judge and helper at the same time. This makes it difficult to be impartial. It is also difficult for the person being appraised. A worker may want to discuss problems, but is likely to be cautious about what they say in case they jeopardise any possible pay rise. One way around this is for the appraisal system to review the performance of the worker only.

Many appraisal schemes have been linked to **performance appraisal**, called **performance management**. This involves observing, measuring and developing the performance of employees. Performance can be 'measured' against criteria such as output, quality and speed.

# Carrying out appraisal

Appraisal has, in the past, been seen as most suitable for employees in management and supervisory positions. Increasingly, clerical, secretarial and manual staff, with skilled or technical jobs, are also being appraised.

Who carries out the appraisal? There is a number of people that might be involved in appraising an individual. Appraisers may be referred to as **raters**. These are people who 'rate' the performance of an individual.

- Superiors. Most appraisals are carried out by the employee's superior. The advantage of this is that the supervisor usually has intimate knowledge of the tasks that a worker has been carrying out and how well they have been done.
- People 'above' the immediate superior can be involved in appraisal in two different ways. They may 'approve' the superior's appraisal of the employee. A manager further up the hierarchy may also directly carry out the appraisal. This is more likely to happen when individuals decide if a worker has the potential for promotion, for example.
- Self appraisal. This is a relatively new idea and not greatly used. Individuals do carry out self appraisal in traditional appraisal schemes, although the superior's decision officially 'counts'. The ratings that the employer has given may be changed, however, in the light of the employee's comments.
- Peer appraisal. It is sometimes argued that appraisal by peers is reliable and valid as they have a more comprehensive view of the employee's job performance. The main problem, though, is that peers may be unwilling to appraise each other. This can be seen as 'grassing'.
- Subordinates. Appraisal by subordinates is another less well used method. It is limited, as subordinates will only know certain aspects of the work of other employees.
- 360 degrees appraisal. This method gathers ratings from a combination of supervisors, peers and subordinates. Self-ratings and customer ratings may also be used. It provides feedback to individuals on how their performance is viewed by business stakeholders (☞ unit 3). It also encourages individuals to self-diagnose their strong and weak areas and identifies where training is needed. The information from 360 degrees appraisal can help a business when making personnel decisions, such as who to

choose for promotion.

Many firms have used appraisal systems only to find that they have to change or abandon them after a short time. Others 'battle' on with the system, but recognise that it is inadequate or disliked. What factors influence the success of an appraisal system?

- Purpose of the system. Effectiveness will be greater if all involved are clear about what the system is for.
- Control. It is vital that the system is controlled by senior and line management and isn't something done simply 'for the personnel department'.
- Openness and participation. The more feedback that appraisees are given about their ratings, the more likely they are to accept the process. Similarly, the more the employee is allowed to take part in the system, the greater the chance of gaining their commitment.
- Appraisal criteria. The criteria must be related to the job, be easy to use and appear fair to the worker.
- Training. Training may be needed in how to appraise and how to conduct interviews.
- Administrative efficiency. Appraisal must be carried out so that it causes as few problems as possible for both parties. It also needs to be confidential.
- Action. Appraisal needs to be supported by follow-up action. Plans that are agreed by appraiser and workers must be checked, to make sure they take place.
- Selection of raters. The choice of rater should be carefully controlled to avoid, for example, individuals nominating only 'friendly raters' to provide them with feedback.
- Anonymity of raters. Ratings should be made anonymously to encourage honest appraisal.
- Training of raters. Raters should be trained to complete rating and appraisal forms accurately.

## Is training becoming more popular?

Ashton and Felstead (2003), in their review of research on training in the UK, suggested a number of reasons to explain the evidence of increased training in the UK over the last five years.

- There has been an improvement in the UK's skills base due to the investment by government to increase numbers in higher education.
- Some employers have played their part in improving skills. Companies with Investors in People and a commitment to training are now training all staff, including the unskilled. This has resulted in the general upskilling of employees in business.
- A group of businesses now state that strategic human resource management is central to business development, and that training is part of that strategy. In addition, a small group of 'leading edge' or high performance organisations use employees' skills as a source of competitive advantage.

However, a group of UK businesses is still not committed to training. They only engage in formal training when they are forced, either by government legislation or customer requirements. For example, some manufacturing firms can only become suppliers to large retail firms when they obtain ISO 9000. Some argue, therefore, that the UK still appears to be struggling to catch up with competitors in Europe in its investment in training. They also suggest that it may be falling behind new competitors from South East Asia.

Pettersford plc is a manufacturer of plastic cartons and other containers. It has a number of plants around the UK. In 2002 it faced rising costs and falling productivity. The business had previously used annual appraisal methods. Every year employees were reviewed to discuss their performance over the year. It was often one a way communication process, with the line manager 'telling' the employee why they had done well or badly, and how they might improve next year. At the end of the appraisal, employees were asked to make their own comments. But only a short time was left for this and usually the employee could not remember issues that had arisen up to 12 months previously.

Faced with the possibility of closure, the business introduced a quarterly performance review for all its factories. It did allow this to be amended if a plant felt that it did not want four, but the business was adamant that it need to get away from the annual reviews. Another change was that each employee nominated two of their work colleagues to comment on their work. At first people were reluctant to criticise, but eventually, as people became more comfortable with the system, the business and employees found constructive criticism and praise useful. The dialogue also had to be more of a two way process, so that employees could express their own views.

The appraisal was backed up by regular meetings with managers, where suggestions at the appraisal could be introduced into the work environment. Employees gave a 'personal commitment' at their review and this was implemented with the help of the line manager and senior staff. Employees also felt that they could take more initiative, by making suggestions at appraisal meetings. Previously they had simply 'keep their heads down' hoping to get it all over quickly.

The business found that productivity rose as a result of the changes. One spokesperson said 'If you give people some recognition for their work, and listen to what they have to say in return, then it's not only the employee who benefits'.

(a) Explain the problems that existed in the old method of appraisal at Pettersford plc.
(b) Identify the methods of appraisal in the new system.
(c) Discuss the advantages and disadvantages of the new appraisal system for (i) employees and (ii) the business.

**Question 5**

## key terms

**Appraisal** - evaluating the usefulness of the employee to the business.
**Induction** - the introduction of a new employee to the business.
**Labour market failure** - the inability of the market to allocate resources, in this case labour, optionally.
**Skills shortages** - where potential employees do not have the skills demanded by employers.

Knowledge...Knowledge...Knowledge

1. Briefly explain the purpose of induction.
2. Why is training important to a business?
3. Give 5 aims of training.
4. State 4 methods which could be used to identify training needs.
5. What is the difference between on-the-job and off-the-job training?
6. Briefly explain 3 methods of off-the-job training.
7. How can training be evaluated?
8. What is meant by performance appraisal?
9. How can appraisal help a business?
10. Who might carry out appraisal in a business?

## Case study INA Bearing Company

In 2001 INA Bearing Company, a Welsh Engineering plant, embarked on a programme of change with retraining at the forefront. Low cost competition from eastern Europe had meant that the factory, which makes engine components, had cut its workforce by 500 since the early 1990s. Faced with the possibility of closure, the management decided to transform the factory into a 'production location of choice' for high tech products by boosting the skills of its remaining workforce. This required a huge amount of investment training and development to create a culture of continuous improvement.

Getting the workforce back to learning while operating around the clock was no small challenge. Time and resources were limited because manufacturing output had to be maintained. Employees had also become cynical about training initiatives in the past which had faltered. The suggestion put to employees was that 'even if this place does close' they now would have better skills and a marketable and portable qualification which would help then to be attractive elsewhere.

The business initially brought in a 5S training programme (sort, straighten, sweep, standardise, self-discipline) to improve the work environment. At the end of training, the workforce told management the areas in which they would enhance the environment. This led to improvements in productivity, quality and health and safety.

The company started an NVQ programme back in 1998, but this did not get off the ground. It was suggested that 'supervisors were left to do the assessing, but they did not have the time, commitment or will so nothing

was done'. So the programme was relaunched. All 200 operators now worked towards NVQ level two in performing manufacturing operations. A local technical college was brought in to provide supervision of the course.

Team leaders also faced problems. They were spending too much time on machines and not enough on their leadership roles. So they were trained in communication skills for team leaders, taking an NVQ level three in management.

INA is committed to employees taking charge of their own learning. It has set up a learning centre at the plant. Employees can now make use of access Learndirect courses and 100 people have signed up for them.

Source: adapted from *People Management*, 6.11.2003.

**(a)** **Identify the reasons why retraining was necessary at the business. (4 marks)**
**(b)** **Explain why the original NVQ programme could have failed. (4 marks)**
**(c)** **Using examples, explain the types of:**
   **(i) on-the-job training;**
   **(ii) off-the-job training;**
   **(iii) e-learning;**
   **that might have taken place at the business.**
   **(12 marks)**
**(d)** **Examine the advantages of training for:**
   **(i) employees at the business;**
   **(ii) the business itself. (10 marks)**
**(e)** **Assess possible training methods that might be effective for a business operating for 24 hours a day. (10 marks)**

## What are equal opportunities?

Units 64 and 65 explained the methods used to recruit and select candidates. Choosing one candidate rather than another is known as DISCRIMINATION. If a man is chosen rather than a woman, when they are both equally qualified, the business has discriminated in favour of the man and against the woman.

Some discrimination is legal and may be considered reasonable. For example, a business may choose a candidate for the post of quality controller in a meat factory because he has 10 years experience, rather than a school leaver. However, if another person with experience did not get the job because she was a woman, or from an ethnic minority, this is illegal in the UK. It could also be said to be unreasonable. The rest of the unit will use the term discrimination in this way. Discrimination occurs not only in selection, but areas such as training, promotion and wages.

EQUAL OPPORTUNITIES mean that everyone has the same chance. In other words, a candidate or employee is not discriminated against because of their sex or race. UK legislation helps to promote this. So do EU laws. These are examples of **individual labour laws** aimed at protecting individuals at work. **Collective labour laws** deal with legislation affecting employee groups such as trade unions (☞ units 73-75).

Why are businesses concerned about equal opportunities? Giving everyone the same chance can affect the productivity, costs and organisation of a business.

## Reasons for discrimination

There are certain groups of individuals in society and in business that are arguably discriminated against. Such groups may include:
- women;
- people from ethnic minorities;
- disabled people;
- older people.

Discrimination may occur because of **unproven** ideas or stereotypes about certain groups, such as the following examples.
- Women might not want to take too much responsibility at work because of home commitments; women who are married are less likely to want to be relocated; women with children may be less reliable than men because their main responsibility is to their children.
- Members of certain ethnic minority groups could be difficult to employ because of problems with religious holidays.
- A person in a wheelchair may be less capable than a non-

disabled person.
- Older people may be less adaptable, are not interested in coping with new technology and might work more slowly.

All these and many other unproven ideas can affect the way people view these groups during recruitment and selection, and when they are employed.

## Women at work

Women form a large and increasing proportion of the working population. In 1979 women accounted for around 38 per cent of all people of working age in employment. By 2003, this had risen to nearly 44 per cent. There is still evidence to suggest that women are discriminated against in the work force.
- There are differences between the earnings of men and women. In 2003 the average hourly earnings of men were £10.04 per hour. For women it was £8.21 per hour.
- Certain industries, such as construction, and certain occupations, such as managers and senior officials, still tend to have male majorities. This is shown in Figure 68.1. In the UK women hold less than one in ten of the top positions in FTSE 100 companies, the police, the judiciary and trade unions.
- Occupations in which women are mainly employed tend to be low paid. Male dominated occupations tend to be more highly paid. For example, in 2002, 75 per cent of working women were in the five lowest paid sectors. In engineering and construction, 97 per cent of modern apprentices are men, earning £115 a week. In social care, 89 per cent of apprentices are women, earning around £60 a week.
- In 2003, 57 per cent of women in employment worked full time. For men, the figure was 91 per cent.
- The rate of employment amongst women with children under five is 54 per cent compared to 72 per cent for women with no children. This perhaps suggests the problem finding jobs for women with young children.

On the other hand, it could be argued that the differences between men and women at work are getting smaller.
- There has been a growth in women's employment opportunities in recent years. The need for a more flexible workforce, equal opportunities legislation, demographic changes and the awareness of the role of women in the workforce have meant that business increasingly look to women to fill vacancies.
- Having children is perhaps less of a constraint than it used to be. Some businesses offer creche facilities or allow work at home to encourage women workers with children. Some women choose to pursue a career instead of having children or return to work after childbirth. Women are remaining in education longer or returning to study. This makes them more qualified for higher grade posts.
- The 'gender gap' in activity rates is getting smaller. The

not to employ the worker. However, employers must make 'reasonable' adjustments for disabled workers. These are adjustments that involve relatively little cost or disruption. They might include:

- changing fixtures, fittings, furniture and equipment, such as modified telephones for people with hearing difficulties or workstations for people in wheel chairs;
- improving access to a building, such as adding a ramp for a wheelchair user;
- changing building features, such as braille in a lift to help a visually impaired employee;
- changing work conditions, such as allowing absences for treatment;
- providing extra training.

**The Disability Rights Commission** The Disability Rights Commission (DRC) is an independent body established by government to eliminate discrimination against disabled people. Its main roles involve:

- providing advice and information for disabled employees, including a helpline;
- supporting disabled people to gain their rights under legislation as well as legal cases;
- organising conferences, campaigns and events to change the law and business policy to protect disabled people;
- providing an independent conciliation service for disabled people.

It also produces a code of practice which outlines the rights of

employees under legislation and how business can meet these requirements.

## Older people

There is evidence to suggest that older people are discriminated against.

- Employment rates fall as people get older, as shown in Figure 68.5. The employment rate is the percentage of the population in a given age group in employment.
- Older workers are more likely to be working part time. This is particularly the case for people over state retirement age. For example, 91 per cent of men aged 16-64 are employed full time compared to just 35 per cent of men aged over 65. For women, 57 per cent aged 16-59 are employed full time compared to 25 per cent working part time. This might be because of choice. But it might also be because employers are less willing to take on older workers full time.
- Older people are less likely to receive training. In 2003, employees aged 16-19 were over twice as likely to have participated in job-related training than those aged 50-59/64.

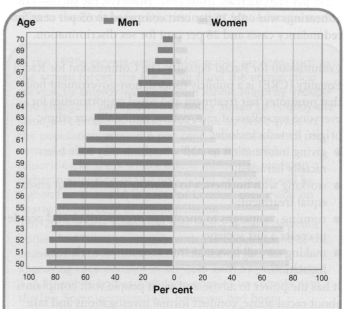

**Figure 68.5** *Employment rates of people aged 50-70 by gender, UK, Spring 2003*
Source: adapted from Labour Force Survey.

## Legislation and guidance

In the past, the main protection for older employees was against redundancy (☞ unit 66). For example, if they were made redundant they were often entitled to severance pay. In difficult periods, older people may be the first to be made redundant. They are sometimes persuaded to accept voluntary redundancy by taking early retirement.

There was also no specific protection against age discrimination when seeking employment and in training or promotion. However, cases taken to an employment tribunal have been won using sex or race discrimination in relation to

---

Val Miles was paralysed from the chest down after a skiing accident. She has now started to work full time again after rehabilitation. But she experienced problems at some of her interviews. In one case, she gave a presentation to the tops of the heads of two interviewers, who were so uncomfortable about making eye contact they looked down all the time. She was so ill at ease she performed badly. At other interviews she has arrived to be told 'there are only a few steps up to the front door'. She has also had to travel long distances to find there is no disabled parking. And some businesses are keen to interview a disabled candidate just so they can meet equal opportunities requirements.

Her experience working for the National Glass Centre has been far better. The interview went well. She was escorted to the lift and shown the disabled toilets. The business operates from a new purpose built building with disabled access.

Source: adapted from *People Management*, 24.1.2002.

(a) Identify discrimination that might have taken place in the article.
(b) Explain how the businesses in the article might make 'reasonable' adjustments to prevent discrimination against disabled people.

age. For example, a case by an employee against the Civil Service bar on people aged over 32 was judged to discriminate against black people, since black employees were older than white employees at the time due to adult immigration.

The EU **Employment Framework Directive** obliges all EU member states to introduce laws preventing age discrimination by 2006. There will, however, be some circumstances where discrimination will be permitted, for example where safety is an issue or to recruit younger workers when a number of employees are nearing retirement age.

Some argue that there are actually advantages to a business in employing workers 'over 40'.
- The over 40s have greater experience and better judgement in decision-making.
- The over 40s have already satisfied many of their needs for salary and status and are able to concentrate more on job responsibilities.
- The over 40s have a greater 'social intelligence' and the ability to understand and influence others.

B&Q, the chain of DIY stores, has recognised the benefits of employing older people, and has adopted a policy of hiring over 50s in its stores.

## Why might businesses have equal opportunities policies?

Certain businesses operate an **equal opportunities policy**. This means that the business is committed to giving all applicants an equal chance of, say, selection, no matter what their sex, sexuality, race, age, marital status, religion or disability. The aim of such a policy is to remove discrimination in all areas of the business, including promotion, training and financial rewards, so that the culture of the organisation is not to exclude any employees whatever their race, colour, nationality or gender. Examples of employers that operate such a policy have included Ford and Kingfisher the retail group.

How will such a policy affect business?
- A business is far more likely to employ the 'best' person for the job if everyone is given an equal opportunity. The quality of applicants may also improve.
- Equal opportunities for training are likely to lead to a better qualified workforce in key positions, although the cost of training could increase.
- Workers may become better motivated if, for example, the chances of promotion are equal. They are also more likely to remain with the business, reducing staff turnover and costs.
- Production may need to be reorganised. This might include more flexible hours, job rotation or even job sharing. For example, an office job could be carried out by a mother in the morning (when children are at school) and by a male in the afternoon. A more flexible workforce may be better able to respond to change.
- There may be extra wage costs. Paying women equal wages

to men will raise the total wage bill.
- Extra facilities may be needed. This can vary from ramps for wheelchairs to children's creches.
- Recruitment, selection and training procedures may have to change.
- The image of the business or jobs in it may have to change. This could improve the image to the customer. Rank Xerox, for example, found that jobs in the business were often seen

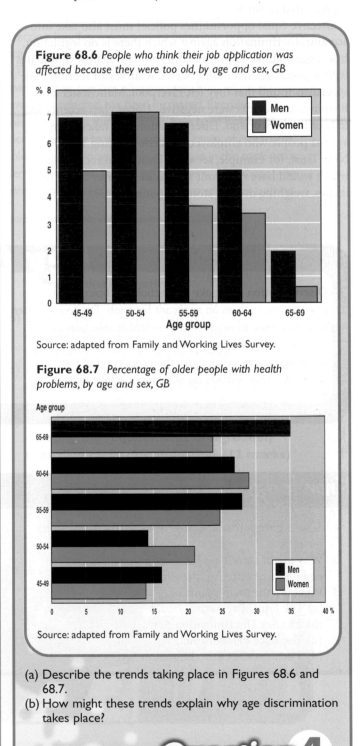

**Figure 68.6** *People who think their job application was affected because they were too old, by age and sex, GB*

Source: adapted from Family and Working Lives Survey.

**Figure 68.7** *Percentage of older people with health problems, by age and sex, GB*

Source: adapted from Family and Working Lives Survey.

(a) Describe the trends taking place in Figures 68.6 and 68.7.
(b) How might these trends explain why age discrimination takes place?

**Question4**

## Why is protection needed?

Why might a business protect its employees? There are certain laws protecting people in the workplace. Legislation has laid down rules about:

- health and safety;
- employment protection (dismissal, redundancy and leave of absence);
- wage protection;
- recruitment, selection and training (☞ units 64-67).
- data about employees.

This legislation provides guidelines and acts as a constraint on how a business makes decisions. In addition, from a purely practical point of view, it makes sense for a business to protect its workers. Satisfied employees are far more likely to help a business achieve its goals. A business may also feel it has a moral obligation to protect employees. As their employer, it should look after their interests in the workplace.

## Health and safety at work

Providing a healthy and safe environment can mean many things. It could include some of the following.

- Providing and maintaining safety equipment and clothing.
- Maintaining workplace temperatures.
- Ensuring adequate work space.
- Ensuring adequate washing and toilet facilities.
- Guaranteeing hygienic and safe conditions.
- Providing breaks in the work timetable.
- Providing protection for the use of hazardous substances.
- Providing protection from violence, threats or bullying.
- Providing a relatively stress free environment.

It is likely that the conditions for a healthy and safe environment will vary depending on the nature of the task carried out. Ensuring the health and safety of a mine worker will require different decisions by a business from protecting an office worker. Although both must be protected from adverse effects of equipment, for example, protection is likely to be different.

Businesses must protect people outside the workplace who might be affected by activities within it, eg those living near a chemical or industrial plant. They must also protect visitors or customers to shops or premises.

## Health and safety legislation

In the UK, laws to protect employees have been passed for over 100 years. There are also many regulations concerning health and safety at work which are updated from time to time as work conditions change. In addition, businesses may follow codes of practice designed to protect workers.

**The Health and Safety at Work Act, 1974** The aim of the **Health and Safety at Work Act, 1974** is to raise the standard of safety and health for all individuals at work, and to protect the public whose safety may be put at risk by the activities of people at work.

Every employer is required to prepare a written statement of their general policy on health and safety. Employees must be advised of what the policy is. Management have the main responsibility for carrying out the policy. In the case of negligence, proceedings can be taken against an individual manager as well as against the business. The Act also places a duty on employees while they are at work to take reasonable care for the safety of themselves and others. The employee is legally obliged to comply with the safety rules drawn up by management. Employers or employees who fail to comply can be taken to court and fined. Part of the Act requires a business to give training, information, instruction and supervision to ensure the health and safety at work of employees.

The Act is backed up by the Health and Safety Executive (HSE) and the Health and Safety Commission (HSC), which are responsible for seeing that the Act is carried out. Health and safety inspectors are appointed to make sure the law is being carried out. They have the power to enter employers' premises, carry out examinations and investigations, take measurements, photographs and recordings, take equipment and materials and examine books and documents. The HSE/HSC have the power to issue **codes of practice** to protect people in various situations, for example:

- the protection of individuals against ionising radiation;
- the control of lead pollution at work;
- time off for training of safety representatives;
- control of substances hazardous to health (various).

The Health and Safety at Work Act is the main Act which allows new regulations to be brought in as appropriate.

**UK and EU regulations** There is a number of regulations relating to health and safety in the UK. Regulations are introduced to cope with new work situations. Increasingly UK regulations are influenced by European Union (EU) directives, which are agreed by member countries of the EU.

The **Working Time Regulations, 1998** were important regulations introduced into the UK as a result of an EU directive which addressed concerns over the problems caused by long work hours. They provided a number of rights for most employees including:

- a maximum working week of 48 hours a week;
- 4 weeks annual paid leave a year;
- 11 consecutive hours' rest in any 24 hour period;
- a 20 minute rest break after 6 hours' work;
- a limit of an average 8 hours' work in any 24 hours for night workers.

The regulations were amended in 2003 to include some groups that were previously excluded, such as 'non-mobile workers in road, rail and sea transport'. In 2003 the UK was the only EU country with an opt-out clause, which allowed employees to work longer than the 48 hour a week limit if they and their employer both agree.

Table 69.1 shows some examples of regulations which affect UK and EU businesses.

---

**Table 69.1** *UK/EU health and safety regulations*

**Manual Handling Operations Regulations, 1992 (Directive 90/269/EEC)** Relate to the transport and handling of loads.

**Workplace (Health, Safety and Welfare) Regulations, 1992 (Directive 89/654/EEC)** Relate to the requirements of conditions at work, such as maintenance, ventilation, space and rest facilities.

**Personal Protective Equipment at Work Regulations, 1992 (Directive 89/656/EEC)** Relate to protective clothing and equipment.

**Health and Safety (Display Screen Equipment) Regulations, 1992 (Directive 90/270/EEC)** Relate to the use of computer screens.

**Safe Use of Work Equipment, Provision and Use of Work Equipment Regulations, 1998 (Directive 89/655/EEC)** Relate to the safe use of equipment and machinery.

**The Management of Health and Safety at Work Regulations, 1999 (Directive 89/391/EEC)** Relate to the assessment of risk and the implementation of health and safety arrangements to keep employees safe.

**The Maternity and Parental Leave Regulations, 1999 (Directive 96/34/EEC)** Relate to time off work for mothers and fathers when children are born.

**Control of Asbestos at Work Regulations, 2002** Relate to the assessment and control of risk associated with asbestos on premises.

**The Control of Substances Hazardous to Health Regulations, 2003** Relate to the handling, use and control of substances used in production which might affect the health of workers, such as nuclear fuel or chemicals.

---

## Employment protection

Unit 66 showed that employees are entitled to a contract of employment when they are first appointed to a job. The contract of employment is an agreement between the employer and the employee on the terms and conditions under which the employee will work. An employee may be able to claim for a breach of contract by the employer. Employees are also protected by legislation against discrimination (☞ unit 68).

The **Employment Relations Act, 1999** stated that employees who have worked for an employer for a year had a right not to be unfairly dismissed. It also aimed to introduce 'family friendly policies', such as parental leave for people adopting a child, and to remove limits on awards for unfair dismissal. Certain people cannot claim unfair dismissal, such as an independent contractor or freelance agent, who are not employees.

There is a number of reasons why employees might be dismissed which may be **unfair** dismissal under the conditions of the Act (and its amendments).

- Because they were trying to become or were a member of a trade union. Alternatively, because they refused to join or make payments to a union.
- On the grounds of pregnancy, even though she was able to do the job.

---

**New and expectant mothers**
The Department of Trade and Industry has estimated that there are around 350,000 pregnant women at work in the UK. More than one in four experience a miscarriage, one in 200 babies are stillborn and 100 premature babies are born each year. In 2001, out of 1,434 potential tribunal cases involving pregnancy or maternity related discrimination, 95 per cent involved some breach of health and safety legislation.

**Work related road travellers**
Every year 3,5000 people are killed and 40,000 are seriously injured according to the Health and Safety Executive. Over a thousand of those killed and 13,000 of those injured involve people at work. They include drivers of heavy goods vehicles, company cars and vans, and dispatch riders who ride bikes or motorcycles.

Employers have a legal duty under The Management of Health and Safety at Work Regulations, 1999. They must assess the risk to employees and carry out measures to ensure their protection. Certain groups of workers have been identified as at risk at work.

Source: adapted from *Labour Research*, March, November, 2003.

(a) Explain why these groups might be most at risk at work.
(b) Suggest ways in which businesses could protect the groups mentioned above.

**Question 1**

- Making workers redundant without following the correct procedure. This is dealt with later.
- As a result of a transfer of a business, such as when one business is bought by another. However, if the business can prove it was for economic, technical or organisational reasons, it may be considered fair.
- For refusing to work on a Sunday. The **Sunday Trading Act, 1994** gives shop workers the right not to be dismissed for refusing to work on Sundays.

There are reasons why dismissal may be **fair**. The employer must have a valid reason and must act 'reasonably' when dealing with this reason.

- The employee is incapable of doing the job or is unqualified.
- 'Misconduct' of the employee, such as persistent lateness (minor) or theft (major).
- The employer is unable to employ the worker. For example, a lorry driver may no longer be employed if he has lost his driving licence.
- Any other substantial reason. For example, false

# The Social Chapter

The European Union's Social Chapter is an attempt to encourage minimum wages and conditions of work in member countries. It was argued that a business may attempt to respond to falling profits or greater competition by cutting costs. This could lead to poor pay and work conditions for employees. To prevent this, member countries outlined an agreement which covered such areas as:

- a limit on hours of work;
- 'fair and reasonable' rewards;
- minimum wages;
- free collective bargaining;
- access to training;
- workers' involvement in company decision making;
- health and safety;
- union recognition;
- equal opportunities.

The UK signed up to the EU Social Chapter in 1997, with the election of a Labour government. The previous Conservative government argued that the conditions:

- restricted a business's ability to reduce wages when necessary;
- did not allow a business to be flexible when employing workers and making them redundant;
- would increase costs.

When the UK signed up, UK laws would have to be changed to comply with the conditions of the Social Chapter. For example, the number of hours to be worked by most employees must be limited to 48 hours, part time and full time workers would be given equal rights, and employees would have a right to paid holidays each year. Other changes would include the introduction of **European works councils (EWC)** in businesses, to negotiate workers' wages with employers, and the setting of a minimum wage as discussed in the previous section.

# Data protection

Businesses keep large amounts of data about their employees. Even small businesses will keep basic information about the earnings of employees and deductions such as pension payments. They might even keep a record of the number of days absent from work.

Large public limited companies will have a huge amount of information about the many employees who work for the organisation. This might include numerical information such as salaries. It might also include written reports, such as an annual review of an employee's progress written by his or her manager. Their application forms are also likely to be kept on record, as well as any disciplinary procedures that have been carried out as a result of their behaviour at work.

Much of the data held by businesses about employees is sensitive, personal information. Increasingly it is being stored on computer files or disks. Businesses must make sure that this information is protected so that it is only available to

---

In 2003 Black & Decker, the tool manufacturing company, introduced software which would allow it to monitor e-mails sent by its employees. A spokesperson for the company said that it had become increasingly aware of the dangers of e-mail misuse as it raises serious issues regarding employee productivity, corporate privacy and legal liability. The software, Mailmeter, will allow the company to generate reports about the amount of e-mail traffic and the domain names of the computers sending and receiving e-mails, without reading the content of e-mails. It is often suggested that using such software helps IT departments to adhere to the law regarding employee privacy.

However, if the business does deem it necessary to analyse e-mail content for disciplinary procedures it must be aware of the data protection law. It must follow strict guidelines if any use of information that is found is to be considered lawful.

Source: adapted from *Computer Weekly*, 28.4.2003.

(a) Explain ways in which the use of the software by Black & Decker might:
   (i) help it comply with the law relating to the protection of employees;
   (ii) lead to the breaking of the law regarding the protection of employees.

Question 4

those with the authority to see it.

The **Data Protection Act, 1998** protects information about employees which is kept by businesses. Any business processing data about employees must comply with a number of principles. There are eight principles put in place to make sure that the information is handled properly. They say that data must be:

- fairly and lawfully processed;
- processed for limited purposes;
- adequate, relevant and not excessive;
- accurate;
- not kept for longer than is necessary;
- processed in line with employees' rights;
- secure;
- not transferred to countries without adequate protection.

Employees have the right to see information that employers keep about them under the Act. They can also request that incorrect information is removed, prevent the processing of information under certain circumstances, stop direct marketing to themselves using the information and claim compensation for misuse.

# To what extent will a business protect its employees?

There are strong arguments to support the protection of

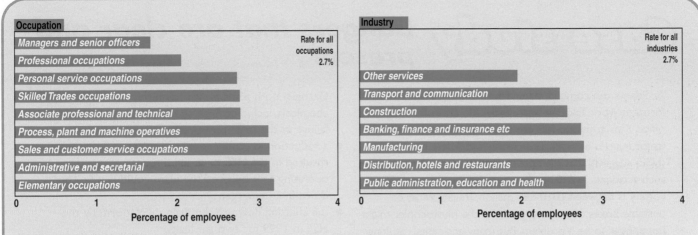

**Figure 69.2** *Percentage of employees absent from work for at least one day in the reference week due to sickness or injury, by occupation and industry, UK, summer 2003, not seasonally adjusted*
Source: adapted from *Labour Force Survey*.

cmployees by their employers.

● Businesses that protect their employees are likely to have a healthy and motivated workforce, free from accidents, injury and illness.

● A business which breaks the law may be ordered to pay compensation and fined. Over the period 1993-2003 a TUC report stated that unions had won over £3 billion injury compensation for workers. In 2001, £305 million was paid out in injury cases for over 39,000 employees.

● The loss of employees due to lack of protection may require costly recruitment of new employees.

● The work of injured employees may need to be covered by part time employees, which is an extra cost.

● Employees off sick or injured may cause disruption, lost production, the missing of deadlines or serious delays. The Labour Force Survey estimated that 40.2 million days were lost pcr ycar due to workplace injury in 2002 compared to 23.9 million in 1998. In 2003, around 3 per cent of all employees reported at least one day's absence. The number of days lost due to sickness or illness in the UK in different occupations and industries is shown in Figure 69.2.

● Poor work conditions may affect the productivity of employees and the business, and profits.

● Businesses that do not protect employees may get a poor reputation, which could affect the quality of future applicants.

However, some businesses still fail to protect their employees adequately. Perhaps the main reason for this is the cost involved in protection. Buying safety equipment, changing work practices to ensure safety, setting up safety courses, ensuring legislation is met, and filling in the many forms associated with ensuring safety are time consuming and costly activities. Small businesses in particular find it difficult to keep up with constant changes in safety laws and requirements. They might even decide that it is worth taking the risk that accidents will not occur or that they will not be found out breaking the law. As long as these things do not happen, they can save money by not spending to protect their workers completely.

*Knowledge* ...owledge... *Knowledge*... *Knowledge*... *Knowledge*... *Know*

1. State 5 types of health and safety dangers that may exist in business.
2. Briefly explain 3 pieces of legislation regarding health and safety at work.
3. Under what circumstances might dismissal be:
   (a) fair;
   (b) unfair?
4. What is the role of an industrial tribunal in protecting the employee at work?
5. 'An employee without a strong case for unfair dismissal may face problems if a tribunal finds against them.' Explain this statement.
6. State 2 pieces of legislation affecting the wages of employees in UK businesses.
7. What does the European Social Chapter aim to achieve?
8. Discuss 2 effects that signing the Social Chapter may have on the business of a country that signed the agreement.
9. What is meant by data protection?
10. State 3 advantages to a business of protecting its workers.

## Assessment criteria/objectives

It is possible to use a range of criteria when assessing the performance of students. This means that examiners or assessors want students to demonstrate a range of different skills. In order to be successful students must:

- understand the skills required by examiners or assessors;
- recognise the skill that is being assessed in a particular question;
- demonstrate all of the skills assessed by the examiner;
- practice skills before the examination.

The criteria used by examiners may fall into the following categories.

**Knowledge** Students have to demonstrate that they:

- understand business theories and concepts;
- recognise and understand business terms;
- interpret information given in a business context.

Students can recognise questions which test knowledge by looking at the command words in the question. Such words are explained in the section above. An example of a question assessing knowledge might be: *What is meant by best practice benchmarking?*

**Application and understanding** This assessment criterion requires students to apply theories and concepts in both familiar and unfamiliar situations. This might involve:

- using a business formula in appropriate circumstances, for example, calculating the current ratio for a business;
- using a theory to explain why a business has chosen a particular course of action, for example, using McGregor's Theory Y to explain why a business has introduced quality circles;
- using a business theory to suggest a suitable course of action for a business, for example, suggesting a chainstore uses loyalty cards to increase repeat sales.

Questions requiring application can again be recognised by looking at the command word. An example of a question requiring application might be: *Explain why the business has cut its research and development budget.*

**Analysis** Students have to demonstrate that they can break down information and understand the implications of what they have been presented with. Students will encounter both qualitative and quantitative information and will need to:

- identify causes and effects and interrelationships, for example, recognise from a graph that sales are falling and could be a result of new competition in the market;
- break down information to identify specific causes or problems, for example, realise that a business is suffering

from inefficiency because according to the information staff motivation has fallen, equipment is worn and working practices are outdated;

- use appropriate techniques to analyse data, for example, use ratio analysis to assess the solvency of a business;
- use appropriate theories, business cases/practices to investigate the question, for example, use elasticity theory to show that raising price may be ineffective.

Questions requiring analysis can be recognised by looking at the command word. An example of a question requiring analysis might be: *Examine the factors which have influenced the firm's decision to close its Cardiff factory.*

**Evaluation** Evaluation involves making a judgment. Evaluation questions are often used to award the highest grades in examinations. Students might be expected to:

- show judgment in weighing up the relative importance of different points or sides of an argument, in order to reach a conclusion;
- comment on the reliability of information or evidence;
- distinguish between fact and opinion;
- distinguish between relevant and irrelevant information;
- draw conclusions from the evidence presented;
- show judgment on the wider issues and implications.

Questions requiring evaluation can be identified by looking at the command word. For example, *To what extent has the decision to delayer the business been successful?*

When evaluating it is often possible for a student to draw a number of different conclusions. Examiners may be less concerned with the particular conclusion drawn. Very often in business studies there is no 'right' answer. They are more interested in whether students have actually made a judgment and also the quality of their argument in support of the judgment.

**Synthesis** Opportunities to demonstrate this particular skill may be limited. Synthesis is required in long written answers such as essays, project work or report writing. It involves bringing together a wide range of information in a clear and meaningful way. In particular, students must:

- develop points and themes in a way which builds on previous material and ends with a rounded conclusion;
- produce an argument in a logical sequence;
- provide a clear summarised argument which draws on all the individual elements.

Examiners will tend to look for evidence of synthesis in essays and report writing questions. The sections below on essay writing and report writing will explain how students can demonstrate synthesis.

**Quality of language** Codes of Practice may require the assessment of candidates' quality of language wherever they

answering than shorter data response questions.

- The case material tends to be hypothetical but usually based on a real life situation.
- The case material tends to focus on a single business.
- The volume of material given is much greater.
- There tends to be some financial information in the case material.
- The case often emphasises analysis and evaluation skills.
- Many of the case questions require an integrated approach when answering. This means that students will need to embrace the full range of the specification in their answers. A single answer may need to address issues such as marketing, production, human resources, finance and external factors all at the same time.
- Questions set usually require students to make decisions or solve problems. For example, a question may require students to suggest a suitable future strategy for a business.
- One question will often require students to use a quantitative technique when answering.
- Examiners often want students to be critical.

## Hints

- Skim read the case material to get a feel for the business, its people, its circumstances and its objectives (see section below on things to think about).
- Read again thoroughly highlighting key information.
- Look at the numerical information and analyse it briefly, without performing any calculations.
- Make brief notes on the key objectives and key themes.
- Read the questions highlighting command words and other key terms.
- Identify some business theories you might consider discussing in your answers. Questions will probably not request specific theories. The onus is on students to introduce relevant theories.
- Reread hints on answering data response questions above.

## Issues to think about when planning answers

- People. Business is about people and your answers need to reflect this. Consider the age, family circumstances, the attitudes and personal interests of the people involved in the case material. What motivates them? What is their background? What are their objectives? What are their strengths and weaknesses? These are some of the people issues which students need to consider when shaping their answers.
- Situation. It is important to think about the context in which the business is set. Examples of issues to consider include the type of business organisation (Ltd, plc or sole trader), the prevailing culture, the type of industry, the nature of competition, the size, its financial position, its age, history and potential. It is often helpful to liken the case material to a business which actually exists in a similar context. However, this may not always be possible.

- Objectives. Answers to questions are bound to be linked to what the business is trying to achieve in its given context. A business may be trying to survive following a recession, it may be trying to break into new markets, it may be trying to raise finance for a big investment project, it may be trying to change its culture or take over another business. It is often useful to consider, and distinguish between, short term and long term objectives.
- Theories. Students should introduce business theories into their answers. There may be little or no guidance as to what theories are required. Students need to be on the lookout for opportunities to introduce some business theory in every answer they write. For example, if a business is considering a price change, price elasticity theory could be introduced. If a business is merging with another, economies of scale may be discussed. If a business is downsizing the effect on staff might be discussed, in which case motivational theories such as Herzberg or Maslow might be applied.
- Be critical. Be prepared to challenge statements or claims made in a case study if relevant and applicable. Students with an enquiring and critical approach will be rewarded.

*Example 1*
Most of the structured questions in decision making/problem solving case studies usually require lengthy answers with analysis and evaluation. Therefore it is important to plan before writing an answer. Below is an extract from part of an extended case study. The case study is about Henshaws Ltd, a components manufacturer for the computer industry. It has faced difficulties in recent years due to escalating costs. It is considering ways of improving efficiency and reducing costs.

*One option currently being considered by Henshaws Ltd is to outsource its marketing activities. The directors of the company have not been impressed with the performance of this department. Their expenditure has consistently exceeded their budget and they seem to get new business and then lose it. In addition, communications between the department and others in the organisation have not been good. Two of the four company directors have long claimed that the company's strength is manufacturing high quality components, although the other two directors argue that the company must avoid clinging to 'past glories' and move forward with the times. A number of marketing agencies have given presentations to the board of directors and a decision whether to outsource marketing is imminent.*

(b) *Assess the likely advantages and disadvantages to Henshaws Ltd of outsourcing its marketing function.*

- To answer this question it is necessary to identify and

analyse 2 or 3 advantages, identify and analyse 2 or 3 disadvantages and then evaluate by making a judgment about whether Henshaws should outsource marketing or not.

● Although the question does not specifically ask for a judgment examiners are probably expecting one. This is because the mark allocation may be quite high.

● A plan should be drafted which might look like this:

Adv.      1. Costs fall
           2. More focus on manufacturing
           3. More effective marketing by specialists

Disadv.   1. Redundancies
           2. Loss of control of a vital function
           3. Long term marketing costs might rise.

Eval.     Yes - outsource because current marketing is expensive, ineffective and is causing problems. Henshaws will then be more focused and able to exploit its strengths.

● In the answer it is necessary to analyse the above advantages and disadvantages in detail explaining their relevance.

● In the evaluation some students may suggest that Henshaws should not outsource its marketing function. This does not matter. Examiners just want students to make a judgment and support it with a coherent and plausible argument. Remember that these case studies are decision making case studies and therefore a decision must be made!

### Example 2

Some quantitative analysis is usually required in extended case studies. It may be quite complex and students often make the mistake of spending too long on this section. The data below contains an extract from an extended case study about a business which is considering a new investment. Arpan Shrinath & Co manufactures training shoes and Arpan is deciding which investment project to go ahead with.

**Project 1.** *Arpan has considered buying a large delivery van and undertaking his own distribution. At the moment he pays a local company to distribute training shoes to his customers. This has proved expensive and often ineffective.*

**Project 2.** *A new moulding machine has just been launched on the market by a German machine manufacturer. It is computer numerically controlled and would help to improve the quality of Arpan's products. It would also be more productive than his existing machine.*

**Project 3.** *Arpan is becoming increasingly concerned that his office staff are working in conditions which are too cramped. Staff frequently complain and he is aware of inefficiencies due to a lack of space. He is considering the construction of a purpose built annex to the factory where office staff can work more effectively.*

*The table below shows the costs and expected returns for each of these projects over a 6 year period.*

| Expected returns | | | | | | | |
|---|---|---|---|---|---|---|---|
| | Cost | Year 1 | Year 2 | Year 3 | Year 4 | Year 5 | Year 6 | Total |
| Project 1 | £15,000 | £4,000 | £4,000 | £4,000 | £4,000 | £4,000 | £4,000 | £24,000 |
| Project 2 | £40,000 | £12,000 | £10,000 | £10,000 | £9,000 | £9,000 | £9,000 | £59,000 |
| Project 3 | £30,000 | £7,000 | £7,000 | £7,000 | £7,000 | £7,000 | £7,000 | £42,000 |

*(c) Calculate the (i)payback; (ii)average rate of return for the 3 investment projects and decide which project is the most attractive. Take into account your results from the calculations and any other information you feel is appropriate.*

● This question requires knowledge and understanding of investment appraisal techniques. Provided students have revised the quantitative techniques required they just need to apply the appropriate formulae.

● It is often helpful to produce calculations (or the results of calculations) in tables. One way in which the answers to the above question might be presented is:

| | Project 1 | Project 2 | Project 3 |
|---|---|---|---|
| Cost | £15,000 | £40,000 | £30,000 |
| Total return | £24,000 | £59,000 | £42,000 |
| Total profit | £9,000 | £19,000 | £12,000 |
| Profit p.a. | £1,500 | £3,167 | £2,000 |
| ARR | 10% | 7.9% | 6.6% |
| Payback | 3.75 years | 3.88 years | 4.29 years |

● According to the calculations above project 1 appears the most attractive. It has the highest ARR and also the shortest payback period.

● There is likely to be other information in the case which will influence the decision here. For example, if customers are complaining about the quality of products, Arpan might decide to buy the new machine to improve quality, even though the projected financial returns are slightly lower.

● This question is likely to offer a high mark allocation. The calculations alone would not generate all the marks. Students must bring in other information from the case, use their own ideas and also evaluate.

● Some thought must be given to the setting out of numerical answers. Good presentation is important. Avoid deletions and sprawling calculations. Space answers generously and underline final answers.

*Example 3*

The final question in an extended case study often requires students to suggest a strategy or give an overall view. The question might also carry higher marks. A possible question might be:

(d) *Taking the whole case into account, do you consider that the board of directors should discontinue production at the Newport factory?*

● Again, planning is very important here. A lengthy answer is required with relevant points being identified, thorough analysis and evaluation. Students need to bring together a range of relevant points and make a decision.

● Timing is also crucial. Students must ensure that they leave sufficient time to plan and write the answer to this final, and important, question properly.

● Students may use some of the material generated in other answers in the case. But obviously repetition must be avoided.

● Again, it probably does not matter in this question whether students suggest that production is discontinued or not. Examiners want to see a well structured, logical argument with a meaningful conclusion drawn.

● Remember to consider the people, the situation, the objectives and to introduce theories.

# Pre-seen case studies

A pre-seen case study is a method of assessment which involves giving students case study material before the day of the examination. This allows students to prepare more thoroughly for the examination by analysing the information and forming ideas in advance.

● Case study material may be issued a number of weeks before the day of the examination.

● The structured questions relating to the case study will not be known until the day of the examination.

● Additional information regarding the case may also be supplied within the question structure.

● The nature of the material provided in the case is likely to be the same as any other case study, but perhaps in more detail. Students should read the previous sections on data response and decision making questions.

### Hints

● The general approach to pre-seen case studies is little different from those which are not pre-seen. The only important difference is that students have a great deal of time to study the data. Again, the hints in previous sections on answering data questions should be read.

● There is much more time to read the material so more time can be spent highlighting key words and terms. Students could also note theories, issues or themes which are relevant.

● Any words, terms or theories which are unfamiliar or

forgotten can be looked up in the text book. For example, if the case contains an extract from a balance sheet, it might be helpful to consult the balance sheet unit to reinforce understanding of balance sheet terms and structure.

● It is helpful to try and predict possible questions which the examiner might set. This will allow students to prepare answers.

● Try to identify trends, patterns and links in the data and account for them.

● Get help from friends and parents.

● When answering the questions in the examination it is very important to answer the ones set. Students should not try to reproduce their own 'model answers'.

# Essay writing

An essay is an assessment method used to find out how students can respond in depth to an open question. It involves writing in continuous prose and provides an opportunity to explain something in detail.

● The quality of grammar, vocabulary, sentence construction and spelling is particularly important.

● A strong emphasis is usually placed on analysis, evaluation and synthesis.

● Essay questions may be integrated and synoptic. This means that students must consider the full range of the specification areas when writing answers. Essays based on one section of a specification or syllabus, such as marketing, may draw on all areas within it.

● The length will vary depending on the time allocated.

● They require a great deal of thought and planning before writing begins.

● The use of real world examples to illustrate points is essential.

● The use of diagrams, such as the Boston Matrix, is encouraged.

● There is rarely a 'right' answer. It is possible for two students to put forward opposing arguments and both be awarded high marks. It is the quality of the argument which is important, not the nature of it.

### Planning

● Read the question very carefully.

● Highlight the command words and other key words to help provide focus.

● Planning could be in two stages. Stage one might involve a 2 or 3 minute session where students jot down an explosion of points and issues they think might be relevant.

● Stage two would then involve sorting points into an appropriate order and planning out a structure which will accommodate an argument.

### Introduction

● It is common to begin with a short introduction where key

terms are defined and the question is put into context. Some general information may also be given. An introduction should be no more than a third of a side long, for example.

The main body
- When writing the main body of an answer it is important to follow the plan and write in detail, ensuring that evidence of analysis and evaluation is provided.
- It is vital to answer the question. It is better to write one side of relevant material than five sides of 'waffle'.
- Never use bullet points in essays.
- Never use subheadings in essays.
- Never write lists in essays. Extra marks are not awarded for identifying a large number of relevant points.
- Remember to include real world examples where appropriate.
- It is inadvisable to switch emphasis during the essay. It is best to stick to the plan.
- Diagrams, graphs and other illustrative material may be used but make sure it is clearly labelled and explained in the text.

Conclusion
- It is important to write a conclusion. It may be a statement which answers the question 'in a nutshell', drawing on the points analysed in the main body.
- Conclusions should not repeat material used elsewhere.
- The best conclusions are those which demonstrate evaluation and synthesis.
- Students are often required to make a judgment or give an opinion. Do not 'sit on the fence'.

*Example*
*It has been argued that the productivity of UK businesses falls well behind that of its overseas rivals. Suggest possible reasons why this might be the case and examine the measures which might be taken by UK businesses to improve productivity?*

- Essay questions can carry a relatively high number of marks.
- The words highlighted in the title are productivity, UK businesses, overseas rivals, suggest possible reasons, examine, measures and improve productivity.
- The following ideas may be suggested for the essay.
    *Define productivity, labour, capital, Rover productivity poor, Nissan good, lack of investment, lack of funds, lack of R & D, dividends too high, too short termist. Standardisation, reengineering, kaizen, JIT, outsourcing, virtual companies, TQM, benchmarking, work study, culture, trade unions, weak management, quality circles, technology, training, labour flexibility, delayering, downsizing.*

- The ideas generated may not be in any particular order. The focus in the above responses appears to be on production and ways of improving efficiency.
- Another 2 or 3 minutes spent planning might deliver the following essay structure.

Introduction
➤ *Define productivity - output in relation to inputs.*
➤ *An example of evidence which might support the statement is the low productivity of Rover compared with, say, Japanese car makers.*
➤ *Suggest that there is a number of approaches to improving productivity, some specific and some strategic.*

Main body
➤ *Analyse 3 possible reasons why productivity is lower in UK.*
➤ *Low investment, therefore inadequate and dated technology.*
➤ *Lack of R & D because the City wants higher dividends NOW.*
➤ *Trade unions may have resisted changes which might improve productivity.*
➤ *Explain that measures designed to improve efficiency might be specific or strategic.*
➤ *Analyse 3 specific measures - JIT, benchmarking and new technology.*
➤ *Analyse 3 strategic measures - kaizen, re-engineering and TQM.*

Conclusion
➤ *Argue that the statement is probably right for the reasons given. Evaluate by saying that one particular reason may be more important eg lack of investment.*
➤ *Argue that the methods employed to improve efficiency depend on the individual firms and their needs.*
➤ *Evaluate by suggesting that particular methods may be more suitable, if, for example, a business has dated machinery new technology may have a very significant impact on productivity.*
➤ *Argue that all measures will require cooperation of staff if they are to be successful.*

- When the essay is finished it is important to read through it and check for errors such as spelling, grammar and punctuation. However, avoid frantic crossing out at the last minute because this tends to have a negative effect on presentation.

# Report writing

A business report is a formal method of communication. It is a written document designed to convey information in a concise but detailed way. A report is written in a structured way so that information is broken down into manageable parts. The end section of the report is very important. It will contain recommendations for action that a business should take.
- A report begins with a formal section showing who the report is for, who has written it, the date it was written and the title.
- A report is broken into a series of sections. Each section

their strengths and weaknesses.
- Make your recommendations and relate these back to your project objectives. It does not matter if the organisation would not necessarily follow your advice; but your recommendation should be firmly backed by evidence from your analysis.
- There will always be more that you could have done, but keep to the time deadline and keep to the word limit.

*Example*
*What is the feasibility of extending a 9-hole golf course to 18 holes?*

This is an example of a project title that a student has negotiated with the local golf club where she plays as a junior member.

**Objectives** For this particular project the student, in discussion with the organisation, might set the following objectives:
- to identify the potential demand for an 18-hole course;
- to explore the local competition for the golf club;
- to examine the financial feasibility of building an 18-hole extension;
- to identify possible sources of finance for the extension to 18 holes;
- to make recommendations to the club on whether they should go ahead.

This is a piece of coursework that provides a reasonable problem for the student to tackle; it has scope for both qualitative and quantitative research and analysis and allows the student to make a clear choice at the end. By negotiating the objectives with the club, the student can hope to receive good access to the necessary people to talk to and the club's financial information. Access to accurate financial data is often the major constraint the students face when carrying out project research.

The scope of the project does not require the student to explore the legal background to expanding the golf course. This is a reasonable limitation that makes the project more manageable and the student would not be penalised for this provided the objectives and limitations of the project are made clear at the start.

**Collecting information** The student might plan to collect a range of data from primary and secondary sources. **Primary research** might include:
- a survey of existing members to establish their demand for an 18-hole course;
- a survey of potential members who might use the course if it had 18 holes;
- interviews with club officials who would be responsible for carrying out the extension;
- identifying the costs of building an extension;

- identifying the costs and availability of different sources of finance;
**Secondary research** might include:
- identification of the demand for golf through national statistics;
- identification of the location, size and facilities of other golf courses in the area;
- looking at the club's existing financial position through its published income and expenditure statements;
- looking at economic trends that might affect the future costs and revenue for a golf club;
- making use of any previous data that the club had collected if this problem had been considered previously.

**Analysis** Once the above research has taken place, the student would be in a position to carry out the following analyses of the information collected:
- a forecast of likely demand for the 18-hole course and thereby of the revenue that the club might generate;
- a forecast of the likely flow of expenditures on the project in order to set up and maintain the extended course;
- a cash flow for the project over the next 5/10 years;
- using the pay-back method or discounted cash flow method, an analysis of the financial benefits of the project when compared to other possible investments;
- a comparison of the costs and benefits of different sources of funding for the extension of the course.

**Evaluation** Before making his/her final recommendation, the student would need to consider the following questions, making use of evidence drawn from the information and analyses presented in the report.
- Does the decision to expand the course fit into the overall strategy of the club?
- On purely financial grounds, is the expansion a viable option? Are there better financial options for the club, eg leaving the money in a high interest bearing account?
- Can the club raise the necessary finance for the expansion? Would the costs of increased borrowing outweigh the benefits?
- How reliable are the forecasts of the demand and revenue figures and the cost and expenditure figures? How accurate is the research on demand? What might change to increase the cost estimates?
- What other external and internal factors would the club need to take into account before making a final decision?

This evaluation would help to provide the basis upon which the student is making their final recommendation as well as pointing forward to other areas that might be considered in a longer report. It should not be seen as a sign of weakness that the report writer asks such questions of their own work. It shows that he or she understands both the strengths and weaknesses of their final decision. It is important to remember that there is no correct answer in report or coursework writing.

# Index

## What is communication?

Communication is about sending and receiving information. Employees, managers and departments communicate with each other every day in business. For example, in a sole trader organisation, the owner may inform the workers verbally that an order for goods has to be sent out in the next two days. In a company, the personnel manager might send a 'memo' to all departments informing them about training courses that are available.

Good communication is vital for the efficient running of a business. A company exporting goods abroad is likely to have major problems if it fails to give the exact time of departure to its despatch department. Similarly, problems will also arise if instructions are not clear and goods are delivered to the wrong address.

Effective communication will only happen if information is sent, received and then understood. Some examples of information and methods of communicating in business might be:

- information on how to fill out expenses claims forms in a memo sent from the accounts department;
- verbal comments made by a manager to an employee informing them that continued lateness is likely to result in disciplinary action by the company;
- employment details given to a new employee on a written contract of employment (☞ unit 66);
- information on sales figures sent from the sales manager to the chief executive by e-mail or saved as a spreadsheet on computer disk;
- face-to-face negotiations between management and employee representatives over possible rewards for agreeing to changes in work practice;
- a group meeting taking place to discuss how quality could be improved in a work section;
- an order for 20 books faxed to a publisher from a bookshop;
- an advertisement for a salesperson placed on a company website on the Internet.

## The communication process

Communication within business can take many forms. There are, however, some common features of all communications that take place in the workplace. Figure 70.1 shows an example.

**Who sends and receives information?** Information must be received and understood by the person or group to whom it was sent. Communication can take place between managers and employees, as well as between representative bodies, such as trade unions. Information is also passed to people and organisations outside the company. For example, company newspapers such as *Ford News* not only inform employees about the firm, but present a picture to the outside world of its operations.

**What message is being communicated?** For communication to be effective the correct **message** must be sent and received. Messages can be sent for a number of reasons.

- To provide information about the company. Management might inform the workforce about production levels achieved during the previous year. Some information is required by law, for example, the business has to tell employees about their conditions of employment.
- To give instructions, for example, to instruct market research to be carried out.
- To persuade people to change attitudes or behaviour, for example, to warn an employee who is consistently late of the likely action.

**What channel is being used?** Communication can be along different routes or CHANNELS in the organisation. Sometimes this can be between a manager and a subordinate (**vertical**) or between two departments (**horizontal**). As well as this **formal** type of communication, information is often passed **informally** between departments and employees. Communication can also be to other people within the organisation (**internal**) or to those outside the organisation (**external**).

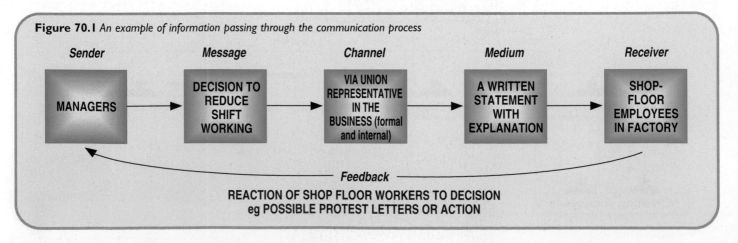

**Figure 70.1** *An example of information passing through the communication process*

| Sender | Message | Channel | Medium | Receiver |
|--------|---------|---------|--------|----------|
| MANAGERS | DECISION TO REDUCE SHIFT WORKING | VIA UNION REPRESENTATIVE IN THE BUSINESS (formal and internal) | A WRITTEN STATEMENT WITH EXPLANATION | SHOP-FLOOR EMPLOYEES IN FACTORY |

Feedback

REACTION OF SHOP FLOOR WORKERS TO DECISION eg POSSIBLE PROTEST LETTERS OR ACTION

**What medium is being used?** Information can be communicated in a variety of ways or through different COMMUNICATION MEDIA. These vary from written methods, such as annual reports, to oral methods such as discussions, to the use of **information and communication (ICT) technology**, such as a fax machine, e-mail or the Internet.

**Feedback** Communication is not complete until the message is received and the receiver confirms that it is understood through feedback of some sort, for example written or verbal confirmation.

# Formal/informal communication

Within a business there are both formal and informal channels of communication. Formal channels are recognised and approved by employers and employee representatives. An example of a formal channel would be a personnel department giving 'notice' to an employee about redundancy.

Informal communication channels can both help and hinder formal communications. Information that is communicated through the **grapevine** (☞ unit 58) may become distorted. This might, in extreme situations, cause industrial relations disputes. However, the grapevine can be acknowledged by management and actively approved of. Some firms issue a 'leak' along the grapevine to see what reaction it might provoke, making changes based on the reaction of employees to proposals, before issuing final instructions. Rumours, such as of a launch of a new product by a competitor, can be useful to a business.

Research has shown that effective communication requires both formal and informal channels. Formal statements can then be supported by informal explanations. A business might inform employees that it is introducing new machinery and then management may discuss this with employees and their representatives to find the best way to do it.

An insurance and risk consulting business, Marsh, carried out a survey of staff in preparation for a programme to align people behind the Marsh brand. Part of the programme involved the HR department conducting a communications survey of around 10,000 employees in eight countries. The Director of European Communications said 'We wanted to find out how people felt emotionally and intellectually about working in the organisation'. It was suggested that six years ago communications with employees was about often about simply 'pumping out newsletters'. However, the company now suggested that in a service business, where people are the brand, communication is absolutely strategic to business operations.

Source: adapted from *People Management*, 30.8.2001.

(a) Identify:
  (i) who is sending and receiving the message at Marsh;
  (ii) the message that is being sent.
(b) Explain whether the message is an internal or external communication.
(c) Explain how a formal and an informal channel might be used in this situation.

**Question 1**

It is also possible to make the distinction between **line** and **staff** communication (☞ unit 58). Line communication has authority behind it. Staff communication does not. An example of staff communication may be where a manager attempts to persuade a worker that it is a 'good idea' to do something.

# Vertical and lateral communication

Information can be communicated downwards, upwards and laterally. These different channels of communication are shown in Figure 70.2. **Downwards** communication has, in the past, been used to tell employees about decisions that have

**Figure 70.2** *Vertical and lateral communication*

already been made. It may be important as it:
● allows decisions by managers to be carried out by employees;
● ensures that action is consistent and co-ordinated;
● reduces costs because fewer mistakes should be made;
● should lead to greater effectiveness and profitability as a result of the above.

There is evidence, however, that the flow of information **upwards** can also help in decision making.
● It helps managers to understand employees' views and concerns.
● It helps managers to keep more in touch with employees' attitudes and values.
● It can alert managers to potential problems.
● It can provide managers with the information that they need for decision making and gives feedback on the effects of previous decisions.
● It helps employees to feel that they are participating and can encourage motivation.
● It provides feedback on the effectiveness of downwards communication and how it can be improved.

**Lateral** communication takes place when people at the same level within an organisation pass information. An example might be a member of the finance department telling the marketing department about funds available for a sales promotion. One problem that firms sometimes face is that departments may become hostile towards each other if they don't understand the problems that each face. The marketing department may want these funds, but this might adversely affect the firm's cash flow.

## Communication networks

Communication takes place between different individuals and parts of a business and between a business and outside bodies. There are advantages and disadvantages to a business of using different types of communication NETWORK.

**The circle** In a circle, sections, departments etc. can communicate with only two others, as shown Figure 70.3a. This type of communication may occur between middle managers from different departments at the same level of the organisation. The main problem with this type of network is that decision making can be slow or poor because of a lack of co-ordination. If middle managers from different departments had been given the task of increasing sales and profits in the short term, they may have difficulty developing a strategy that all would agree on.

**The chain** The chain (Figure 70.3b) is where one person passes information to others, who then pass it on. This approach tends to be the formal approach adopted by hierarchical organisations, such as the Civil Service. The main advantage is that there is a leader/co-ordinator at the top of the hierarchy who can oversee communications downwards and upwards to

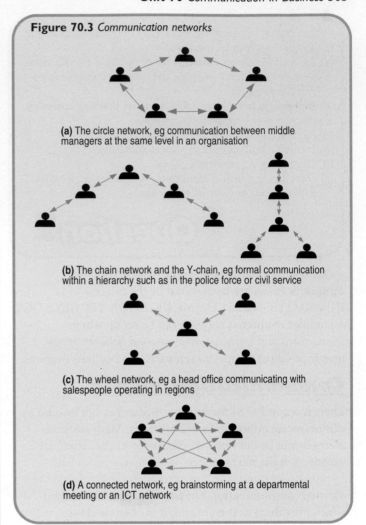

**Figure 70.3** Communication networks

**(a)** The circle network, eg communication between middle managers at the same level in an organisation

**(b)** The chain network and the Y-chain, eg formal communication within a hierarchy such as in the police force or civil service

**(c)** The wheel network, eg a head office communicating with salespeople operating in regions

**(d)** A connected network, eg brainstorming at a departmental meeting or an ICT network

different areas of the business. One problem may be the isolation felt by those at the bottom of the network. Their motivation may be less than others if they feel at the periphery. This network does not encourage lateral communication.

**The wheel** In the wheel pattern (Figure 70.3c) there is a person, group or department that occupies a central position. This network is particularly good at solving problems. If, for example, the North West region of an insurance company had been asked to increase sales by central office, then the North West regional manager would be at the centre of policy initiative communicating with local managers about the best way forward. The leader in this network is the regional manager.

**A connected or 'all channel' network** The 'all channel' communication system (Figure 70.3d) might be used in small group workings. With its participatory style, and more open communication system, the connected network provides the best solutions to complex problems. This type of network might be used, for example, when a department needs to 'brainstorm'. Its disadvantages are that it is slow and that it tends to disintegrate under time pressure to get results when operated in a group.

Which communication network may be most suitable for the following types of message?
(a) An instruction to despatch an order by a certain date.
(b) Discussions about possible extension strategies for a mature product.
(c) A message from head office to local building societies to change mortgage interest rates.
(d) Reacting to a bomb alert in an office block.
(e) Imposing budget cuts in a local authority.
(f) Organising a retirement party.
(g) Developing a brand identity for a consumer product.
Explain your answer in each case.

Question 2

One solution to the problem of passing complex communications has been solved by the use of INFORMATION and COMMUNICATION TECHNOLOGY. A complex connected network can be set up where instructions and information are passed between many people or departments, or even parts of a business overseas.

## Communication media

There is a number of methods or media that can be used to communicate information in businesses. Many of these methods can be delivered via electronic media. These are explained in the next section.

**Written communication** The **letter** is a flexible method which provides a written record. It is often used for communications with others outside the organisation. It can also be used internally where a confidential written record is needed, eg to urge employees against strike action, to announce a redundancy etc.

A **memorandum** is the same as a letter, but is only used for internal communications. It is sent via the internal mail system. Memoranda are useful for many sorts of message, particularly for confirming telephone conversations. Sometimes they are used instead of a telephone. One criticism often made of firms is that they have too many 'memos', when short written notes would do the same job. Some businesses send 'memos' via e-mail. This allows a person to send a message to another person's computer. The memo can then be called up and read by the person receiving it.

**Reports** allow a large number of people to see complex facts and arguments about issues on which they have to make a decision. A written report does not allow discussion or immediate feedback, as does a meeting, and it can be time-consuming and expensive to produce. However, it does have advantages for passing messages to groups. First, people can study the material in their own time, rather than attending a meeting. Second, time that is often wasted at meetings can be better used. Third, the report is presented in an impartial way, so conflict can be avoided.

Routine information can be communicated through the use of **forms**. A well designed form can be filled in quickly and easily. They are simple to file and information is quickly retrieved and confirmed. Examples of forms used in business include expense forms, timesheets, insurance forms, and stock request forms.

The **noticeboard** is a method which cheaply passes information to a large number of people. The drawbacks to noticeboards are that they can become untidy or irrelevant. In addition, they rely on people reading them, which does not always happen.

Larger companies often print an internal **magazine** or **newspaper** to inform employees about a variety of things. These may include staff appointments and retirements, meetings, sports and social events, results and successes, customer feedback, new products or machinery and motivating competitions, eg safety suggestions. The journal usually avoids being controversial. It may not deal with sensitive issues, such as industrial relations (☞ unit 73) or pollution of the environment (☞ unit 112), and may stop short of criticising management policy or products. It is designed to improve communication and morale, and it may be seen by outsiders (especially customers) who might get a favourable impression of the business.

**Face-to-face communication** Face-to-face communication involves an oral message being passed between people talking to each other. Examples might be:
● a message passed between two workers about how long is left before lunch;
● an instruction given to an employee to change jobs in a job rotation scheme (☞ unit 61);
● a warning given by a health and safety officer to a worker.

Group meetings involve face-to-face communication. Meetings can take a number of forms. They may be formal meetings which are legally required, such as the Annual General Meeting of a limited company. They might also be meetings of groups within the business to discuss problems, such as collective bargaining negotiations (☞ unit 74) or meetings of quality circles (☞ unit 83). Team briefings are also a common method of face-to-face communication in business. Many meetings, however, are simply informal discussions taking place to pass information between employees or managers, such as a 'chat' over lunch.

Face-to-face communication has several advantages. It:
● allows new ideas to be generated;
● allows 'on the spot' feedback, constructive criticism and an exchange of views;
● encourages co-operation;
● allows information to be spread quickly among people.

However, face-to-face communication, such as meetings, can have problems, especially if:
● the terms of reference (defining the purpose and power of the meeting) are not clear;
● the people attending are unskilled or unwilling to communicate;

- there is insufficient guidance or leadership to control the meeting;
- body language creates a barrier.

**Oral communication** Oral communication can take place other than in face-to-face situations in a business. The **telephone** is a common method of oral communication between individuals in remote locations or even within an organisation's premises. It provides some of the interactive advantages of face-to-face communication, while saving the time involved in travelling from one place to another. It is, however, more 'distant' and impersonal than an interview for the discussion of sensitive matters and does not provide written 'evidence'. This disadvantage can be overcome by written confirmation.

Sometimes messages can be communicated to groups of employees through a **public address system**. This might operate through loudspeakers placed at strategic points, eg in workshops or yards, where staff cannot be located or reached by telephone.

# Information and communication technology

Rapid developments in technology have greatly changed the way businesses communicate with each other. It is now possible to deliver messages instantly, over great distances and to a number of people at the same time via a variety of electronic media.

**The Internet** The INTERNET is a vast source of information for businesses and individuals who have access to a computer. The introduction of broadband in the UK means that websites containing images and text can be quickly viewed and information can be downloaded. The Internet is useful for external communication, although it might also be useful for internal communication in certain circumstances. For example, businesses can:

- advertise jobs to employees inside and outside the business (☞ unit 64);
- allow people to view financial reports or company mission statements (☞ unit 4);
- allow customers to buy products and pay using credit card details;
- gain market research information (☞ unit 19);

as well as providing stakeholders with a large amount of information about the company.

In February 2004 it was estimated that there were 295 million active Internet users in the world, of which 20 million were in the UK. By far the largest user was the USA, with 141 million users. One major problem is the sending of online junk mail, known as spam. In 2004 it was estimated that 1.2 billion spam messages would be sent worldwide.

**Intranets** Information on the internet is available to the public. This makes it impossible to send confidential messages. A business INTRANET is under the control of the company using it so information sent can be controlled. For example, a company with 150 administration staff may all be linked by an intranet. They can send messages and access common information.

It is suggested that the biggest savings from the intranet will come from the distribution of standard information throughout an organisation. For example, information such as the internal phone numbers, diaries and timetables quickly become out of date. In electronic format, however, they could be revised as soon as a change occurs and made available to all staff through a 'browser'. Intranets may also be extended into 'extranets'. These could include other business stakeholders, such as customers and suppliers, as well as the staff of a business. For example, suppliers mght be able to view their stockholdings held by a company's warehouse to make sure they are provided when required.

**E-mail** Many businesses have e-mail addresses. They allow businesses and individuals to communicate immediately with others via word processed text or images that are contained on a computer. Information sent from one e-mail address, via a computer, modem and telephone to another address is stored by the 'server' - a computer dedicated to storage and network facilities. It stays in that address until it is picked up by the receiver. The advantage of e-mail is that long documents can be immediately sent to other people anywhere in the world without them being there.

**Mobile phones** Many companies and individuals now have mobile phones. These are portable telephones which can be carried around by the user. Telephone calls can be made and received from most areas, often in different countries. There are particularly useful for employees who work outside the office or factory and who move around. Urgent messages can be sent and received immediately. Companies such as Orange and Vodafone offer a variety of services, including receiving and storing messages.

**Answerphones** Answerphones record messages when the receiver is unable to answer the telephone. They allow important messages to be stored and received if, for example, an employee is away from her desk. They also allow messages to be sent from one company or person to another outside normal office hours. The information will be received when work starts the next day. This is particularly useful when there are time differences between countries. Some people find answer phones impersonal and may not leave a message.

**Paging devices** These are devices which are useful for people who work outside a business and move around a lot, such as sales representatives. They may also be used by workers in a large organisation, such as a doctor in a hospital. A 'bleeper' alerts the receiver to a message waiting for him on a prearranged telephone number.

## Working in groups

Working with other people in groups is something that many employees do in business. An employee in a marketing consultancy business may be part of a team developing TV adverts for a client, part of a group set up to think of ideas to improve working methods and may meet with friends for lunch. Only in a small number of cases will individual employees work on their own, as in the case of a freelance journalist. Even an employee delivering goods on his own from a van will interact with staff and management when he returns to the office or factory.

Individuals may behave differently when working in a group than if they were working on their own. For example, an employee on a building site might want to work at a leisurely pace or find ways to avoid carrying out a task immediately. Group pressure could persuade or embarrass the employee into working harder than he would have wished. The group may want to finish the job early or earn any bonus that is available. In this case the employee's behaviour has changed as a result of being a group member. He is behaving in a way that conforms to the GROUP NORM. In other words, he is behaving in a way that is 'normal' for that group.

There is a certain amount of evidence to support the idea that individual behaviour is influenced by the group. The Hawthorne Studies (☞ unit 59) showed that group behaviour can influence workers' motivation. It is possible to identify certain common features of groups that exist in businesses.

- The behaviour of the group influences all members, eg if a decision is made to take industrial action (☞ unit 75).
- Members of the group have some common interests and objectives, eg a production team may want to increase its level of overtime payments.
- Members meet and discuss common interests, eg assembly line workers might discuss the latest changes to working conditions.
- There are rules or norms influencing members' behaviour, eg members of the finance committee of a business are expected to report back to the managing director after each meeting.

It could be argued that, given the emphasis on team work in many modern organisations, it is essential for businesses to understand how people work in groups. If employees in a group do not work 'well' together, this may reduce productivity and make decision making more difficult.

## Types of group

It is possible to distinguish different groups that exist in business. One common method is to divide them into FORMAL and INFORMAL groups.

**Formal groups** These are groups which are set up by a business specifically to carry out tasks. Formal groups are an actual part of the organisation, with arranged meetings and rules determining their behaviour and actions. Examples of formal groups might be management teams that control one aspect of a business, such as the finance department.

Other examples of formal groups might be groups which are set up to deal with certain problems. For example, a unit might be set up by a business to monitor the introduction of new machinery. The group may include the production manager, an engineer, a supervisor and a number of operators. Its task may be to make sure the changeover is as efficient as possible and it would meet to discuss ways in which this could be achieved.

Formal groups can be **temporary** or **permanent**. A temporary group might be a working party to investigate a computerised information system. Permanent groups include standing committees, such as health and safety committees or a trade union, which is a formal group, but not one created by management. The type of group depends on whether the task involved is recurrent or a 'one-off'.

**Informal groups** Informal groups are made up of employees with similar interests. They are not a formal part of the

---

(a) Identify the possible:
 (i) formal;
 (ii) informal;
 groups that the successful candidates might belong to using information in the advertisement.
(b) Explain how belonging to informal groups might help:
 (i) the new employees when settling into their job;
 (ii) the business in its relations with the new employees.

## Exciting Opportunities

The First vacancy is for a person who is dynamic, hardworking, approachable, organised and capable of dealing with the public and their children. They will join the management team and help to develop the future of this growing business, knowledge of the food and beverage industry would also be an advantage. (Hours of business 10am-6pm)

The Second vacancy is for people who like animals and willing to work within their environment. The right person must be outgoing, reliable, friendly and will be expected to work with the public.

Question 1

business itself. They do not have any formal 'rules', although there are often unofficial norms which influence members' behaviour. An example of an informal group might be a casual meeting over lunch between managers in the production, marketing and finance departments to discuss a new product launch. It could also be a group of hospital workers discussing possible job cuts in their rest room.

There are certain reasons why informal groups exist. It is argued that these groups meet the psychological needs (☞ unit 59) of employees. These might be some of the following.
● The need to be with other people.
● Status is determined by membership of various groups. This will also influence the view people have of their personal value and self-esteem.
● Groups offer a feeling of security and mutual support. By doing so, they reduce uncertainty and anxiety.
● The group may act as a problem solver for its members.

The informal groups that develop will be determined, to a large extent, by the physical layout required for work. Distance has a powerful influence on who will interact with whom. In general, the more frequent the interactions, the more likely informal groups are to be formed. Informal groups can have considerable influence on group members and the norms and values that a group develops may or may not support those of the organisation.

It may appear that formal and informal groups are separate. This is not the case. Groups that start off as formal often develop powerful informal relations. 'Part' of a company, as well as being a department, may be a department of friends. Japanese organisations, such as Sony, deliberately encourage this. Informal groupings, such as friendships outside work, can provide useful channels of communication for the organisation. The **grapevine** is a term used for such channels (☞ unit 70). It is also possible to divide groups into primary and secondary groups.

● Primary groups are small groups where people can have regular contact, eg a small department or office.
● Secondary groups are large groups where people have less regular contact, eg a large open-plan office or a large meeting.

A **team** is a particular type of group. Teams are usually put together for a purpose. For example, a business may have team meetings of workers to discuss production problems or have a team of designers developing a new product. Teams are dealt with later in this unit.

## Group decision making

The aims of businesses are to try and create groups that are effective and efficient. If the business can motivate the group to work harder in order to achieve goals, the sense of pride in the group's own competence might create job satisfaction. There is a number of factors that can help group decision making.

**Group members** The characteristics and goals of the individual members of the group will help to determine the group's characteristics and goals. An individual is likely to be influenced more strongly by a small group than by a large group. In a large group the person may feel overwhelmed and, therefore, unable to participate effectively in team decisions.

It has been suggested that the effectiveness of a group depends on the blend of the individual skills and abilities of its members. A group might be most effective if it contains:
● a person of originality and ideas;
● a 'get-up-and-go' person with considerable energy, enthusiasm and drive;
● a quiet, logical thinker, who ponders carefully and criticises the ideas of others.

This is why groups set up to consider new products often draw members from a number of different departments in the business. This means the group will have a wide range of skills and abilities.

**Figure 72.1** *The roles of individuals in groups*

The chairperson-
presides and co-ordinates; balanced, disciplined, good at working through others.

The shaper-
highly strung, dominant, extrovert, passionate about the task itself.

The plant-
introverted, but intellectually dominant and imaginative; a source of ideas for the group.

The monitor-evaluator-
analytically (rather than creatively) intelligent; dissects ideas, spots flaws; possibly aloof.

The resource-investigator-
popular, sociable, extrovert, relaxed; source of new contacts etc. but not an originator.

The company worker-
practical organiser, turning ideas into tasks-scheduling, planning etc; trustworthy and efficient; not a leader, but an administrator.

The team worker-
most concerned with team maintenance; supportive, understanding, diplomatic, popular but uncompetitive.

The finisher-
'chivvies' the team to meet deadlines, attends to details etc. and follows things through; not always popular.

# Case study Tyler Farndon

Sunita Shah is head of human resources at Tyler Farndon, a manufacturer of mobility products for older people and the disabled. When she says 'the future of the business is too important to be left to management alone' both Nick Gregson, the union official, and Gail Anne Knight, the executive director, agree. The business aims to take the thoughts of its mission statement to provide 'excellent products, ethically produced' into the workplace in as many ways as possible.

Sunita, Nick and Gail meet on the works council set up in 2000. Part of their discussions involve the progress of the 'Working together, working better' strategy that the business implemented in an attempt to make sure the employee voice at the organisation was being heard. It is an ambitious project, combining flexible work patterns with elements of a single status organisation, where all employees have the same terms and conditions whether they are union members or not. Staff also receive the same annual wage rises, and a bonus if the business is doing well.

The works council has 20 members. It discusses a number of areas, including production, changes in organisation and the development of the business in future. Decisions made by the council are often accepted by employees in the business as they feel that they have been represented in discussions.

Recently the business has been approached by another company and the possibility of a merger has arisen with a business which specialises in artificial limbs. However, employees feel that the business is doing well and should carry on growing organically. A further option is to transfer some production to an outsourced business and expand into this area itself. Whichever route is taken, the business feels that it would have to be agreed by employees and employers for it to work effectively.

Sunita regularly meets with other departmental managers of the business to review the human resources needs of their departments. The finance manager tends to take the lead in most of these meetings. He argues that the bottom line of the business must be 'to be profitable'. He will often put pressure on the other department heads to 'remain within budget'. Sunita has noticed that the head of R&D often seems to get more than other departments. She wonders whether this is because both the finance and R&D heads joined the company together. They have been with the business a long time and often attend

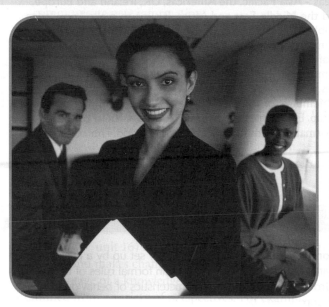

conferences where they discuss trends in the industry.

Gail will have to get any decision approved by the other shareholders in the business. Nick will also have to report any decisions back to his union members at meetings. He feels that some expansion is important. But what type? What if his members disagree and feel that some form of industrial action is necessary? He would then need to consult the head office of the union about procedures. Nick has been approached by some employees who say they have heard that any merger is likely to involve redundancy because of the duplication of skills. They thought that everyone was the same at the business, but now managers seemed to be fighting for a strategy which would benefit them.

**(a) Identify examples of (i) formal and (ii) informal groups suggested in the article. (6 marks)**

**(b) Explain how formal and informal groups have influenced communication at the business. (10 marks)**

**(c) Suggest benefits of team operation and group decision making at the business. (10 marks)**

**(d) Examine potential areas of conflict between members of groups in the business. (12 marks)**

**(e) To what extent do you think that the operation of groups and teams is effective at the business? (12 marks)**

## How are groups represented?

There are many different organisations which represent employees and employers in business. Although they are not part of actual businesses themselves, they influence how firms operate.

**Trade unions** These are perhaps the best known of the representative bodies. A TRADE UNION is an organisation of workers who join together to further their own interests. Trade unions have existed in the UK for over 200 years. Early unions were made up of workers with similar skills and interests, for example the General Union of Operative Spinners set up in 1829.

What features are trade unions likely to have? It is likely that a trade union would:
● register itself as a union;
● become affiliated to the Trades Union Congress (although not all do);
● be independent of employers in negotiations;
● regard collective bargaining (☞ unit 74) and the protection of its members' interests as its main functions;
● be prepared to use industrial action (☞ unit 75) to further its members' interests if agreement cannot be reached with employers or through bodies such as ACAS (☞ unit 74). There are different unions affiliated to the TUC in the UK.
● Large trade unions representing many workers. For example, UNISON the UK's largest union with over 1.3 million members represents public sector workers. AMICUS has over 1 million members in industries such as energy, construction, IT, chemicals and pharmaceuticals, shipbuilding, electronics and telecommunications, food and drink, textiles and paper.
● Unions which have members belonging to a particular business, such as the Nationwide Group Staff Union with over 11,000 members.
● Unions with members mainly from one industry, such as the National Union of Rail, Maritime and Transport Workers (RMT) with around 60,000 members and the Ceramic and Allied Trades Union (CATU).
● Organisations which represent particular occupations and skills. Examples include the Bakers, Food and Allied Workers Union (BFAWU) with around 29,000 members and the General Union of Loom Overlookers with less than 300 members.

**Staff associations** Staff associations represent workers, but tend to perform only some of those functions carried out by trade unions. These might include consultation and bargaining with management. Their members are often made up of workers in a particular business. Examples of staff associations are the Retail Book, Stationery and Allied Trades

Employees Association (RBA) or the Balfour Beatty Group Staff Association. In some cases staff associations develop into trade unions. For example, Unifi, the finance sector union, is made up from members of the Banking, Insurance and Finance Union (BIFU) and the NatWest Staff Association (NWSA). Some associations are affiliated to the TUC, such as the Guinness Staff Association.

**Professional associations** Professional associations perform similar functions to trade unions and are sometimes become TUC members. They represent 'professional' occupations. Examples include the British Dental Association with its 20,000 members, the Prison Officers (POA) Association with around 39,000 members, the Scottish Police Federation with around 15,000 members, and the Professional Footballers' Association with over 3,000 members. Some associations, such as the British Medical Association (BMA), represent their members in collective bargaining with employers. They are also responsible for the setting and maintaining of standards. For example, the BMA insists on certain qualifications before admitting employees to its membership. For this reason professional associations tend to be associated with 'white collar' workers and higher paid groups of employees.

**Employers' organisations** Just as certain bodies represent workers, there are organisations which help and support employers. They are often useful for small firms that may be negotiating with a large union. These organisations give advice to employers about collective bargaining and help with technical problems and overseas trade. They may also provide research and training facilities and act as a pressure group (☞ unit 102) for industries. Examples include the Newspaper Society (NS) and the Engineering Employers' Federation (EEF).

All of the groups mentioned above will aim to protect or further their members' interests. The rest of this unit will concentrate mainly on the role of trade unions, although many of the points dealt with apply to other representative bodies.

## The functions of trade unions

What is the role of a union in a business situation? Unions are an example of a representative body that aims to further its members' interests. It could be argued that this includes some of the following.
● Obtaining satisfactory rates of pay.
● Securing adequate work facilities.
● Ensuring satisfactory work conditions, such as the number of hours worked or the number of breaks in any period of work.

- Negotiating bonuses for achieving targets.
- Obtaining job security for members.
- Negotiating employment conditions, such as contracts of employment or rights relating to redundancy and dismissal.
- Negotiating grievance procedures.
- Negotiating job descriptions and job specifications (☞ unit 64).

Trade unions are responsible for **collective bargaining** in the workplace. They bargain on behalf of their total membership with employers and attempt to obtain the best possible conditions. It is argued that unions are in a far better position to negotiate with management than an individual employee, who will have little bargaining 'power'.

Trade unions are also responsible, along with management, for **industrial relations**. They communicate their members' wishes to employers and try to negotiate the most favourable conditions. However, successful industrial relations means that each party must take into account the wishes of the other when bargaining. It may not be in members' interests for a union to push for a longer work break if this reduces the efficiency of the business, perhaps resulting in job losses in future. However, it may not be in employers' interests to reduce breaks, even if this cuts costs, if it results in worker dissatisfaction.

The ability of trade unions to carry out these functions may depend on the union membership and UNION DENSITY. A small union, with few members, is unlikely to have as much influence as AMICUS with its 1 million plus members. Union density is expressed as:

$$\frac{\text{actual union membership}}{\text{potential union membership}} \times 100$$

If unions only represent a small percentage of all workers in an industry, they might be less likely to have influence. Figure

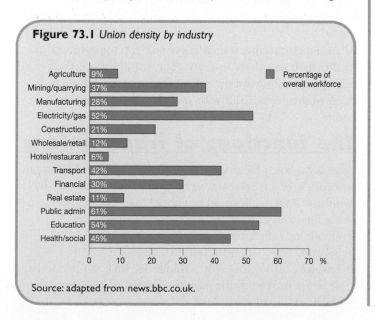

**Figure 73.1** *Union density by industry*

| Industry | Percentage |
|---|---|
| Agriculture | 9% |
| Mining/quarrying | 37% |
| Manufacturing | 28% |
| Electricity/gas | 52% |
| Construction | 21% |
| Wholesale/retail | 12% |
| Hotel/restaurant | 6% |
| Transport | 42% |
| Financial | 30% |
| Real estate | 11% |
| Public admin | 61% |
| Education | 54% |
| Health/social | 45% |

Percentage of overall workforce

Source: adapted from news.bbc.co.uk.

USP is a parcel delivery firm. When it first entered the UK market in 1992 by taking over Carryfast, the UK's largest private parcel delivery business, it only negotiated with T&G union reps at depots, not at national level. In 1997 the company agreed to bargain nationally with representatives of its 2,100 drivers and loaders and to give the union the right to appoint shop stewards who would then negotiate on local issues. The human resources director of USP said that the business wanted to adopt a national set of terms and conditions, which was agreed with the T&G in 1996. The 1997 agreement merely formalised the arrangement.

In 2000 USP signed a three year agreement on pay and conditions. This would help employees to know where they were in the longer term and USP to budget for improvements in terms and conditions, including a union request for a reduction in the working week.

Source: adapted from *People Management*, 13.9.2001.

(a) Identify the functions of the T&G at USP mentioned in the article.
(b) Discuss to what extent changes in the negotiating process at USP might affect the ability of the T&G to carry out its functions.

**Question 1**

73.1 shows union densities in various industries in the UK. It shows that in industries such as public administration union density is high, at over 60 per cent. In the hotel trade it is only 6 per cent. This might suggest that union influence is weak in this industry.

## *Types of union*

There is a number of ways in which unions can be classified. The most common method is to place unions into one of three categories.

- Craft unions are the oldest type of union, developed directly from traditional crafts. Workers with common skills often joined together to form unions. Examples today might be the Musicians Union (MU) or the Bakers, Food and Allied Workers Union (BFAWU).
- Industrial unions. In the past a number of unions have been formed by employees of particular industries, such as coalminers, railway or gas workers. An example of an industrial union is the National Union of Mineworkers (NUM). It is made up of employees with different skills in the mining industry.
- General unions. These unions are made up of workers with a wide range of skills in many different industries. Examples today might be AMICUS, the Union of Shop, Distributive and Allied Workers (USDAW) and the Transport and General Workers Union (T&G).

Although this division appears straightforward, it does have problems.

- It forces unions into one category, whereas many unions often have features common to all classes.
- Very few unions actually fall into the 'craft' category.
- Mergers of unions in recent years have blurred many of these distinctions. This is dealt with later in this unit.

Another way of dividing unions might be into those with more **open** and those with **restricted** recruitment policies. Those with restricted recruitment policies may recruit their membership from employees with certain skills. For example, only musicians tend to join the Musician's Union. Some unions recruit mainly from specific industries, occupations or businesses. Examples might be the National Union of Lock and Metal Workers (NULMW) and the Community and Youth Workers Union (CYWU). This can mean that their membership expands and contracts according to the changing levels of human resource needs in the industry.

More open membership policies tend to be associated with the larger unions. They often seek membership regardless of their members' jobs or industries, such as the T&G, or recruit from a wide variety of related or unrelated industries, such as UNISON, which recruits from public services industries. Such unions organise themselves to deal with different membership needs. This can sometimes lead to conflict, as unions are accused of 'poaching' members from other areas. Many of the larger unions have been formed by the merger of smaller unions with more restricted membership.

## Unions and pay

One criticism often made of unions is that if they negotiate very high wage increases, this can lead to redundancies. Unions can force up wages by:
- negotiating a minimum wage;
- restricting the supply of workers.

In a free market for labour, it is argued that a business can only pay for these higher wages and maintain profits by making workers unemployed.

Against this it could be argued that:
- if there is an increase in productivity by employees, this should pay for higher wages, without the need for job losses;
- other countries have similar unit costs of production to the UK, and pay skilled workers relatively high wages, and yet have not had such high unemployment rates;
- there is evidence in the UK that unemployment still exists even if wages are held down or cut.

## Trade unions and legislation

Much of the legislation that existed in the UK in the 1980s and the early 1990s was the result of the then Conservative government's view of unions. It believed that:
- trade union power was becoming excessive, particularly in wage negotiations;
- unions were often disruptive in preventing changing work practices or the introduction of new machinery;
- unions were increasingly creating industrial stoppages;
- unofficial picketing was disrupting business;

- SHOP STEWARDS were disrupting industry by calling unofficial strikes - strikes not supported by the unions (sometimes called 'wildcat strikes');
- there was undemocratic decision making within unions, especially about industrial action;
- closed shops restricted the rights of employees not to belong to a union;

and that these factors were harming the efficiency of British industry and its ability to compete. Others have argued that it is not trade union power that has made British business uncompetitive, but a lack of good management and poor levels of education and training within the workforce. They suggest that union legislation does not address the long standing issues of UK businesses - the lack of capital investment and the 'laissez-faire' approach of management.

The Labour government, elected in 1997, signed the **European Social Chapter**. This meant that employees were to be given new rights in the workplace. Businesses would also have to take into account new regulations and legislation on working practices and union activities. The government believed that a greater 'partnership' with more cooperation between business and unions would develop. This would involve more union consultation and unity in the workplace.

## The effects of legislation

Trade union activities in the UK are regulated by legislation. This is COLLECTIVE LABOUR LAW as opposed to the **individual labour law** relating to individual employees' work conditions (☞ unit 66).

Legislation between 1980-96 was designed to restrict union power, give employees choice and protect employers. After 1997 some of the legislation remained. But new legislation was introduced to comply with EU regulations. This legislation aimed to give employees greater workplace protection and encourage participation between unions and business. Legislation has focused on a number of areas.

Legal immunity Certain Acts have dealt with whether unions can be sued by a business or individuals as a result of damages caused by their actions. The **1982 Employment Act** made unions liable for any action that was not in 'furtherance' of an industrial dispute. Employers were also able to obtain injunctions. Injunctions are court orders which prevent unions taking action whilst a hearing is taking place. The injunction might be granted if a judge felt a business would suffer if the action continued. The **1990 Employment Act** made unions liable for action induced by any union official, unless written repudiation (a refusal to acknowledge or a disowning) is sent to all members.

Picketing PICKETING involves the rights of workers on strike to assemble and persuade others to help or join them. **Official pickets** (those nominated by unions) can stand outside a workplace to inform the public, employees, suppliers and managers that a strike is taking place.

- A union with regular 'people friendly communications' in the workplace and recruitment that is supported by management.
- Management and unions taking time and effort to make it work.
- A desire on both sides to listen to each other.
- Recognising that both sides win by the partnership's success.

However, some have criticised partnerships in business and suggest a number of factors could lead to the end of the partnership. Faced with difficulties, unions and business may not be as committed to the partnership as they were at the start. They may also 'see' the partnership differently, so that there is conflict over decisions. The gains from the partnership may also be too one sided. Unions may also be cut out from key decisions and managers may prefer to communicate directly with employees.

Negotiations The nature of negotiated agreements between unions and employers has changed in recent years. Unions are far more likely to negotiate on aspects other than pay. These may include facilities for women members or for older or disabled workers, reflecting the changing nature of the workforce.

The 1990s saw a number of agreements:
- at plant or local level rather than national level to take into account the needs of a particular business activity (mainly in the private manufacturing sector);
- over a larger fixed period, so that a business has knowledge of its future costs and can build these into its budgets.

The number workers covered by collective bargaining agreements, where unions agree deals for workers in an industry, fell from 71 per cent in 1984 to just 35 per cent in 2002 (☞ unit 74). This has meant that more agreements have taken place without unions being involved.

Services Unions increasingly offer a wide range of services to employees. These may include:
- insurance schemes;
- pension schemes;
- financial and legal advice;
- discounts on travel and goods;
- education courses;
- mortgage discounts;
- welfare and sickness benefits.

# The TUC

The Trades Union Congress (TUC) is an organisation which represents all major trade unions in the UK. In 2003 its 71 affiliated unions had nearly 7 million members. There were also around 180 unions outside the TUC.

Each year a conference is held and TUC policy is decided. Member unions send delegates to the conference, the number sent depending on the size of the union. The conference also elects the General Council of the TUC. This is responsible for carrying out policy and running TUC affairs in between

conferences. A General Secretary is elected, who is often seen as the mouthpiece of the TUC and is directly involved in TUC negotiations with member unions and government. The TUC has a permanent staff which deals with the day to day issues in between the annual Congress.

In the 1980s and early 1990s the TUC was excluded from consultation by government. Since the mid-1990s, however, it has been involved in a number of new initiatives. For example, it has worked with government and the CBI to encourage **partnerships** in business.

In 2004 the main functions of the TUC were to:
- bring Britain's unions together to draw up common policies and avoid clashes with each other;
- lobby government to implement policies that will benefit people at work;
- campaign on economic and social issues;
- represent working people on public bodies and British workers in international bodies in the European Union and the International Labour Organisation;
- carry out research on employment related issues;
- run training and education programmes for union representatives;
- help unions develop new services for their members;
- build links with other trade union bodies worldwide.

---

In 2002 Amicus, the manufacturing union, refused to sign a draft no-strike agreement with Honda in an attempt to take a tougher industrial relations approach. The union was concerned that the agreement specified binding arbitration to solve disputes and that this would rule out strike action. Derek Simpson, joint general secretary of Amicus, said 'The Honda agreement as it stands is an offspring of agreements done in the 1980s and 1990s' and had 'no place modern industrial relations.' 'Most companies recognise that productive partnerships are based on mutual respect and the right, if necessary, to take industrial action when procedures are exhausted.' Mr Simpson said that under him the union would not seek single union agreements behind the backs of other unions. Supporters of Mr Simpson say that Honda refused to recognise a union until workers used employment legislation to win a legally binding agreement. However, critics argue that workers are worried about the implications of threatening strike action, claiming it will alienate workers and undermine the union's position to represent workers.

Source: adapted from *The Guardian*, 21.9.2002.

(a) Identify the different union practices mentioned in the article.
(b) Examine the reasons for the changing industrial relations approach of Amicus.
(c) Discuss the extent to which Amicus is likely to be successful in its new approach.

Question 4

## The CBI

The Confederation of British Industry (CBI) was formed in 1965. It has a similar role to the TUC, but voices the opinions of employers rather than union members. CBI membership is drawn from private sector industry, service and commercial enterprises, major public sector employers, and some employers' associations, trade associations and Chambers of Commerce.

The internal organisation of the CBI is complex, but it has a ruling council which decides on policy. It also employs permanent staff, headed by the Director General. Detailed policy proposals are examined by standing committees. The CBI is organised to deal with local and area issues through its regional councils. These aim to keep in touch with the needs of small firms and local employers and help them solve their day to day business problems. The membership services of the CBI are wide ranging, both nationally and locally, and are backed up by skilled professional advice from lawyers, accountants and tax specialists.

What role does the CBI have? It attempts to represent its members' interests in a number of ways.

- Government policy. Just like the TUC, it attempts to influence government policy.
- Services. It provides legal, financial and economic advice to its members.
- Local businesses. It provides support and advice to local businesses through its regional offices.
- Through its office in Brussels, the CBI acts in the interests of British industry in the European Union.

- Trade unions. The CBI works with the TUC on consultative bodies such as ACAS (☞ unit 74).
- Other groups. The CBI provides information for a variety of other organisations and the public in general.

## key terms

**Closed shop** - a practice which prevents workers from being employed in a business unless they belong to a trade union.

**Collective labour law** - legislation which affects the rights and conditions workers operating together, ie in pay negotiations, with outcomes which affect all workers involved in the same way.

**Picketing** - involves the rights of workers on strike to assemble and persuade others to help or join them.

**Secondary picketing** - where union members from one place of work picket an unrelated place of work.

**Shop steward** - an elected union official who represents workers' interests in the place in which the shop steward works.

**Trade union** - an organisation of workers that join together to further their own interests.

**Union density** - the actual membership of a trade union as a percentage of the total possible membership.

## Knowledge

1. Explain the difference between a trade union and an employers' organisation.
2. State 6 functions of trade unions.
3. Why are good industrial relations important to a business?
4. What is meant by an 'open' union recruitment policy?
5. Explain 3 reasons why union legislation has taken place.
6. Briefly discuss 3 effects that legislation has had on union activity in business.
7. State 4 factors that have contributed to changes in the organisation and role of trade unions in the UK.
8. What is meant by:
   (a) single union agreements;
   (b) no strike deals;
   (c) union recognition?
9. What are the main functions of:
   (a) the TUC;
   (b) the CBI?

# Case study Eurotunnel

Eurotunnel is the operator of the high speed shuttle service which links the UK to France. It has a 99 year lease to operate the Channel Tunnel link, running freight trains and maintaining the infrastructure. It employs 3,400 people, of which about 1,400 are based in the UK on British contracts. To harmonise the workforce, management set up a company council in 1992.

Until June 2000 the company only recognised the council for consultation. But after the Employment Relations Act, 1999, it signed a recognition agreement with the T&G (Transport and General Workers Union) and a single partnership deal to cover all non-managerial employees and a joint management-union negotiating forum. The company suggested that the threat of industrial action and having to negotiate with many different unions swayed its decision, and the fact that the costs involved of action and negotiations would affect a company already £6.5 billion in debt. There were now two negotiating bodies - the council, representing all employees, and the TU forum, representing union members with sole negotiating rights over pay and conditions.

Two surveys were carried out, one just before recognition and the other 18 months after. Certain results were found.

- About 35 per cent of employees said they were union members in the second survey, but only 12 per cent in the first.
- Over 50 per cent of employees said there was an active union presence in the second survey compared to 6 per cent in the first.
- In the first survey there had been strong support for unions in all sections at Eurotunnel. Most said that unions would improve their pay and benefits (over 70 per cent), work conditions (75 per cent), health and safety, and grievances. In the second survey fewer than a third agreed that the T&G had been effective in representing employee interests and only 10 per cent said that the union had improved pay and benefits.
- Most employees wanted the council to be retained. But this was not a vote to replace the TU forum, as employees agreed the council had largely been ineffective as well.

In 2003 proposals for the EU Information and Consultation of Employees Regulations, 2005, were being discussed. They encouraged a more formal approach to information and consultation. The draft regulations would force employers to establish a framework so that requests by employees for information and consultation must be granted under certain circumstances. The regulations say that existing arrangements must cover all employees in a company. This threatens the use of single union agreements, which do not cover all employees. A further issue is that the arrangements give no automatic participation rights to union representatives, who must stand for election alongside non-union representatives. This might affect the traditional role of unions in collective bargaining.

Source: adapted from *People Management*, 11.9.2003.

(a) **What is meant by the terms:**
   (i) **the traditional role of unions in collective bargaining;**
   (ii) **shop steward? (6 marks)**
(b) **Explain how the role of trade unions changed at Eurotunnel. (8 marks)**
(c) **Examine the reasons for these changes. (12 marks).**
(d) **Discuss to what extent employee representation has been affected as a result of the changes at Eurotunnel. (12 marks)**
(e) **Assess the possible implications for employee representation at Eurotunnel in future. (12 marks)**

## Employer and employee conflict

Conflict can exist between different groups and individuals working in business. One type of conflict which may lead to major problems is between the objectives of employers and employees. Conflict between these two groups may result from a number of factors.

- Rates of pay. Employers could attempt to keep wage costs down to remain competitive, whereas unions could try to maximise employees' rewards.

In July 2003, 250 British Airways staff took part in an unofficial strike. The action was reported as costing BA £40 million. It was in reaction to the introduction of an electronic swipe-card, clocking-in system. Although some colleagues argued it was a small matter, and the public felt largely indifferent, experts suggested that the fact employees were willing to take unofficial action showed the severity of the breakdown in relations. BA staff were concerned that the system, designed to identify busy working periods, would mean the introduction of annualised hours. This could affect the flexibility of working, which staff find useful, especially to retain a balance between home and work life.

A further concern was the increasing monitoring of staff and the distrust that this suggests. Management argued that this was simply a means of turning a paper based system into an electronic one, but workers did not believe them.

It was argued that this was just the straw that broke the camel's back and unrest had been developing for some time. Unions had made concessions in the past to keep airlines in business and were less inclined to do so now. There had been a rise in disputes in other airline industries. Workers at Australian airline Quantas went on strike claiming the business failed to honour agreements to reward workers for improved productivity. Albanian Airlines' workers took strike action in support of improved working conditions. In France, Corsair employees took part in a 24 hour strike over pay.

Source: adapted from *People Management*, 7.8.2003.

(a) Examine the reasons for the sources of conflict between airlines and their employees.

## Question 1

- The introduction of machinery. For example, a business may want to introduce machinery which requires workers to learn new production techniques. Employees, however, may feel that this extra responsibility is an unwanted burden.
- Flexible working (☞ unit 76). Businesses often require a more flexible workforce. A printing works might decide to operate a 24 hour shift, for example, to cope with extra work. Employees may be unwilling to work at night.
- Work conditions. Workers may feel that better canteen facilities are needed, but employers could see this as an unnecessary increase in costs.

The aim of **industrial relations** procedures (☞ unit 73) is to make sure that each party finds an acceptable solution to any conflict that may exist. Successful industrial relations should prevent the need for industrial action (☞ unit 75) by employers' or employees' groups.

## Collective bargaining

COLLECTIVE BARGAINING is one way of minimising conflict in the workplace. It involves determining conditions of work and terms of employment through **negotiations** between employers and employee representatives, such as trade unions. These bodies represent the views of all their members and try to negotiate in their interests. One individual employee working for a large company would have little or no influence in setting their wages or conditions. The representative body has more strength and influence and can negotiate for its membership. Without such a bargaining process, employers and managers would be able to set wages and conditions without taking into account employees' interests.

For collective bargaining to take place:
- employees must be free to join representative bodies, such as trade unions;
- employers must recognise such bodies as representative of workers and agree to negotiate with them;
- such bodies must be independent of employers and the state;
- bodies should negotiate in good faith, in their members' interests;
- employers and employees should agree to be bound by agreements without having to use the law to enforce them.

The result of collective bargaining is a COLLECTIVE AGREEMENT. These agreements are usually written and are signed by the parties and will be binding. Collective agreements can either be **substantive agreements** or **procedural agreements**. Substantive agreements are concerned with terms and conditions of employment. They include pay, work conditions and fringe benefits. Procedural agreements set out how the parties in the bargaining should

relate to each other on certain issues. They include negotiating, redundancy, dismissal, recruitment and promotion procedures.

The number of workers covered by collective agreements fell from 71 per cent in 1984 to 35 per cent in 2002. There were many reasons for this including legislation, union membership, union organisation and the type and nature of employment (☞ unit 73).

Collective bargaining is one method by which a business can achieve greater INDUSTRIAL DEMOCRACY. This is a term which is used in different contexts, but, by analogy with political democracy, generally refers to a situation where workers are entitled to a significant voice in the decisions affecting the business in which they work. This is dealt with again later in this unit.

# Levels of negotiation

Negotiations can take place at a number of different levels.

**International bargaining** Large multinational companies (☞ unit 109) operate in many different countries. Some have considered the possibility of negotiating the same conditions for all employees in the business, no matter what country or factory they work in. This has the advantages that conditions can be standardised and workers in one country will not feel envious of those in another. The major problem of this approach is the inflexibility it causes.

**National level** Employers and employees may agree a deal which applies to all employees. Negotiations may take place to set wage or salary scales, or to discuss national conditions of work. For example, an agreement could be reached on the number of hours that teachers or lecturers should work a year, or their length of holidays, between teachers' unions and the government. A private sector example might be negotiations between the train union RMT and Virgin Trains over health and safety conditions.

**Local level** Discussions may take place at a local level, so that any settlement can reflect local conditions. An example of local negotiations might be wages or salaries based on the area of operation. From time to time the weightings given to local authority workers for working in the London or surrounding areas are revised. These weightings are added to workers' salaries to take into account the higher cost of living in the area. A locally based engineering company may negotiate with regional union representatives about the need to reduce the workforce because of falling sales. Again, this is likely to take place at local level.

**Factory or plant-wide level** Negotiations at factory or plant-wide level can take place over a variety of aspects of work. They may involve the personnel department, departmental managers, shop stewards and employee representatives.

Examples of matters that might be agreed upon could be:

- productivity targets;
- the introduction of new machinery;
- hours of work and flexibility within the plant;
- health and safety conditions.

**Individualised bargaining** Individualised bargaining is where the result of negotiations is the agreement between the employee and the employer in the contract of employment. Union representatives are not involved in negotiations. This means that the employee does not receive advice and does not have the backing of an influential group when discussing terms and conditions. However, it may mean that both sides in the negotiations have greater flexibility.

A report published by train drivers union ASLEF in 2003 argued that there was a need for a far more integrated approach to collective bargaining on the railways. The report, by Keith Ewing of the union-backed Institute of Employment Rights, suggested that such an approach would be far more in the public interest. The current system of negotiations were 'a non-cohesive and incoherent' local bargaining system, where different train operators each negotiated with employees and their representatives at local level. This had led to unacceptable pay differentials, skills shortages and poor staff morale. This in turn had led to a growing number of pay disputes. There was also a lack of procedures for dispute resolution in the current set-up. Ewing said 'It is no more sensible to run an integrated national railway system on the back of a fragmented industrial relations system than it is to run an integrated national railway on the back of a fragmented track and signalling system'.

Source: adapted from *Labour Research*, July 2003.

(a) Identify and describe the types of pay negotiations mentioned in the article.
(b) Discuss whether a change in negotiation methods would be an improvement.

Question 2

# The negotiation process

For negotiation to be successful in collective bargaining, an agreement must be reached which satisfies all parties. This is far more likely to be achieved if a pattern is followed during negotiation.

**The agenda** A meeting between all parties involved in negotiation needs an agenda. This will outline what is to be discussed and all parties must agree to it. The order of items on the agenda may influence the outcome of negotiations. If, for instance, all the employees' claims come first and all the management's points come later, then anything that is agreed at the beginning of the meeting cannot be accepted until the management side is given. An agenda that places management

and employee items in alternate and logical order can make negotiations easier.

**Information** Both parties need 'facts' to support their arguments. Negotiators have to collect the information they need, analyse it and make sure that each member of the negotiating team has a say in its interpretation. Often managers make information about a company's financial position available to representatives before meetings. This ensures that both parties have the correct information on which to base discussions.

**Strategy** It is important for each side in the negotiations to prepare a strategy. This will help them to achieve their objectives. Developing a strategy could include the following stages.

● Agreeing objectives. What do negotiators seek to achieve? The objectives set by employers or unions should, if achieved, lead to improvements. For example, a change in employment rules might improve efficiency or motivation. Negative objectives that emphasise not 'losing ground' are not usually helpful.

● Allocating roles. Who will do what in the negotiations? Negotiators need specific roles. For example, there may be a chairperson to lead the discussion, someone to put the case and a specialist to provide advice. The roles of group members are discussed in unit 72.

● Predict what the other side might do. Strategies are unlikely to remain the same during negotiations. Their chances of success are improved if the negotiators have tried to predict what they will hear from the opposition. Negotiators must be prepared not only to put forward their own arguments, but also to respond to arguments put to them.

**Unity** Because negotiation involves different sets of interests, each team must work out a united position before negotiations begin. If the group's position changes, all members must agree. It is important that a group shows unity at all times during negotiations or its position may become weaker.

**Size of the group** The number of people representing each side will influence the negotiations. The larger the group the greater the problem of managing communications between group members (☞ unit 70). When asked to suggest a number, most experienced negotiators opt for three or four in each group. Meetings of fewer people may be accused of 'fixing' an outcome.

**Stages of the negotiation** Negotiators begin by making it clear that they are representing the interests of others. They often emphasise the strength of their case and start by saying they are unwilling to move from that position. The displays of strength are necessary to convince themselves and the 'opposition' that they are willing to fight for their position. By the time this part of the negotiations starts, both sides should be very clear on the matters that divide them. After the differences have been explored, the next stage is for negotiators to look for solutions that might be more acceptable to each party. Each party will sound out possibilities, float ideas, ask questions and make suggestions. No firm commitments are made at this stage. Negotiations are likely to be more successful if each group is willing to change its position.

**Decision making** The next stage is to come to some agreement. The management may make an offer. The decision about what to offer is the most difficult and important task in the whole process. The offer may be revised, but eventually it will be accepted or rejected. Agreement is usual in all but a small minority of situations. Employees do not really wish to disrupt an organisation. Even if they take strike action, they will eventually return to the firm. The management need the

Korvac and James is a manufacturer of chemicals. It operates from a factory in Newcastle. Despite a number of years of falling sales in the 1990s, it has recently had 2 good years of orders.

This year's pay negotiations are due to take place, and the management has offered a 2 per cent pay increase, which it feels is a good offer given the need to grow in future and the current rate of inflation. The union representative at the factory thinks this is poor given the work by employees to pull the business around. He has suggested to two local union officials who will be involved in negotiations that a 6 per cent increase should be bargained for or strike action should be considered. He feels certain that the company can afford this, although no figures are yet available on this year's profits. The local officials are not so sure. They suggest that other options are available before calling for a vote on strike action. In particular, they are concerned that higher wages will result in redundancies, although they feel in a strong position to argue that increased productivity by workers will pay for any wage increases.

Another unknown factor is the likely installation of new machinery for the next year, which could lead to new grades for certain workers, but also redundancies in some areas.

(a) Write a letter from one of the union officials to the factory representative outlining the steps that should be taken and the strategy that should be adopted before they enter negotiations with management.

**Question 3**

employees to work for them. They have to reach an agreement no matter how long it takes.

**Written statement** Producing a brief written statement before the negotiation has ended will make it clear what both parties have decided, if agreement has been reached.

**Commitment of the parties** So far, agreement has been reached between negotiators only. This is of no value unless the groups represented by the negotiators accept it and make it work.

Employee representatives have to report back to their members and persuade them to accept the agreement. Management representatives may also have to do the same thing. Once the terms have been agreed by both employees and employers, the negotiating process is complete. It is the joint responsibility of both parties to carry out and monitor the agreement.

## Consultation

Negotiation, as we have seen, is an activity by which the two parties make agreements which may cover pay and conditions at work and relations between management and employees. JOINT CONSULTATION, by contrast, is the process where management representatives discuss matters of common interest with employee representatives before negotiating or making a decision. There are three types of consultation.

**Pseudo-consultation** Pseudo-consultation is where management makes a decision and informs employees of that decision through their representatives. Employees have no power to influence these decisions. Some have suggested that it would be more accurately described as information-giving.

**Classical consultation** Classical consultation is a way of involving employees, through their representatives, in discussions on matters which affect them. This allows employees to have an influence on management decisions. Unions may be involved, for example, in restructuring (☞ unit 90).

**Integrative consultation** Pseudo and classical consultation do not directly involve employees in decisions which affect them. Integrative consultation is a more democratic method of decision making. Arguably it is neither consultation nor negotiation. Management and unions discuss and explore matters which are of common concern, such as ways of increasing productivity or methods of changing work practices. The two groups come to a joint decision having used, in many cases, problem solving techniques. An example of an integrative approach to consultation might be the use of quality circles in a number of UK businesses and in foreign firms setting up in the UK.

## The Advisory, Conciliation and Arbitration Service (ACAS)

Sometimes parties fail to reach agreements after consultation and negotiation. In these situations the Advisory, Conciliation and Arbitration Service (ACAS) can be of great value to both sides.

During the period of industrial action in the 1970s, groups of employers and employees called for the setting up of a conciliation and arbitration service, independent of government control and of civil service influence. The result was ACAS, which took up its formal duties in September 1974. ACAS is a public body funded by tax, with over 900 staff employed in 11 regional centres and a head office in London. It has a chief executive and a council made up of 12 members ranging from union members to academics. Its main role is to prevent and resolve problems in the workplace. It provides a wide range of services to employers and employees in business.

**Industrial disputes** ACAS has conciliation duties. It can intervene in industrial disputes (☞ unit 75) at the request of either management or unions. Its role is to try and encourage a settlement that all parties may agree to, using procedures that both parties accept. In 2003 ACAS was called in to 1,353 cases.

**Arbitration and mediation** Arbitration is where both parties in a dispute put forward their case to ACAS. ACAS then independently assesses each case and recommends a final decision. Mediation is where ACAS makes recommendations about a possible solution and leaves the parties to find a settlement.

**Advisory work** ACAS carries out advisory work with employers, trade unions and employers' associations. This can be short visits to answer specific questions or long term, in-depth, projects and surveys. The questions ACAS deal with are wide ranging and can include issues such as contracts of employment, industrial relations legislation, payment systems and personnel policies.

**Codes of practice** ACAS issues codes of practice. These contain practical guidance on how to improve industrial relations between employers and employees.

**Enquiries** ACAS has carried out enquiries into the flexible use of labour, appraisal systems, labour turnover, employee involvement, handling redundancy and the use of quality circles. Much of this research is published by ACAS as advisory booklets. Employers use them to help improve industrial relations and personnel management practices.

**Individual cases** ACAS investigates individual cases of unfair

discrimination and unfair dismissal. The number of cases dealt with has increased from around 4,100 in 1987 to over 95,000 in 2003.

**Tribunals** Employment tribunals hear a wide range of employment disputes, including unfair dismissal and discrimination. ACAS operates independently from the tribunals. Its role is to offer conciliation on disputes, with the aim of settling the matter without a tribunal hearing. This is known as alternative dispute resolution (ADR). The **Employment Rights (Dispute Resolution) Act, 1998** set up an ACAS arbitration scheme designed to find other methods than the courts for solving disputes. In 2003, 77 per cent of the 96,000 complaints to tribunals went no further than the ACAS conciliation stage.

ACAS has developed its services to meet the needs of a changing industrial relations climate. While the bulk of its work continues to be conciliation, mediation and arbitration, it has steadily developed advisory and training services. ACAS has also become more involved in helping business to improve personnel and management practices. These include:

- effective recruitment and selection of employees;
- setting up and operating equal opportunities policies;
- improving communications and joint consultation;
- developing the skills of managers to help them introduce changes in work organisation.

## The Central Arbitration Committee

The **Employment Relations Act, 1999** set out a process for unions to be recognised automatically or where a majority of workers voted for it (☞ unit 73). The **Central Arbitration Committee** (CAC) is a permanent independent body responsible for union recognition. It has a number of functions.

- It judges applications relating to the statutory recognition and derecognition of trade unions when recognition or derecognition cannot be agreed voluntarily.
- It helps to determine disputes between trade unions and employers over the disclosure of information for collective bargaining.
- It handles claims and complaints regarding the establishment and operation of European works councils in Great Britain.
- It provides voluntary arbitration in industrial disputes.

Within its first two years the CAC investigated 127 cases. Union success rate in ballots is high. In 37 ballots ordered by the CAC, employees voted for union recognition in 62 per cent of cases. In the case of union recognition, the CAC would first encourage parties to settle the matter themselves. If this failed it could award recognition or the union could hold a ballot. The CAC has the power to instruct the employer to co-operate with the ballot or risk a fine.

## Employee participation and industrial democracy

Employees are increasingly participating in the operation of businesses and decision making. Decision making is often more accurate and effective when those involved in carrying out instructions have a say in the decision. Many businesses today recognise the value of their employees' views and contributions when deciding on objectives and strategies. The participation of employees in business decision making can take many forms.

**Autonomous work groups** Autonomous working groups and cells are increasingly being used by businesses to improve performance (☞ unit 61). They are groups of employees who operate without direct supervision from superiors, making their own decisions about the allocation of tasks, selection and training of new group leaders and methods of working, for example.

**Teamworking** Team working is where employees work together on tasks rather than individually (☞ unit 72). Teams can take a

---

Merseyrail had a poor history of industrial relations in the 1990s. This resulted in some well publicised stoppages and industrial action when the franchise was operated by MTL. ACAS helped set up a Committee of Enquiry into industrial relations at the company. As a result of its findings, an ACAS-led joint working group was set up. It comprised managers from the company and representatives of train worker unions such as RMT, ASLEF and TSSA. The group's task was to develop proposals that would improve industrial relations. These included awareness policies, and procedures, roles and responsibilities of industrial relations. ACAS also advised the company to bid for a Department of Trade and Industry grant to help improve employer-employee relations, including joint training. The bid was successful.

Logics Resource Services (LRS) had experienced a number of employment tribunal cases at which ACAS had provided conciliation services. The company approached ACAS to develop preventative action. This included a new handbook with discipline and grievance procedures. Once the procedures were agreed, they had to be accepted by staff who were then trained in the new procedures. Problems had occurred in the business as a result of the rapid growth of the company through mergers, which led to a variety of disciplinary systems being in place. The involvement of ACAS led to a legitimising of the new system for employer and employee. The new system resulted in a fall in enquiries regarding disciplinary matters and industrial claims, and also an improvement in employer-employee relations.

Source: adapted from ACAS report, April 2002-March 2003.

(a) Identify the services offered to companies by ACAS using examples from the article.
(b) Examine the benefits to the companies of involving ACAS in discussions.

**Question 4**

Social security managers offered civil servants bonuses and put staff up in hotels to break strikes in job centres and benefit offices in 2001. Staff who agreed to move to sites hit by industrial action were paid an extra £14.22 a day subsistence allowance (around £71.10 a week) to defy the strikes. An overnight allowance of £35 a night was also paid in addition to travelling time, an hour's reduction in the working week and a weekend overtime rate of time-and-a-half plus a day off in lieu. The Secretary of State for Work and Pensions, said 'It is absolutely essential that we do all we can. Millions of vulnerable people depend on us. Hundreds of thousands would be left without money if we don't do all we can because of the strike action. No responsible minister or government could tolerate that.'

Source: adapted from *The Guardian*, 30.10.2001

In 2003 workers at the Trelleborg chemical company in Leicester took strike action. This was in response to management action which introduced tags which had to be worn in break time by staff.

Source: adapted from *Labour Research*, November 2003.

Culina Logistics launched an anti-union recognition campaign using the slogan 'vote no way to the TSSA'. According to the union staff were also 'threatened with derisory pay deals, reductions in breaks, loss of bonus schemes' and job losses if TSSA won recognition.

Source: adapted from *Labour Research*, January 2004.

(a) Identify the methods of industrial action being used by employers.
(b) Explain why employers might justify taking such action.

## Question 1

labour, employers sometimes recruit outside workers or contractors to do their jobs. It has also been suggested that some employers hire 'union busters' to intimidate workers to stop unions winning strike ballots.

**The use of courts** Businesses might challenge the right of unions and their members to take action through the courts. This might prevent the action taking place. They might also claim damages.

## Employees' industrial action

Industrial action used by employees can be wide ranging. It is possible to distinguish between **unorganised** action and **organised** action. R Hyman, in his book *Strikes*, wrote that: '... in unorganised conflict the worker typically responds to the oppressive situation in the only way open to him as an individual ... Such reaction rarely derives from any calculative strategy ... Organised conflict, on the other hand, is far more likely to form part of a conscious strategy to change the

situation which is identified as the source of discontent.'

Unorganised (or unofficial) action by employees can come in a number of forms.
● High labour turnover.
● Poor time keeping.
● High levels of absenteeism.
● Low levels of effort.
● Inefficient work.
● Deliberate time wasting.
● Unofficial strikes not backed by the employees' union.

These are often taken when workers 'down tools' immediately in reaction to employers' actions.

Such action can be disruptive for a business if it continues for a long period of time. The business, however, can use disciplinary procedures against employees and may even be able to terminate contracts in some cases. However, unofficial action may lead to organised action backed by the union. Organised action can take a number of different forms.

**Work to rule or go slow** Organised and group industrial action by trade unions against management can take the form of a WORK TO RULE or GO SLOW. A work to rule means employees do not carry out duties which are not in their employment contract. They may also carry out management orders to the letter. This can result in workers strictly observing the safety and work rules which are normally disregarded. Working to rule does not mean that employees are in breach of contract, simply that they carry out tasks exactly according to their contract. This means that tasks are not carried out efficiently. The impact of train drivers working to rule, for example, could mean that trains are late arriving or are cancelled. Drivers may delay taking trains out until rigorous checks are carried out. A go slow is where employees deliberately attempt to slow down production, whilst still working within the terms of their contract.

**Overtime ban** An overtime ban limits workers' hours to the agreed contract of employment for normal hours. Overtime bans are usually used by trade unions to demonstrate to management that the workforce is determined to take further collective action if their demands are not met. An overtime ban does have a disadvantage for workers as it results in lost earnings. It can lead to a reduction in costs for the business, but may also lead to lost production. It can be especially effective where production takes place overnight, for example on large production lines.

**Sit-ins and work-ins** A SIT-IN or WORK-IN involves a mass occupation of premises by workers. A work-in is where employees continue production with the aim of demonstrating that the factory is a viable concern. It is sometimes used when there is a threat of closure. In a sit-in, production does not continue. The aim is to protest against management decisions and, in the case of factory closure, prevent the transfer of machinery to other factories. A

**Figure 75.3** *Working days lost by principle cause of dispute, UK, 1993-2002*

Legend: Pay, Redundancy, Allocation, Other

Source: adapted from *Labour Market Trends*, Office for National Statistics.

**Figure 75.4** *Proportions of stoppages in progress by duration, UK, 2002*

49%, 18%, 13%, 12%, 2%, 3%, 3%

Legend: 1 day, 2 days, 3 to 4 days, 5 to 10 days, 11 to 20 days, 21 to 50 days, Over 50 days

Source: adapted from *Labour Market Trends*, Office for National Statistics.

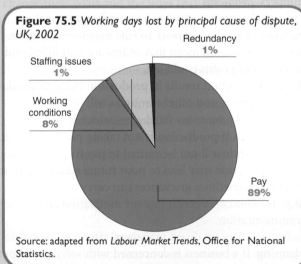

**Figure 75.5** *Working days lost by principal cause of dispute, UK, 2002*

Redundancy 1%
Staffing issues 1%
Working conditions 8%
Pay 89%

Source: adapted from *Labour Market Trends*, Office for National Statistics.

(a) Explain the trends and characteristics of industrial action in the UK over the period 1993-2002.
(b) Analyse why these trends may have taken place.

**Question 2**

**redundancy sit-in** or work-in is a protest against the closure of a plant or company. A **collective bargaining sit-in** may be used instead of other forms of industrial action such as working to rule, overtime bans and all out strikes, to give employees a position of strength in negotiations.

Sit-ins and work-ins mean the illegal occupation of premises by workers. They also allow workers to gain control over the factory. Why are these tactics used? First, they offer some degree of control over the factory or plant being occupied, which is obviously important in redundancy situations where the removal of plant and machinery to other locations is being threatened. Also by working-in or sitting-in, employees are better able to maintain their group solidarity.

**Strikes** The ultimate sanction used by trade unions against employers is the strike or industrial stoppage. Stoppages at work are normally connected with terms and conditions of employment. Strikes can be **official** or **unofficial**. Official strikes are where a union officially supports its members in accordance with union rules during a dispute after a ballot for action has been carried out and agreed by union members. Unofficial strikes have no union backing or support. They have, in the past, been called by shop stewards in particular factories, often in response to a particular incident. Such strikes are likely to be short term, local, unpredictable and disruptive for a business.

There is no single reason that explains the trend in stoppages in the UK. A study of strikes in Britain over an extensive time period was carried out by researchers for the government. They discovered that:

- strikes appear to be over major issues;
- strikes are concentrated in a very small proportion of plants - often the larger ones in certain industries and in certain areas of the country;
- industries and regions that have large factories, on average, tend to experience relatively high numbers of strikes. These strikes occur fairly often.

## Factors influencing the success of employees' industrial action

Whether industrial action by workers and unions is successful in helping them achieve their aims depends on a number of factors.

**Nature and strength of the union** A large union negotiating with a small business is more likely to be able to influence the employer. Where large unions are negotiating with large multinational companies or with the government, action may not always be successful.

It has also been argued that unions are less influential if representation in the industry is split. This was perhaps the case when some mine workers left the NUM to form the Union of Democratic Mineworkers. It may also have been a

## key terms

**Go slow** - the reduction of output by workers whilst still carrying on tasks in their contract of employment.
**Lock-out** - action by employers which prevents employees entering the factory to work.

**Sit-in/Work-in** - the illegal occupation of premises by workers, which allows workers to gain control of the factory.
**Work to rule** - when employees do not carry out duties which are not in their employment contract.

## Case study — Industrial action by council staff and civil service workers

In July 2002 over a million council staff were ready to strike. The action could cripple services such as elderly care, meals on wheels, street cleaning and pest control. The national officer at Unison said 'Our members have voted for industrial action because they are sick of being treated as the poor relations of the public sector. Their case for a realistic pay rise is indisputable'. Union leaders said the action would continue until they got a better pay offer. The T&G and GMB unions said two-thirds of their members had voted in favour of a strike, while the largest town hall union, Unison, had an 80 per cent vote.

Unions wanted a 6 per cent rise. This was rejected as unrealistic by council leaders, who said they did not have the money to increase their 3 per cent offer. A spokesperson for the local government Employers' Organisation said 'The strike action won't achieve anything. You can put a mark on a ballot paper but it can't conjure up more money.'

The services affected would vary from council to council because staff working in privatised services negotiate pay directly with their private employers, rather than joining the national bargaining process which covers most publicly employed council officers. Strikes by Unison in Scotland two years ago saw tonnes of rubbish piling up on the streets, empty offices in Edinburgh and museums and leisure centres closed.

Source: adapted from *The Guardian*, 5.7.2002.

In 2004 up to 90,000 members of the Public and Commercial Services Union (PCS) began a two day strike sparked by workers' anger over pay. This followed the collapse of pay talks, with the threat of further industrial action to come. The strike forced hundreds of job centres and social security offices to close. Up to 5,000 driving tests were also expected to be cancelled as driving examiners joined the picket line. The PCS claimed the strike was the result of the government's refusal to resolve 'appalling' levels of pay and an unacceptable performance appraisal system in the Department for Work and Pensions (DWP).

The union's general secretary claimed that low pay was endemic in the civil service and called on government ministers to intervene in the dispute. He said that civil servants were sick of a lack of recognition. Workers' anger was worsened by reports that a government inquiry into the civil service was to recommend 80,000 job cuts. The PCS general secretary said the union would oppose any moves to cut jobs because vital services such as the New Deal, immigration and customs were carried out by frontline as well as back-office civil servants.

The DWP described the strike as 'indefensible' and said contingency plans were in place to minimise disruption.

Source: adapted from *The Guardian*, 16.2.2004.

(a) Describe the industrial action taken by
 (i) employees and (ii) employers in the two cases. (6 marks)
(b) Examine the reasons for the industrial action. (10 marks)
(c) Explain the possible benefits and problems of industrial action for both sides. (10 marks)

(d) Assess the factors that might affect the relative strengths and weaknesses in the two disputes. (12 marks)
(e) Evaluate the likelihood of success of the industrial action in each case. (12 marks)

## The importance of human resources

Unit 63 explained how the role of the personnel department was to plan human resources. Many businesses have shown a renewed interest in the management of human resources in recent years. They have come to realise the importance of employees and their knowledge and skills as an asset of the business. For example, in 1999 every one of Shell's 105,000 employees around the world were asked for their opinions, which were to be used as an 'agenda for change' in the company. Companies such as ICL have come to recognise the importance of retaining and using workers' knowledge. Siemens, the electronics company, has developed its pension department's team building skills in freezing Arctic Circle conditions. It has also used personality tests to evaluate staff. Companies such as Jaguar and Peugeot have made use of psychological testing of managers.

Businesses also seem to be placing greater emphasis on motivation, customer care and training. In the late 1990s BT's 'for a better life' programme encouraged staff to make their own decisions to benefit the customer. In the early twenty first century there was a growing number of employer and union partnerships and works councils in business aimed at improving industrial relations (☞ units 73 and 74). Many businesses were also moving towards a **flexible workforce**. This is discussed later in this unit.

## Human resources management

One of the most important tasks that involves the personnel department in a business is HUMAN RESOURCE MANAGEMENT (HRM). A business is only likely to achieve its objectives if its employees are used effectively. Planning how best to use human resources will help a business to do this. Human resources management has **strategic** implications. It must be integrated into the strategic and corporate planning of the business (☞ units 16 and 17). It means constantly looking for better ways of using employees to benefit the organisation.

What is involved in the management of human resources? It is often said that it has a 'soft' side and a 'hard' side. This is shown in Figure 76.1.

## The soft side of human resources management

This is mainly concerned with the way in which people are managed. It may include:
● how to motivate and satisfy workers;
● how to develop an organisational culture (☞ unit 15) or approach in employees, for example good relations with customers, flexibility, or quality at all stages of production

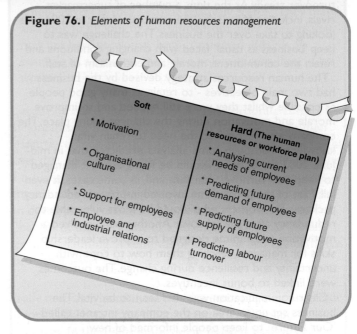

**Figure 76.1** *Elements of human resources management*

Soft
* Motivation
* Organisational culture
* Support for employees
* Employee and industrial relations

Hard (The human resources or workforce plan)
* Analysing current needs of employees
* Predicting future demand of employees
* Predicting future supply of employees
* Predicting labour turnover

(☞ TQM unit 83);
● how to support and develop employees, for example by training or by improving health and safety;
● the most suitable relationships between employer and the employees or their representatives;
● evaluating alternative policies and their likely costs.

There are various methods that a business could use when managing human resources. Take the example of a hotel with a variety of staff working in different jobs.

**Changing business aims into employee goals** The hotel may have decided that its main aim was to provide an excellent service to customers. To achieve this aim, goals would have to be set for the behaviour of employees of the hotel, such as always being polite to the customer. It is likely that staff training in customer care would be used to help employees.

**Examining the environment** There are factors 'outside' a business that could affect human resources management. The hotel would aim to gather as much information as possible to predict the effects of changes in these factors. For example, if health and safety regulations changed that affected the working of the kitchen, staff would need to be aware of these changes and may need training or support to carry them out. Information about external factors can be found from many sources, ranging from industrial journals to competitors' annual reports.

**Analysing the current situation** It is important for the hotel to be aware of current staff needs. It could do this by using:
● questionnaires to staff and customers;
● interviews with staff;

as an important asset. Developing a human resources management policy is likely to have an number of effects on a business.

- A strategic approach is needed. This means that a business must integrate human resources considerations into its overall corporate planning and strategy (☞ units 16 and 17). For example, a business that decides to merge with another company must take into account how the workforce needs to change, whether staff need training and assess how motivation may be affected. Alternatively, the hierarchy of the business could be redesigned to suit the needs of employees.
- The business must develop an organisational culture (☞ unit 15) that sees employees as an important part of the company. Managers who are unprepared to listen to employees' views on improvements will prevent the policy from working effectively.
- Motivation, training and support must be given to staff. Staff must be encouraged in the workplace. Businesses may make use of incentives such as bonuses or non-monetary benefits such as job redesign. Training and support must also be given. Marks & Spencer, for example, has employed counsellors to give advice to single parents on coping with children and work.
- Group involvement and participation. Employees must be made to feel part of the business and be committed to its objectives. They must also be prepared to contribute to improvements in quality and productivity.
- Coordination with other functions. The management of human resources must be built into all parts of the business, including production, marketing and the finance department, and at all levels in the hierarchy.
- Flexible practices and thinking must be encouraged. Workers must be prepared to change jobs, accept new working methods and conditions. This is dealt with in the next section.
- Recruitment, redundancy and redeployment. Businesses must be able to reduce staff if necessary. Cuts in staff may be achieved in a number of ways. Staff may be allowed to leave without being replaced, known as **natural wastage**. A business may ask for **voluntary redundancies**, where workers agree to leave in return for redundancy payments. The company may also offer **early retirement** to workers close to the compulsory retirement age. If there is no longer enough work, workers may be made redundant. It may also be possible to **redeploy** staff within a business. Training should help workers adapt to working in a different job in a business. Moving to another part of the country may be more difficult.

## Advantages of human resources management

There are certain advantages to a business in taking a strategic approach to managing human resources.

- It may allow a business to gain a competitive advantage

In 1999 B&Q opened its first store in China. By 2003 it had 8 stores and aimed to have 58 by 2005. It was not the policy of the business to saturate overseas businesses with too many expats. Rather their role was to transfer skills, to train and coach local successors, and then move on. These individuals maintain links with the UK through B&Q's central international HR team.

B&Q does not simply transfer UK HR policy to other countries such as China. Instead HR management focusses on meeting local requirements. Human resources in China tends to be a policing and administrative function, so finding people with the right experience proved difficult. The company designed an application form asking candidates about their skills and aspirations. Many ignored the form and simply attached a letter with interesting but irrelevant information. So whilst attracting a large number of candidates it was often difficult to assess them. Despite being warned that the process would not work in China, B&Q has successfully introduced performance appraisal. The company also sends between 12 and 15 people to the UK each year for a two week period so they can learn about the business.

Source: adapted from *People Management*, 17.4.2003.

(a) Explain the possible benefits of B&Q's human resource approach in China.
(b) Examine the problems B&Q may have faced with managing human resources in the country.

**Question 2**

over rivals (☞ unit 5). A business which has a well trained, motivated and planned workforce and a human resources policy may be more efficient than competitors.

- It can solve human resources problems that occur in the business such as high rates of turnover and absenteeism.
- Effective human resources management will make the most efficient use of workers and reduce the potential costs of the business.
- A business will be able to anticipate changes to its workforce requirements and plan for these. It will also be able to manage change more effectively (☞ unit 77).
- Industrial relations problems may be prevented if employers and employees are working towards the same goals.
- Human resources management aims to provide long term benefits for the business. Employing part time workers in a crisis may solve a short term problem. But a planned, flexible workforce will give benefits to the business over a longer period.

## The problems of human resources management

There is a number of problems a business will face when managing its employees.

- Problems with predicting the behaviour of people. A business may have filled a position, but after being

appointed the individual may decide he does not want the job. This could mean another costly and time consuming series of interviews for the firm.

- Problems with predicting external events. Sometimes it is difficult to predict exactly how many employees are required. We have seen that many factors can affect human resource planning. For example, the opening up of markets in the Far East, such as China, or the expansion of the EU into eastern Europe in 2004 could have meant changing plans for businesses aiming to break into these markets. It is likely that employees with knowledge of the business and language of these countries would have been in demand.
- Planning has to be constantly monitored. It is unwise for a business to plan its human resource needs and not alter them in the light of changing events. Planning has to be checked, revised and updated as other factors change.
- Human resources management must be well thought out or it is likely to lead to industrial relations problems. Cuts in the workforce or wage reductions that are not negotiated could affect workers' motivation and may even lead to industrial action (☞ unit 75).

## Measurement of personnel effectiveness

A business might evaluate the effectiveness of human resources management by considering some of the following. Similar methods can be used to evaluate the management of change (☞ unit 77).

**Labour turnover** One of the most important tasks in the management of employees is to make sure that labour turnover is minimised and that all vacancies that exist are filled. Labour turnover is a measure of the number of people that **leave** a business in a given period of time as a percentage of the average number of people employed during that period. If labour turnover is high, how will this affect a business? There are likely to be costs as a result. These include:

- the cost of advertising, interviewing and training a new employee;
- a loss of production while the place is filled;
- low morale amongst other employees;
- reorganisation before the place is filled and perhaps after a new worker is hired.

The business will need to identify groups that are likely to leave and be ready to fill any vacancies that occur. Employees may leave because they are ill, retiring or having children. In some cases, they may be dismissed.

These are all unavoidable. However, some workers leave voluntarily because they are not satisfied with the job. It is these workers that a business should be most concerned about. Evidence suggests that those workers who leave voluntarily tend to be younger employees, who are often new recruits. They may be looking for promotion and better pay.

To prevent dissatisfaction, a firm may:

- set up an internal promotion system;
- develop a staff training programme;
- make sure there is good communication between management and workers to avoid grievances and ensure that employees' views are taken into account;
- increase levels of pay.

**Absenteeism** High levels of staff absence may lead to a number of problems for a business. The output and productivity of the business may fall. The business will still have the costs of paying workers who are absent even though they are not working. Constant staff absence may also affect the motivation of other workers in the business. The reputation of the business may suffer if staff absence leads to unfulfilled orders or late deliveries.

A reduction in the number of days that employees are absent may be an indication that human resources management is effective. The motivation of staff may be better. Improved work conditions may have reduced stress and other factors which may lead to absence. Staff may feel more committed to the organisation and more likely to work, when they may have taken time off.

**Labour productivity and turnover per employee** The management of human resources may improve **labour productivity**. Labour productivity is a measure of the output per employee over a period of time. For example, if 20 workers in an engineering company produce 1,000 components in a period of time, their productivity is 50 components ($1,000 \div 20$). If work schedules were changed to create more flexibility and motivation improved so that output increased to 1,200, labour productivity would rise to 60 components ($1,200 \div 20$).

If a large multinational company employs 26,000 staff and has a turnover of £2,000 million a year, the **turnover per head** is nearly £77,000 (£2,000 million $\div$ 26,000). However, if changes to the workforce meant that the company had the same profit next year with only 22,000 workers, turnover per head would be nearly £91,000 (£2,000 million $\div$ 22,000).

**Industrial relations** The management of human resources may also improve industrial relations (☞ unit 73). A business may consider that a reduction in the number of:

- industrial disputes;
- days lost through industrial action;
- grievances against the business by employees;

might indicate effective management. Improvements in staff motivation indicated in appraisal questionnaires, attitude surveys or in meetings may also be an indication of the success of the business's policy.

**Relations with stakeholders** Stakeholders are all the people with an interest in the business. They include employees of the business, such as workers and managers, and shareholders

who may or may not work for the business. They also include people who are affected by the activities of the business, such as clients, customers, suppliers and the general public. An indication of the success of HRM might be found in improved relations with suppliers. It may also be indicated in the views of customers about how the workforce is treated.

**Profitability** The main aim of most private sector businesses is to make profit. Modern approaches to HRM suggest that the management of human resources should be geared towards improving productivity of workers, reducing costs, raising revenue and increasing profit. It is a vital part of the overall strategy of the company rather than a series of processes, such as recruitment, selection and training.

---

**Table 76.1** *Evaluation of human resources management*

- Commitment - employees' loyalty and motivation, assessed by surveys, labour turnover and absenteeism.

- Competence - employees' skills and training - assessed through appraisal systems and skills inventories.

- Congruence - employees and managers sharing the same values, assessed by absence of grievances and conflict.

- Cost effectiveness - employees' efficiency, assessed by cost, output and profit figures

---

Increasing profit may be a result of improvements in HRM.

One model that has been suggested to evaluate the human resources management is the '4Cs model' of the Harvard Business School. This suggests that HRM should be evaluated under four headings as shown in Table 76.1.

**Health and safety** Improvements in the health and safety of employees might be an indication that the personnel department is managing human resources more effectively. This might be shown by a reduction in absenteeism due to illness, as explained earlier. It could also be indicated in a fall in the number of accidents at work. Staff surveys might also indicate that the number of workers who feel that they work in a more 'protected' environment has increased.

## The flexible workforce

Employers have always wanted workers to be as flexible as possible. In the past this has meant paying overtime for extra hours worked, or higher rates for 'shift' work. Faced with competition, businesses attempted to use their existing employees more effectively. Sometimes this could benefit the employee. A single woman with a child may be able to work between the hours of 9am to 3pm each day while her child is at school. Working flexible hours could mean an employee may take time off for personal reasons and still work their required number of hours a week.

---

Tesco is the UK's largest food retailer. It underwent considerable change in order to improve customer service, lower prices, and increase turnover and market share. It attempted to evolve into a customer focussed business in a market where prices were often very similar but service could make the difference. To achieve the change in culture Tesco developed a 'balanced scorecard' in the form of a steering wheel with four quadrants - people, finance, customers and operations. Every store's performance was measured against this. The people quadrant covered issues such as recruitment, retention, employee development and morale.

Section managers who were responsible for recruitment and training showed high levels of commitment to the business. Around 90 per cent said that they worked very hard and felt that their job was challenging. One said 'I believe in the organisation. It looks after staff well, although it expects a great deal and stretches people'.

A survey of staff at four Tesco stores found significant differences with employee's with the HR policies of the business, as shown in Figure 76.2. One explanation for the difference was the extent to which managers put into action the instructions from head office. One of the regional directors of the business said 'One of the biggest challenges we have is getting the right managers into the right stores'.

Source: adapted from *People Management*, 15.5.2003.

(a) Explain how the effectiveness of personnel and human resource management was measured at Tesco.

(b) Evaluate how effective the management of human resources has been.

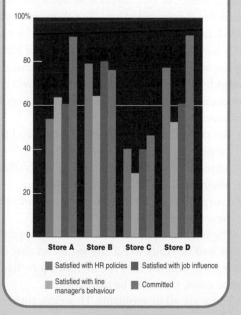

**Figure 76.2** *Survey of employees' commitment and satisfaction with HR policies and line managers' behaviour at four Tesco stores*

- Satisfied with HR policies
- Satisfied with job influence
- Satisfied with line manager's behaviour
- Committed

**Question3**

Training may also be given to workers so they become multi-skilled - able to switch from one job to another if needed. This example of job rotation may perhaps lead to the employee being more motivated. From a firm's point of view, an employee that can change jobs may prevent the need to have temporary workers to cover for illness etc. and so reduce labour costs. An example of this is the 'workstyle' initiative at Birds Eye/Wall's, where team working has been introduced so the workers can change from one process to another and do the work of others in the team if necessary.

In 1985 John Atkinson and The Institute of Manpower Studies developed the idea of the **flexible firm**. They suggested that businesses have a 'core' and a 'periphery', as in Figure 76.3. As a result of increasing competition, firms have attempted to make the workforce as flexible as possible, to increase productivity, reduce costs and react more quickly to change. The business would try to motivate core workers, giving them job security, and employ periphery workers only when needed.

Increasingly employers looked to make plans that allow a business to respond to changes. For example, if a large unexpected order arrives, a business will need workers that can 'get it out on time'. Using a FLEXIBLE WORKFORCE enables a business to react effectively to changes that take place outside the business. Examples of workers that are used by a business might include:

● part time employees, such as cleaners, who only work a few hours a day;
● temporary employees to deal with increases in demand, such as agricultural workers;
● workers on **zero hours contracts** who are employed by the business but only work and are paid when both the business and the employee agree;
● workers who work to annualised hours contracts, where they work a certain number of hours over a year rather than in a week;
● workers who 'bank time', by not working when demand is slack but being asked to work that time at a later date.
● office temporary workers to cover for illness or sickness;
● self-employed workers, such as management consultants, for specialist tasks;
● job sharing, where two workers are employed to do a full time job that may in the past have been carried out by one person.
● outworkers and teleworkers (☞ unit 66).

It has been argued that there are both benefits and disadvantages for these types of employee. On the one hand, a single parent may be able to find work at a convenient time, and job sharing could mean employment for two people, instead of unemployment for one of them. However, the position of flexible staff has often been a source of industrial relations problems for businesses and has led to conflict with trade unions.

In the 1990s individual bargaining increasingly took place. Conditions were negotiated without union involvement and based on the contract of employment. Union recognition and

## Figure 76.3 Organisation of a flexible workforce

**Core Workers**
Full time employees
Perform key tasks
Have skills specific to that business
Have job security

**Periphery Workers**
Part time, temporary or
self-employed workers
Brought into the business
when required

---

Many supermarkets brace themselves for the rush at Christmas. Sainsbury's employed an extra 10,000 staff at Christmas in 2003. Tesco hired an extra 12,000.

---

Eli-Lilly, the pharmaceuticals firm, has a family friendly culture. It encourages term time working, reduced hours and career breaks. This was particularly helpful to single parents. However, certain departments operated the policies differently. It was suggested by Randall Tobias, the chief executive, that 'This is a matter of changing the culture, not only the policy. There are still barriers for women trying to convince management of their commitment and career goals.'

---

The North East Wales Institute of Higher Education (NEWI) employed a pool of workers on zero hours contracts to combat problems of a lack of commitment amongst agency temps. Workers were not guaranteed work, but they have to be available at times that suit the business and the individual. Workers had a right to refuse work and look for another job. NEWI argued that this approach was important as it expected pool members to be flexible, so it was only fair that it was also flexible.

Source: adapted from *People Management*, various.

(a) Comment on the extent to which the practices of the businesses in the cases have (i) increased flexibility and (ii) benefited the businesses.

Question 4

union partnerships with business after the year 2000 may have changed industrial relations, although some argue that flexibility will still be encouraged by both sides.

There has been a number of criticisms of both Atkinson's model and the approach used by business towards human resources, for example, it may be argued that part time workers, contract work and the self employed can not be placed into a single category called 'peripheral work'. Part time workers, for example, may have secure contracts of employment and could be part of the 'core'. It has also been suggested that growth of a flexible workforce has been exaggerated and much has been due to the expansion of the service sector where such employment is common. It has also been suggested that most of the benefits are in favour of the business at the expense of employees. Employees see it as a means of getting them to work harder for less. Although workers have more involvement, management makes all the important decisions. Workers as individuals are ignored as a corporate culture develops and employees feel that they are being manipulated. It is also argued that human resources management takes a lower priority when a business is in difficulty.

## Relocation and outsourcing

In the early twentieth century businesses in the UK attempted to reduce costs and improve the flexibility of employees. Faced with growing competition, but also aided by the development of global markets, the Internet and computer technology, businesses attempted to manage their human resources in more efficient ways.

One method favoured by some companies was to relocate businesses in low cost countries, whilst keeping their head offices in the UK (☞ unit 88). A whole operation might be moved to a country where average earnings were lower than in the UK, employees would be hired in those countries and workers would be made redundant in the UK. This was particularly suitable for operations such as call centres where skills were easily transferrable and there was no need for direct contact with consumers. One of the problems faced with such a reorganisation was control from a distance, although it could be argued that this is no different from the challenges facing a multinational business operating in many countries.

Increasingly businesses have also outsourced operations (☞ unit 90). In some cases this might be to teleworkers working from home, using computers to communicate with employers. Operating from home might reduce costs for the business, although this type of work might only be suitable for certain operations. If these employees were part time or employed on flexible contracts, as explained earlier, this might improve efficiency and reduce costs even further. In some cases businesses have even outsourced entire operations to other businesses which might be able to produce goods or provide services more effectively.

## Knowledge management

Many businesses today see knowledge management (☞ unit 77) as important to their operation. It involves:

● identifying the knowledge of a business, such as the knowledge of employees;
● assessing how the knowledge can be used and planning how to use it effectively;
● ensuring that knowledge is shared by all people in the organisation.

The management of knowledge can have a number of benefits for a business. The speed at which a business gains knowledge and puts it to good use is one way in which it can gain an advantage over its rivals. For example, Sky was the

When Shell in Brazil needed help retrieving broken tools from a borehole, it asked its international colleagues. 24 hours later ideas flooded in from a global knowledge network devoted to wells. Shell was able to save $7 million as a result. The wells network is one of eleven global knowledge communities set up by Shell International Exploration and Production (SIEP). 'This is a very knowledge intensive business because there are so many variables but so many commonalities' says Arjun van Unnik, founder of Shell's New Ways of Working Department. 'Six years ago we had the idea that if we encountered a problem in ... Nigeria, it could be that something similar had happened in the North Sea' and that someone there had the solution. Engineers working in the communities have a culture of sharing knowledge. 'It's all factual stuff' says van Unnik. 'You either extract oil or you don't.'

Initially the communities had 'yellow pages' lists of members. But now they are web-based and online. Some of the communities have up to 4,000 members each. Each has a moderator and a co-ordinator. The co-ordinator has to search for answers to questions. Every few days all the answers will be pulled together and sent by e-mail. As larger communities have developed they have amassed a hugh bank of material. People have started using them as libraries and, using a search engine, can get detailed and precise answers from people who they can contact

Although sharing knowledge is a worthy aim in itself, the real driving force behind the money being spent is 'the bottom line'. Shell has already saved over £134 million and this only takes into account savings which can be quantified. 'There are many other cases where we cannot add precise value to a solution' says van Unnik. For example, a Shell sales company in Singapore beat rivals to a contract after using the network to research Shell's history with the client and those of competitors.

Source: adapted from *People Management*, 27.6.2002.

(a) Explain why knowledge management might be suited to Shell.
(b) Examine how the use of knowledge management might affect Shell.

## Question 5

first company to launch digital television in the UK. It could be argued that this will give it an advantage in future as many customers will have 'signed up' and be unwilling to change to another supplier.

It may also prevent a duplication of services. For example, ICL found that several of its businesses were bidding for the same project at the same time without each knowing about the others' activities. It also found 23 different uncoordinated information services for employees, often providing the same information. Knowledge management could have prevented this waste of resources.

Sometimes people leave a business and take years of knowledge and experience with them. It often exists 'in the head' of the employee, who has found the best way to carry out a task or the most suitable skills to use. Making sure that this knowledge is collected and passed on may prevent

problems for new employees to the job. It will also reduce time and costs for the business.

Unit 77 examines how knowledge management is important in the management of change.

## key terms

**Flexible workforce** - a workforce that can respond (in quantity and type) to changes in demand a business may face.

**Human resources management** - an integrated approach which ensures the efficient management of human resources. It is part of the overall business plan.

## Knowledge

1. Explain the difference between the soft and hard side of human resources management.
2. Briefly describe 5 factors that might affect the managing of human resources by a business.
3. 'A business that does not manage its human resources effectively may face industrial relations problems.' Explain this statement.
4. State:
   (a) 5 implications of taking a strategic approach to HRM;
   (b) 4 advantages of human resources management;
   (c) 4 problems of human resources management;
       for a business.
5. Briefly explain how a business may evaluate its management of human resources.
6. Suggest 3 ways in which a business might reduce labour turnover.
7. State 3 examples of:
   (a) flexible work practices;
   (b) flexible workers.
8. Suggest 3 advantages of:
   (a) a flexible workforce;
   (b) knowledge management.

## Case study A five star strategy

Claridges is one of London's most luxurious hotels. It has changed little in 50 years, retaining the feel of glittering chandeliers and society afternoon tea. But behind the opulent surface there appeared to be human resources issues to be dealt with.

Sara Edwards took over as HR Director in 1998. Claridges was battling to maintain its place in the market. Other hotels offered luxury service. Cheaper hotels were shooting up all the time. Visits were down. Occupancy rates were falling at the hotel, complaints were high and staff turnover was running at 73 per cent. She argued that people weren't enjoying the experience at the hotel and staff weren't

enjoying working there. A staff satisfaction survey revealed the extent of the problems. Only 47 per cent of staff bothered to respond. Of those that did, only 67 per cent said they felt proud to work for the business. Most felt a mistrust of management. As a result, the executive team came up with a new vision for the business, based on seven values. Edwards argued 'If you don't get it right for the employees, you won't get it right with the guests'.

By the end of 2002 staff turnover had fallen to 27 per cent. Pride at working in the hotel had risen to 99 per cent and every member of staff responded to the survey.

What was the secret behind such a change in employees' views? The seven core values of:

● commitment;
● passion;
● team spirit;
● interpersonal relations;
● service perfection;
● maximising resources;
● responsibility of actions;

were at the heart of the matter. They were depicted as a rainbow and this image helped to reinforce the idea that staff should have fun as well as doing their job. This was a novel idea for a hotel that had traditionally been seen as 'straight-laced'.

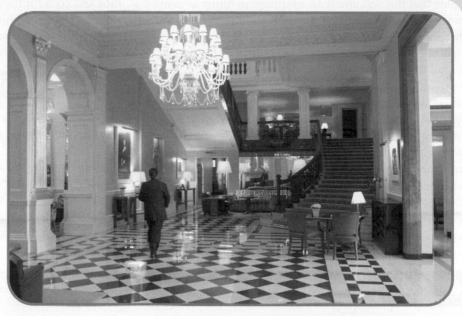

To train staff in the new philosophy, managers were taken off site on an away day. Each was asked to give a five minute performance to demonstrate one of the values. Edwards argued that the business had to do something very significant to show that things were going to be different, but fun as well. A new reward scheme 'Going for Gold' builds on the idea of the 'rainbow values'. Staff demonstrating special value for the business are given a gold card and take a lucky dip. Prizes range from a limo home to a night in a penthouse which would normally cost £3,850.

The 450 employees in the business are now encouraged to look to the future. Internal recruitment used to be rare, but now anyone taken on is viewed as someone who could eventually do a more skilled job. Staff are also encouraged to move across departments to develop their skills. New jobs are advertised in a newsletter. People who do not get the job are given training, as they have shown aspirations to improve.

People who visit the hotel say that they recognise the same faces. This seems to imply that people are staying longer in their jobs. This helps to maintain standards in the business. Another scheme is designed to improve staff pride. Employees are invited to experience staying as guests at the hotel for a night.

One employee who stayed felt that it brought home why Claridges was unique and reminded the employee why they worked at the hotel.

Such reminders were important after the September 11 terrorist attacks in New York. Many hotels experienced falls in trade. Claridges called a meeting and a plan of action was drawn up. Employees were kept informed at all times and redundancies were kept to a minimum.

Source: adapted from *People Management*, 8.4.2004.

**(a) Identify examples of the hard and soft side of human resource management at the hotel. (6 marks)**

**(b) Explain how the flexibility of staff might be improved at the hotel. (10 marks)**

**(c) Explain the factors which may have influenced the change in approach to human resources management. (10 marks)**

**(d) Examine how the changes in the management of human resources may have affected the business. (10 marks)**

**(e) Evaluate the effectiveness of personnel and human resources management at the hotel using appropriate methods. (14 marks)**

## What causes change in business?

Businesses today have to operate in rapidly changing markets and conditions. They can no longer rely on a constant stream of customers, the same production process or the same product over a long period of time. They must constantly be aware of, and be prepared to respond to, changes in a number of areas.

**Developments in technology** Unit 85 shows that the introduction of new technology can affect a business in many ways. There have, for example, been rapid changes in communications technology, production techniques and electronic components in recent years.

**Market changes** Businesses must respond to changes in the markets in which they sell. There may be competition from new businesses. This has been the case in the energy supply market. Former public sector owned gas and electricity suppliers were privatised and markets opened up to competition. New markets have opened up, such as the mobile phone market for companies such as BT. Competition may also come from new businesses entering a market, such as the offering of financial services by supermarkets. Other factors such as the Single European Market, globalisation, the opening up of markets in eastern Europe and China, the introduction of the euro and the expansion of the EU in 2004 were all likely to change how businesses operate.

**Consumer tastes** Businesses must also be prepared for changes in the tastes of consumers. Examples might be the purchase of environmentally friendly products, the desire for greater knowledge about products or the need for more efficient methods of shopping, such as purchasing via the Internet.

**Legislation** Government legislation can force changes in business activity. Taxation of pollution (☞ unit 112) would affect the production methods of many firms. Safety standards, such as EU regulations for VDU users, are also likely to affect how employees operate. Government aid or subsidies may affect the possible location of a business (☞ unit 88). Legislation on the number of hours employees can work may change work practices.

**Changes in the workforce** Population changes will affect the age and make-up of the workforce. The ageing of the population (☞ unit 95) in the UK in the early part of the twenty first century was likely to result in changing recruitment policies for businesses. A falling population is also likely to change how a business plans its human resources.

**Changes in the economy** It is argued that economies go through periods of boom and slump, recession and recovery. This is known as the business cycle (☞ unit 96). Income, spending, saving, investment and economic variables such as unemployment and inflation are all likely to be different at different stages in the cycle.

## The effects of change

The changes illustrated in the last section can have a number of effects on business.

- Product life cycles (☞ unit 24) could become shorter. This means that businesses must constantly be looking to develop new and profitable products or services.
- The role of marketing research is likely to increase. A business must not be 'surprised' by sudden changes in the market. Research and forecasting techniques should help a firm to predict more accurately the situation in future.
- Research and development (☞ unit 87) will be essential in industries where rapid change is taking place. As well as anticipating market changes, a business must be prepared to respond to the needs of the market with new products, which can compete with those of competitors.
- Retraining of managers and 'shop floor' workers might be necessary. This may be to learn skills associated with new technology or to develop skills to meet changing consumer tastes. Examples may be the education of office staff in communications technology, such as e-mail or videoconferencing (☞ unit 70) or the learning of foreign languages by UK business people wishing to enter foreign markets.
- Businesses must take account of changes in their human resource planning (☞ unit 76). This could mean employing a more flexible workforce that could be changed quickly to meet the needs of the business, for example employing part time workers, or the use of job sharing. It might also mean employing workers in low cost countries, such as in call centres abroad.
- A business must develop a culture and organisation which is prepared to respond to change (☞ unit 15).
- Businesses must be aware of competitors' actions and be prepared to react to them. Businesses now benchmark (☞ unit 83) their activities against those of rivals or other companies. Business must also be able to respond to new and emerging markets. These might be new markets abroad or markets for new products within a country.
- Quality is likely to become more important as consumer awareness develops and competition increases. Firms must consider the quality of their products and also their after sales service and customer relations. For example, many businesses have tried to achieve the international ISO 9000 quality standard.
- Changes in equipment. Rapid change often makes

continuously being recreated. Hence, to believe that a senior management team can unilaterally change an existing culture according to some blueprint is mistaken. Organisational culture, according to this view does change, but often slowly and in unpredictable ways. There is also a danger of thinking of organisational culture as a single over-arching idea to which all members of the business subscribe. Organisations, however, may have sub-cultures linked to particular groups. There may be conflict between these subcultures. In addition, even if new culture is established, there is no evidence that simply having a new culture improves performance.

## Different approaches to managing change

Research by John Storey has suggested that the way businesses manage change can be classified into four different approaches.

**A total imposed package** One approach to managing change is for people at the 'top' of the business to plan out major restructuring programmes without consultation with workers or workcr representatives. The main advantage of this method is that a company can have a 'vision' of where it is going. It can compare where it is 'now' with where it was 'then'. It is possible, using this approach, to prepare departmental action plans, set timetables and measure how far change has been achieved. The business can also make changes without having to take into account the wishes of other groups. The disadvantage of planning change from the top is that middle managers, supervisors and employees may not feel involved.

**Imposed piecemeal initiatives** A different approach is to have unplanned or piecemeal initiatives designed to bring about change. Initiatives might be introduced by employers to solve particular problems or only at times when they are needed in the business. Examples of initiatives that might take place are:
- the introduction of team meetings or quality circles (☞ unit 61);
- improvements in technology or channels of communication;
- improvements in incentive payments or rewards;
- improvements in the flexibility of work practices;
- changes in the workforce, such as teleworkers or subcontracting;
- the introduction of performance appraisal.

A problem with piecemeal initiatives is that they sometimes have different objectives. One might be trying to improve management leadership. The other might to trying to encourage greater participation. Another difficulty is that piecemeal initiatives tend to be short lived. In difficult times businesses may decide to drop costly changes.

**Negotiated piecemeal initiatives** Productivity agreements (☞ unit 60) are often used to help change take place. Unions agree to changes in work practices, usually in exchange for extra payments or improved conditions for workers. These negotiated changes tend to be ad-hoc, without any coordinated policy by the business.

**Negotiated total packages** This is where a 'total package' for change is put together. It is negotiated by employers and union representatives. It may be in the form of a 'national deal', which involves changes in work practices for all employees in every plant or office in exchange for increased rewards or improved conditions. In practice this method of managing change was rarely used in Britain before the 1990s. However, the changing roles of trade unions and the likelihood of partnerships between business and unions after the year 2000 may have seen this type of negotiation taking place more often.

---

Remploy is the UK's largest employer of people with disabilities. It manufactures products as diverse as car headrests, furniture and shower units. It has bucked falling industry trends by achieving a five per cent increase in profits largely by embracing changes in those who make a difference - the workforce.

Two years ago the company decided it wanted to increase staff from 12,000 to 25,000 and triple output over a five year period. The personnel director and resource dircctor were asked to work closely to start a major change programme. The idea was that roving internal consultants focus on Remploy sites that had more work than they could cope with. They investigate the 'weakest link' in the production process, then move on to find the next 'weakest link'.

The crux of the change programme was to make sure that every person had a say in how the day to day processes were to be run. This meant that even simple ideas could be shared. For example, one employee suggested sticking coloured tape on the machinists' tables during sewing to improve accuracy and to speed up the process. Staff also wanted to remove a huge overhanging machine so that they could see each other and help to communicate when a constraint in the flow of work had built up.

Assessment is now based on the end product, so that staff have a feeling of ownership and team spirit. Staff morale improved greatly as changes were made with all the factory involved and not just management. The business argues that there were short term benefits but also a long term change in culture. One of the machinists at the company said 'Change is frightening but, because we all have a say, we feel more confident in making those changes'.

Source: adapted from *People Management*, 29.5.2003.

(a) Identify the approach to managing change at Remploy using examples from the article.
(b) Examine the benefits to (i) employees and (ii) the business of such an approach.

**Question 3**

# Evaluating the management of change

Managers will have a clear idea of the improvements to performance that they want from change in business. They may want productivity gains as a result of the use of multi-skilled teams or improved response times to customer demands due to new communication technologies. These are sometimes referred to as **performance indicators**. Performance indicators can be used to evaluate the management of change. Any evaluation strategy will have quantitative and qualitative methods of analysing changes in working practices.

- A rise in output from 10,000 to 15,000 as a result of change or an improvement in average delivery time from two days to 24 hours would be measurable, quantitative improvements.
- Employees' responses to a questionnaire, stating that change had improved their motivation, could be a qualitative method of evaluating the management of change.

# Learning organisations and change

In recent years there has been a growing interest in learning organisations. A LEARNING ORGANISATION (☞ unit 76) is a business which absorbs knowledge, acquires skills and changes its attitudes. Solutions that are found to problems become the 'knowledge' of the business. They then become part of the firm's 'memory' and are used when reacting to future events. For example, a business may find that setting up

a graduate training programme is more effective than trying to headhunt managers from other organisations. It may use this approach when setting up a branch of the business overseas.

There is a number of implications for a business that wants to be a learning organisation.

- Human resource development strategy must be central to business policy.
- A business must constantly change its decision making in the light of new events.
- Employees must be regularly retrained in new working methods. Managers must develop coaching skills.
- Current practices must be questioned and workers must experiment with new solutions.
- Rewards must be geared to finding new solutions and workers must be allowed to manage themselves in work groups.
- There must be communication between all areas of the business.

There are certain advantages of this approach. Such businesses are more likely to grow and develop naturally to meet new demands because learning is integral to the way they operate. The business will not be using outdated plans and procedures to solve problems. Decision making may therefore be more effective. A business may also be better able to cope with change because it can take into account unpredictable events. Because businesses are constantly adapting their approaches to problems there should be less resistance to change from employees. However, an organisation can quickly go back to 'old ways of doing things' unless it constantly makes use of new knowledge. There may also be resistance from some

---

The National Blood Service (NBS) is the body in the UK responsible for ensuring there are sufficient blood reserves to meet the needs of the NHS. In the past it operated 15 autonomous centres, but this was changed to three 'zones' because it was thought to bring greater efficiency and economy. Many NHS workers interpreted this as an attack on the NHS's fundamental values. Now it has been restructured again to remove difficultes.

The three zone system, had been a major problem for people. Management teams had to take on a 'zonal' rather than local responsibility. Some didn't want to adopt the new working practices and 'fifteen into three does not go' it was argued. Leaders did not want to move sideways or downwards and so some left. Back-up from the human resources team was also fragmented across the zones.

People felt threatened by the latest restructuring only three years after the last one. It has helped that the reorganisation has not been as far reaching this time and clearly wasn't done for cost savings.

When the organisation began the restructuring process it started a staff survey. The results at first were as many feared. Directors were not thought to be interested in staff well being or views, workplace stress was not dealt with effectively and workloads were excessive. The survey also

highlighted that terms and conditions were not applied equally. Fortunately much of the scepticism was misplaced. The top ten problems were identified and 300 staff were asked to join focus groups. They then drew up a mission statement and a set of values. This helped the organisation to see staff as a key resource. Now the lines of communication have improved and the culture is starting to change. 'We are getting away from the blame culture and taking best practice from other parts of the service' says a team leader.

Not everyone agrees with this, however. The regional officer of UNISON says that problems in negotiating terms and conditions still hinder the organisation. He says 'It's a bad, old-fashioned industrial relations attitude. There's a complete detachment between the senior management and what happens at ground level'.

Source: adapted from *People Management*, 20.3.2003.

(a) Explain how managing change might be assessed in the organisation.
(b) Discuss to what extent change has been managed well.

managers, who see their control diluted, or workers who do not want to or are not able to learn.

## The management of change and enterprise

Research by Salaman (2002) has suggested that all change programmes can be analysed by focusing on one particular theme - **enterprise**. The idea is that a business should strive to become more enterprising in the way that it is organised and in the way it works. In order to achieve this a business needs to train employees to become more enterprise focused. For example, employees might go 'one step further', by trying to resolve a customer's problem even if it is not their responsibility. Over time individual employees will begin to police their own actions and will be critical of themselves if they don't achieve particular goals that they have set. Previously, employees may have undertaken tasks because of rules and regulations and because of performance or appraisal measures. Now they are more likely to become the guardians of their own performance because training, support and new working styles within the business have developed an enterprising approach in employees.

# key terms

**Learning organisation** - a business in a changing environment that constantly revises its working methods.

## Knowledge

1. State 5 factors that may cause change in a business.
2. How might change affect:
   (a) market research
   (b) research and development;
   in a business?
3. Why is it important for businesses to manage change?
4. Explain 4 ways in which the personnel department can plan human resources to deal with change.
5. What is meant by 'developing an organisational culture for change'?
6. Briefly explain 4 approaches to change.

# Case study  Ringing the changes at BT

BT has a huge property portfolio. It includes a massive infrastructure of wires, cables, junction boxes, buildings and phone boxes. It is managed by people who know that they do an essential job, unglamorous as it might seem. Faced with a debt mountain of £2.38 billion, BT felt the only way to reduce this was to outsource its property operation.

Staff were shocked. The average length of service was 21 years. Most had never worked anywhere else. They had excellent terms and conditions of work, a final salary pension scheme and the ability to work flexibly. In fact, 90 of the employees in the area were homeworkers. How would they all be affected?

BT decided its outsource partner would be Telereal, a company set up between LS Trillium and the Pears Group to bid for BT's property arm. It aimed to set high standards in the way that workers who transferred from BT would be treated. Part of LS Trillium's corporate culture was that 'we couldn't attract the people we needed solely on the strength of pay, so we emphasised the opportunity they would have to shape the business' according to HR director Robbie Wheeler. Wheeler and her team at

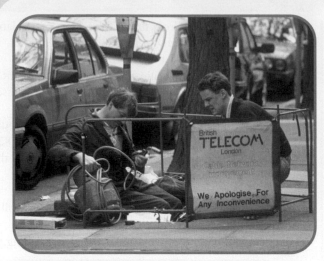

Telereal know that timing is crucial, stating 'When you tell staff something, you have to be sure you can deliver'. The business was used to a corporate emphasis on loyalty.

Telereal started communicating with staff who were transferring from BT about the changes as early as possible. It began by opening a dialogue with BT's HR professionals and the two trade unions involved, CWU and Connect. In the months before the transfer a dedicated helpline was set up, a Internet site was run and a roadshow was taken around the country at which Telereal's MD answered staff questions. This was followed by a further roadshow and audio conferences set up to handle the important question of future pensions.

A key decision made early on by Telereal was to retain the final salary pension scheme. Staff would also transfer initially not to Telereal, which was an unknown name, but to LS Trillium, which had a good property track record and reputation as an employer. Staff who transferred were doing the same work in the same clothes, but for a different business.

So far the results were positive. A survey showed that 80 per cent of staff said they were proud to work for Telereal. Only 2.3 per cent have left. Commitment is high and financial results had exceeded expectations. Having been on the margins at BT, some of the staff who transferred were now an integral part of the new company and experiencing new opportunities.

Source: adapted from *People Management*, 6.11.2003.

**(a) Identify the possible sources of resistance to change mentioned in the article. (4 marks)**

**(b) Explain how the corporate culture of LS Trillium and Telereal might have helped to manage change. (6 marks)**

**(c) What approach to managing change did Telereal use? Explain your answer using examples from the passage. (6 marks)**

**(d) Examine the factors that helped to remove the resistance to change at BT. (12 marks)**

**(d) Assess the extent to which the approach taken by the business might be of benefit in future. (12 marks)**

## What is production?

PRODUCTION takes place when resources, such as raw materials or components, are changed into 'products'. Land, labour, capital and enterprise - the factors of production (☞ unit 1) - are used in the production process. The use of land and a tractor to grow cabbages is an example of production in **primary industry.** An example of **secondary industry** would be the use of wood, plastic, glue, screws, labour, drilling and cutting equipment to manufacture furniture.

Today production is often referred to more generally as those activities that 'bring a product into being'. Activities which are part of **tertiary industry,** such as services, would be included in this definition. A bank might talk about providing a 'product' in the same way as a carpet manufacturer. Examples of products in a bank's product portfolio might include mortgages, current accounts, house insurance and foreign currency. Direct services from the producer to the consumer, such as car repairs or decorating, can also be regarded as production in this sense.

## Features of production

Production takes place when a business takes INPUTS, carries out a PROCESS and produces an OUTPUT or product. Production by a jewellery manufacturer may include the following.

- Inputs are the raw materials and components used by a business. These may include gold, silver and precious stones.
- Processes are the methods used to convert raw materials and components into products. Processes might include designing, cutting, bending, soldering and polishing. Such processes are often performed using machines and tools. For example, metal cutters, specialist jeweller's tools, a soldering iron and a small polishing machine might be used.
- Outputs are the products or services produced when inputs are converted. They might include rings, brooches, bangles, bracelets and necklaces.

## Planning and controlling production

For production to be effective, it needs to be planned and controlled.

**Planning** All businesses, whether small or large, need to plan production. Some large firms employ production planners for this task. A number of factors can influence the plan.
- Demand from customers. Businesses get orders from different customers, for different products, with different specifications, at different times. A business must plan which orders should go out first and which can wait.
- The design of a product might affect planning. For example, the design specifications of a product might state that certain materials must be used or certain processes, like high quality finishing, must be carried out.
- Planning must make sure that there are enough resources available. Many businesses purchase stocks (☞ unit 82) of raw materials and components and keep them until they are needed. Others order 'just in time'.

**Loading** This involves deciding which 'work centres' will carry out which tasks. A work centre may be an employee, a machine, a production cell or a process such as welding.

(a) Using the businesses shown in the photographs, explain what is meant by production.
(b) Explain whether the activities of the businesses are examples of primary, secondary or tertiary production.

**Question 1**

**Sequencing** Production usually involves arranging tasks and processes in a sequence. For many products the order of tasks will rarely change, such as in the production of bread. This is often the case when fairly large numbers of the same product are produced. However, when non-standard or customised products (☞ unit 79) are made, the order in which tasks and processes are arranged may need to change.

**Scheduling** The production schedule will show times when particular tasks and processes should start and finish. This is particularly important when large production projects are being undertaken, such as the construction of a large building. The aim of scheduling is to ensure that resources, such as workers, are not idle whilst waiting for someone else to finish a job before starting their own. **Gantt charts** can be used to help scheduling. A Gantt chart is a visual display showing how tasks might be sequenced over time. The Gantt chart in Figure 78.2 shows the tasks required to produce a batch of 1,000 brackets by an engineering company. The chart shows that:

- cutting begins on Monday and takes two days;
- bending, the longest task, begins on Tuesday. It takes three days and can begin before the entire batch has been cut;
- on Thursday welding begins before the entire batch has finished the bending process. Welding takes two days;
- painting begins on Friday even though the whole batch has not been welded and painting the whole batch takes two days;
- packing, which takes only half a day, cannot begin until Tuesday, when the whole batch has been painted.

**Dispatching** This involves giving instructions about the tasks to be carried out for a particular period. Instructions may be given verbally or in written form.

**Progressing** This is an ongoing monitoring process. It requires supervisors, teams or managers reporting on the progress of jobs. Managers or teams may have to identify problems and help solve them. They should also try to eliminate bottlenecks and encourage workers, when necessary, to speed up the job.

---

W.H. Brakspear & Sons has brewed beer in its Henley brewery, Oxfordshire, since 1799. The brewer markets about six brands of real ale (cask conditioned beer) including XXX Mild, Bitter, Regatta Gold and Old Ale. It owns about 300 tied houses and has used much the same brewing processes since it began.

**Figure 78.1** *Production of beer in the brewery*

## How Real Ale Is Brewed
A step-by-step guide to the technicalities of brewing

**Hot Water**

**Grist Case/Malt Mill** Sieved malt is crushed and fed into the mash tun

**Mash Tun** In the mash tun the grist (crushed malt) is stirred in hot liquor to form a mash

**Copper** The wort is run into a copper (or brew kettle), where it is boiled up with hops for an hour or 90 minutes

**Hop Back** The liquid is strained through the hop back which collects the spent hops

**Cooling**

**Racking** After the ale has matured in conditioning tanks it is racked into casks

**Fermenting Vessel** Yeast is added and fermentation takes place

Source: adapted from the *Good Beer Guide*.

(a) State two examples of inputs used by Brakspear.
(b) Describe two planning activities Brakspear might undertake when brewing beer.

---

| Task | M | Tu | W | Th | F | M | Tu |
|---|---|---|---|---|---|---|---|
| Cutting | ■ | ■ | | | | | |
| Bending | | ■ | ■ | ■ | | | |
| Welding | | | | ■ | ■ | | |
| Painting | | | | | ■ | ■ | |
| Packing | | | | | | | ■ |

**Figure 78.2** *Gantt chart showing the sequence of tasks required to produce a batch of 1,000 metal brackets by an engineering company*

# Added value

A business adds value to raw materials which it uses in the production process. ADDED VALUE can be found in the difference between the cost of purchasing raw materials and the price which the finished goods are sold for. In Figure 78.3 the builder will use inputs such as land, bricks, wood, tiles, frames, glass and other materials to build a house. The total cost of all the inputs is £31,000. The centre of the diagram shows the various processes required in the construction of the house. These include digging, bricklaying, roofing, tiling, plumbing, joining, painting and other tasks. As a result of these processes an output is produced. In this example the output is a house, which is sold by the builder for £89,000. The **value added** in this case is £58,000 (£89,000 - £31,000).

£58,000 is not the **profit** made by the builder. Part of the £58,000 will be used to pay the wages of employees and business overheads such as insurance, motor expenses and tax. So the profit figure will be lower than the value added figure. Value added is the difference between the price at which goods or services are sold and the cost of raw materials. Profit is the difference between the price at which goods or services are sold and all costs of production.

For services, it is sometimes more difficult to see how value is added. A supermarket will buy in a product from a producer or wholesaler. It will sell the product for a higher price to customers than it has paid for it. The difference in price is added value. The retailer is adding value because it is providing a service (making the products available in a convenient location) to the customer.

Figure 78.3 Added value in production

# Production decisions

Businesses make a number of important production decisions. A clothing manufacturer, for example, might decide to produce a new range of casual trousers. This could involve using a new type of cloth, changing the layout of the factory, increasing the size of its warehouse, employing more

Al Brennan runs a paving business in Towcester. Most of his jobs involve paving patios or drives during the summer. He employs two workers between May and October and advertises in the local newspaper and *Yellow Pages*. His most recent job was paving a driveway for a customer in Northampton, which took three days. He charged £1,400 for the job and the costs incurred are shown in Figure 78.4.

Figure 78.4 Costs and profit of Al Brennan on his Northampton job

(a) Describe how Al Brennan adds value in the above case.
(b) Calculate the value added by the business.

**Question 3**

labour and introducing a new quality control system. One production decision will often lead to other decisions having to be made. Decisions made by businesses might include some of the following.

**What to produce** A business must decide what product it wants to produce. The product may be a new product, that no other business has produced, or an adaptation of its own or a competitor's products. For example, 'Little Feet' are foot shaped plastic moulds which keeps two socks together in the wash. The creator, Andrea Marks, based the design on grips used to hold tea towels in kitchens. Many supermarkets now offer financial services such as savings accounts similar to those of banks.

**What production method should be used** Businesses choose how best to make their products. Different businesses might use different production methods, even when they make the same products. For example, TVR and Nissan both

manufacture cars. TVR hand-builds its cars in a small factory in Blackpool. Its production techniques make more use of skilled workers than Nissan's and the car bodies are made from fibre glass. Nissan mass produces cars in factories around the world. It relies more on robots, computers and other machines than TVR and uses metal for the car bodies.

**Where production should be located** Business owners have to decide where best to locate their premises (☞ unit 88). Generally, they will find locations where costs will be lowest. Small business owners may locate near to where they live. Large multinationals (☞ unit 109) may locate production in countries where the government gives them subsidies and grants.

**How large the business should be** Most businesses start off small and then grow. There are many advantages of growing. One is that costs are likely to fall due to economies of scale (☞ unit 81). However, some business owners are content to remain relatively small, to avoid the extra responsibilities growth brings for instance.

**How to ensure quality** Businesses are more likely to be successful if they can produce high quality products. Businesses have to decide how they might improve quality (☞ unit 83). This might involve using more expensive raw materials, training staff to higher levels or introducing a quality system, such as total quality management (TQM).

## key terms

**Input** - the raw materials used in production.
**Output** - the goods or services resulting from production.
**Process** - the method used to convert inputs to final goods or services.
**Production** - the transformation of resources into goods or services.
**Added value** - the difference between the cost of raw materials and the selling price.

## Knowledge

1. State 3 examples of production in the (a) primary (b) secondary and (c) tertiary industries.
2. State 5 features of planning and controlling production.
3. Explain how a cereal manufacturer adds value to production.
4. 'The retailer marked up the wholesale price by 10 per cent.' Explain why this is an example of calculating value added.
5. Why is value added not the same as profit?
6. State 5 questions about production that a business may consider.

# Case study Lafarge

Lafarge, which is quoted on the Paris and New York stock exchange, is one of the world's biggest producers of building materials. It owns Blue Circle, a UK based cement maker, and produces more cement than any other producer in the world. Lafarge has operations in 75 countries, employs over 75,000 worldwide and has over 250,000 shareholders.

**Processes involved in cement production**
- **Blasting**. Raw materials such as limestone and clay are blasted from a quarry. Due to the cost of transporting such a heavy raw material, cement works are usually located very nearby.
- **Crushing**. Large lumps of limestone pass through a crushing machine and are then transported to the plant by conveyer.
- **Raw grinding**. The raw materials then pass through a mill where they are very finely ground into what is called 'raw mix'.
- **Burning**. The raw mix is preheated before it goes into the kiln. Once inside the kiln the raw mix is burnt at 150°C by flames that reach a temperature of 2000°C. This process produces clinker which is cooled by fans as it leaves the kiln. Clinker is the basic material needed to make cement.
- **Grinding**. Additives such as gypsum are combined with the clinker before it is finally ground into cement powder.
- **Storage, packing and dispatch**. The cement is usually stored in huge silos before being dispatched in tankers or bagged.

Lafarge opened a new production line in the Kujawy cement plant, located west of Warsaw, in Poland. The production capacity now amounts to 1.6 million tonnes per year, an annual increase of 500 000 tonnes. With its state-of-the-art technological and environmental standards, Kujawy is among the most modern industrial sites of the Group. The new dry process line, which uses the most environmentally friendly technology, replaces the 3 older wet process lines. The investment in this project amounted to 90 million euros. The new line features a low consumption of fuel (decreased by 60 per cent) and power (decreased by 30 per cent). The decrease in fuel consumption has also allowed a considerable reduction in $CO_2$ emissions. Moreover, dust emissions are seven times lower than previously due to state-of-the-art technology.

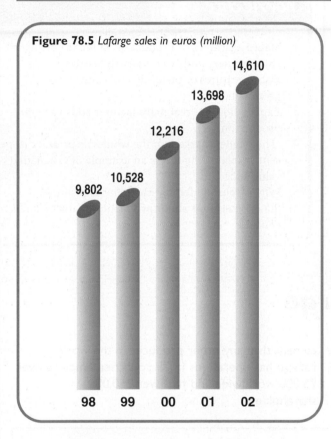

**Figure 78.5** *Lafarge sales in euros (million)*

Lafarge owns over 800 quarries worldwide and was recently refused permission by a Scottish court to quarry up to 600 million tonnes of rock from Roineabhal mountain on the Scottish island of Harris. The proposed site for the quarry was in an area of outstanding natural beauty. The quarry was opposed by most of the islanders and environmentalists said if the quarry were built it would leave a scar six times higher than the cliffs at Dover.

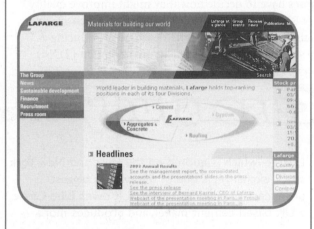

Source: adapted from Lafarge website and *The Guardian*, 10.1.2004.

(a) **Explain how Lafarge is involved in both primary and secondary production. (4 marks)**

(b) **Outline the possible role of a production planner in the manufacturing of cement at Lafarge. (6 marks)**

(c) **Using cement production as an example, explain what is meant by (i) inputs (ii) processes and (iii) outputs. (12 marks)**

(d) **Explain how Lafarge adds value when manufacturing cement. (8 marks)**

(e) **Discuss two production decisions that Lafarge may have made and how they could have affected production. (10 marks)**

## Deciding how to produce

A business must decide on the most suitable method to manufacture its goods or to provide services. It is likely that products which are different will be produced differently. For example, a plastic drinks bottle may be produced using automated machinery, but a wrist watch may be assembled by hand. Products that are similar can also be produced in different ways. The Ford Motor Company and Morgan Cars both produce cars, but different processes are used. Ford builds cars using a production line and semi-skilled labour, but Morgan cars are hand built by skilled workers. There are three important decisions that businesses must make when choosing how to produce. These are shown in Figure 79.1, along with the factors which influence these decisions. In the diagram it is assumed that the firm has already decided 'what' to produce. When deciding how to produce, the objective of the firm will be to minimise the cost per unit of output, ie PRODUCTIVE EFFICIENCY.

**What production method will be used?** Production is sometimes divided into one of three methods. JOB PRODUCTION is where one job is completed at a time before moving on to another. An example might be a costume made for a television play set in the nineteenth century. BATCH PRODUCTION involves dividing the work into a number of different operations. An example would be bread production, where each batch goes through several different baking stages before it is completed. FLOW PRODUCTION involves work being completed continuously without stopping. The production of cars on a production line might be one example.

Some industries may combine different methods of production. For example, a large brewery may produce 'batches' of beer, but then send them to a bottling line for packaging, where flow production is used. Such combinations are particularly common in the food industry.

**What factors of production will be used?** Businesses are often faced with a wide choice between alternative production factors. For example, a builder planning to construct a new house must decide what building materials to buy, which tools to use, which sub-contractors to employ and whether to hire any extra labour. The builder will be faced with a choice in all of these cases. If he decides to hire a labourer, there may be hundreds or even thousands of people to choose from in the area.

**How will the factors of production be combined?** A third production decision concerns the way in which the available production factors should be combined. For example, should an assembly plant invest in a highly automated assembly

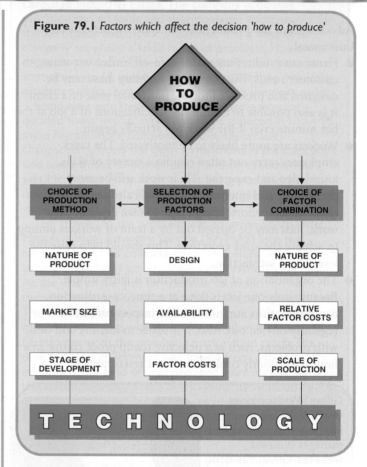

**Figure 79.1** *Factors which affect the decision 'how to produce'*

operation, or employ a large semi-skilled labour force to undertake the work?

There is a relationship between the three decisions concerning how to produce. For example, if a large UK firm produced sheet glass using flow production techniques, it is likely that it would require labour with certain skills and that it may be capital intensive.

## Job production

Job production involves the production of a single product at a time. It is used when orders for products are small, such as 'one-offs'. Production is organised so that one 'job' is completed at a time. There is a wide variety of goods and services which are produced or provided using this method of production. Small scale examples include the baking of a child's birthday cake, a dentist's treatment session or the construction of an extension to a house. On a large scale, examples could include the building of a ship, the construction of the Channel Tunnel or the manufacture of specialised machinery. Job production is found both in manufacturing and the service industries. Because the numbers of units produced is small, the production process tends to be labour intensive. The workforce is usually skilled

# 80 Lean Production

## What is lean production?

LEAN PRODUCTION is an approach to production developed in Japan. Toyota, the Japanese car manufacturer, was the first company to adopt this approach. Its aim is to reduce the quantity of resources used up in production. Lean producers use less of everything, including factory space, materials, stocks, suppliers, labour, capital and time. As a result, lean production raises productivity and reduces costs. The number of defective products is reduced, lead times (☞ unit 82) are cut and reliability improves. Lean producers are also able to design new products more quickly and can offer customers a wider range of products to choose from. Lean production involves using a range of practices designed to reduce waste and to improve productivity and quality.

## Kaizen (continuous improvement)

KAIZEN is perhaps the most important concept in Japanese management. It means continuous improvement. Every aspect of life, including social life, working life and home life, is constantly improved. Everyone in the business is involved. Kaizen is said to be an 'umbrella concept'. A wide range of different production techniques and working practices must be carried out for it to be effective. Figure 80.1 shows examples of the techniques, principles and practices. They should result in ongoing improvements. This approach argues that a day should not pass without some kind of improvement being made somewhere in the business.

There is a number of features of Kaizen which affect a business.

**Continuous improvement** Kaizen has been the main difference between the Japanese and the Western approaches to management in the past. The attempts of Western businesses to improve efficiency and quality have tended to be 'one-offs'. In Figure 80.2 the solid line illustrates the Western approach. Productivity remains the same for long periods of time, then suddenly rises. The increase is followed by another period of stability, before another rise. Increases in productivity may result from new working practices or new technology. The dotted line shows the Japanese approach. Improvements are continuous. They result from changes in production techniques which are introduced gradually.

**Eliminating waste** The elimination of waste (called *muda* in Japan) in business practices is an important part of Kaizen. Waste is any activity which raises costs without adding value to a product. Examples may be:
- time wasted while staff wait around before starting tasks, such as waiting for materials to arrive;
- time wasted when workers move unnecessarily in the workplace, such as walking to a central point in the factory to get tools;
- the irregular use of a machine, such as a machine which is only used once a month for a special order;
- excessive demands upon machines or workers, such as staff working overtime seven days a week which causes them to be tired and work poorly.

Firms that adopt the Kaizen approach train and reward workers to continually search for waste and to suggest how it might be eliminated.

**Implementing continuous improvement** It is often difficult for workers in a business to look for continuous improvement all the time. Japanese businesses tried to solve this problem by introducing the PDCA (Plan, Do, Check, Action) cycle. It is a series of activities that lead to improvement.
- Plan. Businesses must identify where improvement is needed.

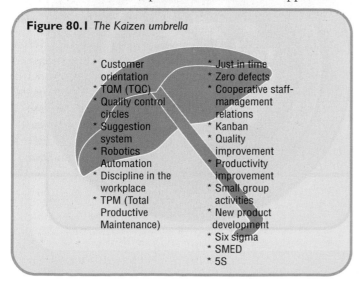

**Figure 80.1** *The Kaizen umbrella*

* Customer orientation
* TQM (TQC)
* Quality control circles
* Suggestion system
* Robotics Automation
* Discipline in the workplace
* TPM (Total Productive Maintenance)

* Just in time
* Zero defects
* Cooperative staff-management relations
* Kanban
* Quality improvement
* Productivity improvement
* Small group activities
* New product development
* Six sigma
* SMED
* 5S

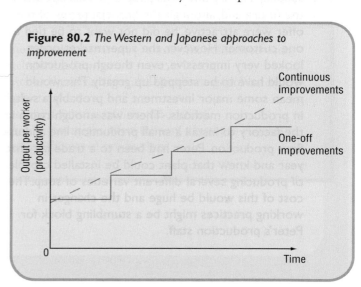

**Figure 80.2** *The Western and Japanese approaches to improvement*

Output per worker (productivity)

Continuous improvements

One-off improvements

Time

Data must be gathered and used to develop a plan which will result in improvement.

- Do. Once the plan has been finalised it must be carried out. The plan is likely to be implemented by workers, on the production line perhaps.
- Check. The next stage in the cycle is to check whether or not there has been an improvement. This task may be carried out by inspectors.
- Action. If the plan has been successful, it must be introduced in all parts of the business.

Julian Richer is a disciple of Kaizen. He heads the hi-fi retailing chain, Richer Sounds, which he set up with just one shop in 1979. In recent years he has earned a reputation for 'wacky' but very effective management ideas. Richer places great emphasis on establishing a rapport with every new member of staff. He invites new employees to his house for three days where they 'work hard and play hard'. They undergo an intensive training course, but also enjoy tennis, badminton, snooker, swimming, dance and films.

Every Richer store offers free coffee and mints to customers and has a mirror which says 'you are looking at the most important person in this shop'. If it is raining when a customer buys a new hi-fi system they are given a free umbrella. Customers' opinions are monitored and staff bonuses are linked to customer satisfaction.

Staff are encouraged to express their ideas. They are given £5 each once a month to visit the pub together and talk about new ideas. Staff with the best customer service records are given the use of four classic cars - Jaguars and Bentleys. There are also five holiday homes which they can book free of charge. Absenteeism is between 1 and 2 per cent less than the national average. If staff are caught stealing from the store they are dismissed instantly. He has a fanatical attention for detail, working from a cardboard worksheet that lists his tasks in minute handwriting.

Richer has a policy of slow growth, arising from past mistakes when he tried to over-reach himself. His policies, plus highly competitive pricing, have earned the business a place in the *Guinness Book of Records* as the world's busiest retailer.

Source: adapted from *The Financial Times*.

(a) Identify Kaizen business techniques or practices which Julian Richer adopts at Richer Sounds. In each case explain your answer.
(b) Explain the possible benefits to Richer Sounds of the Kaizen approach.

## Just-in-time manufacturing

JUST-IN-TIME (JIT) manufacturing is an important part of lean production and the kaizen approach. It was developed in the Japanese shipbuilding industry in the 1950s and 1960s. The industry recognised that a great deal of money was tied up in stocks. Traditionally, one month's supply of steel was held by a shipyard. However, as the industry became more competitive, shipbuilders insisted that steel suppliers deliver orders 'just-in-time', ie a few hours or less before the steel was needed. This reduced the need for high levels of working capital and improved the financial performance of the business. JIT was extended to every stage of production. For example, raw materials were delivered JIT to be made into parts, parts were delivered JIT to be made into goods and goods were produced and delivered JIT to be sold.

JIT was introduced in other Japanese industries, such as the car industry, and then spread to other parts of the world, such as the USA and Europe. JCB has used JIT in its Rochester plant. When JCB excavators are manufactured, every machine on the production line has already been sold. Supplies of components, such as engines from Perkins, and raw materials, such as steel plate, arrive on the day they are needed. JIT manufacturing requires high levels of organisational skills and reliable suppliers.

Table 80.1 shows the advantages and disadvantages of JIT manufacturing.

GD Mountfield is the UK's largest manufacturer of garden machinery. To improve efficiency it needed to reduce stocks, increase productivity and improve delivery performance during the peak 5 month period which accounted for 80 per cent of its sales. Also, space was needed for new products. With many key components bought from foreign suppliers, and heavily seasonal demand, the company held large stocks and used a warehouse to smooth out purchasing, assembly and sales. Even with 70 per cent of floor space allocated to storage, delivery was still inadequate at peak times.

GD Mountfield made a number of changes to the way it operated. To reduce stocks it employed a parts 'regulator', using clearly defined storage locations to give visual control of stock. This ensured that the parts coming in were matched to the number of parts used. The company also began a negotiation process with its suppliers to adopt JIT techniques and improve supplier management. As a result of the changes the company improved its product availability to wholesalers and responded more effectively to demand.

Source: adapted from Bourton Group website.

(a) Explain why GD Mountfield introduced JIT techniques.
(b) Explain why it would be important for GD Mountfield to have good relations with its suppliers when introducing JIT.

overtime eliminated. Paid holiday was increased from four to five weeks.

- Wages were increased in stages from the statutory minimum wage in 1999 to £7.50 per hour in 2003.
- An incentive scheme was introduced which was linked to sales revenue and defects. There was also an attendance bonus scheme. Workers received a £200 bonus if they went three months without being absent. A further £1,000 was paid if staff went a whole year without a day off.

Making the changes was not easy for the management buy-in team. There was a lot of resistance, especially to the training sessions. A massive 76 per cent of the workforce had never received any training at all whilst employed at Gateshead Holdings. The first few training sessions were greeted with a negative attitude. However, after a very powerful motivational speech from Geoff, eventually the workforce started to cooperate as they began to see sense in what the business wanted to do. Geoff also won the respect of the workers because he spent a great deal of the time in the factory helping to deal with problems.

In 2003, the company made a small profit for the first time in eight years. Geoff responded to this by

**Table 80.2** *Staff turnover at Gateshead Holdings, 1995 - 2003*

| 1995 | 1996 | 1997 | 1998 | 1999 | 2000 | 2001 | 2002 | 2003 |
|------|------|------|------|------|------|------|------|------|
| 35% | 39% | 41% | 49% | 34% | 19% | 11% | 9% | 6% |

organising a party for staff and their friends in a special function room at St James Park, home of Newcastle United.

(a) **What evidence is there to suggest that Gateshead Holdings introduced Kaizen between 1999 and 2003? (4 marks)**

(b) **What is the purpose of introducing 5S into the factory? (6 marks)**

(c) **Explain possible reasons for the changes in staff turnover between 1995 and 2003. (8 marks)**

(d) **Examine how waste would be reduced by introducing JIT and Six Sigma. (10 marks)**

(e) **Discuss the most important factors which helped Geoff and his team to transform Gateshead Holdings into a profitable company. (12 marks)**

## Defining size

In the UK there are around four million businesses. Their sizes vary. A company like BP Amoco has operations around the world, employs thousands of people and has a turnover of billions of pounds. A self-employed joiner may operate in a small workshop, employ one other person and have sales of just a few thousand pounds. Most businesses begin on a small scale and then grow. What is the difference between a large firm and a small firm? When does a small firm become large? How might size be measured?

**Turnover** Sales revenue that a business earns could be used to measure size. For example, Royal Bank of Scotland, is a large business. Its turnover in 2002 was £16,815 million.

**The number of employees** A business with thousands of employees may be considered large. IBM, the computer manufacturer, for example, employed over 300,000 people in 2004. The term Small and Medium-sized Enterprises (SMEs) is often used when talking about relatively small firms. The EU uses the following criteria to measure firm size:
- micro firm: maximum of 9 employees;
- small firm: maximum of 49 employees;
- medium firm: maximum of 249 employees;
- large firm: 250 or more employees.

**The amount of capital employed** This measure is based on the amount of money invested in the business. The more money invested the larger the business. For example, in 2003 GUS had capital employed of £2,640 million. EasyNet, in comparison, had capital employed of only £21 million.

**Profit** Businesses which have higher profits than others may be classed as larger businesses. For example, in 2002 Unilever made a pre-tax profit of £2,499 million. Helphire, the company that helps drivers involved in accidents, on the other hand made a pre-tax profit of £5.25 million.

**Market share** It could be argued that a business with a 43 per cent market share (☞ unit 21), is larger than one which has a 9 per cent market share in the same industry. Coca-Cola, for example sells over 50 per cent of all cola drinks worldwide.

**Market capitalisation** This is the current share price multiplied by the number of shares. Table 81.1 shows the largest 5 companies in the UK according to this measure.

According to the EU, a firm is considered to be:
- 'small' if it has a turnover of 7 million euros, a balance sheet total of not more than 5 million euros (ie capital employed), a maximum of 49 employees and is not more than 25 per cent owned by one or more companies satisfying the same criteria;
- medium-sized if it has a turnover of not more than 40 million euros, a balance sheet total of not more than 27 million euros, a maximum of 249 employees and the same 25 per cent criteria as above;
- large if it exceeds the criteria above.

## Problems with measuring size

In practice, measuring the size of a business may not be easy. A

---

Babcock International Group plc is a support services company with four main business divisions in the UK.
- Babcock Defence Services provides a wide range of support and training services to the Royal Navy, British Army and RAF;
- Babcock Engineering Services supports the activities of customers in the defence, marine, oil & gas and supply chain service markets;
- Babcock Infrastructure Services enables customers to reduce costs on their built infrastructure portfolio;
- Babcock Naval Services operates HM Naval Base Clyde in partnership with the MoD, providing the full range of support services.

The company employs several thousand staff and had a turnover of £423.5 million in 2003 (approximately 629.6 million euros at exchange rate of £1=1.48 euros). The value of Babcock's capital employed in 2003 was £87.4 million (approximately 129.9 million euros). In March 2003 the company's share price was 90p and it had 145,580,737 shares in issue.

Source: adapted from Babcock International, *Annual Report and Accounts, 2003*.

(a) Using evidence from the case determine whether Babcock is a small, medium or large business.
(b) In March 2004, Babcock's share price was 130p and the number of shares issued was little changed. Using this as an example, explain why market capitalisation may not always be useful as a measure of business size.

---

| Company | Market capitalisation (£bn) | Industry |
|---|---|---|
| **Table 81.1** *The largest 5 UK firms (market capitalisation), 2004* | | |
| 1. HSBC | £96,271 million | Banking |
| 2. BP | £95.666 million | Oil (integrated) |
| 3. Vodafone | £91,257 million | Telecommunications |
| 4. Glaxo SmithKline | £66,657 million | Pharmaceuticals |
| 5. Royal Bank of Scotland | £50,518 million | Banking |

Source: adapted from *The Sunday Times*, 29.2.2004.

highly automated chemical plant may only employ 45 people, but have a turnover of 50 million euros. According to the number of employees, the EU would class it as a small business. However, according to the level of turnover it could be classed as a large business.

Using the level of profit may also be misleading. A large company may have problems and make only a small profit over a period of time and yet still stay in business. One of the problems of using market capitalisation is that share prices change constantly. This means company size is fluctuating all the time. It is the size of the business relative to its particular sector in an industry that is important. Is it large enough to enjoy the benefits of size in the market? Is it too large or too small in relation to other organisational needs of the business?

## Reasons for growth

In many industries it is rare for a firm to remain exactly the same size for any length of time. Most businesses start small and then grow in size. They may aim to grow for a number of reasons.

- Survival. In some industries firms will not survive if they remain small. Staying small might mean that costs are too high because the firm is too small to exploit economies of scale. In addition, small firms, even if they are profitable, may face a takeover bid from a larger firm.
- Gaining economies of scale. As firms grow in size they will begin to enjoy the benefits of ECONOMIES OF SCALE. This means that unit production costs will fall and efficiency and profits will improve. This is dealt with later in the unit.
- To increase future profitability. By growing and selling larger volumes, a firm will hope to raise profits in the future.
- Gaining market share. This can have a number of benefits. If a firm can develop a degree of monopoly power (☞ unit 93) through growth, it might be able to raise price or control part of the market. Some personnel also enjoy the status and power associated with a high market share. For example, it could be argued that Richard Branson enjoys the publicity which goes with leading a large company like Virgin.
- To reduce risk. Risk can be reduced through diversification. Branching into new markets and new products means that if one product fails success in others can keep the company going. For example, tobacco companies have diversified into breweries to guard against a fall in demand for cigarettes.

## Methods of growth

There is a number of ways in which a company might grow. **Internal growth** is when a firm expands without involving other businesses. ORGANIC GROWTH means that the firm expands by selling more of its existing products. This could be achieved by selling to a wider market, either at home or abroad. It is likely that internal growth will take a long time for many businesses, but will provide a sound base for development. A quicker alternative is **external growth.**

Tesco has become the UK's largest supermarket chain and is continuing to grow. It is increasing the number of stores it operates, and extending its product range rapidly into non-food items. The company sells more DVDs than HMV, more shampoo than Boots, and its £4 jeans outsell Levis, Wrangler and Gap put together. It is developing its smaller outlets, on petrol forecourts for example, growing its online business and is also developing businesses abroad.

**Table 81.2** *Tesco, financial information*

|                    | 1999    | 2000    | 2001    | 2002    | 2003    |
|--------------------|---------|---------|---------|---------|---------|
| Sales              | 18,546  | 20,358  | 22,773  | 25,654  | 28,613  |
| No. of stores      | 821     | 845     | 907     | 979     | 2,291   |
| No. of employees   | 126,914 | 134,896 | 152,210 | 171,794 | 188,182 |
| Dividend per share | 4.12p   | 4.48p   | 4.98p   | 5.60p   | 6.20p   |

Source: adapted from Tesco, *Annual Report and Accounts, 2003.*

(a) What evidence is there to suggest that Tesco has enjoyed strong growth over the last five years?
(b) What do you think might be the main motives for Tesco's growth?

**Question 2**

This can be by ACQUISITION or TAKEOVER of other businesses or by MERGING with them. A takeover is when one company buys control of another. A merger usually means that two companies have agreed to join together and create a new third company. In practice these terms are often used interchangeably. In recent decades merger activity has increased greatly leading to a concentration of ownership in many industries. Mergers and takeovers are discussed in unit 89.

It had also been suggested that companies can attempt to grow in one of three ways. Companies can grow by **acquisition**. For example, AXA, the insurance business, has grown by taking over foreign firms in the US, UK and Japan. However, some companies that have attempt to grow by acquisition have become bigger but not better, and ultimately failed as a result. Examples might be Polly Peck, the food, electronics and textiles group, and Ratners, the jewellery store.

Some companies grow by **innovating** and providing new products. Examples may be Microsoft and Intel. A problem for such companies is that rivals start to copy their ideas, which may slow down growth.

Companies that grow by **robust growth** might include Coca-Cola and Procter & Gamble. They have long term

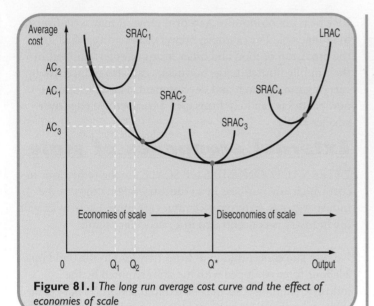

**Figure 81.1** *The long run average cost curve and the effect of economies of scale*

growth as an objective, take consumers' needs into account, are prepared to invest in information technology and value the skills of their workforce.

## Benefits of growth

Earlier in this unit it was argued that firms grow to achieve economies of scale. Economies of scale are the reductions in costs gained by businesses as they increase in size. Unit 38 showed that, in the long run, a firm can build another factory or purchase more machinery. This can cause the average cost of production to fall. In Figure 81.1 a firm is currently producing in a small plant and its short run costs are $SRAC_1$. When it produces an output equal to $Q_1$ its average cost will be $AC_1$. If it raises production to $Q_2$, average costs will rise to $AC_2$. The rise in average costs is a result of **diminshing returns** (☞ unit 53).

If the firm expands the scale of its operations (which it can do in the long run) the same level of output can be produced more efficiently. With a bigger plant, represented by $SRAC_2$, $Q_2$ can be produced at an average cost of just $AC_3$. Long run average costs fall due to economies of scale and will continue to do so until the firm has built a plant which minimises long run average costs. In the diagram this occurs when a plant shown by $SRAC_3$ is built. This is sometimes called the MINIMUM EFFICIENT SCALE of plant. When output reaches $Q^*$ in this plant, long run average costs cannot be reduced any further through expansion. Indeed, if the firm continues to grow it will experience rising average costs due to DISECONOMIES OF SCALE, as in $SRAC_4$ in Figure 81.1. This is dealt with later in the unit.

## Internal economies of scale

What are the different economies of scale a firm can gain? INTERNAL ECONOMIES OF SCALE are the benefits of growth that arise within the firm. They occur for a number of reasons.

Punch Taverns agreed to pay £1.2 billion for rival Pubmaster in 2003. The deal created a group with more than 7,000 managed or tenanted pubs - the largest in the UK. It was argued that Punch Taverns and Pubmaster had a good geographical fit, although there was overlap in Lancashire and the northern home counties. 'They have good concentration in areas where we are not strong like East Anglia, the north east and the south west' said Punch chief executive Giles Thornley. News of the deal was well received in the City. 'There should be good economies of scale in this transaction and so I don't see why it (Punch} shouldn't get stronger as it gets bigger' said Hilary Cook, director of investment strategy at Barclays Stockbrokers. The group did have the resources for further acquisitions, but indicated they were unlikely to be on the same scale as Pubmaster.

Source: adapted from *The Guardian*, 7.11.2003.

(a) Explain the reasons why Punch Taverns may have grown in this way.
(b) Discuss the factors that might affect further expansion in this way.

**Question 3**

**Technical economies** Technical economies arise because larger plants are often more efficient. The capital costs and the running costs of plants do not rise in proportion to their size. For example, the capital cost of a double decker bus will not be twice that of a single decker bus. This is because the main cost (engine and chassis) does not double when the capacity of the bus doubles. Increased size may mean a doubling of output but not cost. The average cost will therefore fall. This is sometimes called the principle of **increased dimensions.** In addition, the cost of the crew and fuel will not increase in proportion to its size.

Another technical economy is that of **indivisibility.** Many firms need a particular item of equipment or machinery, but fail to make full use of it. A small business may pay £400 for a word processor. The cost will be the same whether it is used twice a week by a part time clerical worker or every day. As the business expands, more use will be made of it and so the **average cost** of the machine will fall.

As the scale of operations expands the firm may switch to mass production techniques. Flow production (☞ unit 79), which involves breaking down the production process into a very large number of small operations, allows greater use of highly specialised machinery. This results in large improvements in efficiency as labour is replaced by capital.

Firms often employ a variety of machines which have different capacities. A slow machine may increase production time. As the firm expands and produces more output, it can employ more of the slower machines in order to match the capacity of the faster machines. This is called the **law of multiples.** It involves firms finding a balanced team of

machines so that when they operate together they are all running at full capacity.

**Managerial economies** As the firm grows it can afford to employ specialist managers. In a small business one general manager may be responsible for finance, marketing, production and personnel. The manager may find her role demanding. If a business employs specialists in these fields, efficiency may improve and average costs fall. If specialists were employed in a small firm they would be an indivisibility.

**Financial economies** Large firms have advantages when they try to raise finance. They will have a wider variety of sources from which to choose. For example, sole traders cannot sell more shares to raise extra funds but large public limited companies can. Very large firms will often find it easier to persuade institutions to lend them money since they will have large assets to offer as security. Finally, large firms borrowing very large amounts of money can often gain better interest rates.

In the past the government has recognised the problems facing small firms. A number of schemes have been designed to help small firms raise funds (☞ unit 2).

**Purchasing and marketing economies** Large firms are likely to get better rates when buying raw materials and components in bulk. In addition, the administration costs involved do not rise in proportion to the size of the order. The cost of processing an order for 10,000 tonnes of coal does not treble when 30,000 tonnes are ordered.

A number of marketing economies exist. A large company may find it cost effective to acquire its own fleet of vans and lorries, for example. The cost to the sales force of selling 30 product lines is not double that of selling 15 lines. Again, the administration costs of selling do not rise in proportion to the size of the sale.

**Risk bearing economies** As a firm grows it may well diversify to reduce risk. For example, breweries have diversified into the provision of food and other forms of entertainment in their public houses. Large businesses can also reduce risk by carrying out research and development. The development of new products can help firms gain a competitive edge over smaller rivals.

# External economies of scale

EXTERNAL ECONOMIES OF SCALE are the reductions in cost which any business in an industry might enjoy as the industry grows. External economies are more likely to arise if the industry is concentrated in a particular region.

**Labour** The concentration of firms may lead to the build up of a labour force equipped with the skills required by the industry. Training costs may be reduced if workers have gained skills at another firm in the same industry. Local schools and colleges, or even local government, may offer training courses which are aimed at the needs of the local industry.

**Ancillary and commercial services** An established industry, particularly if it is growing, tends to attract smaller firms trying to serve its needs. A wide range of commercial and support services can be offered. Specialist banking, insurance, marketing, waste disposal, maintenance, cleaning, components and distribution services are just some examples.

**Co-operation** Firms in the same industry are more likely to cooperate if they are concentrated in the same region. They might join forces to fund a research and development centre for the industry. An industry journal might be published, so that information can be shared.

**Disintegration** Disintegration occurs when production is broken up so that more specialisation can take place. When an

---

In 2001 Themutual.net merged with the e-mail specialist KeepAhead. Themutual, which changed from a service provider to a dot.com marketing firm to survive after the dot.com collapse, said the tie-up would enable better exploitation of a promising market in e-mail advertising. KeepAhead invites users to sign up to e-mail newsletters on a range of topics, allowing the formation of a detailed profile of users, and offering advertisers the opportunity to undertake targeted campaigns.

While revenue from banner advertising has collapsed, the e-mail advertising market has strengthened. Managing director of Themutual.net, Ben Heaton, said 'E-mail advertising clearly is an effective medium. It allows advertisers to target the people they want to, and they are willing to pay for it. They are not willing to pay for banner advertising.' The merger will allow the firms to exploit a combined database of 500,000 subscribers, and to pool assets totalling £500,000.

Source: adapted from news.bbc.co.uk.

A reason why some IT companies become dominant is obvious - economies of scale. This is important in computing, because the cost of R&D and the construction of manufacturing plants, are major parts of the price. If it costs $100 million to get a product to market and 100 million are sold, the development cost is $1 each. If you only sell a million, it's $100 each. Microsoft has exploited economies of scale to the hilt. It often launches products at less than half the price of rivals. When PC databases cost around $400-500 each, Microsoft came in with Access at a special offer price of $99. Vermeer sold its web development software, Front Page, for $695. Microsoft bought it and then relaunched it at $149.

Source: adapted from *The Guardian*, 15.2.2003.

(a) Analyse the economies of scale that might be enjoyed by the business in the cases.

**Question 4**

industry is concentrated in an area firms might specialise in the production of one component and then transport it to a main assembly car plant. In the West Midlands a few large car assembly plants exist whilst there are many supporting firms, such as Lucas, manufacturing components ready for assembly.

# The limits to growth

There is a number of factors which might limit the growth of business. If a firm expands the scale of its operations beyond the minimum efficient scale diseconomies of scale may result, leading to rising long run average costs.

Most **internal diseconomies** are caused by the problem of managing large businesses. Communication becomes more complicated and co-ordination more difficult because a large firm is divided into departments. The control of large businesses is also demanding. Thousands of employees, billions of pounds and dozens of plants all mean added responsibility and more supervision. Morale may suffer as individual workers become a minor part of the total workforce. This can cause poor relations between management and the workforce. As shown in Figure 81.1, long run average costs start to rise once a business reaches a certain size. Technical diseconomies also arise. In the chemical industry, construction problems often mean that two smaller plants are more cost effective than one very large one. Also, if a firm employs one huge plant and a breakdown occurs, production will stop. With two smaller plants, production can continue even if one breaks down.

**External diseconomies** might also arise. These may occur from overcrowding in industrial areas. The price of land, labour, services and materials might rise as firms compete for a limited amount. Congestion might lead to inefficiency, as travelling workers and deliveries are delayed.

There are other constraints on the growth of firms.
● Market limitations. The market for high performance power boats is limited due to their high market price, for example. Also, unless a firm is a monopoly, growth will tend to be restricted due to the existence of competitors in the market.
● Lack of funds. Many small firms would like to grow, but are not able to attract enough investors or lenders.
● Geographical limitations. Some products are low value and bulky. High transport costs may discourage the firm from distributing to customers far away. This means it cannot grow. Bread, beer and crisps may fall into this category. However, with improved communication networks, national distributors of these products have entered the market. Also, the provision of services is often limited to local markets. For example, people are not likely to travel very far to have their hair cut.

# Reasons for the survival of small firms

Despite the advantages of large scale production, many firms choose to remain small. Also, small firms sometimes have advantages over larger ones.

**Personal service** As a firm expands it becomes increasingly difficult to deal with individuals. Many people prefer to do business with the owner of the company directly and are prepared to pay higher prices for the privilege. For example, people may prefer to deal directly with one of the partners in an accountancy practice.

**Owner's preference** Some entrepreneurs may be content with the current level of profits. Some will want to avoid the added responsibilities that growth brings. Others will want to remain below the VAT threshold or will not want to risk losing control of their business.

**Flexibility and efficiency** Small firms are more often flexible and innovative. They may be able to react more quickly to changes in market conditions or technology. Management can make decisions quickly, without following lengthy procedures.

**Lower costs** In some cases small firms might have lower costs than larger producers in the same market. For example, large firms often have to pay their employees nationally agreed wage rates. A small firm may be able to pay lower wages to non-union workers.

**Low barriers to entry** In some types of business activity like grocery, painting and decorating, gardening services and window cleaning, the set up costs are relatively low. There is little to stop competitors setting up in business.

**Small firms can be monopolists** Many small firms survive because they supply a service to members of the local community which no other business does. People often use their local shop because it provides a convenient, nearby service, saving them the trouble of travelling.

# The popularity of small firms in the economy

During the past twenty years there has been a growth in the number of small businesses in the UK. Self employment has also grown. What factors have led to these trends?
● Rising unemployment has had an important impact. People with redundancy payments have had the capital to set up in business. In some cases unemployed workers saw self-employment as the only means of support.
● The government and local authorities introduced a number of measures to encourage the development of small businesses. **Business start-up schemes** (☞ unit 2) provided funds for small businesses for an initial period. Tecs and Business Links provided advice on running businesses and obtaining finance. European initiatives have included loans from the European Investment Fund and finance for training from the European Social Fund.

- There have been changes in the structure of the economy The expansion of the tertiary sector has contributed to the growth in small businesses. Many services can be undertaken more effectively on a small scale.

  The growth in the number of small firms has had several effects on the economy.

- Increased flexibility. Smaller firms can adapt to change more quickly because the owners, who tend to be the key decision makers, are close at hand to react to change. For example, a customer may insist that the extension to her house is finished one week before the agreed time. The business owner can put in the extra hours required and perhaps encourage employees to help out. Business owners may also react quickly when some new technology becomes available. This increased flexibility might help the UK economy win more orders from abroad.

- It could be argued that wage levels might fall as a result of more smaller firms. Employees in small businesses often negotiate their own wage rates with the owner. Since they are not in a powerful position on a one to one basis, there may be a tendency for initial wage rates and future wage increases to be relatively lower. This will help to keep business costs down.

- More casual and part time work may have been created. Small firms are often reluctant to employ full time staff because it is more expensive. For example, part time workers may not be entitled to the same level of holiday pay as full time workers. Casual and part time staff also help to improve flexibility. When a business is quiet it can lay off casual staff to reduce costs.

- Staff loyalty may have been improved. In small businesses, relationships between the owners and other staff may be quite good because they are dealing with each other at a personal level. This might improve motivation and productivity as well as staff loyalty.

- Trade union membership may have declined. In small businesses where relatively fewer workers are employed, trade union membership tends to be lower. This might have implications for the rights of workers in small businesses. It might lead to claims that in some cases, staff are being exploited by small business owners.

- Consumers might benefit from the growth in the number of small firms. More small firms often results in more competition and a wider choice in the market. For example, there has been a growth in the number of computer software producers in recent years. This has led to a variety of 'games' and programs for business and personal use.

The contribution made by SMEs (Small and Medium-sized Enterprises) in the UK is shown in Figure 81.2. There were an estimated 3.8 million businesses at the start of 2002, an increase of 1.4 per cent over the year. Almost all of these enterprises, 99.1 per cent, were small with less than 49 employees. Only 27,000 were medium-sized (50-249 employees) and 7,000 were large, with over 250 employees. At the start of 2002, SMEs accounted for more than half of the business turnover and employment in the UK. SMEs employed an estimated 22.7 million people, 43.7 per cent in small enterprises and 11.9 per cent in medium-sized enterprises. The combined turnover of the 3.8 million businesses in the UK was £2,200 billion. Small businesses accounted for 37 per cent of this and medium-sized businesses accounted for 15 per cent.

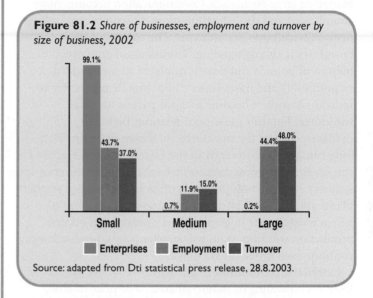

**Figure 81.2** *Share of businesses, employment and turnover by size of business, 2002*

Source: adapted from Dti statistical press release, 28.8.2003.

**Knowledge ...Knowledge...Knowle**

1. How can the size of a firm be measured?
2. State 5 reasons for growth.
3. What is the difference between internal and external growth?
4. Buying firms to grow quickly can sometimes be a problem. Explain this statement.
5. What are the main sources of: (a) internal economies; (b) external economies; (c) diseconomies; of scale?
6. Explain 5 reasons why small firms survive.
7. Describe 5 limitations to growth.
8. Why has there been a growth in the number of small firms in recent years?
9. What effect will the growth in the small firms sector have on the flexibility of employers?

# key terms

**Diseconomies of scale** - rising long run average costs as a firm expands beyond its minimum efficient scale.

**Economies of scale** - the reductions in cost gained by firms as they grow.

**External economies of scale** - the cost reductions available to all firms as the industry grows.

**Internal economies of scale** - the cost reductions enjoyed by a single firm as it grows.

**Merger** - the joining together of two businesses, usually to create a third new company.

**Minimum efficient scale (MES)** - the output which minimises long run average costs.

**Organic growth** - growth achieved through the expansion of current business activities.

**Takeover/acquisition** - the purchase of one business by another.

# Case study Small Firms

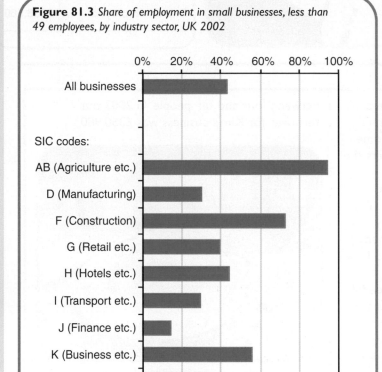

**Figure 81.3** *Share of employment in small businesses, less than 49 employees, by industry sector, UK 2002*

Source: adapted from Dti statistical press release, 28.8.2003.

Ganesh Kumar owns a film production company called Vision Ltd. It makes documentary programmes which it sells to television companies. The programmes are not usually made to order, so the company has to fund the writing, filming and editing of the programmes before any sales are made. In fact funding has always been a problem. Ganesh has struggled for eight years to grow the company but the same obstacle remains. Money lenders and potential investors see the business as high risk. It costs a lot to make a film and there is no guarantee that it will sell. The last production, a documentary about community life in the Scottish Highlands, was sold for £800,000 to two television broadcasters. However, Ganesh had to raise £500,000 to get it made. Most of the firm's capital comes from retained profit and a bank overdraft.

Marcham Uniforms is owned by the Marcham family and produces corporate uniforms and suits. The business was established in 1987 and has been successful under the leadership of Tom Marcham, who owns 30 per cent of the company. Four other family members share in the ownership of the business and also work in the organisation. In 2001, Tom was put under pressure buy his youngest son to expand the business. However, Tom argued that the extra work and responsibility required to grow Marcham Uniforms would not be worth the benefits. Further growth would have meant moving premises, investing in new machinery and taking on more staff in an area where unemployment was virtually nil. Tom suggested that the money the family members were making was more than adequate. He also said that the company's priority was to ensure that the present customers got the best service possible. Some extracts from the balance sheet are shown in Table 81.3.

| Table 81.3 *Extracts from Marcham Uniform's balance sheet* | |
| --- | --- |
| Fixed assets | £220,000 |
| Net current assets | £46,500 |
| Mortgage | (£30,000) |
| **Net assets** | **£236,500** |
| Share capital | £50,000 |
| Reserves | £186,500 |
| **Capital employed** | **£236,500** |

Kim Watson owns a highly specialised business in Fareham, Hampshire. It provides gourmet dinner parties prepared and served in the client's home. Kim offers a planning service where she meets the client and plans the dinner party in detail, discussing menus, for example. She buys food products, wines and spirits from very high quality suppliers and uses a collection of high quality china, cutlery, glassware and table linen. Dinner, up to eight courses, is then prepared and served by a team of highly trained staff according to the requirements of the client. Kim employs three full-time and 4 part-time staff. The dinner parties are truly special occasions and the prices charged reflect this. Kim can charge up to £200 per head excluding wines and spirits. Most parties are for between four and ten people. In 2003 the turnover for Kim's business was £350,980

(a) **Which industrial sectors have an above average number of small firms? (4 marks)**

(b) **What evidence is there to suggest that the three businesses above are SMEs? (8 marks)**

(c) **The finance sector has the smallest number of small firms. It is a sector dominated by some very large banking corporations such as HSBC and the Royal Bank of Scotland. Analyse the economies of scale they might enjoy. (12 marks)**

(d) **Explain why the three firms above might be likely to remain small. (12 marks)**

(e) **Discuss why small firms have managed to survive in such large numbers. (14 marks)**

## Managing materials

Businesses purchase raw materials, semi-finished goods and components. A washing machine manufacturer, for example, may buy electric motors, circuit boards, rubber drive belts, nuts, bolts, sheet metal and a variety of metal and plastic components. These stocks of materials and components are used to produce products which are then sold to consumers and other businesses. Managing the materials is an important part of any business. Materials management involves:

● the purchasing of stocks and their delivery;
● the storing and control of stocks;
● the issue and handling of stocks;
● the disposal of surpluses;
● providing information about stocks.

## Purchasing

Purchasing involves the buying of materials, components, fuel, tools, machinery, equipment, stationery and services by the business. It also includes any method that allows the firm to obtain the goods and services it needs, such as hiring.

The various stages in the purchasing process are shown in Figure 82.1. Purchasing usually begins when the purchasing department is notified of a particular need. For example, a firm's stores or a particular department may send a **requisition form** asking for more stationery.
The purchasing department will then act on this. Most purchases are repeat purchases from regular suppliers. Orders are placed with the supplier at previously agreed prices and delivery accepted under previously arranged terms. New products may need different materials and new suppliers. This will involve a period of search and negotiation, as the buyer tries to find the best deal. If there is a delay in delivery, it is the purchasing department's responsibility to find out why and speed up delivery. Once the goods have arrived the invoice is checked and then payment can be made.

In manufacturing the purchasing department works closely with the production and finance departments. Most purchasing is carried out on behalf of the production department. The finance department needs information about purchases to make payments and record the transactions.

## The importance of purchasing

The importance of purchasing is likely to vary according to the nature and size of the business. In many service industries purchasing is not very important. This is because materials are only a small fraction of the total cost of the final product. For example, hairdressing involves very little purchasing, as production involves a skill and uses few materials. However, a large manufacturer requires a large amount of materials, components etc. and so the firm will employ a purchasing department made up of specialists. In order for the firm to remain competitive the department must obtain the best quality materials, at least cost, and the quickest delivery. Failure to do so may lead to increased cost. The objectives of the purchasing department are:

● to obtain the quality and quantity of goods and materials that the firm requires;
● to purchase goods and materials at the most competitive prices;
● to ensure speedy delivery;
● to arrange delivery at the appropriate site, gate or location;
● to choose reliable suppliers and maintain good relations with them.

Kevin Clarke works in the purchasing department for Compton Engineering, a company that designs, manufactures and services heating systems for office blocks and other large buildings. He has received the requisition form shown in Figure 82.2. It is for some parts for a machine that has just broken down. They have not been ordered before.

**Figure 82.2** *Requisition form for Compton Engineering*

### Compton Engineering - Requisition Form

| Date | Description | Quantity |
|------|-------------|----------|
| 23.4.04 | Gear system CNC cutter - Type 211A | 1 |
| 23.4.04 | Switching mechanism - CNC cutter - Type 211A | 1 |

Authorisation: *F. Gordon*      Date required:   *ASAP (Urgent)*

(a) Describe the process that Kevin might follow when responding to the requisition form.
(b) What features of the process described in (a) might be particularly important in this case?

**Figure 82.1** *Stages in the purchasing process*

REQUISITION → NEGOTIATION → PLACE ORDER → CHASE DELIVERY → CLEAR INVOICE

Question 1

## Knowledge

1. What are the activities involved in materials management?
2. What is meant by purchasing in business?
3. Describe the various stages in the purchasing process.
4. What are the objectives of the purchasing department?
5. What effect can poor purchasing have on a business?
6. What are the advantages of centralised purchasing?
7. What is meant by:
   (a) components;
   (b) finished goods?
8. What are the costs of holding stocks?
9. Why are buffer stocks held by firms?
10. Why do some firms stockpile?
11. Describe the advantages of computerised stock control.

## Case study Prestwick plc

Prestwick plc assembles bicycles in its Glasgow based-based factory. It uses batch production and supplies retailers in Scotland and the north of England. The company has been troubled by stock problems in recent months. One of the difficulties is coping with frequent changes in design. This has resulted in the company being left with stocks of parts that are rapidly going out of date. Another problem is supplier reliability. Some suppliers of bicycle components have let down Prestwick. In extreme cases, supplies of components have failed to arrive, resulting in lost production.

The business is becoming worried about its stock position. The senior management team has met and identified three possible solutions.

- Adopt a JIT approach to stock management.
- Make some of the components themselves.
- Use a computerised stock control system.

(a) **Identify the (i) lead time (ii) minimum stock level (iii) re-order level (iv) re-order quantity for the gear system component in Figure 82.6. (8 marks)**
(b) **Explain the problems associated with holding too much stock. (10 marks)**
(c) **What evidence is there to suggest that Prestwick plc is carrying too much stock? (10 marks)**
(d) **Examine the possible reasons for the stock movement patterns for (i) gear systems and (ii) pedals in Figures 82.6 and 82.7. (12 marks)**
(e) **Evaluate the proposals made by the senior management team to resolve the stock problems. (12 marks)**

**Figure 82.5** *Total stock values for Prestwick plc, 1999-2003*

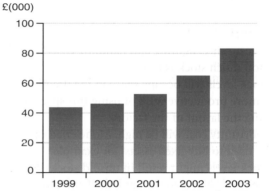

**Figure 82.6** *Stock movements of gear systems - type 23X*

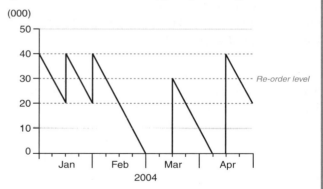

**Figure 82.7** *Stock movements of pedals - type WB12*

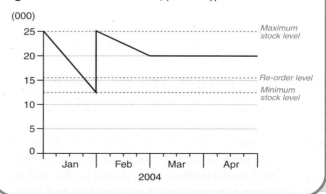

## What is quality?

Consumers, faced with many goods or services at similar prices, are likely to consider QUALITY when making choices. Quality could be described as those features of a product or service that allow it to satisfy customers' wants. Take an example of a family buying a television. They may consider some of the following features:

- physical appearance - they may want a certain style;
- reliability and durability - will it last for 10 years?
- special features - does it have stereo sound?
- suitability - they may want a portable television;
- parts - are spare parts available?
- repairs - does the shop carry out maintenance?
- after sales service - how prompt is delivery?

They may also consider features which they perceive as important, such as:

- image - is the manufacturer's name widely recognised?
- reputation - what do other consumers think of the business or product?

The importance of quality has grown in recent years. Consumers are more aware. They get information through magazines such as *Which?* that contain reports on the quality of certain products. They also have more disposable income and higher expectations than ever before. Legislation and competition have also forced firms to improve the quality of their products.

Businesses, faced with competition, are also concerned about the quality of their:

- design - the ideas and plans for the product or service
- production processes - the methods used to manufacture the goods or provide the services.

Poor designs may lead to problems with the materials and the functions of the finished good or service. It costs time and money to redesign poor products. Clients are unlikely to use businesses with poor designs again. Problems also occur with poor quality production processes. Faulty products are costly for a business. Machinery that breaks down or constantly needs to be repaired will also be expensive. Late delivery and productivity that results from poor quality in production can harm a business's reputation.

## Quality in production

Traditionally, in manufacturing, production departments have been responsible for ensuring quality. Their objectives might have been to make sure that products:

- satisfy consumers' needs;
- work under conditions they will face;
- operate in the way they should;
- can be produced cost effectively;
- can be repaired easily;
- conform to safety standards set down by legislation and independent bodies.

At Kellogg's, the cereal manufacturer, for example, samples of breakfast cereal in the past have been taken from the production line every half hour and tested. The testing took place in a food review room twice a day and was undertaken by a small group of staff. Each sample, about 50 in total, was compared with a 'perfect' Kellogg's sample and given a grade

Kwik-Fit, the car repair and replacement specialist, takes quality seriously. The business aims to give its customers the benefits they really want - fast service, quality products and competitive prices. According to the chairman 'We aren't interested in satisfied customers. We want delighted customers'. 'Our aim is to look after our customers and our people better than anyone else in the automotive parts repair industry'. The business argues that success is due to getting results in five key areas, called 'The Kwik-Fit System':

- identifying and responding to current and future motoring needs;
- developing specialist repair and replacement outfits;
- well-trained and highly motivated staff;
- sophisticated computer systems and management support;
- a distinctive and high-profile brand image.

Kwik-Fit's ability to identify and exploit trends in its markets is illustrated by its Child Safety Scheme which encourages the fitting of child safety seats in cars and the introduction of an interest-free credit plan.

Staff training at Kwik-Fit receives considerable investment - around £2.5 million. All service staff are trained in customer service as well as technical skills. The bold claim 'You can't get

better than a Kwik-Fit fitter' is deliberately made to give staff something to live up to. It's on the overalls of all staff. 'To the public, "You can't get better than a Kwik-Fit fitter" is an advertising slogan' says the chairman. 'To us, it's a philosophy.'

Source: adapted from Bnet website.

(a) What (i) actual and (ii) perceived features might a consumer consider important when using Kwik-Fit's car repair and replacement service?

(b) What evidence is there in the case to suggest that Kwik-Fit takes quality seriously.

**Question 1**

between 1 and 10. 10 was perfect but between 9.8 and 7, although noticeable to the trained eye, was acceptable to the customer. Below 7 the consumer would notice the reduction in quality. The cereals were tested for appearance, texture, colour, taste etc. More sophisticated tests were carried out in a laboratory where the nutritional value of a sample, for example, was measured.

**Quality control** in UK organisations, in the past, often meant inspecting other people's work and the product itself after production had taken place. By today's standards this is not quality control, but a method of finding a poor quality product (or a problem) before it is sold to the consumer. Today businesses are less concerned about 'Has the job been done properly?' than 'Are we able to do the job properly?' In other words inspection is carried out during the production process. This means that problems and poor quality products can be prevented before final production. Such a preventative approach has been used by Japanese businesses and is known as TOTAL QUALITY MANAGEMENT (TQM). It is now being adopted by many companies in the UK.

## Quality assurance

Businesses are increasingly taking into account the needs of customers. QUALITY ASSURANCE is a method of ensuring quality that takes into account customers' views in the production process. This can affect the business in a number of ways. For example, customers may be consulted about their views through market research (☞ unit 19) before a product is manufactured or a service provided. They may also be part of a consultation group involved at the design and manufacturing stage.

Quality assurance attempts to guarantee that quality has been maintained at all stages in the production process. The aim is to stop problems before they occur rather than finding them after they occur.

Businesses also work to quality assurance **codes of practice**. These show that a production process has been carried out to a certain standard and to the required specification. Once a business has been assessed and has achieved a certain standard, it is regularly checked by the awarding organisation to make sure standards are maintained. ISO 9000 is an international standard which businesses seek to achieve.

## Product standards

Businesses also include signs and **symbols** on their products which tell a customer about the product's standards. Examples of such quality symbols include:

- safety goggles which are awarded the BSI kitemark, telling the customer that the product has been independently tested to a specific standard;
- inflatable arm bands which are awarded the CE mark, an EU award. This tells the customer that they have been tested not to deflate during use and carry a safety warning about supervision;
- the Lion Mark, awarded by the British Toy and Hobby

Association (BTHA), which shows that manufacturers have a strict code of practice on toy safety, advertising and counterfeiting.

Some businesses support such guarantees with WARRANTIES. If goods are warranted, it means that the manufacturer will undertake any work necessary arising from a defect in the product 'free of charge'. Warranties are popular with products such as cars and a wide range of electrical appliances.

## Total quality management

Errors are costly for business. It is estimated that about one-third of all the effort of British business is wasted in correcting errors. There are benefits if something is done right the first time. Total quality management (TQM) is a method designed to prevent errors, such as poor quality products, from happening. The business is organised so that the manufacturing process is investigated at every stage. It is argued that the success of Japanese companies is based on their superior organisation. Every department, activity and individual is organised to take into account quality at all times. What are the features of TQM?

**Quality chains** Great stress is placed on the operation of QUALITY CHAINS. In any business a series of suppliers and customers exists. For example, a secretary is a supplier to a manager, who is the customer. The secretarial duties must be carried out to the satisfaction of the manager. The chain also includes customers and suppliers outside the business. The chain remains intact if the supplier satisfies the customer. It is broken if a person or item of equipment does not satisfy the needs of the customer. Failure to meet the requirements in any part of the quality chain creates problems, such as delays in the next stage of production.

**Company policy and accountability** There will only be improvements in quality if there is a company-wide quality policy. TQM must start from the top with the most senior executive and spread throughout the business to every employee. People must be totally committed and take a 'pride in the job'. This might be considered as an example of job enrichment (☞ unit 61). Lack of commitment, particularly at the top, causes problems. For example, if the managing director lacks commitment, employees lower down are unlikely to commit themselves. TQM stresses the role of the individual and aims to make everyone accountable for their own performance. For example, a machine operator may be accountable to a workshop supervisor for his work.

**Control** Consumers' needs will only be satisfied if the business has control of the factors that affect a product's quality. These may be human, administrative or technical factors. This is shown in Figure 83.1. The process is only under control if materials, equipment and tasks are used in the same way every time. Take an example of a firm making

**Figure 83.1** *The systematic approach to quality management*

Good design | Consistent method | Consistent equipment | Consistent materials | Satisfactory instructions

OPERATION AND CONTROL OF PROCESS

CONSISTENTLY SATISFIED CUSTOMER

------ Feedback channel

biscuits. Only by cooking in the same way can the quality be consistent every time. These methods can be documented and used to assess operations. Regular audits must be carried out by the firm to check quality.

Information is then fed back from the customer to the 'operator' or producer, and from the operator to the supplier of inputs, such as raw materials. For example, a retailer may return a batch of vehicles to the manufacturer because the gears were faulty. The manufacturer might then identify the person responsible for fitting the gears. An investigation might reveal that the faulty gears were the responsibility of a component supplier. The supplier can then be contacted and the problem resolved. Quality audits and reviews may lead to suggestions for improvements - a different material, perhaps, or a new piece of equipment.

**Monitoring the process** TQM relies on monitoring the business process to find possible improvements. Methods have been developed to help achieve this. STATISTICAL PROCESS CONTROL (SPC) involves collecting data relating to the performance of a process. Data is presented in diagrams, charts and graphs (☞ unit 10). The information is then passed to all those concerned.

SPC can be used to reduce variability, which is the cause of most quality problems. Variations in products, delivery times, methods, materials, people's attitudes and staff performance often occur. For example, statistical data may show that worker attitudes may have led to variations in output late on Friday afternoon. Discussion might result in a change in the 'clocking on' and 'clocking off' times to solve the problem.

**Teamwork** TQM stresses that teamwork is the most effective way of solving problems. The main advantages are:
● a greater range of skills, knowledge and experience can be used to solve the problem;
● employee morale is often improved;
● problems across departments are better dealt with;

● a greater variety of problems can be tackled;
● team 'ideas' are more likely to be used than individual ones.

TQM strongly favours teamwork throughout the business. It builds trust and morale, improves communications and cooperation and develops interdependence. Many UK firms in the past have suffered due to lack of sharing of information and ideas. Such approaches have often led to division between sections of the workforce.

**Consumer views** Firms using TQM must be committed to their customers. They must be responsive to changes in people's needs and expectations. To do this, information must be gathered on a regular basis and there must be clear communication channels for customers to express their views. Consumers are often influential in setting quality standards. For example, holiday companies issue questionnaires to their customers on the way back from a package holiday. The information can be used to identify the strengths and weaknesses of their operations. Such information can be used to monitor and upgrade quality standards.

**Zero defects** Many business quality systems have a zero defect policy. This aims to ensure that every product that is manufactured is free from defects. A business that is able to guarantee zero defects in customers' orders is likely to gain a good reputation. This could lead to new clients and improved sales.

## Using TQM

TQM helps companies to:
● focus clearly on the needs of customers and relationships between suppliers and customers;
● achieve quality in all aspects of business, not just product or service quality;
● critically analyse all processes to remove waste and inefficiencies:
● find improvements and develop measures of performance;
● develop a team approach to problem solving;
● develop effective procedures for communication and acknowledgement of work (☞ unit 70);
● continually review the processes to develop a strategy of constant improvement.

There are, however, some problems.
● There will be training and development costs of the new system.
● TQM will only work if there is commitment from the entire business.
● There will be a great deal of bureaucracy and documents and regular audits are needed. This may be a problem for small firms.
● Stress is placed on the process and not the product.

## Poka-Yoke

Poka-Yoke (meaning 'inadvertent mistake' and 'prevent' in

Japanese) is a quality assurance technique developed by manufacturing engineer Shigeo Shingo. It aims to eliminate defects in products by preventing or correcting mistakes as early as possible. While visiting the Yamada Electric plant in Japan, Shingo was told about a problem with the assembly of a product that had a switch with two push-buttons supported by springs. Sometimes workers assembling the switch would forget to insert a spring under each push-button. The error would not be found until the product reached a customer, which was embarrassing and expensive.

Shingo suggested a solution that became the first poka-yoke technique. In the old method, workers began by taking two springs out of a large parts box and then assembling the switch. In the new approach, a small dish is placed in front of the parts box and the workers' first task is to take two springs out of the box and place them on the dish. Workers then assemble the switch. If springs remain on the dish, workers know they have forgotten to insert them. Poka-yoke techniques fall into two categories.

● A **prevention** device makes it impossible to make a mistake at all. An example is in the design of a 3.5 inch computer disk. The disk is designed to be asymmetrical, so it will not fit into the disk drive in any other way than the correct one. Prevention devices remove the need to correct a mistake, since one has not been made in the first place.

● A **detection** device warns workers when a mistake has been made, so that the problem can be corrected. The small dish used at the Yamada Electric plant was a detection device. Another example would be an alarm that sounds in a car when the seat belt is not fastened.

## Quality circles

TQM stresses the importance of teamwork in a business. Many businesses have introduced quality circles (☞ unit 61) into their operations. Quality circles are small groups of staff, usually from the same work area, who meet on a regular and voluntary basis. They meet in the employer's time and attempt to solve problems and make suggestions about how to improve various aspects of the business. Issues such as pay and conditions are normally excluded. After discussions, the team will present its ideas and solutions to management. Teams are also involved in implementing and monitoring the effectiveness of solutions. In order for quality circles to be successful certain conditions must exist.

● A steering committee should be set up to oversee the whole quality circle programme.

● A senior manager should ideally chair the committee. Managers must show commitment to the principle of quality circles.

● At least one person on the committee should be accountable for the programme.

● Team leaders should be properly trained.

## Costs of ensuring quality

Firms will want to monitor the costs of quality control

carefully. All businesses are likely to face costs when trying to **maintain** or **improve** the quality of their products and services.

● The cost of designing and setting up a quality control system. This might include the time used to 'think through' a system and the training of staff to use it.

● The cost of monitoring the system. This could be the salary of a supervisor or the cost of an electronic sensor.

● There will be costs if products do not come up to standard. Faulty goods may have to be scrapped or reworked. Product failures might also result in claims against a company, bad publicity and a possible loss of goodwill.

● The cost of improving the actual quality. This may be the cost of new machinery or training staff in new working practices.

● If the whole quality system fails, there may be costs in setting it up again. Time may be needed to 'rethink' or adjust the system. Retraining might also be necessary.

It has been suggested that between 10-20 per cent of the revenue of a business is accounted for by quality related costs. This means that billions of pounds could be saved by UK businesses by cutting such costs. The vast majority of these costs is spent on appraisal and failure, which add very little to the quality of the product. Eliminating failure will also help to reduce appraisal and failure costs.

Although quality control systems are costly, it is argued that their benefits outweigh the costs. The actual quality of the product should be improved, so customers are more likely to purchase the product. Business costs may be cut if faults in products are identified before the product reaches the market. The costs of failure once the product has reached the market are likely to be much higher than those during manufacture.

## Best practice benchmarking

BEST PRACTICE BENCHMARKING (BPB) is a technique used by some businesses to help them discover the 'best' methods of production available and then adopt them. BPB

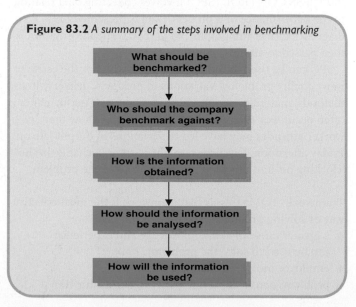

**Figure 83.2** *A summary of the steps involved in benchmarking*

What should be benchmarked?

↓

Who should the company benchmark against?

↓

How is the information obtained?

↓

How should the information be analysed?

↓

How will the information be used?

involves:

- finding out what makes the difference, in the customer's eyes, between an ordinary supplier and an excellent supplier;
- setting standards for business operations based on the best practice that can be found;
- finding out how these best companies meet those standards;
- applying both competitors' standards and their own to meet the new standards and, if possible, exceed them.

Figure 83.2 illustrates the five main steps in BPB. The first step is to **identify** exactly what the company intends to benchmark. Benchmarks that are important for customer satisfaction might include consistency of product, correct invoices, shorter delivery times, shorter lead times and improved after sales service. For example, Motorola, the communications company, has benchmarked the yield and product characteristics of a range of its activities including its assembly, warehousing and purchasing performance.

The second step involves **choosing a company** to set the benchmark against. This may be done by asking customers who they feel is the best in the field. Business analysts, journalists, stockbrokers or industrialists may also be used. Rank Xerox and Centreparc, the leisure group, have used other parts of their own organisations which have developed a reputation for excellence.

In the third step, information can be **gathered** from a number of sources, such as magazines, newspapers, trade association reports, specialist databases, customers and suppliers. Companies in the same industry often share information. An example may be businesses supplying local markets, such as garden centres. The benefits of this are that the worst performers can get advice from the best and perhaps visit their premises.

The **analysis** of information is best done with quantitative techniques (☞ unit 13). For example, a firm might compare numerical data relating to delivery times.

The final stage involves **using** the information. Once standards have been found and set, they must be communicated throughout the business. Improvements must be funded, introduced and monitored. Once a company becomes the best in the field others will begin to benchmark against them. This means the company must continue to benchmark their own process.

## *Independent bodies and trade organisations*

Certain bodies and associations exist that promote quality which are independent of government or businesses seeking to gain quality standards.

**The British Standards Institution** The British Standards Institution (BSI) is an independent organisation that attempts to set quality standards in industry. It performs a number of functions.

---

Bellingham plc supplies high quality, self-service products for worldwide financial institutions and retail markets. These include automatic teller machines, account services and interactive systems designed to provide 24-hour operation. Bellingham aims to be the 'model company' in its industry. It has been involved with benchmarking for a decade and has identified a list of key indicators for comparison with selected high profile companies. At the Basingstoke plant, desk research is carried out and directors and management are asked to nominate the most significant indicators. Further research identifies potential benchmark partners who have relevant data and who are willing to share. Bellingham believes that focusing on high profile companies is justified because they are the ones most familiar with benchmarking and tend to operate best practices. Benchmarking activities at Bellingham have focused on office equipment manufacturers and industries associated with electronics. These have sufficient common ground for discussion and the exchange of data.

Bellingham plc sees benefits in this programme coming from the 'shared knowledge' and likely 'best-in-class' performance comparisons. These will help Bellingham introduce improvement programmes and gain 'world class performance' throughout all its activities.

**Table 83.1** *The top ten benchmarking indicators identified by managers and directors*

1. Product reliability
2. Out-of-box quality
3. Return on assets
4. Revenue growth
5. Levels of inventory
6. Time taken from product concept to market launch measured in months
7. Main line yield (the number of units which pass main line test expressed as a percentage of units produced)
8. Advanced development schedules vs. planned
9. Actual research and development costs vs. planned
10. Manufacturing cycle time measured in days

(a) Describe Bellingham's approach to benchmarking.
(b) What might be the benefits of benchmarking to Bellingham plc?

**Question 2**

---

- Any business can apply to the BSI for an inspection of its product. Those that achieve and maintain a standard can carry the **BSI kitemark**. The kitemark tells the customer that the product has been tested to destruction, to ensure that it meets with certain safety standards. Products that carry a kitemark include some cricket helmets, kitchen units, child car safety seats, door locks, curtains, and sofa and duvet covers. This is shown in Figure 83.3.
- The BSI also issues a number of other product standards. These include BS 4224 for yachts, which shows the product conforms to standards used in yachting and ensures the

tensile strength of yarns, and BS 2724, which sets performance levels for the amount of UV light through sunglasses. BS 7131 grades the pile of carpets according to quality and durability. There are four grades used in the UK - light, medium, heavy and extra heavy.

- The BSI and other independent bodies, such as Lloyds, offer BS EN ISO 9000 registration. The title reflects the European (EN) and international (ISO) recognition for this series. BS EN ISO 9001 gives quality assurance in design, development, production, installation and servicing and is suitable for businesses which have a large element of design in their operations. BS EN ISO 9002 gives quality assurance in production, installation and servicing, for businesses which produce fairly standard products with little or no design. BS EN ISO 9003 gives quality assurance in final inspection and testing. This standard is suitable for small firms or where customers can check quality themselves through inspection.

Firms seeking certification have to show that their methods and procedures meet the recognised standards and comply with requirements. They are inspected on a regular basis to make sure that standards are being maintained. BS EN ISO 9000 certification can help a business to:

- examine and improve systems, methods and procedures to lower costs;
- motivate staff and encourage them to get things right first time;
- define key roles, responsibilities and authorities;
- assure orders are consistently delivered on time;
- highlight product or design problems and develop improvements;
- record and investigate all quality failure and customer complaints and make sure that they do not reoccur;
- give a clear signal to customers that they are taking measures to improve quality;
- produce a documented system for recording and satisfying the training needs of new and existing staff regarding quality.

**The British Electrotechnical Approvals Board** This is a body which inspects domestic electrical equipment. Manufacturers of domestic electrical appliances will be keen for the BEAB to approve their products. Approval can serve as a recognition of quality that customers will recognise.

**The Consumers Association** This is the body which follows up complaints by people about faulty products or services. They also make recommendations about products and services to customers. This takes into account such things as quality, reliability and value for money. Often survey results appear in their *Which?* magazines.

**The Institute of Quality Assurance (IQA)** The Institute of Quality Assurance is the only professional body in the UK whose sole purpose is the promotion and advancement of

quality practices. The IQA has three main objectives.

- To seek the advancement of quality management and practices and help the exchange of related information and ideas.
- To promote the education, training, qualification and development of people involved in quality assurance and the management for quality.
- To provide a range of services to members and, where appropriate, to the community at large.

**The Association of British Travel Agents (ABTA)** The Association of British Travel Agents is a trade association which has drawn up a code of practice for its members. The code aims to improve the trading standards of activities related to the sale of holidays. Travel agents are allowed to register with ABTA if they agree to follow their code of practice.

**The Wool Marketing Board** This allows manufacturers to carry the label shown in Figure 83.3 if their garments are made entirely of pure new wool. Obtaining a trademark is a way for a firm to give quality assurance to customers. If customers know that the quality of a product is guaranteed, they are more likely to buy the product. Also, there is less need to inspect the product, and returns and re-ordering are reduced.

**The British Toy and Hobby Association (BTHA)** developed the Lion Mark as a symbol of toy safety to be displayed on toy packaging. Toy manufacturers that want to include the Lion Mark must take out a licence with the BTHA. The manufacturer must sign a strict code of practice which sets standards relating to toy safety and advertising, as well as counterfeiting and markings on toy guns. The Lion Mark was adapted by the BTHA and the British Association of Toy Retailers (BATR) for shops. If the symbol is displayed in a shop it indicates that the retailer has agreed to a strict code of practice. They agree only to offer safe toys for sale and to ensure staff are briefed on toy safety matters such as age warnings.

A number of laws exist which protect consumers (☞ unit 103) from poor trading practices. They have tended to focus on safety aspects and consumer exploitation. However, increasingly UK laws and EU regulations are taking into account product quality. The laws are enforced by local inspectors, called **Trading Standards Officers.**

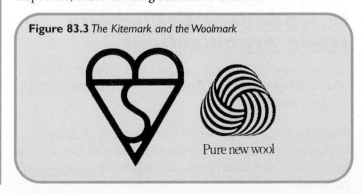

**Figure 83.3** *The Kitemark and the Woolmark*

Pure new wool

KC Stadium, home to Hull City AFC and Hull FC Rugby League, is a state-of-the-art all-seater spectator arena with a capacity of 25,000. It also contains administrative offices, players' accommodation and souvenir shops together with 28 executive boxes, a restaurant overlooking the pitch, hospitality suites and a supporters bar. The stadium will also be used for other local, national and international sporting fixtures, concerts and events. Bison, the UK's leading producer of structural precast products, supplied the main contractor, Birse Construction, with 2,494 terrace units, 16,180 m² of precast prestressed flooring units, 210 m³ of staircases and 440 structural walls.

Bison is committed to customer satisfaction. All Bison manufacturing plants are members of the British Standards Institution Registered Firms Scheme for Quality Assurance to BS EN ISO 9001 for the design and manufacture of precast concrete products. Membership of the scheme ensures that all procedures and disciplines relevant to the design and manufacturing processes are subject to independent approval and periodic review by the BSI. All Bison UK factories have been assessed by the BSI and awarded Certificates of

Assessed Capability under the scheme covering quality assurance for the manufacture of precast concrete products. Bison claims that as a customer you can be sure that all aspects of production, design, detailing and quality control have been independently inspected and have achieved the high level of competence and quality required by the BSI.

Also, Bison Structures Limited has been assessed by the SCQAS (Steel Construction Quality Assurance Scheme Limited) to BS EN ISO 9001. It has been registered for the design, manufacture, supply and erection of structural steelwork for retail, industrial and commercial buildings, car parks, leisure facilities and other private and public sector projects.

Source; adapted from Bison website.

(a) What role does the BSI play in Bison's quality assurance?
(b) Using examples from the case, suggest advantages to Bison of BS EN ISO 9001 registration.

**Question 3**

**Knowledge** ...owledge...Knowledge...Knowledge...Knowledge...Know

1. What is meant by the quality of a product?
2. Explain the difference between actual and perceived quality.
3. Explain the difference between quality control and quality assurance.
4. State 5 implications of TQM for a business.
5. Why is teamwork so important in TQM?
6. What are the costs of ensuring quality?
7. Describe the steps in best practice benchmarking.
8. What is the role of the British Standards Institution?
9. Explain the advantage of manufacturing trademarks to a business.

**key terms**

**Best practice benchmarking** - imitating the standards of an established leader in quality and attempting to better them.
**Quality** - features of a product that allow it to satisfy customers' needs. It may refer to some standard of excellence.
**Quality assurance** - a method of working for businesses that takes into account customers' wants when standardising quality. It often involves guaranteeing that quality standards are met.
**Quality chains** - when employees form a series of links

between customers and suppliers in business, both internally and externally.
**Statistical process control** - the collection of data about the performance of a particular process in a business.
**Total quality management** - a managerial approach which focusses on quality and aims to improve the effectiveness, flexibility, and competitiveness of the business.
**Warranties** - guarantees that faulty products will be repaired or replaced within a period of time.

# Case study Window Care

WindowCare manufactures PVCU windows. It employs 400 people and has grown successively year on year to its present £30 million plus turnover. In 1999 it was one of the UK's fastest growing companies. WindowCare serves two mainstream markets - the residential construction industry and the replacement window and conservatory industry. The PVCU industry's reputation in this sector could have posed problems to the company's success, had WindowCare not set out to prove that its quality was genuine. Hyung Taik Lee, WindowCare's marketing manager, explained that 'we supply replacement windows and products for new buildings, and people had become very wary of PVCU. The industry has a bad reputation - it's known for cowboys and white van man, so proving your product is of good quality has always been an issue.'

Proving that its quality matched up to its claims was exactly what the company set out to do. Hyung Taik Lee says 'We decided that the only way to lose this stigma was to go for the Kitemark'. WindowCare's commitment to gaining approvals provide convincing, third party proof that its products are manufactured to the highest possible standards can be seen in its current list of successes.

- ISO 9002 registration with BSI.
- Kitemark to BS 7412 for plastic windows made from extruded hollow profiles.
- Kitemark to BS 7950/BS 7412 for enhanced security performance of casement and tilt/turn windows for domestic applications.
- Kitemark to BS 5713 for hermetically sealed flat double glazing units.

The hard work has paid off for the company. Concerns about the quality of products, particularly in new build projects, means that specifiers now demand proof that PVCU windows meet stringent standards, and the Kitemark is a recognised mark of quality and integrity. Hyung Taik Lee said 'The NHBC is trying to raise standards to such a degree that it now specifies the Kitemark for windows. We cannot sell into the new build sector without the Kitemark.'

In 2003, in order to reinforce its commitment to quality, WindowCare introduced total quality management (TQM) throughout the whole of its organisation. The company invested a huge £3 million

in a training programme. Although a minority of the directors felt that an investment of £3 million was too high, some of the benefits of introducing TQM have been impressive.

- Staff were organised into teams which improved motivation and encouraged them to solve problems for themselves.
- Defects were reduced to 0.12 per cent, with 0.1 per cent the target for next year.
- Some administrative procedures were streamlined, resulting in a complete elimination of overtime and a reduction in the hours worked by staff from 36 to 35 per week. Basic pay was not cut in line with hours worked.
- BSI inspectors have reduced their visits, resulting in huge savings and less stress.
- Improved communications have resulted from the introduction of quality chains.

**(a) Define the terms (i) kitemark and (ii) zero defects. (4 marks)**

**(b) Describe the benefits to:**
**(i) the business;**
**(ii) its employees;**
**of WindowCare introducing TQM in its organisation. (8 marks)**

**(c) Why might WindowCare be suitable for other companies to benchmark against in future? (8 marks)**

**(d) Examine the factors which may have influenced the introduction of quality techniques at WindowCare. (10 marks)**

**(e) Discuss whether WindowCare should continue to gain ISO accreditation in future. (10 marks)**

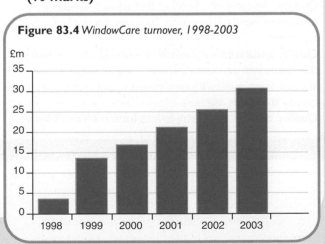

**Figure 83.4** *WindowCare turnover, 1998-2003*

## What is efficiency?

The objective of a business might be to be profitable (☞ unit 4). One way of doing this is to increase efficiency. EFFICIENCY is to do with how well resources, such as raw materials, labour and capital can be used to produce a product or service. Businesses often use costs as an indicator of efficiency. A manufacturer, for example, that finds its **average costs** (☞ unit 38) falling may well be improving efficiency as long as the quality of goods or services does not fall. Generally, as efficiency improves firms become more profitable. However firms may still be profitable without being efficient. This may perhaps be the case with firms that have a great deal of market power. BT, for example, operated profitably in a market free from competition for many years. This does not necessarily mean that increased profits came from being more efficient. Why might businesses want to measure efficiency?

- To improve control of the business. Information about the efficiency of different parts of a business will allow managers to find strengths and weaknesses.
- To make comparisons. The efficiency of different plants can be compared, for example. The efficiency of the business compared to one of its competitors may also be useful.
- To help negotiations. Efficiency indicators can help a business when discussing wage rates, levels of staff and working practices with trade unions, for example.

How might efficiency be measured? Lower average costs or rising profitability are only **indicators** of efficiency. It is difficult to measure efficient business practice as many factors influence it. It is possible, however, to measure the efficiency of a process or an input such as labour or capital.

## Measuring efficiency

How might a business measure the efficiency of a production process or its capital or employees?

**Measuring labour productivity** Labour PRODUCTIVITY can be found by dividing the output over a certain period by the number of workers employed:

$$\text{Labour productivity} = \frac{\text{Output (per period)}}{\text{Number of employees (per period)}}$$

If a small market garden employs 20 pickers who pick 40,000 lettuces a day, their productivity is 2,000 lettuces per worker each day.

This ratio measures the output per employee and is a useful indication of the efficiency of the labour force. There are, however, problems when calculating the ratio. For example, which workers should be counted? Should the maintenance crew, management, and clerical staff be counted, or should the ratio concentrate on direct labour only, ie shopfloor workers? How should part time workers and the long term sick be treated? How can the ratio accommodate a multi-product plant, where an employee's efforts might contribute to the production of more than one product?

What factors may lead to an improvement in labour productivity?

- There may be a change in the amount or quality of another input. For example, tools and equipment may have been replaced by more up to date and effective ones.
- The way in which labour and shifts are organised could be improved.
- Inefficient businesses with low labour productivity may be closed.
- Some of the improvement may result from increased effort from the workforce.
- The number of workers may be cut.

**Measuring capital productivity** A business may be interested in the productivity of its capital. This is becoming increasingly likely as more and more firms become capital intensive. A capital productivity ratio can be calculated by dividing output by the amount of capital employed in a given time period.

$$\text{Capital productivity} = \frac{\text{Output}}{\text{Capital employed}}$$

If a factory employed 10 sewing machinists and the total number of garments sewn in a day was 900, the productivity of capital would be 90 garments per machine each day.

Again, improvements in the productivity of capital may not be the result of more efficient capital alone. For example, the performance of an engine can be improved if it is serviced regularly and used carefully.

The labour and capital productivity ratios above are 'partial factor' productivity ratios. They measure the efficiency of just one input. A firm might want to measure the efficiency of the combined inputs it uses.

$$\text{Multi-factor productivity} = \frac{\text{Output}}{\text{Labour + materials + capital + etc.}}$$

This ratio takes into account that efficiency can be influenced by the quality and effectiveness of all inputs.

**Measuring value added** In recent years some firms have calculated the value added by the business where:

Value added = Sales revenue - external expenditure

This is a measure of overall company performance and shows the money available for reinvestment in the business

and distribution to shareholders.

In the UK productivity for the whole economy can be measured as gross value added (GVA). This is the value of gross domestic product or national income in the economy (☞ unit 101) plus subsidies minus taxes. Labour productivity can then be measured as GVA per head by dividing this figure by employment. The GVA per head in 2001 in the UK, for example, was £37,340.

Assessing business efficiency is a complicated task. A whole variety of measures are required and there is no single indicator which reflects accurately the overall efficiency of a business. A range of financial ratios (☞ unit 56) may also be used to help assess the performance of a business.

UK Coal is Britain's largest producer of coal. It employs around 7,000 people. In 2002, the price of coal was at historically low levels. In addition, demand from UK power stations was falling due to power generators using more gas to generate electricity. The amount of power generated by coal fell from 34 per cent in 2001 to 32 per cent in 2002. This trend was expected to continue. Table 84.1 shows profit/loss before tax, output of coal and number of employees for UK Coal in 2001 and 2002.

Source: adapted from UK Coal, *Annual Reports and Accounts, 2002.*

**Table 84.1** *Profit/loss before tax, output of coal and number of employees for UK Coal in 2001 and 2002*

|  | 2001 | 2002 |
| --- | --- | --- |
| Profit/loss (£000) | -£26,484 | -£83,111 |
| Output (millions of tonnes) | 22.3 | 21.9 |
| Number of employees | 7,376 | 6,902 |

(a) Calculate the labour productivity for UK Coal in 2001 and 2002 and comment on the change over the two years.
(b) The number of employees shown in Table 84.1 includes administrative workers. How might this affect measurements of labour productivity?

**Question 1**

# Work study

WORK STUDY is an attempt to find the 'best' or most 'efficient' way of using labour, machines and materials. The work of F W Taylor (☞ unit 59) is said to have formed the basis of work study methods.

Work study uses two techniques - method study and work measurement. Method study involves identifying all the specific activities in a job, analysing them, and finding the best way to do the job. This could be an existing job or a new one. Method study will allow a firm to:
● identify an optimum way to carry out a task;
● improve the layout of the factory or the workplace;
● minimise effort and reduce fatigue;
● improve the effectiveness of processes;
● improve the use of labour, machines and materials;
● establish the costs of particular activities to help with accounting;
● achieve results in the least time.

Once the best work method has been found, work measurement can be used to find the effort needed to carry out a task to an acceptable standard. The results can be used to design incentive schemes and determine staffing levels.

How is work measurement carried out? One example might be a worker being observed by a work-study assessor. The assessor might watch a worker set up a cutting machine, cut 10 patterns, reset the machine for a different pattern, and cut 10 more patterns, and record the findings. The performance might be rated against a scale of, say, 0 - 100, such as the British Standard Rating Scale (where 100 is the standard performance of an average, experienced, motivated worker). It is possible for an efficient and motivated worker to exceed 100 on this scale. Work-study assessors are often disliked by employees. Some regard these time and motion officers with suspicion and feel threatened. Workers are sometimes expected to work harder in the future as a result of their observations.

**Ergonomics** is also an important feature in work study. Machines and the environment should be adapted so that the individual can achieve the best performance. A study of the working area might concentrate on such things as air temperature, humidity, radiation, noise levels and lighting. A study of the positioning of dials might be used when studying machines. EU legislation has laid down a set of rules relating to the use of VDUs by employees, for example.

# Improving efficiency

There is a variety of methods that a business might choose which could improve efficiency. Some of the main methods are explained in the sections that follow. The aim of the business when introducing changes to improve efficiency is to increase the productivity of factors of production, reduce costs and raise profits. Increasingly businesses are adopting company-wide approaches which involve the whole business in improving efficiency. These strategies are dealt with in unit 17.

# Changes to the workforce

Improvements in efficiency can be made by making labour more productive and reducing labour costs. How can a business make labour more productive?

- Division of labour. If all the tasks involved in constructing a housing estate were carried out by one worker this would be highly inefficient. If tasks are divided between workers, this allows each worker to specialise on the job they do best, such as joinery or plastering (☞ unit 1).
- Incentives. Incentives may motivate workers to be more productive (☞ units 60 and 61). They may be in the form of a reward, such as a bonus.
- Changes in hours and payments. Employees may be asked to work shifts which allow equipment to be run for 24 hours. Flexitime systems allow staff to choose what days they wish to work within limits. Annualised hours (☞ unit 60) mean that workers can be asked to stay at home during slack periods, but work when trading picks up.
- Employing different types of workers may reduce labour costs and increase productivity. Workers who work from home, such as teleworkers who communicate with a business by e-mail or fax are often hired by business. They save on office costs. Part time workers or temporary employees may also reduce costs. Workers who job share might allow a job to be filled by two part time employees.
- Teamwork. This involves employees working closely together in teams when carrying out tasks. For example, quality circles (☞ unit 61) are groups of workers who meet to analyse and solve problems, and then pass on their findings to management. Cell production, where a product is manufactured from start to finish when operations are closely linked, is also more effective if teams carry out the work.
- Training. It is generally agreed that the efficiency of the workforce is linked to the amount and quality of education and training that it receives (☞ unit 67). Some businesses have their own training schemes, such as health and safety, graduate training programmes or Modern Apprenticeships. Some employees follow training courses leading to NVQs.
- Multi-skilling. Multi-skilling (☞ unit 76) is where employees are trained in a variety of operations. It may allow a business to reduce its workforce, as more tasks are carried out by fewer workers.
- Empowerment. This involves giving workers responsibility to make their own decisions and making them feel valued (☞ unit 61). Empowered workers are likely to be better motivated and to make better decisions, which could increase productivity.
- Employees may be involved in job enlargement, job enrichment or job rotation (☞ unit 61). These methods allow individual workers to undertake more tasks than they might otherwise have carried out.

Port Talbot Engineering is a supplier of forged conrods, a car engine component. It employs 200 staff who were being offered terms and conditions (piecework, fixed shift patterns, collective bargaining etc) that were at least 20 years out of date. Recognising that the 'us and them' culture was holding back efficiency improvements and the development of the business, the company decided to implement a new partnership agreement with trade unions and staff representatives.

A consultant was employed to begin the task. The initial approach was to hold a four day workshop with union reps and staff to draft, in outline, the new agreement. The approach adopted by the workshop was to find out what both management and unions would want, given a 'clean slate'. After the workshop all employees were briefed in small groups by in-house people who had been coached in expert and structured delivery. The consultant provided materials for the briefings such as documents to show how individual employees would be affected.

A ballot was held which showed that 64 per cent of the site's workers were in favour of accepting the new proposals. This included single status issues such as grades, shift patterns, sick and holiday pay, overtime payments, and new ways of working such as flexible working and multi-skilling.

The agreement meant that the company could operate more flexibly and meet customer demand more effectively. Improved incentives for the workforce helped to raise productivity by 35 per cent. Four months after the implementation, all performance indicators were positive and all targets were met. The systems implemented at Port Talbot Engineering were also introduced in sister companies.

Source: adapted from various websites.

(a) How might some of the new practices improve flexibility at Port Talbot Engineering?
(b) Why do you think staff at Port Talbot Engineering voted in favour of the new agreement?

## Question 2

# Standardisation

STANDARDISATION involves using uniform resources and activities or producing a uniform product. It can be applied to tools, components, equipment, procedures and business documents.

Changing systems can be very expensive, although there are benefits. A construction firm that builds a range of flats, for example, would benefit if all were fitted with standard cupboards. Savings are made in a number of ways. Bulk purchases can be made, the same tools and procedures could be used for fitting and training time could be reduced. This is an example of internal standardisation. Standardisation can also be more general. For example, efficiency will improve if there are standard components like nuts, bolts, pipes, screws and wire or standard measurements terminology, procedures and equipment.

The creation of the Single European Market in 1992 aimed

# key terms

**Capacity utilisation** – the use that a business makes of its resources.
**Efficiency** - how well inputs, such as raw materials, labour or capital can be changed into outputs, such as goods or services.
**Excess, surplus, spare or unused capacity** – when a business has more resources than it needs to satisfy current demand.

**Productivity** - the ratio of outputs to inputs in a production process, such as the output of a given amount of labour or capital.
**Standardisation** - the use of uniform resources and activities.
**Work study** - a process which investigates the best possible way to use business resources.

# Knowledge ...Knowledge...Knowledge...Knowledge...Knowledge...Know

1. Why might businesses wish to measure efficiency?
2. How might (a) labour productivity and (b) capital productivity be measured?
3. What is meant by multi-factor productivity?
4. What does 'value added' measure?
5. What are the benefits of work study for a business?
6. Describe 4 methods of improving labour productivity.
7. What are the advantages and disadvantages of standardisation?

8. Explain the difference between process and product factory layout.
9. State 3 ways in which a business may be reorganised to improve efficiency.
10. State 5 benefits to a business of improving efficiency.
11. Identify the ways in which a business might improve capacity utilisation.
12. State 3 advantages and 3 disadvantages of operating at full capacity.

# Case study Maritime Navigation Systems

Maritime Navigation Systems (MNS) was originally established to produce navigation systems for the Royal Navy. For 40 years the company did very well. It grew and widened its customer base into Europe. However, in 2002 the company's directors finally accepted that it would have to take measures to reduce capacity and push harder to improve productivity.

In 1998, MNS started to lose customers to foreign competitors. Unfortunately it was unable to generate business from other sources and, gradually, the company started to slide. In 2002, the business made a loss for the first time in its history. MNS reacted by employing a consultant to carry out a work study.

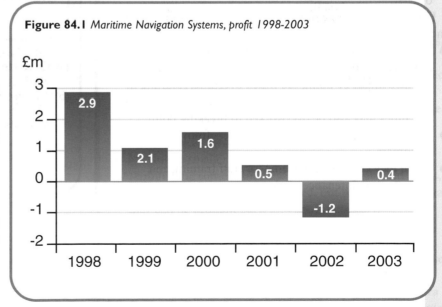

**Figure 84.1** *Maritime Navigation Systems, profit 1998-2003*

The results of the study confirmed the directors' worst suspicions. Its working practices were inflexible and out of date, the company was overstaffed, some machinery was obsolete and the factory layout was inappropriate. A number of recommendations were made by the consultant.

● Move to a smaller factory.
● Reduce staffing from 89 to 60.
● Introduce teamworking, job rotation and multi-skilling.
● Invest £2.4 million in new technology.
● Change the layout of the factory.

The directors agreed that all of the recommendations should be met. In 2002, MNS moved from its large old factory in Gillingham to a smaller, but much newer site, in Rochester. It spent £250,000 on a training programme so that workers could be multi-skilled. It offered voluntary redundancy and retirement packages to 20 of the staff and reduced staffing to 69. Finally, it bought some new machinery and sold off obsolete and unwanted machinery and equipment.

The results of the 'shake-up' were encouraging. In 2003, when relocation and redundancy costs were stripped out, MNS returned to profit. There were dramatic changes in labour productivity and capital utilisation. It also appeared that worker motivation

had improved. Staff seemed to prefer teamworking and the initial fears about having to do more than one job had all but faded. Figure 84.1 shows profit for MNS between 1998 and 2002. Table 84.4 shows some production data for 2002-2003.

**(a)** Using this case as an example, explain what is meant by capacity utilisation. (4 marks)
**(b)** Calculate (i) labour productivity and (ii) capital utilisation for MNS in 2002 and 2003. (8 marks)
**(c)** Explain how the changes identified in (b) will benefit MNS. (8 marks)
**(d)** Explain what is meant by a work study and how it benefited MNS. (8 marks)
**(e)** Explain how multi-skilling and teamworking might have helped to improve labour productivity at MNS. (10 marks)
**(f)** MNS could have chosen other ways to increase capacity utilisation. Discuss whether it chose the best options. (12 marks)

**Table 84.4** *Output, staff employed and factory capacity 2002 and 2003*

|                    | 2002  | 2003  |
| ------------------ | ----- | ----- |
| Output (systems)   | 2,300 | 2,200 |
| Staff employed     | 89    | 69    |
| Capacity (systems) | 6,000 | 3,000 |

## The nature and impact of technology

One of the most significant factors affecting how businesses have operated in the twentieth century has been the impact of new TECHNOLOGY. It is easy to see its impact when we consider some of the changes that have taken place in business.

- New products, such as camcorders, compact discs, laptop computers and services such as direct purchasing from television.
- New production processes, such as robotic welding, and computer controlled cutting machines.
- New materials such as silicon chips for computer circuit boards and polystyrene for packaging.
- Changes in business operations and new skills. For example, as a result of automatic cash tills in banking, many staff have been retrained to sell financial services.

There are many ways in which technology can be defined. One approach is to say that it is 'a creative process which uses human, scientific and material resources to solve problems and generate better efficiency'. Some examples make this clear. A business that uses video conferencing to communicate with branches spread all over the country is using technology. So is a plant which uses lasers to detect faults in products as they move along the production line.

How does technological progress take place? It is usually by means of **invention** and **innovation**. Invention is the discovery of something new. Some examples include the laser beam in 1960 by Dr. Charles Townes, the micro-processor in 1971 by Marcian Hoff in the USA and the Rubik Cube in 1975 by Professor Erno Rubik in Hungary. Inventions are then developed into products. The laser beam has been used for cutting in industry, micro-surgery in hospitals and spectacular lighting shows in displays.

Inventions are sometimes made by creative people 'outside' business. For example, the ball point pen was invented by a sculptor, and the pneumatic tyre by a veterinary surgeon! Today, most research is carried out by teams of people working for a business, university or the government. The rewards to inventors can be very high indeed, if their inventions can be used commercially and patented (☞ unit 87).

In business, innovation is the commercial exploitation of an invention. An invention is not usually in a form that consumers will buy. The product must be developed to meet consumers' needs, so that it can be sold profitably by business. UK firms have, perhaps, been reluctant to do this in the past. For example, the first working computers were developed in the 1930s. Since then Japan and America have led the world in hardware production and computer research. Enormous investment is often required to innovate once a technical breakthrough has been achieved.

One aspect of new technology is that new materials are developed. The new Mercedes CLS Coupe, launched in March 2004 at the Geneva Motor Show, came with scratch-resistant, nanotechnology-based paint as standard. The new clear lacquer top coat, which provides gloss and weatherproofing properties, is the result of a four-year collaboration between Mercedes and US-based automotive coatings supplier PPG Industries. Scratch-resistant coatings already existed, but they had no elasticity. They crack when exposed to the extreme temperatures that cars must withstand. PPG's new coating, called Ceramiclear, remains elastic when heated.

Most paintwork scratches are caused by minute particles of dust or sand that become lodged in car wash brushes. After 40 wash cycles, scratches on a vehicle using Ceramiclear were about half the width and depth of those in conventional paintwork. The coating retained about 80 per cent of its gloss compared with 20 per cent with a standard clearcoat. The new paint will also protect against degradation caused by ultraviolet radiation or salt and chemicals, but not deliberate vandalism. Mercedes was able to introduce the new coating without making any changes to its production process. Eventually, the scratch-resistant paint will be applied to the entire Mercedes range.

Source: adapted from *The Engineer*, 5.3.2004.

(a) Using this case as an example, explain the difference between innovation and invention.
(b) How will Mercedes and PPG Industries benefit from collaboration on the project?

## Question 1

## Applications in the primary sector

Primary industry has been affected by the introduction of new technology in a number of ways. In agriculture the use of tractors, combine harvesters, lifting equipment, grain drying machines and automatic milking and feeding apparatus have helped to increase output, reduce time and waste, and improve conditions. Agrochemicals and pesticides have raised crop yields. Biological research has helped to develop plants and crops which are more resistant to disease and more attractive to consumers. Genetically modified foods are argued to have better resistance to disease. In extractive

industries, such as mining, cutting, lifting and tunnelling machines have all led to increased output. There have also been improvements in safety equipment and mining conditions for workers. The extraction of oil now takes place on large oil rigs with computer controlled drilling equipment. This improves the speed and accuracy of production. In fishing, the introduction of refrigerated boats has helped to improve productivity. Forestry has benefited from cutting, lifting and haulage equipment.

One problem with the use of more efficient technology is that resources are used up more quickly. It may be possible to control this in the case of **renewable resources**, such as timber, by replanting and managed forestry. However, unless new forms of power can be developed, there are likely to be problems in future with extracting large amounts of the world's finite resources such as coal and oil. There have also been criticisms of genetically modified food and its possible effects on humans.

## Applications in the secondary sector

New technology has led to major changes in manufacturing. Many factories and production lines employ complex mechanical, electrical and electronic systems. Even smaller manufacturing businesses have benefited from the introduction of new equipment and processes. Examples of new technology can be found in a number of areas.

**Robots** Robots are increasingly used on assembly and production lines. They have some form of arm, which moves to instructions given by a computer. Repetitive tasks, such as installing components, can be carried out many times with great accuracy. Such tasks may lead to boredom, lack of motivation, tiredness and human error if undertaken by employees. Robots may also increase the flexibility of a business. For example, in 1998 small robots, each with its own set of paint cans, were installed in the paint shop of the Volkswagen-Audi car plant in Germany. The robot could be activated at a few minutes' notice when a customer wants a colour which is not included in the current program. Using the robot means that customer demand for less popular colours can be satisfied without having to clean out the pipes of the main painting apparatus, which would be costly.

**Computer aided design** COMPUTER AIDED DESIGN (CAD) is now used by businesses in the design process, before a product is manufactured. Examples of products designed using CAD include vehicle bodies, plastic containers to hold milk and oil, furniture and clothing. Designing on computer allows a business to produce accurate drawings, which can be viewed in 3D and altered cheaply and quickly for a client. Designs can be accurately measured and tested on computer for faults, such as unsuitable components or dimensions, which might have caused problems during manufacture.

**Computer numerically controlled machines** Products can be manufactured using COMPUTER NUMERICALLY CONTROLLED (CNC) machines. Instructions are given to the CNC machine by the operator. The machine then carries out its instructions, controlled by a computer. An example might be a CNC milling machine which is used to cut out a mould of a mouse in plastic. The computer controls the cutting to produce the shape of a mould. In the textile industry computer controlled sewing, cutting and printing machines are used. Some CNC machines make use of probes and **coordinate measuring machines** (CMM). These are designed to make simple or complex measurements, check batches or components one at a time and inspect geometric or irregular shapes. CMMs are accurate to within a few microns. CNC machines can produce shapes and cut quickly and accurately. They can also carry out repetitive tasks without human error. The instructions can be changed easily to carry out different tasks. For example, JCB uses CNC machines to cut a wide range of patterns from metal plates for its mechanical diggers.

**Computer aided manufacture** In many factories computers are used to design products and the information is then fed

**Figure 85.1** *Computer integrated manufacture*

Order

Order processing
Costing
Accounting

(CAD)
Computer
Aided
Design

Planning,
scheduling,
stock control,
quality control

(CAM)
Computer
Aided
Manufacture

CNC
lathe

Robot

Robot

CNC
miller

AGV

Transfer
station

Robot

Automatic
storage and
retrieval

CMM

Product

## Trayport

Edmund Hor bought the name Trayport for £100 and started looking for IT contract work. He had worked as a commodities and foreign exchange trader while at university, so it was no surprise when his first client was an energy broker. As a result of this work, a software application called Global Vision was developed. It was designed for online trading of energy and commodities such as coal, gas and metals. An eighth version of the software has been launched to cater for currency and credit derivatives. Trayport claims that 2,700 trading screens worldwide run its software. Its sales have grown from £207,000 in 2000 to £3.1 million in 2002, when the company reported a profit.

## Empower Interactive

If you have ever played Who Wants To Be A Millionaire? on a mobile phone or sent a text message, it is likely that you have used Empower's SMS (short messaging service) technology. SMS was originally designed to send short messages between two phones. However, because of the delay in launching third generation phones, Empower is responding to the demand for more complex uses. It has high profile customers such as Orange and BT. The company managed to raise £20 million from institutional investors and sales have risen by 221 per cent to £1.6 million in 2002. The company has made significant losses since it was formed, but expected to break even in 2005.

## Molecular Profiles

This company came out of Nottingham University and provides research support for the pharmaceutical and chemical industries. It investigates the level of contamination in drugs, helping manufacturers to improve their processes. It can also identify counterfeit drugs so that companies can take action against the producer. The firm's sales grew by 181 per cent a year from 2000 from £160,000 to £1.3 million in 2002. However, they are beginning to flatten out.

Source: adapted from *The Sunday Times*, 28.9.2003.

(a) **Why do you think the technology companies are described as 'innovators'? (4 marks)**

(b) **Identify the most important sector in the Tech Track 100 and suggest reasons why it dominates the technology industry at this level. (6 marks)**

(c) **Comment on the profitability of technology companies and explain two reasons for the pattern. (8 marks)**

(d) **How might these technology companies benefit (i) consumers, (ii) other businesses and (iii) the economy? (12 marks)**

(e) **Discuss possible reasons why technology companies might have been the subject of adverse publicity. (12 marks)**

## What are resources?

Businesses use resources in production. These are the factors of production in business activity - land, labour, capital and enterprise. This unit deals with land and the materials and resources used by businesses. There are many different materials used in business products. Some are manufactured into other materials or components, which are then used to make different products.

- Silk, a natural resource, is used in the textile industry. Silk fibres are made by caterpillars and are used to make a silk yarn. The yarn is then woven into a fabric. This fabric can be dyed or printed on and used in the manufacture of scarves or shirts, for example.
- Lycra is a SYNTHETIC fibre made from chemicals. It is usually combined with other materials such as wool, nylon, cotton or silk to produce clothes, for example. It allows clothing to stretch and recover its shape.
- Sugar is made by a variety of processes from the natural materials sugar cane or beet. It can be added as a sweetener to products such as jam. When sugar is processed it produces BY-PRODUCTS. These are materials which are created as a 'side effect' of the process. For example, raw sugar is separated from syrup, called molasses, in sugar production. This molasses is used in the food industry and as animal feed.
- Pine is a natural wood used in the production of many items, including tables and chairs, beds, toilet roll holders, children's toys and CD racks.
- Medium density fibreboard (MDF) is produced from waste wood, such as pine or spruce, left over after wooden products are made. Cuttings are combined with water, wax and resin to produce MDF boards. The boards are then used to make products such as furniture, shelving, toys, display stands and flooring.
- Plastics are manufactured from chemicals. Pigments can be added to change their colour and plasticisers make them more bendy. Plastics include polythene (made into bottles, crates and carrier bags), ABS (kettles and telephone bodies), polystyrene (packaging and model kits) and acrylic (as a glass substitute in baths, spectacles and street signs).
- Metals may be natural materials found in rocks, such as iron, copper or tin. Carrying out processes can change metal. Heating iron while blowing oxygen on it produces steel. Joining metals into alloys gives the new metal the combined advantages of the original metals. Brass is an alloy of copper, which conducts electricity, and zinc, which is hard but brittle. An alloy of aluminium and copper resists corrosion and is used for outdoor window frames and motor car parts, as it is lightweight and can be shaped.

## Waste

In the production of many goods or services some materials are wasted. WASTE also results from production processes. Waste is any material which is no longer useful in a particular production process and has to be disposed of. The **Special Waste Regulations, 1996** classifies different types of waste.

Unilever is a large international supplier of food, personal care and home care products. A summary of its products is shown below.
- Savoury and dressings. Some of the company's best selling brands in this category include Knorr soups and noodles, Bertolli's pasta sauces and Hellmann's salad dressings.
- Spreads and cooking products. This sector is responsible for producing brands such as Blueband, Flora, Brunch Boursin and Crème Bonjour.
- Ice cream and frozen foods. Unilever produces Cornettos, Magnums and Soleros for the ice cream market. It also owns the Findus and Bird's Eye range of frozen ready meal solutions.
- Health & wellness beverages. Two popular brands in this category are Slim.Fast and Lipton's drinks which include Lipton Ice Tea, Lipton Brisk and a range of leaf teas.
- Home care and professional cleaning. Unilever is a world leader in this sector which includes hygiene and cleaning products such as Snuggle, Comfort, Omo, Persil, Surf, Skip, Domestos, Cif and many others.
- Personal care. This sector accounts for around 25 per cent of Unilever's turnover. It includes brands such as Dove, Sunsilk, Pond's, Lux, Axe, Rexona and Signal toothpaste.

Figure 86.1 shows the contribution to turnover made by each of these sectors.

**Figure 86.1** *Turnover by category - Unilever 2002*

**Turnover by category %**
- ■ Savoury and Dressings
- □ Spreads and cooking products
- ■ Health & wellness and beverages
- □ Ice cream and frozen foods
- □ Home care and professional cleaning
- ■ Personal care
- ■ Other operations

25, 1, 19, 13, 9, 15, 18

Source: adapted from Unilever, *Annual Report and Accounts, 2002.*

(a) State six examples of natural resources that Unilever might use in production.
(b) To what extent do Unilever make use of plastics in its operations?

**Question 1**

different. However, like all other businesses, it produces waste and is obliged to deal with it according to environmental legislation. BOC's performance with regard to waste management and other environmental issues is overseen by the SHEQ (social, health, environment and quality) Department. BOC reported the following in 2002.

- A special global environmental working party was set up to develop the group's environmental and waste management practices. Its aim was to develop the best environmental operating practices in the world.
- Many BOC businesses have ISO 14001 environmental certification.
- A fuel efficiency programme was implemented to reduce fuel consumption costs and carbon dioxide emissions. In the UK alone, BOC operates over 2,000 large delivery vehicles. The programme has resulted in an annual saving of more than £340,000.
- BOC incurred no fines or prosecutions for breach of any environmental regulation. It was also compliant with external standards. However, it was unable to comply with all internal codes or practices.
- BOC patented systems to recover carbon dioxide from other company's productive processes and put it to constructive use. For example, carbon dioxide is infused in drip-irrigation water or used to enrich atmospheres to enhance growth.
- The development of technology that is more

energy efficient is a priority at BOC. This helps to support customers meet their carbon dioxide emission reduction targets.

- The UK-based BOC Foundation for the Environment, which was set up in 1990, has so far supported more than 110 projects focusing on waste management, water quality and pollution control.

BOC has had some criticism. The US Environmental Protection Agency named BOC as a potentially responsible party for clean-up costs at a number of hazardous waste sites. Liability for the restoration of the sites may be legally imposed without regard to the quantity of waste contributed. However, the cost was expected to be insignificant.

**(a) Identify five types of waste that BOC generates. (5 marks)**

**(b) Define the terms (i) waste management; (ii) hazardous waste. (6 marks)**

**(c) How might BOC benefit from having ISO 14001 environmental certification? (6 marks)**

**(d) Explain three ways in which BOC disposes of its waste. (9 marks)**

**(e) What evidence is there in the case to suggest that BOC takes waste management seriously? (12 marks)**

**(f) Discuss how different stakeholders might benefit from BOC's approach to waste management. (12 marks)**

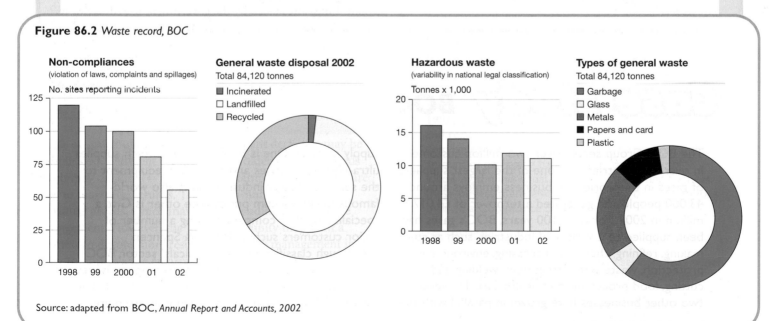

**Figure 86.2** *Waste record, BOC*

**Non-compliances**
(violation of laws, complaints and spillages)
No. sites reporting incidents

**General waste disposal 2002**
Total 84,120 tonnes
- Incinerated
- Landfilled
- Recycled

**Hazardous waste**
(variability in national legal classification)
Tonnes x 1,000

**Types of general waste**
Total 84,120 tonnes
- Garbage
- Glass
- Metals
- Papers and card
- Plastic

Source: adapted from BOC, *Annual Report and Accounts, 2002*

## Product choice

New businesses have to decide what product to manufacture or what service to provide. Once a business is established, it is unlikely to supply exactly the same product or service indefinitely. Over time businesses modify products, withdraw declining products and introduce new ones. They tend to extend product lines and may even diversify into completely different product areas. Decisions to launch new products or adapt existing ones are often complex and can be uncertain. Most businesses will carry out marketing research before making these decisions. This will help to evaluate the likely success of a new product before production begins.

What influences the products a firm chooses to produce?

**The approach of the business** Some businesses may be **product orientated** (☞ unit 18). The nature of the product itself (what it could do and its quality) would be enough to make sure that it sold. For example, when cars were first produced they were unique and a novelty and so the product sold itself. Many firms recognise the need to design products that meet consumers' wishes. These are **market orientated firms**. Increasingly businesses are becoming **asset-led**. They are launching products based on the strengths of the business. For example, a company with a strong brand name for a product may develop other related products (☞ unit 27).

**Competitors' behaviour** In order to survive in a competitive market, businesses must supply products which customers prefer at the expense of those supplied by competitors. This may mean developing products which are not available, or copying rivals' ideas and improving them.

**Technology** New inventions and innovations often result in new products. For example research has resulted in mobile telephones, satellite television, with pay per view options, and digital television, with improved picture quality and interactive options. New materials have been created which have led to improved products. Kevlar is a fibre which is used in the manufacture of bullet proof vests because of its resistance to impact. Carbon fibre racing cycles have been created which are lighter and faster than traditional cycles. Totally new products may be created. DVD players play films stored on discs similar to CDs. However, they contain far more information.

**Management** The choice of product is often made by senior management. It is a crucial decision because it may decide the fate of a company.

**Financial viability** Do the benefits of new or adapted goods or services outweigh the costs? The benefit to the firm might be the revenue it gains from selling the product. Accountants often act as a **constraint** on production decisions. They are unlikely to approve funds for products which will make long term losses.

## Approaches to product development

Businesses may prefer to develop a new product which is unique. In practice this is difficult. New product development is expensive and highly risky. As a result most 'new' products tend to be adapted from those which already exist. Product ideas can come from a number of sources.

**Ideas from customers** The most successful firms will be those which provide products which match the wants of customers. Thus it makes sense to listen to the views of customers when forming ideas for new products. The marketing department is likely to play an important role. Questionnaires and interviews can be used to gather data from customers (☞ unit 19). However, it is often argued that less structured methods are more appropriate for collecting new ideas. The use of **focus groups**, where 7 to 10 participants sit to discuss and share ideas about new products, is one approach. Another

(a) What factors might have influenced the development of the products above?

**Question 1**

country by quotas. One way to avoid these restrictions is to produce and sell products in the country which imposes the restriction. These goods are then classified as domestic output and avoid tariffs or quotas. Many Japanese companies have located in the EU because it imposes tariffs on products entering the EU from foreign countries. In recent years it could be argued that protectionism has declined. Countries such as India, Japan, China and Russia have allowed foreign products to enter their countries.

- Legislation and bureaucracy. Businesses want to avoid countries which impose restrictive laws and time consuming bureaucracy when locating operations. They are more likely to locate in countries where there is a liberal approach to issues like health and safety, the environment and employment legislation.
- The growth of ICT has also affected international location. It is now possible for a UK company with its main market in the UK to have its head office in the UK, its orders department in a low cost country in Asia and its production in the far east or eastern Europe. The immediate communication through e-mail or other media makes it possible to run such an organisation efficiently.
- Political stability. Businesses will tend to reduce risk by avoiding the location of plants in countries where the political system is unstable or there is the possibility of military action.
- The labour force. The cost of labour in different countries may affect the location decision of a business. Multinationals have set up production operations in Asia, where wages are comparatively low. The quality of the workforce is also a key factor. Companies will locate plants in countries where the workforce is flexible, cooperative, highly motivated, well trained and talented.
- Market opportunities and transport costs. Some businesses locate plants in countries where they see selling opportunities. When trying to enter a new market, it may be more cost effective to supply the market from within. In particular, if the products are bulky like motor cars, shipping costs from one side of the world to markets on the other side can reduce profit margins. For example, the growth of the Chinese economy in the period 2000-04 created market opportunities for businesses that did not exist previously when the government operated a closed economic system. Opportunities were also likely to take place with the expansion of the EU in 2004 (☞ unit 107).
- Financial incentives. Businesses may be attracted to a particular country or area if cash or other financial incentives are offered if they locate there. Some of the regional aid available in parts of Europe may have influenced the location of Asian multinationals in the 1990s.
- Globalisation. It has been suggested that businesses are facing globalised markets (☞ unit 109). Selling into a global market, rather than a single country or area, is likely to be more effective if a business produces and sells in many different countries. For example, it may be able to

take into account regional characteristics in its products or establish a corporate brand image.
- Corporate image. Some multinationals (☞ unit 109) set

A number of businesses have shifted their service jobs to India because labour costs are roughly one-third of what they would be in the UK. Large corporations such as BT, Lloyds, TSB, Abbey, British Airways and HSBC are all taking advantage of the low-cost services in India. Officials in Delhi expect IT-enabled services, which include call centres, to grow by 65 per cent a year. This is not surprising when you consider that staff in a typical call centre, located in one of the Software Technology Parks in India (STPIs), gets paid 10,000 rupees (£132) a month. Staff are also well qualified, many with university degrees.

STPIs play an important role in attracting foreign businesses. They are responsible for granting licenses to Indian companies that want to export IT services. STPIs have also pushed hard to develop the infrastructure. They have set up broadband networks right across India. STPI-licensed companies do not have to pay corporation tax in India. This has encouraged entry into the industry and helped to supply IT services to the growing band of foreign companies looking for cheap locations.

Bangalore is one of the cities to have benefited most of all from the boom in IT exporting. The invasion of foreign customers began in 1984 when Texas Instruments, the US IT company, arrived. It was attracted by Bangalore's concentration of high-quality graduates, specialising in software design, and low salaries. Since then Bangalore has developed into the self-styled IT capital of India. Today, Bangalore has some excellent colleges and produces 40,000 engineering graduates each year. However, this success has brought with it some problems. Water and power shortages are common and the traffic is horrendous.

**Figure 88.2** *IT export growth in India*

Per cent %

Share in India's exports

1997/8 — 2002/3

$m

Value of IT exports

1997/8 — 2002/3

Source: adapted from *The Sunday Times*, 9.11.2003.

(a) Describe the location factors that have attracted foreign businesses to India.
(b) Examine the possible benefits of foreign companies being attracted to India for cities such as Bangalore.

Question 4

up parts of their business in other countries, but keep their head offices and take back profits to the home country. Others have head offices and operations in many different countries. They use labour from the country in which they operate. They reinvest profits in that country and develop infrastructure. This approach could allow a business to improve its corporate image (☞ unit 15), as it is seen as providing benefits to the countries in which it operates.

● The introduction of the single European currency (☞ unit 107) may have influenced business location after the year 2000. Multinational companies may have located inside Europe to gain the benefits of simplified accounting, pricing and marketing.

## Inward investment

INWARD INVESTMENT is the flow of foreign funds into a country for the purposes of setting up business operations. In the 1990s the UK attracted billions of pounds of inward investment from foreign companies setting up production

plants in the country. The success of the UK in attracting this investment was largely the work of national, regional and local agencies. Examples included English Partnerships, the Commission for the New Towns, the Mersey Partnership and the West Midlands Development Agency. These played vital roles in attracting overseas investment in new factories and decisions by foreign firms to invest in existing operations. For example, English Partnerships played a key role in attracting Samsung Electronics, the Korean firm, to invest in a £450 million multi-product complex in Teeside.

Inward investment can have a number of benefits to UK industry.

● Foreign businesses which locate in the UK will need supplies, perhaps from UK suppliers of components and specialist commercial services.

● Businesses will recruit workers. Retailers, cinemas, restaurants and other local businesses will gain from the extra spending.

● Some UK businesses may already supply the overseas business. If production is switched to the UK then transport costs may fall and profits rise.

● UK businesses may learn about new production methods and working practices.

● If UK businesses make a good impression with overseas investors, this might generate publicity which could lead to further investment in the UK.

## key terms

**Assisted areas** – areas that are designated as having problems by the UK or EU and are eligible for support in a variety of forms.

**Brownfield site** – areas of land which were once used for urban development.

**Enterprise zones** – small inner city areas designated by the government which qualify for financial assistance.

**Footloose industries** – those industries which are neither influenced by their market or the source of raw materials when deciding where to locate.

**Green belt** – areas designated by government, usually in agricultural areas, where the development of business is prohibited.

**Greenfield sites** – areas of land, usually on the outskirts of towns and cities, where businesses develop for the first time.

**Industrial inertia** – the tendency for firms in the same industry to locate in the same region even when the original locational advantages have disappeared.

**Inward investment** – the setting up of business, or investment in business, by a company from another country.

**Regional policy** – measures used by central and local government to attract businesses to 'depressed' areas.

**Site factors** – factors affecting the choice of a plot or premises rather than an area.

## Knowledge Knowledge...Knowle

1. Under what circumstances will transport costs be particularly influential in business location?
2. State 3 types of business that will benefit from locating close to the market.
3. Give 4 methods of communication that may influence a location decision.
4. For what type of business activity is land an important factor in influencing location?
5. Why might it be important to transfer existing employees when relocating?
6. Give 3 problems that a business might have in transferring its existing labour force to a new location.
7. How might the geographical distribution of labour affect location?
8. Identify the help which the UK government and the EU gives to businesses when locating in the UK.
9. Describe 6 factors which might be important when locating a business operation overseas.
10. State 3 examples of inward investment.

# Case study  *Business location in Cumbria*

To some, Cumbria might be an unlikely location to set up a new business or develop an existing one. Sparsely populated, slightly isolated in the far North west and apparently offering little in the way of modern urban infrastructure, there appears to be little to attract business activity. However, there is plenty of evidence to suggest that businesses are impressed with the area.

- Cumbria is England's second largest county, covering 6,810 square kilometres (2,629 miles).
- Situated in the north-west of England, the county represents 48 per cent of the region's land mass.
- Around half the county is designated as National Park or Areas of Outstanding Natural Beauty.
- The total population of Cumbria is 490,000 with 63 per cent of the inhabitants of working age.
- There are 204,000 households in Cumbria.

Cumbria is well represented in all business sectors. Around 23 per cent of the total workforce is employed in manufacturing, with this figure rising to 38 per cent in some parts of Cumbria. Table 88.1 lists the main national and international companies with operations in Cumbria.

The Research, Development and Advanced Technologies sector has seen significant growth and offers huge potential to investors as advances in telecommunications and IT, give companies the freedom to locate in a high quality environment. Expanding fields in Cumbria include small and medium sized enterprises and research centres in specialist areas such as bio-technologies, genetics and health care treatments, marine technologies, terrestrial ecology, paper and film technologies and waste management control.

As in most other regions, the service sector is the biggest. In Cumbria it accounts for two thirds of the working population, creating a high level of office-based, computer and IT skills. Customer Service Centres are a growing industry with operations at the Barrow BT Call Centre and mail order centres at Lakeland Limited, Hawkshead Countrywear and Historical Collections.

Around 15 per cent of the Cumbrian workforce is employed in tourist related industries and Cumbria receives nearly 15 million visitors a year with over £400 million being generated in direct tourist related spending.

**Table 88.1**

| COMPANY | SECTOR |
|---|---|
| BAE Systems | *marine engineering* |
| British Nuclear Fuels Ltd | *nuclear fuels* |
| Breed UK | *car safety restraints* |
| Carnaud MetalBox | *cans/containers* |
| Carrs Milling Plc | *food manufacture* |
| Corus | *rail track and steel manufacture* |
| James Cropper Plc | *paper manufacture* |
| Eastman Chemicals | *chemicals* |
| Eddie Stobart Ltd | *transport and distribution* |
| Enesco European | *giftware* |
| Farley Health Products | *baby foods* |
| Glaxo SmithKline | *pharmaceuticals* |
| Iggesund Board | *paper and board manufacture* |
| Kangol | *clothing* |
| Kimberley Clark | *paper manufacture* |
| K Shoes | *footwear manufacture* |
| Lawson Mardon Packaging | *flexible packaging* |
| Nestlé | *food manufacture* |
| New Balance Athletic Shoes | *footwear manufacture* |
| Pirelli | *tyre manufacture* |
| Robert McBride | *detergent manufacturer* |
| Sealy United Kingdom | *bed manufacture* |
| UCB Films | *films for labels, securities and packaging* |
| United Biscuits | *food manufacture* |
| James Walker | *fluid sealing technology* |

Examples of three businesses located in the region are shown over the page.

**Eddie Stobart** A private company with headquarters in Carlisle, Eddie Stobart Ltd is the UK's largest transport and logistics organisation. Chairman and Chief Executive, Edward Stobart, believes the Cumbrian location has played a vital role in the company's success. The Group's strategic position is adjacent to the M6, linking Scotland with the rest of the UK motorway network. From 100 vehicles in 1991 to a fleet that numbers 700 today, 20 depots nationally and 3 million square feet of warehousing, Eddie Stobart Ltd is constantly expanding. New opportunities include property and development, mail order and retail, and there are even plans for a new rail service and roadside restaurants. This growth has led to more jobs, where the emphasis is on training to achieve maximum efficiencies. This is proof that Cumbria provides the place and the people to transport a business forward.

**Farley's** Farley's is part of the largest baby food manufacturers in Britain and owned by H.J. Heinz. To produce the highest quality baby foods, the highest quality environment is essential. The clean air, clean water and committed workforce have all contributed to Farley's continued success. The company is market leader in the UK and has worldwide exports. In 1998, Heinz demonstrated its commitment to the plant with a £3.5 million investment programme. Farley's is surrounded by Lakeland fells, close to the market town of Kendal and dual carriageway creating a fast link with the M6 motorway. So the healthy Cumbrian environment is not just good for people, it's good for business.

**Kimberly** Clark Kimberly-Clark is the global number one in facial tissues, bathroom tissues, hand towels and wipes. Mill Manager, Peter Taylor, credits the adaptability of the highly skilled workforce and the low operating costs in Cumbria which maintains his company's competitiveness, as key factors for success. The Barrow-based paper mill is expanding rapidly as a result of this success. To help meet increasing demand, the company invested £15 million in 1997/98 for a new mill and machinery.

Source: adapted from Cumbrian Inward Investment Agency website.

(a) **British Nuclear Fuel has a power station at Sellafield in Cumbria. Why might this have been chosen as a site? (6 marks)**

(b) **What are likely to be important location factors for a logistics company like Eddie Stobart? Explain your answer. (8 marks)**

(c) **Explain the advantages to a footloose business of locating in Cumbria. (8 marks)**

(d) **Analyse the advantages and disadvantages of locating a small hotel, catering for hill walkers, in Whitehaven which is situated on the Cumbrian coast. (10 marks)**

(e) **Do you think Cumbria is likely to qualify for any regional aid? Explain your answer. (8 marks)**

(f) **Discuss whether or not a blue chip company would consider moving its head office from London to Cumbria. (10 marks)**

## Reasons for mergers and takeovers

Mergers and takeovers take place when firms join together and operate as one organisation. Why do some businesses act in this way?

- It is a quick and easy way to expand the business (☞ unit 14). For example, if a supermarket chain wanted to open another twenty stores in the UK, it could find sites and build new premises. A quicker way could be to buy a company that already owns some stores and convert them.
- Buying a business is often cheaper than growing internally. A business may calculate that the cost of internal growth is £80 million. However, it might be possible to buy another company for £55 million on the stock market. The process of buying the company might inflate its price, but it could still work out much cheaper.
- Some businesses have cash available which they want to use. Buying another business is one way of doing this.
- Mergers have taken place for defensive reasons. A business might buy another to consolidate its position in the market. Also, if a firm can increase its size through merging, it may avoid being the victim of a takeover itself.
- In response to economic changes. For example, some businesses may have merged before the introduction of the euro in 1999 in certain European countries or before the expansion of the EU in 2004.
- Merging with a business in a different country is one way in which a business can gain entry into foreign markets. It may also avoid restrictions that prevent it from locating in a country or avoid paying tariffs on goods sold in that country (☞ unit 100).
- The globalisation of markets (☞ unit 109) has encouraged mergers between foreign businesses. This could allow a company to operate and sell worldwide, rather than in particular countries or regions.
- A business may want to gain economies of scale (☞ unit 81). Firms can often lower their costs by joining with another firm. This is dealt with later in this unit.
- Some firms are asset strippers. They buy a company, sell off profitable parts, close down unprofitable sections and perhaps integrate other activities into the existing business.
- Management may want to increase the size of the company. This is because the growth of the business is their main objective.

## Merger activity

In the late 1990s and early twenty first century both the number and value of mergers reached record levels. What might have been the reasons for this 'merger boom'?

- There was growth in the UK economy and a buoyant stock market. Higher profits attracted companies to buy shares in

or take over other businesses. Companies were also prepared to pay higher prices, which raised the value of mergers and takeovers.
- Faced with greater competition in providing services, there was a number of mergers between financial institutions. Examples of mergers in the financial sector include Lloyds Bank and the TSB and The Royal and Sun Alliance insurance companies.
- Deregulation and liberalisation freed markets. For example, deregulation of the communications industry in the USA allowed an 'alliance' between AT&T and BT. Deregulation of electricity in the UK led to the creation of 14 electricity companies in 1990. By 1998, 12 had either merged together or been bought by outside businesses, mainly because the merged companies would be better able to compete.
- Improvements in information and communication technology (☞ unit 70) meant that it was far easier for businesses to deal with each other. Before, companies in different parts of the country, or in different countries, may have been reluctant to merge because of problems with passing information. Private company intranets greatly reduced this problem.
- A growing number of large businesses merged. For example, BP's takeover of Amoco in 1998 was the UK's largest industrial takeover. It was suggested that the merger would lead to cost savings of 6 per cent.
- Many firms adopted a company strategy of 'going global'. They wanted operations in many countries and many markets.
- Companies were 'bargain hunting' by taking over companies in Asia. Economic problems in that part of the world meant that companies could be bought relatively cheaply.

It appears that the merger boom peaked in 2000 in the UK. Figure 89.1 shows the merger and acquisition activity between 1995 and 2003. Activity was greatest in 2000. However, both

**Figure 89.1** *Quarterly volume of merger and acquisition activity, UK*

Source: adapted from KPMG Corporate Finance.

the number of deals and their value fell after that. By 2004 many investment bankers thought that activity would begin to rise again, with America leading the way. For example, in February 2004 Comcast, the US cable giant, made a £28.6 billion hostile bid for Disney.

## Types of merger or integration

As Figure 89.2 shows, mergers can be classed in a number of ways. Not all mergers fit neatly into these categories, however. HORIZONTAL INTEGRATION occurs when two firms which are in exactly the same line of business and the same stage of production join together. The merger between BP and Amoco, the two oil companies is an example of a horizontal merger. The benefits of mergers between firms at the same stage of operation include:
● a 'common' knowledge of the markets in which they operate;
● less likelihood of failure by moving into a totally new area;
● similar skills of employees;
● less disruption.

VERTICAL INTEGRATION can be FORWARD VERTICAL INTEGRATION or BACKWARD VERTICAL INTEGRATION. Consider a firm which manufactures and assembles mountain bikes. If it were to acquire a firm which was a supplier of tyres for the bikes, this would be an example of backward vertical integration. The two firms are at different stages of production. The main motives for such a merger are to guarantee and control the supply of components and raw materials and to remove the profit margin the supplier would demand. Forward vertical integration involves merging with a firm which is in the next stage of production rather than the previous stage. For example, the mountain bike manufacturer may merge with a retail outlet selling bikes. Again this eliminates the profit margin expected by the firm in the next stage of production. It also gives the manufacturer confidence when planning production, knowing that there are retail outlets in which to sell. Vertical mergers tend to be rare in the UK.

LATERAL INTEGRATION involves the merging of two firms with related goods which do not compete directly with each other. Production techniques or the distribution channels may be similar. Cadbury-Schweppes is perhaps an example. The two companies used similar raw materials and had similar markets, but did not compete with each other directly.

There are some motives for firms in completely different lines of business to join together. This type of merger is called a CONGLOMERATE or DIVERSIFYING MERGER. A firm might fear a loss of market share due to greater competition. As a result it may try to explore new and different opportunities.

**Figure 89.2** *A summary of the methods of integration*

BACKWARD VERTICAL (Previous stage of production)

LATERAL (similar production techniques)

TYPES OF INTEGRATION

HORIZONTAL (same line of business/same stage of production)

DIVERSIFYING OR CONGLOMERATE (different line of business)

FORWARD VERTICAL (Next stage of production)

---

One of the most high profile mergers to take place in 2003 was between the two ITV broadcasting companies, Granada and Carlton. The £4.6 billion merger took a long time before it was finalised. It was subject to lengthy investigation by the Competition Commission. The Commission found that the proposed merger would be expected to operate against the public interest in two areas.
● Its impact on Channel TV, SMG and Ulster TV in relation to networking arrangements and the sale of their advertising airtime.
● The sale of Carlton's and Granada's advertising airtime and, in particular, the share of discount deals struck with advertisers and media buyers.

After wide consultation and an unusually large number of hearings with interested parties, the Commission concluded that the expected adverse effects of the merger could be remedied if Carlton and Granada agreed to a package of safeguards and conditions.

Carlton and Granada believe that the merged group will be in a better position to compete with the BBC and BSkyB in the future. The following benefits were expected.
● Viewers will benefit from better programmes with improved quality and choice, more premieres, more event entertainment and more dramas.
● Advertisers will benefit from the greater ability of the merged group to improve audience share and commercial impacts, particularly to the key demographic groups. This will allow advertisers to increase the size and efficiency of their reach.
● Shareholders will benefit from a simpler and clearer structure, greater efficiency and lower costs. Shareholders will also benefit from significant synergies together with the increased scale and cash flow of the merged group.

Source: adapted from Competition Commission press release, 7.10.2003 and *The Guardian*.

(a) What type of merger is taking place in the example? Explain your answer.
(b) Who is likely to benefit most from the merger?

**Question 1**

Pressman Associates is a property development company. It was born out of a construction company called Pressman Construction in 2001. Carl Pressman, the owner of both companies, decided to focus on property development when he realised that a lot of his construction company's time was being wasted on doing things that other companies could do for him - more effectively and efficiently. He sold off all the physical assets of Pressman Construction and opened an office in Newcastle.

Working from his quayside location, he searches for suitable sites, draws up plans for properties, builds large detached houses and sells them at lucrative prices. Carl is able to do this almost without leaving his office. Building plots are found by a specialist estate agent, plans are drawn up by architects, legal issues such as planning and contracts are dealt with by a solicitor, the dwellings are constructed by builders and fitted by a number of subcontractors. The properties are finally marketed and sold by another firm of estate agents. Carl co-ordinates all of these activities from his office. However, he employs a project manager to oversee construction. Working in this way Carl can undertake a number of developments all at the same time.

(a) What evidence is there in the case to suggest that Pressman Associates is a virtual company?
(b) Explain the benefits to Pressman Associates of operating in this way.

**Question 2**

orientated managers. Executives must be leaders who can influence and reinforce employees' values and beliefs.

## Agile manufacturing

Some have suggested that businesses need an approach to cope with turbulent markets, competition, changing tastes, fast growth in technology and increasing consumer expectations. Today, customers want to buy products which are custom made and tailored to individual needs. All these trends have led to the development of AGILE MANUFACTURING.

The main aim of agile manufacturing is for a business to be able to perform effectively in a changing market. It will allow customised products to be made with short lead times and without rising costs. Agile manufacturers will be able to adopt new technologies more quickly and have a high degree of flexibility. This will allow large and rapid changes in output, product mixes and delivery dates.

How will a business be able to do this? An agile manufacturer will need flexible people, a reduction in rigid structural hierarchies, broader-based training, flexible production technologies and computer-integrated manufacturing (☞ unit 85). Radical changes in organisation will also be needed. Figure 90.1 shows the differences in approach of three production methods. Agile manufacturers need short term relationships with suppliers. This will allow

**Figure 90.1** *The organisation of three production methods*

**Mass production**  **Lean production**  **Virtual production**

Many remote external suppliers

Many internal links in supply chain

Complete set of internal business processes

Closer relationships with fewer suppliers

More focused: fewer internal links in supply chain

Short-term collaborations

Electronic links

Non-competitive business processes outsourced

Core competences only

supply contracts to be set up and ended quickly to cope with changes in technology and demand. There is evidence of this happening already, with a growing number of joint ventures across industries. They will also make greater use of OUTSOURCING. This involves finding a contractor to supply components or to carry out processes that a business may have undertaken. Car manufacturers often outsource production. Brakes, brakepads, electronics, mirrors, windows and seats are all produced by outside suppliers. It leaves the business able to concentrate on its 'core' areas. This growth in outsourcing will require quick and effective communication

In 2002 GlaxoSmithKline (GSK), the pharmaceuticals group, was considering outsourcing its entire information technology operation. The company was negotiating with a number of IT suppliers, including IBM, EDS and CSC, asking them to come up with cost-saving plans. The suppliers were told to consider all options, including moving some of the IT work offshore, which could mean substantial job losses.

The IT operation at the company is huge. It involves 66,000 desktop computers which are used for tasks including payroll operations and scientists' research work. A GSK spokesperson said 'It is not just about costs. It is to do with improving services and increasing quality and efficiency'. Outsourcing IT functions is becoming increasingly popular. The Inland Revenue has a 10 year, £2.8 billion deal with EDS and the Royal Mail announced in October it planned to outsource its IT services to CSC in a £1.5 billion contract.

One fear was that the changes could affect staff morale within GSK. In recent months the company had been hit by the departure of three of its six most senior scientists.

Source: adapted from *The Guardian*, 5.9.2002.

(a) Examine the possible effects of outsourcing on the stakeholders of:
(i) GlaxoSmithKline;
(ii) IT companies.

**Question 3**

with suppliers and workers. Improved communications technology (☞ unit 70) will allow this.

These ideas have led to term the VIRTUAL COMPANY. It refers to a group of closely linked separate 'entities' which can quickly disband and reform to cope with a turbulent environment.

## The learning organisation

In his book *The Fifth Disciple*, Peter Senge put forward the idea of the learning organisation. According to a definition in the IRS Management Review, a learning organisation is one 'that facilitates the learning of all its members and thus continually transforms itself'. It has been argued that to compete in the uncertain and changing conditions of the global market place, a business needs to be able to learn.

There are two types of learning. **Learning how** involves processes designed to transfer and improve skills that will improve performance. **Learning why** involves looking at how things are happening using diagnostic skills.

An example of its operation took place in 1998 when Reed Elsevier, the publishing group, began to prepare for the 'age of the Internet'. The Reed Elsevier Technology Group (RETG) was set up to educate other parts of the group about new technologies. The aim was to ensure that Reed Elsevier's different business units acquired technological expertise themselves. When part of the company acquired some new technological knowledge RETG passed it around the whole organisation. This ensured that something was only learnt once and time was not wasted.

## Knowledge management

The aim of knowledge management (☞ unit 77) is to unlock the information held by individual members of the workforce and share it throughout the company. If this can be done, efficiency should improve. For example, the marketing department may find that customers are unhappy with the stitching on a shirt. If this knowledge was passed to the production department, it may help to reduce returns. Information and communication technology has a vital role to play in the storage, manipulation and presentation of information to all staff in the organisation.

## Kaizen

Kaizen means continuous improvement. It is a company wide strategy designed to eliminate waste in business and lead to continual improvement in all aspects of a firm's operations. All staff in the organisation are trained to be on the lookout, all of the time, for ways of making improvements. If small improvements are made continually, their impact over long periods of time will be great. In addition, the company will always be moving forward. Kaizen includes a wide range of different production techniques and working practices, such as quality circles, suggestion schemes, automation, discipline in the workplace, just-in-time manufacturing and zero defects. Businesses which have adopted Kaizen in the UK

BP, the oil company, and Bovis Lend Lease, a project management and construction company, established Global Alliance in 1996. Its aim was to improve capital productivity in BP's retail site development process. The Alliance has run a successful 'Lessons Learnt' initiative for several years and its knowledge sharing system (called 'konnect') gives all its staff access to lessons learned and expertise worldwide. Knowledge management is not a separate business activity. It is the result of numerous daily acts of searching for better ways of doing things. In 2002, the new challenge for the Alliance was to cut the total cost of the standard service station by more than 25 per cent and reduce construction time by 2 weeks.

The Alliance met the challenge by using Foresight Review and standard value management techniques such as focus on function not on product,' and involvement of experienced staff to get the benefit of their individual and collective knowledge.

**Foresight Review**
This three-phase approach to identifying possible sources of cost savings and efficiency improvements was undertaken by a multidisciplinary team of eight. It included representatives from design and innovation, project management, commercial, procurement and external suppliers and contractors. Further knowledge and experience was brought in on an ad-hoc basis from Bovis Lend Lease. The team met for four half-day sessions and worked through the following phases.
● Understanding the challenge and identifying the focus areas.
● Brainstorming ideas and alternatives, including experience from previous projects.
● An analysis and evaluation of proposed solutions.
By following this process, sharing knowledge, learning from past successes and developing ideas creatively, a new approach was developed which cut the cost of building service stations by 29-33 per cent, substantially beating the 25 per cent target.

Source: adapted from LfE case study, 2003.

(a) Using this case as an example, explain what is meant by knowledge management.
(b) Explain how the approach used by BP to share knowledge in its organisation might affect the business.

## Question 4

have enjoyed enormous efficiency gains. For example, GSM Graphic Arts of Thirsk, which makes metal and plastic labels for the motor and electronics industries, operates Kaizen in its factory. In 10 years, GSM improved many aspects of its operations, attracted high profile customers, such as Nissan, GM and Ford, and saw employment grow from 17 to 200.

## Michael Porter - competitive advantage

Michael Porter suggested that businesses could achieve a competitive advantage over rivals by following one of three generic strategies (☞ unit 94). One of these strategies is cost leadership. A cost leader will be the firm with the lowest unit

costs. Low costs may be achieved through the mass production of a fairly standardised product, exploiting economies of scale, automating and reducing overheads.

## The flexible labour force

In the past many UK businesses felt that their workforces were too inflexible. Labour productivity in many industries was significantly lower than in other countries. Workforces were uncooperative, resistant to change and lacking in motivation. In order to compete with overseas competition firms needed to improve the flexibility of the workforce (☞ unit 76). Methods of improving flexibility included:

- training workers in a number of tasks so that they can be switched around at short notice;
- allowing staff to choose their hours of work between certain limits;
- using temporary staff to cope with seasonal demand;
- using part time staff or workers on or zero hours contracts to cope with fluctuations in demand;
- encouraging staff to solve their own work problems;
- allowing staff to plan their own work schedules;
- encouraging staff to share information, help each other and check each other's work;
- the use of annualised hours schemes (☞ unit 60).

It was argued that a business with a flexible workforce would be more efficient in a number of ways. They could operate more freely if workers can be switched from one task to another. Fluctuations in demand could be dealt with more comfortably. The use of overtime payments could almost be eliminated. Stores, offices and other premises could also stay open for longer hours.

## Criticisms

There are certain criticisms of modern production and management theories.

- After implementing strategies such as downsizing, delayering, reengineering and outsourcing, a number of businesses have found problems. For example, two thirds of the companies identified by Tom Peters as standard-bearers of excellence in 1982 were in trouble five years later. Michael Hammer admitted that 70 per cent of the firms that claimed to have 'reengineered' themselves failed to improve their market position.
- Michael Hammer admitted that a flaw existed in his own theory. In an article published in *The Wall Street Journal* in November 1996, he reported to have told a business conference that he had forgotten about one factor - people. He said: 'I was reflecting my engineering background and was insufficiently appreciative of the human dimension. I've learned that is critical'.
- Reengineering in many businesses has simply meant downsizing. Businesses have tried to cut jobs without appreciating the long term effect of their actions. Job cuts have led to a stressed out, insecure and demotivated workforce.
- Peter Drucker and other management theorists emphasise the role of people as a firm's main asset and the corporation as a social as well as a commercial institution. Approaches which seek to remove employees with important business knowledge may have an adverse effect on the business. This is perhaps why knowledge management was said to be important for businesses in the early twenty first century.
- Many new management theories have been described as 'fads' or 'bandwagons'. They have failed to deliver improvements in profit or positive change. Business may simply use whatever theory happens to be in fashion at the time.

## key terms

**Agile manufacturing** - a strategy which allows a business to react to rapidly changing conditions.

**Delayering** - the removal of managerial layers in the hierarchical structure.

**Downsizing** - the process of reducing capacity, usually by laying off staff.

**Outsourcing** - the contracting out of work to other businesses that might otherwise have been performed within the organisation.

**Reengineering** - redesigning business processes, such as product design, to improve efficiency in the organisation.

**Virtual company** - a company which has outsourced every business activity.

Knowledge...nowledge...Knowle

1. What is meant by a company-wide strategy to improve efficiency?
2. Describe four of Tom Peters' characteristics of good performing companies.
3. State 4 benefits of downsizing.
4. State (i) 2 advantages and (ii) 2 disadvantages: of delayering.
5. State 4 possible effects on businesses of reengineering.
6. Suggest 2 ways in which a business may become more agile in manufacturing.
7. Give 4 examples of labour flexibility.
8. What is the aim of Kaizen?
9. What is the difference between knowledge management and the learning organisation?
10. Suggest 2 criticisms of modern management theories to improve efficiency.

# Case study Gregsons

Gregsons is a large mail order company, selling a wide variety of electrical goods such as kettles, irons, food blenders, microwave ovens, TVs, music systems and computers. Its products are advertised heavily in daily newspapers, magazines and on TV. The business sells on price, by offering well known brand names at prices that are typically 20 per cent below those of other outlets. The company operates from a site in Staffordshire where it owns a warehouse and an office block. It is organised into five departments.

● Finance and HR.
● Marketing.
● Goods inward.
● Order-picking and dispatch.
● Logistics.

In 2000 Gregsons attempted to diversify into furniture by mail order. However, this was unsuccessful and it withdrew from the operation after two years at a cost of £5.6 million. In 2002 the directors decided to embark on a new strategy. They decided to improve efficiency across the whole organisation and increase sales by going online. A number of strategic initiatives were implemented.

**Reengineering.** The entire ordering process was reengineered. Before, orders were received by post or over the telephone and dealt with manually. A new system was introduced which could cope simultaneously with telephone orders and online orders and process them automatically. A voice recognition system is now used for telephone orders. Mail orders are still accepted, but order forms were redesigned to be read by computer. The IT system installed to run the process also allows customers to track their order status on the Internet. Staffing in the department was cut from 120 to 32. However, many of the staff were retrained to work in a new customer services function. The purpose of this function was to deal swiftly and sympathetically with customer complaints and to try to sell more products by developing relationships with customers once an order had been dispatched successfully.

**Flexibility.** More flexible working practices were introduced. Staff would be able to choose 80 per cent of their hours of work in return for being on call at certain times. One problem that Gregsons experienced was a surge in demand immediately after a TV advert.

**Table 90.3** *Key performance indicators 2001 and 2004*

|  | 2001 | 2004 |
| --- | --- | --- |
| Lead time | 10 days | 3 days |
| Order-picking errors | 7,350 | 2,100 |
| Absenteeism | 8.70% | 5.60% |
| Customer complaints | 1,290 | 320 |
| Sales revenue | £231m | £275m |
| Wage bill | £34m | £28m |

This often meant that staff were overworked for a period and mistakes were made with order picking and dispatch. Vehicle drivers were also included in this arrangement. Staff would also be trained in more tasks and encouraged to solve their own problems.

**Delayering.** A delayering process was undertaken. Three management and supervisory layers were 'stripped out'. The purpose of this was to cut costs, improve communications, empower staff and speed up the decision making process. It was also felt that delayering was necessary to help introduce the flexible working practices described above. It was expected that delayering would cut the wage bill by several million pounds per year once voluntary redundancy and early retirement payments had been met.

In 2004, by monitoring a number of key performance indicators, Gregsons was able to conclude that its new strategy was beginning to generate some very encouraging results. Table 90.3 shows some performance data.

(a) **Identify two benefits to Gregsons of delayering. (6 marks)**
(b) **Using this case as an example, explain what is meant by reengineering. (8 marks)**
(c) **Identify elements of Tom Peters' 8 key characteristics of good performing companies in the Gregsons case. (10 marks)**
(d) **Analyse the possible advantages and disadvantages to Gregsons of the flexible working practices introduced. (12 marks)**
(e) **To what extent might the increase in sales revenue be attributed to the new efficiency strategy? (14 marks)**

## Operational research

Businesses constantly make decisions. The production department may have to find the cheapest way to carry out a task. The marketing department may have to choose between two advertising campaigns. Unit 11 explained the steps involved in decision making. Businesses can use a number of **quantitative techniques** to help them make decisions and to solve problems that arise. These OPERATIONAL RESEARCH (OR) methods were developed by American scientists in the 1960s. They were based on problem solving methods used in Second World War operations, such as the most effective way to destroy submarines. OR methods use models (or simplified real world situations) to investigate solutions to the problems businesses may face. However, such models are only aids to decision making - the decision itself will still need to be taken and might involve other quantitative and qualitative data which is not included in the model. The types of decision where such models might be used include the following.

- Where should a new plant be sited?
- In what order should a new product be assembled?
- Which method of distribution has the cheapest transport costs?
- How should resources be allocated in production?
- How should the launch of a new product be organised?
- How can customer waiting time be reduced in busy retail outlets?
- How can a building project be timetabled?

This unit deals with network and cost-benefit analysis, and simulation, while the next looks at linear programming, transportation and the economic order quantity.

## Critical path analysis

CRITICAL PATH ANALYSIS or NETWORK ANALYSIS is a technique which allows a business to:

- estimate the minimum time that could be taken to complete a possibly complex operation;
- identify whether resources are being used efficiently;
- anticipate any tasks that may or may not cause delays in the operation.

Critical path analysis is used in many industries, particularly manufacturing and construction. For example, a builder may consider the use of network analysis when planning the sequence of tasks to build a new house. In such industries the time and resources used are vital to the project.

Take a simple operation, such as painting a window frame, that a builder might carry out. This could involve many different tasks, for example:

- preparing the woodwork;
- applying the undercoat;
- waiting for the undercoat to dry;
- applying the gloss.

**Figure 91.1** *A network diagram showing the sequence of activities in painting a window frame*

This is shown in Figure 91.1 as a network diagram.

There are certain features in Figure 91.1 that are important when constructing any network.

- The circles are called **nodes.** They show the start or finish of a task. The arrows show the tasks involved in painting the window. They use up resources as they are carried out. For example, even waiting for paint to dry uses up resources, such as time. The activities are **dependent** on each other. So the undercoat cannot be applied until the woodwork has been prepared.
- Nodes contain information. Figure 91.1 shows that nodes are divided into three sections. In the left hand semi-circle the **node number** is written. This makes it possible to follow tasks more easily through the network. The number in the top right is the **earliest starting time** (EST). This shows the earliest time that the next task can begin. The number in the bottom right is the **latest finishing time** (LFT). This shows the latest time that the previous task can finish without delaying the next task.
- Arrows show the **order** in which the tasks take place. They often have letters next to them to show what the order is. The length of time each task takes is placed below the arrow.

## Constructing a network

Figure 91.1 is a rather simple example of a network. In practice operations in business may be more complex with many different tasks, some of which can be carried out at the same time as others. For example, the tasks involved in producing an advertising campaign for a company could be:

- A - plan the advertising campaign;
- B - make a TV video;
- C - make a poster;
- D - test market the TV video;
- E - test suitability of poster;
- F - present campaign to the board of directors;
- G - communicate the campaign to all company personnel.

The estimated length of time for each task and the order, ie the tasks that **depend** upon others being completed, are shown in Table 91.1. The total estimated time is 49 hours, but

**Table 91.1** *The order and times of tasks when producing an advertising campaign*

| Tasks | Order/dependency | Estimated time (hours) |
|---|---|---|
| A | Must be done first | 4 |
| B | Can only start when A is complete | 6 |
| C | Can only start when A is complete | 7 |
| D | Can only start when B is complete | 8 |
| E | Can only start when C is complete | 10 |
| F | Can only start when D and E are complete | 9 |
| G | Must wait for D, E and F to be completed | 5 |

this is not important because activities B and C, and D and E can be done at the same time by different employees.

Figure 91.2 shows the network for the marketing campaign summarised in Table 91.1. The tasks, node numbers and time durations are all included.

Once the network has been constructed it is possible to 'fill-in' the earliest start times and latest finishing times, and then show the critical path. This will tell the business how long it will take to launch the advertising campaign, and indicate where delays could take place.

**Figure 91.2** *The network for the marketing campaign*

**Earliest start time** Assuming that the **earliest time** task A can be started is hour 0 then tasks B and C cannot start for 4 hours (0 + 4), ie until task A has been completed. These are shown in the top right of nodes 1 and 2.

Task D cannot start until A and B have been completed, this takes 10 hours (0+4+6) which is shown in node 3. Task E cannot start for 11 hours (0+4+7) and is shown in node 4. Task F cannot start until E and D are complete. The EST for task F is 21 (0 + 4 + 7 + 10). It is important to choose the longest route when calculating the ESTs. The route A,B,D is

**Figure 91.3** *The ESTs for the tasks in the marketing campaign*

only 18 (0 + 4 + 6 + 8). The EST of the longer route (21) is shown in node 5. The EST in the final node also shows the time it takes to complete the whole marketing campaign. It is 35 hours (0 + 4 + 7 + 10 + 9 + 5) and is shown in node 7. All this information is shown in Figure 91.3.

**Latest finish time** The next step is to identify the **latest finish time** (LFT) of each task without extending the project duration. We must start at node 7 and work back. Task G must be completed by the 35th hour. This LFT is shown in the bottom right of node 7. To calculate the LFT for task F, we subtract the time it takes to perform task F from the previous LFT, ie 30 (35 - 5). This LFT is shown in node 6. The LFTs for tasks D and E are 21 (30 - 9), as shown in node 5. For task B the LFT is 13 (21 - 8) and for task C 11 (21 - 10). The LFT for task A is 4, following the route that will give the earliest time, ie C (11-7=4) rather than B which would give (13-6=7). The LFTs for all tasks are shown in Figure 91.4.

**Figure 91.4** *The ESTs, the LFTs and the critical path for the marketing campaign*

---- Critical path

**The critical path** Once all the LFTs have been identified it is possible to outline the CRITICAL PATH. This can be drawn through the nodes where the ESTs and the LFTs are the **same.** This means that there can be no delays between completing the preceding tasks and starting the next ones on this path without prolonging the total time of the marketing campaign. The critical path for the campaign, A, C, E, F, G, is shown by a dotted line in Figure 91.4. It is critical because any task on this path which is delayed will delay the whole campaign beyond the 35 hours identified earlier as the minimum time.

**The float** What about tasks which do not lie on the critical path, ie B and D? B and D together could be delayed up to 3 hours without prolonging the campaign's completion time. This is called the **float.** We have already seen that the critical path is the longest route through the network. Activities C and E take longer than B and D by 3 hours, so speeding up activities B and D will not help the business to finish earlier.

● The **total float** is found by subtracting the EST and the duration from the LFT. So for task B it would be:

13-6-4=3.

This is the total float up to that activity (B).

● The **free float** is found by subtracting the EST at the start

**Table 91.2** The duration, EST, LFT and floats for each task in the marketing campaign

(Hours)

| Task | Duration | EST | LFT | Total Float | Free Float |
|------|----------|-----|-----|-------------|------------|
| A | 4 | 0 | 4 | 0* | 0 |
| B | 6 | 4 | 13 | 3 | 0 |
| C | 7 | 4 | 11 | 0* | 0 |
| D | 8 | 10 | 21 | 3 | 3 |
| E | 10 | 11 | 21 | 0* | 0 |
| F | 9 | 21 | 30 | 0* | 0 |
| G | 5 | 30 | 35 | 0* | 0 |

of the task and the duration from the EST at the end. So for task B this would be:

$$10 - 6 - 4 = 0.$$

This is the free float for that task. It shows that task B can be delayed, but this will interfere with other tasks, ie D. Table 91.2 shows the total float after each task in the marketing campaign. The tasks without a float (shown by a *) are 'critical' - any delay in these and the whole campaign will be prolonged. Only non-critical tasks have a float.

It is important for a business to know how much float there is. If tasks in the operations could be delayed without delaying the whole job, then resources in these tasks, (such as labour, machinery etc.), could be used more productively elsewhere or shared between tasks. It is also important when tasks may take days or weeks. If an operation is delayed, a business will not be too worried if there is some float, only if the float disappears.

Figure 91.5 shows a network for the installation of a new piece of machinery. The times shown are for the number of days taken.

**Figure 91.5**

(a) Calculate the earliest start time for each task.
(b) Calculate the latest finish time for each task and the minimum time for the whole project.
(c) Determine the critical path.
(d) Identify the amount of total float and free float in a table.
(e) Determine the critical path if task D took 12 days.

# A more complex network

Sometimes it is necessary to include a **dummy activity** or task in a network diagram. Take an example made up of four tasks A, B, C and D. Assume that task C cannot start until tasks A and B have been completed. Task D can only start when B has been completed. The network in Figure 91.6 appears to represent this sequence of tasks. However, the diagram also shows that task D cannot start until A and B have been completed, yet this is not a requirement in our example. In order to show a **dependency** the network can be redrawn using a dummy activity as shown in Figure 91.7. The dummy task is shown by a dotted line and now the diagram shows that task D is only dependent upon the completion of task B. Dummy activities do not use up any time - they always have a time duration of zero.

Let's look at a network which involves a variety of tasks and a dummy activity. Table 91.3 and Figure 91.8 show tasks involved in the assembly of a vehicle engine. The earliest start times and latest finish times have been calculated using the

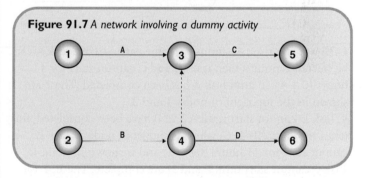

**Figure 91.6** A network diagram representing four tasks A, B, C and D

**Figure 91.7** A network involving a dummy activity

**Table 91.3** Tasks and their estimated time involved in assembling a vehicle engine

| Task | Order/dependency | Estimated time (hours) |
|------|------------------|------------------------|
| A | Can start at the same time as B | 2 |
| B | Can start at the same time as A | 2 |
| C | Must follow A | 6 |
| D | Must follow A | 3 |
| E | Must follow B | 1 |
| F | Must follow B | 8 |
| G | Must follow C | 2 |
| H | Must follow D,E | 1 |
| J | Cannot start until C,H have finished | 3 |
| K | Cannot start until C,H have finished | 3 |
| L | Must follow G,J | 4 |

The operation is complete when F, K and L have finished.

**Figure 91.8** A network involving a dummy activity

-------- Critical path

**Table 91.4**

| Task | Duration | EST | LFT | Total Float | Free Float |
|------|----------|-----|-----|-------------|------------|
| A | 2 | 0 | 2 | 0* | 0 |
| B | 2 | 0 | 6 | 4 | 0 |
| C | 6 | 2 | 8 | 0* | 0 |
| D | 3 | 2 | 7 | 2 | 0 |
| E | 1 | 2 | 7 | 4 | 2 |
| F | 8 | 2 | 15 | 5 | 5 |
| G | 2 | 8 | 11 | 1 | 1 |
| H | 1 | 5 | 8 | 2 | 2 |
| J | 3 | 8 | 11 | 0* | 0 |
| K | 3 | 8 | 15 | 4 | 4 |
| L | 4 | 11 | 15 | 0* | 0 |

method in Figures 91.3 and 91.4 earlier. There are certain features about this network.

● A dummy activity or task links J and K to the completion of C. This is because whilst J and K are dependent upon C finishing, they are also dependent upon H finishing. It would be impossible to illustrate these dependencies in the network without the use of a dummy line, which shows a logical connection, but does not show any time passing.

● The critical path through the network is shown by a broken (blue) line, linking activities A,C,J and L. Notice that these are the nodes where the ESTs and LFTs are equal. It is also the route with the longest ESTs, as explained earlier in this unit.

● The minimum time to complete the assembly of the engine would be 15 hours.

● The float in the network is shown in Table 91.4.

# Advantages of critical path analysis

The major advantage of critical path analysis is that it provides decision makers with a picture of a problem which may be easier to interpret. It can be used to suit a range of circumstances and help solve a variety of business problems.

● Reduce the time lost between tasks, ensuring that projects run smoothly.

● Encourage forward planning. The process ensures that all the tasks in a particular operation have been identified and timed from start to finish. The construction of the

Ashington Ltd uses batch production to make a range of ready meals for supermarkets and other retailers. It has recently introduced lean production methods to speed up changeover times between batches. The aim of the company in the first year of the new system was to get changeover times below 15 minutes. The tasks needed to re-set one machine, when switching from one product to another, are shown in Figure 91.9. The times shown are for the number of minutes taken.

**Figure 91.9**

(a) Calculate the earliest start times and latest finishing times for each task.
(b) Identify the critical path.
(c) Does Ashington achieve its aim when switching production on this machine?

**Question 2**

network forces decision makers to consider all aspects of a project.

● Improve efficiency in production. The level of working capital can be minimised by ordering and receiving materials and components 'just-in-time'. By identifying float and critical activities, resources such as labour and capital can be used more effectively.

● Control cash flow. This is achieved by not ordering supplies too early and only making purchases when they are required.

# Disadvantages of critical path analysis

Despite the advantages of critical path analysis, there are drawbacks.

● The construction of a network alone will not guarantee the smooth completion of a project. The co-operation and commitment of the entire team of staff is needed to ensure that each task is completed according to the estimated duration. Staff should also be consulted when management decides how long tasks will take.

● Some projects are immense. Network diagrams may become complex and unmanageable. Computers may be used to manage information more effectively.

● Network analysis will only be helpful if the data used to construct diagrams is reliable. If the task durations are inaccurate or the order of tasks is wrong, then the ESTs, LFTs and the critical path will all be misleading.

---

A toy manufacturer has designed a new wooden toy. The construction of the toy involves 9 activities A to J. The order and the duration of tasks are shown in the network diagram illustrated in Figure 91.10. The time durations shown are in minutes.

**Figure 91.10** Network diagram for the construction of a new wooden toy

(a) What is the minimum construction time for the new toy?
(b) What is the critical path?
(c) If task D and task H were each delayed by one minute what would be the effect on:
  (i) the minimum construction time;
  (ii) the critical path?
(d) Explain how critical path analysis might benefit the toy manufacturer.

**Question 3**

# Queueing and simulation

SIMULATIONS are models which try to reproduce in a dynamic way what is going on in reality. Business simulations, such as business games, have become common tools in management training and Business Studies teaching. But simulations can also be used to look at a very specific problem, such as queueing. People who are kept waiting in queues may look for a different place to buy goods and services. Queues also waste resources, such as time spent dealing with customer complaints.

Such problems often result when customers arrive at random. Examples may be people using a cashpoint or a public telephone, patients arriving at casualty or cars arriving at a toll booth. It is the random element which causes the problem. If people used these items regularly it would be easy to decide on the number of staff required to deal with customers without causing delay. This assumes, however, that the service time is constant. This is not always the case. Where the service time is variable, such as at a supermarket checkout, a problem will exist.

Take an example of how a simulation can be used to reduce queuing at checkouts in a supermarket. A number of variables need to be considered:

● The number of customers arriving at the checkouts.
● The number of checkouts in operation.
● The frequency of arrival at checkouts.
● The length of time each customer takes at the checkout.

A simulation will allow a business to work out the number of checkouts it must operate at different times of the day to keep queues at a minimum.

The first stage is to collect information about how the system operates at present. The supermarket collected information about 100 customers who 'checked out' between 5.00pm and 5.30pm. Table 91.5 shows this information.

**Table 91.5** Information relating to customers arriving at a supermarket checkout

| Time between arrivals at checkout (mins) | Frequency (per cent) | Cumulative frequency | Time at check out (mins) | Frequency (per cent) | Cumulative frequency |
|---|---|---|---|---|---|
| 0 | 8 | 8 | 1 | 7 | 7 |
| 1 | 20 | 28 | 2 | 25 | 32 |
| 2 | 32 | 60 | 3 | 32 | 64 |
| 3 | 21 | 81 | 4 | 16 | 80 |
| 4 | 9 | 90 | 5 | 12 | 92 |
| 5 | 10 | 100 | 6 | 8 | 100 |

Table 91.5 also shows the **cumulative frequency** (☞ unit 13) of people at the checkout. The information forms the basis of a model which will try to simulate the arrival of customers at checkouts. Random numbers are used to indicate the time between arrivals and the length of time spent at the checkout. Random numbers are obtained from computers and have no pattern provided they are used in a random way. For example a random series of 50 numbers may be:

20 84 27 38 66 19 60 10 51 20
35 16 74 58 72 79 98 09 47 07
98 82 69 63 23 70 80 88 86 23
94 67 94 34 03 77 89 30 49 51
04 54 32 55 94 82 08 19 20 73

**Table 91.6** Cumulative frequencies and allocated random numbers

| Time between arrivals (mins) | Cumulative frequency | Random numbers | Time at check out (mins) | Cumulative frequency | Random numbers |
|---|---|---|---|---|---|
| 0 | 8 | 01 - 08 | 1 | 7 | 01 - 07 |
| 1 | 28 | 09 - 28 | 2 | 32 | 08 - 32 |
| 2 | 60 | 29 - 60 | 3 | 64 | 35 - 64 |
| 3 | 81 | 61 - 81 | 4 | 80 | 65 - 80 |
| 4 | 90 | 82 - 90 | 5 | 92 | 81 - 92 |
| 5 | 100 | 91 -100 | 6 | 100 | 93 -100 |

The random numbers are allocated to the 'Time between arrivals' and the 'Time spent at the checkout', according to the cumulative frequencies as shown in Table 91.6. The

simulation can now begin, using the random numbers in the order they are shown above:

Random number 20 - customer 1 arrives after 1 minute
Random number 84 - customer 1 takes 5 minutes to be served
Random number 27 - customer 2 arrives 1 minute after customer 1
Random number 38 - customer 2 takes 3 minutes to be served

Random number 66 - customer 3 arrives 3 minutes after customer 2
Random number 19 - customer 3 takes 2 minutes to be served

The simulation can be recorded as shown in Table 91.7. It is assumed that there is just one checkout in operation to start with.

**Table 91.7** *The results of the simulation showing the arrival times, waiting times, service times, and the leaving times of customers*

| Customer | Random number Arrival | Random number Service time | Simulated times Between arrival (mins) | Simulated times Service time (mins) | Arrived at | Served at | Leaves at | Cust wait (mins) | Checkout wait (mins) |
|---|---|---|---|---|---|---|---|---|---|
| 1 | 20 | 84 | 1 | 5 | 5.01 | 5.01 | 5.06 | 0 | 1 |
| 2 | 27 | 38 | 1 | 3 | 5.02 | 5.06 | 5.09 | 4 | 0 |
| 3 | 66 | 19 | 3 | 2 | 5.05 | 5.09 | 5.11 | 4 | 0 |
| 4 | 60 | 10 | 2 | 2 | 5.07 | 5.11 | 5.13 | 4 | 0 |
| 5 | 51 | 20 | 2 | 2 | 5.09 | 5.13 | 5.15 | 4 | 0 |
| 6 | 35 | 16 | 2 | 2 | 5.11 | 5.15 | 5.17 | 4 | 0 |
| 7 | 74 | 58 | 3 | 3 | 5.14 | 5.17 | 5.20 | 3 | 0 |
| 8 | 72 | 79 | 3 | 4 | 5.17 | 5.20 | 5.24 | 3 | 0 |
| 9 | 98 | 09 | 5 | 2 | 5.22 | 5.24 | 5.26 | 2 | 0 |
| 10 | 47 | 07 | 2 | 1 | 5.24 | 5.26 | 5.27 | 2 | 0 |

With just one checkout in operation, the average customer waiting time is about three minutes - this might be considered acceptable. Also, the checkout has been working constantly. Let us now run the simulation with two checkouts in operation. The results are shown in Table 91.8.

**Table 91.8** *Results from simulation with two checkouts employed (the random numbers are excluded)*

| Customer | Simulated times Between arrival (mins) | Simulated times Service time (mins) | Arrived at | Checkout number | Served at | Leaves at | Cust. wait (mins) | Checkout wait (mins) |
|---|---|---|---|---|---|---|---|---|
| 1 | 1 | 5 | 5.01 | 1 | 5.01 | 5.06 | 0 | 1 |
| 2 | 1 | 3 | 5.02 | 2 | 5.02 | 5.05 | 0 | 2 |
| 3 | 3 | 2 | 5.05 | 2 | 5.05 | 5.07 | 0 | 0 |
| 4 | 2 | 2 | 5.07 | 1 | 5.07 | 5.09 | 0 | 1 |
| 5 | 2 | 2 | 5.09 | 1 | 5.09 | 5.11 | 0 | 0 |
| 6 | 2 | 2 | 5.11 | 2 | 5.11 | 5.13 | 0 | 4 |
| 7 | 3 | 3 | 5.14 | 1 | 5.14 | 5.17 | 0 | 3 |
| 8 | 3 | 4 | 5.17 | 2 | 5.17 | 5.21 | 0 | 4 |
| 9 | 5 | 2 | 5.22 | 1 | 5.22 | 5.24 | 0 | 5 |
| 10 | 2 | 1 | 5.24 | 2 | 5.24 | 5.25 | 0 | 3 |

With two checkouts in operation, customers are never kept waiting. However, both checkouts are waiting for customers on many occasions. The results from this simulation can help the supermarket decide whether it wants to operate one or two checkouts. The final decision will also depend on its

policy towards customer queueing and staff productivity. For example, if its policy is to keep staff fully employed then it will use just one checkout. Simulations like this may appear cumbersome, but the use of a computer will help speed up the process. They are used quite commonly in business. Other OR techniques are too complex to deal with problems like queueing and congestion. However, simulations are only as good as the data upon which they are based. Inaccurate data could lead to incorrect conclusions being drawn. Also, the data may be expensive to collect in the first place.

A warehouse receives lorry loads of corn from local farmers. It currently operates one tipping facility. Table 91.9 shows the arrival intervals of successive lorries and the times taken to tip their loads.

**Table 91.9** *Information regarding the arrival of lorries at a warehouse and the time it takes to tip their loads*

| Time between arrivals (mins) | Frequency (per cent) | Cumulative frequency | Tipping time (mins) | Frequency (per cent) | Cumulative Frequency |
|---|---|---|---|---|---|
| 3 | 5 | 5 | 10 | 12 | 12 |
| 4 | 10 | 15 | 11 | 20 | 32 |
| 7 | 45 | 60 | 12 | 30 | 62 |
| 10 | 30 | 90 | 13 | 28 | 90 |
| 13 | 10 | 100 | 14 | 10 | 100 |

(a) Use a simulation to show the (i) arrival time and (ii) waiting time of 10 lorries which begin arriving at 9.00am. Use the random numbers in the text on the previous page.
(b) Using another simulation, show the effect of operating two tipping facilities.
(c) Do you think a second tipping facility would be a worthwhile investment? Explain your answer.
(d) Explain one possible disadvantage of using simulation in this case.

**Question 4**

# Cost-benefit analysis

Many decisions in business are 'financial' decisions. When considering different courses of action decision makers often weigh up the financial costs against the financial benefits. Normally, a business will choose the course of action which generates the greatest net financial benefit. Recently, some firms have begun to consider the costs and benefits of their decisions to the rest of society. Take an example of a chemical company. It is likely to face the 'private' costs of machinery etc., but may also generate pollution into the atmosphere. Pollution is one example of negative externalities (☞ unit 112) or external costs. Similarly, the business will aim to sell its product to earn revenue (a private benefit), but may build a factory and a new road which eases traffic congestion in the area (an external benefit). We can say:

Social costs = private/financial costs + external costs.
Social benefit = private/financial benefit + external benefit.

$$\frac{A}{Q} = \sqrt{\frac{HPA}{2C}}$$

$$= \sqrt{\frac{0.05 \times £10 \times 5,000}{2 \times £8}}$$

$$= \quad 12.5 \text{ orders per year}$$

**Limitations** The assumptions on which the economic order quantity formula is based may be unrealistic in practice. The price of many materials, particularly commodities like oil, copper, coffee and cotton, tends to fluctuate with changing market conditions. Businesses are unlikely to have unlimited storage space. Materials, such as perishable goods, may deteriorate if left for a period of time. Changes in these assumptions may lead to different costs for a business, which might affect the EOQ. On the other hand, it could be argued that assumptions are not important, as long as a business realises the limitations and finds the predictions of the model useful.

Moss Peters Ltd assembles domestic drying machines. It buys components from all over Europe and is keen to minimise storage costs. One component, the drum, is bought from Northern Spain. Moss Peters has just acquired a new warehouse where it hopes to hold larger quantities of certain key components. The drum is one of these components and the purchasing manager has been asked to review the economic order quantity now that there is almost unlimited space for its storage. The drums cost £40 to buy and Moss Peters uses 40,000 of them each year. The acquisition costs are £50 and the holding cost is 8 per cent of the average stock value.

(a) Calculate the economic order quantity for the drums.
(b) Calculate the total cost of holding and acquiring the drums for one year (do not include the cost of the actual drums).
(c) What would happen to the economic order quantity if the price of the drums rose to £45?

## Question 3

## key terms

**Blending** - a graphical approach to linear programming which deals with resource allocation subject to constraints.
**Economic order quantity (EOQ)** - the level of stock order which minimises ordering and stock holding costs.
**Linear programming** - a technique which shows practical problems as a series of mathematical equations which can then be manipulated to find the optimum or best solution.

**Transportation** - a method designed to solve problems where there are a number of different points of supply and demand, such as a number of manufacturers distributing their products to a number of different wholesalers.

## Knowledge ...Knowledge...Knowledge...Knowledge...Knowledge...Know

1. State 5 problems that operational research methods could be used to investigate.
2. Why are blending and transportation examples of linear programming?
3. Explain briefly two problems that businesses might have when using blending.
4. What does the use of blending show a business?

5. What types of problem does the transportation technique help to solve?
6. What does the use of transportation show a business?
7. Why might a business want to calculate its economic order quantity?
8. State 2 problems with calculating the economic order quantity.

# Case study Westmoore Metal Products

Westmoore Metal Products (WMP) is a medium sized engineering company. It employs 45 staff and operates cell production in its factory. Each cell concentrates on a particular family of products. One such cell, the metal rod cell, makes two of the most popular products. These are high precision steel rods for an Austrian customer which makes machine tools. Their component codes are MK and MG.

The metal rod cell contains three machines and employs five staff. The staff organise their own work patterns, but must keep the cell operating for 15 hours per day, 6 days per week. The three machines include a CNC lathe, a CNC milling machine and a vertical profile projector (an inspection machine). To manufacture the MK and MG three key processes are required - turning, milling and inspection. The vertical profile projector is used by other cells for some of the week. The amount of time each process takes and the capacity available is summarised in Table 92.9. The profit made by each component is £100 for the MK and £80 for the MG.

Westmoore introduced cell production about 5 years ago. One of the problems it had in the factory was a lack of space. In the past the company tended to hold quite high levels of stocks. Westmoore imported most of its steel from northern Spain. Although it is some of the cheapest steel in the world, lead times are long and delivery very unreliable. Thus, the high stock holdings occupy a lot of factory space. At the moment WMP orders about 80 tonnes of steel at a time from its Spanish supplier.

In order to keep stock holding costs to a minimum at WMP, a newly recruited cost accountant has suggested using the economic order quantity (EOQ) to determine the amount of stock to purchase when placing a new order. This takes into account the acquisition cost per order (C), the total number of tonnes used each year (A), the

holding cost as a percentage of the average stock value (H) and the price of each tonne (P).

**(a) Write out the problem above as three equations showing the constraints. (3 marks)**

**(b) Draw the constraints on a graph. (6 marks)**

**(c) (i) On the graph identify the point which maximises profit. (2 marks)**

**(ii) State how many of each component should be produced to maximise profit. (1 mark)**

**(d) Calculate the weekly profit made from the two components at the profit maximising point. (4 marks)**

**(e) Assuming that C = £100, A = 500 tonnes, H = 20 per cent and P = £200, calculate (i) the EOQ and (ii) the number of orders to be placed during the year. (6 marks)**

**(f) Using the information in (e), evaluate whether WMP's current ordering policy is cost effective. (8 marks)**

**Table 92.9** *Time constraints for the three engineering processes*

| | | Turning | Milling | Inspection |
|---|---|---|---|---|
| Hours needed to | MK | 1.5 | 4 | 2 |
| produce one unit | MG | 4.5 | 2 | 2 |
| Total hours per week available | | 90 | 80 | 50 |

## Markets and the external environment

A market is any situation where buyers come into contact with sellers to exchange goods and services (☞ unit 1). The markets in which a business sells its products are part of the EXTERNAL ENVIRONMENT in which the business operates. Businesses do not operate in a vacuum. There are factors outside the business that may affect its decisions.

- The state of competition. A new competitor entering a market could lead to a reduction in the sales of existing firms.
- The labour market. The availability of low priced labour may influence the location of a business.
- Economic factors and the state of the economy. If people have more money to spend, this may encourage businesses to produce new products. If exchange rates are stable, a business may be more willing to trade on foreign markets.

Paul Merrick runs an instrument repair business. He has been successful in the local area, particularly amongst semi-professional musicians and parents wanting repairs to their children's guitars and violins. His speciality is the repair of acoustic instruments. Music retail shops can often deal with electric instruments, but may charge high prices for time consuming work on acoustic instruments.

Paul now wants to set up a workshop rather than work from home. He is likely to have to borrow money and interest rates are forecast to rise soon. The business might be eligible for a grant if Paul employs some people in the workshop, but he is unsure. He knows a few school leavers who would be keen to work for him, but they would need training. He would want to pay more than the minimum wage to motivate them, but he is aware this will raise his costs and also that there are restrictions on the length of time that employees can work. However, Paul feels that there is a growing demand, particularly in the case of cheaper instruments which tend to break more easily. And people seem to have more money to spend on leisure activities these days.

Source: adapted from company information.

(a) Using examples from the case, identify the external factors affecting the business.
(b) A friend has approached Paul. She discussed the possibility of buying guitars from the USA and selling them in this country. What external factors might Paul take into account before making a decision?

- Government objectives and government policy. If the government offers training funds, a business may be willing to employ young workers for a period. The reduction of interest rates means that businesses may borrow as they have less to pay back.
- Legislation. There might be laws that affect the product, eg controls on the ingredients that can be used in food.
- Population. The size, age and sex distribution of the population can affect demand for a product, eg an increase in the birth rate would affect firms marketing baby products.
- Social factors, eg an increase in the amount of crime directed against businesses will affect firms differently. A few, such as security firms, may benefit. Others may find that their costs increase due to, for example, higher insurance premiums.
- Political factors. A shop may change its opening hours because of the influence of a local pressure group.
- Environmental factors. Increased consumer awareness has led many firms to re-evaluate their impact upon the environment. An environmentally friendly business may spend more on waste disposal.
- Technology. The rate of change of technology may influence the type of good produced, eg the development of the microchip has made possible a whole new range of products.

One of the most important influences of markets on businesses is the way in which they help to determine prices. In all markets, buyers (often referred to as consumers) demand goods and services from sellers who supply them. It is the interaction of demand and supply within markets that determines the prices of goods or services.

## Demand

Demand is the amount of a product that consumers are willing and able to purchase at any given price. Demand is concerned with what consumers are actually able to buy (what they can afford to and would buy), rather than what they would like to buy. So, for example, we could say that the demand for cars in the UK market at an average price of £9,000 might be 130,000 a year.

Table 93.1 shows a **demand schedule** for button

**Table 93.1** *The demand schedule for button mushrooms*

| Price per kilo (£) | Quantity demanded (000 kilos) |
| --- | --- |
| 0.50 | 100 |
| 1.00 | 80 |
| 1.50 | 60 |
| 2.00 | 40 |
| 2.50 | 20 |

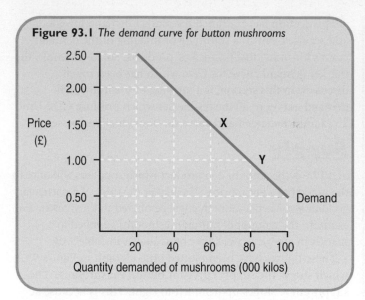

**Figure 93.1** *The demand curve for button mushrooms*

**Figure 93.2** *The effect of changes in income on the demand curve for compact discs*

mushrooms. These figures can be used to draw a **demand curve** as in Figure 93.1. In practice, demand curves are not a straight line, but are usually drawn in this way for simplicity.

The curve shows the quantity of a good or service that will be demanded at any given price. As with nearly all such curves, it slopes downwards from left to right. This is because the quantity demanded is likely to be higher at lower prices and lower at higher prices - **ceteris paribus** (assuming no other things change). In Table 93.1 more button mushrooms are bought at a price of £0.50 than at a price of £2.50.

A change in the price of a good or service will lead to a change in the quantity demanded. This is shown on the demand curve as a movement along (up or down) the curve. In Figure 93.1, a fall in price from £1.50 to £1, for example, will result in a movement along the curve from point X to point Y.

This will result in a rise in the quantity demanded from 60,000 to 80,000 kilos. The demand curve itself has not moved from its original position. Price changes only lead to an **extension** (rise) or **contraction** (fall) in the quantity demanded.

# Changes in demand

As well as price, there is a number of other factors which might affect the demand for a product. Unlike price, a change in any of these factors might cause the whole demand curve to **shift**. This might result in an increase in the demand for a good. The result is that more of a product will be demanded at any given price. Alternatively, it may result in a fall in demand, so less is demanded at any given price.

**Income** It is reasonable to assume that the higher the incomes of consumers, the more they will be able to buy. When incomes in the country as a whole increase, the demand for products will increase. However, the rise in income is unlikely to be the same for everyone. Some consumers will have large increases in income. Others will find that their incomes do not increase at all. Thus, demand

for a product will only increase if the incomes of those consumers buying the product increase.

Assume that consumers of compact discs have had a rise in their income. The demand for compact discs increases as a result. This is shown in Figure 93.2 as a shift to the right of the demand curve from D to $D_1$. The demand for compact discs has increased at any given price level. In Figure 93.2, demand has risen from OQ to $OQ_1$. On the other hand, if consumers' incomes were to fall, this would cause the demand for compact discs to fall at any given price. The result of this would be a shift of the demand curve to the left from D to $D_2$ in Figure 93.2. Demand will have fallen from OQ to $OQ_2$.

**The price of and demand for other goods** The demand for one product often depends on the price of and demand for another. For example, the demand for one brand of tea bags can be influenced by the price of other brands. A rise in the price of one brand is likely to cause an increase in the demand for others. This is often true of products which have close **substitutes**, such as canned drinks. An increase in the price of cassette tapes may result in a shift in demand from D to $D_1$ in Figure 93.2. Fewer tapes would be bought if prices rose, leading perhaps to increased demand for compact discs.

**Complementary** goods are those which are used together. Examples include cars and petrol, and DVD players and DVDs. An increase in the price of one will affect the demand for the other. A fall in the price of compact disc players may lead to a shift in demand from D to $D_1$ in Figure 93.2. More players would be bought and so the quantity demanded of discs would also rise.

**Changes in tastes and fashions** Some products are subject to changes in tastes and fashions. Skateboards, for example, were bought in huge quantities in the1970s. They then went out of fashion for a number of years only to come back into favour again. It is more usual for a company to stop producing products which have gone out of fashion altogether. Other products have shown more gradual changes in demand. In

recent years, the demand for red meat has gradually declined as tastes have changed, often in response to health concerns. This has caused the demand curve for red meat to shift to the left. This means that at any given price, less red meat is now demanded than in previous years. The growth in CD sales over the last decade has shifted the demand curve to the right. Some have suggested that the demand curve for compact discs may shift to the left in the future as internet access to music becomes more popular.

**Changes in population** As well as changes in population levels, changes in the structure of population can affect demand. The increase in the proportion of over 65s in the population of Western industrialised countries will have an effect upon the demand for a number of products. They include winter-sun holidays, sheltered housing and leisure facilities. This means that, other things staying the same, the demand curve for products associated with the old will shift to the right, with more being demanded at any given price.

**Advertising** Successful advertising and promotion will shift the demand curve to the right, with more being demanded at any given price. A successful advertising campaign for CDs could have this effect.

**Legislation** Government legislation can affect the demand for a product. For example, a law requiring all cyclists to wear helmets would lead to an increase in the demand for cycling helmets at any given price.

This section has examined the market demand for goods and services. This is a summing or totalling of the demand curves for individual businesses' products. So, for example, the market demand curve for CDs, which has been much discussed in this section, is a totalling of the individual demand curves of all the businesses which produce CDs. Unit 25 examines the demand curve for individual businesses.

## Supply

SUPPLY is the amount of a product which suppliers will offer to the market at a given price. The higher the price of a particular good or service, the more that will be offered to the market. For example, the amount of button mushrooms supplied to a market in any given week may be as shown in Table 93.3.

These figures have been plotted onto a graph in Figure 93.3, which shows the supply curve for button mushrooms. The supply curve slopes up from left to right. This is because at higher prices a greater quantity will be supplied to the market and at lower prices less will be supplied.

A change in price will cause a movement either up or down the supply curve. The curve will not change its position assuming that all other factors remain the same. There is a number of other factors that may affect supply other than price. Changes in these factors will cause the whole supply curve to shift.

**Costs of production** A fall in the costs of production due, for

---

**Table 93.3** The supply schedule for button mushrooms

| Price per kilo (£) | Quantity supplied (000 kilos) |
| --- | --- |
| 0.50 | 20 |
| 1.00 | 40 |
| 1.50 | 60 |
| 2.00 | 80 |
| 2.50 | 100 |

---

**Table 93.2** The demand schedule for ice cream at a local theme park

| Price (£) | Quantity demanded |
| --- | --- |
| 0.80 | 2,000 |
| 0.90 | 1,600 |
| 1.00 | 1,200 |
| 1.10 | 800 |
| 1.20 | 400 |

Table 93.2 shows the monthly demand schedule based on the average price of ice creams at a local theme park. It has been predicted that the following changes to the market will occur:
● incomes will rise so that there will be 500 more bought at each level;
● the prices of substitute goods (ice lollies etc.) are likely to rise so that there would be another 500 bought at each price level.
(a) Draw the original demand curve from the figures in the table.
(b) Show the combined effect on the demand curve of the changes in the market.

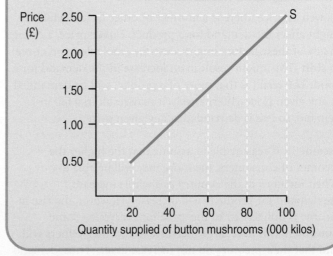

**Figure 93.3** The supply curve for button mushrooms

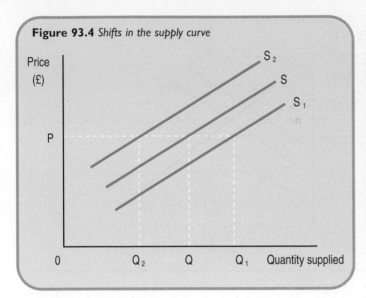

**Figure 93.4** *Shifts in the supply curve*

frost can reduce the supply of strawberries, from say S to $S_2$ in Figure 93.4.

It was shown earlier in this unit that the market demand curve is a summing of individual firms' demand curves. Similarly, the market supply curve is an adding up of the supply curves of individual firms.

## Price and output determination

How does the interaction of demand and supply determine the market price and output? Market prices are set where the plans of consumers are matched with those of suppliers. The point at which the demand and supply curves intersect is known as the EQUILIBRIUM PRICE. This is shown in Figure 93.5. The equilibrium price of button mushrooms is £1.50. The figure is drawn from Tables 93.1 and 93.3. At this price 60,000 mushrooms will be produced.

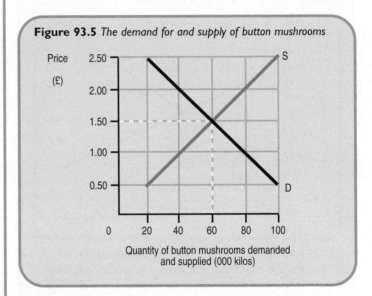

**Figure 93.5** *The demand for and supply of button mushrooms*

example, to new technology will mean that more can be offered at the same price. This will cause the supply curve to shift to the right as shown in Figure 93.4, from S to $S_1$. A rise in the costs of production would cause the supply curve to shift to the left, from S to $S_2$. A rise in raw material costs or wage costs could lead to such a shift.

**Changes in production** Where it is possible to shift production from one area to another, the price of other products can influence the quantity supplied. For example, many farmers are able to produce a wide range of crops on their land. A rise in the price of broccoli, might encourage farmers not only to produce more broccoli, but less of other crops such as turnips. The broccoli price change has affected the quantity of turnips supplied to the market. So a rise in the price of broccoli would shift the supply curve for turnips to the left, in Figure 93.4 from S to $S_2$.

**Legislation** A new anti-pollution law might increase production costs causing the supply curve to shift to the left. Similarly, a tax on a product would shift the supply curve to the left.

**The objectives of firms** Firms might seek to increase their profit levels and their market share. This might reduce the overall level of supply as other firms are forced out of business. The result of this would be a shift of the supply curve in Figure 93.4 from S to $S_2$.

**Expectations** If businesses expect future prices to rise they may restrict current supplies. This would be shown as a shift to the left of the supply curve in Figure 93.4, from S to $S_2$. Similarly, if businesses expect worsening trading conditions they might reduce current supply levels in anticipation of this.

**The weather** The weather can influence the supply of agricultural products. For example, in the UK a late spring

## Changes in demand and supply

Shifts in the demand or supply curves will cause a change in the market price.

**Changes in demand** Assume that there has been a rise in income which has resulted in an increase in demand. The effect of this, as shown in Figure 93.6a, is a shift in the demand curve to the right, all things remaining the same, from D to $D_1$. This leads to an increase in quantity demanded from OQ to $OQ_1$. This increase in demand raises the equilibrium price from OP to $OP_1$. As a result, the quantity supplied extends as well, as producers will supply more at the higher price.

If demand falls, due to lower incomes, from D to $D_2$, this leads to a fall in quantity demanded from OQ to $OQ_2$. The equilibrium price falls from OP to $OP_2$ and at this lower price suppliers will supply less.

**Figure 93.6** *The effect on equilibrium price of an increase in demand and supply*

(a)

(b)

**Figure 93.7** *The demand for and supply of organically grown broccoli*

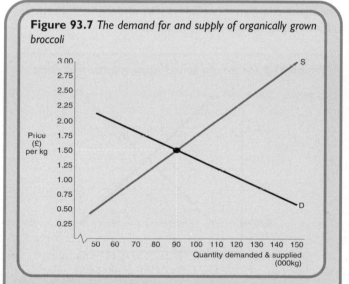

(a) What is the equilibrium price of organic broccoli?
(b) Explain the effect that the following factors will have on: (i) the equilibrium price of organic broccoli; (ii) the demand for organic broccoli or the supply of organic broccoli by businesses in the market.
● A reduction in the average incomes of consumers purchasing organic vegetables.
● Improved organic farming methods leading to a reduction in the cost of producing organic broccoli.
● All types of organic vegetables becoming increasingly popular with greater health consciousness amongst food consumers.
● A fall in the price of non-organic broccoli.

# Question3

**Changes in supply** Figure 93.6b shows the effect on the equilibrium price of changes in supply. An increase in supply may have been as a result of lower labour costs. This shifts the supply curve from S to $S_1$. The equilibrium price falls from OP to $OP_1$ as the supply curve shifts from S to $S_1$. Consumers are more willing and able to buy goods at the lower price and so the quantity demanded rises as well from

OQ to $OQ_1$.

If supply is cut, the supply curve moves to the left from S to $S_2$. The equilibrium price rises from OP to $OP_2$. Consumers are less willing to buy products at this higher price and so the quantity demanded falls from OQ to $OQ_2$.

# Excess demand and excess supply

EXCESS DEMAND occurs when the demand for a product is greater than its supply. This can be illustrated using the demand for and supply of mushrooms shown in Figure 93.8. At a price of £0.50 per kilo, 100,000 kilos of button mushrooms are demanded, but only 20,000 kilos are supplied by businesses. This means that there is an excess demand of 80,000 kilos (100,000 - 20,000). This excess demand will result in a shortage of mushrooms, with many consumers being left disappointed.

EXCESS SUPPLY occurs when the supply of a product is greater than the demand for it. In Figure 93.8, at a price of £2.50, 100,000 kilos of button mushrooms are supplied by businesses, but only 20,000 are demanded. This means that there is an excess supply of 80,000 kilos of button mushrooms. This excess supply will result in a surplus (sometimes referred to as a glut) of button mushrooms. This

**Figure 93.8** *The excess demand for and supply of button mushrooms*

will mean a huge quantity of unsold button mushrooms for businesses, with no immediate buyers.

It can be seen in Figure 93.8 that it is only at the equilibrium price, £1.50, that there is no excess demand or supply. At this price all products supplied to the market are purchased and all buyers able to afford the price of £1.50 per kilo will be able to purchase their intended quantity.

## key terms

**Excess demand** - a situation where the quantity demanded of a product is greater than the quantity supplied at a given price.

**Excess supply** - a situation where the quantity supplied of a product is greater than the quantity demanded at a given price.

**External environment** - the factors outside a business that may influence its decisions. .

**Supply** - the quantity of products which suppliers make available to the market at any given price.

**Equilibrium price** - the price at which the quantity demanded is equal to the quantity supplied.

**Table 93.4** *The demand for and supply of sunflower oil*

| Price per litre (£) | Quantity demanded (Million litres) | Quantity supplied (Million litres) |
|---|---|---|
| 0.50 | 800 | 500 |
| 0.75 | 700 | 600 |
| 1.00 | 600 | 700 |
| 1.25 | 500 | 800 |

(a) Draw the demand and supply diagram for sunflower oil using the figures in Table 93.4.
(b) What is the equilibrium price for sunflower oil?
(c) What will be the excess demand or excess supply of sunflower oil at the following prices?
   (i) £0.60;
   (ii) £0.90;
   (iii) £0.70;
   (iv) £1.15.

Question 4

## Knowledge

1. State 6 external factors that may affect a business's decisions.
2. What happens to the amount consumers are willing and able to buy as the price of a product falls?
3. State 4 factors that cause the market demand to move to the right.
4. What happens to the amount that businesses are willing to offer to the market as price increases?
5. State 4 factors that cause the market supply curve to shift to the left.
6. What effect will a shift in demand to the left have on equilibrium price and the supply by businesses in a market?
7. What effect will a shift in supply to the right have on equilibrium price and the demand by consumers in a market?
8. What problems will excess supply cause for some businesses in a market?

# Case study The price of oil

**Figure 93.9** *The price of oil*

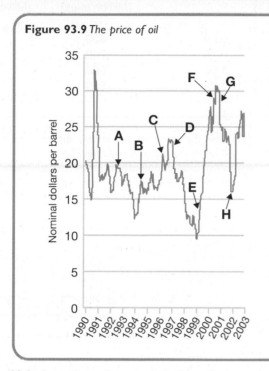

A OPEC production reaches 25.3 million barrels per day, the highest in over a decade.

B Nigerian oil workers' strike.

C Extremely cold weather in the US and Europe.

D Iraq begins exporting oil under United Nations Security Council Resolution 986.

E OPEC pledges additional production cuts for the third time since March 1998. Total pledge cuts amount to about 4.3 million barrels per day.

F USA releases 30 million barrels of oil from the Strategic Petroleum Reserve (SPR) over 30 days to bolster oil supplies, particularly heating oil in the Northeast.

G Weak world demand largely as a result of economic recession in the United States and OPEC overproduction.

H OPEC oil production cuts, unrest in Venezuela, and rising tension in the Middle East.

Figure 93.9 shows how the price of oil has fluctuated between 1990 and 2003. The price of oil on world markets is affected by many factors, as shown in the Figure.

One of the factors is the actions of OPEC, the Organisation of Petroleum Exporting Countries. This is an organisation made up of countries around the world which produce oil and sell it to businesses and other organisations in other countries. It has eleven members including Iran, Iraq, Saudi Arabia, Venezuela, Nigeria and Libya, whose economies rely heavily on income from oil exports. OPEC's primary mission is to 'achieve stable prices which are fair and reasonable for producers and consumers.'

OPEC countries meet to agree on the amount of production and supply of oil onto the world market. For example, in February 2004 OPEC agreed to stop overproducing crude at once, and then cut quotas by 1 million barrels. One problem with this is that countries do not always agree. Even when they do, some countries go back on the agreement. Another problem is that countries producing oil who are not OPEC members, such as Russia or Norway, might expand production when OPEC is trying to cut it.

Source: adapted from OPEC website and www.cbsnews.com.

(a) **Who are likely to be the (i) demanders and the (ii) suppliers of oil? (6 marks)**

(b) **Suggest factors which are likely to affect the (i) demand for and (ii) supply of oil in world markets. (10 marks)**

(c) **Explain, using examples from the data, how changes in demand and supply over the period 1990-2003 have:**
   (i) **raised the price of oil;**
   (ii) **reduced the price of oil. (12 marks)**

(d) **Assess the extent to which OPEC is likely to be able to influence the world price of oil. (12 marks)**

## Markets and competition

Unit 93 showed how the prices of products and services can be determined by demand and supply. In market economies, the forces of demand and supply will influence prices in a wide range of different markets. These could be markets divided by geographical boundaries including:

- local markets, such as the market for houses in South London;
- regional markets, such as the market for out of town entertainment in the North West of England;
- national markets, such as the market for personal computers in the UK;
- international markets, such as foreign exchange markets.

On the other hand they could be markets differentiated by use including:

- highly specialised markets, such as the market for water polo playing equipment;
- non-specialist markets, such as the market for potatoes.

The degree of competition in a market will affect how prices are determined. Assessing the level of competition in a market is not as easy as it sounds. Two businesses operating a local bus route, for example, may seem to have little competition except each other. In fact they face competition from other forms of transport such as trains, mini buses and taxis. A new chocolate bar will face **direct** competition from other chocolate bars. But it will also face **indirect** competition

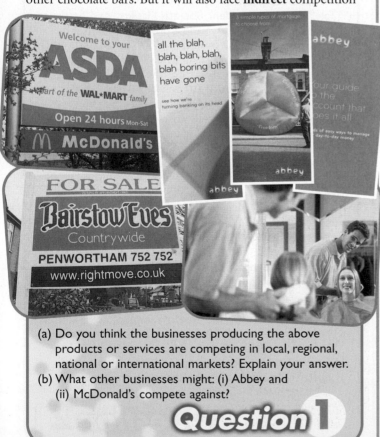

(a) Do you think the businesses producing the above products or services are competing in local, regional, national or international markets? Explain your answer.

(b) What other businesses might: (i) Abbey and (ii) McDonald's compete against?

**Question 1**

from other forms of confectionery, such as crisps or sweets.

## Degrees of competition

The amount of competition that exists in a market is known as the MARKET STRUCTURE. There is a number of widely recognised MODELS OF COMPETITION with different market structures. They vary according to:

- the amount of knowledge consumers have about different products;
- the ease with which firms can set up and compete within the market;
- the number of firms operating within the market;
- the extent to which rival products are different;
- the amount of control which businesses exert within their markets;
- the extent to which individual businesses can determine the price of their goods and services.

## Perfect competition

The model of PERFECT COMPETITION assumes businesses produce products which are exactly the same. Consumers have 'perfect knowledge' of the market. They are aware of what is being offered by all businesses. There are no barriers to prevent firms from setting up and there is a large number of firms in competition with one another.

Businesses in such markets are known as PRICE TAKERS. Each individual firm has no influence over the price which it charges for its products. If a firm were to charge a higher price than others then no consumers would buy its products, since every product is exactly the same and they would know exactly where to go to buy an alternative. A firm that charged a price below that of others would be forced out of business.

In reality, it is not easy to identify markets which conform to the model of perfect competition. However, there are some which have many of the characteristics of a perfectly competitive market. One example in the UK could be agriculture. There are large numbers of farmers providing farm produce for the market. Farming businesses tend, generally, to be small scale and are unable to influence market price. Furthermore, it is likely that one vegetable will be much the same as another on a different farm. Information about this market is also available in trade journals.

One advantage for businesses of operating in conditions of perfect competition is that they have a strong incentive to operate efficiently. Inefficient businesses are forced out of perfectly competitive markets.

However, there are certain problems.

- Businesses only make what are known as 'normal profits'. Normal profits are relatively modest. They are only just enough to prevent new businesses being attracted to the market and existing businesses from leaving the market. Businesses operating under normal competition making

larger than normal profits would quickly see these profits eroded by the entrance of new businesses into the market forcing prices, and therefore profits, down.

- Businesses operating under perfect competition are not able to control their prices. This is because of the competitiveness of the markets in which they operate. Such businesses have little control over their own destinies. They are completely governed by market conditions.

It is for the above reasons that businesses prefer to operate in conditions that are less competitive than perfect competition. Wherever possible, the majority of businesses attempt to exert some control over the degree of competition in markets in which they operate.

## Monopoly

MONOPOLY occurs when one business has total control over a market and is the only seller of the product. This **pure monopoly** should not be confused with a **legal monopoly**, which occurs in the UK when a firm controls 25 per cent or more of a market.

Monopolists are likely to erect barriers to prevent others from entering their market. They will also exert a strong influence on the price which they charge for their product. However, because monopolists are the only supplier of a product, it does not mean that they can charge whatever they want. If they raise the price a great deal demand will fall to some extent. Because of the influence monopolists have on their price, they are often called **price makers**.

Although there are many businesses in the UK which exert a great deal of power in the markets in which they operate, few, if any, could be described as being a pure monopoly. In the past, however, certain businesses have come close to exerting pure monopoly power. Before competitors such as Transco were able to supply gas to consumers, British Gas enjoyed a monopoly position in the gas market. It was the sole supplier of piped gas in the UK. On the other hand, it could be argued that British Gas was operating in the energy market and therefore faced competition from electricity and oil companies. One of the main reasons why British Gas no longer exerts such control over the market for gas is that the government introduced **legislation** to increase competition in markets where monopolies previously existed (☞ unit 103).

From a business's point of view monopoly has certain advantages and problems. To some extent these are the reverse of the benefits and problems of perfect competition. For example, monopolies tend to make 'abnormal' profits compared to competitive businesses. However, there may be little or no incentive for a large business to innovate if it faces a lack of competition. It may therefore be less efficient and profitable than it is capable of being, resulting in bureaucracy, inefficient management and a lower dividend for shareholders.

## Monopoly, perfect competition and consumers

Businesses often attempt to restrict competition in the markets in which they operate. This allows them to have a greater control of prices and to become more profitable. In addition, governments seek to regulate markets in order to control monopolies and protect consumers. This might suggest that competition is better for consumers than monopoly. However, under certain circumstances, consumers may benefit from monopolies.

**Prices** It might be expected that prices for consumers would be higher under monopolies than under perfect competition. However, monopolies can sometimes provide consumers with lower prices than businesses operating under competitive conditions. This is because the large size of many monopoly businesses allows them to gain economies of scale (☞ unit 81). Cost savings gained by operating on a large scale may allow monopolies to earn large profits. They might then set prices either lower than or the same as low profit making businesses operating under perfect competition.

**Choice** It could be argued that a large number of businesses competing against each other will lead to greater choice of products for customers. However, there are conditions where competition does not lead to wider choice for consumers. For

---

In January 2004 TelePassport Telecommunications, the first private telephone operator in Cyprus, pledged to reduce call rates by 15 per cent after gaining approval from the Telecommunications Regulator. Previously the only telephone company had been CyTA, a government controlled company.

TelePassport's president, Socratis Hasikos, said 'Statistics show that in 1998 CyTA made a profit of £50 million which increased to £62 million in 1999 and in 2001 reached £91 million. According to CyTA they expected to reap a profit of £107 million from the period 1998-2002, yet they earned a profit of £218 million. How can this be possible if they are not over-charging their customers? Now, they must present their costs and expenses to the Telecommunications Regulator, who has given them 15 days to do so.' He believed that CyTA delayed presenting its expenses because 'they have been paying out too much money and need to earn it back by charging more, or they have simply been ripping off customers'.

It was suggested that the entry of Cyprus into the EU would open the door to healthy competition for CyTA. Hasikos argues 'Our aim is not to attack CyTA, but to offer customers a better service at cheaper rates. Competition need not be negative, but could push CyTA into also lowering their prices.'

Source: adapted from www.xak.com.

(a) Identify and explain the type of model of competition before the entry of TelePassport Telecommunications into the market in Cyprus.
(b) Examine how (i) businesses and (ii) consumers are likely to be affected by the change in competition that is taking place in Cyprus.

## Question 2

example, many believe that a wider choice of channels operated by an increasing range of television companies is not improving choice. This is because competing businesses tend to replicate the products of their competitors. In the US, consumers are faced with vast numbers of channels offering what many regard as low quality programmes.

**Innovation** Businesses in competitive markets have the incentive to innovate as they try to differentiate their products from those of competitors. However, the relatively large profits made by monopolies allow them to invest heavily in research and development, which could lead to innovations. Smaller businesses facing intense competition may not be able to finance this research.

## Monopolistic competition

This is a market model where there is **imperfect** competition. This means that there is some restriction on competition.

MONOPOLISTIC COMPETITION exists where a large number of relatively small firms compete in an industry. There are few BARRIERS TO ENTRY, so that it is fairly easy for firms to set up and to leave these markets.

Each firm has a product that is **differentiated** from the others. This is achieved through **branding**, when a product is given an identity of its own (☞ unit 27). A business will face competition from a wide range of other firms competing in the same market with similar, but differentiated, products.

Firms operating under these conditions are not price takers, but they will only have a limited degree of control over the prices they charge. There are few markets of this kind in the UK. Two examples might be legal services and the manufacture of certain types of clothing.

## Oligopoly

When there are many firms, but only a few dominate the market, OLIGOPOLY is said to exist. Examples include the markets for petrol, beer, detergents, paint and sweets. The majority of businesses in the UK operate under this type of competition.

Under oligopoly, each firm will have a differentiated product, often with a strong brand identity. Several brands may be competing in the same market. Brand loyalty amongst customers is encouraged by advertising and promotion. Firms in such markets are often said to compete in the form of non-price competition. Prices are often stable for long periods, disturbed only by short price wars.

Although brand loyalty does allow some price control, businesses often follow the price of the market leaders. This means that they tend to be interdependent.

Barriers to entry exist. If it was easy for new firms to enter the industry, they would set up and take the market share of the few large producers. Examples of barriers to entry might be:

● legal restrictions, such as patents which prevent other businesses copying products for a period of time;

**Figure 94.1** *The world's biggest automotive markets in 2001*

- **USA** (17.5m vehicles, 8.4m cars)
- **Japan** (5.9m vehicles, 4.3m cars)
- **Germany** (3.6m vehicles, 3.3m cars)
- **United Kingdom** (2.8m vehicles, 2.5m cars)
- **France** (2.7m vehicles, 2.3m cars)
- **Italy** (2.6m vehicles, 2.4m cars)
- **China** (2.4m vehicles, 717,000 cars)
- **Spain** (1.8m vehicles, 1.5m cars)
- **Canada** (1.6m vehicles, 869,000 cars)
- **Korea** (1.5m vehicles, 1.1m cars)

**Figure 94.2** *Top passenger car brands in the UK by sales, 2003*

- **Ford** (378,942)
- **Vauxhall/General Motors** (326,436)
- **Renault** (189,427)
- **Peugeot** (184,940)
- **Volkswagen** (178,953)
- **Citroen** (117,602)
- **Toyota** (117,531)
- **Nissan** (105,798)
- **MG Rover** (95,848)
- **BMW** (93,822)
- **Mercedes Benz** (93,625)
- **Honda** (81,858)
- **Fiat** (74,823)
- **Audi** (70,824)
- **Mini** (41,510)
- **Land Rover** (41,056)
- **Volvo** (39,062)
- **Mazda** (37,854)
- **Skoda** (36,548)
- **Seat** (34,293)

**Table 94.1** *The World's Top 10 automotive manufacturers, 2002*

| Company | Region of origin | Global vehicle sales |
|---|---|---|
| General Motors | (US) | 8.5m |
| Ford | (US) | 7.0m |
| Toyota | (Japan) | 6.2m |
| Volkswagen | (Europe) | 5.0m |
| DaimlerChrysler | (US) | 4.5m |
| PSA Peugeot-Citroen | (Europe) | 3.3m |
| Honda | (Japan) | 2.8m |
| Nissan | (Japan) | 2.7m |
| Renault | (Europe) | 2.4m |
| Fiat | (Europe) | 2.1m |

Source: adapted from www.mind-advertising.com.

(a) Which of the models of competition do you think best describes the motor vehicle market? Explain your answer using examples from the data.

(b) What influence might any one of the top twenty car manufacturers be likely to have on the price of cars in the UK market?

**Question 3**

- high start up costs, such as the cost of manufacturing;
- the promotion or advertising required, for example, in the tobacco or soap powder industries;
- arrangements between businesses, for example in the 1990s newsagents could not stock ice creams by other producers in certain manufacturers' freezers (known as freezer exclusivity);
- collusion between businesses in cartels, which act together to prevent new entrants.

**Table 94.2** *A summary of the characteristics of models of competition*

|  | Perfect competition | Monopolistic competition | Oligopoly | Monopoly |
|---|---|---|---|---|
| Barriers to entry | None | Few | Many | Almost impossible for new firms to enter the market |
| Number of of firms | Many | Many | A few | One |
| Influence over price | None | Some | Strong | Very strong |
| Differentiated product | No | Yes | Strong brands | No competition; not necessary |

# Porter's five forces analysis

The models of competition outlined above provide a useful means of describing markets. It can be argued, however, that they project businesses as being largely passive, simply accepting the constraints of their market structures. Michael Porter (1980) in his book *Competitive Strategy*, suggested that in certain circumstances businesses can influence the markets in which they operate. He outlined five forces that determine the extent to which businesses are able to manage competition within their markets.

**Rivalry among competitors** Porter argues that competitive rivalry is the main force that affects the ability of businesses to influence markets. This includes:

- the number of competitors - the more competitors the less likely it is that a business will be able to have influence;
- their ability to differentiate products - a promotional campaign by a business to differentiate its product will increase its influence;
- the rate of growth of the market - in a fast growing market competition may be less intense and individual firms will have more scope to influence the market;
- the existence of barriers to exit - competition may be intense in markets where businesses are deterred from leaving the market. Exit barriers may include the costs of

high redundancy payments or losses as a result of having to sell machinery at reduced prices.

**The threat of new entrants** The number of businesses in a market may not always be a useful guide to competition in that market. This may also depend on the ability of businesses to enter the market. If it is easy for businesses to enter markets then competition is likely to be greater. This will restrict the ability of a business to influence the market. It is possible that businesses may be prevented or deterred from entering markets due to barriers to entry. For example, the need to invest heavily in new plant and machinery or to match high levels of promotional spending could deter new businesses from entering a market.

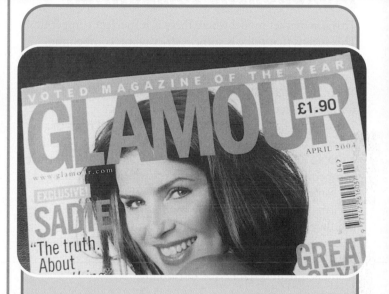

*Glamour* magazine is leader of the women's monthly magazine market. Its closest rival, *Cosmopolitan*, is one pound more expensive. *Glamour* is seen by many as being younger, funkier and more celebrity orientated, with stars such as Jennifer Lopez on its front cover. *InStyle* and *Company*, although experiencing sales increases, cannot match the 537,474 sales achieved by Glamour. The older women's market is not looking quite so healthy with declining or static sales for *Good Housekeeping* and *Prima*. The so-called 'middle youth market' has *Red*, *She* and *Eve* competing for customers, while the market for more intelligent upmarket women's glossies is fought for between *Marie Claire* and *Vogue*.

Source: adapted from *The Guardian*, 13.2.2003.

(a) Using Porter's five force analysis, examine *Glamour's* ability to manage competition in the market for women's monthly magazines.

Question 4

**The threat of substitute products** This depends upon the extent to which businesses can differentiate their products from those of competitors. A business which struggles to differentiate its products is likely to face intense competition. This is why businesses spend large sums of money attempting to make their products different or seem different from those of competitors. For example, the success of a chain of pizza restaurants may depend on its ability to appear to offer a style of pizza that others do not.

**The bargaining power of customers** Where customers are strong, there is likely to be more competition between producers and their influence will tend to be weaker. The factors affecting the power of consumers may be:
- the number of customers;
- whether they act together;
- their importance, for example, large supermarket chains have had great influence over food manufacturers;
- their ability to switch products;
- regularity of purchases, for example, consumers on holiday are often 'one-off' purchasers prepared to pay a higher price.

**The bargaining power of suppliers** Powerful suppliers can increase the costs of a business and decrease the extent to which it can control its operations. The power of suppliers is likely to depend upon the number of suppliers able to supply a business and the importance in the production process of the product being supplied. For example, if a JIT manufacturer can easily switch supplier, the producer will have greater control of the production process.

## key terms

**Barriers to entry** - factors that might deter or prevent businesses from entering a market.

**Market structure** - the characteristics of a market which determine the behaviour of firms operating within it.

**Model of competition** - a simplified theory to explain the types of competition between businesses.

**Monopolistic competition** - a market structure with freedom of entry and exit, differentiated products and a large number of small firms competing.

**Monopoly** - a market structure in which only one firm supplies the entire output, there is no competition and barriers to entry exist.

**Oligopoly** - a market structure with a small number of dominant firms, producing heavily branded products with some barriers to entry.

**Perfect competition** - a market structure with perfect knowledge, many buyers and sellers, freedom of entry and exit and a homogeneous product.

**Price taker** - a firm that is unable to influence the price at which it sells its products.

## Knowledge

1. Explain the difference between a local and an international market.
2. What determines the amount of discretion firms have in making their pricing decisions?
3. What is the difference between a price taker and a price maker?
4. What are the 4 models of market competition?
5. Under what conditions might a firm be unable to influence the price it sets for its product?

**Figure 95.3** *Economic activity rates of males and females, UK, percentages*

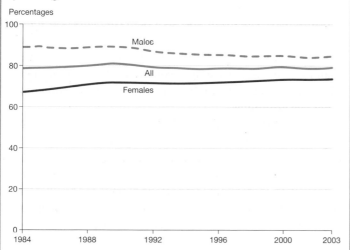

**Figure 95.4** *Economic activity rates of male and females by age, UK, percentages*

Source: adapted from *Social Trends*, Office for National Statistics.

(a) Identify the trends taking place in the data.
(b) Comment on the advert in the light of these trends.

Question2

# Geographical distribution of population and business

The movement of people between countries is called migration. The location and movement of people within a country may also affect businesses. In the 1990s and after the year 2000 there were a number of trends in the UK population that could have affected businesses.

- Urban and rural location. In Great Britain, almost 90 per cent of people lived in urban areas in the 1990s. In recent years this trend has been reversed in certain parts of the country. For example, there have been noticeable declines in the population of some inner cities. The South East of England experienced the largest net percentage gain in population. In future some cities might see an increase in population as a result of inner city centre developments, such as those in Liverpool to coincide with its status as European Capital of Culture in 2008.
- Age and location. In general, younger people are more likely to live in urban areas than older people. In the 1990s 41 per cent of the population under 30 lived in urban areas, compared to 36 per cent in rural areas.
- Age and migration. Young people tend to have higher mobility than older people.

How might businesses have been affected? It is possible that businesses may react to demand by younger people in cities. For example, in Inner London house builders have responded to these changes by building houses and flats suited to the needs of younger people. Their marketing of these developments has been geared to the needs of younger buyers. The movement out from cities may encourage support businesses or entertainment to locate in semi-rural or urban fringe areas. Examples may be multiplex cinemas, shopping malls and family orientated pubs.

# Other changes in the structure of the population

**Households** One of the most significant changes in the structure of the population has been changes in the households within which people live. Increasingly people are living in smaller units, especially one person households, and less in extended and nuclear family groups. This has been the result of increases in the number of divorces and older people living longer after their partners have died. Businesses may be able to cater for the needs of people in these groups by developing fast, microwavable food, single accommodation or singles holidays, for example.

**Ethnic minority groups** The age structure of ethnic minority groups may vary. For example, people from black groups other than Black African and Black Caribbean are more likely than people from the Chinese group to have been born in the UK. Certain ethnic groups have a younger age structure. 45 per cent of Bangladeshis in the UK are under the age of 16, for instance.

1. What does the population growth rate show?
2. Suggest 3 effects of a growing population on businesses.
3. State 3 factors that affect population size and growth.
4. What happens to population if net migration is negative?
5. How might immigration affect businesses?
6. State 2 factors that might cause a fall in the birth rate.

7. How might a fall in the birth rate affect a business?
8. State 2 benefits to a business of an ageing population.
9. How might a larger proportion of women than men affect population?
10. State 2 other features of the structure of population that might affect a business.

**Figure 95.5** *Divorces, UK, thousands*

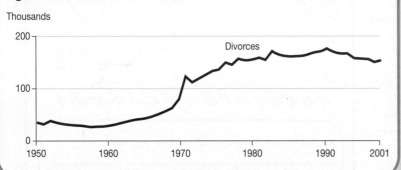

**Table 95.3** *Households by size, UK, percentages*

| | 1971 | 1981 | 1991 | 2001 | 2003 |
|---|---|---|---|---|---|
| One person | 18 | 22 | 27 | 29 | 29 |
| Two people | 32 | 32 | 34 | 35 | 35 |
| Three people | 19 | 17 | 16 | 16 | 15 |
| Four people | 17 | 18 | 16 | 14 | 14 |
| Five people | 8 | 7 | 5 | 5 | 5 |
| Six or more | 6 | 4 | 2 | 2 | 2 |

Source: adapted from *Social Trends*, Office for National Statistics.

(a) Identify the trends taking place in the data.
(b) Examine how these trends might have affect businesses in the UK.

**Question 3**

# key terms

**Birth rate** - the number of live births per thousand of the population.
**Death rate** - the number of deaths per thousand of the population.
**Demographic factors** - features of the size, location and distribution of the population.
**Dependency ratio** - the proportion of dependants or non-workers to workers.

**Net migration** - the difference between the number of people entering a country (or region) and the number leaving it.
**Population structure** - the breakdown of the people in a country into groups based on differences in age, gender, geographical location etc.

# Case study The future of the UK population

The UK population is predicted to increase more rapidly than before and peak at more than 65 million in 2051. Almost all the growth will be among older people and the working age population will start to decline within the next twenty years. This will leave the UK increasingly dependent on immigrants to maintain its economic vitality. 'Immigration is one part of ensuring the continued success of the UK economy and supporting an ageing population,' said Beverley Hughes the then Home Office Minister.

The number of people of working age is expected to rise to 37.8 million by 2011. Partly this is due to the raising of the retirement age for women to 65. By 2021 the working population will be 39.4 million, but after it will start to fall.

The total UK population is predicted to increase to 64.8 million in 2031. The number of children under 16 is projected to fall by 7.4 per cent from 2002 to 2014. The number of people of state pensionable age is projected to increase by 11.9 per cent from 2002 to 2011. These projections suggest a big change in the balance between generations. In 2002 there were about 850,000 more children than pensioners. From 2007 pensioners will be in the majority and by 2031 they will exceed the number of children by about 4 million.

Source: adapted from *The Guardian*, 2003.

**(a) Outline the main population trends in the UK from the data. (8 marks)**

**(b) Explain possible reasons to explain why these trends have occurred. (10 marks)**

**(c) Examine the effects of each of these trends on the supply of labour to businesses. (10 marks)**

**(d) Assess, in future, how businesses might change their products and services to take advantage of these trends. (12 marks)**

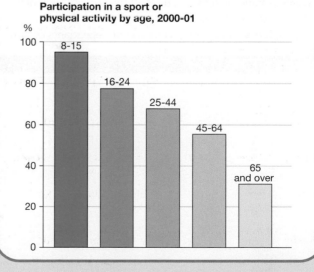

**Figure 95.6** *Population data, UK*
Source: adapted from Office for National Statistics.

*Interest in television programme type by age, 2002*

|  | 16-24 | 25-64 | 65 and over |
|---|---|---|---|
| News | 83 | 94 | 97 |
| Factual | 69 | 87 | 84 |
| Drama | 75 | 80 | 87 |
| Entertainment | 89 | 76 | 70 |
| Regional | 50 | 72 | 85 |
| Current affairs | 57 | 68 | 79 |
| Educational | 45 | 61 | 52 |
| Sports | 51 | 54 | 53 |
| Arts | 30 | 33 | 43 |
| Children's | 41 | 33 | 17 |
| Religious | 11 | 19 | 51 |

## The economy and government

Unit 93 explained that a number of external factors can affect businesses. One of these factors is the economy in which the businesses operate. Changes in the economy can affect how businesses make decisions. For example, a growing economy, with increased spending by consumers, may encourage a business to expand production. Governments often attempt to influence the economy in order to achieve their objectives. The activities of government can also influence businesses (☞ unit 105).

## The business cycle

Economies tend to grow over a period of time. This is known as **economic growth** (☞ unit 101). Growth can be measured by changes in national income. National income is the total amount of income, output or spending in the economy. It can be measured in a number of ways, including GROSS DOMESTIC PRODUCT (GDP) and GROSS NATIONAL PRODUCT (GNP).

Output does not grow smoothly. It tends to fluctuate, going through 'ups and downs'. These short term fluctuations are known as the BUSINESS CYCLE. It is argued that all economies go through these cycles which illustrate fluctuations in the level of activity in the economy.

Figure 96.1 shows a traditional business cycle. There are four parts to the business cycle, indicated on the diagram. The broken line shows the long-term path of economic growth.

**Boom** In a BOOM (also called a peak) consumer spending and investment will be high. Many businesses will experience high levels of demand from people with increasing incomes. Profits should be high for most firms and wages might be rising. Output will be high and the economy will be growing

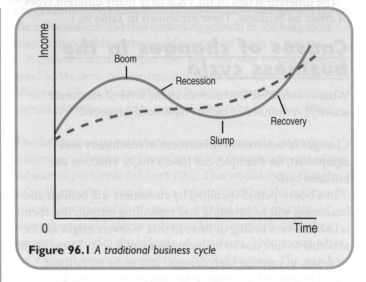

**Figure 96.1** A traditional business cycle

steadily. Business and consumer confidence is also likely to be high.

**Recession** A RECESSION (also called a downturn, downswing or economic slowdown) is where incomes and output start to fall. Business might experience a fall in demand for their products and a decline in profit. Some might start to lay off workers.

**Slump** A SLUMP (also called a depression) occurs at the bottom of the cycle. Unemployment is likely to be high and confidence, spending, investment and profits low. Many firms may be forced out of business. Sometimes, when growth is taking place, but only very slowly, this is also called a recession.

**Recovery** A RECOVERY (also called an expansion or upswing) is where income starts to rise again after a slump. Output will begin to increase as spending and confidence

**Table 96.1** Effects of the business cycle

|  | Sales | Output | Wages | Profit | Confidence | Unemployment | Spending | Prices | Imports | Start-ups/ closures | Investment/stocks |
|---|---|---|---|---|---|---|---|---|---|---|---|
| **Boom** | High | High | Rising fast | High | Strong | Low | Strong | Rises above average | Rise above average | Many start ups/ few closures | High |
| **Recession** | Falling | Falling | Rises slow down | Falling or losses | Weakening | Rising | Falling | Rises slow down | Falling | Start ups fall/ closures increase | Falling |
| **Slump** | Low | Low | Little or no rise | Losses | Weak | High | Weak | Rises below average, none or may fall | Low | Few start ups/ many closures | Low |
| **Recovery** | Rising | Rising | May rise | Rising | Rising | Falling | Start to rise | Start to rise | May rise | Start ups rise/ fewer closures | Start to rise |

1. What are the 4 main parts of the business cycle?
2. State 3 factors that might cause the business cycle.
3. Explain 5 effects of a boom on business.
4. State 4 government objectives.
5. Give an example of:
   (a) taxation on the price of a product;
   (b) taxation on income;
   (c) taxation on profits.
6. How might an increase in government spending affect a business producing hospital beds?
7. What effect would cutting interest rates have on business borrowing?

# Case study   Signs of UK recovery?

Recovery or not? In December 2003 and January 2004 there was debate about the extent to which recovery had started in the UK economy, and even if there was likely to be recovery at all.

There were some encouraging signs that recovery was about to take place. Telecom equipment companies were enthusiastic about signs that big phone companies were starting to spend money again to upgrade their technologies and their stock. The share price of Marconi for example had risen by six per cent. Other areas buoyed by the prospect of a pick up in investment included media companies and music companies such as EMI.

On 8 January 2004 the Bank of England decided not to raise interest rates further. This followed the strongest demand for three years for exports in December 2003 according to the Confederation of British Industry (CBI). Export prospects had been boosted by the growth in the US since mid-2003. Whilst accepting that manufacturers were still struggling, the CBI argued that it was clear that conditions for industry were improving after the tough times since the collapse of the IT boom at the end of the Millennium. It pointed to annual growth of about 2 per cent. Doug Gooden, CBI head of economic analysis, said 'manufacturers are still facing a really tough uphill battle, with over a third saying order books remain below normal'.

Businesses reported stronger domestic demand also, with orders expected to feed through into the first increase in output in a year. However, manufacturers were unlikely to raise prices which had remained low due to competitive pressures in the recession periods of previous years.

The Organisation for Economic Cooperation and Development (OECD) suggested that recovery could be delayed unless interest rates were cut further. This would boost confidence among consumers and businesses. It forecast that any recovery would be slow to materialise.

The International Monetary Fund (IMF), however, cast doubt on growth predictions. Gordon Brown, the Chancellor of the Exchequer, had predicted growth of 3-3.5 per cent in 2004. The IMF suggested that it would be closer to 2.5 per cent. The Bank of England had a mixture of good and bad news. It predicted growth of just under 3 per cent and said that consumers were borrowing and spending again. However, it argued that many consumers were in debt and spending could be affected by changes in circumstances and levels of interest rates in future.

Source: adapted from news.bbc.co.uk, www.guardian.co.uk, uk.news.yahoo.com.

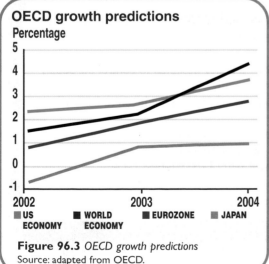

**OECD growth predictions**
Percentage

**Figure 96.3** OECD growth predictions
Source: adapted from OECD.

(a) **Identify the conditions that UK businesses might have faced in recession periods mentioned in the article. (6 marks)**
(b) **Describe how changes in investment might bring about recovery using phone companies as an example. (6 marks)**
(c) **Describe two other factors that might have led to recovery in the UK economy. (8 marks)**
(d) **Suggest how recovery might affect UK businesses. (10 marks)**
(e) **Discuss whether recovery was likely to take place. (10 marks)**

## Interest rates

Businesses and people sometimes need to borrow money. A company might buy new machinery and not have enough funds in the business to pay for it. Consumers sometimes borrow to spend at Christmas or to take holidays and pay the money back later. INTEREST RATES are the cost or price of this borrowing. For example, if a business borrowed £10,000 at an interest rate of 5 per cent a year, assuming it did not pay off any of the loan it would be charged £500 in interest per year.

There are many different interest rates in the economy. Borrowing takes place in a number of ways. A business might have an overdraft facility at the bank and pay interest at 7-9 per cent a year. Interest rates on a mortgage to buy a house might be 6 per cent. Credit cards often charge higher rates, for example between 12-15 per cent.

## Variations in interest rates

Interest rates change over time. Figure 97.1 shows changes in interest rates in the UK from 1990 to 2004. It shows that interest rates have been relatively stable over the period 1993-2003 and that interest rates after the year 2000 have been historically low.

What determines interest rates? In any market, such as the market for mortgages, interest rates are determined by the demand for and supply of money. Borrowers, such as businesses and consumers, will demand money and lenders, such as banks and other financial institutions, will supply it. If borrowers demand more money for mortgages, the interest rate (the price of borrowing) will rise, just like prices of goods rise when people demand more (☞ unit 93).

Many markets in the UK are influenced by the rate of interest set by the central bank in the UK - the Bank of England. The Bank of England has the power to control interest rates charged by banks such as HSBC, Abbey and NatWest to their customers. If the Bank of England increases interest rates, then the base rates of banks will follow. Other interest rates of banks will then follow the base rate. Banks charge higher rates of interest on short term borrowing than the base rate and pay lower rates on savings. They hope to make profit by earning more on loans than they pay on savings. Rates of interest on other forms of borrowing tend to follow changes in bank base rates so as to remain competitive, although there is no direct link.

## Interest rates and consumer spending

Changes in interest rates can affect consumer spending in a number of ways.

- Higher interest rates increase the cost of borrowing to consumers. Consumers then tend to cut back on taking out loans and using overdrafts and credit cards. This can affect a wide variety of businesses, particularly those selling goods on credit, such as cars or electrical goods. It might also affect businesses selling 'luxury goods' such as jewellery or yachts. Businesses selling basic consumer goods might not be affected by small changes in interest rates.

- Higher interest rates lead to higher mortgage payments. This might affect businesses in two ways. Consumers with higher mortgage payments will have less money to spend on other goods. Also, higher payments mean that people may be less willing to take out a mortgage to buy property, affecting businesses involved in construction and houses for sale. Businesses which rent housing, however, might benefit, if people switch to renting property.

**Figure 97.1** *Changes in base interest rates in the UK, 1990-2003*
Source: adapted from Bank of England.

**Table 97.1** *Changes in National Insurance contributions*

|  | Last Year | This Year |
|---|---|---|
| **Employers' National Insurance contributions** | | |
| Earnings £89-£595 | 9.3% on excess over £89 | 12.8% on excess over £89 |
| Earnings over £595 | 12.8% | 11.8% |

Source: adapted from *The UK Pocket Tax Book*, PricewaterhouseCoopers.

years, using his building as collateral. However, he needed more than the bank was prepared to offer. So he had to borrow the rest at a variable rate of interest, which might change in future.

Josh had recently heard about possible increases in interest rates by the Bank of England. The interest rate in early 2004 was 3.75 per cent, but there was a lot of pressure on the Bank of England to raise this rate. This would determine rates of interest in other money markets and force them up as well. Josh was worried about the effect of a rise on his own business and his customers.

Most of Belmont's parts are brought in from Italy. This is part of the EU, with no trade restrictions. The euro had recently been worth 1.26 euros against the pound.

Josh is now considering buying products from the USA. The value of the pound against the dollar is strong. Between 2003 and 2004 it had risen from £1 = $1.6 to £1 = $1.8. This has made imports to the UK cheaper, but UK exports more expensive in the USA.

Josh has found some interesting new wheels which he hopes to incorporate into his designs. He has been assured that when the designs come out he will be able to sell them to US importers of British goods. But he has been worried about stories in the paper recently about US trade restrictions on EU imports. He is concerned that customs duties will raise the price and lower sales of his cycles in the USA.

Josh had also noticed a slowdown in spending, from both customers and businesses, and felt that indirect and direct taxation might have something to do with this.

*Answer either A or B*

*A - Interest rates*
(a) **What is meant by the following phrases which apply to Belmont Cycles?**
  (i) **Fixed and variable rates of interest. (4 marks)**
  (ii) **The decision by the Bank of England to raise interest rates. (4 marks)**
(b) **Explain how interest rates affected the choice of finance of the business. (8 marks)**
(c) **Examine how rises in interest rates in future might affect borrowing and investment by the business. (12 marks)**
(d) **Discuss the extent to which a possible rise in interest rates might affect:**
  (i) **the exchange rate;**
  (ii) **the imports and exports of the business. (12 marks)**

*B - Taxation*
(a) **What is meant by the following phrases which apply to Belmont Cycles?**
  (i) **Direct and indirect taxation. (4 marks)**
  (ii) **Customs duties will raise the price of cycles. (4 marks)**
(b) **Explain how business rates may have influenced the decision to move to new premises. (8 marks)**
(c) **Examine how the changes in Table 97.1 might affect:**
  (i) **the costs of the business;**
  (ii) **the operation of the business at the new location. (12 marks)**
(d) **Discuss the extent to which changes in taxation might have affected the consumer and business customers of Belmont. (12 marks)**

## What is inflation?

INFLATION can be defined as a persistent tendency for prices to rise. It occurs when there is a general increase in the price level, not just if one business raises its prices. So, if inflation is 3 per cent for example, then prices are rising on average by 3 per cent over the period of a year.

To what extent is this a problem? Low levels of inflation, below 5 per cent, are likely to be considered acceptable in many countries. Governments, consumers and businesses do not suffer the difficulties of high inflation, such as rising costs, and gain benefits of some inflation, such as a fall in the value of repayments on borrowing. Rates of around 10 per cent or more, as experienced by the UK in the early 1990s, may lead to greater problems. HYPER-INFLATION, such as the inflation rate of 1,500 per cent in Tajikistan in 1995, can cause serious difficulties.

Governments may try to reduce the rate of inflation from 5 per cent to 2 per cent for example. This does not mean that prices are falling, just that the rate of inflation is slowing down. DEFLATION is a situation where average prices actually fall over a period. Governments also set target rates of inflation. They aim for rates that are lower than or the same as those of their main international competitors. The UK government in the early twenty-first century set target rates mainly around 2 per cent per annum.

## The causes of inflation

What causes inflation? Certain arguments may be put forward.

**Money** Some believe that inflation is caused by increases in the MONEY SUPPLY. This is the total amount of money circulating in the economy. This view is often associated with the group of economists known as **monetarists** (☞ unit 105).

Supporters of this idea argue that any increase in the money supply which is not in line with growth in the output of the economy will lead to inflation. Take, for example, an increase in the money supply of 10 per cent. In the short term, consumer spending would increase, but the output of producers would not be able to expand as quickly. Instead, there would be an increase in prices. Supporters of this view argue strongly that it is important for governments to ensure that the rate of growth of the money supply is kept in line with the rate of growth of output or there will be inflation.

It has been suggested that the excessive inflation levels in some Eastern European and South American countries has been inflamed by governments simply printing money to cope with price rises. This has led to further price rises as the money supply has increased over and above any output rise. In the UK the independence of the Bank of England is said to be a factor which may have influenced the low levels of inflation in the late 1990s and early twenty first century.

Governments could no longer make the Bank increase the money supply before an election in order to gain public support.

**Demand** Too much spending or **demand** can lead to inflation. This is known as DEMAND-PULL INFLATION. The result is similar to that described under changes in the money supply, but the cause is different. Demand-pull inflation comes about when there is excessive spending in the economy. This expenditure leads to an increase in demand which cannot be matched by the level of supply. Because demand is greater than supply, prices rise. The increase in demand can be due to:
● a rise in consumer spending;
● firms investing in more machinery;
● government expenditure increasing;
● more exports being bought abroad.

Some economists argue that inflation in the UK at the end of the 1980s and early 1990s was caused by earlier tax cuts, leading to increases in consumer expenditure.

**Increasing costs** Another argument is that rising costs lead to inflation. This is known as COST-PUSH INFLATION, as rising costs force firms to push up their prices. What causes costs to increase?
● Rises in wages and salaries. There may be an increase in labour costs as workers and unions push for and receive an increase in their wages.
● Tax increases. Increases in indirect taxes, such as VAT (☞ unit 97), can raise the price of products. They can also increase the costs of production, which causes firms to raise their prices.
● Profits. A push by firms to raise profit levels, due to pressure from shareholders, can increase production costs.
● Imports. An increase in costs can be 'imported' from abroad (☞ unit 100). The prices of imported raw materials or semi-finished products, such as components, may rise. This could increase the price of home produced goods which use these in production. A rise in the price of imported finished goods can more directly lead to inflation, as it adds to the general level of prices. For example, a sudden fall in reserves of raw materials such as oil will force up the price. Businesses importing oil or using oil in their production process will have to pay higher costs.

Rises in wages or the price of imports are said to be examples of **supply shocks** because they affect the firms' costs and the supply of their products. It was argued that the high levels of inflation experienced by the UK in the 1970s and early 1980s was due to huge oil price rises. In the 1990s the UK had relatively low inflation rates. Some argued that one of the factors affecting this was the reduced power of trade

unions and their inability to negotiate high wage rises.

**Expectations** Some economists believe that employees expecting inflation to occur can actually be a cause of inflation. This is because workers pressing for a pay rise tend to build in an **anticipated** amount of inflation into their claim. For example, if they expect inflation to be four per cent, and want a two per cent pay rise, they will demand a six per cent pay increase. If awarded, this would give them a two per cent **real** increase in wages and a six per cent **money** increase. If this was the average for all businesses in the economy, they would be faced with a six per cent increase in their wage costs. This increase in costs may lead businesses to increase their prices, and inflation can occur. If expectations of inflation are reduced, wage costs may be kept down. It is also argued that increases in wages in line with increases in productivity do not lead to higher costs, and higher prices as a result.

---

Inflation is likely to fall following falling costs facing manufacturers and lower global demand for products. 'Small and medium sized manufacturers are facing extreme pressure from the global slowdown in demand' said a vice-chair of the Confederation of British Industry. The falling costs were accounted for by lower fuel prices arising out of the tumbling price of oil. In addition, many businesses were in the process of shedding labour leading to lower wage costs. 'Falling prices at the factory gate should spell lower prices in the shops. The rate of inflation should dip back down to 2.3 per cent' said one leading commentator.

Source: adapted from *The Guardian*, 14.8.2002.

(a) Using data from the article, identify two reasons why inflation was considered likely to fall.
(b) Explain whether you think deflation might occur following the events described in the article.

---

## Effects of inflation on business

Reducing inflation is one of the main economic objectives of UK governments (☞ unit 96). The UK government has had strong support from the Confederation of British Industry (CBI) and other business groups in following this approach. Why is inflation seen as such a problem? There is a number of effects that relatively high rates of inflation might have on business, and on consumer demand and confidence.

**Increasing costs** Inflation leads to an increase in business costs. Examples might be:
● increases in the cost of components or raw materials;
● increases in wages and salaries of employees to keep pace with inflation;
● increasing energy costs;

● rising 'service' costs, such as the cost of calling out technicians.
    If a business cannot pass on these costs to consumers as higher prices or 'absorb' the costs in greater productivity, profits can fall. Higher prices are likely to mean fewer sales. Whether this results in a fall in turnover depends on the response of consumers to a rise in price (☞ unit 25). Businesses may be able to raise the prices of essential products a great deal with little fall-off in sales.

**Shoe leather costs** During periods of price stability firms are likely to have good knowledge of the price that they will pay for various goods and services. Such purchases might include delivery vehicles, premises insurance, computer equipment and stationery. However, during periods of rising prices firms may be less able to recognise a 'reasonable' price. They may need to spend more time shopping around for the best price (hence the term shoe leather costs). The extra time spent on this can be extremely expensive for some small firms.

**Menu costs** This refers to the time and money which firms have to spend on changing their price lists. It is a problem for firms displaying their price either on the actual product or on its packaging. Some firms, such as those distributing their goods via vending machines, are particularly affected.

**Wage negotiating** When inflation is high, firms will be under strong pressure to upgrade wages and salaries in line with expected levels of inflation. As well as the increased wage costs there will be some administrative costs in these changes. Conflict between employees and employers can result from disagreements about the extent to which wages need to be raised to compensate for inflation.

**Reduced purchasing power** When prices are rising the REAL VALUE of money will fall. This is the value taking into account inflation. A consumer with £200 to spend will be able to buy far less if prices are increasing. So will a business aiming to purchase £20,000 worth of raw materials. There is said to be a fall in their **purchasing power**.

    In periods of inflation, sales of certain goods are particularly affected. Businesses that produce 'luxury' goods, such as designer footwear, are likely to suffer as consumers switch to more essential products. Producers of goods and services sold to groups that are badly hit by inflation may also lose sales. It is argued that fixed income groups, such as pensioners, are affected most because their earnings do not always keep pace with inflation.

    Businesses unable to increase their turnover in line with their costs will suffer similar effects. This may be the case, for example, with a local retailer with a geographically 'fixed' market, who is unable to raise prices for fear of losing customers to a local superstore. Profits will decline as costs, which are not covered by increased turnover, rise.

**Borrowing and lending** Inflation redistributes money from

lenders to borrowers. A business that has borrowed £20,000 is likely to pay back far less in real terms over a ten year period if inflation is high. Those businesses that owe a large amount of money stand to gain in periods of high inflation as the value of their debts may be 'wiped out'. Businesses that have saved will lose out. Interest rates may fail to keep up with inflation, especially when inflation reaches levels of 10 per cent or more. So, if interest rates are 10 per cent and inflation is 20 per cent, the saver will lose 10 per cent of the real value of savings, but the borrower will find the value to be paid back falls 10 per cent a year.

**Investment** Views are divided as to the effects of inflation upon investment decisions. Some argue that, in the short term at least, it might increase the amount of investment undertaken by firms. This is because the real rate of interest (taking into account the rate of inflation) is often low during inflationary periods as inflation figures get close to, or exceed, the rate of interest. This makes investment using borrowed money relatively cheap.

Others believe that businesses are less likely to go ahead with investment projects. This is because inflation makes entrepreneurs less certain about the future and less willing to take risks.

**Uncertainty** Uncertainty may affect decisions other than investment that a business makes. Firms are often unwilling to enter into long term transactions in inflationary periods. Take, for example, a business ordering stocks of sheet metal in March to be delivered in June and paid for in August. Inflation of 24 per cent a year may mean that the price of the good increases by 12 per cent during this period. The firm supplying the sheet metal will receive the amount quoted in March when the payment is made in August. However, by August the value of this money will have declined as a result of the inflation.

**Unemployment, growth and trade** It is sometimes argued that inflation can actually cause unemployment and lower economic growth. The uncertainty that inflation creates in the minds of business people means they are less willing to take risks, invest in new ventures, expand production or hire workers. Also, if UK inflation rates are higher than those of competitors, UK products would be relatively more expensive in markets abroad, whilst foreign products would be relatively cheaper in the UK. An inability to compete on price in both domestic and foreign markets could mean the loss of many jobs. It could also result in a deterioration in the balance of payments (☞ unit 100) as the number of exports sold abroad falls and the number of imports coming into the country increases.

**The value of assets** The monetary value of assets increases in inflationary periods. Consumers who own antiques or scarce items may find their values soar. The money value of houses, factories, offices and machinery also rises. A business owning an office can sell it for a higher price. Of course, it will have to pay a higher price for any other office it wants to buy.

A footloose business in an area of high demand may be able to sell a factory or a set of offices for a high price and move to an area where property is cheaper. This is true at any time, but in periods of inflation the gains to be made are larger because the difference between prices will be greater.

## Measuring inflation

Inflation in the UK has been measured by the RETAIL PRICE INDEX. This is an **index** which is constructed to provide an accurate figure on the changes in the prices of goods and services each month. It is based upon a 'basket' of goods and services which is meant to represent the typical purchases of consumers throughout the UK. This basket of goods and services includes a range of items, such as foodstuffs, electrical items and petrol.

Index numbers can be used as indicators of changes and allow comparisons to be made. The Retail Price Index chooses a base year from which changes in prices can be calculated. Average prices are given a value of 100 in the base year. If the

**Table 98.1** *Inflation in selected countries, 2003*

**Percentage changes on previous 12 months**

| Country | |
|---|---|
| UK | 2.1% |
| USA | 1.6% |
| Japan | 0.9% |
| Germany | 1.3% |
| Czech Republic | 0.6% |
| Hungary | 5.3% |
| Turkey | 45.2% |
| Zimbabwe | 134.5% |
| Venezuela | 31.2% |
| Ukraine | -1.2% |
| Switzerland | 0.5% |
| Italy | 2.4% |
| Spain | 3.0% |

Source: adapted from *The World Factbook*, 2003.

(a) Describe the UK's inflation rate relative to that of its international competitors during the period.
(b) Explain how inflation in the UK in 2003 may have affected the following UK businesses.
  (i) A small firm that considered investing in a new machine and had to borrow £20,000.
  (ii) A manufacturer of drinks machines for sports and leisure centres which had to buy parts from a variety of sources overseas.
  (iii) An exporter of men's suits to the USA.

**Question 2**

index in the following year is 102, then on average prices may be said to have risen by 2 per cent. Table 98.3 shows the changes in the Retail Price Index.

The Retail Price Index (RPI) is a **weighted index** (☞ unit 13). This means that the importance attached to some goods and services included in the index is higher than for others. For example, petrol will tend to have a higher weighting in the index than soap. This is because petrol represents a higher proportion of the monthly expenditure of consumers than soap. The effect of this on the index is that a two per cent change in the price of petrol will have more impact upon the Retail Price Index than a two per cent rise in the price of soap.

The RPIX is another measure of inflation. It removes mortgage payments from the RPI figure, to take out any overemphasis of inflation when house prices are rising.

In 2003 the UK government announced that it would use a new price index as the main measure of inflation, called the CONSUMER PRICE INDEX (CPI). It is similar to the retail price index. But it is more sensitive to changes in household spending and allows better comparison with inflation in other countries. The main differences are that the CPI:

● excludes some housing items in the RPIX such as council tax, mortgage interest payments, house depreciation, buildings insurance, estate agents' fees and conveyancing fees;

● covers all private households, whereas the RPIX excludes the top 4 per cent by income and pensioner households who gain at least three quarters of their income from state benefits;

● includes the residents of institutional households such as student hostels and foreign visitors to the UK. So it covers some items that are not in the RPI, such as unit trust and stockbrokers' fees, university accommodation fees and foreign students' university tuition fees.

Also, different methods are used in the CPI and RPI to adjust prices for new cars and personal computers. Figure 98.1 shows how inflation would be measured by both the RPIX and the CPI over the period 1989-2003.

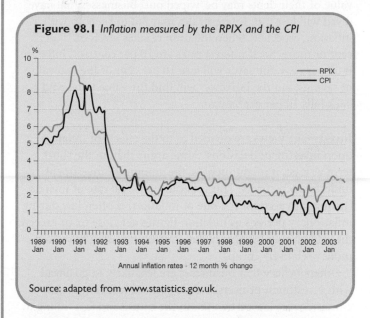

**Figure 98.1** *Inflation measured by the RPIX and the CPI*

Annual inflation rates - 12 month % change

Source: adapted from www.statistics.gov.uk.

**Table 98.2** *Percentage changes in retail prices on year earlier, 2002*

| | | | |
|---|---|---|---|
| Food | 3.6 | Personal goods | 2.5 |
| Catering | 4.1 | and services | |
| Alcoholic drink | 2.2 | Motoring expenditure | -1.3 |
| Tobacco | 3.3 | Fares and other | 2.5 |
| Housing | -1.4 | travel costs | |
| Fuel and light | 3.7 | Leisure goods | -1.9 |
| Household services | 4.1 | | |
| Leisure services | 6.7 | | |
| Clothing and footwear | -5.3 | | |

Source: adapted from *Labour Market Trends*, Office for National Statistics.

(a) Identify the product with the: (i) largest percentage increase; (ii) smallest percentage increase; (ii) largest percentage decrease in prices in 2002.
(b) Suggest the possible effects on:
 (i) customers buying these products;
 (ii) businesses producing these products;
 (iii) other businesses.

**Question 3**

Knowledge ...owledge...Knowle

1. How is inflation measured in the UK?
2. Describe the main causes of inflation.
3. What is imported inflation?
4. List 3 ways in which (a) a business and (b) consumers might be affected by inflation.
5. How might inflation lead to unemployment?
6. What is meant by the Consumer Price Index?

**Table 98.3** *The Retail Price Index, Jan 1987 = 100*

| 1990 | 1991 | 1992 | 1993 | 1994 | 1995 | 1996 | 1997 | 1998 | 1999 | 2000 | 2001 | 2002 | 2003 |
|---|---|---|---|---|---|---|---|---|---|---|---|---|---|
| 126.2 | 133.8 | 138.5 | 140.7 | 144.1 | 149.1 | 152.7 | 157.5 | 162.9 | 165.4 | 170.3 | 173.3 | 176.2 | 181.3 |

Source: adapted from *Labour Market Trends*, Office for National Statistics.

# key terms

Consumer Price Index - an indicator of changes in average prices of a range of goods typically bought by consumers in the UK. Currently used to measure inflation in the UK.

Cost-push inflation - inflation which occurs as a result of businesses facing increased costs, which are then passed on to consumers in the form of higher prices.

Deflation - a situation where prices are falling.

Demand-pull inflation - inflation which occurs as a result of excessive spending in the economy.

Hyper-inflation - a situation where inflation levels are very high.

Inflation - a continuing or persistent tendency for prices to rise.

Money supply - the total amount of money circulating in the economy.

Real value - any value which takes into account the rate of inflation.

Retail Price Index - an indicator of the changes in average prices of a range of goods typically bought by consumers in the UK.

# Case study A spending spree?

Shoppers were snapping up everything from handbags to sofas at the Cribbs Causeway shopping centre on the outskirts of Bristol in 2003. The MetroCentre in Gateshead last Saturday enjoyed its busiest day in three years. Retailers from one end of the country to the other witnessed a wave of spending not seen since the heady days of the late 1980s. Official figures which showed retail sales up 6.9 per cent on the previous year came as no surprise to John Edwards, commercial director at Cribbs Causeway, a centre with 140 stores. 'Sales are very strong' he said. 'They are 13 per cent up so far. All our retailers tell us they are doing well, from Eissenger Klassiker and New Look through to Marks & Spencer and John Lewis.'

Some analysts of the market argue that the strength of the spending boom can be explained by retailers cutting prices as a consequence of ferocious competition. 'Its an endless cycle of sales and special offers and special events. The only winner at the moment is the consumer.' Others are concerned that this increased consumer spending might lead to higher inflation. This was what happened in the late 1980s as consumers embarked upon a debt crazed frenzy of spending. A UK based economist said it was easy to understand why consumers were on a spending spree. 'Money is cheap, and people are taking advantage of that. The conditions for borrowing are the best most people have seen for a generation.'

Source: adapted from *The Guardian*, 24.5.2003.

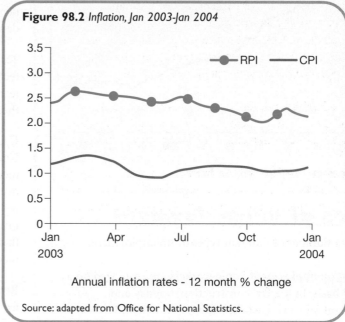

**Figure 98.2** *Inflation, Jan 2003-Jan 2004*

Annual inflation rates - 12 month % change

Source: adapted from Office for National Statistics.

(a) Describe the reasons for the spending spree highlighted in the article. (4 marks)

(b) Using data from the article, explain the possible causes of inflation. (6 marks)

(c) If inflation rises following the spending spree, examine how this might affect retailers such as those in the article. (10 marks)

(d) Discuss the extent to which the spending spree identified in the article might be expected to lead to a rise in inflation. (10 marks)

# 99 Unemployment and Business

## What is unemployment?

UNEMPLOYMENT is concerned with people being out of work. It can measured as the **number** of people who are unemployed. So, for example, in the UK in October 2003, 1.47 million people were unemployed. Figure 99.1 illustrates the **rate of unemployment** in the UK between 1993 and 2002. This shows the number of people who are unemployed as a percentage of those who are either in employment or not in employment.

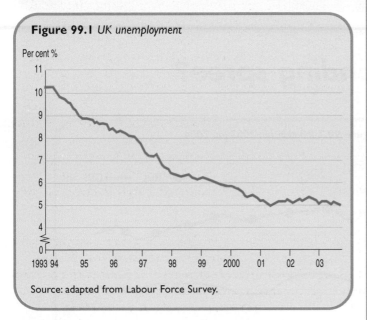

**Figure 99.1** *UK unemployment*

Per cent %

Source: adapted from Labour Force Survey.

## Types of unemployment

There is a number of different types of unemployment.

**Seasonal unemployment** Some workers are employed on a seasonal basis. In the UK construction, holiday and agricultural industries, workers are less in demand in winter because of the climate. Seasonal unemployment can therefore be high. In summer it may fall, as these workers are hired. It is difficult in practice for governments to 'solve' this type of unemployment, which may always occur. In producing unemployment statistics, governments often adjust the figures to allow for seasonal factors.

**Search and frictional unemployment** These two types of unemployment are very similar. FRICTIONAL UNEMPLOYMENT occurs when people are moving between jobs. Usually it only lasts for a short amount of time. For example, an electrician who had been working in the North East may have a few weeks 'off' before starting a new job in London. It is not seen as a serious problem by government. SEARCH UNEMPLOYMENT, however, can last longer. This type of unemployment occurs when people are searching for a new job. The greater the information on job opportunities, the lower search unemployment is likely to be.

**Structural unemployment** STRUCTURAL UNEMPLOYMENT is caused by changes in the structure of a country's economy which affect particular industries and occupations. Examples include the decline of the coal and steel industries in the second half of the twentieth century. Between 1963 and the mid-1990s almost half a million jobs were lost in the coal mining industry. This indicates the size of the problem in the UK. Because certain industries have traditionally been located in particular parts of the country, their decline can have a dramatic effect upon those regions. As a result, structural unemployment is closely linked with regional unemployment. It may also result from changes in demand for the goods and services produced by particular sectors of the economy. For example, there has been a decline in demand for natural fibres such as jute as a result of the development of synthetic products.

**Technological unemployment** This occurs when new technology replaces workers with machines. For example, new technology introduced to the newspaper industry has meant the loss of many print workers' jobs.

**Cyclical or demand-deficient unemployment** CYCLICAL UNEMPLOYMENT results from the cycles which occur in most economies. These ups and downs in economic activity over a number of years are known as the business cycle (☞ unit 96). In a recession, at the 'bottom' of a business cycle, unemployment results from a lack of demand. It is argued that demand is not high enough to employ all labour, machines, land, offices etc. in the economy.

**Real wage unemployment** Unit 104 explains how the demand for workers by businesses and the supply of workers is influenced by the **real wage rate**. Relatively high real wages mean that workers will want to supply more labour than businesses want to employ. This results in unemployment. In other words, it is argued that workers 'price themselves' out of jobs. There are vacancies, but businesses will only be willing to pay wages which are lower than workers are prepared to accept.

**Voluntary and involuntary unemployment** Some suggest that unemployment can be voluntary or involuntary. Voluntary unemployment occurs when workers refuse to accept jobs at existing wage rates. Involuntary unemployment occurs when there are not enough jobs in the economy at existing wage rates. Economists sometimes talk about the **natural rate of unemployment**. This is the percentage of workers who are voluntarily unemployed.

In October, 2001 Britain's jobless rate rose for the first time in a year. The number unemployed increased by 4,300 to 951,000, government figures showed. Manufacturing firms, struggling with the slowdown in the global economy, had already laid off 123,000 employees in the three months leading up to this rise in unemployment.

This had the effect of leaving employment in the manufacturing sector at just 3.8 million, the lowest since records began. Part time workers, particularly women, bore the brunt of the job losses, with 68,000 female part time workers losing their jobs.

Source: adapted from *The Guardian*, 15.11.2001.

(a) Explain three types of unemployment that may occur in the manufacturing sector.
(b) What type of unemployment in the manufacturing sector is suggested in the article? Explain your answer.

## Effects of unemployment on business

High levels of unemployment have a number of effects on businesses. The majority of the effects of unemployment are harmful for businesses. However, there are some businesses which may be unaffected by unemployment. A small minority may even benefit.

**Demand** The obvious effect of unemployment is that people are not earning income and are likely to have less to spend. Businesses will suffer a loss of demand for their products and reduced profits as a result. Producers of goods, such as clothing and household furniture, and providers of services, such as insurance and holidays, are all likely to suffer.

**Organisation** Unemployment can have a number of effects on the internal organisation of a business. It may mean that a firm can no longer afford to recruit new members of staff because of low demand for its products. New, often young, recruits to a firm will no longer be coming through. In addition, new posts which arise may be filled through retraining of existing staff rather than recruitment. This can lead to significant changes in the age profile of an organisation's employees.

Redundancies are also a common feature of a period of high unemployment. Whilst the work of some who are made redundant will not be replaced, the responsibilities and roles of others may be added to the job descriptions of those who remain with the firm. This can lead to increasing demands on existing employees.

During periods of high unemployment, some firms reorganise their internal structure. This may mean the loss of

a whole tier in the hierarchy or the changing of individual job descriptions. Businesses, such as IBM, have removed large numbers of middle managers in such restructuring exercises.

**Payments** Businesses may be faced with making redundancy payments to workers. These tend to vary between firms depending upon the average length of service of the employee.

The cost of any reorganisation caused by redundancies will also have to be borne by firms. Such costs may include lost productivity after a reorganisation as employees struggle to cope with new responsibilities.

**Labour supply** It may be easier for firms to recruit new employees during a period of high unemployment. This is because there is a larger pool of people to choose from, with more applicants for each available post. In addition, because of the increased competition for new jobs, people may be prepared to work for less money. In this way firms can lower their labour costs.

**Output** During periods of unemployment, many firms reduce their level of output to compensate for falling demand. This can lead to excess capacity and under-utilisation of capital equipment. In addition, falling levels of demand can interrupt the flow of production, causing production and stock control problems (☞ unit 82).

**Government spending** High levels of unemployment mean that government spending on social security will be high. Also, the government will lose revenue from tax and National Insurance contributions which people would have paid had they been in employment. To make up for this the government may borrow, increase taxation or reduce other items of spending.

**Increased trade and reduced costs** The services offered by some firms depend upon other firms going out of business. Firms specialising in receiverships and pawnbrokers may see an increase in the demand for their services. Firms also benefit from 'trading down', ie buying cheaper alternatives. Retailers and manufacturers selling goods aimed at lower income segments of the market tend to do well during periods of unemployment. Supermarkets, in particular, have benefited. It has been argued that this is because consumers spend more on home entertainment and less on going out during periods of high unemployment.

**Social issues** Research into unemployment has shown that it has a number of possible 'side effects'. These can have consequences for businesses. The suggested side effects include poverty and stress for those individuals, families and communities that have high levels of unemployment. They also include higher levels of vandalism and crime. This can lead to higher insurance premiums for businesses, disruption

to businesses caused by crime and, in some cases, loss of custom and the need to relocate premises.

## Measuring unemployment

How many people are unemployed? In the UK the main measure used as an indicator of unemployment in is the International Labour Force measure (ILO). This is based on a survey of people. To be unemployed, a person has to be out of work, have looked for work in the last four weeks and be able to start work in the next two weeks. It is a useful measure because it allows comparisons with unemployment rates in other countries, as other countries use this measure.

Another measure sometimes used only in the UK is the claimant count measure. This is based on the number of people claiming unemployment-related benefits, including jobseekers' allowance and National Insurance credits. People must declare that they are out of work and be capable of, available for and actively seeking work during the week the claim was made. A problems with this measure is that it excludes those who do not claim benefit and might be looking for work.

A certain number of people in the UK are said to be underemployed. They might not be seeking work for a variety reasons, including looking after children or because they have retired.

## key terms

**Cyclical unemployment** - unemployment resulting from the ups and downs (cycles) which occur in most economies.
**Frictional/search unemployment** - unemployment caused by people moving from one job to another.
**Structural unemployment** - unemployment caused by changes in the structure of the economy.
**Unemployment** - the number of people looking for work who are unable to obtain a job.

---

In November 2002 the TUC highlighted a significant increase in the level of unemployment in London, making it Britain's most severely affected region. 3.5 per cent of manufacturing jobs in London were lost in the year to June. 23,000 service sector jobs were lost during the same period and more jobs were likely to go in finance and banking. The rate of unemployment in London was 7.5 per cent, almost 1 per cent higher than any other region, and compared to the national average of 5.3 per cent. London's total of 287,000 unemployed is more than the totals for Wales and Scotland combined, more than the entire Midlands and more than the North West and North East combined.

Mick Connolly, Regional Secretary for the TUC London Region said 'Unemployment is a personal tragedy and an economic waste. There are problems of unemployment throughout Britain ... but the media, many policy makers and some politicians seem blind to the level of unemployment in London. The government's own figures show the true extent of the problem ... Is it any wonder that a huge proportion of children in London are raised in poverty when nearly 300,000 workers who live in London are unemployed.'

Six London boroughs have unemployment levels of more than 6 per cent, as shown in Figure 99.2.

Source: adapted from www.brent.gov.uk.

(a) Examine the effects of unemployment in London boroughs on:
  (i)  businesses in the boroughs;
  (ii)  people in the boroughs;
  (iii) local government.

**Figure 99.2** *Unemployment in London boroughs, 2002*

10.4%  12.2%  12.3%  11.7%  10.3%  10.7%

Haringey  Hackney  Tower Hamlets  Newham  Southwark  Lewisham

**Question 2**

*Knowledge*...*Knowledge*...*Knowledge*...*Knowledge*...*Knowledge*...*Know*

1. What are the different types of unemployment?
2. Why is frictional unemployment not regarded as a problem by government?
3. What are the possible negative effects of unemployment on firms?
4. What are the possible positive effects of unemployment on firms?
5. State 2 methods of measuring unemployment.

# Case study  Unemployment in Manton, Nottinghamshire

In 1996 the coal mine at Manton in North Nottinghamshire was closed down. Manton was just one of a number of coal mines throughout the former mining areas of Britain that was closed down during the 1990s. This programme of pit closures resulted in thousands of miners losing their jobs. The effect was dramatic upon the former mining towns and villages and areas of the country, including south Wales, South Yorkshire, North Nottinghamshire, County Durham and parts of Scotland with large numbers of coal miners.

In Manton and surrounding areas the number of people registered as unemployed was close to 4,000 by the end of 1996. 'The community was dying on its feet' said Josie Potts whose husband lost his job when the mine closed.

By 2003 there was greater optimism in Manton amongst many. A number of new employers were moving to the area. B&Q's announcement of a 25 hectare distribution system would create 1,000 new jobs, for example. John Mann the MP for the area announced 'The transformation is so phenomenal. The number of unemployment claimants has fallen to 1,000'. He hopes that his constituency will be the first in the area to have full employment.

Not all are quite so impressed with developments in Manton and surrounding areas. Professor Steve Fothergill of the Coalfield Communities Campaign acknowledges that the number of unemployment claimants is lower, but thinks this may be obscuring a deeper problem. 'In many mining communities we have diverted huge numbers off job seekers' allowance, for example, onto other benefits, or even outside the benefits system altogether'.

Source: adapted from *The Guardian*, 6.12.2003.

(a) **Using an example, suggest the main type of unemployment referred to in the article. (4 marks)**
(b) **Explain the possible effects on the following businesses in the Manton area of the closure of the pit.**
   (i)  **A road haulage business.**
   (ii) **A restaurant.**
   (iii) **A garden centre. (14 marks)**
(c) **Explain why the official unemployment figures might mask a deeper problem of unemployment in areas such as Manton. (10 marks)**
(d) **Assess the possible effects on businesses in the Manton area of B&Q's decision to build a distribution centre there. (12 marks)**

## The balance of payments

Business transactions often take place across country borders. A UK manufacturer may buy components from the USA. Japanese businesses may use British insurance companies. A UK business may invest in a land reclamation project in a developing country.

All these transactions would be shown in a country's BALANCE OF PAYMENTS. It is a record of transactions between one country and the rest of the world. The balance of payments is usually divided into sections.

**The current account** The current account of the balance of payments is also divided into a number of sections.

- **Trade in goods.** Examples of traded goods might be computers, machine tools and chemicals. Goods which are manufactured in a country and sold abroad are called EXPORTS. Goods which are brought into a country from abroad are known as IMPORTS. An export from the UK, where goods are sold abroad, earns money for UK businesses. Money flows into the UK, so UK exports are recorded as **credits**. An import to the UK, where UK consumers or businesses buy goods from abroad, leads to an outflow of money from the UK. UK imports are recorded as **debits**. The difference between the value of exports and imports of goods is shown as TRADE IN GOODS on the balance of payments.
- **Trade in services.** Examples of traded services might be banking, shipping, travel and tourism, and insurance. Services which are sold abroad are exports and services bought from abroad are imports. Passenger tickets sold abroad for travel on a UK airline is an export of a service for the UK. The UK business earns money which flows into the UK. It appears as a credit. A UK business which insures with a foreign company is an example of an import of a service to the UK. The UK business spends abroad and money flows out of the UK. It appears as a debit. The difference between the value of exports and imports of goods is shown as TRADE IN SERVICES.
- **Income.** Income may be compensation paid to employees working abroad. Income sent home to the UK by a British computer programmer working in Saudi Arabia would appear as a credit under income on the UK accounts as money is entering the UK. Income may also be investment income. This is the interest, profit and dividends earned by companies abroad or foreign firms in a country. Profits sent to Japan made by a Japanese car firm in the UK would appear as a debit on the UK accounts.
- **Current transfers.** These include central government transfers. They also include gifts from individuals abroad to a country or gifts to foreign countries. For example, a payment to the EU by the UK government would be

shown as a debit under current transfers on the UK current account, as money is leaving the UK.

The difference between the value of money entering a country (credits) and the value of money leaving a country (debits) for:

- trade in goods and services;
- income to/from abroad;
- transfers;

is called the CURRENT BALANCE. We can say that:

Current balance = sales of exports and services, income earned from abroad and transfers to a country *minus* purchases of imports and services, income going abroad and transfers from a country

**Capital account** This involves the transfer of ownership of assets, transfers of funds associated with the purchase and sale of assets and the cancellation of liabilities. Examples include transfers from the EU regional fund (☞ unit 88) and the forgiveness of debt. This is a small part of the balance of payments account compared to the current and financial accounts.

---

Jobson plc is a UK based multinational business. It has plants in Singapore, the USA, the UK and Australia. It specialises in the manufacture and distribution of a wide variety of food and drink products. Below are some of its transactions over the past 12 months.

- Profits from plants in Singapore, Malaysia and Ireland taken back to the UK.
- Buying shares in a French drinks producing firm.
- Exporting £30 million of soft drinks to EU nations from its UK plant.
- Holding a conference for senior managers from all of its plants in Bermuda.
- Paying for a team of Japanese management consultants to help with the restructuring of its London headquarters.
- Buying new production machinery from Germany for its UK plant.
- Investing £50 million on upgrading production facilities in its USA, Singapore and Australian factories.

Explain which of the above would be shown as:
(a) exports of services;
(b) imports of services;
(c) exports of goods;
(d) imports of goods;
(e) transactions in liabilities;
(f) the purchase or sale of assets;
in the UK's balance of payments account.

**Question 1**

**The financial account** This covers the flow of money for transactions in **financial assets and liabilities**. For example, a foreign business may buy shares (an asset) in a UK company. Money would flow into the UK and would be shown as a credit on the financial account. Note that any dividend earned by the foreign business on the shares would be shown as a debit under investment income on the UK's current account as money is leaving the country. A transaction in liabilities on the UK accounts would be a UK business borrowing from a foreign bank. This would appear as a credit on the financial account, as money is flowing into the UK.

## Balance of payments problems and business

The balance of payments must always 'balance'. Take a situation where a country has a **current account deficit**. This also means that outflows of money are greater than inflows to that country from trade in goods and services, income and transfers.

Where does the money come from to finance this deficit? The UK may, for example, borrow from foreign banks or sell its assets abroad to bring money back in. The Bank of England (☞ unit 105) could sell some of the country's gold or foreign currency reserves. Whatever happens, the deficit on the current account would be made up by a surplus on the capital account and financial account. In practice, if the values do not actually balance a **balancing item** is added. This is a figure for errors and omissions. It is large or small enough so that the accounts always balance.

Although the accounts always balance, individual parts of the balance of payments may not. What if the current account deficit carried on for a long period? This could lead to a number of problems for the UK government and for UK business.

● The country as a whole will get more and more into debt. Other countries may refuse to lend more money, and may insist upon repayment of any debt. Third World and Eastern European countries have faced such problems over the past few decades.

● Loss of jobs. If consumers buy imports, they will not buy home produced goods or services. Thus opportunities for job creation are lost. Similarly, low levels of exports mean the demand by businesses for employees will be lower.

● UK businesses may become dependent on imports of components and raw materials. This may mean that costs are dependent upon the exchange rate value of the pound sterling. This is dealt with later in this unit. It may also make the UK economy more vulnerable to IMPORTED INFLATION (☞ unit 98).

Figure 100.1 shows the current account of the UK over the period 1980-2002. For most of the period the current balance was in deficit. This was because the UK tends to be a **net importer** of goods. In other words, it imports more goods than it exports. Although the UK exports a large amount of services (it is a **net exporter**), this is not enough to offset the deficit on the trade in goods (known as the **balance of trade**).

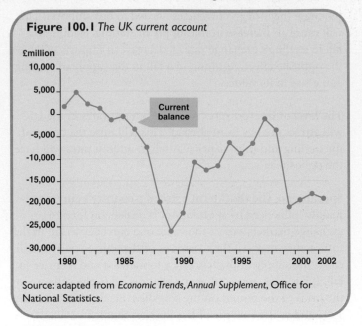

**Figure 100.1** *The UK current account*

£million

Current balance

Source: adapted from *Economic Trends, Annual Supplement*, Office for National Statistics.

## Exchange rates

An EXCHANGE RATE is the price of one country's currency in relation to that of another. So, for example, an exchange rate £1 = $2 means that one pound is worth two dollars. Alternatively, one dollar is worth 50 pence.

Exchange rates are determined on foreign exchange markets throughout the world. If an exchange rate is **freely floating,** then changes in the demand for or supply of a currency will result in a change in that country's exchange rate. For example, a fall in the demand for sterling will cause its value to fall. This is the same type of analysis that was used to show the effect of changes in the demand for and supply of goods on prices in unit 93. A **fixed** exchange rate system is where countries do not allow the values of their currencies to change against each other's.

If the value of a currency falls in relation to the value of another currency then the exchange rate is said to have DEPRECIATED. Under a system of fixed exchange rates the currency will be DEVALUED by the government or controlling organisation. If the value of the currency rises against that of another currency then it is said to have **appreciated** (or to have been revalued).

There is a number of factors that can affect the exchange rate of a currency.

**The volume of exports** An increase in exports by UK firms will mean that more pounds are required to buy these exports. This will result in an increase in the demand for sterling and cause the value of sterling to rise. A decrease in UK exports will have the opposite effect, resulting in a fall in the demand for sterling and a fall in its value.

**The volume of imports** An increase in imports coming into the UK will mean that more sterling has to be sold in order to

purchase the foreign currencies needed to buy imports. This will cause an increase in the supply of sterling, leading to a fall in sterling's exchange rate. A decrease in imports will have the opposite effect, resulting in a fall in the supply of sterling and a rise in its value.

**The level of interest rates** A rise in interest rates in the UK will attract savings from abroad. This will raise the demand for sterling and thus its price. A fall in interest rates will have the opposite effect.

**Speculation** The short term price of a country's currency is mainly influenced by speculation. If dealers on foreign exchange markets expect the value of a currency to fall in the future, they may sell their reserves of that currency. This will cause the supply of that currency to increase and its price to fall. It has been argued that speculation led to the collapse in the price of the pound on the so-called 'Black Wednesday' in 1992 and to the collapse of the Russian rouble in 1998. If, however, speculators expect the value of a currency to rise in the future, then they will begin purchasing that currency leading to an increase in its value.

**Government intervention** Governments may intervene on foreign exchange markets. They may try to influence the price of either their own currency or that of another country. For example, the UK government may attempt to raise the value of the pound by purchasing it on foreign exchange markets. Governments may also raise interest rates in order to increase the value of the pound.

**Investment and capital flows** An inflow of funds for long-term investment in the UK will cause the demand, and therefore the price, of sterling to rise. Similarly an outflow of investment funds will cause the supply of sterling to rise and its price to fall, other factors remaining the same. Thus, French investment in a UK water bottling plant would cause a rise in the exchange rate.

Capital flows are largely determined by the rate of interest. Thus an increase in UK interest rates would lead to an inflow of funds into the UK and a rise in the value of sterling. Such inflows of funds following interest rate changes tend to be short term money moving from one of the world's financial centres to another in search of the highest rate of return.

---

Discuss the likely effects on the value of the pound against the Japanese yen of the following:
(a) increases in the number of UK residents visiting Japan;
(b) the yen coming under speculative selling pressure as an election comes nearer;
(c) an increase in UK aircraft sales to Japan;
(d) UK interest rates increased to 6 per cent whilst Japanese interest rates remain at 4 per cent.

**Question 2**

---

# Exchange rates and business

The main reason why exchange rates are so important to businesses is because of their influence on the price of imports and exports. All but a very few small firms use at least some goods and services imported from abroad. Increasingly, large numbers of businesses are finding that they have to export their products in order to grow or survive. Thus the majority of firms are affected in some way by exchange rates.

**The effect of falling exchange rates** A fall in the exchange rate (a **depreciation** or **devaluation**) will affect the price of a business's exports and the price it pays for imports. Look at Table 100.1 which shows the effects of a fall in the value of the pound from £1 = $2 to £1 = $1.60. Note that if the value of a currency falls against another currency it becomes **weaker**. Less of another currency will be exchanged for one unit of that currency.

**Table 100.1** *The effects of a fall in the value of the pound on the price of exports and imports*

| | Exchange rate | UK price | USA price |
|---|---|---|---|
| Exported goods | £1 = $2 | £10 | $20 |
| | £1 = $1.60 | £10 | $16 |
| Imported goods | £1 = $2 | £10 | $20 |
| | £1 = $1.60 | £12.50 | $20 |

At an exchange rate of £1 = $2, a book priced at £10 that is exported to the USA would cost Americans $20. If the value of the pound fell to £1 = $1.60, Americans would now be able to buy the same book for $16. So a fall in the exchange rate can make UK exports cheaper.

What about imports to the UK? A picture frame priced at $20 imported to the UK would cost £10 before the depreciation of the exchange rate. If the exchange rate fell to £1 = $1.60, the picture frame would now cost £12.50 ([$2÷$1.60]x£10) or ($20÷1.60). So a fall in the exchange rate can cause the price of imports to rise.

The overall effect should be beneficial for UK businesses. The price paid for UK exports should fall, allowing businesses to sell more in export markets. The price paid by UK businesses and consumers for imports should rise. This might encourage them to switch their purchases from foreign goods to UK products.

There are problems, however, for firms if exchange rates are falling.
- Rising import prices mean that the amount paid for any inputs, such as raw materials or components bought in from abroad, will rise.
- Rising import prices can lead to imported inflation and the

associated problems of this for businesses (☞ unit 98).

- Uncertainty over future prices of raw materials and components can result.
- Constant price changes may affect foreign demand for products as they are unsettling for customers.

**The effect of rising exchange rates** A rise in exchange rates means that a currency becomes **stronger** against another currency. So more of another currency will be exchanged for the unit of that currency. This is the opposite effect to devaluation. A rise in the exchange rate can cause the price of exports to rise and the price of imports to fall. For example, in Table 100.1 an increase in the exchange rate from £1=$1.60 to £1=$2 will cause the price of a £10 export to rise from $16 to $20 and the price of a $20 import to fall from £12.50 to £10.

The overall effect is likely to be negative. Not only will it become more difficult for UK firms to compete on price in export markets, but it will put pressure on them in UK markets, as they struggle to compete with lower priced imported goods. However, a rise in the exchange rate could allow UK businesses to buy cheaper imports from abroad.

**The stability of exchange rates** Unstable exchange rates can make it very difficult for firms to plan for the future. A rise in the exchange rate, for example, could turn a previously profitable export order into a loss maker. A devaluation, on the other hand, could mean that exports which looked unprofitable could now earn a profit for the firm.

In 2000 Ford announced that it was likely to axe car production at its Dagenham plant. This would lead to more than 3,000 workers being 'out in the cold'. One of the problems was the old style of the Fiesta. Ford had been overtaken in Europe by a number of manufacturers bringing out new models for the twenty first century. The old Ford Escort had been replaced by the Ford Focus, which was doing well. However, Ford suggested that it could not be successful on one car alone. Perhaps the biggest problem had been the rising value of the pound against the euro. Like all manufacturers with plants in the UK, Ford had a difficulty with the strength of the pound against the euro.

Source: adapted from *The Guardian*, 30.4.2000.

(a) Explain, using an example, what is meant by the rising value of the pound against the euro.
(b) Examine how this might have affected Ford.

## Question 3

## How much are businesses affected?

Not all businesses are affected to the same extent by changes in exchange rates.

**The response of consumers** Some products have a strong brand identity. Even if their prices increase, consumers do not reduce the amount purchased by a great deal. Unit 25 refers to these products as having an **inelastic** demand. What effect will a fall in the value of the pound from £1=1.8 euros to £1=1.5 euros have on UK businesses exporting such goods?

A firm selling 1,000 books to Germany each month for 5 euros each at an exchange rate of £1 = 1.8 euros, would receive 5,000 euros (£2,777) in revenue. If the exchange rate fell to £1 = 1.5 euros, and the demand for books was price inelastic, then the business may be able to keep the price at 5 euros. At this new exchange rate the 5,000 euros would be worth £3,333 (5,000÷ 1.5). Thus, revenue would increase by £556.

Firms with products which are sensitive to price changes are likely to feel the impact of even minor exchange rate changes. If export prices rise the volume of sales will fall by a greater degree, and the overall revenue for exports will fall. If export prices fall, revenue should be greater because the increase in quantity sold is relatively greater than the fall in price.

**The degree of control over prices** Not all businesses have the same degree of control over the price at which their products are sold. Those with a high degree of control over their prices can adopt market based methods of pricing, such as customer value pricing (☞ unit 26). They might decide not to allow exchange rate changes to alter the price of their exports, although their sales revenue may change. For example, a business selling sportswear with a strong degree of brand loyalty amongst its customers might be unwilling to alter its price as a result of relatively small exchange rate fluctuations. This is because prices will have been carefully chosen to suit particular markets. In this case, only a large rise in the exchange rate, which threatened profits, would cause a pricing re-think.

The Reconstruction Company rebuilds cars such as Land Rovers and exports them to countries such as South Africa and Australia. It has exported 5 reconditioned vehicles for use on game reserves, selling each one for 120,000 rand. The exchange rate at the time was £1=10 rand.

(a) Calculate the earnings in rands and in pounds for the business.
(b) The exchange rate fell over the next year to £1=9.6 rand. The South African companies still needed vehicles and were not likely to find a supplier at this price and at short notice. The Reconstruction Company decided to keep its price the same in rand. It sells another 5 vehicles. Calculate the effect of this on the revenue of the business.

## Question 4

## What is economic growth?

ECONOMIC GROWTH is an indication of the change in the goods and services produced by an economy. One way an economy can tell if growth is taking place is to examine its GDP or GNP figures (☞ unit 96). These show how much money is flowing around the economy. A rise from one year to the next is usually an indication of growth. Growth is measured in **real** terms, in other words, it takes into account the rate of inflation (☞ unit 98).

If economic growth is taking place, there are likely to be favourable trading conditions for business. Many new businesses set up and continue to grow. In periods of growth, businesses may find a healthy demand for their products. Businesses will tend to suffer when growth is zero or even negative. Negative growth may be an indication of recession in an economy (☞ unit 96). This will have the opposite effect to a period of growth, with declining sales and many firms going out of business.

The growth rate of one country compared to others is also important. Figure 101.1 shows the growth rates in the UK compared to other countries over the period 1990-2001. The UK has performed relatively well against competitors in western and eastern europe, as well as Japan. However, it has lagged behind some countries in Asia and a little behind the USA.

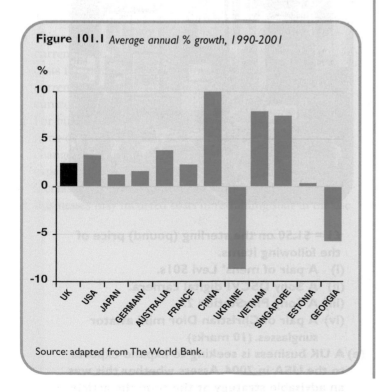

**Figure 101.1** *Average annual % growth, 1990-2001*

Source: adapted from The World Bank.

## The business cycle

Unit 96 explained how economies move through periods of 'up and downs' over time. This can be shown by the use of the **business cycle** or **trade cycle**. At the top of the cycle, in a boom, growth will be high. As output and income fall, the economy moves into recession. At the bottom of the cycle, in a trough, firms fail and unemployment is high. As the economy recovers, output and income start to rise again.

Figure 101.2 shows changes in GDP at constant prices since 1955 in the UK. The trends in the figures show that the performance of the UK economy has broadly been similar to the traditional business cycle (☞ unit 96). For example, the early 1990s saw a period of recession, with annual growth rates of minus 2 per cent or more at times. In the mid to late 1990s there was a recovery, with growth rates over 4 per cent. Annual growth rates slowed in the early twenty first century in the UK, as in many other countries. In 2002 it was estimated to be around 1.5 per cent.

**Figure 101.2** *Quarterly year on year growth of UK GDP at constant prices (%)*

Source: adapted from Datastream/ICV.

## Factors affecting growth

There is a number of factors that can lead to economic growth.

**Land** Land includes all natural resources such as forests, lakes and oil and coal deposits, as well as land itself. It is possible for countries to experience economic growth through more effective exploitation of their natural resources. Saudi Arabia, for example, has generated the vast majority of its wealth from its oil reserves and the UK has benefited from North Sea oil.

**Labour force/population** Increasing the quantity of the labour force can contribute to economic growth.

**Table 101.1** *Individual bankruptcies and company liquidations, 1989-2002*

|  | 1989 | 1990 | 1991 | 1992 | 1993 | 1994 | 1995 | 1996 | 1997 | 1998 | 1999 | 2000 | 2001 | 2002 |
|---|---|---|---|---|---|---|---|---|---|---|---|---|---|---|
| Bankruptcies | 8,138 | 12,058 | 22,632 | 32,106 | 31,016 | 25,634 | 21,933 | 21,803 | 19,892 | 19,647 | 21,611 | 21,550 | 23,447 | 24,292 |
| Total company liquidations | 10,456 | 15,051 | 21,827 | 24,425 | 20,708 | 16,728 | 14,536 | 13,461 | 12,610 | 13,203 | 14,280 | 14,317 | 14,972 | 16,305 |

Source: adapted from *Annual Abstract of Statistics*, Office for National Statistics

(a) Describe the main trends taking place in the table.
(b) To what extent does the information suggest that there is a business cycle?

**Question 1**

- One relatively easy way of increasing the labour force is to encourage immigration. The success of the US economy has been partly attributed to the effects of immigration.
- Changes in the demography (☞ unit 95) of a country can be important. More young people will swell the size of the workforce, but an increase in the birth rate will create more dependants for a number of years. The UK is at present experiencing an ageing of its population, resulting in a relative decline in the number of people of working age.
- One of the biggest increases in the UK's workforce over the last thirty years has come about through the increasing participation of women in work. At any given time, there are usually large numbers of women willing to enter the workforce should suitable employment become available.

Whilst the quantity of labour in a country can be important, the quality of it tends to be especially significant in influencing growth rates. A well trained, well educated workforce, which is flexible and able to respond to change, can help to provide favourable trading conditions for businesses, leading to growth.

**Investment and technology** Economic growth requires an increase in the capital stock of the economy. This means the development of and investment in new technology (☞ unit 85) and the updating of capital equipment. Technological development also allows new products to be created. It is not just the quantity of investment in an economy which is important. Investment needs to be directed into growth industries whose products are likely to be in high demand in the future.

**Government policy** Governments can use a combination of fiscal, monetary, exchange rate and supply side policies to stimulate growth (☞ unit 105). The policies a government chooses will reflect its views about the operation of the economy. The choice of policy is important. Even if an economy has great natural resources, a well trained workforce and high levels of investment it may be held back by inappropriate government policy.

**Competitive advantage** Michael Porter has suggested that countries must have strategies that attempt to create a competitive advantage (☞ unit 5) in international trade. This, he suggests, can be done by building up the competitive advantage of particular sectors of the economy, rather than attempting to compete in all sectors. For example, Singapore has been successful in achieving growth as a result of its trading policy despite a relatively weak agricultural sector.

## The effects of economic growth on business

The majority of firms benefit from a growing economy. There are some, such as pawnbrokers and scrap-metal dealers who perhaps do better in recessions, but these tend to be exceptions. If a business is operating in a growing economy, experiencing economic growth rates of 3 per cent per annum or more, this is likely to have a number of effects upon it. Not all of them, however, are positive.

**Sales revenue** Consumer spending should be high during a period of economic growth. This will increase the demand for many firms' products and should lead to an increase in sales revenue. If a firm is able to keep its costs under control, this should also mean an increase in profits.

**Expansion** An increase in the demand for a firm's products generated by a sustained period of economic growth may lead to expansion. Some businesses are forced into expanding where they find that they cannot meet demand. Others plan their expansion well in advance. Expansion may involve some or all of the following:
- recruiting new staff;
- raising finance;
- increasing the size of premises;
- moving to new premises;
- purchasing more assets, for example, production facilities, machinery or office equipment;
- taking over competitors.

**Security** In a healthy business climate, a business is likely to feel more secure in its decisions. It will be able to order from suppliers with greater confidence. This may lead to a better and more effective relationship. Businesses should also be able to hire employees without concern about being forced to lay them off within a short period of time. This may result in a

firm committing itself more to the workforce, for example, by investing in training programmes.

**Planning for the future** Economic growth should provide businesses with more confidence in planning for the future. Higher profit levels, for example, should help to provide investment funds for new projects. Year to year or even day to day survival is likely to become less of an issue as a firm seeks to consolidate its future position. However, confidence in planning for the future will hinge upon how long the business expects the growth to last. Due to the UK's past record of rapidly moving from boom to slump, there is evidence that many British businesses have not, in the past, regarded a period of economic growth as sufficient reason to undertake investment projects.

**Increasing costs** It is not unusual for high economic growth rates to be accompanied by rising costs. Land costs often rise during such periods. This was especially evident in the South East of England during the period 2000-2002, when property prices spiralled. Labour costs may also increase as employees and trade unions seek to benefit from the success of their business.

# The effects of lack of growth on business

A lack of growth or negative growth in the economy can have a number of effects on business.

**Changes in consumer demand** Many firms will face a fall in the demand for their products. This is because the incomes of consumers tend to fall during such periods, forcing them into cutting back on spending. The effect of this is not spread evenly amongst firms. For some the impact can be dramatic, leading to redundancies and even closure. The construction industry is notoriously vulnerable to recessions. Producers of consumer goods tend to suffer less in a recession than producers of goods for industrial markets.

**Confidence** There tends to be a general lack of confidence amongst businesses during a recession. This can lead to investment projects being cancelled and orders being lost. Some businesses will be affected not only for the period of the recession itself, but also in the longer term. It may also lead to a loss of profitability and competitiveness.

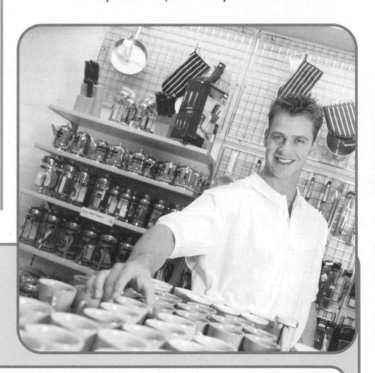

Capthorn Ltd manufactures a variety of household products. It has seen a steady increase in turnover and profits in recent years. Faced with the challenges of a new millennium in the year 2000, it was considering expanding the business. However, it was likely to have to make a choice about which products to promote and in which areas to launch new products.

**Table 101.2** *Individual consumption expenditure at current market prices*

£ million

| | 2000 | 2001 | 2002 |
|---|---|---|---|
| Furniture, furnishings, carpets and coverings | 13,758 | 14,934 | 17,897 |
| Household textiles | 4,465 | 4,677 | 5,317 |
| Household appliances | 4,948 | 6,054 | 5,859 |
| Glassware, tableware and utensils | 4,431 | 4,657 | 5,226 |
| Tools and equipment for house and garden | 2,722 | 2,960 | 3,154 |
| Goods and services for household maintenance | 5,343 | 5,587 | 5,824 |
| **All furnishings, household equipment and maintenance** | **35,667** | **38,869** | **43,277** |

Source: adapted from *Annual Abstract of Statistics*, Office for National Statistics.

(a) Discuss whether and how the business should expand in future.
(b) Explain the possible effects of the strategy you have advised.

**Question2**

**Effect on small firms** Small firms tend to be especially vulnerable to recession. They often do not have the finance to withstand periods of negative cash flow (☞ unit 46) which occur during such times. Also, small firms tend to rely upon banks. This means that they may suffer as banks are reluctant to lend during recessions. Banks also tend to call in loans at short notice.

**Possible benefits** Those firms which survive during a recession may benefit from a reduction in competition, as their rivals go out of business. This should put them in a position to gain a greater share of the market, especially when the economy picks up again. The recession may also force businesses to become leaner and fitter operations. Government policies designed to bring an economy out of recession can be an advantage to many firms. For example, interest rates are often reduced to help bring a recession to an end.

Occasionally a slowdown helps to speed things up for a business. Great Universal Stores (GUS) consists of a range of businesses, including Burberry's, the coat manufacturer, Argos, the town centre catalogue company, the GUS catalogue company and Experian, the credit rating agency. It is this last, less well known, part of GUS that is responsible for over 40 per cent of the company's profits. Experian is involved in checking the credit ratings of hundreds of thousands of consumers applying to stores, car showrooms, mortgage businesses and others offering credit and loans.

Following much lower levels of economic growth in the US economy many had predicted serious difficulties for GUS. But a combination of factors has led to a revival in the business' fortunes despite the grim economic circumstances. New managers at Burberry and Argos performed minor miracles in making the businesses sharper with more sought after brands and identities. In addition, the slowdown in the US economy meant that business was booming for Experian. Because of difficulties in the US economy, car showrooms, stores and other credit providers were being far more careful about making credit available to consumers. Hence there were more credit checks and better profits for Experian and GUS.

Source: adapted from *The Guardian*, 12.4.2001.

(a) Describe the relationship between economic growth in the US and the performance of GUS.
(b) Explain how some businesses may be unaffected by or may perform better during periods of lower levels of economic growth.

**Question 3**

## key terms

**Economic growth** - an indication of the change in the output or income of an economy. It is usually measured by a change in national income figures (GDP or GNP).

## Knowledge ...Knowledge...Knowledge...Knowled

1. What does a business cycle show?
2. How might land contribute to economic growth?
3. In what ways might a firm be affected by demographic change?
4. How might a business benefit from economic growth?
5. What problems might economic growth cause for a business?
6. Why are small firms especially vulnerable to recession?

# Case study SkyTravel

Sky Travel, a travel firm based in Bristol, was considering expanding the range of holidays which it would offer to the public in the next summer season. It already offered packages to traditional destinations such as the Greek Islands, the Costa del Sol and the Balearic Islands. It wished to expand into the long haul market, offering holidays to destinations previously out of the reach of mass tourism. Such destinations were likely to include India, Thailand and Bali.

A firm of economic consultants had been employed to provide the business with a report on future economic conditions. Before the consultants had presented the report, there had been concern expressed about the expansion plan by the firm's chief accountant, Errol Lee. He was worried about the building up of debt. He believed that economic conditions were such that it was unlikely sufficient revenue could be generated in the current year to finance expansionary plans.

Anne Doyle, the marketing director, who had been carefully researching the market for long haul flights, felt that consumer demand for long haul flights to some of these exotic locations might dry up just as quickly as it had initially grown. There was growing evidence of fickle behaviour amongst consumers of such holidays. In addition, concern about the link between sunbathing and skin cancer was leading to a trend towards taking holidays in countries with more moderate climates. The firm's personnel director, John Bryden, also expressed doubts about the extent to which staff currently employed in comfortable Mediterranean locations would cope if transferred to potentially much more difficult long haul destinations. He was particularly concerned about political unrest in Indonesia, of which Bali is a region, the sometimes dramatic changes in the Thai economy and possible terrorist activity.

At the next board meeting a number of these concerns were discussed, but the managing director, Chris Boughie, insisted that no decision could be made until the presentation by the economic consultants which was to take place the next day.

That evening, all directors watched the evening news in the comfort of their homes. The main stories were the redundancies to be made by several leading firms, rising unemployment and a large current account deficit on the balance of payments.

They arrived at work the next day in a gloomy mood. Erica Harper, a young economist working for the firm of

consultants, gave the presentation. 'It could be argued that the UK faces a prolonged period of low growth at the moment. Industrial output is down, unemployment is rising and there has been an upsurge in business failures. However, indicators suggest that growth will begin to increase after 2-3 years as government policies to stimulate growth begin to take effect. This should lead to much improved trading conditions as incomes begin to rise. Sky Travel should be aware that at least 70 per cent of its current and potential customers are unlikely to be influenced by current economic conditions and will continue to take holidays once, twice or even more times a year to destinations served by the business.'

(a) **Identify the factors which may have influenced Sky Travel's decision to expand its business. (4 marks)**
(b) **Using evidence from the article, explain how low growth rates affected businesses in the economy at the time. (8 marks)**
(c) **Examine the factors that may act as a constraint on the decision of the business to expand. (10 marks)**
(d) **Explain why a percentage of the business's clients may not be affected by changes in the economic climate when making a decision to book holidays. (6 marks)**
(e) **Advise Sky Travel on whether it should go ahead with its expansion plans. (12 marks)**

## Business and social constraints

Businesses affect the societies in which they operate. A sole trader running a small grocery store may benefit local residents by opening for a few hours on a Sunday. On the other hand such a business may have negative effects. Canned drinks bought from the shop may be left in the street. Opening on a Sunday may lead to more traffic in the area. Decisions made by a multinational company (☞ unit 109) can have a huge impact in many different countries. For example, it may decide to relocate its factory from one country to another. This is likely to lead to a fall in income and employment in the country that the company has left. The new location may gain from more jobs, the building of infrastructure, such as roads, and perhaps spending on health care and community projects.

These examples show that businesses do not operate in isolation. The decisions they make can affect a range of other groups and individuals. The businesses can be seen as part of the societies in which they operate. As a result, governments often pass laws and set regulations to control the conduct of businesses.

Such laws tend to set the legal minimum in terms of the way in which businesses behave. However, do businesses have any further responsibilities to society? Should businesses consider the implications of their decisions upon society and not just take into account whether these decisions help the business to achieve its objectives? For example, a cement factory may have emissions within legal limits. The local community might argue that the emissions cause health problems amongst children and the elderly in the area. Should the business try to reduce the emissions?

Some would argue that businesses are self-regulating. They do not need to be controlled by government. If they ignore the views of society, consumers will not buy their products. They will lose trade and perhaps go out of business. Others argue that, without external regulation, businesses may have negative effects upon society. People who are adversely affected by business activity may not be in a position to influence the business. The children and elderly people living near the cement factory may not buy cement. The young and old may not be able to exert any outside pressure by complaining to the management of the business.

## Business and stakeholders

One way of considering the impact of businesses upon society is to view all of the groups affected by the behaviour of a business as **stakeholders** (☞ unit 3). The stakeholders in a business are likely to include customers, employees, shareholders, suppliers, government, local communities and businesses, financial institutions and other creditors.

Businesses have tended to be influenced mainly by customers, employees and shareholders. Increasingly, however, other groups are affecting business behaviour. For example, some businesses will only supply their products to other businesses that have an ethical or environmental policy. Some pension companies will not invest in businesses that sell arms. This suggests that businesses need to have a greater SOCIAL RESPONSIBILITY to groups beyond those immediately involved in the business.

## Business ethics

The way in which businesses respond to issues such as the sale of arms or health risks from pollution may depend on their ETHICS. Ethics are the **values** and **beliefs** which influence how individuals, groups and societies behave. For example, an electricity generating business may be operating within legal emissions limits. However, it may feel that it has to change its production methods to reduce emissions even further because it believes businesses should work towards a cleaner environment.

In part the ethics of a business will depend upon the values of its employees. However, the ethical stance of the business is likely to be determined by the values of senior managers, directors and other important stakeholders. It will also be influenced by codes of conduct which may operate in the industry. The term ETHICAL is used to refer to businesses which explicitly recognise the importance of social responsibility and the need to consider the effects of its actions upon stakeholders. It is possible that a business following an ethical policy may:
- attract customers and employees who agree with its policy;
- have to change its operations to fit in with this policy, for

Cadbury is a business proud of its work in the community and has won many awards from within the business world for its work. However, in 2003 the company was criticised by a number of health groups for its Get Active campaign. Vouchers were available on its chocolate bars that could be used to provide more sports equipment for schools. Some felt that a business marketing products which are inherently unhealthy and in a climate of rising concerns about obesity in young people should not be engaging in marketing to schools. Others thought that schools needed all the help they could get in purchasing sports equipment and helping young people to lead more healthy lives.

Source: adapted from *The Observer*, 21.3.2004.

(a) Discuss to what extent businesses using vouchers to provide school equipment might be said to be acting in an ethical way.

## Question 1

example approving certain suppliers;
- have to set a policy for all the business in areas such as recruitment and marketing.

## *Business and the environment*

It is possible that the activities of business can have certain beneficial effects on the environment. For example, a new factory may be built in a derelict area. The new premises may be landscaped, improving the view. A grass area built might have a bench which could be used by pedestrians. Businesses are becoming more and more aware of the need to consider the environment in their operations. Many critics of certain business activities suggest that they have a negative effect on the environment in the surrounding area. Some of the negative effects of business activity include:

- air pollution caused by the discharge of emissions into the atmosphere and traffic visiting retail outlets;
- water pollution as a result of the dumping of waste;
- congestion from employees going to work or consumers visiting retail outlets;
- noise from factories and traffic;
- destruction of natural habitats from the building of premises.

How might these effects be controlled?

- Laws can be passed which make it illegal for firms to pollute the environment. For example, various environmental protection acts and regulations set limits on the quantities of gas emissions (☞ unit 112).
- Increased fuel prices in the UK have been justified by

governments on the grounds that consumers should pay prices which accurately reflect the impact of car use on the environment. High taxes on petrol are designed to reduce car use. In 1996 the UK government introduced a **landfill tax**. This taxed businesses for dumping waste on a landfill site. It was designed to discourage waste and encourage recycling and reuse of materials.

- Firms could be forced by law to compensate those affected by business activities. For example, it is common for airports to provide grants for nearby housing to buy double glazing.
- Government could offer grants, tax allowances or subsidies to business to encourage the reduction of external costs. For example, a subsidy might be given to a business undertaking an environmentally friendly project, but not to another business with a project that could cause environmental damage. Subsidies may also be given by businesses, for example, to employees who share a car or cycle to work.
- Charging road users could be useful in reducing pollution and congestion. This method of control is used in European countries such as France and Italy. Similarly, vehicles entering city areas may be charged for travelling at certain times of the day.
- In the USA, pollution permits have been introduced. They allow businesses a certain amount of emissions. If a business reduces its emissions below a certain level it can save its allowance for later or even sell it to another firm.
- Businesses and government may work together to control

**GREEN TYRES FOR YOUR VEHICLE**

○ SAFE
○ GREAT VALUE FOR MONEY
○ ENVIRONMENTALLY FRIENDLY

The next time you change the tyres on your vehicle, it's worth considering the environmental benefits of quality British- manufactured retreaded tyres.
Every retread sold extends the tyre's natural life, thereby saving natural resources and helping reduce the scrap tyre mountain. In addition, each retreaded tyre requires **4.5** gallons less oil than a new tyre.

**For your nearest Green Tyre Dealer
www.greentyres.com**

RETREAD MANUFACTURERS ASSOCIATION
2ND FLOOR, FEDERATION HOUSE,
STATION ROAD, STOKE-ON-TRENT,
STAFFORDSHIRE. ST4 2TJ
tel: 01782 417777 fax: 01782417766
email: retreads@ukonline.co.uk

*RETREADING IS RECYCLING*

**Enhance and Preserve your Environment** the **Green** shop
PRODUCTS FOR A SUSTAINABLE FUTURE

Quality Environmentally Friendly Interior Paints and Finishes

- Auro Natural Paint
- Green Paints
- Earthborn Clay Paints
- Lime Earth Paints
- OS Colour Wood Treatments
- Holkham Linseed Paint
- La Tienda Pigments
100's of other environmental products from solar torches to books and bodycare.

Go online or phone for a catalogue to see our full range

**www.greenshop.co.uk**
tel: 01452 770629

Look at the adverts.
(a) Explain how the businesses in these operations might be acting in the interests of the environment.

(b) Suggest how this might affect the businesses.

**Question 2**

their effects on the environment by sharing best practice, producing environmental codes of practice or developing waste strategies.

In many areas, businesses are becoming responsible for regulating their own behaviour. The ethics of a business can affect the extent to which it controls its impact on the environment. Some businesses have adopted their own stringent codes of practice and policies to control their activities. It is likely that attempts to control the effect on the environment by businesses will lead to:

●  increased costs in the short term;
●  the attraction of customers who agree with the policy of the business;
●  a change in production methods.

## Business and law

Governments often pass laws which are designed to control the conduct of businesses. Often governments will introduce laws when businesses have a record of failing to meet minimum standards or where it is anticipated that they will be unable to meet such standards. Laws act as a substitute for self regulation by businesses. The regulation of business activity by legislation falls into a number of categories.

●  How businesses treat consumers in general and their customers in particular. Such laws attempt to ensure that consumers are not misled or customers are not treated unfairly by businesses. Unit 103 provides more details about consumer protection laws. Unit 28 provides information about restrictions on advertising.
●  How businesses treat their employees. These laws are designed to protect the rights of employees and to ensure that they are treated fairly. Laws in this area include those relating to the terms and conditions of employees (☞ unit 66), equal opportunities (☞ unit 68) and the protection of employees in work (☞ unit 69).
●  The ways in which businesses affect the wider communities within which they operate. For example, as explained earlier, legislation sets limits on the quantities of certain emissions which businesses are allowed to release into the atmosphere. The aim is to set limits on maximum amounts of pollution and control the harmful effects of businesses on the environment. Other laws governing business activity in this area include planning regulations which impose restrictions on where businesses may locate.
●  Legislation which affects the information that businesses must maintain and produce. For example, Companies Acts (☞ unit 6) regulate the information that must be contained on company accounts. There are also restrictions on the information that can be kept about clients and the operation of computers (☞ unit 69).

Although laws can control the behaviour of businesses, there are some problems with this method of control. First, businesses can obey the 'letter of the law' rather than the 'spirit of the law'. This might mean, for example, a business adopting practices which are legal, but which do not greatly reduce negative externalities. Second, legislation which only applies within national boundaries may not affect businesses in other countries. For example, legislation governing the behaviour of the UK or EU nuclear industry would have had no impact on the Chernobyl disaster in Eastern Europe. This led to radioactive materials being deposited in the UK and other Western European countries.

In 2004 UK business was bracing itself for the impact of EU regulation regarding working time. The EU Working Time Directive states that an employee should work only a 48 hour week. They should rest 11 consecutive hours per day and have a rest break when the day is longer than six hours, a minimum of one rest day per week and four weeks' holiday. Night working must not average out at more than eight hours at a stretch.

Previously the UK had negotiated an opt-out clause from the directive, so that UK businesses did not have to comply. However, within 18 months UK businesses that did not comply would face sanctions. These included fines for the company. Directors may also be taken to court if their company transgresses.

It was argued that the directive prevents exploitation of workers. Another benefit is the reduction in 'dead time'. It is suggested that 61 per cent of UK employees find themselves with dead time on their hands of around an hour a week. This is time they could have been spending better.

However, all companies and employees might not benefit. For example, a company that gets extra work might previously have asked its employees to work a little longer. Now it will have to employ another worker, who could be part time. This part time worker may not have the skills of the employee who previously would have worked overtime to do the job. A UK manufacturing business argued 'If you look at the sort of person we employ, which are semi-skilled individuals, they would tend to increase their earning capabilities through the provision of overtime or additional shifts. If their working time is restricted, they need to look at increasing their hourly rate to get them back to where they are currently in terms of take-home pay.'

Source: adapted from *The Guardian*, 25.3.2004.

(a) Why might legislation have been introduced on the length of the working week?
(b) Discuss whether such legislation is in the interests of (i) employees and (ii) businesses.

**Question 3**

## Business and technology

Technological innovations and developments influence the operation of businesses in a number of ways. For example, robots and computers have been increasingly used in the manufacture of goods and the provision of services. Computer based technologies have been used to store,

retrieve and manipulate information. Generally it might be argued that the introduction of technology has improved the efficiency of businesses (☞ unit 85).

As well as affecting the ways in which businesses operate, such technologies can have an effect upon society.

● Many new technologies have reduced the need for businesses to employ so many people. This is because businesses have been able to reduce unit costs by replacing labour with new technology. For society as a whole this could be beneficial. The same level of income or more is being generated by fewer employees. The problem here is who benefits from the new technology. Consumers may benefit from relatively cheaper goods and services and increased quality. However, those who have lost their jobs may be faced with a dramatic loss of income and experience many of the problems associated with unemployment. Thus whilst new technologies can benefit some, others can be left worse off.

● The introduction of new labour saving technology should leave people with increased leisure time, as computers and other machines perform production and service tasks once carried out by workers. Increased leisure time would leave people with time to devote to activities such as sports and the arts and involve them undertaking less work. On the other hand, it could be argued that the increased use of new technologies has led to a surge of economic activity and to increases in working hours for many employees.

● New technologies have led to a significant increase in the choices available to consumers. A range of products has become available which were previously unheard of or out of the reach of consumers. So, for example, digital cameras, laptop computers and satellite television are now widely in use.

● Many believe that the introduction of new technologies, in particular information and communication technology, have enabled the economies of developed nations, such as the US and the UK, to continue growing. This has led to higher income levels amongst consumers and increased life expectancies associated with advances in medical technology. However, it should be noted that the increased incomes in the developed economies of the West have been far from equally shared. Many groups in society continue not to benefit from increased income and divisions between the rich and poor continue to widen.

## Pressure groups

PRESSURE GROUPS are groups without the direct political power to achieve their aims, but whose aims lie within the sphere of politics. They usually attempt to influence local government, central government, businesses and the media. They aim to have their views taken into account when any decisions are made. Such influence can occur directly, through contact with politicians, local representatives and business people, or indirectly by influencing public opinion.

The use of pressure groups is one way in which

stakeholders can exert influence over those making decisions within a business. Pressure groups can represent stakeholders directly involved with the business, such as employees or shareholders. They can also represent those not directly involved in the business, such as local communities or consumer groups.

There are many different types of pressure group and many ways of classifying them. One way is to divide groups into those which have a single cause and those which have a number of different causes.

● Single cause groups include the Campaign for Nuclear Disarmament (CND), Survival International and the NSPCC. Such groups mainly try to promote one cause.

● Multi-cause groups include trade unions, Greenpeace and the Confederation of British Industry. Pressure groups falling into this category tend to campaign on a number of issues. Trade unions, for example, have campaigned on a variety of issues, including the rights of the unemployed and improving the pay and conditions of their members.

Over the last few decades there has been a huge increase in the number of pressure groups and in the scale of their activities. Inevitably this has brought them into much closer contact with businesses. As a result there are now a number of groups which focus their activities upon businesses in general or particular businesses and industries.

● Environmental groups such as Friends of the Earth campaign to prevent businesses from polluting the environment.

● Consumer groups, such as the Consumers' Association seek to protect the rights of consumers in general. Others include The Football Supporters' Federation and rail users' groups.

● Local community groups may, for example, seek to prevent particular business developments or influence the policies of individual firms which operate in their local area.

● Employee groups, such as trade unions and professional associations, try to influence firms on issues such as conditions of work and pay levels.

Pressure groups vary in size. Some, like a local group aiming to divert a by-pass, may be made up of a few local people. Others are national organisations such as Greenpeace or the Royal Society for the Protection of Birds, or international groups such as Amnesty International.

## Factors influencing the success of pressure groups

The success of any group, no matter how large or small, will depend on a number of factors.

● Finance and organisational ability. A pressure group with large funds will be able to spend on well organised campaigns. This has been a tactic employed by trade unions and professional groups. A well financed pressure group may also be able to employ full time professional campaigners. Such people are likely to organise more effective campaigns than enthusiasts devoting some of

their spare time to such an activity.

● Public sympathy. Capturing the imagination of the public will play an important role in the ability of a pressure group to succeed. The Campaign for Real Ale has been effective in this respect. Almost single handedly they caused a change in the types of beer available in public houses and in the brewing methods of the big brewing companies. As with many successful campaigns, CAMRA's ability to present a clear and simple message to the public was vital.

● Access to politicians. Pressure groups which have access to politicians are able to apply pressure for changes in the law. For example, the International League for the Protection of Horses persuaded the government to ban the export of live horses for human consumption within the EU. Their contacts with politicians were vital in this campaign. The process of applying pressure on politicians is known as lobbying. It has become dominated by skilled professional lobbyists, the fees of whom are out of the range of all but the wealthiest of groups.

● Reputation. Gaining a favourable reputation amongst politicians can be important. The British Medical Association, for example, has a good reputation amongst a variety of politicians and is therefore often consulted on a variety of health matters by the government.

## The effects of pressure groups on business

There is a number of ways in which pressure groups can affect firms.

● Pressure groups often seek to influence the behaviour of members of the public about a particular product, business or industry. Friends of the Earth attempts to persuade the public to use cars less and public transport or bicycles more in order to reduce emissions into the atmosphere. This campaign, if successful, would have important implications for a wide range of firms involved in the transport industry.

● Political parties, through their representatives in Parliament, are able to pass laws which regulate the activities of businesses. Therefore it is not surprising that many pressure groups devote resources to lobbying politicians. An example of this is the attempt by the anti-smoking group, Action on Smoking and Health (ASH), to change the law so that all advertising of tobacco is made illegal.

In 2004 a controversial study by the RAC (Royal Automobile Club) Foundation suggested that Britain's busiest roads needed £20 billion of improvements over a ten year period to avert gridlock for millions of motorists. The RAC Foundation is an independent body, established in 1999 to carry out research into motoring issues and to take on the role of protecting the interests of the motorist. The Foundation carries out regular opinion surveys of RAC Members and has, in the course of its campaigning work, taken up many of the issues which they have raised.

The organisation claimed that drivers in Britain endure 'the worst conditions in Europe' and demanded greater government expenditure on widening schemes and bypasses. Edmund King, the foundation's executive director, said taking into account that roads account for 93 per cent of all journeys, '£20 billion over 10 years is very little. It's half what the motorist pays in tax every year'. The government pledged £7 billion in 2003 for roadbuilding. But the RAC said this was insufficient and published a wish-list of more than 30 additional schemes.

Environmentalists attacked the list as unnecessary. Steve Hounsham of the pressure group Transport 2000 said 'Roadbuilding on this scale is as old-fashioned and doomed as the dinosaurs. The future belongs to sustainable transport. The RAC should be supporting better public transport and better opportunities for walking and cycling.' Critics also accused the RAC of outdated 'predict and provide' thinking, which would just encourage more vehicles onto roads and damage the environment.

Source: adapted from *The Guardian*, 13.1.2004 and www.rac.co.uk.

(a) Using examples, explain why the groups in the article might be described as pressure groups.
(b) Examine the factors which may influence the success of the pressure groups in the article.
(c) Discuss how the success of the groups might affect:
 (i) road users;
 (ii) government.

Question 4

# Consumer protection and the European Union

Increasingly the European Union (☞ unit 107) is affecting legislation in member countries. The EU's aim is to harmonise (make the same) consumer laws. It is responsible for a series of directives which all EU nations implement as laws and regulations. Examples include:

- EU directive, Unfair Terms in Consumer Contracts, in April 1993, which led to the **Unfair Terms in Consumer Contracts Regulations, 1994** in the UK. This directive sought to prevent consumers being locked into unfair contracts which undermined their rights;
- the EU directive which led to **The General Product Safety Regulations, 1994** in the UK. These state that all products supplied to customers must be safe;
- EU directives 88/314 and 88/315 leading to the **Price Marking Order, 1991** which states that the selling price of goods must be indicated in writing;
- **Telecommunications (Data Protection and Privacy) Regulations, 1999** which prevent people and businesses from receiving unwanted direct marketing telephone calls or faxes;
- **Consumer Protection (Distance Selling) Regulations, 2000** which relate to sales over the Internet. They require a seller to provide information on the main characteristics of the goods, the price, including any taxes and delivery costs, payment arrangements, guarantees and where to address complaints about the goods;
- **Electronic Commerce (EC Directive) Regulations, 2002** which deal with the protection of consumers involved in e-commerce. For example, online selling and advertising is subject to UK legislation and online traders must give clear information about who they are and how to complete transactions;
- The **Sale and Supply of Goods to Consumers Regulations, 2002** provide minimum rights on faulty goods, such as rights to refunds, compensation and replacements. They are designed to encourage people to shop 'across borders', in other EU countries, knowing there is protection if something is wrong with goods they buy.

# Effects of protection on business

The increase in the number of consumer laws and the concern about protecting consumers has a number of possible implications for firms.

- Increases in costs. Improving the safety of a good or ensuring that measuring equipment is more accurate can increase the costs of a firm. For example, an electrical firm producing table lamps may find that its product contravened legislation. The firm would have to change or improve the components used to make the lamps or re-design the lamp itself. Such changes would be likely to raise the firm's costs.

- Quality control. Many firms have needed to improve their quality control procedures as a result of legislation. For example, firms involved in bagging or packaging goods must ensure that the correct quantities are weighed out. Failure to do so could result in prosecution. In addition, businesses must be careful not to sell substandard or damaged products.
- Dealing with customer complaints. Many businesses now have a customer service or customer complaints department to deal with customers. These allow firms to deal with problems quickly and efficiently and to 'nip problems in the bud' - dealing with any problems before the customer turns to the legal system.
- Changes in business practice. Attempts to ensure that customers are treated fairly by a business may place pressure on it to become more market orientated (☞ unit 18). The firm would attempt to ensure that it is actually meeting the needs of those people it is attempting to serve. Such a change, for example, may lead to greater use of market research.

---

In December 2003 the UK government unveiled plans for revised consumer credit laws. They would include a regulation of 'loan sharks' who targeted the most vulnerable in society. These people often had to borrow large amounts, urgently and were charged high interest rates and extreme penalties for non-payment.

A new range of measures would be introduced. They included undercover officers to investigate loan companies and recover illegal profits. They would also make it easier for people to understand loans. The size of 'small print', stating the terms of agreements, was to be increased. And all businesses must present information in a standardised form, stating what people owe, how much they will pay, the length of the agreement, total charges, penalties and rights to cancel. The Office of Fair Trading (OFT) was given powers to make surprise raids on loan companies and to fine lenders acting against the law. It could also refuse to give a trading licence or vary the length of time for which the licence was granted.

Source: adapted from *The Independent*, 9.12.2003.

(a) Examine the implications of suggested changes to consumer credit legislation for:
   (i) consumers;
   (ii) businesses.

**Question 2**

# Monopolies and mergers

It is argued, by some, that competition between businesses benefits consumers. Such arguments have been one influence upon government's attempts to control monopolies and mergers.

In some cases just one business, a monopolist (☞ unit 94),

controls the market for a particular good or service although this is rare in the UK. Such market strength puts this firm in a position where it has the potential to exploit its consumers. It can also prevent other businesses from competing against it.

A LEGAL MONOPOLY in UK law is defined as any business which has over 25 per cent market share. An example may be Microsoft, in its production of operating systems for computers.

A merger is the joining together of two or more firms. Examples of mergers between well known companies in the UK in 2003 included:

- HSBC acquired Bank of Bermuda for £770 million, as part of a strategy to expand its private banking and fund administration operations;
- Warner Village, the chain of 36 cinemas, was acquired by SBC International Cinemas for £225 million, and the sites would be renamed as Vue;
- Selfridges, the department store group, accepted a £600 million takeover bid from the Wittington Canada private holding company;
- Holland & Barrett acquired Health & Diet Group from Royal Numico of the Netherlands for £7.5 million, gaining 49 GNC health food stores in the UK;
- Oasis Stores, the fashion retailer, was acquired by Baugur of Iceland for £152 million;
- Ryanair acquired the Buzz budget airline from KLM for £16 million;
- Gala, the operator of 166 bingo clubs and 28 casinos, was acquired by venture capital groups Cinven and Candover for £1.24 billion.

Some criticisms of monopolies and mergers for consumers and businesses include the following.

- They raise prices in order to make excess profits.
- They fix prices. When a small group of firms control the market for a product, it is believed that they may act in unison to fix prices at an artificially high level.
- They force competition out. It has been suggested that monopolists sometimes pursue pricing or promotional strategies designed to force competitors out of the market.
- They prevent new firms from entering markets.
- They carry out a range of practices to restrict competition. Examples include putting pressure on retailers not to stock the goods of rival firms and attempting to prevent suppliers from doing business with new entrants to the market.

There are, however, a number of arguments which support the continued existence of monopolies.

- Because monopolies often operate on a large scale, they are able to benefit from economies of scale (☞ unit 81). The cost advantages from this can allow monopolies to set prices lower than would be the case if there were a number of firms competing, and still make profits.
- Monopolies can use their large profits to undertake research and development projects. Many of these projects, which result in technological and scientific breakthroughs,

could not be afforded by smaller firms.

- Monopolies are much better placed to survive in international markets. It is argued that this is only possible if a firm operates on a large scale.

## Restrictive trade practices

Anti-competitive or RESTRICTIVE TRADE PRACTICES prevent competition between businesses. Examples of restrictive practices include the following.

- A business which is a dominant supplier in a particular market may set a minimum price for the re-sale of its products. Such firms may also seek to ensure that retailers stock their products alone. In return, retailers are often given exclusive rights to sell this product within a particular area.
- Firms forming agreements to fix prices and/or limit the supply of a product. Such agreements between firms are often referred to as COLLUSION.
- A dominant supplier requiring retailers to stock the full range of its product lines.

It is usually argued that consumers suffer as a result of these practices. For example, if two businesses join together to fix prices so that another business is forced to close, this will restrict consumers' choice. Such practices may benefit those businesses taking part, but will be against the interest of those that are faced with the restrictive practices.

## Legislation in the UK

Certain legislation in the UK is designed to protect consumers from the problems created by monopolies, mergers and restrictive practices.

**Fair Trading Act, 1973** This Act defined what constitutes a monopoly or merger in the UK. A monopoly is said to exist if a business has a 25 per cent share of the market or greater. A merger is said to exist if the combined total assets of businesses that joined together were greater than a certain value, ie £70 million in 2004. It also set up the **Office of Fair Trading (OFT)**. This was set up as a body to oversee all policy relating to competition and consumer protection. The current role of the OFT is discussed in the next section.

**Competition Act, 1998** This Act:

- prohibits agreements, cartels or practices which prevent, restrict or distort competition;
- prohibits conduct which amounts to abuse of a dominant position;

although the government can grant exemptions. It also set up the **Competition Commission**. The current role of the Competition Commission is discussed later.

**Enterprise Act, 2002** This Act replaced the provisions of the Fair Trading Act. Many of its new provisions were complementary to those of The Competition Act, which remained in force. The Act:

## Government policy

Unit 96 considered how and why governments seek to influence the economy. Governments use a variety of methods of intervention, including legislation, spending and taxation. Part of the government's involvement in the economy is the use of policies to control economic variables such as inflation, unemployment and trade. The use of these different policies can affect businesses.

## Fiscal policy

Fiscal policy aims to manage the level of total spending or aggregate demand in the economy. The government can use fiscal policy in a number of ways to achieve its objectives.
- It can boost total spending in the economy when there is unemployment (☞ unit 99).
- If there is inflation in the economy, linked to the level of demand (☞ unit 98), fiscal policy can be used to reduce demand in the economy as a whole.
- If there is a current balance deficit the government could raise taxes or cut spending on imports.
- It may try to redistribute income. It may spend money or reduce tax on low income groups to give them more disposable income.

Fiscal policy may involve governments making the following changes.

**Changes in government spending** If the economy needs a boost, government expenditure can be raised. For example, spending on building new hospitals can create jobs, income and increased spending by the people in those jobs. On the other hand, if the economy needs to be slowed down, government expenditure can be lowered. This may also be used to control inflation.

**Changes in direct taxation** **Direct taxes** are those which are levied directly on individuals or businesses. Income tax rates, as part of a fiscal policy, can be lowered in order to encourage consumers to buy more goods and services. This should raise the level of spending in the economy. Corporation tax, a tax on company profits, may be cut to encourage businesses to invest and increase output. Raising income tax is likely to have the opposite effect, ie to lower the level of aggregate demand. This could be used to cut disposable income and control inflation.

**Changes in indirect taxation** **Indirect taxes** are taxes on goods or services. The main indirect tax in the UK is VAT. Governments raise indirect taxes as part of fiscal policy in order to raise the price of goods and services and discourage spending. Indirect taxes are also used by governments as a means of raising revenue in order to

finance spending plans. There is much debate as to whether it is individual businesses or consumers who have to pay for indirect taxes. Take the example of a 2 per cent increase in VAT. If this was passed on to consumers in the form of a 2 per cent price rise, then consumers would be paying for it. However, firms might be reluctant to pass on the price rise to consumers because of fears of falling demand for their product. In this case, they might only raise the price by 1 per cent and pay the other 1 per cent VAT increase themselves. This would lead to a 1 per cent increase in their costs.

If a government spends more than it receives in revenue from taxation and other sources, then it is said to have a **budget deficit**. This will mean it has to borrow money from a variety of sources, such as individual members of the public or banks. This is will increase the PUBLIC SECTOR NET CASH REQUIREMENT (PSNCR). Governments may have budget surpluses, ie higher revenue than spending. In this case the government is able to pay off past debts.

## Monetary policy

Monetary policy (☞ unit 96) is also used to manage the level of aggregate demand in the economy, with a particular emphasis upon controlling the money supply. Monetary policy can be used to:

---

Nearly 1,000 cinemas in the western Indian state Maharashtra, including the entertainment capital Bombay which makes Bollywood films, called off a three-week strike in April 2004. Cinema owners said that the government had accepted their demand for a 10 per cent cut in tax on tickets. During the strike cinemas lost an estimated £130,000 per day - twice as much as the government.

The government had placed a 55 per cent entertainment tax on each ticket sold in Maharashtra, one of the highest in India. RV Vidhani, chairman of the cinema halls owners' association, said the government's acceptance of only one of its demands was 'like a drop in the ocean'. But they had to accept it in the face of stiff competition from multiplexes, which did not pay entertainment tax.

Source: adapted from news.bbc.co.uk.

(a) Identify the type of taxation mentioned in the article.
(b) Examine the possible effects of a reduction in taxation on:
   (i)    cinemas in Maharashtra;
   (ii)   cinema goers;
   (iii)  other businesses;
   (iv)   government revenue.

**Question 1**

- expand the economy by allowing more money to circulate and increase spending;
- control spending and restrict increases in money flowing around the economy which may lead to price rises;
- control spending on imports if there is a current balance deficit.

The government has used a variety of methods in the past to control the money supply.

**Changing interest rates** An increase in interest rates can reduce the money supply (☞ unit 97). If interest rates increase, the cost of borrowing rises. This could reduce the amount that businesses and consumers borrow from banks and building societies.

**Restricting bank loans** By restricting the ability of banks to give out loans, the size of the money supply can be regulated. The BANK OF ENGLAND could instruct banks to keep a higher proportion of their assets in reserve. This means that they are able to lend less. The government may also sell financial securities. This will reduce the size of the bank's assets and leave banks with less to lend out.

**Credit or hire purchase restrictions** The government can place controls on the amount of credit and hire purchase agreements which banks and other financial institutions are allowed to give to businesses and consumers. Over the last 25 years the UK government has encouraged competition in financial markets. This has led to an explosion in the amount of credit available and made restricting credit more difficult.

**Independent central banks** In certain countries, such as Germany, the central bank has responsibility for control of inflation and the money supply. Governments in the UK traditionally controlled interest rates directly. In 1997, control of interest rates passed to the Monetary Policy Committee of the Bank of England. It is argued that an independent bank is in a better position to control monetary policy. For example, it will not allow a government to increase the money supply before an election to finance spending in order to win votes.

An increase in interest rates and restrictions of loans and credit are aimed at controlling the money supply and inflation. However, this will also affect spending and may reduce output, employment and imports.

## Exchange rate policy

The exchange rate is the price of one currency in relation to another (☞ unit 100). The value of the pound, for instance, can be shown against a variety of other currencies, such as the dollar, the yen or the euro. Some governments take the view that the exchange rate should be left to find its own market value. Such governments do not try to intervene in foreign currency markets to influence the exchange rate.

Other governments seek directly to influence exchange rates. This involves the buying and selling of the currency on foreign exchange markets to influence its price. A government may want to:

- support the currency to prevent its value from falling. This might involve buying up currency to restrict its supply. A fall in the exchange rate may raise the price of imported products, possibly leading to **imported inflation** (☞ unit 98);
- allow the value of the currency to fall to improve the competitiveness of businesses in export markets. A fall in the value of a currency should make exports relatively cheaper;
- 'shadow' or follow another currency. For example, the British government has tried to shadow the value of the euro (☞ unit 107). This is so that UK businesses operating within the single European market do not experience variations in prices compared to those of European competitors.

There is a link between monetary policy, explained in the previous section, and exchange rate policy. Changes in interest rates have an effect on the value of a country's currency. An increase in US interest rates, for example, will tend to raise the value of the dollar. Higher interest rates attract short term investors who buy the currency. This increases the demand for the dollar. As a result its price rises. Lower US interest rates cause short term investors to move assets elsewhere. They will sell the dollar and buy other currencies with which to invest. This increases the supply of the dollar and lowers its price.

## Protectionism

This involves the use of controls to restrict the amount of imports coming into a country. TARIFFS are a tax on imports. They raise the price of imports and, hopefully, discourage consumers from buying them. For example, there is a Common External Tariff (☞ unit 107) on goods entering

---

The Bank of England's Monetary Policy Committee decided to keep interest rates at 4 per cent after twice raising the interest rate in the last six months. The Bank made clear its desire not to give a shock to consumers at a time when they were heavily in debt. Prior to the decision not to raise interest rates, union leaders warned about possible job losses arising from a further increase in interest rates. Roger Lyons of the union Amicus warned that higher rates would hurt businesses and debt burdened households. 'High rates will harm business first and then cast a shadow over millions of people who've borrowed money in the past couple of years and who aren't used to paying higher rates on their loans.'

Source: adapted from *The Guardian*, 4.3.2004.

(a) Why do you think the Bank of England decided not increase interest rates at the time the article was written?
(b) Explain how an increase in interest rates might affect a retail business.

**Question 2**

## The European Union

The European Union, then known as the European Economic Community, was set up in 1958. The six member countries (West Germany, France, Italy, Belgium, the Netherlands and Luxembourg) committed themselves, in the Treaty of Rome, to establishing a **Common Market**.

By the late 1990s the EU consisted of 15 countries. They included the original six plus countries such as the UK, Spain, Eire, Greece and Sweden. At that time other countries such as Slovenia, Hungary and Bulgaria were hoping to join in future. On May 1st 2004 ten new countries joined the EU. These countries were Hungary, Poland, the Czech Republic, Slovakia, Slovenia, Estonia, Latvia, Lithuania, Malta and Cyprus.

A COMMON MARKET exists when a group of countries forms a CUSTOMS UNION, with free trade between member countries, and establish a common external tariff on imports of goods and services from outside. Free trade should take place in goods and services, as well as factors of production such as land, labour and capital. For example, it should be possible for a worker from Denmark to work in Newcastle on the same terms as in her home country. Also, a German company should be able to buy land in London to develop offices. In practice, the free movement of factors of production has proved a lot more difficult than mobility of goods and services.

A common external tariff is placed on all imports into a customs union. If tariffs were different for different EU countries, this might lead to problems. Say Germany had a 10 per cent tariff and France a 20 per cent tariff. An American firm exporting to France could bring products in through Germany, paying the lower tariff, and then import them into France paying no extra tax. To avoid this, a common external tariff harmonises all tariffs on imports. This means the tariff is the same for imported products into all member countries.

There are some advantages to businesses operating in countries belonging to a customs union or common market.

- Firms operating within customs unions have free access to markets which would otherwise be protected by tariffs or quotas. In this way British firms, for example, have access to all other EU markets.
  For many firms this provides them with the opportunity to operate in EU markets in much the same way that they would at home. A Blackburn based firm would operate in Berlin or Bilbao in much the same way as it would in Brighton or Birmingham.
- Firms will have access to the most appropriate factors of production. A British firm might purchase cheap land in Southern Portugal for a new factory location, skilled designers from Italy or capital equipment from France.
- Customs unions provide firms with large markets to sell to.

The bigger the market a firm is selling to, the greater the economies of scale it is able to benefit from.

- Businesses operating within a common market will be protected from competition from outside this area by an external business. Such protection allows businesses to be sheltered from the potentially damaging effects of competition such as price wars.
- Increased competition from European firms may act as an incentive for British firms to increase efficiency and standards.

There are, however, disadvantages for businesses operating within a customs union or common market.

- Before Britain joined the EU, British firms could buy goods and services from the lowest cost producers around the world. Foodstuffs were imported in huge quantities from New Zealand and the USA in this way. Since joining the EU, however, British firms have had to pay far more for foodstuffs from New Zealand and Australia because of the common external tariff.
- Whilst a British based firm will have free access to other EU markets, businesses based in these markets will also have access to the UK market. Such competition may reduce the market share which domestic businesses have established.
- Protection from external tariffs is not always beneficial to firms operating from within a common market. This is because being sheltered from external competition may result in less incentive for a firm to become more efficient. In the long run, this may lead to a deterioration in the firm's performance.

---

P Clark Ltd, a Stafford based firm specialising in the manufacture of hi-tech exercise machines, had enjoyed enormous success in the US market with its rowing machines and running tracks. However, it could not have failed to notice a fall in its share of the UK market as a result of competition from Italian and French firms.

It had been poised to enter the European market for over a year, but had been held up by recurrent production difficulties which meant that it could barely satisfy the demand for its products in the UK and US markets. With free access to EU markets, and unlike in the US no tariff barriers to overcome, it had begun planning for the launch of its products in Europe. Its initial plan was to increase production by 50 per cent. If successful, its long term plan was to open a new manufacturing and distribution plant in a suitable EU location.

(a) In what ways will P Clark be able to benefit from operating within a common market?
(b) What problems has operating from within a common market brought it?

**Question 1**

- Firms may have to adapt their marketing strategies to suit the needs of consumers in each country within the customs union. For example, surveys have found that of the thousands of products commonly sold in European supermarkets, only a small proportion are widely on sale in identical format in at least the four largest countries.

## EU policies and business

The European Union has economic policies which are designed to help businesses within member countries. These policies vary from employee protection (☞ unit 68) and consumer protection (☞ unit 103) to transport and energy policies (☞ unit 112). Here we will concentrate on three policies and their effects on business.

**The Common Agricultural Policy (CAP)** This policy operates in all EU countries and accounted for approximately half of the EU's £60 billion budget in 2003. Article 39 of the Treaty of Rome states 5 objectives of agricultural policy:
- to increase the productivity of agriculture;
- to ensure a fair standard of living for farmers;
- to stabilise markets;
- to guarantee supplies;
- to ensure fair prices.

The CAP aims to achieve this. Farmers are guaranteed a fixed minimum price by the EU for their produce. The EU will buy up any amount that farmers produce at this price. Farmers could, of course, always sell on world markets if the market price was higher. If the market price drops below the minimum, however, CAP maintains the price to farmers, thus guaranteeing their income.

For farmers the CAP guarantees them a price for their produce so that they are not at the mercy of fluctuations in price. This means that fewer farmers will go out of business during difficult years and, to some extent, their incomes will be guaranteed.

The CAP has a number of problems associated with it.
- Overproduction. The setting of high, guaranteed prices has often caused excess supplies (☞ unit 93) of a variety of agricultural products. Any excess supply is purchased by EU authorities. They prevent it from being sold on markets by storing it, resulting in butter mountains, wine lakes etc.
- High prices. The minimum price set by the EU for agricultural products as part of CAP is very often higher than the price which would have resulted without their intervention. It is consumers and businesses such as food retailers who suffer as a result of these high prices.
- Purchasing excess supplies of agricultural products is expensive for the EU. It is possible that the money spent on this could be better diverted to projects such as providing grants to firms engaged in producing new high technology products.
- The EU cannot use all its agricultural products, so it sells them cheaply to developing countries. This undercuts farmers in developing countries who are unable to compete with heavily subsidised imports.

- 70 per cent of CAP's funds go to only 20 per cent of Europe's farms. Small farmers are the main losers in this. The biggest beneficiaries have been larger farmers. For example, in the UK in 2002 five farms received more than £1 million per year in subsidies.

Attempts have been made to reform the CAP. In order to prevent over production farmers are now paid to 'set aside' land and to leave it fallow. In addition, reforms have made to encourage farmers to produce what the market requires rather than paying them to produce crops that are already overproduced.

**The Regional Fund** This provides funds to member states to help reduce unemployment in depressed parts of the EU. It also aims to encourage development in areas on the edge of the EU, such as Southern Italy and Northern Ireland. For example, construction firms may win contracts to build new roads, or industrial units could be financed through the Regional Fund. Similarly, firms may receive investment grants if they locate in particular parts of the EU. This is dealt with in more detail in unit 88

**The Social Chapter** The **Maastricht Treaty** was signed by all EU member states in December 1992. One section of this treaty is the Social Chapter. The aim of the Social Chapter is to standardise working conditions throughout the EU so that all workers within the community are guaranteed basic rights. These include the following.
- A minimum wage to be paid to all workers.
- A maximum working week.
- A minimum paid holiday per year.

---

In the recent round of Common Agricultural Policy negotiations there were two main pressures on EU ministers. First, there was the issue of the enlargement of the EU to include agricultural economies such as Poland and Slovakia. Hardly anyone believed that the 10 new states could join on the same terms as existing members. Second, the EU was coming under fire during international trade talks for its lavish farm subsidies. These were causing difficulties for farmers in developing countries. During the October 2002 summit to discuss CAP reforms there was a high profile fall out between Tony Blair and the French President Jacques Chirac. Mr Blair reportedly told Mr Chirac that the French concern for Africa would sound hollow if it blocked further CAP reform.

Source: adapted from *The Guardian*, 26.6.2003.

(a) Why might the enlargement of the EU create pressures to reform the CAP?
(b) Explain how farmers in developing countries might be affected by the CAP.

**Question 2**

- The freedom to join a union.
- Access to appropriate training.
- The right to be consulted and informed about company plans.
- The protection of young workers.

The UK initially opted out of the Social Chapter, when all other EU nations signed it. However, the UK signed up to the Social Chapter after the election of a Labour government in 1997. What might be the implications of the Social Chapter for businesses?

- Workers may be better motivated. This should make them more effective and productive employees, able to raise the efficiency of the firm for which they work.
- Industrial relations may improve as employees are involved in making company decisions and consulted about the work which they carry out.
- It may raise the labour costs of those firms currently employing workers at wages below the minimum level set out in the Chapter. Those firms expecting their employees to work longer than maximum may also find their costs rise as they are required to employ more people.
- Higher labour costs may make it more difficult for EU based firms to compete with businesses in low wage countries, such as China or South Korea.

## *The Single European Market*

A major event in the EU's move towards free trade was the signing of the Single European Act in 1986, which established a SINGLE EUROPEAN MARKET which came into being on 31 December 1992. Despite the existence of a customs union for over 30 years, there were still many non-tariff barriers to trade in the EU. This Act aimed to remove those barriers between EU member countries. The effects of this should be to encourage the freer movement of people, goods, services and capital. Three categories of barriers were removed.

- Barriers which prevented entry into markets. For example, differing technical standards were required of products by different member states. This made it difficult for firms to enter certain markets. Also, the practice of public sector contracts being given only to domestic firms prevented free trade.
- Barriers which caused firms' costs to rise. Often complex documents were needed in order to move goods from one country to another. Also, there were long delays waiting to get exports through customs posts.
- Barriers which lead to the market being distorted. Such barriers are said to prevent firms from competing on equal terms. They included differing rates of VAT in EU countries and subsidies given by EU governments to domestic industries.

Not all firms have been affected to the same degree by the Single Market. In some industries, very few barriers to trade existed between EU countries before December 1992. Firms operating in such industries have seen little or no changes to their situation. However, in other industries, where trade barriers were high, the Single Market has resulted in major changes for those firms operating within them. What effects has the Single Market had on firms in member countries?

- Product standards. Firms have, for example, had to alter their products so that they meet new product standards. Many firms have had to improve the safety aspects of their products in order to meet new EU regulations.
- Harmonisation of tariffs and taxes. There have been attempts to harmonise VAT rates throughout the EU. For businesses this may mean that the selling prices of their products rise or fall in line with VAT rate changes. In the UK, a number of products such as childrens' clothes and books, which had previously not attracted any VAT, were faced with the prospect of this tax if the UK was to fall into line with other EU countries. Attempts have also been made to harmonise EXCISE DUTIES on products such as petrol, tobacco and spirits. This has affected the price at which these products are sold and, therefore, the businesses marketing them.
- Ease of trading. The reduction in the number of customs posts, and the amount of paperwork which is required for goods traded between EU countries, should save businesses time and reduce costs.

---

The European Union yesterday condemned Microsoft for an abuse of its near monopoly. It ordered it to change its business practices and pay a record fine of nearly £333 million. After a five year investigation, Mario Monti, the EU Competition Commissioner, said the world's second largest company must now offer its Windows operating system without its digital media player to PC manufacturers. The Windows operating system is found in 90 per cent of PCs worldwide. 'Today's decision restores conditions for fair competition and establishes clear principles', Mr Monti said. 'Dominant companies have a special responsibility to ensure that the way they do business doesn't prevent competition on merit and does not harm consumers and innovation'.

Microsoft's rivals welcomed the decision. Lee Patch, vice president of legal affairs at Sun Microsystems, said the decision would lead to increased competition in the server market. 'We want to be able to have products competing on their merits rather than on the basis of whether they can effectively communicate with Microsoft's desktops,' he said. Microsoft legal counsel Brad Smith said that the company would appeal and the issue is therefore likely to be bogged down in the courts for five years.

Source: adapted from *The Guardian*, 25.3.2004.

(a) Explain why the EU Competition Commissioner might have argued that Microsoft's practice with regard to its media player was an abuse of its dominant position.
(b) Why might the EU wish to promote more competitive practices?

**Question3**

# The single European currency

EUROPEAN MONETARY UNION (EMU) became a reality in January, 1999 when a single European currency was introduced. At the time, some of the member states of the EU signed up to the single European currency, known as the euro. The UK was not one of them, preferring to leave a decision about whether to join to a later date.

Participating countries fixed their exchange rates so that they could not move against each other and against the euro. On 1st January 2002 actual euro notes and coins were introduced in 12 of the EU's 15 member states at the time. The UK, Denmark and Sweden continued with their own currencies. In the participating countries, known as 'euroland' or the 'euro zone', the old national currencies were withdrawn during the first three months of 2002.

In order to manage the single currency a European Central Bank (ECB), based in Frankfurt, was established. Amongst other things the European Central Bank is responsible for setting interest rates (☞ unit 97) throughout the participating countries.

It has been argued that European Monetary Union will have a number of benefits for businesses within the euro zone.

**A reduction in transactions costs** It is expensive for a business to change currencies when trading abroad. There are administration expenses in exchanging the currencies and possible charges. The costs of exchanging one currency for another are eliminated if all trading between countries is done in euros. For example, a French business exporting telecommunications equipment to Italy will no longer have to convert Italian lira into French francs. It has been estimated that the savings made from the introduction of the single European currency would be between 0.25 to 0.5 percent of national income for a member country.

**A reduction in uncertainty** The uncertainties of trading are reduced for those businesses within the euro zone. It has been argued that greater stability within the euro zone would lead to greater confidence amongst businesses, thus leading to more trade between member countries.

One reason for stability is because there is no possibility of exchange rate fluctuations. Fluctuations in exchange rates can make it difficult for importers and exporters to know what price they will receive or have to pay for future transactions. For example, a Spanish business that received the value of 500,000 lire instead of 600,000 for a sale as a result of a fall in the value of the pound will find that its profit margins are cut. Some businesses try to hedge against rising prices by stockpiling stocks of components, which can be expensive.

It is also argued that the control of monetary policy by the ECB is less likely to lead to sudden, large changes in interest rates, for example. The control of interest rates to restrict inflation should also lead to more stable conditions in which businesses may operate. Businesses may also have a greater choice of finance if the euro encourages more investors in stock exchanges.

**Transparent prices** Pricing all products and services in one currency makes price differentials for products in different countries more obvious. This may show that a company is offering good value for money in the products it is selling. Companies that charge different prices in different countries may decide to reduce their prices to be more competitive, or to round up prices, which may increase profits. Companies will also be able to see the prices of competitors more easily.

**Merger activity** The introduction of a single currency will make cross-border mergers between businesses in member countries easier. They will each have the same pricing and accounting system, which should help the coordination of the business.

There is, however, a number of potential problems with the single currency for businesses in member countries.

**Costs** The initial conversion which all businesses needed to make was costly. It affected businesses in a number of ways. Accounting systems changed to take into account the new currency. New pricing led to redesigned packaging, advertising and display material. Staff needed to be trained to use the new currency. In addition, there was a general 'levelling up' of prices as businesses converted their prices from the old national currencies into the euro. Businesses must constantly review prices due to price transparency.

**The impact of the ECB** The European Central Bank's central role in setting interest rates and controlling monetary policy (☞ unit 105) for all nations within the euro zone could have a damaging effect upon some businesses. This is because the interest rates and monetary policy pursued by the ECB will reflect the needs of the member countries as a whole. If there are inflationary pressures in the euro zone the ECB is likely to pursue tight monetary polices, such as the raising of interest rates. However, there may be particular countries within the euro zone which do not have inflationary pressures, but which are seeking to avoid recession. Such countries would also be subject to tight monetary policies, but for them it would be inappropriate. These policies could help drive these countries into recession with damaging effects for business.

# Effects of the euro on non-member countries

Businesses in countries which remained outside the euro zone in the early twenty first century, such as the UK, were far less likely to enjoy the benefits or incur the costs of operating within the zone. There was great debate about whether and

under what conditions the UK might join the euro zone in future at the time.

For businesses outside the euro zone, the introduction of the euro has had a number of effects.

- Businesses trading with the member states now have to quote their prices in euros and be able to make transactions in this currency.
- The uncertainties of dealing with a number of different EU nations, all with their own separate currencies, have been reduced.
- There have been some reduction in transactions costs, although not as great as for members' businesses.
- UK businesses selling into the euro zone may be at a competitive disadvantage against competitors that share the same currency.
- The competitiveness of businesses may depend on the value of their country's currency against the euro. For example, if the value of the Swedish krone against the euro fell, this may make Swedish exports to countries in the euro zone more attractive.

It is suggested that the UK businesses most affected by the euro zone are:

- exporters and importers who would need to quote in euros;
- UK multinationals (☞ unit 109) who adopted the euro as their trading currency. This had an effect upon businesses supplying them. It meant that even businesses trading entirely in the UK were asked to price, invoice and accept payment in euros;
- banks who are asked to provide euros, make payments in

euros and open euro accounts;

- some retailers, perhaps in tourist areas, who need to quote prices in euros;
- subsidiaries of multinationals in the euro zone who are asked to deal in euros.

## The expansion of the EU

On May 1st 2004 the EU expanded to include ten new countries. These were Hungary, Poland, the Czech Republic, Slovakia, Slovenia, Estonia, Latvia, Lithuania, Malta and Cyprus. Figure 107.1 shows details of all members of the EU in 2004.

There is a number of implications of EU expansion.

- All of the new nations seeking membership of the EU are poorer than existing members. This will inevitably place a strain on the EU's budget. Cyprus, for example, the wealthiest of the new member countries, has a national income per head that is a fifth below the EU average. In countries such as Lithuania and Estonia, the differential is significantly greater. The poorer countries may not be in a position to contribute greatly to EU funds, whilst requiring large amounts in payments to help their development. This could affect businesses operating in existing EU countries.
- By including countries such as Poland, Slovakia and Malta in the EU there may need to be significant changes to policies. Many of the new member countries have economies that are more agriculturally based than those of existing members. The CAP may need to change to prevent large sums being paid to economies that are more agriculturally based.

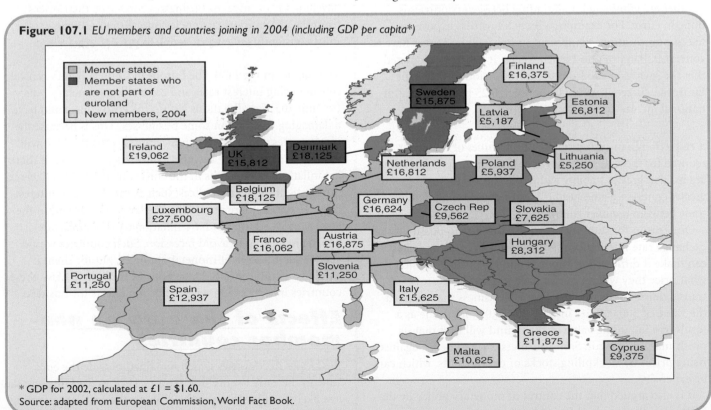

**Figure 107.1** *EU members and countries joining in 2004 (including GDP per capita\*)*

Member states
Member states who are not part of euroland
New members, 2004

Finland £16,375
Sweden £15,875
Latvia £5,187
Estonia £6,812
Ireland £19,062
UK £15,812
Denmark £18,125
Netherlands £16,812
Poland £5,937
Lithuania £5,250
Belgium £18,125
Germany £16,624
Czech Rep £9,562
Slovakia £7,625
Luxembourg £27,500
France £16,062
Austria £16,875
Hungary £8,312
Slovenia £11,250
Portugal £11,250
Spain £12,937
Italy £15,625
Greece £11,875
Cyprus £9,375
Malta £10,625

\* GDP for 2002, calculated at £1 = $1.60.
Source: adapted from European Commission, World Fact Book.

- Enlargement will increase the size of the EU market from 370 million to 450 million. This will provide a huge increase in the potential number of customers for many EU businesses and offer further opportunities for them to enjoy economies of scale.
- Including eastern European countries within the EU should generate greater economic and political stability within them. This will provide improved investment opportunities within these countries for existing EU businesses.
- The eventual adoption of the euro by these countries could lead to major benefits. The area would also operate as a strong trading bloc with the rest of the world.
- Many more countries will now be involved in the decision making process involving EU regulations and legislation. Such legislation affecting employees and employers will now need to take into account the concerns of many. This might affect the type and style of regulation. The decision making process is likely to become more involved, which may lead to delays.

## key terms

**CAP** - the Common Agricultural Policy of the European Community. It is designed to stabilise EC agricultural markets by fixing minimum prices for agricultural products.

**Customs union/Common market** - a group of countries with free trade between them and a common external tariff.

**European Monetary Union** - the adoption of a single currency by members of the EU.

**Excise duties** - taxes levied on fuel, alcohol, tobacco and betting.

**Single European Market** - an agreement by EU countries to remove all barriers to trade.

## Knowledge Knowledge...Knowle

1. Why is the EU said to be a customs union?
2. What is the Common Agricultural Policy?
3. What changes have occurred as a result of the Single Market?
4. State 5 implications of the Single Market for British businesses.
5. State 3 benefits of a single currency for businesses in member countries.
6. State 2 problems of a single currency for businesses in member countries.
7. Explain 3 effects that the single European currency might have on businesses in non-member countries.
8. What effects might EU enlargement have on businesses in existing member countries?

## Case study   EU enlargement and UK businesses

Countries joining the EU in 2004 have been identified as targets for businesses in the East Midlands. In a report on new business opportunities, the regional development agency, Emda, highlighted Poland, Estonia, Latvia and Lithuania, and future candidates such as Romania. The main industries recommended for targeting were environmental technologies and food processing. The report urges quick action in new countries where opportunities exist. Emda's EU enlargement projects manager, Helen Whitehead, said 'There will be greater potential to export to the accession states, but because forging relationships with local partners is often fundamental to winning business, there's real mileage in developing a presence there sooner rather than later'.

Source: adapted from news.bbc.co.uk, 23.4.2004.

In 2003 it was announced that Stansted would get two new runways as part of the government's 30 year plan for air travel in the UK. Expansion was to cope with the increasing amount of air traffic expected to come through the UK. A sixth terminal at Heathrow was also being considered, although a series of environmental conditions would have to be met to keep within EU limits on pollution.

Source: adapted from news.bbc.co.uk, 16.12.2003.

It has been estimated that the UK could gain as many as 80,000 nurses under EU expansion. Up to 20 per cent of nursing staff from countries joining the EU could decide to come to the UK for better pay. The increase in the UK's nursing workforce could stop the rising cost of agency staff, used to fill vacant posts in hospitals. However, nursing leaders in Europe argue that the transfer of staff could lead to major difficulties in the new EU member states, many of which could have staffing shortages of their own.

Source: adapted from *The Guardian*, 20.4.2004.

The Lovebytes digital arts festival in Sheffield is the longest-running event of its kind in Britain. It has grown from an afternoon of presentations in a converted garage, to a six-week-long internationally renowned event of digital art and culture. The festival largely continues because of EU funding. But with EU expansion, the worry is that the financial support the festival receives will move to Eastern Europe.

Source: adapted from *The Guardian*, 13.3.2003.

According to one study, the gain of EU expansion to the existing EU countries will be about £6 billion and approximately £15 billion to the newcomers of EU enlargement. The Home Office, however, believed that 5,000-13,000 people a year would enter the UK from new member states. There was criticism by some that large numbers of workers from new member states would flood into the UK, claiming benefits. The government acted by introducing restrictions. For example, migrants from the new member states will have to get a work registration certificate from their employers, rather than applying for work permits before they arrive in Britain. It was suggested that this would allow the government to monitor whether the numbers were getting too big and will pave the way for identity cards, which would be issued to all EU nationals living in the UK.

Source: adapted from *The Guardian*, 23.2.2004 and www.bbc.co.uk, 23.2.2004.

The new member states were bracing themselves for the impact of UK travellers in 2004. Previously UK airlines wanting to fly into these European countries had to complete mountains of bureaucracy to obtain a licence. 'This is all swept away come 1 May,' explained a spokesperson for the Civil Aviation Authority. An expanded free trade zone would create cut throat competition and low prices to attract the punters. In April, EasyJet planned to launch flights from Britain to Budapest in Hungary and Ljubljana in Slovenia, with prices starting from as little as £6.99 one way.

Source: adapted from *The Guardian*, 29.2.2004.

In September 2003 Sweden rejected the euro by 56 - 44 per cent. The rejection in Sweden also makes it less likely that Britain and Denmark will scrap their own currencies. It opens up the prospect of a two-speed, or even multi-speed, Europe, in which some share a currency, others defence policies, and others border controls or perhaps environmental standards.

Source: adapted from *The Guardian*, 2.9.2003.

**(a) How might the decision by Sweden affect businesses in that country? (6 marks)**

**(b) Explain how being a member of the EU affects UK businesses using examples from the articles. (12 marks)**

**(c) Examine how EU enlargement might affect:**
  **(i)   businesses in the UK; (10 marks)**
  **(ii)  businesses in the new member countries. (10 marks)**

**(d) Discuss to what extent further enlargement of the EU might be in the interests of UK businesses. (12 marks)**

## Business competitiveness in international markets

Unit 107 explained how the European Union might affect businesses in member and non-member countries. This unit examines the effects of international trading in other areas around the world and the effects of trading conditions on businesses. There is a number of factors that might influence the competitiveness of businesses trading in international markets.

**The existence of trade barriers** Some countries and groups of countries, known as TRADING BLOCS, such as the EU (☞ unit 107), erect trade barriers. These are designed to prevent businesses based outside the trading areas from competing with those who are members of the trading area.

Tariffs (☞ unit 100), a tax on imports, are one form of restriction. The effect of a tariff on products exported to countries which impose them is to increase the price charged by businesses or to lower their profit margins.

Quotas may also be used, which restrict the amount of a product that can be exported to a particular country or trading bloc. For individual businesses, quotas can mean that they can only export small quantities of their products, or indeed none at all, to countries which impose them. It is easier for businesses exporting abroad to compete with local businesses when they do not have to pay a tariff or have quotas imposed upon them.

**The costs of production** For some businesses their ability to compete in international markets depends upon their ability to have the same or lower costs of production than their international competitors. Lower costs of production allow businesses to have lower prices and therefore undercut their competitors. Because of the importance of labour costs these have traditionally been taken to indicate the competitiveness of a country and the businesses operating within it.

**The behaviour of businesses** Keeping production costs low and matching or beating competitors' prices are important in many markets. However, it is increasingly the view of business commentators such as Michael Porter that competitiveness in international markets depends upon how businesses behave. Competitiveness may depend on the extent to which businesses innovate and produce new products desired by consumers. Those businesses which produce quality goods and services, which meet the needs of consumers and stand out from those offered by competitors, are likely to be successful in international markets. The ability of businesses to produce innovative products and make good use of new technology will depend on their ability to recruit and train suitable employees.

**Trading agreements** In certain international markets, trade agreements regulate competition. For example, countries may belong to The World Trade Organisation, which is committed to increasing free trade. This is discussed in the next section. Another example is Mercosur, a free trade area agreed between Brazil, Paraguay, Argentina and Uruguay.

---

Ten South-East Asian countries signed an accord to turn their very different states into an integrated, tariff free trading and economic community by 2020. It will resemble the European Union in its earlier years.

At a summit, on the Indonesian resort island of Bali, the Association of South-East Asian Nations (ASEAN) agreed to eliminate tariff and non tariff barriers, standardise customs procedures, gradually reduce capital controls and abolish visas in a region that is home to 500 million people. The member states of ASEAN are Brunei, Indonesia, Thailand, the Philippines, Malaysia, Singapore, Cambodia, Burma and Vietnam.

In a further development at the summit the ASEAN agreed to complete deals with China, India and Japan by 2012. The pact with China would create by far the world's largest free trade zone.

Source: adapted from *The Guardian*, 8.10.2003.

(a) Identify the changes taking place in the article which might affect international competitiveness.
(b) Explain how these changes might affect businesses in ASEAN nations.

**Question 1**

---

## Developed economies

Western Europe and, in particular, the EU (☞ unit 107) is an important market for British firms. However, there are many other parts of the world which are significant trading partners for the UK. Particularly important are the US, Japan and Canada. They provide large export markets and have rival firms operating in the UK market. The way these countries trade with the UK and the EU is largely determined by two organisations - the G7/G8 countries and the World Trade Organisation.

**G7/G8 countries** The G7 (Group of seven) nations are the seven leading industrial countries - Germany, Japan, US, UK, France, Italy and Canada. Between them they are responsible for over two-thirds of the world's total output, and a similar proportion of its expenditure. Their main aim is to promote growth in the world economy. In 2002 Russia became a full member, and the group is now referred to as the G8 countries.

The success of G8 nations in reaching agreements has implications for firms trading in all parts of the world. For

example, the break-up of G8 nations into rival trading groups centred around Europe, North America and the Pacific Rim could lead to a reduction in the quantity of goods and services traded. This may result in a reduction in business opportunities for firms. The failure of G8 nations to reach agreement on promoting economic growth could have similar effects.

Trading agreements between non-EU G8 nations can also affect EU-based firms. For example, the US, Canada and Mexico formed the North American Free Trade Agreement (NAFTA). This is a regional trading bloc similar to the EU. Such regional trade blocs place barriers in the way of external firms seeking to export into them. Trade barriers of this kind can be damaging to firms wishing to enter such markets.

**The World Trade Organisation (WTO)** The WORLD TRADE ORGANISATION (WTO) was set up in 1995. Its aim is to promote free trade and to prevent protectionist measures by member countries. The WTO is made up of 147 countries (in 2004) that account for around 90 per cent of world trade. It has a number of roles, including being responsible for policing the world trade system. For example, it has annual reviews and also oversees individual members' trade policies.

All countries that join the WTO must agree to abide by its decisions. At the heart of the WTO system (known as the multilateral trading system) are agreements which are negotiated and signed by the majority of the world's trading nations. These agreements are the legal rules for international commerce. They are like contracts which guarantee member countries important trade rights. They also force governments to keep their trade policies within agreed limits.

Major conferences held by the WTO can last for years. At these conferences negotiations take place and agreements are made on major policies to promote trade. For example:

- the Uruguay Round, signed in 1995, agreed to phase out the 'multi-fibre agreement' which had previously protected the textiles industries of certain countries, removed voluntary export restraint and introduced rules on intellectual property rights, such as copyright and patents, to prevent them being copied;
- the DOHA Agenda in Qatar, which was due to end by January 2005, discussed anti-dumping rules to prevent cheap goods flooding developing countries, trade issues relating to e-commerce and tariff cutting for example.

The reason the WTO is important is because of its potential for increasing the amount of trade in the world. Such an increase in trade, many believe, can lead to greater prosperity. Indeed, the increase in the wealth of many nations has, perhaps, been due to the success of the WTO in lowering trade barriers. There are concerns that, without the WTO, the world could divide up into trading blocs resulting in a reduction in trade and possibly a worldwide depression. For individual firms, the WTO makes it more likely that they can operate in export markets on equal terms with locally based companies.

**Japan and the USA** Many of the world's largest and most famous businesses, such as Exxon Mobil, Toyota and Microsoft, are based in Japan and the USA. In addition to these famous large businesses there are many small and medium sized businesses producing innovative and highly sought after products. Despite a severe economic problems in the late 1990s and early twentieth century, the growth of the Japanese economy in the post war years was arguably the most dramatic economic miracle of the twentieth century. The USA has the largest economy in the world. For UK businesses this means that non-EU developed economies represent both opportunities and threats.

- Opportunities. These arise because the income levels in these countries and the size of their markets provide numerous openings for UK businesses.
- Threats. These arise because many businesses based in non-EU developed nations are renowned for their innovation, use of new technology and general ability to gain a competitive advantage over rivals. Consequently, businesses originating in these countries are able to challenge UK businesses both in domestic and international markets.

## *Eastern Europe*

The fall of the communist governments of eastern Europe and the countries' attempts to move to market economies in the 1990s and early twentieth century presented many opportunities for UK and EU businesses.

Countries such as the Czech Republic, Russia, Poland and Hungary have introduced the operation of markets into their economies (☞ unit 9). In 1992, East Germany united with West Germany to form one country. This meant that businesses in the former East Germany were faced with the prospect of competing in a market economy with domestic and foreign businesses.

Prior to the dramatic economic changes of the 1990s, most products in this part of the world were provided by state-owned monopolies. These were protected from overseas competition by trade barriers. Today, most of these state-owned monopolies have been privatised and investment from foreign firms is positively encouraged.

A number of eastern European countries joined the EU in 2004 (☞ unit 107). Those countries which were new members of the EU, such as Poland and Latvia, may grow and develop in ways which are different to the eastern European countries such as Russia, Bulgaria, Romania and Hungary that remained outside the EU.

For British firms, the changes in eastern Europe have presented a number of opportunities. Many UK firms see these economies as largely untapped export markets for their products.

- The opening up of these markets has provided western-based firms with access to a huge number of consumers. They can be used as a manufacturing base for western firms, taking advantage of workforces and land prices

Russian companies in the market for 'juice' were expecting an increasing threat from foreign multinationals in 2004. Attracted by the potential for growth and recovery from the financial crisis of the late 1990s, they were slowly returning to eastern Europe.

Multinationals have the financial 'clout' that local businesses cannot compete with. But they must have the right strategy. In Russia, for example, multinationals tend to sell to the 'super premium sector'. This has more limited demand, restricted to higher income consumers in major cities. Examples of businesses setting up included the following.

● Coca-Cola started local production of Minute Maid in 2002 in Ukraine, reducing its production costs and making it a more price-competitive option. It was in direct competition to Wimm Bill Dann (WBD), the Russian market leader. In Russia, the company added more flavours to its locally produced Minute Maid range in order to attract a wider range of consumers.
● In Hungary, PepsiCo launched its Toma fruit juice brand in 2001.
● In 2002, the Russian company Nidan-Ekofruct became the official distributor of Capri-Sonne juice drinks, bottled under the license from German company Wild.
● In 2002, Danone took a 4 per cent shareholding of WBD when it floated in New York.

It was estimated that the growing health trend and the impact of multinationals would raise juice sales by around 58 per cent between 2003-2008. The joining of the EU by countries such as Poland and Czech Republic was expected to raise levels of disposable income and living standards in the region. As a result it was predicted that consumers would buy better quality juices.

Source: adapted from www.euromonitor.com.

(a) Examine how changes in eastern Europe might affect:
  (i) eastern European businesses;
  (ii) multinationals from countries such as the UK.

**Question 2**

which are relatively cheaper than those in western Europe.
● There are opportunities for joint ventures (☞ unit 89) with former state-owned firms. This allows British and other western firms to combine their international business skills with local knowledge of markets and trading conditions.
● Businesses and individual entrepreneurs have the opportunity to sell their expertise and skills to Eastern European businesses.

Although there are many opportunities for UK businesses in eastern Europe, some businesses based in these countries also represent an increasing threat. Countries such as the Czech Republic adapted more effectively to the demands of a market economy than other countries. Consequently, the businesses based in more successful former communist countries are beginning to rival their western counterparts.

This is a trend which is likely to continue in future years.

There is also a number of problems with trading in eastern Europe.

**Bureaucracy** Many of the institutions and regulations under the old planned system are still in existence. These can present a number of obstacles. For example, there are huge delays in receiving permits and licences for western businesses wishing to set up and trade in some of these countries. With membership of the EU, many of the former bureaucratic obstacles may no longer exist for the new EU member countries.

**Political instability** Since their transition to market economies, there has been political instability in a number of these countries. This ranges from full scale war, as in Bosnia and Kosovo, to weak and fragile governments. Such instability may be off-putting for potential business investors. They may argue that their businesses are unlikely to flourish in the 'turmoil' which results from such instability. Many believe that membership of the EU will create greater stability in the new eastern European member states (☞ unit 107).

**Low incomes** Although eastern Europe represent a huge potential market for western-based businesses, opportunities are likely to be limited whilst average incomes remain low. The bulk of the population of these countries is unlikely to be able to afford many of the products manufactured by western-based firms. This could, however, be less of a problem over time if businesses in these countries develop and earnings increase.

**Infrastructure** The INFRASTRUCTURE of a country includes roads, railways, schools, airports, hospitals and office accommodation. In many ways the infrastructure of the eastern European nations is of a high standard. For example, the hospitals and public transport in some of these countries are better than those found in some western countries. However, there are also problems. Poor telecommunication systems, banking services and law enforcement are all problems which may affect the prospects of western firms.

## Developing economies

These economies are almost always found in the southern hemisphere. They are often known as 'the South', Third World Countries, developing countries or low and middle income countries.

Their main features are that they have poorly developed infrastructures and low average incomes per head of population. However, it is difficult to place countries in the South into one single group. This is because some have developed a wide range of industries which can compete with those in the West. Such countries are sometimes known as the Newly Industrialised Countries (NICs). Others are hardly developing at all. They continue to struggle with a range of

The world is transfixed by China. In a few days in 2004:

- Korea's INI Steel Company launched a $500 million steel project in the Dalian development zone;
- France's Saint Gobain invested another $70 million in one of its existing glass production lines;
- Germany's Siemens opened its fortieth office in China, to develop software applications in Nanjing, and warned that it could shift thousands of jobs from Europe and America to China;
- Finnish paper giant Stora Enso invested $1.6 billion in a pulp-paper project in South China.

In the past businesses had struggled to make profit in China, but not now. For example, microprocessors made previously were the wrong type and sales were poor as a result. In 2004 Infineon, the giant German producer, makes plenty of profit. As a result China will get 30 per cent of the German firm's $1.2 billion investment total over the next three years.

What makes China special? Size is one thing - it has 1.3 billion people and a $1.23 trillion economy. Its middle class is growing and consumption is booming. There is also low inflation, cheap and plentiful labour, urbanisation driving demand, and a savings rate of 30 per cent providing easy capital. It is said that 'China is a manufacturer's dream'.

Source: adapted from news.bbc.co.uk, 19.2.2004.

---

A US report in 2004 said that China had made great strides since joining the WTO in 2001. But deregulation had stopped and in many sectors import barriers made it difficult for foreign businesses to operate in China. Tariffs had been reduced but officials were accused of tweaking technical standards on issues such as safety or packaging to the detriment of foreign firms. Counterfeiting and piracy also took place as intellectual property rights were still inadequate.

Source: adapted from news.bbc.co.uk, 1.4.2004.

**(a) Suggest factors that might have affected businesses in the region in 2002/04. (8 marks)**
**(b) Analyse how these factors might have affected the international competitiveness of businesses based in:**
   **(i)   Asia; (10 marks)**
   **(ii)  the EU. (10 marks)**
**(c) Recommend possible strategies that businesses might take in these situations. (12 marks)**

In 2003 the Sars virus terrified millions in Asia and threatened the economies of several nations in the region. Although the disease originated in China, consumers in Japan and other Asian nations were taking no chances as it was suggested that Sars may be airborne. The UN revised its growth forecast for Asia down from 5.4 to 5 per cent, partly because of a fall in tourism caused by Sars. Morgan Stanley estimated that the virus will shave more than $15 billion off the output of Asia's economies. Singapore estimated that Sars could knock one per cent off the island's GDP (worth $875 million). The government in Singapore announced a series of measures for the hardest hit industries. 'It's having a negative impact but people need to put it in perspective' said Gerard Lyons of Standard Chartered Bank. 'In the short term it dents sentiment and it dents spending, but if Sars is contained, the impact could be short term.'

The impact of Sars was felt by airlines that would normally be carrying people to and from China, Hong Kong and Singapore. Potential travellers were staying at home and this was affecting business. For example, Hong Kong carrier Cathay Pacific was forced to cut more than 40 per cent of its flights. The airline business said it was losing $3 million a day while the outbreak persisted.

Hotels were also suffering from the Sars outbreak. Bookings were down and staff at hotels in Hong Kong were being encouraged to take annual leave. In the tourist resort of Phuket in Thailand, hotels faced a 30 per cent fall in demand. In Vietnam, restaurants were asking staff to take early holidays because customers were so reluctant to eat out.

Tourists to Japan used to laugh at the sight of people wearing face masks in the street. But this Japanese custom was increasingly being adopted as a prudent measure elsewhere in Asia as fears of Sars grew around the world. Hakujuji, the face mask business in Japan found its products flying off the shelves. Yoshi Izumi of the company said 'people are buying five or six masks at the same time. Most are families travelling overseas, others work in airports and some have relatives in China where good masks are harder to get hold of.' Profits were being made from the Sars outbreak in other ways. In China, sales of traditional medicines were rising. In Thailand home delivery pizza businesses and shopping websites were getting more business as people did not want to mingle with crowds.

Source: adapted from *The Guardian*, 22.4.2003.

## What is globalisation?

GLOBALISATION is the term used to describe the growing **integration** of the world's economy. It is suggested that as globalisation takes place, national economies are becoming integrated into a single 'global economy' with similar characteristics. There are interrelationships throughout the world between related businesses, between competitors and between businesses and consumers. Decisions taken in one part of the world affect other parts. Businesses base decisions on what is happening in the 'world market' rather than national markets.

Evidence of the integration of the world's economy can perhaps be seen in businesses that design and market their products to a world market, such as Coca-Cola. This product is sold in many countries throughout the world. Consumers in different countries recognise the product easily and have similar tastes for the product. Coca-Cola is able to market its products worldwide. It has close relationships with businesses in other countries, some of which manufacture Coca-Cola products.

Three important aspects of globalisation might be identified.

**The growing importance of international trade** Businesses and consumers are increasingly relying on overseas markets and suppliers. Over a six year period between 1997 and 2003 world trade rose by 50 per cent. The value of air freight out of the UK doubled over a 10 year period to 2003.

**The rise of the multinational business** The operation of multinational companies (MNCS) can be seen in many countries around the world. Familiar products and brand names appear worldwide. Examples might be Microsoft, Nokia, Exxon Mobil, Coca-Cola, PepsiCo, McDonald's, General Motors, Ford, Intel, Sony, Nike and IBM. It has been suggested that multinationals are bigger than some nations. Figures sometimes quoted include 'Fifty one of the world's top 100 economies are corporations' and that 'MNCs make up twenty nine of the world's 100 largest economic entities'. However, there is great debate about the size and impact of multinationals. This is dealt with later in this unit.

**The emergence of businesses which think globally about their strategy** Such businesses base their strategic decisions (☞ unit 17) on the global market rather than national markets. For example, a business may make parts for a product in several different countries and assemble them in another because this is the most cost effective and efficient method to get the product to its consumers. They will tend to make use of their business's **competitive advantage** by locating production wherever it is most efficient. This means

businesses with widely spread networks of research, component production, assembly and distribution. Asea Brown Boveri (ABB), the world's leading supplier of power and automation technology, is an example of a global business. It employed 115,00 people in 2004 and operated in 100 countries around the world.

## Factors affecting globalisation

It could be argued that certain factors have contributed to the growth of globalisation.

● Technological change has played an important role in globalising the world's economy. More powerful computers and communications technology (☞ unit 70) have allowed the easy transfer of data. The Internet has revolutionised the way in which consumers purchase products.

● The cost of transportation and communication has fallen. For example, an survey in Australia in 2002 found that over the period 1990-2002 air freight rates declined by 25 per cent. This may have reduced the cost of goods transported to and from the country. The costs of videoconferencing and Internet-related communications have also fallen (☞ unit 70).

● The deregulation of business. Throughout the 1980s, 1990s and early twenty first century many businesses were privatised in countries throughout the world. In the UK the privatisation of former state owned monopolies (☞ unit 7) allowed competition. The removal of restrictions on foreign businesses operating in eastern European and Asian countries (☞ unit 108) also increased the ability of businesses to operate globally. New markets were opened up to foreign competition.

● The liberalisation of trade. Trade protection has been reduced due to the operation of organisations such as the World Trade Organisation (WTO) (☞ unit 108). For example, reduction of restrictions on trade in textiles is likely to have opened up markets in Asia and the West.

● Consumer tastes and their responses have changed. Consumers in many countries are more willing to buy foreign products. Examples might include cars from Korea and Malaysia which are now purchased in Europe. It could also be argued that consumers around the world increasingly have similar tastes. Some food products are sold in many countries with little difference to their ingredients.

● The growth of emerging markets and competition. New markets have opened up in countries that have seen a growth in their national income. Examples might include countries in South East Asia and the more successful countries in eastern Europe. As businesses in these countries have become more successful, they have been able to compete in western economies.

Unilever is an Anglo-Dutch business formed in 1930. It is one of the world's largest producers of consumer goods and is known for its branded food and drinks, detergents and personal products. Such brands include Birds Eye Wall's, Surf, Vaseline, Mentadent, Magnum, Flora and Brooke Bond. Unilever employs around 265,000 people worldwide.

Unilever is one of the world's leading suppliers of fast moving consumer goods in foods, homecare and personal care products. The company operates with two global divisions - Foods and Home and Personal Care. This structure allows improved focus on foods and home and personal care activities at both the regional and global levels.

Unilever attempts to 'meet the needs of people everywhere.' It states that 'Every day, all around the world, 150 million people choose to make our brands part of their lives'. Its world famous brands include Lipton's teas, Findus frozen products, Magnum ice cream and Surf washing powder.

**Speaking the local language**
We think globally when it comes to strategy, product innovation and creative ideas. But when regional and local marketing teams put these plans and ideas into action, they have the freedom to tailor their approach for local consumers and create joint promotional opportunities with, for example, local retailers. Across the world, the brand message is consistent, while its execution has a uncompromisingly local flavour.

**Creating the world's best creative partnerships for growth**
We are working closer than ever before with our brand agencies. Acting as strategic partners, they are fully involved in developing our brands and their rewards are increasingly linked to the major contribution they make to brand growth.

Source: adapted from www.unilever.com.

(a) Using examples from the data, explain why Unilever might be described as a multinational company.
(b) Using examples from the data, explain how the business might interact with the countries in which it operates.
(c) Suggest reasons why the business may operate as a multinational organisation.

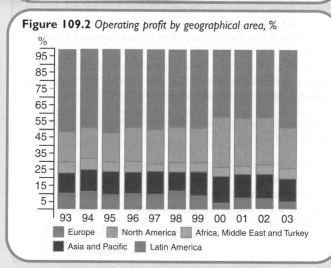

**Figure 109.1** *Turnover by geographical area, %*

Legend: Europe, North America, Africa, Middle East and Turkey, Asia and Pacific, Latin America

**Figure 109.2** *Operating profit by geographical area, %*

Legend: Europe, North America, Africa, Middle East and Turkey, Asia and Pacific, Latin America

**Figure 109.3** *Operating profit by product, %*

Legend: Foods, Home care, Personal care, Speciality chemicals, Other operations

**Question3**

in-time stock control and management methods such as quality control circles have been successfully used by Japanese firms in foreign countries. Such techniques have also been adopted by home based firms. These raise the standards of local firms who become aware of these new developments.

The process by which multinationals benefit countries in this respect is known as **technology transfer.**

Technology transfer can be especially important to developing countries, which may lack technical expertise and know-how. However, this is not always the case. Managers

and supervisors are often brought in from the multinationals' home country, with little training being given to locally recruited staff. As a consequence locals may be employed in low skilled jobs.

**Social responsibility** Multinationals have often been criticised, especially in their dealings with low income economies. The Union Carbide disaster in Bhopal, India, when hundreds were killed by the release of poisonous gases into the atmosphere, raised serious doubts about the safety measures used by multinationals in low income economies.

They have also been accused of marketing harmful products. One example was the aggressive selling of milk powder to mothers with new born babies when medical research indicated that breast feeding is far more likely to benefit infant health. In addition, environmentalists are concerned about the impact of multinationals on tropical rainforests and other natural resources. On the other hand, large multinationals are in a better position to finance projects that protect the environment from their activities. They also tend to offer better pay than local firms in developing economies.

**Government control** Because of the size and financial power of many multinationals, there are concerns about the ability of governments to control them. For example, they may be able to avoid paying corporation tax in particular countries.

Taxation can be avoided by the use of TRANSFER PRICING. This involves declaring higher profits in those countries with lower taxation levels, thus reducing the overall tax bill. A company may charge subsidiary branches in low taxation countries low prices for components bought in from overseas branches of the same firm. This means that costs in the low tax country are kept low and high profits can be declared. Similarly, subsidiary branches in high tax countries are charged high prices for components bought in from overseas branches. This means little or no profit is recorded.

## Globalisation - an alternative view

Few would dispute that globalisation is a reality in today's world. However, critics such as the Global Justice Movement and Globalise Resistance oppose the way in which globalisation is taking place and argue for a form of globalisation that is less damaging to society and the environment.

Opponents of the current form of globalisation argue that it is driven by the needs of the most powerful in the world, including rich nations and multinational businesses. They

believe that organisations such as the IMF and WTO work mainly to further the interests of powerful countries and businesses. They also suggest that it will lead to further concentrations of power and wealth with multinational businesses that will make ever larger profits. This process will be at the cost of increased environmental damage and greater inequalities of income. The effects in the short term will be seen most clearly in poorer, developing nations. They point to statistics such as:

- 2.8 billion of the world's 6 billion people live on less than £1.40 per day;
- the gap between the richest 20 per cent and the poorest 20 per cent of the world's population has doubled since the 1960s;
- the assets of the world's top three wealthiest people exceeded the total GNP of the 48 poorest countries in the world (with a combined population of 600 million).

## key terms

**Globalisation** - the integration of the world's economy.
**Hypercompetition** - the disruption of existing markets by flexible, fast moving businesses.
**Multinational** - a company which owns or controls production or service facilities outside the country in which it is based.
**Transfer pricing** - a system operated by multinationals. It is an attempt to avoid relatively high tax rates through the prices which one subsidiary charges another for components and finished products.

## Knowledge

1. What is meant by a global market?
2. State 3 important aspects of globalisation.
3. Suggest 5 factors which have contributed to the growth of globalisation.
4. How might globalisation affect the location of a business?
5. Why might globalisation increase competition for businesses?
6. For what reasons do firms become multinationals?
7. What are the potential benefits of multinationals?
8. What problems might be created by multinationals?

## What are business ethics?

Ethics are a set of values and beliefs which influence how individuals, groups and society behave. BUSINESS ETHICS are concerned with how such values and beliefs operate in business. They help firms to decide what actions are right or wrong in certain circumstances. Ethics might influence the following business decisions.

- Should products which might damage the health of consumers be withdrawn from the market?
- What efforts, if any, should be made to ensure that business activities do not damage the environment?
- Should money be spent on wheelchair access to workplaces and retail outlets?
- Should a firm reject a bribe given to secure an overseas contract?
- Should part time staff be offered the same employment rights as full time staff?
- Should a workplace creche be provided for working mothers?
- Should a contribution be made to a local charity?

A business that says 'yes' to some or all of these questions might be described as ethical. A firm which is ethical with regard to society as a whole and the community within which it is based might also be described as 'socially responsible'. **Corporate responsibility** (☞ unit 111) is the term used to describe attempts by individual businesses to behave in an ethical manner.

Different individuals and groups have different viewpoints. It is these which can determine what they see as ethical business behaviour. For example, a firm polluting a river might only be able to take action against further pollution through savings made by job losses. What is ethical behaviour in this case - preventing the pollution or saving jobs?

To some extent the law attempts to ensure that businesses act ethically. However, obeying the 'letter' of the law does not necessarily mean that a firm is behaving in an ethical way. For example, some would regard water companies which pump untreated sewerage into the sea as unethical, even if the activity is legal. This is due to the possible pollution and health problems associated with such an activity.

There have been a number of businesses that could be described as acting unethically in the past. Examples which some believe fall into this category include BA for the 'dirty tricks' which it allegedly used against its competitor Virgin Airlines and Exxon for the safety standards on its oil tanker Exxon Valdez which sank in Alaskan waters. Other examples may include the large salary increases given to the chief executives of privatised companies, insider share dealing in the City of London, the trade of some businesses with countries that have oppressive regimes, or the trade in arms. Individuals within businesses also act 'unethically'. A well

publicised example is the behaviour of Robert Maxwell, former owner of Maxwell Communications

## YOU GET EXCELLENT COFFEE. YOU DON'T GET COCAINE.

The coffee growers of Latin America face a problem. Either they get paid a fair price for their coffee, or they face bankruptcy and may have to turn their land over to the illegal production of the coca plant for cocaine.

Cafédirect helps avoid this problem, because more of the money you pay for Cafédirect roast and ground coffee goes directly to the growers.

The result? They continue to produce high quality Arabica coffee for Cafédirect.

## Cafédirect. Fair trade. Excellent coffee.

(a) Would you describe the above as ethical behaviour? Explain your answer.
(b) Why might the (i) owners and (ii) customers of Cafédirect be concerned about Latin American coffee workers?

## Question 1

Corporation. After his death, it was found that he had been supporting his business empire with money 'borrowed' from his employees' pension fund.

The ethical behaviour of businesses is, to some extent, controlled by laws and regulation. Increasingly, however, businesses and industries are placing greater emphasis on developing their own codes of conduct and practice. For example, the Chemical Industries Association has a Responsible Care programme which includes the requirement that individual chemical businesses must be open about giving relevant information to interested parties. They must also work closely with local communities in achieving required levels of performance. A number of businesses, including PepsiCo, Apple and Kodak, have stopped selling their products in Burma, a country with a record of human rights abuse.

# The benefits of ethical behaviour

There are certain advantages for businesses in behaving in an ethical or socially responsible way.

**Consumers' views** Increasing numbers of consumers are taking into account a firm's 'behaviour' when buying products. As a result, ethical behaviour can be good for sales. Body Shop is a good example of this. A feature of the Body Shop's marketing is that its products are not tested on animals. The company has also lent support to groups helping firms in the world's poorest countries. This stance has perhaps helped the Body Shop become a successful business. There is a number of other firms which have responded in a similar way. The Co-operative Bank, for example, has conducted a wide ranging campaign. It refuses to invest money in or finance a variety of concerns. These range from countries with poor human rights records to companies using exploitative factory farming methods. This policy was introduced as a result of a survey carried out amongst the bank's customers, which found that they regarded a clear ethical policy as important for the bank.

**Improvements in the recruitment and retention of staff**
Firms with an ethical approach believe that they will be more able to recruit well qualified and motivated staff. In addition,

---

Clerical Medical uses its Evergreen Investment Trust to invest in 'ethical' businesses. It uses the following guidelines to help make investment decisions.

### Industry exposure

Investments considered appropriate will typically have interests in one or more of the following areas:

| | |
|---|---|
| Air quality/emissions control | Pollution analysis |
| Drinking water purification | Recycling |
| Energy conservation | Site remediation |
| Environmental assessment | Waste reduction/disposal |
| Geothermal energy | Wastewater treatment |
| Natural gas | Wind power |

### Share Selection Criteria
The fund manager will seek to avoid companies which are involved in:
1  The production, sale or distribution of fur products.
2  The production, sale or distribution of cosmetics where animal testing may be involved.

3  The manufacture of ozone depleting chemicals (CFCs and halons).
4  The manufacture or distribution of harmful pesticides.
5  The supply of tropical hardwood.
6  The production, processing or sale of meat products.
Other types of company, which would normally be ineligible for an ethical portfolio, will also be avoided as they are inconsistent with Evergreen's objectives. These are companies which are involved in:
7  The manufacture or provision of armaments.
8  Companies involved in repressive regimes to a total extent of no more than 10% of group turnover. Fot this purpose "repressive regimes" are those listed by the Ethical Investment Research Service (EIRIS).
9  The provision of gambling services.
10 The production of tobacco products.
11 The production or distribution of pornography.

Source: Clerical Medical, Evergreen Trust Investment information.

---

Anita Roddick the founder of the Body Shop believes that 'it is a basic responsibility of business to be open and honest about its environmental and social impacts'. Alongside Greenpeace, the Body Shop has backed a global campaign encouraging organisations to use clean, renewable energy and so fight global warming. Employees of the Body Shop are encouraged to participate in campaigns designed to have a positive impact upon communities. Nicky Amos, the company's head of corporate responsibility says 'The Body Shop's integrity is based on what we do, rather than what we say. We ask ourselves what we can do that's different, and we will demonstrate our campaigns to our employees and customers. Employees must have the opportunity to get directly involved in a campaign. We provide a half day each month for people to participate in a project of their choice.'

Source: adapted from *People Management*, 10.7.2003.

(a) Why might these companies be said to be acting in an ethical manner?
(b) Using information above discuss the benefits to these businesses of an ethical stance.

ethical firms argue that they are able to retain their staff better if they adopt a more caring approach to employees. Polaroid in the US, for example, has subsidised child-care expenses for their lower paid workers. Marks and Spencer provide their staff with a range of benefits, over and above those usually provided in the retail sector. They have benefited by achieving one of the lowest rates of staff turnover in the UK. This has cut their recruitment and retraining costs.

**Improvements in employee motivation** Firms which behave in an ethical manner believe that their employees are more committed to their success as a result. They may be prepared to work harder to allow the business to achieve its aims.

## Effects of ethical behaviour

What effect will acting in an ethical way have on a business?

**Increasing costs** Ethical behaviour can result in an increase in costs for a firm. An ethical firm may, for example, be forced to turn down cheaper supplies from a firm which tests its products on animals. Similarly, costs may be raised by pollution reducing filters put on coal-fired power stations.

**Loss of profit** Firms may be forced to turn down profitable business due to their ethical stance. A business, for example, may reject a profitable investment opportunity in a company which produces animal fur, as this is against its ethical policy. However, the ethical firm would hope that the gains it makes from its policy, by attracting increased numbers of customers, would outweigh these costs.

**Conflict** When a firm's overall profitability comes into conflict with its ethical policy, problems may result. In such cases the shareholders of a firm may object to the ethical policy as the return on their investment is harmed.

**Business practice** A firm seeking to act more ethically may need to alter the way in which it approaches a huge range of business matters. Such a firm might, for example, need to consider the impact of its activities on the environment (☞ unit 112), whether or not its recruitment policy was providing equal opportunities for all applicants regardless of age, sex, ethnic background or disability (☞ unit 68), the extent to which its advertisements are offensive or in poor taste, and the protection given to consumers buying their products (☞ unit 69).

**Relations with suppliers** Some suppliers will only supply products to businesses that meet ethical criteria. This might include agreeing not to trade with certain countries or businesses that deal in arms, that exploit workers or that abuse human rights.

## Should businesses be expected to act ethically?

There is considerable debate about how businesses should

Mobile phone firm O$_2$ is taking measures to ensure that all the mobile phone manufacturers it deals with are complying with its own social and corporate responsibility polices. O$_2$ does not make phones itself. But it does provide the network on which they operate and it sells their handsets through its retail outlets. David Varney, the company's chairman, said the move was designed to protect the reputation of the company. Varney argued that there is 'a new risk for corporations - which is a risk to reputations'. He was particularly concerned about the damage to reputation caused by manufacturers which use illegally mined quantities of a substance called 'coltan' which is present in nearly all mobile phones. As the prices of coltan increased, some manufacturers had taken to using illegally mined coltan from the Democratic Republic of Congo. As a result, the habitat of endangered gorillas was being destroyed.

Varney warned that ordering manufacturers to produce 'coltan free' phones could be 'seriously compromising' to the business, but it was in discussions with manufacturers about how to address the problem.

Source: adapted from *People Management*, 15.5.2003.

(a) Explain why O$_2$ might be said to be acting ethically in this situation.
(b) Discuss the likely effects of the actions of the business on:
  (i)  the business itself;
  (ii)  its suppliers;
  (iii) its competitors.

**Question 3**

actually behave.

Some argue that businesses have a responsibility to act ethically. Those who hold this view stress the fact that firms do not operate in isolation. They are a part of society and have an impact upon the lives of those communities in which they operate. As such they should act in a responsible manner and consider the possible effects of any decisions they make. This means that profit making should not be the only criterion used when making decisions. Other factors which firms might consider include the effect of their decisions upon the environment, jobs, the local community, consumers, competitors, suppliers and employees.

Others argue that businesses should not be expected to act ethically. There are two main views in support of this argument. The first is from supporters of free market economics (☞ unit 9). They argue that the primary responsibility of businesses is to produce goods and services in the most efficient way, and make profit for shareholders. Firms should attempt to do this in any way they can,

providing it is legal. Only by doing this will the general good of everyone be served. If firms are expected to act 'ethically', then consumers may suffer because the ethical behaviour could lead to inefficiency, higher costs and higher prices.

A second argument is that in most cases it is naive to expect businesses to act ethically. Whenever there is a conflict between acting ethically and making greater profits, the vast majority of firms will choose the latter. Those firms which do act in an ethical manner only do so because it is profitable. This view is often held by those who favour government intervention to regulate business. They argue that it is necessary for the government to force firms to behave responsibly through a variety of laws which it must enforce.

## Are businesses becoming more ethical?

It could be argued that businesses are increasingly taking a more 'caring' attitude. The growth of companies producing health care products which are not animal tested, the use of recyclable carrier bags and the sale of organically grown vegetables by many retailers could all be an indication of this. Some pension funds and a number of investment schemes are now termed 'green'. They will only invest savers' money in companies which promote the environment.

Others argue that ethical attitudes have failed to penetrate the boardrooms of the UK and that firms continue to act unethically in a variety of ways. An extensive survey undertaken by the University of Westminster found that junior executives and women took the moral 'high ground', with more concern about green issues, staff relations and trade with countries that had records of abusing human rights. This was in contrast to the greed driven motives of company directors, the majority of whom were old and male. One respondent summed up the climate. 'In general, business ethics does not come very high in the scale of human behaviour. Professional standards and levels of caring sometimes leave a lot to be desired.'

One explanation for the findings of the survey is that business culture (☞ unit 15) continues to be driven by short term profit. This suggests that the stakeholders such as shareholders and directors hold most influence in setting the objectives of the business. These groups tend to be most interested in the profit of the business.

---

Mr Richard Branson and his Virgin Atlantic airline won near record libel damages of £610,000 at the end of a two year 'dirty tricks' legal battle against British Airways. In charging BA with going 'beyond the limits of commercially acceptable practice', Mr Branson listed details of its rival's campaign to discredit Virgin. These included:

- the illegal use of Virgin Atlantic's computer information;
- the poaching of Virgin passengers by bogus Virgin representatives;
- the shredding of documents relating to Virgin activities;
- the spreading of hostile and discreditable stories to destabilise Virgin.

BA, which also had to meet several million pounds in legal costs, apologised 'unreservedly' to Mr Branson in court for alleging that Virgin Atlantic, in claiming BA was conducting a 'dirty tricks' campaign, was only seeking publicity.

Sir Colin Marshall, BA's chief executive and deputy chairman, said his airline was taking steps to ensure 'regrettable incidents' undertaken by BA employees did not occur again.

In a special message to BA staff intended to bolster morale, Sir Colin said the 'overwhelming majority' of the airline's workforce had no involvement whatsoever in the campaign against Virgin. He urged them not to be distracted by the publicity surrounding the affair.

Mr Branson also demanded BA directors give a full explanation of a separate covert activity targeted at Virgin which, he alleged, was carried out by private investigators.

Source: adapted from *The Financial Times.*

(a) What elements of BA's behaviour could be termed
   (i) illegal;
   (ii) unethical?
(b) Which view about the behaviour of the firms might BA's actions lend support to? Explain your answer.

**Question 4**

**Business ethics** - the influence of values and beliefs upon the conduct and operation of businesses.

---

**Knowledge**

1. Give 5 examples which might indicate a business is behaving ethically.
2. Give 5 examples which might indicate a business is behaving unethically.
3. Why might firms draw up a code of ethics?
4. Briefly explain 5 effects that ethical behaviour may have on businesses.
5. 'Businesses should not be expected to act ethically.' Explain the 2 sides to this argument.

continues, however. Some pressure groups, frustrated in their attempts to change corporate behaviour, have called for greater democracy in the corporate decision making process. This would involve stakeholders being involved as a matter of routine in decisions that have a direct effect upon them.

## Barriers to corporate responsibility

There is a number of incentives for businesses to behave in a responsible manner. They might attract more customers as a result of their stance or avoid penalties from legislation. However, there are certain reasons why businesses may fail to act in a responsible manner.

**Costs and profit** Responsible behaviour can raise the costs of businesses. Some businesses may consider that the costs of accepting corporate responsibility are too great. For example, a business which uses the cheapest overseas contractors, regardless of how it treated its workforce, may find that it is able to achieve lower production costs. This could enable the business to price its product more competitively than rival products and possibly make higher profits. Similarly, a local garage may find it cheaper to dispose of engine oil in a local stream than to pay for it to be disposed of in an environmentally friendly manner.

**Values and beliefs** The values and beliefs of the senior managers and employees of a business may not correspond with what the majority of others in a society regard as responsible. For example, a public house or bar which continued to serve alcoholic drinks to a drunken customer may be regarded as irresponsible. However, the manager or employee of the business may regard this as the concern of the customer and a matter in which he should not become involved. This view may lead him to continue serving alcoholic drinks to the customer. In this case the business is not accepting the responsibility of possible problems that the customer may have, nor the potential danger to others as a result.

**Information available to consumers, governments and pressure groups** In the absence of useful information about the behaviour of a business it is difficult for interested parties to monitor its activities. For example, the nuclear industry has been accused by pressure groups of being secretive about its activities. Nuclear industry representatives have argued that this is due to defence and national security reasons. However, this secrecy has made it difficult for consumers and pressure groups to make judgments about its behaviour. For other businesses it is the complexity and scope of their activities that makes it difficult to evaluate their actions. Multinationals, in particular, because of their global activities, can be very difficult to monitor. Other businesses are involved in such technically complex work that it can be difficult for consumers, governments and pressure groups to understand

issues relevant to their behaviour. Businesses involved in genetic modification may fall into this category.

## Implications of taking corporate responsibility

To some extent a business which takes greater corporate responsibility will face similar challenges to those which follow a more ethical approach (☞ unit 110). A business accepting greater corporate responsibility might have to change some of the following to take into account the effects of its actions.

● The aims and objectives of the business.
● Operating methods, which might lead to increasing costs.
● The relationship with employees. This might involve changing work practices.
● The relationship with other stakeholders, including suppliers and people in the local community.
● Changing the organisation of the business.
● Taking into account the needs of consumers when making marketing decisions.
● Providing help to bodies and organisations outside the business.

---

American Apparel is a Los Angeles based business that specialises in the manufacture of T-shirts. It is the largest company in the business in the US. American Apparel operates in an industry renowned for 'sweatshops'. These are manufacturing units where business methods in some countries include, the use of child labour, enforced prison labour, starvation wages and 16 hour working days. The President of American Apparel has always adopted an anti-sweatshop mentality. His workers receive much higher than average wages, English classes and health insurance.

Source: adapted from *Metro*, 9.10.2003.

*Levi Strauss & Co. Global Sourcing and Operating Guidelines*

'Our Global Sourcing and Operating Guidelines help us to select business partners who follow workplace standards and business practices that are consistent with our company's values. These requirements are applied to every contractor who manufactures or finishes products for Levi Strauss & Co. Trained inspectors closely audit and monitor compliance among approximately 600 cutting, sewing, and finishing contractors in more than 60 countries.'

Source: www.itglwf.org/doc/Levis.doc.

(a) Suggest why there might not be barriers to corporate responsibility in these businesses.
(b) Explain how taking a greater corporate responsibility has affected these businesses.

# Social auditing

A business that produces its final accounts must have them **audited** by law. An audit is a check to make sure the financial performance of the business is accurately shown in its accounts.

Social auditing (☞ unit 37) is the process by which a business organisation attempts to assess the impact of the entire range of its activities on stakeholders. It might try to produce a set of 'social accounts' to evaluate its performance against a set of non-financial criteria. This might include its effect on the environment and its attempts to meet social obligations to employees. Social auditing may involve:

- identifying the social objectives and ethical values of the organisation;
- defining the stakeholders of the business;
- establishing social performance indicators;
- measuring performance, keeping records and preparing social accounts;
- submitting the accounts to an independent audit and publishing the results.

The social audit might include details such as:

- the salary difference between the highest and lowest paid employee;
- health and safety information;
- the extent to which employees feel valued;
- the views of consumers about whether the business is living up to its ideals.

# The benefits of social auditing

Increasingly businesses are carrying out their own social audit. Some publish the results in their Annual Report and Accounts. Businesses as wide ranging as The Co-operative Bank, Ben & Jerry's, the US ice cream manufacturer, and St Lukes, the ethical advertising agency, have carried out social audits. Why might they be seen as useful?

- They provide valuable information to pressure groups and consumers about the corporate responsibility of a business. Consumers can take account of this information, often issued through press reports, when making purchasing decisions. Pressure groups can use them as the basis for further enquiries.
- They allow the managers of a business to gain a complete picture of the impact of the business's activities. Especially in large businesses, managers may be unaware of some practices which they would regard as undesirable. This can allow the business to make better informed decisions about the impact of its activities upon stakeholders.
- A business can use a social audit as a means of preventing future criticism of its activities. By opening up its activities to scrutiny a business can deflect suspicions which some stakeholders may have about less than responsible behaviour. The use of an independent social audit is especially valuable. There can be a lack of credibility associated with social audits which are generated from within the business itself. It is also important that a business commits itself to full publication of an independent social audit. Edited versions are unlikely to persuade more critical stakeholders.

- A business will be able to identify the extent to which it is meeting some of its non-financial objectives. For example, a social audit may indicate a growing agreement with the corporate culture of the business (☞ unit 15).
- Shareholders can use social audits to raise questions about a business's activities at annual shareholder meetings.
- Governments can use social audits of a range of businesses in a particular industry as one means of assessing the need for legislation or regulation of businesses in the industry.

As businesses are subjected to increasing levels of scrutiny and as consumers and pressure groups have access to more information about business behaviour, it is likely that an increasing number of businesses will use social audits.

# Corporate responsibility - an alternative view

Many businesses, especially larger multinational businesses, claim to be enthusiastic supporters of corporate responsibility. They publicise these claims, producing glossy brochures which refer to their good work in a range of areas. They produce **social** and **environmental** audits, detailing how their spending is benefiting society or improving the environment.

However, critics have suggested this is merely 'window dressing', offering a positive, but perhaps misleading picture of the overall business position. In practice, corporate responsibility may apply mainly to superficial and less important aspects of business activity. A corporate accountability specialist at Friends of the Earth argues that 'Glossy corporate social responsibility reports are filled with references to commitments, dialogue, transparency, partnerships and stakeholders. The company is there to do good, they suggest, and a smiling ethnic face on the front cover completes the picture. But read these reports and you realise their focus is nearly always on the superficial aspects of business; lots of detail on trees planted and light bulbs changed, but rarely anything about the social and environmental impacts of the core business of the company.'

It could be argued, therefore, that in some cases social audits and a stress on corporate responsibility may simply be used to deflect attention away from other aspects of business, such as unethical activities or business practices which harm the environment.

A further problem with social audits is that the businesses themselves select what to include and measure. This means that there is no standard or regulated method of assessing the impact of their activities. For example, what if a business shows that it has reduced pollution greatly in an audit, but continues to use a supplier which pays very low wages which is not disclosed? To what extent is it acting in a socially responsible way?

The Cooperative Bank is famed for its ethical stance. It uses a number of criteria against which to assess its performance. For example in 2001 it set a number of SMART indicators. It reported that 'Of the 65 targets set last year, the bank has fully achieved 43, made acceptable progress against 15 and has not yet achieved 7. Broadly speaking, the bank is satisfied with these latest results; particularly considering how far it has progressed since 1997. But, of course, there is always room for improvement, which is why in this section there are also details of the 62 new targets set for 2002.'

Examples of its performance against indictors included the following.

'Maintain the continued growth in profits and the reductions in the cost/income ratio as envisaged in the bank's Strategic Plan 2001-2003, whilst at the same time adhering to the culture and the principles of 'co-operation.' **TARGET ACHIEVED**

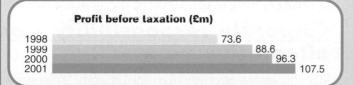

**Profit before taxation (£m)**

| | |
|---|---|
| 1998 | 73.6 |
| 1999 | 88.6 |
| 2000 | 96.3 |
| 2001 | 107.5 |

'Encourage and increase the level of support given to ethnic minority and disability groups as part of the community involvement policy.' **TARGET ACHIEVED**

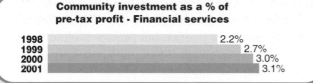

**Community investment as a % of pre-tax profit - Financial services**

| | |
|---|---|
| 1998 | 2.2% |
| 1999 | 2.7% |
| 2000 | 3.0% |
| 2001 | 3.1% |

**Water consumption at bank metered sites (cubic metres)**

| | Major occupancies | Network | Total |
|---|---|---|---|
| 1999 | 43,421 | 20,261 | 63,682 |
| 2000 | 40,082 | 17,341 | 57,423 |
| 2001 | 37,721 | 14,449 | 52,170 |

■ Major occupancies ■ Network

'In line with Building Research Establishment best practice, undertake to reduce water consumption across all major occupancies to 9m³ per employee by 2005.' **ACCEPTABLE PROGRESS**

Source: adapted from www.co-operativebank.co.uk.

(a) Using examples from the data and other suggestions, explain what might be included in (i) an audit, (ii) a social audit, (iii) an environmental audit.
(b) Explain how producing a social audit might be useful to the Cooperative Bank in future.
(c) Discuss to what extent the Cooperative Bank might be operating in a socially responsible way.

**Question 3**

## key terms

**Corporate responsibility** - the willingness of a business to accept responsibility for its actions and their impact on a range of stakeholders.

## Knowledge...Knowledge...Knowle

1. Give an example of a business acting with corporate responsibility.
2. State 4 ways in which corporate responsibility may be encouraged.
3. Why might legislation to control companies be a problem?
4. State 3 possible barriers to corporate responsibility.
5. What might be involved in social auditing for a business?
6. What details might be included in a social audit?
7. How might a business benefit from a social audit?
8. How might other stakeholders benefit from a social audit?

# Case study *Centrica*

Do socially responsible companies win the war for talent? Certainly many of the businesses which stress corporate social responsibility (CSR) argued that they do. But firms often do little to measure the effect of their activities on their ability to recruit, retain and motivate employees.

It has been suggested that CSR is often an intuitive approach and could become 'an expensive exercise in compliance that has minimal impact' unless businesses are careful. One business that has risen to the challenge, however, is Centrica. Over three years it has participated in a research project which scrutinises how corporate community involvement and wider corporate citizenship can contribute to business success by enhancing employee morale, motivation, commitment and performance.

Centrica's Cardiff call centre has been involved with Business in the Community's 'Cares' volunteering project for three years. Employees have devoted a total of around 1,000 hours to helping a range of local charities and causes, including the Cystic Fibrosis Trust and Ty Hafan Children's Hospice. In one project, volunteers cleared 7.5 million tonnes of rubbish in an attempt to encourage the return of freshwater wildlife. In another, managers acted as consultants to local businesses in areas such as web design.

Improvements in employee retention, absenteeism levels, positive customer relations and job satisfaction were all found as a result of the 'Cares' project. The retention rate for employees participating in the project was 99.6 per cent, 19.6 per cent over target. Six employees were also chosen for an initiative to develop team leaders to achieve promotion. The project developed their skills, making them candidates for promotion in the company.

But has the programme proved cost effective? Certainly at Centrica. Previously the company had spent on team building exercises. Now these were replaced with 'Cares' at a fraction of the cost. Employee satisfaction ratings increased in four areas - customer focus went up four points, performance and development improved by one point, management impact increased by three and satisfaction about working life rose two.

Anne Minto, Centrica's group HR director says 'We look at corporate responsibility as a core part of our overall strategy. We can't expect to thrive as a business unless we involve ourselves in the communities we operate in and respond to the needs of people within them'.

Centrica is by no means the only business to take corporate responsibility seriously. Marks & Spencer recently developed its CSR activities to create employability amongst disadvantaged groups. The 'Ready to Work' programme offered 600 work experience placements to people affected by homelessness. Employees in the business acted as 'mentors' or buddies to help and give advice. The company had already piloted schemes for people with learning and physical difficulties. The company says 'Our focus on employability has delivered real, measurable benefits to the people who have taken part in our work placements - many of whom now have jobs with us or with other employers'. It also argues 'Our workers have benefited too. Those that had responsibility as a buddy have fed back to us that their personal and management skills have developed as a result'.

Source: adapted from *People Management*, 18.12.2003.

(a) **What may have influenced corporate responsibility at Centrica? (6 marks)**

(b) **Using examples, explain why the businesses in the article might be said to be acting in a socially responsible manner. (10 marks)**

(c) **Explain how Centrica might make use of the information in the article to produce a social audit. (10 marks)**

(d) **Assess the impact which corporate responsibility at the businesses in the article might have had on;**
   **(i)  the businesses themselves;**
   **(ii) the employees in the businesses;**
   **(iii) other stakeholders. (12 marks)**

(e) **Discuss to what extent corporate responsibility might be 'an expensive exercise in compliance that has minimal impact' at Centrica. (12 marks)**

## The costs and benefits of business activity

When businesses produce and sell products or services it is relatively easy for them to see the costs involved and the benefits they will gain. These costs are known as PRIVATE COSTS. They might include such things as the wages paid to employees, the cost of an advertising campaign or the purchase of raw materials. The PRIVATE BENEFITS to the business and its owners include the total revenue earned from sales, any resulting profit and the dividends paid to shareholders.

A business may find, however, that it creates other costs. Take a factory producing cement which is located in a small 'scenic' town. The firm may dispose of some of its waste in a local river or discharge dust into the atmosphere. Lorries making deliveries to the factory may disturb the local residents. The factory may be sited close to a local beauty spot, ruining the view. These are all examples of spillover effects or EXTERNALITIES. So the costs to the whole of society, the SOCIAL COSTS, are made up of the private costs of the business plus **negative externalities** (the costs to the rest of society). Social and environmental audits (☞ unit 111) take into account the social costs of business activity.

There may also be **positive externalities** which result from the business. It may create other jobs in the area for companies producing components or design a factory that complements the landscape. The firm may create skills which can be used for other jobs in the area. We can say that SOCIAL BENEFITS to

society are the private benefits to business plus positive externalities (the benefits to the rest of society).

There are obvious problems that result from negative externalities. Many externalities affect the environment. Furthermore, when firms set their prices these usually only reflect the private costs of production. Prices will not, therefore, reflect the cost of pollution, noise etc. As a result of this firms may not be concerned about negative externalities as they do not have to pay for them. For example, a chemical company may produce toxic waste from its production process. It might be faced with two choices - disposing of this waste in a nearby river without treating it, or treating it and removing any toxins. The first measure would cost next to nothing, but the second measure could be relatively expensive. The rational choice for the firm, assuming this is legal, is to dispose of the waste untreated in the river. However, for other users of the river, such as anglers and water sports enthusiasts, this decision would have serious effects.

In order to assess the impact of business activity, cost - benefit analysis is sometimes used, particularly for large projects (☞ unit 91).

## Environmental costs

There are many different types of negative externality that may result from business activity. Some are dealt with in other units, eg consumer exploitation (☞ unit 103) and employee exploitation (☞ units 68 and 69). This section will focus on environmental costs.

**Air pollution** This is pollution from factories, machines or vehicles emitting poisonous gases into the atmosphere. We need only look into the sky above some factories to see evidence of this. Other forms of air pollution may be catastrophes such as at the Chernobyl nuclear plant in 1986, when massive quantities of radioactive materials were released into the atmosphere and surrounding countryside. The results were seen in many countries in Europe.

What are the main causes of air pollution?
- Acid rain. Thousands of acres of forests have been destroyed by acid rain, as a result of sulphur dioxide emissions into the atmosphere.
- Chlorofluorocarbons (CFCs). The use by some firms of CFCs in aerosols and refrigerators has contributed to the breakdown of the earth's ozone layer. The ozone layer acts as a filter for the sun's rays. Without it, exposure to sunlight can increase the risk of skin cancer.
- Carbon dioxide ($CO_2$) and other gases. There has been a growing awareness that the release of $CO_2$, and other gases such as methane and nitrous oxide, into the atmosphere is causing a 'greenhouse effect'. The build-up of these gases is associated with the rise in the use of cars and with the generation of electricity with fossil fuels such as coal.

In 1991 Shell, the owner of the Brent Spar oil platform, was looking for ways to dispose of the structure. With the approval of the UK government, it decided to sink it in a deep part of the Atlantic. Sinking it in its place of operation in the North Sea would have caused a hazard to shipping and would have caused further environmental damage to an already polluted area. In 1995 the platform was towed to the Atlantic for sinking. Pressure from groups such as Greenpeace led to Shell abandoning the plan to dump the platform. In 1998 Shell decided to dismantle the platform and use the parts to construct a ferry quay in Norway. Shell had already spent £20 million preparing the platform for sinking. It would cost £26 million for the recycling of the structure.

Using examples from the article, outline the possible:
(a) private costs;
(b) negative externalities;
(c) positive externalities;
of the proposed methods of disposal of the Brent Spar oil platform.

## Question 1

Scientists argue that the 'greenhouse effect' could result in the earth's atmosphere warming up (**global warming**) to such an extent that the polar ice caps melt. This could lead to significant areas of land being submerged by rising sea levels. The 'greenhouse effect', many scientists believe, has also been responsible for the climatic extremes experienced in parts of the world.

Figure 112.1 shows the emissions of air pollutants in the UK. It suggests that concern over their effect on the environment has led to an effort to cut emissions.

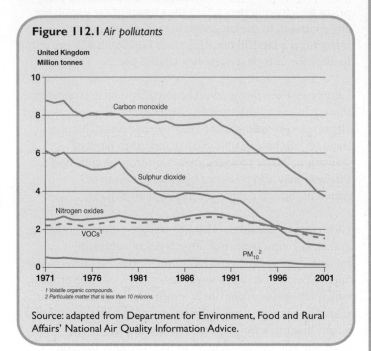

**Figure 112.1** *Air pollutants*

United Kingdom
Million tonnes

1 Volatile organic compounds.
2 Particulate matter that is less than 10 microns.

Source: adapted from Department for Environment, Food and Rural Affairs' National Air Quality Information Advice.

**Water pollution** Water pollution can occur in a number of ways. Many industries, such as brewing and chemical manufacturing, use water in production. Their plants are usually located by rivers and it is fairly easy, therefore, for them to dispose of waste into nearby water. It is also possible for our drinking water from reservoirs to be polluted by chemicals used in agricultural production. People are starting to drink bottled water or have water filters fitted to their water supply in the home as a result.

The sea has also been polluted over many years. Industries sited near to the coast have used the sea as a dump for their waste. The effluence and cargo of ships are also sometimes dropped into the sea. The North Sea, for example, is one of the most polluted seas in the world as a result of years of discharges from a variety of industries. These have included sewage and the by-products of chemical production. A number of beaches in the UK are unsafe for bathing, according to the European Union, which grades the quality of beaches. Table 112.1 shows that there has been some success in reducing water pollution in England in recent years.

**Congestion and noise** Business activity has resulted in more roads becoming congested with traffic. For example, many firms now transport their goods by rail rather than road. Recent estimates have put the cost of this congestion on British roads as high as £15 billion.

Some business activity can also result in noise pollution. For example, a decision by an airport to open a new runway would affect noise levels experienced by local residents.

**Destruction of the environment** One example of this is logging and associated industries, which have been responsible for the destruction of sections of the Amazonian rainforests. Another example might include the effects of new buildings in a rural area. A new housing estate in a village, for example, may deprive villagers and visitors of previously unspoilt countryside. It may also increase noise and congestion levels in the village.

**Table 112.1** *Water pollution indicators, England*

|  | 1990 | 1995 | 2000 | 2002 |
|---|---|---|---|---|
| **Chemical quality of rivers and canals (percentage of total river length)** | | | | |
| Good | 43 | 55 | 64 | 65 |
| Fair | 40 | 35 | 29 | 28 |

|  | 1998 | 2000 | 2002 |
|---|---|---|---|
| **Compliance with EU bathing water standards (percentages)** | | | |
|  | 90 | 95 | 99 |

Source: adapted from Department for Environment, Food and Rural Affairs and Environment Agency.

In 1989 the oil tanker, the Exxon Valdez, crashed onto a reef in Prince William Sound in Southern Alaska, USA. The accident covered one of the world's cleanest and most beautiful stretches of coastline with 11 million gallons of crude oil. Exxon spent an initial $2 billion on the clean up and also paid $300 million in compensation to 11,000 individuals. Additionally, following legal action, $5 billion in damages was awarded by a court to the local fishing communities in 1994.

There is disagreement about the longer term effects of the Exxon Valdez disaster. An Exxon company statement said 'the environment in Prince William Sound is healthy, robust and thriving.' Environmentalists, however, point to respiratory illnesses, brain tumours and cancers amongst the local population linked to the oil spills and the clean up. They also point to the pollution remaining on the coast and the failure of fish stocks, including herrings, to return to the area.

Source: adapted from *The Independent*, 25.3.2004.

(a) Describe the costs associated with the Exxon Valdez crash.

**Question 2**

**Waste disposal** Many business operations result in waste products (☞ unit 86). This may be in the form of waste chemicals resulting from the manufacture of plastics or waste materials from the manufacture of wooden products. The packaging used in products can also be waste and needs to be disposed of.

It has been suggested that some water operators in the UK impose external costs. If a company does not maintain its pipes and leaks occur, this can result in hosepipe bans. It also means that it has to take more water from reservoirs and rivers because of the waste water it has created by leakages.

The impact on the environment of business is not always negative. In derelict urban areas, for example, businesses have converted rundown buildings into office space and have landscaped waste land around the site. Also, some of the buildings may be thought to have architectural merit.

# Controlling environmental costs

Because of concern about the impact of business on the environment, attention has been focused on how pollution, congestion and other environmental costs can be controlled. There is a number of ways this can be done.

**Government regulation** Various pieces of legislation exist in the UK and Europe to prevent the pollution of the environment by business activity. For example, in the UK **The Environment Act, 1995** set up the Environment Agency to the monitor and control pollution. It also set up regulations concerning contaminated land, abandoned mines, national parks, air quality and waste. EU directives often become regulations in the UK. For example, the **Air Quality Limit Values Regulations, 2003** sets targets for reductions in levels of ozone in the air by 2010.

Some countries have government bodies designed to control pollution. For example, in the US the Environment Protection Agency attempts to ensure US businesses do not contravene legislation. There are also agreements between countries to control pollution. The Kyoto Protocol agreed to limit greenhouse gas emissions between 2008 and 2012 to 5.2 per cent of their 1990 levels. In certain cases voluntary agreements between governments and manufacturers also take place.

**Taxation** The aim of taxation in this context is to ensure that the social cost of any pollution caused by a firm is paid for. This means that the government must estimate the actual cost to society of different types of pollution. As a result prices would more accurately reflect the true cost of using environmental resources. So, for example, a firm which produced a £5 product with 'environmentally unfriendly' packaging might be taxed 50p for this packaging, raising the price to £5.50. There are two advantages to this. First, the tax revenue might be used to minimise the impact of this packaging on the environment. Second, it might act as an incentive for the firm to produce more environmentally sensitive packaging, so that the tax is either reduced or removed.

In this example the consumer pays for the environmentally unfriendly packaging in the form of a price rise. Some would argue that the firm itself should pay for such costs. In this way, the price would remain at £5.00, but the firm would be taxed 50 pence for externalities created by its packaging. The consumer would not directly suffer as a result of the taxation.

Increases in fuel prices in the UK have been justified by governments on the grounds that consumers should pay prices which accurately reflect the impact of car use on the environment. In the late 1990s the UK government introduced a **landfill tax**. This taxed businesses £15 per tonne in 2004 for dumping waste in a landfill site.

**Compensation** Firms could be forced by law to compensate those affected by externalities. For example, it is common for airports to provide grants to nearby residents. This allows them to purchase double glazing and other types of insulation, which provides protection from aircraft noise. Business may also be forced by court action to pay compensation to people affected by their actions.

**Government subsidies** This involves governments offering grants, tax allowances and other types of subsidy to businesses in order to encourage them to reduce externalities. Such subsidies can allow environmentally desirable projects, which otherwise might not be profitable, to go ahead. For example, a business may be given a grant so that it can build a recycling plant for plastics. This should encourage domestic and industrial users to recycle rather than dump plastic products.

Government subsidies could also be used to encourage more environmentally friendly habits amongst consumers. For example, many councils are attempting to encourage the use of bicycles through schemes such as setting up cycle lanes and giving grants to employees wishing to use bicycles for travelling to and from work.

**Road pricing and charges** Charging road users could be used to reduce pollution and congestion. There is a long history of charging for motorways in European countries such as France, Spain and Italy. In the UK the first toll motorway was opened in 2004, with travellers and business users paying to travel around Birmingham to reduce traffic on the M6. In 2003 a £5 charge was introduced on most vehicles entering the centre of London.

**Park and ride schemes** These are also designed to encourage a reduction in car use in city areas. They are often run by local authorities. Car users, for a fee, can park their cars outside the city areas and are taken by bus or rail into and out of the city. A single bus, if full, reduces traffic in the city area and also reduces the need for inner city car parking spaces.

**Pollution permits** In the USA pollution permits have been introduced. These allow businesses a certain amount of emissions. If the business reduces its pollution below a certain level, it can save the allowance for later or even sell it. Some have argued that Western economies should adopt the same approach to developing countries as they pollute the atmosphere across the world.

**Working together** It may be possible for business and/or government to work together to control the effect of business action on the environment. Examples might be:
● the sharing of best practice on environmental controls;
● producing environmental codes of practice;
● developing waste strategies.

**Education** Governments and other agencies, such as charities, could try to influence consumers and producers through educational and promotional campaigns.

**Consumer pressure** Consumers have forced a number of firms to consider the impact of their activities on the environment. There is evidence that a new breed of consumer is emerging, who considers factors other than price and quality when buying products. Such consumers take into account the effect on the environment and society of those products which they purchase. So, for example, such a consumer may not buy aerosols containing CFCs, furniture made from trees which have been chopped down in the Amazon rainforest or cosmetics which have been tested on animals.

Although this approach has influenced a wide range of firms, it does have one major problem. Consumers often do not have sufficient information with which to evaluate the impact of business activity upon the environment. Such information is often not disclosed to members of the public. Also, many firms have not been slow to realise that presenting themselves as being environmentally conscious can be very good for sales. However, the actual record of such firms with regard to the environment may well fall short of the claims which they make for themselves. For example, a battery producing company placed an environmentally friendly label on its products. However, this had to be removed when it was revealed that batteries use up more energy in their construction than they create in their use.

**Environmental audits** An environmental audit is one method by which consumers have a fairer chance of assessing the environmental impact of a firm. This could be much like the financial audits which all companies are at present required to have by law. An environmental audit can be one part of a wider social audit (☞ unit 111). This perhaps indicates the growing pressure put on firms to be concerned about their impact on the environment.

## Business and environmemental policies

With public concern increasing about the dangers of damaging the environment, pressure is building on many firms to become more environmentally friendly. Adopting such environmental policies can affect businesses in a number of ways.
● They may need to change production techniques or the materials which they use. Such changes may range from

---

Electricity prices in the UK could rise as a result of plans to cut carbon dioxide emissions beyond EU targets. The UK energy minister, Stephen Timms, said 'Our suggestion is that industrial electricity prices will increase ... by something like 6 per cent, not just in the UK but in major European industrial economies. The comparable figure for domestic bills would be about 3 per cent ... '.

The government had plans to cut carbon dioxide emissions by a fifth by 2010 in preparation for a new EU scheme on emissions trading to start in 2005. The initiative introduces caps on the amount of carbon dioxide emitted by industry. The scheme would force EU companies to pay to pollute. It will be mandatory for around 12,000 factories, of which 2,000 are in the UK. Under the scheme, the government would set emission limits on industry and allow companies to trade the right to produce emissions. Carbon emission limits for power stations have been cut so that, by 2007, their allocations will be 2.75 million tonnes of carbon dioxide below the government's updated energy projections for the sector..

Britain only imports around 2 per cent of its electricity and exports much less than that. The government said the fact that UK producers do not face competition from generators not affected by the EU scheme means they are better placed to absorb the costs of reducing their emissions.

The overall number of allowances for UK industry have been set at level beyond the Kyoto Protocol commitment. Industry voiced its displeasure at this. 'Emissions trading is the right approach, but if we go too far and other countries don't make similar commitments, we are going to put our hard-pressed manufacturers in an extremely difficult position in global markets' said Digby Jones, the director general of the Confederation of British Industry. But Friends of the Earth pointed out that the UK will not be introducing the toughest limits in Europe. It said some countries, such as Spain and Ireland, will have to take tougher action simply to meet Kyoto targets. Germany was also expected to follow the UK in going further than its Kyoto target.

Source: adapted from *The Guardian*, 19.1.2004.

(a) Explain the types of control on environmental costs mentioned in the article.
(b) Discuss to what extent the competitiveness of UK industry would be affected by these controls.

**Question 3**

the simple, such as the use of recycled paper in offices, to the complex, such as the installation of new recycling plants.

- Businesses may have to change their operations. For example, they may have to seek different methods of waste disposal. They may have to reduce or alter the packaging used in products. They may consider reducing the size of company cars or encouraging transport on trains by representatives.

- Firms may find that their costs increase. For example, a firm previously dumping waste products into the sea would find it more expensive to process this waste. Similarly, a firm which encouraged its employees to use bicycles rather than cars on company business might find that this takes employees longer and is, therefore, more expensive. Such increases in costs may well be passed on to customers in the form of higher prices.

- Some activities which improve a firm's environmental practices may lead to lower rather than higher costs. For example, a firm which sought to improve its energy efficiency might insulate the workplace, turn down heating appliances and turn off unused lights. Such actions are likely to reduce fuel bills and thus reduce costs. Encouraging employees to re-use items, such as paper clips, envelopes and elastic bands, is likely to have a similar effect.

- Business might be forced to work together more closely to reduce their impact on the environment. For example, businesses might work with suppliers to avoid charges on pollution, congestion or waste disposal. Industry bodies may be set up by businesses in certain areas to monitor environmental effects and work to develop solutions.

- There may need to be a change in its ethical stance (☞ unit 110). This may have a knock-on effect on other aspects of a firm's activities and lead to a re-examination of a number of its business practices.

- There is growing evidence that consumers are attracted to firms with environmentally friendly policies. Adopting such policies may lead to an increase in sales and possibly in profit levels.

- Research and development expenditure may need to increase as a firm seeks to find new, more environmentally friendly, products and production processes. Such an increase in expenditure may go on testing and creating new packaging materials or materials to be used in production.

## Conservation

All businesses depend, to a greater or lesser degree, on the use of non-renewable resources (☞ unit 86). These are resources which cannot be replaced and which might in some cases, with current usage, run out within the next 100 years. Such resources range from raw materials, like oil, iron, copper and aluminium, to living creatures.

Conservation ranges from banning the use of such

Congestion charging is a way of ensuring that those using valuable and congested road space make a financial contribution. It encourages the use of other modes of transport and is also intended to ensure that, for those who have to use the roads, journey times are quicker and more reliable.

The London scheme requires drivers to pay £5 per day if they wish to drive in central London during the scheme's hours of operation.

The following explains why the Mayor has decided to introduce congestion charging in central London.

- London suffers the worst traffic congestion in the UK and amongst the worst in Europe.
- Drivers in central London spend 50 per cent of their time in queues.
- Every weekday morning, the equivalent of 25 busy motorway lanes of traffic tries to enter central London.
- It has been estimated that London loses between £2 and 4 million every week in terms of lost time caused by congestion.

Not surprisingly, Londoners say congestion is one of the biggest issues facing the capital.

Surveys have shown that Londoners do not want to see congestion clogging up roads, threatening businesses and damaging London's status as a thriving world city.

Source: adapted from www.cclondon.com.

It was argued that the London congestion charge cut traffic so effectively that London faced a cash crisis because drivers were avoiding the charging zone. Figures suggested that so many cars kept out of central London after the charge was introduced in February 2003 that traffic levels fell by around 40 per cent. The lack of drivers paying £5 to enter the zone meant that Transport for London's budget for the scheme would be £65 million short by the end of the financial year, according to the mayor's estimates.

Source: adapted from *The Guardian*, 13.6.2003.

(a) Examine how the London congestion charge might affect:
(i) businesses;
(ii) individuals;
(iii) local government in London.

**Question 4**

resources altogether, to encouraging businesses to use them sparingly. There is a number of measures which seek to conserve non-renewable resources.

- Recycling schemes. Bottle banks set up to help the recycling of glass are now a common sight in supermarket car parks. Not only do glass recycling schemes help to conserve natural resources, but they can be profitable for those companies involved. Recycling

schemes also exist in the paper, plastics and aluminium industries.

● Multilateral agreements. These are agreements between a number of countries which seek to limit the use of natural resources. Agreements now exist which place limits on the amount of fishing and whaling which countries are allowed to carry out. In addition, some countries now have import bans on commodities such as ivory which come from endangered species.

● Government subsidies. These have been used to encourage farmers to conserve the countryside through retaining features such as dry stone walls and hedgerows, for example.

## Business opportunities

The growth in the importance of conservation and the management of waste (☞ unit 86) in recent years has led to a huge expansion in commercial opportunities in the provision of waste management services. Examples of businesses that have grown as a result of these trends include:

● chemical treatments such as metal precipitation, pH adjustment and acid/alkali neutralisation, cyanide treatment and ammonia stripping and recovery;
● special waste transfer stations where a wide range of waste material can be dealt with;
● domestic refuse collection on behalf of local authorities;
● clearing contaminated land;
● waste transportation from business sites to disposal or treatment points;
● clinical waste disposal on behalf of hospitals, dentists and veterinary surgeons;
● laboratory chemicals packing and disposal;
● dry waste disposal services;
● on-site treatment technologies;
● water jetting and air conveyancing;
● backtrack services to help businesses recycle and recover difficult and special wastes;
● drainage systems and support services;
● integrated waste management services;
● sewer surveying services.

---

**Table 112.2** *Management of municipal waste by method, England*

**Thousand tonnes**

|  | 1996/97 | 1998/99 | 2000/01 | 2001/02 |
|---|---|---|---|---|
| Landfill | 20,631 | 21,534 | 22,039 | 22,317 |
| Incineration with energy from waste | 1,446 | 2,117 | 2,391 | 2,459 |
| Recycled/composted | 1,750 | 2,525 | 3,446 | 3,907 |
| Other | 761 | 160 | 182 | 140 |
| Total | 24,588 | 26,337 | 28,057 | 28,823 |

Source: adapted from Department for Environment, Food and Rural Affairs.

---

**Table 112.3** *Electricity generated from renewable sources, UK*

**GWh**

|  | 1991 | 1996 | 2001 | 2002 |
|---|---|---|---|---|
| Wind and wave | 9 | 499 | 965 | 1,256 |
| Solar photo-voltaics | - | - | 2 | 3 |
| Hydro | 4,624 | 3,393 | 4,055 | 4,788 |
| Landfill gas | 208 | 708 | 2,507 | 2,679 |
| Sewage sludge digestion | 328 | 410 | 363 | 397 |
| Municipal solid waste combustion | 151 | 490 | 929 | 958 |
| Other biofuels | 1 | 197 | 777 | 870 |
| Wastes | 88 | 417 | 479 | 494 |
| Total | 5,409 | 6,102 | 10,077 | 11,444 |

Source: adapted from Department of Trade and Industry.

---

(a) Describe the methods used to improve conservation and protect the environment in the tables.
(b) Comment on the extent to which these methods have been successful.

## Question 5

---

## key terms

**Externalities** - occur when private costs are different to social costs and private benefits are different to social benefits.
**Private benefits** - the benefit of an activity to an individual or a business.
**Private costs** - the cost of an activity to an individual or a business.
**Social benefits** - the benefit of an activity to society as well as to a business.
**Social costs** - the cost of an activity to society as well as to a business.

## Studying and assessment

Study skills are the skills that a student needs to plan, organise and carry out their work effectively. They also help a student to answer questions and carry out tasks which are designed to test their abilities. Units 113 and 114 are set out like a manual. They provide guidance and examples to help students when working in term time or when taking examinations. Examples are shown in italics. The units could be used:

- at the start of the course to get ideas on the best way to study;
- constantly throughout the course when studying;
- before examinations during revision preparation.

## Action planning

Studying is more effective if there is a **plan** or **strategy**. An action plan can be formally written out, but it does not have to be. For any piece of work, it is important for a student to plan:

- how long it will take, bearing in mind any deadline;
- where the student will work;
- when the student will work;
- in what order tasks will be carried out;
- factors likely to affect the work, such as unforeseen occurrences.

A plan can be made for an individual piece of work, work over a term, coursework or project work, revision or an entire scheme of work. It is important for a student to develop a **routine** of work that is effective. It is also important for students to be **committed** to complete the plan. The table below shows a possible action plan that may be used for study, work or revision.

| | |
|---|---|
| Title and nature of work | What needs to be done? What is the focus? How will it be judged? |
| Start and finish date | What is the deadline? How long will it take? |
| Collecting information | Where from? How can it be obtained? What help is needed? How long will it take? How will it be used? |
| Carry out the work | Where? When? How long? Who with? What order? Continuous or broken down? Help needed? What factors might affect the work? Possible changes? |
| Review | Did the plan work? Was the outcome successful? How could it have been done better? Was everything covered? |

## Time management

An important part of the action plan is planning how long to study or work. Certain factors must be considered when deciding how much time to take when studying.

**When to start and when to finish** There is a deadline for most pieces of work. This is the date by which it has to be completed. It is important to start early enough and to leave enough time to finish the work. Some people work faster than others. This will affect the time they allocate.

**How long the work will take** Some pieces of work will take longer than others. Short answer questions will perhaps take less time than an essay. A piece of coursework or project work may take months. So will revision. Some people work quicker than others, which may reduce the time taken.

**How long to work** The length of time spent on work can affect its quality.

- Spending a greater amount of time preparing and planning may improve a piece of work.
- The time spent writing may also improve work.
- Working for too long can be tiring and work may suffer. Sometimes it is better to take a short break.
- Some work, such as coursework and revision, can not be done all at once and must be broken up.
- It is useful to try to break up revision, by learning as you go along. There is likely to be too much to learn in one session at the end. Spreading the work also allows practice.

**When to study** This will depend on the time available. Some people have a free choice of time. They could work in free time in the day, at lunchtime, in the evening or at weekends. People with part time jobs or with great commitments may find it more difficult. They may have to work when they can. Sometimes there may be free time which could be usefully used, such as travelling to school or college on a bus or train. Students should also consider that it may not be useful to work:

- late at night because they are tired;
- after strenuous exercise because it may be difficult to concentrate;
- when they are doing lots of other things.

## Where to study

It is important to consider where to work. Some students will work better in certain environments than others. Should you work at home or in a different place such as school, a library or another person's house? Issues to consider might be:

- the availability of materials. A library will have books you can use. It may also have a facility to find book titles,

newspapers and magazines, perhaps on CD Rom, and access to the Iinternet. If you keep all your materials at home, it may be better to work there;

- ease of access. Working at home allows easy access to drinks and food. Some people may also want to take a break to watch television or do something else;
- comfortable or not? Working in a familiar environment, such as home, can make work easier. Other people prefer to work in a more 'academic' atmosphere;
- alone or in a group? Some people prefer to work alone. Others like to work with someone else, even if they are doing their own work. Sometimes group activities demand that people work together;
- silent or not? Some people prefer to work in silence as they concentrate better. Working in a library would allow this. Others prefer things to be happening around them.

## Other learning considerations

There are other factors that students may want to take into consideration when working.

- Some people prefer to sit on a hard chair. Some prefer to be more comfortable and sit on a soft or relaxing chair.
- Some people like to listen to music whilst they are working. Others prefer silence.
- Some people prefer bright lighting so that everything is clear. Others work better in dimmed lighting.
- Some people prefer to carry out several tasks or activities at once. Others prefer to do one task and then move on to another.
- Some people prefer to eat or chew while they are working as it helps them to concentrate. Others don't.
- Some people learn better by moving around from time to time and some by standing up.

## Learning and memory strategies

Different people learn in different ways. Some people learn and remember more easily when they hear something. Others prefer to see it written down and to read it. Some prefer a diagram or picture. Each of these styles of learning may be useful in different circumstances. If a student finds learning something difficult in one way, he or she might try another.

**Written methods** In many cases students will have to read information and take notes. This is often the most common form of learning on a course at advanced level.

A possible technique used to read information is to:

- choose a section of written material that you will read and quickly scan through it to get the overall idea;
- read the material more slowly;
- put the written material aside and recite the key ideas or points that you have read;
- check that you have covered the main points;
- if you have missed anything, re-read the information.

Often in work or for revision students have to condense large amounts of information into shorter note form. This makes it easier to remember. Steps to note taking may involve the following:

- reading the information and making sure that you understand it first;
- dividing up the information into topic headings and subheadings;
- making suitable notes that are clear and easy to read, and are in a logical order;
- underlining or highlighting important words or key phrases that will trigger memory of the point;
- using page references to the written material;
- leaving space for additions;
- creating an index for your notes, either using a card system or a computer package and updating the order.

Once you have a set of notes you can use the reading technique above to make sure you understand them or for revision.

*Example*

*In 1999 The European Commission was poised to open an investigation into BP Amoco's proposed $26bn merger with Atlantic Richfield (Arco). EU sources said the merger, which would further tighten the oligopolistic structure of the oil market, had to be examined in the context of other anti-trust investigations involving the sector - notably the Exxon-Mobil project. Competition authorities in Brussels and the US were worried that these and other deals would enhance the power of a small number of oil companies in the exploration and production of oil and gas worldwide. If the two mergers went through, the top three oil majors - including the Anglo Dutch group Shell - would account for close to 50 per cent of crude oil production by publicly quoted western companies, bankers estimated.*

*EU officials had serious doubts about the BP Amoco-Arco merger. One problem involved the high joint share BP Amoco-Arco would have in pipeline transportation of natural gas in the UK sector of the North Sea. The potential blocks to the approval of Exxon-Mobil were greater. As well as its doubts about the global structure of the industry, Brussels identified numerous problems affecting Europe as a whole, as well as the EU member states. One was that the deal could harm competition in the onshore production and distribution of low calorific gas in the Netherlands and Germany, where the two companies jointly had a high market share. The Commission said that it was determined not to let the merger damage the consumer benefits expected to flow from the liberalisation of the European gas market.*

*Oil mergers*

- *Possible investigation by European Commission of BP Amoco -Arco and Exxon-Mobil mergers.*
- *Concern that the mergers would increase oligopolistic nature of oil market. If mergers went through, BP Amoco-Arco, Exxon- Mobil and Shell would have nearly 50 per cent of crude oil production.*

**(a) Mind maps**

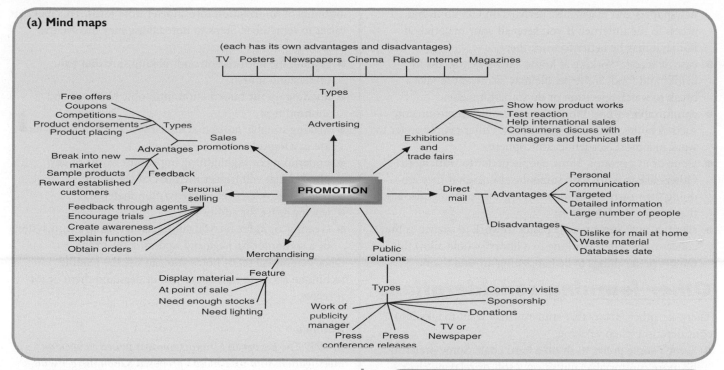

- *Problem of BP Amoco-Arco merger. Domination of natural gas pipelines.*
- *Problems of Exxon-Mobil merger. Harm to competition, transport of low calorific gas in Holland and Germany and possible benefits of market liberalisation (lower prices, better choice etc.)*

**Oral methods** It is sometimes easier to remember or understand something if you hear it. When you meet people do you remember their name? If so you may have a strong oral memory. Strategies for learning might include:

- answering questions asked by another person;
- making oral notes onto a tape recorder which are played back regularly;
- constantly repeating phrases or key words, perhaps in an order;
- make up a **mnemonic**, rhyme or phrase which can be repeated. For example, PEST analysis stands for the Political, Economic, Social and Technological factors that affect a business.

**Pictorial/visual** When you meet people do you remember their face? If so you may have a strong visual memory. Visual material can provide an instant 'picture' of information. Sometimes it is easier to see relationships by visual representation. Visual information may make use of some of the note taking techniques explained above. It may also make use of photographs. Examples of visual presentation include the following.

(a) Mind maps. *Promotion methods.*
(b) Family trees. *The sources of funds.*
(c) Flow diagrams. *The stages in the design process.*
(d) Horizontal family trees. *Herzberg's two-factor theory.*

**(b) Family trees**

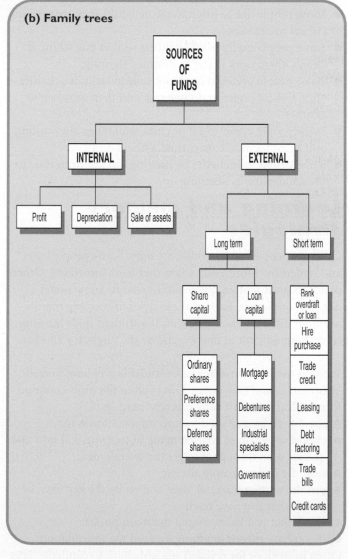

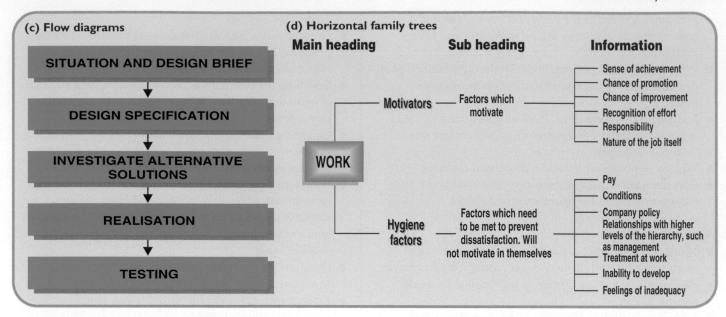

**(c) Flow diagrams**

SITUATION AND DESIGN BRIEF

↓

DESIGN SPECIFICATION

↓

INVESTIGATE ALTERNATIVE SOLUTIONS

↓

REALISATION

↓

TESTING

**(d) Horizontal family trees**

Main heading    Sub heading    Information

WORK

Motivators — Factors which motivate
- Sense of achievement
- Chance of promotion
- Chance of improvement
- Recognition of effort
- Responsibility
- Nature of the job itself

Hygiene factors — Factors which need to be met to prevent dissatisfaction. Will not motivate in themselves
- Pay
- Conditions
- Company policy
- Relationships with higher levels of the hierarchy, such as management
- Treatment at work
- Inability to develop
- Feelings of inadequacy

(e) Block diagrams. *Calculating profit and loss.*

(f) Method of loci. This involves taking a room you know and imagining certain key words in parts of the room. *Types of integration.*

**Learning by doing** You may think that you know something or know how to do it. But you might only find out if you test yourself by doing something. It may be possible to test yourself by using:

● classroom or homework activities you have already completed earlier in the course;
● activities in textbooks or workbooks;
● applying ideas in a project or a piece of coursework;
● past examination questions;
● your own activities.

## Key skills

**Key skills** allow a student to learn, select and apply important competences. Key skills at advanced level include

communication, application of number, information technology, working with others, improving own learning and performance, and problem solving. All of these skills can be developed by a student taking a course in Business Studies. Some examples of each key skill are shown below.

**Communication**

● Debates. *The extent to which business ethics should influence profit.*
● Role play. *An interview scenario or a meeting with a pressure group.*
● Group discussions. *How a business might promote a new product.*
● Interviews. *A one-to-one interview with a manager about a business problem.*
● Oral presentations. *The results of marketing research.*
● Passing information. *A memo to staff about reorganisation following the introduction of new technology.*
● Written analysis. *A report recommending action to solve*

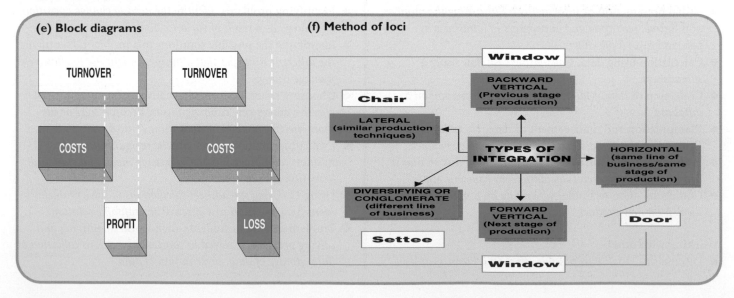

**(e) Block diagrams**

TURNOVER    TURNOVER

COSTS    COSTS

PROFIT    LOSS

**(f) Method of loci**

Window

Chair

BACKWARD VERTICAL (Previous stage of production)

LATERAL (similar production techniques)

TYPES OF INTEGRATION

HORIZONTAL (same line of business/same stage of production)

DIVERSIFYING OR CONGLOMERATE (different line of business)

FORWARD VERTICAL (Next stage of production)

Settee    Door

Window

*problems identified in the profit and loss account and a balance sheet or a strategy to deal with entry into foreign markets.*

- Written and visual presentations. *Producing a business plan or charts showing the market share of businesses in an industry.*
- Summarising information. *Producing a business organisational chart or a summary of performance from financial ratio data.*
- Written responses. *A letter to a dissatisfied customer.*
- Communication using technology. *An e-mail to the manager showing sales figures on a spreadsheet.*

## Application of number

- Numerical calculations. *Calculating the depreciation of assets using different methods or calculating labour turnover.*
- Planning information. *Preparing information for a sales revenue budget.*
- Interpreting results. *Identifying gearing problems from ratios.*
- Numerical analysis. *Investment appraisal using various methods.*
- Graphical analysis. *Identifying stock problems from a chart.*
- Construction of graphs. *Constructing a break-even chart.*
- Construction of tables. *Constructing a balance sheet.*
- Collection and presentation of data. *Sales figures used to produce product life cycle diagrams or market research information showing customers' responses.*
- Forecasting. *Estimating future sales figures from a trend.*

## Information technology

- Searching for information. *Finding information on a CD Rom or an Internet website.*
- Reviewing and selecting information. *Selecting appropriate information from the Internet to show accidents at work.*
- Written presentation and manipulation of information. *Writing a report using appropriate software on the impact on the business of the euro.*
- Visual presentation of information. *Illustrating the number of full time, part time and outworkers in a business as percentages in a pie chart.*
- Calculation using data. *Calculating cash flow using a spreadsheet.*
- Collection of data. *Marketing research information on a database.*
- Manipulation and management of data. *Updating stock figures over time on a spreadsheet to show stock balances.*
- Transfer of data. *Storing cost information on disk so that it can be used for financial calculations by someone else.*
- Communication technology. *Sending an e-mail containing ideas for a new product.*

## Working with others

- Discussions. *To discuss possible effect on a business of lean production methods.*
- Group debates. *Should multinational businesses take their profits back to the 'home' country or spend it in foreign countries in which they operate?*
- Searching for information. *When dealing with a great deal of information such as changes in government legislation over a period.*
- Collecting information. *When dealing with a great deal of information such as the effects of government policy on a business over a year.*
- Summarising. *When a great deal of information has to be summarised, each group member could take one aspect. For example, when looking at changes in a business, summaries of marketing, production and approaches to human resources could be made.*
- Question practice and cross checking. *Using another person to ask questions or to check your answers.*
- Brainstorming. *Developing possible promotional methods using brainstorming sessions.*
- Using outside sources of information. *Discussing the effects of pedestrianisation of a town on a local retailer.*

## Improving own learning performance

- Identifying areas to improve. *Knowledge, memory, time management, work and resource management, such as where to find information and what resources to use, interpreting questions, answering questions, working with others, the work environment, motivation.*
- Evaluating work. *Own evaluation, others' opinions, evaluation against criteria, past experience of problems.*
- Identifying methods of improvement. *More practice, changing the method of learning, identifying strengths and applying to other areas, reorganisation of environment such as changing the place or time of work, changing attitudes, changing resources.*
- Identifying help. *Resources, other people, self-help.*

## Problem solving

- Identifying problems. *Identify the need to change operations or strategy as a result of variance analysis.*
- Identifying the possible solutions to a problem. *Identifying the different strategies that a business might use to effectively manage change.*
- Choosing solutions from alternatives. *Choosing the most effective advertising campaign using decision trees or the most effective method of work using critical path analysis.*
- Evaluating solutions. *Evaluate the reorganisation of a business to improve productivity using mean and standard deviation calculations.*
- Using IT. *Using spreadsheet calculations to solve problems by identifying the most cost effective or profitable solution.*
- Problem solving in students' own work. *Identifying and solving problems involved in coursework, such as collection of data, storage of data, presentation of data.*

# Case study Dangers that are clear and present

Accidents can come in many different ways, shapes and forms at work. Take the apparently safe environment of the office. Slips, trips and falls are the single largest cause of major injuries at work. The Health and Safety Executive (HSE) suggests that the cost to employees each year of such accidents is £300 million and the overall cost to society is between £810-840 million. Trailing wires or unstable boxes of stationery left on the photocopier might not appear to be a problem. But many accidents, resulting in lost days work, are caused as a result of such apparently innocent situations.

Accidents can take many forms. Examples in the local authority offices of Westminster City Council include a woman who tripped on a box and fell onto a filing cabinet, damaging her cheekbone and the corner of her eye socket. Another female employee fell on a workstation cable and shattered her arm. Neither returned to work. And there is also the problem of constantly ringing phones causing stress and distracting employees.

The Health and Safety at Work Regulations, 1999 require employees to carry out risk assessment to assess health risks in office. But are risks being assessed? According to the HSE, only 39 per cent of organisations undertake risk assessment of workstations. There are also the risks of using chemicals, such as toner in photocopiers. And there is the issue of lifting heavy loads.

Businesses face problems if they do not look after their employees. The largest pay-out ever as compensation for injuries at work to a UNISON union member was £600,000 as a result of a disabling accident. Another member received £35,000 after lifting items that were too heavy. In most cases employees say that they would give back the money to regain their health.

But what about the risks of potentially dangerous activities such as the storage and handling of fuel? BP has ordered its drivers not to deliver fuel as a result of concerns over the safety of its employees in the past.

An investigation was launched into BP in 2000 as a result of safety breaches in the past, such as by the HSE in 2000 into
- seven major alerts in 14 months at the

Grangemouth plant, which has highly flammable chemicals, including fires, an exploding pipe and the failure of the main power cable;
- a reduction in staffing levels at a plant in Essex which resulted in the HSE ordering the business to stop operating as it believed the plant could not be shut down in an emergency;
- the shutting down of the main oil platform by the HSE in 1999 for two gas leaks.

In April 1999, the business was prosecuted after two contractors were overcome by nitrogen fumes.

BP stated that unfortunately accidents do occur. But it argued that even in attempts to cut costs, it never compromises safety. And if an accident happens the business investigates and works with authorities to make sure it never happens again.

Source: adapted from *The Observer*, 1.10.2000 and 10.12.2000.

**(a) Identify the types of risk to employees mentioned in the article. (6 marks)**

**(b) Explain how:**
   **(i) the Health and Safety Executive;**
   **(ii) legislation;**
   **may affect the organisations mentioned in the article. (8 marks)**

**(c) Examine the problems which (i) employees and (ii) organisations may face as a result of accidents at work. (12 marks)**

**(d) Recommend changes which the organisations in the article might make to prevent accidents taking place. (12 marks)**

**(e) Discuss the extent to which organisations are likely to protect their employees. (12 marks)**